Excel® 2021/Microsoft® 365 Programming by Example

EXCEL® 2021/MICROSOFT® 365 PROGRAMMING BY EXAMPLE

Julitta Korol

MERCURY LEARNING AND INFORMATION
Dulles, Virginia
Boston, Massachusetts
New Delhi

Publisher: David Pallai
Mercury Learning and Information
22841 Quicksilver Drive
Dulles, VA 20166
info@merclearning.com
www.merclearning.com
(800) 232-0223

Julitta Korol. *Excel® 2021/Microsoft® 365 Programming by Example.*
ISBN: 978-1-68392-886-7

222324321 This book is printed on acid-free paper in the United States of America.

Library of Congress Control Number: 2022947022

To my niece, Jowita

CONTENTS

Acknowledgments

First, I'd like to express my gratitude to everyone at Mercury Learning and Information. A sincere thank-you to my publisher, David Pallai, for offering me the opportunity to update this book to the new 2021 version and tirelessly keeping things on track during this long project.

A whole bunch of thanks go to the editorial team for working so hard to bring this book to print. In particular, I would like to thank the copyeditor for the thorough review of my writing, Jennifer Blaney, for her production expertise and keeping track of all the edits and file processing issues, and the compositor, for all the composition efforts that gave this book its pleasant look and feel.

Finally, I'd like to acknowledge readers like you who cared enough to post reviews of the previous edition of this book online. Your invaluable feedback has helped me improve the quality of this work by including the material that matters to you most. Please continue to inspire me with your ideas and suggestions.

INTRODUCTION

If you ever wanted to open a new worksheet without using built-in commands or create a custom, fully automated form to gather data and store the results in a worksheet, you've picked up the right book. This book shows you what's doable with Microsoft® Excel® 2021 beyond the standard user interface. This book's purpose is to teach you how to delegate many time-consuming and repetitive tasks to Excel by using its built-in language, VBA (Visual Basic for Applications). By executing special commands and statements and using several Excel's built-in programming tools, you can work smarter than you ever thought possible. I will show you how.

When I first started programming in Excel (circa 1990), I was working in a sales department, and it was my job to calculate sales commissions and send the monthly and quarterly statements to our sales representatives spread all over the United States. As this was a very time-consuming and repetitive task, I became immensely interested in automating the whole process. In those days, it wasn't easy to get started in programming on your own. There weren't as many books written on the subject; all I had was the built-in documentation that was hard to read. Nevertheless, I succeeded; my first macro worked like magic. It automatically calculated our salespeople's commissions and printed out nicely formatted statements. While the computer was busy performing the same tasks repeatedly, I was free to deal with other more interesting projects.

Many years have passed since that day, and Excel is still working like magic for me and a great number of other people who took time to familiarize themselves with its programming interface. If you'd like to join these people and have Excel do magical things for you as well, this book provides an easy step-by-step introduction to VBA and other technologies that work nicely with Microsoft Excel. Besides this book, there is no extra cost to you; all the tools you need are built into Excel. If you have not yet discovered them, *Excel 2021 / Microsoft 365 Programming by Example* will lead you through the process of creating your first macros, VBA procedures, web queries and power queries, and XML documents, from start to finish. Along the way, there are detailed, practical "how-to" examples and plenty of illustrations. The book's approach is to learn by doing. There's no better way than step by step. Simply turn on the computer, open this book, launch Microsoft Excel, and do all the guided Hands-On exercises. But before you get started, allow me to give you a short overview of the things you'll be learning as you progress through this book.

Excel 2021 / Microsoft 365 Programming by Example is divided into 8 parts (29 chapters) that progressively introduce you to programming Microsoft Excel 2021 as well as controlling other applications with Excel.

Part I introduces you to Visual Basic for Applications (VBA), the programming language for Microsoft Excel. In this part of the book, you acquire the fundamentals of VBA that you will use over and over again in building real-life spreadsheet applications. Part I chapters are also the subject of a standalone book "Microsoft Excel 2021 Programming Pocket Primer," available from Mercury Learning and Information (ISBN: 978-1-68392-892-8). If you already worked through the pocket primer book, you could skip chapters 1-9 and begin from Chapter 10.

PART I CONSISTS OF THE FOLLOWING NINE CHAPTERS:

Chapter 1—Excel Macros: A Quick Start in Excel VBA Programming
In this chapter, you learn how you can introduce automation into your Excel worksheets by simply using the built-in macro recorder. You learn about different phases of macro design and execution. You also learn about macro security.

Chapter 2—Excel Programming Environment: A Quick Overview of Its Tools and Features
In this chapter, you learn almost everything you need to know about working with the Visual Basic Editor window, commonly referred to as VBE. Some of the programming tools that are not covered here are discussed and used in Chapter 9.

Chapter 3 — Excel VBA Fundamentals: A Quick Reference to Writing VBA Code
In this chapter, you are introduced to the basic VBA concepts, such as Microsoft Excel object model and its objects, properties, and methods. You also learn concepts that allow you to store various pieces of information for later use.

Chapter 4—Excel VBA Procedures: A Quick Guide to Writing Function Procedures
In this chapter, you learn how to write and execute function procedures. You also

learn how to provide additional information to your procedures before they are run. You are introduced to working with some useful built-in functions and methods that allow you to interact with your VBA procedure users.

Chapter 5—Adding Decisions to Excel VBA Programs: A Quick Introduction to Conditional Statements
In this chapter, you learn how to control your program flow with several different decision-making statements.

Chapter 6—Adding Repeating Actions to Excel VBA Programs: A Quick Introduction to Looping Statements
In this chapter, you learn how you can repeat certain groups of statements using procedure loops.

Chapter 7—Storing Multiple Values in Excel VBA Programs: A Quick Introduction to Working with Arrays
In this chapter, you learn the concept of static and dynamic arrays, which you can use for holding various values. You also learn about built-in array functions.

Chapter 8—Keeping Track of Multiple Values in Excel VBA Programs: A Quick Introduction to Creating and Using Collections
In this chapter, you learn how to use your custom collection object to track and manipulate data in your VBA procedures.

Chapter 9—Excel Tools for Testing and Debugging: A Quick Introduction to Testing VBA Programs
In this chapter, you begin using built-in debugging tools to test your programming code and trap errors.

The above nine chapters will give you the fundamental techniques and concepts you will need to continue your Excel VBA learning path. The skills obtained in Excel VBA Primer are very portable. They can be utilized in programming other Microsoft 365 applications that also use VBA as their native programming language such as Access, Word, PowerPoint, Outlook, and others.

While VBA offers numerous built-in functions and statements for working with the file system, you can also perform file and folder manipulation tasks via objects and methods included in the Windows Script Host installed by default on computers running the Windows operating system. Additionally, you can open and manipulate files directly via the low-level file I/O (input/output) functions. In Part II of this book, you discover various methods of working with files and folders, and learn how to programmatically open, read, and write three types of files.

PART II CONSISTS OF THE FOLLOWING THREE CHAPTERS:

Chapter 10—File and Folder Manipulation with VBA
In this chapter, you learn about numerous VBA statements used in working with Windows files and folders.

Chapter 11—File and Folder Manipulation with Windows Script Host (WSH)
In this chapter, you learn how the Windows Script Host works together with VBA and allows you to get information about files and folders.

Chapter 12—Using Low-Level File Access
In this chapter, you learn how to get in direct contact with your data by using the process known as low-level file I/O. You also learn about various types of file access.

The VBA programming language goes beyond Excel. It can be used to program any application that supports this language. In Part III of the book, you learn how other applications expose their objects to VBA.

PART III CONSISTS OF THE FOLLOWING TWO CHAPTERS:

Chapter 13—Using Excel VBA to Interact with Other Applications
In this chapter, you learn how you can launch and control other applications from within VBA procedures written in Excel. You also learn how to establish a reference to a Type library and use and create Automation objects.

Chapter 14—Using Excel with Microsoft Access
In this chapter, you learn about accessing Microsoft Access data and running Access queries and functions from VBA procedures. If you are interested in learning more about Access programming with VBA using the same step-by-step approach as presented in this book, I recommend another book of mine titled *Access 2021/Microsoft 365 Programming by Example* (Mercury Information and Learning, 2022).

In Part IV of this book, you learn how to create desired interface elements for your users via Ribbon customizations and the creation of dialog boxes and custom forms. You will also learn how to format worksheets with VBA, handle printing and email tasks, and control Excel with event-driven programming.

PART IV CONSISTS OF THE FOLLOWING SIX CHAPTERS:

Chapter 15—Event-Driven Programming
In this chapter, you learn about the types of events that can occur when you are running VBA procedures in Excel. You gain a working knowledge of writing event procedures and handling various types of events.

Chapter 16—Using Dialog Boxes
In this chapter, you learn about working with Excel built-in dialog boxes programmatically.

Chapter 17—Creating Custom Forms
In this chapter, you learn how to use various controls for designing user-friendly forms. This chapter has a hands-on application you build from scratch.

Chapter 18—Formatting Worksheets with VBA
In this chapter, you learn how to perform worksheet formatting tasks with VBA by applying visual features such as data bars, color scales, and icon sets. You also learn how to produce consistent-looking worksheets by using document themes and styles.

Chapter 19—Context Menu Programming and Ribbon Customizations
In this chapter, you learn how to add custom options to Excel built-in context (shortcut) menus and how to work programmatically with the Ribbon interface and Backstage View.

Chapter 20—Printing and Sending Email from Excel
In this chapter, you learn how to control printing and emailing your workbooks via VBA code.

Some Excel 2021 features are used more frequently than others; some are only used by Excel power users and developers. In Part V of the book, you work with Excel tools for data analysis. You gain experience in programming advanced Excel features such as Excel tables, PivotTables, PivotCharts, and get introduced to the Power Query feature that allows you to create powerful queries that simplify data import and transformation.

PART V CONSISTS OF THE FOLLOWING THREE CHAPTERS:

Chapter 21—Using and Programming Excel Tables
In this chapter, you learn how to work with Excel tables. You will learn how to retrieve information from an Access database, convert it into a table, and enjoy

database-like functionality in the spreadsheet. You will also learn how tables are exposed through Excel's object model and manipulated via VBA.

Chapter 22—Programming PivotTables and PivotCharts
In this chapter, you learn how to work with two powerful Microsoft Excel objects that are used for data analysis: PivotTable and PivotChart. You will learn how to use VBA to manipulate these two objects to quickly produce reports that allow you or your users to easily examine large amounts of data pulled from an Excel worksheet range or from an external data source such as an Access database.

Chapter 23—Getting and Transforming Data in Excel 2021
In this chapter, you are introduced to data import, transformation and shaping features available in the Get & Transform section of the Excel's 2021 Data tab. You work with Query Editor and Advanced Editor and learn formulas and functions written in the M expression language while bringing together data from various sources.

While VBA provides a very comprehensive Object Model for automating worksheet tasks, some of the processes and operations that you may need to program are an integral part of the Windows operating system and cannot be controlled via VBA. In Part VI of the book, you start by learning how to programmatically work with VBA projects, modules, and procedures. Next, you are introduced to the Windows API library of functions that will come to your rescue when you need to overcome the limitations of the native VBA library.

PART VI CONSISTS OF THE FOLLOWING TWO CHAPTERS:

Chapter 24—Programming the Visual Basic Editor (VBE)
In this chapter, you learn how to use numerous objects, properties, and methods from the Microsoft Visual Basic for Applications Extensibility Object Library to control the Visual Basic Editor to gain full control over Excel.

Chapter 25—Calling Windows API functions from Excel VBA
In this chapter, you are introduced to the Windows API library. After learning basic Windows API concepts, you are shown how to declare and utilize API functions from VBA.

As your Excel VBA procedures become more complex, you may find that your code is scattered all over the place and is difficult to maintain. Copying code from place to place and modifying procedures to include more arguments and enhancements because of the changing requirements sooner or later will result in creating a coding mess that is difficult to handle. Before you go this route, you should know that Excel has a special feature known as a *class module* that allows you to create code that is self-contained and reusable.

PART VII CONSISTS OF THE FOLLOWING CHAPTER:

Chapter 26—Creating Classes in VBA
In this chapter, you will learn how coding in a standalone class module can help you organize your code into more manageable objects that can easily be reused and adjusted when necessary. Here you learn about creating and using custom objects, declaring class members, defining class properties, and writing property procedures and class methods. You also learn how to use event procedures in a class module. These advanced topics are covered in custom application that you will build from scratch.

Thanks to the Internet and intranets, your worksheet data can be easily accessed and shared with others 24/7. Excel is capable of both capturing data from the Web and publishing it to the Web.

In Part VIII of the book, you are introduced to using Excel VBA with HTML (the Hypertext Markup Language), XML (the Extensible Markup Language), and calling a new type of a Web service, known as the REST API.

PART VIII CONSISTS OF THE FOLLOWING THREE CHAPTERS:

Chapter 27—HTML Programming and Web Queries
In this chapter, you learn how to create hyperlinks and publish HTML files using VBA. You also learn how to activate and work with one of Excel legacy features known as a Web query.

Chapter 28—Using XML in Excel 2021
In this chapter, you learn how to use Extensible Markup Language with Excel. You learn about enhanced XML support in Excel 2021 and many objects and technologies that are used to process XML documents.

Chapter 29—Excel and REST API
In this chapter, you explore several external libraries that will help you build more advanced VBA applications. You learn about a Dictionary object and how it compares to the native VBA Collection object. You learn about regular expressions and

how to use them to extract data. Finally, you are introduced to the JSON format and learn the basics of making HTTP GET requests to pull data from a RESTful web service.

INTENDED AUDIENCE

This book is designed for Excel users who want to expand their knowledge and learn what can be accomplished with Excel beyond the provided user interface.

Consider this book as a sort of private course that you can attend in the comfort of your office or home. Some courses have prerequisites, and this is no exception. *Excel 2021 / Microsoft 365 Programming by Example* does not explain how to select options from the Ribbon or use shortcut keys. The book assumes that you can easily locate in Excel the options that are required to perform any of the tasks already preprogrammed by the Microsoft team. With the basics already mastered, this book will take you to the next learning level where your custom requirements and logic are rendered into the language that Excel can understand. Let your worksheets perform magical things for you and let the fun begin.

THE COMPANION FILES

The example files for all the hands-on activities in this book are available in the companion files. These companion files may also be downloaded by contacting the publisher at info@merclearning.com. Digital versions of this title are available at *academiccourseware.com* and numerous other digital vendors.

Part I

Excel VBA Primer

The Excel VBA Primer is divided into nine chapters that progressively introduce you to programming Microsoft Excel using the 2021 version of the product. These chapters present the fundamental techniques and concepts that you need to master before you can take further steps in Excel programming.

Chapter 1

Excel Macros A Quick Start in Excel VBA Programming

Visual Basic for Applications (VBA) is the programming language built into all Microsoft® Office® applications, including Microsoft Excel®. By learning some basic VBA commands, you can start automating many of the mundane routine tasks that you perform in Excel. In this chapter, you acquire the fundamentals of VBA by recording macros and using the Visual Basic Editor to examine and edit the VBA code behind the recorded macro.

MACROS AND VBA

Macros are programs that store a series of commands. When you create a macro, you simply combine a sequence of keystrokes into a single command that you can later "play back." Because macros can reduce the number of steps required to complete tasks, using macros can significantly decrease the time you spend creating, formatting, modifying, and printing your Excel worksheets. You can create macros by using Microsoft Excel's built-in recording tool (Macro Recorder), or you can write them from scratch using Visual Basic Editor, a special development environment built into Excel. You can combine recorded macros with your own programming code to create unique VBA applications that meet your everyday needs. Whether you write or record your programming code in Excel, you'll be utilizing the powerful programming language—Visual Basic for Applications—commonly known as VBA.

Microsoft Excel comes with dozens of built-in, time-saving features that allow you to work faster and smarter. Before you decide to automate a worksheet task with a recorded macro or programming code written from scratch, make sure there is not already a built-in feature that you can use to perform that task. Consider writing your own VBA code or recording a macro when you find yourself performing the same series of actions multiple times or when Excel does not provide a built-in tool to do the job.

Just by learning how to handle Excel's macro recorder and use basic VBA statements and constructs to enhance your macros, you'll be able to automate any part of your worksheet. For example, you can automate data entry by recording a macro that enters headings in a worksheet or replaces column titles with new labels. Adding a little bit of conditional logic to your VBA code will allow you to automatically check for duplicate entries in a specified range of your worksheet. With a macro, you can quickly apply formatting to several worksheets, as well as combine different formats, such as fonts, colors, borders, and shading. Macros will save you keystrokes when it comes to setting print areas, margins, headers, and footers, and selecting special options for printouts.

Excel Macro-Enabled File Formats

When a workbook contains programming code, it should be saved in one of the following macro-enabled file formats:

- Excel Macro-Enabled Workbook (.xlsm)
- Excel Binary Workbook (.xlsb)
- Excel Macro-Enabled Template (.xltm)

If you attempt to save the workbook in a file format that is incompatible with the type of content it includes, Excel will warn you with a message as shown in Figure 1.1.

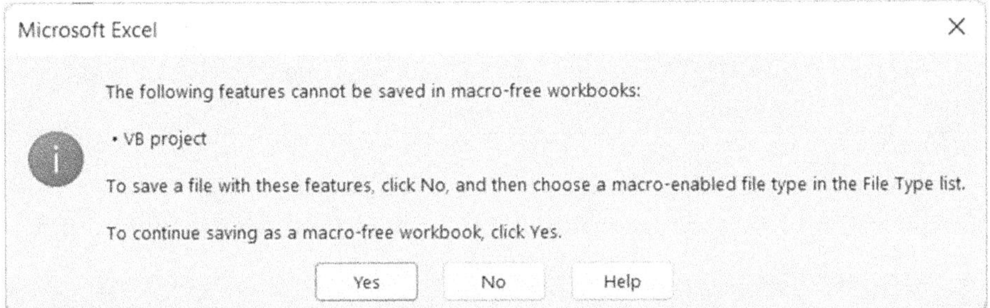

FIGURE 1.1 When a workbook contains programming code, you must save it in a macro-enabled file type instead of a regular .XLSX workbook file.

Macro Security Settings

Because macros can contain malicious code designed to put a virus on a user's computer, it is important to understand different security settings that are available in Excel. It is also critical that you run up-to-date antivirus software on your computer. Antivirus software installed on your computer will scan the workbook file you are attempting to open if the file contains macros. The default macro security setting is to disable all macros with notification, as shown in Figure 1.2.

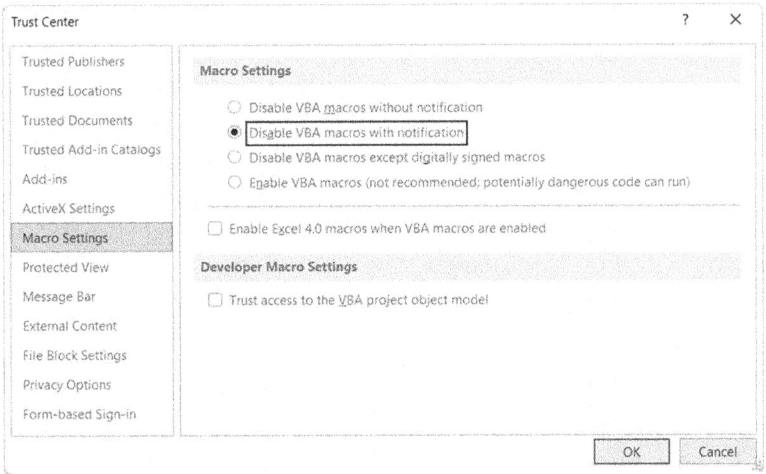

FIGURE 1.2 The Macro Settings options in the Trust Center allow you to control how Excel should deal with macros when they are present in an open workbook. To open Trust Center's Macro Settings, choose File | Options | Trust Center | Trust Center Settings and click the Macro Settings link.

NOTE	*VBA macros are the macros you create using the Excel built-in language – VBA. You will be working with these macros throughout this book. Excel 4.0 macros are legacy Excel macros. Introduced in 1992, they are commonly referred to as XLM 4.0 macros. They are still in Excel for backward compatibility reasons. Using these macros is discouraged as they can hide malicious code in Excel formulas.*

If VBA macros are present in a workbook you are trying to open, you will receive a security warning message just under the Ribbon, as shown in Figure 1.3.

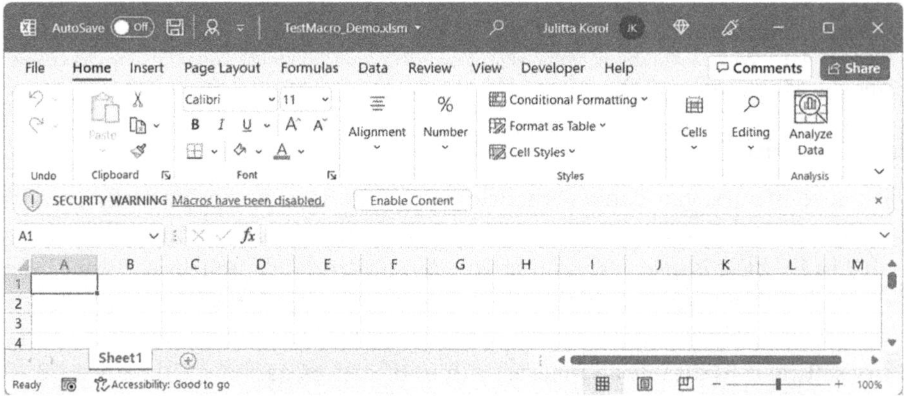

FIGURE 1.3 Upon opening a workbook with VBA macros, Excel brings up a security warning message.

To use the disabled components, you should click the Enable Content button on the message bar. This will add the workbook to the Trusted Documents list in your registry. The next time you open this workbook you will not be alerted to macros. If you need more information before enabling content, you can click the message text displayed in the security message bar to activate the Backstage View, where you will find an explanation of the active content that has been disabled, as shown in Figure 1.4. Clicking the Enable Content button in the Backstage View presents two options:

- Enable All Content

  This option provides the same functionality as the Enable Content button in the security message bar. This will enable all the content and make it a trusted document.

- Advanced Options

  This option brings up the Microsoft Office Security Options dialog shown in Figure 1.5. This dialog provides options for enabling content for the current session only.

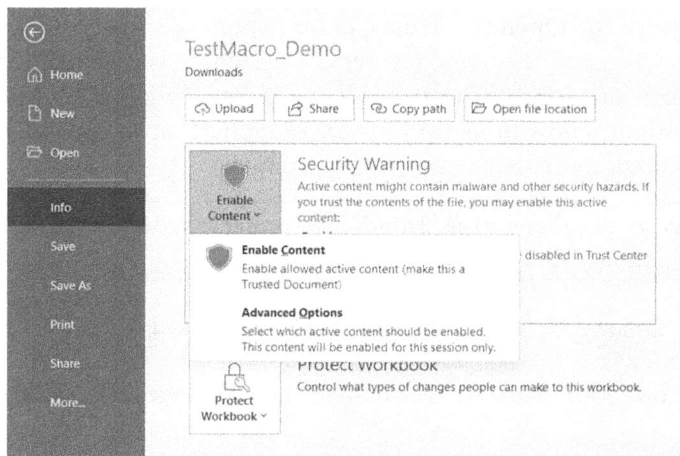

FIGURE 1.4 The Backstage View in Excel.

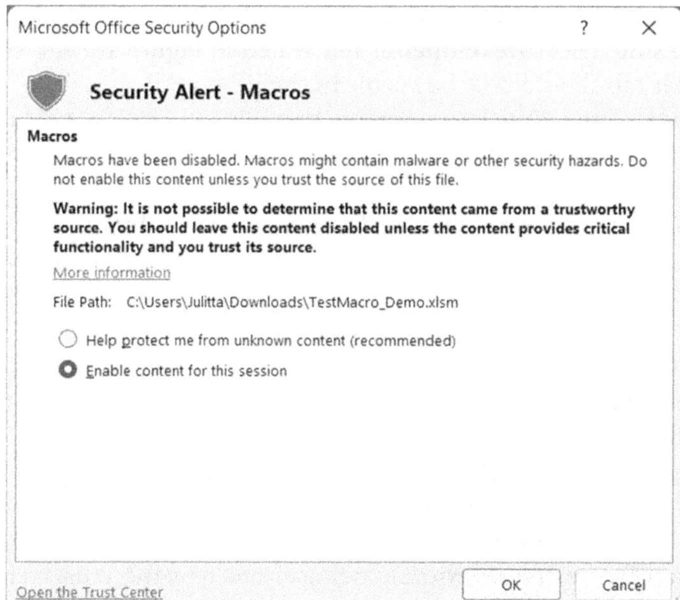

FIGURE 1.5 Disabled macros can be enabled for the current session in the Microsoft Office Security Options dialog.

ENABLING THE DEVELOPER TAB IN EXCEL

To make it easy to work with macro-enabled workbooks while working with this book's exercises, you will permanently trust your workbooks with recorded macros or VBA code by placing them in a folder on your local drive that you mark as trusted. Notice the Open the Trust Center hyperlink shown in Figure 1.5. This hyperlink will open the Trust Center dialog where you can set up a trusted folder. You can also activate the Trust Center by selecting File | Options.

Let's take a few minutes now to set up your Excel application so you can run VBA macros on your computer without security prompts.

NOTE	*Please note files for the "Hands-On" project may be found in the companion files.*

Hands-On 1.1 Setting Up Excel for Macro Development

1. Create a folder on your hard drive named **C:\VBAPrimerExcel2021_ByExample**.
2. Launch Excel and open a blank workbook.
3. Choose **File | Options**.
4. In the Excel Options dialog, click **Customize Ribbon**. In the Main Tabs listing on the right-hand side, select **Developer** as illustrated in Figure 1.6 and click **OK**. The Developer tab should now be visible in the Ribbon.
5. In the Code group of the Developer tab on the Ribbon, click the **Macro Security** button, as shown in Figure 1.7. The Trust Center dialog appears as depicted in Figure 1.2.
6. In the left pane of the Trust Center dialog, click **Trusted Locations.**
   The Trusted Locations dialog already shows several predefined trusted locations that were created when you installed Excel. For this book, we will add a custom location to this list.
7. Click the **Add new location** button.
8. In the Path text box, type the name of the folder you created in Step 1 of this Hands-On as shown in Figure 1.8.
9. Click **OK** to close the Microsoft Office Trusted Location dialog.
10. Notice that the Trusted Locations list in the Trust Center now includes the C:\ **VBAPrimerExcel2021_ByExample** folder as a trusted location. Files placed in a trusted location can be opened without being checked by the Trust Center security feature.
11. Click **OK** to close the Trust Center dialog box.

Your Excel application is now set up for easy macro development as well as opening files containing macros. You should save all the files created in the book's Hands-On exercises into your trusted C:\VBAPrimerExcel2021_ByExample folder.

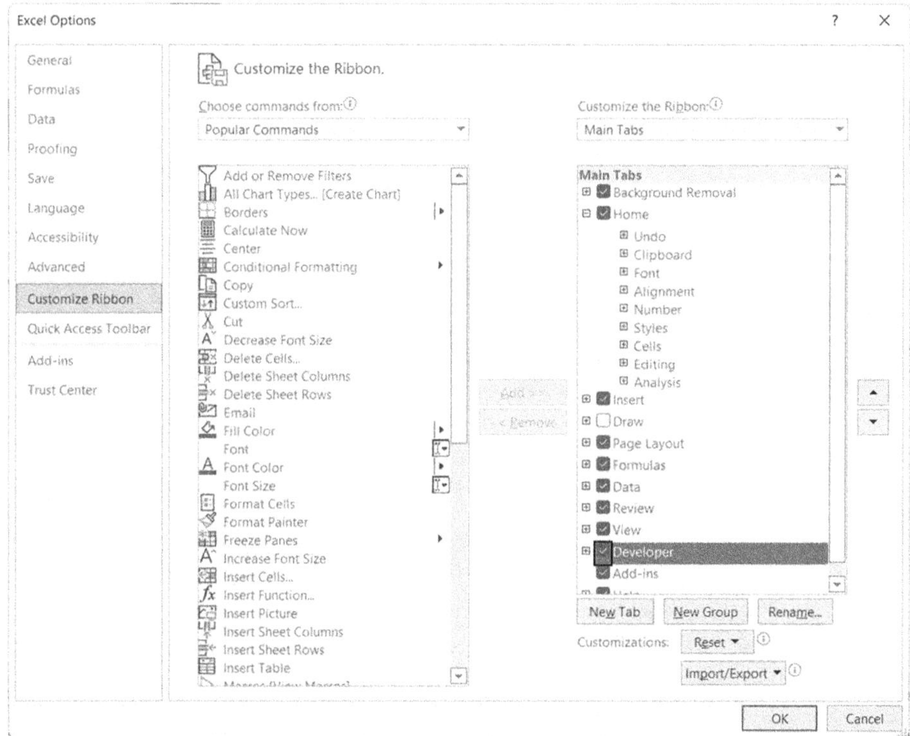

FIGURE 1.6 To enable the Developer tab on the Ribbon, use the Excel Options dialog and select Customize Ribbon.

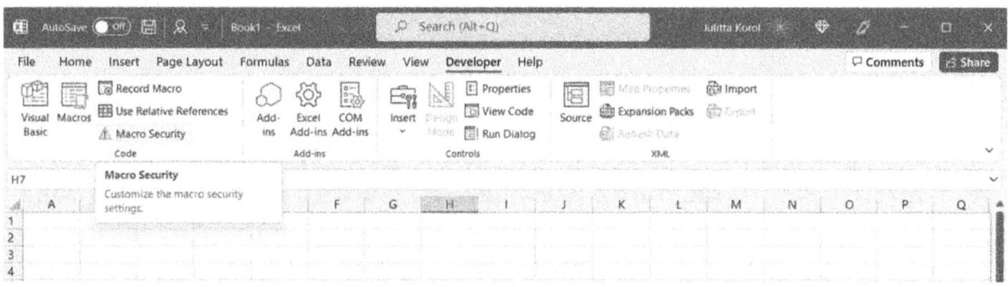

FIGURE 1.7 Use the Macro Security button in the Code group on the Developer tab to customize the macro security settings.

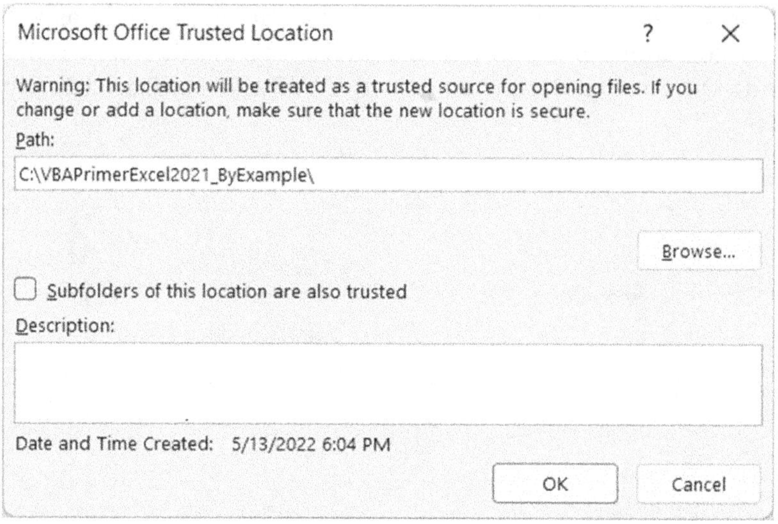

Microsoft Office Trusted Location

Warning: This location will be treated as a trusted source for opening files. If you change or add a location, make sure that the new location is secure.

Path:

C:\VBAPrimerExcel2021_ByExample\

Browse...

Subfolders of this location are also trusted

Description:

Date and Time Created: 5/13/2022 6:04 PM

OK Cancel

FIGURE 1.8 Designating a Trusted Location folder for this book's programming examples.

USING THE BUILT-IN MACRO RECORDER

In this section, we will go through the process of recording several short macros that perform data entry and formatting tasks in an Excel worksheet. You will learn how to plan your macros, record your keystrokes, edit, and improve your recorded macro code, run your macros, and learn basic troubleshooting techniques that will get you back on track in case you encounter errors while running your macros. You will also learn how to save your macros, rename them, combine them, and print them.

Planning a Macro

Before you create a macro, take a few minutes to consider what you want to do. The easiest way to plan your macro is to manually perform all the actions that the macro needs to do. As you enter the keystrokes, write them down on a piece of paper exactly as they occur. Don't leave anything out. Like a voice recorder, Excel's macro recorder records every action you perform. If you do not plan your macro prior to recording, you may end up with unnecessary actions that will not only slow it down but also require more editing later to make it work as intended. Although it's easier to edit a macro than it is to erase unwanted passages from a voice recording, performing only the actions you want recorded will save you editing time and trouble later.

Suppose you are asked to programmatically create the worksheet depicted in Figure 1.9. No worries. Getting started is very easy with the macro recorder. Let's begin by identifying the tasks required to complete this worksheet.

Task 1	Insert a new sheet into a workbook and name it Employee Wages.
Task 2	Enter column headings into first row of the worksheet and apply required formatting (column size, font styles).
Task 3	Enter employee data (Full Name, Hourly Rate, Hours Worked).
Tasks 4 and 5	Enter formulas to fill in the employee First and Last Name columns.
Task 6	Enter formulas to calculate employee total wages.
Task 7	Apply formatting to the completed worksheet.

Instead of recording one macro to complete your assignment, you will create a separate macro for each task. This approach will give you a chance to learn how to combine code from several simpler macros and how to create a master macro. Let's get started.

	A	B	C	D	E	F	G
1	Employee Name	First Name	Last Name	Hourly Rate	Hours Worked	Total Wages	
2	James Rogers	James	Rogers	15	7	$105.00	
3	Martha Lambert	Martha	Lambert	13.4	6	$80.40	
4	Eugene Zelnik	Eugene	Zelnik	21.42	10	$214.20	
5	Enrique Martinez	Enrique	Martinez	16.5	11	$181.50	
6	Wanda Pasterniak	Wanda	Pasterniak	35	21	$735.00	
7	Bruce Smith	Bruce	Smith	28.33	14	$396.62	
8							

FIGURE 1.9 A sample worksheet to be created and formatted with the help of the Excel built-in macro recorder.

Hands-On 1.2 Getting Things Ready for Macro Recording

1. Open a new workbook and save it as **Chap01_ExcelPrimer.xlsm** in your trusted **VBAPrimerExcel2021_ByExample** folder. You must save the file in the macro-enabled file format (.xlsm) to allow for storing macros. Keep this file open as you will use it to record all the macros in this chapter.

Recording a Macro

Before you record a macro, you need to decide whether you want to record the positioning of the active cell. If you want the macro to always start in a specific location on the worksheet, turn on the macro recorder first and then select the cell you want to start in. If the location of the active cell does not matter, select a single cell first and then turn on the macro recorder.

Hands-On 1.3 Inserting and Naming a Worksheet (Macro Task 1)

1. Choose **Developer | Record Macro.**
2. In the Record Macro dialog box, enter the name **Insert_NewSheet** for the macro, as shown in Figure 1.10. Do not dismiss this dialog box until you are instructed to do so.

SIDEBAR *Macro Names*

If you forget to enter a name for the macro, Excel assigns a default name, such as *Macro1*, *Macro2*, and so on. Macro names can contain letters, numbers, and the underscore character, but the first character must be a letter. For example, *Report1* is a correct macro name, while *1Report* is not. Spaces are not allowed. If you want a space between the words, use the underscore.

3. Select **This Workbook** in the **Store macro in** list box.

SIDEBAR *Storing Macros*

Excel allows you to store macros in three locations:

- Personal Macro Workbook—Macros stored in this location will be available each time you work with Excel. You can find the Personal Macro Workbook in the XLStart folder. If this workbook doesn't already exist, Excel creates it the first time you select this option.
- New Workbook—Excel will place the macro in a new workbook.
- This Workbook—The macro will be stored in the workbook you are currently using.

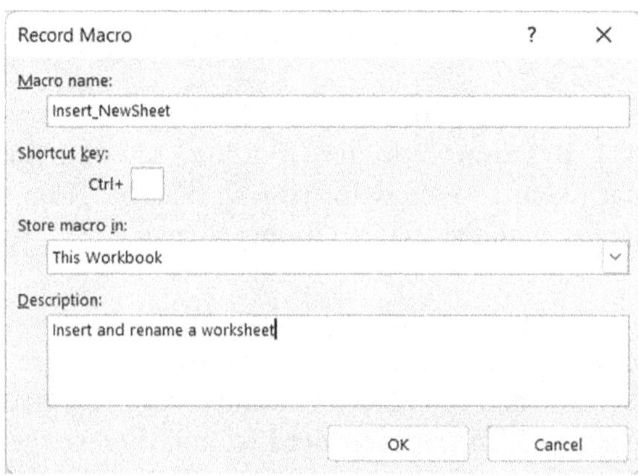

FIGURE 1.10 When you record a new macro, you must name it. In the Record Macro dialog box, you can also supply a shortcut key, a storage location, and a description for your macro.

4. In the Description box, enter the following text: **Insert and rename a worksheet**.
5. Choose **OK** to close the Record Macro dialog box.
   The Stop Recording button shown in Figure 1.11 appears in the status bar. Do not click this button until you are instructed to do so. When this button appears in the status bar, the workbook is in the recording mode.

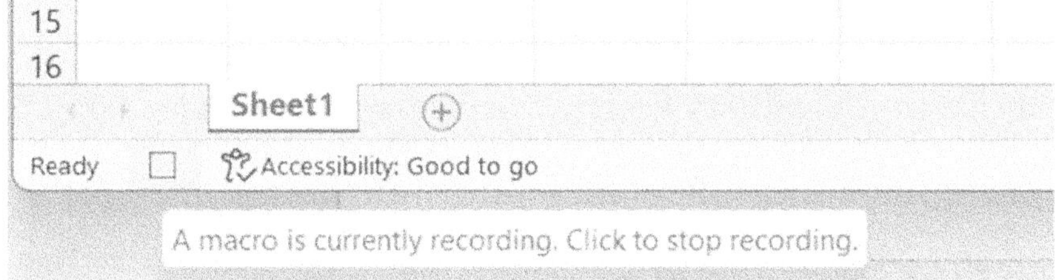

FIGURE 1.11 The Stop Recording button in the status bar indicates that the macro recording mode is active.

   The Stop Recording button remains in the status bar while you record your macro. Only the actions finalized by pressing Enter or clicking OK are recorded. If you press the Esc key or click Cancel before completing the entry, the macro recorder does not record that action.
6. Add a new sheet to the current workbook. You can do this by either right clicking the Sheet1 tab and choosing **Insert | Worksheet | OK**, or simply clicking the plus button to the right of the Sheet1 tab.
7. Rename the new sheet **Employee Wages**.
8. Click the **Stop Recording** button in the status bar as shown in Figure 1.11 or choose **View | Macros | Stop Recording**. When you stop the macro recorder, the status bar displays a button that allows you to record another macro (see Figure 1.12).

FIGURE 1.12 Excel status bar with the macro recording button turned off.

You have now recorded your first macro. Excel has written all the necessary statements to execute the actions you performed. Let's continue recording all the remaining actions to complete the tasks that we defined earlier. After that you will have a chance to review the recorded macro code and try out your macros.

Hands-On 1.4 Inserting Column Headings and Applying Formatting (Macro Task 2)

1. Choose **View | Macros | Record Macro** (or you may click the **Begin recording** button located in the status bar).
2. Enter **Insert_Headings** as the name for your macro.
3. Ensure that **This Workbook** is selected in the **Store macro in** list box.
4. Click **OK**.
   Excel turns on the macro recorder. All your Excel actions from now on are being recorded.
5. Select **cell A1** and enter the first heading: **Employee Name**.
6. Move to cell **B1** and enter: **First Name**.
7. Enter the remaining headings in cells **C1: F1** (**Last Name, Hourly Rate, Hours Worked, Total Wages**).
8. Select **A1:F1** and apply the bold formatting to the selection by pressing the **B** button in the Font group of the Ribbon's Home tab.
9. With the range **A1:F1** still selected, choose **Home | Cells | Format | Autofit Column Width**.
10. Click the **Stop Recording** button in the status bar as shown in Figure 1.11 or choose **View | Macros | Stop Recording**.
11. You have just recorded your second macro. The Employee Wages worksheet should now have the required headings in Row 1.

SIDEBAR ***Using Relative or Absolute References in Macros***

The Excel macro recorder can record your actions using absolute or relative cell references (see Figure 1.13).

- To have your macro execute the recorded action in a specific cell, no matter what cell is selected during the execution of the macro, use absolute cell addressing. Absolute cell references have the following form: $A$1, $C$5, etc. By default, the Excel macro recorder uses absolute references. Before you begin to record a new macro, make sure the Use Relative References option is not selected when you click the Macros button as shown in Figure 1.13.
- To have your macro perform the action in any cell, be sure to select the Use Relative References option before you choose the Record Macro op-

tion. Relative cell references have the following form: A1, C5, etc. The Excel macro recorder will continue to use relative cell references until you exit Microsoft Excel or click the Use Relative References option again.

- During the process of recording your macro, you may use both methods of cell addressing. For example, you may select a specific cell (e.g., $A$4), perform an action, and then choose another cell relative to the selected cell (e.g., C9, which is located five rows down and two columns to the right of the currently active cell $A$4). Relative references automatically adjust when you copy them, and absolute references don't.

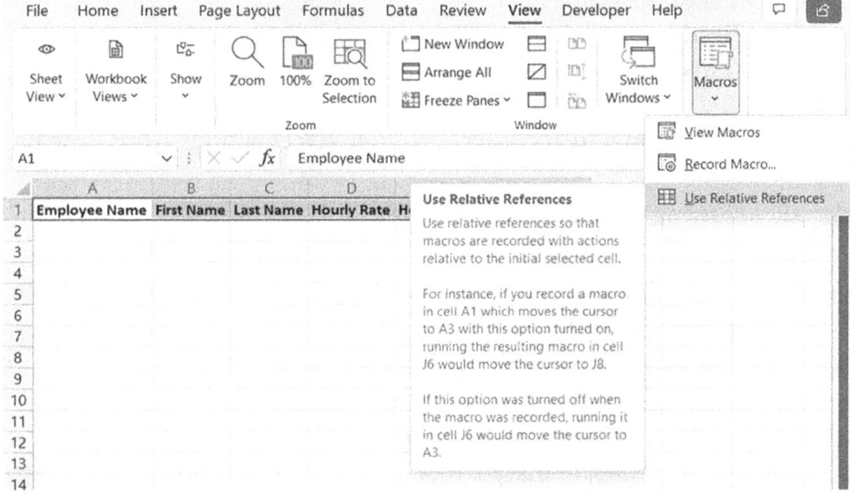

FIGURE 1.13 Excel macro recorder can record your actions using absolute or relative cell references. To make your selection, use the Macros drop-down on the Ribbon's View tab.

Hands-On 1.5 Entering Employee Data (Macro Task 3)

1. Choose **View | Macros | Record Macro** (or you may click the **Begin recording** button located in the status bar).
2. Enter **Insert_EmployeeData** as the name for your macro.
3. Ensure that **This Workbook** is selected in the **Store macro in** list box.
4. Click **OK**.
   Excel turns on the macro recorder. All your Excel actions from now on are being recorded.
5. Enter employee data in columns **A**, **D**, and **E** as shown in Figure 1.9.
   Leave the First Name, Last Name, and Total Wages columns blank as they will be filled in later.

6. Click the **Stop Recording** button in the status bar as shown in Figure 1.11 or choose **View | Macros | Stop Recording**.
   You have just recorded the third macro. The static data entry has been completed. We will now proceed to record macros that use formulas to fill the remaining columns of the worksheet.

Hands-On 1.6 Entering Formulas to Fill in Employee First Name (Macro Task 4)

1. Choose **View | Macros | Record Macro** (or you may click the **Begin recording** button, located in the status bar).
2. Enter **Get_FirstName** as the name for your macro.
3. Ensure that **This Workbook** is selected in the **Store macro in** list box.
4. Click **OK**.
   Excel turns on the macro recorder. All your Excel actions from now on are being recorded.
5. Enter the following formula in cell B2:
   ```
   =LEFT(A2,FIND(" ", A2)-1)
   ```
6. Copy the formula down to cells B3:B7 by dragging the selection handle in the bottom right corner of cell B2.
   Excel fills in the first names of all employees.
7. Click the **Stop Recording** button in the status bar as shown in Figure 1.11 or choose **View | Macros | Stop Recording**.
   You have just recorded a macro that makes use of a formula to retrieve employee first names from their full name. The next macro will populate the last name column using another formula.

Hands-On 1.7 Entering Formulas to Fill in Employee Last Name (Macro Task 5)

1. Choose **View | Macros | Record Macro** (or you may click the **Begin recording** button located in the status bar).
2. Enter **Get_LastName** as the name for your macro.
3. Ensure that **This Workbook** is selected in the **Store macro in** list box.
4. Click **OK**.
   Excel turns on the macro recorder. All your Excel actions from now on are being recorded.
5. Enter the following formula in cell **C2**:
   ```
   =RIGHT(A2,LEN(A2)-FIND(" ", A2))
   ```

6. Copy the formula down to cells **C3:C7** by dragging the selection handle in the bottom right corner of cell C2.
   Excel fills in the last names of all employees.
7. Click the **Stop Recording** button in the status bar as shown in Figure 1.11 or choose **View | Macros | Stop Recording**.
   You have just recorded a macro that makes use of a formula to retrieve employee last names from their full name. We have one more column to fill in before we can apply the final formatting to this worksheet.

Hands-On 1.8 Entering Formulas to Calculate Employee Total Wages (Macro Task 6)

1. Choose **View | Macros | Record Macro** (or you may click the **Begin recording** button located in the status bar).
2. Enter **CalculateWages** as the name for your macro.
3. Ensure that **This Workbook** is selected in the **Store macro in** list box.
4. Click **OK**.
   Excel turns on the macro recorder. All your Excel actions from now on are being recorded.
5. Select cells **F2:F7** and type the formula shown here. Press **Ctrl+Ent**er to ensure that formula is entered into the selected range F2:F7.

```
=D2*E2
```

6. Apply Currency format to cells **F2:F7**.
7. Click the **Stop Recording** button in the status bar as shown in Figure 1.11 or choose **View | Macros | Stop Recording**.
   In the next macro you will complete the worksheet by applying desired formatting.

Hands-On 1.9 Applying Table Format (Macro Task 7)

1. Choose **View | Macros | Record Macro** (or you may click the **Begin recording** button located in the status bar).
2. Enter **FormatTable** as the name for your macro.
3. Ensure that **This Workbook** is selected in the **Store macro in** list box.
4. Click **OK**.
   Excel turns on the macro recorder. All your Excel actions from now on are being recorded.

5. Select all data in the Employee Wages worksheet and choose **Home | Styles | Format as a Table**. Select any of the predefined table styles from the drop-down.
6. Select cell **A1**.
7. Click the **Stop Recording** button in the status bar as shown in Figure 1.11 or choose **View | Macros | Stop Recording**.
   You have now completed recording a set of macros that create and format a worksheet. Now that Excel has given us some code to work with, let's locate and examine it.

Editing Recorded Macros

Before you can modify your macro, you must find the location where the macro recorder placed its code. As you recall, when you turned on the macro recorder, you selected `ThisWorkbook` for the location. To find the location of your macros, you will use the Macro dialog box as instructed in Hands-On 1.10.

Hands-On 1.10 Examining the Macro Code

1. Choose **View | Macros | View Macros**.
   You should see all seven macros you recorded earlier (see Figure 1.14).

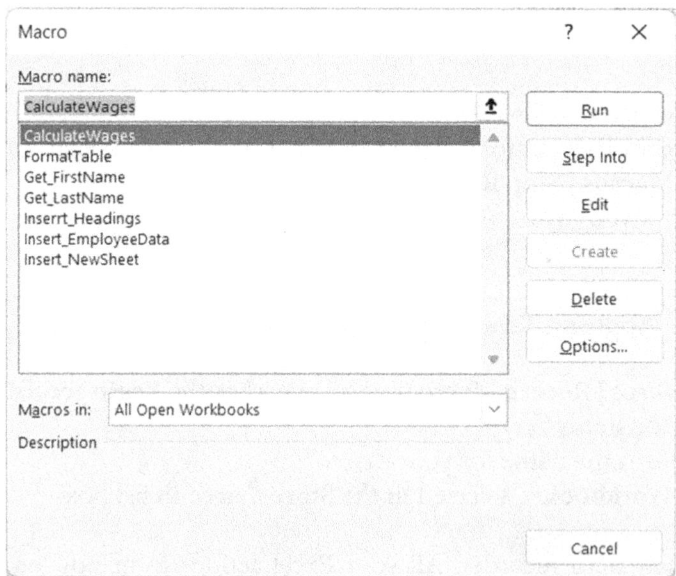

FIGURE 1.14 In the Macro dialog box, you can select a macro to run, debug (Step Into), edit, or delete. You can also set macro options.

2. Select the **Insert_NewSheet** macro name and click the **Edit** button.
   Excel opens a special window called Visual Basic Editor (also known as VBE), as shown in Figure 1.15. This window is your VBA programming environment. Using the keyboard shortcut Alt+F11, you can quickly switch between the Microsoft Excel application window and the Visual Basic Editor window. Now take a moment and try switching between both windows. When you are done, ensure that you are back in the VBE window.
3. Close the Visual Basic Editor window by using the key combination **Alt+Q** or choosing **File | Close and Return to Microsoft Excel.**
   Don't worry if the Visual Basic Editor window seems a bit confusing right now. As you work with the recorded macros and start writing your own VBA procedures from scratch, you will become familiar with all the elements of this screen.
4. In the Microsoft Excel application window, choose **Developer | Visual Basic** to switch again to the programming environment.

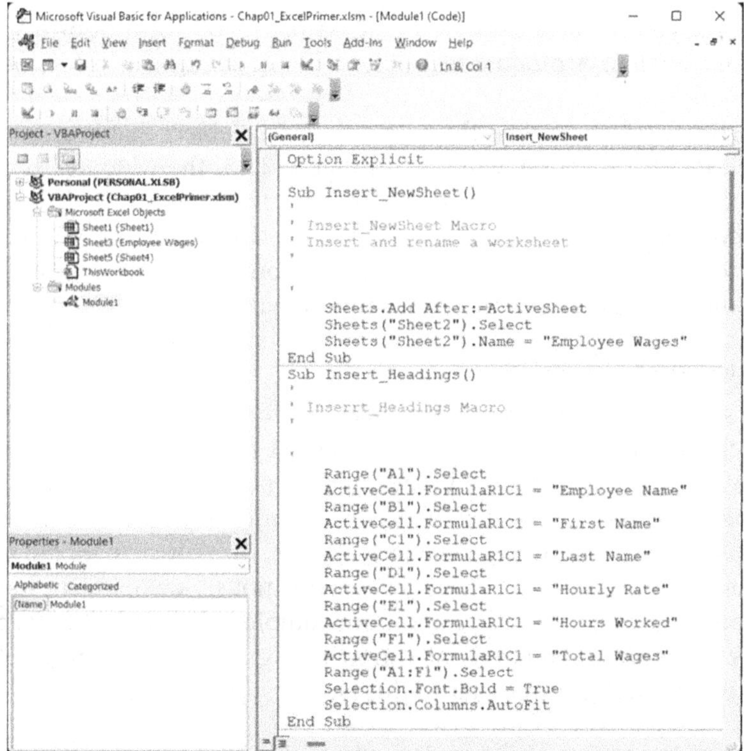

FIGURE 1.15 The Visual Basic Editor window is used for editing macros as well as writing new procedures in the Visual Basic for Applications language.

Notice the menu bar and toolbar in the Visual Basic Editor window look different than those in the Microsoft Excel window. As you can see, there is no Ribbon interface. The Visual Basic Editor uses the old Excel style menu bar and toolbar, which provide tools required for programming and testing your recorded macros as well as VBA procedures that you can write from scratch. As you work through the individual chapters of this book, you will feel very comfortable in using these tools.

The main part of the Visual Basic Editor window is a docking surface for various windows that you will find extremely useful while creating and testing your VBA procedures.

In Figure 1.15, you can see three windows that are docked in the Visual Basic Editor window: the Project Explorer window, the Properties window, and the Code window.

The Project Explorer window that appears in the left panel, shows an open Modules folder. Excel records your macro actions in special worksheets called Module1, Module2, and so on. These modules are stored in the Modules folder. Later in this book, you will also use modules to write the code of your own VBA procedures from scratch. A module resembles a blank document in Microsoft Word.

The Properties window displays the properties of the object that is currently selected in the Project Explorer window. In Figure 1.15, the Module1 object is selected in the Project - VBAProject window, and therefore the Properties - Module1 window displays the properties of Module1. Notice that the only available property for the module is the Name property. You can use this property to change the name of Module1 to a more meaningful name.

SIDEBAR ***Macro or Procedure?***

A macro is a series of commands or functions recorded with the help of a built-in macro recorder or entered manually in a Visual Basic module. The term "macro" is often replaced with the broader term "procedure." Although the words can be used interchangeably, many programmers prefer "procedure." While macros allow you to mimic keyboard actions, true procedures can also execute actions that cannot be performed using the mouse, keyboard, or menu options. In other words, procedures are more complex macros that incorporate language structures found in the traditional programming languages. You will learn about these structures later in this book.

The Module1 (Code) window displays the code of all macros you recorded earlier. Note that the following code may not exactly match the code in your Code window. Excel records all actions while the recorder is on, so you may see more, or fewer statements recorded.

```
Sub Insert_NewSheet()
'
' Insert_NewSheet Macro
' Insert and rename a worksheet
'

'
    Sheets.Add After:=ActiveSheet
    Sheets("Sheet2").Select
    Sheets("Sheet2").Name = "Employee Wages"
End Sub
Sub Insert_Headings()
'
' Insert_Headings Macro
'

'
    Range("A1").Select
    ActiveCell.FormulaR1C1 = "Employee Name"
    Range("B1").Select
    ActiveCell.FormulaR1C1 = "First Name"
    Range("C1").Select
    ActiveCell.FormulaR1C1 = "Last Name"
    Range("D1").Select
    ActiveCell.FormulaR1C1 = "Hourly Rate"
    Range("E1").Select
    ActiveCell.FormulaR1C1 = "Hours Worked"
    Range("F1").Select
    ActiveCell.FormulaR1C1 = "Total Wages"
    Range("A1:F1").Select
    Selection.Font.Bold = True
    Selection.Columns.AutoFit
End Sub
Sub Insert_EmployeeData()
'
' Insert_EmployeeData Macro
'

'
    Range("A2").Select
    ActiveCell.FormulaR1C1 = "James Rogers"
    Range("D2").Select
    ActiveCell.FormulaR1C1 = "15"
```

```
    Range("E2").Select
    ActiveCell.FormulaR1C1 = "7"
    Range("A3").Select
    ActiveCell.FormulaR1C1 = "Martha Lambert"
    Range("D3").Select
    ActiveCell.FormulaR1C1 = "13.4"
    Range("E3").Select
    ActiveCell.FormulaR1C1 = "6"
    Range("A4").Select
    ActiveCell.FormulaR1C1 = "Eugene Zelnik"
    Range("D4").Select
    ActiveCell.FormulaR1C1 = "21.42"
    Range("E4").Select
    ActiveCell.FormulaR1C1 = "10"
    Range("A5").Select
    ActiveCell.FormulaR1C1 = "Enrique Martinez"
    Range("D5").Select
    ActiveCell.FormulaR1C1 = "16.5"
    Range("E5").Select
    ActiveCell.FormulaR1C1 = "11"
    Range("A6").Select
    ActiveCell.FormulaR1C1 = "Wanda Pasterniak"
    Range("D6").Select
    ActiveCell.FormulaR1C1 = "35"
    Range("E6").Select
    ActiveCell.FormulaR1C1 = "21"
    Range("A7").Select
    ActiveCell.FormulaR1C1 = "Bruce Smith"
    Range("D7").Select
    ActiveCell.FormulaR1C1 = "28.33"
    Range("E7").Select
    ActiveCell.FormulaR1C1 = "14"
    Range("A8").Select
End Sub
Sub Get_FirstName()
'
' Get_FirstName Macro
'

'
    Range("B2").Select
    ActiveCell.FormulaR1C1 = "=LEFT(RC[-1],FIND("" "", RC[-1])-1)"
    Range("B2").Select
    Selection.Copy
    Range("B3:B7").Select
    ActiveSheet.Paste
```

```
    Application.CutCopyMode = False
End Sub
Sub Get_LastName()
'
' Get_LastName Macro
'

'
    Range("C2").Select
    ActiveCell.FormulaR1C1 = "=RIGHT(RC[-2], LEN(RC[-2])-FIND(
      "" "", RC[-2]))"
    Range("C2").Select
    Selection.Copy
    Range("C3:C7").Select
    ActiveSheet.Paste
    Application.CutCopyMode = False
End Sub
Sub CalculateWages()
'
' CalculateWages Macro
'

'
    Range("F2").Select
    Application.CutCopyMode = False
    ActiveCell.FormulaR1C1 = "=RC[-2]*RC[-1]"
    Range("F2").Select
    Selection.AutoFill Destination:=Range("F2:F7"),
        Type:=xlFillDefault
    Range("F2:F7").Select
    Selection.NumberFormat = "$#,##0.00"
End Sub
Sub FormatTable()
'
' FormatTable Macro
'

'
    Range("A1:F7").Select
    Application.CutCopyMode = False
    ActiveSheet.ListObjects.Add(xlSrcRange,
      Range("$A$1:$F$7"), , xlYes).Name = _
        "Table1"
    Range("Table1[#All]").Select
```

```
    ActiveSheet.ListObjects("Table1").
      TableStyle = "TableStyleLight14"
    Range("Table1[[#Headers],[Employee Name]]").Select
End Sub
```

For now, let's focus on finding answers to two questions:

- How do you read the macro code?
- How can you edit macros?

Notice that each macro code you recorded is located between the `Sub` and `End Sub`. These words are known as keywords. You read the code line by line from top to bottom. You can edit the recorded macros by deleting or modifying existing code or typing new instructions in the Code window.

Macro Comments

Look at the recorded macro code. The lines that begin with a single quote denote comments. By default, comments appear in green. When the macro code is executed, Visual Basic ignores the comment lines. Comments are often placed within the macro code to document the meaning of certain lines that aren't obvious. Comments can also be used to temporarily disable certain blocks of code that you don't want to execute. This is often done while testing and troubleshooting your macros.

Let's add some comments to the CalculateWages macro to make the code easier to understand.

Hands-On 1.11 Adding Comments to the Macro Code

1. Make sure that the Visual Basic Editor screen shows the Code window with the CalculateWages macro.
2. Click after the `Range("F2:F7").Select` and press **Enter**.
3. In the empty line you just created, type the following comment. Be sure to start with a single quote.

   ```
   ' Apply Currency Format
   ```

4. Press **Ctrl+S** to save the changes in Chap01_ExcelPrimer.xlsm or choose **File | Save Chap01_ExcelPrimer.xlsm.**

All macro procedures begin with the keyword `Sub` and end with the keywords `End Sub`. The `Sub` keyword is followed by the macro name and a set of parentheses. Between the keywords `Sub` and `End Sub` are statements that Visual Basic executes each time you run your macro. Visual Basic reads the lines from top to bottom, ignoring the statements preceded with a single quote (see the information about comments) and stops when it reaches the keywords `End Sub`. Notice that the recorded macro contains many periods. The periods appear in almost every line of code and are used to join various elements of the Visual Basic for Applications language. How do you read the instructions written in this language? They are read from the right side of the last period to the left. Here are a few statements from the Insert_Headings macro and a description of what they mean:

Code Segment	Description
`Range("A1:F1").Select`	Select cells A1 to F1.
`Selection.Columns.AutoFit`	Extend the column width so that all entries fit.
`ActiveCell.FormulaR1C1 = "Hourly Rate"`	Let the formula of the active cell be "Hourly Rate."
`Selection.Font.Bold = True`	Applies bold format to all selected cells.

Cleaning Up the Macro Code

As you review and analyze your macro code line by line, you may notice that Excel recorded a lot of information that you didn't intend to include. For example, if you used the Font dialog box to apply bold formatting to the heading cells in your Insert_Headings macro, in addition to setting the font style to bold, Excel also recorded the current state of other options on the Font tab—strikethrough, superscript, subscript, outline font, shadow, underline, theme color, tint and shade, and theme font as shown below:

```
With Selection.Font
     .Name = "Calibri Light"
     .FontStyle = "Bold"
     .Size = 9
     .Strikethrough = False
     .Superscript = False
     .Subscript = False
     .OutlineFont = False
     .Shadow = False
     .Underline = xlUnderlineStyleNone
     .ThemeColor = xlThemeColorLight1
     .TintAndShade = 0
     .ThemeFont = xlThemeFontMajor
End With
```

When you use dialog boxes, Excel always records all the settings. These additional instructions make your macro code longer and more difficult to understand.

Therefore, when you finish recording your macro, it is a good idea to go over the recorded statements and delete the unnecessary lines of code. In the above code snippet, different font settings are applied to the selection of cells. This is done with the special block of code that begins with the keyword `With` and ends with the keyword `End With`. Assume you just wanted to change the font name, style, and size of the selected cells. In this case you can simply delete all the other settings that were recorded, and you are left with the following code:

```
With Selection.Font
     .Name = "Calibri Light"
     .FontStyle = "Bold"
     .Size = 9
End With
```

This makes your macro code easier to understand as only the settings you selected are shown.

Notice that each setting in the `With...End With` block begins with a period. If you wanted to list each setting separately you would write them as:

```
Selection.Font.Name = "Calibri Light"
Selection.Font.FontStyle = "Bold"
Selection.Font.Size = 9
```

Using the `With...End With` block, you simply write the repeating code once. Simply move the repeating code `Selection.Font` to the right of the `With` keyword and end the entire block with `End With`.

As you work more with Excel macro recorder and learn more about VBA statements you will be able to make your recorded macros much cleaner.

Running a Macro

You can run your macros from either the Microsoft Excel window or the Visual Basic Editor window. When you execute a macro from the VBE screen, Visual Basic executes the macro behind the scenes. You can't see when Visual Basic performed a specific action. To watch Visual Basic at work, you must run your macro from the Macro dialog box or arrange your screen in such a way that the Microsoft Excel and Visual Basic windows can be viewed at the same time. Two monitors attached to your computer will help you greatly in the development work when you need to observe actions performed by your code.

After you create a macro, you should run it at least once to make sure it works correctly. Later in this chapter you will learn other ways to run macros, but for now, let's use the Macro dialog box.

Hands-On 1.12 Running a Macro Using the Macro Dialog Box

1. Make sure that the Chap01_ExcelPrimer.xlsm workbook is open.
2. Delete the **Employee Wages** worksheet so we can start from scratch.
3. Choose **View | Macros | View Macros**.
4. In the Macro dialog box, click the **Insert_NewSheet** macro name.
5. Click **Run** to execute the macro.
   The Insert_NewSheet macro inserts a blank worksheet and renames it Employee Wages.
   Now, let's proceed to run the remaining macros. All macros should be run in the order they were recorded.
6. Choose **View | Macros | View Macros**.
7. In the Macro dialog box, click the **Insert_Headings** macro name.
8. Click **Run** to execute the macro.
9. Run the remaining macros: **Insert_EmployeeData**, **Get_FirstName**, **Get_LastName**, **CalculateWages**, and **FormatTable**.

After running all macros, you should see the completed and formatted Employee Wages worksheet.

Quite often, you will notice that your macro does not perform as expected the first time you run it. Perhaps during the macro recording you selected the wrong font or forgot to change the cell color or maybe you just realized it would be better to include an additional step. Don't panic. Excel makes it possible to modify the macro without forcing you to go through the tedious process of re-cording your keystrokes again.

Testing and Debugging a Macro

When you modify a recorded macro, it is quite possible that you will introduce some errors. For example, you may delete an important line of code, or you may inadvertently remove or omit a necessary period. To make sure that your macro continues to work correctly after your modifications, you need to run it again.

Hands-On 1.13 Running a Macro from the VBE Screen

1. In the Excel window, with the Employee Wages worksheet active, choose **Developer | Visual Basic**.
2. In the Visual Basic Editor Code window, place the pointer in any line of the **Insert_NewSheet** macro code (except for a comment line), and choose **Run | Run Sub/UserForm**.

You should see the Microosft Visual Basic error message dialog: *"Run-time error '9' Subscript out of range"* (see Figure 1.16). Visual Basic cannot find Sheet2 that the macro references, so it displays an error.

Before you run macros, you must make sure that your macro can run in the worksheet that is currently selected. Click the **End** button in the error dialog box, and make sure that you select the correct worksheet before you try to run the macro again. In this case, you should either delete the Employee Wages worksheet, or insert a new workbook and rerun the macro.

3. When running a macro from a VBE screen, to see the result of your macro, you must switch to the Microsoft Excel window. To do this, press **Alt+F11**. Various errors can popup during your macro execution. For example, if your macro code had a `With...End With` block and you happened to omit the period in `With Selection.Font`, Visual Basic will generate the "*Run time error '424' — Object required*" message when running this line of code. Instead of pressing the **End** button to end your macro, you can use the **Debug** button in the message box, so you can correct your macro code right away. When you press Debug, you will be placed in the Code window. At this time, Visual Basic will activate break mode and will use the yellow highlighter to indicate the line it had trouble executing. As soon as you correct your error, Visual Basic may announce, "*This action will reset your project, proceed anyway?*" Click **OK** to this message. Although you can edit code in break mode, some edits prevent continuing execution. After correcting the error, run the macro again, as there may be more errors to be fixed before the macro can run smoothly.
4. Switch back to the Visual Basic Editor screen by pressing **Alt+F11**.

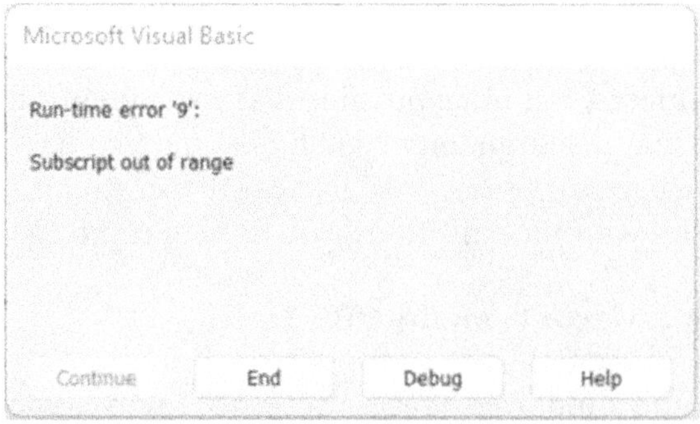

Microsoft Visual Basic

Run-time error '9':

Subscript out of range

Continue | End | Debug | Help

FIGURE 1.16 The Visual Basic Editor displays an error message when it encounters an error while executing a macro. The error may be caused by an incorrect statement or incorrect setup of worksheet environment prior to running a macro.

Saving and Renaming a Macro

The macros you recorded in this chapter are in a Microsoft Excel workbook. All macros are automatically saved when you save the workbook.

Hands-On 1.14 Saving Macros and Running Macros from Another Workbook

1. Close the **Chap01_ExcelPrimer.xlsm** workbook.
2. Open a brand-new workbook and press **Alt+F8** to open the Macro dialog box. Notice that there is no trace of your macros in the Macro dialog box. If you'd like to run the macros you recorded earlier in this chapter in another workbook, you need to open the file that stores these macros.
3. Close the Macro dialog box and save the open workbook file as **Chap01_ExcelPrimer2.xlsx** in your trusted **C:\VBAPrimerExcel2021_ByExample** folder. You will not have any macros in this workbook, so saving it in Excel's default file format will work just fine.
4. Open the **C:\VBAPrimerExcel2021_ByExample\Chap01_ExcelPrimer.xlsm** workbook file.
5. Activate **Sheet1** in the **Chap01_ExcelPrimer2.xlsx** workbook.
6. Press **Alt+F8** to activate the Macro dialog box. Notice that Excel displays macros in all open workbooks.
7. Run each of the macros listed in this dialog box in the order you have recorded them.
   Your macros go to work again. You should end up with the Employee Wages worksheet formatted to your liking.
8. Close the **Chap01_ExcelPrimer2.xlsx** workbook file. Do not save the changes. Do not close the Chap01_ExcelPrimer.xlsm workbook file. We will work with it in the next section.

When you add additional actions to your macro, you may want to change the macro name to better indicate its purpose. The name of the macro should communicate its function as clearly as possible. To change the macro name, you don't need to press a specific key. In the Code window, simply delete the old macro name and enter the new name following the `Sub` keyword.

Printing Macro Code

If you want to document your macro or perhaps study the macro code when you are away from the computer, you can print your macros. You can print the entire module sheet where your macro is stored or indicate a selection of lines to print. Let's print the entire module sheet that contains your macros.

Hands-On 1.15 Printing Macro Code

1. Switch to the Visual Basic Editor window and double-click **Module1** in the Project Explorer window to activate the module containing your macros.
2. Choose **File | Print**.
3. In the Print - VBAProject dialog box, the Current Module option button should be selected.
4. Click **OK** to print the entire module sheet.
   If you'd like to print only a certain block of programming code, perform the following steps:
5. In the module sheet, highlight the code you want to print.
6. Choose **File | Print**.
7. In the Print - VBAProject dialog box, the Selection option button should be selected.
8. Click **OK** to print the highlighted code.

IMPROVING YOUR RECORDED MACROS

After you record your macro, you may realize that you'd like the macro to perform additional tasks. Adding new instructions to the macro code is not very difficult if you are already familiar with the Visual Basic language. In most situations, however, you can do this more efficiently when you delegate the extra tasks to the macro recorder. You may argue that Excel records more instructions than are necessary. However, one thing is for sure—the macro recorder does not make mistakes. If you want to add additional instructions to your macro using the macro recorder, you must record a new macro, copy the sections you want, and paste them into the correct location in your original macro. Note that Microsoft Excel places the newly recorded macro in a new module sheet.

At times you may need to modify your macro code by removing some statements. Before you start deleting unnecessary lines of code, think of how you can use the comment feature that you've recently learned. You can comment out the unwanted lines and run the macro with the commented code. If the Visual Basic Editor does not generate errors, you can safely delete the commented lines. By following this path, you will never find yourself recording the same keystrokes more than once. And, if the macro does not perform correctly, you can remove the comments from the lines that may be needed after all.

When you create macros with the macro recorder, you can quickly learn the VBA equivalents for the Excel commands and dialog box settings. Then you can look up the meaning and the usage of these Visual Basic commands in the online help. It's obvious that the more instructions Visual Basic needs to read, the slower your macro will execute. Eliminating extraneous commands will speed up your macro. Learning the right word or expression in any language takes time. You'll learn about Visual Basic objects, properties, and methods in Chapter 3, "Excel VBA Fundamentals."

SideBar ***Including Additional Instructions***

To include additional instructions in the existing macro, add empty lines in the required places of the macro code by pressing Enter, and type in the necessary Visual Basic statements. If the additional instructions are keyboard actions or menu commands, you may use the macro recorder to generate the necessary code and then copy and paste these code lines into the original macro.

Want to add more improvements to your macro? How about a message to notify you when Visual Basic has finished executing the last macro line? This sort of action cannot be recorded, as Excel does not have a corresponding Ribbon command or shortcut menu option. However, using the Visual Basic for Applications language, you can add new instructions to your macro by hand. Let's see how this is done.

Hands-On 1.16 Adding Visual Basic Statements to the Recorded Macro Code

1. In the Code window containing the code of the **FormatTable** macro, click in front of the `End Sub` keywords and press **Enter**.
2. Place your cursor on the empty line and type the following statement:

```
MsgBox "Your worksheet is ready."
```

3. Press Ctrl+S to save the changes made in your macro code.

   When you run this macro next time around, you should see a message box with your programmed message text. You must click the OK button in the message box to discard this message. MsgBox is one of the most frequently used built-in VBA functions. You will learn more about its usage in Chapter 4, "Excel VBA Procedures."

CREATING A MASTER MACRO

In this chapter, you recorded several macros that required that you execute them in the order they were recorded. Instead of running your macros one by one, it is more convenient to have one master macro that will perform all the required tasks in the correct order. Let's see how this is done in the next Hands-On.

Hands-On 1.17 Creating a Master Macro Procedure

1. Switch to the Microsoft Visual Basic for Application window and select **VBAProject (Chap01_ExcelPrimer.xlsm)** in the Project Explorer window.
2. Choose **Insert | Module** to add a new module to the selected VBA project.
3. In the Properties window select **Module2** next to the (Name) property and rename it **MasterProcedure.**
4. In the Code window on your right, enter the following procedure:

```
Sub CreateEmployeeWorksheet()
    Insert_NewSheet
    Insert_Headings
    Insert_EmployeeData
    Get_FirstName
    Get_LastName
    CalculateWages
    FormatTable
End Sub
```

5. Press **Ctrl+S** to save the changes.
6. Choose **File | Close and Return to Microsoft Excel.**
7. In the Microsoft Excel window, choose **File | New | Blank workbook.**
8. Choose **View | Macros | View Macros** to display the Macro dialog box.
9. Select the **CreateEmployeeWorksheet** macro name and click **Run.**
   Excel runs your code and displays a message box that you added in the previous Hands-On.
10. Click **OK** to dismiss the message box.
11. Close the Excel workbook you just created without saving it.
    In this Hands-On you learned how easy it is to combine stand-alone macros into a master macro. All you need to do is list the macro names on separate lines between the `Sub` and `End Sub` keywords and name your macro. You could also copy all the code of the recorded macros into a new macro; however, this will make the macro code more difficult to troubleshoot. It is much easier to

understand and work with shorter macros. When referencing macro names in other macros any misspelling of a macro name will cause a compile error *"Sub or Function not defined"* when you attempt to run your macro.

In Chapter 9 of this book, you will learn about different types of errors and techniques that will allow you to test your macros using Excel built-in tools.

VARIOUS METHODS OF RUNNING MACROS

So far in this chapter, you have learned a couple of methods of running macros. You already know that you can run a macro from the VBE screen or a Macro dialog box in the Microsoft Excel application window.

In the VBE screen you can run your macro / Visual Basic code in one of the following ways:

- Press F5 on the keyboard
- Choose Run | Run Sub/UserForm
- Choose Tools | Macros
- Click the Run Sub/UserForm (F5) button on the Standard toolbar as shown in Figure 1.17.

In this section, you will learn three cool methods of macro execution that will allow you to run your macros using a keyboard shortcut, toolbar button, or worksheet button. Let's get started.

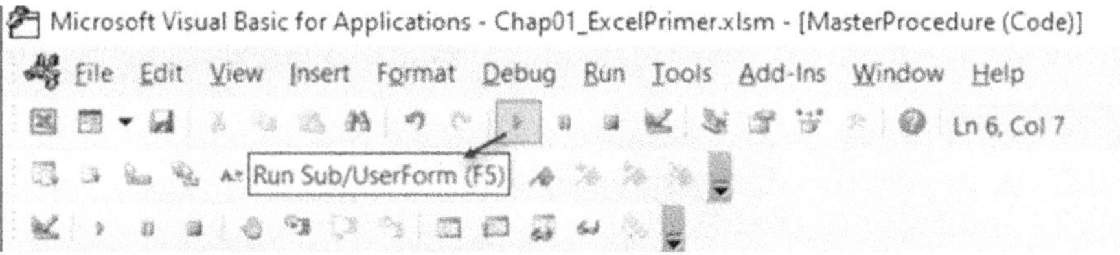

FIGURE 1.17 The Visual Basic code can also be run from the toolbar button.

Running the Macro Using a Keyboard Shortcut

A popular method to run a macro is by using an assigned keyboard shortcut. It is much faster to press Ctrl+Shift+I than it is to activate the macro from the Macro dialog box. Before you can use the keyboard shortcut, you must assign it to your macro. Let's learn how this is done.

Hands-On 1.18 Assigning a Macro to a Keyboard Shortcut

1. In the Excel application window, press **Alt+F8** to open the Macro dialog box.
2. In the list of macros, click the **CreateEmployeeWorksheet** macro, and then choose the **Options** button.
3. When the Macro Options dialog box appears, the cursor is in the Shortcut key text box.
4. Hold down the **Shift** key and press the letter **I** on the keyboard. Excel records the keyboard combination as Ctrl+Shift+I. The result is shown in Figure 1.18.

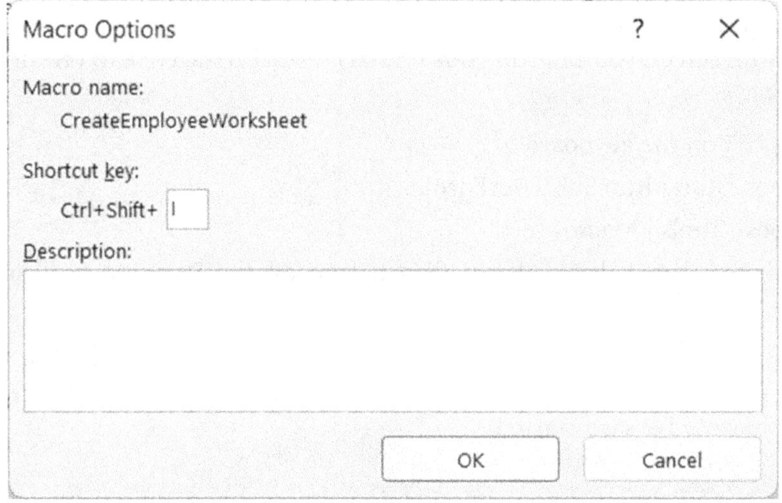

FIGURE 1.18 Using the Macro Options dialog box, you can assign a keyboard shortcut for running a macro.

5. Click **OK** to close the Macro Options dialog box.
6. Click **Cancel** to close the Macro dialog box and return to the worksheet.
7. To run your macro using the newly assigned keyboard shortcut, open a new workbook and press **Ctrl+Shift+I.**

   Your macro goes to work, and your worksheet is ready to use.
8. Close the workbook with the employee worksheet you just created without saving it.

SIDEBAR ***Avoid Shortcut Conflicts***

If you assign to your macro a keyboard shortcut that conflicts with a Microsoft Excel built-in shortcut, Excel will run your macro if the workbook containing the macro code is currently open.

Running the Macro from the Quick Access Toolbar

You can add your own buttons to the built-in Quick Access toolbar. Let's see how it is done to run a macro from Excel.

Hands-On 1.19 Running a Macro from the Quick Access Toolbar

1. In the Microsoft Excel window, click the **Customize Quick Access Toolbar** button (the downward-pointing arrow in the title bar) and choose **More Commands** as shown in Figure 1.19.

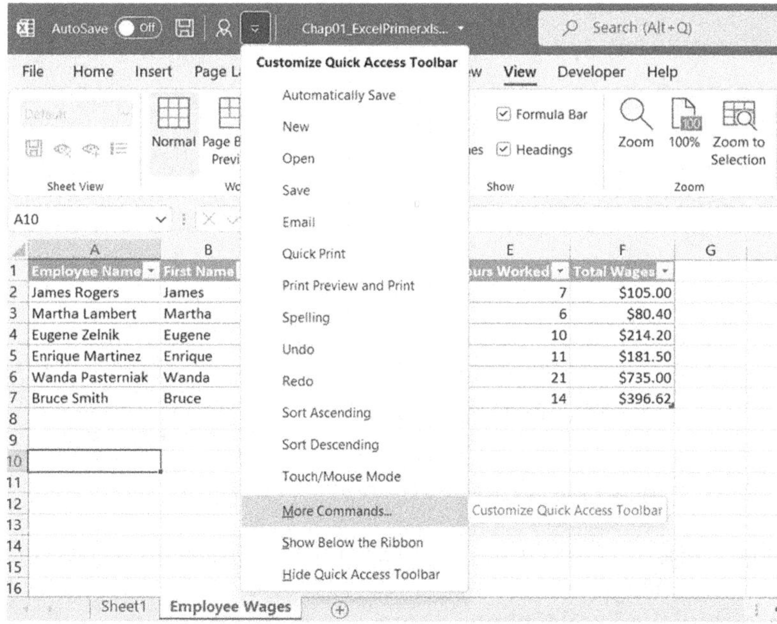

FIGURE 1.19 Adding a new button to the Quick Access toolbar (Step 1).

The Excel Options dialog box appears with the page titled Customize the Quick Access Toolbar.

2. In the Choose commands from drop-down list box, select **Macros.**
3. Select **CreateEmployeeWorksheet** in the list box on the left-hand side.
4. Click the **Add** button to move the CreateEmployeeWorksheet macro to the list box on the right-hand side.
   The current selections are shown in Figure 1.20.
5. To change the button image for your macro, click the **Modify** button.
6. In the button gallery, select any button you like and click **OK.**

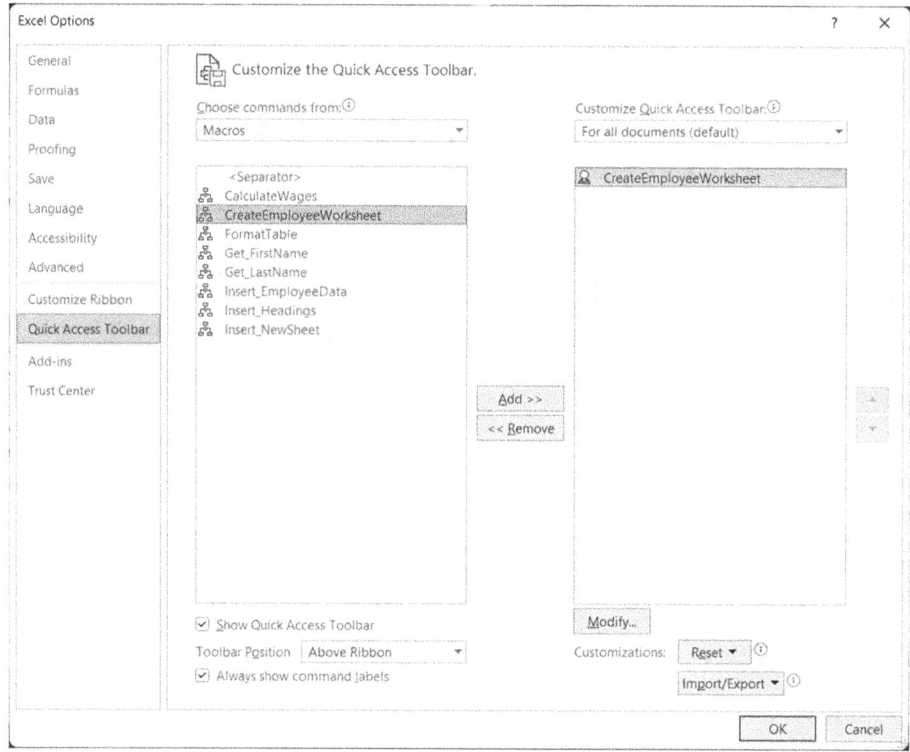

FIGURE 1.20 Adding a new button to the Quick Access toolbar (Step 2).

7. After closing the gallery window, make sure that the image to the left of the macro name has changed.
8. Click **OK** to close the Excel Options dialog.
   You should now see a new button on the Quick Access toolbar as shown in Figure 1.21. This button will be available for any open workbook.

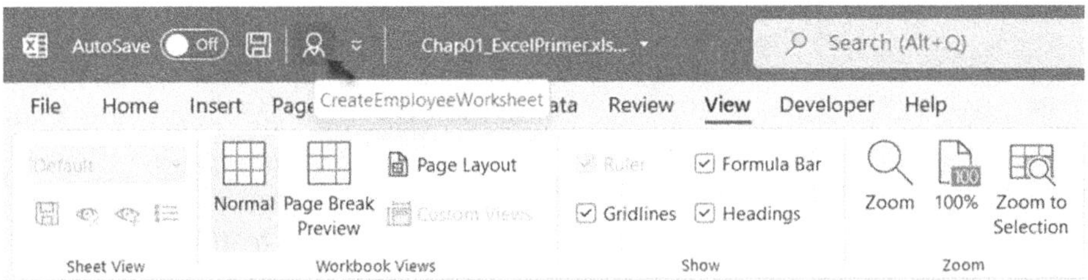

FIGURE 1.21 A custom button placed on the Quick Access toolbar will run the specified macro (Step 3).

9. Click the macro button you've just added to run the macro assigned to it. Again, your macro goes to work; however, this time it runs into a problem. Recall that previously before you ran it you opened a new blank workbook. To run this macro from any workbook, you need to modify it.
10. Click the **End** button in the error dialog box.
11. Switch to the Visual Basic Editor screen and modify the **Insert_NewSheet** macro as shown in Figure 1.22.

```
Sub Insert_NewSheet()
'
' Insert_NewSheet Macro
' Insert and rename a worksheet
'

'
    Sheets.Add After:=ActiveSheet
    ActiveSheet.Name = Application.InputBox("Enter the name for your worksheet:", "Rename This Sheet")

End Sub
```

FIGURE 1.22 The recorded Insert_NewSheet macro was modified to correct issues encountered during its execution.

To allow the user to name the sheet during the macro execution you can use the Excel InputBox method discussed in detail in Chapter 4.

12. Save the workbook and return to the Microsoft Excel window.
13. Click the macro button on the Quick Access toolbar (see Figure 1.21).
    Excel adds a new worksheet to the active workbook and prompts you for the name of the worksheet.
14. Enter any name for the newly created worksheet and click **OK**.

NOTE	*If you clicked the Cancel button instead of typing in the name for the worksheet, Visual Basic will run into an issue and you will see the Application-defined or object-defined run time error 1004. Click End to close the error message and you will be returned to the Microsoft Excel application window. Manually delete the empty sheet that was added to the workbook and execute the macro again this time entering the name for the sheet when prompted. You will learn how to handle the Cancel button in Chapter 9.* *After you supply the worksheet name, the Visual Basic continues to execute the remaining macros in your master procedure. The execution fails again when the program reaches the FormatTable procedure. What's wrong with this macro code? It worked perfectly well when you recorded it. Oftentimes issues with recorded code arise with the named ranges. A line of the FormatTable procedure assigns the name 'Table1' to the table range. Because you are running the master procedure inside the workbook where the 'Table1' name already exists, the Visual Basic throws the error – "Select method of range class failed". Table names within the workbook must be unique. For your code to run correctly you must revise the FormatTable procedure.*

15. Click the **Debug** button in the error message dialog and Visual Basic will highlight the line of code it cannot execute.
16. Exit the break mode by choosing **Run | Reset.**
17. Modify the **FormatTable** procedure as shown in Figure 1.23.

```
Sub FormatTable()
'
' FormatTable Revised Macro
'

'
Dim strTableName As String
strTableName = InputBox("Enter the name for your table:", "Name your table range")


    ActiveSheet.ListObjects.Add(xlSrcRange, Range("$A$1:$F$7"), , xlYes).Name = strTableName
    ActiveSheet.ListObjects(strTableName).TableStyle = "TableStyleLight14"
    Range("A1").Select
    MsgBox "Your worksheet is ready."
End Sub
```

FIGURE 1.23 The recorded macro FormatTable was modified to correct issues encountered during its execution.

The first line of code in the revised procedure declares *strTableName* variable to hold the name of the table supplied by the InputBox function on the next line.

You will learn about variables and their types, declarations, and assignments in Chapter 3. The third line creates a new list object and assigns it a name stored in the *strTableName* variable. Every time you run the procedure and are prompted for a table name you must enter a unique name.

After adding and assigning a name to the table object, the macro again refers to the *strTableName* variable to assign a predefined formatting style to the table. The procedure then selects cell A1 in the active worksheet and displays a message to the user.

18. After making changes to the **FormatTable** procedure save your code and return to the Microsoft Excel application window.
19. Run the procedure again by clicking the button on the Quick Access toolbar.
    The master procedure should now run as expected.

Running the Macro from a Worksheet Button

Sometimes it makes the most sense to place a macro button right on the worksheet, where it cannot be missed. Let's go over the steps that will attach the WhatsInACell macro to a worksheet button.

Hands-On 1.20 Running a Macro from a Button Placed on a Worksheet

1. Copy **Chap01_Supplement.xlsm** workbook from the companion files to your **C:\VBAPrimerExcel2021_ByExample** folder.
2. Open the copied workbook file in Excel.
3. Choose **Developer | Insert**. The Forms toolbar appears, as shown in Figure 1.24.

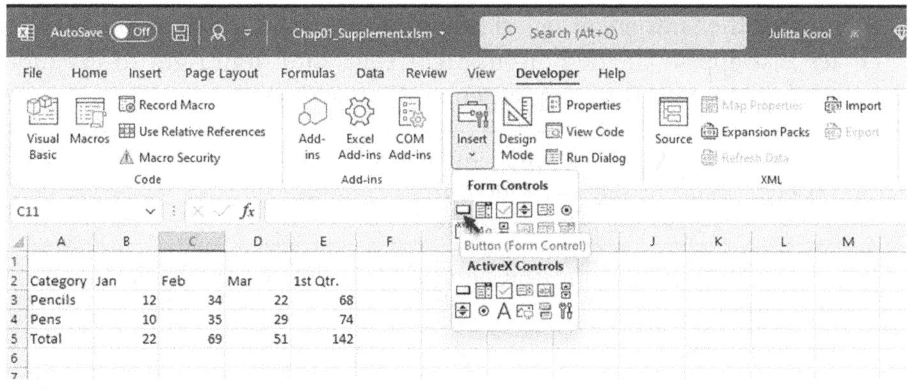

FIGURE 1.24 Adding a button to a worksheet.

4. In the Form Controls area, click the first image, which represents a button.
5. Click anywhere in the empty area of the worksheet. When the Assign Macro dialog box appears, choose the **WhatsInACell** macro and click **OK**.
6. Excel creates a button with the default label 'Button 1'. To change the button's label, click inside the button, delete the default text and type **Format Cells**. If the text does not fit, do not worry; you will resize the button in Step 7. When the button is selected, it looks like the one shown in Figure 1.25. If the selection handles are not displayed, right-click **Button 1** on the worksheet and choose **Edit Text** on the shortcut menu. Select the default text and enter the new label.

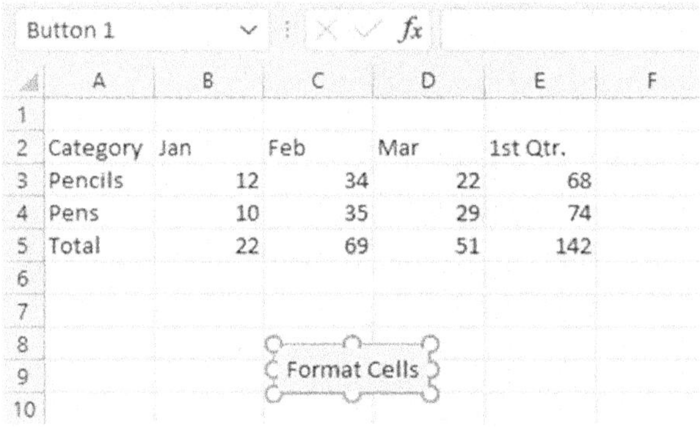

Button 1

	A	B	C	D	E	F
1						
2	Category	Jan	Feb	Mar	1st Qtr.	
3	Pencils	12	34	22	68	
4	Pens	10	35	29	74	
5	Total	22	69	51	142	
6						
7						
8						
9			Format Cells			
10						

FIGURE 1.25 A button with an attached macro.

7. When you're done renaming the button, click outside the button to exit the edit mode.
   Because the text you entered is longer than the default button text, let's resize the button so that the entire text is visible.
8. Right-click the button you've just renamed to select it, point to one of the tiny circles that appear in the button's right edge, and drag right to expand the button until you see the complete entry, Format Cells.

NOTE	*If you left click the button inadvertently, there is nothing you can do to stop the macro from running. You can resize the button after the macro has run.*

9. When you're done resizing the button, click outside the button to exit the selection mode.

10. To run your macro, click the button you just created.
    Your macro goes to work, and your worksheet is now formatted as shown in Figure 1.26.

FIGURE 1.26 The worksheet was formatted with a macro attached to the Format Cells button.

Let's remove the formatting you just applied by running the RemoveFormats macro.

11. Press **Alt+F8** to open the Macro dialog box. Select the **RemoveFormats** macro and click the **Run** button.
12. On your own, create another button on this worksheet that will be used for running the RemoveFormats macro.
13. Save your workbook with a different file name so that the original workbook can be reused again in case you'd like to revisit the button creation process.

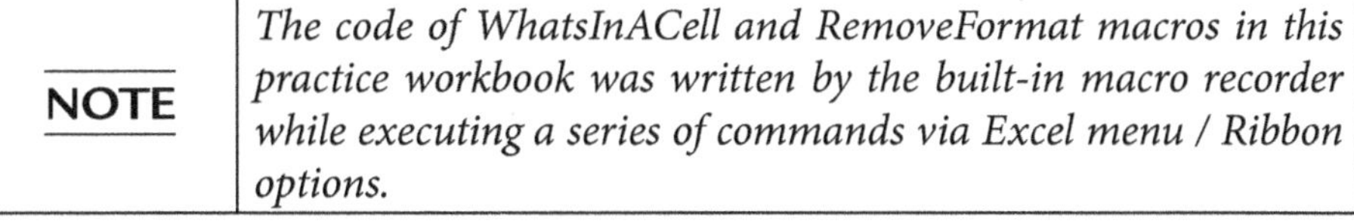

NOTE	*The code of WhatsInACell and RemoveFormat macros in this practice workbook was written by the built-in macro recorder while executing a series of commands via Excel menu / Ribbon options.*

You can also run macros from a hyperlink, or a button placed in the Ribbon. These techniques are not introduced in this book because they require the understanding of the advanced topic of Ribbon Customizations.

SUMMARY

In this chapter, you have learned how to create macros by recording your selections in the Microsoft Excel application window. You also learned how to view, read, and modify the recorded macros in the Visual Basic Editor window. In addition, you tried various methods of running macros. This chapter has also explained macro security issues that you should be aware of when opening workbooks containing macro code.

The next chapter focuses on using the Visual Basic Editor window.

Chapter 2

Excel Programming Environment

A Quick Overview of its Tools and Features (VBE)

Now that you know how to record, run, and edit macros, let's spend some time in the Visual Basic Editor window (also known as VBE) and become familiar with its features. With the tools located in the VBE window, you can:

- Write your own VBA procedures.
- Create custom forms.
- View and modify object properties.
- Test VBA procedures and locate errors.

The Visual Basic Editor window can be accessed in the following ways:

- Choose Developer | Code | Visual Basic.
- Choose Developer | Controls | View Code.
- Press Alt+F11.

UNDERSTANDING THE PROJECT EXPLORER WINDOW

The Project Explorer window displays a hierarchical list of currently open projects and their elements. A VBA project can contain the following elements:

- Worksheets
- Charts
- ThisWorkbook—The workbook where the project is stored
- Modules—Special sheets where programming code is stored
- Classes—Special modules that allow you to create your own objects
- Forms
- References to the other projects

With the Project Explorer you can manage your projects and easily move between projects that are loaded into memory. You can activate the Project Explorer window in one of three ways:

- From the View menu by selecting Project Explorer.
- From the keyboard by pressing Ctrl+R.
- From the Standard toolbar by clicking the Project Explorer button as shown in Figure 2.1.

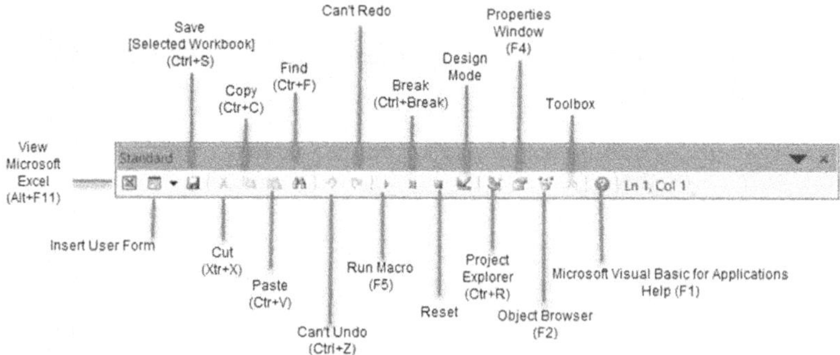

FIGURE 2.1 Buttons on the Standard toolbar provide a quick way to access many of the Visual Basic Editor features.

The Project Explorer window contains three buttons as shown in Figure 2.2. The first button from the left (View Code) displays the Code window for the selected module. The middle button (View Object) displays either the selected sheet in the Microsoft Excel Object folder or a form located in the Forms folder.

The button on the right (Toggle Folders) hides and/or activates the display of folders in the Project Explorer window.

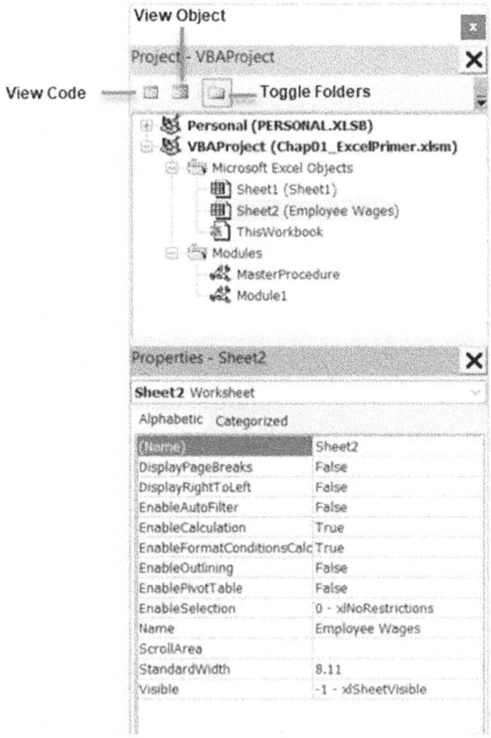

FIGURE 2.2 The Project Explorer window displays a list of currently open projects. The Properties window displays the settings for the object currently selected in the Project Explorer.

UNDERSTANDING THE PROPERTIES WINDOW

The Properties window allows you to review and set properties of various objects in your project. The name of the currently selected object is displayed in the Object box located just below the Properties window's title bar. For example, Figure 2.2 displays the properties of the Sheet1 object. Properties of the object can be viewed alphabetically or by category by clicking the appropriate tab.

- Alphabetic tab—Lists alphabetically all properties for the selected object. You can change the property setting by selecting the property name and typing or selecting the new setting.

- Categorized tab—Lists all properties for the selected object by category. You can collapse the list so that you see the categories, or you can expand a category to see the properties. The plus sign (+) icon to the left of the category name indicates that the category list can be expanded. The minus sign (–) indicates that the category is currently expanded.

The Properties window can be accessed in three ways:

- From the View menu by selecting Properties Window.
- From the keyboard by pressing F4.
- From the toolbar by clicking the Properties Window button.

UNDERSTANDING THE CODE WINDOW

The Code window is used for Visual Basic programming as well as viewing and modifying the code of recorded macros and existing VBA procedures. Each module can be opened in a separate Code window. There are several ways to activate the Code window:

- From the Project Explorer window, choose the appropriate UserForm or module, and click the View Code button.
- From the menu bar, choose View | Code.
- From the keyboard, press F7.

In Figure 2.3, you will notice at the top of the Code window two drop-down list boxes that allow you to move quickly within the Visual Basic code. In the Object box on the left side of the Code window, you can select the object whose code you want to view. The box on the right side of the Code window lets you quickly choose a procedure or event procedure to view. When you open this box, the names of all procedures located in a module are sorted alphabetically. If you select a procedure in the Procedures/Events box, the cursor will jump to the first line of this procedure.

By dragging the split bar shown in Figure 2.3 down to a selected position in the Code window, you can divide the Code window into two panes. You can then view different sections of a long procedure or a different procedure in each pane. This two-pane display in the Code window is often used for copying or cutting and pasting sections of code between procedures of the same module.

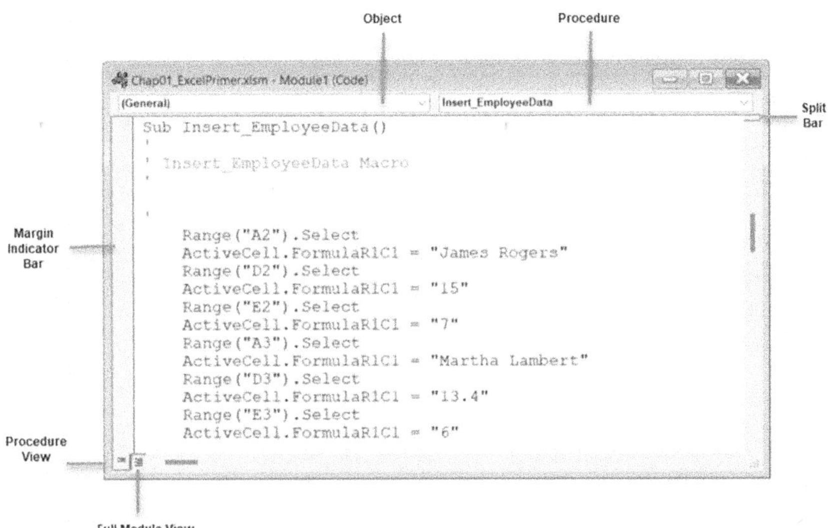

FIGURE 2.3 The Visual Basic Code window has several elements that make it easy to locate procedures and review the VBA code.

To return to the one-window display, simply drag the split bar all the way to the top of the Code window.

At the bottom left of the Code window, there are two icons. The Procedure View icon displays one procedure at a time in the Code window. To select another procedure, use the Procedures/Events box. The Full Module View icon displays all the procedures in the selected module. Use the vertical scrollbar to scroll through the module's code.

The margin indicator bar is used by Visual Basic Editor to display helpful indicators during editing and debugging. If you'd like to take a quick look at some of these indicators, skim through Chapter 9, "Excel Tools for Testing and Debugging."

SETTING THE VBE OPTIONS

There are several other windows that are frequently used in the Visual Basic environment.

Figure 2.4 displays the list of windows that can be docked in the Visual Basic Editor window. You will learn how to use some of these windows in Chapter 3 (Object Browser, Immediate window) and Chapter 9 (Locals window, Watch window).

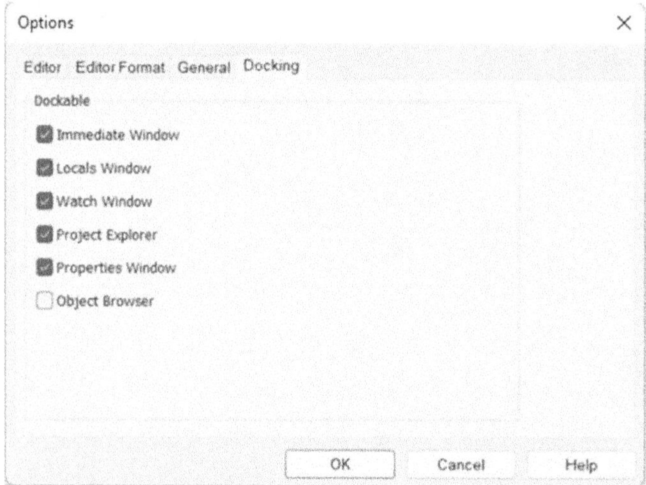

FIGURE 2.4 The Docking tab in the Tools | Options dialog box allows you to choose which windows you want to be dockable in the Visual Basic Editor screen.

SYNTAX AND PROGRAMMING ASSISTANCE

Figure 2.5 shows the Edit toolbar in the VBE window that contains several buttons that let you enter correctly formatted VBA instructions with speed and ease. If the Edit toolbar isn't currently docked in the Visual Basic Editor window, you can turn it on by choosing View | Toolbars | Edit.

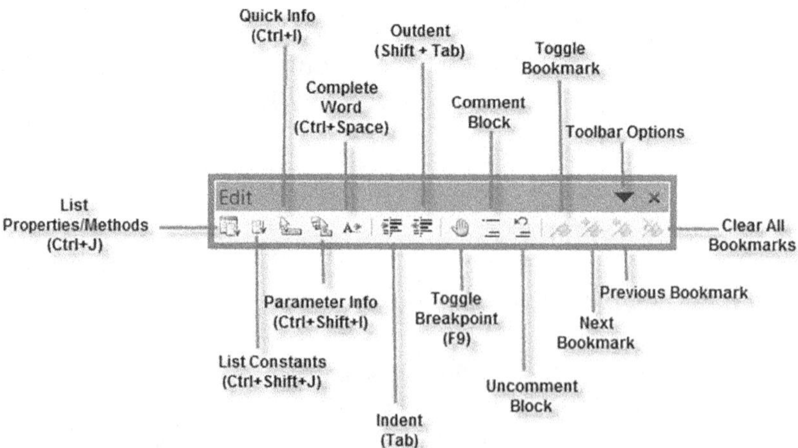

FIGURE 2.5 Buttons located on the Edit toolbar make it easy to write and format VBA instructions.

Writing procedures in Visual Basic requires that you use hundreds of built-in instructions and functions. Because most people cannot memorize the correct syntax of all the instructions that are available in VBA, the IntelliSense® technology provides you with syntax and programming assistance on demand when entering instructions. You can have special windows pop up and guide you through the process of creating correct VBA code.

List Properties/Methods

Each object can contain several properties and methods. When you enter the name of the object and a period that separates the name of the object from its property or method in the Code window, a pop-up menu may appear. This menu lists the properties and methods available for the object that precedes the period as shown in Figure 2.6. To turn on this automated feature, choose Tools | Options. In the Options dialog box, click the Editor tab, and make sure the Auto List Members check box is selected.

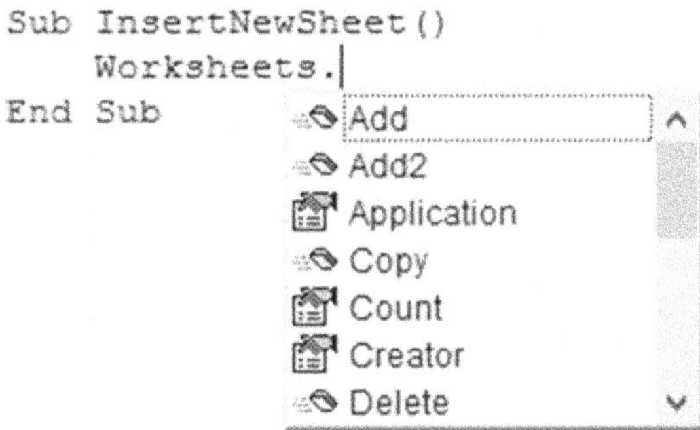

FIGURE 2.6 While you are entering the VBA instructions, Visual Basic suggests properties and methods that can be used with the object.

To choose an item from the pop-up menu that appears, start typing the name of the property or method that you want to select. When Excel highlights the correct item name, press Enter to insert the item into your code and start a new line. Or, if you want to continue writing instructions on the same line, press the Tab key instead. You can also double-click the item to insert it in your code. To close the pop-up menu without inserting an item, simply press Esc. When you press Esc to remove the pop-up menu, Visual Basic will not display it again for the same object. To display the Properties/Methods pop-up menu again, you can:

- Press Ctrl+J.
- Use the Backspace key to delete the period and type the period again.

- Right-click in the Code window and select List Properties/Methods from the shortcut menu.
- Choose Edit | List Properties/Methods.
- Click the List Properties/Methods button on the Edit toolbar.

List Constants

A *constant* is a value that indicates a specific state or result. Excel has many predefined, built-in constants. You will learn about constants, their types, and usage in Chapter 3.

Suppose you want your program to turn on the Page Break Preview of your worksheet. In the Microsoft Excel application window, the View tab lists four types of workbook views:

- The Normal View is the default view for most tasks in Excel.
- Page Layout View allows you to view the document as it will appear on the printed page.
- Page Break Preview allows you to see where pages will break when the document is printed.
- Custom Views allows you to save the set of display and print settings as a custom view.

The first three view options are represented by a built-in constant. Microsoft Excel constant names begin with the characters "xl." As soon as you enter in the Code window the instruction:

```
ActiveWindow.View =
```

a pop-up menu will appear with the names of valid constants for the property, as shown in Figure 2.7.

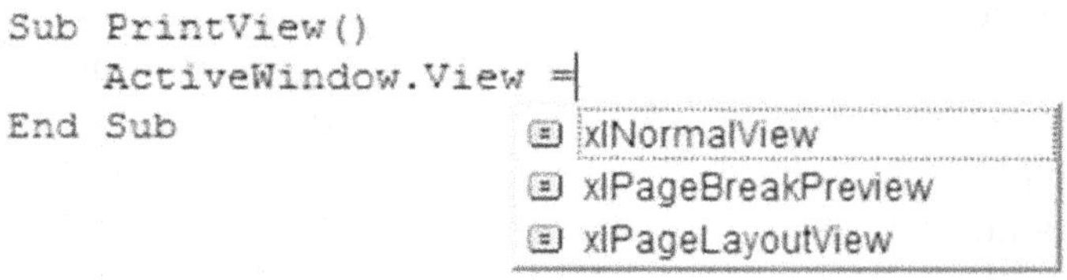

```
Sub PrintView()
    ActiveWindow.View =
End Sub
                    xlNormalView
                    xlPageBreakPreview
                    xlPageLayoutView
```

FIGURE 2.7 The List Constants pop-up menu displays a list of constants that are valid for the property entered.

To work with the List Constants pop-up menu, use the same techniques as for the List Properties/Methods pop-up menu outlined in the preceding section.

The List Constants pop-up menu can be activated by pressing Ctrl+Shift+J or clicking the List Constants button on the Edit toolbar.

Parameter Info

If you've had a chance to work with Excel worksheet functions, you already know that many functions require one or more arguments (or *parameters*). For example, here's the syntax for the most common worksheet function:

```
SUM(number1,number2, ...)
```

where `number1, number2,` ... are 1 to 30 arguments that you can add up.

Like functions, VBA methods may require one or more arguments. If a method requires an argument, you can see the names of required and optional arguments in a tooltip box that appears just below the cursor as soon as you type the beginning parenthesis as illustrated in Figure 2.8. In the tooltip, the current argument is displayed in bold. When you supply the first argument and enter the comma, Visual Basic displays the next argument in bold. Optional arguments are surrounded by square brackets [ ].

You can open the Parameter Info tooltip using the keyboard. To do this, enter the method or function name, follow it with the left parenthesis, and press Ctrl+Shift+I. You can also click the Parameter Info button on the Edit toolbar or choose Edit | Parameter Info.

```
Sub PrintView()
    ActiveWindow.View = xlPageBreakPreview
    ActiveWorkbook.SaveAs
End Sub            SaveAs([Filename], [FileFormat], [Password], [WriteResPassword], [ReadOnlyRecommended], [CreateBackup], [AccessMode As
                   XlSaveAsAccessMode = xlNoChange], [ConflictResolution], [AddToMru], [TextCodepage], [TextVisualLayout], [Local])
```

FIGURE 2.8 A tooltip displays a list of arguments utilized by a VBA method.

The Parameter Info feature makes it easy for you to supply correct arguments to a VBA method. In addition, it reminds you of two other things that are very important for the method to work correctly: the order of the arguments and the required data type of each argument. You will learn about data types in Chapter 3.

Quick Info

When you select an instruction, function, method, procedure name, or constant in the Code window and then click the Quick Info button on the Edit toolbar (or press Ctrl+I), Visual Basic displays the syntax of the highlighted item, as well as the value of a constant, as depicted in Figure 2.9. The Quick Info feature can be turned on or off using the Options dialog box. To use the feature, click the Editor tab and choose the Auto Quick Info option.

```
Sub PrintView()
    ActiveWindow.View = xlPageBreakPreview
    ActiveWorkbook.SaveA xlPageBreakPreview = 2 el_ByExample\CopyChap02_ExcelPrimer.xlsm")
End Sub
```

FIGURE 2.9 The Quick Info feature displays a list of arguments required by a selected method or function, a value of a selected constant, or the type of the selected object or property.

Complete Word

Another way to increase the speed of writing VBA procedures in the Code window is with the Complete Word feature. As you enter the first few letters of a keyword and press Ctrl+Spacebar or click the Complete Word button on the Edit toolbar, Visual Basic will fill in the remaining letters by completing the keyword entry for you. For example, when you enter the first four letters of the keyword Application (Appl) in the Code window and press Ctrl+Spacebar, Visual Basic will complete the rest of the word, and in the place of "Appl," you will see the entire word "Application."

Indent/Outdent

If the Auto Indent option is turned on, you can automatically indent the selected lines of code by the number of characters specified in the Tab Width text box. The default entry for Auto Indent is four characters. You can easily change this setting via the Options dialog box (by selecting the Editor tab; see Figure 2.4).

Why would you want to use indentation in your code? When you indent certain lines in your VBA procedures, you make them more readable and easier to understand. Indenting is especially recommended for entering lines of code that make decisions or repeat actions. You will learn how to create these kinds of Visual Basic instructions in Chapters 5 and 6, "Adding Decisions to Excel VBA Programs" and "Adding Repeating Actions to Excel VBA Programs." Let's spend a few minutes learning how to apply the indent and outdent features to the lines of code in the WhatsInACell macro that you worked with in Chapter 1.

Hands-On 2.1 Indenting/Outdenting Visual Basic Code

1. Open the **Chap01_Supplement.xlsm** workbook that you worked with in Chapter 1.
2. Press **Alt+F11** to switch to the VBE window.
3. Choose **View** | **Toolbars** | **Edit** to gain access to the Editing toolbar. If the toolbar pops up in the middle of the screen, double-click its title bar to get it docked at the top of the VBE window.
4. In the Project Explorer window, select the **Chap01_Supplement.xlsm**VBA project and activate the **Module1** that contains the code of the **WhatsInACell** macro.

5. Select the block of code located between the keyword `With` and `End With`.
6. Click the **Indent** button (see Figure 2.5) on the Edit toolbar or press **Tab** on the keyboard. The selected block of instructions will move four spaces to the right if you are using the default setting in the Tab Width box in the Options dialog box (Editor tab).
7. Click the **Outdent** button on the Edit toolbar or press **Shift+Tab** to return the selected lines of code to the previous location in the Code window.
8. Close the **Chap01_Supplement.xlsm** workbook.

The Indent and Outdent options are also available from the Edit menu.

Comment Block/Uncomment Block

In Chapter 1, you learned that a single quote placed at the beginning of a line of code denotes a comment. Not only do comments make it easier to understand what the procedure does, but also, they are very useful in testing and troubleshooting VBA code.

For example, when you execute your code, it may not run as expected. Instead of deleting the lines that may be responsible for the problems you encounter, you may want to skip those lines of code for now and return to them later. By placing a single quote at the beginning of the line you want to avoid, you can continue checking the other parts of your procedure.

- To comment a few lines of code, simply select the lines and click the Comment Block button on the Edit toolbar (see Figure 2.5).
- To turn the commented code back into VBA instructions, select the lines and click the Uncomment Block button on the Edit toolbar (see Figure 2.5).

If you don't select text and click the Comment Block button, the single quote is added only to the line of code where the cursor is currently located.

USING THE OBJECT BROWSER

You can move easily through the myriad of VBA elements and features by examining the capabilities of the Object Browser. To access the Object Browser, use any of the following methods in the VBE window:

- Press F2.
- Choose View | Object Browser.
- Click the Object Browser button on the toolbar.

The Object Browser allows you to browse through the objects that are available to your VBA procedures, as well as view their properties, methods, and events. With the aid of the Object Browser, you can move quickly between procedures in your own VBA projects, as well as search for objects and methods across object type libraries.

The Object Browser window is divided into three sections as illustrated in Figure 2.10. The top of the window displays the Project/Library drop-down list box with the names of all libraries and projects that are available to the currently active VBA project. A library is a special file that contains information about the objects in an application. New libraries can be added via the References dialog box (Tools | References). The entry for <All Libraries> lists the objects of all libraries that are installed on your computer. When you select the library called Excel, you will see only the names of the objects that are exclusive to Microsoft Excel. In contrast to the Excel library, the VBA library lists the names of all the objects in Visual Basic for Applications.

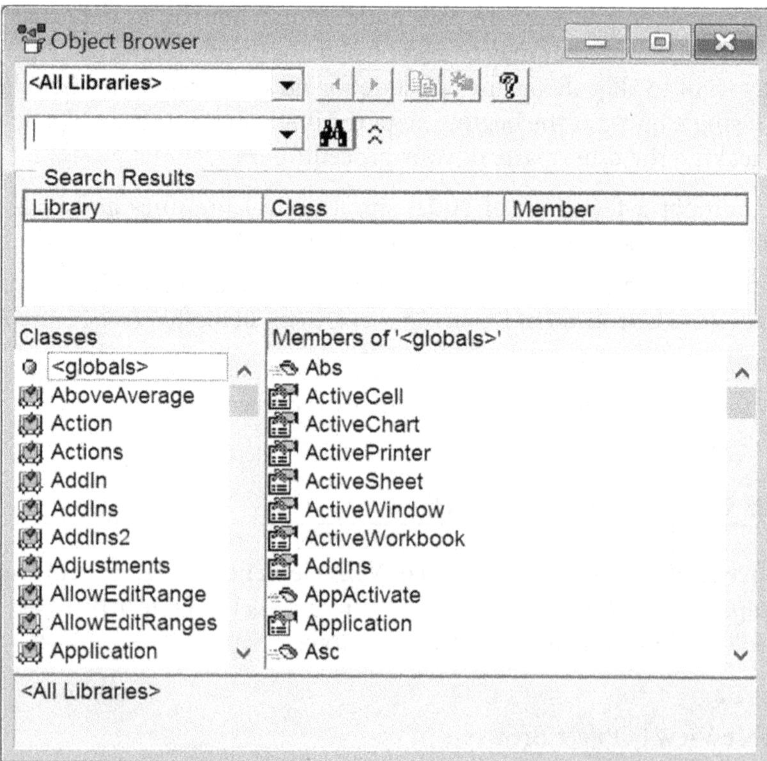

FIGURE 2.10 The Object Browser window allows you to browse through all the objects, properties, and methods available to the current VBA project.

Below the Project/Library drop-down list box is a Search text box that you'll use to quickly find information in a library. This field remembers the last four items for which you searched. To find only whole words, you can right-click anywhere in the Object Browser window and choose Find Whole Word Only from the shortcut menu.

The Search Results section of the Object Browser displays the library, class, and member elements that met the criteria entered in the Search text box as shown in Figure 2.11.

When you type the search text and click the Search button (the binoculars icon), Visual Basic expands the Object Browser dialog box to show the Search Results area. You can hide or show the Search Results by clicking the button located to the right of the Search button.

FIGURE 2.11 Searching for answers in the Object Browser.

The Classes list box displays the available object classes in the selected library. If you select a VBA project, this list shows objects in the project. In Figure 2.11, the Application object class is selected. When you highlight a class, the list on the right-hand side (Members) shows the properties, methods, and events available for that class. By default, members are listed alphabetically. You can, however, organize the members list by group type (properties, methods, or events) using the Group Members command from the Object Browser shortcut menu.

If you select a VBA project in the Project/Library list box, the Members list box will list all the procedures available in this project. To examine the code of a procedure, simply double-click its name. If you select a VBA library, you will see a listing of Visual Basic built-in functions and constants. If you need more information on the selected class or a member, click the question mark button at the top of the Object Browser window.

The bottom of the Object Browser window displays a code template area with the definition of the selected member. If you click the green hyperlink text in the code template, you can quickly jump to the selected member's class or library in the Object Browser window. Text displayed in the code template area can be copied to the Windows clipboard and then pasted to a Code window. If the Code window is visible while the Object Browser window is open, you can save time by dragging the highlighted code template and dropping it into the Code window.

You can easily adjust the size of the various sections of the Object Browser window by dragging the dividing horizontal and vertical lines.

Now that you've discovered the Object Browser, you may wonder how you can put it to use in VBA programming. Let's assume that you placed a text box in the middle of your worksheet. How can you make Excel move this text box so that it is positioned at the top left-hand corner of the sheet? Hands-On 2.2 should provide the answer to this question.

Hands-On 2.2 Writing a VBA Procedure to Move a Text Box on the Worksheet

1. Open a new workbook.
2. Choose **Insert | Text |Text Box**.
3. Now draw a box in the middle of the sheet and enter any text as shown in Figure 2.12.
4. Select any cell outside the text box area.
5. Press **Alt+F11** to activate the Visual Basic Editor window.
6. Choose **Insert | Module** to add a new module sheet.
7. In the Properties window, enter the new name for this module: **Manipulations**.

8. Choose **View | Object Browser** or press **F2**.
9. In the Project/Library list box, click the drop-down arrow and select the **Excel** library.
10. Enter **textbox** as the search text in the Search box as shown in Figure 2.13, and then click the **Search** button. Make sure you don't enter a space in the search string.

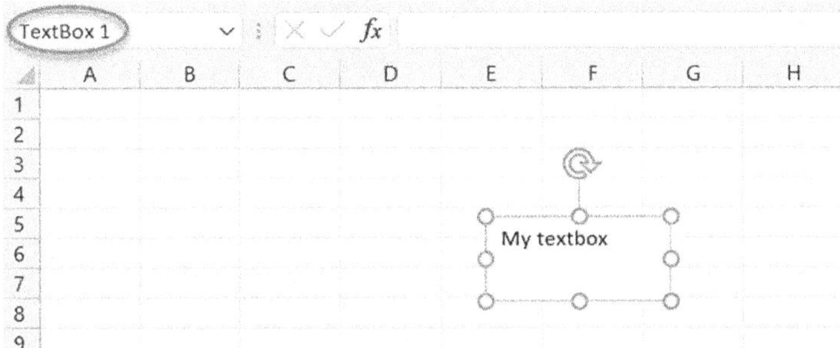

FIGURE 2.12 Excel displays the name of the inserted object in the Name box above the worksheet.

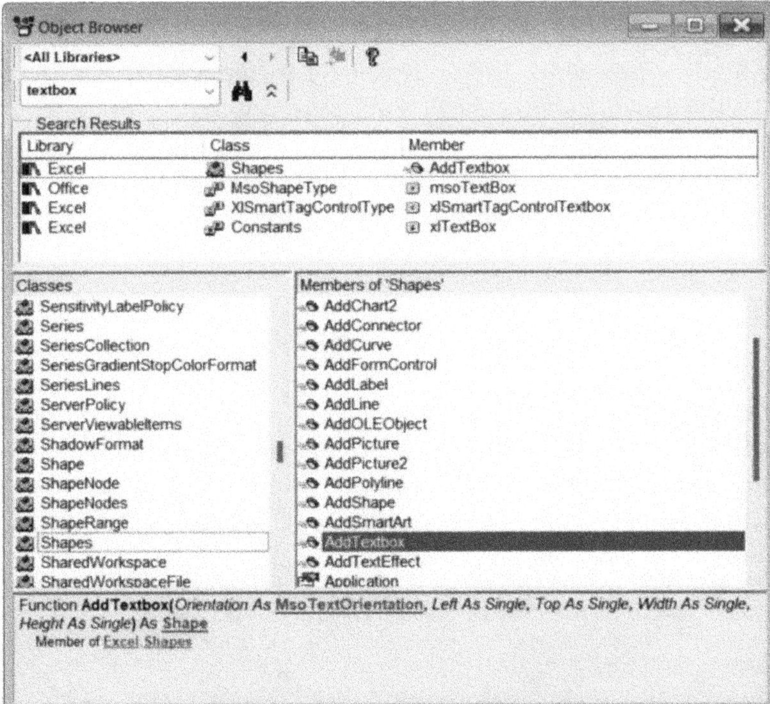

FIGURE 2.13 Using the Object Browser window, you can find the appropriate VBA instructions for writing your own procedures.

Visual Basic searches the Excel library and displays the search results. It appears that the Shapes object shown in Figure 2.13 is in control of our text box operations. Looking at the members list, you can quickly determine that the `AddTextbox` method is used for adding a new text box to a worksheet. The code template at the bottom of the Object Browser shows the correct syntax for using this method. If you select the `AddTextbox` method and press F1, you will see the Help window with more details on how to use this method. The Help window tells us that the Left and Top properties determine the position of the text box in a worksheet.

11. Close the Object Browser window and the Help window if they are open. Double-click the **Manipulations** module and enter the MoveTextBox procedure, as shown here:

```
Sub MoveTextBox()
   With ActiveSheet.Shapes("TextBox 1")
       .Select
       .Left = 0
       .Top = 0
   End With
End Sub
```

The MoveTextBox procedure selects TextBox 1 in the collection of Shapes. TextBox 1 is the default name of the first object placed in the worksheet. Each time you add a new object to your worksheet, Excel assigns a new number (index) to it. Instead of using the object name, you can refer to the member of a collection by its index. For example, instead of:

```
With ActiveSheet.Shapes("TextBox 1")
```

enter:

```
With ActiveSheet.Shapes(1)
```

12. Choose **Run | Run Sub/UserForm** to execute this procedure.
13. Press **Alt+F11** to switch to the Microsoft Excel application window. The text box should be positioned at the top left-hand corner of the worksheet.
14. Save the workbook file as **Chap02_ExcelPrimer.xlsm**. Keep this file open as you will continue to work with it in Hands-On 2.3.

Let's manipulate another object with Visual Basic.

Hands-On 2.3 Writing a VBA Procedure to Move a Circle on the Worksheet

1. Place a small circle in the same worksheet where you originally placed the text box in Hands-On 2.2. Use the **Oval** shape in the Basic Shapes area of the **Insert | Illustrations | Shapes** tool. Hold down the **Shift** key while drawing on the worksheet to create a perfect circle.
2. Click outside the circle to deselect it.
3. Press **Alt+F11** to activate the Visual Basic Editor screen.
4. In the Manipulations Module's Code window, write a VBA procedure that will place the circle inside the text box. Keep in mind that Excel numbers objects consecutively. The first object is assigned a number 1, the second object a number 2, and so on. The type of object—whether it is a text box, a circle, or a rectangle—does not matter.
5. The MoveCircle procedure shown here demonstrates how to move a circle to the top left-hand corner of the active worksheet:

   ```
   Sub MoveCircle()
      With ActiveSheet.Shapes(2)
          .Select
          .Left = 0
          .Top = 0
      End With
   End Sub
   ```

   Moving a circle is like moving a text box or any other object placed in a worksheet. Notice that instead of referring to the circle by its name, Oval 2, the procedure uses the object's index.
6. Run the MoveCircle procedure.
7. Press **Alt+F11** to return to the Microsoft Excel window.
8. The circle should now appear on the top of the text box.

Locating Procedures with the Object Browser

In addition to locating objects, properties, and methods, the Object Browser is a handy tool for locating and accessing procedures written in various VBA projects. The Hands-On 2.4 exercise demonstrates how you can find quickly which procedures are stored in the selected project.

Hands-On 2.4 Using Object Browser to Locate VBA Procedures

1. In the Object Browser, select **VBAProject** from the Project/Library drop-down list as shown in Figure 2.14.

The left side of the Object Browser displays the names of objects that are included in the selected project. The Members list box on the right shows the names of all the available procedures.

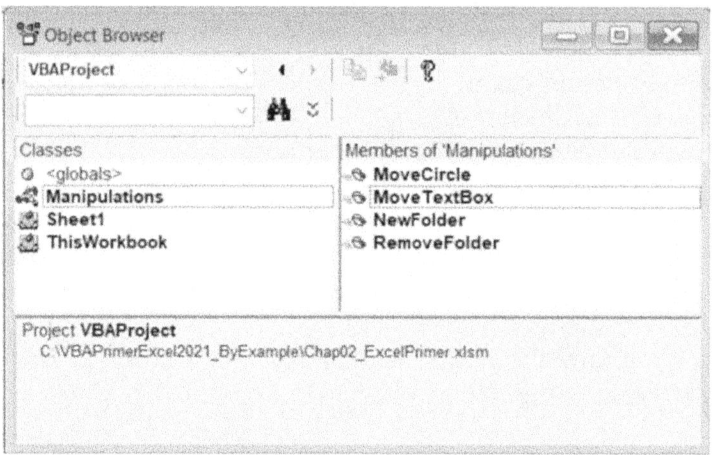

FIGURE 2.14 The Object Browser lists all the procedures available in a VBA project.

2. In the Members list, double-click the **MoveCircle** procedure.
3. Excel locates the selected procedure in the Code window.

USING THE VBA OBJECT LIBRARY

In the previous examples, you used the properties of objects that are members of the Shapes collection in the Excel object library. While the Excel library contains objects specific to using Microsoft Excel, the VBA object library provides access to many built-in VBA functions that are general in nature. They allow you to manage files, set the date and time, interact with users, convert data types, deal with text strings, or perform mathematical calculations. In the following Hands-On 2.5 exercise, you will use one of the built-in VBA functions to create a new Windows subfolder without leaving Excel.

Hands-On 2.5 Writing a VBA Procedure to Create a Folder in Windows

1. Press **Alt+F11** to return to the Manipulations module, where you entered the MoveTextBox and MoveCircle procedures.

2. On a new line, type the name of the new procedure: **Sub NewFolder()**.
3. Press **Enter**. Visual Basic will enter the ending keywords `End Sub`.
4. Press **F2** to activate the Object Browser.
5. Click the drop-down arrow in the Project/Library list box and select **VBA**.
6. Enter **file** as the search text in the Search box and press the **Search** button.
7. Scroll down in the Members list box and highlight the **MkDir** method as shown in Figure 2.15.

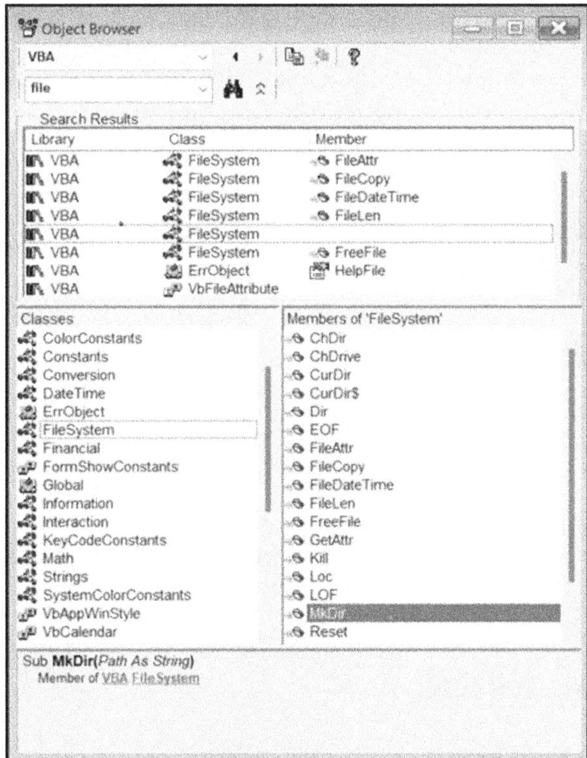

FIGURE 2.15 When writing procedures from scratch, consult the Object Browser for names of the built-in VBA functions.

8. Click the **Copy** button (the middle button in the top row) in the Object Browser window to copy the selected method name to the Windows clipboard.
9. Return to the Manipulations Code window and paste the copied instruction inside the procedure NewFolder.
10. Enter a space, followed by **"C:\Study"**. Be sure to enter the name of the entire path in quotes. The NewFolder procedure should look like this:

```
Sub NewFolder()
   MkDir "C:\Study"
End Sub
```

11. Position the insertion point within the code of the NewFolder procedure and choose **Run | Run Sub/UserForm** to execute the NewFolder procedure.
    When you run the NewFolder procedure, Visual Basic creates a new folder on drive C. To see the folder, activate Windows Explorer.

    After creating a new folder, you may realize that you don't need it after all. Although you could easily delete the folder while in Windows Explorer, how about getting rid of it programmatically? The Object Browser displays many other methods that are useful for working with folders and files. The `RmDir` method is just as simple to use as the `MkDir` method.
12. To remove the Study folder from your hard drive, you could replace the `MkDir` method with the `RmDir` method, and then rerun the NewFolder procedure. However, let's write a new procedure called RemoveFolder in the Manipulations Code window, as shown here:

```
Sub RemoveFolder()
   RmDir "C:\Study"
End Sub
```

    The `RmDir` method allows you to remove unwanted folders from your hard disk.
13. Position the insertion point within the code of the RemoveFolder procedure and choose **Run | Run Sub/UserForm** to execute the RemoveFolder procedure. Check Windows Explorer to see that the Study folder is gone.

USING THE IMMEDIATE WINDOW

The Immediate window is used for trying out various instructions, functions, and operators present in the Visual Basic language before using them in your own VBA procedures. It is a great tool for experimenting with your new language.

The Immediate window allows you to type VBA statements and test their results immediately without having to write a procedure. The Immediate window is like a scratch pad. Use it to try out your statements. If the statement produces the expected result, you can copy the statement from the Immediate window into your procedure (or you can drag it right onto the Code window if it is visible).

The Immediate window can be moved anywhere on the Visual Basic Editor screen, or it can be docked so that it always appears in the same area of the screen. The docking setting can be turned on and off on the Docking tab in the Options dialog box (Tools | Options).

- To quickly access the Immediate window, simply press Ctrl+G while in the Visual Basic Editor screen.
- To close the Immediate window, click the Close button in the top right-hand corner of the window.

Before you start creating full-fledged VBA procedures (this awaits you in the next chapter!), begin with some warm-up exercises to build up your VBA vocabulary. How can you do this quickly and painlessly? How can you try out some of the newly learned VBA statements? Here is a short, interactive language exercise: Enter a simple VBA instruction and Excel will check it out and display the result in the next line. Let's begin by setting up your exercise screen.

Hands-On 2.6 Entering and Executing VBA Statements in the Immediate Window

1. In the Visual Basic Editor window, choose **View | Immediate Window**.
2. Arrange the screen so that both the Microsoft Excel window and the Visual Basic window are placed side by side as presented in Figure 2.16 or use a setup with two monitors displaying Excel windows on separate screens.

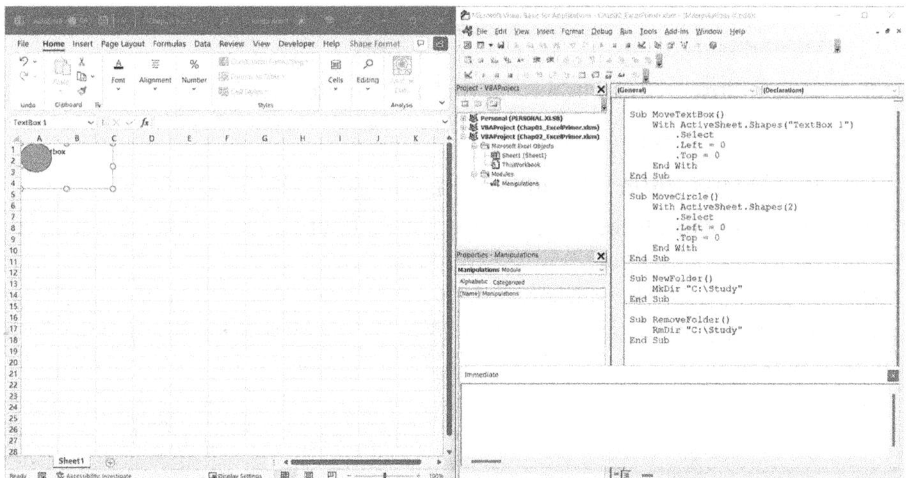

FIGURE 2.16 By positioning the Microsoft Excel and Visual Basic windows side by side you can watch the execution of the instructions entered in the Immediate window.

3. In the VBE screen, press Ctrl+G to activate the Immediate window.
4. In the Immediate window, type the following instruction and press **Enter**:

```
Worksheets.Add
```

   When you press the Enter key, Visual Basic gets to work. If you entered the foregoing VBA statement correctly, VBA adds a new sheet in the current workbook. The Sheet2 tab at the bottom of the workbook should now be highlighted.
5. In the Immediate window, type another VBA statement and be sure to press **Enter** when you're done:

```
Range("A1:A4").Select
```

   As soon as you press **Enter**, Visual Basic highlights the cells A1, A2, A3, and A4 in the active worksheet.
6. Enter the following instruction in the Immediate window:

```
[A1:A4].Value = 55
```

   When you press **Enter**, Visual Basic places the number 55 in every cell of the specified range, A1:A4. This statement is an abbreviated way of referring to the Range object. The full syntax is more readable:

```
Range("A1:A4").Value = 55
```

7. Enter the following instruction in the Immediate window:

```
Selection.ClearContents
```

   When you press **Enter**, VBA deletes the results of the previous statement from the selected cells. Cells A1:A4 are now empty.
8. Enter the following instruction in the Immediate window:

```
ActiveCell.Select
```

   When you press **Enter**, Visual Basic makes cell A1 active.

   Figure 2.17 shows all the instructions entered in the Immediate window in this exercise. Every time you pressed the Enter key, Excel executed the statement on the line where the cursor was located. If you want to execute the same instruction again, click anywhere in the line containing the instruction and press Enter.

```
Immediate
Worksheets.Add
Range("A1:A4").Select
[A1:A4].Value = 55
Selection.ClearContents
ActiveCell.Select
```

FIGURE 2.17 Instructions entered in the Immediate window are executed as soon as you press the Enter key.

For more practice you may want to rerun the statements shown in Figure 2.17. Execute the instructions one by one by clicking in the appropriate line and pressing the Enter key.

Obtaining Information in the Immediate Window

So far you have used the Immediate window to perform actions. These actions could have been performed manually by clicking the mouse in various areas of the worksheet and entering data.

Instead of simply performing actions, the Immediate window also allows you to ask questions. Suppose you want to find out which cells are currently selected, the value of the active cell, the name of the active sheet, or the number of the current window. When working in the Immediate window, you can easily get answers to these and other questions.

In the preceding exercise, you entered several instructions. Let's return to the Immediate window to ask some questions. Excel remembers the instructions entered in the Immediate window even after you close this window. Note that the contents of the Immediate window are automatically deleted when you exit Microsoft Excel.

Hands-On 2.7 Obtaining Information in the Immediate Window

1. Click the mouse in the second line of the Immediate window where you previously entered the instruction `Range("A1:A4").Select`.
2. Press **Enter** to have Excel reselect cells A1:A4.
3. Click in the new line of the Immediate window, enter the following question, and press **Enter**:

   ```
   ?Selection.Address
   ```

When you press Enter, Excel will not select anything in the worksheet. Instead, it will display the result of the instruction on a separate line in the Immediate window. In this case, Excel returns the absolute address of the cells that are currently selected ($A$1:$A$4).

The question mark (?) tells Excel to display the result of the instruction in the Immediate window. Instead of the question mark, you can use the Print keyword, as shown in the next step.

4. In a new line in the Immediate window, enter the following statement and press **Enter**:

```
Print ActiveWorkbook.Name
```

Excel enters the name of the active workbook on a new line in the Immediate window.

How about finding the name of the application?

5. In a new line in the Immediate window, enter the following statement and press **Enter**:

```
?Application.Name
```

Excel will reveal its full name: Microsoft Excel.

The Immediate window can also be used for a quick calculation.

6. In a new line in the Immediate window, enter the following statement and press **Enter**:

```
?12/3
```

Excel shows the result of the division on the next line. But what if you want to know right away the result of 3+2 and 12*8?

Instead of entering these instructions on separate lines, you can enter them on one line, as in the following example:

```
?3+2:?12*8
```

Notice the colon separating the two blocks of instructions. When you press the Enter key, Excel displays the results 5, 96 on separate lines in the Immediate window.

The following lists all the instructions you entered in the Immediate window, including Excel's answers to your questions:

```
Worksheets.Add
Range("A1:A4").Select
[A1:A4].Value = 55
```

```
Selection.ClearContents
ActiveCell.Select
?Selection.Address
$A$1:$A$4
Print ActiveWorkbook.Name
Book2
?Application.Name
Microsoft Excel
?12/3
 4
?3+2:?12*8
 5
 96
```

To delete the instructions from the Immediate window, make sure that the selection point is in the Immediate window, press Ctrl+A to highlight all the lines, and then press Delete.

WORKING WITH WORKSHEET CELLS AND RANGES

When you are ready to write your own VBA procedure to automate a spreadsheet task, you will most likely begin searching for instructions that allow you to manipulate worksheet cells. You will need to know how to select cells, how to enter data in cells, how to assign range names, how to format cells, and how to move, copy, and delete cells. Although these tasks can be easily performed with the mouse or keyboard, mastering these techniques in Visual Basic for Applications requires a little practice. You must use the Range object to refer to a single cell, a range of cells, a row, or a column. There are three properties that allow you to access the Range object: the Range property, the Cells property, and the Offset property.

Using the Range Property

The Range property returns a cell or a range of cells. The reference to the range must be in an A1-style and in quotation marks (for example, "A1"). The reference can include the range operator, which is a colon (for example, "A1:B2"), or the union operator, which is a comma (for example, "A5", "B12").

Hands-On 2.8 Using the Range Property to Select Worksheet Cells

To render this into VBA:	Enter this in the Immediate window:
Select a single cell (e.g., A5).	`Range("A5").Select`
Select a range of cells (e.g., A6:A10).	`Range("A6:A10").Select`
Select several nonadjacent cells (e.g., A1, B6, C8).	`Range("A1, B6, C8").Select`
Select several nonadjacent cells and cell ranges (e.g., A11:D11, C12, D3).	`Range("A11:D11, C12, D3").Se-lect`

Using the Cells Property

You can use the Cells property to return a single cell. When selecting a single cell, this property requires two arguments. The first argument indicates the row number and the second one is the column number. Arguments are entered in parentheses. When you omit arguments, Excel selects all the cells in the active worksheet. Let's try out a couple of statements in Hands-On 2.9.

Hands-On 2.9 Using the Cells Property to Select Worksheet Cells (Part I)

To render this into VBA:	Enter this in the Immediate window:
Select a single cell (e.g., A5).	`Cells(5, 1).Select`
Select a range of cells (e.g., A6:A10).	`Range(Cells(6, 1), Cells(10, 1)).Select`
Select all cells in a worksheet.	`Cells.Select`

Notice how you can combine the Range property and the Cells property:

```
Range(Cells(6, 1), Cells(10, 1)).Select
```

In this example, the first Cells property returns cell A6, while the second one returns cell A10. The cells returned by the Cells properties are then used as a reference for the Range object. As a result, Excel will select the range of cells where the top cell is specified by the result of the first Cells property and the bottom cell is defined by the result of the second Cells property.

A worksheet is a collection of cells. You can also use the Cells property with a single argument that identifies a cell's position in the collection of a worksheet's cells. Excel numbers the cells in the following way: Cell A1 is the first cell in a worksheet, cell B1 is the second one, cell C1 is the third one, and so on. Cell 16384 is the last cell in the first worksheet row. Now let's write some practice statements in Hands-On 2.10.

Hands-On 2.10 Using the Cells Property to Select Worksheet Cells (Part II)

To render this into VBA:	Enter this in the Immediate window:

Select cell A1.	`Cells(1).Select`
	or
	`Cells.Item(1).Select`

Select cell C1.	`Cells(3).Select`
	or
	`Cells.Item(3).Select`

Select cell XFD.	`Cells(16384).Select`
	or
	`Cells.Item(16384).Select`

Notice that the word Item is a property that returns a single member of a collection. Because Item is the default member for a collection, you can refer to a worksheet cell without explicitly using the Item property.

Now that you've discovered two ways to select cells (Range property and Cells property), you may wonder why you should bother using the more complicated Cells property. It's obvious that the Range property is more readable; after all, you used the Range references in Excel formulas and functions long before you decided to learn about VBA. Using the Cells property is more convenient, however, when it comes to working with cells as a collection. Use this property to access all the cells or a single cell from a collection.

Using the Offset Property

Another very flexible way to refer to a worksheet cell is with the Offset property. Quite often when automating worksheet tasks, you may not know exactly where a specific cell is located. How can you select a cell whose address you don't know? The answer: Have Excel select a cell based on an existing selection.

The Offset property calculates a new range by shifting the starting selection down or up a specified number of rows. You can also shift the selection to the right or left a specified number of columns. In calculating the position of a new range, the Offset property uses two arguments. The first argument indicates the row offset and the second one is the column offset. Let's try out some examples in Hands-On 2.11.

Hands-On 2.11 Selecting Cells Using the Offset Property

To render this into VBA:	Enter this in the Immediate window:
Select a cell located one row down and three columns to the right of cell A1.	`Range("A1").Offset(1, 3).Select`
Select a cell located two rows above and one column to the left of cell D15.	`Range("D15").Offset(-2, -1).Select`
Select a cell located one row above the active cell. If the active cell is in the first row, you will get an error message.	`ActiveCell.Offset(-1, 0).Select`

In the first example, Excel selects cell D2. As soon as you enter the second example, Excel chooses cell C13.

If cells A1 and D15 are already selected, you can rewrite the first two statements in the following way:

```
Selection.Offset(1, 3).Select
Selection.Offset(-2, -1).Select
```

Notice that the third example in the practice table displays zero (0) in the position of the second argument. Zero entered as a first or second argument of the Offset property indicates a current row or column. The instruction `ActiveCell.Offset(-1, 0).Select` will cause an error if the active cell is located in the first row.

Using the Resize Property

When working with the Offset property, you may occasionally need to change the size of a selection of cells. Suppose that the starting selection is A5:A10. How about shifting the selection two rows down and two columns to the right and then changing the size of the new selection? Let's say the new selection should highlight cells C7:C8. The Offset property can take care of only the first part of this task. The second part requires another property. Excel has a special Resize property. You can combine the Offset property with the Resize property to answer the foregoing question. Before you combine these two properties, let's proceed to Hands-On 2.12 to learn how you can use them separately.

Hands-On 2.12 Writing a VBA Statement to Resize a Selection of Cells

1. Arrange the screen so that the Microsoft Excel window and the Visual Basic window are side by side.

2. Activate the Immediate window and enter the following instructions:

```
Range("A5:A10").Select
Selection.Offset(2, 2).Select
Selection.Resize(2, 4).Select
```

The first instruction selects range A5:A10. Cell A5 is the active cell. The second instruction shifts the current selection to cells C7:C12. Cell C7 is located two rows below the active cell A5 and two columns to the right of A5. Now the active cell is C7.

The last instruction resizes the current selection. Instead of range C7:C12, cells C7:F8 are selected.

Like the Offset property, the Resize property takes two arguments. The first argument is the number of rows you intend to include in the selection, and the second argument specifies the number of columns. Hence, the instruction `Selection.Resize(2, 4).Select` resizes the current selection to two rows and four columns.

The last two instructions can be combined in the following way:

```
Selection.Offset(2, 2).Resize(2, 4).Select
```

In this statement, the Offset property calculates the beginning of a new range, the Resize property determines the new size of the range, and the Select method selects the specified range of cells.

SIDEBAR *Recording a Selection of Cells*

By default, the macro recorder selects cells using the Range property. If you turn on the macro recorder and select cell A2, enter any text, and select cell A5, you will see the following lines of code in the Visual Basic Editor window:

```
Range("A2").Select
ActiveCell.FormulaR1C1 = "text"
Range("A5").Select
```

You can have the macro recorder use the Offset property if you tell it to use relative references. To do this, click View | Macros | Use Relative References, and then choose Record Macro. The macro recorder produces the following lines of code:

```
ActiveCell.Offset(-1, 0).Range("A1").Select
ActiveCell.FormulaR1C1 = "text"
ActiveCell.Offset(3, 0).Range("A1").Select
```

When you record a procedure using the relative references, the procedure will always select a cell relative to the active cell. The first and third lines in this set of instructions reference cell A1, even though nothing was said about cell A1. As you remember from Chapter 1, the macro recorder has its own way of getting things done. To make things simpler, you can delete the reference to `Range("A1")`:

```
ActiveCell.Offset(-1, 0).Select
ActiveCell.FormulaR1C1 = "text"
ActiveCell.Offset(3, 0).Select
```

After recording a procedure using the relative reference, make sure Use Relative References is not selected if your next macro does not require the use of relative addressing.

Using the End Property

If you often must quickly access certain remote cells in your worksheet, you may already be familiar with the following keyboard shortcuts: End+up arrow, End+down arrow, End+left arrow, and End+right arrow. In VBA, you can use the End property to quickly move to remote cells. Let's move around the worksheet by writing statements listed in Hands-On 2.13.

Hands-On 2.13 Selecting Cells Using the End Property

To render this into VBA:	Enter this in the Immediate window:
Select the last cell in any row.	`ActiveCell.End(xlToRight).Select`
Select the last cell in any column.	`ActiveCell.End(xlDown).Select`
Select the first cell in any row.	`ActiveCell.End(xlToLeft).Select`
Select the first cell in any column.	`ActiveCell.End(xlUp).Select`

Notice that the End property requires an argument that indicates the direction you want to move. Use the following Excel built-in Direction Enumeration constants to jump in the specified direction: `xlToRight`, `xlToLeft`, `xlUp`, `xlDown`.

Moving, Copying, and Deleting Cells

In the process of developing a new worksheet model, you often find yourself moving and copying cells and deleting cell contents. Visual Basic allows you to automate these worksheet editing tasks with three simple-to-use methods: Cut,

Copy, and Clear. And now let's do some hands-on exercises to get some practice in the most frequently used worksheet operations.

Hands-On 2.14 Moving, Copying, and Deleting Cells

To render this into VBA:	Enter this in the Immediate window:
Move the contents of cell A5 to cell A4.	`Range("A5").Cut Destination:=Range("A4")`
Copy a formula from cell A3 to cells D5:F5.	`Range("A3").Copy Destination:=Range("D5:F5")`
Delete the contents of cell A4.	`Range("A4").Clear` or `Range("A4").Cut`

Notice that the first two methods in the table require a special argument called `Destination`. This argument specifies the address of a cell or a range of cells where you want to place the cut or copied data. In the last example, the `Cut` method is used without the `Destination` argument to remove data from the specified cell.

The `Clear` method deletes everything from the specified cell or range, including any applied formats and cell comments. If you want to be specific about what you delete, use the following methods:

- `ClearContents`—Clears only data from a cell or range of cells
- `ClearFormats`—Clears only applied formats
- `ClearComments`—Clears all cell comments from the specified range
- `ClearNotes`—Clears notes and sound notes from all the cells in the specified range
- `ClearHyperlinks`—Removes all hyperlinks from the specified range
- `ClearOutline`—Clears the outline for the specified range

WORKING WITH ROWS AND COLUMNS

Excel uses the EntireRow and EntireColumn properties to select the entire row or column. Let's now write the statements in Hands-On 2.15 to quickly select entire rows and columns.

Hands-On 2.15 Selecting Entire Rows and Columns

To render this into VBA:	Enter this in the Immediate window:
Select an entire row where the active cell is located.	`Selection.EntireRow.Select`
Select an entire column where the active cell is located.	`Selection.EntireColumn.Select`

When you select a range of cells you may want to find out how many rows or columns are included in the selection. Let's have Excel count rows and columns in `Range("A1:D15")`.

1. Type the following VBA statement in the Immediate window and press **Enter**:

   ```
   Range("A1:D15").Select
   ```

   If the Microsoft Excel window is visible, Visual Basic will highlight the range A1:D15 when you press Enter.

2. To find out how many rows are in the selected range, enter the following statement:

   ```
   ?Selection.Rows.Count
   ```

   As soon as you press **Enter**, Visual Basic displays the answer on the next line. Your selection includes 15 rows.

3. To find out the number of columns in the selected range, enter the following statement:

   ```
   ?Selection.Columns.Count
   ```

   As soon as you press **Enter**, Visual Basic tells you that the selected `Range("A1:D15")` occupies the width of four columns.

4. In the Immediate window, position the cursor anywhere within the word Rows or Columns and press **F1** to find out more information about these useful properties.

Obtaining Information about the Worksheet

How big is an Excel worksheet? How many columns and rows does it contain? If you ever forget the details, use the Count property as shown in Hands-On 2.16.

Hands-On 2.16 Counting Rows and Columns

To render this into VBA:	Enter this in the Immediate window:
Find out the total number of rows in an Excel worksheet.	`?Rows.Count`
Find out the total number of columns in an Excel worksheet.	`?Columns.Count`

A Microsoft Excel worksheet has 1,048,576 rows and 16,384 columns.

ENTERING DATA AND FORMATTING CELLS

The information entered in a worksheet can be text, numbers, or formulas. To enter data in a cell or range of cells, you can use either the Value property or the Formula property of the Range object.

- Using the Value property:

```
ActiveSheet.Range("A1:C4").Value = "=4 * 25"
```

- Using the Formula property:

```
ActiveSheet.Range("A1:C4").Formula = "=4 * 25"
```

In both examples, cells A1:C4 display 100—the result of the multiplication 4 * 25. Let's proceed to some practice in Hands-On 2.17.

Hands-On 2.17 Using VBA Statements to Enter Data in a Worksheet

To render this into VBA:	Enter this in the Immediate window:
Enter in cell A5 the following text: Amount Due	`Range("A5").Formula = "Amount Due"`

Enter the number 123 in cell D21.	`Range("D21").Formula = 123`
	or
	`Range("D21").Value = 123`

Enter in cell B4 the following formula: = D21 * 3	`Range("B4").Formula = "=D21 * 3"`

Returning Information Entered in a Worksheet

In some Visual Basic procedures, you will undoubtedly need to return the contents of a cell or a range of cells. Although you can use either the Value or Formula property, this time the two Range object's properties are not interchangeable.

- The Value property displays the result of a formula entered in a specified cell. If, for example, cell A1 contains a formula = 4 * 25, then the instruction

  ```
  ?Range("A1").Value
  ```

  will return the value of 100.
- If you want to display the formula instead of its result, you must use the Formula property:

  ```
  ?Range("A1").Formula
  ```

  Excel will display the formula (= 4 * 25) instead of its result (100).

Finding Out about Cell Formatting

A frequent spreadsheet task is applying formatting to a selected cell or a range. Your VBA procedure may need to find out the type of formatting applied to a worksheet cell. To retrieve the cell formatting, use the NumberFormat property:

```
?Range("A1").NumberFormat
```

Upon entering the foregoing statement in the Immediate window, Excel displays the word "General," which indicates that no special formatting was applied to the selected cell. To change the format of a cell to dollars and cents using VBA, enter the following instruction:

```
Range("A1").NumberFormat = "$#,##0.00"
```

If you enter 125 in cell A1 after it has been formatted using this code, cell A1 will display $125.00. You can look up the available format codes in the Format Cells dialog box in the Microsoft Excel application window as shown in Figure 2.18.

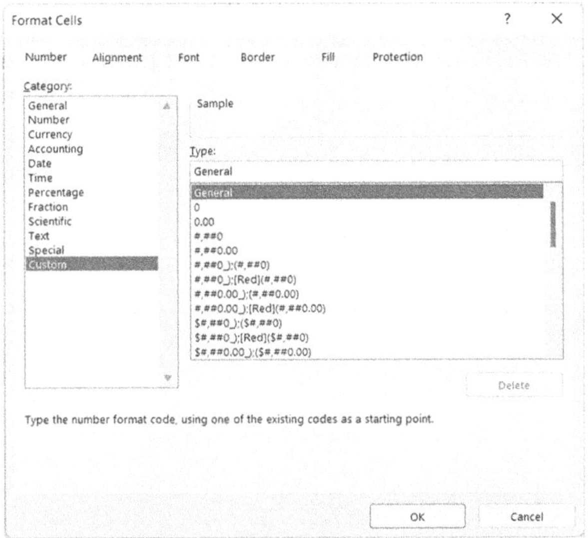

FIGURE 2.18 You can apply different formatting to selected cells and ranges using format codes, as displayed in the Custom category in the Format Cells dialog box. To quickly bring up this dialog box, press the Alt, H, F, and M keys one at a time.

WORKING WITH WORKBOOKS AND WORKSHEETS

Now that you've got your feet wet working with worksheet cells and ranges, it's time to move up one level and learn how you can control a single workbook, as well as an entire collection of workbooks. You cannot prepare a new worksheet if you don't know how to open a new workbook. You cannot remove a workbook from the screen if you don't know how to close a workbook. You cannot work with an existing workbook if you don't know how to open it. These important tasks are handled by the following VBA methods: `Add`, `Open`, and `Close`. The next series of drills in Hands-On 2.18 and 2.19 will give you the language skills necessary for dealing with workbooks and worksheets.

Hands-On 2.18 Working with Workbooks

To render this into VBA:	Enter this in the Immediate window:
Open a new workbook.	`Workbooks.Add`
Find out the name of the first workbook.	`?Workbooks(1).Name`
Find out the number of open workbooks.	`?Workbooks.Count`

To render this into VBA:	Enter this in the Immediate window:
Activate the second open workbook.	`Workbooks(2).Activate`
Close the Chap01_ExcelPrimer.xlsm workbook and save the changes.	`Workbooks("Chap01_ExcelPrimer.xlsm").Close SaveChanges:=True`
Open the Chap01_ExcelPrimer.xlsm workbook. Type the correct path to the file location on your computer.	`Workbooks.Open "C:\VBAExcel2021Primer_ByExample\Chap01_ExcelPrimer.xlsm"`
Activate the Chap01_ExcelPrimer.xlsm workbook.	`Workbooks("Chap01_ExcelPrimer.xlsm").Activate`
Save the active workbook as NewChap.xlsm.	`ActiveWorkbook.SaveAs Filename:= "NewChap.xlsm"`
Close the first workbook.	`Workbooks(1).Close`
Close the active workbook without saving recent changes to it.	`ActiveWorkbook.Close SaveChanges:=False`
Close all open workbooks.	`Workbooks.Close`

If you worked through the last example in Hands-On 2.18, all workbooks are now closed. Before you experiment with worksheets, make sure you have opened a new workbook.

When you deal with individual worksheets, you must know how to add a new worksheet to a workbook, select a worksheet or a group of worksheets, name a worksheet, and copy, move, and delete worksheets. In Visual Basic, each of these tasks is handled by a special method or property.

Hands-On 2.19 Working with Worksheets

To render this into VBA:	Enter this in the Immediate window:
Add a new worksheet.	`Worksheets.Add`
Find out the name of the first worksheet.	`?Worksheets(1).Name`
Select a sheet named Sheet3.	`Worksheets(3).Select`
Select sheets 1, 3, and 4.	`Worksheets(Array(1,3,4)).Select`
Activate a sheet named Sheet1.	`Worksheets("Sheet1").Activate`
Move Sheet2 before Sheet1.	`Worksheets("Sheet2").Move Before:=Worksheets("Sheet1")`
Rename worksheet Sheet2 to Expenses.	`Worksheets("Sheet2").Name = "Expenses"`
Find out the number of worksheets in the active workbook.	`?Worksheets.Count`
Remove the worksheet named Expenses from the active workbook.	`Worksheets("Expenses").Delete`

Notice the difference between the `Select` and `Activate` methods:

- The `Select` and `Activate` methods can be used interchangeably if only one worksheet is selected.
- If you select a group of worksheets, the `Activate` method allows you to decide which one of the selected worksheets is active. As you know, only one worksheet can be active at a time.

SIDEBAR ***Sheets Other than Worksheets***

In addition to worksheets, the collection of workbooks contains chart sheets. To add a new chart sheet to your workbook, use the `Add` method:

```
Charts.Add
```

To count the chart sheets, use:

```
?Charts.Count
```

WORKING WITH WINDOWS

When you work with several Excel workbooks and need to compare or consolidate data or you want to see different parts of the same worksheet, you are bound to use the options available from the Microsoft Excel Window menu: New Window and Arrange.

In Hands-On 2.20 you will learn how to work with Windows using VBA.

Hands-On 2.20 Working with Windows

To render this into VBA:	Enter this in the Immediate window:
Show the active workbook in a new window.	`ActiveWorkbook.NewWindow`
Display on screen all open workbooks.	`Windows.Arrange`
Activate the second window.	`Windows(2).Activate`
Find out the title of the active window.	`?ActiveWindow.Caption`
Change the active window's title to My Window.	`ActiveWindow.Caption = "My Window"`

When you display windows on screen, you can decide how to arrange them. The `Arrange` method has many arguments, as shown in Table 2.1. The argument that allows you to control the way the windows are positioned on your screen is called `ArrangeStyle`. If you omit the `ArrangeStyle` argument, all windows are tiled.

TABLE 2.1 Arguments of the `Arrange` method of the Windows object.

Constant	Value	Description
`xlArrangeStyleTiled`	1	Windows are tiled (the default value).
`xlArrangeStyleCascade`	7	Windows are cascaded.
`xlArrangeStyleHorizontal`	2	Windows are arranged horizontally.
`xlArrangeStyleVertical`	3	Windows are arranged vertically.

Instead of the names of constants, you can use the value equivalents shown in Table 2.1.

To cascade all windows, use the following VBA instruction:

```
Windows.Arrange ArrangeStyle:=xlArrangeStyleCascade
```

or simply:

```
Windows.Arrange ArrangeStyle:=7
```

WORKING WITH THE EXCEL APPLICATION

The Application object represents the Excel application itself. By controlling the Application object, you can perform many tasks, such as saving the way your screen looks at the end of a day's work or quitting the application. As you know, Excel allows you to save the screen settings by using the Save Workspace button on the View tab. The task of saving the workspace can be easily performed with VBA:

```
Application.SaveWorkspace "Project"
```

This instruction saves the screen settings in the workspace file named Project. The next time you need to work with the same files and arrangement of windows, simply open the Project.xlwx file so Excel will bring up the correct files and restore your screen with those settings. And now let's write some statements that use the Application object.

Hands-On 2.21 Working with the Excel Application

To render this into VBA:	Enter this in the Immediate window:
Check the name of the active application.	`?Application.Name`
Change the title of the Excel application to My Application.	`Application.Caption = "My Application"`
Change the title of the Excel application back to Microsoft Excel.	`Application.Caption = "Microsoft Excel"`
Find out what operating system you are using.	`?Application.OperatingSystem`
Find out the name of a person or firm to whom the application is registered.	`?Application.OrganizationName`
Find out the name of the folder where the Excel executable file (Excel.exe) resides.	`?Application.Path`
Quit working with Microsoft Excel.	`Application.Quit`

SUMMARY

This chapter has given you an overview of the Visual Basic Editor window. You learned many basic VBA terms and practiced them by executing single statements in the Immediate window.

In the next chapter, you will learn how the data can be stored for later use in variables. You will also explore VBA data types and constants.

Chapter 3

EXCEL VBA FUNDAMENTALS

A QUICK REFERENCE TO WRITING VBA CODE

In programming, just as in life, certain things need to be done at once while others can be put off until later. When you postpone a task, you may enter it in your mental or paper "to-do" list and classify it by its type or importance. When you delegate the task or finally get around to doing it yourself, you cross it off the list. This chapter shows you how your VBA procedures can memorize important pieces of information for use in later statements or calculations. You will learn how a procedure can keep a "to-do" entry in a variable, how variables are declared, and how they relate to data types and constants.

EXCEL OBJECTS, PROPERTIES, AND METHODS

You can create procedures that control many features of Microsoft Excel using Visual Basic for Applications. You can also control many other applications. The power of Visual Basic comes from its ability to control and manage various objects. But what is an object?

An *object* is a thing you can control with VBA. Workbooks, a worksheet, a range in a worksheet, a chart, and a toolbar are just a few examples of the objects you may want to control while working in Excel. Excel contains a multitude of objects that you can manipulate in different ways. All these objects are organized in a hierarchy. Some objects may contain other objects. For example, Microsoft Excel is an Application object. The Application object contains other objects, such as workbooks or command bars. The Workbook object may contain other objects, such as worksheets or charts. In this chapter, you will learn how to control the following Excel objects: Range, Window, Worksheet, Workbook, and Application. You begin by learning about the Range object. You can't do much work in spreadsheets unless you know how to manipulate ranges of cells.

Certain objects look alike. For example, if you open a new workbook and examine its worksheets, you won't see any differences. A group of like objects is called a *collection*. A Worksheets collection includes all worksheets in a workbook. Collections are also objects. In Microsoft Excel, the most frequently used collections are:

- Workbooks collection—represents all currently open workbooks.
- Worksheets collection—represents all the Worksheet objects in the specified or active workbook. Each Worksheet object represents a worksheet.
- Sheets collection—represents all the sheets in the specified or active workbook. The Sheets collection can contain Chart or Worksheet objects.
- Windows collection—represents all the Window objects in Microsoft Excel. The Windows collection for the Application object contains all the windows in the application, whereas the Windows collection for the Workbook object contains only the windows in the specified workbook.

When you work with collections, you can perform the same action on all the objects in the collection.

Each object has some characteristics that allow you to describe the object. In Visual Basic, the object's characteristics are called *properties*. For example, a Workbook object has a Name property, and the Range object has such properties as Column, Font, Formula, Name, Row, Style, and Value. The object properties can be set. When you set an object's property, you control its appearance or its position. Object properties can take on only one specific value at any one time. For example, the active workbook can't be called two different names at the same time.

The most difficult part of Visual Basic is to understand the fact that some properties can also be objects. Let's consider the Range object. You can change the appearance of the selected range of cells by setting the Font property. But the font can have a different name (Times New Roman, Arial, ...), different size (10, 12, 14, ...), and different style (bold, italic, underline, ...). These are font properties. If the font has properties, then the font is also an object.

Properties are great. They let you change the look of the object, but how can you control the actions? Before you can make Excel carry out some tasks, you need to know another term. Objects have methods. Each action you want the object to perform is called a *method*. The most important Visual Basic method is the `Add` method, which you can use to add a new workbook or worksheet. Objects can use various methods. For example, the Range object has special methods that allow you to clear the cell contents (`ClearContents` method), clear just formats (`ClearFormats` method), and clear both contents and formats (`Clear` method). Other methods allow objects to be selected, copied, or moved.

Methods can have optional parameters that specify how the method is to be carried out. For example, the Workbook object has a method called `Close`. You can close any open workbook using this method. If there are changes to the workbook, Microsoft Excel will display a message prompting you to save the changes. You can use the `Close` method with the `SaveChanges` parameter set to False to close the workbook and discard any changes that have been made to it, as in the following example:

```
Workbooks("Chap01_Excel.xlsm").Close SaveChanges:=False
```

MICROSOFT EXCEL OBJECT MODEL

When you learn new things, theory can give you the necessary background, but how do you really know what's where? All the available Excel objects as well as their properties and methods can be looked up in the online Excel Object Model Reference that you can access by choosing Help | Microsoft Visual Basic for Applications Help in the Visual Basic Editor window. Figure 3.1 illustrates the Excel Object Model Reference in the online help. This page can be accessed via the following link:

https://docs.microsoft.com/en-us/office/vba/api/overview/Excel/object-model

Objects are listed alphabetically for easy perusal, and when you click the object, you will see object subcategories that list the object's properties, methods, and events. Reading the object model reference is a great way to learn about Excel objects and collections of objects. The time you spend here will pay big dividends later when you need to write complex VBA procedures from scratch. A good way to get started is to always look up objects that you come across in Excel programming texts or example procedures. Now take a few minutes to familiarize yourself with the main Excel object—Application. This object allows you to specify application-level properties and execute application-level methods. You saw several examples of working with the Application object in Chapter 2.

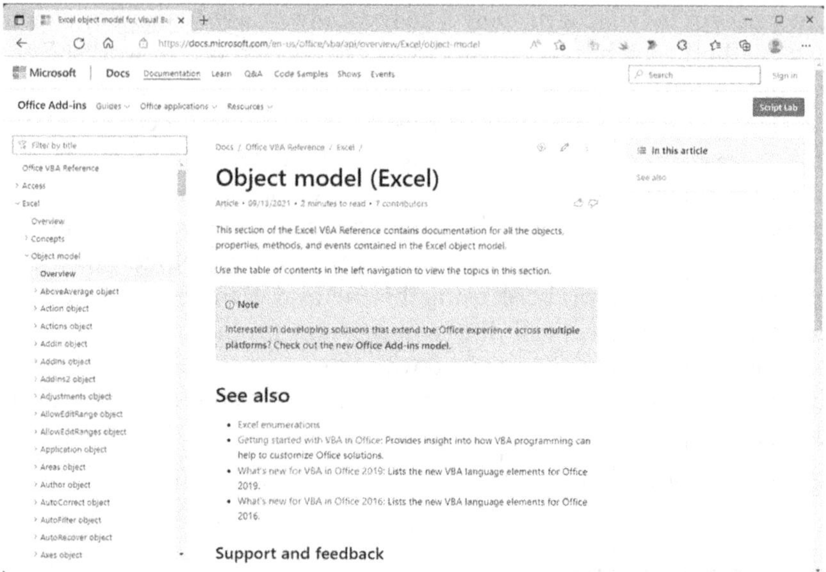

FIGURE 3.1 In your VBA programming work, always refer to the Excel Object Model Reference that contains documentation for all the objects, properties, methods, and events contained in the Excel object model.

WRITING SIMPLE AND COMPLEX VBA STATEMENTS

Now that you know the basic elements of VBA (objects, properties, and methods), it's time to start using them. But how do you combine objects, properties, and methods into correct language structures? Every language has grammar rules that people follow to make themselves understood. Whether you communicate in English, Spanish, French, or another language, you apply certain rules to your writing and speech. In programming, we use the term *syntax* to specify language rules. You can look up the syntax of each object, property, or method in the online help or in the Object Browser window.

To make sure Excel always understands what you mean, just stick to the following rules:

Rule #1: Referring to the property of an object

If the property does not have arguments, the syntax is as follows:

```
Object.Property
```

Object is a placeholder. It is where you should place the name of the actual object that you are trying to access. Property is also a placeholder. Here you place the name of the object's characteristics. For example, to refer to the value entered in cell A4 on your worksheet, you can write the following instruction:

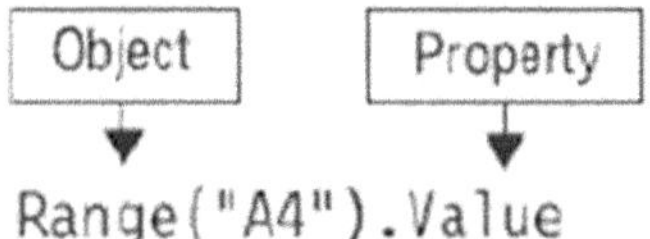

Notice that there is a period between the name of the object and its property.

When you need to access the property of an object that is contained within several other objects, you must include the names of all objects in turn, separated by the dot operator, as shown here:

```
ActiveSheet.Shapes(2).Line.Weight
```

This example references the Weight property of the Line object and refers to the second object in the collection of Shapes located in the active worksheet.

Some properties require one or more arguments. For example, when using the Offset property, you can select a cell relative to the active cell. The Offset property requires two arguments. The first argument indicates the row number (`rowOffset`), and the second one determines the column number (`columnOffset`).

In this example, assuming the active cell is A1, `Offset(3, 2)` will reference the cell located three rows down and two columns to the right of cell A1. In other words, cell C4 is referenced. Because the arguments placed within parentheses are often difficult to understand, it's common practice to precede the value of the argument with its name, as in the following example:

```
ActiveCell.Offset(rowOffset:=3, columnOffset:=2)
```

Notice that a colon and an equal sign must always follow the named arguments. When you use the named arguments, you can list them in any order. The foregoing instruction can also be written as follows:

```
ActiveCell.Offset(columnOffset:=2, rowOffset:=3)
```

The revised instruction does not change the meaning; you are still referencing cell C4 assuming that A1 is the active cell. However, if you transpose the arguments in a statement that does not use named arguments, you will end up referencing another cell. For example, the statement `ActiveCell.Offset(2, 3)` will reference cell D3 instead of C4.

Rule #2: Changing the property of an object

```
Object.Property = Value
```

Value is a new value that you want to assign to the property of the object. The value can be:

- A number. The following instruction enters the number 25 in cell A4.

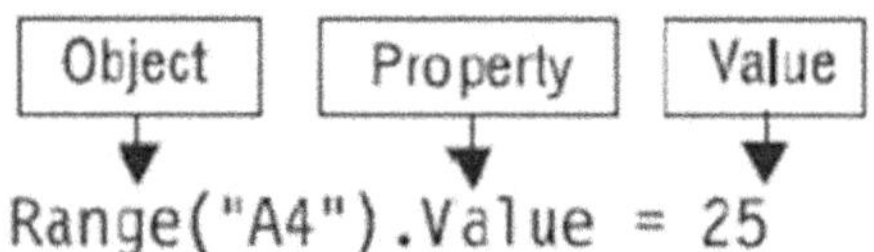

- Text entered in quotes. The following instruction changes the font of the active cell to Times New Roman.

```
ActiveCell.Font.Name = "Times New Roman"
```

- A logical value (True or False). The following instruction applies bold formatting to the active cell.

```
ActiveCell.Font.Bold = True
```

Rule #3: Returning the current value of the object property

```
Variable = Object.Property
```

Variable is the name of the storage location where Visual Basic is going to store the property setting. You will learn about variables later in this chapter.

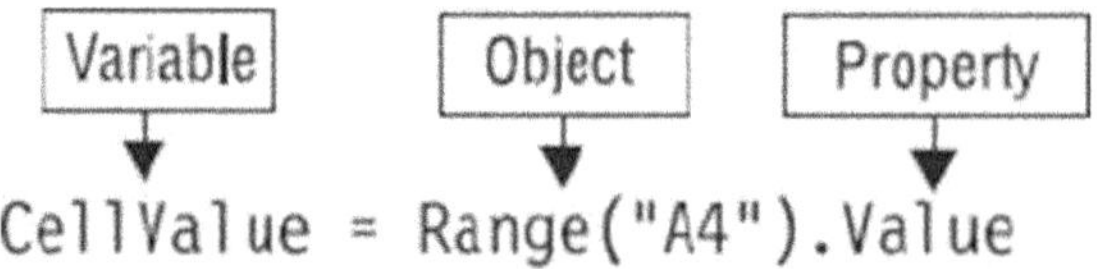

This instruction saves the current value of cell A4 in the variable named `CellValue`.

Rule #4: Referring to the object's method

If the method does not have arguments, the syntax is as follows:

```
Object.Method
```

Object is a placeholder. It is where you should place the name of the actual object that you are trying to access. Method is also a placeholder. Here you place the name of the action you want to perform on the object. For example, to clear the contents in cell A4, use the following instruction:

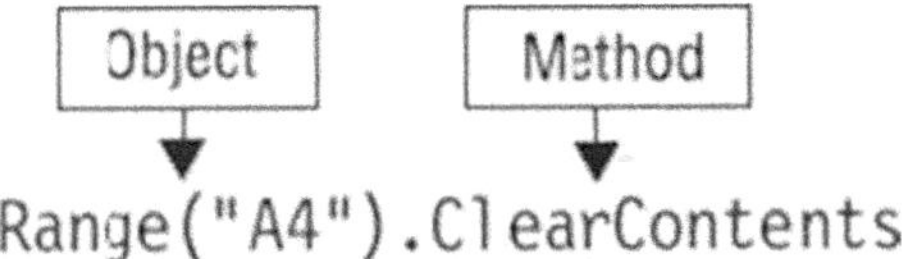

If the method requires arguments, the syntax is as follows:

```
Object.Method (argument1, argument2, ... argumentN)
```

For example, using the `GoTo` method, you can quickly select any range in a workbook. The syntax of the `GoTo` method is shown here:

```
Object.GoTo(Reference, Scroll)
```

The `Reference` argument is the destination cell or range. The `Scroll` argument can be set to True to scroll through the window or to False to not scroll through the window. For example, the following VBA statement selects cell P100 in Sheet1 and scrolls through the window:

```
Application.GoTo _
    Reference:=Worksheets("Sheet1").Range("P100"), _Scroll:=True
```

The foregoing instruction did not fit on one line, so it was broken into sections using the special line continuation character (the underscore), described in the next section.

Suppose you want to delete the contents of cell A4. To do this manually, you would select cell A4 and press the Delete key on your keyboard. To perform the same operation using Visual Basic, you first need to find out how to make Excel select an appropriate cell. Cell A4, like any other worksheet cell, is represented by the Range object. Visual Basic does not have a Delete method for deleting contents of cells. Instead, you should use the `ClearContents` method, as in the following example:

```
Range("A4").ClearContents
```

Notice the dot operator between the name of the object and its method. This instruction removes the contents of cell A4. However, how do you make Excel delete the contents of cell A4 located in the first sheet of the Chap03_ExcelPrimer.xlsm workbook? Let's also assume that there are several workbooks open. If you don't want to end up deleting the contents of cell A4 from the wrong workbook or worksheet, you must write a detailed instruction so that Visual Basic knows where to locate the necessary cell:

```
Application.Workbooks("Chap03_ExcelPrimer.xlsm")
.Worksheets("Sheet1").Range("A4").ClearContents
```

The foregoing instruction should be written on one line and read from right to left as follows: Clear the contents of cell A4, which is part of a range located in a worksheet named Sheet1 contained in a workbook named Chap03_ExcelPrimer.xlsm, which in turn is part of the Excel application. Be sure to include the letter "s" at the end of the collection names: Workbooks and Worksheets. All references to the names of workbooks, worksheets, and cells must be enclosed in quotation marks.

Breaking Up Long VBA Statements

When you start writing complete VBA procedures from scratch, you will need to know how to break up a long VBA statement into two or more lines to make your procedure more readable. Visual Basic has a special line continuation character that can be used at the end of a line to indicate that the next line is a continuation of the previous one, as in the following example:

```
Selection.PasteSpecial _
   Paste:=xlValues, _
   Operation:=xlMultiply, _
   SkipBlanks: =False, _
   Transpose:=False
```

The line continuation character is the underscore (_). You must precede the underscore with a space.

You can use the line continuation character in your code before or after:

- Operators; for example: &, +, Like, NOT, AND
- A comma
- An equal sign
- An assignment operator (:=)

You cannot use the line continuation character between a colon and an equal's sign. For example, the following use of the continuation character is not recognized by Visual Basic:

```
Selection.PasteSpecial Paste: _
   =xlValues, Operation: _
   =xlMultiply, SkipBlanks: _
```

```
   =False, Transpose: _
   =False
```

Also, you may not use the line continuation character within text enclosed in quotes. For example, the following usage of the underscore is invalid:

```
MsgBox "To continue the long instruction, use the _
   line continuation character."
```

Instead, break it up as follows:

```
MsgBox "To continue the long instruction, use the " & _
       "line continuation character."
```

SAVING RESULTS OF VBA STATEMENTS

In Chapter 2, while working in the Immediate window, you tried several Visual Basic instructions that returned some information. For example, when you entered `?Rows.Count`, you found out that there are 1,048,576 rows in a worksheet. However, when you write Visual Basic procedures outside of the Immediate window, you can't use the question mark. If you want to know the result after executing an instruction, you must tell Visual Basic to memorize it. In programming, results returned by Visual Basic instructions can be written to variables. Since variables can hold various types of data, the next section focuses on introducing you to VBA data types. Once you understand the basics of data types, it will be easy to tackle the variable part.

INTRODUCING DATA TYPES

When you create Visual Basic procedures, you have a purpose in mind: You want to manipulate data. Because your procedures will handle different kinds of information, you should understand how Visual Basic stores data. The *data type* determines how the data is stored in the computer's memory. For example, data can be stored as a number, text, date, object, and so on. If you forget to tell Visual Basic the type of your data, it assigns the Variant data type. The Variant type can figure out on its own what kind of data is being manipulated and then take on that type.

The Visual Basic data types are shown in Table 3.1. In addition to the built-in data types, you can define your own data types. Because data types take up different amounts of space in the computer's memory, some of them are more expensive than others. Therefore, to conserve memory and make your procedure run faster, you should select the data type that uses the least number of bytes and, at the same time, can handle the data that your procedure has to manipulate.

TABLE 3.1 VBA data types.

Data Type (Name)	Size (Bytes)	Description
Boolean	2	Stores a value of True (0) or False (–1).
Byte	1	A number in the range of 0 to 255.
Integer	2	A number in the range of –32,768 to 32,767. The type declaration character for Integer is the percent sign (%).
Long (Long integer)	4	A number in the range of –2,147,483,648 to 2,147,483,647. The type declaration character for Long is the ampersand (&).
LongLong (LongLong integer)	8	Stored as a signed 64-bit (8-byte) number ranging in value from –9,223,372,036,854,775,808 to 9,223,372,036,854,775,807. The type declaration character for LongLong is the caret (^). LongLong is a valid declared type only on 64-bit platforms.
LongPtr (Long integer on 32-bit systems; LongLong integer on 64-bit systems)	4 on 32-bit 8 on 64-bit	Numbers ranging in value from –2,147,483,648 to 2,147,483,647 on 32-bit systems; –9,223,372,036,854,775,808 to 9,223,372,036,854,775,807 on 64-bit systems. Using LongPtr enables writing code that can run in both 32-bit and 64-bit environments.
Single (single-precision floating-point)	4	Single-precision floating-point real number ranging in value from –3.402823E38 to –1.401298E–45 for negative values and from 1.401298E–45 to 3.402823E38 for positive values. The type declaration character for Single is the exclamation point (!).
Double (double-precision floating-point)	8	Double-precision floating-point real number in the range of –1.79769313486231E308 to –4.94065645841247E–324 for negative values and 4.94065645841247E–324 to 1.79769313486231E308 for positive values. The type declaration character for Double is the number sign (#).
Currency (scaled integer)	8	(scaled integer) Monetary values used in fixed-point calculations: –922,337,203,685,477.5808 to 922,337,203,685,477.5807. The type declaration character for Currency is the at sign (@).

Data Type (Name)	Size (Bytes)	Description

Decimal	14	96-bit (12-byte) signed integer scaled by a variable power o f 10. The power of 10 scaling factor specifies the number of digits to the right of the decimal point, and ranges from 0 to 28.
		With no decimal point (scale of 0), the largest value is
		+/-79,228,162,514,264,337,593,543,950,335.
		With 28 decimal places, the largest value is
		+/-7.9228162514264337593543950335. The smallest nonzero value is +/-0.0000000000000000000000000001.
		You cannot declare a variable to be of type Decimal. You must use the Variant data type. Use the `CDec` function to convert a value to a decimal number:
		`Dim numDecimal As Variant`
		`numDecimal = CDec(0.02 * 15.75 * 0.0006)`

Date	8	Date from January 1, 100, to December 31, 9999, and times from 0:00:00 to 23:59:59. Date literals must be enclosed within number signs (#)—for example: #January 1, 2019#
String (variable-length)	10 bytes + string length	A variable-length string can contain up to approximately 2 billion characters. The type declaration character for String is the dollar sign ($).
String (fixed-length)	Length of string	A fixed-length string can contain 1 to approximately 65,400 characters.
Object	4	Object variable used to refer to any Excel object. Use the `Set` statement to declare a variable as an Object.
Variant (with numbers)	16	Any numeric value up to the size of a Double.
Variant (with characters)	22 bytes + string length	Any valid nonnumeric data type in the same range as for a variable-length string.

(Contd.)

<table>
<tr><th>Data Type (Name)</th><th>Size (Bytes)</th><th>Description</th></tr>
<tr><td>User-Defined (using Type)</td><td>One or more elements</td><td>A data type you define using the <code>Type</code> statement. User-defined data types can contain one or more elements of a data type, an array, or a previously defined user-defined type—for example:

<code>Type custInfo</code>
<code> custFullName as String</code>
<code> custTitle as String</code>
<code> custBusinessName as String</code>
<code> custFirstOrderDate as Date</code>
<code>End Type</code></td></tr>
</table>

NOTE	*For more information about data types see the online help at: https://docs.microsoft.com/en-us/office/vba/language/reference/user-interface-help/data-type-summary*

USING VARIABLES

A *variable* is simply a name that is used to refer to an item of data. Each time you want to remember a result of a VBA instruction, think of a name that will represent it. For example, if the number 1,048,576 must remind you of the total number of rows in a worksheet (a very important piece of information when you want to bring external data into Excel), you can make up a name such as AllRows, NumOfRows, or TotalRows, and so on. The names of variables can contain characters, numbers, and some punctuation marks, except for the following:

, # $ % & @ !

The name of a variable cannot begin with a number or contain a space. If you want the name of the variable to include more than one word, use the underscore (_) as a separator. Although the name of a variable can contain as many as 254 characters, it's best to use short and simple variable names. Using short names will save you typing time when you need to refer to the variable in your Visual Basic procedure. Visual Basic doesn't care whether you use uppercase or lowercase letters in variable names, but most programmers use lowercase letters. For variable names that are made up of one or more words, you may want to use title case, as in the names NumOfRows and First_Name.

SIDEBAR *Reserved Words Can't Be Used for Variable Names*

You can use any label you want for a variable name, except for the reserved words that VBA uses. Visual Basic statements and certain other words that have a special meaning in VBA cannot be used as names of variables. For example, words such as Name, Len, Empty, Local, Currency, or Exit will generate an error message if used as a variable name.

SIDEBAR *Meaningful Variable Names*

Give variables names that can help you remember their roles. Some programmers use a prefix to identify the type of a variable. A variable name that begins with "str" (for example, strName) can be quickly recognized within the code of your procedure as the one holding the text string.

How to Create Variables

You can create a variable by declaring it with a special command or by just using it in a statement. When you declare your variable, you make Visual Basic aware of the variable's name and data type. This is called *explicit variable declaration.* There are several advantages to explicit variable declaration:

- Explicit variable declaration speeds up the execution of your procedure. Because Visual Basic knows the data type, it reserves only as much memory as is necessary to store the data.
- Explicit variable declaration makes your code easier to read and understand because all the variables are listed at the very beginning of the procedure.
- Explicit variable declaration helps prevent errors caused by misspelled variable names. Visual Basic automatically corrects the variable name based on the spelling used in the variable declaration.

If you don't let Visual Basic know about the variable prior to using it, you are implicitly telling VBA that you want to create this variable. Variables declared implicitly are automatically assigned the Variant data type (see Table 3.1 in the previous section). Although implicit variable declaration is convenient (it allows you to create variables on the fly and assign values without knowing in advance the data type of the values being assigned), it can cause several problems, as outlined here:

- If you misspell a variable name in your procedure, Visual Basic may display a runtime error or create a new variable. You are guaranteed to waste some time troubleshooting problems that could have been easily avoided had you declared your variable at the beginning of the procedure.
- Because Visual Basic does not know what type of data your variable will store, it assigns it a Variant data type. This causes your procedure to run slower because Visual Basic must check the data type every time it deals with your variable. Because a Variant can store any type of data, Visual Basic must reserve more memory to store your data.

How to Declare Variables

You declare a variable with the `Dim` keyword. `Dim` stands for dimension. The `Dim` keyword is followed by the name of the variable and then the variable type.

Suppose you want the procedure to display the age of an employee. Before you can calculate the age, you must tell the procedure the employee's date of birth. To do this, you declare a variable called `DateOfBirth`, as follows:

```
Dim DateOfBirth As Date
```

Notice that the `Dim` keyword is followed by the name of the variable (`DateOfBirth`). This name can be anything you choose, if it is not one of the VBA keywords. Specify the data type the variable will hold by placing the `As` keyword after its name, followed by one of the data types from Table 4.1. The Date data type tells Visual Basic that the variable `DateOfBirth` will store a date. To store the employee's age, declare the `age` variable as follows:

```
Dim age As Integer
```

The `age` variable will store the number of years between today's date and the employee's date of birth. Because `age` is displayed as a whole number, this variable has been assigned the Integer data type.

You may also want your procedure to keep track of the employee's name, so you declare another variable to hold the employee's first and last name:

```
Dim FullName As String
```

Because the word "Name" is on the VBA list of reserved words, using it in your VBA procedure would guarantee an error. To hold the employee's full name, call the variable `FullName` and declare it as the String data type, because the data it will hold is text.

Declaring variables is regarded as a good programming practice because it makes programs easier to read and helps prevent certain types of errors.

SIDEBAR *Informal Variables*

Variables that are not explicitly declared with `Dim` statements are said to be implicitly declared. These variables are automatically assigned a data type called Variant. They can hold numbers, strings, and other types of information. You can create a variable by simply assigning some value to a variable name anywhere in your VBA procedure. For example, you will implicitly declare a variable in the following way:

```
DaysLeft = 100
```

Now that you know how to declare your variables, let's look at a procedure that uses them:

```
Sub AgeCalc()
  ' variable declaration
  Dim FullName As String
  Dim DateOfBirth As Date
  Dim age As Integer

  ' assign values to variables
  FullName = "John Smith"
  DateOfBirth = #01/03/1981#

  ' calculate age
  age = Year(Now())-Year(DateOfBirth)

  ' print results to the Immediate window
  Debug.Print FullName & " is " & age & " years old."
End Sub
```

The variables are declared at the beginning of the procedure in which they are going to be used. In this procedure, the variables are declared on separate lines. If you want, you can declare several variables on the same line, separating each variable name with a comma, as shown here:

```
Dim FullName As String, DateOfBirth As Date, age As Integer
```

Notice that the `Dim` keyword appears only once at the beginning of the variable declaration line.

When Visual Basic executes the variable declaration statements, it creates the variables with the specified names and reserves memory space to store their values. Then specific values are assigned to these variables.

To assign a value to a variable, begin with a variable name followed by an equal sign. The value entered to the right of the equals sign is the data you want to store in the variable. The data you enter here must be of the type determined by the variable declaration. Text data should be surrounded by quotation marks, and dates by the # characters.

Using the data supplied by the `DateOfBirth` variable, Visual Basic calculates the age of an employee and stores the result of the calculation in the `age` variable. Then the full name of the employee as well as the age is printed to the Immediate window using the instruction `Debug.Print`. When the Visual Basic procedure has executed, you must view the Immediate window to see the results.

Let's see what happens when you declare a variable with the incorrect data type. The purpose of the following procedure is to calculate the total number of rows in a worksheet and then display the results in a dialog box.

```
Sub HowManyRows()
  Dim NumOfRows As Integer

  NumOfRows = Rows.Count

  MsgBox "The worksheet has " & NumOfRows & " rows."
End Sub
```

A wrong data type can cause an error. In the foregoing procedure, when Visual Basic attempts to write the result of the `Rows.Count` statement to the variable `NumOfRows`, the procedure fails, and Excel displays the message "*Run-time error 6—Overflow*." This error results from selecting an invalid data type for that variable. The number of rows in a spreadsheet does not fit the Integer data range. To correct the problem, you should choose a data type that can accommodate a larger number:

```
Sub HowManyRows2()
  Dim NumOfRows As Long

  NumOfRows = Rows.Count
  MsgBox "The worksheet has " & NumOfRows & " rows."
End Sub
```

You can also correct the problem caused by the assignment of the wrong data type in the first example by deleting the variable type (`As Integer`). When you rerun the procedure, Visual Basic will assign to your variable the Variant data type. Although Variants use up more memory than any other variable type and slow down the speed at which your procedures run (because Visual Basic must do extra work to check the Variant's context), when it comes to short procedures, the cost of using Variants is barely noticeable.

SIDEBAR ***What Is the Variable Type?***

You can quickly find out the type of a variable used in your procedure by right clicking the variable name and selecting Quick Info from the shortcut menu.

SIDEBAR ***Concatenation***

You can combine two or more strings to form a new string. The joining operation is called *concatenation*. You have seen examples of concatenated strings in the foregoing AgeCalc and HowManyRows2 procedures. Concatenation is represented by an ampersand character (&). For instance, `"His name is " & FirstName` will produce the following string: His name is John. The name of the person is determined by the contents of the `FirstName` variable. Notice that there is an extra space between "is" and the ending quote: "His name is ."

Concatenation of strings also can be represented by a plus sign (+). However, many programmers prefer to restrict the plus sign to operations on numbers to eliminate ambiguity.

Specifying the Data Type of a Variable

If you don't specify the variable's data type in the `Dim` statement, you end up with an untyped variable. Untyped variables in VBA are always Variant data types. It's highly recommended that you create typed variables. When you declare a variable of a certain data type, your VBA procedure runs faster because Visual Basic does not have to stop to analyze the Variant variable to determine its type.

Visual Basic can work with many types of numeric variables. Integer variables can hold only whole numbers from –32,768 to 32,767. Other types of numeric variables are Long, Single, Double, and Currency. Long variables can hold whole numbers in the range –2,147,483,648 to 2,147,483,647. Unlike the Integer and Long variables, the Single and Double variables can hold decimals. String variables are used to refer to text. When you declare a variable of String data type, you can tell Visual Basic how long the string should be—for instance:

```
Dim extension As String * 3
```

declares a fixed-length String variable named `extension` that is three characters long. If you don't assign a specific length, the String variable will be dynamic. This means that Visual Basic will make enough space in computer memory to handle whatever amount of text is assigned to it.

After you declare a variable, you can store only the type of information in it that you determined in the declaration statement. Assigning string values to numeric variables or numeric values to string variables results in the error message "Type mismatch" or causes Visual Basic to modify the value. For example, if your variable was declared to hold whole numbers and your data uses decimals, Visual Basic will disregard the decimals and use only the whole part of the number. When you run the MyNumber procedure shown here, Visual Basic modifies the data to fit the variable's data type (Integer), and instead of 23.11 the variable ends up holding a value of 23.

```
Sub MyNumber()
  Dim myNum As Integer
  myNum = 23.11
  MsgBox myNum
End Sub
```

If you don't declare a variable with a `Dim` statement, you can still designate a type for it by using a special character at the end of the variable name. To declare the `FirstName` variable as String, you can append the dollar sign to the variable name:

```
Dim FirstName$
```

This declaration is the same as `Dim FirstName As String`. The type declaration characters are shown in Table 3.2.

TABLE 3.2 Type declaration characters.

Data Type	Character
Integer	%
Long	&
Single	!
Double	#
Currency	@
String	$

Notice that the type declaration characters can be used only with six data types. To use the type declaration character, append the character to the end of the variable name.

In the AgeCalc2 procedure here we use two type declaration characters shown in Table 3.2.

```
Sub AgeCalc2()
  ' variable declaration
  Dim FullName$
  Dim DateOfBirth As Date
  Dim age%

  ' assign values to variables
  FullName$ = "John Smith"
  DateOfBirth = #1/3/1981#

  ' calculate age
  age% = Year(Now()) - Year(DateOfBirth)

  ' print results to the Immediate window
Debug.Print FullName$ & " is " & age% & " years old."
End Sub
```

SIDEBAR ***Declaring Typed Variables***

The variable type can be indicated by the `As` keyword or a type symbol. If you don't add the symbol type or the `As` command, the variable will be the default data type Variant.

Assigning Values to Variables

Now that you know how to name and declare variables and have seen examples of using variables in complete procedures, let's gain experience using them. In Hands-On 3.1, we will begin by creating a variable and assigning it a specific value.

NOTE	*Please note files for the "Hands-On" project may be found in the companion files.*

Hands-On 3.1 Writing a VBA Procedure with Variables

1. Open a new workbook and save it as **C:\VBAPrimerExcel2021_ByExample\Chap03_ExcelPrimer.xlsm**.
2. Activate the Visual Basic Editor window.
3. In the Project Explorer window, select the new project VBAProject (Chap03_ExcelPrimer.xlsm) and in the Properties window change its name to **Chapter3**.

4. Choose **Insert | Module** to add a new module to the **Chapter3 (Chap03_ExcelPrimer.xlsm)** VBA project.
5. While the Module1 is selected, use the Properties window to change its name to **Variables.**
6. In the Code window, enter the CalcCost procedure shown here:

```
Sub CalcCost()
  slsPrice = 35
  slsTax = 0.085

  Range("A1").Formula = "The cost of calculator"
  Range("A4").Formula = "Price"
  Range("B4").Formula = slsPrice
  Range("A5").Formula = "Sales Tax"
  Range("A6").Formula = "Cost"
  Range("B5").Formula = slsPrice * slsTax
  cost = slsPrice + (slsPrice * slsTax)

  With Range("B6")
    .Formula = cost
    .NumberFormat = "0.00"
  End With

  strMsg = "The calculator total is $" & cost & "."
  Range("A8").Formula = strMsg
End Sub
```

The foregoing procedure calculates the cost of purchasing a calculator using the following assumptions: The price of a calculator is $35 and the sales tax equals 8.5%.

The procedure uses four variables: `slsPrice`, `slsTax`, `cost`, and `strMsg`. Because none of these variables have been explicitly declared, they all have the same data type—Variant. The variables `slsPrice` and `slsTax` were created by assigning some values to variable names at the beginning of the procedure. The `cost` variable was assigned a value that is a result of a calculation: `slsPrice + (slsPrice * slsTax)`. The cost calculation uses the values supplied by the `slsPrice` and `slsTax` variables. The `strMsg` variable puts together a text message to the user. This message is then entered as a complete sentence in a worksheet cell. When you assign values to variables, place an equal sign after the name of the variable. After the equals sign, you should enter the value of the variable. This can be a number, a formula, or text surrounded by quotation marks. While the values assigned to the variables `slsPrice`, `slsTax`, and `cost` are easily understood, the value stored in the `strMsg` variable is a little more involved. Let's examine the contents of the `strMsg` variable.

```
strMsg = "The calculator total is $ " & cost & "."
```

- The string `"The calculator total is "` is surrounded by quotation marks. Notice that there is an extra space before the ending quotation marks.
- The dollar sign inside the quotes is used to denote the Currency data type. Because the dollar symbol is a character, it is surrounded by the quotes.
- The & character allows another string or the contents of a variable to be appended to the string. The & character must be used every time you want to append a new piece of information to the previous string.
- The `cost` variable is a placeholder. The actual cost of the calculator will be displayed here when the procedure runs.
- The & character attaches yet another string.
- The period is surrounded by quotes. When you require a period at the end of a sentence, you must attach it separately when it follows the name of the variable.

SIDEBAR ***Variable Initialization***

When Visual Basic creates a new variable, it initializes the variable. Variables assume their default value. Numerical variables are set to zero (0), Boolean variables are initialized to False, String variables are set to the empty string (""), and Date variables are set to December 30, 1899.

Now let's execute the CalcCost procedure.

7. Position the cursor anywhere within the CalcCost procedure and choose **Run | Run Sub/UserForm.**
   When you run this procedure, Visual Basic may display the following message: "*sAS*." If this happens, click **OK** to close the message box. Visual Basic will select the `slsPrice` variable and highlight the name of the CalcCost procedure. The title bar displays "Microsoft Visual Basic – Chap03_ExcelPrimer.xlsm [break]." The Visual Basic break mode allows you to correct the problem before you continue. Later in this book, you will learn how to fix problems in break mode. For now, exit this mode by choosing **Run | Reset**. Now go to the top of the Code window and delete the statement `Option Explicit` that appears on the first line. The `Option Explicit` statement means that all variables used within this module must be formally declared. You will learn about this statement in

the next section. When the `Option Explicit` statement is removed from the Code window, choose **Run | Run Sub/UserForm** to rerun the procedure. This time, Visual Basic goes to work with no objections.

8. After the procedure has finished executing, press **Alt+F11** to switch to Microsoft Excel.
   The result of the procedure should match Figure 3.2.

	A	B	C	D
1	The cost of calculator			
2				
3				
4	Price	35		
5	Sales Tax	2.975		
6	Cost	37.98		
7				
8	The calculator total is $37.975.			
9				

Sheet1

FIGURE 3.2 The VBA procedure can enter data and calculate results in a worksheet.

Cell A8 displays the contents of the `strMsg` variable. Notice that the cost entered in cell B6 has two decimal places, while the cost in `strMsg` displays three decimals. To display the cost of a calculator with two decimal places in cell A8, you must apply the required format not to the cell but to the `cost` variable itself.

VBA has special functions that allow you to change the format of data. To change the format of the `cost` variable, you will now use the `Format` function. This function has the following syntax:

```
Format(expression, format)
```

where `expression` is a value or variable that you want to format, and `format` is the type of format you want to apply.

9. In the VBE window, select the entire code of the CalcCost procedure and copy and paste it below the current procedure on the first empty line. Add some spacing between the two procedures by pressing Enter two times after the first procedure End Sub keywords.
10. Change the name of the copied procedure to CalcCost_Modified.
11. Change the calculation of the `cost` variable in the CalcCost procedure:

```
cost = Format(slsPrice + (slsPrice * slsTax), "0.00")
```

12. Replace the `With...End With` block of instructions with the following:

```
Range("B6").Formula = cost
```

13. Replace the statement `Range("B5").Formula = slsPrice * slsTax` with the following instruction:

```
Range("B5").Formula = Format((slsPrice * slsTax), "0.00")
```

14. Rerun the modified procedure.
After running the procedure, the text displayed in cell A8 shows the cost of the calculator formatted with two decimal places.

After trying out the CalcCost procedure, you may wonder why you should bother declaring variables if Visual Basic can handle undeclared variables so well. The CalcCost procedure is very short, so you don't need to worry about how many bytes of memory will be consumed each time Visual Basic uses the Variant variable. In short procedures, however, it is not the memory that matters but the mistakes you are bound to make when typing variable names. What will happen if the second time you use the `cost` variable you omit the "o" and refer to it as `cst`?

```
Range("B6").Formula = cst
```

What will you end up with if instead of `slsTax` you use the word `Tax` in the formula?

```
Cost = Format(slsPrice + (slsPrice * Tax), "0.00")
```

The result of the CalcCost procedure after introducing these two mistakes is shown in Figure 3.3.

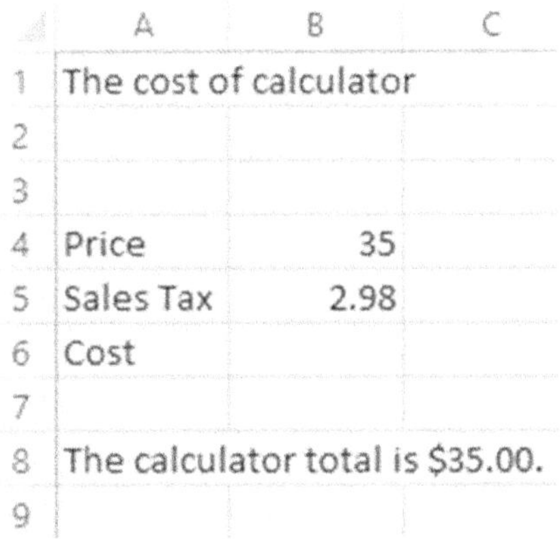

	A	B	C
1	The cost of calculator		
2			
3			
4	Price	35	
5	Sales Tax	2.98	
6	Cost		
7			
8	The calculator total is $35.00.		
9			

FIGURE 3.3 Misspelling variable names will produce incorrect results.

Notice that in Figure 3.3 cell B6 does not show a value because Visual Basic does not find the assignment statement for the `cst` variable. Because Visual Basic does not know the sales tax, it displays the price of the calculator (see cell A8) as the total cost. Visual Basic does not guess. It simply does what you tell it to do. This brings us to the next section, which explains how to make sure this kind of error doesn't occur.

NOTE	*If you have made changes in the variable names as described earlier, be sure to replace the names of the variables* `cst` *and* `tax` *with* `cost` *and* `slsTax` *in the appropriate lines of the VBA code before you continue.*

Forcing Declaration of Variables

Visual Basic has the `Option Explicit` statement that automatically reminds you to formally declare all your variables. This statement must be entered at the top of each of your modules. The `Option Explicit` statement will cause Visual Basic to generate an error message when you try to run a procedure that contains undeclared variables as demonstrated in Hands-On 3.2.

Hands-On 3.2 Writing a VBA Procedure with Explicitly Declared Variables

This Hands-On requires prior completion of Hands-On 3.1.

1. Return to the Code window where you entered the CalcCost procedure.
2. At the top of the module window (in the first line), type **Option Explicit** and press **Enter**. Excel will display the statement in blue.
3. Run the CalcCost procedure. Visual Basic displays the error message "*Compile error: Variable not defined.*"
4. Click **OK** to exit the message box.
   Visual Basic highlights the name of the variable `slsPrice`. Now you must formally declare this variable. When you declare the `slsPrice` variable and rerun your procedure, Visual Basic will generate the same error as soon as it encounters another variable name that was not declared.
5. Choose **Run | Reset** to reset the VBA project.
6. Enter the following declarations at the beginning of the CalcCost procedure:

```
' declaration of variables
Dim slsPrice As Currency
Dim slsTax As Single
Dim cost As Currency
Dim strMsg As String
```

The revised CalcCost procedure is shown here:

```
Sub CalcCost()
   ' declaration of variables
   Dim slsPrice As Currency
   Dim slsTax As Single
   Dim cost As Currency
   Dim strMsg As String

   slsPrice = 35
   slsTax = 0.085
   Range("A1").Formula = "The cost of calculator"
   Range("A4").Formula = "Price"
   Range("B4").Formula = slsPrice
   Range("A5").Formula = "Sales Tax"
   Range("A6").Formula = "Cost"
   Range("B5").Formula = Format((slsPrice * slsTax), "0.00")
   cost = Format(slsPrice + (slsPrice * slsTax), "0.00")
   Range("B6").Formula = cost
   strMsg = "The calculator total is $" & cost & "."
   Range("A8").Formula = strMsg
End Sub
```

7. Rerun the procedure to ensure that Excel no longer displays the error.

Option Explicit in Every Module

To automatically include `Option Explicit` in every new module you create, follow these steps:

- Choose **Tools | Options.**
- Make sure that the **Require Variable Declaration** check box is selected in the **Options** dialog box (Editor tab).
- Choose **OK** to close the Options dialog box.

From now on, every new module will be added with the `Option Explicit` statement in line 1. If you want to require variables to be explicitly declared in a previously created module, you must enter the `Option Explicit` statement manually by editing the module yourself.

`Option Explicit` forces formal (explicit) declaration of all variables in a module. One big advantage of using `Option Explicit` is that any mistyping of the variable name will be detected at compile time (when Visual Basic attempts to translate the source code to executable code). If included, the `Option Explicit` statement must appear in a module before any procedures.

Understanding the Scope of Variables

Variables can have different ranges of influence in a VBA procedure. The term *scope* defines the availability of a variable to the same procedure, other procedures, and other VBA projects.

Variables can have the following three levels of scope in Visual Basic for Applications:

- Procedure-level scope
- Module-level scope
- Project-level scope

Procedure-Level (Local) Variables

From this chapter, you already know how to declare a variable by using the `Dim` keyword. The position of the `Dim` keyword in the module sheet determines the scope of a variable. Variables declared with the `Dim` keyword placed within a VBA procedure have a *procedure-level scope.*

Procedure-level variables are frequently referred to as *local variables*. Local variables can be used only in the procedure in which they were declared. Undeclared variables always have a procedure-level scope. A variable's name must be unique within its scope. This means that you cannot declare two variables with the same name in the same procedure. However, you can use the same variable name in different procedures. In other words, the CalcCost procedure can have the `slsTax` variable, and the ExpenseRep procedure in the same module can have its own variable called `slsTax`. Both variables are independent of each other.

Module-Level Variables

Local variables help save computer memory. As soon as the procedure ends, the variable dies and Visual Basic returns the memory space used by the variable to the computer. In programming, however, you often want the variable to be available to other VBA procedures after the procedure in which the variable was declared has finished running. This situation requires that you change the scope of a variable. Instead of a procedure-level variable, you want to declare a module-level variable. To declare a module-level variable, you must place the `Dim` keyword at the top of the module sheet before any procedures (just below the `Option Explicit` keyword). For instance, to make the `slsTax` variable available to any other procedure in the Variables module, declare the `slsTax` variable in the following way:

```
Option Explicit
Dim slsTax As Single

Sub CalcCost()
...Instructions of the procedure...
End Sub
```

In the foregoing example, the `Dim` keyword is located at the top of the module, below the `Option Explicit` statement. Before you can see how this works, you need another procedure that uses the `slsTax` variable. In Hands-On 3.3, we will write a new VBA procedure named ExpenseRep.

Hands-On 3.3 Writing a VBA Procedure with a Module-Level Variable

1. In the Code window, cut the declaration line **Dim slsTax As Single** in the Variables module from the CalcCost procedure and paste it at the top of the module sheet below the `Option Explicit` statement.
2. In the same module where the CalcCost procedure is located, enter the code of the ExpenseRep procedure as shown here:

```
Sub ExpenseRep()
  Dim slsPrice As Currency
  Dim cost As Currency

  slsPrice = 55.99

  cost = slsPrice + (slsPrice * slsTax)
  MsgBox slsTax
  MsgBox cost
End Sub
```

The ExpenseRep procedure declares two Currency type variables: `slsPrice` and `cost`. The `slsPrice` variable is then assigned a value of 55.99. The `slsPrice` variable is independent of the `slsPrice` variable that is declared within the CalcCost procedure.

The ExpenseRep procedure calculates the cost of a purchase. The cost includes the sales tax stored in the `slsTax` variable. Because the sales tax is the same as the one used in the CalcCost procedure, the `slsTax` variable has been declared at the module level.

3. Run the **ExpenseRep** procedure.
   Because you have not yet run the CalcCost procedure, Visual Basic does not know the value of the `slsTax` variable, so it displays zero in the first message box.
4. Run the **CalcCost** procedure.
   After Visual Basic executes the CalcCost procedure that you revised in Hands-On 3.2, the contents of the `slsTax` variable equals 0.085. If `slsTax` were a local variable, the contents of this variable would be empty upon the termination of the CalcCost procedure.

   When you run the CalcCost procedure, Visual Basic erases the contents of all the variables except for the `slsTax` variable, which was declared at a module level.
5. Run the **ExpenseRep** procedure again.
   As soon as you attempt to calculate the cost by running the ExpenseRep procedure, Visual Basic retrieves the value of the `slsTax` variable and uses it in the calculation.

SIDEBAR ***Private Variables***

When you declare variables at a module level, you can use the `Private` keyword instead of the `Dim` keyword—for instance:

```
Private slsTax As Single
```

Private variables are available only to the procedures that are part of the module where they were declared. Private variables are always declared at the top of the module after the `Option Explicit` statement.

Project-Level Variables

Module-level variables that are declared with the `Public` keyword (instead of `Dim`) have project-level scope. This means that they can be used in any Visual Basic for Applications module. When you want to work with a variable in all the procedures in all the open VBA projects, you must declare it with the `Public` keyword—for instance:

```
Option Explicit
Public slsTax As Single

Sub CalcCost()
  ...procedure statements...
End Sub
```

Notice that the `slsTax` variable declared at the top of the module with the `Public` keyword will now be available to any other procedure in the VBA project.

SIDEBAR ***Keeping the Project-Level Variable Private***

To prevent a project-level variable's contents from being referenced outside its project, you can use the `Option Private Module` statement at the top of the module sheet, just below the `Option Explicit` statement and before the declaration line—for example:

```
Option Explicit
Option Private Module
Public slsTax As Single

Sub CalcCost()
... procedure statements...
End Sub
```

Lifetime of Variables

In addition to scope, variables have a lifetime. The *lifetime* of a variable determines how long a variable retains its value. Module-level and project-level variables preserve their values as long as the project is open. Visual Basic, however, can reinitialize these variables if required by the program's logic. Local variables declared with the Dim statement lose their values when a procedure has finished. Local variables have a lifetime while a procedure is running, and they are reinitialized every time the program is run. Visual Basic allows you to extend the lifetime of a local variable by changing the way it is declared.

Finding a Variable Definition

When you find an instruction in a VBA procedure that assigns a value to a variable, you can quickly locate the definition of the variable by selecting the variable name and pressing Shift+F2 or choosing View | Definition. Visual Basic will jump to the variable declaration line. Press Ctrl+Shift+F2 or choose View | Last Position to return your mouse pointer to its previous position.

Determining a Data Type of a Variable

You can find out the type of a variable by using one of the VBA built-in functions. The `VarType` function returns an integer indicating the type of a variable. Figure 3.4 displays the `VarType` function's syntax and the values it returns. Let's try using the `VarType` function in the Immediate window.

Hands-On 3.4 Using the Built-In VarType Function

1. In the Visual Basic Editor window, choose **View | Immediate Window**.
2. Type the following statements that assign values to variables:

```
age = 18
birthdate = #1/1/1981#
firstName = "John"
```

3. Now ask Visual Basic what type of data each of the variables holds:

```
?VarType(age)
```

When you press **Enter**, Visual Basic returns 2. As shown in Figure 3.4, the number 2 represents the Integer data type. If you type:

```
?VarType(birthdate)
```

VarType(*varname*)

The required *varname* argument is a Variant containing any variable except a variable of a user-defined type.

Return values

Either one of the following constants or the summation of a number of them is returned.

Constant	Value	Description
vbEmpty	0	Empty (uninitialized)
vbNull	1	Null (no valid data)
vbInteger	2	Integer
vbLong	3	Long integer
vbSingle	4	Single-precision floating-point number
vbDouble	5	Double-precision floating-point number
vbCurrency	6	Currency value
vbDate	7	Date value
vbString	8	String
vbObject	9	Object
vbError	10	Error value
vbBoolean	11	Boolean value
vbVariant	12	Variant (used only with arrays of variants)
vbDataObject	13	A data access object
vbDecimal	14	Decimal value
vbByte	17	Byte value
vbLongLong	20	LongLong integer (valid on 64-bit platforms only)
vbUserDefinedType	36	Variants that contain user-defined types
vbArray	8192	Array (always added to another constant when returned by this function)

FIGURE 3.4 With the built-in `VarType` function, you can learn the data type the variable holds.
Source: *https://docs.microsoft.com/en-us/office/vba/Language/Reference/user-interface-help/vartype-function*

Visual Basic returns 7 for Date. If you make a mistake in the variable name (let's say you type birthday, instead of birthdate), Visual Basic returns zero (0). If you type:

```
?VarType(firstName)
```

Visual Basic tells you that the value stored in the variable `firstName` is a String type (8).

USING CONSTANTS

The contents of a variable can change while your procedure is executing. If your procedure needs to refer to unchanged values repeatedly, you should use constants. A *constant* is like a named variable that always refers to the same value. Visual Basic requires that you declare constants before you use them. Declare constants by using the `Const` statement, as in the following examples:

```
Const dialogName = "Enter Data" As String
Const slsTax = 8.5
Const ColorIdx = 3
```

A constant, like a variable, has a scope. To make a constant available within a single procedure, declare it at the procedure level, just below the name of the procedure—for instance:

```
Sub WedAnniv()
  Const Age As Integer = 25
  MsgBox (Age)
End Sub
```

If you want to use a constant in all the procedures of a module, use the `Private` keyword in front of the `Const` statement—for instance:

```
Private Const driveLetter As String = "C:"
```

The `Private` constant has to be declared at the top of the module, just before the first `Sub` statement. If you want to make a constant available to all modules in the workbook, use the `Public` keyword in front of the `Const` statement—for instance:

```
Public Const NumOfChars As Integer = 255
```

The `Public` constant must be declared at the top of the module, just before the first `Sub` statement. When declaring a constant, you can use any one of the following data types: Boolean, Byte, Integer, Long, Currency, Single, Double, Date, String, or Variant.

Like variables, several constants can be declared on one line if separated by commas—for instance:

```
Const Age As Integer = 25, City As String = "Denver"
```

Using constants makes your VBA procedures more readable and easier to maintain. For example, if you refer to a certain value several times in your procedure, use a constant instead of the value. This way, if the value changes (for example, the sales tax goes up), you can simply change the value in the declaration of the `Const` statement instead of tracking down every occurrence of that value.

Built-In Constants

Both Microsoft Excel and Visual Basic for Applications have a long list of predefined constants that do not need to be declared. These built-in constants can be looked up using the Object Browser window. Let's proceed to Hands-On 3.5, where we open the Object Browser to look at the list of Excel constants.

Hands-On 3.5 Viewing Excel Constants in the Object Browser

1. In the Visual Basic Editor window, choose **View | Object Browser**.
2. In the Project/Library list box, click the drop-down arrow and select **Excel**.
3. Enter **constants** as the search text in the Search box and press **Enter** or click the **Search** button. Visual Basic shows the result of the search in the Search Results area.
4. Scroll down in the Classes list box to locate and then select **Constants** as shown in Figure 3.5. The right side of the Object Browser window displays a list of all built-in constants that are available in the Microsoft Excel object library. Notice that the names of all the constants begin with the prefix "xl."
5. To look up VBA constants, choose **VBA** in the Project/Library list box (see Figure 3.6). Notice that the names of the VBA built-in constants begin with the prefix "vb."

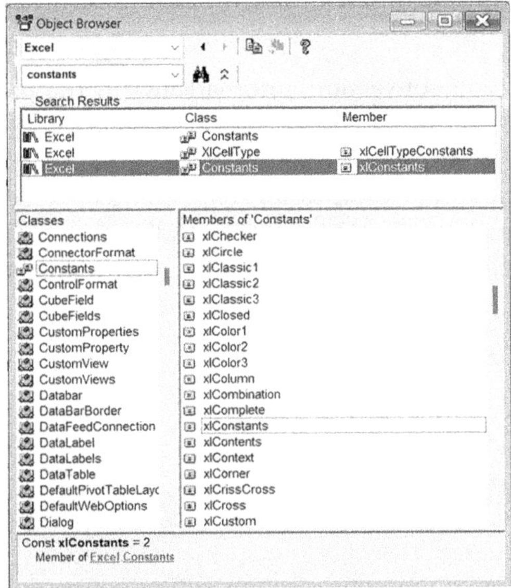

FIGURE 3.5 Use the Object Browser to look up any built-in constant.

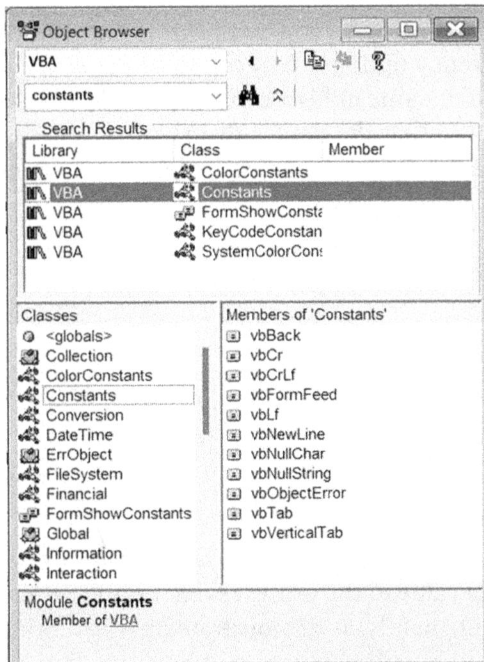

FIGURE 3.6 The names of VBA constants begin with the "vb" prefix.

CONVERTING BETWEEN DATA TYPES

While VBA handles a lot of data type conversion automatically in the background, it also provides several data conversion functions (see Table 3.3) that allow you to convert one data type to another. These functions should be used in situations where you want to show the result of an operation as a specific data type rather than the default data type. For example, instead of showing the result of your calculation as an integer or single-precision or double-precision number, you may want to use the `CCur` function to force currency arithmetic, as in the following example procedure:

```
Sub ShowMoney()
  'declare variables of two different types
  Dim myAmount As Single
  Dim myMoneyAmount As Currency

  myAmount = 345.34

  myMoneyAmount = CCur(myAmount)
  Debug.Print "Amount = $" & myMoneyAmount
End Sub
```

When using the `CCur` function, currency options are recognized depending on the locale setting of your computer. The same holds true for the `CDate` function. By using this function, you can ensure that the date is formatted according to the locale setting of your system. Use the `IsDate` function to determine whether a return value can be converted to date or time.

```
Sub ConvertToDate()
  'assume you have entered  Jan 1 2021 in cell A1
  Dim myEntry As String
  Dim myRangeValue As Date

  myEntry = Sheet2.Range("A1").Value
  If IsDate(myEntry) Then
      myRangeValue = CDate(myEntry)
  End If
  Debug.Print myRangeValue
End Sub
```

In cases where you need to round the value to the nearest even number, you will find the `CInt` and `Clng` functions quite handy, as demonstrated in the following procedure:

```
Sub ShowInteger()
```

```
    'declare variables of two different types
    Dim myAmount As Single
    Dim myIntAmount As Integer

    myAmount = 345.64

    myIntAmount = CInt(myAmount)
    Debug.Print "Original Amount = " & myAmount
    Debug.Print "New Amount = " & myIntAmount
End Sub
```

As you can see in the code of the foregoing procedures, the syntax for the VBA conversion functions is as follows:

```
conversionFunctionName(variablename)
```

where `variablename` is the name of a variable, a constant, or an expression (like x + y) that evaluates to a specific data type.

TABLE 3.3 VBA data type conversion functions.

Conversion Function	Return Type	Description
CBool	Boolean	Any valid string or numeric expression
CByte	Byte	0 to 255
CCur	Currency	-922,337,203,685,477.5808 to 922,337,203,685,477.5807
CDate	Date	Any valid date expression
CDbl	Double	-1.79769313486231E308 to --4.94065645841247E-324 for negative values; 4.94065645841247E-324 to 1.79769313486232E308 for positive values.
CDec	Decimal	+/-79,228,162,514,264,337,593,543,950,335 for zero-scaled numbers—that is, numbers with no decimal places. For numbers with 28 decimal places, the range is +/-7.9228162514264337593543950335. The smallest possible nonzero number is 0.0000000000000000000000000001.
CInt	Integer	-32,768 to 32,767; fractions are rounded.
CLng	Long	-2,147,483,648 to 2,147,483,647; fractions are rounded.

(Contd.)

<table>
<tr><th>Conversion Function</th><th>Return Type</th><th>Description</th></tr>
<tr><td>CLngLng</td><td>LongLong</td><td>–9,223,372,036,854,775,808 to 9,223,372,036,854,775,807; fractions are rounded. (Valid on 64-bit platforms only.)</td></tr>
<tr><td>CLngPtr</td><td>LongPtr</td><td>–2,147,483,648 to 2,147,483,647 on 32-bit systems; –9,223,372,036,854,775,808 to 9,223,372,036,854,775,807 on 64-bit systems. Fractions are rounded for 32-bit and 64-bit systems.</td></tr>
<tr><td>CSng</td><td>Single</td><td>–3.402823E38 to –1.401298E-45 for negative values; 1.401298E-45 to 3.402823E38 for positive values.</td></tr>
<tr><td>CStr</td><td>String</td><td>Returns for CStr depend on the expression argument.
<table>
<tr><td>If Expression Is</td><td>CStr returns</td></tr>
<tr><td>Boolean</td><td>A string containing True or False</td></tr>
<tr><td>Date</td><td>A string containing a date in the short date format of your system</td></tr>
<tr><td>Null</td><td>A runtime error</td></tr>
<tr><td>Empty</td><td>A zero-length string ("")</td></tr>
<tr><td>Error</td><td>A string containing the word "Error" followed by the error number</td></tr>
<tr><td>Other numeric</td><td>A string containing the number</td></tr>
</table></td></tr>
<tr><td>Cvar</td><td>Variant</td><td>Same range as Double for numerics. Same range as String for nonnumeric.</td></tr>
</table>

Hands-On 3.6 Using Data Type Conversion Functions in VBA

1. Select **Insert | Module** to insert a new module into the Chapter3 (**Chap03_ExcelPrimer.xslm**) project.
2. Use the Properties window to rename the module to **DataTypeConversion**.
3. Enter the code of the procedures introduced in this section: **ShowMoney**, **ConvertToDate**, and **ShowInteger**.
4. Insert a new worksheet into current workbook and enter **Jan 1 2021** in cell **A1**.
5. Run each procedure and check the results in the Immediate window.

USING STATIC VARIABLES IN VBA PROCEDURES

A variable declared with the `Static` keyword is a special type of local variable. Static variables are declared at the procedure level. Unlike local variables declared with the `Dim` keyword, static variables do not lose their contents when the program is not in their procedure. For example, when a VBA procedure with a static variable calls another procedure, after Visual Basic executes the statements of the called procedure and returns to the calling procedure, the static variable still retains the original value. The CostOfPurchase procedure shown in Hands-On 3.7 demonstrates the use of the static variable named `allPurchase`. Notice how this variable keeps track of the running total.

Hands-On 3.7 Writing a VBA Procedure with a Static Variable

1. In the Code window of the Variables module, write the following procedure:

```
Sub CostOfPurchase()
  ' declare variables
  Static allPurchase
  Dim newPurchase As String
  Dim purchCost As Single

  newPurchase = InputBox("Enter the cost of a purchase:")
  purchCost = CSng(newPurchase)
  allPurchase = allPurchase + purchCost

  ' display results
  MsgBox "The cost of a new purchase is: " & newPurchase
  MsgBox "The running cost is: " & allPurchase
End Sub
```

The foregoing procedure begins with declaring a static variable named `allPurchase` and two other local variables: `newPurchase` and `purchCost`. The `InputBox` function used in this procedure displays a dialog box and waits for the user to enter the value. As soon as you input the value and click OK, Visual Basic assigns this value to the variable `newPurchase`.

The `InputBox` function is discussed in detail in Chapter 4. Because the result of the `InputBox` function is always a string, the `newPurchase` variable was declared as the String data type. You can't, however, use strings in mathematical calculations. That's why the next instruction uses a type conversion function (`CSng`) to translate the text value into a numeric variable of the Single data type.

The `CSng` function requires one argument—the value you want to translate. To find out more about the `CSng` function, position the insertion point anywhere within the word `CSng` and press F1. The number obtained as the result of the `CSng` function is then stored in the variable `purchCost`.

The next instruction, `allPurchase = allPurchase + purchCost`, adds to the current purchase value the new value supplied by the `InputBox` function.

2. Position the cursor anywhere within the `CostOfPurchase` procedure and press **F5**. When the dialog box appears, enter a number. For example, enter **100** and click **OK** or press **Enter**. Visual Basic displays the message "The cost of a new purchase is: 100." Click **OK** in the message box. Visual Basic displays the second message "The running cost is: 100."
3. When you run this procedure for the first time, the content of the `allPurchase` variable is the same as the content of the `purchCost` variable.
4. Rerun the same procedure. When the input dialog appears, enter another number. For example, enter **50** and click **OK** or press **Enter**. Visual Basic displays the message "The cost of a new purchase is: 50." Click **OK** in the message box. Visual Basic displays the second message "The running cost is: 150."
5. When you run the procedure the second time, the value of the static variable is increased by the new value supplied in the dialog box. You can run the `CostOfPurchase` procedure as many times as you want. The `allPurchase` variable will keep the running total for as long as the project is open.

USING OBJECT VARIABLES IN VBA PROCEDURES

The variables that you've learned in the preceding sections are used to store data. Storing data is the main reason for using "normal" variables in your procedures. In addition to the normal variables that store data, there are special variables that refer to the Visual Basic objects. These variables are called *object variables*. In Chapter 2, you worked with several objects in the Immediate window. Now you will learn how you can represent an object with the object variable.

Object variables don't store data; instead, they tell where the data is located. For example, with the object variable you can tell Visual Basic that the data is in cell E10 of a worksheet. Object variables make it easy to locate data. When writing Visual Basic procedures, you often need to write long instructions, such as:

```
Worksheets("Sheet2").Range(Cells(1, 1), Cells(10, 5).Select
```

Instead of using long references to the object, you can declare an object variable that will tell Visual Basic where the data is located. Object variables are declared similarly to the variables you already know. The only difference is that after the `As` keyword, you enter the word `Object` as the data type—for instance:

```
Dim myRange As Object
```

The foregoing statement declares the object variable named `myRange`.

Well, it's not enough to declare the object variable. You also must assign a specific value to the object variable before you can use this variable in your procedure. Assign a value to the object variable by using the `Set` keyword. The `Set` keyword must be followed by the equals sign and the value that the variable will refer to—for example:

```
Set myRange = Worksheets("Sheet2").Range(Cells(1, 1), Cells(10, 5))
```

This statement assigns a value to the object variable `myRange`. This value refers to cells A1:E10 in Sheet1. If you omit the word `Set`, Visual Basic will respond with an error message—"*Run-time error 91: Object variable or With block variable not set.*"

Again, it's time to see a practical example.

Hands-On 3.8 Writing a VBA Procedure with Object Variables

1. In the Code window of the Variables module, write the following procedure:

```
Sub UseObjVariable()
  Dim myRange As Object
  Sheets.Add
  Set myRange = Worksheets("Sheet2").Range(Cells(1, 1), _
      Cells(10, 5))
  myRange.BorderAround Weight:=xlMedium

  With myRange.Interior
    .ColorIndex = 6
    .Pattern = xlSolid
  End With

  Set myRange = Worksheets("Sheet2").Range(Cells(12, 5), _
      Cells(12, 10))
  myRange.Value = 54

  Debug.Print IsObject(myRange)
End Sub
```

Let's examine the code of the UseObjVariable procedure line by line. The procedure begins with the declaration of the object variable `myRange`. The next statement sets the object variable `myRange` to the range A1:E10 on Sheet2. From now on, every time you want to reference this range, instead of using the entire object's address, you'll use the shortcut—the name of the object variable. The purpose of this procedure is to create a border around the range A1:E10. Instead of writing a long instruction:

```
Worksheets("Sheet2").Range(Cells(1, 1), _
        Cells(10, 5)).BorderAround Weight:=xlMedium
```

you can take a shortcut by using the name of the object variable:

```
myRange.BorderAround Weight:=xlMedium
```

The next series of statements changes the color of the selected range of cells (A1:E10). Again, you don't need to write the long instruction to reference the object that you want to manipulate. Instead of the full object name, you can use the `myRange` object variable. The next statement assigns a new reference to the object variable `myRange`. Visual Basic forgets the old reference, and the next time you use `myRange`, it refers to another range (E12:J12).

After the number 54 is entered in the new range (E12:J12), the procedure shows you how you can make sure that a specific variable is of the Object type. The instruction `Debug.Print  IsObject(myRange)` will enter True in the Immediate window if `myRange` is an object variable. `IsObject` is a VBA function that indicates whether a specific value represents an object variable.

2. Position the cursor anywhere within the UseObjVariable procedure and press F5.

SIDEBAR ***The Advantages of Using Object Variables***

- They can be used instead of the actual object.
- They are shorter and easier to remember than the actual values to which they point.
- You can change their meaning while your procedure is running.

Using Specific Object Variables

The object variable can refer to any type of object. Because Visual Basic has many types of objects, it's a good idea to create object variables that refer to a specific object to make your programs more readable and faster. For instance, in the UseObjVariable procedure (see the previous section), instead of the generic object variable (`Object`), you can declare the `myRange` object variable as a Range object:

```
Dim myRange As Range
```

If you want to refer to a specific worksheet, then you can declare the Worksheet object:

```
Dim mySheet As Worksheet
Set mySheet = Worksheets("Marketing")
```

When the object variable is no longer needed, you can assign Nothing to it. This frees up memory and system resources:

```
Set mySheet = Nothing
```

SUMMARY

This chapter introduced several new VBA concepts, such as data types, variables, and constants. You learned how to declare various types of variables and define their types. You also saw the difference between a variable and a constant. Now that you know what variables are and how to use them, you can create VBA procedures that allow you to manipulate data in more meaningful ways than you saw in previous chapters.

In the next chapter, you will expand your VBA knowledge by learning how to write custom function procedures. In addition, you will learn about built-in functions that will allow your VBA procedure to interact with users.

Chapter 4

Excel VBA Procedures

A Quick Guide to Writing Function Procedures

Earlier in this book you learned that a procedure is a group of instructions that allows you to accomplish specific tasks when your program runs. In this book you get acquainted with the following types of VBA procedures:

- **Subroutine procedures** (*subroutines*) perform some useful tasks but don't return any values. They begin with the keyword `Sub` and end with the keywords `End Sub`. Subroutines can be recorded with the macro recorder or written from scratch in the Visual Basic Editor window. In Chapter 1, you learned various ways to execute this type of procedure.
- **Function procedures** (*functions*) perform specific tasks that return values. They begin with the keyword `Function` and end with the keywords `End Function`. In this chapter, you will create your first function procedure. Function procedures can be executed from a subroutine or accessed from a worksheet just like any Excel built-in function.
- **Property procedures** are used with custom objects. Use them to set and get the value of an object's property or set a reference to an object. Property procedures are an advanced feature of VBA and are covered in Chapter 26.

In this chapter, you will learn how to create and execute custom functions. In addition, you find out how variables are used in passing values to subroutines and functions. Later in the chapter, you will take a thorough look at the two most useful VBA built-in functions: `MsgBox` and `InputBox`.

UNDERSTANDING FUNCTION PROCEDURES

With the hundreds of built-in Excel functions, you can perform a wide variety of calculations automatically. However, there will be times when you may require a custom calculation. With VBA programming, you can quickly fulfill this special need by creating a function procedure. You can build any functions that are not supplied with Excel. Among the reasons for creating custom VBA functions are the following:

- analyze data and perform calculations
- modify data and report information
- take a specific action based on supplied or calculated data

Creating a Function Procedure

Like Excel functions, function procedures perform calculations and return values. The best way to learn about functions is to create one, so let's get started. After setting up a new VBA project, you will create a simple function procedure that sums two values.

NOTE	*Please note files for the "Hands-On" project may be found in the companion files.*

Hands-On 4.1 Writing a Simple Function Procedure

1. Open a new Excel workbook and save it as **C:\ VBAPrimerExcel_ByExample\ Chap04_ExcelPrimer.xlsm.**
2. Switch to the Visual Basic Editor window and select **VBAProject (Chap04_ExcelPrimer.xlsm).**
3. In the Properties window, change the name of the project name to **ProcAndFunctions.**
4. Select the **ProcAndFunctions (Chap04_ExcelPrimer.xlsm)** project in the Project Explorer window and choose **Insert | Module.**
5. In the Properties window, change the Module1 name to **Sample1.**
6. In the Project Explorer window, highlight **Sample1** and click anywhere in the Code window. Choose **Insert | Procedure.** The Add Procedure dialog box appears.
7. In the Add Procedure dialog box, make the entries shown in Figure 4.1:
   Name: **SumItUp**

Type: **Function**
Scope: **Public**

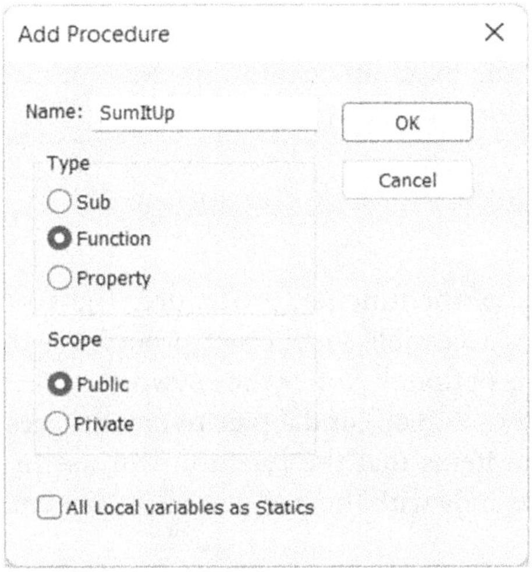

FIGURE 4.1 When you use the Add Procedure dialog box, Visual Basic automatically creates the procedure type you choose.

8. Click **OK** to close the Add Procedure dialog box. Visual Basic enters an empty function procedure that looks like this:

```
Public Function SumItUp()

End Function
```

9. Modify the function declaration as follows:

```
Public Function SumItUp(m,n)

End Function
```

The purpose of this function is to add two values. Instead of passing the actual values to the function, you can make the function more flexible by providing it with the arguments in the form of variables. By doing this, your custom function will be able to add any two numbers that you specify. Each of the passed-in variables (`m`, `n`) represents a value. You will supply the values for each of these variables when you run this function.

10. Type the following statement between the `Public Function` and `End Function` statements:

```
SumItUp = m + n
```

This statement instructs Visual Basic to add the value stored in the `n` variable to the value stored in the `m` variable and return the result to the `SumItUp` function. To specify the value that you want the function to return, type the function name followed by the equals sign and the value you want it to return. In the foregoing statement, set the name of the function equal to the total of m + n. The completed custom function procedure is shown here:

```
Public Function SumItUp(m,n)
  SumItUp = m + n
End Function
```

The first statement declares the name of the function procedure. The `Public` keyword indicates that the function is accessible to all other procedures in all other modules. The `Public` keyword is optional. Notice the keyword `Function` followed by the name of the function (`SumItUp`) and a pair of parentheses. In the parentheses, you will list the data items that the function will use in the calculation. Every function procedure ends with the `End Function` statement.

SIDEBAR ***About Function Names***

Function names should suggest the role that the function performs and must conform to the rules for naming variables (see Chapter 3).

SIDEBAR ***Scoping VBA Procedures***

In the previous chapter, you learned that the variable's scope determines which modules and procedures it can be used in. Like variables, VBA procedures have scope. A procedure scope determines whether it can be called by procedures in other modules. By default, all VBA procedures are public. This means they can be called by other procedures in any module. Because procedures are public by default, you can skip the `Public` keyword if you want. And if you replace the `Public` keyword with the `Private` keyword, your procedure will be available only to other procedures in the same module, not to procedures in other modules.

VARIOUS METHODS OF RUNNING FUNCTION PROCEDURES

Unlike a subroutine, a function procedure can be executed in just two ways: You can use it in a worksheet formula, or you can call it from another procedure. In the following sections, you will learn special techniques for executing functions.

Running a Function Procedure from a Worksheet

A custom function procedure is like an Excel built-in function. If you don't know the exact name of the function or its arguments, you can use the Formula palette to help enter the required function in a worksheet as shown in Hands-On 4.2.

Hands-On 4.2 Executing a Function Procedure from within an Excel Worksheet

1. Switch to the Microsoft Excel window and select any cell.
2. Click the **Insert Function** (*fx*) button on the Formula bar. Excel displays the Insert Function dialog box. The lower portion of the dialog box displays an alphabetical listing of all the functions in the selected category.
3. In the category drop-down box, select **User Defined**. In the function name box, locate and select the **SumItUp** function that was created in Hands-On 4.1. When you highlight the name of the function in the function name box (Figure 4.2), the bottom part of the dialog box displays the function's syntax: SumItUp(m,n).

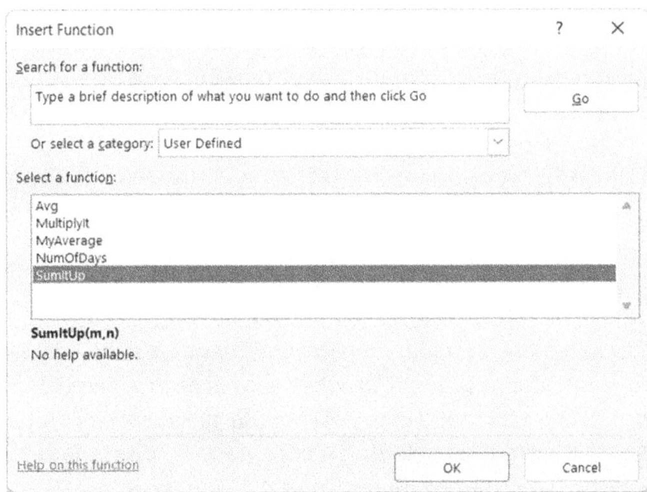

FIGURE 4.2 VBA custom function procedures are listed under the User Defined category in the Insert Function dialog box. They also appear in the list of all Excel built-in functions when you select All in the category drop-down.

4. Click **OK** to begin writing a formula. The Function Arguments dialog box appears, as shown in Figure 4.3. This dialog displays the name of the function and each of its arguments: `m` and `n`.

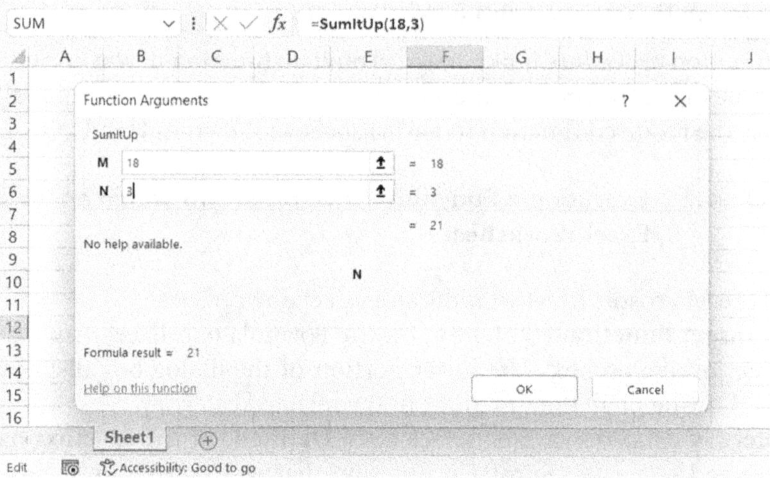

FIGURE 4.3 The Formula palette feature is helpful in entering any worksheet function, whether built-in or custom-made with VBA programming.

5. Enter the values for the arguments as shown in Figure 4.3 or enter your own values. As you type the values in the argument text boxes, Excel displays the values you entered and the current result of the function. Because both arguments (`m` and `n`) are required, the function will return an error if you skip either one of the arguments.
6. Click **OK** to exit the Function Arguments dialog.
   Excel enters the `SumItUp` function in the selected cell and displays its result.
7. To edit the function, select the cell that displays the function's result and click the **Insert Function** (*fx*) button to access the Function Arguments dialog box. Enter new values for the function's `m` and `n` arguments and click **OK**.

NOTE	*To edit the arguments' values directly in the cell, double-click the cell containing the function and make the necessary changes. You may also set up the* `SumItUp` *function to perform calculations based on the values entered in cells. To do this, in the Function Arguments dialog box shown in Figure 4.3, simply enter cell references instead of values. For example, enter C1 for the* `m` *argument and C2 for the* `n` *argument. When you click OK, Excel will display zero (0) as the result of the function. On the worksheet, enter the values in cells C1 and C2 and your custom function will recalculate the result just like any other built-in Excel function.*

Running a Function Procedure from Another VBA Procedure

To execute a custom function, write a VBA subroutine and call the function when you need it. The following procedure calls the `SumItUp` function and prints the result of the calculation to the Immediate window.

Hands-On 4.3 Executing a Function from a VBA Procedure

1. In the same module where you entered the code of the `SumItUp` function procedure, enter the RunSumItUp procedure.

```
Sub RunSumItUp()
  Dim m As Single, n As Single
  m = 37
  n = 3459.77

  Debug.Print SumItUp(m,n)
  MsgBox "Open the Immediate Window to see the result."
End Sub
```

   Notice how the foregoing subroutine uses one `Dim` statement to declare the `m` and `n` variables. These variables will be used to feed the data to the function. The next two statements assign the values to those variables. Next, Visual Basic calls the `SumItUp` function and passes the values stored in the `m` and `n` variables to it. When the function procedure statement `SumItUp = m + n` is executed, Visual Basic returns to the RunSumItUp subroutine and uses the `Debug.Print` statement to print the function's result to the Immediate window. Finally, the `MsgBox` function informs the user where to look for the result. You can find more information about using the `MsgBox` function later in this chapter.

2. Place the mouse pointer anywhere within the **RunSumItUp** procedure and press **F5** to run it.

ENSURING AVAILABILITY OF YOUR CUSTOM FUNCTIONS

Your custom VBA function is available only while the workbook where the function is stored is open. If you close the workbook, the function is no longer available. To make sure that your custom VBA functions are available every time you work with Microsoft Excel, you can do one of the following:

- Store your functions in the Personal macro workbook.
- Save the workbook with your custom VBA function in the XLStart folder.
- Set up a reference to the workbook containing your custom functions.

SIDEBAR *A Quick Test of a Function*

After you write your custom function, you can quickly try it out in the Immediate window. To display the value of a function, open the Immediate window and type a question mark (?) followed by the function name. Remember to enclose the function's arguments in parentheses.

For example, type:

```
? SumItUp(54, 367.24)
```

and press Enter. Your function procedure runs, using the values you passed for the `m` and `n` arguments. The result of the function appears on a line below:

```
421.24
```

PASSING ARGUMENTS TO FUNCTION PROCEDURES

Procedures (both subroutines and functions) often take arguments. *Arguments* are one or more values needed for a procedure to do something. Arguments are entered within parentheses. Multiple arguments are separated with commas.

Having used Excel for a while, you already know that Excel's built-in functions can produce different results based on the values you supply to them. For example, if cells A4 and A5 contain the numbers 5 and 10, respectively, the `Sum` function `=SUM(A4:A5)` will return 15, unless you change the values entered in the specified cells. Just like you can pass any values to Excel's built-in functions, you can pass values to custom VBA procedures.

Let's see how you can pass some values from a subroutine procedure to the `SumItUp` function. We will write a procedure that collects the user's first and last name. Next, we will call the `SumItUp` function to get the sum of characters in a person's first and last name.

Hands-On 4.4 Passing Arguments to Functions (Example 1)

1. Type the following NumOfCharacters subroutine in the same module (Sample1) where you entered the `SumItUp` function:

```
Sub NumOfCharacters()
  Dim f As Integer
  Dim l As Integer

  f = Len(InputBox("Enter first name:"))
```

```
    l = Len(InputBox("Enter last name:"))
    MsgBox SumItUp(f,l)
End Sub
```

2. Place the mouse pointer within the code of the NumOfCharacters procedure and press **F5**. Visual Basic displays the input box asking for the first name. This box is generated by the following function: `InputBox("Enter first name:")`. For more information on the use of this function, see the section titled "Using the InputBox Function" later in this chapter.
3. Enter any name, and press **Enter** or click **OK**. Visual Basic takes the text you entered and supplies it as an argument to the `Len` function. The `Len` function calculates the number of characters in the supplied text string. Visual Basic places the result of the `Len` function in the `f` variable for further reference. After that, Visual Basic displays the next input box, this time asking for the last name.
4. Enter any last name, and press **Enter** or click **OK**.
   Visual Basic passes the last name to the `Len` function to get the number of characters. Then that number is stored in the `l` variable. What happens next? Visual Basic encounters the `MsgBox` function. This function tells Visual Basic to display the result of the `SumItUp` function. However, because the result is not yet ready, Visual Basic jumps quickly to the `SumItUp` function to perform the calculation using the values saved earlier in the `f` and `l` variables. Inside the function procedure, Visual Basic substitutes the `m` argument with the value of the `f` variable and the `n` argument with the value of the `l` variable. Once the substitution is done, Visual Basic adds up the two numbers and returns the result to the `SumItUp` function.

   There are no more tasks to perform inside the function procedure, so Visual Basic returns to the subroutine and provides the `SumItUp` function's result as an argument to the `MsgBox` function. Now a message appears on the screen displaying the total number of characters.
5. Click **OK** to exit the message box.
   You can run the NumOfCharacters procedure as many times as you'd like, each time supplying different first and last names.

To pass a specific value from a function to a subroutine, assign the value to the name of the function. For example, the `NumOfDays` function shown here passes the value of 7 to the subroutine `DaysInAWeek`.

```
Function NumOfDays()
  NumOfDays = 7
End Function
```

```
Sub DaysInAWeek()
  MsgBox "There are " & NumOfDays & " days in a week."
End Sub
```

Specifying Argument Types

In the preceding section, you learned that functions perform some calculations based on data received through their arguments. When you declare a function procedure, you list the names of arguments inside a set of parentheses. Argument names are like variables. Each argument name refers to whatever value you provide at the time the function is called. When a subroutine calls a function procedure, it passes the required arguments as variables to it. Once the function does something, the result is assigned to the function name. Notice that the function procedure's name is used as if it were a variable.

Like variables, functions can have types. The result of your function procedure can be String, Integer, Long, and so on. To specify the data type for your function's result, add the keyword `As` and the name of the desired data type to the end of the function declaration line—for example:

```
Function MultiplyIt(num1, num2) As Integer
```

Let's look at an example of a function that returns an Integer number, although the arguments passed to it are declared as Single data types in a calling subroutine.

Hands-On 4.5 Passing Arguments to Functions (Example 2)

1. Add a new module to the **ProcAndFunctions (Chap04_ExcelPrimer.xlsm)** project and change the module's name to **Sample2**.
2. Activate the **Sample2** module and enter the HowMuch subroutine as shown here:

```
Sub HowMuch()
  Dim num1 As Single
  Dim num2 As Single
  Dim result As Single

  num1 = 45.33
  num2 = 19.24

  result = MultiplyIt(num1, num2)
  MsgBox result
End Sub
```

3. Enter the **MultiplyIt** function procedure below the HowMuch subroutine:

```
Function MultiplyIt(num1, num2) As Integer
  MultiplyIt = num1 * num2
End Function
```

Because the values stored in the variables `num1` and `num2` are not whole numbers, you may want to assign the Integer data type to the result of the function to ensure that the result is a whole number. If you don't assign the data type to the `MultiplyIt` function's result, the HowMuch procedure will display the result in the data type specified in the declaration line of the result variable. Instead of 872, the result of the multiplication will be 872.1492.

4. Run the HowMuch procedure.

How about passing different values each time you run the procedure? Instead of hardcoding the values to be used in the multiplication, you can use the `InputBox` function to ask the user for the values at runtime—for example:

```
num1 = InputBox("Enter a number:")
```

The InputBox function is discussed in detail in a later section of this chapter.

Passing Arguments by Reference and by Value

In some procedures, when you pass arguments as variables, Visual Basic can suddenly change the value of the variables. To ensure that the called function procedure does not alter the value of the passed-in arguments, you should precede the name of the argument in the function's declaration line with the keyword `ByVal`. Let's look at the following example.

Hands-On 4.6 Passing Arguments to Functions (Example 3)

1. Add a new module to the **ProcAndFunctions (Chap04_ExcelPrimer.xlsm)** project and change the module's name to **Sample3**.
2. Activate the **Sample3** module and type the procedures shown here:

```
Sub ThreeNumbers()
  Dim num1 As Integer, num2 As Integer, num3 As Integer
  num1 = 10
  num2 = 20
  num3 = 30

  MsgBox MyAverage(num1, num2, num3)
  MsgBox num1
```

```
  MsgBox num2
  MsgBox num3
End Sub

Function MyAverage(ByVal num1, ByVal num2, ByVal num3)
  num1 = num1 + 1

  MyAverage = (num1 + num2 + num3) / 3
End Function
```

To prevent the function from altering values of arguments, use the keyword `ByVal` before the arguments' names (see the "Know Your Keywords: ByRef and ByVal" sidebar).

3. Run the ThreeNumbers procedure.

The ThreeNumbers procedure assigns values to three variables and then calls the `MyAverage` function to calculate and return the average of the numbers stored in these variables. The function's arguments are the variables `num1`, `num2`, and `num3`. Notice that all of the function arguments are preceded with the keyword `ByVal`. Also, notice that prior to the calculation of the average, the `MyAverage` function changes the value of the `num1` variable. Inside the function procedure, the `num1` variable equals 11 (10 + 1). Therefore, when the function passes the calculated average to the ThreeNumbers procedure, the `MsgBox` function displays the result as 20.3333333333333 and not 20, as expected. The next three `MsgBox` functions show the contents of each of the variables. The values stored in these variables are the same as the original values assigned to them—10, 20, and 30.

What will happen if you omit the keyword `ByVal` in front of the `num1` argument in the `MyAverage` function's declaration line? The function's result will still be the same, but the contents of the `num1` variable displayed by `MsgBox num1` is now 11. The `MyAverage` function has not only returned an unexpected result (20.3333333333333 instead of 20) but also modified the original data stored in the `num1` variable. To prevent Visual Basic from permanently changing the values supplied to the function, use the `ByVal` keyword.

SIDEBAR ***Know Your Keywords: ByRef and ByVal***

Because any of the variables passed to a function procedure (or a subroutine) can be changed by the receiving procedure, it is important to know how to protect the original value of a variable. Visual Basic has two keywords that give or deny permission to change the contents of a variable—`ByRef` and `ByVal`. By default, Visual Basic passes information into a function procedure (or a subroutine) by reference (`ByRef` keyword), referring to the original data specified in the function's argument at the time the function is called. So, if the function alters the value of the argument, the original value is changed. You will get this result if you omit the `ByVal` keyword in front of the `num1` argument in the `MyAverage` function's declaration line. If you want the function procedure to change the original value, you don't need to explicitly insert the `ByRef` keyword, because passed variables default to `ByRef`. When you use the `ByVal` keyword in front of an argument name, Visual Basic passes the argument by value. This means that Visual Basic makes a copy of the original data and passes that copy to a function. If the function changes the value of an argument passed by value, the original data does not change—only the copy changes. That's why when the `MyAverage` function changed the value of the `num1` argument, the original value of the `num1` variable remained the same.

Using Optional Arguments

At times you may want to supply an additional value to a function. Let's say you have a function that calculates the price of a meal per person. Sometimes, however, you'd like the function to perform the same calculation for a group of two or more people. To indicate that a procedure argument is not always required, precede the name of the argument with the `Optional` keyword. Arguments that are optional come at the end of the argument list, following the names of all the required arguments.

Optional arguments must always be the Variant data type. This means that you can't specify the optional argument's type by using the `As` keyword. In the preceding section, you created a function to calculate the average of three numbers. Suppose that sometimes you'd like to use this function to calculate the average of two numbers. You could define the third argument of the `MyAverage` function as optional.

To preserve the original `MyAverage` function, let's create the `Avg` function to calculate the average for two or three numbers.

Hands-On 4.7 Writing Functions with Optional Arguments

1. Add a new module to the **ProcAndFunctions (Chap04_ExcelPrimer.xlsm)** project and change the module's name to **Sample4**.

2. Activate the **Sample4** module and enter the function procedure Avg shown here:

```
Function Avg(num1, num2, Optional num3)
  Dim totalNums As Integer

  totalNums = 3

  If IsMissing(num3)Then
    num3 = 0
    totalNums = totalNums - 1
  End If

  Avg = (num1+num2+num3)/totalNums
End Function
```

Let's take a few minutes to analyze the `Avg` function. This function can take up to three arguments. The arguments `num1` and `num2` are required. The argument `num3` is optional. Notice that the name of the optional argument is preceded with the `Optional` keyword. The optional argument is listed at the end of the argument list. Because the type of the `num1`, `num2`, and `num3` arguments is not declared, Visual Basic treats all these arguments as Variants. Inside the function procedure, the `totalNums` variable is declared as an Integer and then assigned a beginning value of 3. Because the function has to be capable of calculating an average of two or three numbers, the handy built-in function `IsMissing` checks for the number of supplied arguments. If the third (optional) argument is not supplied, the `IsMissing` function puts in its place the value of zero (0), and at the same time it deducts the value of 1 from the value stored in the `totalNums` variable. Hence, if the optional argument is missing, `totalNums` is 2. The next statement calculates the average based on the supplied data, and the result is assigned to the name of the function.

The `IsMissing` function allows you to determine whether the optional argument was supplied. This function returns the logical value true if the third argument is not supplied, and it returns false when the third argument is given. The `IsMissing` function is used here with the decision-making statement `If...Then`. (See Chapter 5 for a detailed description of decision-making statements used in VBA.) If the `num3` argument is missing (`IsMissing`), then (`Then`) Visual Basic supplies a zero for the value of the third argument (`num3 = 0`) and reduces the value stored in the argument `totalNums` by one (`totalNums = totalNums - 1`).

3. Now call this function from the Immediate window like this:

```
?Avg(2,3)
```

As soon as you press **Enter**, Visual Basic displays the result: 2.5. If you enter the following:

```
?Avg(2,3,5)
```

this time the result is 3.3333333333333.

As you've seen, the `Avg` function allows you to calculate the average of two or three numbers. You decide which values and how many values (two or three) you want to average. When you start typing the values for the function's arguments in the Immediate window, Visual Basic displays the name of the optional argument enclosed in square brackets.

How else can you run the `Avg` function? On your own, run this function from a worksheet. Make sure you run it with two and then with three arguments.

TESTING A FUNCTION PROCEDURE

To test whether a custom function does what it was designed to do, write a simple subroutine that will call the function and display its result. In addition, the subroutine should show the original values of arguments. This way, you'll be able to quickly determine when the values of arguments were altered. If the function procedure uses optional arguments, you'll also need to check those situations in which the optional arguments may be missing.

LOCATING BUILT-IN FUNCTIONS

VBA comes with numerous built-in functions. These functions can be looked up in the Visual Basic online help:

https://docs.microsoft.com/en-us/office/vba/Language/Reference/functions-visual-basic-for-applications

Take, for example, the `MsgBox` or `InputBox` function. One of the features of a good program is its interaction with the user. When you work with Microsoft Excel, you interact with the application by using various dialog boxes. When you make a mistake, a dialog box comes up and displays a message informing you of the error. When you write your own procedures, you can also inform the users about an unexpected error or the result of a specific calculation. You do this with the help of the MsgBox function. So far you have seen a simple implementation of this function. In the next section, you will find out how to control the way your message looks. You will also learn how to get information from the user with the InputBox function.

GETTING TO KNOW THE MSGBOX FUNCTION

The MsgBox function that you have used thus far was limited to displaying a message to the user in a simple one-button dialog box. You closed the message box by clicking the OK button or pressing the Enter key. You create a simple message box by following the MsgBox function name with the text enclosed in quotation marks. In other words, to display the message "The procedure is complete." you write the following statement:

```
MsgBox "The procedure is complete."
```

You can quickly try out the foregoing instruction by entering it in the Immediate window. When you type this instruction and press Enter, Visual Basic displays the message box shown in Figure 4.4.

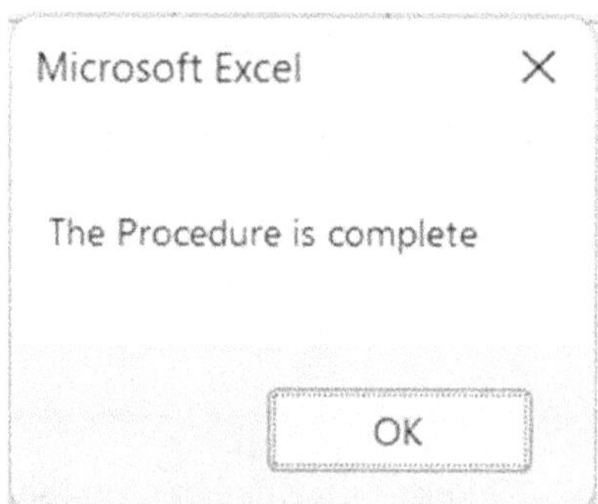

FIGURE 4.4 To display a message to the user, place the text as the argument of the MsgBox function.

The MsgBox function allows you to use other arguments that make it possible to set the number of buttons that should be available in the message box or change the title of the message box from the default, "Microsoft Excel." You can also assign your own help topic.

The syntax of the MsgBox function is as follows:

```
MsgBox (prompt [, buttons] [, title], [, helpfile, context])
```

Notice that while the `MsgBox` function has five arguments, only the first one, `prompt`, is required. The arguments listed in square brackets are optional. When you enter a long text string for the `prompt` argument, Visual Basic decides how to break the text so it fits the message box. Let's do some exercises in the Immediate window to learn various text formatting techniques.

Hands-On 4.8 Formatting Text for Display in the MsgBox Function

1. Enter the following instruction in the Immediate window. Be sure to enter the entire text string on one line, and then press **Enter**.

```
MsgBox "All processes completed successfully. Now connect an
    external storage device to your computer. The following
   procedure will copy the workbook file to the attached device."
```

As soon as you press **Enter**, Visual Basic shows the resulting dialog box (Figure 4.5).

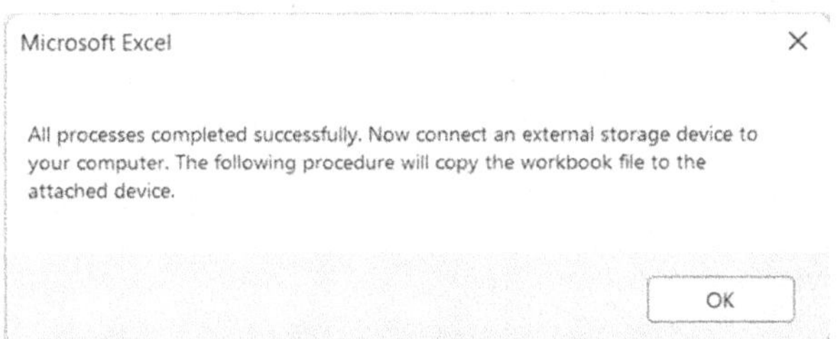

FIGURE 4.5 This long message will look more appealing when you take the text formatting into your own hands.

When you write a VBA procedure that requires long messages, you can break your message text into several lines using the VBA `Chr` function. The `Chr` function takes one argument (a number from 0 to 255), and it returns a character represented by this number. For example, `Chr(13)` returns a carriage return character (this is the same as pressing the Enter key), and `Chr(10)` returns a linefeed character (useful for adding spacing between the text lines).

```
Sub LongTextMessage()
   MsgBox "All processes completed successfully. " & Chr(13) _
    & "Now connect an external storage device to " & Chr(13) _
    & "your computer. The following procedure " & Chr(13) _
    & "will copy the workbook file to the attached device."
End Sub
```

Figure 4.6 depicts the message box after running the LongTextMessage procedure.

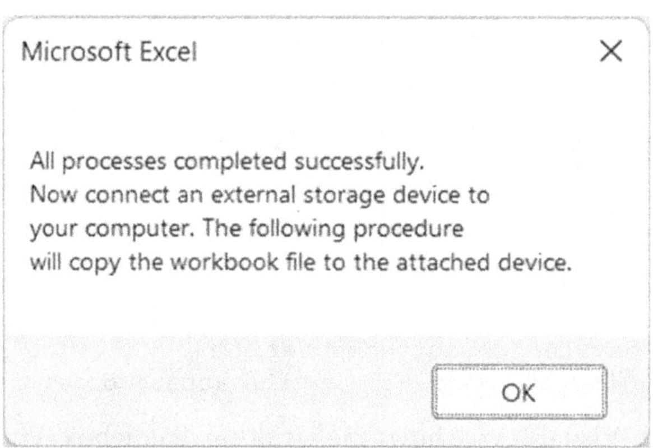

FIGURE 4.6 You can break a long text string into several lines by using the `Chr(13)` function.

You must surround each text fragment with quotation marks. The `Chr(13)` function indicates a place where you'd like to start a new line. The string concatenation character (&) is used to add a carriage return character to a concatenated string.

Quoted text embedded in a text string requires an additional set of quotation marks, as shown in the revised statement here:

```
Sub LongTextMessageRev()
    MsgBox "All processes completed successfully. " & _
        Chr(13) _
    & "Now connect an external storage device to " & _
        Chr(13) & "your computer. " & _
    "The following procedure ""TestProc()""" & _
        Chr(13) & "will copy the workbook file " & _
    "to the attached device."
End Sub
```

When you enter exceptionally long text messages on one line, it's easy to make a mistake. As you recall, Visual Basic has a special line continuation character (an underscore _) that allows you to break a long VBA statement into several lines. Unfortunately, the line continuation character cannot be used in the Immediate window.

2. Add a new module to the **ProcAndFunctions (Chap04_ExcelPrimer.xlsm)** project and change the module's name to **Sample5**.

3. Activate the **Sample5** module and enter the **LongTextMessage** and **LongTextMessageRev** subroutines as shown earlier. Be sure to precede each line continuation character (_) with a space.
4. Execute each procedure.

   Notice that the text entered on several lines is more readable, and the code is easier to maintain.

   To improve the readability of your message, you may want to add more spacing between the text lines by including blank lines. To do this, use two `Chr(13)` or two `Chr(10)` functions, as shown in the following step.
5. Enter the following LongTextMessage2 procedure and run it:

```
Sub LongTextMessage2()
    MsgBox "All processes completed successfully. " & _
        Chr(10) & Chr(10) _
    & "Now connect an external storage device " & _
        Chr(13) & Chr(13) _
    & "to your computer. The following procedure " & _
        Chr(10) & Chr(10) _
    & "will copy the workbook file to the attached device."
End Sub
```

   Figure 4.7 displays the message box generated by the LongTextMessage2 procedure.

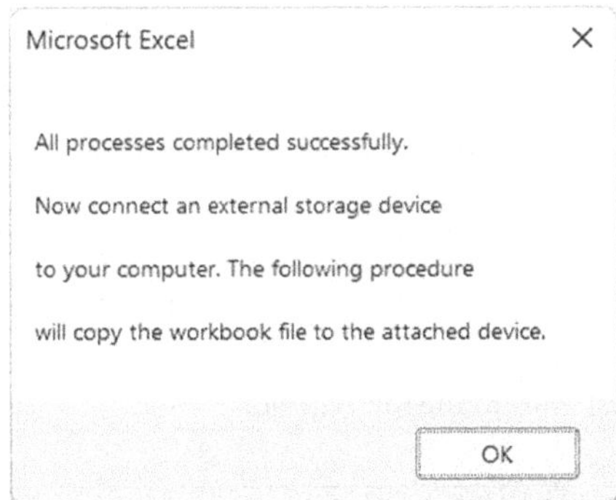

FIGURE 4.7 You can increase the readability of your message by increasing spacing between the selected text lines.

Now that you've mastered the text formatting techniques, let's take a closer look at the next argument of the `MsgBox` function. Although the `buttons` argument is optional, it is frequently used. The `buttons` argument specifies how many and what types of buttons you want to appear in the message box. This argument can be a constant or a number, as shown in Table 4.1. If you omit this argument, the resulting message box includes only the OK button, as you've seen in the preceding examples.

TABLE 4.1 Settings for the `MsgBox buttons` argument.

Constant	Value	Description
Button settings		
`vbOKOnly`	0	Displays only an OK button. This is the default.
`vbOKCancel`	1	OK and Cancel buttons.
`vbAbortRetryIgnore`	2	Abort, Retry, and Ignore buttons.
`vbYesNoCancel`	3	Yes, No, and Cancel buttons.
`vbYesNo`	4	Yes and No buttons.
`vbRetryCancel`	5	Retry and Cancel buttons.
Icon settings		
`vbCritical`	16	Displays the Critical Message icon.
`vbQuestion`	32	Displays the Question Message icon.
`vbExclamation`	48	Displays the Warning Message icon.
`vbInformation`	64	Displays the Information Message icon.
Default button settings		
`vbDefaultButton1`	0	The first button is the default.
`vbDefaultButton2`	256	The second button is the default.
`vbDefaultButton3`	512	The third button is the default.
`vbDefaultButton4`	768	The fourth button is the default.
Message box modality		
`vbApplicationModal`	0	The user must respond to the message before continuing to work in the current application.
`vbSystemModal`	4096	All applications are suspended until the user responds to the message box.
Other MsgBox display settings		
`vbMsgBoxHelpButton`	16384	Adds Help button to the message box.
`vbMsgBoxSetForeground`	65536	Specifies the message box window as the foreground window.
`vbMsgBoxRight`	524288	Text is right aligned.
`vbMsgBoxRtlReading`	1048576	Text appears as right-to-left reading on Hebrew and Arabic systems.

When should you use the `buttons` argument? Suppose you want the user of your procedure to respond to a question with Yes or No. Your message box may then require two buttons. If a message box includes more than one button, one of them is considered a default button. When the user presses Enter, the default button is selected automatically. Because you can display various types of messages (critical, warning, information), you can visually indicate the importance of the message by including in the `buttons` argument the graphical representation (icon) for the chosen message type.

In addition to the type of message, the `buttons` argument can include a setting to determine whether the message box must be closed before a user switches to another application. It's quite possible that the user may want to switch to another program or perform another task before responding to the question posed in your message box. If the message box is application modal (`vbApplication Modal`), the user must close the message box before continuing to use your application. On the other hand, if you want to suspend all the applications until the user responds to the message box, you must include the `vbSystemModal` setting in the `buttons` argument.

The `buttons` argument settings are divided into five groups: button settings, icon settings, default button settings, message box modality, and other `MsgBox` display settings. Only one setting from each group can be included in the `buttons` argument. To create a `buttons` argument, you can add up the values for each setting you want to include. For example, to display a message box with two buttons (Yes and No), the question mark icon, and the No button as the default button, look up the corresponding values in Table 4.1 and add them up. You should arrive at 292 (4 + 32 + 256).

Let's go back to the Immediate window for more testing of the capabilities of the `MsgBox` function.

Hands-On 4.9 Using the MsgBox Function with Arguments (Example 1)

1. To quickly see the message box using the calculated message box argument, enter the following statement in the Immediate window, and press Enter:

```
MsgBox "Do you want to proceed?", 292
```

The resulting message box is shown in Figure 4.8.

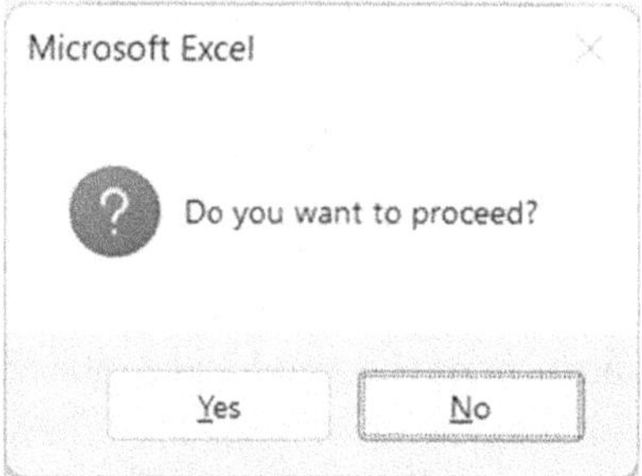

FIGURE 4.8 You can specify the number of buttons to include in the message box by using the optional `buttons` argument.

When you derive the `buttons` argument by adding up the constant values, your procedure becomes less readable. There's no reference table where you can check the hidden meaning of 292. To improve the readability of your `MsgBox` function, it's better to use the constants instead of their values.

2. Now enter the following revised statement on one line in the Immediate window and press Enter.

```
MsgBox "Do you want to proceed?", vbYesNo + vbQuestion +
vbDefaultButton2
```

This statement (which must be entered on one line) produces the same result shown in Figure 4.8 and is more readable.

The following example shows how to use the `buttons` argument inside the Visual Basic procedure.

Hands-On 4.10 Using the MsgBox Function with Arguments (Example 2)

1. Add a new module to the **ProcAndFunctions (Chap04_ExcelPrimer.xlsm)** project and change the module's name to **Sample6**.
2. Activate the **Sample6** module and enter the MsgYesNo subroutine shown here, and then run it:

```
Sub MsgYesNo()
  Dim question As String
  Dim myButtons As Integer

  question = "Do you want to open a new workbook?"
  myButtons = vbYesNo + vbQuestion + vbDefaultButton2
```

```
   MsgBox question, myButtons
End Sub
```

In the foregoing subroutine, the `question` variable stores the text of your message. The settings for the `buttons` argument is placed in the `myButtons` variable. Instead of using the names of constants, you can use their values, as in the following:

```
myButtons = 4 + 32 + 256
```

However, by specifying the names of the `buttons` argument's constants, you make your procedure easier to understand for yourself and others who may work with this procedure in the future.

The `question` and `myButtons` variables are used as arguments for the `MsgBox` function. When you run the procedure, you see the result displayed, as shown in Figure 4.8. Notice that the No button is selected. It's the default button for this dialog box. If you press Enter, Excel removes the `MsgBox` from the screen. Nothing happens because your procedure does not have any more instructions following the `MsgBox` function.

To change the default button, use the `vbDefaultButton1` setting instead.

The third argument of the `MsgBox` function is `title`. While this is also an optional argument, it's very handy, as it allows you to create procedures that don't provide visual clues to the fact that you programmed them with Microsoft Excel. Using this argument, you can set the title bar of your message box to any text you want.

Suppose you want the MsgYesNo procedure to display in its title the text "New workbook." The following MsgYesNo2 procedure demonstrates the use of the `title` argument:

```
Sub MsgYesNo2()
   Dim question As String
   Dim myButtons As Integer
   Dim myTitle As String

   question = "Do you want to open a new workbook?"
   myButtons = vbYesNo + vbQuestion + vbDefaultButton2
   myTitle = "New workbook"

   MsgBox question, myButtons, myTitle
End Sub
```

The text for the `title` argument is stored in the variable `myTitle`. If you don't specify the value for the `title` argument, Visual Basic displays the default text, "Microsoft Excel."

Notice that the arguments are listed in the order determined by the `MsgBox` function. If you would like to list the arguments in any order, you must precede the value of each argument with its name:

```
MsgBox title:=myTitle, prompt:=question, buttons:=myButtons
```

The last two optional arguments—`helpfile` and `context`—are used by programmers who are experienced with using help files in the Windows environment.

The `helpfile` argument indicates the name of a special help file that contains additional information you may want to display to your VBA procedure user. When you specify this argument, the Help button will be added to your message box.

Returning Values from the MsgBox Function

When you display a simple message box dialog with one button, clicking the OK button or pressing the Enter key removes the message box from the screen. However, when the message box has more than one button, your procedure should detect which button was pressed. To do this, you must save the result of the message box in a variable. Table 4.2 shows values that the `MsgBox` function returns.

TABLE 4.2 Values returned by the `MsgBox` function.

Button Selected	Constant	Value
OK	vbOK	1
Cancel	vbCancel	2
Abort	vbAbort	3
Retry	vbRetry	4
Ignore	vbIgnore	5
Yes	vbYes	6
No	vbNo	7

Let's revise the MsgYesNo2 procedure to show which button the user has chosen.

Hands-On 4.11 Using the MsgBox Function with Arguments (Example 3)

1. Activate the **Sample6** module and enter the MsgYesNo3 subroutine as shown here:

```
Sub MsgYesNo3()
  Dim question As String
  Dim myButtons As Integer
  Dim myTitle As String

  Dim myChoice As Integer

  question = "Do you want to open a new workbook?"
  myButtons = vbYesNo + vbQuestion + vbDefaultButton2
  myTitle = "New workbook"
  myChoice = MsgBox(question, myButtons, myTitle)

  MsgBox myChoice
End Sub
```

In the foregoing procedure, we assigned the result of the `MsgBox` function to the variable `myChoice`. Notice that the arguments of the `MsgBox` function are now listed in parentheses:

```
myChoice = MsgBox(question, myButtons, myTitle)
```

2. Run the **MsgYesNo3** procedure.
   When you run the MsgYesNo3 procedure, a two-button message box is displayed. When you click on the Yes button, the statement `MsgBox myChoice` displays the number 6. When you click the No button, the number 7 is displayed.

SIDEBAR ***MsgBox Function with or without Parentheses?***

Use parentheses around the `MsgBox` function's argument list when you want to use the result returned by the function. By listing the function's arguments without parentheses, you tell Visual Basic that you want to ignore the function's result. Most likely, you will want to use the function's result when the `MsgBox` contains more than one button.

GETTING TO KNOW THE INPUTBOX FUNCTION

The `InputBox` function displays a dialog box with a message that prompts the user to enter data. This dialog box has two buttons—OK and Cancel. When you click OK, the `InputBox` function returns the information entered in the text box. When you select Cancel, the function returns the empty string (""). The syntax of the `InputBox` function is as follows:

```
InputBox(prompt [, title] [, default] [, xpos] [, ypos]
    [, helpfile, context])
```

The first argument, `prompt`, is the text message that you want to display in the dialog box. Long text strings can be entered on several lines by using the `Chr(13)` or `Chr(10)` functions (see examples of using the `MsgBox` function earlier in this chapter). All the remaining `InputBox` arguments are optional.

The second argument, `title`, allows you to change the default title of the dialog box. The default value is "Microsoft Excel."

The third argument of the `InputBox` function, `default`, allows the display of a default value in the text box. If you omit this argument, the empty edit box is displayed.

The following two arguments, `xpos` and `ypos`, let you specify the exact position where the dialog box should appear on the screen. If you omit these arguments, the box appears in the middle of the current window. The `xpos` argument determines the horizontal position of the dialog box from the left edge of the screen. When omitted, the dialog box is centered horizontally. The `ypos` argument determines the vertical position from the top of the screen. If you omit this argument, the dialog box is positioned vertically approximately one-third of the way down the screen. Both `xpos` and `ypos` are measured in special units called *twips*. One twip is equivalent to approximately 0.0007 inches.

The last two arguments, `helpfile` and `context`, are used in the same way as the corresponding arguments of the `MsgBox` function discussed earlier in this chapter.

Now that you know the meaning of the `InputBox` function's arguments, let's look at some examples of using this function.

Hands-On 4.12 Using the InputBox Function (Example 1)

1. Add a new module to the **ProcAndFunctions (Chap04_ExcelPrimer.xlsm)** project and change the module's name to **Sample7**.

2. Activate the **Sample7** module and enter the Informant subroutine shown here:

```
Sub Informant()
  InputBox prompt:="Enter your place of birth:" & Chr(13) _
      & " (e.g., Boston, Great Falls, etc.) "
End Sub
```

This procedure displays a dialog box with two buttons, as shown in Figure 4.9. The input prompt is displayed on two lines.

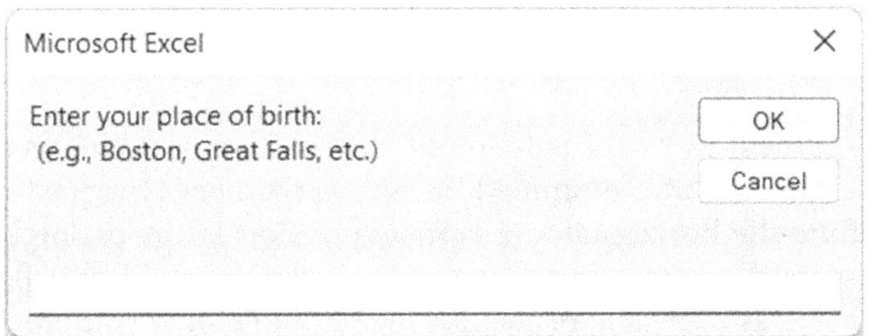

FIGURE 4.9 A dialog box generated by the Informant subroutine.

As with the `MsgBox` function, if you plan on using the data entered by the user in the dialog box, you should store the result of the `InputBox` function in a variable.

3. Type the Informant2 procedure shown here to assign the result of the `InputBox` function to the variable `town`:

```
Sub Informant2()
  Dim myPrompt As String
  Dim town As String

  Const myTitle = "Enter data"

  myPrompt = "Enter your place of birth:" & Chr(13) _
      & "(e.g., Boston, Great Falls, etc.)"
  town = InputBox(myPrompt, myTitle)

  MsgBox "You were born in " & town & ".", , "Your response"
End Sub
```

Notice that this time the arguments of the `InputBox` function are listed within parentheses. Parentheses are required if you want to use the result of the `InputBox` function later in your procedure. The Informant2 subroutine uses a constant to specify the text to appear in the title bar of the dialog box.

Because the constant value remains the same throughout the execution of your procedure, you can declare the input box title as a constant. However, if you'd rather use a variable, you still can. When you run a procedure using the `InputBox` function, the dialog box generated by this function always appears in the same area of the screen. To change the location of the dialog box, you must supply the `xpos` and `ypos` arguments, as explained earlier.

4. Run the Informant2 procedure.
5. To display the dialog box in the top left-hand corner of the screen, modify the `InputBox` function in the Informant2 procedure as follows and then run it:

```
town = InputBox(myPrompt, myTitle, , 1, 200)
```

Notice that the argument `myTitle` is followed by two commas. The second comma marks the position of the omitted `default` argument. The next two arguments determine the horizontal and vertical position of the dialog box. If you omit the second comma after the `myTitle` argument, Visual Basic will use the number 1 as the value of the `default` argument. If you precede the values of arguments by their names (for example, `prompt:=myPrompt, title:=myTitle, xpos:=1, ypos:=200`), you won't have to remember to place a comma in the place of each omitted argument.

What will happen if you enter a number instead of the name of a town? Because users often supply incorrect data in an input dialog box, your procedure must verify that the supplied data can be used in further data manipulations. The `InputBox` function itself does not provide a facility for data validation. To validate user input, you must learn additional VBA instructions that are presented in the next chapter.

Determining and Converting Data Types

The result of the `InputBox` function is always a string. If the user enters a number, the string value the user entered should be converted to a numeric value before your procedure can use this number in mathematical computations. Visual Basic can convert values from one data type to another.

NOTE	*Refer to Chapter 3 for more information about using the* `VarType` *function to determine the data type of a variable and common data type conversion functions.*

Let's try out a procedure that suggests what type of data the user should enter by supplying a default value in the InputBox dialog.

Hands-On 4.13 Using the InputBox Function (Example 2)

1. Activate the **Sample7** module in the **ProcAndFunctions (Chap04_ExcelPrimer.xlsm)** project and enter the following AddTwoNums procedure:

```
Sub AddTwoNums()
  Dim myPrompt As String
  Dim value1 As String
  Dim value2 As Integer
  Dim mySum As Single

  Const myTitle = "Enter data"

  myPrompt = "Enter a number:"
  value1 = InputBox(myPrompt, myTitle, 0)
  value2 = 2
  mySum = value1 + value2

  MsgBox "The result is " & mySum & _
      " (" & value1 & " + " & CStr(value2) + ")", _
       vbInformation, "Total"
End Sub
```

The AddTwoNums procedure displays the dialog box shown in Figure 4.10. Notice that this dialog box has two special features that are obtained by using the `InputBox` function's optional `title` and `default` arguments. Instead of the default title "Microsoft Excel," the dialog box displays a text string defined by the contents of the `myTitle` constant. The zero entered as the default value in the edit box suggests that the user enter a number instead of text. Once the user provides the data and clicks OK, the user's input is assigned to the variable `value1`.

```
value1 = InputBox(myPrompt, myTitle, 0)
```

2. Run the AddTwoNums procedure, supply any number when prompted, and then click **OK**.

FIGURE 4.10 To suggest that the user enter a specific type of data, you may want to provide a default value in the edit box.

The data type of the variable `value1` is String.

3. You can check the data type easily if you follow the foregoing instruction in the procedure code with this statement:

```
MsgBox VarType(value1)
```

When Visual Basic runs the foregoing line, it will display a message box with the number 8. Recall from Chapter 3 (Table 3.3) that this number represents the String data type.

The statement `mySum = value1 + value2` adds the value stored in the `value2` variable to the user's input and assigns the result of the calculation to the variable `mySum`. Because the `value1` variable's data type is String, prior to using this variable's data in the computation, Visual Basic goes to work behind the scenes to perform the data type conversion. Visual Basic understands the need for conversion. Without it, the two incompatible data types (String and Integer) would generate a Type mismatch error. The procedure ends with the `MsgBox` function displaying the result of the calculation and showing the user how the total was derived. Notice that the `value2` variable must be converted from Integer to String data type using the `CStr` function to display it in the message box:

```
MsgBox "The result is " & mySum & _
    " (" & value1 & " + " & CStr(value2) + ")", _
    vbInformation, "Total"
```

SIDEBAR ***Define a Constant***

To ensure that all the title bars in a particular VBA procedure display the same text, assign the title text to a constant. By doing this you will save time by not having to type the title text more than once.

USING THE INPUTBOX METHOD

In addition to the built-in `InputBox` VBA function, there is also the Excel `InputBox` method. If you activate the Object Browser window and type "input-box" in the search box and press Enter, Visual Basic will display two occurrences of `InputBox`—one in the Excel library and the other one in the VBA library, as shown in Figure 4.11.

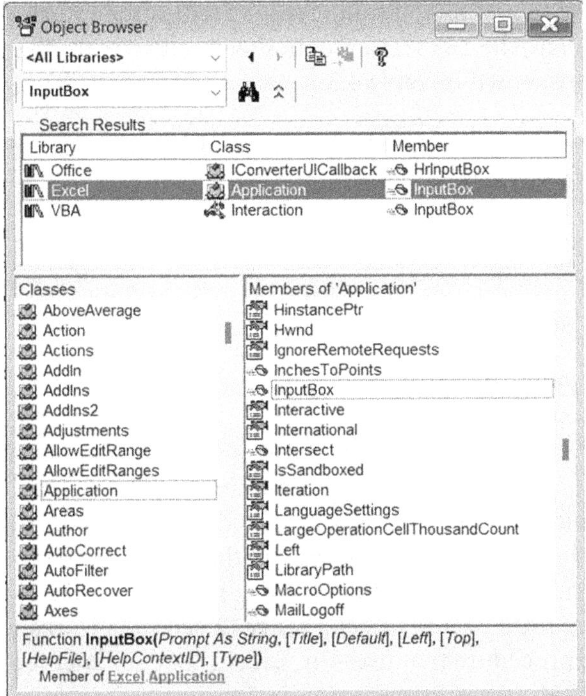

FIGURE 4.11 Don't forget to use the Object Browser when researching Visual Basic functions and methods.

The `InputBox` method available in the Microsoft Excel library has a slightly different syntax than the `InputBox` function that was covered earlier in this chapter. Its syntax is:

```
expression.InputBox(prompt, [title], [default], [left], [top], _
[helpfile], [helpcontextID], [type])
```

All bracketed arguments are optional. The `prompt` argument is the message to be displayed in the dialog box, `title` is the title for the dialog box, and `default` is a value that will appear in the text box when the dialog box is initially displayed.

The `left` and `top` arguments specify the position of the dialog box on the screen. The values for these arguments are entered in points. Note that one-point equals 1/72 inch. The arguments `helpfile` and `helpcontextID` identify the name of the help file and the specific number of the help topic to be displayed when the user clicks the Help button.

The last argument of the `InputBox` method, `type`, specifies the return data type. If you omit this argument, the `InputBox` method will return text. The values of the `type` argument are shown in Table 4.3.

TABLE 4.3 Data types returned by the `InputBox` method.

Value	Type of Data Returned
0	A formula
1	A number
2	A string (text)
4	A logical value (True or False)
8	A cell reference, as a Range object
16	An error value (for example, #N/A)
64	An array of values

You can allow the user to enter a number or text in the edit box if you use 3 for the `type` argument. This value is obtained by adding up the values for a number (1) and a string (2), as shown in Table 4.3. The `InputBox` method is quite useful for VBA procedures that require a user to select a range of cells in a worksheet.

Let's look at an example procedure that uses the Excel `InputBox` method.

Hands-On 4.14 Using the Excel InputBox Method

1. Close the Object Browser window if you opened it before.
2. In the **Sample7** module, enter the following **WhatRange** procedure:

```
Sub WhatRange()
  Dim newRange As Range
  Dim tellMe As String

  tellMe = "Use the mouse to select a range:"
  Set newRange = Application.InputBox(prompt:=tellMe, _
      Title:="Range to format", _
      Type:=8)
  newRange.NumberFormat = "0.00"
  newRange.Select
End Sub
```

The WhatRange procedure begins with a declaration of an object variable—`newRange`. As you recall from Chapter 3, object variables point to the location of the data. The range of cells that the user selects is assigned to the object variable `newRange`. Notice the keyword `Set` before the name of the variable:

```
Set newRange = Application.InputBox(prompt:=tellMe, _
  Title:="Range to format", _Type:=8)
```

The `Type` argument (`Type:=8`) enables the user to select any range of cells. When the user highlights the cells, the next instruction:

```
newRange.NumberFormat = "0.00"
```

changes the format of the selected cells. The last instruction selects the range of cells that the user highlighted.

3. Press **Alt+F11** to activate the Microsoft Excel Application window, and then press **Alt+F8** and choose **WhatRange** procedure and run it.
   Visual Basic displays a dialog box prompting the user to select a range of cells in the worksheet.
4. Use the mouse to select any cells you want. Figure 4.12 shows how Visual Basic enters the selected range reference in the edit box as you drag the mouse to select the cells.

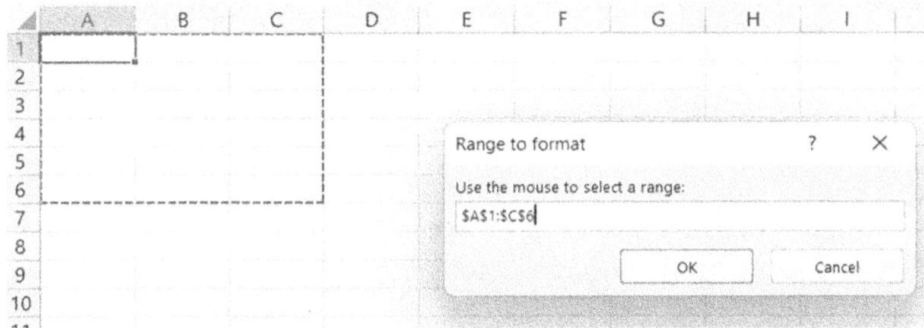

FIGURE 4.12 Using Excel's `InputBox` method, you can get the range address from the user.

5. When you're done selecting cells, click **OK** in the dialog box.
   The selected range is now formatted. To check this out, enter a whole number in any of the selected cells. The number should appear formatted with two decimal places.
6. Rerun the procedure, and when the dialog box appears, click **Cancel**.
   When you click the Cancel button or press Esc, Visual Basic displays an error message—*"Object Required."* When you click the Debug button in the error dialog box, Visual Basic will highlight the line of code that caused the error. Because you don't want to select anything when you cancel the dialog box, you must find a way to ignore the error that Visual Basic displays. Using a special statement, `On Error GoTo` *labelname*, you can take a detour when an error occurs. This instruction has the following syntax:

```
On Error GoTo labelname
```

This instruction should be placed just below the variable declaration lines. `Labelname` can be any word you want, except for a Visual Basic keyword. If an error occurs, Visual Basic will jump to the specified label, as shown in Step 8 ahead.

7. Choose **Run | Reset** to cancel the procedure you were running.
8. Modify the **WhatRange** procedure so it looks like the **WhatRange2** procedure shown here:

```
Sub WhatRange2()
  Dim newRange As Range
  Dim tellMe As String

  On Error GoTo VeryEnd

  tellMe = "Use the mouse to select a range:"
  Set newRange = Application.InputBox(prompt:=tellMe, _
      Title:="Range to format", _
      Type:=8)
  newRange.NumberFormat = "0.00"
  newRange.Select

  VeryEnd:
End Sub
```

9. Run the modified procedure and click **Cancel** as soon as the input box appears. Notice that this time the procedure does not generate the error when you cancel the dialog box. When Visual Basic encounters the error, it jumps to the `VeryEnd` label placed at the end of the procedure. The statements placed between `On Error Goto VeryEnd` and the `VeryEnd` labels are ignored. In Chapter 9 you will find other examples of trapping errors in your VBA procedures.

SIDEBAR ***Subroutines and Functions: Which Should You Use?***

Create a subroutine when...	Create a function when...
You want to perform some actions.	You want to perform a simple calculation more than once.
You want to get input from the user.	You must perform complex computations.
You want to display a message on the screen.	You must call the same block of instructions more than once.
	You want to check if a certain expression is True or False.

SUMMARY

In this chapter, you learned the difference between subroutine procedures that perform actions and function procedures that return values. While you can create subroutines by recording or typing code directly into the Visual Basic module, function procedures cannot be recorded because they can take arguments. You must write them manually. You learned how to pass arguments to functions and determine the data type of a function's result. You increased your repertoire of VBA keywords with the `ByVal`, `ByRef`, and `Optional` keywords. You also learned how, with the help of parameters, subprocedures can pass values back to the calling procedures. After working through this chapter, you should be able to create some custom functions of your own that are suited to your specific needs. You should also be able to interact easily with your procedure users by employing the `MsgBox` and `InputBox` functions as well as the Excel `InputBox` method.

The next chapter will introduce you to decision making. You will learn how to change the course of your VBA procedure based on the results of the conditions that you supply.

Chapter 5

Adding Decisions to Excel VBA Programs

A Quick Introduction to Conditional Statements

Visual Basic for Applications, like other programming languages, offers special statements that allow you to include decision points in your own procedures. But what is decision making? Suppose someone approaches you with the question, "Do you like the color red?" After giving this question some thought, you'll answer "yes" or "no." If you're undecided or simply don't care, you might answer "maybe" or "perhaps." In programming, you must be decisive. Only "yes" or "no" answers are allowed. In programming, all decisions are based on supplied answers. If the answer is positive, the procedure executes a specified block of instructions. If the answer is negative, the procedure executes another block of instructions or simply doesn't do anything. In this chapter, you will learn how to use VBA conditional statements to alter the flow of your program. Conditional statements are often referred to as "control structures," as they give you the ability to control the flow of your VBA procedure by skipping over certain statements and "branching" to another part of the procedure.

RELATIONAL AND LOGICAL OPERATORS

You make decisions in your VBA procedures by using conditional expressions inside the special control structures. A *conditional expression* is an expression that uses one of the relational operators listed in Table 5.1, one of the logical operators listed in Table 5.2, or a combination of both. When Visual Basic encounters a conditional expression in your program, it evaluates the expression to determine whether it is true or false.

TABLE 5.1 Relational operators in VBA.

Operator	Description
=	Equal to
<>	Not equal to
>	Greater than
<	Less than
>=	Greater than or equal to
<=	Less than or equal to

TABLE 5.2 Logical operators in VBA.

Operator	Description
AND	All conditions must be true before an action can be taken.
OR	At least one of the conditions must be true before an action can be taken.
NOT	Used for negating a condition. If a condition is true, NOT makes it false. If a condition is false, NOT makes it true.

USING IF...THEN STATEMENT

The simplest way to get some decision making into your VBA procedure is to use the `If...Then` statement. Suppose you want to choose an action depending on a condition. You can use the following structure:

```
If condition Then statement
```

For example, to delete a blank row from a worksheet, first check if the active cell is blank. If the result of the test is true, go ahead and delete the entire row that contains that cell:

```
If ActiveCell = "" Then Selection.EntireRow.Delete
```

If the active cell is not blank, Visual Basic will ignore the statement following the `Then` keyword.

Sometimes you may want to perform several actions when the condition is true. Although you could add other statements on the same line by separating them with colons, your code will look clearer if you use the multiline version of the `If...Then` statement, as shown here:

```
If condition Then
  statement1
  statement2
  statementN
End If
```

For example, to perform some actions when the value of the active cell is greater than 50, you can write the following block of instructions:

```
If ActiveCell.Value > 50 Then
    MsgBox "The exact value is " & ActiveCell.Value
    Debug.Print ActiveCell.Address & ": " & ActiveCell.Value
End If
```

In this example, the statements between the `Then` and the `End If` keywords are not executed if the value of the active cell is less than or equal to 50. Notice that the block `If...Then` statement must end with the keywords `End If`.

How does Visual Basic make a decision? It evaluates the condition it finds between the `If...Then` keywords. Let's try to evaluate the following condition: `ActiveCell.Value > 50`.

NOTE	*Please note files for the "Hands-On" project may be found in the companion files.*

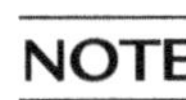

Hands-On 5.1 Evaluating Conditions in the Immediate Window

1. Open a new Microsoft Excel workbook.
2. Select any cell in a blank worksheet and enter **50**.
3. Switch to the Visual Basic Editor window.
4. Activate the Immediate window.
5. Type the following statement, and press **Enter** when you're done:

```
? ActiveCell.Value > 50
```

When you press Enter, Visual Basic writes the result of this test—false. When the result of the test is false, Visual Basic will not bother to read the statement following the `Then` keyword in your code. It will simply go on to read the next line of your procedure, if there is one. If there are no more lines to read, the procedure will end.

6. Now change the operator to less than or equal to, and have Visual Basic evaluate the following condition:

```
? ActiveCell.Value <= 50
```

This time, the test returns true, and Visual Basic will jump to whatever statement or statements it finds after the `Then` keyword.

7. Close the Immediate window.

Now that you know how Visual Basic evaluates conditions, let's try the `If...Then` statement in a VBA procedure.

Hands-On 5.2 Writing a VBA Procedure with a Simple If...Then Statement

1. Open a new workbook and save it as **C:\VBAPrimerExcel2021_ByExample\Chap05_ExcelPrimer.xlsm**.
2. Switch to the Visual Basic Editor screen and rename the VBA project **Decisions**.
3. Insert a new module in the **Decisions (Chap05_ExcelPrimer.xlsm)** project and rename this module **IfThen**.
4. In the IfThen module, enter the following procedure:

```
Sub SimpleIfThen()
  Dim weeks As String
  weeks = InputBox("How many weeks are in a year?", "Quiz")
  If weeks <> 52 Then MsgBox "Try Again"
End Sub
```

The SimpleIfThen procedure stores the user's answer in the variable named `weeks`. The variable's value is then compared to the number 52. If the result of the comparison is true (that is, if the value stored in the variable `weeks` is not equal to 52), Visual Basic will display the message "Try Again."

5. Run the SimpleIfThen procedure and enter a number other than 52.
6. Rerun the SimpleIfThen procedure and enter the number **52**.

When you enter the correct number of weeks, Visual Basic does nothing. The procedure simply ends. It would be nice to display a message when the user guesses right.

7. Enter the following instruction on a separate line before the `End Sub` keywords:

```
If weeks = 52 Then MsgBox "Congratulations!"
```

8. Run the SimpleIfThen procedure again and enter **52**.

When you enter the correct answer, Visual Basic does not execute the statement `MsgBox "Try Again."` When the procedure is executed, the statement to the right of the `Then` keyword is ignored if the result from evaluating the supplied condition is false. As you recall, a VBA procedure can call another procedure. Let's see whether it can also call itself.

9. Modify the first `If` statement in the SimpleIfThen procedure as follows:

```
If weeks <> 52 Then MsgBox "Try Again": SimpleIfThen
```

We added a colon and the name of the SimpleIfThen procedure to the end of the existing `If...Then` statement. If the user enters the incorrect answer, he will see a message, and as soon as he clicks the OK button in the message box, the input box will appear again, and he will get another chance to supply the correct answer. The user will be able to keep on guessing for a long time. In fact, he won't be able to exit the procedure gracefully until he supplies the correct answer. If he clicks Cancel, he will have to deal with the unfriendly error message "*Type mismatch.*" You saw in the previous chapter how to use the `On Error GoTo labelname` statement to go around the error, at least temporarily until you learn more about error handling in Chapter 9. For now, you may want to revise your SimpleIfThen procedure as follows:

```
Sub SimpleIfThen()
  Dim weeks As String
  On Error GoTo VeryEnd
  weeks = InputBox("How many weeks are in a year:", "Quiz")
  If weeks <> 52 Then MsgBox "Try Again": SimpleIfThen
  If weeks = 52 Then MsgBox "Congratulations!"
  VeryEnd:
End Sub
```

10. Run the SimpleIfThen procedure a few times by supplying incorrect answers. The error trap that you added to your procedure allows the user to quit guessing without having to deal with the ugly error message.

SIDEBAR *Two Formats for the* `If...Then` *Statement*

The `If...Then` statement has two formats—single line and multiline. The single-line format is good for short or simple statements like:

```
If secretCode <> 01W01 Then MsgBox "Access denied"
```

Or

```
If secretCode = 01W01 Then alpha = True : beta = False
```

Here, `secretCode`, `alpha`, and `beta` are the names of variables. In the first example, Visual Basic displays the message "Access denied" if the value of `secretCode` is not equal to 01W01. In the second example, Visual Basic sets the value of `alpha` to true and `beta` to false when the `secretCode` variable is equal to 01W01. Notice that the second statement to be executed is separated from the first by a colon. The multiline `If...Then` statement is clearer when there are more statements to be executed when the condition is true or when the statement to be executed is extremely long, as in the following example:

```
If ActiveSheet.Name = "Sheet1" Then
  ActiveSheet.Move after:= Sheets(Worksheets.Count)
End If
```

Here, Visual Basic examines the active sheet name. If it is Sheet1, the condition `ActiveSheet.Name = "Sheet1"` is true, and Visual Basic proceeds to execute the line following the `Then` keyword. As a result, the active sheet is moved to the last position in the workbook.

SIDEBAR ***If Block Instructions and Indenting***

To make the `If` blocks easier to read and understand, use indentation. Compare the following:

```
If condition Then                  If condition Then
   action                             action
End If                             End If
```

In the `If...Then` block statement on the right, you can easily see where the block begins and where it ends.

USING IF...THEN...ELSE STATEMENT

Now you know how to display a message or take an action when one or more conditions are true or false. What should you do, however, if your procedure needs to take one action when the condition is true and another action when the condition is false? By adding the `Else` clause to the simple `If...Then` statement, you can direct your procedure to the appropriate statement depending on the result of the test.

The `If...Then...Else` statement has two formats—single line and multiline. The single-line format is as follows:

```
If condition Then statement1 Else statement2
```

The statement following the `Then` keyword is executed if the condition is true, and the statement following the `Else` clause is executed if the condition is false—for example:

```
If Sales > 5000 Then Bonus = Sales * 0.05 Else MsgBox "No Bonus"
```

If the value stored in the variable `Sales` is greater than 5000, Visual Basic will calculate the bonus using the following formula: `Sales * 0.05`. However, if the variable `Sales` is not greater than 5000, Visual Basic will display the message "No Bonus."

The `If...Then...Else` statement should be used to decide which of the two actions to perform. When you need to execute more statements when the condition is true or false, it's better to use the multiline format of the `If...Then...Else` statement:

```
If condition Then
  statements to be executed if condition is True
Else
  statements to be executed if condition is False
End If
```

Notice that the multiline (block) `If...Then...Else` statement ends with the `End If` keywords. Use the indentation shown in the previous section to make this block structure easier to read. Here's a code example that uses the foregoing syntax:

```
If ActiveSheet.Name = "Sheet1" Then
  ActiveSheet.Name = "My Sheet"
  MsgBox "This sheet has been renamed."
Else
  MsgBox "This sheet name is not default."
End If
```

If the condition (`ActiveSheet.Name = "Sheet1"`) is true, Visual Basic will execute the statements between `Then` and `Else` and ignore the statement between `Else` and `End If`. If the condition is false, Visual Basic will omit the statements between `Then` and `Else` and execute the statement between `Else` and `End If`. Let's look at the complete procedure example.

Hands-On 5.3 Writing a VBA Procedure with an If...Then...Else Statement

1. Insert a new module into the **Decisions (Chap05_ExcelPrimer.xlsm)** project.
2. Change the module name to **IfThenElse**.

3. Enter the following WhatTypeOfDay procedure and then run it:

```
Sub WhatTypeOfDay()
  Dim response As String
  Dim question As String
  Dim strmsg1 As String, strmsg2 As String
  Dim myDate As Date

  question = "Enter any date in the format mm/dd/yyyy:" _
    & Chr(13)& " (e.g., 11/22/2021)"
    strmsg1 = "weekday"
    strmsg2 = "weekend"
    response = InputBox(question)
    myDate = Weekday(CDate(response))
    If myDate >= 2 And myDate <= 6 Then
      MsgBox strmsg1
    Else
      MsgBox strmsg2
    End If
End Sub
```

The foregoing procedure asks the user to enter any date. The user-supplied string is then converted to the Date data type with the built-in `CDate` function. Finally, the `Weekday` function converts the date into an integer that indicates the day of the week. The day of the week constants are listed in Table 5.3. The integer is stored in the variable `myDate`. The conditional test is performed to check whether the value of the variable `myDate` is greater than or equal to 2 (`>=2`) and less than or equal to 6 (`<=6`). If the result of the test is true, the user is told that the supplied date is a weekday; otherwise, the program announces that it's a weekend.

4. Run the procedure from the Visual Basic window. Run it a few times, each time supplying a different date. Check the Visual Basic answers against your desktop or wall calendar.

TABLE 5.3 Values returned by the built-in `Weekday` function.

Constant	Value
vbSunday	1
vbMonday	2
vbTuesday	3
vbWednesday	4
vbThursday	5
vbFriday	6
vbSaturday	7

USING IF...THEN...ELSEIF STATEMENT

Quite often you will need to check the results of several different conditions. To join a set of `If` conditions together, you can use the `ElseIf` clause. Using the `If...Then...ElseIf` statement, you can supply more conditions to evaluate than is possible with the `If...Then...Else` statement discussed earlier.

Here's the syntax of the `If...Then...Else` statement:

```
If condition1 Then
  statements to be executed if condition1 is True
ElseIf condition2 Then
  statements to be executed if condition2 is True
ElseIf condition3 Then
  statements to be executed if condition3 is True
ElseIf conditionN Then
statements to be executed if conditionN is True
Else
  statements to be executed if all conditions are False
End If
```

The `Else` clause is optional; you can omit it if there are no actions to be executed when all conditions are false. Your procedure can include any number of `ElseIf` statements and conditions. The `ElseIf` clause always comes before the `Else` clause. The statements in the `ElseIf` clause are executed only if the condition in this clause is true.

Let's look at the following code example:

```
If ActiveCell.Value = 0 Then
  ActiveCell.Offset(0, 1).Value = "zero"
ElseIf ActiveCell.Value > 0 Then
  ActiveCell.Offset(0, 1).Value = "positive"
ElseIf ActiveCell.Value < 0 Then
  ActiveCell.Offset(0, 1).Value = "negative"
End if
```

This example checks the value of the active cell and enters the appropriate label (zero, positive, negative) in the adjoining column. Notice that the `Else` clause is not used. If the result of the first condition (`ActiveCell.Value = 0`) is false, Visual Basic jumps to the next `ElseIf` statement and evaluates its condition (`ActiveCell.Value > 0`). If the value is not greater than zero, Visual Basic skips to the next `ElseIf` and the condition `ActiveCell.Value < 0` is evaluated.

Let's see how the `If...Then...ElseIf` statement works in a complete procedure.

Hands-On 5.4 Writing a VBA Procedure with an If...Then...ElseIf Statement

1. Insert a new module into the current VBA project.
2. Rename the module **IfThenElseIf.**
3. Enter the following WhatValue procedure:

```
Sub WhatValue()
  Range("A1").Select
  If ActiveCell.Value = 0 Then
    ActiveCell.Offset(0, 1).Value = "zero"
  ElseIf ActiveCell.Value > 0 Then
    ActiveCell.Offset(0, 1).Value = "positive"
  ElseIf ActiveCell.Value < 0 Then
    ActiveCell.Offset(0, 1).Value = "negative"
  End If
End Sub
```

Because you need to run the WhatValue procedure several times to test each condition, let's have Visual Basic assign a temporary keyboard shortcut to this procedure.

4. Open the Immediate window and type the following statement:

```
Application.OnKey "^+y", "WhatValue"
```

When you press **Enter**, Visual Basic runs the `OnKey` method that assigns the WhatValue procedure to the key sequence Ctrl+Shift+Y. This keyboard shortcut is only temporary—it will not work when you restart Microsoft Excel. To assign the shortcut key to a procedure, use the Options button in the Macro dialog box accessed from Developer | Macros in the Microsoft Excel window.

5. Now switch to the Microsoft Excel window and activate **Sheet2.**
6. Type **0** (zero) in cell A1 and press **Enter**. Then press **Ctrl+Shift+Y**.
7. Visual Basic calls the WhatValue procedure and enters "zero" in cell B1.
8. Enter any number greater than zero in cell A1 and press **Ctrl+Shift+Y**.
Visual Basic again calls the WhatValue procedure. Visual Basic evaluates the first condition, and because the result of this test is false, it jumps to the `ElseIf` statement. The second condition is true, so Visual Basic executes the statement following `Then` and skips over the next statements to the `End If`. Because there are no more statements following the `End If`, the procedure ends. Cell B1 now displays the word "positive."
9. Enter any number less than zero in cell A1 and press **Ctrl+Shift+Y**.

This time, the first two conditions return false, so Visual Basic goes to examine the third condition. Because this test returns true, Visual Basic enters the word "negative" in cell B1.

10. Enter any text in cell A1 and press **Ctrl+Shift+Y**.

Visual Basic's response is "positive." However, this is not a satisfactory answer. You may want to differentiate between positive numbers and text by displaying the word "text." To make the WhatValue procedure smarter, you need to learn how to make more complex decisions by using nested `If...Then` statements.

NESTED IF...THEN STATEMENTS

You can make more complex decisions in your VBA procedures by placing an `If...Then` or `If...Then...Else` statement inside another `If...Then` or `If...Then...Else` statement.

Structures in which an `If` statement is contained inside another `If` block are referred to as nested `If` statements. The following TestConditions procedure is a revised version of the WhatValue procedure created in the previous section. The WhatValue procedure has been modified to illustrate how nested `If...Then` statements work.

```
Sub TestConditions()
    Range("A1").Select
    If IsEmpty(ActiveCell) Then
        MsgBox "The cell is empty."
    Else
        If IsNumeric(ActiveCell.Value) Then
            If ActiveCell.Value = 0 Then
                ActiveCell.Offset(0, 1).Value = "zero"
            ElseIf ActiveCell.Value > 0 Then
                ActiveCell.Offset(0, 1).Value = "positive"
            ElseIf ActiveCell.Value < 0 Then
                ActiveCell.Offset(0, 1).Value = "negative"
            End If
        Else
            ActiveCell.Offset(0, 1).Value = "text"
        End If
    End If
End Sub
```

To make the TestConditions procedure easier to understand, each `If...Then` statement is shown with different formatting. You can now clearly see that the procedure uses three If...Then blocks. The first If block (in bold) checks whether the active cell is empty. If this is true, the message is displayed, and Visual Basic skips over the Else part until it finds the matching End If. This statement is located just before the End Sub keywords. If the active cell is not empty, the IsEmpty(ActiveCell) condition returns false, and Visual Basic runs the single underlined If block following the Else formatted in bold. This (underlined) If...Then...Else statement is said to be nested inside the first If block (in bold). This statement checks if the value of the active cell is a number. Notice that this is done with the help of another built-in function—IsNumeric. If the value of the active cell is not a number, the condition is false, so Visual Basic jumps to the statement following the underlined Else and enters "text" in cell B1. However, if the active cell contains a number, Visual Basic runs the double-underlined If block, evaluating each condition and making the appropriate decision. The first If block (in bold) is called the outer If statement. This outer statement contains two inner If statements (single and double underlined).

USING THE SELECT CASE STATEMENT

To avoid complex nested If statements that are difficult to follow, you can use the Select Case statement instead. The syntax of this statement is as follows:

```
Select Case testexpression
  Case expressionlist1
    statements if expressionlist1 matches testexpression
  Case expressionlist2
    statements if expressionlist2 matches testexpression
  Case expressionlistN
    statements if expressionlistN matches testexpression
  Case Else
    statements to be executed if no values match
testexpression
End Select
```

You can place any number of Case clauses to test between the keywords Select Case and End Select. The Case Else clause is optional. Use it when you expect that there may be conditional expressions that return false. In the Select Case statement, Visual Basic compares each expressionlist with the value of testexpression.

Here's the logic behind the Select Case statement. When Visual Basic encounters the Select Case clause, it makes note of the value of testexpression. Then it proceeds to test the expression following the first Case clause.

If the value of this expression (`expressionlist1`) matches the value stored in `testexpression`, Visual Basic executes the statements until another `Case` clause is encountered and then jumps to the `End Select` statement. If, however, the expression tested in the first `Case` clause does not match `testexpression`, Visual Basic checks the value of each `Case` clause until it finds a match. If none of the `Case` clauses contain the expression that matches the value stored in `testexpression`, Visual Basic jumps to the `Case Else` clause and executes the statements until it encounters the `End Select` keywords. Notice that the `Case Else` clause is optional. If your procedure does not use `Case Else` and none of the `Case` clauses contain a value matching the value of `testexpression`, Visual Basic jumps to the statements following `End Select` and continues executing your procedure.

Let's look at an example of a procedure that uses the `Select Case` statement. In Chapter 4, you learned quite a few details about the `MsgBox` function, which allows you to display a message with one or more buttons. You also learned that the result of the `MsgBox` function can be assigned to a variable. Using the `Select Case` statement, you can now decide which action to take based on the button the user pressed in the message box.

Hands-On 5.5 Writing a VBA Procedure with a Select Case Statement

1. Insert a new module into the current VBA project.
2. Rename the new module **SelectCase**.
3. Enter the following TestButtons procedure:

```
Sub TestButtons()
  Dim question As String
  Dim bts As Integer
  Dim myTitle As String
  Dim myButton As Integer

  question = "Do you want to open a new workbook?"
  bts = vbYesNoCancel + vbQuestion + vbDefaultButton1
  myTitle = "New Workbook"
  myButton = MsgBox(prompt:=question, _
      buttons:=bts, _
      title:=myTitle)
  Select Case myButton
    Case 6
          Workbooks.Add
```

```
    Case 7
          MsgBox "You can open a new book manually later."
    Case Else
          MsgBox "You pressed Cancel."
  End Select
End Sub
```

The first part of the TestButtons procedure displays a message with three buttons: Yes, No, and Cancel. The value of the button selected by the user is assigned to the variable myButton. If the user clicks Yes, the variable `myButton` is assigned the `vbYes` constant or its corresponding value—6. If the user selects No, the variable `myButton` is assigned the constant `vbNo` or its corresponding value—7. Lastly, if Cancel is pressed, the contents of the variable `myButton` will equal `vbCancel`, or 2. The `Select Case` statement checks the values supplied after the `Case` clause against the value stored in the variable `myButton`. When there is a match, the appropriate `Case` statement is executed.

The TestButtons procedure will work the same if you use the constants instead of button values:

```
Select Case myButton
  Case vbYes
    Workbooks.Add
  Case vbNo
    MsgBox "You can open a new book manually later."
  Case Else
    MsgBox "You pressed Cancel."
End Select
```

You can omit the `Else` clause. Simply revise the `Select Case` statement as follows:

```
Select Case myButton
  Case vbYes
    Workbooks.Add
  Case vbNo
    MsgBox "You can open a new book manually later."
  Case vbCancel
    MsgBox "You pressed Cancel."
End Select
```

4. Run the TestButtons procedure three times, each time selecting a different button.

Using Is with the Case Clause

Sometimes a decision is made based on a relational operator, listed in Table 5.1, such as whether the test expression is greater than, less than, or equal to. The `Is` keyword lets you use a conditional expression in a `Case` clause. The syntax for the `Select Case` clause using the `Is` keyword is shown here:

```
Select Case testexpression
  Case Is condition1
    statements if condition1 is True
  Case Is condition2
    statements if condition2 is True
  Case Is conditionN
    statements if conditionN is True
End Select
```

Although using `Case Else` in the `Select Case` statement isn't required, it's always a good idea to include one, just in case the variable you are testing has an unexpected value. The `Case Else` statement is a good place to put an error message. For example, let's compare some numbers:

```
 Select Case myNumber
Case Is <=10
  MsgBox "The number is less than or equal to 10."
Case 11
  MsgBox "You entered eleven."
Case Is >=100
  MsgBox "The number is greater than or equal to 100."
Case Else
  MsgBox "The number is between 12 and 99."
End Select
```

Assuming that the variable `myNumber` holds 120, the third `Case` clause is true, and the only statement executed is the one between the `Case Is >=100` and the `Case Else` clause.

Specifying a Range of Values in a Case Clause

In the preceding example you saw a simple `Select Case` statement that uses one expression in each `Case` clause. Many times, however, you may want to specify a range of values in a `Case` clause. Do this by using the `To` keyword between the values of expressions, as in the following example:

```
Select Case unitsSold
  Case 1 To 100
```

```
      Discount = 0.05
    Case Is <= 500
      Discount = 0.1
    Case 501 To 1000
      Discount = 0.15
    Case Is > 1000
      Discount = 0.2
  End Select
```

Let's analyze the foregoing `Select Case` block with the assumption that the variable `unitsSold` currently holds the value 99. Visual Basic compares the value of the variable `unitsSold` with the conditional expression in the `Case` clauses. The first and third `Case` clauses illustrate how to use a range of values in a conditional expression by using the `To` keyword. Because `unitsSold` equals 99, the condition in the first `Case` clause is true; thus, Visual Basic assigns the value 0.05 to the variable `Discount`. How about the second `Case` clause, which is also true? Although it's obvious that 99 is less than or equal to 500, Visual Basic does not execute the associated statement `Discount = 0.1`. The reason for this is that once Visual Basic locates a `Case` clause with a true condition, it doesn't bother to look at the remaining `Case` clauses. It jumps over them and continues to execute the procedure with the instructions that may be following the `End Select` statement.

Specifying Multiple Expressions in a Case Clause

You may specify multiple conditions within a single `Case` clause by separating each condition with a comma, as shown in the following code example:

```
Select Case myMonth
  Case "January", "February", "March"
    Debug.Print myMonth & ": 1st Qtr."
  Case "April", "May", "June"
    Debug.Print myMonth & ": 2nd Qtr."
  Case "July", "August", "September"
    Debug.Print myMonth & ": 3rd Qtr."
  Case "October", "November", "December"
    Debug.Print myMonth & ": 4th Qtr."
End Select
```

SIDEBAR *Multiple Conditions with the* `Case` *Clause*

The commas used to separate conditions within a `Case` clause have the same meaning as the OR operator used in the `If` statement. The `Case` clause is true if at least one of the conditions is true.

Nesting means placing one type of control structure inside another control structure. You will see more nesting examples with the looping structures discussed in Chapter 7.

WRITING A VBA PROCEDURE WITH MULTIPLE CONDITIONS

The SimpleIfThen procedure that you worked with earlier evaluated only a single condition in the `If...Then` statement. This statement, however, can take more than one condition. To specify multiple conditions in an `If...Then` statement, use the logical operators AND and OR (listed in Table 5.2 at the beginning of this chapter). Here's the syntax with the AND operator:

```
If condition1 AND condition2 Then statement
```

In the foregoing syntax, both `condition1` and `condition2` must be true for Visual Basic to execute the statement to the right of the `Then` keyword—for example:

```
If sales = 10000 AND salary < 45000 Then SlsCom = Sales * 0.07
```

In this example:

```
Condition1 sales = 10000
Condition2 salary < 45000
```

When AND is used in the conditional expression, both conditions must be true before Visual Basic can calculate the sales commission (`SlsCom`). If either of these conditions is false, or both are false, Visual Basic ignores the statement after `Then`.

When it's good enough to meet only one of the conditions, you should use the OR operator. Here's the syntax:

```
If condition1 OR condition2 Then statement
```

The OR operator is more flexible. Only one of the conditions has to be true before Visual Basic can execute the statement following the `Then` keyword.

Let's look at this example:

```
If dept = "S" OR dept = "M" Then bonus = 500
```

In this example, if at least one condition is true, Visual Basic assigns 500 to the `bonus` variable. If both conditions are false, Visual Basic ignores the rest of the line.

Now let's look at a complete procedure example. Suppose you can get a 10% discount if you purchase 50 units of a product, each priced at $7.00. The IfThenAnd procedure demonstrates the use of the AND operator.

Hands-On 5.6 Writing a VBA Procedure with Multiple Conditions

1. Enter the following procedure in the IfThen module of the **Decisions (Chap05_ExcelPrimer.xlsm)** project:

```
Sub IfThenAnd()
  Dim price As Single
  Dim units As Integer
  Dim rebate As Single

  Const strmsg1 = "To get a rebate you must buy an additional "
  Const strmsg2 = "Price must equal $7.00"

  units = Range("B1").Value
  price = Range("B2").Value

  If price = 7 AND units >= 50 Then
    rebate = (price * units) * 0.1
    Range("A4").Value = "The rebate is: $" & rebate
  End If

  If price = 7 AND units < 50 Then
    Range("A4").Value = strmsg1 & 50 - units & " unit(s)."
  End If

  If price <> 7 AND units >= 50 Then
    Range("A4").Value = strmsg2
  End If

  If price <> 7 AND units < 50 Then
    Range("A4").Value = "You didn't meet the criteria."
  End If
End Sub
```

The IfThenAnd procedure just shown has four `If...Then` statements that are used to evaluate the contents of two variables: `price` and `units`. The AND operator between the keywords `If...Then` allows more than one condition to be tested. With the AND operator, all conditions must be true for Visual Basic to run the statements between the `Then...End If` keywords. Because the

IfThenAnd procedure is based on the data entered in worksheet cells, it's more convenient to run it from the Microsoft Excel window.

2. Switch to the Microsoft Excel application window and choose **Developer | Macros**.
3. In the Macro dialog box, select the **IfThenAnd** macro and click the **Options** button.
4. While the cursor is blinking in the Shortcut key box, press **Shift+I** to assign the shortcut key Ctrl+Shift+I to your macro, and then click **OK** to exit the Macro Options dialog box.
5. Click **Cancel** to close the Macro dialog box.
6. Enter the sample data in a worksheet as shown in Figure 5.1.

	A	B	C
1	units	200	
2	price	7	
3			
4			

FIGURE 5.1 Sample test data in a worksheet.

7. Press **Ctrl+Shift+I** to run the IfThenAnd procedure.
8. Change the values of cells B1 and B2 so that every time you run the procedure, a different `If...Then` statement is true.

USING CONDITIONAL LOGIC IN FUNCTION PROCEDURES

To get more practice with the `Select Case` statement, let's use it in a function procedure. As you recall from Chapter 4, function procedures allow you to return a result to a subroutine. Suppose a subroutine must display a discount based on the number of units sold. You can get the number of units from the user and then run a function to determine which discount applies.

Hands-On 5.7 Writing a Function Procedure with a Select Case Statement

1. Enter the following subroutine in the **SelectCase** module:

```
Sub DisplayDiscount()
  Dim unitsSold As Integer
  Dim myDiscount As Single
```

```
  unitsSold = InputBox("Enter the number of units sold:")
  myDiscount = GetDiscount(unitsSold)
  MsgBox myDiscount
End Sub
```

2. Enter the following function procedure:

```
Function GetDiscount(unitsSold As Integer)
  Select Case unitsSold
    Case 1 To 200
      GetDiscount = 0.05
    Case Is <= 500
      GetDiscount = 0.1
    Case 501 To 1000
      GetDiscount = 0.15
    Case Is > 1000
      GetDiscount = 0.2
  End Select
End Function
```

3. Place the cursor anywhere within the code of the DisplayDiscount procedure and press **F5** to run it. Run the procedure several times, entering values to test each `Case` statement.

   The DisplayDiscount procedure passes the value stored in the variable `unitsSold` to the `GetDiscount` function. When Visual Basic encounters the `Select Case` statement, it checks whether the value of the first `Case` clause expression matches the value stored in the `unitsSold` parameter. If there is a match, Visual Basic assigns a 5% discount (0.05) to the function name, and then jumps to the `End Select` keywords. Because there are no more statements to execute inside the function procedure, Visual Basic returns to the calling procedure—DisplayDiscount. Here it assigns the function's result to the variable `myDiscount`. The last statement displays the value of the retrieved discount in a message box.

SUMMARY

Conditional statements, which were introduced in this chapter, let you control the flow of your procedure. By testing the truth of a condition, you can decide which statements should be run and which should be skipped over. In other words, instead of running your procedure from top to bottom, line by line, you can execute only certain lines. If you are wondering what kind of conditional statement you should use in your VBA procedure, here are a few guidelines:

- If you want to supply only one condition, the simple `If...Then` statement is the best choice.
- If you need to decide which of two actions to perform, use the `If...Then...Else` statement.
- If your procedure requires two or more conditions, use the `If...Then...ElseIf` or `Select Case` statements.
- If your procedure has a great number of conditions, use the `Select Case` statement. This statement is more flexible and easier to comprehend than the `If...Then...ElseIf` statement.

Some decisions must be repeated. For example, you may want to repeat the same actions for each cell in a worksheet or each sheet in a workbook. The next chapter teaches you how to perform the same steps repeatedly.

Chapter 6 ADDING REPEATING ACTIONS TO EXCEL VBA PROGRAMS

A QUICK INTRODUCTION TO LOOPING STATEMENTS

Now that you've learned how conditional statements can give your VBA procedures decision-making capabilities, it's time to go a step further. Not all decisions are easy. Sometimes you will need to perform several statements multiple times to arrive at a certain condition. On other occasions, however, after you've reached the decision, you may need to run the specified statements as long as a condition is true or until a condition becomes true. In programming, performing repetitive tasks is called *looping*. VBA has various looping structures that allow you to repeat a sequence of statements several times. In this chapter, you will learn how to loop through your code.

INTRODUCING LOOPING STATEMENTS

A loop is a programming structure that causes a section of program code to execute repeatedly. VBA provides several structures to implement loops in your procedures: `Do...While`, `Do...Until`, `For...Next`, `For...Each`, and `While...Wend`.

Understanding Do...While and Do...Until Loops

Visual Basic has two types of `Do` loop statements that repeat a sequence of statements either as long as or until a certain condition is true. The `Do...While` loop lets you repeat an action as long as a condition is true. This loop has the following syntax:

```
Do While condition
  statement1
  statement2
```

```
    statementN
Loop
```

When Visual Basic encounters this loop, it first checks the truth value of the condition. If the condition is false, the statements inside the loop are not executed. Visual Basic will continue to execute the program with the first statement after the `Loop` keyword. If the condition is true, the statements inside the loop are run one by one until the `Loop` statement is encountered. The `Loop` statement tells Visual Basic to repeat the entire process again, as long as the testing of the condition in the `Do...While` statement is true. Let's now see how you can put the `Do...While` loop to good use in Microsoft Excel.

In Chapter 5, you learned how to make a decision based on the contents of a cell. Let's take it a step further and see how you can repeat the same decision for a number of cells. Our task is to apply bold formatting to any cell in a column, as long as it's not empty.

NOTE	*Please note files for the "Hands-On" project may be found in the companion files.*

Hands-On 6.1 Writing a VBA Procedure with a Do...While Statement

1. Open a new workbook and save it as **C:\VBAPrimerExcel_ByExample\Chap06_ExcelPrimer.xlsm**.
2. Switch to the Visual Basic Editor screen and change the name of the new project to **Repetition**.
3. Insert a new module into the Repetition project and change its name to **DoLoops**.
4. Enter the following procedure in the DoLoops module:

```
Sub ApplyBold()
  Do While ActiveCell.Value <> ""
    ActiveCell.Font.Bold = True
    ActiveCell.Offset(1, 0).Select
  Loop
End Sub
```

5. Press **Alt+F11** to switch to the Microsoft Excel application window, activate Sheet1, and then enter any data (text or numbers) in cells **A1:A7**.
6. When finished with the data entry, select cell **A1**.
7. Choose **Developer | Macros**. In the Macro dialog box, double-click the **ApplyBold** procedure (or highlight the procedure name and click **Run**).

When you run the ApplyBold procedure, Visual Basic first evaluates the condition in the `Do While` statement—`ActiveCell.Value <>""`. The condition says: Perform the following statements as long as the value of the active cell is not an empty string (""). Because you have entered data in cell A1 and made this cell active (see Steps 5 to 6), the first test returns true. So Visual Basic executes the statement `ActiveCell.Font.Bold = True`, which applies the bold formatting to the active cell. Next, Visual Basic selects the cell in the next row (the Offset property is discussed in Chapter 3). Because the statement that follows is the `Loop` keyword, Visual Basic returns to the `Do While` statement and again checks the condition. If the newly selected active cell is not empty, Visual Basic repeats the statements inside the loop. This process continues until the contents of cell A8 are examined. Because this cell is empty, the condition is false, so Visual Basic skips the statements inside the loop. Because there are no more statements to execute after the `Loop` keyword, the procedure ends. Let's look at another `Do...While` loop example.

The `Do...While` loop has an alternative syntax that lets you test the condition at the bottom of the loop in the following way:

```
Do
  statement1
  statement2
  statementN
Loop While condition
```

When you test the condition at the bottom of the loop, the statements inside the loop are executed at least once. Let's take a look at an example:

```
Sub SignIn()
  Dim secretCode As String
  Do
    secretCode = InputBox("Enter your secret code:")
    If secretCode = "sp1045" Then Exit Do
  Loop While secretCode <> "sp1045"
End Sub
```

Notice that by the time the condition is evaluated, Visual Basic has already executed the statements one time. In addition to placing the condition at the end of the loop, the SignIn procedure shows how to exit the loop when a condition is reached. When the `Exit Do` statement is encountered, the loop ends immediately.

Another handy loop, `Do...Until`, allows you to repeat one or more statements until a condition becomes true. In other words, `Do...Until` repeats a block of code as long as something is false. Here's the syntax:

```
Do Until condition
  statement1
  statement2
  statementN
Loop
```

Using the foregoing syntax, you can now rewrite the previous ApplyBold procedure in the following way:

```
Sub ApplyBold2()
  Do Until IsEmpty(ActiveCell)
    ActiveCell.Font.Bold = True
    ActiveCell.Offset(1, 0).Select
  Loop
End Sub
```

The first line of this procedure says to perform the following statements until the first empty cell is reached. As a result, if the active cell is not empty, Visual Basic executes the two statements inside the loop. This process continues as long as the condition `IsEmpty(ActiveCell)` evaluates to false. Because the ApplyBold2 procedure tests the condition at the beginning of the loop, the statements inside the loop will not run if the first cell is empty. You will get the chance to try out this procedure in the next section.

Like the `Do...While` loop, the `Do...Until` loop has a second syntax that lets you test the condition at the bottom of the loop:

```
Do
   statement1
   statement2
   statementN
Loop Until condition
```

If you want the statements to execute at least once, place the condition on the line with the `Loop` statement no matter what the value of the condition.
Let's try out an example procedure that deletes empty sheets from a workbook.

Hands-On 6.2 Writing a VBA Procedure with a Do...Until Statement

1. Enter the DeleteBlankSheets procedure, as shown here, in the DoLoops module that you created earlier.

```
Sub DeleteBlankSheets()
  Dim myRange As Range
  Dim shcount As Integer
  shcount = Worksheets.Count
  Do
    Worksheets(shcount).Select
    Set myRange = ActiveSheet.UsedRange
    If myRange.Address = "$A$1" And _
        Range("A1").Value = "" Then
        Application.DisplayAlerts = False
        Worksheets(shcount).Delete
        Application.DisplayAlerts = True
    End If
    shcount = shcount - 1
  Loop Until shcount = 1
End Sub
```

2. Press **Alt+F11** to switch to the Microsoft Excel window and manually insert three new worksheets into the current workbook. In one of the sheets, enter text or number in cell **A1**. On another sheet, enter some data in cells **B2** and **C10**. Do not enter any data on the third inserted sheet.
3. Run the DeleteBlankSheets procedure.

When you run this procedure, Visual Basic deletes the selected sheet whenever two conditions are true—the UsedRange property address returns cell A1 and cell A1 is empty. The UsedRange property applies to the Worksheet object and contains every nonempty cell on the worksheet, as well as all the empty cells that are among them. For example, if you enter something in cells B2 and C10, the used range is $B$2:$C$10. If you later enter data in cell A1, the UsedRange will be $A$1:$C$10. The used range is bounded by the farthest upper-left and farthest lower-right nonempty cell on a worksheet.

Because the workbook must contain at least one worksheet, the code is executed until the variable `shcount` equals one. The statement `shcount = shcount - 1` makes sure that the `shcount` variable is reduced by one each time the statements in the loop are executed. The value of `shcount` is initialized at the beginning of the procedure with the following statement:

```
Worksheets.Count
```

Notice also that when deleting sheets, Excel normally displays the confirmation dialog box. If you'd rather not be prompted to confirm the deletion, use the following statement:

```
Application.DisplayAlerts = False
```

When you are finished, turn the system messages back on with the following statement:

```
Application.DisplayAlerts = True
```

SIDEBAR ***Counters***

A *counter* is a numeric variable that keeps track of the number of items that have been processed. The DeleteBlankSheets procedure just shown declares the variable `shcount` to keep track of sheets that have been processed. A counter variable should be initialized (assigned a value) at the beginning of the program. This ensures that you always know the exact value of the counter before you begin using it. A counter can be incremented or decremented by a specified value. See other examples of using counters with the `For...Next` loop later in this chapter.

Avoiding Infinite Loops

If you don't design your loop correctly, you get an infinite loop—a loop that never ends. You will not be able to stop the procedure by using the Esc key. The following procedure causes the loop to execute endlessly because the programmer forgot to include the test condition:

```
Sub SayHello()
  Do
    MsgBox "Hello."
  Loop
End Sub
```

To stop the execution of the infinite loop, you must press Ctrl+Break. When Visual Basic displays the message box that says, "Code execution has been interrupted," click End to end the procedure.

Executing a Procedure Line by Line

When you run procedures that use looping structures, it's sometimes hard to see whether the procedure works as expected. Occasionally, you'd like to watch the procedure execute in slow motion so that you can check the logic of the program. Let's examine how Visual Basic allows you to execute a procedure line by line.

Hands-On 6.3 Executing a Procedure Line by Line

1. Insert a new sheet into the current workbook and enter any data in cells **A1:A5**.
2. Select cell **A1** and choose **Developer | Macros**.
3. In the Macro dialog box, select the **ApplyBold** procedure and click the **Step Into** button.
   The VBE screen will appear with the name of the procedure highlighted in yellow, as shown in Figure 6.1. Notice the yellow arrow in the margin indicator bar of the Code window.

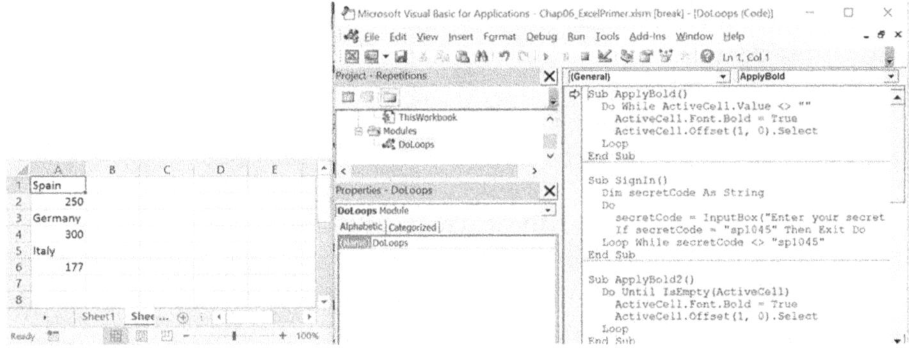

FIGURE 6.1 Watching the procedure code execute line by line.

4. Arrange the screens side by side as shown in Figure 6.1.
5. Make sure cell **A1** is selected and that it contains data.
6. Click the title bar in the Visual Basic window to move the focus to this window, and then press **F8**. The yellow highlight in the Code window jumps to this line:

```
Do While ActiveCell.Value <> ""
```

7. Continue pressing **F8** while watching both the Code window and the worksheet window.

NOTE	*You will find more information related to stepping through VBA procedures in Chapter 9.*

Understanding While...Wend Loop

The `While...Wend` loop is functionally equivalent to the `Do...While` loop. This statement is a carryover from earlier versions of Microsoft Basic and is included in VBA for backward compatibility. The loop begins with the keyword `While` and ends with the keyword `Wend`. Here's the syntax:

```
While condition
  statement1
  statement2
  statementN
Wend
```

The condition is tested at the top of the loop. The statements are executed as long as the given condition is true. Once the condition is false, Visual Basic exits the loop.

Let's look at an example of a procedure that uses the `While...Wend` looping structure. We will change the row height of all nonempty cells in a worksheet.

Hands-On 6.4 Writing a VBA Procedure with a While...Wend Statement

1. Insert a new module into the current VBA project. Rename the module **WhileLoop.**
2. Enter the following procedure in the WhileLoop module.

```
Sub ChangeRHeight()
  While ActiveCell <> ""
    ActiveCell.RowHeight = 28
    ActiveCell.Offset(1, 0).Select
  Wend
End Sub
```

3. Switch to the Microsoft Excel window and enter some data in cells **B1:B4** of any worksheet.
4. Select cell **B1** and choose **Developer | Macros.**
5. In the Macro dialog, select the **ChangeRHeight** procedure and click **Run.**

The ChangeRHeight procedure sets the row height to 28 when the active cell is not empty. The next cell is selected by using the Offset property of the Range object. The statement `ActiveCell.Offset(1, 0).Select` tells Visual Basic to select the cell that is located one row below (1) the active cell and in the same column (0).

Understanding For...Next Loop

The `For...Next` loop is used when you know how many times you want to repeat a group of statements. The syntax of a `For...Next` loop looks like this:

```
For counter = start To end [Step increment]
   statement1
   statement2
  statementN
Next [counter]
```

The code in the brackets is optional. `Counter` is a numeric variable that stores the number of iterations. `Start` is the number at which you want to begin counting, and `end` indicates how many times the loop should be executed.

For example, if you want to repeat the statements inside the loop five times, use the following `For` statement syntax:

```
For counter = 1 To 5
  Your statements go here
Next
```

When Visual Basic encounters the `Next` keyword, it will go back to the beginning of the loop and execute the statements inside the loop again, as long as `counter` hasn't reached the value in `end`. As soon as the value of `counter` is greater than the number entered after the `To` keyword, Visual Basic exits the loop. Because the variable `counter` automatically changes after each execution of the loop, sooner or later the value stored in `counter` exceeds the value specified. By default, every time Visual Basic executes the statements inside the loop, the value of the variable `counter` is increased by one. You can change this default setting by using the `Step` clause. For example, to increase the variable `counter` by three, use the following statement:

```
For counter = 1 To 5 Step 3
  Your statements go here
Next counter
```

When Visual Basic encounters the foregoing instruction, it executes the statements inside the loop twice. The first time in the loop, `counter` equals 1. The second time in the loop, `counter` equals 4 (3 + 1). After the second time inside the loop, `counter` equals 7 (4 + 3). This causes Visual Basic to exit the loop. Note that the `Step` increment is optional and isn't specified unless it's a value other than 1. You can also place a negative number after `Step`. Visual Basic will then decrement this value from `counter` each time it encounters the `Next` keyword. The name of the variable (`counter`) after the `Next` keyword is also optional. However, it's good programming practice to make your `Next` keywords explicit by including `counter`.

How can you use the `For...Next` loop in a Microsoft Excel worksheet? Suppose in your sales report you'd like to include only products that were sold in a particular month. When you imported data from a Microsoft Access table, you also got rows with the sold amount equal to zero. How can you quickly eliminate those "zero" rows? Although there are many ways to solve this problem, let's see how you can handle it with a `For...Next` loop.

Hands-On 6.5 Writing a VBA Procedure with a For...Next Statement

1. In the Visual Basic window, insert a new module into the current project and rename it **ForNextLoop**.
2. Enter the following procedure in the ForNextLoop module:

```
Sub DeleteZeroRows()
  Dim totalR As Integer
  Dim r As Integer

  Range("A1").CurrentRegion.Select
  totalR = Selection.Rows.Count
  Range("B2").Select

  For r = 1 To totalR - 1
    If ActiveCell = 0 Then
          Selection.EntireRow.Delete
          totalR = totalR - 1
    Else
          ActiveCell.Offset(1, 0).Select
    End If
  Next r
End Sub
```

Let's examine the DeleteZeroRows procedure line by line. The first two statements calculate the total number of rows in the current range and store this number in the variable `totalR`. Next, Visual Basic selects cell B2 and encounters the `For` keyword. Because the first row of the worksheet contains the column headings, decrease the total number of rows by one (`totalR - 1`). Visual Basic will need to execute the instructions inside the loop six times. The conditional statement (`If...Then...Else`) nested inside the loop tells Visual Basic to make a decision based on the value of the active cell. If the value is equal to zero, Visual Basic deletes the current row and reduces the value of `totalR` by one. Otherwise, the condition is false, so Visual Basic selects the next cell. Each time Visual Basic completes the loop, it jumps to the `For` keyword to compare the value of `r` with the value of `totalR - 1`.

3. Switch to the Microsoft Excel window and insert a new worksheet. Enter the data shown here:

	A	B
1	Product Name	Sales (in Pounds)
2	Apples	120
3	Pears	0
4	Bananas	100
5	Cherries	0
6	Blueberries	0
7	Strawberries	160

4. Choose **Developer | Macros.**
5. In the Macro dialog, select the **DeleteZeroRows** procedure and click **Run.** When the procedure ends, the sales worksheet does not include products that were not sold.

SIDEBAR ***Paired Statements***

`For` and `Next` must be paired. If one is missing, Visual Basic generates the following error message: "For without Next."

Understanding For...Each...Next Loop

When your procedure needs to loop through all of the objects of a collection or all of the elements in an array (arrays are covered in Chapter 7), the `For Each... Next` loop should be used. This loop does not require a counter variable. Visual Basic can figure out on its own how many times the loop should execute.

Let's take, for example, a collection of worksheets. To remove a worksheet from a workbook, you must first select it and then choose Home | Cells | Delete | Delete Sheet. To leave only one worksheet in a workbook, you need to use the same command several times, depending on the total number of worksheets. Because each worksheet is an object in a collection of worksheets, you can speed up the process of deleting worksheets by using the `For Each...Next` loop. This loop looks like the following:

```
For Each element In Group
  statement1
  statement2
  statementN
Next [element]
```

In the foregoing syntax, `element` is a variable to which all the elements of an array or collection will be assigned. This variable must be of the Variant data type for an array and an Object data type for a collection. `Group` is the name of a collection or an array.

Let's now see how to use the `For Each...Next` loop to remove some worksheets.

Hands-On 6.6 Writing a VBA Procedure with a For Each... Next Statement

1. Insert a new module into the current project and rename it **ForEachNextLoop**.
2. Type the following procedure in the **ForEachNextLoop** module:

```
Sub RemoveSheets()
  Dim mySheet As Worksheet

  Application.DisplayAlerts = False

  Workbooks.Add
  Sheets.Add After:=ActiveSheet, Count:=3

  For Each mySheet In Worksheets
    If mySheet.Name <> "Sheet1" Then
        ActiveWindow.SelectedSheets.Delete
    End If
  Next mySheet

  Application.DisplayAlerts = True
End Sub
```

   Visual Basic will open a new workbook, add three new sheets after the default Sheet1 (ActiveSheet), and proceed to delete all the sheets except for Sheet1. Notice that the variable `mySheet` represents an object in a collection of worksheets. Therefore, this variable has been declared of the specific object data type Worksheet. The first instruction, `Application.DisplayAlerts = False`, makes sure that Microsoft Excel does not display alerts and messages while the procedure is running. The `For Each...Next` loop steps through each worksheet and deletes it as long as it is not Sheet1. When the procedure ends, the workbook has only one sheet—Sheet1.

3. Position the insertion point anywhere within the RemoveSheets procedure code and press **F5** to run it.

Exiting Loops Early

Sometimes you may not want to wait until the loop ends on its own. It's possible that a user has entered the wrong data, a procedure has encountered an error, or perhaps the task has been completed and there's no need to do additional looping. You can leave the loop early without reaching the condition that normally terminates it. Visual Basic has two types of `Exit` statements:

- The `Exit For` statement is used to end either a `For...Next` or a `For Each... Next` loop early.
- The `Exit Do` statement immediately exits any of the VBA `Do` loops.

The following procedure demonstrates how to use the `Exit For` statement to leave the `For Each...Next` loop early.

Hands-On 6.7 Writing a VBA Procedure with an Early Exit from a For Each...Next Statement

1. Enter the following procedure in the **ForEachNextLoop** module:

```
Sub EarlyExit()
  Dim myCell As Variant
  Dim myRange As Range

  Set myRange = Range("A1:H10")
  For Each myCell In myRange
      If myCell.Value = "" Then
          myCell.Value = "empty"
      Else
          Exit For
      End If
  Next myCell
End Sub
```

   The EarlyExit procedure examines the contents of each cell in the specified range—A1:H10. If the active cell is empty, Visual Basic enters the text "empty" in the active cell. When Visual Basic encounters the first nonempty cell, it exits the loop.

2. Open a new workbook and enter a value in any cell within the specified range—**A1:H10**.
3. Choose **Developer | Macros**.
4. In the Macro dialog, select the **EarlyExit** procedure and click **Run**.

Using a Do...While Statement

The next example procedure demonstrates how to display today's date and time in Microsoft Excel's status bar for 10 seconds.

Hands-On 6.8 Writing a VBA Procedure with a Do...While Statement

1. Enter the following procedure in the **DoLoops** module:

```
Sub TenSeconds()
  Dim stopme

  stopme = Now + TimeValue("00:00:10")

  Do While Now < stopme
    Application.DisplayStatusBar = True
    Application.StatusBar = Now
  Loop

  Application.StatusBar = False
End Sub
```

   In the TenSeconds procedure, the statements inside the `Do...While` loop will be executed as long as the time returned by the `Now` function is less than the value of the variable called `stopme`. The variable `stopme` holds the current time plus 10 seconds. (See the online help for other examples of using the built-in `TimeValue` function.)

   The statement `Application.DisplayStatusBar` tells Visual Basic to turn on the status bar display. The next statement places the current date and time in the status bar. While the time is displayed for 10 seconds, the user cannot work with the system (the mouse pointer turns into the hourglass). After the 10 seconds are over (that is, when the condition `Now < stopme` evaluates to true), Visual Basic leaves the loop and executes the statement after the `Loop` keyword. This statement returns the default status bar message "Ready."

2. Press **Alt+F11** to switch to the Microsoft Excel application window.
3. Choose **Developer | Macros**. In the Macro dialog box, double-click the **TenSeconds** macro name (or highlight the macro name and click **Run**).
   Observe the date and time display in the status bar. The status bar should return to "Ready" after 10 seconds.

USING LOOPS AND CONDITIONALS

Let's combine the looping statements and some conditional logic to write a procedure that checks whether a certain sheet is part of a workbook.

Hands-On 6.9 Writing a VBA Procedure with Loops and Conditionals

1. Enter the following procedures in a new module:

```
Sub IsSuchSheet(strSheetName As String)
  Dim mySheet As Worksheet
  Dim counter As Integer

  counter = 0

  Workbooks.Add
  Sheets.Add After:=ActiveSheet, Count:=3
  For Each mySheet In Worksheets
      If mySheet.Name = strSheetName Then
          counter = counter + 1
          Exit For
      End If
  Next mySheet

  If counter = 1 Then
      MsgBox strSheetName & " exists."
  Else
      MsgBox strSheetName & " was not found."
  End If
End Sub

Sub FindSheet()
  Call IsSuchSheet("Sheet4")
End Sub
```

The IsSuchSheet procedure uses the `Exit For` statement to ensure that we exit the loop as soon as the sheet name passed in the procedure argument is found in the workbook. The FindSheet procedure is used to show you how to call one procedure from another.

2. To execute the IsSuchSheet procedure, run the FindSheet procedure.

SUMMARY

In this chapter, you learned how to repeat certain groups of statements using procedure loops. While working with several types of looping statements, you saw how each loop performs repetitions in a slightly different way. As you gain programming experience, you'll find it easier to choose the appropriate flow control structure for your task.

The next chapter will show you how arrays are used to work with larger sets of data.

Chapter 7

STORING MULTIPLE VALUES IN EXCEL VBA PROGRAMS

A QUICK INTRODUCTION TO WORKING WITH ARRAYS

In previous chapters, you worked with many VBA procedures that used variables to hold specific information about an object, property, or value. For each single value that you wanted your procedure to manipulate, you declared a variable. But what if you have a series of values? If you had to write a VBA procedure to deal with larger amounts of data, you would have to create enough variables to handle all the data. Can you imagine the nightmare of storing in your program currency exchange rates for all the countries in the world? To create a table to hold the necessary data, you'd need at least three variables for each country: country name, currency name, and exchange rate. Fortunately, Visual Basic has a way to get around this problem. By clustering the related variables together, your VBA procedures can manage a large amount of data with ease. In this chapter, you'll learn how to manipulate lists and tables of data with arrays.

UNDERSTANDING ARRAYS

An *array* is a special type of variable that represents a group of similar values that are of the same data type (String, Integer, Currency, Date, etc.). The two most common types of arrays are one-dimensional arrays (lists) and two-dimensional arrays (tables). A one-dimensional array is sometimes referred to as a *list*. A shopping list, a list of the days of the week, and an employee list are examples of one-dimensional arrays or, simply, numbered lists. Each element in the list has an index value that allows accessing that element. For example, in the following illustration we have a one-dimensional array of six elements indexed from 0 to 5:

(0)	(1)	(2)	(3)	(4)	(5)

You can access the third element of this array by specifying index (2). By default, the first element of an array is indexed zero. You can change this behavior by using the `Option Base 1` statement or by explicitly coding the lower bound of your array as explained further in this chapter.

All elements of the array must be of the same data type. In other words, one array cannot store both strings and integers. Following are two examples of one-dimensional arrays: a one-dimensional array called cities that is populated with text (String data type—$) and a one-dimensional array called lotto that contains six lottery numbers stored as integers (Integer data type—%).

A one-dimensional array: cities$

cities(0)	Baltimore
cities(1)	Atlanta
cities(2)	Boston
cities(3)	Washington
cities(4)	New York
cities(5)	Trenton

A one-dimensional array: lotto%

lotto(0)	25
lotto(1)	4
lotto(2)	31
lotto(3)	22
lotto(4)	11
lotto(5)	5

As you can see, the contents assigned to each array element match the Array type. If you want to store values of different data types in the same array, you must declare the array as Variant. You will learn how to declare arrays in the next section.

A two-dimensional array may be thought of as a table or matrix. The position of each element in a table is determined by its row and column numbers. For example, an array that holds the yearly sales for each product your company sells has two dimensions (the product name and the year). The following is a diagram of an empty two-dimensional array.

(0,0)	(0,1)	(0,2)	(0,3)	(0,4)	(0,5)
(1,0)	(1,1)	(1,2)	(1,3)	(1,4)	(1,5)
(2,0)	(2,1)	(2,2)	(2,3)	(2,4)	(2,5)
(3,0)	(3,1)	(3,2)	(3,3)	(3,4)	(3,5)
(4,0)	(4,1)	(4,2)	(4,3)	(4,4)	(4,5)
(5,0)	(5,1)	(5,2)	(5,3)	(5,4)	(5,5)

You can access the first element in the second row of this two-dimensional array by specifying indexes (1, 0). Following are two examples of a two-dimensional array: an array named yearlyProductSales@ that stores yearly product sales using the Currency data type (@) and an array named exchange (of Variant data type) that stores the name of the country, its currency, and the U.S. dollar exchange rate.

A two-dimensional array: yearlyProductSales@

Walking Cane (0,0)	$25,023 (0,1)
Pill Crusher (1,0)	$64,085 (1,1)
Electric Wheelchair (2,0)	$345,016 (2,1)
Folding Walker (3,0)	$85,244 (3,1)

A two-dimensional array: exchange

Japan (0,0)	Japanese Yen (0,1)	108.83 (0,2)
Australia (1,0)	Australian Dollar (1,1)	1.28601 (1,2)
Canada (2,0)	Canadian Dollar (2,1)	1.235 (2,2)
Norway (3,0)	Norwegian Krone (3,1)	6.4471 (3,2)
Europe (4,0)	Euro (4,1)	0.816993 (4,2)

In these examples, the yearlyProductSales@ array can hold a maximum of 8 elements (4 rows * 2 columns = 8) and the exchange array will allow a maximum of 15 elements (5 rows * 3 columns = 15).

Although VBA arrays can have up to 60 dimensions, most people find it difficult to picture dimensions beyond 3-D. A three-dimensional array is an array of two-dimensional arrays (tables) where each table has the same number of rows and columns. A three-dimensional array is identified by three indexes: table, row, and column. The first element of a three-dimensional array is indexed (0, 0, 0).

Declaring Arrays

Because an array is a variable, you must declare it in a similar way that you declare other variables (by using the keywords `Dim`, `Private`, or `Public`). For fixed-length arrays, the array bounds are listed in parentheses following the variable name. If a variable-length, or dynamic, array is being declared, the variable name is followed by an empty pair of parentheses.

The last part of the array declaration is the definition of the data type that the array will hold. An array can hold any of the following data types: Integer, Long, Single, Double, Variant, Currency, String, Boolean, Byte, or Date. Let's look at some examples:

Array Declaration (one-dimensional)	Description
`Dim cities(5) as String`	Declares a 6-element array, indexed 0 to 5
`Dim lotto(1 to 6) as String`	Declares a 6-element array, indexed 1 to 6
`Dim supplies(2 to 11)`	Declares a 10-element array, indexed 2 to 11
`Dim myIntegers(-3 to 6)`	Declares a 10-element array, indexed –3 to 6 (the lower bound of an array can be 0, 1, or negative)
`Dim dynArray() as Integer`	Declares a variable-length array whose bounds will be determined at runtime (see examples later in this chapter)

Array Declaration (two-dimensional)	Description
`Dim exchange(4,2) as Variant`	Declares a two-dimensional array (five rows by three columns)
`Dim yearlyProductSales(3, 1) as Currency`	Declares a two-dimensional array (four rows by two columns)
`Dim my2Darray(1 to 3, 1 to7) as Single`	Declares a two-dimensional array (three rows indexed 1 to 3 by seven columns indexed 1 to 7)

Array Declaration (three-dimensional)	Description
`Dim exchange(2, 1 to 6, 4) as Variant`	Declares a three-dimensional array (the first dimension has three elements, the second dimension has six elements indexed 1 to 6, and the third dimension has five elements)

When you declare an array, Visual Basic automatically reserves enough memory space. The amount of the memory allocated depends on the array's size and data type. When you declare a one-dimensional array named lotto with six elements, Visual Basic sets aside 12 bytes—2 bytes for each element of the array (recall that the size of the Integer data type is 2 bytes, and hence 2 * 6 = 12).

The larger the array, the more memory space is required to store the data. Because arrays can eat up a lot of memory and impact your computer's performance, it's recommended that you declare arrays with only as many elements as you think you'll use.

SIDEBAR ***What Is an Array Variable?***

An array is a group of variables that have a common name. While a typical variable can hold only one value, an array variable can store many individual values. You refer to a specific value in the array by using the array name and an index number.

SIDEBAR ***Subscripted Variables***

The numbers inside the parentheses of the array variables are called *subscripts*, and each individual variable is called a subscripted variable or element. For example, cities(5) is the sixth subscripted variable (element) of the array cities().

Array Upper and Lower Bounds

By default, VBA assigns zero (0) to the first element of the array. Therefore, number 1 represents the second element of the array, number 2 represents the third, and so on. With numeric indexing starting at 0, the one-dimensional array cities(5) contains six elements numbered from 0 to 5. If you'd rather start counting your array's elements at 1, you can explicitly specify a lower bound of the array by using an `Option Base 1` statement. This instruction must be placed in the declaration section at the top of a VBA module before any `Sub` statements. If you don't specify `Option Base 1` in a procedure that uses arrays, VBA assumes that the statement `Option Base 0` is to be used and begins indexing your array's elements at 0. If you'd rather not use the `Option Base 1` statement and still have the array indexing start at a number other than 0, you must specify the bounds of an array when declaring the array variable. The bounds of an array are its lowest and highest indices. Let's look at the following example:

```
Dim cities(3 To 6) As Integer
```

The foregoing statement declares a one-dimensional array with four elements. The numbers enclosed in parentheses after the array name specify the lower (3) and upper (6) bounds of the array. The first element of this array is indexed 3, the second 4, the third 5, and the fourth 6. Notice the keyword `To` between the lower and the upper indexes.

Initializing and Filling an Array

After you declare an array, you must assign values to its elements. This is often referred to as "initializing an array," "filling an array," or "populating an array." The three methods you can use to load data into an array are discussed in this section.

Filling an Array Using Individual Assignment Statements

Assume you want to store the names of your six favorite cities in a one-dimensional array named cities. After declaring the array with the `Dim` statement:

```
Dim cities(5) as String
```

or

```
Dim cities$(5)
```

you can assign values to the array variable like this:

```
cities(0) = "Baltimore"
cities(1) = "Atlanta"
cities(2) = "Boston"
cities(3) = "San Diego"
cities(4) = "New York"
cities(5) = "Denver"
```

Filling an Array Using the Array Function

VBA's built-in function `Array` returns an array of Variants. Because Variant is the default data type, the `As Variant` clause is optional in the array variable declaration:

```
Dim cities() as Variant
```

or

```
Dim cities()
```

Notice that you don't specify the number of elements between the parentheses.

Next, use the `Array` function as shown here to assign values to your cities array:

```
cities = Array("Baltimore", "Atlanta", "Boston", "San Diego",
      "New York", "Denver")
```

When using the `Array` function for array population, the lower bound of an array is 0 or 1 and the upper bound is 5 or 6, depending on the setting of `Option Base` (see the previous section titled "Array Upper and Lower Bounds").

Filling an Array Using For...Next Loop

The easiest way to learn how to use loops to populate an array is by writing a procedure that fills an array with a specific number of integer values. Let's look at the example procedure here:

```
Sub LoadArrayWithIntegers()
  Dim myIntArray(1 To 10) As Integer
  Dim i As Integer

  'Initialize random number generator
  Randomize

  'Fill the array with 10 random numbers between 1 and 100
  For i = 1 To 10
    myIntArray(i) = Int((100 * Rnd) + 1)
  Next

  'Print array values to the Immediate window
  For i = 1 To 10
    Debug.Print myIntArray(i)
  Next
End Sub
```

The foregoing procedure uses a `For...Next` loop to fill `myIntArray` with 10 random numbers between 1 and 100. The second loop is used to print out the values from the array. Notice that the procedure uses the `Rnd` function to generate a random number. This function returns a value less than 1 but greater than or equal to 0. You can try it out in the Immediate window by entering:

```
x=rnd
?x
```

Before calling the `Rnd` function, the LoadArrayWithIntegers procedure uses the `Randomize` statement to initialize the random-number generator. To become more familiar with the `Randomize` statement and `Rnd` function, be sure to follow up with the Excel online help.

USING A ONE-DIMENSIONAL ARRAY

Having learned the basics of array variables, let's write a couple of VBA procedures to make arrays a part of your new skill set. The procedure in Hands-On 7.1 uses a one-dimensional array to programmatically display a list of six North American cities.

NOTE	*Please note files for the "Hands-On" project may be found in the companion files.*

Hands-On 7.1 Using a One-Dimensional Array

1. Open a new workbook and save it as **C:\VBAPrimerExcel2021_ByExample\Chap07_ExcelPrimer.xlsm.**
2. Switch to the Microsoft Visual Basic Editor window and rename the VBA project **Arrays.**
3. Insert a new module into the Arrays (Chap07_ExcelPrimer.xlsm) project and rename this module **StaticArrays.**
4. In the StaticArrays module, enter the following FavoriteCities procedure:

```
' start indexing array elements at 1
Option Base 1
Sub FavoriteCities()
  'now declare the array
  Dim cities(6) As String

  'assign the values to array elements
  cities(1) = "Baltimore"
  cities(2) = "Atlanta"
  cities(3) = "Boston"
  cities(4) = "San Diego"
  cities(5) = "New York"
  cities(6) = "Denver"

  'display the list of cities
  MsgBox cities(1) & Chr(13) & cities(2) & Chr(13) _
      & cities(3) & Chr(13) & cities(4) & Chr(13) _
      & cities(5) & Chr(13) & cities(6)
End Sub
```

Before the FavoriteCities procedure begins, the default indexing for an array is changed. Notice that the position of the `Option Base 1` statement is at the top of the module window before the `Sub` statement. This statement tells Visual Basic to assign the number 1 instead of the default 0 to the first element of the array. The array `cities()` of String data type is declared with six elements. Each element of the array is then assigned a value. The last statement uses the `MsgBox` function to display the list of cities. When you run this procedure in Step 5, the city names will appear on separate lines in the message box, as shown in Figure 7.1. You can change the order of the displayed data by switching the index values.

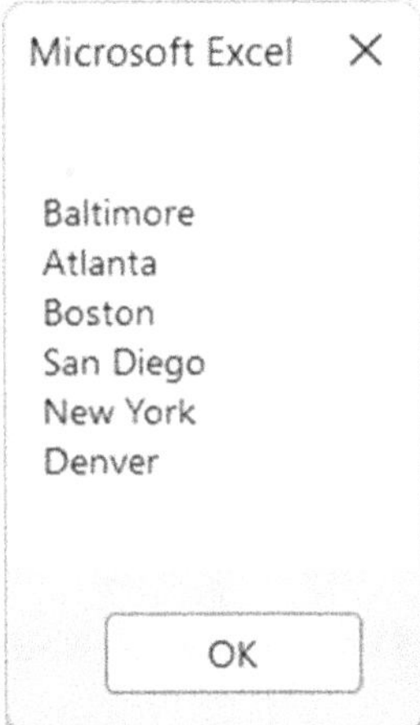

FIGURE 7.1 You can display the elements of a one-dimensional array with the `MsgBox` function.

5. Position the insertion point anywhere within the procedure code and press **F5** to run the FavoriteCities procedure.
6. On your own, modify the FavoriteCities procedure so that it displays the names of the cities in the reverse order (from 6 to 1).

USING A TWO-DIMENSIONAL ARRAY

Now that you know how to programmatically produce a list (a one-dimensional array), it's time to take a closer look at how you can work with tables of data. The following procedure creates a two-dimensional array that will hold the country name, currency name, and exchange rate for three countries.

Hands-On 7.2 Storing Data in a Two-Dimensional Array

1. In the **StaticArrays** module, enter the following procedure:

```
Sub Exchange()
  Dim t As String
  Dim r As String
  Dim Ex(3, 3) As Variant

    t = Chr(9)   ' tab
    r = Chr(13)  ' Enter
```

```
        Ex(1, 1) = «Japan»
        Ex(1, 2) = «Yen»
        Ex(1, 3) = 104.57
        Ex(2, 1) = «Mexico»
        Ex(2, 2) = «Peso»
        Ex(2, 3) = 11.2085
        Ex(3, 1) = «Canada»
        Ex(3, 2) = "Dollar"
        Ex(3, 3) = 1.2028
        MsgBox "Country " & t & t & "Currency" & t & "per US$" _
          & r & r _
          & Ex(1, 1) & t & t & Ex(1, 2) & t & Ex(1, 3) & r _
          & Ex(2, 1) & t & t & Ex(2, 2) & t & Ex(2, 3) & r _
          & Ex(3, 1) & t & t & Ex(3, 2) & t & Ex(3, 3) & r & r _
          & "* Sample Exchange Rates for Demonstration Only", , _
          "Exchange"
    End Sub
```

2. Run the Exchange procedure.
3. When you run the Exchange procedure, you will see a message box with the exchange information presented in three columns, as shown in Figure 7.2.

FIGURE 7.2 The text displayed in a message box can be custom formatted.

USING A DYNAMIC ARRAY

The arrays introduced thus far in this chapter were static. A *static array* is an array of a specific size. Use a static array when you know in advance how big the array should be. The size of the static array is specified in the array's declaration statement. For example, the statement `Dim Fruits(9) As String` declares a static array called Fruits that is made up of 10 elements (assuming you have not changed the default indexing to 1). But what if you're not sure how many elements your array will contain? If your procedure depends on user input, the number of user-supplied elements might vary every time the procedure is executed. How can you ensure that the array you declare is not wasting memory? After you declare an array, VBA sets aside enough memory to accommodate the array. If you declare an array to hold more elements than what you need, you'll end up wasting valuable computer resources. The solution to this problem is making your arrays dynamic.

A *dynamic array* is an array whose size can change. You use a dynamic array when the array size is determined each time the procedure is run. A dynamic array is declared by placing empty parentheses after the array name:

```
Dim Fruits() As String
```

Before you use a dynamic array in your procedure, you must use the `ReDim` statement to dynamically set the lower and upper bounds of the array. For example, initially you may want to hold five fruits in the array:

```
Redim Fruits(1 To 5)
```

The `ReDim` statement redimensions arrays as the code of your procedure executes and informs Visual Basic about the new size of the array. This statement can be used several times in the same procedure.

The example procedure in Hands-On 7.3 will dynamically load data entered in a worksheet into a one-dimensional array.

Hands-On 7.3 Loading Worksheet Data into an Array

1. Insert a new module into the Arrays project and rename it **DynamicArrays**.
2. In the **DynamicArrays** module, enter the following procedure:

```
Sub LoadArrayFromWorksheet()
  Dim myDataRng As Range
  Dim myArray() As Variant
  Dim cnt As Integer
  Dim i As Integer
  Dim cell As Variant
  Dim r As Integer
  Dim last As Integer

  Set myDataRng = ActiveSheet.UsedRange
```

```
    'get the count of nonempty cells (text and numbers only)
    last = myDataRng.SpecialCells(xlCellTypeConstants, 3).Count

    If IsEmpty(myDataRng) Then
        MsgBox "Sheet is empty."
        Exit Sub
    End If

    ReDim myArray(1 To last)

    i = 1

    'fill the array from worksheet data
    'reformat all numeric values
    For Each cell In myDataRng
        If cell.Value <> "" Then
            If IsNumeric(cell.Value) Then
                myArray(i) = Format(cell.Value, "$#,#00.00")
            Else
                myArray(i) = cell.Value
            End If
            i = i + 1
        End If
    Next

    'print array values to the Immediate window
    For i = 1 To last
        Debug.Print myArray(i)
    Next
    Debug.Print "Items in the array: " & UBound(myArray)
  End Sub
```

3. Switch to the Microsoft Excel application window of the Chap07_ExcelPrimer.xlsm workbook and enter some data in **Sheet2**. For example, enter your favorite fruits in cells A1:B6 and numbers in cells D1:D9.
4. Choose **Developer | Macros**. In the Macro dialog box, choose **LoadArray-FromWorksheet**, and click **Run**.

   When the procedure completes, check the data in the Immediate window. You should see the entries you typed in the worksheet. The numeric data should appear formatted with the currency format.

USING ARRAY FUNCTIONS

You can manipulate arrays with five built-in VBA functions: `Array`, `IsArray`, `Erase`, `LBound`, and `UBound`. The following sections demonstrate the use of each of these functions in VBA procedures.

The Array Function

The `Array` function allows you to create an array during code execution without having to dimension it first. This function always returns an array of Variants. Using the `Array` function, you can quickly place a series of values in a list.

The CarInfo procedure shown here creates a fixed-size, one-dimensional, three-element array called auto.

Hands-On 7.4 Using the Array Function

1. Insert a new module into the current project and rename it **Array_Function**.
2. Enter the following **CarInfo** procedure:

```
Option Base 1

Sub CarInfo()
  Dim auto As Variant
  auto = Array("Ford", "Black", "1999")
  MsgBox auto(2) & " " & auto(1) & ", " & auto(3)
  auto(2) = "4-door"
  MsgBox auto(2) & " " & auto(1) & ", " & auto(3)
End Sub
```

3. Run the CarInfo procedure.

The IsArray Function

Using the `IsArray` function, you can test whether a variable is an array. The `IsArray` function returns either true, if the variable is an array, or false, if it's not an array. Here's an example.

Hands-On 7.5 Using the IsArray Function

1. Insert a new module into the current project and rename it **IsArray_Function**.
2. Enter the code of the **IsThisArray** procedure, as shown here:

```
Sub IsThisArray()
  ' declare a dynamic array
```

```
    Dim sheetNames() As String
        Dim totalSheets As Integer
    Dim counter As Integer

    ' count the sheets in the current workbook
    totalSheets = ActiveWorkbook.Sheets.Count

    ' specify the size of the array
    ReDim sheetNames(1 To totalSheets)

    ' enter and show the names of sheets
    For counter = 1 To totalSheets
      sheetNames(counter) = _
         ActiveWorkbook.Sheets(counter).Name
      MsgBox sheetNames(counter)
    Next counter

    ' check if this is indeed an array
    If IsArray(sheetNames) Then
      MsgBox "The sheetNames variable is an array."
    End If
  End Sub
```

3. Run the IsThisArray procedure.

The Erase Function

When you want to remove the data from an array, you should use the `Erase` function. This function deletes all the data held by static or dynamic arrays. In addition, the `Erase` function reallocates all the memory assigned to a dynamic array. If a procedure has to use the dynamic array again, you must use the `ReDim` statement to specify the size of the array.

The following example shows how to erase the data from the array cities.

Hands-On 7.6 Using the Erase Function

1. Insert a new module into the current project and rename it **Erase_Function.**
2. Enter the code of the FunCities procedure shown here:

```
' start indexing array elements at 1
Option Base 1

Sub FunCities()
' declare the array
Dim cities(1 To 5) As String
```

```
' assign the values to array elements
cities(1) = "Las Vegas"
cities(2) = "Orlando"
cities(3) = "Atlantic City"
cities(4) = "New York"
cities(5) = "San Francisco"

' display the list of cities
  MsgBox cities(1) & Chr(13) & cities(2) & Chr(13) _
    & cities(3) & Chr(13) & cities(4) & Chr(13) _
    & cities (5)
Erase cities

' show all that were erased
MsgBox cities(1) & Chr(13) & cities(2) & Chr(13) _
  & cities(3) & Chr(13) & cities(4) & Chr(13) _
  & cities (5)
End Sub
```

After the `Erase` function deletes the values from the array, the `MsgBox` function displays an empty message box.

3. Run the FunCities procedure.

The LBound and UBound Functions

The `LBound` and `UBound` functions return whole numbers that indicate the lower bound and upper bound of an array.

Hands-On 7.7 Using the LBound and UBound Functions

1. Insert a new module into the current project and rename it **L_and_UBound_Function**.
2. Enter the code of the **FunCities2** procedure shown here:

```
Sub FunCities2()
  ' declare the array
  Dim cities(1 To 5) As String

  ' assign the values to array elements
  cities(1) = "Las Vegas"
  cities(2) = "Orlando"
  cities(3) = "Atlantic City"
  cities(4) = "New York"
  cities(5) = "San Francisco"
```

```
        ' display the list of cities
    MsgBox cities(1) & Chr(13) & cities(2) & Chr(13) _
      & cities(3) & Chr(13) & cities(4) & Chr(13) _
      & cities (5)
    ' display the array bounds
    MsgBox "The lower bound: " & LBound(cities) & Chr(13) _
      & "The upper bound: " & UBound(cities)
End Sub
```

3. Run the FunCities2 procedure.

TROUBLESHOOTING ERRORS IN ARRAYS

When working with arrays, it's easy to make a mistake. If you try to assign more values than there are elements in the declared array, VBA will display the error message "Subscript out of range," as shown in Figure 7.3.

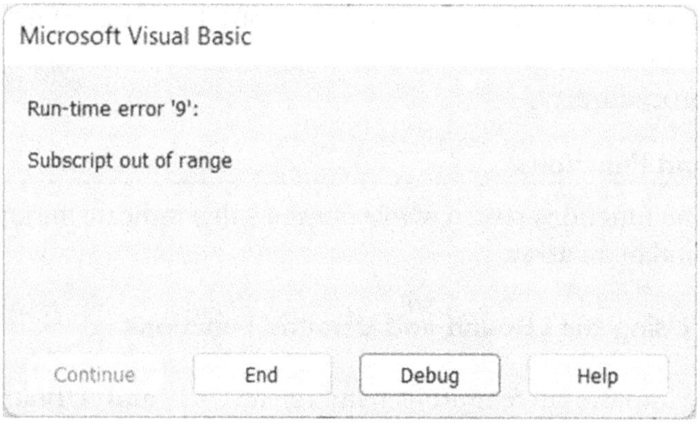

Microsoft Visual Basic

Run-time error '9':

Subscript out of range

Continue End Debug Help

FIGURE 7.3 This error was caused by an attempt to access a nonexistent array element.

Suppose you declare a one-dimensional array that consists of six elements, and you are trying to assign a value to the seventh element. When you run the procedure, Visual Basic can't find the seventh element, so it displays the error message. When you click the Debug button, Visual Basic will highlight the line of code that caused the error.

To fix this type of error, you should begin by looking at the array's declaration statement. Once you know how many elements the array should hold, it's easy to figure out that the culprit is the index number that appears in the parentheses in the highlighted line of code. In the example shown in Figure 7.4, once we replace the line of code `cities(7) = "Denver"` with `cities(6) = "Trenton"` and press F5 to resume the procedure, the procedure will run as intended.

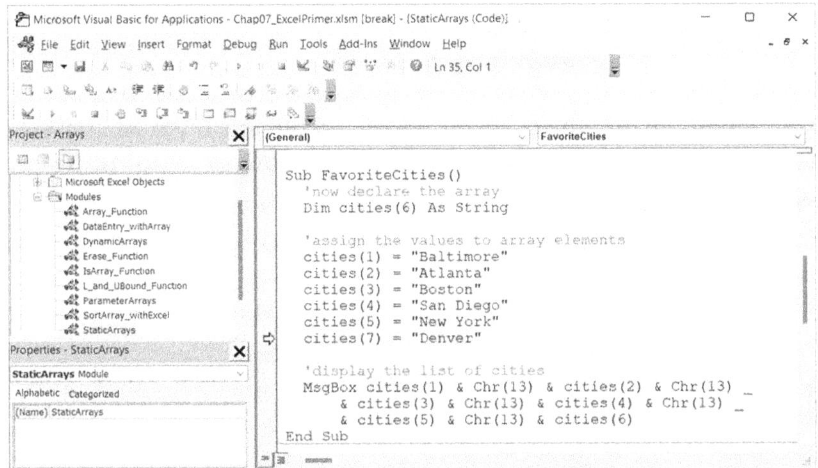

FIGURE 7.4 When you click the Debug button in the error message, Visual Basic highlights the statement that triggered the error.

Another frequent error you may encounter while working with arrays is *Type mismatch*. To avoid this error, keep in mind that each element of an array must be of the same data type. If you attempt to assign to an element of an array a value that conflicts with the data type of the array declared in the `Dim` statement, you'll obtain the Type mismatch error during code execution. To hold values of different data types in an array, declare the array as Variant.

USING THE PARAMARRAY KEYWORD

Values can be passed between subroutines or functions as required or optional arguments. If the passed argument is not absolutely required for the procedure to execute, the argument's name is preceded by the keyword `Optional`. Sometimes, however, you don't know in advance how many arguments you want to pass. A classic example is addition. You may want to add together two numbers. Later, you may use 3, 10, or 15 numbers.

Using the keyword `ParamArray`, you can pass an array consisting of any number of elements to your subroutines and function procedures.

The following AddMultipleArgs function will add up as many numbers as you require. This function begins with the declaration of an array, `myNumbers`.

Notice the use of the `ParamArray` keyword. The array must be declared as an array of type Variant, and it must be the last argument in the procedure definition.

Hands-On 7.8 Passing an Array to Procedures Using the ParamArray Keyword

1. Insert a new module into the current project and rename it **ParameterArrays**.
2. In the ParameterArrays module, enter the following **AddMultipleArgs** function procedure:

```
Function AddMultipleArgs(ParamArray myNumbers() As Variant)
  Dim mySum As Single
  Dim myValue As Variant
  For Each myValue in myNumbers
    mySum=mySum+myValue
  Next
  AddMultipleArgs = mySum
End Function
```

3. To try out the AddMultipleArgs function, activate the Immediate window and type the following instruction:

```
?AddMultipleArgs(1, 23.24, 3, 24, 8, 34)
```

When you press **Enter**, Visual Basic returns the total of all the numbers in the parentheses: 93.24. You can supply an unlimited number of arguments. To add more values, enter additional values inside the parentheses and press Enter. Notice that each function argument must be separated by a comma.

DATA ENTRY WITH AN ARRAY

Earlier in this chapter you learned how to use various Array functions. The following procedure demonstrates how the simple `Array` function can speed up data entry.

Hands-On 7.9 Using the Array Function to Enter Headings in a Worksheet

1. Insert a new module into the current project and rename it **DataEntry_withArray**.

2. In the EnterData_Array module, enter the following **ColumnHeads** procedure:

```
Sub ColumnHeads()
  Dim heading As Variant
  Dim cell As Range
  Dim i As Integer
  i = 0
  heading = Array("First Name", "Last Name", _
    "Position", "Salary")
  Workbooks.Add

  For Each cell In Range("A1:D1")
    cell.Formula = heading(i)
  i = i + 1
  Next

  Columns("A:D").Select
  Selection.Columns.AutoFit
  Range("A1").Select
End Sub
```

3. Switch to Microsoft Excel window and run the ColumnHeads procedure.

SORTING AN ARRAY WITH EXCEL

We all find it easier to work with sorted data. Some operations on arrays, like finding maximum and minimum values, require that the array is sorted. Once it is sorted, you can find the maximum value by assigning the upper bound index to the sorted array, as in the following:

```
y = myIntArray(UBound(myIntArray))
```

The minimum value can be obtained by reading the first value of the sorted array:

```
x = myIntArray(1)
```

So, how can you sort an array? This section demonstrates how you can use Excel to get your array data into the sorted order. An easy way to sort an array is copying your array values to a new worksheet, and then using the Excel built-in `Sort` function. After completing the sort, you can load your sorted values back into a VBA array. This technique is the simplest since you can use a macro recorder to get your Sort statement started for you. And, with a large array, it is also faster than the classic bubble sort routine that is commonly used with arrays.

Hands-On 7.10 Using Excel to Sort a VBA Array

1. Insert a new module into the current project and rename it **SortArray_withExcel**.
2. In the SortArray_withExcel module, enter the following **SortArrayWithExcel** procedure:

```
Sub SortArrayWithExcel()
  Dim myIntArray() As Integer
  Dim i As Integer
  Dim x As Integer
  Dim y As Integer
  Dim r As Integer
  Dim myDataRng As Range

  'initialize random number generator
  Randomize

  ReDim myIntArray(1 To 10)

  ' Fill the array with 10 random numbers between 1 and 100
  For i = 1 To 10
      myIntArray(i) = Int((100 * Rnd) + 1)
     Debug.Print "aValue" & i & ":" & vbTab & myIntArray(i)
  Next

  'write array to a worksheet
  Worksheets.Add

  r = 1   'row counter
  With ActiveSheet
    For i = 1 To 10
        Cells(r, 1).Value = myIntArray(i)
        r = r + 1
    Next i
  End With

  'Use Excel Sort to order values in the worksheet
  Set myDataRng = ActiveSheet.UsedRange

  With ActiveSheet.Sort
    .SortFields.Clear
    .SortFields.Add Key:=Range("A1"), _
      SortOn:=xlSortOnValues, Order:=xlAscending, _
```

```
        DataOption:=xlSortNormal
      .SetRange myDataRng
      .Header = xlNo
      .MatchCase = False
      .Apply
    End With

    'free the memory used by array by using Erase statement
    Erase myIntArray

    ReDim myIntArray(1 To 10)

    'load sorted values back into an array

    For i = 1 To 10
      myIntArray(i) = ActiveSheet.Cells(i, 1).Value
    Next

    'write out sorted array to the Immediate Window

    i = 1
    For i = 1 To 10
      Debug.Print "aValueSorted: " & myIntArray(i)
    Next

    'find minimum and maximum values stored in the array
    x = myIntArray(1)
    y = myIntArray(UBound(myIntArray))
    Debug.Print "Min value=" & x & vbTab; "Max value=" & y
  End Sub
```

The SortArrayWithExcel procedure populates a dynamic array with 10 random Integer values and prints out this array to an Immediate window and a new worksheet. Next, the values entered in the worksheet are sorted in ascending order using the Excel Sort object. The sort statements have been generated by the macro recorder and then modified for this procedure's needs. Once sorted, the `Erase` statement is used to free the memory used by the dynamic array. Before reloading the array with the sorted values, the procedure redeclares the array variable using the `ReDim` statement. The last statements in the procedure demonstrate how to retrieve the minimum and maximum values from the array variable.

3. Switch to Microsoft Excel window and run the SortArrayWithExcel procedure.

SUMMARY

In this chapter, you learned how you can use arrays in complex VBA procedures that require many variables. You worked with examples of procedures that demonstrated how to declare and use a one-dimensional array (list) and a two-dimensional array (table). You saw the difference between static and dynamic arrays and practiced using five built-in VBA functions that are frequently used with arrays: `Array`, `IsArray`, `Erase`, `LBound`, and `UBound`. You also learned how to use a new keyword—`ParamArray`—and perform sorting of an array with Excel.

In the next chapter, you will learn how to use collections instead of arrays to manipulate large amounts of data.

Chapter 8

Keeping Track of Multiple Values in Excel VBA Programs

A Quick Introduction to Creating and Using Collections

In the previous chapter, you learned how arrays are used to manipulate multiple items quickly and easily. Instead of creating several variables to keep track of your data, you only needed to declare one variable. Using arrays instead of defining individual variables saves you from writing many lines of repetitive code. As you have seen so far, in programming there are many ways of performing the same task. The method you use depends on your needs. So, it is with storing multiple values. In addition to arrays, you can maintain your items of data while your program is running by using a special type of object – the collection. Like arrays, collections are used for grouping variables.

Because collections have built-in properties and methods that allow you to add, remove, and count their elements, they make working with multiple data items much easier than arrays. Collections can also be used to hold objects. This is a more advanced feature of object-oriented programming that we'll cover in Chapter 26. In this chapter, we will focus on learning the basic skills of using collections for tracking and maintaining data in your VBA procedures.

WORKING WITH BUILT-IN COLLECTIONS

A set of similar objects is known as a collection. In Microsoft Excel, for example, all open workbooks belong to the collection of Workbooks, and all the sheets in a workbook are members of the Worksheets collection. Collections are objects that contain other objects. No matter what collection you want to work with, you can do the following:

- Refer to a specific object in a collection by using an index value. For example, to refer to the second object in the collection of Worksheets, use either of the following statements:

  ```
  Worksheets(2).Select
  ```

  Or

  ```
  Worksheets("Sheet2").Select
  ```

- Determine the number of items in the collection by using the `Count` property. For example, when you enter in the Immediate window the statement:

  ```
  ?Worksheets.Count
  ```

  VBA will return the total number of worksheets in the current workbook.
- Insert new items into the collection by using the `Add` method. For example, when you enter in the Immediate window the statement:

  ```
  Worksheets.Add
  ```

  VBA will insert to the current workbook a new worksheet. The Worksheets collection now contains one more item.
- Cycle through every object in the collection by using the `For Each…Next` loop.

  Suppose that you opened a workbook containing five worksheets with the following names: "Daily wages," "Weekly wages," "Monthly wages," "Yearly salary," and "Bonuses." To delete the worksheets that contain the word "wages" in the name, you could write the following procedure:

  ```
  Sub DeleteSheets()
    Dim ws As Worksheet
    Application.DisplayAlerts = False
     For Each ws In Worksheets
             If InStr(ws.Name, "wages") Then
  ```

```
            ws.Delete
                End If
        Next
        Application.DisplayAlerts = True
    End Sub
```

The statement `Application.DisplayAlerts = False` is used to suppress some prompts and messages that Excel displays while the code is running. In this case, we want to suppress the confirmation message that Excel displays when worksheets are deleted. The `InStr` function is very useful for string comparisons as it allows you to find one string within another. The statement `InStr(ws.Name, "wages")` tells Excel to determine if the worksheet name (stored in ws object variable) contains the string of characters "wages."

CREATING YOUR OWN COLLECTION

Collection is an object; it is a data type in VBA. To create a user-defined collection, begin by declaring an object variable of the Collection type:

```
Dim collection_name As Collection
Set collection_name = New Collection
```

Or

```
Dim collection_name As New Collection
```

Notice the **New** keyword. VBA uses this keyword to create a new instance of an object. The collection_name is the name of your collection. You can use any name if it is not one of the reserved words Excel uses for its own collections or other internal operations.

You can define more than one collection but each collection you define should have a distinct name so you can easily reference it in your code. Collections can be defined at the top of the standard module or within a procedure. They can also be defined in class modules which are often used in more advanced Excel VBA programming. Unlike arrays, collections do not require you to predefine their size. Once you define the object variable of the Collection type you are ready to begin adding items to the collection.

Adding Objects to a Custom Collection

After you've declared the Collection object, you can insert new items into the collection by using the `Add` method. The `Add` method looks like this:

```
object.Add item[, key, before, after]
```

You are required to specify only the object and the item. All arguments in the square brackets are optional. The object is the collection name. This is the same name that was used in the declaration of the Collection object. The item is the object that you want to add to the collection. For example, if the name of your collection is `colFruits`, the following statement adds several new items to it:

```
colFruits.Add "Apple"
colFruits.Add "Pear"
colFruits.Add "Strawberry"
colFruits.Add "Blueberry"
colFruits.Add "Orange"
colFruits.Add "Peach"
```

Although other arguments are optional, they are quite useful. It's important to understand that the items in a collection are automatically assigned numbers starting with 1. However, they can also be assigned a unique key value. Instead of accessing a specific item with an index (1, 2, 3, and so on), you can assign a key for that object at the time an object is added to a collection. For instance, if you are creating a collection of custom sheets, you could use a sheet name as a key. To identify an individual in a collection of students or employees, you could use their ID numbers as a key. For example, here's how you can add *James Allen* to `colPeople` collection, using his EmployeeID as a key:

```
Dim colPeople As New Collection
colPeople.Add "James Allen", Key:="123456"
```

If you want to specify the position of the object in the collection, you should use either a `before` or `after` argument (do not use both). The `before` argument is the object before which the new object is added. The `after` argument is the object after which the new object is added.

For example, to add *Kiwi* to the `colFruits` collection so that it appears after the second item, use the following statement:

```
colFruits.Add "Kiwi", , , 2
```

or

```
colFruits.Add "Kiwi", After:=2
```

Notice that if you are not using the named argument `After`, you must place a comma for each of the preceding optional arguments that you are not specifying.

To enter *Cherry* in the first position, use the named `Before` argument:

```
colFruits.Add "Cherry", Before:=1
```

Using the optional `Before` or `After` arguments you can easily add elements in any position.

Each element of a collection can be a different data type. Please note that arrays can support different data types only if they are defined as Variants. To store a date item in your collection, use the following statement:

```
colFruits.Add #12/10/2021#, Key:="InvoiceDate"
```

To store a number in your collection, the following statement can be used:

```
colFruits.Add 100.99, Key:="InvoiceTotal"
```

Determining the Number of Items in your Collection

Use the `Count` property to find out the number of items in your collection. To determine the current number of fruit items in the `colFruits`, write the following statement:

```
Debug.Print colFruits.Count
```

Accessing Items in a Collection

To refer to a specific item in your collection, use its index or key value.

For example, to find out the names of the first collection item, use this statement:

```
Debug.Print colFruits.Item(1)
```

Because the `Item` method is a default method of the collection, you may omit it from the statement, as shown here:

```
Debug.Print colFruits(1)
```

If you know the item key, then you can quickly retrieve it like this:

```
Debug.Print colPeople("123456")
```

By using the Key to access a collection item you can go to it directly without the need to iterate through all the items. Excel VBA does not provide a built-in method to check if the Key exists, but you can write your own function to return a Boolean value of True if the key exists. Here's how you would do it:

```
Function KeyExists(colName As Collection, _
        key As String) As Boolean
    On Error GoTo EndHere
    IsObject (colName.Item(key))
    KeyExists = True

EndHere:
End Function
```

The `IsObject` is a built-in VBA function that returns `True` if the passed to it expression (i.e., key name) represents an object variable. The statement `OnError GoTo EndHere` tells Excel to jump to the line `EndHere:` : if the result of the `IsObject` function is `False`. The error handling statements introduced here are covered in detail in Chapter 9.

Removing Items from a Collection

Removing an item from your custom collection is as easy as adding an item. To remove an item, use the `Remove` method in the following format:

```
object.Remove index
```

`object` is the name of the custom collection that contains the object you want to remove. `index` is an expression specifying the position of the object in the collection. To remove the third fruit item from the `colFruits`, you simply write the following statement:

```
colFruits.Remove 3
```

Collections are reindexed automatically when an item is removed. Therefore, to remove all items from a custom collection you can use 1 for the `Index` argument, as in the following example:

```
Do While colFruits.Count > 0
  colFruits.Remove Index:=1
Loop
```

Another way to remove all objects from your collection is by using the `For Each...Next` loop. For example, to remove all objects from the `colFruits`, use the following looping structure:

```
Dim m As Variant

For Each m in colFruits
```

```
 colFruits.Remove 1
Next
```

Note that the control variable used in the `For Each...Next` loop must be declared as Variant or Object. Because collections are reindexed, the preceding statement will remove the first item of the collection on each iteration. After the loop completes, `colFruits` should have zero items. However, to be sure, use the `Count` property to find out.

```
Debug.Print colFruits.Count
```

You can also remove all items from a collection by setting the collection object variable to a new collection, like this:

```
Set colFruits = New Collection
```

Updating Items in a Collection

When you add an item to your collection that has a basic data type such as string, integer, long, currency, or date, your collection will be read-only. This means you will not be able to change the value of the item. Excel will display an error if you try to assign a value to an existing item in your collection:

```
' this statement will produce Run-time error 424 'Object required'
colFruits(4) = "Cranberry"
```

Therefore, if your procedure requires that the values are updated, you should group your items into an array. If you want to stick with the collection, to change an item, remove the item and add a new one. The only time that the collection is updatable is when it references objects and this is a subject for the advanced VBA.

Let's proceed to the first Hands-On in this chapter where you put all your knowledge about collections into a VBA procedure.

NOTE	*Please note files for the "Hands-On" project may be found in the companion files.*

Hands-On 8.1 Creating and Manipulating a Custom Collection (Example 1)

1. Start Excel and create a new macro-enabled workbook named **Chap08_ExcelPrimer.xlsm** in your **C:\VBAPrimerExcel2021_ByExample** folder.
2. Press **Alt+F11** to switch to the Visual Basic Editor window.

3. Choose **Insert | Module** to add a new standard module.
4. In the Module1 Code window, enter the following **WorkWith_**Collection, **Display_Items** and **KeyExists** procedures.

```
Sub WorkWith_Collection()
    Dim colFruits As New Collection
    Dim itm As Variant
    Dim strColItems As String

    colFruits.Add "Apple"
    colFruits.Add "Pear"
    colFruits.Add "Strawberry"
    colFruits.Add "Blueberry"
    colFruits.Add "Orange"
    colFruits.Add "Peach"
    colFruits.Add "Kiwi", , , 2
    colFruits.Add "Mango", , 5
    colFruits.Add "Cherry", Before:=1
    colFruits.Add 100.99, Key:="InvoiceTotal"
    colFruits.Add #12/10/2021#, Key:="InvoiceDate"

    Debug.Print "Total Items in colFruits: " & colFruits.Count

    'call a procedure to display all items in the collection
    Display_Items colFruits, itm

    colFruits.Remove 3
   Debug.Print "New Total Items in colFruits: " & colFruits.Count

    For Each itm In colFruits
        strColItems = strColItems & ", " & itm
    Next

    ' remove a comma and a space from the beginning of
    ' the strColItems variable
    strColItems = Mid(strColItems, 3, Len(strColItems))
    Debug.Print strColItems

    'Find if keys exist and if not display a message
    'and go to the next line

    If KeyExists(colFruits, "InvoiceDate") And _
        KeyExists(colFruits, "InvoiceTotal") Then
    Debug.Print "Invoiced on: " & colFruits("InvoiceDate") & _
       vbCrLf & "Total: " & colFruits("InvoiceTotal")
```

```
    Else
        MsgBox "Provided key(s) not found."
    End If

    ' Remove all items from collection one by one
    For Each itm In colFruits
        colFruits.Remove 1
    Next
    Debug.Print "Total Items in colFruits: " & colFruits.Count

End Sub

Sub Display_Items(col As Collection, myItm As Variant)

    For Each myItm In col
        Debug.Print myItm
    Next
End Sub

Function KeyExists(colName As Collection, _
        key As String) As Boolean

    On Error GoTo EndHere

    IsObject (colName.Item(key))
    KeyExists = True

EndHere:
End Function
```

5. Position the pointer anywhere within the WorkWith_Collection procedure and choose **Run | Run Sub/UserForm** to execute it.
6. Press **Ctrl+G** to open the Immediate Window and check the output of the procedure.

   The WorkWith_Collection procedure performs various operations on the declared collection object variable `colFruits`. If you plan on using the same collection in other procedures in the same module, you will need to move its variable declaration statement to the top of the module.

Returning a Collection from a Function

Collections like arrays can be used as parameters or return values to functions or subroutine procedures. In Hands-On 8.2, you will collect entries from the user via the VBA InputBox function and store them into an array. Next, you will pass that array to a function and return a collection with the same items. Let's see how this is done.

Hands-On 8.2 Creating and Manipulating a Custom Collection (Example 2)

1. Choose **Insert | Module** to add a new standard module to the current VBA project.
2. In the Code window, enter the code shown as follows.
   Notice that the `allItems` variable is declared at the top of the module (above all the procedure code). This placement will make this variable available to all the procedures in this module.

```
Dim allItems As String

Sub ShowCollItems()
    Dim coll As Collection
    Dim myArray As Variant
    Dim itm As Variant

    ' get items from user input
    If AskForItems <> "" Then
        Debug.Print allItems
        ' extract items from the user input string (allItems)
        ' and place them in an array
        myArray = Split(allItems, ",")
       Debug.Print "Array has " & UBound(myArray) + 1 & " items."

        ' call function to create a collection from the array
        Set coll = CreateCollection(myArray)

        ' iterate through the collection to display each item
        For Each itm In coll
          Debug.Print itm
        Next
       Debug.Print "Total items in the collection: " & coll.Count
    End If
End Sub

Function AskForItems() As String
  allItems = InputBox("Enter your items separated by a comma", _
        "Demo - Get User Input", _
        "item1, item2")
```

```
    If allItems = "" Then
      AskForItems = ""
    Else
      AskForItems = allItems
    End If
End Function

Function CreateCollection(arrMyItems As Variant) As Collection
    Dim coll As New Collection
    Dim i As Integer
    For i = 0 To UBound(arrMyItems)
        coll.Add arrMyItems(i)
    Next i
    'Return a collection
    Set CreateCollection = coll
End Function
```

3. Position the pointer anywhere within the ShowCollItems procedure and choose **Run | Run Sub/UserForm** to execute it.
4. Press **Ctrl+G** to open the Immediate Window and check the output of the procedure.

Let's review the previous code. The main procedure ShowCollItems declares three variables that we need for working with the array and collection. Notice that you don't need to use the `New` keyword to declare the collection because the collection is created inside the CreateCollection function. The declared object variable `coll` will be assigned a collection received from this function. In addition to the CreateCollection function, the ShowCollItem procedure relies on following functions: AskForItems and Split.

The custom function procedure AskForItems populates the allItems string variable (declared on the top of the module) with the values obtained from the user via the VBA `InputBox` function. The user is requested to input values as a comma-delimited string (each item must be separated by a comma). If the user does not enter any values and presses Cancel instead, the function will return an empty string to the calling procedure (ShowCollItems). If items are entered, then the entire string will be returned. If the string returned from the AskForItems function is not empty, we continue running the statements within the If block. If the string is empty, the procedure ends.

Within the If block, we print the contents of the allItems variable to the Immediate window. Next, we use the built-in VBA `Split` function to extract the values from the allItems string using a comma delimiter and return an array (myArray). We use the `UBound` function to find the number of items in the array.

Because by default arrays are zero-based, we need to add 1 to the count to get the correct number of items. Refer to the previous chapter on arrays if you'd like to add code here to list the items in the myArray variable.

The next set of statements focuses on creating a collection. To do this we set the coll variable to the result obtained from the CreateCollection function. We call the CreateCollection function and pass it the myArray variable. Notice that myArray is a Variant and the CreateCollection function was defined to expect the parameter of the Variant type. Inside the CreateCollection function we start by declaring the coll variable of the Collection type. We also need a counter (i) to loop through the items of the array variable that we passed to this function. Note that the parameter name that the CreateCollection function expects can be any name you define.

Using the For...Next loop we loop through the items of the array starting from zero and add each array item to the collection. Once we are done looping, we pass the entire collection to the calling procedure – ShowCollItems. The coll is an object variable so we need to use the `Set` keyword to return it from the function:

```
'Return a collection
Set CreateCollection = coll
```

Now we are back again in the ShowCollItems procedure, this time returning a collection. To view the collection items, we use the `For each Next` loop to print each item to the Immediate window. Note that the `itm` iterator must be defined as Variant. The procedure ends by printing the total number of collection items.

USING CUSTOM AND BUILT-IN COLLECTIONS TOGETHER

Let's apply our knowledge of custom collections to working with the Excel built-in collection of worksheets. As worksheets can contain various objects, you may need to collect different values stored within them. The GetNotes procedure in Hands-On 8.3 declares a custom collection object named colNotes. We will use this collection to store notes that you insert in various worksheets of the active workbook.

NOTE	*Currently in Excel for Microsoft 365 notes are used for making notes and annotations about the data in a worksheet. Notes look like yellow stickies and were formerly called. comments. The comments are still in Excel, but they look different and are used when you want to discuss the data. Comments have a Reply box which allows you to discuss the data with other people. Comments are now threaded which means that when people reply to the comment, you can see several comments connected together, forming a conversation. In the following Hands-On you will work with notes.*

Hands-On 8.3 Using a Custom Collection Object

1. Right-click any cell in Sheet1 of the Chap8_ExcelPrimer.xlsm workbook and choose **New Note** from the shortcut menu. You can also enter a note by choosing Review | Notes | New Note. Type any text you want for your note. Click outside the note box to exit the edit mode. Add two new sheets to the workbook. Use the same technique to enter two notes in Sheet2. Enter different text for each note. Add a note in any cell on Sheet3. You should now have four notes in three worksheets.
2. Click the **File tab** and choose **Options**. In the Excel Options window's General section, in the area named "Personalize your copy of Microsoft Office," you should see a text box with your name. Delete your name and enter **Joan Smith**, and then click **OK**. Now, enter one note anywhere on Sheet2 and one note anywhere on Sheet3. These notes should be automatically stamped with Joan Smith's name. When you're done entering the note text, return to the Excel Options window and change the User name text box entry back to the way it was (your name).
3. Switch to the Visual Basic Editor and add a new module to the current project.
4. Use the Properties box to rename the module. Enter **MyCollection** next to the **Name** property.
5. In the MyCollection module, enter the GetNotes procedure, as shown here:

```
Sub GetNotes()
  Dim sht As Worksheet
  Dim colNotes As New Collection
  Dim myNote As Comment
  Dim i As Integer
```

```
    Dim t As Integer
    Dim strName As String

    strName = InputBox("Enter author's name:")
    For Each sht In ThisWorkbook.Worksheets
      sht.Select
      i = ActiveSheet.Comments.Count
      For Each myNote In ActiveSheet.Comments
          If myNote.Author = strName Then
            MsgBox myNote.Text
            If colNotes.Count = 0 Then
              colNotes.Add Item:=myNote, key:="first"
            Else
              colNotes.Add Item:=myNote, Before:=1
            End If
        End If
      Next
      t = t + i
    Next
    If colNotes.Count <> 0 Then MsgBox colNotes("first").Text
      MsgBox "Total notes in workbook: " & t & Chr(13) & _
      "Total notes in collection: " & colNotes.Count
      Debug.Print "Notes by " & strName
    For Each myNote In colNotes
      Debug.Print Mid(myNote.Text, Len(myNote.Author) + 2, _
        Len(myNote.Text))
    Next
  End Sub
```

The foregoing procedure begins by declaring the custom collection object called colNotes. Next, the procedure prompts for an author's name and then loops through all the worksheets in the active workbook to locate this author's notes. Only notes entered by the specified author are added to the custom collection.It is important to note that we are working here with the note feature that is compatible with previous versions of Excel. To use the new comments feature using the Excel VBA you will need to declare myNote as CommentThreaded and make other changes in the procedure. Look for the example in the companion files.

The procedure assigns a key to the first note and then adds the remaining notes to the collection by placing them before the note that was added last (notice the use of the `before` argument). If the collection includes at least one note, the procedure displays a message box with the text of the note that was identified with the special `key` argument. Notice how the `key` argument is used in referencing an item in a collection. The procedure then prints the text of all the notes included in the collection to the Immediate window.

Text functions (`Mid` and `Len`) are used to get only the text of the note without the author's name. Next, the total number of notes in a workbook and the total number of notes in the custom collection are returned by the Count property.

6. Run the GetNotes procedure twice each time, supplying a different name of the author (your name and Joan Smith). Check the procedure results in the Immediate window.

Now let's modify the GetNotes procedure that you prepared in the previous Hands-On. At the end of the procedure, we'll display the contents of the items that are currently in the colNotes collection one by one and ask the user whether the item should be removed from the collection. If for any reason your name does not appear in the notes you entered after you've saved your workbook, enter Author for the name of the author. To resolve the issue of the author's name being sometimes removed from your notes, review the options available from File | Info. Choose Check for Issues next to the Inspect Workbook section and select Inspect Document to launch Document Inspector. Make sure that Comments are not selected.

Hands-On 8.4 Removing Items from the Custom ColNotes Collection

1. Add the following line to the declaration section of the GetNotes procedure:

```
Dim response As Integer
```

This statement declares the variable called `response`. You will use this variable to store the result of the `MsgBox` function.

2. Locate the following statement in the GetNotes procedure:

```
For Each myNote In colNotes
```

Precede the foregoing statement with the following line of code:

```
myID = 1
```

3. Locate the following statement in the GetNotes procedure:

```
Debug.Print Mid(myNote.Text, Len(myNote.Author) + 2, _
   Len(myNote.Text))
```

Enter the following block of instructions below that statement:

```
response = MsgBox("Remove this note?" & Chr(13) _
& Chr(13) & myNote.Text, vbYesNo + vbQuestion)
If response = 6 Then
    colNotes.Remove Index:=myID
End If
```

4. Enter the following statements at the end of the procedure before the `End Sub` keywords:

```
Debug.Print "These notes remain in the collection:"
For Each myNote in colNotes
    Debug.Print Mid(myNote.Text, Len(myNote.Author) + 2, _
             Len(myNote.Text))
Next
```

The revised GetNotes procedure, named GetNotes2, is shown here. The procedure removes the specified notes from the custom collection. It does not delete the notes from the worksheets.

```
Sub GetNotes2()
  Dim sht As Worksheet
  Dim colNotes As New Collection
  Dim myNote As Comment
  Dim i As Integer
  Dim t As Integer
  Dim strName As String
  Dim response As Integer

  strName = InputBox("Enter author's name:")
  For Each sht In ThisWorkbook.Worksheets
    sht.Select
    i = ActiveSheet.Comments.Count
            For Each myNote In ActiveSheet.Comments
      If myNote.Author = strName Then
        MsgBox myNote.Text
        If colNotes.Count = 0 Then
          colNotes.Add Item:=myNote, key:="first"
        Else
          colNotes.Add Item:=myNote, Before:=1
        End If
      End If
    Next
    t = t + i
  Next
```

```
    If colNotes.Count <> 0 Then MsgBox colNotes("first").Text

       MsgBox "Total notes in workbook: " & t & Chr(13) & _
       "Total notes in collection:" & colNotes.Count
       Debug.Print "Notes by " & strName

       For Each myNote In colNotes
        Debug.Print Mid(myNote.Text, Len(myNote.Author) + 2, _
          Len(myNote.Text))
        response = MsgBox("Remove this note?" & Chr(13) _
          & Chr(13) & myNote.Text, vbYesNo + vbQuestion)
        If response = 6 Then
          colNotes.Remove index:=1
        End If
       Next

       MsgBox "Total notes in workbook: " & t & Chr(13) & _
       "Total notes in collection: " & colNotes.Count
       Debug.Print "These notes remain in the collection:"

       For Each myNote In colNotes
          Debug.Print Mid(myNote.Text, Len(myNote.Author) + 2, _
          Len(myNote.Text))
       Next
  End Sub
```

5. Run the GetNotes2 procedure and remove one of the notes displayed in the message box.
6. To delete all notes from the workbook, run the following code:

```
Sub DeleteWorkbookNotes()
  Dim myComment As Comment
  Dim sht As Worksheet

  For Each sht In ThisWorkbook.Worksheets
      For Each myComment In sht.Comments
          myComment.Delete
      Next
  Next
End Sub
```

COLLECTIONS VERSUS ARRAYS

As you have seen so far, both collections and arrays provide a very convenient way for storing and manipulating groups of similar items. Most people find collections easier to use and master than arrays. However, before you decide which grouping structure you should use for storing items in your program, examine your needs. Arrays are usually faster and more convenient to use if you know ahead of time the number of items you are going to store. If the number of elements varies and you often need to add and remove elements, collections may be more efficient to use.

Let's do some feature comparison: collections versus arrays.

- Custom collections you create use 1 by default as a first element. Arrays by default are zero-based. You need to use the `Option Base 1` statement to force the numbering of array items to start at position 1.
- You don't need to specify the size of your collection upfront as collections are dynamically allocated. Arrays, on the other hand, require that you define their size and if you need to change the array size further in your procedure you must use the `ReDim` keyword. Each time you re-dimension the array, Access takes up more resources.
- It's very easy to add or remove items from the collection with the `Add` and `Remove` methods. With arrays, before you can add or remove items, you need to find the size of the array by using its upper and lower bounds.
- You can add new items to a collection in any position. To perform the same task using arrays you must write more code.
- Collections can store items of different data types. Arrays can only store items of different data types when they are declared as a Variant.
- You can use the For and For Each loop to access items in a collection while with arrays you must first set and verify the upper and lower bounds to iterate through the items.
- Collections allow you to use Keys to access a particular item directly, while arrays don't provide this feature.

WATCHING THE EXECUTION OF YOUR VBA PROCEDURES

To help you understand what's going on when your code runs and how one procedure passes information to a function and receives back function result, let's walk through the ShowCollItems procedure you created in Hands-On 8.2. Treat this exercise as a brief introduction to the debugging techniques that are covered in detail in the next chapter.

Hands-On 8.5 Code Walkthrough

1. In the VBE Editor screen locate the ShowCollItems procedure.
2. Set a breakpoint by clicking in the left margin next to the following line of code, as shown in Figure 8.1:

```
If AskForItems <> "" Then
```

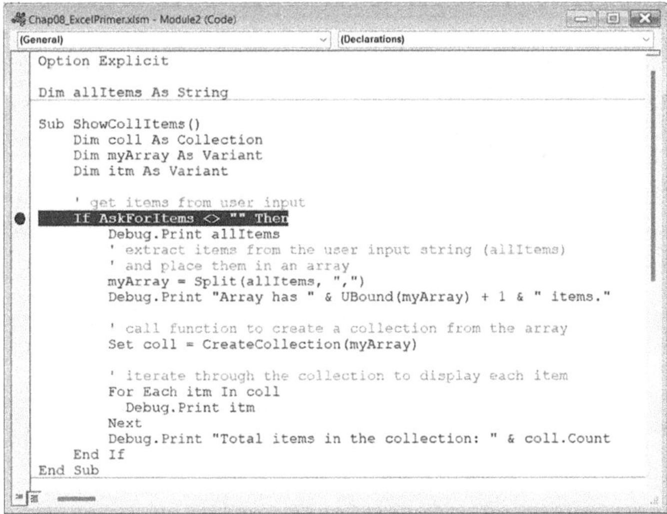

FIGURE 8.1 A red circle in the margin indicates a breakpoint. The statement with a breakpoint is displayed as white text on a red background.

3. Choose **View | Immediate window** and position the window next to the procedure as shown in Figure 8.2.
4. Click anywhere within the code of the ShowCollItems procedure and press **F5** or choose **Run | Run Sub/User Form**.

   Visual Basic should now jump to the line where you set a breakpoint (see Figure 8.2).

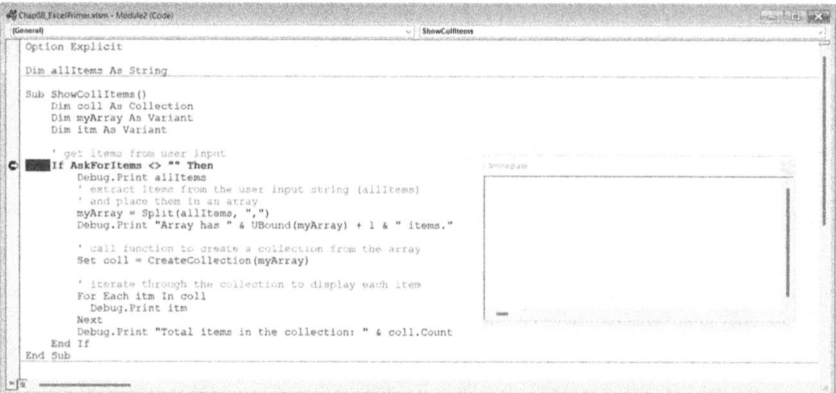

FIGURE 8.2 When Visual Basic encounters a breakpoint while running a procedure, it switches to the Code window and displays a yellow arrow in the margin to the left of the statement at which the procedure is suspended.

5. Step through the code one statement at a time by pressing **F8**.
   Visual Basic runs the current statement which in this case is a call to the AskForItems function procedure. The yellow highlight moves to the line with the name of this function as shown in Figure 8.3.

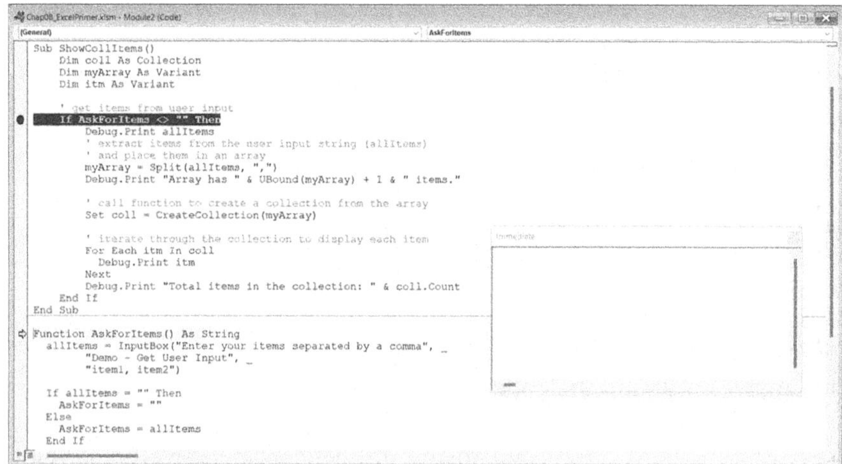

FIGURE 8.3 When you press the F8 key you activate a step mode when each press of the key jumps to the next line of code, allowing you to step through the procedure.

6. Press **F8** again and the highlight should move to the first line of the function procedure. Press **F8** again to execute this line.
   You should now be presented with the Input box where you need to enter the

items you want to include in the array (see Figure 8.4).

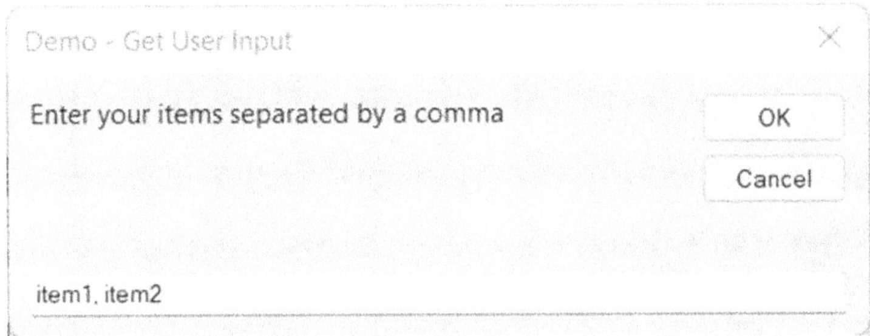

FIGURE 8.4 The Function procedure asks for items separated by a comma. These items will be used to fill an array variable.

7. Enter four names of your best friends or family members or any items you want separated by a comma and click **OK**. Clicking Cancel will terminate the procedure.
   When you click OK you should see the Immediate window filled with the data you entered (see Figure 8.5). All Debug statements in your procedures wrote results to the Immediate window while the code was executing.

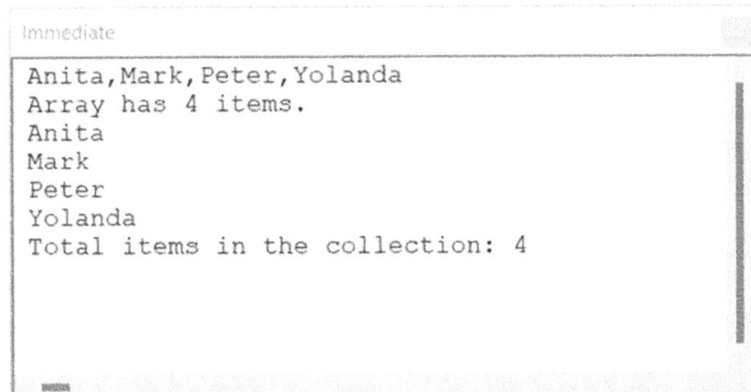

FIGURE 8.5 The Immediate Window is populated with the data generated by the Debug Print statements.

This was a quick run through the VBA procedure. To go slower and gain more understanding of what's happening in the code, you need to put in more breakpoints next to the lines where you would like Visual Basic to temporarily stop the code execution.

8. Erase all data in the Immediate window by clicking anywhere within it, then press **Ctrl+A**, and then **Delete**.
   Let's add more breakpoints and execute the procedure again.

9. Add the breakpoints as shown in Figure 8.6.

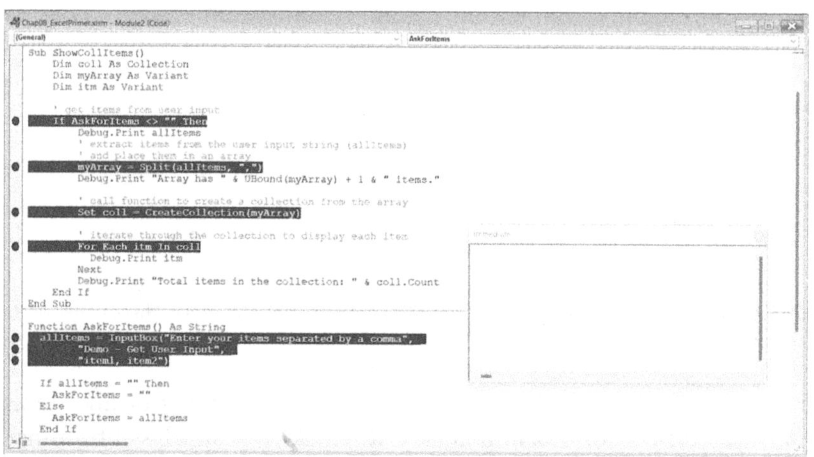

FIGURE 8.6 Adding multiple breakpoints on important lines in VBA procedures allows you to better troubleshoot your own or someone else's code.

10. Position the cursor within the ShowCollItems procedure and press F5. Keep pressing F5 to quickly execute the code between the set breakpoints. At any time when you need to step line by line, press the F8 key. While your procedure execution is in the break mode with the yellow highlight on some code statement, you can use the Immediate window to find out the contents of your variables or issue other commands that will allow you to check the returned values. For example, after you type entries in the dialog box, you can find the contents of the `allItems` variable by typing `?allItems` in the Immediate window and pressing Enter.

11. Keep pressing **F8** to execute the function procedure step by step. The yellow highlight should eventually move to the line that tells Visual Basic to return the `allItems` variable from this function:

```
AskForItems = allItems
```

12. Press **F8** until the execution moves to the ShowAllItems procedure. Press **F8** and you should see the output of the **`Debug.Print allItems`** statement in the Immediate window.

13. Press **F8** again when the yellow highlight reaches the line that uses the `Split` function to extract items from the `allItems` string variable into the `myArray` varriable:

```
myArray = Split(allItems, ",")
```

14. Press **F8** to fill the `myArray` variable.
15. Find the first element of the `myArray` variable by typing the following in the Immediate window and pressing Enter:

    ```
    ?myArray(0)
    ```

    You should see the first item you entered.
16. Continue pressing the **F8** key and examining each line of code until the execution moves to the CreateCollection function procedure.
17. Press **F8** again to move to the For Next loop within the CreateCollection procedure. Let's use the Immediate Window to find out what was passed to this function.
18. In the Immediate Window, type **`?Ubound(arrMyItems)`** and press **Enter**. You should see the count of the total items you entered. Recall that arrays are zero based by default so the actual count is **`?Ubound(arrMyItems) + 1`**.
19. Press **F8** until you are out of the loop that adds individual array items to the coll object variable.
20. When you reach the last statement of the CreateCollection procedure (**`Set CreateCollection = coll`**), type **`?coll.count`** to return the total number of items in your collection.
21. Press **F8** to pass the collection back to the calling procedure (**ShowAllItems**) and exit the function by pressing **F8** again.
    Now you should be positioned on the next statement in the ShowAllItems procedure. This statement will loop through the collection as you continue pressing **F8**. All collection items and the total count will be written to the Immediate window.
22. Press F8 until you reach the end of the procedure. The code execution will stop. You can repeat this entire walkthrough again for more practice before we clear the breakpoints in the next step.
23. Select **Debug | Clear All Breakpoints**.
24. Choose **File | Save** to save the changes in the workbook.
25. Choose **File | Close and Return to Microsoft Excel**.
26. Close the Chap08_ExcelPrimer.xlsm workbook.

SIDEBAR ***VBA Debugging Tools***

Visual Basic provides many debugging tools to help you analyze how your application operates, as well as to locate the source of errors in your procedures. See the next chapter for details on working with these tools.

SUMMARY

This chapter walked you through the process of building your own custom collection object that can be used to track and manipulate data in your VBA program. You also learned how to build an array and convert it into a collection. After making some comparisons between collections and arrays you learned how to analyze your VBA procedures by stepping through the programming code. As your procedures become more complex, you will need to start using special tools for tracing errors, which are covered in the next chapter.

Chapter 9

EXCEL TOOLS FOR TESTING AND DEBUGGING

A QUICK INTRODUCTION TO TESTING VBA PROGRAMS

It does not take much for an error to creep into your VBA procedure. The truth is that no matter how careful you are, it is rare that all your VBA procedures will work correctly the first time. There are three types of errors in VBA: syntax errors, logic errors, and runtime errors. This chapter introduces you to the Visual Basic Editor tools that are available for you to use in the process of analyzing the code of your VBA procedures and locating the source of errors.

TESTING VBA PROCEDURES

Because most of the procedures we wrote earlier were quite short, finding errors wasn't very difficult. However, locating the source of errors in longer and more complex procedures is more tedious and time-consuming. Fortunately, Visual Basic Editor provides a set of handy tools that can make the process of tracking down your VBA problems easier, faster, and less frustrating. Bugs are errors in computer programs. Debugging is the process of locating and fixing those errors by stepping through the code of your procedure or checking the values of variables.

When testing your VBA procedure, use the following guidelines:

- To analyze your procedure, step through your code one line at a time by pressing F8 or choose Debug | Step Into.
- To locate an error in a specific place in your procedure, use a breakpoint.

- To monitor the value of a variable or expression used by your procedure, add a watch expression.
- To get to sections of code that interest you, set up a bookmark to jump quickly to the desired location.

Each of these guidelines is demonstrated in a hands-on scenario in this chapter.

STOPPING A PROCEDURE

While testing your VBA procedure you may want to halt its execution. This can be done simply by pressing the Esc key, which causes Visual Basic to stop your program and display the message shown in Figure 9.1. VBA also offers other methods of stopping your procedure. When you stop your procedure, you enter what is called a break mode.

To enter break mode, do one of the following:

- Press the Ctrl+Break key combination
- Set one or more breakpoints
- Insert the Stop statement into your procedure code
- Add a watch expression

A break occurs when the execution of your VBA procedure is suspended. Visual Basic remembers the values of all variables and the statement from which the execution of the procedure should resume when the user decides to continue by clicking Run Sub/UserForm on the toolbar (or the Run menu option with the same name), or by clicking the Continue button in the dialog box. The error dialog box shown in Figure 9.1 informs you that the procedure was halted. The buttons in this dialog are described in Table 9.1.

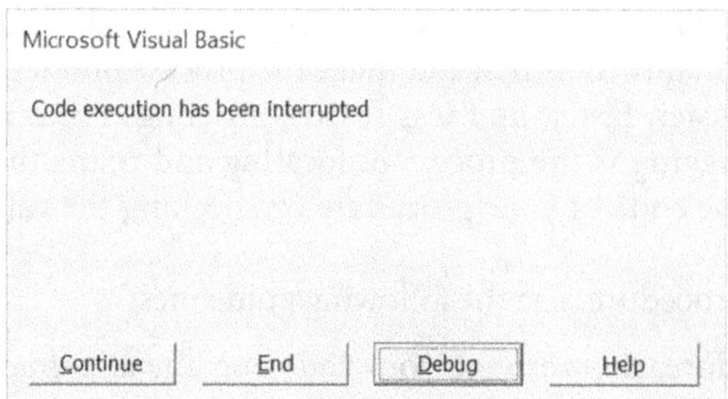

FIGURE 9.1 This message appears when you press Esc or Ctrl+Break while your VBA procedure is running.

TABLE 9.1 Error dialog buttons.

`Continue`	Click this button to resume code execution. This button will be grayed out if an error was encountered.
`End`	Click this button if you do not want to troubleshoot the procedure at this time. VBA will stop code execution.
`Debug`	Click this button to enter break mode. The Code window will appear, and VBA will highlight the line at which the procedure execution was suspended. You can examine, debug, reset, or step through the code.
`Help`	Click this button to view the online help that explains the cause of this error message.

You can prevent application users from halting your procedure by including the following statement in the procedure code:

```
Application.EnableCancelKey = xlDisabled
```

When the user presses Esc or Ctrl+Break while the procedure is running, nothing happens. The Application object's EnableCancelKey property disables these keys.

USING BREAKPOINTS

If you know more or less where you can expect a problem in the code of your procedure, suspend code execution on a given line by pressing F9 to set a breakpoint on that line. When VBA gets to that line while running your procedure, it will immediately display the Code window. At this point, you can step through the procedure code line by line by pressing F8 or choosing Debug | Step Into. To see how this works, let's look at the following scenario. Assume that during the execution of the ChangeCode procedure in Hands-On 9.1, the following line of code could get you in trouble:

```
ActiveCell.FormulaR1C1 "=VLOOKUP(RC[1],Codes.xlsx!R1C1:R6C2,2)"
```

NOTE	*Please note files for the "Hands-On" project may be found in the companion files.*

Hands-On 9.1 Setting Breakpoints in a VBA Procedure

1. Copy the **Chap09_ExcelPrimer.xlsm** and **Codes.xlsx** workbooks from the companion files to your **C:\VBAPrimerExcel2021_ByExample** folder.
2. Start Microsoft Excel and open both these files (**Chap09_ExcelPrimer.xlsm**, **Codes.xlsx**) from the **C:\VBAPrimerExcel2021_ByExample** folder.

3. Examine the data in both workbooks. It should look like Figures 9.2 and 9.3.

	A	B	C	D
1	Teacher	Position	Amount	Code
2	Ann Marie Smith	A	6500	227.163-23-220
3	Barbara Kaufman	A	6500	227.163-14-100
4	John Frederick	A	6500	211.163-23-330
5	Katherine Stein	B	6300	211.163-23-330
6	Christine Martin	B	6300	211.163-23-330
7	Mark O'Brian	B	6300	211.163-23-220
8	Jorge Rodriguez	B	6300	227.163-11-100
9				

FIGURE 9.2 The data entered in column D of this worksheet will be used to look up the equivalent code from the column B in Codes.xlsx workbook (see Figure 9.3).

4. Close the **Codes.xlsx** workbook. Leave the other file open.
5. With Chap09_ExcelPrimer.xlsm active, switch to the Visual Basic Editor window.
6. In the Project Explorer, open the Modules folder in the **Debugging (Chap09_ExcelPrimer.xlsm)** project and double-click the **Breaks** module.
   The Breaks Module Code window lists the following `ChangeCode` procedure:

	A	B	C
1	211.163-23-220	65	
2	211.163-23-330	73	
3	211.163-28-330	78	
4	227.163-11-100	67	
5	227.163-14-100	62	
6	227.163-23-220	66	
7			
8			
9			

Sheet1

FIGURE 9.3 The ChangeCode procedure uses this code table for lookup purposes.

```
Sub ChangeCode()
    Workbooks.Open  Filename:="C:\VBAPrimerExcel2021_ByExample\
Codes.xlsx"
  Windows("Chap09_ExcelPrimer.xlsm").Activate
  Columns("D:D").Insert Shift:=xlToRight
  Range("D1").Formula = "Simple Code"
  Columns("D:D").SpecialCells(xlBlanks).Select
  ActiveCell.FormulaR1C1 = "=VLookup(RC[1],Codes.
xlsx!R1C1:R6C2,2)"
  Selection.FillDown
```

```
    With Columns("D:D")
      .EntireColumn.AutoFit
      .Select
    End With
  Selection.Copy
  Selection.PasteSpecial Paste:=xlValues
  Rows("1:1").Select
    With Selection
      .HorizontalAlignment = xlCenter
      .VerticalAlignment = xlBottom
      .Orientation = xlHorizontal
    End With
  Workbooks("Codes.xlsx").Close
End Sub
```

7. In the `ChangeCode` procedure, click anywhere on the line containing the following statement:

```
ActiveCell.FormulaR1C1 = "=VLookup(RC[1],Codes.
xlsx!R1C1:R6C2,2)"
```

8. Set a breakpoint by pressing **F9** (or choosing **Debug | Toggle Breakpoint** or clicking in the margin indicator to the left of the line).
   When you set the breakpoint, Visual Basic displays a red circle in the margin. At the same time, the line that has the breakpoint is indicated as white text on a red background as in Figure 9.4. The color of the breakpoint can be changed on the Editor Format tab in the Options dialog box (Tools menu).

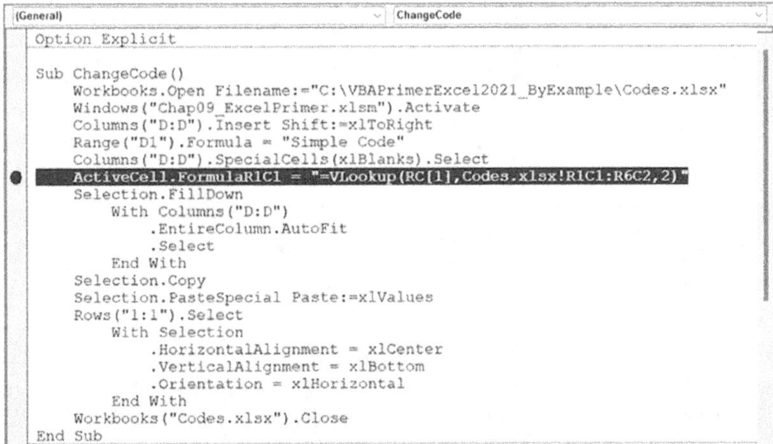

FIGURE 9.4 The line of code where the breakpoint is set is displayed in the color specified on the Editor Format tab in the Options dialog box.

9. Press **F5** to run the ChangeCode procedure.
   When you run the procedure, Visual Basic will execute all the statements until it encounters the breakpoint. Figure 9.5 shows the yellow arrow in the margin to the left of the statement at which the procedure was suspended, and the statement inside a box with a yellow background. The arrow and the box indicate the current statement or the statement that is about to be executed. If the current statement also contains a breakpoint, the margin displays both indicators overlapping one another (the circle and the arrow).

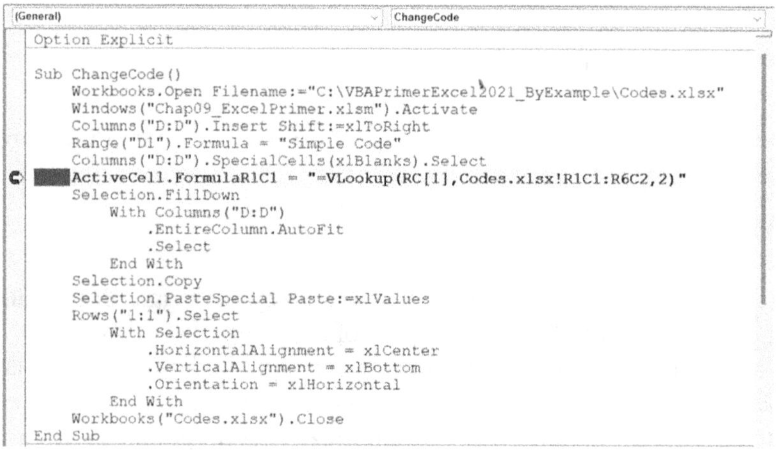

```
(General)                                    ChangeCode
Option Explicit

Sub ChangeCode()
    Workbooks.Open Filename:="C:\VBAPrimerExcel2021_ByExample\Codes.xlsx"
    Windows("Chap09_ExcelPrimer.xlsm").Activate
    Columns("D:D").Insert Shift:=xlToRight
    Range("D1").Formula = "Simple Code"
    Columns("D:D").SpecialCells(xlBlanks).Select
    ActiveCell.FormulaR1C1 = "=VLookup(RC[1],Codes.xlsx!R1C1:R6C2,2)"
    Selection.FillDown
        With Columns("D:D")
            .EntireColumn.AutoFit
            .Select
        End With
    Selection.Copy
    Selection.PasteSpecial Paste:=xlValues
    Rows("1:1").Select
        With Selection
            .HorizontalAlignment = xlCenter
            .VerticalAlignment = xlBottom
            .Orientation = xlHorizontal
        End With
    Workbooks("Codes.xlsx").Close
End Sub
```

FIGURE 9.5 When Visual Basic encounters a breakpoint, it displays the Code window and indicates the current statement.

While in break mode, you can change code, add new statements, execute the procedure one line at a time, skip lines, set the next statement, use the Immediate window, and more. When Visual Basic is in break mode, all the options on the Debug menu are available. If you change certain code while you work in break mode, VBA will prompt you to reset the project by displaying the following error message: "*This action will reset your project, proceed anyway?*" You can click OK to stop the program's execution and proceed editing your code or click Cancel to delete the new changes and continue running the code from the point at which it was suspended.

10. Press **F5** (or choose **Run Sub/UserForm**) to continue running the procedure.
    Visual Basic leaves break mode and continues to run the procedure statements until it reaches the end of the procedure. When the procedure finishes executing, Visual Basic does not automatically remove the breakpoint. Notice that the line of code with the `VLookup` function is still highlighted in red.

In this example you have set only one breakpoint. Visual Basic allows you to set any number of breakpoints in a procedure. This way, you can suspend and continue the execution of your procedure as you please. You can analyze the code of your procedure and check the values of variables while execution is suspended. You can also perform various tests by typing statements in the Immediate window.

11. Remove the breakpoint by choosing **Debug | Clear All Breakpoints** or by pressing **Ctrl+Shift+F9** or by clicking on the red circle in the margin area to remove the breakpoint.
    All the breakpoints are removed. If you had set several breakpoints in a given procedure and would like to remove only one or some of them, click on the line containing the breakpoint that you want to remove and press F9 (or choose Debug | Clear Breakpoint or simply click the red dot in the margin). You should clear the breakpoints when they are no longer needed. The breakpoints are automatically removed when you close the file.
12. Switch to the Microsoft Excel application window and notice that a new column with the looked-up codes, like the one in Figure 9.6, was added on Sheet1 of the Chap09_ExcelPrimer.xlsm workbook.

	A	B	C	D	E
1	Teacher	Position	Amount	Simple Code	Code
2	Ann Marie Smith	A	6500	66	227.163-23-220
3	Barbara Kaufman	A	6500	62	227.163-14-100
4	John Frederick	A	6500	73	211.163-23-330
5	Katherine Stein	B	6300	73	211.163-23-330
6	Christine Martin	B	6300	73	211.163-23-330
7	Mark O'Brian	B	6300	65	211.163-23-220
8	Jorge Rodriguez	B	6300	67	227.163-11-100
9					

FIGURE 9.6 This worksheet was modified by the ChangeCode procedure in Hands-On 9.1.

When to Use a Breakpoint

Consider setting a breakpoint if you suspect that your procedure never executes a certain block of code.

In break mode, you can quickly find out the contents of the variable at the cursor in the Code window by holding the mouse pointer over it. For example, in the VarValue procedure shown in Figure 9.7, the breakpoint has been set on the `Workbooks.Add` statement. When Visual Basic encounters this statement, the Code window (break mode) appears. Because Visual Basic has already executed the statement that stores the name of ActiveWorkbook in the variable `strName`, you can quickly find out the value of this variable by resting the mouse pointer over its name. The name of the variable and its current value appear in a tooltip frame.

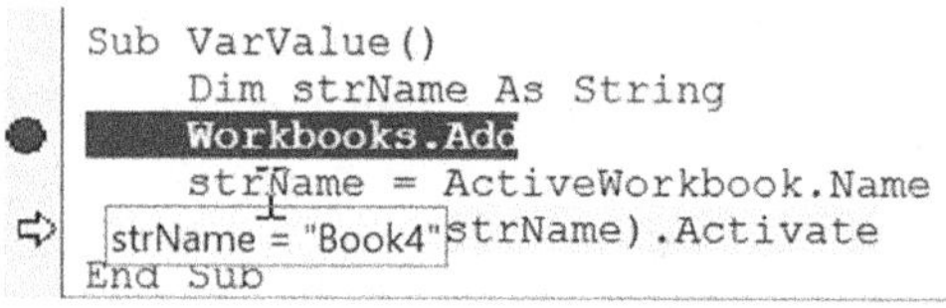

```
Sub VarValue()
    Dim strName As String
    Workbooks.Add
    strName = ActiveWorkbook.Name
 strName = "Book4" strName).Activate
End Sub
```

FIGURE 9.7 In break mode, you can find out the value of a variable by resting the mouse pointer on that variable.

NOTE	*To show the values of several variables used in a procedure at once, you should use the Locals window, which is discussed later in this chapter.*

USING THE IMMEDIATE WINDOW IN BREAK MODE

Once the procedure execution is suspended and the Code window appears, you can activate the Immediate window and type VBA instructions to find out, for instance, which cell is currently active or the name of the active sheet. You can also use the Immediate window to change the contents of variables in order to correct values that may be causing errors.

Figure 9.8 shows the suspended ChangeCode procedure and the Immediate window with the questions that were asked of Visual Basic while in break mode.

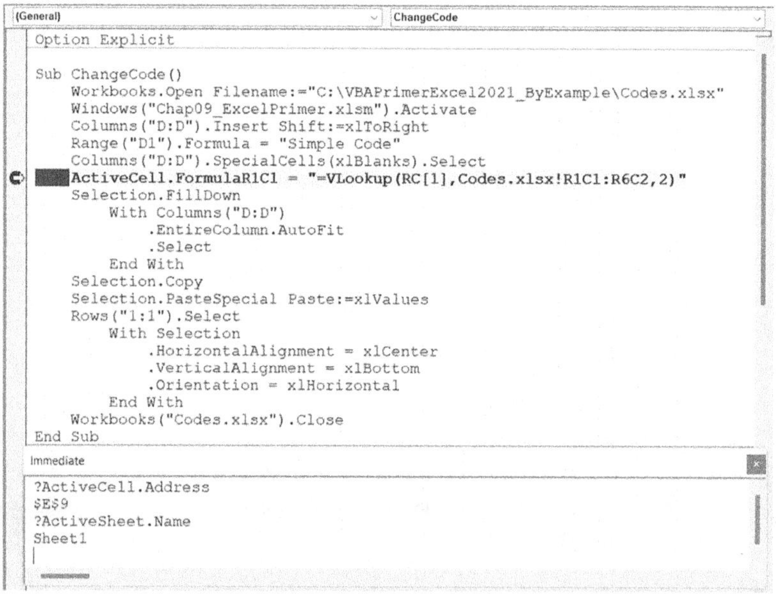

```
(General)                                    ChangeCode
Option Explicit

Sub ChangeCode()
    Workbooks.Open Filename:="C:\VBAPrimerExcel2021_ByExample\Codes.xlsx"
    Windows("Chap09_ExcelPrimer.xlsm").Activate
    Columns("D:D").Insert Shift:=xlToRight
    Range("D1").Formula = "Simple Code"
    Columns("D:D").SpecialCells(xlBlanks).Select
    ActiveCell.FormulaR1C1 = "=VLookup(RC[1],Codes.xlsx!R1C1:R6C2,2)"
    Selection.FillDown
        With Columns("D:D")
            .EntireColumn.AutoFit
            .Select
        End With
    Selection.Copy
    Selection.PasteSpecial Paste:=xlValues
    Rows("1:1").Select
        With Selection
            .HorizontalAlignment = xlCenter
            .VerticalAlignment = xlBottom
            .Orientation = xlHorizontal
        End With
    Workbooks("Codes.xlsx").Close
End Sub
Immediate
?ActiveCell.Address
$E$9
?ActiveSheet.Name
Sheet1
```

FIGURE 9.8 When the code execution is suspended, you can find the values of your variables and execute additional commands by entering appropriate statements in the Immediate window.

USING THE STOP AND ASSERT STATEMENTS

Sometimes you won't be able to test your procedure right away. If you set up your breakpoints and then close the file, Excel will remove your breakpoints, and the next time you are ready to test your procedure, you'll have to begin by setting up breakpoints again. To postpone the task of testing your procedure until you reopen the file, insert a `Stop` statement into your code wherever you want to halt a procedure. Figure 9.9 shows a `Stop` statement before the `For Each...Next` loop. Visual Basic will suspend the execution of the StopExample procedure when it encounters the `Stop` statement. The screen will display the Code window in break mode.

```
(General)                                    StopExample
Sub StopExample()
    Dim curCell As Range
    Dim num As Integer

    ActiveWorkbook.Sheets(1).Select
    ActiveSheet.UsedRange.Select
    num = Selection.Columns.Count
    Selection.Resize(1, num).Select
    Stop
    For Each curCell In Selection
        Debug.Print curCell.Text
    Next
End Sub
```

FIGURE 9.9 You can insert a Stop statement anywhere in the code of your VBA procedure. The procedure will halt when it gets to the Stop statement, and the Code window will appear with the line highlighted.

Although the `Stop` statement has the same effect as setting a breakpoint, it has one disadvantage—all `Stop` statements stay in the procedure until you remove them. When you no longer need to stop your procedure, you must locate and remove all the `Stop` statements.

A very powerful and easy-to-apply debugging technique is utilizing `Debug.Assert` statements. Assertions allow you to write code that checks itself while running. By including assertions in your programming code, you can verify that a particular condition or assumption is true. Assertions give you immediate feedback when an error occurs. They are great for detecting logic errors early in the development phase instead of hearing about them later from your end users. The fact that your procedure ran on your system without generating an error does not mean that there are no bugs in that procedure. Don't assume anything—always test for validity of expressions and variables in your code. The `Debug.Assert` statement takes any expression that evaluates to True or False and activates the break mode when that expression evaluates to False. The syntax for `Debug.Assert` is shown here:

```
Debug.Assert condition
```

where `condition` is a VBA code or expression that returns True or False. If `condition` evaluates to False or 0 (zero), VBA will enter break mode. For example, when running the following looping structure, the code will stop executing when the variable `i` equals 50:

```
Sub TestDebugAssert()
  Dim i As Integer

  For i = 1 To 100
    Debug.Assert i <> 50
  Next
End Sub
```

Keep in mind that `Debug.Assert` does nothing if the condition is False or zero. The execution simply stops on that line of code and the VBE screen opens with the line containing the false statement highlighted so that you can start debugging your code. You may need to write an error handler to handle the identified error. Error-handling procedures are discussed later in this chapter.

While you can stop the code execution by using the `Stop` statement (see the previous section), `Debug.Assert` differs from the `Stop` statement in its conditional aspect; it will stop your code only under specific conditions. Conditional breakpoints can also be set by using the Watch window (see the next section).

After you have debugged and tested your code, comment out or remove the `Debug.Assert` statements from your final code. The easiest way to do this is to use Edit | Replace in the VBE editor screen. To comment out the statements, enter Debug.Assert in the Find What box. In the Replace With box, enter an apostrophe followed by Debug.Assert.

To remove the `Debug.Assert` statements from your code, enter `Debug.Assert` in the Find What box. Leave the Replace With box empty but be sure to mark the Use Pattern Matching check box.

USING THE WATCH WINDOW

Many errors in procedures are caused by variables that assume unexpected values. If a procedure uses a variable whose value changes in various locations, you may want to stop the procedure and check the current value of that variable.

Visual Basic offers a special Watch window that allows you to keep an eye on variables or expressions while your procedure is running.

To add a watch expression to your procedure, perform the following:

- In the Code window, select the variable whose value you want to monitor.
- Choose **Debug | Add Watch.**

The screen will display the Add Watch dialog box, as shown in Figure 9.10. The Add Watch dialog box contains three sections, which are described in Table 9.2.

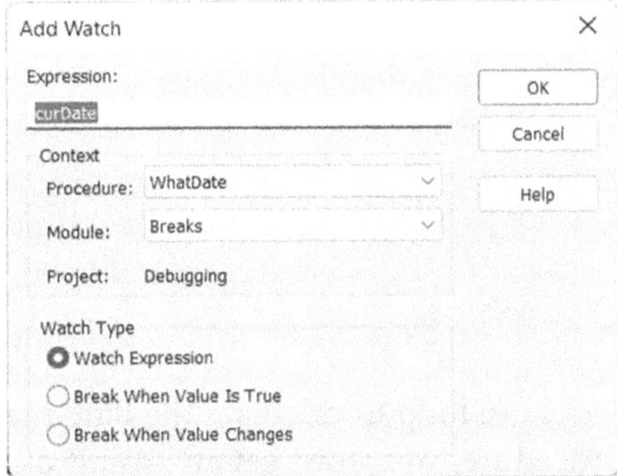

FIGURE 9.10 The Add Watch dialog box allows you to define conditions that you want to monitor while a VBA procedure is running.

TABLE 9.2 Add Watch dialog options.

`Expression`	Displays the name of a variable that you have highlighted in your procedure. If you opened the Add Watch dialog box without selecting a variable name, type the name of the variable you want to monitor in the Expression text box.
`Context`	In this section you should indicate the name of the procedure that contains the variable and the name of the module where this procedure is located.
`Watch Type`	Specifies how to monitor the variable. If you choose the Watch Expression option button, you will be able to read the value of the variable in the Watch window while in break mode. If you choose Break When Value Is True, Visual Basic will automatically stop the procedure when the variable evaluates to true (nonzero). The last option button, Break When Value Changes, stops the procedure each time the value of the variable or expression changes.

You can add a watch expression before running a procedure or after execution of your procedure has been suspended. The difference between a breakpoint and a watch expression is the breakpoint always stops a procedure in a specified location and the watch stops the procedure only when the specified condition (Break When Value Is True or Break When Value Changes) is met. Watches are extremely useful when you are not sure where the variable is being changed. Instead of stepping through many lines of code to find the location where the variable assumes the specified value, you can simply put a watch expression on the variable and run your procedure as normal. Let's see how this works.

Hands-On 9.2 Watching the Values of VBA Expressions

1. The Breaks Module Code window lists the following WhatDate procedure:

```
Sub WhatDate()
  Dim curDate As Date
  Dim newDate As Date
  Dim x As Integer

  curDate = Date
  For x = 1 To 365
    newDate = Date + x
  Next
End Sub
```

   The WhatDate procedure uses the `For...Next` loop to calculate the date that is `x` days in the future. If you run this procedure, you won't get any result unless you insert the following instruction in the code of the procedure:

```
MsgBox "In " & x & " days, it will be " & NewDate
```

2. In this example, however, you don't care to display the individual dates, day after day. What if all you want to do is to stop the program when the value of the variable `x` reaches 211? In other words, what date will be 211 days from now? To get the answer, you could insert the following statement into your procedure:

```
If x = 211 Then MsgBox "In " & x & " days it will be " & NewDate
```

   Introducing new statements into your procedure just to get an answer about the value of a certain variable when a specific condition occurs will not always be viable. Instead of adding `MsgBox` or other debug statements to your procedure code that you will later need to delete, you can use the Watch window and avoid extra code maintenance. If you add watch expressions to the procedure, Visual Basic will stop the `For...Next` loop when the specified condition is met, and you'll be able to check the values of the desired variables.

3. Choose **View | Watch Window**.
4. An empty Watches window should appear. This window is divided into four areas: Expression, Value, Type and Context. The Expression column

will list all the watch expressions that you'll set in this Hands-On. The Value column will list the value of the expression at the time of transition into break mode. The Type column will list the expression type and the Context column will list the context of the watch expression. Let's set a few watches for the WhatDate procedure.

5. Choose **Debug | Add Watch**.
6. In the Expression text box, enter the following expression: **x = 211**. In the Context section, choose **WhatDate** from the Procedure combo box and **Breaks** from the Module combo box. In the Watch Type section, select the **Break When Value Is True** option button.
7. Click **OK** to close the Add Watch dialog box. You have now added your first watch expression.
   Visual Basic places your expression x = 211 in the first line of the Watches window. Notice that the Value column will show <Out of context> entry. This entry will change as you run your procedure. Now let's add another expression to the Watch window for tracking the current date.
8. In the Code window, position the insertion point anywhere within the name of the `curDate` variable.
9. Choose **Debug | Add Watch** and click **OK** to set up the default watch type with Watch Expression.
   Notice that a new line is added to the Watches window with the curDate variable in the Expression column. Let's add another variable to the Watches window.
10. In the Code window, position the insertion point anywhere within the name of the `newDate` variable.
11. Choose **Debug | Add Watch** and click **OK** to set up the default watch type with Watch Expression.
    Notice that newDate now appears in the Expression column of the Watch window. After performing the foregoing steps, the WhatDate procedure contains the following three watches:

    x = 211—Break When Value is True
    curDate—Watch Expression
    newDate—Watch Expression
12. Position the insertion point anywhere inside the code of the WhatDate procedure, and press **F5**.
    Figure 9.11 shows the Watches window when Visual Basic stops the procedure when `x` equals 211.

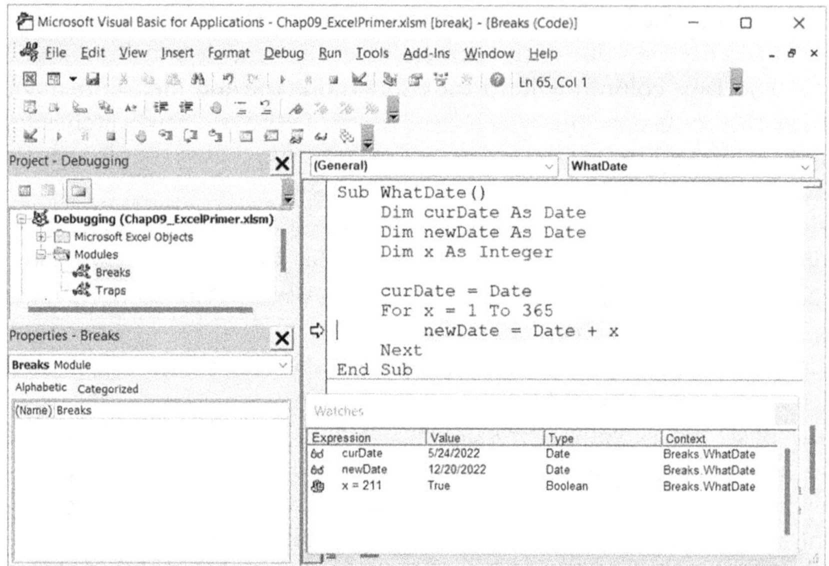

FIGURE 9.11 Using the Watches window.

Notice that the value of the variable `x` in the Watch window is the same as the value that you specified in the Add Watch dialog. In addition, the Watch window shows the value of both variables—`curDate` and `newDate`. The procedure is in break mode. You can press F5 to continue or you can ask another question, such as "What date will be in 277 days?" The next step shows how to do this.

13. Choose **Debug | Edit Watch** and enter the following expression: **x = 277**.
14. Click **OK** to close the Edit Watch dialog box.
    Notice that the Watch window now displays a new value for the expression. `x` is now False.
15. Press **F5** to continue running the procedure.
    The procedure stops again when the value of `x` equals 277. The value of `curDate` is the same; however, the `newDate` variable now contains a new value—a date that is 277 days from now. You can change the value of the expression again or finish running the procedure.
16. Press **F5** to finish running the procedure.
    When your procedure is running and a watch expression has a value, the Watch window displays the value of the watch expression. If you open the Watch window after the procedure has finished, you will see <out of context> instead of the variable values. In other words, when the watch expression is out of context, it does not have a value.

Removing Watch Expressions

To remove the watch expressions, click on the expression in the Watch window that you want to remove, and press Delete. You may now remove all the watch expressions you had defined in the preceding example.

USING QUICK WATCH

In break mode you can check the value of an expression for which you have not defined a watch expression by using the Quick Watch dialog box displayed in Figure 9.12.

FIGURE 9.12 The Quick Watch dialog box shows the value of the selected expression in a VBA procedure.

The Quick Watch dialog box can be accessed in the following ways:

- While in break mode, position the insertion point anywhere inside the name of a variable or expression you wish to watch.
- Choose Debug | Quick Watch.
- Press Shift+F9.

The Add button in the Quick Watch dialog box allows you to add the expression to the Watch window. Let's find out how to work with this dialog box.

Hands-On 9.3 Using the Quick Watch Dialog Box

1. Make sure that the WhatDate procedure you entered in the previous Hands-On exercise does not contain any watch expressions. See the section called "Removing Watch Expressions" for instructions on how to remove a watch expression from the Watch window.
2. In the WhatDate procedure, position the insertion point on the name of the variable x.
3. Choose **Debug | Add Watch.**

4. Enter the following expression: **x = 50**.
5. Choose the **Break When Value Is True** option button and click **OK**.
6. Run the WhatDate procedure.
   Visual Basic will suspend procedure execution when `x` equals 50. Notice that the Watch window does not contain the `newDate` or the `curDate` variables. To check the values of these variables, you can position the mouse pointer over the appropriate variable name in the Code window, or you can invoke the Quick Watch dialog box.
7. In the Code window, position the mouse pointer inside the `newDate` variable and press **Shift+F9**.
   The Quick Watch dialog shows the name of the expression and its current value.
8. Click **Cancel** to return to the Code window.
9. In the Code window, position the mouse pointer inside the `curDate` variable and press **Shift+F9**.
   The Quick Watch dialog now shows the value of the variable `curDate`.
10. Click **Cancel** to return to the Code window.
11. Press **F5** to continue running the procedure.
12. In the Watch window, highlight the line containing the expression x = 50 and press **Delete** to remove it.
13. Close the Watch window.

USING THE LOCALS WINDOWS AND THE CALL STACK DIALOG BOX

During the execution of a VBA procedure you can keep an eye on all the declared variables and their current values, by choosing View | Locals Window before you run the procedure. Figure 9.13 shows a list of variables and their corresponding values in the Locals window which is displayed while Visual Basic is in the break mode.

The Locals window contains three columns. The Expression column displays the names of variables that are declared in the current procedure. The first row displays the name of the module preceded by the plus sign. When you click the plus sign, you can check if any variables have been declared at the module level. For class modules, the system variable `Me` is defined. For standard modules, the first variable is the name of the current module. The global variables and variables in other projects are not accessible from the Locals window.

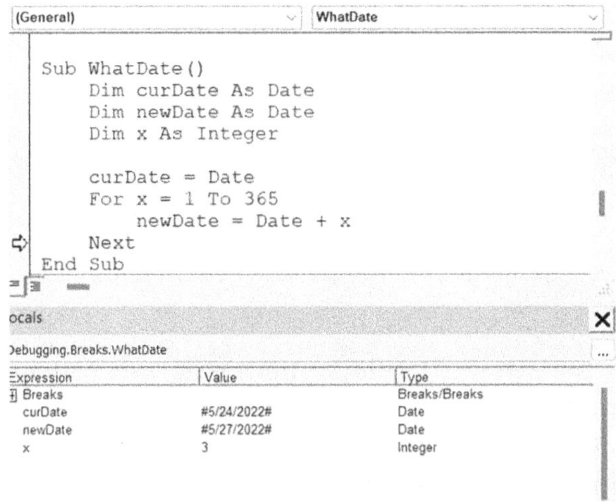

FIGURE 9.13 The Locals window displays the current values of all the declared variables in the current VBA procedure.

The second column shows the current values of variables. In this column, you can change the value of a variable by clicking it and typing the new value. After changing the value, press Enter to register the change. You can also press Tab, Shift+Tab, or the up or down arrows, or click anywhere within the Locals window after you've changed the variable value. The third column displays the type of each declared variable.

To observe the values of variables in the Locals window, perform the following Hands-On exercise.

Hands-On 9.4 Using the Locals and Call Stack Windows

1. Choose **View | Locals Window**.
2. Click anywhere inside the WhatDate procedure and press **F8**.
   By pressing F8, you place the procedure in break mode. The Locals window displays the name of the current module and the local variables and their beginning values.
3. Press **F8** a few more times while keeping an eye on the Locals window.
   The Locals window also contains a button with three dots. This button opens the Call Stack dialog box shown in Figure 9.14, which displays a list of all active procedure calls. An active procedure call is a procedure that is started but not completed. You can also activate the Call Stack dialog box by choosing **View | Call Stack**. This option is available only in break mode.

FIGURE 9.14 The Call Stack dialog box displays a list of the procedures that are started but not completed.

The Call Stack dialog box is especially helpful for tracing nested procedures. Recall that a nested procedure is a procedure that is being called from within another procedure. If a procedure calls another, the name of the called procedure is automatically added to the Calls list in the Call Stack dialog box. When Visual Basic has finished executing the statements of the called procedure, the procedure name is automatically removed from the Call Stack dialog box. You can use the Show button in the Call Stack dialog box to display the statement that calls the next procedure listed in the dialog box.

4. Press **F5** to continue running the WhatDate procedure.
5. Close the Locals window.

NAVIGATING WITH BOOKMARKS

In the process of analyzing or reviewing your VBA procedures, you will often find yourself jumping to certain areas of code. Using the built-in bookmark feature, you can easily mark the spots in your code that you want to navigate between.

To set up a bookmark:

- Click anywhere in the statement that you want to define as a bookmark.
- Choose **Edit | Bookmarks | Toggle Bookmark** or click the **Toggle Bookmark** button on the Edit toolbar as illustrated in Figure 9.15.
- Visual Basic will place a rounded blue rectangle in the left margin beside the statement.

Once you've set up two or more bookmarks, you can jump between the marked locations of your code by choosing Edit | Bookmarks | Next Bookmark or simply by clicking the Next Bookmark button on the Edit toolbar. You can remove bookmarks at any time by choosing Edit | Bookmarks | Clear All Bookmarks or by clicking the Clear All Bookmarks button on the Edit toolbar. To remove a single bookmark, click anywhere in the bookmarked statement and choose Edit | Bookmarks | Toggle Bookmark or click the Toggle Bookmark button on the Edit toolbar.

(General) ChangeCode

Edit

Toggle Bookmark

```
Option Explicit

Sub ChangeCode()
    Workbooks.Open Filename:="C:\V[illegible]cel2021_ByExample\Codes.xlsx"
    Windows("Chap09_ExcelPrimer.xl[illegible]ate
    Columns("D:D").Insert Shift:=xlToRight
    Range("D1").Formula = "Simple Code"
    Columns("D:D").SpecialCells(xlBlanks).Select
    ActiveCell.FormulaR1C1 = "=VLookup(RC[1],Codes.xlsx!R1C1:R6C2,2)"
    Selection.FillDown
        With Columns("D:D")
            .EntireColumn.AutoFit
            .Select
        End With
    Selection.Copy
    Selection.PasteSpecial Paste:=xlValues
    Rows("1:1").Select
        With Selection
            .HorizontalAlignment = xlCenter
            .VerticalAlignment = xlBottom
            .Orientation = xlHorizontal
        End With
    Workbooks("Codes.xlsx").Close
End Sub
```

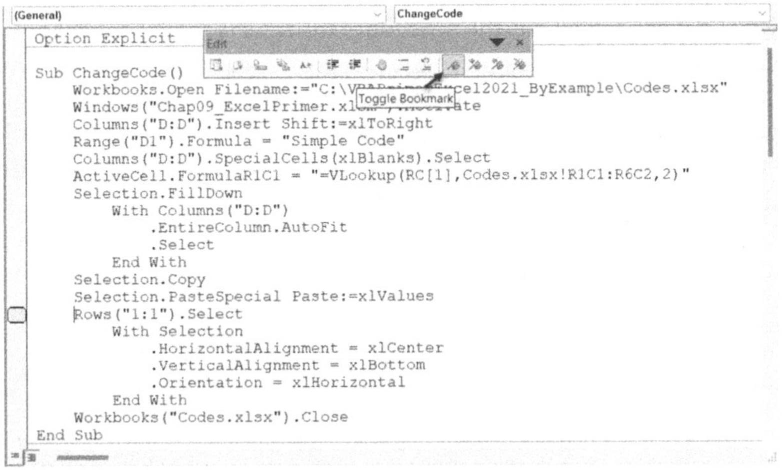

FIGURE 9.15 Using bookmarks you can quickly jump between often-used sections of your procedures.

TRAPPING ERRORS

No one writes bug-free programs the first time. When you create VBA procedures, you must determine how your program will respond to errors. Many unexpected errors happen during runtime. For example, your procedure may try to give a workbook the same name as an open workbook. Runtime errors are often discovered by users who attempt to do something that the programmer has not anticipated. If an error occurs when the procedure is running, Visual Basic displays an error message and the procedure is stopped. Most often, the error message that VBA displays is quite cryptic to the user. You can prevent users from seeing many runtime errors by including error-handling code in your VBA procedures. This way, when Visual Basic encounters an error, instead of displaying a default error message, it will show a much friendlier and more comprehensive error message.

In programming, mistakes and errors are not the same thing. A mistake, such as a misspelled or missing statement, a misplaced quote or comma, or assigning a value of one type to a variable of a different (and incompatible) type, can be removed from your program through proper testing and debugging. But even though your code may be free of mistakes, this does not mean that errors will not occur. An error is the result of an event or an operation that doesn't work as expected. For example, if your VBA procedure accesses a particular file on disk and someone has deleted this file or moved it to another location, you'll get an error no matter what. An error prevents the procedure from carrying out a specific task.

To implement error handling, place the `On Error` statement in your procedure. This statement tells VBA what to do if an error occurs while your program is running. VBA uses the `On Error` statement to activate an error-handling procedure that will trap runtime errors. Depending on the type of procedure, you can exit the error trap by using one of the following statements: `Exit Sub`, `Exit Function`, `Exit Property`, `End Sub`, `End Function`, or `End Property`. You should write an error-handling routine for each procedure. Table 9.3 shows how the `On Error` statement can be used.

TABLE 9.3 `On Error` statement options.

`On Error GoTo Label`	Specifies a label to jump to when an error occurs. This label marks the beginning of the error-handling routine. An error handler is a routine for trapping and responding to errors in your application. The label must appear in the same procedure as the `On Error` statement.
`On Error Resume Next`	When a runtime error occurs, Visual Basic ignores the line that caused the error, and does not display an error message but continues the procedure with the next line.
`On Error GoTo 0`	Turns off error trapping in a procedure. When VBA runs this statement, errors are detected but not trapped within the procedure.

Using the Err Object

Your error-handling code can utilize various properties and methods of the Err object. For example, to check which error occurred, check the value of Err.Number. The Number property of the Err object will tell you the value of the last error that occurred, and the Description property will return a description of the error. You can also find the name of the application that caused the error by using the Source property of the Err object (this is very helpful when your procedure launches other applications). After handling the error, use the `Err.Clear` statement to reset Err.Number back to zero.

To test your error-handling code you can use the `Raise` method of the Err object. For example, to raise the "Disk not ready" error, use the following statement:

```
Err.Raise 71
```

The OpenToRead procedure shown here demonstrates the use of the `Resume Next` and `Error` statements, as well as the `Err` object.

Hands-On 9.5 Writing a VBA Procedure with Error-Handling Code

1. Insert a new module into the Testing project and rename it **Traps**.
2. In the Traps module Code window, enter the Archive procedure as shown here:

```
Sub OpenToRead()
Dim myFile As String
Dim myChar As String
Dim myText As String
Dim FileExists As Boolean

FileExists = True

On Error GoTo ErrorHandler

myFile = InputBox("Enter the name of file to open:")
Open myFile For Input As #1
If FileExists Then
' loop until the end of file (EOF)
    Do While Not EOF(1)
      ' get one character
      myChar = Input(1, #1)
      ' store in the variable myText
      myText = myText + myChar
    Loop
    Debug.Print myText
    ' close the file
    Close #1
End If
Exit Sub

ErrorHandler:
  FileExists = False
  Select Case Err.Number
    Case 76
    MsgBox "The path you entered cannot be found."
    Case 53
    MsgBox "This file can't be found on the " & _"specified drive."
    Case 75
      Exit Sub
    Case Else
      MsgBox "Error " & Err.Number & " :" & _Error(Err.Number)
```

```
    Exit Sub
  End Select
  Resume Next
End Sub
```

The purpose of the OpenToRead procedure is to read the contents of the user-supplied text file character by character. When the user enters a filename, various errors can occur. For example, the filename or the path may be wrong, or the user may try to open a file that is already open. To trap these errors, the error-handling routine at the end of the OpenToRead procedure uses the Number property of the Err object.

There are several methods of reading a text file. In this example, to read data from a text file, the procedure uses the Windows Low-Level File I/O (Input / Output) method. Therefore, to open the file for reading, we need to use the `Open` statement, like this:

```
Open myFile For Input As #1
```

Here's the general syntax of the Open statement, followed by an explanation of each component:

```
Open pathname For mode[Access access][lock] As [#]filenumber
     [Len=reclength]
```

The `Open` statement has three required arguments: `pathname`, `mode`, and `filenumber`. `Pathname` is the name of the file you want to open. The filename may include the name of a drive and folder.

- `Mode` is a keyword that determines how the file was opened. Sequential files can be opened in one of the following modes: Input, Output, or Append. Use Input to read the file, Output to write to a file overwriting any existing file and Append to write to a file by adding to any existing information.
- The optional `Access` clause can be used to specify permissions for the file (Read, Write, or Read Write).
- The optional `Lock` argument determines which file operations are allowed for other processes. For example, if a file is open in a network environment, `lock` determines how other people can access it. The following `lock` keywords can be used: Shared, Lock Read, Lock Write, or Lock Read Write.
- `Filenumber` is a number from 1 to 511. This number is used to refer to the file in subsequent operations. You can obtain a unique file number using the Visual Basic built-in `FreeFile` function.

- The last element of the `Open` statement, `reclength`, specifies the buffer size (total number of characters) for sequential (text) files, or the record size for random-access files (text files where data is stored in records of equal length and fields separated by commas).

If the specified file exists, the procedure uses the `Do...While` loop to tell Visual Basic to execute the statements inside the loop until the end of the file has been reached. The end of the file is determined by the result of the `EOF` function. The `Input` function is used to return the specified number of characters:

```
myChar = Input(1, #1)
```

`#1` is the file number that was used in the process of opening the file with the `Open` statement.

Each character being read is stored in the `myChar` variable. Next, the `myChar` variable is appended to the `myText` variable, like this:

```
myText = myText + myChar
```

The procedure then writes the contents of the myText variable to the Immediate window using the Debug.Print statement. When the file has been read, we must close it using the Close statement:

```
Close #1    ' close the file
```

The Err object contains information about runtime errors. If an error occurs while the procedure is running, the statement `Err.Number` will return the error number. If errors 76, 53, or 75 occur, Visual Basic will display user-friendly messages stored inside the `Select...Case` block and then proceed to the `Resume Next` statement, which will send it to the line of code following the one that caused the error. If another error occurs, Visual Basic will return its error code (Err.Number) and error description (Error (Err.Number)). At the beginning of the procedure, the variable `FileExists` is set to True. This way, if the program doesn't encounter an error, all the instructions inside the `If FileExists Then` block will be executed. However, if VBA encounters an error, the value of the `FileExists` variable will be set to False (see the first statement in the error-handling routine just below the `ErrorHandler` label). This way, Visual Basic will not cause another error while trying to read a file that caused the error on opening. Notice the `Exit Sub` statement before the `ErrorHandler` label. Put the `Exit Sub` statement just above the error-handling routine because you don't want Visual Basic to carry out the error handling if there are no errors.

To test the OpenToRead procedure and better understand error trapping, we will need a text file (see Step 3).

3. Use Windows Notepad to prepare a text file. Enter any text you want in this file. When done, save the file as **C:\VBAPrimerExcel2021_ByExample\Vacation.txt**.
4. Run the OpenToRead procedure three times in step mode by using the F8 key, each time supplying one of the following:
   - Name of the C:\VBAPrimerExcel2021_ByExample\Vacation.txt file
   - Filename that does not exist on drive C
   - Path that does not exist on your computer (e.g., K:\Test)

Setting Error Trapping Options in a VBA Project

You can specify the error-handling settings for your current Visual Basic project by choosing Tools | Options and selecting the General tab (shown in Figure 9.16).

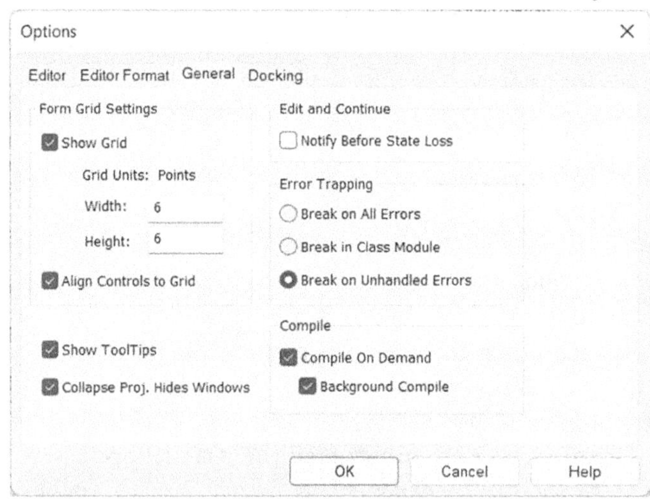

FIGURE 9.16 Setting the Error Trapping options in the Options dialog box will affect all instances of Visual Basic started after you change the setting.

The Error Trapping area located on the General tab determines how errors are handled in the Visual Basic environment. The following options are available:

- Break on All Errors

  This setting will cause Visual Basic to enter the break mode on any error, whether an error handler is active or whether the code is in a class module (class modules are covered in Chapter 26).

- Break in Class Module

  This setting will trap any unhandled error in a class module. Visual Basic will activate a break mode when an error occurs and will highlight the line of code in the class module that produced this error.

- Break on Unhandled Errors

  This setting will trap errors for which you have not written an error handler. The error will cause Visual Basic to activate a break mode. If the error occurs in a class module, the error will cause Visual Basic to enter break mode on the line of code that called the offending procedure of the class.

STEPPING THROUGH THE VBA CODE

Stepping through the code means running one statement at a time. This allows you to check every line in every procedure that is encountered. To start stepping through a procedure from the beginning, place the insertion point anywhere inside the code of your procedure and choose Debug | Step Into or press F8. Figure 9.17 shows the Debug menu, which contains several options that allow you to execute a procedure in step mode. When you run a procedure one statement at a time, Visual Basic executes each statement until it encounters the `End Sub` keywords. If you don't want Visual Basic to step through every statement, you can press F5 at any time to run the rest of the procedure without stepping through it.

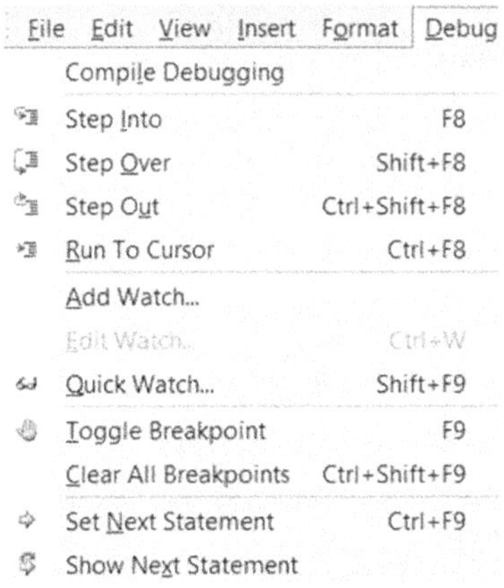

File Edit View Insert Format Debug

Compile Debugging	
Step Into	F8
Step Over	Shift+F8
Step Out	Ctrl+Shift+F8
Run To Cursor	Ctrl+F8
Add Watch...	
Edit Watch...	Ctrl+W
Quick Watch...	Shift+F9
Toggle Breakpoint	F9
Clear All Breakpoints	Ctrl+Shift+F9
Set Next Statement	Ctrl+F9
Show Next Statement	

FIGURE 9.17 The Debug menu offers many commands for stepping through VBA procedures.

Let's step through a procedure line by line.

Hands-On 9.6 Stepping through a VBA Procedure

1. Place the insertion point anywhere inside the code of the procedure whose execution you wish to trace. For example, try out the OpenToRead procedure you prepared in Hands-On 9.5.
2. Press **F8** or choose **Debug | Step Into**.
   Visual Basic executes the current statement and automatically advances to the next statement and suspends execution. While in break mode, you can activate the Immediate window, Watches window, or Locals window to see the effect of a particular statement on the values of variables and expressions. And if the procedure you are stepping through calls other procedures, you can activate the Call Stack window to see which procedures are currently active.
3. Press **F8** again to execute the selected statement.
   After executing this statement, Visual Basic will select the next statement, and the procedure execution will be halted again.
4. Continue stepping through the procedure by pressing **F8** or press **F5** to continue the code execution without stopping.
   You can also choose **Run | Reset** to stop the procedure at the current statement without executing the remaining statements.

Stepping Over a Procedure and Running to Cursor

When you step over procedures (Shift+F8), Visual Basic executes each procedure as if it were a single statement. This option is particularly useful if a procedure contains calls to other procedures and you don't want to step into these procedures because they have already been tested and debugged, or you want to concentrate only on the new code that has not yet been debugged.

Suppose that the current statement in MyProcedure (see Hands-On 9.7) calls the SpecialMsg procedure. If you choose Debug | Step Over (Shift+F8) instead of Debug | Step Into (F8), Visual Basic will quickly execute all the statements inside the SpecialMsg procedure and select the next statement in the calling procedure (MyProcedure). During the execution of the SpecialMsg procedure, Visual Basic continues to display the Code window with the current procedure.

Hands-On 9.7 Stepping over a Procedure

1. In the Breaks Module Code window, locate the following procedure:

```
Sub MyProcedure()
  Dim strName As String
```

```
  Workbooks.Add
  strName = ActiveWorkbook.Name
  ' choose Step Over to avoid stepping through the
  ' lines of code in the called procedure - SpecialMsg
  SpecialMsg strName
  Workbooks(strName).Close
End Sub

Sub SpecialMsg(n As String)
  If n = "Book2" Then
    MsgBox "You must change the name."
  End If
End Sub
```

2. Add a breakpoint at the following statement:

```
SpecialMsg strName
```

3. Place the insertion point anywhere within the code of MyProcedure, and press **F5** to run it.
   Visual Basic halts execution when it reaches the breakpoint.
4. Press **Shift+F8** or choose **Debug | Step Over**.
   Visual Basic quickly runs the SpecialMsg procedure and advances to the statement immediately after the call to the SpecialMsg procedure.
5. Press **F5** to finish running the procedure without stepping through its code.
6. Remove the breakpoint you set in Step 2.
   Stepping over a procedure is particularly useful when you don't want to analyze individual statements inside the called procedure. Another command on the Debug menu, Step Out (Ctrl+Shift+F8), is used when you step into a procedure and then decide that you don't want to step all the way through it. When you choose this option, Visual Basic will execute the remaining statements in this procedure in one step and proceed to activate the next statement in the calling procedure. In the process of stepping through a procedure, you can switch between the Step Into, Step Over, and Step Out options. The option you select depends on which code fragment you wish to analyze at a given moment. The Debug menu's Run To Cursor (Ctrl+F8) command lets you run your procedure until the line you have selected is encountered. This command is useful if you want to stop the execution before a large loop or intend to step over a called procedure. Now, let's suppose you want to execute MyProcedure to the line that calls the SpecialMsg procedure.
7. Click inside the statement `SpecialMsg strName`.

8. Choose **Debug | Run To Cursor**. Visual Basic will stop the execution of the MyProcedure code when it reaches the specified line.
9. Press **Shift+F8** to step over the SpecialMsg procedure.
10. Press **F5** to execute the remaining statements in the procedure.

Setting the Next Statement

At times, you may want to rerun previous lines of code in the procedure or skip over a section of code that is causing trouble. In each of these situations, you can use the Set Next Statement option on the Debug menu. When you halt execution of a procedure, you can resume the procedure from any statement you want. Visual Basic will skip execution of the statements between the selected statement and the statement where execution was suspended. Suppose that in MyProcedure (see the code of this procedure in the preceding section) you have set a breakpoint on the statement calling the SpecialMsg procedure. To skip the execution of the SpecialMsg procedure, you can place the insertion point inside the statement `Workbooks (strName).Close` and press Ctrl+F9 (or choose Debug | Set Next Statement).

Keep in mind that you can't use the Set Next Statement option unless you have suspended the execution of the procedure.

While skipping lines of code can be very useful in the process of debugging your VBA procedures, it should be done with care. When you use the Next Statement option, you tell Visual Basic that this is the line you want to execute next. All lines in between are ignored. This means that certain things that you may have expected to occur don't happen, which can lead to unexpected errors.

Showing the Next Statement

If you are not sure from which statement the execution of the procedure will resume, you can choose Debug | Show Next Statement and Visual Basic will place the cursor on the line that will run next. This is particularly useful when you have been looking at other procedures and are not sure where execution will resume. The Show Next Statement option is available only in break mode.

Stopping and Resetting VBA Procedures

At any time while stepping through the code of a procedure in the Code window, you can:

- Press F5 to execute the remaining instructions without stepping through.
- Choose Run | Reset to finish the procedure without executing the remaining statements.

When you reset your procedure, all the variables lose their current values. Numeric variables assume the initial value of zero, variable-length strings are initialized to a zero-length string (""), and fixed-length strings are filled with the character represented by the ASCII character code 0 or Chr(0). Variant variables are initialized to Empty, and the value of object variables is set to Nothing.

TERMINATING A PROCEDURE BASED ON A CONDITION

You may recall, in Chapter 1 (see Hands-On 1.20) we ran into an error while executing the Insert_NewSheet macro. We modified this macro to prompt the user for the sheet name using the Excel InputBox method. However, to make this macro error-proof, we need to ensure that the macro will not fail if the user clicks Cancel or enters a space or several blank spaces for the worksheet name. Let's address this problem now that you have more Excel VBA knowledge under your belt. Here is the Insert_NewSheet procedure as we modified it in Chapter 1.

```
Sub Insert_NewSheet()
'
' Insert_NewSheet Macro
' Insert and rename a worksheet
'

    Sheets.Add After:=ActiveSheet
    ActiveSheet.Name = Application.InputBox _
     ("Enter the name for your worksheet:", "Rename This Sheet")

End Sub
```

The `InputBox` method is a member of the Excel Application object and this requires that you precede its name with the name of the object (`Application`). Note that the following code uses the line continuation character (an underscore) to break up the long statement that you may end up with when supplying the arguments to this method. You will find the list of arguments and their descriptions in Chapter 4. One of the arguments we absolutely must add to the `InputBox` method to get the expected results with the Cancel button is called 'type' and it specifies the return data type. When the user clicks Cancel the `Application.InputBox` method returns *False*. Therefore, we need to introduce some conditional logic to test for the return type. We also need to prevent the user from feeding us blank spaces for the sheet name. By now you should be familiar with writing VBA conditional statements. Conditional logic will allow you to make many enhancements to your recorded macro code. Let's look at the revised Insert_NewSheet procedure.

```
Option Explicit

Sub Insert_NewSheet()
'
' Insert_NewSheet Macro revised
' Insert and rename a worksheet
'
  Dim userInput As Variant

  userInput = Application.InputBox _
   ("Enter the name for your worksheet:", _
     "Rename This Sheet", , , , , , 2)

  If userInput = False Then
     MsgBox ("You pressed the Cancel button." & _
         "The procedure will terminate.")
     sFlag = True
     Exit Sub
  ElseIf userInput = "" Or Trim(userInput) = "" Then
     MsgBox "Please enter the sheet name or press Cancel to exit."
     Insert_NewSheet

  Else
     Sheets.Add After:=ActiveSheet
     ActiveSheet.Name = userInput
  End If
End Sub
```

Note that we will now store the user supplied sheet name in the `userInput` variable. This variable is declared as `Variant` data type because the `InputBox` method can return different types of data and we want Excel to handle it for us. We begin by asking the user for the input. First, we must define the message that the user will see. Next, we specify the text that appears in the title bar of the dialog box. We don't care about the five arguments that follow, so you will see commas as their placeholders, or you can forgo commas when you specify the names for your arguments as shown in Chapter 4 procedures.

Recall that you can use named arguments to make your methods easier to understand. What we care about is the last argument. The value of 2 specifies that we expect to get a string (text). Once the result of the user interaction with the `InputBox` is in the `userInput` variable, it's time for the `if` statements. If the contents of the variable are `False`, then we want to display a message to the user and terminate the procedure. You already know that you can exit early from a VBA procedure by using the `Exit Sub` statement. Before terminating the procedure, however, you may want to store some vital piece of information in additional variables. In the case of the Insert_NewSheet procedure, we need to remember that we exited the procedure, so we don't run other procedures that may depend on this one. Recall that our Insert_NewSheet procedure is a part of a larger master procedure which will also need to be terminated. The `sFlag` variable would hold a Boolean value of `True` if the user clicked Cancel and `False` otherwise. You are free to choose names for your variables. Notice that the `sFlag` variable is not declared anywhere in the Insert_NewSheet procedure. Since we must use it also in the CreateEmployeeWorksheet master procedure, we need a project-level scope declaration.

Recall from Chapter 3 that public variables can be used in any module. Here is the perfect opportunity to utilize them. Figure 9.18 shows the revised CreateEmployeeWorksheet procedure from Chapter 1. Notice the declaration of the `sFlag` variable at the top of the module. The first line of code in the procedure makes sure that `sFlag` is set to `False` when we start. When the Insert_NewSheet procedure has finished running, the `sFlag` will be `True` if the user clicked Cancel. Again, we can use the `Exit Sub` statement to stop further code execution. And if `sFlag` is False we will continue with the remaining statements.

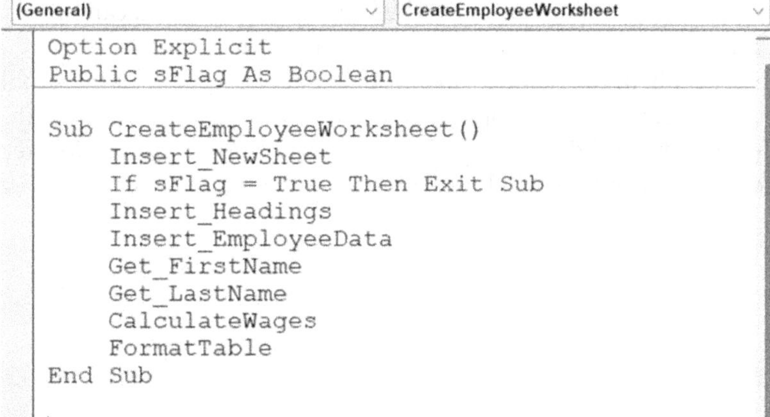

```
Option Explicit
Public sFlag As Boolean

Sub CreateEmployeeWorksheet()
    Insert_NewSheet
    If sFlag = True Then Exit Sub
    Insert_Headings
    Insert_EmployeeData
    Get_FirstName
    Get_LastName
    CalculateWages
    FormatTable
End Sub
```

FIGURE 9.18 The revised CreateEmployeeWorksheet procedure uses a public variable of Boolean data type.

Note that the Insert_NewSheet procedure also checks in the `Elseif` clause whether the user clicked OK without supplying any data or entered a space or several spaces. The VBA Trim function removes the leading and trailing spaces from a supplied text string. If the value of the `userInput` variable is an empty string (""), then we display a message to the user and call the procedure again. This way the user has a chance to either enter the required data or click Cancel. Finally, if everything looks good, then we execute the statements in the `Else` clause. A new worksheet is inserted after the current sheet and is renamed with the text stored in the `userInput` variable.

Hands-On 9.8 Working with all the Debugging Tools

1. The revised Chap01_ExcelPrimer.xlsm file can be found in the companion files (Chap01_ExcelPrimer_Revised_in_Chapter9.xlsm). Be sure to run the CreateEmployeeWorksheet master procedure at least three times to check all the conditions used in the Insert_NewSheet procedure.

SUMMARY

In this chapter, you learned how to trap errors and test your VBA procedures to make sure they behave as planned. You debugged your code by stepping through it using breakpoints and watches. You learned how to work with the Immediate window in break mode, and you found out how the Locals window can help you monitor the values of variables and how the Call Stack dialog box can be helpful in keeping track of where you are in a complex program.

By using the built-in debugging tools, you can quickly pinpoint the problem spots in your procedures. Try to spend more time getting acquainted with the Debug menu options and debugging tools discussed in this chapter. Mastering the art of debugging can save you hours of trial and error.

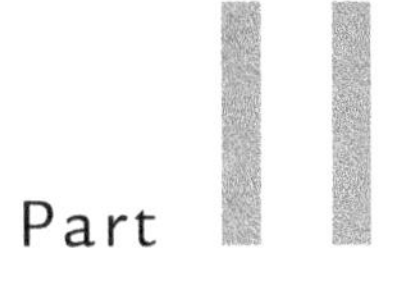

MANIPULATING FILES AND FOLDERS WITH VBA

While VBA offers a large number of built-in functions and statements for working with the file system, you can also perform file and folder manipulation tasks via objects and methods included in the installations of Windows. In addition, you can open and manipulate files directly via the low-level file I/O functions.

In this part of the book, you discover various methods of working with files and folders, and learn how to programmatically open, read, and write three types of files.

Chapter 10 File and Folder Manipulation with VBA

In the course of your work, you've surely accessed, created, renamed, copied, and deleted hundreds of files and folders. However, you've probably never performed these tasks programmatically. So, here's your chance. This chapter focuses on VBA functions and instructions that specifically deal with files and folders. By using these functions, you'll be able to:

- Find out the name of the current folder (`CurDir` function)
- Change the name of a file or folder (`Name` function)
- Check whether a file or folder exists on a disk (`Dir` function)
- Find out the date and time a file was last modified (`FileDateTime` function)
- Get the size of a file (`FileLen` function)
- Check and change file attributes (`GetAttr` and `SetAttr` functions)
- Change the default folder or drive (`ChDir` and `ChDrive` statements)
- Create and delete a folder (`MkDir` and `RmDir` statements)
- Copy and delete a file or folder (`FileCopy` and `Kill` statements)

MANIPULATING FILES AND FOLDERS

This section discusses a set of VBA functions used to perform operations on files and folders.

Finding Out the Name of the Active Folder

When you work with files, you often need to find out the name of the current folder. You can get this information easily with the `CurDir` function, which looks like this:

```
CurDir([drive])
```

Note that `drive` is an optional argument. If you omit `drive`, VBA uses the current drive. The `CurDir` function returns a file path as Variant. To return the path as String, use `CurDir$` (where $ is the Type declaration character for a string).

To see this function in action, let's perform a couple of exercises in the Immediate window.

NOTE	*Please note files for the "Hands-On" project may be found in the companion files.*

Hands-On 10.1 Using the CurDir Function

NOTE	*Create a new folder on your computer named VBAExcel2021_ByExample and designate it as a trusted folder (see Chapter 1 for details). We will use this folder to store workbook files created in Chapters 10–27.*

1. Open a new workbook and save it as **Chap10_VBAExcel2021.xlsm** in your **C:\VBAExcel2021_ByExample** folder.
2. Switch to Microsoft Visual Basic Editor and press **Ctrl+G** to activate the Immediate window. Type the following statement, and press **Enter**:

   ```
   ?CurDir
   ```

   When you press Enter, Visual Basic displays the name of the current folder. For example:

   ```
   C:\
   ```

3. If you have a second disk drive (or a CD-ROM drive), you can find out the current folder on drive D, as follows:

   ```
   ?CurDir("D:\")
   ```

NOTE	*If you supply a letter for a drive that does not exist, Visual Basic will display the following error message: "Device unavailable."*

4. To store the name of the current disk drive in a variable called `myDrive`, type the following statement and press **Enter**:

   ```
   myDrive = Left(CurDir$,1)
   ```

   When you press Enter, Visual Basic stores the letter of the current drive in the variable `myDrive`. Notice how the `CurDir$` function is used as the first argument of the `Left` function. The `Left` function tells Visual Basic to extract the leftmost character from the string returned by the `CurDir$` function and store it in the `myDrive` variable.

5. To check the contents of the variable `myDrive`, type the following statement and press **Enter**:

   ```
   ?myDrive
   ```

   To return the letter of the drive followed by the colon, type the following instructions, pressing **Enter** after each line:

   ```
   myDrive = Left(CurDir$,2)
   ?myDrive
   ```

Changing the Name of a File or Folder

To rename a file or folder, use the `Name` function, as follows:

```
Name old_pathname As new_pathname
```

`Old_pathname` is the current path and name of a file or folder that you want to rename. `New_pathname` specifies the new path and name of the file or folder.

Using the `Name` function, you can move a file from one folder to another (you can't move a folder). Here are some precautions to consider while working with the `Name` function:

- The filename in `new_pathname` cannot refer to an existing file.

  Suppose you'd like to change the name of the system.txt file to test.txt. This is easily done with the following statement:

```
Name "c:\system.txt" As "c:\test.txt"
```

  However, if the file c:\test.txt already exists on drive C, Visual Basic will display the following error message: "File already exists." Similarly, the "File not found" error message will appear if the file you want to rename does not exist. Try the above statement in the Immediate window (replace the example names with the actual names of your files and folders).

- If `new_pathname` already exists, and it's different from `old_pathname`, the `Name` function moves the specified file to a new folder and changes its name, if necessary.

  ```
  Name "c:\system.txt" As "d:\test.txt"
  ```

  If the test.txt file doesn't exist in the root directory on drive D, Visual Basic moves the c:\system.txt file to the specified drive; however, it does not rename the file.
- If `new_pathname` and `old_pathname` refer to different directories and both supplied filenames are the same, the `Name` function moves the specified file to a new location without changing the filename.

  ```
  Name "d:\test.txt" As "c:\VBAExcel2021_ByExample\test.txt"
  ```

  The above instruction moves the test.txt file to the DOS folder on drive C.

SIDEBAR ***Renaming an Open File***

You must close an open file before renaming it. Also note that the filename cannot contain the wildcard characters (*) or (?).

Checking the Existence of a File or Folder

The `Dir` function, which returns the name of a file or folder, has the following syntax:

```
Dir[(pathname[, attributes])]
```

Notice that both arguments of the `Dir` function are optional. `Pathname` is the name of a file or folder. You can use one of the constants or values in Table 10.1 for the `attributes` argument:

TABLE 10.1 File attributes

Constant	Value	Attribute Name
vbNormal	0	Normal
vbHidden	2	Hidden
vbSystem	4	System
vbVolume	8	Volume Label
vbDirectory	16	Directory or Folder

The `Dir` function is often used to check whether a file or folder exists on a disk. If a file or folder does not exist, the empty string ("") is returned (see Step 3 in Hands-On 10.2).

Let's try out the `Dir` function in several exercises in the Immediate window.

Hands-On 10.2 Using the `Dir` Function

1. In the Immediate window, type the following statement and press Enter:

```
?Dir("C:\", vbNormal)
```

As soon as you press Enter, Visual Basic returns the name of the first file in the specified folder. A normal file (`vbNormal`) is any file that does not have a Hidden, Volume Label, Directory, Folder, or System file attribute.

2. To return the names of other files in the current directory, type the `Dir` function without an argument and press **Enter**:

```
?Dir
```

3. Enter the following instructions in the Immediate window and examine their results as you press **Enter**:

```
myfile = Dir("C:\", vbHidden)
?myfile
myfile = Dir
?myfile
```

4. Type the following instruction on one line in the Immediate window and press Enter:

```
If Dir("C:\stamp.bat") = "" Then Debug.Print "File not found."
```

Because the stamp.bat file doesn't exist on drive C, Visual Basic prints the message "File not found" in the Immediate window.

The `Dir` function allows you to use the wildcards in the specified pathname—an asterisk (*) for multiple characters and a question mark (?) for a single character. For example, to find all Control Panel files in the WINDOWS\System32 folder, you can look for all the MSC files, as shown below (the lines in italics show what Visual Basic might return as you call the `Dir` function):

```
?Dir("C:\WINDOWS\System32\*.msc", vbNormal)
azman.msc
?dir
certlm.msc
?dir
certmgr.msc
```

Now let's try out a couple of complete procedures that use the `Dir` function. How about writing the names of files in the specified directory to the Immediate window and a spreadsheet? We'll make our output consistent by using the `LCase$` function, which causes the names of files to appear in lowercase.

Hands-On 10.3 Using the `Dir` Function in a Procedure

1. Open the Visual Basic Editor window in the **Chap10_VBAExcel2021.xlsm** workbook.
2. Rename the VBA project **FileMan_VBA**.
3. Insert a new module into the FileMan_VBA (Chap10_VBAExcel2021.xlsm) project, and rename it **DirFunction**.
4. Enter the MyFiles procedure in the Code window as shown below:

```
Sub MyFiles()
    Dim myfile As String
    Dim mpath As String
    Dim myPrompt As String

    myPrompt = "Enter pathname, "
    myPrompt = myPrompt & "e.g. C:\VBAExcel2021_ByExample"
    mpath = InputBox(myPrompt)
    If Right(mpath, 1) <> "\" Then mpath = mpath & "\"

    myfile = Dir(mpath & "*.*")
    If myfile <> "" Then Debug.Print "Files in the " & _
        mpath & " folder:"
    Debug.Print LCase$(myfile)
    If myfile = "" Then
        MsgBox "No files found."
        Exit Sub
    End If
    Do While myfile <> ""
        myfile = Dir
        Debug.Print LCase$(myfile)
    Loop
End Sub
```

The MyFiles procedure shown above asks the user for the pathname. If the path does not end with the backslash, the `Right` function appends the backslash to the end of the pathname string. Next, Visual Basic looks for all the files (*) in the specified path. If there are no files, a message is displayed. If files exist, the filenames are written to the Immediate window.

5. Run the MyFiles procedure.
6. To output the filenames to a worksheet, enter the GetFiles procedure in the same module where you entered the MyFiles procedure, and then run it:

```
Sub GetFiles()
    Dim myfile As String
    Dim nextRow As Integer

    nextRow = 1
    With Worksheets("Sheet1").Range("A1")
        myfile = Dir("C:\VBAExcel2021_ByExample\*.*", vbNormal)
        .Value = myfile
        Do While myfile <> ""
            myfile = Dir
            .Offset(nextRow, 0).Value = myfile
            nextRow = nextRow + 1
        Loop
    End With
End Sub
```

The GetFiles procedure obtains the names of files located in the specified directory of drive C and writes each filename to a worksheet.

Finding Out the Date and Time the File Was Modified

If your procedure must check when a file was last modified, use the `FileDateTime` function in the following form:

```
FileDateTime(pathname)
```

`Pathname` is a string that specifies the file you want to work with. The pathname may include the drive and folder where the file resides. The function returns the date and timestamp for the specified file. The date and time format depends on the regional settings selected in the Windows Control Panel. Let's practice using this function in the Immediate window.

Hands-On 10.4 Using the `FileDateTime` Function

1. Enter the following statement in the Immediate window:

```
?FileDateTime("C:\VBAExcel2021_ByExample\Chap10_VBAExcel2021.
xlsm")
```

When you press Enter, Visual Basic returns the date and timestamp in the following format:

```
6/11/2022 8:43:22 PM
```

To return the date and time separately, use the `FileDateTime` function as an argument of the `DateValue` or `TimeValue` functions. For instance, enter the following statements on one line in the Immediate Window:

```
?DateValue(FileDateTime("C:\VBAExcel2021_ByExample\
Chap10_VBAExcel2021.xlsm"))
?TimeValue(FileDateTime("C:\VBAExcel2021_ByExample\
Chap10_VBAExcel2021.xlsm"))
```

The `Date` function returns the current system date as it is set in the Date and Time Properties dialog box accessed in the Windows Control Panel.

Finding Out the Size of a File (the FileLen Function)

To check the size of a file, use the `FileLen` function in the following form:

```
FileLen(pathname)
```

The `FileLen` function returns the size of a specified file in bytes. If the file is open, Visual Basic returns the size of the file when it was last saved.

Returning and Setting File Attributes (the GetAttr and SetAttr Functions)

Files and folders can have attributes such as read-only, hidden, system, and archive. To find out the attributes of a file or folder, use the `GetAttr` function, which returns an integer that represents the sum of one or more of the constants shown in Table 10.2. The only argument of this function is the name of the file or folder you want to work with:

```
GetAttr(pathname)
```

TABLE 10.2 File and folder attributes.

Constant	Value	Attribute
vbNormal	0	Normal (other attributes are not set).
vbReadOnly	1	Read-only (file or folder can't be modified).
vbHidden	2	Hidden (file or folder isn't visible under normal setup).
vbSystem	4	System file.
vbDirectory	16	The object is a directory.
vbArchive	32	Archive (the file has been modified since it was last backed up).

To find out whether a file has any of the attributes shown in Table 10.2, use the `AND` operator to compare the result of the `GetAttr` function with the value of the constant. If the function returns a nonzero value, the file or folder specified in the pathname has the attribute for which you are testing.

Hands-On 10.5 Returning File Attributes with the GetAttr Function

1. Insert a new module into the project **FileMan_VBA (Chap10_VBAExcel2021.xlsm)**, and rename it **GetAttrFunction**.
2. Enter the following GetAttributes procedure and run it.

```
Sub GetAttributes()
    Dim attr As Integer
    Dim msg As String
    Dim strFileName As String

    strFileName = InputBox("Enter the complete file name:", _
        "Drive\Folder\Filename")
    If strFileName = "" Then Exit Sub
    attr = GetAttr(strFileName)

    msg = ""

    If attr And vbReadOnly Then msg = msg & "Read-Only (R)"
    If attr And vbHidden Then msg = msg & Chr(10) & "Hidden (H)"
    If attr And vbSystem Then msg = msg & Chr(10) & "System (S)"
    If attr And vbArchive Then msg = msg & Chr(10) & "Archive (A)"
    MsgBox msg, , strFileName
End Sub
```

The opposite of the `GetAttr` function is the `SetAttr` function, which allows you to set the attributes for files or folders that are closed. Its syntax is:

```
SetAttr pathname, attributes
```

`Pathname` is a string that specifies the file or folder that you want to work with. The second argument, attributes, is one or more constants that specify the attributes you want to set. See Table 10.2 previously in this chapter for the list of available constants.

Suppose you have a file called C:\stamps.txt and you want to set two attributes: read-only and hidden. You can do this with the `SetAtrr` function, as shown in the next exercise.

Hands-On 10.6 Setting File Attributes with the `SetAttr` Function

1. To set the file attributes, type the following instruction in the Immediate window, and press **Enter** (replace C:\stamps.txt with the name of a file that exists on your disk):

```
SetAttr "C:\stamps.txt", vbReadOnly + vbHidden
```

2. To find out what attributes were set in Step 1, type the following instruction in the Immediate window and press **Enter** (check the returned value against Table 10.2):

```
?GetAttr("C:\stamps.txt")
```

Changing the Default Folder or Drive (the ChDir and ChDrive Statements)

You can easily change the default folder by using the `ChDir` statement, as follows:

```
ChDir pathname
```

In the statement above, pathname is the name of the new default folder. Pathname may include the name of the disk drive. If pathname doesn't include a drive designation, the default folder will be changed on the current drive. The current drive will not be changed. Suppose the default folder is C:\WINDOWS. The statement:

```
ChDir "D:\MyFiles"
```

changes the default folder to D:\MyFiles; however, the current drive is still drive C.

To change the current drive, use the `ChDrive` statement in the following format:

```
ChDrive drive
```

The `drive` argument specifies the letter of the new default drive.

For instance, to change the default drive to drive D or E, use the following statements:

```
ChDrive "D"
ChDrive "E"
```

If you refer to a nonexistent drive, you will get the message "Device unavailable."

Creating and Deleting Folders (the MkDir and RmDir Statements)

You can create a new folder using the following syntax of the `MkDir` statement:

```
MkDir pathname
```

`Pathname` specifies the new folder you want to create. If you don't include the name of the drive, Visual Basic will create the new folder on the current drive.

To delete a folder you no longer need, use the `RmDir` function. This function has the following syntax:

```
RmDir pathname
```

`Pathname` specifies the folder you want to delete. `Pathname` may include the drive name. If you omit the name of the drive, Visual Basic will delete the folder on the current drive if a folder with the same name exists. Otherwise, Visual Basic will display the error message "Path not found."

Let's run through some examples in the Immediate window.

Hands-On 10.7 Creating and Deleting Folders with the `MkDir` and `RmDir` Statements

1. Type the following instruction in the Immediate window and press **Enter** to create a folder called Mail on drive C:

```
MkDir "C:\Mail"
```

2. To change the default folder to C:\Mail, enter the following statement and press **Enter**:

```
ChDir "C:\Mail"
```

3. To find out the name of the active folder, enter the following statement and press **Enter**:

```
?CurDir
```

4. To delete the C:\Mail folder that was created in Step 1, enter the following statements and press **Enter**:

```
ChDir "C:\"
RmDir "C:\Mail"
```

SIDEBAR ***RmDir Removes Empty Folders***

You cannot delete a folder if it still contains files. You should first delete the files with the `Kill` statement (discussed later in this chapter).

Copying Files (the FileCopy Statement)

To copy files between folders, use the `FileCopy` statement shown below:

```
FileCopy source, destination
```

The first parameter of this statement, `source`, specifies the name of the file that you want to copy. The name may include the drive in which the file resides. The second parameter, `destination`, is the name of the destination file and may include the drive and folder designation. Both parameters are required.

Suppose you want to copy a file specified by a user to a folder called C:\Abort. Hands-On 10.8 demonstrates how to do this.

Hands-On 10.8 Copying Files with the `FileCopy` Statement

1. Insert a new module into the project **FileMan_VBA (Chap10_VBAExcel2021.xlsm)**, and rename it **FileCopyAndKill.**
2. In the module's Code window, enter the following **CopyToAbortFolder** procedure:

```
Sub CopyToAbortFolder()
  Dim folder As String
  Dim source As String
  Dim dest As String
  Dim msg1 As String
  Dim msg2 As String
  Dim p As Integer
  Dim s As Integer
  Dim i As Long

  On Error GoTo ErrorHandler

  folder = "C:\Abort"
  msg1 = "The selected file is already in this folder."
  msg2 = "was copied to"
  p = 1
  i = 1
  ' get the name of the file from the user
  source = Application.GetOpenFilename
  ' don't do anything if cancelled
  If source = "False" Then Exit Sub
   ' get the total number of backslash characters "\" in the
source
  ' variable's contents
  Do Until p = 0
```

```
    p = InStr(i, source, "\", 1)
    If p = 0 Then Exit Do
    s = p
    i = p + 1
  Loop
  ' create the destination filename
  dest = folder & Mid(source, s, Len(source))
    ' create a new folder with this name
    MkDir folder
    ' check if the specified file already exists in the
    ' destination folder
    If Dir(dest) <> "" Then
      MsgBox msg1
    Else
    ' copy the selected file to the C:\Abort folder
      FileCopy source, dest
      MsgBox source & " " & msg2 & " " & dest
    End If
    Exit Sub
  ErrorHandler:
    If Err = "75" Then
      Resume Next
    End If
    If Err = "70" Then
      MsgBox "You can't copy an open file."
    Exit Sub
  End If
End Sub
```

The procedure `CopyToAbortFolder` uses the Excel application method called `GetOpenFilename` to get the name of the file from the user. This method causes the built-in Open dialog box to pop up. Using this dialog box, you can choose any file, in any directory, and on any disk drive. If the user cancels, Visual Basic returns the value "False" and the procedure ends. If the user selects a file and clicks Open, the selected file will be assigned to the variable `source`.

For the purpose of copying, you'll only need the filename (without the path), so the `Do...Until` loop finds out the position of the last backslash (\) in the file stored in the variable `source`, the first argument of the `FileCopy` statement. Next, Visual Basic prepares a string of characters and assigns it to the variable `dest`, the second argument of the `FileCopy` statement. This variable holds the string obtained by concatenating the name of the destination folder (C:\Abort) with the user-specified filename preceded by a backslash (\).

The `MkDir` function creates a new folder called C:\Abort if it doesn't exist on drive C. If such a folder already exists, Visual Basic will need to deal with error 75. This error will be caught by the error-handler code included at the end of the procedure. Notice that the error handler is a fragment of code that begins with the label ErrorHandler followed by a colon.

When Visual Basic encounters the `Resume Next` statement, it will continue to execute the procedure from the instruction following the instruction that caused the error. This means that the statement `MkDir` folder won't be executed.

Next, the procedure checks whether the selected file already exists in the destination folder. If the file already exists there, the user will get the message stored in the variable `msg1`. If the file does not exist in the destination folder and the file is not currently open, Visual Basic will copy the file to the specified folder and notify the user with the appropriate message. If the file is open, Visual Basic will encounter runtime error 70 and run the corresponding instructions in the ErrorHandler section of the procedure.

3. Run the **CopyToAbortFolder** procedure several times, each time selecting files from different folders.
4. Try to copy a file that was copied before by this procedure to the C:\Abort folder.
5. Try to copy an open file while using the **CopyToAbortFolder** procedure.
6. Run the procedure **MyFiles** prepared earlier in this chapter to write to the Immediate window the contents of the Abort folder.

	*Do not delete the C:\Abort folder and files that you have copied to it. You'll delete both the folder and the files in the next section using a VBA procedure.*

Deleting Files (the Kill Statement)

You already know from one of the earlier sections in this chapter that you can't delete a folder if it still contains files. To delete the files from any folder, use the following `Kill` statement:

```
Kill pathname
```

`Pathname` specifies the names of one or more files that you want to delete. Optionally, `pathname` may include the drive and folder name where the file resides. To enable quick deletion of files, you can use the wildcard characters (* or ?) in the `pathname` argument.

You can't delete a file that is open. If you worked through the exercises in the preceding section, your hard drive now contains the folder C:\Abort with several files.

Let's write a VBA procedure to dispose of this folder and the files contained in it.

Hands-On 10.9 Deleting Files with the `Kill` Statement

1. Insert a new module into the project **FileMan_VBA(Chap10_VBAExcel2021.xlsm)**, and rename it **KillStatement**.
2. Enter the code of the RemoveMe procedure, as shown below:

```
Sub RemoveMe()
  Dim folder As String
  Dim myFile As String

  ' assign the name of folder to the folder variable
  ' notice the ending backslash "\"
  folder = "C:\Abort\"
  myFile = Dir(folder, vbNormal)

  Do While myFile <> ""
    Kill folder & myFile
    myFile = Dir
  Loop
  RmDir folder
End Sub
```

3. Run the RemoveMe procedure. When the procedure ends, check Windows Explorer to see that the Abort folder was removed.

SIDEBAR ***Obtaining Information about Recent Files***

Excel has a `RecentFiles` property that can be used to return a `RecentFiles` collection that represents the list of recently used files. Let' try it out in the Immediate Window:

```
?Application.RecentFiles(1).Name
\VBAExcel2021_ByExample\Chap10_VBAExcel2021.xlsm
?Application.RecentFiles.Count
50
```

The first statement in the above code snippet returns the name of the most recent file.

The second statement displays the total count of recent files.

SUMMARY

In the course of this chapter, you learned about and tried out functions and statements that allow you to work use VBA with the filesystem. You found out how to manage files and folders by using functions, such as the `CurDir` function to get the name of the current folder. You learned how to use the `GetAttr` and `SetAttr` functions to check and change file attributes. You also learned about creating, copying, and deleting files and folders by using the statements `MkDir`, `FileCopy`, and `RmDir`. Finally, you retrieved information about the recent files using the properties and methods of the Excel `RecentFiles` object.

In the next chapter, we will look at Windows Script Host (WSH), an invaluable ActiveX tool that lets you control and retrieve information from the Windows operating system.

Chapter 11 File and Folder Manipulation with Windows Script Host (WSH)

There is a hidden treasure in your computer called Windows Script Host (WSH) that allows you to create little programs that control the Windows operating system and its applications, as well as retrieve information from the operating system. WSH is an ActiveX control that can be used to create scripts that perform simple or complex operations that a long time ago could only be performed by writing batch files (.bat). WSH is a scripting language. A *script* is a set of commands that can be run automatically. Scripts can be created and run directly from the command prompt by using the Command Script Host (Cscript.exe) or from Windows by using the Windows Script Host (Wscript.exe). In the following sections of this chapter, you will learn how the Windows Script Host works together with VBA.

REFERENCING THE MICROSOFT SCRIPTING RUNTIME

WSH has its own object hierarchy. Using the `CreateObject` function, you can refer to WSH objects from your VBA procedure. Before you start writing VBA procedures that utilize WSH objects, let's look at some of the objects you will be able to control.

SIDEBAR ***Useful Operations You Can Perform with WSH***

- Work with and manipulate Windows drives, folders, and files using the FileSystemObject
- Retrieve information about Windows; access the Windows registry; read and set environment variables; retrieve user, domain, and computer name
- Launch other applications
- Display dialog boxes and retrieve user input
- Create and manage shortcuts on your Windows desktop

To explore various features of the Windows Script Host library, let's begin by creating a reference to the Microsoft Scripting Runtime.

NOTE	*Please note files for the "Hands-On" project may be found in the companion files.*

Hands-On 11.1 Controlling Objects with Windows Script Host (WSH)

1. Open a new workbook and save it as **C:\VBAExcel2021_ByExample\Chap11_VBAExcel2021.xlsm.**
2. Switch to the Visual Basic Editor window and choose **Tools | References.** Click the checkbox next to **Microsoft Scripting Runtime**, as in Figure 11.1, then click **OK** to close the References dialog box.

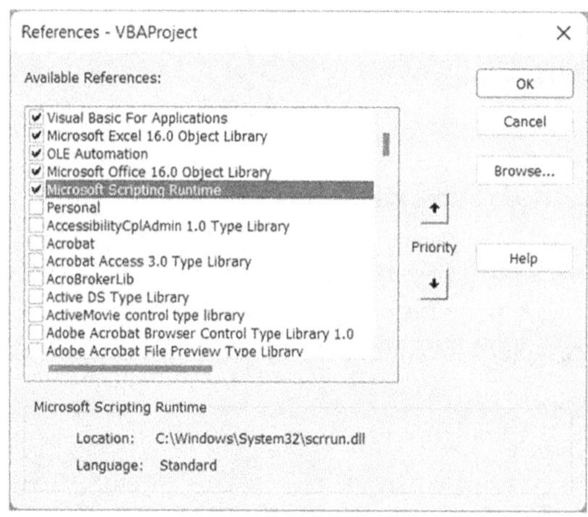

FIGURE 11.1 Creating a reference to the Microsoft Scripting Runtime.

3. Press **F2** to open the Object Browser.
4. In the <All Libraries> combo box, choose **Scripting**. You will see a list of objects that are part of the Windows Script Host library, as shown in Figure 11.2.

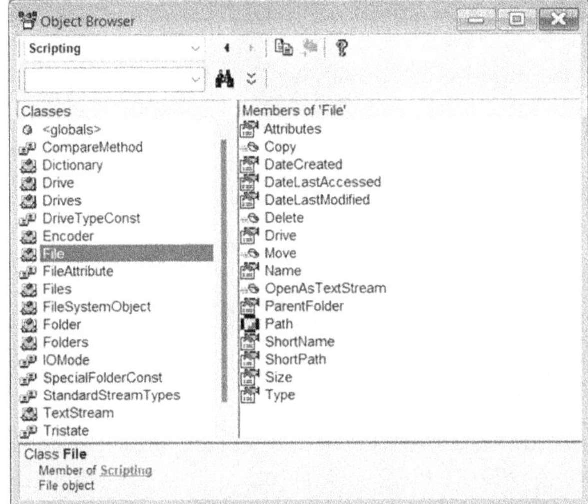

FIGURE 11.2 After establishing a reference to the Microsoft Scripting Runtime, the Object Browser displays many objects that allow you to work with disks, folders, files, and their contents.

Windows Script Host allows you to quickly obtain answers to such questions as "On which disk can I locate a particular file?" (`GetDrive` method), "What is the extension of a filename?" (`GetExtensionName` method), "When was this file last modified?" (DateLastModified property), and "Does this folder or file exist on a given drive?" (`FolderExists` and `FileExists` methods).

5. Close the Object Browser.

FINDING INFORMATION ABOUT FILES WITH WSH

Windows Script Host exposes an object called `FileSystemObject`. This object has several methods for working with the filesystem. Let's see how you can obtain some information about a specific file.

Hands-On 11.2 Using WSH to Obtain File Information

1. In the Visual Basic Editor window, activate the Properties window and change the name of VBAProject (Chap11_VBAExcel2021.xlsm) to **FileMan_WSH**.

2. Insert a new module into the FileMan_WSH project and rename it **WSH**.
3. In the WSH module's Code window, enter the following FileInfo procedure (you may need to change the path to the Windows folder to make it run on your computer):

```
Sub FileInfo()
  Dim objFs As Object
  Dim objFile As Object
  Dim strMsg As String

  Set objFs = CreateObject("Scripting.FileSystemObject")
  Set objFile = objFs.GetFile("C:\WINDOWS\System.ini")
  strMsg = "File name: " & _
      objFile.Name & vbCrLf
  strMsg = strMsg & "Disk: " & _
  objFile.Drive & vbCrLf
  strMsg = strMsg & "Date Created: " & _
      objFile.DateCreated & vbCrLf
  strMsg = strMsg & "Date Modified: " & _
      objFile.DateLastModified & vbCrLf
  MsgBox strMsg, , "File Information"
End Sub
```

The FileInfo procedure shown above uses the `CreateObject` VBA function to create an ActiveX object (FileSystemObject) that is a part of the Windows Script Host library. This object provides access to a computer's filesystem.

```
Dim objFs As Object
Set objFs = CreateObject("Scripting.FileSystemObject")
```

The above code declares an object variable named `objFs`. Next, it uses the `CreateObject` function to create an ActiveX object and assigns the object to an object variable. The statement

```
Set objFile = objFs.GetFile("C:\WINDOWS\System.ini")
```

creates and returns a reference to the File object for the System.ini file in the C:\WINDOWS folder and assigns it to the `objFile` object variable. The File object has many properties that you can read. For example, the statement `objFile.Name` returns the full name of the file.

The statement `objFile.Drive` returns the drive name where the file is located. The statements `objFile.DateCreated` and `objFile.DateLastModified` return the date the file was created and when it was last modified. This procedure can be modified easily so that it also returns the type of file, its attributes, and the name of the parent folder. Try to modify this procedure on your own by adding the following instructions to the code: `objFile.Type`, `objFile.Attributes`, `objFile.ParentFolder`, and `objFile.Size`. Check the Object Browser for other things you can learn about the file by referencing the File object.

4. Run the **FileInfo** procedure.

Methods and Properties of FileSystemObject

You can access the computer's filesystem using `FileSystemObject`. This object offers a number of methods, some of which are shown below:

- `FileExists`—Returns True if the specified file exists

```
Sub FileExists()
  Dim objFs As Object
  Dim strFile As String
  Set objFs = CreateObject("Scripting.FileSystemObject")
  strFile = InputBox("Enter the full name of the file: ")
  If objFs.FileExists(strFile) Then
    MsgBox strFile & " was found."
  Else
    MsgBox "File does not exist."
  End If
End Sub
```

- `GetFile`—Returns a File object
- `GetFileName`—Returns the filename and path
- `GetFileVersion`—Returns the file version
- `CopyFile`—Copies a file

```
Sub CopyFile()
  Dim objFs As Object
  Dim strFile As String
  Dim strNewFile As String

  strFile = "C:\Hello.doc"
  strNewFile = "C:\VBAExcel2021_ByExample\Hello.doc"

  Set objFs = CreateObject("Scripting.FileSystemObject")
  objFs.CopyFile strFile, strNewFile
  MsgBox "A copy of the specified file was created."
  Set objFs = Nothing
```

```
End Sub
```

- `MoveFile`—Moves a file
- `DeleteFile`—Deletes a file

```
Sub DeleteFile()
  ' This procedure requires that you set up
  ' a reference to Microsoft Scripting Runtime
  ' Object Library by choosing Tools | References
  ' in the VBE window
  Dim objFs As FileSystemObject
  Set objFs = New FileSystemObject

  objFs.DeleteFile "C:\VBAExcel2021_ByExample\Hello.doc"
  MsgBox "The requested file was deleted."
End Sub
```

- `DriveExists`—Returns True if the specified drive exists

```
Function DriveExists(disk)
  Dim objFs As Object
  Dim strMsg As String
  Set objFs = CreateObject("Scripting.FileSystemObject")
  If objFs.DriveExists(disk) Then
    strMsg = "Drive " & UCase(disk) & " exists."
  Else
    strMsg = UCase(disk) & " was not found."
  End If
  DriveExists = strMsg
' run this function from the worksheet
' by entering the following in any cell :
=DriveExists("E:\")
End Function
```

- `GetDrive`—Returns a Drive object

```
Sub DriveInfo()
  Dim objFs As Object
  Dim objDisk As Object
  Dim infoStr As String
  Dim strDiskName As String
  strDiskName = InputBox("Enter the drive letter:", _
      "Drive Name", "C:\")

  Set objFs = CreateObject("Scripting.FileSystemObject")
  Set objDisk = objFs.GetDrive(objFs.
GetDriveName(strDiskName))
  infoStr = "Drive: " & UCase(strDiskName) & vbCrLf
```

```
  infoStr = infoStr & "Drive letter: " & _
      UCase(objDisk.DriveLetter) & vbCrLf
  infoStr = infoStr & "Drive Type: " & objDisk.DriveType &
vbCrLf
  infoStr = infoStr & "Drive File System: " & _
      objDisk.FileSystem & vbCrLf
  infoStr = infoStr & "Drive SerialNumber: " & _
      objDisk.SerialNumber & vbCrLf
  infoStr = infoStr & "Total Size in Bytes: " & _
      FormatNumber(objDisk.TotalSize / 1024, 0) & " Kb" &
vbCrLf
  infoStr = infoStr & "Free Space on Drive: " & _
      FormatNumber(objDisk.FreeSpace / 1024, 0) & " Kb" &
vbCrLf
  MsgBox infoStr, vbInformation, "Drive Information"
End Sub
```

- `GetDriveName`—Returns a string containing the name of a drive or network share

```
Function DriveName(disk) As String
  Dim objFs As Object
  Dim strDiskName As String

  Set objFs = CreateObject("Scripting.FileSystemObject")
  strDiskName = objFs.GetDriveName(disk)
  DriveName = strDiskName
' run this function from the Immediate window
' by entering ?DriveName("C:\")
End Function
```

- `FolderExists`—Returns True if the specified folder exists

```
Sub DoesFolderExist()
  Dim objFs As Object
  Set objFs = CreateObject("Scripting.FileSystemObject")
  MsgBox objFs.FolderExists("C:\Program Files")
End Sub
```

- `GetFolder—Returns a Folder object`

```
Sub FilesInFolder()
  Dim objFs As Object
  Dim objFolder As Object
  Dim objFile As Object

  Set objFs = CreateObject("Scripting.FileSystemObject")
  Set objFolder = objFs.GetFolder("C:\")
```

```
  Workbooks.Add
  For Each objFile In objFolder.Files
      With ActiveCell
          .Formula = objFile.Name
          .Offset(0, 1).Range("A1").Formula = objFile.Type
          .Offset(1, 0).Range("A1").Select
      End With
  Next
  Columns("A:B").AutoFit
End Sub
```

- `GetSpecialFolder`—Returns the path to the operating system folders:

  0—Windows folder

  1—System folder

  2—Temp folder

```
Sub SpecialFolders()
  Dim objFs As Object
  Dim strWindowsFolder As String
  Dim strSystemFolder As String
  Dim strTempFolder As String

  Set objFs = CreateObject("Scripting.FileSystemObject")
  strWindowsFolder = objFs.GetSpecialFolder(0)
  strSystemFolder = objFs.GetSpecialFolder(1)
  strTempFolder = objFs.GetSpecialFolder(2)

  MsgBox strWindowsFolder & vbCrLf _
      & strSystemFolder & vbCrLf _
      & strTempFolder, vbInformation + vbOKOnly, _
      "Special Folders"
End Sub
```

- `CreateFolder`—Creates a folder

```
Sub MakeNewFolder()
  Dim objFs As Object
  Dim objFolder As Object
  Set objFs = CreateObject("Scripting.FileSystemObject")
  Set objFolder = objFs.CreateFolder("C:\TestFolder")
  MsgBox "A new folder named " & _
      objFolder.Name & " was created."
End Sub
```

- `CopyFolder`—Creates a copy of a folder

```
Sub MakeFolderCopy()
  Dim objFs As FileSystemObject
  Set objFs = New FileSystemObject
  If objFs.FolderExists("C:\TestFolder") Then
    objFs.CopyFolder "C:\TestFolder", "C:\FinalFolder"
    MsgBox "The folder was copied."
  End If
End Sub
```

- `MoveFolder`—Moves a folder
- `DeleteFolder`—Deletes a folder

```
Sub RemoveFolder()
  Dim objFs As Object
  Dim objFolder As Object
  Set objFs = CreateObject("Scripting.FileSystemObject")

  If objFs.FolderExists("C:\TestFolder") Then
      objFs.DeleteFolder "C:\TestFolder"
      MsgBox "The folder was deleted."
  End If
End Sub
```

- `CreateTextFile`—Creates a text file (see the example procedure later in this chapter)
- `OpenTextFile`—Opens a text file

```
Sub ReadTextFile()
    Dim objFs As Object
    Dim objFile As Object
    Dim strContent As String
    Dim strFileName As String

    strFileName = "C:\VBAExcel2021_ByExample\Vacation.txt"
    Set objFs = CreateObject("Scripting.FileSystemObject")
    Set objFile = objFs.OpenTextFile(strFileName)
    Do While Not objFile.AtEndOfStream
       strContent = strContent & objFile.ReadLine & vbCrLf
    Loop

    objFile.Close
    Set objFile = Nothing
    ActiveWorkbook.Sheets(1).Select
    Range("A1").Formula = strContent
```

```
        Columns("A:A").Select
        With Selection
            .ColumnWidth = 62.43
            .Rows.AutoFit
        End With
    End Sub
```

The FileSystemObject has only one property. The Drives property returns a reference to the collection of drives. Using this property you can create a list of drives on a computer, as shown below:

```
Sub DrivesList()
  Dim objFs As Object
  Dim colDrives As Object
  Dim strDrive As String
  Dim Drive As Variant

  Set objFs = CreateObject("Scripting.FileSystemObject")
  Set colDrives = objFs.Drives

  For Each Drive In colDrives
    strDrive = "Drive " & Drive.DriveLetter & ": "
    Debug.Print strDrive
  Next
End Sub
```

Properties of the File Object

With `File` object you to access all the properties of a specified file. The following lines of code create a reference to the `File` object:

```
Set objFs = CreateObject("Scripting.FileSystemObject")
Set objFile = objFs.GetFile("C:\My Documents\myFile.doc")
```

You will find an example of using the `File` object in the `FileInfo` procedure that was created earlier in this chapter.

These are the properties of the `File` object:

- Attributes—Returns file attributes (compare this property to the `GetAttr` VBA function explained in Chapter 10, “File and Folder Manipulation with VBA”).
- DateCreated—File creation date.
- DateLastAccessed—File last-access date.
- DateLastModified—File last-modified date.
- Drive—Drive name followed by a colon.

- Name—Name of the file.
- ParentFolder—Parent folder of the file.
- Path—Full path of the file.
- Size—File size in bytes (compare this property to the `FileLen` VBA function introduced in Chapter 10).
- Type—File type. This is the text that appears in the Type column in Windows Explorer, e.g., configuration settings, application, and shortcut.

Properties of the Folder Object

The `Folder` object provides access to all of the properties of a specified folder. The following lines of code create a reference to the `Folder` object:

```
Set objFs = CreateObject("Scripting.FileSystemObject")
Set objFolder = objFs.GetFolder("C:\My Documents")
```

The `Folder` object has the following properties:

- Attributes—Folder attributes
- DateCreated—Folder creation date
- Drive—Returns the drive letter of the folder where the specified folder resides
- Files—Collection of files in the folder

```
Sub CountFilesInFolder()
  Dim objFs As Object
  Dim strFolder As String
  Dim objFolder As Object
  Dim objFiles As Object

  strFolder = InputBox("Enter the folder name:")
  If Not IsFolderEmpty(strFolder) Then
      Set objFs = CreateObject("Scripting.FileSystemObject")
      Set objFolder = objFs.GetFolder(strFolder)
      Set objFiles = objFolder.Files
      MsgBox "The number of files in the folder " & _
          strFolder & " = " & objFiles.Count
  Else
      MsgBox "Folder " & strFolder & " has 0 files."
  End If
End Sub
```

The above procedure calls the `IsFolderEmpty` function (see the next code example).

- IsRootFolder—Returns True if the folder is the root folder
- Name—Name of the folder
- ParentFolder—Parent folder of the specified folder
- Path—Full path to the folder
- Size—Folder size in bytes

```
Function IsFolderEmpty(myFolder)
  Dim objFs As Object
  Dim objFolder As Object

  Set objFs = CreateObject("Scripting.FileSystemObject")
  Set objFolder = objFs.GetFolder(myFolder)
  IsFolderEmpty = (objFolder.Size = 0)
End Function
```

- SubFolders—Collection of subfolders in the folder
- Type—Folder type, e.g., file folder or Recycle Bin

Properties of the Drive Object

The `Drive` object provides access to the properties of the specified drive on a computer or a server. The following lines of code create a reference to the `Drive` object:

```
Set objFs = CreateObject("Scripting.FileSystemObject")
Set objDrive = objFs.GetDrive("C:\")
```

The `Drive` object has the following properties:

- AvailableSpace—Available space in bytes
- FreeSpace—Same as AvailableSpace
- DriveLetter—Drive letter (without the colon)
- DriveType—Type of drive:

0—Unknown
1—Removable
2—Fixed
3—Network
4—CD-ROM
5—RAM disk

```
Sub Removable_DriveLetter()
    Dim objFs As Object
    Dim colDrives As Object
    Dim Drive As Object
    Dim counter As Integer
    Const Removable = 1

    Set objFs = CreateObject("Scripting.FileSystemObject")
    Set colDrives = objFs.Drives
    counter = 0
    For Each Drive In colDrives
        If Drive.DriveType = Removable Then
            counter = counter + 1
         Debug.Print "The Removable Drive: " & Drive.DriveLetter
        End If
    Next
    MsgBox "There are " & counter & " Removable drives."
End Sub
```

- `FileSystem`—Filesystem such as FAT, NTFS, or CDFS
- `IsReady`—Returns True if the appropriate media (CD-ROM) is inserted and ready for access

```
Function IsCDROMReady(strDriveLetter)
  Dim objFs As Object
  Dim objDrive As Object

  Set objFs = CreateObject("Scripting.FileSystemObject")
  Set objDrive = objFs.GetDrive(strDriveLetter)

  IsCDROMReady = (objDrive.DriveType = 4) And _
      objDrive.IsReady = True
  ' run this function from the Immediate window
  ' by entering: ?IsCDROMReady("D:")
End Function
```

- `Path`—Path of the root folder
- `SerialNumber`—Serial number of the drive
- `TotalSize`—Total drive size in bytes

CREATING A TEXT FILE USING WSH

Windows Script Host (WSH) offers three methods for creating text files: `CreateTextFile`, `OpenTextFile`, and `OpenAsTextStream`. The syntax of each of these methods and example procedures are shown below.

- `CreateTextFile object.CreateTextFile(filename[, overwrite[, unicode]])`
- `Object` is the name of the FileSystemObject or the Folder object.
- `Filename` is a string expression that specifies the file to create.
- `Overwrite` (optional) is a Boolean value that indicates whether you can overwrite an existing file. The value is True if the file can be overwritten and False if it can't be overwritten. If omitted, existing files are not overwritten.
- `Unicode` (optional) is a Boolean value that indicates whether the file is created as a Unicode or ASCII file. The value is True if the file is created as a Unicode file and False if it's created as an ASCII file. If omitted, an ASCII file is assumed.

```
Sub CreateFile_Method1()
  Dim objFs As Object
  Dim objFile As Object

  Set objFs = CreateObject("Scripting.FileSystemObject")
  Set objFile = _ objFs.CreateTextFile("C:\VBAExcel2021_
ByExample\Phones.txt", True)
  objFile.WriteLine ("Margaret Kubiak: 212-338-8778")
  objFile.WriteBlankLines (2)
  objFile.WriteLine ("Robert Prochot: 202-988-2331")
  objFile.Close
End Sub
```

The above procedure creates a text file to store the names and phone numbers of two people. Because there is a Boolean value of True in the position of the `overwrite` argument, the Phones.txt file will be overwritten if it already exists in the specified folder.

- `OpenTextFile object.OpenTextFile(filename[, iomode[, create[, format]]])`
- `Object` is the name of the `FileSystemObject`.
- `Filename` is a string expression that identifies the file to open.

- `Iomode` (optional) is a Boolean value that indicates whether a new file can be created if the specified filename doesn't exist. The value is True if a new file is created and False if it isn't created. If omitted, a new file isn't created. The `Iomode` argument can be one of the following constants:

  ForReading (1)

  ForWriting (2)

  ForAppending (8)

- `Create` (optional) is a Boolean value that indicates whether a new file can be created if the specified filename doesn't exist. The value is True if a new file is created and False if it isn't created. If omitted, a new file isn't created.
- `Format` (optional) is one of three Tristate values used to indicate the format of the opened file. If omitted, the file is opened as ASCII.

  `TristateTrue`—Open the file as ASCII.

  `TristateFalse`—Open the file as Unicode.

  `TristateUseDefault`—Open the file using the system default.

```
Sub CreateFile_Method2()
  Dim objFs As Object
  Dim objFile As Object

  Const ForWriting = 2

  Set objFs = CreateObject("Scripting.FileSystemObject")
  Set objFile = _
objFs.OpenTextFile("C:\VBAExcel2021_ByExample\Shopping.txt", _
      ForWriting, True)

  objFile.WriteLine ("Bread")
  objFile.WriteLine ("Milk")
  objFile.WriteLine ("Strawberries")
  objFile.Close
End Sub
```

- `OpenAsTextStream object.OpenAsTextStream([iomode, [format]])`
- `Object` is the name of the File object.
- `Iomode` (optional) indicates input/output mode. This can be one of three constants:

ForReading (1)

ForWriting (2)
ForAppending (8)

- `Format` (optional) is one of three Tristate values used to indicate the format of the opened file. If omitted, the file is opened as ASCII.

  `TristateTrue`—Open the file as ASCII.

  `TristateFalse`—Open the file as Unicode.

  `TristateUseDefault`—Open the file using the system default.

```
Sub CreateFile_Method3()
  Dim objFs As Object
  Dim objFile As Object
  Dim objText As Object
  Const ForWriting = 2
  Const ForReading = 1

  Set objFs = CreateObject("Scripting.FileSystemObject")
  objFs.CreateTextFile "New.txt"
  Set objFile = objFs.GetFile("New.txt")
  Set objText = objFile.OpenAsTextStream(ForWriting, _
      TristateUseDefault)

  objText.Write "Wedding Invitation"
  objText.Close
  Set objText = objFile.OpenAsTextStream(ForReading, _
      TristateUseDefault)
  MsgBox objText.ReadLine
  objText.Close
End Sub
```

PERFORMING OTHER OPERATIONS WITH WSH

WSH makes it possible to manipulate any Automation object installed on your computer. In addition to accessing the filesystem through `FileSystemObject`, WSH allows you to perform such tasks as handling WSH and ActiveX objects, mapping and unmapping printers and remote drives, manipulating the registry, creating Windows and Internet shortcuts, and accessing the Windows NT Active Directory service.

The WSH object model is made of the following three main objects:

- WScript

- WshShell
- WshNetwork

The following sections demonstrate how you can take advantage of the Wsh-Shell object to write procedures to start other applications and create shortcuts.

Running Other Applications

Suppose you want to start up Windows Notepad from your VBA procedure. The procedure that follows shows you how easy it is to run an application using the WshShell object that is a part of Windows Script Host. If you'd rather launch the built-in calculator, just replace the name of the Notepad application with Calc.

Hands-On 11.3 Running Other Applications Using the WSH Object

1. Insert a new module into the project FileMan_WSH (Chap11_VBAExcel2021.xlsm) and rename it **WSH_Additional**.
2. Enter the RunNotepad procedure in the WSH_Additional module's Code window, as shown below:

```
Sub RunNotepad()
  Dim WshShell As Object
  Set WshShell = CreateObject("WScript.Shell")
  WshShell.Run "Notepad"
  Set WshShell = Nothing
End Sub
```

The above procedure begins by declaring and creating a WshShell object:

```
Dim WshShell As Object
Set WshShell = CreateObject("WScript.Shell")
```

The next statement uses the `Run` method to run the required application:

```
WshShell.Run "Notepad"
```

Using the same concept, it is easy to run Windows utility applications such as Calculator or Explorer:

```
WshShell.Run "Calc"
WshShell.Run "Explorer"
```

The last line in the procedure destroys the `WshShell` object because it is no longer needed:

```
Set WshShell = Nothing
```

3. Execute the RunNotepad procedure.

Instead of launching an empty application window, you can start your application with a specific document, as shown in the following procedure:

```
Sub OpenTxtFileInNotepad()
  Dim WshShell As Object
  Set WshShell = CreateObject("WScript.Shell")
  WshShell.Run "Notepad C:\VBAExcel2021_ByExample\Vacation.txt"
  Set WshShell = Nothing
End Sub
```

If the specified file cannot be found, Visual Basic will prompt you whether you want to create the file. If the path contains spaces, the pathname must be enclosed in double quotes, or the `Run` method will raise a runtime error. For example, to open "C:\My Files\my text file.txt" file in Notepad, use the following statement:

```
WshShell.Run "Notepad " & """C:\My Files\my text file.txt"""
```

or use the ANSI (American National Standards Institute) equivalent for double quote marks as shown below:

```
WshShell.Run "Notepad " & Chr(34) & _
        "C:\My Files\my text file.txt" & Chr(34)
```

The above statement uses the VBScript function `Chr` to convert an ANSI value to its character equivalent. 34 is the ANSI value for double quotes.

To open a Web page, pass the Web page address to the `Run` method, as in the following:

```
Sub Launch_MSN()
Dim WshShell As Object
Set WshShell = CreateObject("WScript.Shell")

WshShell.Run "https://msn.com"
Set WshShell = Nothing
End Sub
```

The following statement invokes a Control Panel:

```
WshShell.Run "Control.exe"
```

The Control Panel has various property sheets. The following statement will open the System property page with the Hardware tab selected:

```
WshShell.Run "Control.exe Sysdm.cpl, ,2"
```

The parameters after the name of the Control Panel property page (identified by the .cpl extension) specify which page is selected. To select the General tab on this property page, replace 2 with 0 (zero).

Note that the `Run` method has two optional arguments that allow you to specify the window style and whether the system should wait until the executed process completes. For example, you can launch Notepad in the minimized view as shown below:

```
WshShell.Run "Notepad", vbMinimizedFocus
```

Because the second optional parameter is not specified, the `Run` method executes the command (Notepad.exe) and immediately terminates the process. If the second parameter is set to True, the `Run` method will create a new process, execute the command, and wait until the process terminates:

```
WshShell.Run "Notepad", vbMinimizedFocus, True
```

If you run the above statement with the second parameter set to True, you will not be able to work with Excel until you close Notepad.

Obtaining Information about Windows

Windows stores various kinds of information in environment variables. You can use the Environment property of the `WshShell` object to access these variables. Depending on which version of operating system you are using, the environment variables are grouped into System, User, Volatile, and Process categories. You can use the name of the category as the index of the Environment property. The following procedure demonstrates how to retrieve the values of several environment variables from the Process category:

```
Sub ReadEnvVar()
  Dim WshShell As Object
  Dim objEnv As Object

  Set WshShell = CreateObject("WScript.Shell")
  Set objEnv = WshShell.Environment("Process")

  Debug.Print "Path=" & objEnv("PATH")
  Debug.Print "System Drive=" & objEnv("SYSTEMDRIVE")
  Debug.Print "System Root=" & objEnv("SYSTEMROOT")
  Debug.Print "Windows folder=" & objEnv("Windir")
  Debug.Print "Operating System=" & objEnv("OS")
  Set WshShell = Nothing
End Sub
```

Retrieving Information about the User, Domain, or Computer

You can use the properties of the WshNetwork object of WSH to retrieve the user's name, domain name, or the computer name, as shown in the procedure below:

```
Sub GetUserDomainComputer()
  Dim WshNetwork As Object
  Dim myData As String

  Set WshNetwork = CreateObject("WScript.Network")
  myData = myData & "Computer Name: " _
      & WshNetwork.ComputerName & vbCrLf
  myData = myData & "Domain: " _
      & WshNetwork.UserDomain & vbCrLf
  myData = myData & "User Name: " _
      & WshNetwork.UserName & vbCrLf

  MsgBox myData
End Sub
```

Creating Shortcuts

When you start distributing your VBA applications, users will certainly request that you automatically place a shortcut to your application on their desktop. VBA does not provide a way to create Windows shortcuts. Luckily for you, you now know how to work with WSH, and you can use its Shell object to create shortcuts to applications or Web sites without any user intervention. The `WshShell` object exposes the `CreateShortcut` method, which you can use in the following way:

```
Set myShortcut = WshShell.CreateShortcut(pathname)
```

`Pathname` is a string indicating the full path to the shortcut file. All shortcut files have the .lnk extension, which must be included in the pathname. The `CreateShortcut` method returns a shortcut object that exposes a number of properties and one method:

- TargetPath—The `TargetPath` property is the path to the shortcut's executable.

  ```
  WshShell.TargetPath = ActiveWorkbook.FullName
  ```

- WindowStyle—The `WindowStyle` property identifies the window style used by a shortcut.

  1—Normal window

  3—Maximized window

  7—Minimized window

  ```
  WshShell.WindowStyle = 1
  ```

- Hotkey—The `Hotkey` property is a keyboard shortcut. For example, Alt+F, Shift+G, Ctrl-Shift+Z, etc.

  ```
  WshShell.Hotkey = "Ctrl+Alt+W"
  ```

- IconLocation—The `IconLocation` property is the location of the shortcut's icon. Because icon files usually contain more than one icon, you should provide the path to the icon file followed by the index number of the desired icon in this file. If not specified, Windows uses the default icon for the file.

  ```
  WshShell.IconLocation = "notepad.exe, 0"
  ```

- Description—The `Description` property contains a string value describing a shortcut.

  ```
  WshShell.Description = "Mercury Learning Web Site"
  ```

- WorkingDirectory—The `WorkingDirectory` property identifies the working directory used by a shortcut.

  ```
  strWorkDir = WshShell.SpecialFolders("Desktop")
  WshShell.WorkingDirectory = strWorkDir
  ```

- `Save`—`Save` is the only method of the `Shortcut` object. After using the `CreateShortcut` method to create a `Shortcut` object and set the Shortcut object's properties, the `CreateShortcut` method must be used to save the `Shortcut` object to disk.

  Creating a shortcut is a three-step process:

1. Create an instance of a `WshShortcut` object.
2. Initialize its properties (shown above).
3. Save it to disk with the `Save` method.

The following Hands-On creates a WshShell object and uses the `CreateShortcut` method to create two shortcuts: a Windows shortcut to the active Microsoft Excel workbook file and an Internet shortcut to the Mercury Learning and Information Web site. Both shortcuts are placed on the user's desktop.

Hands-On 11.4 Creating Shortcuts Using the WshShell Object

1. In the WSH_Additional module created in the previous Hands-On exercise, enter the `CreateShortcut` procedure as shown below:

```
Sub CreateShortcut()
    ' this script creates two desktop shortcuts
    Dim WshShell As Object
    Dim objShortcut As Object
    Dim strWebAddr As String

    strWebAddr = "http://www.merclearning.com"

    Set WshShell = CreateObject("WScript.Shell")

    ' create an Internet shortcut
    Set objShortcut = WshShell.CreateShortcut(WshShell. _
        SpecialFolders("Desktop") & "\Mercury Learning.url")
    With objShortcut
        .TargetPath = strWebAddr
        .Save
    End With

    ' create a file shortcut
    ' you cannot create a shortcut to unsaved workbook file
    Set objShortcut = WshShell.CreateShortcut(WshShell. _
        SpecialFolders("Desktop") & "\" & ActiveWorkbook.Name &
          ".lnk")
    With objShortcut
        .TargetPath = ActiveWorkbook.FullName
        .Description = "Discover Mercury Learning"
        .WindowStyle = 7
        .Save
    End With

    Set objShortcut = Nothing
    Set WshShell = Nothing
End Sub
```

The above procedure uses the `SpecialFolders` property of the `WshShell` object to return the path to the Windows desktop.

2. Run the **CreateShortcut** procedure.
3. Switch to your desktop and click the Mercury Learning shortcut.
4. Close the active workbook file and test the shortcut to this file that you should now have on your desktop.

SIDEBAR ***Using the SpecialFolders Property***

You can find out the location of a special folder on your machine using the SpecialFolders property. The following special folders are available: AllUsers-Desktop, AllUsersPrograms, AllUsersStartMenu, AllUsersStartup, Desktop, Favorites, Fonts, MyDocuments, NetHood, PrintHood, Programs, Recent, SendTo, StartMenu, Startup, and Templates. If the requested special folder is not available, the SpecialFolders property returns an empty string.

Listing Shortcut Files

The following procedure prints to the Immediate window the list of all shortcut files found on the desktop. You can easily modify this procedure to list other special folders (StartMenu, Recent, and others as listed in the sidebar) or enumerate all folders by removing the conditional statement. Notice that the procedure uses the `InStrRev` function to check whether the file is a shortcut. This function has the same syntax as the `InStr` function, except that it returns the position of an occurrence of one string within another, from the end of string.

```
Sub ListShortcuts()
    Dim objFs As Object
    Dim objFolder As Object
    Dim wshShell As Object
    Dim strLinks As String
    Dim s As Variant
    Dim f As Variant

    Set wshShell = CreateObject("WScript.Shell")
    Set objFs = CreateObject("Scripting.FileSystemObject")
    strLinks = ""

    For Each s In wshShell.SpecialFolders
        Set objFolder = objFs.GetFolder(s)
        strLinks = strLinks & objFolder.Name _
            & " Shortcuts:" & vbCrLf
```

```
        If objFolder.Name = "Desktop" Then
            For Each f In objFolder.Files
                If InStrRev(UCase(f), ".LNK") Then
                    strLinks = strLinks & f.Name & vbCrLf
                End If
            Next
        End If
        Exit For
    Next
    Debug.Print strLinks
End Sub
```

SUMMARY

In the course of this chapter, you learned how to use the Windows Script Host (WSH) to access the `FileSystemObject` and perform other operations, such as launching applications and creating Windows shortcuts with the `WshShell` object.

In the next chapter, you will learn how to use VBA to work with three types of files: sequential, random access, and binary.

Chapter 12

Using Low-Level File Access

In addition to opening files within a particular application, your VBA procedures are capable of opening other types of files and working with their contents. This chapter will put you in direct contact with your data by introducing you to the process known as low-level file I/O (input/output).

FILE ACCESS TYPES

There are three types of files used by a computer:

- *Sequential access files* are files where data is retrieved in the same order as it is stored, such as files stored in the CSV format (comma-delimited text), TXT format (text separated by tabs), or PRN format (text separated by spaces). Sequential access files are often used for writing text files such as error logs, configuration settings, and reports. Sequential access files have the following modes: Input, Output, and Append. The mode specifies how you can work with a file after it has been opened.
- *Random-access files* are text files where data is stored in records of equal length and fields separated by commas. Random-access files have only one mode: Random.
- *Binary access files* are graphic files and other non-text files. Binary files can only be accessed in a Binary mode.

WORKING WITH SEQUENTIAL FILES

The hard drive of your computer contains hundreds of sequential files. Configuration files, error logs, HTML files, and all sorts of plain text files are all sequential files. These files are stored on disk as a sequence of characters.

The beginning of a new text line is indicated by two special characters: the carriage return and the linefeed. When you work with sequential files, start at the beginning of the file and move forward character by character, line by line, until you encounter the end of the file. Sequential access files can be easily opened and manipulated by just about any text editor.

Reading Data Stored in Sequential Files

Let's take one of the sequential files already present on your computer and read its contents with VBA straight from the VBE window. You can read any other text file you want. To read data from a file, open the file with the `Open` statement. Here's the general syntax of this statement, followed by an explanation of each component:

```
Open pathname For mode[Access access][lock] As [#]filenumber
```

The `Open` statement has three required arguments: `pathname`, `mode`, and `filenumber`. `Pathname` is the name of the file you want to open. The filename may include the name of a drive and folder.

- `Mode` is a keyword that determines how the file was opened. Sequential files can be opened in one of the following modes: Input, Output, or Append. Use Input to read the file, Output to write to a file overwriting any existing file, and Append to write to a file by adding to any existing information.
- The optional `Access` clause can be used to specify permissions for the file (Read, Write, or Read Write).
- The optional `Lock` argument determines which file operations are allowed for other processes. For example, if a file is open in a network environment, `lock` determines how other people can access it. The following `lock` keywords can be used: Shared, Lock Read, Lock Write, or Lock Read Write.
- `Filenumber` is a number from 1 to 511. This number is used to refer to the file in subsequent operations. You can obtain a unique file number using the Visual Basic built-in `FreeFile` function.

- The last element of the `Open` statement, `reclength`, specifies the buffer size (total number of characters) for sequential files, or the record size for random-access files.

Taking the preceding into consideration, to open Vacation.txt or any other sequential file in order to read its data, use the following instruction:

```
Open "C:\VBAPrimerExcel2021_ByExample\Vacation.txt"
For Input As #1
```

If a file is opened for input, it can only be read from. After you open a sequential file, you can read its contents with the `Line Input #` or `Input #` statements or by using the `Input` function. When you use sequential access to open a file for input, the file must already exist.

SIDEBAR ***What Is a Sequential File?***

A sequential file is one in which the records must be accessed in the order they occur in the file. This means that before you can access the third record, you must first access record number 1 and then record number 2.

Reading a File Line by Line

To read the contents of a sequential file line by line, use the following `Line Input #` statement:

```
Line Input #filenumber, variableName
```

`#filenumber` is the file number that was used in the process of opening the file with the `Open` statement. `VariableName` is a String or Variant variable that will store the line being read. The statement `Line Input #` reads a single line in an open sequential file and stores it in a variable. Bear in mind that the `Line Input #` statement reads the sequential file one character at a time, until it encounters a carriage return (Chr(13)) or a carriage return-linefeed sequence (Chr(13) & Chr(10)). These characters are omitted from the text retrieved in the reading process.

The ReadMe procedure that follows demonstrates how you can use the `Open` and `Line Input #` statements to read the contents of the Vacation.txt file line by line. Apply the same method for reading other sequential files.

NOTE	*Please note files for the "Hands-On" project may be found in the companion files.*

Hands-On 12.1 Reading File Contents with the Open and Line Input # Statements

1. Open a new workbook and save it as C:\VBAExcel2021_ByExample\Chap12_VBAExcel2021.xlsm.
2. Switch to the Visual Basic Editor and use the Properties window to rename VBAProject (Chap12_VBAExcel2021.xlsm) **FileMan_IO**.
3. Insert a new module in the FileMan_IO project and rename it **SeqFiles**.
4. In the SeqFiles module's Code window, enter the ReadMe procedure shown below:

```
Sub ReadMe(strFileName As String)
  Dim rLine As String
  Dim i As Integer

  ' line number

  i = 0

  On Error GoTo ExitHere
  Open strFileName For Input As #1

  ' stay inside the loop until the end of file is reached
  Do While Not EOF(1)
     i = i + 1
     Line Input #1, rLine
     MsgBox "Line " & i & " in " & strFileName & " reads: " _
       & Chr(13) & Chr(13) & rLine
  Loop
  MsgBox i & " lines were read."
  Close #1
  Exit Sub
ExitHere:
  MsgBox "File " & strFileName & " could not be found."
End Sub
```

- The ReadMe procedure opens the specified text file in the Input mode as file number 1 in order to read its contents. If the specified file cannot be opened (because it may not exist), Visual Basic jumps to the label ExitHere and displays a message box.
- If the file is successfully opened, we can proceed to read its content. The `Do...While` loop tells Visual Basic to execute the statements inside the loop until the end of the file has been reached. The end of the file is determined

by the result of the `EOF` function. The `EOF` function returns a logical value of True if the next character to be read is past the end of the file. Notice that the `EOF` function requires one argument—the number of the open file you want to check. This is the same number used in the `Open` statement. Use the `EOF` function to ensure that Visual Basic doesn't read past the end of the file.

- The `Line Input #` statement stores each line's contents in the variable `rLine`. Next, a message is displayed that shows the line number and its contents. Visual Basic exits the `Do...While` loop when the result of the `EOF` function is true. Before VBA ends the procedure, two more statements are executed. A message is displayed with the total number of lines that have been read, and the file is closed.

5. To run the procedure, open the Immediate window, type the following statement, and press **Enter** to execute:

```
ReadMe "C:\VBAPrimerExcel2021_ByExample\Vacation.txt"
```

Reading Characters from Sequential Files

Suppose that your procedure needs to check how many commas appear a file. Instead of reading entire lines, you can use the `Input` function to return the specified number of characters. Next, the `If` statement can be used to compare the obtained character against the one you are looking for. Before you write a procedure that does this, let's review the syntax of the `Input` function:

```
Input(number, [#]filenumber)
```

Both arguments of the `Input` function are required; `number` specifies the number of characters you want to read, and `filenumber` is the same number that the `Open` statement used to open the file. The `Input` function returns all the characters being read, including commas, carriage returns, end-of-file markers, quotes, and leading spaces.

Hands-On 12.2 Reading Characters from Sequential Files

1. Enter the CountChar procedure below in the SeqFiles module.

```
Sub CountChar(strFileName As String, srchChar As String)
  Dim counter As Integer
  Dim char As String
```

```
    counter = 0
    Open strFileName For Input As #1

    Do While Not EOF(1)
        char = Input(1, #1)
        If char = srchChar Then
            counter = counter + 1
        End If
    Loop
    If counter <> 0 Then
        MsgBox "Characters (" & srchChar & ") found: " & counter
    Else
        MsgBox "The specified character (" & srchChar & _
          ") has not been found."
    End If
    Close #1
End Sub
```

2. To run the procedure, open the Immediate window, type the following statement, and press **Enter** to execute:

```
CountChar "C:\VBAPrimerExcel2021_ByExample\Vacation.txt", "."
```

- As there are no periods in the Vacation.txt file, you should get a message that the specified character was not found.

3. Run the procedure again after replacing the period character with any other character you'd like to find.

- The `Input` function allows you to return any character from the sequential file. If you use the Visual Basic function `LOF` (length of file) as the first argument of the `Input` function, you'll be able to quickly read the contents of the sequential file without having to loop through the entire file. The `LOF` function returns the number of bytes in a file. Each byte corresponds to one character in a text file. The following ReadAll procedure shows how to read the contents of a sequential file to the Immediate window:

```
Sub ReadAll(strFileName As String)
    Dim all As String

    Open strFileName For Input As #1
    all = Input(LOF(1), #1)
    Debug.Print all
```

```
  Close #1
End Sub
```

4. To execute the above procedure, open the Immediate window, type the following statement, and press **Enter**:

```
ReadAll "C:\VBAPrimerExcel2021_ByExample\Vacation.txt"
```

Instead of printing the file contents to the Immediate window, you can read it into a text box placed in a worksheet, like the one in Figure 12.1. Let's take a few minutes to write this procedure.

Hands-On 12.3 Printing File Contents to a Worksheet Text Box

1. Enter the WriteToTextBox procedure below in the SeqFiles module.

```
Sub WriteToTextBox(strFileName As String)
  Dim sh As Worksheet
  Set sh = ActiveSheet

  On Error GoTo CloseFile:

  Open strFileName For Input As #1
  sh.Shapes.AddTextbox(msoTextOrientationHorizontal, _
    10, 10, 300, 200).Select

  Selection.Characters.Text = Input(LOF(1), #1)
CloseFile:
  Close #1
End Sub
```

- Notice that the statement `On Error GoTo CloseFile` activates error trapping. If an error occurs during the execution of a line of the procedure, the program will jump to the error-handling routine that follows the CloseFile label. The statement `Close #1` will be executed, whether or not the program encounters an error. Before the file contents are placed in a worksheet, a text box is added using the `AddTextbox` method of the Shapes object.

2. To execute the above procedure, open the Immediate window, type the following statement, and press **Enter**:

```
WriteToTextBox "C:\VBAPrimerExcel2021_ByExample\Vacation.txt"
```

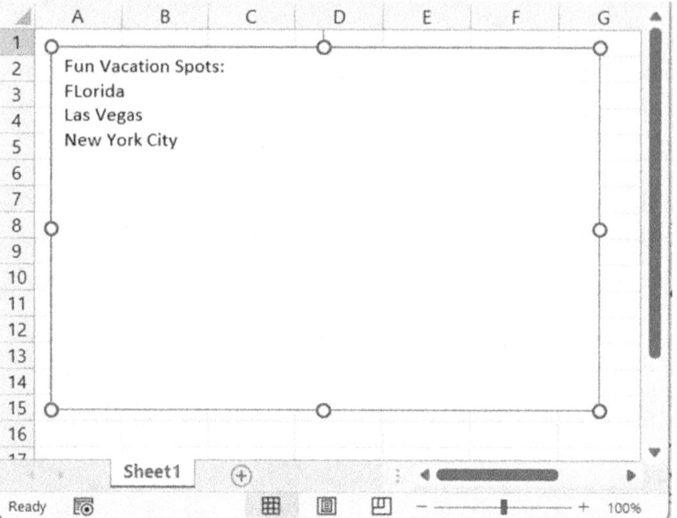

FIGURE 12.1 The contents of a text file are displayed in a text box placed in an Excel worksheet.

Reading Delimited Text Files

In some text files (usually files saved in CSV, TXT, or PRN format), data entered on each line of text is separated (or delimited) with a comma, tab, or space character. These types of files can be read faster with the `Input #` statement instead of the `Line Input #` statement introduced earlier in this chapter. The `Input #` statement allows you to read data from an open file into several variables. This function looks like the following:

```
Input #filenumber, variablelist
```

`Filenumber` is the same file number that was used in the `Open` statement. `Variablelist` is a comma-separated list of variables that you will want to use to store the data being read. You can't use arrays or object variables. You can, however, use a user-defined variable (explained later in this chapter). An example of a sequential file with comma-delimited values is shown below:

```
Smith,John,15
Malloney,Joanne,28
Ikatama,Robert,15
```

Note that in this example there are no spaces before or after the commas. To read text formatted in this way, you must specify one variable for each item of data: last name, first name, and age. Let's try it out.

Hands-On 12.4 Reading a Comma-Delimited (CSV) File with the Input # Statement

1. Open a new workbook and enter the data shown in the worksheet in Figure 12.2:

	A	B	C	D
1	Smith	John	15	
2	Malloney	James	28	
3	Ikatama	Robert	15	
4				

FIGURE 12.2 You can create a comma-delimited file from an Excel workbook.

2. Click the **File** tab on the Ribbon, then click **Save As**. Switch to the **C:\VBAExcel2021_ByExample** folder. In the Save as type drop-down box, select **CSV (Comma delimited) (*.csv)**. Change the filename to **Winners.csv** and click **Save**.
3. Excel will display a message that some features will be lost if you save the file as CSV. Click **Yes** to use that format.

NOTE	*The CSV file type does not support workbooks that contain multiple sheets. If you added more sheets to the workbook and try to save the workbook as a comma-delimited file (CSV), Excel will display a warning message.*

4. Close the Winners.csv file. Click **No** when prompted to save changes.
5. Activate the Chap12_VBAExcel2021.xlsm workbook and switch to the Visual Basic Editor.
6. In the Project Explorer window, double-click the **SeqFiles** module in the FileMan_IO project and enter the Winners procedure as shown below:

```
Sub Winners()
  Dim lname As String
  Dim fname As String
  Dim age As Integer

  Open "C:\VBAExcel2021_ByExample\Winners.csv" For Input As #1
  Do While Not EOF(1)
      Input #1, lname, fname, age
      MsgBox lname & ", " & fname & ", " & age
  Loop
```

```
  Close #1
End Sub
```

- The above procedure opens the Winners.csv file for input and sets up a `Do...While` loop that runs through the entire file until the end of file is reached. The `Input #1` statement is used to write the contents of each line of text into three variables: `lname`, `fname`, and `age`. Then a message box displays the contents of these variables. The procedure ends by closing the Winners.csv file.

7. Run the Winners procedure.

Writing Data to Sequential Files

To write data to a sequential file, open the file in Append or Output mode. The differences between these modes are explained below:

- Append mode—Use it to add data to the end of an existing text file. For example, if you open the Readme.txt file in Append mode and add to this file the text "Thank you for reading this document," Visual Basic won't delete or alter the text that is currently in the file but will add the new text to the end of the file.
- Output mode—In Output mode, Visual Basic will delete the data that is currently in the file. If the file does not exist, a brand-new file will be created. For example, if you open the Readme.txt file in Output mode and attempt to write some text to it, the previous text that was stored in this file will be removed. If you don't back up the file prior to writing the data, this mistake may be quite costly. *You should open an existing file in Output mode only if you want to replace its entire contents with new data.*

Here are some examples of when to open a file in Append mode or Output mode:

- To create a brand-new text file called C:\VBAExcel2021_ByExample\Readme.txt, open the file in Output mode as follows:

```
Open "C:\VBAExcel2021_ByExample\Readme.txt" For Output As #1
```

- To add new text to the end of C:\VBAExcel2021_ByExample\Readme.txt, open the file in Append mode as follows:

```
Open "C:\VBAExcel2021_ByExample\Readme.txt" For Append As #1
```

- To replace the contents of an existing file C:\VBAExcel2021_ByExample\Winners.csv with a list of new winners, first prepare a backup copy of the original file, then open the original file in Output mode:

```
FileCopy "C:\VBAExcel2021_ByExample\Winners.csv",
    "C:\VBAExcel2021_ByExample\Winners.old"
Open "C:\VBAExcel2021_ByExample\Winners.csv" For Output As #1
```

SIDEBAR ***Can't Read and Write at the Same Time***

You cannot perform read and write operations simultaneously on an open sequential file. The file must be opened separately for each operation. For instance, after data has been written to a file that has been opened for output, the file must be closed before being opened for input.

SIDEBAR ***Advantages and Disadvantages of Sequential Files***

Although sequential files are easy to create and use, and don't waste any space, they have several disadvantages. For example, you can't easily find one specific item in the file without having to read through a large portion of the file. Also, you must rewrite the entire file to change or delete an individual item in the file. And as stated above, sequential files must be opened for reading and again for writing.

Using Write # and Print # Statements

Now that you know both methods (Append and Output) for opening a text file with the intention of writing to it, let's look at the `Write #` and `Print #` statements that will allow you to send data to the file.

When you read data from a sequential file with the `Input #` statement, you usually write data to this file with the `Write #` statement. This statement looks like this:

```
Write #filenumber, [outputlist]
```

`Filenumber` specifies the number of the file you're working with. It is the only required argument of the `Write #` statement. `outputlist` is the text you want to write to the file and can be a single text string or a list of variables that contain data that you want to write. If you specify only the `filenumber` argument, Visual Basic will write a single empty line to the open file.

To illustrate how data is written to a file, let's prepare a text file with the first name, last name, birthdate, and the number of siblings for three people.

Hands-On 12.5 Using the Write # Statement to Write Data to a File

1. In the SeqFiles module, enter the DataEntry procedure as shown below:

```
Sub DataEntry()
  Dim lname As String
  Dim fname As String
  Dim birthdate As Date
  Dim sib As Integer

  Open "C:\VBAExcel2021_ByExample\Friends.txt" For Output As #1
  lname = "Smith"
  fname = "Gregory"
  birthdate = #1/2/1963#
  sib = 3
  Write #1, lname, fname, birthdate, sib

  lname = "Conlin"
  fname = "Janice"
  birthdate = #5/12/1948#
  sib = 1
  Write #1, lname, fname, birthdate, sib

  lname = "Kaufman"
  fname = "Steven"
  birthdate = #4/7/1957#
  sib = 0
  Write #1, lname, fname, birthdate, sib

  Close #1
End Sub
```

The above procedure creates a brand-new file named C:\VBAExcel2021_ByExample\Friends.txt, opens it for output, then writes to it three records.

The data written to the file is stored in variables. Notice that the strings are delimited with double quotes ("") and the birthdate is surrounded by pound signs (#).

2. Run the DataEntry procedure.
3. Locate the Friends.txt file created by the DataEntry procedure and open it using Windows Notepad.

   - The Friends.txt file opened in Notepad looks as follows:

```
"Smith","Gregory",#1963-01-02#,3
```

```
"Conlin","Janice",#1948-05-12#,1
"Kaufman","Steven",#1957-04-07#,0
```

- The `Write #` statement in the DataEntry procedure automatically inserted commas between the individual data items in each record and placed the carriage return-linefeed sequence (Chr(13) & Chr(10)) at the end of each line of text so that each new record starts in a new line. Each line of text shows one record—each record begins with the last name and ends with the number of siblings.
- To show the data separated by columns, instead of commas, write the data with the `Print #` statement. For example, if you replace the `Write #` statement in the DataEntry procedure with the `Print #` statement, Visual Basic will write the data as follows:

```
Smith Gregory 1/2/63 3
Conlin Janice 5/12/48 1
Kaufman Steven 4/7/57 0
```

Although the `Print #` statement has the same syntax as the `Write #` statement, `Print #` writes data to the sequential file in a format ready for printing. The variables in the list may be separated with semicolons or spaces. To print out several spaces, you should use the `Spc(n)` instruction, where *n* is the number of spaces. Similarly, to enter a word in the fifth column, you should use the instruction `Tab(5)`. Let's look at some formatting examples:

- To add an empty line to a file, use the `Write #` statement with a comma: `Write #,`
- To enter the text "fruits" in the fifth column: `Write #1, Tab(5); "fruits"`
- To separate the words "fruits" and "vegetables" with five spaces: `Write #1, "fruits"; Spc(5); "vegetables"`

WORKING WITH RANDOM-ACCESS FILES

When a file contains structured data, open the file in random-access mode. A file opened for random access allows you to:

- Read and write data at the same time
- Quickly access a particular record

In random-access files, all records are of equal length, and each record has the same number of fixed-size fields. The length of a record or field must be determined prior to writing data to the file. If the length of a string that is being written to a field is less than the specified size of the field, Visual Basic automatically enters spaces at the end of the string to fill in the entire size of the field. If the text being written is longer than the size of the field, the text that does not fit will be truncated.

SIDEBAR ***What Is a Random-Access File?***

A random-access file is one in which data is stored in records that can be accessed without having to read every record preceding it.

To find out how to work with random-access files, let's create a small database for use in a foreign language study. This database will contain records made up of two fields: an English term and its foreign language equivalent.

Hands-On 12.6 Creating a Random-Access Database with a User-Defined Data Type

1. Insert a new module into the FileMan_IO project in Chap12_VBAExcel2021.xls and rename it **RandomFiles**.
2. Enter the following statements just below the `Option Explicit` statement at the top of the RandomFiles module:

```
' create a user-defined data type called Dictionary
Type Dictionary
  en As String * 16 ' English word up to 16 characters
  sp As String * 20 ' Spanish word up to 20 characters
End Type
```

- In addition to the built-in data types introduced in Chapter 4 and listed in Table 4.1, Visual Basic allows you to define a nonstandard data type using a `Type...End Type` statement placed at the top of the module. This nonstandard data type is often referred to as a user-defined data type. The user-defined data type can contain items of various data types (String, Integer, Date, and so on). When you work with files opened for random access, you often create a user-defined variable because such a variable provides you with easy access to the individual fields of a record.
- The user-defined type called Dictionary that you just defined contains two items declared as String with the specified size. The `en` item can ac-

cept up to 16 characters. The size of the second item (`sp`) cannot exceed 20 characters. By adding up the lengths of both items, you will get a record length of 36 characters (16 + 20).

SIDEBAR *Understanding the Type Statement*

The `Type` command allows you to create a custom group of mixed variable types called a "user-defined data type." This statement is generally used with random-access files to store data as fields within records of a fixed size. Instead of declaring a separate variable for each field, cluster the fields into a user-defined variable using the `Type` statement. For example, define a record containing three fields in the following way:

```
Type MyRecord
  country As String * 20
  city As String * 14
  rank As Integer
End Type
```

Once the general type is defined, you must give a name to the variable that will be of that type:

```
Dim myInfo As MyRecord
```

Access the interior variables (`country`, `city`, `rank`) by using the following format:

```
Variable_name.Interior_variable_name
```

For example, to specify the city, enter:

```
MyInfo.city = "Warsaw"
```

3. Enter the EnglishToSpanish procedure as shown below:

```
Sub EnglishToSpanish()
  Dim d As Dictionary
  Dim recNr As Long
  Dim choice As String
  Dim totalRec As Long

  recNr = 1
  ' open the file for random access
  Open "C:\VBAExcel2021_ByExample\Translate.txt" _
      For Random As #1 Len = Len(d)

  Do
```

```
    ' get the English word
    choice = InputBox("Enter an English word", "ENGLISH")
    d.en = choice
    ' exit the loop if cancelled
    If choice = "" Then Exit Do
    choice = InputBox("Enter the Spanish equivalent of " _
        & d.en, "SPANISH EQUIVALENT  " & d.en)
    If choice = "" Then Exit Do
    d.sp = choice

    ' write to the record
    Put #1, recNr, d
    ' increase record counter
    recNr = recNr + 1
  'ask for words until Cancel
  Loop Until choice = ""

  totalRec = LOF(1) / Len(d)
  MsgBox "This file contains " & totalRec & " record(s)."
  ' close the file
  Close #1
End Sub
```

- The EnglishToSpanish procedure begins with the declaration of four variables. The variable `d` is declared as a user-defined type called Dictionary. This type was declared earlier with the `Type` statement (see Step 2 above).
- After the initial value is assigned to the variable `RecNr`, Visual Basic opens the Translate.txt file for random access as file number 1. The `Len(d)` instruction tells Visual Basic that the size of each record is 36 characters. (The variable `d` contains two elements: `sp` is 20 characters and `en` is 16 characters. Consequently, the total size of a record is 36 characters.) Next, Visual Basic executes the statements inside the `Do...Until` loop.
- The first statement in the loop prompts you to enter an English word and assigns it to the variable `choice`. The value of this item is then passed to the first element of the user-defined variable `d` (`d.en`). When you cancel or stop entering data, Visual Basic exits the `Do` loop and executes the final statements in the procedure that calculate and display the total number of records in the file. The last statement closes the file.
- When you enter an English word and click OK, you will be prompted to supply a foreign language equivalent. If you do not enter a word, Visual Basic will exit the loop and continue with the remaining statements. If you do enter the foreign language equivalent, Visual Basic will assign it

to the variable `choice` and then pass it to the second element of the user-defined variable `d` (`d.sp`). Next, Visual Basic will write the entire record to the file using the following statement:

```
Put #1, recNr, d
```

- After writing the first record, Visual Basic will increase the record counter by one and repeat the statements inside the loop. The EnglishToSpanish procedure allows you to enter any number of records into your dictionary. When you quit supplying the words, the procedure uses the `LOF` and `Len` functions to calculate the total number of records in the file, and displays the message:

```
"This file contains " & totalRec & " record(s)."
```

- After displaying the message, Visual Basic closes the text file (Translate.txt).
- Creating a random-access file is only the beginning. Next, we create the VocabularyDrill procedure to illustrate how to work with records in a file opened for random access. Here you will learn statements that allow you to quickly find the appropriate data in your file.

4. Run the EnglishToSpanish procedure. When prompted, enter data as shown in Figure 12.3. For example, enter the word **mother**. When prompted for a Spanish equivalent of mother, enter **madre**.

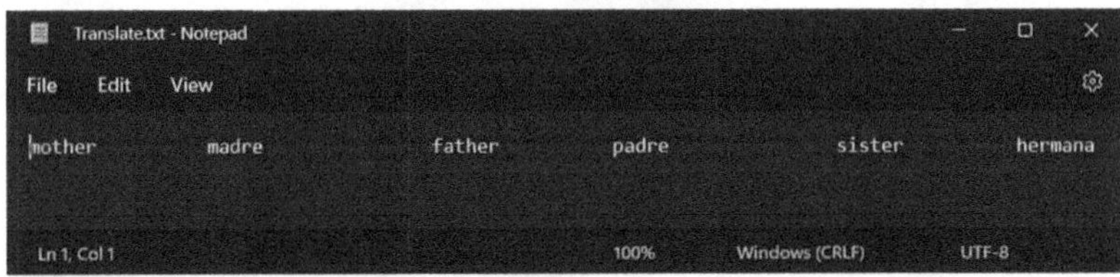

FIGURE 12.3 The contents of a random-access file opened in Notepad.

5. Below the EnglishToSpanish procedure, enter the VocabularyDrill procedure as shown here:

```
Sub VocabularyDrill()
  Dim d As Dictionary
  Dim totalRec As Long
  Dim recNr As Long
  Dim randomNr As Long
  Dim question As String
```

```
    Dim answer As String

    ' open a random access file
    Open "C:\VBAExcel2021_ByExample\Translate.txt" _
        For Random As #1 Len = Len(d)

    ' print the total number of bytes in this file
    Debug.Print "There are " & LOF(1) & " bytes in this file."

    ' find and print the total number of records
    recNr = LOF(1) / Len(d)
    Debug.Print "Total number of records: " & recNr

    Do
      ' get a random record number
      randomNr = Int(recNr * Rnd) + 1
      Debug.Print randomNr

      ' find the random record
      Seek #1, randomNr

      ' read the record
      Get #1, randomNr, d
      Debug.Print Trim(d.en); " "; Trim(d.sp)

      ' assign answer to a variable
      answer = InputBox("What's the Spanish equivalent?", d.en)

      ' finish if cancelled
      If answer = "" Then Close #1: Exit Sub
      Debug.Print answer
          ' check if the answer is correct
          If answer = Trim(d.sp) Then
              MsgBox "Congratulations!"
          Else
              MsgBox "Invalid Answer!!!"
          End If
  ' keep on asking questions until Cancel is pressed
    Loop While answer <> ""

    ' close file
    Close #1
End Sub
```

- After declaring variables, the VocabularyDrill procedure opens a file for random access and tells Visual Basic the length of each record: `Len = Len(d)`.

Next, two statements print in the Immediate window the total number of bytes and records in the open file. The number of bytes is returned by the `LOF(1)` statement. The number of records is computed by dividing the entire file (`LOF`) by the length of one record—`Len(d)`. Next, Visual Basic executes the statements inside the loop until the Esc key is pressed or Cancel is clicked.

- The first statement in the loop assigns the result of the `Rnd` function to the variable `randomNr`. The next statement writes this number to the Immediate window. The instruction:

```
Seek #1, randomNr
```

- moves the cursor in the open file to the record number specified by the variable `randomNr`. The next instruction reads the contents of the found record. To read the data in a file opened for random access, you must use the `Get` statement.
- The instruction:

```
Get #1, randomNr, d
```

- tells Visual Basic the record number (`randomNr`) to read and the variable (`d`) into which data is being read. The first record in a random-access file is at position 1, the second record at position 2, and so on. *Omitting a record number causes Visual Basic to read the next record.* The values of both elements of the user-defined type dictionary are then written to the Immediate window. The `Trim(d.en)` and `Trim(d.sp)` functions print the values of the record being read without the leading and trailing spaces that the user may have entered.
- Next, Visual Basic displays an input box with a prompt to supply the foreign language equivalent of the word shown in the input box title. The word is assigned to the variable `answer`. If you press the Esc key instead of clicking OK, Visual Basic closes the file and ends the procedure. Otherwise, Visual Basic prints your answer to the Immediate window and notifies you whether your answer is correct. You can press the Esc key or click the Cancel button in the dialog box whenever you want to quit the vocabulary drill.
- If you decide to continue and click OK, a new random number will be generated, and the program will retrieve the English word and ask you for the Spanish equivalent.

- You can modify the VocabularyDrill procedure so that every incorrectly translated word is written to a worksheet. Also, you may want to write all the records from the Translate.txt file to a worksheet so that you always know the contents of your dictionary.

6. Run the VocabularyDrill procedure. When prompted, type the Spanish equivalent of the English word shown in the title bar of the input box. Press Cancel to exit the vocabulary drill.
7. Press Alt+F11 to activate the Microsoft Excel application screen.

- Steps 8 to 9 demonstrate the process of opening random-access files in Excel.

8. Click the **File** tab on the Ribbon, then click **Open**. Switch to the **C:\VBAExcel2021_ByExample** folder. Select **All Files (*.*)** in the Files of type drop-down box, and double-click the **Translate.txt** file. Excel displays the Text Import Wizard shown in Figure 12.4.

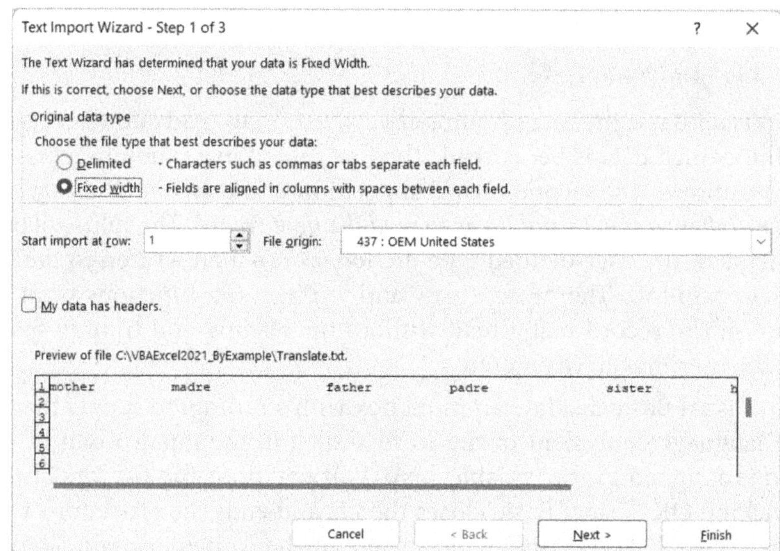

FIGURE 12.4 The contents of a random-access file on attempt to open it with Microsoft Excel. Notice that Excel correctly recognizes the original data type—the data in a random-access file is of a fixed width.

9. Click **Finish** to load your translation data file into Excel.
10. Close the Translate.txt file.

SIDEBAR ***Advantages and Disadvantages of Random-Access Files***

Unlike sequential files, data stored in random-access files can be accessed very quickly. Also, these files don't need to be closed before writing into them and reading from them, and they don't need to be read or written to in order. Random-access files also have some disadvantages. For example, they often store the data inefficiently. Because they have fixed-length fields and records, the same number of bytes is used regardless of the number of characters being stored. So, if some fields are left blank or contain strings shorter than the declared field size, you may waste a lot of space.

WORKING WITH BINARY FILES

Unlike random-access files that store data in records of fixed length, binary files store records with variable lengths. For example, the first record may contain 10 bytes, the second record may have only 5 bytes, while the third record may have 15 bytes. This method of storing data saves a lot of disk space because Visual Basic doesn't need to add additional spaces to the stored string to ensure that all the fields are of the same length.

Just like random-access files, binary files can be opened for simultaneous read and write operations. However, because binary file records are of variable length, it is more difficult to manipulate these files. In order to retrieve the data correctly, you must store information about the size of each field and record.

To work with binary files, you will use the following four statements:

- The `Get` statement is used to read data. This statement has the following syntax:

  ```
  Get [#]filenumber, [recnumber], varname
  ```

- The `filenumber` argument is the number used in the `Open` statement to open a file. The optional `recnumber` argument is the record number in random-access files, or the byte number in binary access files, at which reading begins. If you omit `recnumber`, the next record or byte after the last `Get` statement is read. You must include a comma for the skipped `recnumber` argument. The required `varname` argument specifies the name of the variable that will store this data.

- The `Put` statement allows you to enter new data into a binary file. This statement has the following syntax:

```
Put [#]filenumber, [recnumber], varname
```

- The `filenumber` argument is the number used in the `Open` statement to open a file. The optional `recnumber` argument is the record number in random-access files, or the byte number in binary access files, at which writing begins. If you omit `recnumber`, the next record or byte after the last `Put` statement is written. You must include a comma for the skipped `recnumber` argument. The required `varname` argument specifies the name of the variable containing data to be written to disk.
- The `Loc` statement returns the number of the last byte that was read. (In random-access files, the `Loc` statement returns the number of the record that was last read.)
- The `Seek` statement moves the cursor to the appropriate position inside the file.

To quickly master the usage of the above statements, let's try the procedure in Hands-On 12.7.

Hands-On 12.7 Mastering the Get and Put Statements

1. Add a new module to the current VBA project and name it **BinaryFiles**.
2. In the **BinaryFiles** module, enter the procedure located in the **RandomData.txt** file in the companion files.
3. Run the **RandomData** procedure.
4. Open the DataSample file created by the RandomData procedure and examine its contents.

When entering data to a binary file, use the following guidelines:

- Before writing a string to a binary file, assign the length of the string to an Integer type variable. Usually the following block of instructions can be used:

```
string_length = Len(variable_name)
Put #1, , string_length
Put #1, , variable_name
```

- When reading data from binary files, first read the string length and then the string contents. To do this, use the `Get` statement and the `String` function:

```
Get #1, , string_length
variable_name = String(string_length, " ")
Get #1, , variable_name
```

SideBar ***Advantages and Disadvantages of Binary Access Files***

In comparison with sequential and random-access files, binary files are the smallest of all. Because they use variable-length records, they can conserve disk space. Like files opened for random access, you can simultaneously read and write to a file opened for binary access. One big disadvantage of binary access files is that you must know precisely how the data is stored in the file to retrieve or manipulate it correctly.

SUMMARY

This chapter has given you a working knowledge of writing to and retrieving data from three types of files: sequential, random access, and binary.

The next chapter introduces you to more automating tasks. You will learn how to use VBA to control other applications. You will also learn various methods of starting applications and find out how to manipulate them directly from Microsoft Excel.

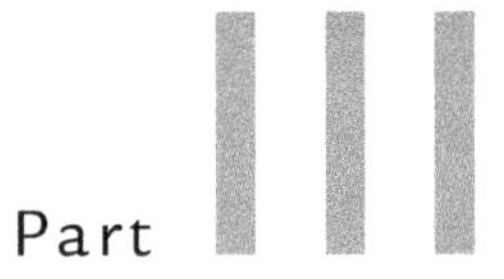

Part III Controlling Other Applications with VBA

The VBA programming language goes beyond Excel. It is used by other Microsoft 365 applications such as Word, PowerPoint, Outlook, OneNote, and Access and is also supported by a number of non-Microsoft products. The VBA skills you acquire in Excel can be used to program any application that supports this language.

In this part of the book, you learn how other applications expose their objects to VBA.

Chapter 13

Using Excel VBA to Interact with Other Applications

One of the nicest things about the VBA language is that you can use it to launch and control other Microsoft 365 applications. For example, you can create or open a Word document straight from your VBA procedure without ever leaving Excel or seeing the Word user interface. You can also start and manipulate a number of non-Office programs by using built-in VBA functions. This chapter shows you various methods of launching other programs and transferring data between them.

LAUNCHING APPLICATIONS USING THE SHELL FUNCTION

Under the Windows operating system, you can start a program in various ways. This section assumes that you are familiar with the manual techniques of launching applications and you are eager to experiment with additional techniques of starting applications by writing programming code.

Let's begin with the simplest of all—the `Shell` function, which allows you to start any program directly from a VBA procedure. Suppose that your procedure must open the Windows Notepad. To launch Notepad, all you need is one statement between the keywords `Sub` and `End Sub`. Or better yet, you can type the following statement in the Immediate window and press Enter to see the result immediately:

```
Shell "notepad.exe", vbMaximizedFocus
```

Here, notepad.exe is the name of the program you want to start. This name should include the complete path (the drive and folder name) if you have any concerns that the program may not be found. Notice that the program name is in double quotes. The second argument of the `Shell` function is optional. This argument specifies the window style. In this example, Notepad will appear in a maximized window. If the window style is not specified, the program will be minimized with focus. Table 13.1 lists the window style constants and appearance options.

TABLE 13.1 Window styles used in the `Shell` function

Window Style Constant	Value	Window Appearance
`vbHide`	0	Window is hidden and the focus is passed to the hidden window. Not applicable on Macintosh platforms.
`vbNormalFocus`	1	Window has focus and is restored to its original size and position.
`vbMinimizedFocus`	2	Window is displayed as an icon with focus.
`vbMaximizedFocus`	3	Window is maximized with focus
`vbNormalNoFocus`	4	Window is restored to its most recent size and position and the currently active window remains active.
`vbMinimizedNoFocus`	6	Window is displayed as an icon. The currently active window remains active.

If the `Shell` function is successful in launching the specified executable file, it will return a number called a Task ID which uniquely identifies the application that has been launched. If the `Shell` function cannot start the specified program, Visual Basic generates an error. The `Shell` function works asynchronously. That means that Visual Basic starts the program specified by the `Shell` function, and immediately after launching, it returns to the procedure to continue with the execution of the remaining instructions without giving you a chance to work with the application. If you want to work with the program launched by the `Shell` function, do not enter any other statements in the procedure after the `Shell` function.

Let's see how to use the `Shell` function to launch the Control Panel.

NOTE	*Please note files for the "Hands-On" project may be found in the companion files.*

Hands-On 13.1 Using the Shell Function to Activate the Control Panel

1. Open a new workbook and save it as **C:\VBAExcel2021_ByExample\Chap13_VBAExcel2021.xlsm**.
2. Switch to the Visual Basic Editor window and insert a new module in the Chap13_VBAExcel2021.xlsm VBA project.
3. Rename the VBA project **WorkWApplets**, and change the module name to **Shell_Function**.
4. In the Shell_Function Code window, enter the StartPanel procedure as shown below:

```
Sub StartPanel()
  Shell "Control.exe", vbNormalFocus
End Sub
```

5. Run the above procedure.
   When you run the StartPanel procedure, the Control Panel window is opened automatically on top of any other windows. The Control Panel contains several tools represented by individual icons. As you know, there is a program behind every icon that is activated when the user double-clicks the icon or selects the icon with the arrow keys and then presses Enter. As a rule, you can check what filename is driven by an icon by looking at the icon's properties. Unfortunately, the icons in the Control Panel have the Properties option disabled. You can, however, find out the name of the Control Panel file by creating a shortcut. For example, before you create a procedure that changes the regional settings in your computer, let's find out the name of the file that activates this tool.
6. In the Control Panel window, click the **Clock, Language, and Region** icon or link. Right-click the **Region** link and choose **Create Shortcut** from the shortcut menu.
7. If asked, click **Yes** to place the shortcut on the desktop.
8. Close the Control Panel window.
9. Switch to your desktop and right-click the **Region** shortcut icon. Next, choose **Properties** from the shortcut menu. In Windows 11, you must choose Show More Options to reveal the Properties item in the menu.
10. In the Properties window, click the **Shortcut** tab and then click the **Change Icon** button to bring up the Change Icon window shown in Figure 13.1.

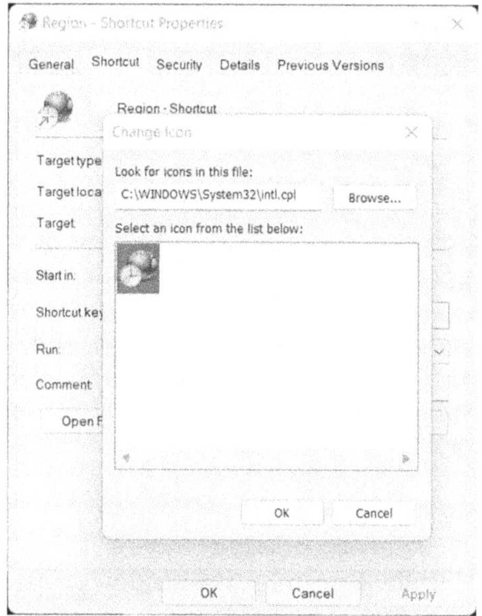

FIGURE 13.1 Each Control Panel tool icon file has a .cpl extension.

11. Write down the name of the CPL file (Control Panel Library) or DLL file (Dynamic Link Library) listed at the top of the Change Icon window and close all the windows that were opened in this exercise. Some of the files that activate Control Panel tools are listed in Table 13.2.

TABLE 13.2 Sample files that activate Control Panel tools

Icon in the Control Panel	CPL or DLL File
Accessibility Options	access.cpl
Phone and Modem Options	telephon.cpl or modem.cpl
Add/Remove Programs	appwiz.cpl
Network and Dial-up Connections	ncpa.cpl users
32-Bit ODBC	odbccp32.cpl
System	sysdm.cpl
Mail	mlcfg32.cpl
User Accounts	userpasswords, userpasswords2
Date/Time	timedate.cpl
Regional Options	intl.cpl
Internet Options	inetcpl.cpl

Icon in the Control Panel	CPL or DLL File
Sounds and Multimedia Properties	mmsys.cpl
Display	desk.cpl
Mouse	main.cpl

12. In the ShellFunction Code window, enter the ChangeSettings procedure as shown below:

```
Sub ChangeSettings()
  Dim nrTask
  nrTask = Shell("Control.exe intl.cpl", vbMinimizedFocus)
  Debug.Print nrTask
End Sub
```

The ChangeSettings procedure demonstrates how to launch the Control Panel's Regional Settings icon using the `Shell` function. Notice that the arguments of the `Shell` function must appear in parentheses if you want to use the returned value later in your procedure.

13. To open the Control Panel window with the Languages tab activated, revise the above procedure as follows:

```
nrTask = Shell("Control.exe intl.cpl 0,1", vbMinimizedFocus)
```

The first tab in the window has an index of 0, the second an index of 1, and so on.

14. Run the ChangeSettings procedure several times, each time supplying a different CPL file according to the listing presented in Table 13.2. You may want to modify the above procedure as follows:

```
Sub ChangeSettings2()
  Dim nrTask
  Dim iconFile As String
  iconFile = InputBox("Enter the name of the control " & _
    "icon CPL or DLL file:")
  nrTask = Shell("Control.exe " & iconFile, vbMinimizedFocus)
  Debug.Print nrTask
End Sub
```

If a program you want to launch is a Microsoft application, it's more convenient to use the Visual Basic `ActivateMicrosoftApp` method than the `Shell` function. This method is available from the Microsoft Excel Application object. For example, to launch PowerPoint from the Immediate window, all you need to do is type the following instruction and press Enter:

```
Application.ActivateMicrosoftApp xlMicrosoftPowerPoint
```

Notice that the `ActivateMicrosoftApp` method requires a constant to indicate which program to start. The above statement starts Microsoft PowerPoint if it is not already running. If the program is already open, this instruction does not open a new occurrence of the program; it simply activates the already running application. You can use the constants shown in Table 13.3 with the `Activate-MicrosoftApp` method.

TABLE 13.3 `ActivateMicrosoftApp` method constants

Application Name	Constant
Access	xlMicrosoftAccess
FoxPro	xlMicrosoftFoxPro
Mail	xlMicrosoftMail
PowerPoint	xlMicrosoftPowerPoint
Project	xlMicrosoftProject
Schedule	xlMicrosoftSchedulePlus
Word	xlMicrosoftWord

MOVING BETWEEN APPLICATIONS

Because the user can work simultaneously with several applications in the Windows environment, your VBA procedure must know how to switch between the open programs. Suppose that in addition to Microsoft Excel, you have two other applications open: Microsoft Word and Windows Explorer. To activate an already open program, use the `AppActivate` statement using the following syntax:

```
AppActivate title [, wait]
```

Only the `title` argument is required. This is the name of the application as it appears in the title bar of the active application window or its task ID number as returned by the `Shell` function.

The optional argument `wait` is a Boolean value (True/False) that specifies when Visual Basic activates the application. The value of False in this position immediately activates the specified application, even if the calling application does not have the focus. If you place True in the position of the `wait` argument, the calling application waits until it has the focus before it activates the specified application.

For example, here's how you can activate Microsoft Word:

```
AppActivate "Microsoft Word"
```

Notice that the name of the application is surrounded by double quotation marks. You can also use the return value of the `Shell` function as the argument of the `AppActivate` statement:

```
' run Microsoft Word
Sub RunWord()
    Dim ReturnValue As Variant
    ReturnValue = Shell("C:\Program Files\Microsoft Office\" & _
        "root\office16\WINWORD.EXE /w", 1)
    ' activate Microsoft Word
    AppActivate ReturnValue
End Sub
```

In the RunWord procedure, the "/w" startup switch after the "Winword.exe" will start a new instance of Word with a blank document.

The `AppActivate` statement is used for moving between applications and requires that the program is already running. This statement merely changes the focus. The specified application becomes the active window. The `AppActivate` statement will not start an application running.

CONTROLLING ANOTHER APPLICATION WITH THE SENDKEYS STATEMENT

Now that you know how to use VBA statements to start a program and switch between applications, let's see how one application can communicate with another. The simplest way for an application to get control of another is by means of the `SendKeys` statement. This statement allows you to send a series of keystrokes to the active application window. You can send a key or a combination of keys and achieve the same result as if you worked directly in the active application window using the keyboard. The `SendKeys` statement looks as follows:

```
SendKeys string [, wait]
```

The required argument, `string`, is the key or key combination that you want to send to the active application. For example, to send a letter "f," use the following instruction:

```
SendKeys "f"
```

To send the key combination Alt+f, use:

```
SendKeys "%f"
```

The percent sign (%) is the symbol used for the Alt key.

To send a combination of keys, such as Shift+Tab, use the following statement:

```
SendKeys "+{TAB}"
```

The plus sign (+) denotes the Shift key.

To send other keys and combinations of keys, see Table 13.4.

The `SendKeys` statement's second argument, `wait`, is optional. `Wait` is a logical value that is True or False. If False (default), Visual Basic returns to the procedure immediately upon sending the keystrokes. If `wait` is True, Visual Basic returns to the procedure only after the sent keystrokes have been executed.

To send characters that aren't displayed when you press a key, use the codes in Table 13.4. Remember to enclose these codes in quotes. For example:

```
SendKeys "{BACKSPACE}"
```

TABLE 13.4 Keycodes used with the `SendKeys` statement

Key	Code
Backspace	{BACKSPACE}{BS}{BKSP}
Break	{BREAK}
Caps Lock	{CAPSLOCK}
Del or Delete	{DELETE}{DEL}
Down Arrow	{DOWN}
End	{END}
Enter	{ENTER} or ~
Esc	{ESC}
Help	{HELP}
Home	{HOME}
Ins or Insert	{INSERT}{INS}
Left Arrow	{LEFT}
Num Lock	{NUMLOCK}
Page Down	{PGDN}
Page Up	{PGUP}
Print Screen	{PRTSC}

Key	Code
Right Arrow	{RIGHT}
Scroll Lock	{SCROLLLOCK}
Tab	{TAB}
Up Arrow	{UP}
F1	{F1}
F2	{F2}
F3	{F3}
F4	{F4}
F5	{F5}
F6	{F6}
F7	{F7}
F8	{F8}
F9	{F9}
F10	{F10}
F11	{F11}
F12	{F12}
F13	{F13}
F14	{F14}
F15	{F15}
F16	{F16}
Shift	+
Ctrl	^
Alt	%

Note that you can only send keystrokes to applications that were designed for the Microsoft Windows operating system.

You can use the `SendKeys` statement to activate a Ribbon tab. For example, to activate the Insert tab and select the Insert Picture command, use the following keys:

```
SendKeys "%np"
```

To view the list of keys assigned to individual Ribbon tabs, press the Alt key. You should see the Ribbon mappings as shown in Figure 13.2. After pressing the key for the tab you'd like to activate, the Ribbon will now display the access keys assigned to individual commands, as illustrated in Figure 13.3.

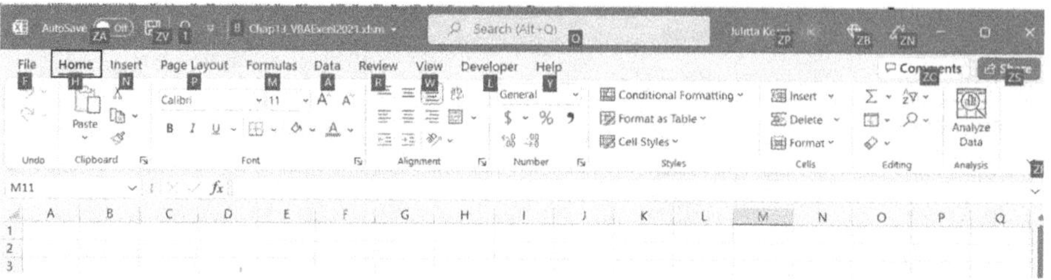

FIGURE 13.2 Each Ribbon tab has an access key that can be used with the SendKeys statement to activate a particular tab.

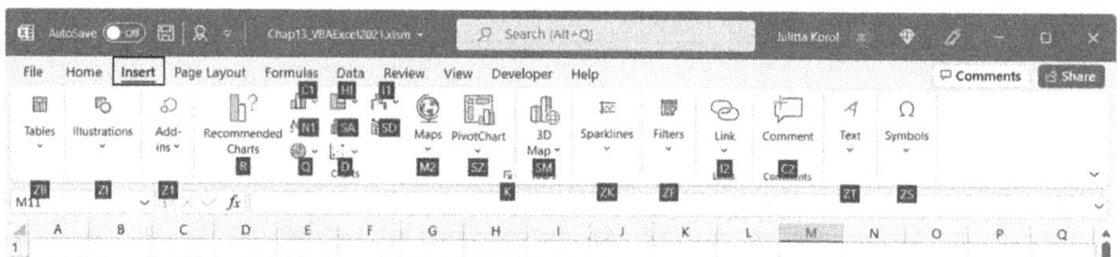

FIGURE 13.3 Each icon/command in the Ribbon has an access key that can be used to activate a particular command using the SendKeys statement.

SIDEBAR *SendKeys and Reserved Characters*

Some characters have a special meaning when used with the SendKeys statement. These keys are: plus sign (+), caret (^), tilde (~), and parentheses ( ). To send these characters to another application, you must enclose them in braces {}. To send braces, enter {{} and {}}.

Let's create a VBA procedure that will SendKeys statements to locate all the files with the .xlsm extension on your computer. The example procedure uses keystrokes that work under Windows 11. The procedure compatible with Windows 8 and 10 is included in the companion files (see Chap13_SendKeys_Windows_8_10.txt).

Hands-On 13.2 Using the SendKeys Statement in a VBA Procedure

1. Insert a new module into the WorkWApplets (Chap13_VBAExcel2021.xlsm) project and rename it **SendKeysStatement**.
2. Enter the Find_Files_Win11 function procedure, as shown below:

```
' Execute from Immediate window with the following statement
' Find_Files_Win11 "C:\VBAExcel2021_ByExample", "*.xlsm"
```

```
Function Find_Files_Win11(strSearchFolder As String, _
        strFilter As String)

    ' Launch File Explorer
    Shell "Explorer", vbMaximizedFocus

    ' delay the execution by 3 seconds
    Application.Wait (Now + TimeValue("0:00:03"))

    ' select and change address bar to a specific folder
    ' using Windows 11 shortcut Alt+D
    SendKeys "%d" & strSearchFolder & "~", True

    ' delay the execution by 3 seconds
    Application.Wait (Now + TimeValue("0:00:03"))

    ' activate the search box in the file explorer
    ' using Windows 11 shortcut (Alt+E)
    SendKeys "^e"

    ' delay the execution by 3 seconds
    Application.Wait (Now + TimeValue("0:00:03"))

    ' enter file extension to search for in the search box
    SendKeys strFilter, True

    ' delay the execution by 3 seconds
    Application.Wait (Now + TimeValue("0:00:03"))

    'Press Enter key to execute the search
    SendKeys "~", True

End Function
```

3. Execute the above function from the Immediate Window:

```
Find_Files_Win11 "C:\VBAExcel2021_ByExample", "*.xlsm"
```

Observe what happens in the Search Results window as your VBA procedure sends keystrokes that activate the Search function.

SIDEBAR ***SendKeys Statement Is Case Sensitive***

When you send keystrokes with the `SendKeys` statement, bear in mind that you must distinguish between lower- and uppercase characters. Therefore, to send the key combination Ctrl+d, you must use ^d, and to send Ctrl+Shift+d, you should use: ^+d.

Using VBA to Work with Microsoft PowerShell

Microsoft PowerShell is a powerful automation, scripting, and development language often used by system administrators to manage and automate desktop and server environments. Both the `Shell` and SendKeys methods already introduced in this chapter can be quite useful to launch and execute commands using PowerShell. Let's look at a few examples. The procedure below opens the PowerShell window where you can begin to manually write various PowerShell commands:

```
Sub Open_PowerShell1()

Shell "powershell.exe -noexit", vbNormalFocus

End Sub
```

When you launch PowerShell using the `-noexit` switch, the PowerShell console window stays open so you can work in it. You can now enter any PowerShell command. If you are new to PowerShell, you can get a full list of available commands by typing `Get-Command` and pressing Enter. For a more detailed information on each command, type `Get-Help` followed by the command from the listing you just obtained. For example, type `Get-Help Write-Output` and press Enter. At this point, you should see the syntax for the `Write-Output` command as well as some remarks. To exit the PowerShell console window, simply type `Exit` and press Enter.

Now let's look at another example, in which you will issue a command to get your computer information.

```
Sub GetComputerInfo_PowerShell()

Shell "powershell.exe -noexit -command Get-ComputerInfo",
vbNormalFocus

End Sub
```

Again, we kept the PowerShell console window open so we can see the results of the `Get-ComputerInfo` command.

Oftentimes, when working with PowerShell in VBA you will need to write longer commands, so it will be easier to store them in strings, as in our next example:

```
Sub CreateFolder_PowerShell()
    Dim sCmdPs As String
    Dim sFolderName As String
```

```
    sFolderName = "'C:\PowerShell_Test'"
    sCmdPs = "-noexit -command New-Item " & sFolderName
    sCmdPs = sCmdPs & "-ItemType Directory"

    Shell "powershell.exe " & sCmdPs, vbNormalFocus

    Application.Wait (Now + TimeValue("0:00:05"))
    SendKeys "exit~"
End Sub
```

In the above procedure, we issue a `New-Item` command to create a folder on a computer and after five seconds delay, we exit the PowerShell console window by using the `SendKeys` method.

There is a lot more to discover about PowerShell. You can start by reading the documentation at:

https://docs.microsoft.com/en-us/powershell/

OTHER METHODS OF CONTROLLING APPLICATIONS

Although you can pass commands to another program by using the `SendKeys` statement, to gain full control of another application you must resort to other methods. There are two standard ways in which applications can communicate with one another. Using Automation, you can write VBA procedures that control other applications by referencing another application's objects, properties, and methods. There is also an older data-exchange technology called DDE (Dynamic Data Exchange), however, it is a slow and difficult to work with. DDE is a protocol that allows you to dynamically send data between two programs by creating a special channel for sending and receiving information. It should be used only to communicate with older applications that do not support Automation. DDE is not covered in this book.

Understanding Automation

When you communicate with another application, you may require more functionality than simply activating it for sending keystrokes. For example, you may want to create and manipulate objects within that application. You can embed an entire Word document in a Microsoft Excel worksheet. Because both Excel and Word support Automation, you can write a VBA procedure in Excel to manipulate Word objects, such as documents or paragraphs. The applications that support Automation are called *Automation servers* or *Automation objects*. The applications that can manipulate a server's objects are referred to as *Automation controllers*. Some applications can be only a server or a controller, and others can act in both of these roles. Beginning with the Office 2000 release, all Microsoft Office / Microsoft 365 applications can act as Automation servers and controllers. The Automation controllers can be all sorts of ActiveX objects installed on your computer.

Understanding Linking and Embedding

Object linking and embedding (OLE) allows you to create compound documents. A *compound document* contains objects created by other applications. For example, if you embed a Word document in a Microsoft Excel worksheet, Excel only needs to know the name of the application that was used to create this object and the method of displaying the object on the screen. Compound documents are created by either linking or embedding objects. When you use the manual method to embed an object, you first need to copy it in one application and then paste it into another. The main difference between a linked object and an embedded object is in the way the object is stored and updated. The embedded object becomes a part of the destination file. Because the embedded object is not connected with the original data, the information is static. When the data changes in the source file, the embedded object is not updated. To change the embedded data, you must double-click it. This will open the object for editing in the source program. Of course, the source program must be installed on the computer. When you embed objects, all the data is stored in the destination file. This causes the file size to increase considerably. When you embed an object in Excel, the Formula bar displays:

```
=EMBED("Word.Document.12","")
```

The number following Word.Document denotes the version of Word you are using. Version 8 indicates that we are bringing an object from Word 2007 or newer. If your source program is a Word version prior to 2007, the formula bar displays:

```
=EMBED("Word.Document.8","")
```

Under Windows 11 / Microsoft 365, you may also see the following:

```
=EMBED("Document","")
```

When you double-click the linked object, the source application is launched.

Linking objects is a dynamic operation. This means that the linked data is updated automatically when the data in the source file changes. Because the destination document contains only information on how the object is linked with the source document, object linking doesn't increase the size of a destination file. The following formula is used to link an object in Microsoft Excel:

```
=Word.Document.12|'C:\VBAExcel2021_ByExample\Hello.docx'!''''
```

The InsertLetter procedure shown below demonstrates how to programmatically embed a Word document in an Excel worksheet. You should replace the reference to C:\Hello.docx with your own document name.

Hands-On 13.3 Writing a Procedure to Embed a Word Document in a Worksheet

1. Insert a new module into the WorkWApplets (Chap13_VBAExcel2021.xlsm) VBA project and rename it **OLE**.
2. In the OLE module Code window, enter the InsertLetter procedure as shown below:

```
Sub InsertLetter()
    Workbooks.Add
    ActiveSheet.Shapes.AddOLEObject _
    Filename:="C:\VBAExcel2021_ByExample\Hello.docx"
End Sub
```

The InsertLetter procedure uses the `AddOLEObject` method. This method creates an OLE object and returns the Shape object that represents the new OLE object. Additional arguments that the `AddOLEObject` method can use are listed in the VBA online documentation.

3. Run the InsertLetter procedure.
The procedure opens a new workbook and embeds the indicated Word document in it.

If you'd rather link a document, you must specify an additional argument, `Link`, and set it to `True`, as shown below:

```
Sub InsertLetter_Link()
    Workbooks.Add
    ActiveSheet.Shapes.AddOLEObject _
   Filename:="C:\VBAExcel2021_ByExample\Hello.docx", Link:=True
End Sub
```

SIDEBAR ***Objects—Linking or Embedding***

Use object embedding rather than linking if:

- You don't mind if the size of a document increases, or you have enough disk space and memory to handle large files.
- You will never need the source file or use source text in other compound documents.
- You want to send the document to other people by email or on a disk, and you want to make sure that they can read the data without any problems.

COM and Automation

The driving force behind Automation is the Component Object Model (COM), which determines the rules for creating objects by the server application and specifies the methods that both the server and the control application must apply when using these objects. The COM standard contains a collection of functions that are made available as Automation interfaces. When a server application creates an object, it automatically makes available an interface that goes along with it. This interface includes properties, methods, and events that can be recognized by the object. The controller application doesn't need to know the internal structure of the object in order to control it; it only needs to know how to manipulate the object interface that is made available by the server application.

Understanding Binding

For a controller application to communicate with the Automation object (server), you must associate the object variable that your VBA procedure uses with the actual Automation object on the server. This process is known as *binding*. There are two types of binding: *late binding* and *early binding*. Your choice of binding will have a great impact on how well your application performs.

Late Binding

When you declare a variable As Object or As Variant, Visual Basic uses *late binding*. Late binding is also known as *runtime binding*. Late binding simply means that Visual Basic doesn't associate your object variable with the Automation object at design time but waits until you actually run the procedure. Because the declaration As Object or As Variant is very general in nature, Visual Basic cannot determine at compile time that the object your variable refers to has the properties and methods your VBA procedure is using.

The following declaration results in late binding of the specified object:

```
Dim mydoc As Object
```

The advantage of late binding is that all the Automation objects know how to use it. The disadvantage is that there is no support for built-in constants. Because Visual Basic does not know at design time the Type Library to which your object is referring, you must define constants in your code by looking up the values in the application's documentation. Also, querying an application at runtime can slow down the performance of your solution.

NOTE	*The main difference between late binding and early binding is how you declare your object variables. Late binding makes it possible to access objects in a Type Library of another application without first establishing a reference to the object library. Use late binding if you are uncertain that your users will have the referenced type libraries installed on their machines.*

Let's write a VBA procedure that uses late binding. The purpose of this procedure is to print out a Word document. Be sure to modify the filename so that you can actually print a Word document that exists on your hard disk.

Hands-On 13.4 Printing a Word Document with VBA

1. Insert a new module into the WorkWApplets (Chap13_VBAExcel2021.xlsm) VBA project and rename it **Automation**.
2. In the Automation module Code window, enter the PrintWordDoc procedure as shown below:

```
Sub PrintWordDoc()
  Dim objWord As Object
  Set objWord = CreateObject("Word.Application")

  With objWord
    .Visible = True
    .Documents.Open "C:\VBAExcel2021_ByExample\Hello.docx"
    .Options.PrintBackground = False
    .ActiveDocument.PrintOut
    .Documents.Close
    .Quit
  End With

  Set objWord = Nothing
End Sub
```

3. Run the PrintWordDoc procedure.
   You should get a printout of your document.
   For more information on the Word PrintOut method, check out:
   https://docs.microsoft.com/en-us/office/vba/api/word.application.printout

Early Binding

When you declare object variables as specific object types, Visual Basic uses *early binding*, also known as *compile-time binding*. This means that Visual Basic associates your object variable with the Automation object while the procedure source code is being translated into executable code. The general syntax looks like this:

```
Dim objectVariable As Application.ObjectType
```

In the above syntax, `Application` is the name of the application as it appears in the Object Browser's Project/Library drop-down list (for example, Word and Excel). `ObjectType` is the name of the object class type (for example, application, document, workbook, and worksheet). The following declarations result in early binding:

```
Dim mydoc As Word.Document
Dim mydoc As Excel.Worksheet
```

Early binding allows you to take full advantage of many of the debugging tools that are available in the VBE window. For example, you can look up external objects, properties, and methods with the Object Browser. Visual Basic Auto Syntax Check, Auto List Members, and Auto Quick Info (all discussed in Chapter 2) can help you write your code faster and with fewer errors. In addition, early binding allows you to use built-in constants as arguments for methods and property settings. Because these constants are available in the Type Library at design time, you do not need to define them. The handy built-in syntax checking, IntelliSense features, or support for built-in constants aren't available with late binding. Although VBA procedures that use early binding execute faster, some very old Windows applications can only use late binding.

NOTE	*In order to use early binding, you must first establish a reference to the object library (see the following section). Use early binding when you are certain that your users will have the referenced type libraries installed on their machines.*

Establishing a Reference to a Type Library

If you decide to use early binding to connect to another application via Automation, start by establishing a reference to the object library whose objects you are planning to manipulate. Follow the steps outlined in Hands-On 13.5 to create a reference to the Microsoft Word object library.

Hands-On 13.5 Setting Up a Reference to a Type Library

1. Activate the Visual Basic Editor window.
2. Select the current project in the Project Explorer window, and choose **Tools | References.**
   In the References dialog box, choose the name of the application in the Available References list box. For this example, click the checkbox next to **Microsoft Word 16.0 Object Library or its earlier release** (see Figure 13.4). Scroll down in the Available References list box to locate this object library.

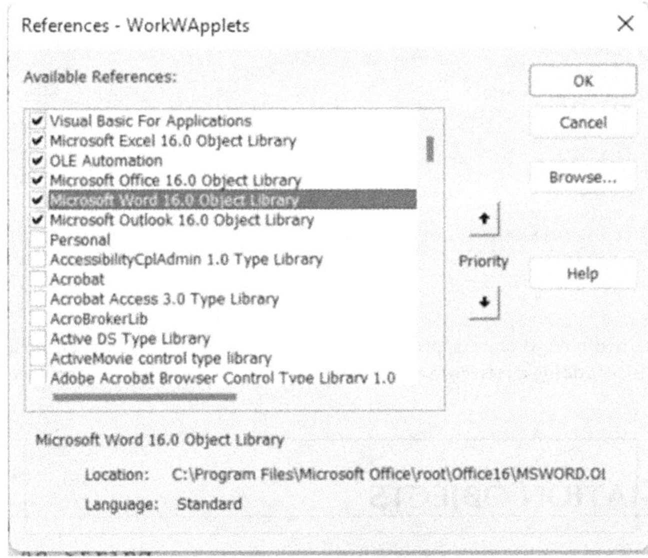

FIGURE 13.4 Setting a reference to the required object library is one of the steps you need to complete before attempting to manipulate objects of another application.

3. Click **OK** to close the References dialog box.

The References dialog box lists the names of the references that are available to your VBA project. The references that are not used are listed alphabetically.

The references that are checked are listed by priority. For example, in Excel, the Microsoft Excel 16.0 object library has a higher priority than the Microsoft Word 16.0 object library. When a procedure references an object, Visual Basic searches each referenced object library in the order in which the libraries are displayed in the References dialog box. After setting a reference to the required object library, you can browse the object properties and methods by using the Object Browser (see Figure 13.5).

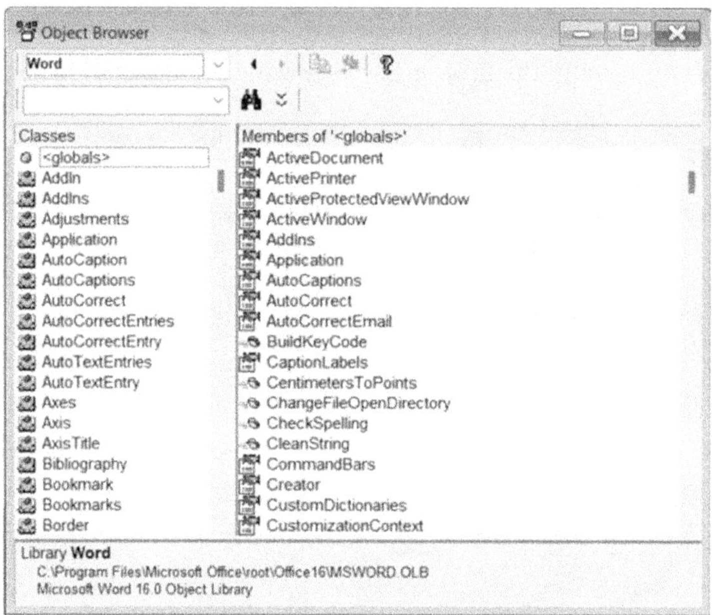

FIGURE 13.5 All of the Microsoft Word objects, properties, and methods can be accessed from a Microsoft Excel VBA project after adding a reference to the Microsoft Word 16.0 object library (see Figure 13.4).

CREATING AUTOMATION OBJECTS

To create an Automation object in your VBA procedure, follow these steps:

- Declare an object variable using the `Dim…As Object` or `Dim…As Application.ObjectType` clause (see the topics on using late and early binding in the preceding sections).
- If you are using early binding, use the References dialog box to establish a reference to the Application object type library.

- If the Automation object doesn't exist yet, use the `CreateObject` function. If the Automation object already exists, establish the reference to the object by using the `GetObject` function.
- Assign the object returned by the `CreateObject` or `GetObject` function to the object variable by using the `Set` keyword.

Using the CreateObject Function

To create a reference to the Automation object from a VBA procedure, use the `CreateObject` function with the following syntax:

```
CreateObject(class)
```

The argument `class` is the name of the application you want to reference. This name includes the object class type as discussed earlier (see the section on early binding). The Automation object must be assigned to the object variable by using the `Set` keyword, as shown below:

```
Set variable_name = CreateObject(class)
```

For example, to activate Word using the Automation object, include the following declaration statements in your VBA procedure:

```
' early binding
Dim wordAppl As Word.Document
Set wordAppl = CreateObject("Word.Application")
```

Or

```
' late binding
Dim wordAppl As Object
Set wordAppl = CreateObject("Word.Application")
```

As a rule, use the `CreateObject` function when there is no current instance of the object. If the instance of the object is already running, a new instance is created. To use the current instance, use the `GetObject` function.

Sometimes you may be required to open a Word document programmatically and write some data to it straight from Excel. The following example uses early binding to create a new Word document using Automation.

Hands-On 13.6 Creating a New Word Document with VBA

1. In the Visual Basic Editor screen, select the **WorkWApplets (Chap13_Excel2021.xlsm)** VBA project and choose **Tools | References**.

2. If the **Microsoft Word 16.0 object library** or an earlier object library is not selected in the Available References list box, locate this object library and click the checkbox to select it. Click **OK** when done.
3. In the Automation module Code window, enter the **WriteLetter** procedure as shown below:

```
Sub WriteLetter()
  Dim wordAppl As Word.Application
  Dim strFolder As String
  Dim strFileName As String
  Dim flag As Boolean

  On Error GoTo ErrorHandler
  flag = True
  strFolder = "C:\VBAExcel2021_ByExample\"
  strFileName = "Invite.docx"

  Set wordAppl = CreateObject("Word.Application")

  With wordAppl
     .Visible = True
     .StatusBar = "Creating a new document..."
     .Documents.Add
     .ActiveDocument.Paragraphs(1).Range.InsertBefore "Invitation"
     .StatusBar = "Saving document..."
     .ActiveDocument.SaveAs2 _
          Filename:=strFolder & strFileName
     .StatusBar = "Exiting Word..."
     .Quit
  End With
ExitHere:
    If flag Then MsgBox "The Document file " & _
        strFileName & Chr(13) & "was saved in " & _
        Left(strFolder, Len(strFolder) - 1) & ".", _
        vbInformation, "Document Created and Saved"
    Set wordAppl = Nothing
    Exit Sub
ErrorHandler:
  If Err.Number <> 0 Then
     MsgBox Err.Number & ":" & Err.Description
     flag = False
  End If
  Resume ExitHere
End Sub
```

The WriteLetter procedure begins with the declaration of the object variable of the specific object type (`Word.Application`). Recall that this type of declaration (early binding) requires that you establish a reference to the Microsoft Word object library (discussed earlier in this chapter). The Automation object returned by the `CreateObject` function is assigned to the object variable called `class`. Because the applications launched by Automation don't appear on the screen, the statement:

```
wordAppl.Visible = True
```

will make the launched Word application visible so that you can watch VBA at work.

The remaining statements of this procedure open a new Word document (the `Add` method), enter text in the first paragraph (the `InsertBefore` method), save the document in a disk file (the `SaveAs2` method), and close the Word application (the `Quit` method). Each statement is preceded by an instruction that changes the message displayed in the status bar at the bottom of the Word application window. When the Word application is closed, `the` instruction:

```
Set wordAppl = Nothing
```

will clear the object variable to reclaim the memory used by the object.

4. To run the procedure, switch to the Microsoft Excel application window and choose **View | Macros | View Macros**. Select the **WriteLetter** procedure in the list of macros and click **Run**.

Using the GetObject Function

If you are certain that the Automation object already exists or is already open, consider using the `GetObject` function. The function looks like this:

```
GetObject([pathname][, class])
```

The `GetObject` function has two arguments that are optional; however, one of the arguments must be specified. If `pathname` is omitted, `class` is required. For example:

```
Excel.Application
Excel.Sheet
Excel.Chart
Excel.Range
Word.Application
Word.Document
PowerPoint.Application
```

- To create an Excel object based on the Report.xls workbook and force the object to be an Excel 97–2003 version worksheet, you could use the following declaration:

```
' late binding
Dim excelObj As Object
Set  excelObj  =  GetObject("C:\VBAExcel2021_ByExample\Report.
xls", "Excel.Sheet.8")
```

NOTE	*Use "Excel.Sheet.12" for Microsoft Office Excel 2007–2021 Worksheet.*

- To set the object variable to a specific Word document, you would use:

```
 ' early binding
Dim wordObj As Word.Application
Set  wordObj  =  GetObject("C:\VBAExcel2021_ByExample\Invite.
docx")
```

- To access a running Office application object, leave the first argument out:

```
Dim excelObj As Object
Set excelObj = GetObject(, "Excel.Application")
```

When the `GetObject` function is called without the first argument, it returns a reference to an instance of the application. If the application isn't running, an error will occur.

Opening an Existing Word Document

The CenterText procedure that follows demonstrates the use of the `GetObject` function to access the Invite.doc file. As you recall, this file was created earlier in this chapter by the WriteLetter procedure. The CenterText procedure will center the first paragraph in the specified Word document.

Hands-On 13.7 Opening and Modifying a Word Document with VBA

This Hands-On uses the Word document file (Invite.doc) created in Hands-On 13.7.

1. In the Automation module Code window, enter the CenterText procedure as shown below:

```
Sub CenterText()
  Dim wordDoc As Word.Document
  Dim wordAppl As Word.Application
  Dim strDoc As String
  Dim myAppl As String

  On Error GoTo ErrorHandler

  strDoc = "C:\VBAExcel2021_ByExample\Invite.docx"
  myAppl = "Word.Application"

  ' first find out whether the specified document exists
  If Not DocExists(strDoc) Then
    MsgBox strDoc & " does not exist." & Chr(13) & Chr(13) _
        & "Please run the WriteLetter procedure to create " & _
        strDoc & "."
        Exit Sub
  End If

  ' now check if Word is running
  If Not IsRunning(myAppl) Then
      MsgBox "Word is not running -> will create " & _
      "a new instance of Word. "
      Set wordAppl = CreateObject("Word.Application")
      Set wordDoc = wordAppl.Documents.Open(strDoc)
  Else
   MsgBox "Word is running -> will get the specified document. "
      ' bind the wordDoc variable to a specific Word document
      Set wordDoc = GetObject(strDoc)
  End If
  ' center the 1st paragraph horizontally on page
  With wordDoc.Paragraphs(1).Range
      .ParagraphFormat.Alignment = wdAlignParagraphCenter
  End With
  wordDoc.Application.Quit SaveChanges:=True
  Set wordDoc = Nothing
  Set wordAppl = Nothing
  MsgBox "The document " & strDoc & " was reformatted."
  Exit Sub
ErrorHandler:
  MsgBox Err.Description, vbCritical, "Error: " & Err.Number
End Sub
```

The CenterText procedure uses a custom function named `DocExists` (see code in Step 2) to check for the existence of the specified document. Another custom function, `IsRunning` (see code in Step 3), checks whether a copy of Microsoft Word is already running. Based on the findings, either the `CreateObject` or `GetObject` function is used. If an error occurs, the error number and error description are displayed.

2. In the Automation module Code window, enter the `DocExists` function procedure as shown below:

```
Function DocExists(ByVal mydoc As String) As Boolean
  On Error Resume Next
  If Dir(mydoc) <> "" Then
    DocExists = True
  Else
    DocExists = False
  End If
End Function
```

3. In the Automation module Code window, enter the `IsRunning` function procedure as shown below:

```
Function IsRunning(ByVal myAppl As String) As Boolean
  Dim applRef As Object
  On Error Resume Next

  Set applRef = GetObject(, myAppl)
  If Err.Number = 429 Then
    IsRunning = False
  Else
    IsRunning = True
  End If
  ' clear the object variable
  Set applRef = Nothing
End Function
```

4. In the Visual Basic Editor window, position the pointer anywhere within the code of the CenterText procedure, then choose **Debug | Step Into**.
5. When a yellow highlight appears on the `Sub CenterText` line, press **F8**. Keep on pressing F8 to execute the procedure step by step.
   Notice how Visual Basic jumps to the appropriate function procedure to find out whether the specified Word document exists and whether the Word application is running.

Using the New Keyword

Instead of using the `CreateObject` function to assign a reference to another application, you can use the `New` keyword. The `New` keyword tells Visual Basic to create a new instance of an object, return a reference to that instance, and assign the reference to the object variable being declared. For example, you can use the `New` keyword in the following way:

```
Dim objWord As Word.Application
Set objWord = New Word.Application

Dim objAccess As Access.Application
Set objAccess = New Access.Application
```

Object variables declared with the `New` keyword are always early bound. Using the `New` keyword is more efficient than using the `CreateObject` function. Each time you use the `New` keyword, Visual Basic creates a new instance of the application. The `New` keyword can also be used to create a new instance of the object at the same time that you declare its object variable. For example:

```
Dim objWord As New Word.Application
```

Notice that when you declare the object variable with the `New` keyword in the `Dim` statement, you do not need to use the `Set` statement. However, this method of creating an object variable is not recommended because you lose control over when the object variable is actually created. Using the `New` keyword in the declaration statement causes the object variable to be created even if it isn't used. Therefore, if you want control over when the object is created, always declare your object variables using the following syntax:

```
Dim objWord As Word.Application
Set objWord = New Word.Application
```

The `Set` statement can be placed further in your code where you need to use the object. The following section demonstrates how to use the `New` keyword to create a new instance of Microsoft Outlook and write your contact addresses to an Excel worksheet.

Using Automation to Access Microsoft Outlook

To access Outlook's object model directly from Excel, begin by establishing a reference to the Microsoft Outlook 16.0 or earlier object library. The example procedure that follows will insert your Outlook contact information into an Excel spreadsheet.

Hands-On 13.9 Bringing Outlook Contacts to Excel

1. Establish a reference to the **Microsoft Outlook 16.0** (or earlier) object library.

2. In the Automation module Code window, enter the GetContacts procedure as shown below:

```
Sub GetContacts()
  Dim objOut As Outlook.Application
  Dim objNspc As Namespace
  Dim objItem As ContactItem
  Dim r As Integer ' row index
  Dim Headings As Variant
  Dim i As Integer ' array element
  Dim cell As Variant

  r = 2
  Set objOut = New Outlook.Application
  Set objNspc = objOut.GetNamespace("MAPI")

  Headings = Array("Full Name", "Street", "City", _
      "State", "Zip Code", "E-Mail")
  Workbooks.Add
  Sheets(1).Activate
  For Each cell In Range("A1:F1")
      cell.FormulaR1C1 = Headings(i)
      i = i + 1
  Next
  For Each objItem In objNspc.GetDefaultFolder _
      (olFolderContacts).Items
      With ActiveSheet
          .Cells(r, 1).Value = objItem.FullName
          .Cells(r, 2).Value = objItem.BusinessAddress
          .Cells(r, 3).Value = objItem.BusinessAddressCity
          .Cells(r, 4).Value = objItem.BusinessAddressState
         .Cells(r, 5).Value = objItem.BusinessAddressPostalCode
          .Cells(r, 6).Value = objItem.Email1Address
      End With
      r = r + 1
  Next objItem

  Set objItem = Nothing
  Set objNspc = Nothing
  Set objOut = Nothing
  MsgBox "Your contacts have been dumped to Excel."
End Sub
```

The GetContacts procedure starts by declaring an object variable called `objOut` to hold a reference to the Outlook application. This variable is defined by a specific object type (`Outlook.Application`); therefore, VBA will use early binding. Notice that in this procedure, we use the `New` keyword discussed earlier to create a new instance of an Outlook Application object, return a reference to that instance, and assign the reference to the `objOut` variable being declared.

In order to access contact items in Outlook, you also need to declare object variables to reference the Outlook Namespace and Item objects. The Namespace object represents the message store known as MAPI (Messaging Application Programming Interface). The Namespace object contains folders (Contacts, Journal, Tasks, etc.), which in turn contain items. An item is an instance of Outlook data, such as an email message or a contact.

After writing column headings to the worksheet using the `For Each...Next` loop, the procedure uses another `For Each...Next` loop to iterate through the Items collection in the Contacts folder. The `GetDefaultFolder` method returns an object variable for the Contacts folder. This method takes one argument, the constant representing the folder you want to access. After all the contact items are written to an Excel spreadsheet, the procedure releases all object variables by setting them to `Nothing`.

3. Run the GetContacts procedure.

When you run the GetContacts procedure, you may get a warning message that the program is trying to access email addresses. Choose Allow access for 1 minute and click Yes to allow the operation. Upon the successful execution of the procedure, click OK to the message and switch to the Microsoft Excel application window to view your Outlook contacts in a new workbook file that was created by the GetContacts procedure.

SUMMARY

In this chapter, you learned how to launch, activate, and control other applications from VBA procedures. You learned how to send keystrokes to another application by using the `SendKeys` method and how to manually and programmatically link and embed objects. Additionally, you used Automation to create a new Word document from Excel and accessed this document later to change some formatting. You also learned how to retrieve your contact addresses from Microsoft Outlook and place them in an Excel worksheet. You expanded your knowledge of VBA statements with two new functions—`CreateObject` and `GetObject`—and learned how and when to use the `New` keyword.

In the next chapter, you will learn various methods of controlling Microsoft Access from Excel.

Chapter 14 USING EXCEL WITH MICROSOFT ACCESS

In Chapter 13, you learned about controlling Microsoft Word and Outlook from Excel via Automation. This chapter shows you how to programmatically use Microsoft Access from Excel as well as how to retrieve Access data into an Excel worksheet by using the following methods:

- Automation
- DAO (Data Access Objects)
- ADO (ActiveX Data Objects)

Before you learn how to use Excel VBA to perform various tasks in an Access database, let's briefly examine the data access methods that Microsoft Access uses to gain programmatic access to its objects.

OBJECT LIBRARIES

A Microsoft Access database consists of various types of objects stored in different object libraries. In this chapter, you will be accessing objects, properties, and methods from several libraries that are listed below.

- The Microsoft Access 16.0 object library

  This library, shown in Figure 14.1, provides objects that are used to display data and work with Microsoft Access. The library is stored in the MSACC.OLB file and can be found in the C:\Program Files\Microsoft Office\root\office16 folder. After setting up a reference to this library in the References dialog box (this is covered in the next section), you will be able to look up this library's objects, properties, and methods in the Object Browser.

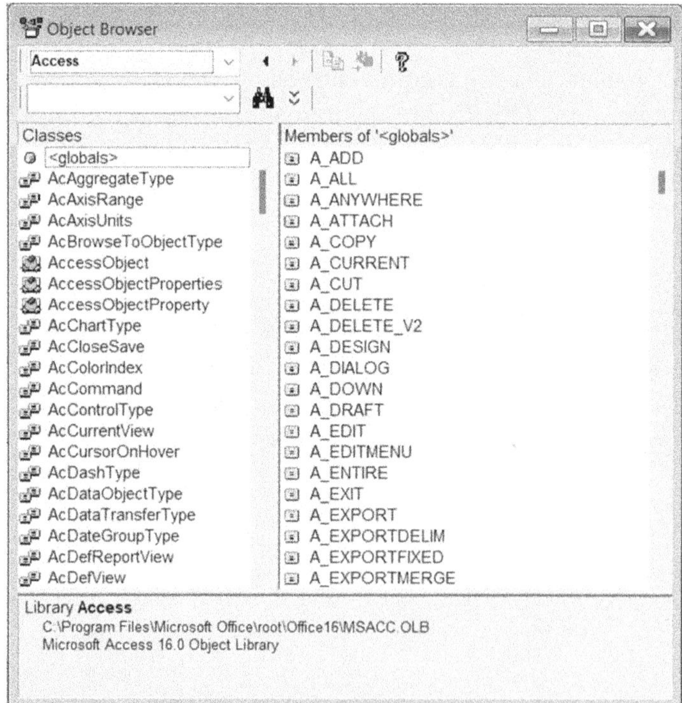

FIGURE 14.1 The Microsoft Access 16.0 object library.

NOTE	*On 32-bit systems, look for files mentioned in this section in the Program Files (x86) folder.*

- The Microsoft DAO 3.6 object library

  Data Access Objects (DAO) that are provided by this library allow you to determine the structure of your database and manipulate data using VBA. This library is stored in the DAO360.dll file and can be found in the C:\Program Files\Common Files\Microsoft Shared\DAO folder. After setting up a reference to this library in the References dialog box (this is covered in the next section), you will be able to look up the library's objects, properties, and methods in the Object Browser (see Figure 14.2).

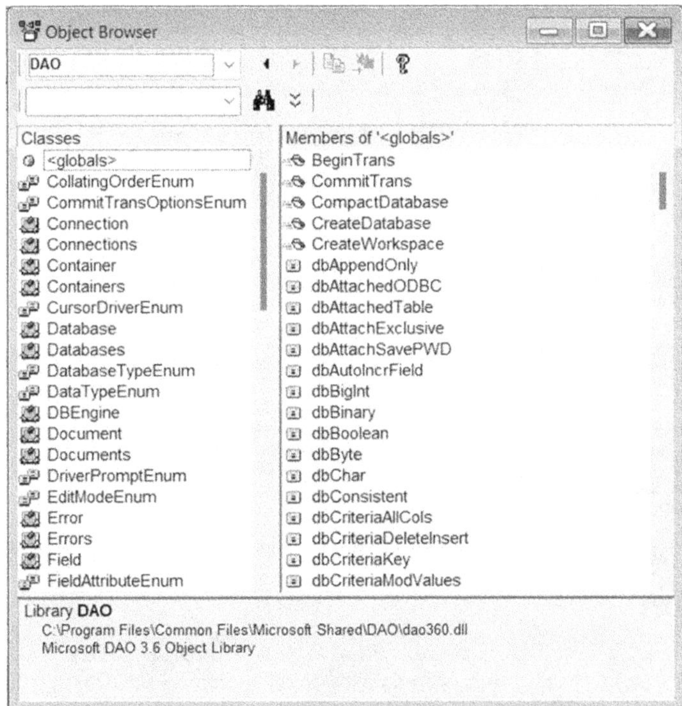

FIGURE 14.2 The Microsoft DAO 3.6 object library.

- The Microsoft ActiveX Data Objects 6.1 library (ADODB)

  ActiveX Data Objects (ADO) provided by this library let you access and manipulate data using the OLE DB provider. ADO objects make it possible to establish a connection with a data source in order to read, insert, modify, and delete data in an Access database. This library is stored in MSADO15.dll and can be found in the C:\Program Files\Common Files\System\ado folder. After setting up a reference to this library in the References dialog, you will be able to access this library's objects, properties, and methods in the Object Browser (see Figure 14.3).

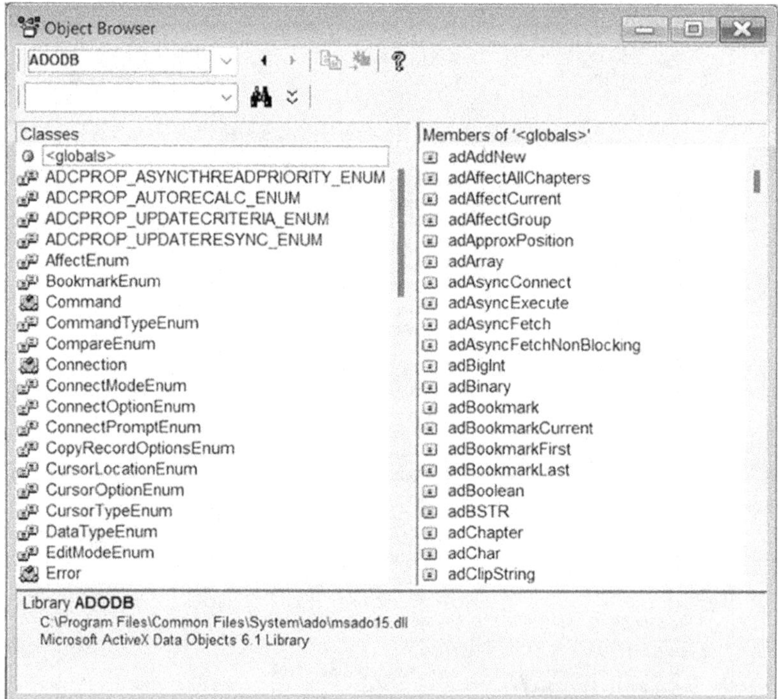

FIGURE 14.3 The Microsoft ActiveX Data Objects 6.1 library (ADODB).

- The Microsoft ADO Ext. 6.0 for DDL and Security library (ADOX)

  Objects that are stored in this library allow you to define the database structure and security. For example, you can define tables, indexes, and relationships, as well as create and modify user and group accounts. This library, shown in Figure 14.4, is stored in MSADOX.dll and can be found in the C:\Program Files\Common Files\System\ado folder. After setting up a reference to this library in the References dialog box, you will be able to look up this library's objects, properties, and methods in the Object Browser.

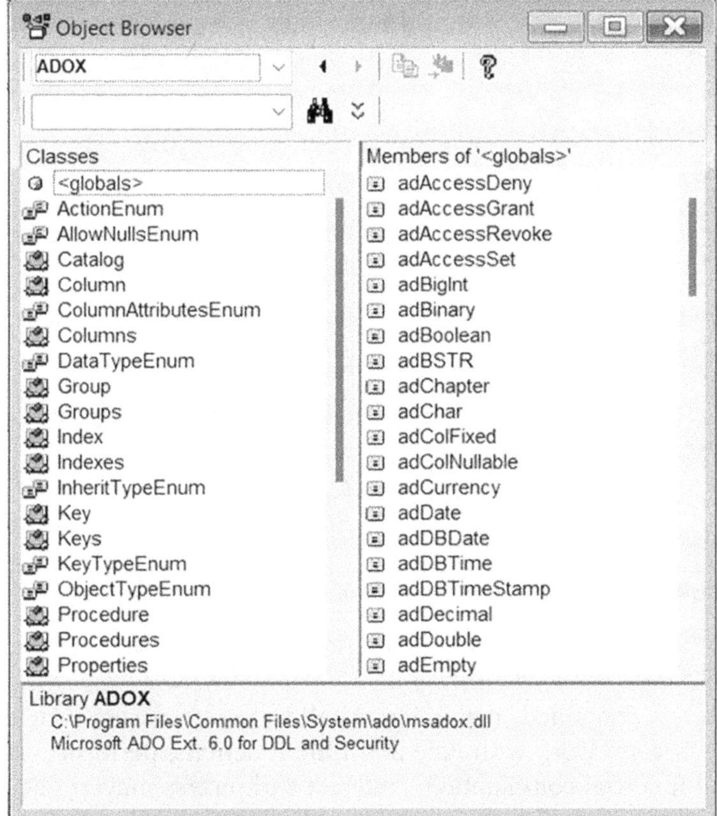

FIGURE 14.4 The Microsoft ADO Ext. 6.0 for DDL and the Security library (ADOX).

- The Microsoft Jet and Replication Objects 2.6 library (JRO)

  Objects contained in this library, shown in Figure 14.5, are used in the replication of a database. This library is stored in MSJRO.dll and can be found in the C:\Program Files\Common Files\System\ado folder. After setting up a reference to this library in the References dialog box, you will be able to look up this library's objects, properties, and methods in the Object Browser. Database replication is no longer supported in Access 2013-2021.

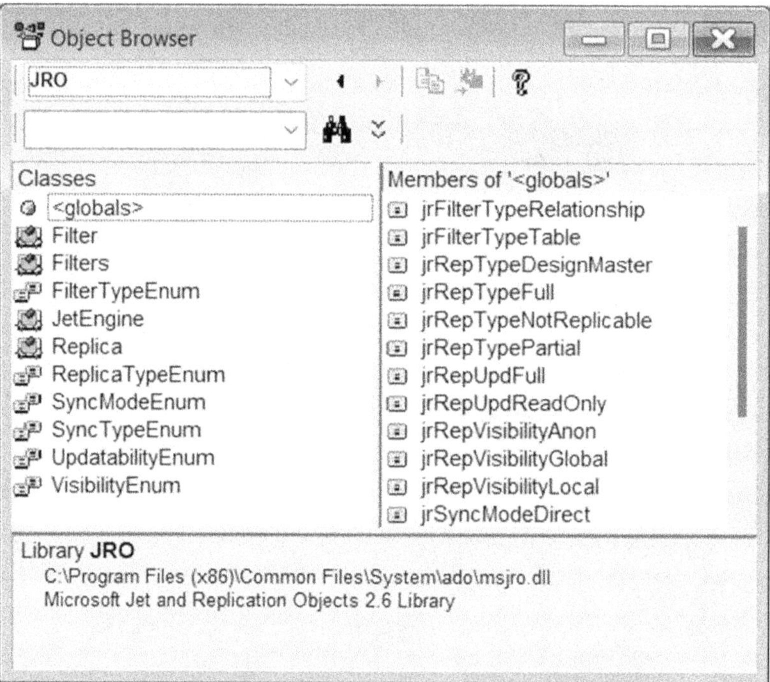

FIGURE 14.5 The Microsoft Jet and Replication Objects 2.6 library (JRO).

- The Visual Basic for Applications object library (VBA)

  Objects contained in this library allow you to access your computer's file system, work with date and time functions, perform mathematical and financial computations, interact with users, convert data, and read text files. This library is stored in the VBE7.dll file located in the C:\Program Files\Common Files\Microsoft Shared\VBA\VBA7.1 folder. The reference to this library is automatically set when you install Excel. This library, shown in Figure 14.6, is shared between all Microsoft 365 applications.

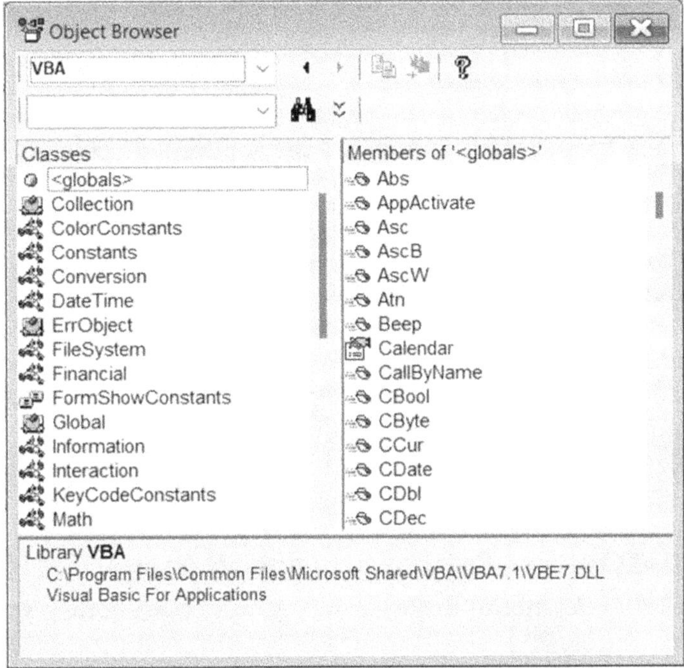

FIGURE 14.6 The Visual Basic for Applications object library (VBA).

Setting Up References to Object Libraries

To work with Microsoft Access 2021 objects, begin by creating a reference to the Microsoft Access 16.0 object library.

NOTE	*Please note files for the "Hands-On" project may be found in the companion files.*

Hands-On 14.1 Establishing a Reference to the Access Object Library

1. Start Microsoft Excel and open a new workbook. Save the file as **C:\VBAExcel2021_ByExample\Chap14_VBAExcel2021.xlsm**.
2. Activate the Visual Basic Editor window, and choose **Tools | References** to open the References dialog box. This dialog displays a list of all the type libraries that are available on your computer based on the applications you have installed.

3. Locate **Microsoft Access 16.0 Object Library** in the list of entries and select its checkbox.
4. Close the References dialog box.
   Once you've created a reference to the Microsoft Access type library, you can use the Object Browser to view a list of the application's objects, properties, and methods (see Figure 14.1 in the previous section).
5. Use the References dialog box to set up references to other object libraries that will be accessed in this chapter's exercises. You will find the list of libraries at the beginning of this chapter. You can skip setting up the reference to the Microsoft Jet and Replication Objects 2.6 library (JRO), as it will not be used here. If you are interested in database replication, there are many older books on Microsoft Access VBA programming that cover this subject, including those of mine: Access 2010 Programming by Example with VBA, XML, and ASP (ISBN: 978-1-936420-0-2-5) and *Access 2007 Programming by Example with VBA, XML, and ASP* (ISBN 1-59822-042-X)

SIDEBAR ***Advantages of Creating a Reference to a Microsoft Access Object Library***

When you set a reference to the Microsoft Access object library, you gain the following:

- You can look up Microsoft Access objects, properties, and methods in the Object Browser.
- You can run Microsoft Access functions directly in your VBA procedures.
- You can declare the object variable of the Application type instead of the generic Object type. Declaring the object variable as `Dim objAccess As Access.Application` (early binding) is faster than declaring it as `Dim objAccess As Object` (late binding).
- You can use Microsoft Access built-in constants in your VBA code.
- Your VBA procedure will run faster.

CONNECTING TO ACCESS

The example procedures in this chapter use various methods of connecting to Microsoft Access. Each method is discussed in detail as it first appears in the procedure (see the next section titled "Opening an Access Database"). You can establish a connection to Microsoft Access by using one of the following three methods:

- Automation
- Data Access Objects (DAO)
- ActiveX Data Objects (ADO)

OPENING AN ACCESS DATABASE

In order to access data in a database, you need to open it. How you open a database depends largely on which method you selected to establish a database connection.

Using Automation to Connect to an Access Database

When working with Microsoft Access from Excel (or another application) using Automation, you must take the following steps:

1. Set a reference to the Microsoft Access 16.0 object library. (Refer to the section titled "Setting up References to Object Libraries" earlier in this chapter.)
2. Declare an object variable to represent the Microsoft Access Application object:

   ```
   Dim objAccess As Access.Application
   ```

   In the declaration line above, objAccess is the name of the object variable, and `Access.Application` qualifies the object variable with the name of the Visual Basic object library that supplies the object.
3. Return the reference to the Application object and assign that reference to the object variable. Return the reference to the Application object using the `CreateObject` function, `GetObject` function, or the `New` keyword as demonstrated below. Notice that you must assign the reference to the object variable with the `Set` statement.

   - Use the `CreateObject` function to return a reference to the Application object when there is no current instance of the object. If Microsoft Access is already running, a new instance is started, and the specified object is created.

     ```
     Dim objAccess As Object
     Set objAccess = CreateObject("Access.Application.16")
     ```

- Use the `GetObject` function to return a reference to the Application object to use the current instance of Microsoft Access or to start Microsoft Access and have it load a file.

```
Dim objAccess As Object
Set objAccess = GetObject(,"Access.Application.16")
```

or

```
Set objAccess = GetObject("C:\VBAExcel2021_ByExample\" & _
    "Northwind 2007.accdb")
```

- Use the New keyword to declare an object variable, return a reference to the Application object, and assign the reference to the object variable, all in one step.

```
Dim objAccess As New Access.Application
```

- It is also possible to declare an object variable using the two-step method, which gives more control over the object:

```
Dim objAccess As Access.Application
Set objAccess = New Access.Application
```

SIDEBAR ***Arguments of the GetObject Function***

The first argument of the `GetObject` function, `pathname`, is optional. It is used when you want to work with an object in a specific file. The second argument, `class`, specifies which application creates the object and what type of object it is. When the first argument is optional and the second argument is required, you must place a comma in the position of the first argument, as shown below:

```
Dim objAccess As Object
Set objAccess = GetObject(, "Access.Application.16")
```

Because the first argument (`pathname`) of the `GetObject` function is omitted, a reference to an existing instance of the Microsoft Access application class is returned.

```
Dim objAccess As Object
Set objAccess = GetObject("C:\VBAExcel2021_ByExample\" & _
    "Northwind 2007.accdb")
```

When the first argument of the `GetObject` function is the name of a database file, a new instance of the Microsoft Access application is activated or created with the specific database.

SIDEBAR *Using the New Keyword*

- When you declare the object variable with the `New` keyword, the Access application does not start until you begin working with the object variable in your VBA code.
- When you use the `New` keyword to declare the Application object variable, a new instance of Microsoft Access is created automatically and you don't need to use the `CreateObject` function.
- Using the `New` keyword to create a new instance of the Application object is faster than using the `CreateObject` function.

Because you may have more than one version of Microsoft Access installed, include the version number in the argument of the `GetObject` or `CreateObject` function. The seven most recent versions of Microsoft Access are shown below:

Microsoft Access 2016/2021	Access.Application.16
Microsoft Access 2013	Access.Application.15
Microsoft Access 2010	Access.Application.14
Microsoft Access 2007	Access.Application.12
Microsoft Access 2003	Access.Application.11
Microsoft Access 2002	Access.Application.10
Microsoft Access 2000	Access.Application.9
Microsoft Access 97	Access.Application.8
Microsoft Access 95	Access.Application.7

Once you've created a new instance of the Application class by using one of the methods outlined in Step 3 above, you can open a database or create a new database with the help of `OpenCurrentDatabase`. You can close the Microsoft Access database that you opened through Automation by using the `CloseCurrentDatabase` method.

Now let's look at an example procedure that opens an Access database straight from an Excel VBA procedure.

Hands-On 14.2 Opening an Access Database Using Automation

This Hands-On requires that you establish a reference to the Microsoft Access 16.0 object library (see Hands-On 14.1). Make sure you have a copy of the Northwind 2007.accdb database in the VBAExcel2021_ByExample folder.

1. Switch to the Visual Basic Editor window and rename VBAProject (Chap14_VBAExcel2021.xlsm) to **AccessFromExcel**.
2. Insert a new module into the AccessFromExcel project and rename it **Automation.**
3. In the Automation module Code window, enter the AccessViaAutomation procedure as shown below:

```
Sub AccessViaAutomation()
  Dim objAccess As Access.Application
  Dim strPath As String

  On Error Resume Next

  Set objAccess = GetObject(, " Access.Application.16")
  If objAccess Is Nothing Then
      ' Get a reference to the Access Application object
      Set objAccess = New Access.Application
  End If

  strPath = "C:\VBAExcel2021_ByExample\Northwind 2007.accdb"

  ' Open the Employees table in the Northwind database
  With objAccess
      .OpenCurrentDatabase strPath
      .DoCmd.OpenTable "Employees", acViewNormal, acReadOnly
      If MsgBox("Do you want to make the Access " & vbCrLf _
          & "Application visible?", vbYesNo, _
          "Display Access") = vbYes Then
          .Visible = True
          MsgBox "Notice the Access Application icon " _
          & "now appears on the Windows taskbar."
      End If
      ' Close the database and quit Access
      .CloseCurrentDatabase
      .Quit
  End With

  Set objAccess = Nothing
End Sub
```

This procedure uses a current instance of Access if it is available. If Access isn't running, a runtime error will occur and the object variable will be set to `Nothing`. By placing the `On Error Resume Next` statement inside this procedure, you can trap this error. Therefore, if Access isn't running, a new instance of Access will be started. This particular example uses the `New` keyword to start a new instance of Access.

As mentioned earlier, instead of creating a new object instance with the `New` keyword, you can use the `CreateObject` function to start a new instance of an automation server, as illustrated below:

```
Set objAccess = GetObject(, " Access.Application.16")
If objAccess Is Nothing Then
  Set objAccess = CreateObject(, " Access.Application.16")
End If
```

Once Access is opened and the Northwind database is loaded with the OpenCurrentDatabase method, we issue a command to open the Employees table in read-only mode. The procedure then asks the user whether to make the Access application window visible. If the user selects Yes to this prompt, the `Visible` property of the Access Application object is set to True and the user is prompted to look for the Access icon on the taskbar. After selecting OK in response to the message, the Northwind database is closed with the CloseCurrentDatabase method and the Access `Application` object is closed with the `Quit` method. After closing the object, the object variable is set to the Nothing keyword to free the memory resources used by the variable. You can prevent an instance of Microsoft Access from closing by making an object variable a module-level variable rather than declaring it at the procedure level. Under these circumstances, the connection to the database will remain open until you close the Automation controller (Excel) or use the `Quit` method in your VBA code.

4. Run the above procedure by stepping through its code with the **F8** key. Be sure to check the Access interface before running the statement that closes Access. At the top of the Access window just below the Ribbon you should see a familiar security warning message. Access, like Excel, automatically disables all potentially harmful database content. To let Access know that you trust the database, click the **Options** button and then select the **Enable this content** option button. To permanently trust the Northwind 2007 database for this chapter's exercises, choose **File | Options | Trust Center** and then proceed to designate the C:\VBAExcel2021_ByExample folder as a trusted location. (See Chapter 1 for more information on trusted locations.)

SIDEBAR *Opening a Secured Microsoft Access Database*

If the Access database is secured with a password, the user will be prompted to enter the correct password. You must use Data Access Objects (DAO) or ActiveX Data Objects (ADO) to programmatically open a password-protected Microsoft Access database. The following example uses the `DBEngine` property of the Microsoft Access object to specify the password of the database. For this procedure to work, you must set up a reference to the Microsoft DAO 3.6 object library, as explained in the beginning of this chapter. You should also replace the name of the database file with your own Access database that you have previously secured with password "test."

```
Sub OpenSecuredDB()
  Static objAccess As Access.Application
  Dim db As DAO.Database
  Dim strDb As String

  strDb = "C:\VBAExcel2021_ByExample\Med.mdb"
  Set objAccess = New Access.Application
  Set db = objAccess.DBEngine.OpenDatabase(Name:=strDb, _
      Options:=False, _
      ReadOnly:=False, _
      Connect:=";PWD=test")
  With objAccess
      .Visible = True
      .OpenCurrentDatabase strDb
  End With
  db.Close
  Set db = Nothing
End Sub
```

Using DAO to Connect to an Access Database

To connect to a Microsoft Access database using Data Access Objects (DAO), you must first set up a reference to the Microsoft DAO 3.6 object library in the References dialog box (see the section titled "Setting up References to Object Libraries" earlier in this chapter). The example procedure shown below uses the `OpenDatabase` method of the `DBEngine` object to open the Northwind database and then proceeds to read the names of its tables.

Hands-On 14.3 Opening an Access Database with DAO

1. Insert a new module into the AccessFromExcel VBA project and rename it **Examples_DAO**.
2. In the Examples_DAO module Code window, enter the DAO_OpenDatabase procedure as shown below:

```
Sub DAO_OpenDatabase(strDbPathName As String)
  Dim db As DAO.Database
  Dim tbl As Variant

  Set db = DBEngine.OpenDatabase(strDbPathName)

  MsgBox "There are " & db.TableDefs.Count & _
      " tables in " & strDbPathName & "." & vbCrLf & _
      " View the names in the Immediate window."

  For Each tbl In db.TableDefs
      Debug.Print tbl.Name
  Next

  db.Close
  Set db = Nothing
  MsgBox "The database has been closed."
End Sub
```

The `DBEngine` object allows you to initialize the standard Access database engine known as ACE and open a database file. You can open a file in the .accdb or older .mdb Microsoft Access file format. Once the database is open, the DAO_OpenDatabase procedure retrieves the total number of tables from the `TableDefs` collection. A `TableDefs` collection contains all stored `TableDef` objects in a Microsoft Access database. Next, the procedure iterates through the `TableDefs` collection, reading the names of tables and printing them out to the Immediate window. All these operations occur behind the scenes; notice that the Access application window is not visible to the user. Finally, the procedure uses the Close method to close the database file.

3. To run the DAO_OpenDatabase procedure, type either of the following statements in the Immediate window and press **Enter**:

   DAO_OpenDatabase "C:\VBAExcel2021_ByExample\Northwind 2007.accdb"

   DAO_OpenDatabase "C:\VBAExcel2021_ByExample\Northwind.mdb"

   Notice that when the procedure finishes, the Immediate window contains the list of all the database tables.

Using ADO to Connect to an Access Database

Another method of establishing a connection with an Access database is using ActiveX Data Objects (ADO). You must begin by setting up a reference to the Microsoft ActiveX Data Objects 6.1 library or a `lower` version. The example procedure ADO_OpenDatabase connects to the Northwind database using the `Connection` object.

Hands-On 14.4 Opening an Access Database with ADO

1. Insert a new module into the AccessFromExcel VBA project and rename it **Examples_ADO**.
2. In the Examples_ADO module Code window, enter the ADO_OpenDatabase procedure as shown below:

```
Sub ADO_OpenDatabase(strDbPathName)
  Dim con As New ADODB.Connection
  Dim rst As New ADODB.Recordset
  Dim fld As ADODB.Field
  Dim iCol As Integer
  Dim wks As Worksheet

  ' connect with the database
    con.Open _
      "Provider = Microsoft.ACE.OLEDB.12.0;" _
       & "Data Source=" & strDbPathName

  ' open Recordset based on the SQL statement
    rst.Open "SELECT * FROM Employees " & _
      "WHERE City = 'Redmond'", con, _
      adOpenForwardOnly, adLockReadOnly

  ' enter data into an Excel worksheet in a new workbook
  Workbooks.Add
  Set wks = ActiveWorkbook.Sheets(1)
  wks.Activate

  'write column names to the first worksheet row
  For iCol = 0 To rst.Fields.Count - 1
      wks.Cells(1, iCol + 1).Value = rst.Fields(iCol).Name
  Next

  'copy records to the worksheet
  wks.Range("A2").CopyFromRecordset rst
```

```
    'autofit the columns to make the data fit
    wks.Columns.AutoFit

    'release object variables
    Set wks = Nothing

    ' close the Recordset and connection with Access
    rst.Close
    con.Close

    ' destroy object variables to reclaim the resources
    Set rst = Nothing
    Set con = Nothing
End Sub
```

In the above procedure we open the Access database via the `Open` method. The `Open` method requires a connection string argument that contains the name of the data provider. The data source name is the full name of the database file you want to open.

After establishing a connection to the Northwind database, you can use the `Recordset` object to access its data. Recordset objects are used to manipulate data at the record level. The `Recordset` object is made up of records (rows) and fields (columns). To obtain a set of records, you need to use the `Open` method and specify information such as the source of records for the recordset. The source of records can be the name of a database table, a query, or the SQL statement that returns records. After specifying the source of records, you must indicate the connection with the database (con) and two constants, one of which defines the type of cursor (`adOpenForwardOnly`) and the other the lock type (`adLockReadOnly`). The `adOpenForwardOnly` constant tells VBA to create the forward-only recordset, which scrolls forward in the returned set of records. The second constant, `adLockReadOnly`, specifies the type of the lock placed on records during editing; the records are read-only, which means that you cannot alter the data. Next, the procedure iterates through the entire recordset and its Fields collection to print the contents of all the fields to an Excel worksheet. After obtaining the data, the `Close` method closes the recordset and another `Close` method is used to close the connection with the Access database.

3. To run the ADO_OpenDatabase procedure, type either of the following statements in the Immediate window and press **Enter**:

```
ADO_OpenDatabase "C:\VBAExcel2021_ByExample\Northwind 2007.accdb"
ADO_OpenDatabase "C:\VBAExcel2021_ByExample\Northwind.mdb"
```

4. Activate the Microsoft Excel application window to view the worksheet with the procedure results.
5. Close the created Excel files without saving them.

PERFORMING ACCESS TASKS FROM EXCEL

After connecting to Microsoft Access from Excel you can perform different tasks within the Access application. This section demonstrates in particular how to use VBA code to:

- Create a new Access database
- Open an existing database form
- Create a new database form
- Open a database report
- Run an Access function

Creating a New Access Database with DAO

If you want to programmatically transfer Excel data into a new Access database, you may need to create a database from scratch by using VBA code. The following example procedure demonstrates how this is done using Data Access Objects (DAO).

Hands-On 14.5 Creating a New Access Database

1. In the Examples_DAO module Code window, enter the NewDB_DAO procedure as shown below:

```
Sub NewDB_DAO()
  Dim db As DAO.Database
  Dim tbl As DAO.TableDef
  Dim strDb As String
  Dim strTbl As String

  On Error GoTo Error_CreateDb_DAO
  strDb = "C:\VBAExcel2021_ByExample\ExcelDump.mdb"
  strTbl = "tblStates"
  ' Create a new database named ExcelDump
  Set db = DBEngine.CreateDatabase(strDb, dbLangGeneral)
```

```
    ' Create a new table named tblStates
    Set tbl = db.CreateTableDef(strTbl)

    ' Create fields and append them to the Fields collection
    With tbl
      .Fields.Append .CreateField("StateID", dbText, 2)
      .Fields.Append .CreateField("StateName", dbText, 25)
      .Fields.Append .CreateField("StateCapital", dbText, 25)
    End With

    ' Append the new tbl object to the TableDefs
    db.TableDefs.Append tbl
    ' Close the database
    db.Close
    Set db = Nothing
    MsgBox "There is a new database on your hard disk. " _
        & Chr(13) & "This database file contains a table " _
        & "named " & strTbl & "."
Exit_CreateDb_DAO:
    Exit Sub
Error_CreateDb_DAO:
    If Err.Number = 3204 Then
        ' Delete the database file if it
        ' already exists
        Kill strDb
        Resume
    Else
        MsgBox Err.Number & ": " & Err.Description
        Resume Exit_CreateDb_DAO
    End If
End Sub
```

The `CreateDatabase` method of the `DBEngine` object is used to create a new database named ExcelDump.mdb. The `CreateTableDef` method of the `Database` object is then used to create a table named tblStates.

Before a table can be added to a database, the fields must be created and appended to the table. The procedure creates three text fields (dbText) that can store 2, 25, and 25 characters each. As each field is created, it is appended to the `Fields` collection of the `TableDef` object using the Append method.

Once the fields have been created and appended to the table, the table itself is added to the database with the `Append` method. Because the database file may already exist in the specified location, the procedure includes the error-handling routine that will delete the existing file so the database creation process can go on. Because other errors could occur, the `Else` clause includes statements that will display the error and its description and allow an exit from the procedure.

2. Run the NewDB_DAO procedure.
3. Launch Microsoft Access and open the **ExcelDump.mdb** file. Next, open the table named **tblStates**. The result of this procedure is shown in Figure 14.7.

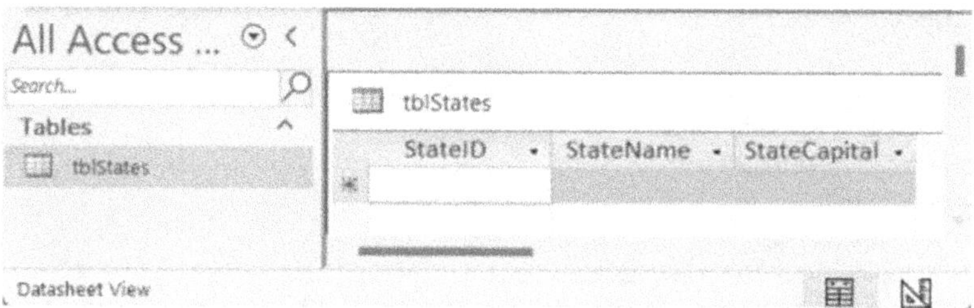

FIGURE 14.7 This Microsoft Access database table was created by an Excel VBA procedure.

4. Close the Access application.

Opening an Access Form

You can open a Microsoft Access form from Microsoft Excel. You can also create a new Access form. The following example uses Automation to connect to Access.

Hands-On 14.6 Opening an Access Form from a VBA Procedure

1. Insert a new module into the AccessFromExcel VBA project and rename it **Database_Forms.**
2. In the Database_Forms module Code window, enter the following module-level declaration and the DisplayAccessForm procedure as shown below:

```
Dim objAccess As Access.Application

Sub DisplayAccessForm()
  Dim strDb As String
  Dim strFrm As String

  strDb = "C:\VBAExcel2021_ByExample\Northwind.mdb"
  strFrm = "Customers"
  Set objAccess = New Access.Application
  With objAccess
      .OpenCurrentDatabase strDb
```

```
        .DoCmd.OpenForm strFrm, acNormal
        .DoCmd.Restore
        .Visible = True
    End With
End Sub
```

In the above procedure, the `OpenCurrentDatabase` method is used to open the sample Northwind database. The Customers form is opened in normal view (`acNormal`) with the `OpenForm` method of the `DoCmd` object. To display the form in design view, use the `acDesign` constant. The Restore method of the DoCmd object ensures that the form is displayed on the screen in a window and not minimized. The Visible property of the Access `Application` object (objAccess) must be set to True for the form to become visible.Notice that the Access.`Application` object variable (objAccess) is declared at the top of the module. For this procedure to work correctly, you must set up a reference to the Microsoft Access object library.

3. Switch to the Microsoft Excel application window and press **Alt+F8** to display the Macro dialog box. Highlight the **DisplayAccessForm** macro name and click **Run**. Figure 14.8 shows the Customers form after it's been opened.

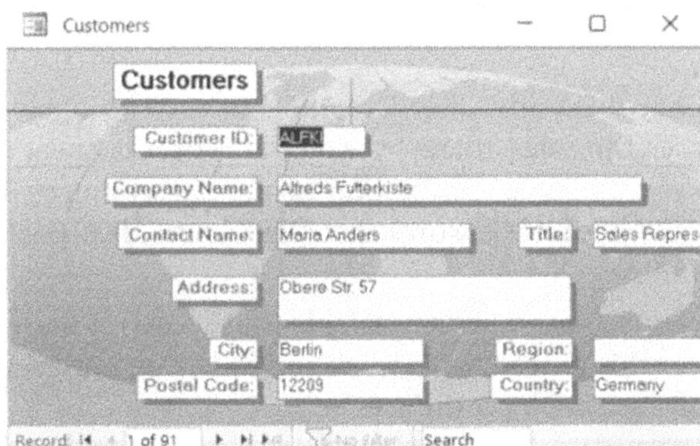

FIGURE 14.8 A Microsoft Access form can be opened using an Excel VBA procedure.

4. Close the Customer Details form and exit Microsoft Access.

Opening an Access Report

The following procedure demonstrates how you can display an existing Access report straight from Excel.

Hands-On 14.7 Opening an Access Report

1. Insert a new module into the AccessFromExcel VBA project and rename it **Database_Reports.**
2. In the Database_Reports module Code window, enter the module-level declaration and the DisplayAccessReport procedure as shown below:

```
Dim objAccess As Access.Application

Sub DisplayAccessReport()
  Dim strDb As String
  Dim strRpt As String
  strDb = "C:\VBAExcel2021_ByExample\Northwind.mdb"
  strRpt = "Sales Totals by Amount"

  Set objAccess = New Access.Application
  With objAccess
      .OpenCurrentDatabase (strDb)
      .DoCmd.OpenReport strRpt, acViewPreview
      .DoCmd.Maximize
      .Visible = True
  End With
End Sub
```

In this procedure, the `OpenCurrentDatabase` method is used to open the sample Northwind database. The Sales Totals by Amount report is opened in print preview mode with the `OpenReport` method of the `DoCmd` object. The Maximize method of the `DoCmd` object ensures that the form is displayed on the screen in a full-size window.

Notice that the Access.`Application` object variable (objAccess) is declared at the top of the module. For this procedure to work correctly, you must set up a reference to the Microsoft Access object library.

Switch to the Microsoft Excel application window and press **Alt+F8** to display the Macro dialog box. Highlight the `DisplayAccessReport` macro name and click **Run**. Figure 14.9 shows the report after it's been opened and displayed in print preview mode.

3. Close the Print Preview window and exit Microsoft Access.

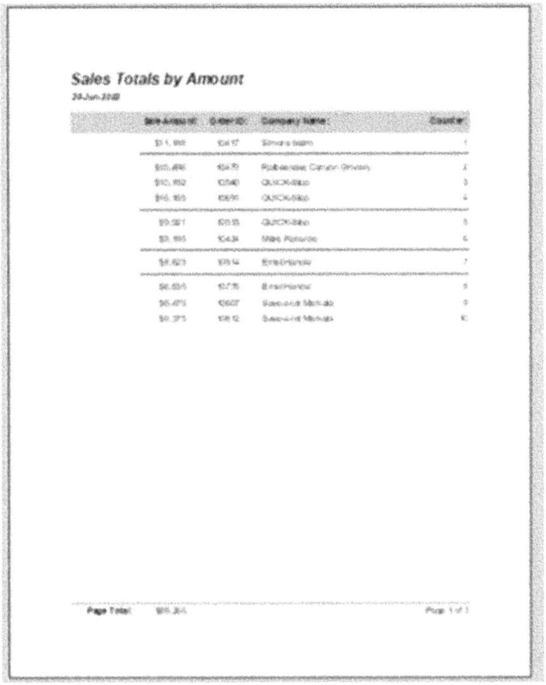

FIGURE 14.9 A Microsoft Access report can be opened using an Excel VBA procedure.

The example procedure below is more versatile, as it allows you to display any Access report in any Access database. Notice that this procedure takes two string arguments: the name of the Access database and the name of the report. Make sure that the following declaration is present at the top of the module:

```
Dim objAccess As Access.Application

Sub GetReport(strDb As String, strRpt As String)
  Set objAccess = New Access.Application

  With objAccess
      .OpenCurrentDatabase (strDb)
      .DoCmd.OpenReport strRpt, acViewPreview
      .DoCmd.Maximize
      .Visible = True
  End With
End Sub
```

You can run the above procedure from the Immediate window or from a subroutine, as shown below:

- Running the GetReport procedure from the Immediate window:

```
' type the following statement on one line
' in the Immediate window and press Enter

Call GetReport("C:\VBAExcel2021_ByExample\Northwind.mdb",
"Invoice")
```

- Running the GetReport procedure from a subroutine:

```
' Enter the following procedure in the Code window and run it

Sub ShowReport()
  Dim strDb As String
  Dim strRpt As String

  strDb = InputBox("Enter the name of the database (full path):
")
  strRpt = InputBox("Enter the name of the report:")
  Call GetReport(strDb, strRpt)
End Sub
```

Creating a New Access Database with ADO

In Hands-On 14.5 you created a new database called ExcelDump.mdb by using Data Access Objects (DAO). Creating a new Access database from a VBA procedure is also possible and just as easy by using ActiveX Data Objects (ADO). All you need is the `Catalog` object of the `ADOX` object library and its `Create` method. The `Catalog` object represents the entire database. This object contains such database elements as tables, fields, indexes, views, and stored procedures.

In the following Hands-On, we will create an Access database named ExcelDump2.accdb.

Hands-On 14.8 Creating a New Access Database with ADO

1. In the Visual Basic Editor window, choose **Tools | References** and ensure that the **Microsoft ADO Ext. 6.0 for DDL and Security Library** is selected.
2. Click **OK** to exit the References dialog box.

3. In the Examples_ADO module's Code window, enter the CreateDB_ViaADO procedure as shown below:

```
Sub CreateDB_ViaADO()
  Dim cat As ADOX.Catalog
  Set cat = New ADOX.Catalog

  cat.Create "Provider=Microsoft.ACE.OLEDB.12.0;" & _
      "Data Source=C:\VBAExcel2021_ByExample\ExcelDump2.accdb;"

  Set cat = Nothing
End Sub
```

The above procedure uses the ADOX `Catalog` object's `Create` method to create a new Access database. Notice that we created an Access 2021 database. To create a database file in the .mdb format, make sure you change the Provider string and the filename.

4. Run the CreateDB_ViaADO procedure and switch to File Explorer to check out the database file that this procedure has created.

Running a Select Query

The most popular types of queries that are executed in the Access user interface are Select and Parameter queries. You can run these queries easily from within an Excel VBA procedure. To place the data returned by the query into an Excel worksheet, use the `CopyFromRecordset` method of the `Range` object. Let's work with a procedure that executes an Access select query.

Hands-On 14.9 Running an Access Select Query

1. Insert a new module into the AccessFromExcel VBA project and rename it **Database_Queries.**
2. Choose **Tools | References** and ensure that the Microsoft ActiveX Data Objects 6.1 and **Microsoft ADO Ext. 6.0 for DDL and Security** libraries are selected.
3. Click **OK** to exit the References dialog box.
4. In the Database_Queries module Code window, enter the RunAccessQuery procedure as shown below:

```
Sub RunAccessQuery(strQryName As String)
  Dim cat As ADOX.Catalog
  Dim cmd As ADODB.Command
  Dim rst As ADODB.Recordset
  Dim i As Integer
```

```
  Dim strPath As String

  strPath = "C:\VBAExcel2021_ByExample\Northwind.mdb"

  Set cat = New ADOX.Catalog
  cat.ActiveConnection = _
      "Provider=Microsoft.ACE.OLEDB.12.0;" & _
      "Data Source=" & strPath

  Set cmd = cat.Views(strQryName).Command
  Set rst = cmd.Execute

  Sheets.Add

  For i = 0 To rst.Fields.count - 1
      Cells(1, i + 1).Value = rst.Fields(i).Name
  Next
  With ActiveSheet
      .Range("A2").CopyFromRecordset rst
      .Range(Cells(1, 1), _
          Cells(1, rst.Fields.count)).Font.Bold = True
      .Range("A1").Select
  End With

  Selection.CurrentRegion.Columns.AutoFit
  rst.Close

  Set cmd = Nothing
  Set cat = Nothing
End Sub
```

The example procedure RunAccessQuery begins by creating an object variable that points to the `Catalog` object. Next the `ActiveConnection` property of the `Catalog` object defines the method of establishing the connection to the database:

```
Set cat = New ADOX.Catalog
cat.ActiveConnection =  "Provider=Microsoft.ACE.OLEDB.12.0;" &
_ "Data Source=" & strPath
```

The `Command` object in the ADODB object library specifies the command that you want to execute in order to obtain data from the data source. This procedure attempts to access a specific query in a database whose name will be supplied at runtime.

```
Set cmd = cat.Views(strQryName).Command
```

The `Views` collection, which is a part of the ADOX object library, contains all `View` objects of a specific catalog. A *view* is a filtered set of records, or a virtual table created from other tables or views.

After gaining access to the required query in the database, you can run the query in the following way:

```
Set rst = cmd.Execute
```

The `Execute` method of the `Command` object allows you to activate a specific query, an SQL statement, or a stored procedure. The returned set of records is then assigned to the object variable of the type `Recordset` using the `Set` keyword. After creating the set of records, these records are placed in an Excel worksheet using the `CopyFromRecordset` method (this method is discussed in more detail later in this chapter).

5. To run the above procedure, type the following statement in the Immediate window and press **Enter**:

```
RunAccessQuery("Current Product List")
```

6. Switch to the Microsoft Excel application window to view the results obtained by executing the RunAccessQuery procedure, as shown in Figure 14.10.

	A	B
1	ProductID	ProductName
2	3	Aniseed Syrup
3	40	Boston Crab Meat
4	60	Camembert Pierrot
5	18	Carnarvon Tigers
6	1	Chai
7	2	Chang
8	39	Chartreuse verte
9	4	Chef Anton's Cajun Seasoning
10	48	Chocolade
11	38	Côte de Blaye
12	58	Escargots de Bourgogne
13	52	Filo Mix
14	71	Fløtemysost
15	33	Geitost
16	15	Genen Shouyu

FIGURE 14.10 The results of running an Access query from an Excel VBA procedure are placed in a worksheet.

Running a Parameter Query

When you want to obtain a different set of data based on the provided criteria, you will want to utilize parameter queries. This section demonstrates how you can run a Microsoft Access parameter query and place the resulting data in a Microsoft Excel worksheet. Let's write a procedure to run the Employee Sales by Country query and retrieve records for the period beginning 7/1/96 and ending 7/31/96.

Hands-On 14.10 Running an Access Parameter Query

1. In the Database_Queries module Code window, enter the RunAccessParamQuery procedure as shown below:

```
Sub RunAccessParamQuery()
  Dim cat As ADOX.Catalog
  Dim cmd As ADODB.Command
  Dim rst As ADODB.Recordset
  Dim i As Integer
  Dim strPath As String
  Dim StartDate As String
  Dim EndDate As String

  strPath = "C:\VBAExcel2021_ByExample\Northwind.mdb"
  StartDate = "7/1/96"
  EndDate = "7/31/96"

  Set cat = New ADOX.Catalog
   cat.ActiveConnection  =  "Provider=Microsoft.ACE.OLEDB.12.0;"
& _
      "Data Source=" & strPath
  Set cmd = cat.Procedures("Employee Sales by Country").Command

  cmd.Parameters("[Beginning Date]")  = StartDate
  cmd.Parameters("[Ending Date]")  = EndDate

  Set rst = cmd.Execute

  Sheets.Add
  For i = 0 To rst.Fields.count - 1
      Cells(1, i + 1).Value = rst.Fields(i).Name
  Next
  With ActiveSheet
      .Range("A2").CopyFromRecordset rst
```

```
        .Range(Cells(1, 1), Cells(1, rst.Fields.count)) _
            .Font.Bold = True
        .Range("A1").Select
    End With
    Selection.CurrentRegion.Columns.AutoFit

    rst.Close
    Set cmd = Nothing
    Set cat = Nothing
End Sub
```

To run parameter queries in the Microsoft Access database, you need to access the `Command` object of the `Procedures` collection of the ADOX Catalog object:

```
Set cmd = cat.Procedures("Employee Sales by Country").Command
```

Because the Microsoft Access Employee Sales by Country query requires two parameters that define the beginning and ending dates, you need to define these parameters by using the `Parameters` collection of the `Command` object:

```
cmd.Parameters("[Beginning Date]") = StartDate
cmd.Parameters("[Ending Date]") = EndDate
```

After setting up the parameters, the query is executed using the following statement:

```
Set rst = cmd.Execute
```

The set of records returned by this query is assigned to the object variable of type `Recordset` and then copied to a worksheet using the `CopyFromRecordset` method (this method is discussed in more detail later in this chapter).

2. Run the above procedure.
   Because the parameter values are hardcoded in the procedure, you are not prompted for input. On your own, modify the RunAccessParamQuery procedure so that you can provide the parameter values at runtime.
3. Switch to the Excel application window to view the results obtained by executing the RunAccessParamQuery procedure.

Calling an Access Function

You can run a built-in Microsoft Access function from Microsoft Excel through Automation. The following example procedure calls the `EuroConvert` function to convert 1,000 Spanish pesetas to Euro dollars. The `EuroConvert` function uses fixed conversion rates established by the European Union.

```
Sub RunAccessFunction()
  Dim objAccess As Object

  On Error Resume Next
  Set objAccess = GetObject(, "Access.Application")

  ' if no instance of Access is open, create a new one
  If objAccess Is Nothing Then
      Set objAccess = CreateObject("Access.Application")
  End If
  MsgBox "For 1000 Spanish pesetas you will get " & _
      objAccess.EuroConvert(1000, "ESP", "EUR") & _
      " euro dollars. "
  Set objAccess = Nothing
End Sub
```

RETRIEVING ACCESS DATA INTO AN EXCEL WORKSHEET

There are numerous ways of bringing external data into Excel. This section shows you different techniques of putting Microsoft Access data into an Excel worksheet. While you have worked with some of these methods earlier in this book, the following sections discuss these methods in greater detail.

- Using the `GetRows` method
- Using the `CopyFromRecordset` method
- Using the `TransferSpreadsheet` method
- Using the `OpenDatabase` method
- Creating a text file
- Creating a query table
- Creating an embedded chart from Access data

Retrieving Data with the GetRows Method

To place Microsoft Access data into an Excel spreadsheet, you can use the `GetRows` method. This method returns a two-dimensional array where the first subscript is a number representing the field, and the second subscript is the number representing the record. Record and field numbering begins with 0.

The following example demonstrates how to use the `GetRows` method in a VBA procedure. We will run the Invoices query in the Northwind database and return records to a worksheet.

Hands-On 14.11 Retrieving Access Data Using the GetRows Method

1. Insert a new module into the AccessFromExcel VBA project and rename it **Method_GetRows**.
2. Choose **Tools | References** and ensure that **Microsoft DAO 3.6 Object Library** is selected.
3. Click **OK** to exit the References dialog box.
4. In the Method_GetRows module Code window, enter the GetData_withGetRows procedure as shown below:

```
Sub GetData_withGetRows()
  Dim db As DAO.Database
  Dim qdf As DAO.QueryDef
  Dim rst As DAO.Recordset
  Dim recArray As Variant
  Dim i As Integer
  Dim j As Integer
  Dim strPath As String
  Dim a As Variant
  Dim countR As Long
  Dim strShtName As String

  strPath = "C:\VBAExcel2021_ByExample\Northwind.mdb"
  strShtName = "Returned records"

  Set db = DBEngine.OpenDatabase(strPath)
  Set qdf = db.QueryDefs("Invoices")
  Set rst = qdf.OpenRecordset

  rst.MoveLast
  countR = rst.RecordCount
  a = InputBox("This recordset contains " & _
      countR & " records." & vbCrLf _
      & "Enter number of records to return: ", _
      "Get Number of Records")

  If a = "" Or a = 0 Then Exit Sub
  If a > countR Then
      a = countR
      MsgBox "The number you entered is too large." & vbCrLf _
          & "All records will be returned."
  End If
```

```
  Workbooks.Add
  ActiveWorkbook.Worksheets(1).Name = strShtName
  rst.MoveFirst
      With Worksheets(strShtName).Range("A1")
        .CurrentRegion.Clear
        recArray = rst.GetRows(a)
        For i = 0 To UBound(recArray, 2)
            For j = 0 To UBound(recArray, 1)
                .Offset(i + 1, j) = recArray(j, i)
            Next j
        Next i
        For j = 0 To rst.Fields.count - 1
            .Offset(0, j) = rst.Fields(j).Name
            .Offset(0, j).EntireColumn.AutoFit
        Next j
      End With
  db.Close
End Sub
```

After opening an Access database with the `OpenDatabase` method of the `DBEngine` object, the GetData_withGetRows procedure illustrated above runs the Invoices query using the following statement:

```
Set qdf = db.QueryDefs("Invoices")
```

In the Microsoft DAO 3.6 object library the `QueryDefs` object represents a select or action query. *Select queries* return data from one or more tables or queries, while action queries allow you to add, modify, or delete records.

After executing the query, the procedure places the records returned by the query in the object variable of type `Recordset` using the `OpenRecordset` method, as shown below:

```
Set rst = qdf.OpenRecordset
```

Next, the record count is retrieved using the `RecordCount` method and placed in the `countR` variable. Notice that to obtain the correct record count, the record pointer must first be moved to the last record in the recordset by using the `MoveLast` method:

```
rst.MoveLast
countR = rst.RecordCount
```

The procedure then prompts the user to enter the number of records to return to the worksheet. You can cancel at this point by clicking the Cancel button in the input dialog box or you can type the number of records to retrieve. If you enter a number that is greater than the record count, the procedure will retrieve all the records.

Before retrieving records, you must move the record pointer to the first record by using the `MoveFirst` method. If you forget to do this, the record pointer will remain on the last record and only one record will be retrieved.

The procedure then goes on to activate the Returned records worksheet and clear the current region. The records are first returned to the Variant variable containing a two-dimensional array by using the `GetRows` method of the `Recordset` object. Next, the procedure loops through both dimensions of the array to place the records in the worksheet starting at cell A2. When this is done, another loop will fill in the first worksheet row with the names of fields and autofit each column so that the data is displayed correctly.

5. Run the GetData_withGetRows procedure. When prompted for the number of records, type **10** and click **OK**. Next, switch to the Microsoft Excel application window to view the results.
6. Close the Excel workbook created in this Hands-on exercise.

   The `GetRows` method can also be used with ActiveX Data Objects as demonstrated in the GetData_withGetRows_ADO procedure included in the companion files. To try out this procedure, ensure that the References dialog box has the Microsoft ActiveX Data Objects 6.1 and **Microsoft ADO Ext. 6.0 for DDL and Security** libraries checked.

Retrieving Data with the CopyFromRecordset Method

To retrieve an entire recordset into a worksheet, use the `CopyFromRecordset` method of the `Range` object. This method can take up to three arguments: `Data`, `MaxRows`, and `MaxColumns`. Only the first argument, `Data`, is required. This argument can be the `Recordset` object. The optional arguments, `MaxRows` and `MaxColumns`, allow you to specify the number of records (`MaxRows`) and the number of fields (`MaxColumns`) that should be returned.

If you omit the `MaxRows` argument, all the returned records will be copied to the worksheet. If you omit the `MaxColumns` argument, all the fields will be retrieved.

The following procedure uses the ADO objects and the `CopyFromRecordset` method to retrieve all the records from the Northwind database Products table.

Hands-On 14.12 Retrieving Access Data Using the `CopyFromRecordset` Method

1. Insert a new module into the AccessFromExcel VBA project and rename it **Method_CopyFromRecordset.**
2. In the Method_CopyFromRecordset module Code window, enter the GetProducts procedure as shown below.

NOTE	*For this procedure to work correctly, you must create a reference to the Microsoft ActiveX Data Objects 6.1 library. (Refer to the instructions on setting up a reference to object libraries earlier in this chapter.)*

```
Sub GetProducts()
    Dim conn As New ADODB.Connection
    Dim rst As ADODB.Recordset
    Dim strPath As String

    strPath = "C:\VBAExcel2021_ByExample\Northwind.mdb"

    conn.Open "Provider=Microsoft.ACE.OLEDB.12.0;" _
        & "Data Source=" & strPath & ";"
    conn.CursorLocation = adUseClient

    ' Create a Recordset from all the records
    ' in the Products table

    Set rst = conn.Execute(CommandText:="Products", _
        Options:=adCmdTable)

    rst.MoveFirst

    ' transfer the data to Excel
    ' get the names of fields first
    With Worksheets("Sheet3").Range("A1")
        .CurrentRegion.Clear
        For j = 0 To rst.Fields.Count - 1
            .Offset(0, j) = rst.Fields(j).Name
        Next j
        .Offset(1, 0).CopyFromRecordset rst
        .CurrentRegion.Columns.AutoFit
    End With
    rst.Close
    conn.Close
```

```
    Set rst = Nothing
    Set conn = Nothing
End Sub
```

The above procedure copies all the records from the Products table in the Northwind database into an Excel worksheet. If you want to copy fewer records, use the MaxRows argument as follows:

```
.Offset(1, 0).CopyFromRecordset rst, 5
```

The above statement tells Visual Basic to copy only five records. The `Offset` method causes the records to be entered in a spreadsheet, starting with the second spreadsheet row. To send all the records to the worksheet using the data from only two table fields, use the following statement:

```
.Offset(1, 0).CopyFromRecordset rst, , 2
```

The above statement tells Visual Basic to copy all the data from the first two columns. The comma between the rst and the number 2 is a placeholder for the omitted MaxRows argument.

3. Run the GetProducts procedure and switch to the Excel application window to view the results.

Retrieving Data with the TransferSpreadsheet Method

It is possible to use the `TransferSpreadsheet` action of the Microsoft Access DoCmd object to import or export data between the current Access database (.mdb) and a spreadsheet file. Using this method, you can also link the data in an Excel spreadsheet to the current Access database. With a linked spreadsheet, you can view and edit the spreadsheet data with Access while still allowing complete access to the data from your Excel spreadsheet application. The `TransferSpreadsheet` method carries out the `TransferSpreadsheet` action in Visual Basic and has the following syntax:

```
DoCmd.TransferSpreadsheet [transfertype][, spreadsheettype],
    tablename, filename [, hasfieldnames][, range]
```

The `transfertype` argument can be one of the following constants: `acImport` (default setting), `acExport`, or `acLink`. These constants define whether data has to be imported, exported, or linked to the database. The `spreadsheettype` argument can be one of the constants shown in Table 14.1.

TABLE 14.1 `Spreadsheettype` argument constants

spreadsheettype Constant Name	Value
acSpreadsheetTypeExcel3 (default setting)	0
acSpreadsheetTypeExcel4	6
acSpreadsheetTypeExcel5	5
acSpreadsheetTypeExcel7	5
acSpreadsheetTypeExcel8	8
acSpreadsheetTypeExcel9	8
acSpreadsheetTypeExcel12	9
acSpreadsheetTypeExcel12XML	10
acSpreadsheetTypeLotusWK1	2
acSpreadsheetTypeLotusWK3	3
acSpreadsheetTypeLotusWK4	7

It is not difficult to guess that the `spreadsheettype` argument specifies the spreadsheet name and the version number.

The `tablename` argument is a string expression that specifies the name of the Access table you want to import spreadsheet data into, export spreadsheet data from, or link spreadsheet data to. Instead of the table name, you may also specify the name of the select query whose results you want to export to a spreadsheet.

The `filename` argument is a string expression that specifies the filename and path of the spreadsheet you want to import from, export to, or link to.

The `hasfieldnames` argument is a logical value of True (–1) or False (0). True indicates that the first worksheet row contains the field names. False denotes that the first row contains normal data. The default setting is False (no field names in the first row).

The `range` argument is a string expression that specifies the range of cells or the name of the range in the worksheet. This argument applies only to importing. If you omit the `range` argument, the entire spreadsheet will be imported. Leave this argument blank if you want to export, unless you need to specify the worksheet name.

The ExportData example procedure shown below, exports data from the Shippers table in the Northwind database to the Shippers.xls spreadsheet using the `TransferSpreadsheet` method.

Hands-On 14.13 Retrieving Data with the `TransferSpreadsheet` Method

1. Insert a new module into the AccessFromExcel VBA project and rename it **Method_TransferSpreadsheet**.
2. In the Method_TransferSpreadsheet module Code window, enter the ExportData procedure as shown below:

```
Sub ExportData()
  Dim objAccess As Access.Application
  Set objAccess = CreateObject("Access.Application")

  objAccess.OpenCurrentDatabase filepath:= _
      "C:\VBAExcel2021_ByExample\Northwind.mdb"

  objAccess.DoCmd.TransferSpreadsheet _
      TransferType:=acExport, _
      SpreadsheetType:=acSpreadsheetTypeExcel12, _
      TableName:="Shippers", _
      Filename:="C:\VBAExcel2021_ByExample\Shippers.xls", _
      HasFieldNames:=True, _
      Range:="Sheet1"

  objAccess.Quit
  Set objAccess = Nothing
End Sub
```

   The ExportData procedure uses Automation to establish a connection to Microsoft Access. The database is opened using the OpenCurrentDatabase method. The TransferSpreadsheet method of the DoCmd object is used to specify that the data from the Shippers table should be exported into an Excel spreadsheet named Shippers.xls and placed in Sheet1 of this workbook. The first row of the worksheet is to be used by field headings. When data is retrieved, the Access application is closed and the object variable pointing to the Access application is destroyed.

3. Switch to the Excel application window and choose **View | Macros | View Macros**. In the Macros dialog box, select the **ExportData** procedure and click **Run**.
4. Open the Shippers.xls file created by the ExportData procedure to view the retrieved data. When asked to verify that the file is not corrupted or is from a trusted source, click **OK**.

Using the OpenDatabase Method

The `OpenDatabase` method is the easiest way to get database data into a Microsoft Excel spreadsheet. This method, which applies to the workbooks, requires that you specify the name of a database file that you want to open.

The following example procedure demonstrates how to open the Northwind database using the `OpenDatabase` method of the `Workbooks` collection.

```
Sub OpenAccessDatabase()
    On Error Resume Next

    Workbooks.OpenDatabase _
        Filename:="C:\VBAExcel2021_ByExample\Northwind.mdb"
    Exit Sub
End Sub
```

When you run the above procedure, Excel will display a dialog box listing all the tables and queries in the database (see Figure 14.11). After selecting from the list, a new workbook is opened with the worksheet showing data from the selected table or query.

The `OpenDatabase` method has four optional arguments, listed in Table 14.2, which you can use to further qualify the data that you want to retrieve.

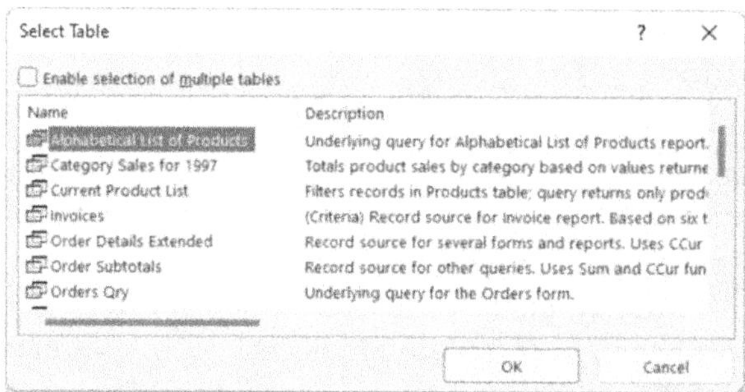

FIGURE 14.11 Database data stored in a table or query can be easily retrieved into an Excel workbook using the `OpenDatabase` method.

TABLE 14.2 Optional arguments for the OpenDatabase method

Optional Argument Name	Data Type	Description
`CommandText`	Variant	The SQL query string. See Hands-On 14.14 for an example of using this argument.
`CommandType`	Variant	The command type of the query. Specify one of the following constants: `xlCmdCube`, `xlCmdList`, `xl-CmdSql`, `xlCmdTable`, or `xlCmdDefault`.

Optional Argument Name	Data Type	Description
`BackgroundQuery`	Variant	Use True to have Excel perform queries for the report asynchronously (in the back ground). The default value is False.
`ImportDataAs`	Variant	Specifies the format of the query. Use `xlQueryTable` or `xlPivotTableReport` to generate a query table or a PivotTable report from the retrieved database data.

Let's write a procedure that creates a PivotTable report from the retrieved customer records.

Hands-On 14.14 Retrieving Access Data into a PivotTable with the `OpenDatabase` Method

1. Insert a new module into the AccessFromExcel VBA project and rename it **Method_OpenDatabase**.
2. In the Method_OpenDatabase module Code window, enter the CountCustomersByCountry procedure as shown below:

```
Sub CountCustomersByCountry()
  On Error Resume Next

  Workbooks.OpenDatabase _
      Filename:="C:\VBAExcel2021_ByExample\Northwind.mdb", _
      CommandText:="Select * from Customers", _
      CommandType:=xlCmdSql, _
      BackgroundQuery:=True, _
      ImportDataAs:=xlPivotTableReport
  Exit Sub
End Sub
```

3. Switch to the Excel application window and choose **View | Macros | View Macros**. Select the **CountCustomersByCountry** procedure and click **Run**. When you run the procedure, Excel opens a new workbook and displays a PivotTable Field List window listing the fields that are available in the Customers table (see Figure 14.12).

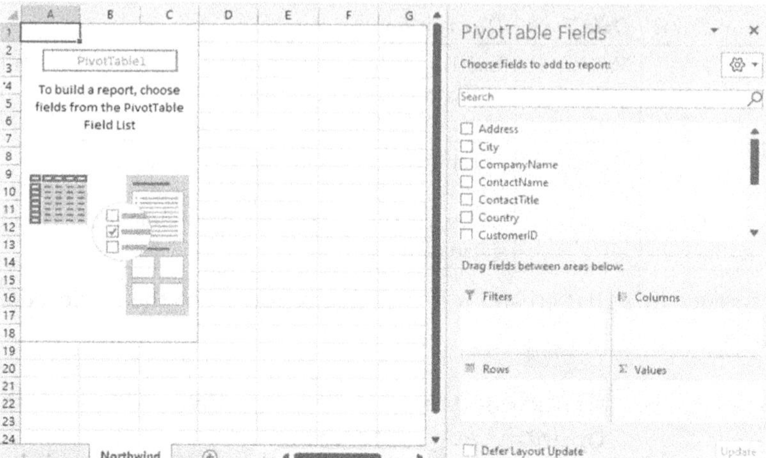

FIGURE 14.12 Using the `OpenDatabase` method's optional arguments, you can specify that the database data be retrieved into a specific format, such as a PivotTable report or a query table.

4. Drag the Country and CustomerID fields from the PivotTable Fields and drop them in the Row Labels area. Drag the CustomerID field and drop it in the Values area. Figure 14.13 displays the completed PivotTable report.

FIGURE 14.13 A PivotTable report based on the data retrieved from the Northwind database's Customers table.

5. Close the workbook with the PivotTable report.

Creating a Text File from Access Data

You can create a comma- or tab-delimited text file from Access data by using a VBA procedure in Excel. Text files are particularly useful for transferring large amounts of data to a spreadsheet.

The example procedure below illustrates how to use ADO recordset to create a tab-delimited text file.

Hands-On 14.15 Creating a Text File from Access Data

1. Insert a new module into the AccessFromExcel VBA project and rename it **TextFiles**.
2. In the TextFiles module Code window, enter the CreateTextFile procedure as shown below.

NOTE	*For this procedure to work correctly, you must create a reference to the Microsoft ActiveX Data Objects 6.1 library. (Refer to the instructions on setting up a reference to object libraries earlier in this chapter.)*

```
Sub CreateTextFile()
  Dim strPath As String
  Dim conn As New ADODB.Connection
  Dim rst As ADODB.Recordset
  Dim strData As String
  Dim strHeader As String
  Dim strSQL As String
  Dim fld As Variant

  strPath = "C:\VBAExcel2021_ByExample\Northwind.mdb"
  conn.Open "Provider=Microsoft.ACE.OLEDB.12.0;" _
      & "Data Source=" & strPath & ";"
  conn.CursorLocation = adUseClient

  strSQL = "SELECT * FROM Products WHERE UnitPrice > 50"
 Set rst = conn.Execute(CommandText:=strSQL, Options:=adCmdText)

  ' save the recordset as a tab-delimited file
  strData = rst.GetString(StringFormat:=adClipString, _
      ColumnDelimeter:=vbTab, RowDelimeter:=vbCr, _
    nullExpr:=vbNullString)

  For Each fld In rst.Fields
    strHeader = strHeader + fld.Name & vbTab
  Next
```

```
  Open "C:\VBAExcel2021_ByExample\ProductsOver50.txt" For Output
As #1
  Print #1, strHeader
  Print #1, strData
  Close #1
  rst.Close
  conn.Close

  Set rst = Nothing
  Set conn = Nothing
End Sub
```

Before the text file can be created, we retrieve the necessary records from the Access database using the `GetString` method of the Recordset object. This method returns a set of records into a string and is faster than looping through the recordset. The `GetString` method has the following syntax:

```
variant = recordset.GetString(StringFormat, NumRows, _
      ColumnDelimiter,  RowDelimiter, NullExpr)
```

The first argument (StringFormat) determines the format for representing the recordset as a string. Use the `adClipString` constant for this argument. The second argument (NumRows) specifies the number of recordset rows to return. If blank, `GetString` will return all the rows. The third argument (ColumnDelimiter) specifies the delimiter for the columns within the row (the default is a tab—vbTab). The fourth argument (RowDelimiter) specifies a row delimiter (the default is a carriage return—vbCr). The fifth argument (NullExpr) specifies an expression to represent `NULL` values (the default is an empty string—`vbNullString`).

Once we have all the data in a String variable, the procedure loops through the fields in the recordset to retrieve the names of columns. The `GetString` method can only handle the data requests, so if you need the data with the headings you need to get this info separately. We store the names of fields in a separate String variable.

Next, the procedure creates a text file with the following statement:

```
Open "C:\VBAExcel2021_ByExample\ProductsOver50.txt" For Output As #1
```

You should already be familiar with this method of creating text files, as it was discussed in detail in Chapter 12.

Next, we use the Print statement to write both the heading and the data string to the text file. Now that the file has the data, we can close it with the Close statement.

3. Run the CreateTextFile procedure. The procedure creates the ProductsOver50.txt file in the root directory of your C drive.
4. Now let's open the ProductsOver50.txt file. In the Open dialog box, select **All Files (*.*)** in the Files of type drop-down list. Next, select the **ProductsOver50.txt** file and click **Open**. The Text Import Wizard (Step 1 of 3) dialog box will open with the Delimited option button selected. Click **Next** to preview the structure of this file. Click **Finish** to show the data in a worksheet.

In Chapter 11, "File and Folder Manipulation with Windows Script Host (WSH)," you learned how to work with text files using the `FileSystemObject`. The CreateTextFile2 procedure in the companion files demonstrates how to use this object to create a text file named ProductsOver20.txt.

Creating a Query Table from Access Data

If you want to work in Excel with data that comes from external data sources and you know that the data you'll be working with often undergoes changes, you may want to create a query table. A *query table* is a special table in an Excel worksheet that is connected to an external data source, such as a Microsoft Access database, SQL Server® database, Web page, or a text file. To retrieve the most up-to-date information, the user can easily refresh the query table. Microsoft Excel offers a special option for obtaining data from external data sources: Simply choose Data | Get Data | From Other Sources | From Microsoft Query.

By querying an external database, you can bring in data that fits your requirements exactly. For example, instead of bringing all product information into your worksheet for review, you may want to specify criteria that the data must meet prior to retrieval. Thus, instead of bringing in all the products from an Access table, you can retrieve only products with a unit price greater than $20.

In VBA, you can use the `QueryTable` object to access external data. Each `QueryTable` object represents a worksheet table built from data returned from an external data source, such as an SQL Server or a Microsoft Access database. To create a query programmatically, use the `Add` method of the QueryTables collection object. This method requires three arguments that are explained in the following Hands-On exercise that uses the `QueryTable` object programmatically.

Hands-On 14.16 Creating a Query Table from Access Data

1. Insert a new module into the AccessFromExcel VBA project and rename it **QueryTable**.

2. In the QueryTable module Code window, enter the CreateQueryTable procedure as shown below:

```
Sub CreateQueryTable()
  Dim myQryTable As Object
  Dim myDb As String
  Dim strConn As String
  Dim Dest As Range
  Dim strSQL As String

  myDb = "C:\VBAExcel2021_ByExample\Northwind.mdb"
  strConn = "OLEDB;Provider=Microsoft.ACE.OLEDB.12.0;" _
      & "Data Source=" & myDb & ";"
  Workbooks.Add
  Set Dest = Worksheets(1).Range("A1")
  Sheets(1).Select
  strSQL = "SELECT * FROM Products WHERE UnitPrice > 20"
  Set myQryTable = ActiveSheet.QueryTables.Add(strConn, _
      Dest, _
      strSQL)
  With myQryTable
      .RefreshStyle = xlInsertEntireRows
      .Refresh False
  End With
End Sub
```

The CreateQueryTable procedure uses the following statement to create a query table on the active sheet:

```
Set myQryTable = ActiveSheet.QueryTables.Add(strConn, Dest, strSQL)
```

`strConn` is a variable that provides a value for the first argument of the `QueryTables` method—`Connection`. This is a required argument of the Variant data type that specifies the data source for the query table.

`Dest` is a variable that provides a value for the second argument—Destination. This is a required argument of the `Range` data type that specifies the cell where the resulting query table will be placed.

`strSQL` is a variable that provides a value for the third argument—`SQL`. This is a required argument of the String data type that defines the data to be returned by the query.

When you create a query using the `Add` method, the query isn't run until you call the Refresh method. This method accepts one argument—`BackgroundQuery`. This is an optional argument of the `Variant` data type that allows you to determine whether control should be returned to the procedure when a database connection has been established and the query has been submitted (True) or after the query has been run and all the data has been retrieved into the worksheet (False).

The CreateQueryTable procedure only retrieves from the Northwind database's Products table those products whose UnitPrice field is greater than 20. Notice that the control is returned to the procedure only after all the relevant records have been fetched.

The `RefreshStyle` method determines how data is inserted into the worksheet. The following constants can be used:

- `xlOverwriteCells`—Existing cells are overwritten with the incoming data.
- `xlInsertDeleteCells`—Cells are inserted or deleted to accommodate the incoming data.
- `xlInsertEntireRows`—Entire rows are inserted to accommodate incoming data.

3. Run the CreateQueryTable procedure. When this procedure completes, you should see a new workbook. The first sheet in this workbook will contain the data you specified in the query (see Figure 14.14).

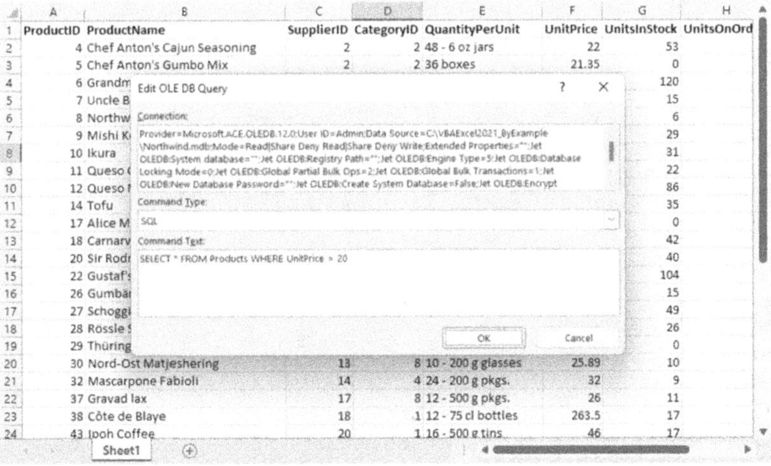

FIGURE 14.14 To modify the SQL statement for the query table, right-click anywhere within the returned data and choose Edit Query.

Creating an Embedded Chart from Access Data

Using VBA, you can easily create a chart based on the data retrieved from a Microsoft Access database. Charts are created by using the `Add` method of the `Charts` collection.

Let's spend some time now creating a procedure that fetches data from the Northwind database and creates an embedded chart.

Hands-On 14.17 Creating an Embedded Chart from Access Data

1. Insert a new module into the AccessFromExcel VBA project and rename it **ChartingData**.
2. In the ChartingData module Code window, enter the ChartData_withADO procedure as shown below:

```
Sub ChartData_withADO()
  Dim conn As New ADODB.Connection
  Dim rst As New ADODB.Recordset
  Dim mySheet As Worksheet
  Dim recArray As Variant
  Dim strQueryName As String
  Dim i As Integer
  Dim j As Integer

  strQueryName = "Category Sales for 1997"
  ' Connect with the database
  conn.Open _
      "Provider=Microsoft.ACE.OLEDB.12.0;" _
      & "Data Source=C:\VBAExcel2021_ByExample\Northwind.mdb;"
  ' Open Recordset based on the SQL statement
      rst.Open "SELECT * FROM [" & strQueryName & "]", conn, _
      adOpenForwardOnly, adLockReadOnly

  Workbooks.Add
  Set mySheet = Worksheets("Sheet1")
  With mySheet.Range("A1")
    recArray = rst.GetRows()
    For i = 0 To UBound(recArray, 2)
        For j = 0 To UBound(recArray, 1)
            .Offset(i + 1, j) = recArray(j, i)
        Next j
    Next i
    For j = 0 To rst.Fields.count - 1
        .Offset(0, j) = rst.Fields(j).Name
        .Offset(0, j).EntireColumn.AutoFit
```

```
        Next j
    End With
    rst.Close
    conn.Close
    Set rst = Nothing
    Set conn = Nothing

    mySheet.Activate
    Charts.Add
    ActiveChart.ChartType = xl3DColumnClustered
    ActiveChart.SetSourceData _
        Source:=mySheet.Cells(1, 1).CurrentRegion, _
        PlotBy:=xlRows
    ActiveChart.Location Where:=xlLocationAsObject, _
        Name:=mySheet.Name

    With ActiveChart
        .HasTitle = True
        .ChartTitle.Characters.Text = "Category Sales for 2018"
        .Axes(xlCategory).HasTitle = True
        .Axes(xlCategory).AxisTitle.Characters.Text = ""
        .Axes(xlValue).HasTitle = True
        .Axes(xlValue).AxisTitle. _
            Characters.Text = mySheet.Range("B1") & "($)"
        .Axes(xlValue).AxisTitle.Orientation = xlUpward
    End With
End Sub
```

The above procedure uses ActiveX Data Objects (ADO) to retrieve data from an Access database query. The data rows are retrieved using the `GetRows` method of the `Recordset` object. As you already know from earlier examples in this chapter, the `GetRows` method retrieves data into a two-dimensional array. Once the data is placed in an Excel worksheet, a chart is added with the Add method. The `SetSourceData` method of the `Chart` object sets the source data range for the chart, like this:

```
ActiveChart.SetSourceData Source:=mySheet.Cells(1, 1)
    .CurrentRegion, PlotBy:=xlRows
```

Source is the range that contains the source data that we have just placed on the worksheet beginning at cell A1. PlotBy will cause the embedded chart to plot data by rows.

Next, the Location method of the `Chart` object specifies where the chart should be placed. This method takes two arguments: Where and Name. The Where argument is required. You can use one of the following constants for this argument: xlLocationAsNewSheet, xlLocationAsObject, or xlLocationAutomatic. The Name argument is required if Where is set to xlLocationAsObject. In this procedure, the Location method specifies that the chart should be embedded in the active worksheet:

```
ActiveChart.Location Where:=xlLocationAsObject, Name:=mySheet.Name
```

Next, a group of statements formats the chart by setting various properties.

3. Run the ChartData_withADO procedure.
   The resulting chart is shown in Figure 14.15.

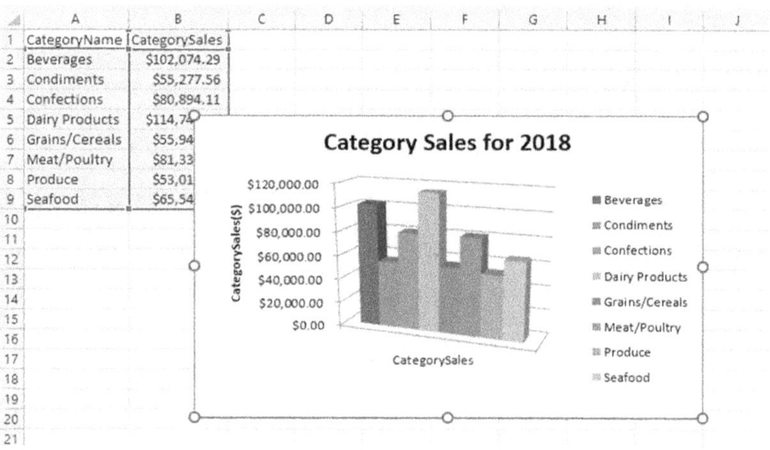

FIGURE 14.15 You can create an embedded chart programmatically with VBA based on the data retrieved from a Microsoft Access table, a query, or an SQL statement.

TRANSFERRING THE EXCEL WORKSHEET TO AN ACCESS DATABASE

Many of the world's biggest databases began as spreadsheets. When the time comes to build a database application from your worksheet, you can resort to a tedious manual method to have the data transferred, or you can use your recently acquired VBA programming skills to automatically turn your worksheets into database tables. Once in a database format, your Excel data can be used in advanced company-wide reports or as a standalone application (needless to say, the latter requires that you possess database application design skills).

The remaining sections of this chapter demonstrate how to link and import Excel worksheets to an Access database. Prior to moving your Excel data to

Access, it is a good idea to clean up your data as much as possible so that the transfer operation goes smoothly. Keep in mind that each worksheet row you'll be transferring will become a record in a table, and each column will function as a table field. For this reason, the first row of the worksheet range that you are planning to transfer to Access should contain field names. There should be no gaps between the columns of data that you want to transfer. In other words, your data should be contiguous. If the data you want to transfer represents a large number of columns, you should produce a printout of your data first and examine it so that there are no surprises later. If the first column contains the field names, it is recommended that you use the built-in Transpose feature to reposition your data so that it goes down rather than from left to right. The key to smooth data import is to make your spreadsheet look as close as possible to a database table.

Linking an Excel Worksheet to an Access Database

You can link an Excel spreadsheet to a Microsoft Access database by using the `TransferSpreadsheet` method. (Refer to the "Retrieving Data with the `TransferSpreadsheet` Method" section earlier in this chapter for the details on working with this method.) The example procedure shown below links the worksheet shown in Figure 14.16 to the Northwind database.

Hands-On 14.18 Linking an Excel Worksheet to an Access Database

1. Insert a new sheet into the Chap14_VBAExcel2021.xlsm workbook and rename it **mySheet**.
2. Prepare the worksheet data as shown in Figure 14.16. The data can be copied from the SampleData_ForLinkingInAccess.xlsx file in the companion files.

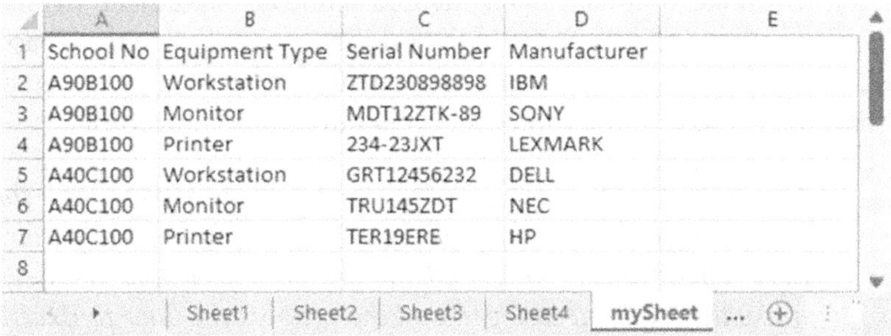

	A	B	C	D	E
1	School No	Equipment Type	Serial Number	Manufacturer	
2	A90B100	Workstation	ZTD230898898	IBM	
3	A90B100	Monitor	MDT12ZTK-89	SONY	
4	A90B100	Printer	234-23JXT	LEXMARK	
5	A40C100	Workstation	GRT12456232	DELL	
6	A40C100	Monitor	TRU145ZDT	NEC	
7	A40C100	Printer	TER19ERE	HP	
8					

Sheet1 | Sheet2 | Sheet3 | Sheet4 | mySheet | ...

FIGURE 14.16 The LinkExcel_ToAccess VBA procedure links this worksheet to the Northwind database in Microsoft Access.

3. Switch to the Visual Basic Editor screen and insert a new module into the AccessFromExcel VBA project. Rename this module **ExcelToAccess**.
4. In the ExcelToAccess module Code window, enter the LinkExcel_ToAccess procedure as shown below:

```
Sub LinkExcel_ToAccess()
  Dim objAccess As Access.Application
  Dim strTableName As String
  Dim strBookName As String
  Dim strPath As String

  On Error Resume Next

  strPath = ActiveWorkbook.Path
  strBookName = strPath & "\Chap14_VBAExcel2021.xlsm"
  strTableName = "Linked_ExcelSheet"

  Set objAccess = New Access.Application

  With objAccess
      .OpenCurrentDatabase "C:\VBAExcel2021_ByExample\" & _
       "Northwind 2007.accdb"
      .DoCmd.TransferSpreadsheet acLink, _
          acSpreadsheetTypeExcel12Xml, _
          strTableName, strBookName, True, "mySheet!A1:D7"
      .Visible = True
  End With
  Set objAccess = Nothing
End Sub
```

After opening the Access database with the `OpenCurrentDatabase` method, the procedure uses the `TransferSpreadsheet` method of the Microsoft Access `DoCmd` object to create a linked table named Linked_ExcelSheet from the specified range of cells (A1:D7) located in the mySheet worksheet in the Chap14_VBAExcel2021.xlsm file. Notice that the True argument in the `DoCmd` statement indicates that the first row of the spreadsheet contains column headings.

NOTE	*You cannot add, change, or delete the data in Access tables that are linked to Excel workbooks in Access. If you need to perform these operations, you should import the Excel data to Access, make the required changes, and then export the data to Excel in the .xls file format.*

5. Run the LinkExcel_ToAccess procedure. When the procedure finishes execution, take a look at the linked table, shown in Figure 14.17.

6. Close the Linked_ExcelSheet table in Access and exit the application.

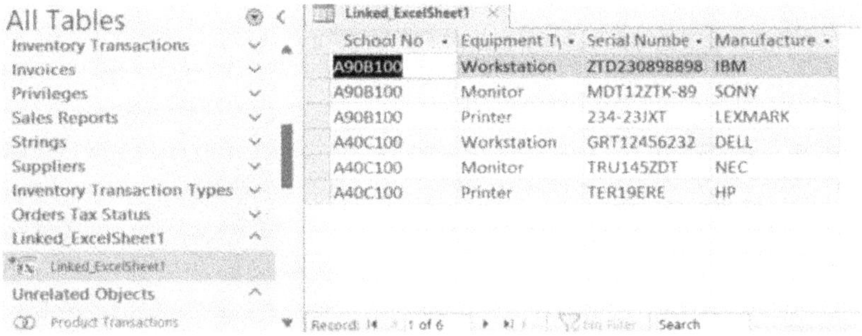

FIGURE 14.17 The Microsoft Excel spreadsheet is linked to a Microsoft Access database.

Importing an Excel Worksheet to an Access Database

In the previous section, you learned how to link your Excel worksheet to an Access database. Importing your worksheet data is just as easy. You can even use the same VBA procedure you used for linking with only minor changes; simply modify the name, replace the `acLink` constant with `acImport`, change the table name, and you are done.

Placing Excel Data in an Access Table

What if, rather than linking or importing your Excel worksheet, you wanted to create an Access table from scratch and load it with the data sitting in a worksheet? Using several programming techniques that you've already acquired in this book, you can easily accomplish this task.

Let's write a VBA procedure that dynamically creates an Access table based on the Excel worksheet presented in Figure 14.16 (see "Linking an Excel Worksheet to an Access Database").

Hands-On 14.19 Creating an Access Table and Populating It with the Worksheet Data

This Hands-On requires the worksheet data prepared in Hands-On 14.18 (see Figure 14.16).

1. In the ExcelToAccess module Code window, enter the AccessTbl_From_ExcelData procedure as shown below:

```
Sub AccessTbl_From_ExcelData()
  Dim conn As ADODB.Connection
```

```
Dim cat As ADOX.Catalog
Dim myTbl As ADOX.Table
Dim rstAccess As ADODB.Recordset
Dim rowCount As Integer
Dim i As Integer

On Error GoTo ErrorHandler

' connect to Access using ADO
Set conn = New ADODB.Connection
conn.Open "Provider = Microsoft.ACE.OLEDB.12.0;" & _
    "Data Source = C:\VBAExcel2021_ByExample\Northwind.mdb;"

' create an empty Access table
Set cat = New Catalog
cat.ActiveConnection = conn
Set myTbl = New ADOX.Table
myTbl.Name = "TableFromExcel"
cat.Tables.Append myTbl

' add fields (columns) to the table
With myTbl.Columns
  .Append "School No", adVarWChar, 7
  .Append "Equipment Type", adVarWChar, 15
  .Append "Serial Number", adVarWChar, 15
  .Append "Manufacturer", adVarWChar, 20
End With
Set cat = Nothing

MsgBox "The table structure was created."

' open a recordset based on the newly created
' Access table

Set rstAccess = New ADODB.Recordset
With rstAccess
  .ActiveConnection = conn
  .CursorType = adOpenKeyset
  .LockType = adLockOptimistic
  .Open myTbl.Name
End With

' now transfer data from Excel worksheet range

With Worksheets("mySheet")
  rowCount = Range("A2:D7").Rows.count
```

```
        For i = 2 To rowCount + 1
            With rstAccess
              .AddNew     ' add a new record to an Access table
              .Fields("School No") = Cells(i, 1).Text
              .Fields("Equipment Type") = Cells(i, 2).Value
              .Fields("Serial Number") = Cells(i, 3).Value
              .Fields("Manufacturer") = Cells(i, 4).Value
              .Update     ' update the table record
            End With
        Next i
    End With

    MsgBox "Data from an Excel worksheet was loaded into the table."

    ' close the Recordset and Connection object and remove them
    ' from memory
    rstAccess.Close
    conn.Close
    Set rstAccess = Nothing
    Set conn = Nothing

    MsgBox "Open the Northwind database to view the table."
AccessTbl_From_ExcelDataExit:
    Exit Sub
ErrorHandler:
    MsgBox Err.Number & ": " & Err.Description
    Resume AccessTbl_From_ExcelDataExit
End Sub
```

Notice that this procedure connects to the Access database using ActiveX Data Objects (ADO). After the connection is established, the procedure creates a new Access table by using the `Catalog` and `Table` objects from the ADOX object library. Next, the fields are added to the table based on the names of the worksheet columns. Each text field specifies the maximum number of characters that it can accept. If the worksheet cell's length is larger than the specified field size, the error-handling routine will display the Access built-in message appropriate for this error and the procedure will end. The final task in the procedure is the data transfer operation. To perform this task, the procedure opens a recordset based on the newly created table. Because we need to add records to the table, the procedure uses an `adOpenKeyset` cursor type. The `For...Next` loop is used to move through the Excel data rows, placing information found in each worksheet cell into the corresponding table field. Notice that a new record is added to an Access table with the `AddNew` method of the `Recordset` object. After copying data from all cells in each row, the procedure uses the `Update` method of the `Recordset` object to save the table record.

2. Run the AccessTbl_From_ExcelData procedure.
3. Open the Northwind.mdb database file to view the procedure results.

SUMMARY

This chapter presented numerous examples of getting Excel data into a Microsoft Access database and retrieving data from Microsoft Access into a worksheet. You learned how to control an Access application from an Excel VBA procedure, performing such tasks as opening Access forms and reports, creating new forms, running select and parameter queries, and calling Access built-in functions. In addition, this chapter has shown you techniques for creating text files, query tables, and charts from the Access data. You also learned how to place Excel data in an Access database by using linked, imported, and dynamic Access tables.

In the next chapter, you will learn how event programming can help you build spreadsheet applications that respond to or limit user actions.

Part IV

Enhancing the User Experience

The Ribbon interface in Excel enables you to create superb-looking worksheets.

In this part of the book, you learn how to create desired interface elements for your users via Ribbon customizations and how to create dialog boxes and custom forms. You will also learn how to format spreadsheets with VBA and control Excel with event-driven programming.

Chapter 15 Event-Driven Programming

How do you disable a built-in shortcut menu when a user clicks on a worksheet cell? How do you display a custom message before a workbook is opened or closed? How can you validate data entered in a cell or range of cells?

To gain complete control over Microsoft Excel, you must learn how to respond to events. Learning how to program events will allow you to implement your own functionality in an Excel application. The first thing you need to know about this subject is what an event is. An *event* is an action recognized by an object. An event is something that happens to objects that are part of Microsoft Excel. Once you learn about events in Excel, you will find it easier to understand events that occur to objects in Word or another Microsoft 365 application.

Events can be triggered by an application user (such as you), another program, or the system itself. So, how can you trigger an event? Suppose you right-clicked a worksheet cell. This particular action would display a built-in shortcut menu for a worksheet cell, allowing you to quickly access the most frequently used commands related to worksheet cells. But what if this particular built-in response isn't appropriate under certain conditions? You may want to entirely disallow right-clicking in a worksheet or perhaps ensure that a custom menu appears on a cell shortcut menu when the user right-clicks any cell. The good news is you can use VBA to write code that can react to events as they occur. The following Microsoft Excel objects can respond to events:

- Worksheet
- Chart sheet
- Query table
- Workbook
- Application

You can decide what should happen when a particular event occurs by writing an *event procedure.*

INTRODUCTION TO EVENT PROCEDURES

A special type of VBA procedure, an *event procedure*, is used to react to specific events. That procedure contains VBA code that handles a particular event. Some events may require a single line of code, while others can be more complex. Event procedures have names, which are created in the following way:

```
ObjectName_EventName()
```

The parameters that need to be sent to the procedure are placed in the parentheses after the name of the event. The programmer cannot change the name of the event procedure.

Before you can write an event procedure to react to an Excel event, you need to know:

- The names of an object and event to which you want to respond.

  Figure 15.1 illustrates how objects that respond to events display a list of events in the Procedure drop-down list in the Code window. Also, you can use the Object Browser to find out event names, as shown in Figure 15.2.

- The place where you should put the event code.

  Some events are coded in a standard module; others must be entered in a class module. While workbook, chart sheet, and worksheet events are available for any open sheet or workbook, to create event procedures for an embedded chart, query table, or the Application object, you must first create a new object using the `With Events` keywords in the class module.

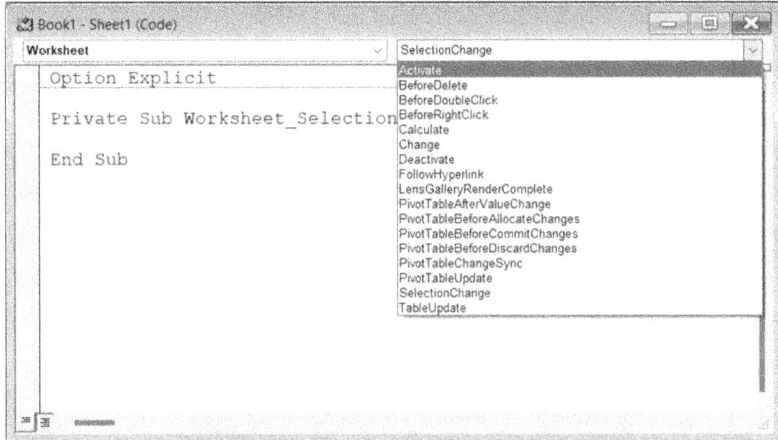

FIGURE 15.1 You can find out the event names in the Code window.

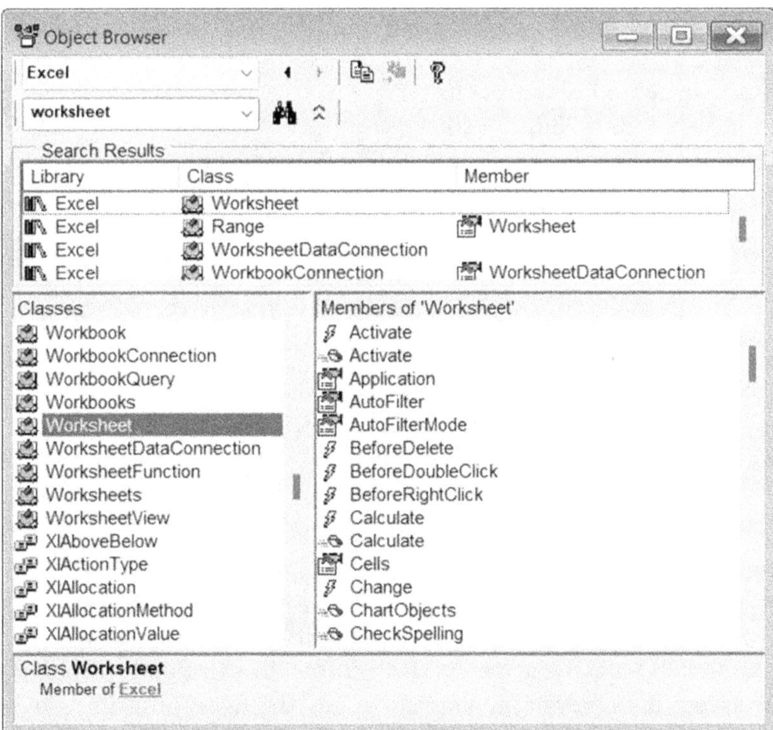

FIGURE 15.2 You can also find out the event names in the Object Browser.

WRITING YOUR FIRST EVENT PROCEDURE

At times you will want to trigger a certain operation when a user invokes an Excel command. For example, when the user attempts to save a workbook you may want to present him with the opportunity to copy the active worksheet to another workbook. Your first event procedure in this chapter explores this scenario. Once this event procedure is written, its code will run automatically when a user attempts to save the workbook file in which the procedure is located.

NOTE	*Please note files for the "Hands-On" project may be found in the companion files.*

Hands-On 15.1 Writing an Event Procedure

1. Open a new workbook and save it as **C:\VBAExcel2021_ByExample\Chap15_VBAExcel2021.xlsm.**
2. Change the name of **Sheet1** in the Chap15_VBAExcel2021.xlsm workbook to **Test.**
3. Type anything in cell **A1** and press **Enter.**
4. Switch to the Visual Basic Editor screen.
5. In the Project Explorer, double-click **ThisWorkbook** in the Microsoft Excel Objects folder under VBAProject (Chap15_VBAExcel2021.xlsm).
6. In the ThisWorkbook Code window, enter the following Workbook_BeforeSave event procedure:

```
Private Sub Workbook_BeforeSave(ByVal SaveAsUI As Boolean, _
    Cancel As Boolean)
  If MsgBox("Would you like to copy " & vbCrLf _
    & "this worksheet to " & vbCrLf _
    & "a new workbook?", vbQuestion + vbYesNo) = vbYes Then
    Sheets(ActiveSheet.Name).Copy
  End If
End Sub
```

The above event procedure uses a `MsgBox` function to display a two-button dialog box asking the user whether the current worksheet should be copied to another workbook. If the user clicks the Yes button, Visual Basic will open a new workbook and copy the active worksheet to it. The original workbook file will not be saved. If, however, the user clicks No, the Excel built-in save event will be triggered. If the workbook has never been saved before, you will be presented with the Save As dialog box where you can specify the filename, the file format, and its location.

7. Switch to the Microsoft Excel application window, click the **File** tab, and choose **Save**.

   The Workbook_BeforeSave event procedure that you wrote in Step 6 will be triggered at this time. Click **Yes** to the message box. Excel will open a new workbook with the copy of the current worksheet.

8. Close the workbook file created by Excel without saving any changes. Do not close the Chap15_VBAExcel2021.xlsm workbook.

9. Click the **File** tab and choose **Save** to save Chap15_VBAExcel2021.xlsm.

   Notice that again you are prompted with the dialog box. Click **No** to the message. Notice that the workbook file is now being saved.

   But what if you wanted to copy the worksheet file to another workbook and also save the original workbook file? Let's modify our Workbook_BeforeSave procedure to make sure the workbook file is saved regardless of whether the user answered Yes or No to the message.

10. Change the Workbook_BeforeSave procedure as follows:

```
Private Sub Workbook_BeforeSave(ByVal SaveAsUI As Boolean, _
    Cancel As Boolean)

  Dim wkb As Workbook
  Set wkb = ActiveWorkbook

  Cancel = False
  If MsgBox("Would you like to copy " & vbCrLf _
      & "this worksheet to " & vbCrLf _
      & "a new workbook?", vbQuestion + vbYesNo) = vbYes Then
      Sheets(ActiveSheet.Name).Copy
  wkb.Activate
  End If
End Sub
```

   To continue with the saving process, you need to set the `Cancel` argument to `False`. This will trigger the Excel built-in save event. Because copying will move the focus to the new workbook that does not contain the customized Workbook_BeforeSave procedure, you need to activate the original workbook after performing the copy. We can get back pretty easily to the original workbook by setting a reference to it at the beginning of the event procedure and then issuing the `wkb.Activate` statement.

NOTE	*If you'd rather call your own saving procedure, set the* `Cancel` *property to* `True` *and type the name of your custom save procedure. Here's a short event procedure example:*
	`Private Sub Workbook_BeforeSave(ByVal SaveAsUI As Boolean, _`
	`    Cancel As Boolean)`
	`  ' abort the built-in save event`
	`  Cancel = True`
	`  ' call your own saving procedure`
	`  MyCustomSaveProcedure`
	`End Sub`

11. Type anything in the **Test** worksheet in the Chap15_VBAExcel2021.xlsm file, then click the **Save** button on the Quick Access toolbar.

When you click Yes or No in response to the message box, Excel proceeds to save the workbook file (you should see the flashing message in the status bar). If you clicked Yes, Excel also copies the Test worksheet to another workbook. After all these tasks are completed, Excel activates the Chap15_VBAExcel2021.xlsm workbook.

12. If you answered Yes in the previous step, close the workbook file created by Excel without saving any changes. Do not close Chap15_VBAExcel2021.xlsm.

Now that you know how to use the `Cancel` argument, let's look at the other argument of the Workbook_BeforeSave event—`SaveAsUI`. This argument allows you to handle the situation when the user chooses the Save As option. Suppose that in our procedure example we want to prompt the user to copy the current worksheet to another workbook only when the Save option is selected. In cases when the file has not yet been saved or the user wants to save the workbook with a different filename, the default Save As dialog box will pop up and the user will not be bothered with the copy prompt. The following step takes this situation into consideration.

13. Modify the Workbook_BeforeSave event procedure as follows:

```
Private Sub Workbook_BeforeSave(ByVal SaveAsUI As Boolean, _
    Cancel As Boolean)

  If SaveAsUI = True Then Exit Sub
  Dim wkb As Workbook
  Set wkb = ActiveWorkbook

  Cancel = False
```

```
  If MsgBox("Would you like to copy " & vbCrLf _
      & "this worksheet to " & vbCrLf _
      & "a new workbook?", vbQuestion + vbYesNo) = vbYes Then
    Sheets(ActiveSheet.Name).Copy
    wkb.Activate
  End If
End Sub
```

14. Switch to the Chap15_VBAExcel2021 application window, click the **File** tab, and choose **Save As | Excel Macro-Enabled Workbook.**

Notice that you are not prompted to copy the current worksheet to another workbook. Instead, Excel proceeds to run its own built-in Save As process. When the Save As dialog box appears, click **Cancel.**

ENABLING AND DISABLING EVENTS

You can use the Application object's `EnableEvents` property to enable or disable events. If you are writing a VBA procedure and don't want a particular event to occur, set the `EnableEvents` property to `False`.

To demonstrate how you can prevent a custom event procedure from running, we will write a procedure in a standard module that will save the workbook after making some changes in the active sheet. We will continue working with the Chap15_VBAExcel2021 file because it already contains the Worksheet_BeforeSave event procedure we want to block in this demonstration.

Hands-On 15.2 Disabling a Custom Event Procedure

This Hands-On requires prior completion of Hands-On 15.1.

1. Choose **Insert | Module** to add a standard module to VBAProject (Chap15_VBAExcel2021.xlsm) and rename it **StandardProcedures.**
2. In the module's Code window, enter the following EnterData procedure:

```
Sub EnterData()
  With ActiveSheet.Range("A1:B1")
    .Font.Color = vbRed
    .Value = 15
  End With
  Application.EnableEvents = False
  ActiveWorkbook.Save
  Application.EnableEvents = True
End Sub
```

Notice that prior to calling the `Save` method of the `ActiveWorkbook` property, we have disabled events by setting the `EnableEvents` property of the `Application` object to `False`. This will prevent the Workbook_BeforeSave event procedure from running when Visual Basic encounters the statement to save the workbook. We don't want the user to be prompted to copy the worksheet while running the EnterData procedure. When Visual Basic has completed the saving process, we want the system to respond to the events as we programmed them, so we enable the events with the `Application.EnableEvents` statement set to `True`.

3. Switch to the Chap15_VBAExcel2021.xlsm application window and choose **View | Macros | View Macros.** In the Macro dialog box, select **EnterData** and click **Run.**

   Notice that when you run the EnterData procedure, you are not prompted to copy the worksheet before saving. This indicates that the code you entered in the Hands-On 15.1 Workbook_BeforeSave event procedure is not running.

4. Close the Chap15_VBAExcel2021 workbook.

EVENT SEQUENCES

Events occur in response to specific actions. Events also occur in a predefined sequence. Table 15.1 demonstrates the sequence of events that occur while opening a new workbook, adding a new worksheet to a workbook, and closing the workbook.

TABLE 15.1 Event sequences

Action	Object	Event Sequence
Opening a new workbook	Workbook	NewWorkbook ↓ WindowDeactivate ↓ WorkbookDeactivate ↓ WorkbookActivate ↓ WindowActivate
Inserting a new sheet into a workbook	Workbook	WorkbookNewSheet ↓ SheetDeactivate ↓ SheetActivate

Action	Object	Event Sequence
Closing a workbook	Workbook	WorkbookBeforeClose ↓ WindowDeactivate ↓ WorkbookDeactivate ↓ WorkbookActivate ↓ WindowActivate

WORKSHEET EVENTS

A Worksheet object responds to such events as activating and deactivating a worksheet, calculating data in a worksheet, making a change to a worksheet, and double-clicking or right-clicking a worksheet. Table 15.2 lists some of the events to which the Worksheet object can respond.

TABLE 15.2 Worksheet events (a partial listing)

Worksheet Event Name	Event Description
`Activate`	This event occurs upon activating a worksheet.
`Deactivate`	This event occurs when the user activates a different sheet.
`SelectionChange`	This event occurs when the user selects a worksheet cell.
`Change`	This event occurs when the user changes a cell formula.
`Calculate`	This event occurs when the user recalculates the worksheet.
`BeforeDoubleClick`	This event occurs when the user double-clicks a worksheet cell.
`BeforeRightClick`	This event occurs when the user right-clicks a worksheet cell.

Let's try out these events to get the hang of them.

Worksheet_Activate()

This event occurs upon activating a worksheet.

Hands-On 15.3 Writing the Worksheet_Activate() Event Procedure

1. Open a new workbook and save it as **Chap15_WorksheetEvents.xlsm** in your **VBAExcel2021_ByExample** folder.
2. Insert a new worksheet to the current workbook.
3. Switch to the Visual Basic Editor window.

4. In the Project Explorer window, double-click **Sheet2** under VBAProject (Chap15_WorksheetEvents.xlsm) in the Microsoft Excel Objects folder.
5. In the **Sheet2** Code window, enter the code shown below:

```
Dim shtName As String

Private Sub Worksheet_Activate()
  shtName = ActiveSheet.Name
  Range("B2").Select
End Sub
```

The example procedure selects cell B2 each time the sheet is activated. Notice that the `shtName` variable is declared at the top of the module.

6. Switch to the Microsoft Excel application window and activate **Sheet2**. Notice that when Sheet2 is activated, the selection is moved to cell B2. Excel also stores the sheet name in the `shtName` variable that was declared at the top of the module. We will need this value as we work with other event procedures in this section.

Worksheet_Deactivate()

This event occurs when the user activates a different sheet in a workbook.

Hands-On 15.4 Writing the Worksheet_Deactivate() Event Procedure

This Hands-On exercise uses the Chap15_WorksheetEvents workbook created in Hands-On 15.3.

1. Switch to the Visual Basic Editor window. In the Sheet2 Code window, enter the Worksheet_Deactivate procedure as shown below:

```
Private Sub Worksheet_Deactivate()
  MsgBox "You deactivated " & _
    shtName & "." & vbCrLf & _
    "You switched to " & _
    ActiveSheet.Name & "."
End Sub
```

The example procedure displays a message when Sheet2 is deactivated.

2. Switch to the Microsoft Excel application window and click the **Sheet2** tab. The Worksheet_Activate procedure that you created in Hands-On 15.3 will run first. Excel will select cell B2 and store the name of the worksheet in the `shtName` global variable declared at the top of the Sheet2 code module.

3. Now click any other sheet in the active workbook.
   Notice that Excel displays the name of the worksheet that you deactivated and the name of the worksheet you switched to.

Worksheet_SelectionChange(ByVal Target As Range)

This event occurs when the user selects a worksheet cell.

Hands-On 15.5 Writing the Worksheet_SelectionChange() Event Procedure

1. In the current workbook, insert a new worksheet.
2. Switch to the Visual Basic Editor window. In the Project Explorer window, double-click **Sheet3** under VBAProject (Chap15_WorksheetEvents.xlsm) in the Microsoft Excel Objects folder.
3. In the Sheet3 Code window, enter the Worksheet_SelectionChange procedure as shown below:

```
Private Sub Worksheet_SelectionChange(ByVal Target As Range)
  Dim myRange As Range

  On Error Resume Next
  Set myRange = Intersect(Range("A1:A10"), Target)
  If Not myRange Is Nothing Then
     MsgBox "Data entry or edits are not permitted."
  End If
End Sub
```

   The example procedure displays a message if the user selects any cell in `myRange`.
4. Switch to the Microsoft Excel application window and activate **Sheet3**. Click on any cell within the specified range A1:A10.
   Notice that Excel displays a message whenever you click a cell in the restricted area.

Worksheet_Change(ByVal Target As Range)

This event occurs when the user changes a cell formula.

Hands-On 15.6 Writing the Worksheet_Change() Event Procedure

1. In the Visual Basic Editor window, activate the Project Explorer window and double-click **Sheet1** in the Microsoft Excel Objects folder of Chap15_WorksheetEvents.xlsm.

2. In the **Sheet1** Code window, enter the Worksheet_Change event procedure as shown below:

```
Private Sub Worksheet_Change(ByVal Target As Range)
  Application.EnableEvents = False
    Target = UCase(Target)
    Columns(Target.Column).AutoFit
  Application.EnableEvents = True
End Sub
```

The example procedure changes what you type in a cell to uppercase. The column where the target cell is located is then auto sized.

3. Switch to the Microsoft Excel application window and activate **Sheet1**. Enter any text in any cell.

Notice that as soon as you press the **Enter** key, Excel changes the text you typed to uppercase and auto sizes the column.

Worksheet_Calculate()

This event occurs when the user recalculates the worksheet.

Hands-On 15.7 Writing the Worksheet_Calculate() Event Procedure

1. Add a new sheet to the Chap15_WorksheetEvents workbook.
2. In cell A2 of the newly added sheet, enter **1**, and in cell B2, enter **2**. Enter the following formula in cell C2: = **A2+B2**.
3. Switch to the Visual Basic Editor window, activate the Project Explorer window, and double-click the sheet you added in Step 1.
4. In the Code window, enter the code of the Worksheet_Calculate procedure as shown below:

```
Private Sub Worksheet_Calculate()
  MsgBox "The worksheet was recalculated."
End Sub
```

5. Switch to the Microsoft Excel application window and modify the entry in cell B2 on the sheet you added in Step 1 by typing any number.

Notice that after leaving Edit mode, the Worksheet_Calculate event procedure is triggered and you are presented with a custom message.

Worksheet_BeforeDoubleClick(ByVal Target As Range, Cancel As Boolean)

This event occurs when the user double-clicks a worksheet.

Hands-On 15.8 Writing the Worksheet_BeforeDoubleClick() Event Procedure

1. Enter any data in cell **C9** on **Sheet2** of the Chap15_WorksheetEvents workbook.
2. In the Visual Basic Editor window, activate the Project Explorer window and open the Microsoft Excel Objects folder. Double-click **Sheet2**.
3. In the **Sheet2** Code window, type the code of the procedure as shown below:

```
Private Sub Worksheet_BeforeDoubleClick(ByVal _
     Target As Range, Cancel As Boolean)
  If Target.Address = "$C$9" Then
    MsgBox "No double-clicking, please."
    Cancel = True
  Else
    MsgBox "You may edit this cell."
  End If
End Sub
```

The example procedure disallows in-cell editing when cell C9 is double-clicked.

4. Switch to the Microsoft Excel application window and double-click cell **C9** on Sheet2.
   The Worksheet_BeforeDoubleClick event procedure cancels the built-in Excel behavior, and the user is not allowed to edit the data inside the cell. However, the user can get around this restriction by clicking on the formula bar or pressing F2. When writing event procedures that restrict access to certain program features, write additional code that prevents any workaround.

Worksheet_BeforeRightClick(ByVal Target As Range, Cancel As Boolean)

This event occurs when the user right-clicks a worksheet cell.

Hands-On 15.9 Writing the Worksheet_BeforeRightClick() Event Procedure

1. In the Visual Basic Editor window, activate the Project Explorer window and double-click **Sheet2** in the Microsoft Excel Objects folder.
2. In the **Sheet2** Code window, enter the code of the Worksheet_BeforeRightClick procedure as shown below:

```
Private Sub Worksheet_BeforeRightClick(ByVal _
    Target As Range, Cancel As Boolean)
```

```
  With Application.CommandBars("Cell")
    .Reset
    If Target.Rows.Count > 1 Or _
        Target.Columns.Count > 1 Then
        With .Controls.Add(Type:=msoControlButton, _
            before:=1, temporary:=True)
          .Caption = "Print..."
          .OnAction = "PrintMe"
        End With
    End If
  End With
End Sub
```

The example procedure adds a Print option to the cell shortcut menu when the user selects more than one cell on the worksheet.

3. Insert a new module into the current project and enter the PrintMe procedure as shown below:

```
Sub PrintMe()
  Application.Dialogs(xlDialogPrint).Show arg12:=1
End Sub
```

The PrintMe procedure is called by the Worksheet_BeforeRightClick event when the user selects the Print option from the shortcut menu. Notice that the `Show` method of the Dialogs collection is followed by a named argument: `arg12:=1`. This argument will display the Print dialog box with the preselected option button "Selection" in the Print area of the dialog box. Excel dialog boxes are covered in the next chapter.

4. Switch to the Microsoft Excel application window and right-click on any single cell in Sheet2.
   Notice that the shortcut menu appears with the default options.
5. Now select at least two cells in the Sheet2 worksheet and right-click the selected area.
   You should see the Print option as the first menu entry. Click the **Print** option and notice that instead of the default "Print active sheet," the Print dialog displays "Print Selection."
6. Save and close the Chap15_WorksheetEvents.xlsm workbook file.

NOTE	*The Worksheet_BeforeRightClick event procedure relies on the* `CommandBar` *object to customize Excel's built-in context menu. Before Excel 2010, the* `CommandBar` *object was the only way to create, modify, or disable context menus. Excel 2021 continues to support* `CommandBars` *collection for compatibility; however, you should rely on the RibbonX model (as discussed in Chapter 19) to add your own customizations to context menus.*

WORKBOOK EVENTS

Workbook object events occur when the user performs such tasks as opening, activating, deactivating, printing, saving, and closing a workbook. Workbook events are not created in a standard VBA module. To write code that responds to a particular workbook you can:

- Double-click the ThisWorkbook object in the Visual Basic Editor's Project Explorer.
- In the Code window that appears, open the Object drop-down list on the left-hand side and select the Workbook object.
- In the Procedure drop-down list (the one on the right), select the event you want. The selected event procedure stub will appear in the Code window as shown below:

```
Private Sub Workbook_Open()
  [place your event handling code here]
End Sub
```

Table 15.3 lists some of the events to which the Workbook object can respond.

TABLE 15.3 Workbook events (a partial listing)

Workbook Event Name	Event Description
`Activate`	This event occurs when the user activates the workbook. This event will not occur when the user activates the workbook by switching from another application.
`Deactivate`	This event occurs when the user activates a different workbook within Excel. This event does not occur when the user switches to a different application.
`Open`	This event occurs when the user opens a workbook.

(Contd.)

Workbook Event Name	Event Description
BeforeSave	This event occurs before the workbook is saved. The SaveAsUI argument is read-only and refers to the Save As dialog box. If the workbook has not been saved, the value of SaveAsUI is True; otherwise, it is False.
BeforePrint	This event occurs before the workbook is printed and before the Print dialog appears. The example procedure places the full workbook's name in the document footer prior to printing if the user clicks Yes in the message box.
BeforeClose	This event occurs before the workbook is closed and before the user is asked to save changes.
NewSheet	This event occurs after the user creates a new sheet in a workbook.
WindowActivate	This event occurs when the user shifts the focus to any window showing the workbook.
WindowDeactivate	This event occurs when the user shifts the focus away from any window showing the workbook.
WindowResize	This event occurs when the user opens, resizes, maximizes, or minimizes any window showing the workbook.

Let's try out the above events to get the hang of them.

Workbook_Activate()

This event occurs when the user activates the workbook. This event will not occur when the user activates the workbook by switching from another application.

Hands-On 15.10 Writing the Workbook_Activate() Event Procedure

1. Open a new workbook and save it as **Chap15_WorkbookEvents.xlsm** in your **C:\VBAExcel2021__ByExample** folder.
2. Switch to the Visual Basic Editor window. In the Project Explorer window, double-click **ThisWorkbook** in the Microsoft Excel Objects folder.
3. In the ThisWorkbook Code window, type the Workbook_Activate procedure as shown below:

```
Private Sub Workbook_Activate()
  MsgBox "This workbook contains " & _
    ThisWorkbook.Sheets.Count & " sheets."
End Sub
```

The example procedure displays the total number of worksheets when the user activates the workbook containing the Workbook_Activate event procedure.

4. Switch to the Microsoft Excel application window and open a new workbook.
5. Activate the Chap15_WorkbookEvents workbook. Excel should display the total number of sheets in this workbook.

Workbook_Deactivate()

This event occurs when the user activates a different workbook within Excel. This event does not occur when the user switches to a different application.

Hands-On 15.11 Writing the Workbook_Deactivate() Event Procedure

1. In the Visual Basic Editor window, activate the Project Explorer window and double-click **ThisWorkbook** in the Microsoft Excel Objects folder under VBAProject (Chap15_WorkbookEvents.xlsm).
2. In the ThisWorkbook Code window, type the Workbook_Deactivate procedure as shown below:

```
Private Sub Workbook_Deactivate()
  Dim cell As Range
  For Each cell In ActiveSheet.UsedRange
    If Not IsEmpty(cell) Then
        Debug.Print cell.Address & ":" & cell.Value
    End If
  Next
End Sub
```

The example procedure will print to the Immediate window the addresses and values of cells containing entries in the current workbook when the user activates a different workbook.

3. Switch to the Microsoft Excel application window and make some entries on the active sheet. Next, activate a different workbook.
   This action will trigger the Workbook_Deactivate event procedure.
4. Switch to the Visual Basic Editor screen and open the Immediate window to see what entries were reported.

Workbook_Open()

This event occurs when the user opens a workbook.

Hands-On 15.12. Writing the Workbook_Open() Event Procedure

1. Double-click the **ThisWorkbook** object in the Microsoft Excel Objects folder under VBAProject (Chap15_WorkbookEvents.xlsm).
2. In the ThisWorkbook Code window, type the Workbook_Open procedure as shown below:

```
Private Sub Workbook_Open()
  ActiveSheet.Range("A1").Value = Format(Now(), "mm/dd/yyyy")
  Columns("A").AutoFit
End Sub
```

   The example procedure places the current date in cell A1 when the workbook is opened.

3. Save and close Chap15_WorkbookEvents.xlsm and then reopen it.
   When you open the workbook file again, the Workbook_Open event procedure will be triggered, and the current date will be placed in cell A1 on the active sheet.

Workbook_BeforeSave(ByVal SaveAsUI As Boolean, Cancel As Boolean)

This event occurs before the workbook is saved. The `SaveAsUI` argument is read-only and refers to the Save As dialog box. If the workbook has not been saved, the value of `SaveAsUI` is True; otherwise, it is False.

Hands-On 15.13 Writing the Workbook_BeforeSave() Event Procedure

1. In the Visual Basic Editor screen, activate the Project Explorer window and open the Microsoft Excel Objects folder under VBAProject. (Chap15_WorkbookEvents.xlsm). Double-click **ThisWorkbook**.
2. In the ThisWorkbook Code window, type the Workbook_BeforeSave procedure as shown below:

```
Private Sub Workbook_BeforeSave(ByVal _
    SaveAsUI As Boolean, Cancel As Boolean)
  If SaveAsUI = True And _
    ThisWorkbook.Path = vbNullString Then
    MsgBox "This document has not yet " _
      & "been saved." & vbCrLf _
    & "The Save As dialog box will be displayed."
  ElseIf SaveAsUI = True Then
```

```
      MsgBox "You are not allowed to use " _
        & "the SaveAs option. "
      Cancel = True
    End If
End Sub
```

The example procedure displays the Save As dialog box if the workbook hasn't been saved before. The workbook's pathname will be a null string (`vbNullString`) if the file has not been saved before. The procedure will not let the user save the workbook under a different name—the SaveAs operation will be aborted by setting the `Cancel` argument to `True`. The user will need to choose the Save option to have the workbook saved.

3. Switch to the Microsoft Excel application window and activate any sheet in the Chap15_WorkbookEvents.xlsm workbook.
4. Make an entry in any cell of this workbook, click the **File** tab, and choose **Save As | Excel Macro-Enabled Workbook.**
   The Workbook_BeforeSave event procedure will be activated, and the `ElseIf` clause gets executed. Notice that you are not allowed to save the workbook by using the SaveAs option.

Workbook_BeforePrint(Cancel As Boolean)

This event occurs before the workbook is printed and before the Print dialog appears.

Hands-On 15.14 Writing the Workbook_BeforePrint() Event Procedure

1. In the Visual Basic Editor window, activate the Project Explorer window and double-click the **ThisWorkbook** object in the Microsoft Excel Objects folder under VBAProject (Chap15_WorkbookEvents.xlsm).
2. In the ThisWorkbook Code window, type the Workbook_BeforePrint event procedure as shown below:

```
Private Sub Workbook_BeforePrint(Cancel As Boolean)
  Dim response As Integer
  response = MsgBox("Do you want to " & vbCrLf & _
      "print the workbook's full name in the footer?", _
      vbYesNo)
  If response = vbYes Then
    ActiveSheet.PageSetup.LeftFooter = _
        ThisWorkbook.FullName
```

```
  Else
      ActiveSheet.PageSetup.LeftFooter = ""
  End If
End Sub
```

The example procedure places the workbook's full name in the document footer prior to printing if the user clicks Yes in the message box.

3. Switch to the Microsoft Excel application window and activate any sheet in the Chap15_WorkbookEvents.xlsm workbook.
4. Enter anything you want in any worksheet cell.
5. Click the **File | Print** and click the **Print** button.

Excel will ask you if you want to place the workbook's name and path in the footer.

Workbook_BeforeClose(Cancel As Boolean)

This event occurs before the workbook is closed and before the user is asked to save changes.

Hands-On 15.15 Writing the Workbook_BeforeClose() Event Procedure

1. In the Visual Basic Editor window, activate the Project Explorer window and double-click **ThisWorkbook** in the Microsoft Excel Objects folder under VBAProject (Chap15_WorkbookEvents.xlsm).
2. In the ThisWorkbook Code window, type the Workbook_BeforeClose event procedure as shown below:

```
Private Sub Workbook_BeforeClose(Cancel As Boolean)
  If MsgBox("Do you want to change " & vbCrLf _
      & " workbook properties before closing?", _
      vbYesNo) = vbYes Then
    Application.Dialogs(xlDialogProperties).Show
  End If
End Sub
```

The example procedure displays the Properties dialog box if the user responds Yes to the message box.

3. Switch to the Microsoft Excel application window and close the Chap15_WorkbookEvents.xlsm workbook.

Upon closing, you should see a message box asking you to view the Properties dialog box prior to closing. After viewing or modifying the workbook properties, the procedure closes the workbook. If there are any changes that you have not yet saved, you are given the chance to save the workbook, cancel the changes, or abort the closing operation altogether.

Workbook_NewSheet(ByVal Sh As Object)

This event occurs after the user creates a new sheet in a workbook.

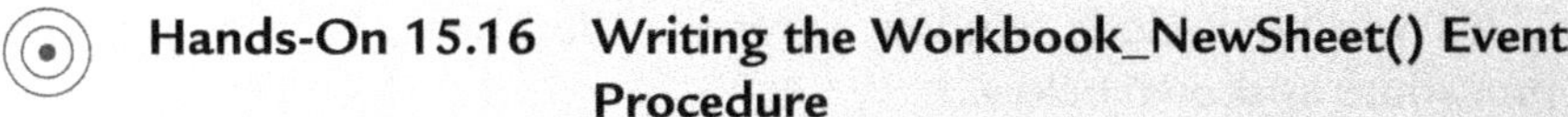

Hands-On 15.16 Writing the Workbook_NewSheet() Event Procedure

1. Open a new workbook and save it as **Chap15_WorkbookEvents2.xlsm** in your **C:\VBAExcel2021__ByExample** folder.
2. Switch to the Visual Basic Editor window, and in the Project Explorer window, double-click **ThisWorkbook** in the Microsoft Excel Objects folder under VBAProject (Chap15_WorkbookEvents2.xlsm).
3. In the ThisWorkbook Code window, type the Workbook_NewSheet event procedure as shown below:

```
Private Sub Workbook_NewSheet(ByVal Sh As Object)
  If MsgBox("Do you want to place  " & vbCrLf _
      & "the new sheet at the beginning " & vbCrLf _
      & "of the workbook?", vbYesNo) = vbYes Then
        Sh.Move before:=ThisWorkbook.Sheets(1)
  Else
    Sh.Move After:=ThisWorkbook.Sheets( _
        ThisWorkbook.Sheets.Count)
    MsgBox Sh.Name & _
         " is now the last sheet in the workbook."
  End If
End Sub
```

The example procedure places the new sheet at the beginning of the workbook if the user responds Yes to the message box; otherwise, the new sheet is placed at the end of the workbook.

4. Switch to the Microsoft Excel application window and click the **New Sheet Button (+)** (at the bottom of the screen). Excel will ask where to place the new sheet.

Let's try out some of the events related to operations on workbook windows.

Workbook_WindowActivate(ByVal Wn As Window)

This event occurs when the user shifts the focus to any window showing the workbook.

Hands-On 15.17 Writing the Workbook_WindowActivate() Event Procedure

1. In the Visual Basic Editor window, activate the Project Explorer window and double-click the **ThisWorkbook** object in the Microsoft Excel Objects folder under VBAProject (Chap15_WorkbookEvents2.xlsm).
2. In the ThisWorkbook Code window, enter the Workbook_WindowActivate event procedure as shown below:

```
Private Sub Workbook_WindowActivate(ByVal Wn As Window)
  Wn.GridlineColor = vbYellow
End Sub
```

The example procedure changes the color of the worksheet gridlines to yellow when the user activates the workbook containing the code of the Workbook_WindowActivate procedure.

3. Switch to the Microsoft Excel application window and open a new workbook.
4. Arrange Microsoft Excel workbooks vertically on the screen, by choosing **View | Arrange All** to open the Arrange Windows dialog. Select the **Vertical** option button and click **OK**. When you activate the worksheet of the workbook in which you entered the code of the Workbook_WindowActivate event procedure, the color of the gridlines should change to yellow.

Workbook_WindowDeactivate(ByVal Wn As Window)

This event occurs when the user shifts the focus away from any window showing the workbook.

Hands-On 15.18 Writing the Workbook_WindowDeactivate() Event Procedure

1. In the Visual Basic Editor window, activate the Project Explorer window and double-click the **ThisWorkbook** object in the Microsoft Excel Objects folder under VBAProject (Chap15_WorkbookEvents2.xlsm).
2. In the ThisWorkbook Code window, enter the Workbook_WindowDeactivate procedure as shown below:

```
Private Sub Workbook_WindowDeactivate(ByVal Wn As Window)
  MsgBox "You have just deactivated " & Wn.Caption
End Sub
```

The example procedure displays the name of the deactivated workbook when the user switches to another workbook from the workbook containing the code of the Workbook_WindowDeactivate procedure.

3. Switch to the Microsoft Excel application window and open a new workbook.

   Excel displays the name of the deactivated workbook in a message box.

Workbook_WindowResize(ByVal Wn As Window)

This event occurs when the user opens, resizes, maximizes, or minimizes any window showing the workbook.

Hands-On 15.19 Writing the Workbook_WindowResize() Event Procedure

1. In the Visual Basic Editor window, activate the Project Explorer window and double-click the **ThisWorkbook** object in the Microsoft Excel Objects folder under VBAProject (Chap15_WorkbookEvents2.xlsm).
2. In the ThisWorkbook Code window, enter the Workbook_WindowResize procedure as shown below:

```
Private Sub Workbook_WindowResize(ByVal Wn As Window)
  If Wn.WindowState <> xlMaximized Then
      Wn.Left = 0
      Wn.Top = 0
  End If
End Sub
```

   The example procedure moves the workbook window to the top left-hand corner of the screen when the user resizes it.

3. Activate the Chap15_WorkbookEvents2.xlsm workbook in the Excel application window.
4. Click the **Restore Window** button to the right of the menu bar.
5. Move the Chap15_WorkbookEvents2.xlsm window to the middle of the screen by dragging its title bar.
6. Change the size of the active window by dragging the window borders in or out.

   As you complete the sizing operation, the workbook window should automatically jump to the top left-hand corner of the screen.

7. Click the **Maximize** button to restore the Chap15_WorkbookEvents2.xlsm workbook window to its full size.

An Excel workbook can respond to a number of other events. Some of them are listed in Table 15.4. For a complete list of the events and their usage, go to *https://docs.microsoft.com/en-us/office/vba/api/excel.workbook* and expand the Events topic in the left pane.

TABLE 15.4 Additional workbook events

Workbook Event Name	Event Description
`SheetActivate`	This event occurs when the user activates any sheet in the workbook. The SheetActivate event occurs also at the application level when any sheet in any open workbook is activated.
`SheetDeactivate`	This event occurs when the user activates a different sheet in a workbook.
`SheetSelectionChange`	This event occurs when the user changes the selection on a worksheet. This event happens for each sheet in a workbook.
`SheetChange`	This event occurs when the user changes a cell formula.
`SheetCalculate`	This event occurs when the user recalculates a worksheet.
`SheetBeforeDoubleClick`	This event occurs when the user double-clicks a cell on a worksheet.
`SheetBeforeRightClick`	This event occurs when the user right-clicks a cell on a worksheet.
`NewChart`	This event occurs when a new chart is created in the workbook.
`AfterSave`	This event occurs after the workbook is saved.
`AddinInstall`	This event occurs after the workbook is installed as an add-in.
`AddinUninstall`	This event occurs when the workbook is uninstalled as an add-in.
`SheetFollowHyperlink`	This event occurs when you click any hyperlink in Microsoft Excel.

PIVOTTABLE EVENTS

In Excel, PivotTable reports provide a powerful way of analyzing and comparing large amounts of information stored in a database. By rotating rows and columns of a PivotTable report, you can see different views of the source data or see details of the data that interests you the most. When working with PivotTable reports programmatically, you can determine when a PivotTable report opened or closed the connection to its data source by using the PivotTableOpenConnection and PivotTableCloseConnection workbook events and determine when the PivotTable was updated via the SheetPivotTableUpdate event. Table 15.5

lists events related to PivotTable reports. If you haven't worked with PivotTables programmatically, Chapter 22, "Programming PivotTables and PivotCharts," will get you started writing VBA code for creating and manipulating PivotTables and PivotCharts. You will find it easier to delve into the PivotTable event programming after working through Chapter 22.

TABLE 15.5 Workbook events related to PivotTable reports

Workbook Event Name	Event Description
`PivotTableOpenConnection`	Occurs after a PivotTable report opens the connection to its data source. This event requires that you declare an object of type Application or Workbook using the `WithEvents` keyword in a class module (see examples of using this keyword further in this chapter).
`PivotTableCloseConnection`	Occurs after a PivotTable report closes the connection to its data source. This event requires that you declare an object of type Application or Workbook using the `WithEvents` keyword in a class module (see examples of using this keyword further in this chapter).

`SheetPivotTableUpdate`
 	
The `SheetPivotTableUpdate` event procedure takes the following two arguments:
 	
`Sh` – the selected sheet
`Target` – the selected PivotTable report
	This event occurs after the sheet of the PivotTable report has been updated. This event requires that you declare an object of type Application or Workbook using the `WithEvents` keyword in a class module (see examples of using this keyword at the end of this chapter).
	
	Note: The example event procedure shown below, along with other procedures related to the PivotTable reports, can be found in the Chap15_PivotReport-Events.xlsm downloadable file.
	
	`Private Sub pivTbl_SheetPivotTableUp-`
	`date( _`
	`  ByVal Sh As Object, _`
	`  ByVal Target As PivotTable)`
	`  MsgBox Target.Name & _`
	`  " report has been updated." & vbCrLf _`
	`  & "The PivotReport is located in cells`
	`    " & _`
	`  Target.DataBodyRange.Address`
	
	`End Sub`

(Contd.)

Workbook Event Name	Event Description

`SheetPivotTableChangeSync`
 	
This event takes the following two arguments:
 	
`Sh` – the worksheet that contains the PivotTable
 	
`Target` – the PivotTable that was changed
	This event occurs after changes to a PivotTable. For example, after making changes to a PivotTable you can write code to display a message:
	
	`Private Sub _`
	`  Workbook_SheetPivotTableChangeSync( _`
	`  ByVal Sh As Object, _`
	`  ByVal Target As PivotTable)`
	
	`  MsgBox "Thanks for working with " & _`
	`     "PivotTable (" & Target.Name & _`
	`     ") on " & Sh.Name & _`
	`     " worksheet."`
	`End Sub`
	
	Note: The example event procedure shown above can be found in the Chap15_PivotReportEvents.xlsm downloadable file.

`SheetPivotTableAfterValueChange`	This event occurs after a cell or range of cells (that contain formulas) inside a PivotTable are edited or recalculated. This event will not occur when a PivotTable is refreshed, sorted, filtered, or dilled down on.
`SheetPivotTableBeforeDiscardChanges`	This event occurs immediately before changes to a PivotTable are discarded. It is used with the PivotTable's OLAP (online analytical processing) data source.
`SheetPivotTableBeforeCommitChanges`	This event occurs immediately before changes are committed against the OLAP data source for a PivotTable.
`SheetPivotTableBeforeAllocateChanges`	This event occurs immediately before changes are applied to the PivotTable's OLAP data source.

CHART EVENTS

As you know, you can create charts in Excel that are embedded in a worksheet or located on a separate chart sheet. In this section, you will learn how to control chart events no matter where you've decided to place your chart. Before you try out selected chart events, perform the tasks in Hands-On 15.20.

Hands-On 15.20 Creating Charts for Trying Out Chart Events

1. Open a new Excel workbook and save it as **Chap15_ChartEvents.xlsm**.
2. Enter sample data as shown in Figure 15.3.
3. Select cells **A1:D5** and choose **Insert | Charts | Insert Column Chart | 2-D | Clustered Column**.

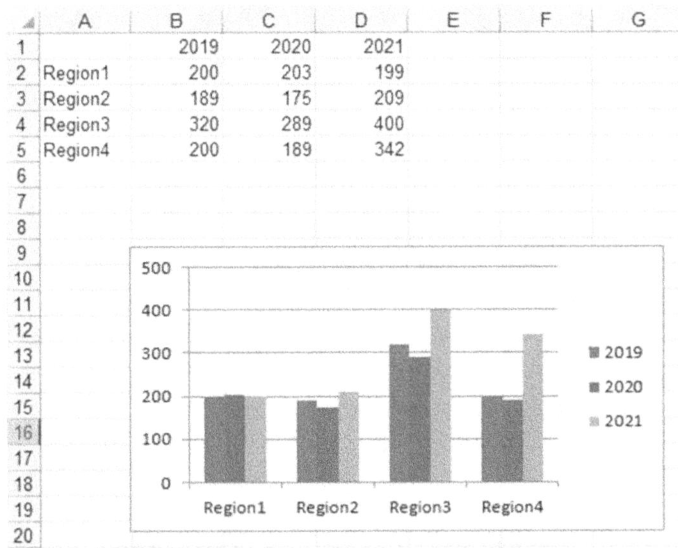

	A	B	C	D
1		2019	2020	2021
2	Region1	200	203	199
3	Region2	189	175	209
4	Region3	320	289	400
5	Region4	200	189	342

FIGURE 15.3 Column chart embedded in a worksheet.

4. Resize the chart as shown in Figure 15.3.
5. Using the same data, create a line chart on a separate chart sheet, as shown in Figure 15.5. To add a new chart sheet, right-click any sheet tab in the workbook and choose **Insert**. In the Insert dialog box, select **Chart** and click **OK**. On the Chart Design tab, click the **Select Data** button. Excel will display the Select Data Source dialog box. At this point, click the **Sheet1** tab and select cells **A1:D5**. Excel will fill in the Chart data range box in the dialog box as in Figure 15.4. Click **OK** to complete the chart. Now, change the chart type to Line chart with Markers by choosing the **Change Chart Type** button in the Chart Design tab. In the Change Chart Type dialog box, select **Line chart** in the left pane, and click the button representing the **Line chart with Markers**. Click **OK** to close the dialog box. Add a legend to the chart using the Add Chart Element button on the Chart Design tab.
6. Change the name of the chart sheet to **Sales Analysis Chart**.

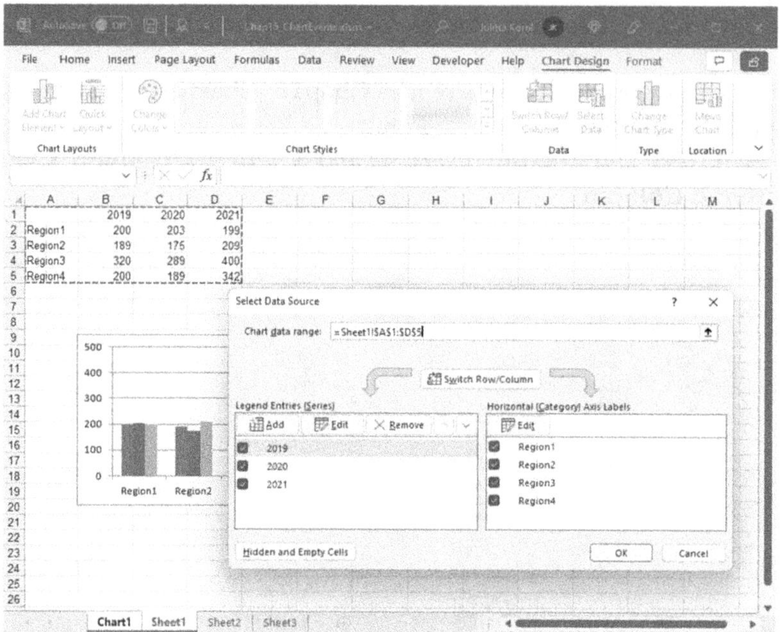

FIGURE 15.4 Creating a chart in a chart sheet.

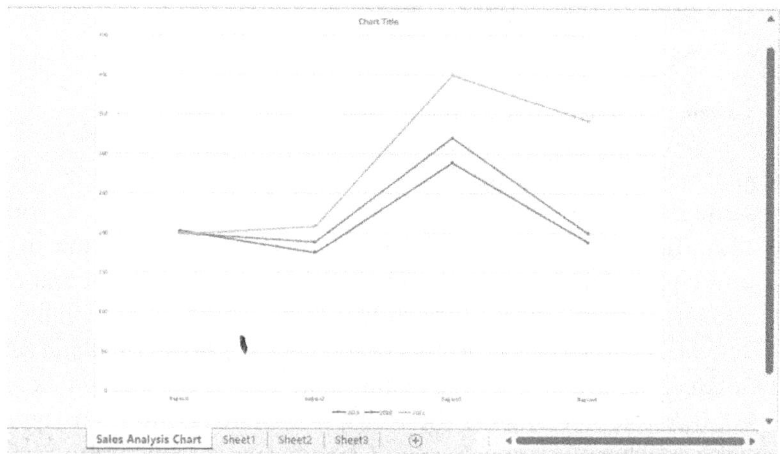

FIGURE 15.5 Line chart placed in a chart sheet.

Writing Event Procedures for a Chart Located on a Chart Sheet

Excel charts can respond to a number of events, as shown in Table 15.6.

TABLE 15.6 Chart events

Chart Event Name	This event occurs when ...
`Activate`	The user activates the chart sheet.
`Deactivate`	The user deactivates the chart sheet.
`Select`	The user selects a chart element.
`SeriesChange`	The user changes the value of a chart data point. The Chart object should be declared in the class module using the `WithEvents` keyword.
`Calculate`	The user plots new or changed data on the chart.
`Resize`	The user changes the size of the chart. The Chart object should be declared in the class module using the `WithEvents` keyword.
`BeforeDoubleClick`	An embedded chart is double-clicked, before the default double-click action.
`BeforeRightClick`	An embedded chart is right-clicked, before the default right-click action.
`MouseDown`	A mouse button is pressed while the pointer is over a chart.
`MouseMove`	The position of a mouse pointer changes over a chart.
`MouseUp`	A mouse button is released while the pointer is over a chart.

We will start by writing event procedures that control a chart placed on a separate chart sheet as shown in Figure 15.5. Events for a chart embedded in a worksheet like the one in Figure 15.3 require using the `WithEvents` keyword and are explained in the section titled "Writing Event Procedures for Embedded Charts."

Chart_Activate()

This event occurs when the user activates the chart sheet.

Chart_Deactivate()

This event occurs when the user deactivates the chart sheet.

Chart_Select(ByVal ElementID As Long, ByVal Arg1 As Long, ByVal Arg2 As Long)

This event occurs when the user selects a chart element.

`ElementID` returns a constant representing the type of the selected chart element. Arguments `Arg1` and `Arg2` are used in relation to some chart elements. For example, the chart axis (`ElementID` = 21) can be specified as Main Axis (`Arg1 = 0`) or Secondary Axis (`Arg1 = 1`), while the axis type is specified by `Arg2`, which can be one of the following three values: `0` – Category Axis, `1` – Value Axis, and `3` – Series Axis.

Chart_Calculate()

This event occurs when the user plots new or changed data on the chart.

Chart_BeforeRightClick()

This event occurs when the user right-clicks the chart.

Chart_MouseDown(ByVal Button As Long, ByVal Shift As Long, ByVal x As Long, ByVal y As Long)

This event occurs when a mouse button is pressed while the pointer is over a chart.

The `Button` argument determines which mouse button was pressed (MouseDown event) or released (MouseUp event): 1 – left button, 2 – right button, and 4 – middle button. The `Shift` argument specifies the state of the Shift, Ctrl, and Alt keys: 1 – Shift was selected, 2 – Ctrl was selected, 4 – Alt was selected. The `x`, `y` arguments specify the mouse pointer coordinates.

Hands-On 15.21 Writing Event Procedures for a Chart Sheet

1. In the Visual Basic Editor window, activate the Project Explorer window and open the Microsoft Excel Objects folder under **VBAProject (Chap15_ChartEvents.xlsm)**.
2. Double-click the chart object **Chart1 (Sales Analysis Chart)**.
3. In the Code window, enter the code of the following event procedures:

```
Private Sub Chart_Activate()
  MsgBox "You've activated the chart sheet."
End Sub

Private Sub Chart_Deactivate()
  MsgBox "It looks like you want to leave the " _
      & "chart sheet."
End Sub

Private Sub Chart_Select(ByVal ElementID As Long, _
    ByVal Arg1 As Long, ByVal Arg2 As Long)
  If Arg1 <> 0 And Arg2 <> 0 Then
    MsgBox ElementID & ", " & Arg1 & ", " & Arg2
  End If
  If ElementID = 4 Then
    MsgBox "You've selected the chart title."
  ElseIf ElementID = 24 Then
```

```
      MsgBox "You've selected the chart legend."
    ElseIf ElementID = 12 Then
      MsgBox "You've selected the legend key."
    ElseIf ElementID = 13 Then
      MsgBox "You've selected the legend entry."
    End If
  End Sub

  Private Sub Chart_Calculate()
    MsgBox "The data in your spreadsheet has " & vbCrLf _
        & "changed. Your chart has been updated."
  End Sub

  Private Sub Chart_BeforeRightClick(Cancel As Boolean)
    Cancel = True
  End Sub

  Private Sub Chart_MouseDown(ByVal Button As Long, _
      ByVal Shift As Long, ByVal x As Long, ByVal y As Long)
    If Button = 1 Then
      MsgBox "You pressed the left mouse button."
    ElseIf Button = 2 Then
      MsgBox "You pressed the right mouse button."
    Else
      MsgBox "You pressed the middle mouse button."
    End If
  End Sub
```

4. Activate the chart sheet and perform the actions that will trigger the event procedures that you've written. For example, click the chart legend and notice that this action triggers two events: Chart_MouseDown and Chart_Select.

Writing Event Procedures for Embedded Charts

To capture events raised by a chart embedded in a worksheet, you must first create a new object in the class module using the keyword `WithEvents`.

The `WithEvents` keyword allows you to specify an object variable that will be used to respond to events triggered by an ActiveX object. This keyword can only be used in class modules in the declaration section. In the following example procedure, we will learn how to use the `WithEvents` keyword to capture the Chart_Activate event for the embedded chart you created in Hands-On 15.20.

Hands-On 15.22 Writing the Chart_Activate() Event Procedure for an Embedded Chart

1. Activate the Visual Basic Editor window. In the Project Explorer, select **VBAProject (Chap15_ChartEvents.xlsm)**.
2. Choose **Insert | Class Module**.
   In the Class Modules folder, you will see a module named Class1.
3. In the Properties window, rename Class1 to **clsChart**.
4. In the clsChart class module Code window, type the following declaration:

   ```
   Public WithEvents xlChart As Excel.Chart
   ```

   The above statement declares an object variable that will represent the events generated by the Chart object.

   The `Public` keyword will make the object variable `xlChart` available to all modules in the current VBA project. Declaring an object variable using the `WithEvents` keyword exposes all of the events defined for that particular object type. After typing the above declaration, the `xlChart` object variable is added to the drop-down Object list in the upper-left corner of the Code window, and the events associated with this object variable appear in the Procedure drop-down listbox in the upper-right corner of the Code window.
5. Open the Object drop-down listbox and select the **xlChart** variable.
   The Code window should now show the skeleton of the xlChart_Activate event procedure:

   ```
   Private Sub xlChart_Activate()

   End Sub
   ```

6. Add your VBA code to the event procedure. In this example, we will add a statement to display a message box. After adding this statement, your VBA procedure should look like the following:

   ```
   Private Sub xlChart_Activate()
     MsgBox "You've activated a chart embedded in  " & _
         ActiveSheet.Name & "."
   End Sub
   ```

   After entering the code of the event procedure, you need to inform Visual Basic that you are planning on using it (see Step 7).

7. In the Project Explorer window, double-click the object named **ThisWorkbook**, and enter in the first line of the ThisWorkbook Code window the statement to create a new instance of the class named `clsChart`:

   ```
   Dim myChart As New clsChart
   ```

   This instruction declares an object variable named `myChart`. This variable will refer to the xlChart object located in the class module `clsChart`. The `New` keyword tells Visual Basic to create a new instance of the specified object.

   Before you can use the `myChart` object variable, you must write a VBA procedure that initializes it (see Step 8).

8. Enter the following procedure in the ThisWorkbook Code window to initialize the object variable `myChart`:

   ```
   Sub InitializeChart()

   ' you must run this procedure before event procedures
   ' written in clsChart class module can be triggered for
   ' the chart embedded in Sheet1

   ' connect the class module with the Excel chart object
     Set myChart.xlChart = _
         Worksheets("Sheet1").ChartObjects(1).Chart
   End Sub
   ```

9. Run the InitializeChart procedure.

   After running this procedure, the event procedures entered in the `clsChart` class module will be triggered in response to an event. Recall that right now the `clsChart` class module contains the Chart_Activate event procedure. Later on you may want to write in the `clsChart` class module additional event procedures to capture other events for your embedded chart.

10. Activate the Microsoft Excel application window and click the embedded chart in Sheet1.

    At this time, the xlChart_Activate event procedure that you entered in Step 6 above should be triggered.

11. Save and close the Chap15_ChartEvents.xlsm workbook file.

EVENTS RECOGNIZED BY THE APPLICATION OBJECT

If you want your event procedure to execute no matter which Excel workbook is currently active, you must create the event procedure for the `Application` object. Event procedures for the `Application` object have a global scope. This means that the procedure code will be executed in response to a certain event as long as the Microsoft Excel application remains open.

Some events for the Application object are listed in Table 15.7. For a complete list of events and their usage, go to Application.AfterCalculate event (Excel) | Microsoft Docs.

Similar to an embedded chart, event procedures for the `Application` object require that you create a new object using the `WithEvents` keyword in a class module.

TABLE 15.7 Partial listing of Application events

Application Event Name	Event Description
`AfterCalculate`	This event occurs whenever all pending calculations and all of the resultant calculation activities have been completed and there are no outstanding queries.
`NewWorkbook`	This event occurs when the user creates a new workbook.
`ProtectedViewWindowActivate`	This event occurs when a Protected View window is activated.
`ProtectedViewWindowBeforeClose`	This event occurs immediately before a Protected View window or a workbook in a Protected View window opens.
`ProtectedViewWindowBeforeEdit`	This event occurs immediately before editing is enabled on the workbook in the specified Protected View window.
`ProtectedViewWindowDeactivate`	This event occurs when a Protected View window is deactivated.
`ProtectedViewWindowOpen`	This event occurs when a workbook is opened in a Protected View.
`ProtectedViewWindowResize`	This event occurs when any Protected View window is resized.
`WorkbookOpen`	This event occurs when the user opens a workbook.
`WorkbookActivate`	This event occurs when the user shifts the focus to an open workbook.
`WorkbookDeactivate`	This event occurs when the user shifts the focus away from an open workbook.
`WorkbookNewSheet`	This event occurs when the user adds a new sheet to an open workbook.

Application Event Name	Event Description
`WorkbookNewChart`	This event occurs when a new chart is created in any open workbook. If multiple charts are inserted or pasted, the event will occur for each chart in the insertion order. If a chart object or chart sheet is moved from one location to another, the event will not occur. However, the event will occur if the chart is moved between a chart object and a chart sheet.
`WorkbookBeforeSave`	This event occurs before an open workbook is saved.
`WorkbookBeforePrint`	This event occurs before an open workbook is printed.
`WorkbookBeforeClose`	This event occurs before an open workbook is closed.
`WorkbookAddInInstall`	This event occurs when the user installs a workbook as an add-in.
`WorkbookAddInUninstall`	This event occurs when the user uninstalls a workbook as an add-in.
`WorkbookAfterSave`	This event occurs after the workbook is saved.
`WorkbookRowsetComplete`	This event occurs when the user either drills through the recordset or invokes the rowset action on an OLAP PivotTable.
`SheetActivate`	This event occurs when the user activates a sheet in an open workbook.
`SheetDeactivate`	This event occurs when the user deactivates a sheet in an open workbook.
`SheetFollowHyperlink`	This event occurs when the user clicks any hyperlink in Microsoft Excel.
`SheetPivotTableAfterValueChanged`	This event occurs after a cell or range of cells that contain formulas inside a PivotTable are edited or recalculated.
`SheetPivotTableBeforeAllocateChanges`	This event occurs before changes are applied to a PivotTable.
`SheetPivotTableBeforeCommitChanges`	This event occurs before changes are committed against the OLAP data source for a PivotTable (immediately before Excel executes a COMMIT TRANSACTION).
`SheetPivotTableBeforeDiscardChanges`	This event occurs before changes to a PivotTable are discarded.

Application Event Name	Event Description
SheetPivotTableUpdate	This event occurs after the sheet of the PivotTable report has been updated.
SheetSelectionChange	This event occurs when the user changes the selection on a sheet in an open workbook.
SheetChange	This event occurs when the user changes a cell formula in an open workbook.
SheetCalculate	This event occurs when the user recalculates a worksheet in an open workbook.
SheetBeforeDoubleClick	This event occurs when the user double-clicks a worksheet cell in an open workbook.
SheetBeforeRightClick	This event occurs when the user right-clicks a worksheet cell in an open workbook.
WindowActivate	This event occurs when the user shifts the focus to an open window.
WindowDeactivate	This event occurs when the user shifts the focus away from the open window.
WindowResize	This event occurs when the user resizes an open window.
WorkbookPivotTableCloseConnection	This event occurs after a PivotTable report connection has been closed.
WorkbookPivotTableOpenConnection	This event occurs after a PivotTable report connection has been opened.
WorkbookAfterXmlExport	This event occurs after Microsoft Excel saves or exports data from any open workbook to an XML data file.
WorkbookAfterXmlImport	This event occurs after an existing XML data connection is refreshed or new XML data is imported into any open Microsoft Excel workbook.
WorkbookBeforeXmlExport	This event occurs before Microsoft Excel saves or exports data from any open workbook to an XML data file.
WorkbookBeforeXmlImport	This event occurs before an existing XML data connection is refreshed or new XML data is imported into any open Microsoft Excel workbook.
WorkbookSync	This event occurs when the local copy of a workbook that is part of a document workspace is synchronized with the copy on the server. This event has been deprecated; it's used only for backward compatibility.

Let's try a couple of event procedures for the `Application` object.

Hands-On 15.23 Writing Event Procedures for the Application Object

1. Open a new workbook and save it as **Chap15_ApplicationEvents.xlsm** in **C:\VBAExcel2021__ByExample**.
2. Switch to the Visual Basic Editor window, and in the Project Explorer's window select **VBAProject (Chap15_ApplicationEvents.xlsm)**.
3. Choose **Insert | Class Module**.
4. In the Properties window, change the class module name to **clsApplication**.
5. In the clsApplication Code window, type the following declaration statement:

```
Public WithEvents App As Application
```

This statement uses the `WithEvents` keyword to declare an Application object variable.

6. Below the declaration statement, enter the event procedures as shown below:

```
Private Sub App_WorkbookOpen(ByVal Wb As Workbook)
  If Wb.FileFormat = xlCSV Then
    If MsgBox("Do you want to save this " & vbCrLf _
        & "file as an Excel workbook?", vbYesNo, _
        "Original file format: " _
        & "comma delimited file") = vbYes Then
      Wb.SaveAs FileFormat:=xlWorkbookNormal
    End If
  End If
End Sub

Private Sub App_WorkbookBeforeSave(ByVal _
    Wb As Workbook, ByVal SaveAsUI As Boolean, _
    Cancel As Boolean)
  If Wb.Path <> vbNullString Then
    ActiveWindow.Caption = Wb.FullName & _
        " [Last Saved: " & Time & "]"
  End If
End Sub

Private Sub App_WorkbookBeforePrint(ByVal _
    Wb As Workbook, Cancel As Boolean)
  Wb.PrintOut Copies:=2
```

```
End Sub

Private Sub App_WorkbookBeforeClose(ByVal _
    Wb As Workbook, Cancel As Boolean)
  Dim r As Integer
  Dim p As Variant

  Sheets.Add
  r = 1
  For Each p In Wb.BuiltinDocumentProperties
    On Error GoTo ErrorHandle
    Cells(r, 1).Value = p.Name & " = " & _
        ActiveWorkbook.BuiltinDocumentProperties _
        .Item(p.Name).Value
    r = r + 1
  Next
  Exit Sub
ErrorHandle:
    Cells(r, 1).Value = p.Name
    Resume Next
End Sub

Private Sub App_SheetSelectionChange(ByVal Sh _
    As Object, ByVal Target As Range)

  If Selection.Count > 1 Or _
       (Selection.Count < 2 And _
      IsEmpty(Target.Value)) Then
    Application.StatusBar = Target.Address
  Else
    Application.StatusBar = Target.Address & _
        "(" & Target.Value & ")"
  End If
End Sub

Private Sub App_WindowActivate(ByVal _
    Wb As Workbook, ByVal Wn As Window)
  Wn.DisplayFormulas = True
End Sub
```

7. After you've entered the code of the above event procedures in the class module, choose **Insert | Module** to insert a standard module into your current VBA project.
8. In the newly inserted standard module, create a new instance of the `clsApplication` class and connect the object located in the class module

clsApplication with the object variable `App` representing the Application object, as shown below:

```
Dim DoThis As New clsApplication

Public Sub InitializeAppEvents()
  Set DoThis.App = Application
End Sub
```

Recall that you declared the `App` object variable to point to the Application object in Step 5 above.

9. Now place the mouse pointer within the InitializeAppEvents procedure and press **F5** to run it.

   As a result of running the InitializeAppEvents procedure, the App object in the class module will refer to the Excel application. From now on, when a specific event occurs, the code of the event procedures you've entered in the class module will be executed.

   If you don't want to respond to events generated by the Application object, you can break the connection between the object and its object variable by entering in a standard module (and then running) the following procedure:

   ```
   Public Sub CancelAppEvents()
     Set DoThis.App = Nothing
   End Sub
   ```

   When you set the object variable to `Nothing`, you release the memory and break the connection between the object variable and the object to which this variable refers. When you run the CancelAppEvents procedure, the code of the event procedures written in the class module will not be automatically executed when a specific event occurs.

   Now let's proceed to try triggering the application events you coded in the class module.

10. Switch to the **Chap15_ApplicationEvents** workbook in the Excel application window. Click the **File** tab and choose **New**. Select **Blank Workbook** and click **Create**.
11. Click the **File** tab and choose **Save As**. Save the workbook opened in Step 10 as **TestBeforeSaveEvent.xlsx**.
12. Type anything in Sheet1 of the TestBeforeSaveEvent.xlsx workbook and save this workbook.

    Notice that Excel writes the full name of the workbook file and the time the workbook was last saved in the workbook's title bar as coded in the WorkbookBeforeSave event procedure (see Step 6). Every time you save this workbook file, Excel will update the last saved time in the workbook's title bar.

13. Look at the code in other event procedures you entered in Step 6 and perform actions that will trigger these events.
14. Close the Chap15_ApplicationEvents.xlsm file and other workbooks if they are currently open.

QUERY TABLE EVENTS

A query table is a table in an Excel worksheet that represents data returned from an external data source, such as an SQL Server database, a Microsoft Access database, a Web page, or a text file. Excel provides two events for the QueryTable object: BeforeRefresh and AfterRefresh. These events are triggered before or after the query table is refreshed. You can create a query table as a standalone object or as a list object whose data source is a query table. The list object is discussed in detail in Chapter 21, "Using and Programming Excel Tables."

When you retrieve data from an external data source such as Access or SQL Server using the controls available on the Excel Ribbon's Data tab, Excel creates a query table that is associated with a list object. The resulting table is easier to use thanks to a number of built-in data management features available on the Ribbon. The next Hands-On demonstrates how to create a query table associated with a list object and enable the QueryTable object's BeforeRefresh and AfterRefresh events. You must have Microsoft Access and a sample Northwind 2007.accdb database installed on your computer.

Hands-On 15.24 Writing Event Procedures for a Query Table

1. Open a new Microsoft Excel workbook and save it as **Chap15_QueryTableEvents.xlsm** in your **C:\VBAExcel2021__ByExample** folder.
2. Choose the **Data** tab. In the Get & Transform Data group, click the **Get Data** and select **From Other Sources | From Microsoft Query**.
3. In the Choose Data Source dialog box, select **<New Data Source>** and click **OK**.
4. In Step 1 of the Create New Data Source dialog box, enter **SampleDb** as the data source name, as shown in Figure 15.6.
5. In Step 2 of the Create New Data Source dialog box, select **Microsoft Access Driver (*.mdb, *.accdb)** from the drop-down list.
6. In Step 3 of the Create New Data Source dialog box, click the **Connect** button.

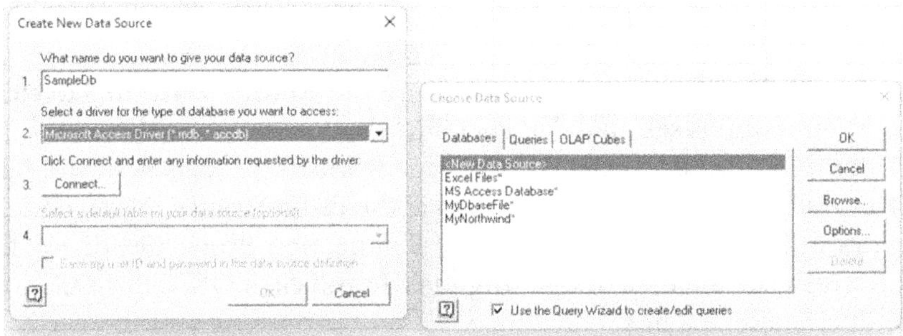

FIGURE 15.6 Use the Create New Data Source dialog box to specify the data source that will provide data for the query table.

7. In the ODBC Microsoft Access Setup dialog box, click the **Select** button.
8. In the Select Database dialog box, navigate to the C:\VBAExcel2021_ByExample folder and select the **Northwind 2007.accdb** file, then click **OK** to close the Select Database dialog box.
9. In Step 4 of the Create New Data Source dialog box, select the **Inventory on Order** table in the drop-down listbox, as shown in Figure 15.7.

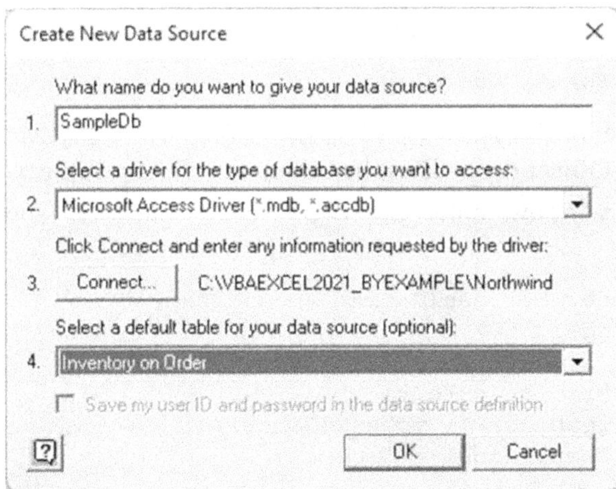

FIGURE 15.7 Use Step 4 of the Create New Data Source dialog to specify a default table for your data source.

10. Click **OK** to close the Create New Data Source dialog box.
11. In the Choose Data Source dialog box, the SampleDb data source name should now be highlighted. Click **OK**.
12. In the Query Wizard–Choose Columns dialog box, click the button with the greater than sign (>) to move all the fields from the Inventory on Order table to the Columns in your query box.

13. Click the **Next** button until you get to the Query Wizard–Finish dialog box.
14. In the wizard's Finish dialog box, make sure the **Return Data to Microsoft Excel** option button is selected and click **Finish**.
15. In the Import Data dialog box, the current worksheet cell is selected. Click cell **A1** in the current worksheet to change the cell reference. Next, click the **Properties** button. Excel will display the Connection Properties dialog box. Check **Refresh the data when opening the file** and click **OK**. Click **OK** to exit the Import Data dialog box.

    After completing the above steps, the data from the **Inventory on Order** table in the Northwind 2007 database should be placed in the active worksheet.

    To write event procedures for a QueryTable object, you must create a class module and declare a QueryTable object by using the `WithEvents` keyword. Let's continue.
16. Save the changes in the **Chap15_QueryTableEvents.xlsm** workbook.
17. Switch to the Visual Basic Editor window and insert a class module into VBAProject (Chap15_QueryTableEvents.xlsm).
18. In the Properties window, rename the class module **clsQryTbl**.
19. In the clsQryTbl Code window, type the following declaration statement:

```
Public WithEvents qryTbl As QueryTable
```

    After you've declared the new object (qryTbl) by using the `WithEvents` keyword, it appears in the Object drop-down listbox in the class module.
20. In the clsQryTbl Code window, enter the two event procedures shown below:

```
Private Sub qryTbl_BeforeRefresh(Cancel As Boolean)
  Dim Response As Integer

  Response = MsgBox("Are you sure you " _
      & " want to refresh now?", vbYesNoCancel)
  If Response = vbNo Then Cancel = True
End Sub

Private Sub qryTbl_AfterRefresh(ByVal Success As Boolean)
  If Success Then
    MsgBox "The data has been refreshed."
  Else
    MsgBox "The query failed."
  End If
End Sub
```

The BeforeRefresh event of the QueryTable object occurs before the query table is refreshed. The AfterRefresh event occurs after a query is completed or canceled. The Success argument is True if the query was completed successfully.

Before you can trigger these event procedures, you must connect the object that you declared in the class module (qryTbl) to the specified QueryTable object. This is done in a standard module as shown in Step 21.

21. Insert a standard module into VBAProject (Chap15_QueryTableEvents.xlsm) and rename it **QueryTableListObj**.
22. In the **QueryTableListObj** Code window, enter the declaration line and the procedure as shown below:

```
Dim sampleQry As New clsQryTbl

Public Sub Auto_Open()
 ' connect the class module and its objects with the Query object

 Set sampleQry.qryTbl = ActiveSheet.ListObjects(1).QueryTable
End Sub
```

This procedure creates a new instance of the QueryTable class (clsQryTbl) and connects this instance with the first list object on the active worksheet.

NOTE	*A query table associated with a list object can only be accessed through the* `ListObject.QueryTable` *property. This query table is not a part of the* `Worksheet.QueryTables` *collection. To find out whether a query table exists on a worksheet, be sure to check both the* `QueryTables` *and* `ListObjects` *collections. This can be done easily by entering in the Immediate window the following statements:*
	`?ActiveSheet.ListObjects.Count`
	`?ActiveSheet.QueryTables.Count`

23. Run the Auto_Open procedure.
After you run this initialization procedure, the object that you declared in the class module points to the specified QueryTable object.

NOTE	*The next time you want to work with the QueryTable object in this workbook file, you won't need to run the Auto_Open procedure. This procedure will run automatically upon opening the workbook file.*

24. Switch to the Microsoft Excel application window. In the worksheet where you placed the **Inventory on Order** table from the Microsoft Access database, choose **Data | Refresh All.** Excel will now trigger the qryTbl_BeforeRefresh event procedure and you should see the custom message box. If you click **Yes**, the data in the worksheet will be refreshed with the existing data in the database. Excel will then trigger the qryTbl_AfterRefresh event procedure and another custom message will be displayed.
25. Close the Chap15_QueryTableEvents.xlsm workbook file.

OTHER EXCEL EVENTS

There are two events in Excel that are not associated with a specific object: the OnTime and OnKey events. These events are accessed using the methods of the Application Object: `OnTime` and `OnKey`.

OnTime Method

The OnTime event uses the `OnTime` method of the Application object to trigger an event at a specific time. The syntax is:

```
Application.OnTime(EarliestTime, Procedure, LatestTime, Schedule)
```

The `Procedure` parameter is the name of the VBA procedure to run. The `EarliestTime` parameter is the time you would like the procedure to run. Use the `TimeValue` function to specify time as shown in the examples below. `LatestTime` is an optional parameter that allows you to specify the latest time the procedure can be run. Again, you can use the `TimeValue` function to specify a time for this parameter. The `Schedule` parameter allows you to clear a previously set OnTime event. Set this parameter to False to cancel the event. The default value for `Schedule` is True.

For example, you can have Excel run the specified procedure at 4:00 p.m. as shown below:

```
Application.OnTime TimeValue("4:00PM"), "YourProcedureName"
```

To cancel the above event, run the following code:

```
Application.OnTime TimeValue("4:00PM"), "YourProcedureName", , False
```

To schedule the procedure five minutes after the current time, use the following code:

```
Application.OnTime Now + TimeValue("00:05:00"), "YourProcedureName"
```

The `Now` function returns the current time. Therefore, to schedule the procedure to occur in the future (a certain amount from the current time), you need to set the value of the `EarliestTime` parameter to:

```
Now + TimeValue(time)
```

To trigger your procedure on July 4, 2022, at 12:01 a.m., type the following statement on one line in the Immediate window and press Enter:

```
Application.OnTime DateSerial(2022, 7, 4) +
       TimeValue("00:00:01"), "YourProcedureName"
```

OnKey Method

You can use the Application object's `OnKey` method to trigger a procedure whenever a particular key or key combination is pressed. The syntax of the `OnKey` method is as follows:

```
Application.OnKey(Key, Procedure)
```

where `Key` is a string indicating the key to be pressed and `Procedure` is the name of the procedure you want to execute. If you pass an empty string ("") as the second parameter for the `OnKey` method, Excel will ignore the keystroke.

The key parameter can specify a single key or any key combined with Shift, Alt, and/or Ctrl. For a letter, or any other character key, use that character. To specify a key combination, use the plus sign (+) for Shift, percent sign (%) for Alt, and caret (^) for Ctrl in front of the keycode.

For example, to run your procedure when you press Ctrl-a, you would write the following statement:

```
Application.OnKey "^a", "YourProcedureName"
```

Special keys are entered using curly braces: {Enter}, {Down}, {Esc}, {Home}, {Backspace}, {F1} or {Right}. See the list of keycodes in Table 13.4 (Chapter 13). For example, to run the procedure named "NewFolder" when the user presses Alt-F10, use the following code:

```
Application.OnKey "%{F10}", "NewFolder"
```

To cancel an OnKey event and return the key to its normal function, call the `OnKey` method without the `Procedure` parameter:

```
Application.OnKey "%{F10}"
```

The above code will return the key combination Alt+F10 to its default function in Excel, which is to display the Selection and Visibility pane on the right side of the Excel screen.

While using the `OnKey` method is a quick way to assign a shortcut to execute a VBA procedure or macro, a better way is to use the Options button in the Macro dialog to assign a Ctrl+key combination to a procedure.

When using the OnKey events, keep in mind that reassigning frequently used Excel shortcuts (such as Ctrl+P for Print) to perform other customized processes may make you an unpopular developer among your users.

SUMMARY

In this chapter, you gained hands-on experience with events and event-driven programming in Excel. These are invaluable skills, whether you are planning to create spreadsheet applications for others to use or simply automating your worksheet daily tasks. Excel provides many events to which you can respond. By writing event procedures, you can change the way objects respond to events. Your event procedures can be as simple as a single line of code displaying a custom message, or more complex with code that includes decision-making statements and other programming structures. When a certain event occurs, Visual Basic will simply run an appropriate event procedure instead of responding in the standard way. You've learned that some event procedures are written in a standard module (workbook, worksheet, and standalone chart sheet) while others (embedded chart, application, and query table) require that you create a new object by using the `WithEvents` keyword in a class module. You've also learned that you can enable or disable events using the `EnableEvents` property. In the final section of this chapter you worked with two `Application` object methods to execute procedures at a specific time or in response to the user pressing a key or a key combination.

The next chapter takes you through the process of accessing Excel dialog boxes with VBA.

Chapter 16 USING DIALOG BOXES

In Chapters 4 and 5, you learned how to use the built-in `InputBox` function to collect single items of data from the user during the execution of your VBA procedure. But what if your procedure requires more data at runtime? The user may want to supply all the data at once or make appropriate selections from a list of items. If your procedure must collect data, you can:

- Use the collection of built-in dialog boxes
- Create a custom form

This chapter teaches you how to display the built-in dialog boxes from your VBA procedures. In Chapter 17, you will design your own custom forms from scratch.

EXCEL DIALOG BOXES

Before you start creating your own forms, you should spend some time learning how to take advantage of dialog boxes that are built into Excel and are therefore ready for you to use. I'm not talking about your ability to manually select appropriate options, but how to call these dialog boxes from your own VBA procedures.

Microsoft Excel has a special collection of built-in dialog boxes that are represented by constants beginning with `xlDialog`, such as `xlDialogClear`, `xlDialogFont`, `xlDialogDefineName`, and `xlDialogOptionsView`. These built-in dialog boxes, some of which are listed in Table 16.1, are Microsoft Excel objects that belong to the built-in collection of dialog boxes. Each Dialog object represents a built-in dialog box.

TABLE 16.1 Frequently used built-in dialog boxes

Dialog Box Name	Constant
New	`xlDialogNew`
Open	`xlDialogOpen`
Save As	`xlDialogSaveAs`
Page Setup	`xlDialogPageSetup`
Print	`xlDialogPrint`
Fonts	`xlDialogFont`

To display a dialog box, use the `Show` method in the following format:

```
Application.Dialogs(constant).Show
```

For example, the following statement displays the Fonts dialog box:

```
Application.Dialogs(xlDialogFont).Show
```

Figure 16.1 shows a list of constants identifying Excel built-in dialog boxes, which is available in the Object Browser window after selecting the Excel library and searching for xlDialog.

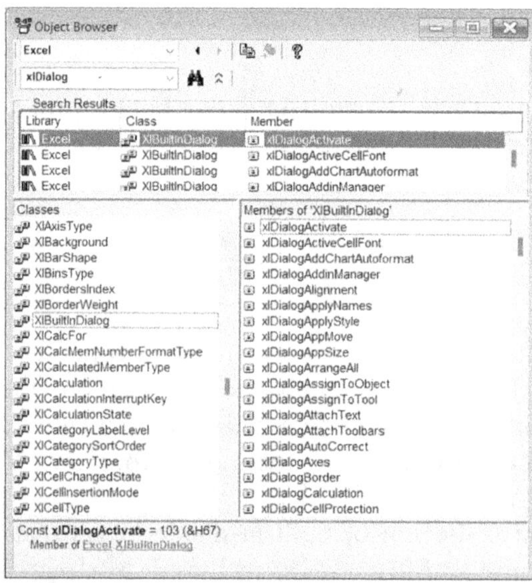

FIGURE 16.1 Constants prefixed with "xlDialog" identify Excel built-in dialog boxes.

Let's practice displaying some of the Excel dialog boxes straight from the Immediate window.

NOTE	*Please note files for the "Hands-On" project may be found in the companion files.*

Hands-On 16.1 Using Excel Dialog Boxes from the Immediate Window

1. Open a new workbook and save it as **C:\VBAExcel2021_ByExample\Chap16_VBAExcel2021.xlsm**.
2. Switch to the Visual Basic Editor window and open the Immediate window.
3. In the Immediate window, type the following statement and press **Enter**:

   ```
   Application.Dialogs(xlDialogFont).Show
   ```

   The above instruction displays the Fonts dialog box.

   After displaying a built-in dialog box, you can select an appropriate option, and Excel will format the selected cell or range, or the entire sheet. Although you can't modify the looks or behavior of a built-in dialog box, you can decide which initial setting the built-in dialog box will display when you show it from your VBA procedure. If you don't change the initial settings, VBA will display the dialog box with its default settings.
4. Press **Cancel** to exit the Fonts dialog box.
5. In the Immediate window, type the following statement and press **Enter**:

   ```
   Application.Dialogs(xlDialogFontProperties).Show
   ```

   The above instruction displays the Format Cells dialog box with the Font tab active.
6. Press **Cancel** to exit the Format Cells dialog box.
7. In the Immediate window, type the following statement and press **Enter**:

   ```
   Application.Dialogs(xlDialogDefineName).Show
   ```

   The above statement displays the Define Name dialog box where you can define a name for a cell or a range of cells.
8. Press **Close** to exit the Define Name dialog box.
9. In the Immediate window, type the following statement and press **Enter**:

   ```
   Application.Dialogs(xlDialogOptionsView).Show
   ```

   The above instruction opens the Excel Options dialog box with the Advanced options displayed, as shown in Figure 16.2.

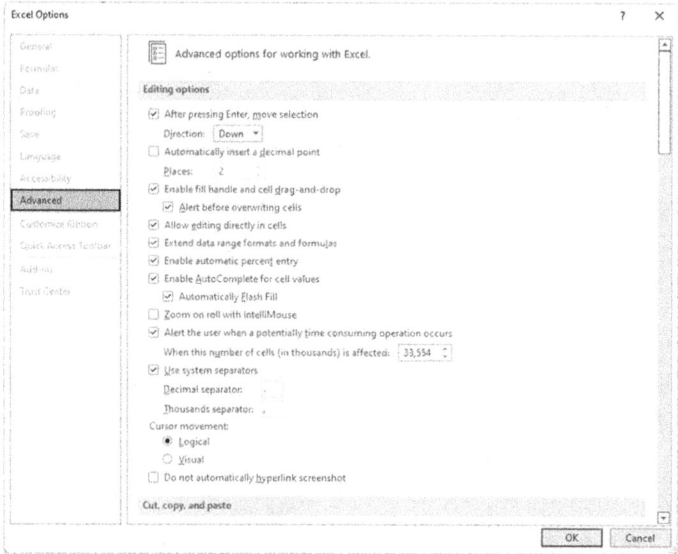

FIGURE 16.2 The advanced settings available in the Excel Options dialog box are identified by the xlDialogOptionsView constant.

10. Press **Cancel** to exit the Excel Options dialog box.
11. Type the following statement in the Immediate window and press **Enter**:

```
Application.Dialogs(xlDialogClear).Show
```

Excel shows the Clear dialog box with four option buttons: All, Formats, Contents, and Comments. Normally, the Contents option button is selected when Excel displays this dialog box. But what if you wanted to invoke this dialog with a different option selected as the default? To do this, you can include a list of arguments. Arguments are entered after the `Show` method. For example, to display the Clear dialog box with the first option button (All) selected, you would enter the following statement.

```
Application.Dialogs(xlDialogClear).Show 1
```

Excel often numbers the available options. Therefore, All = 1, Formats = 2, Contents = 3, Comments = 4, and Hyperlinks = 5.

12. Press **Cancel** to close the Clear dialog box.

SIDEBAR *Built-In Dialog Box Argument Lists*

The built-in dialog box argument lists are available at *https://docs.microsoft.com/en-us/office/vba/excel/Concepts/Controls-DialogBoxes-Forms/built-in-dialog-box-argument-lists* (see Figure 16.3).

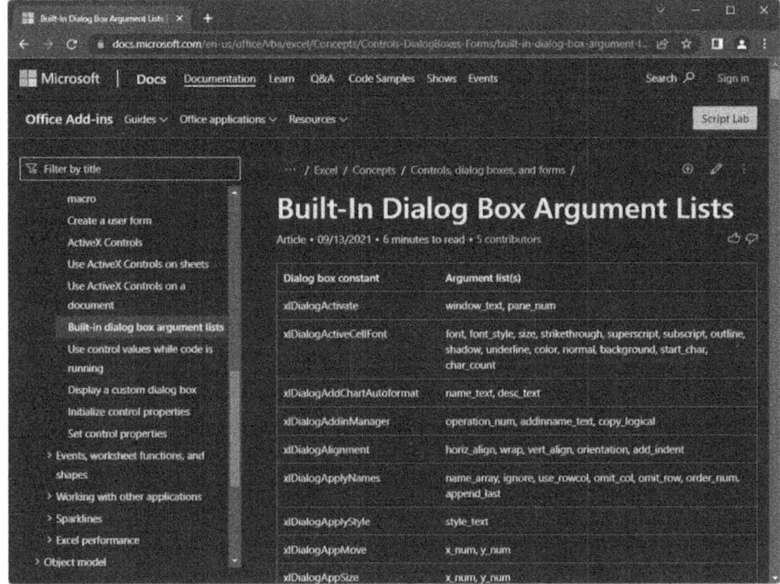

FIGURE 16.3 Microsoft Excel built-in dialog box arguments list.

13. To display the Fonts dialog box in which the Arial 14-point font is already selected, type the following instruction in the Immediate window and press **Enter**:

```
Application.Dialogs(xlDialogFont).Show "Arial", 14
```

14. Press **Cancel** to close the Fonts dialog box.
15. To specify only the font size, enter a comma in the position of the first argument:

```
Application.Dialogs(xlDialogFont).Show , 8
```

16. Press **Cancel** to close the Fonts dialog box.
17. Type the following instruction in the Immediate window and press **Enter**:

```
Application.Dialogs(xlDialogDefineName).Show "John", "=$A$1"
```

The above statement displays the Define Name dialog box, enters "John" in the Names in workbook text box, and places the reference to cell A1 in the Refers to box. The `Show` method returns True if you click OK and False if you cancel.

18. Press **Close** to close the Define Name dialog box.

FILE OPEN AND FILE SAVE AS DIALOG BOXES

FileDialog is a very powerful dialog object. This object allows you to display the File Open and File Save As dialog boxes from your VBA procedures. Because the `FileDialog` object is a part of the Microsoft Office 16.0 object library, it is available to all Microsoft 365 applications. You can also use two methods of the `Application` object (`GetOpenFilename` and `GetSaveAsFilename`) to display File Open and File Save As dialog boxes without actually opening or saving any files (this is discussed later in this chapter). Let's practice using the `FileDialog` object from the Immediate window.

Hands-On 16.2 Using the FileDialog Object from the Immediate Window

1. To display the File Open dialog box, type the following statement in the Immediate window and press **Enter**:

```
Application.FileDialog(msoFileDialogOpen).Show
```

2. Press **Cancel** to close the File Open dialog box.
3. To display the File Save As dialog box, type the following statement and press **Enter**:

```
Application.FileDialog(msoFileDialogSaveAs).Show
```

4. Press **Cancel** to close the File Save dialog box.
   In addition to File Open and File Save As dialog boxes, the `FileDialog` object is capable of displaying a dialog box with a list of files or a list of files and folders. Let's take a quick look at these dialog boxes.
5. Type the following statement in the Immediate window and press **Enter** to display the Browse dialog box.

```
Application.FileDialog(msoFileDialogFilePicker).Show
```

6. Press **Cancel** in the dialog box to return to the Immediate window.
7. Type the following statement in the Immediate window and press **Enter**:

```
Application.FileDialog(msoFileDialogFolderPicker).Show
```

   Excel displays a dialog box with a list of directories.
8. Press **Cancel** in the dialog box to return to the Immediate window.

The constants that the FileDialog object uses are listed in Table 16.2. The "mso" prefix denotes that the constant is a part of the Microsoft Office object model.

TABLE 16.2 FileDialog object's constants

Constant Name	Value
`msoFileDialogOpen`	1
`msoFileDialogSaveAs`	2
`msoFileDialogFilePicker`	3
`msoFileDialogFolderPicker`	4

Filtering Files

When you choose File | Open and click Browse, Excel displays the Open dialog box listing Excel files. You can control the types of files that are displayed in this window via the drop-down box located to the right of the File name drop-down box, or you can do this programmatically by using the `Filters` property. If the filter you need is not listed in the Open dialog, you can add it to the filters list. Filters are stored in the `FileDialogFilters` collection for the `FileDialog` object.

In the following Hands-On, you will create a simple procedure that returns the list of default file filters to an Excel worksheet.

Hands-On 16.3 Writing a List of Default File Filters to an Excel Worksheet

1. In the Project Explorer window, select **VBAProject (Chap16_VBAExcel2021.xlsm)**.
2. In the Properties window, rename the project **VBA_Dialogs**.
3. Insert a new module into the VBA_Dialogs (Chap16_VBAExcel2021.xlsm) project and rename it **DialogBoxes**.
4. In the DialogBoxes Code window, enter the ListFilters procedure as shown below:

```
Sub ListFilters()
  Dim fdf As FileDialogFilters
  Dim fltr As FileDialogFilter
  Dim c As Integer

  Set fdf = Application.FileDialog(msoFileDialogOpen).Filters

  Workbooks.Add
```

```
  Cells(1, 1).Select
  Selection.Formula = "List of Default filters"
  With fdf
    c = .Count
    For Each fltr In fdf
      Selection.Offset(1, 0).Formula = fltr.Description & _
          ": " & fltr.Extensions
      Selection.Offset(1, 0).Select
    Next
  MsgBox c & " filters were written to a worksheet."
  End With
End Sub
```

The above procedure declares two object variables. The `fdf` object variable returns a reference to the `FileDialogFilters` collection of the `FileDialog` object, and the `fltr` object variable stores a reference to the FileDialogFilter object. The `Count` property of the `FileDialogFilters` collection returns the total number of filters.

Next, the procedure iterates through the `FileDialogFilters` collection and retrieves the description and extension of each defined filter.

5. Run the ListFilters procedure.
When the procedure completes, you should see a list of preset filters in the worksheet of a new workbook.

Using the `Add` method of the `FileDialogFilters` collection, you can easily add your own filter to the default filters. The following modified ListFilters procedure (ListFilters2) demonstrates how to add a filter to filter out temporary files (*.tmp). The last statement in this procedure will open the File Open dialog box so that you can check for yourself that the custom filter Temporary files (*.tmp) has indeed been added to the list of filters in the drop-down list.

```
Sub ListFilters2()
  Dim fdf As FileDialogFilters
  Dim fltr As FileDialogFilter
  Dim c As Integer

  Set fdf = Application.FileDialog(msoFileDialogOpen).Filters

  Workbooks.Add
  Cells(1, 1).Select
  Selection.Formula = "List of Default filters"
  With fdf
    c = .Count
    For Each fltr In fdf
```

```
        Selection.Offset(1, 0).Formula = fltr.Description & _
            ": " & fltr.Extensions
        Selection.Offset(1, 0).Select
      Next
      MsgBox c & " filters were written to a worksheet."
      .Add "Temporary Files", "*.tmp", 1
      c = .Count
      MsgBox "There are now " & c & " filters." & vbCrLf _
          & "Check for yourself."
      Application.FileDialog(msoFileDialogOpen).Show
    End With
  End Sub
```

You can remove all the preset filters using the `Clear` method of the FileDialogFilters collection. For example, you could modify the ListFilters2 procedure to clear the built-in filters prior to adding the custom filter—Temporary files (*.tmp).

Selecting Files

When you select a file in the Open File dialog box, the selected filename and path is placed in the FileDialogSelectedItems collection. Use the SelectedItems property to return the FileDialogSelectedItems collection. By setting the AllowMultiSelect property of the FileDialog object to True, a user can select one or more files by holding down the Shift or Control keys while clicking filenames.

The following procedure demonstrates how to use the above-mentioned properties. This procedure will open a new workbook and insert a listbox control. The user will be allowed to select more than one file. The selected files will then be loaded into the listbox control, and the first filename will be highlighted.

Hands-On 16.4 Loading Files into a Worksheet Listbox Control

1. In the DialogBoxes module Code window, enter the ListSelectedFiles procedure as shown below:

```
Sub ListSelectedFiles()
  Dim fd As FileDialog
  Dim myFile As Variant
  Dim lbox As Object

  Application.FileDialog(msoFileDialogOpen).Filters.Clear
  Set fd = Application.FileDialog(msoFileDialogOpen)
  With fd
      .AllowMultiSelect = True
```

```
        If .Show Then
          Workbooks.Add
        Set lbox = Worksheets(1).Shapes. _
            AddFormControl(xlListBox, _
            Left:=20, Top:=60, Height:=40, Width:=300)
        lbox.ControlFormat.MultiSelect = xlNone
        For Each myFile In .SelectedItems
          lbox.ControlFormat.AddItem myFile
        Next
        Range("B4").Formula = _
            "You've selected the following " & _
            lbox.ControlFormat.ListCount & " files:"
        lbox.ControlFormat.ListIndex = 1
      End If
    End With
End Sub
```

The above procedure uses the following statement to clear the list of filters in the File Open dialog box to ensure that only the preset filters are listed:

```
Application.FileDialog(msoFileDialogOpen).Filters.Clear
```

Next, the reference to the FileDialog object is stored in the object variable `fd`:

```
Set fd = Application.FileDialog(msoFileDialogOpen)
```

Prior to displaying the File Open dialog box, we set the `AllowMultiSelect` property to True so that users can select more than one file.

Next, the `Show` method is used to display the File Open dialog box. This method does not open the files selected by the user. When the user clicks the Open button, the names of the files are retrieved from the `SelectedItems` collection via the `SelectedItems` property and placed in a listbox on a worksheet.

2. Run the ListSelectedFiles procedure. When the File Open dialog box appears on the screen, switch to the VBAExcel2021_ByExample folder, select a couple of files (hold down the Shift or Ctrl key to choose contiguous or nonadjacent files), and then click **Open**.
The selected files are not opened. The procedure simply loads the names of the files you selected in a listbox control that has been added to a worksheet (see Figure 16.4).

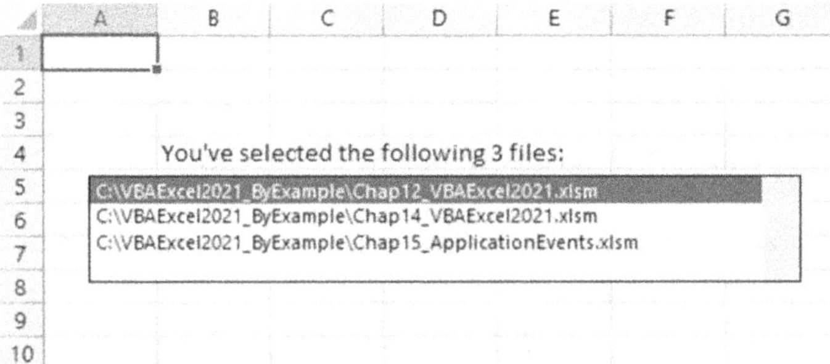

FIGURE 16.4 User-selected files are loaded into a listbox control placed in a worksheet by the ListSelectedFiles procedure.

If you'd like to immediately carry out the File Open operation when the user clicks the Open button, you must use the `Execute` method of the `FileDialog` object. The OpenRightAway procedure shown below demonstrates how to open the user-selected files right away.

```
Sub OpenRightAway()
  Dim fd As FileDialog
  Dim myFile As Variant

  Set fd = Application.FileDialog(msoFileDialogOpen)
  With fd
    .AllowMultiSelect = True
    If .Show Then
      For Each myFile In .SelectedItems
        .Execute
      Next
    End If
  End With
End Sub
```

GETOPENFILENAME AND GETSAVEASFILENAME METHODS

For many years now, Excel has offered its programmers two handy VBA methods for displaying the File Open and File Save As dialog boxes: `GetOpenFilename` and `GetSaveAsFilename`. These methods are available only in Excel and can still be used in Excel if backward compatibility is required. The `GetOpenFilename` method displays the Open dialog box, where you can select the name of a file to open. The `GetSaveAsFilename` method shows the Save As dialog box. Let's try out these methods from the Immediate window.

Using the GetOpenFilename Method

Let's open a file using the `GetOpenFilename` method.

Hands-On 16.5 Using the GetOpenFilename Method

1. Type the following statement in the Immediate window and press **Enter**:

```
Application.GetOpenFilename
```

The above statement displays the Open dialog box where you can select a file. The `GetOpenFilename` method gets a filename from the user without opening the specified file. This method has four optional arguments. The most often used are the first and third arguments, shown in Table 16.3.

TABLE 16.3 Arguments of the `GetOpenFilename` method

Argument Name	Description
`FileFilter`	This argument determines what appears in the dialog box's Save as type field. For example, the filter excel files (*.xls), .xls displays the following text in the Save As drop-down list of files: excel files. The first part of the filter, excel files (.xls), determines the text to be displayed. The second part, .xls, specifies which files are displayed. The filter parts are separated by a comma.
`title`	This is the title of the dialog box. If omitted, the dialog box will appear with the default title "Open."

2. Click **Cancel** to close the dialog box opened in Step 1.
3. To see how arguments are used with the `GetOpenFilename` method, enter the following statement in the Immediate window (be sure to enter it on one line and press **Enter**):

```
Application.GetOpenFilename("excel macro-enabled files(*.xlsm),
*.xlsm"),,"Highlight the File"
```

Notice that the Open dialog box now has the text "Highlight the File" in the titlebar. Also, the Files of type drop-down listbox is filtered to display only the specified file type.

4. Click **Cancel** to close the dialog box opened in Step 3.
The `GetOpenFilename` method returns the name of the selected or specified file. This name can be used later by your VBA procedure to open the file. Let's see how this is done.
5. In the Immediate window, type the following statement and press **Enter**:

```
yourFile = Application.GetOpenFilename
```

This statement displays the Open dialog box. The file you select while this dialog box is open will be stored in the `yourFile` variable.

6. Select an Excel file and click **Open**.
   Notice that Excel did not open the selected file. All it did is remember its name in the `yourFile` variable. Let's check this out.
7. In the Immediate window, type the following statement and press **Enter**:

   ```
   ?yourFile
   ```

   Excel prints the name of the selected file in the Immediate window. Now that you have a filename, you can write a statement to actually open this file (see the next step).
8. In the Immediate window, type the following statement and press **Enter**:

   ```
   Workbooks.Open Filename:=yourFile
   ```

   Notice that the file you picked is now opened in Excel.
9. Close the file you opened in Step 8.

NOTE	*The* `GetOpenFilename` *method returns False if you cancel the dialog box by pressing the Esc key or clicking Cancel.*

Using the GetSaveAsFilename Method

Having mastered the `GetOpenFilename` method, let's examine a similar method that allows you to save a file. We will continue to work in the Immediate window.

Hands-On 16.6 Using the GetSaveAsFilename Method

1. Open a new workbook and switch to the Visual Basic Editor window.
2. In the Immediate window, type the following statement and press **Enter**.

   ```
   yourFile = Application.GetSaveAsFilename
   ```

   The above statement displays the Save As dialog box. The suggested filename is automatically entered in the File name box at the bottom of this dialog box. The `GetSaveAsFilename` method is convenient for obtaining the name of the file the workbook should be saved as. The filename that the user enters in the File name box will be stored in the `yourFile` variable.
3. Type **Test1.xlsx** in the File name box and click **Save**.
   When you click the Save button, the `GetSaveAsFilename` method will store the filename and its path in the `yourFile` variable. You can check out the value

of the `yourFile` variable in the Immediate window by entering the following statement and pressing Enter:

```
?yourFile
```

To actually save the file you have to enter a different statement, as demonstrated in the next step.

4. In the Immediate window, type the following statement and press **Enter**:

```
ActiveWorkbook.SaveAs yourFile
```

Now the workbook file opened in Step 1 has been saved as Test1.xlsx.

5. To close the Test1.xlsx file, type the following statement in the Immediate window and press **Enter**:

```
Workbooks("Test1.xlsx").Close
```

NOTE

Because the file we are working with does not contain any VBA code, we have saved it with the "xlsx" extension instead of using the macro-enabled file format (xlsm).

When using the `GetSaveAsFilename` *method, you can specify the filename, file filter, and custom title for the dialog box:*

```
yourFile = Application.GetSaveAsFilename("Test1.xlsx", _
 "Excel files(*.xlsx), *.xlsx",,"Name of your file")
```

SUMMARY

In this chapter, you learned how to use VBA statements to display various built-in dialog boxes. You also learned how to select files by using the `FileDialog` object. You ended this chapter by familiarizing yourself with older methods of displaying the File Open and File Save As dialog boxes that you will encounter often in VBA procedures written in older versions of Excel.

In the next chapter, you will learn how to create and display your custom dialog boxes with user forms.

Chapter 17 Creating Custom Forms

Although ready to use and convenient, the built-in dialog boxes will not meet all of your VBA application's requirements. Apart from displaying a dialog box on the screen and specifying its initial settings, you can't control the dialog box's appearance. You can't decide which buttons to add, which ones to remove, and which ones to move around. Also, you can't change the size of a built-in dialog box. Therefore, if you're looking to provide a custom interface, you need to create a user form.

CREATING FORMS

A user form is like a custom dialog box. You can add various controls to the form, set properties for these controls, and write VBA procedures that respond to form and control events. Forms are separate objects that you add to a VBA project by choosing Insert | UserForm from the Visual Basic Editor. Forms can be shared across applications. For example, you can reuse the form you designed in Microsoft Excel, Microsoft Word, or another application that uses Visual Basic Editor.

To create a custom form, follow these steps:

1. Press **Alt+F11** or select **Developer | Visual Basic** to switch to the Visual Basic Editor window.
2. Choose **Insert | UserForm**.

A new folder called Forms appears in the Project Explorer window. This folder contains a blank UserForm object. The work area automatically displays the form and the Toolbox with the necessary tools for adding controls (see Figure 17.1).

The Properties window (see Figure 17.1) displays seven properties that you can set: Appearance, Behavior, Font, Misc, Picture, Position, and Scrolling. To list form properties by category, click the Categorized tab in the Properties window. To find out information about a specific property, click the property name and press F1. The online help will be launched with the property description topic.

After adding a new form to your VBA project, you should assign a unique name to it by setting the Name property. You can also set the form's title by using the Caption property.

All VBA applications that use the Visual Basic Editor share features for creating custom forms. You can share your forms by exporting and importing form files or by dragging a form object to another project. To import or export a form file, choose File | Import File or File | Export File. Before you export a form file, be sure to select it in the Project Explorer window. Before dragging a form to a different VBA application, arrange the VBE windows so that you can see the Project Explorer window in both applications, then drop the form on the name of another project in the Project Explorer.

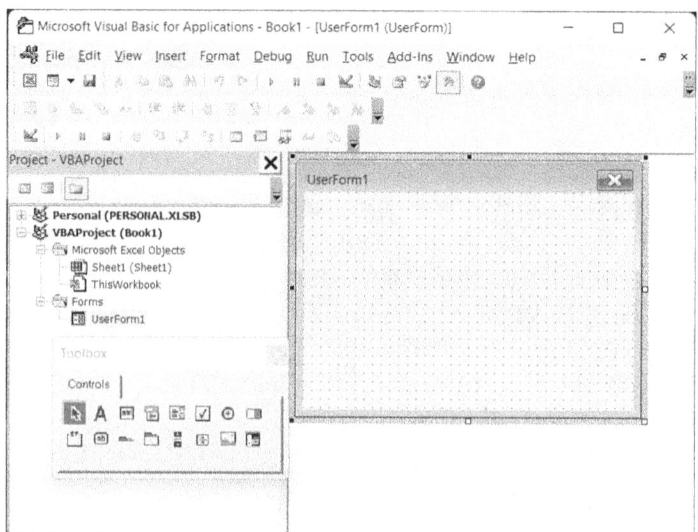

FIGURE 17.1 A new form can be added to the open VBA project by selecting UserForm from the Insert menu.

Tools for Creating User Forms

When you design a form, you insert appropriate controls into it to make it useful. The Toolbox (Figure 17.2) contains standard Visual Basic buttons for all the controls that you can add to a form. It may also contain additional controls that have been installed on your computer. Controls available in the Toolbox are known as ActiveX controls. These controls can respond to specific user actions, such as clicking a control or changing its value.

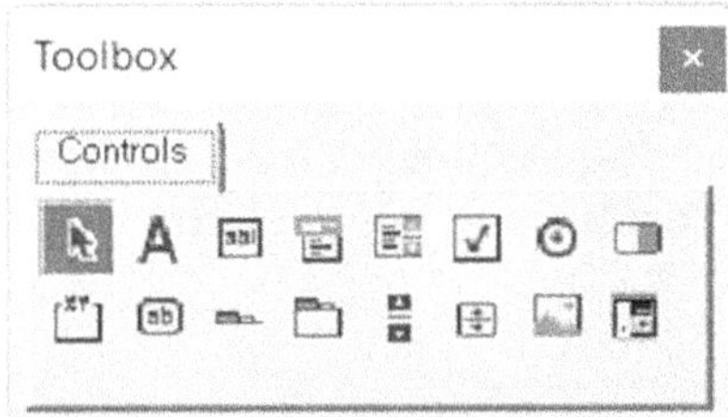

FIGURE 17.2 The Toolbox displays the controls that can be added to your custom form.

You will work with the Toolbox controls throughout the remaining sections of this chapter. If you have other applications installed on your computer that contain ActiveX controls that you'd like to use, you can also place them in the Toolbox. Let's take a few minutes and add a Date and Time Picker ActiveX control to the Toolbox. This control is one of several controls included in the Microsoft Windows Common Controls 6.0 located in the MSCOMCT2.OCX file.

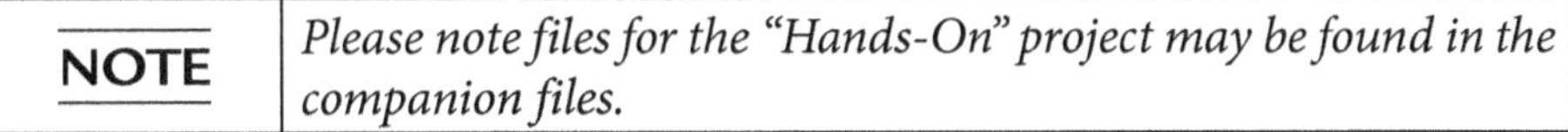

NOTE	*Please note files for the "Hands-On" project may be found in the companion files.*

Hands-On 17.1 Adding an ActiveX Date and Time Picker Control to the Toolbox

1. Open a new workbook and save it as **C:\VBAExcel2021ByExample\Chap17_VBAExcel2021.xlsm**.
2. Switch to the Visual Basic Editor window and select **VBAProject (Chap17_VBAExcel2021.xlsm)** in the Project Explorer window. Use the Properties window to rename the project **VBA_Forms**.
3. Choose **Insert | UserForm** to add a new form to the selected project.
   A default user form named UserForm1 appears with the accompanying Toolbox.

4. Right-click the **Controls** tab in the Toolbox and choose **New Page** from the shortcut menu.
   A New Page tab appears in the Toolbox.
5. Right-click the **New Page** tab in the Toolbox and choose **Rename**. If this option is not available, make sure you right clicked the New Page tab.
6. In the Caption box, type **Extra Controls** as the new name.
7. In the Control Tip Text box, type the following description: **Additional ActiveX Controls.**
8. Click **OK** to return to the Toolbox.
9. Right-click anywhere within the new page area and choose **Additional Controls** from the shortcut menu. If this option is not available, make sure you are right clicking the page area in the Toolbox and not the Extra Controls tab itself.

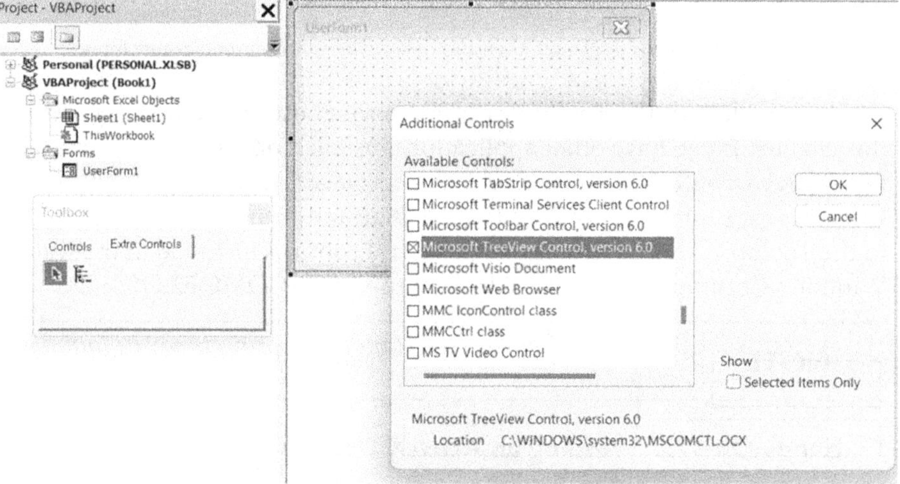

FIGURE 17.3 You can add to the Toolbox additional ActiveX controls that are installed on your computer.

10. When the Additional Controls dialog box appears, click the checkbox next to **Microsoft TreeView Control, Version 6.0,** or any other control from the list of choices (see Figure 17.3).
11. Click **OK** to close the Additional Controls dialog box.
12. The selected control now appears on the Extra Controls page in the Toolbox.

Default Toolbox Controls

The standard Visual Basic controls are described below. You will use many of these controls in this chapter's Hands-On projects.

Select Objects

Select Objects is the only item in the Toolbox that doesn't draw a control. Use it to resize or move a control that has already been drawn on a form.

Label

The Label control is often used to add captions, titles, headings, and explanations to your forms. You can use the label to assign a title to those controls that don't have the Caption property (for example, text boxes, listboxes, scrollbars, and spin buttons). You can define an accelerator (shortcut) key for the label. For example, by pressing Alt and a specified letter, you can activate the control that was added to the form immediately after adding the Label control and setting its Accelerator property. To add a title or a keyboard shortcut to an existing control, add a Label control and type a letter from its caption in its Accelerator property in the Properties window. Next, choose View | Tab Order, and make sure that the name of the label appears before the name of the control that you want to activate with the assigned keyboard shortcut. You will learn how to use the Tab Order dialog box later in this chapter (see Figure 17.6).

Text Box

Text boxes are the most popular form controls because they can be used to either display or request data from the user. You can enter text, numbers, cell references, or formulas in them. By changing the setting of the `MultiLine` property, you can enter more than one line of text in a text box. The text lines can automatically wrap when you set the `WordWrap` property. If you set the `EnterKeyBehavior` property to True when the `MultiLine` property is also set to True, you'll be able to start a new line in the text box by pressing Enter. Another property, `EnterFieldBehavior`, determines whether the text is selected when the user selects the text field. Setting this property to 0 (fmEnterFieldBehaviorSelectAll) will select the text within the field. Setting this property to 1 (fmEnterFieldBehaviorRecallSelect) will only select the text that the user selected the last time he activated this field. If you want to limit the number of characters the user can enter in a text box, you can do this by specifying the exact number of characters in the `MaxLength` property.

Frame

Frames allow you to visually organize and logically group various controls placed on the form. Later in this chapter, you will find an example of the Info Survey form that uses two frames. One of them organizes Hardware and Software option buttons into one logical group; the second frame groups the checkboxes related to the computer type (see Figure 17.4).

Command Button

A command button carries out a command when it is clicked. In this chapter, you will learn how to execute VBA procedures from command buttons.

Option Button

An option button lets you select one of a number of options. Option buttons usually appear in groups of two or more buttons surrounded by a frame control. Only one option button can be selected. When you select a new option button, the previously selected option button is automatically deselected. To activate or deactivate an option button, set its `Value` property to True or False. True means that the option is activated; False indicates that the option is deactivated.

Check Box

Checkboxes are used for turning specific options on and off. Unlike option buttons, you can select one or more checkboxes. If the checkbox is selected, its `Value` property is set to True; if the checkbox is not selected, its `Value` property is set to False.

Toggle Button

A toggle button looks like a command button and works similarly to an option button. When you click a toggle button, the button stays pressed. The next click on the button returns it to the normal (unpressed) state. The pressed toggle button has its `Value` property set to True. The unpressed toggle button has its `Value` property set to False.

Listbox

Instead of prompting the user to enter a specific value in a text box, sometimes it's better to present a list of available choices from which to select. The listbox reduces the possibility of data entry errors. The listbox entries can be typed in a worksheet, or they can be loaded directly from a VBA procedure using the `AddItem` method. The `RowSource` property indicates the source of data displayed in the listbox. For example, the reference $A$1: $B$8 will display in the listbox the contents of the specified range of cells.

The listbox can display one or more columns when you set the `ColumnCount` property. Another property, `ColumnHeads`, can be set to True to display the column titles in the listbox.

The user may select more than one item in the listbox if the `MultiSelect` property is set to True.

Combo Box

The combo box is a control that combines a text box with a listbox. This control is often used to save space on the form. When you click the down arrow located to the right of the combo box, the box will drop open to reveal a number of items from which to choose. You may enter a new value if you set the `MatchRequired` property to False. The `ListRows` property determines how many items will appear when the user drops down the list. The `Style` property determines the type of combo box. To select an item from the list, use 0 (fmStyleDropDownCombo). Set the Style property to 2 (fmStyleDropDownList) to limit the user's selection to the items available in the combo box.

Scrollbar

This control allows you to place horizontal and vertical scrollbars on your form. Although normally used to navigate windows, scrollbars can be used on your form to enter values in a predefined range. The current value of the scrollbar is set or returned by the `Value` property. The scrollbar's `Max` property lets you set its maximum value. The `Min` property determines the minimum value. The `LargeChange` property determines by what value the `Value` property should change when the user clicks inside the scrollbar. When programming the behavior of the scrollbar, don't forget to set the `SmallChange` property that determines how the `Value` property changes when you click one of the scroll arrows.

Spin Button

The spin button works similarly to a scrollbar. You can click an arrow to increment or decrement a value. The spin button is often used with a text box. The user can then type the exact value in the text box or select a value by using the arrows. The technique of using the spin button with a text box is discussed later in this chapter.

 *Image Control*

The image control lets you display a graphical image on a form. This control supports the following file formats: *.bmp, *.cur, *gif, *.ico, *.jpg, and *.wmf. Like other controls in the Toolbox, the image control has a number of properties that you can set. For example, you can control the appearance of the picture with the `PictureSizeMode` property. This property has three settings:

- 0 (fmPictureSizeModeClip) crops the part of a picture that does not fit within the picture frame.
- 1 (fmPictureSizeModeStretch) stretches the picture horizontally or vertically until it fills the entire frame area.
- 3 (fmPictureSizeModeZoom) enlarges the picture without distorting its proportions.

 *MultiPage Control*

The `MultiPage` control displays a series of tabs at the top of the form. Each tab acts as a separate page. Using the `MultiPage` control, you can design forms that contain two or more pages. You can place a different set of controls on each form page to make the data more readable. It's much easier to click a form tab than move around in a long form using scrollbars. By default, each `MultiPage` control appears on your form with two pages. New pages can be added by using the shortcut menu or the `Add` method from within a VBA procedure.

TabStrip Control

Although the TabStrip and MultiPage controls look almost alike, each has a different function. The TabStrip lets you use the same controls for displaying multiple sets of the same data. Suppose that the form shows students' exams. Each student has to pass an exam in the same subjects. Each subject can be placed on a separate page (tab), and each tab will contain the same controls to collect data, such as the grade received and the date of the exam. When you activate any subject tab, you will see the same controls. Only the data in these controls will change.

RefEdit Control

This control is specific to forms created in Microsoft Excel, as it allows you to select a cell or a range of cells in a worksheet and pass it to your VBA procedure. You can see how this control works by taking a look at some of the built-in dialog boxes in Excel. For example, the Consolidate dialog box accessed from the Data tab's Data Tools group has a RefEdit control labeled Reference that lets you specify the range of data that you want to consolidate. To temporarily hide the dialog box while selecting a range of cells, click the button on the right of the RefEdit control.

Placing Controls on a Form

When you create a custom form, you place various controls that are available in the Toolbox on an empty form. The type of control you select depends on the type of data the control will have to store and the functionality of your form. The Toolbox can be moved around on the screen.You can also change its size, or close it when all controls are already on the form and all you want to do is work with their properties. The Toolbox display can be toggled on and off by choosing View | Toolbox. To add a new control to a form, first click the control image in the Toolbox and then click the form or draw a frame. Clicking on a form (without drawing a frame) will place a control in its default size. The standard settings of each control can be looked up in the Properties window. For example, the standard text box size is 18 x 72 points (see the Height and Width properties of the text box). After placing a control on a form, the Select Object button (represented by the arrow) becomes the active control in the Toolbox. When you double-click a control in the Toolbox, you can draw as many instances of that control as you want. For example, to quickly place three text boxes on your form, double-click the text box control in the Toolbox and then click three times on the form.

Setting Grid Options

When you drag a control on a form, Visual Basic adjusts the control so that it aligns with the form's grid. You can set the grid to your liking by using the Options dialog box.

To access grid options, perform the following:

1. Choose **Tools | Options**.
2. Click the **General** tab in the Options dialog box.

The Form Grid Settings area lets you turn off the grid, adjust the grid size, and decide whether you want the controls aligned to the grid.

SAMPLE APPLICATION: INFO SURVEY

As you already know, the best way to understand a complex feature is to apply it in a real-life project. In this section, you will create a custom form for a coworker who requested that you streamline the tedious process of entering survey data into a spreadsheet. While working with this form (Figure 17.4), you will have the chance to experiment with many controls and their properties. Also, you will learn how to transfer data from your custom form to a worksheet (Figure 17.5).

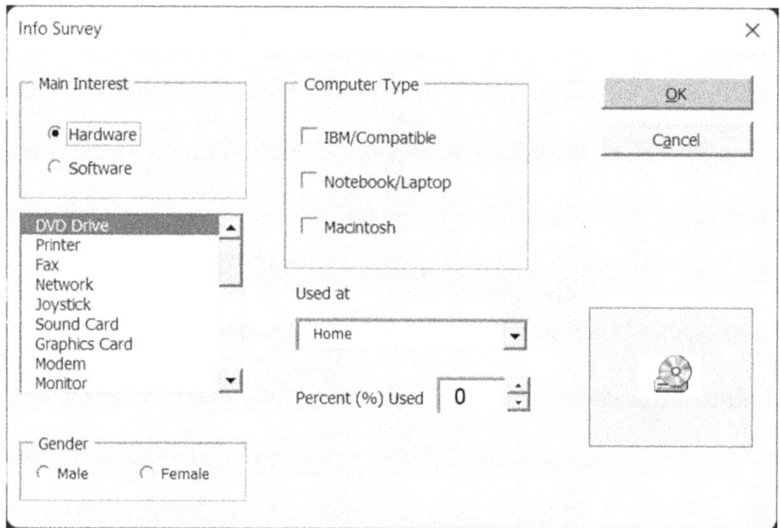

FIGURE 17.4 The Info Survey custom form allows the user to quickly enter data by making appropriate selections from various controls placed on the form.

	A	B	C	D	E	F	G	H	I	J	K
1											
2	Description	Hardware	Software	IBM Compatible	Notebook/Laptop	Macintosh	Used at	Percent (%) Used	Male	Female	Survey
3	Network	*		*			work	100	*		
4	Word Processing		*		*		home	50		*	
5	Graphics Card	*		*			work/home	100			
6	Accounting Programs		*		*		work/home/school	35	*		
7	Scanner	*				*	home	25		*	
8	Imaging Software		*			*	Work/home	10		*	
9	Mouse	*			*		Home	1			
10	Finance Programs		*		*		Work	50	*		
11	Printer	*		*			School	20		*	
12	Monitor	*		*			Work/home/school	15	*		
13	CAD Systems		*	*			Work/home	22		*	
14	Imaging Software		*	*		*	Work/home	22		*	
15											

FIGURE 17.5 Each time the Info Survey form is used, the user's selections are written to the worksheet.

Setting Up the Custom Form

Before you can begin programming, you need to perform several tasks. The tasks listed below are described in Hands-On 17.1.

1. Step 1 (Hands-On 17.1a): Insert a new form into your VBA project and set up this form's initial properties like the Name and Caption properties that will allow you to identify the form.
2. Step 2 (Hands-On 17.1b): Adjust the size of the form so that all controls required by the application can be easily placed on the form and the form does not look crowded.
3. Step 3 (Hands-On 17.1c): Place the required controls on the form.
4. Step 4 (Hands-On 17.1d): Adjust other properties of the form and its controls.
5. Step 5 (Hands-On 17.1e): Set the tab order of the controls on the form.
6. Step 6 (Hands-On 17.1f): Prepare a worksheet to receive the data.
7. Step 7 (Hands-On 17.1g): Display the completed custom form.
8. Step 8 (Hands-On 17.1h): Write a procedure to initialize the form.
9. Step 9 (Hands-On 17.1i): Write a procedure that populates the listbox control.
10. Step 10 (Hands-On 17.1j): Write procedures that control option buttons.
11. Step 11 (Hands-On 17.1k): Write a procedure that synchronizes text box with the spin button control.
12. Step 12 (Hands-On 17.1l): Write a procedure that closes the form.
13. Step 13 (Hands-On 17.1m): Write a procedure that transfers data to a worksheet.
14. Step 14 (Hands-On 17.1n): Start using the completed InfoSurvey application.

Inserting a New Form and Setting Up the Initial Properties

Follow the step below to get started with the Info Survey application.

Hands-On 17.1a Inserting a New Form (Step 1)

1. Choose **Insert | UserForm** to add a blank form to the VBA_Forms (Chap17_VBAExcel2021.xlsm) project.
2. In the Properties window, double-click the **Name** property and type **InfoSurvey** to change the default form name.
   We will use this name later on to refer to this UserForm object in VBA procedures.

3. Double-click the **Caption** property and type the new title for the form: **Info Survey**.
   The name Info Survey will appear in your form's titlebar.
4. Double-click the **BackColor** property, click the **Palette** tab, and select a color for the form background.

Changing the Size of the Form

When a default form inserted in your project is too large or too small to fit all the controls properly, you can change its size by using the mouse or by setting the form properties in the Properties window.

To resize the form with the mouse, click on an empty part of the form. Notice that several selection handles appear around the form. Place the mouse pointer over any selection handle located in the middle of a side, drag the handle to the position you want, and then release the mouse button.

You can also place the mouse pointer over the selection handle located at the undocked corner and drag the handle to the position you want. Release the mouse button.

To resize the form using the Properties window, you will need to enter new values for the form's Height and Width.

NOTE	*Each new form has a default size of 180 x 240. The form's dimensions are in points. One point equals 1/72 inch.*

Click in the form's title bar. In the Properties window, double-click the Height property and enter a new value. Do the same for the Width property if you need to adjust the form's width as well. To avoid extra work, figure out how much space you really need and resize the form before adding the desired controls.

After setting the initial properties for our custom Info Survey form, let's adjust the size of the form so that all the controls that we need to place on this form will fit nicely.

Hands-On 17.1b Adjusting the Size of the Form (Step 2)

1. Click the form's titlebar (where the words "Info Survey" appear).
2. In the Properties window, double-click the **Height** property and enter the value **252.75**.
3. In the Properties window, double-click the **Width** property and enter the value **405.75**.

Adding Buttons, Checkboxes, and Other Controls to a Form

Now we are ready to proceed with placing the required controls on the Info Survey form. We will model this form after Figure 17.4.

The UserForm toolbar contains a number of useful shortcuts for working with forms, such as making controls the same size, centering a control horizontally or vertically, aligning control edges, and grouping and ungrouping controls. To display this toolbar, choose View | Toolbars | UserForm.

Hands-On 17.1c Adding Buttons, Checkboxes, and Other Controls to a Form (Step 3)

1. Click the **Frame** control in the Toolbox.
   The mouse pointer changes to a cross accompanied by the symbol of the selected control.
2. Point to the upper left-hand side of the form, then click and drag the mouse to draw a small rectangle.
   When you release the mouse button, you will see a small rectangle titled Frame1. When the frame is selected, various selection handles will appear in its sides, and the Properties window's titlebar will display Properties-Frame1.
3. In the Properties window, double-click the **Caption** property and replace the selected default caption, Frame1, with **Main Interest**.
4. Click the **Option Button** control in the Toolbox. Next, click inside the Main Interest frame that you've just added to your form. Click and drag the mouse to the right until you see a rectangle with the default label OptionButton1.
5. In the Properties window, change the option button's Caption property to **Hardware**.
6. Use the method presented in Step 4 to add another option button to the Main Interest frame. Change the Caption property of this option button to **Software**.
   The option buttons are used whenever the user must select one choice from a group of mutually exclusive choices. If the user can select more than one choice, checkboxes are used.
7. Click the **List Box** control in the Toolbox.
   The mouse pointer will change to a cross accompanied by the symbol of the selected control.
8. Click below the Main Interest frame and drag the mouse down and to the right to draw a listbox.

When you release the mouse button, you will see a white rectangle. Figure 17.4 shows the listbox populated with hardware entries.

9. Insert a frame below the listbox. Change the frame's Caption property to **Gender**. Add two option buttons inside this frame and change the first button's Caption property to **Male** and the second one to **Female** (see Figure 17.4).
10. Click the **Frame** control in the Toolbox and draw a rectangle to the right of the frame labeled Main Interest.
11. Change the Caption property of the new frame to **Computer Type**.
12. Click the **Check Box** control in the Toolbox and click inside the empty frame that you have just added. The CheckBox1 control should appear inside the frame.
13. Change the Caption property of the CheckBox1 control to **IBM/Compatible**.
14. Place two more checkboxes inside the frame labeled Computer Type. Use the Caption property to assign the following titles to these checkboxes: **Notebook/ Laptop** and **Macintosh**. The result should match Figure 17.4.
    Unlike option buttons, which are mutually exclusive, checkboxes allow the user to activate one or more options simultaneously. The checkbox can be checked, unchecked, or unavailable at a time. An unavailable checkbox has its label grayed out and is therefore inactive (cannot be selected). The checked box has an x in front of its caption. The checkbox that has the focus is indicated by a dotted line around the caption.

    Use option buttons when only one option can be selected at a given time. Use checkboxes to have the user select any number of options that apply.
15. Click the **Label** control in the Toolbox.
16. Click the empty space below the frame labeled Computer Type. The Label1 control should appear.
17. Change the Caption property of Label1 to **Used at**.
18. Click the **Combo Box** control in the Toolbox.
19. Click the empty space below the Used at label and drag the mouse to draw a rectangle. Release the mouse button.
    The combo box displays a list of available choices only after you click the down arrow placed at the right of this control. The combo box is sometimes referred to as a drop-down list and is used to save valuable space on the screen. Although the user can only see one element of the list at a given time, the current selection can be quickly changed by clicking on the arrow button.
20. Click the **Label** control in the Toolbox.

21. Click on the empty part of the form just below the Used at combo box. A label control will appear. Change the Caption property for this label to **Percent (%) Used**.
22. Click the **Text Box** control in the Toolbox.
23. Click to the right of the Percent (%) Used label control to place a default size text box.
24. Click the **Spin Button** control in the Toolbox, and then click to the right side of the text box control. A default size spin button will appear. The result is shown in Figure 17.4.

    The spin button has two arrows that are used to increment or decrement a value in a given range. The maximum value is determined by the setting of the Max property, and the minimum value is set with the Min property. The spin button has the same properties as the scrollbar, with two differences. The spin button does not have a scroll box, and it lacks the LargeChange property. A text box is usually placed next to the spin button. This allows the user to enter a value directly into the text box or use the spin buttons to determine the value. If the spin button must work with the text box, your VBA procedure must ensure that the value of the text box and the spin button are synchronized. In this example, you will use the spin button to indicate the percent of interest that the user has in the selected hardware or software product.
25. Double-click the **Command Button** control in the Toolbox. Recall that by double-clicking the control in the Toolbox, you indicate that you want to create more than one control using the selected tool.
26. Click in the top right-hand corner of the form. This will cause CommandButton1 to appear.
27. Click below CommandButton1. CommandButton2 will appear.
28. Change the Caption property of CommandButton1 to **OK** and CommandButton2 to **Cancel**.

    Most custom forms have two command buttons, OK and Cancel, which enable the user to accept the data entered on the form or dismiss the form. In this example, the OK button will transfer the data entered on the form to a worksheet. The user will be able to click the Cancel button when he's done inputting the data. To make the buttons respond to user actions, you will write appropriate VBA procedures later in this chapter.
29. Click the **Image** control in the Toolbox.
30. Click the mouse below the Cancel button and drag the mouse to draw a rectangle. Release the mouse button. The result is shown in Figure 17.4.

    The form will display a different picture depending on whether the Hardware or Software option button is selected. The images will be loaded by a VBA procedure.

31. Click the titlebar, or click on any empty area of the form to select it.
32. Press **F5** or choose **Run | Run Sub/UserForm** to display the form as the user will see it. Visual Basic switches to the active sheet in the Microsoft Excel window and displays the custom form you designed.
    If you forget to select the form, the Macro dialog box will appear. Close the dialog box and repeat Steps 31 and 32.
33. Click the **Close** button (x) in the top right-hand corner of the form to close the form and return to the Visual Basic Editor.

Note that the OK and Cancel buttons placed on the form aren't functional yet. They require VBA procedures to make them work. After you've added controls to the form, use the mouse or the Format menu commands to adjust the alignment and spacing of the controls.

The Info Survey form design is complete. Now you should feel comfortable designing any form you want. When working with controls, it is worthwhile to learn some shortcuts. For example, here's how you can quickly copy and move controls:

- To copy a control, click the Select Objects tool in the Toolbox and select the control (a selected control will have handles at its sides), hold down the Ctrl key, position the mouse pointer inside the control, and press the left mouse button. Drag the pointer to the position you want and release the mouse button. Then change the control's Caption property.
- To select an entire group of controls, click the Select Objects tool in the Toolbox and start drawing a rectangle around the group of controls that you want to move together. When you release the mouse button, all the controls will be selected. (You can also select more than one control by holding down the Ctrl key while clicking each of the controls you want to select—don't just read about it, try it out now!)
- To move the selected group of controls to another position on the form, click within the selected area and drag the mouse to the desired position.

Changing Control Names and Properties

After you have placed controls on your form but before you begin to write procedures to control the form, you should assign your own names to the controls. Although Visual Basic automatically assigns a default name to each control (OptionButton1, OptionButton2, and so on), these names are difficult to distinguish in a procedure that may reference objects of the same class that have almost identical names. Assigning meaningful names to the controls placed on your form makes VBA procedures referencing these controls much more readable.

Before you change the Name property, make sure that the title bar of the Properties window displays the correct type of the control. For example, to assign a new name to the frame control, click the frame control on the form. When the Properties window displays "Properties-Frame1," double-click the Name property and type the new name in place of the highlighted default name. Do not confuse the name of the control with the control's title (caption). For example, on the Info Survey form, the default name of the frame control is Frame1, but the title of this control is Main Interest. The control's title can be changed by setting the Caption property. While the control's caption allows the user to identify the purpose of the control and may suggest the type of data expected, it is the name of the control that will be used in the code of your VBA procedures to make things happen.

Let's go back to our form to make adjustments to the controls' properties.

Hands-On 17.1d Naming Form Controls (Step 4)

1. Assign names to the controls placed on the Info Survey form as shown below. To assign a new name to a control, perform these steps:
   - Click the appropriate control on the form.
   - Double-click the Name property in the Properties window.
   - Type the corresponding name as shown in the Name Property column.

Object Type	Name Property
First option button	optHard
Second option button	optSoft
Listbox	lboxSystems
Third option button	optMale
Fourth option button	optFemale
First checkbox	chkIBM
Second checkbox	chkNote
Third checkbox	chkMac
Combo box	cboxWhereUsed

(Contd.)

Object Type	Name Property
Text box	txtPercent
Spin button	spPercent
First command button	cmdOK
Second command button	cmdCancel
Image	picImage

The controls that you placed on the Info Survey form are objects. Each of these objects has its own properties and methods. You've just changed the Name property for all the objects that will be referenced later from within VBA procedures. The control properties can be set during the design phase of your custom form or at runtime (that is, when your VBA procedure is executed).

Let's set some properties for selected controls.

2. Change the object properties as shown in the following table.
   To set a property, click a control on the form, locate the desired property in the Properties window, and type the new value in the space to the right of the property name. For example, to set the ControlTipText property of the lboxSystems control, click the listbox control on the Info Survey form and locate the ControlTipText property in the Properties window. In the right-hand column of the Properties window, type the text you want to display when the user positions the mouse pointer over the listbox control—in this case, **Select only one item**.

Object Name	Property	Change to:
lboxSystems	ControlTipText	Select only one item.
spPercent	Max	100
spPercent	Min	0
cmdOK	Accelerator	O
cmdCancel	Accelerator	C
picImage	PictureSizeMode	0-fmPictureSizeModeClip

   The Accelerator property indicates which letter in the object name can be used to activate the control with the keyboard shortcut combination. The specified letter will appear underlined in the object's caption (title). For example, after displaying the form, you will be able to quickly select OK by pressing Alt+O.

The remaining properties of the Info Survey form objects will be set directly from VBA procedures.

Setting the Tab Order

The user can move around a form by using the mouse or the Tab key. Because many users prefer to navigate through the form using the keyboard, it is important to determine the order in which each control on the form is activated. Follow these steps to set the tab order in the Info Survey form.

Hands-On 17.1e Setting the Tab Order in a Form (Step 5)

1. In the Forms folder in the Project Explorer window, double-click the **InfoSurvey** form.
2. Choose **View | Tab Order**.
   The Tab Order dialog box appears. This box displays the names of all the controls on the Info Survey form in the order that they were added. The right side of the dialog box has buttons that allow you to move the selected control up or down. To move a control, click its name and click the **Move Up** or **Move Down** button until the control appears in the position you want.
3. Rearrange the order of controls of the Info Survey form as shown in Figure 17.6.

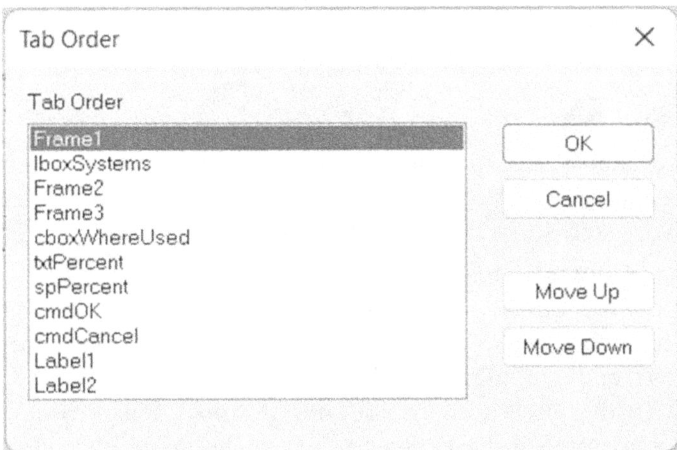

FIGURE 17.6 The Tab Order dialog box lets you organize the controls on the form in the order you would like to access them.

4. Close the Tab Order dialog box by clicking **OK**.
5. Activate the Info Survey user form and tab through the controls. Press the **Tab** key to move forward. Press **Shift+Tab** to move backward.

6. Close the Info Survey form.
   If you'd like to change the order in which the controls are activated, reopen the Tab Order dialog box, and make the appropriate changes.

Preparing a Worksheet to Store Custom Form Data

After you select appropriate options on the custom form and click OK, the selected data will be transferred to a worksheet. However, before this happens, we need to prepare a worksheet to accept the data and give the user an easy interface for launching your form. Follow the steps below to get your worksheet ready.

Hands-On 17.1f Preparing a Worksheet to Store Custom Form Data (Step 6)

1. Activate the Microsoft Excel window.
2. Double-click the **Sheet1** tab in the Chap17_VBAExcel2021.xlsm workbook and type the new name for this sheet: **Info Survey**.
3. Enter the column headings as shown in Figure 17.5 earlier in this chapter.
4. Select row 1 through column K and change the background of all cells to your favorite color (use the Fill Color button in the Font section of the Home tab). You may also want to change the background color of column K as shown in Figure 17.5.

   The easiest way to launch a custom form from a worksheet is by clicking a button. The remaining steps walk you through the process of adding the Survey button to your Info Survey worksheet.
5. Choose **Developer | Controls | Insert.**
6. Click the **Button** control on the Form Controls toolbar. Click in cell K2 to place a button. When the Assign Macro dialog box appears, type **DoSurvey** in the Macro name box, and click **OK**. You will write this procedure later.
7. When you return to the worksheet, the button (Button1, if it is your first button) to which you assigned the DoSurvey macro should still be selected. Type the new name for this button: **Survey**. If the button is not selected, use the right mouse button to select it. Choose **Edit Text** from the shortcut menu, and type **Survey** for the button's new name. To exit Edit mode, click outside the button.
8. Save the changes you've made to Chap17_VBAExcel2021.xlsm.

Displaying a Custom Form

Each UserForm has a `Show` method that allows you to display the form to the user. In the example below, you will prepare the DoSurvey procedure. Recall that in the previous section you assigned the DoSurvey procedure to the Survey button placed in the Info Survey worksheet.

Hands-On 17.1g Displaying a Custom Form (Step 7)

1. In the Visual Basic Editor window, select the **VBA_Forms (Chap17_VBAExcel2021.xlsm)** VBA project in the Project Explorer window and choose **Insert | Module**.
2. In the Properties window, change the new module's name to **ShowSurvey**.
3. Enter the following procedure to display the custom form:

```
Sub DoSurvey()
  InfoSurvey.Show
End Sub
```

   Notice that the `Show` method is preceded by the name of the form object as it appears in the Forms folder (InfoSurvey).
4. Save the changes made to the Chap17_VBAExcel2021.xlsm workbook.
5. Switch to the Microsoft Excel window and click the **Survey** button. The Info Survey form appears.

NOTE	*If an error message appears after you click the Survey button, you have not assigned the required macro to this button as instructed in Step 6 (Hands-On 17.1f). To correct this problem, click OK to the message, right-click the Survey button, and choose Assign Macro from the shortcut menu. Click the DoSurvey macro name in the listbox, and click OK. Now click the Survey button to display the form.*

6. Close the Info Survey form by clicking the **Close** button (x) in the top right-hand corner of the form.

Before we can utilize this form we need to program in some events. This is a good time to go back to Chapter 15 if you skipped it. In this chapter, we will only look at the events related to creating and using UserForm.

Understanding Form and Control Events

In addition to having properties and methods, each form and control has a predefined set of events. An *event* is some type of action, such as clicking a mouse button, pressing a key, selecting an item from a list, or changing a list of items available in a listbox. Events can be triggered by the user or the system.

To specify how a form or control should respond to events, you write event procedures. When you design a custom form, you should anticipate and program events that can occur at runtime (while the form is being used). The most popular event is the Click event. Every time a command button is clicked, it triggers the appropriate event procedure to respond to the Click event for that button. A form itself can respond to more than 20 separate events, including Click, DblClick, Activate, Initialize, and Resize. Table 17.1 lists events that are recognized by various form controls. If a control recognizes a specific event, the table cell displays "Y"; otherwise, it is blank. Take a few minutes now to familiarize yourself with the names of the events. For example, take a look at the AddControl event in the table. You can see at a glance that this event is only available for three objects: UserForm, Frame, and MultiPage control.

TABLE 17.1 Form and control events

Event Name	User Form	Label	Text Box	Combo Box	Checkbox	Option Button	Toggle Button	Frame	Command Button	TabStrip Control	MultiPage Control	ScrollBar	Spin Button	Image	RefEdit
Activate	Y														
AddControl	Y							Y			Y				
AfterUpdate			Y	Y	Y	Y	Y					Y	Y		Y
BeforeDragOver	Y	Y	Y	Y	Y	Y	Y	Y	Y	Y	Y	Y	Y	Y	Y
BeforeDropOrPaste	Y	Y	Y	Y	Y	Y	Y	Y	Y	Y	Y	Y	Y	Y	Y
BeforeUpdate			Y	Y	Y	Y	Y					Y	Y		Y
Change			Y	Y	Y	Y	Y			Y	Y	Y	Y		Y
Click	Y	Y		Y	Y	Y	Y	Y	Y	Y	Y			Y	
DblClick	Y	Y	Y	Y	Y	Y	Y	Y	Y	Y	Y			Y	Y
Deactivate	Y														
DropButtonClick			Y	Y											Y
Enter			Y	Y	Y	Y	Y	Y	Y	Y	Y	Y	Y		Y

Event Name	User Form	Label	Text Box	Combo Box	Checkbox	Option Button	Toggle Button	Frame	Command Button	TabStrip Control	MultiPage Control	ScrollBar	Spin Button	Image	RefEdit
Error	Y	Y	Y	Y	Y	Y	Y	Y	Y	Y	Y	Y	Y	Y	Y
Exit			Y	Y	Y	Y	Y	Y	Y	Y	Y	Y	Y		Y
Initialize	Y														
KeyDown	Y		Y	Y	Y	Y	Y	Y	Y	Y	Y	Y	Y		Y
KeyPress	Y		Y	Y	Y	Y	Y	Y	Y	Y	Y	Y	Y		Y
KeyUp	Y		Y	Y	Y	Y	Y	Y	Y	Y	Y	Y	Y		Y
Layout	Y							Y			Y				
MouseDown	Y	Y	Y	Y	Y	Y	Y	Y	Y	Y	Y			Y	Y
MouseMove	Y	Y	Y	Y	Y	Y	Y	Y	Y	Y	Y			Y	Y
MouseUp	Y	Y	Y	Y	Y	Y	Y	Y	Y	Y	Y			Y	Y
QueryClose	Y														
RemoveControl	Y							Y							
Resize	Y										Y				
Scroll	Y							Y			Y	Y			
SpinDown													Y		
SpinUp													Y		
Terminate	Y														
Zoom	Y							Y			Y				

Each form you create contains a form module for storing VBA event procedures. To access the form module to write an event procedure or to find out the events recognized by a specific control, you can:

- Double-click a control.
- Right-click the control and choose View Code from the shortcut menu.
- Click the View Code button in the Project Explorer window.
- Double-click any unused area of the UserForm.

When you execute any of the above actions, a Code window will open for the form as shown in Figure 17.7. Notice the title in the Microsoft Visual Basic title bar: Chap17_VBAExcel2021.xlsm-InfoSurvey(Code). A form module contains a general section as well as individual sections for each control placed on the form. The general section is used for declaration of form variables or constants.

```
UserForm                                   Initialize
Private Sub UserForm_Initialize()
'select the Hardware option
    optHard.Value = True
'turn off the Software option and all
    optSoft.Value = False
    chkIBM.Value = False
    chkNote.Value = False
    chkMac.Value = False
    'display a zero in the text box
    txtPercent.Value = 0
' call ListHardware procedure
    Call ListHardware
'populate the combo box
    With Me.cboxWhereUsed
        .AddItem "Home"
        .AddItem "Work"
        .AddItem "School"
        .AddItem "Work/home"
        .AddItem "Home/school"
        .AddItem "Work/home/school"
    End With
 'select the first element in the list box
    Me.cboxWhereUsed.ListIndex = 0
'load a picture file for the Hardware option
    Me.picImage.Picture = LoadPicture("C:\VBAExcel2021_ByExample\cd.bmp")
End Sub
```

Activate, AddControl, BeforeDragOver, BeforeDropOrPaste, Click, DblClick, Deactivate, Error, Initialize, KeyDown, KeyPress, KeyUp, Layout, MouseDown, MouseMove, MouseUp, QueryClose, RemoveControl, Resize, Scroll, Terminate, Zoom

FIGURE 17.7 The combo box above the Code window lists the available event procedures for the UserForm.

You can access the desired section by clicking the down arrow to the right of the combo box in the upper-right corner. This combo box, the Procedure box, displays the event procedures that are recognized by the control selected in the combo box on the left. Events that already have procedures written for them appear in bold.

Writing VBA Procedures to Respond to Form and Control Events

Before you can accomplish specific tasks with a custom form, you must usually write several VBA procedures. As mentioned earlier, each form created in the Visual Basic Editor has a module for storing procedures used by that form. Before displaying a custom form, you may want to set initial values for controls. To set the initial values, or default values, that the controls will have every time the form is displayed, write an Initialize event procedure for a user form. The Initialize event occurs when the form is loaded but before it's shown on the screen.

Writing a Procedure to Initialize the Form

Suppose that you want the Info Survey form to appear with the following initial settings:

- The Hardware button is selected in the Main Interest frame.

- The listbox below contains the items that correspond to the selected Hardware option button.
- None of the Computer Type checkboxes are selected.
- The combo box below the Used at label displays the first available item, and the user cannot add a new item to the combo box.
- The text box next to the spin button displays the initial value of zero (0).
- The image control displays a picture related to the selected Hardware option button.

Hands-On 17.1h Writing a Procedure to Initialize the Form (Step 8)

1. In the Project Explorer window, double-click the **InfoSurvey** form.
2. Double-click the background of the form to open the Code window for the active form.
   When you double-click the form or a control, the Code window opens to the form or control's Click event. In the procedure definition, Visual Basic automatically adds the keyword `Private` before the `Sub` keyword. Private procedures can be called only from the current form module. In other words, a procedure that is in another module of the current project cannot call this particular (Private) procedure.

   Note that there are two combo boxes above the Code window. The combo box on the left displays the names of all form objects. The combo box on the right shows the event procedures recognized by the selected form object.
3. Click the down arrow in the Procedure box on the right and select the **Initialize** event. Visual Basic displays the InfoSurveyUserForm_Initialize procedure in the Code window:

```
Private Sub UserForm_Initialize()

End Sub
```

4. Type the form's initial settings between the `Private Sub` and `EndSub` keywords. The complete UserForm_Initialize procedure is shown below:

```
Private Sub UserForm_Initialize()
'select the Hardware option
  optHard.Value = True
'turn off the Software option and all the check boxes
  optSoft.Value = False
  chkIBM.Value = False
```

```
  chkNote.Value = False
  chkMac.Value = False
  'display a zero in the text box
  txtPercent.Value = 0
'call ListHardware procedure
  Call ListHardware
'populate the combo box
  With Me.cboxWhereUsed
      .AddItem "Home"
      .AddItem "Work"
      .AddItem "School"
      .AddItem "Work/home"
      .AddItem "Home/school"
      .AddItem "Work/home/school"
  End With
'select the first element in the list box
  Me.cboxWhereUsed.ListIndex = 0
'load a picture file for the Hardware option
  Me.picImage.Picture = LoadPicture("C:\VBAExcel2021_ByExample\
cd.bmp")
End Sub
```

To simplify the event procedure code, you can use the `Me` keyword instead of the actual form name. For example, instead of using the statement:

```
InfoSurvey.cboxWhereUsed.ListIndex = 0
```

you can save time typing by using the following statement:

```
Me.cboxWhereUsed.ListIndex = 0
```

This technique is especially useful when the form name is long. Notice also that the first element of the listbox has the index number zero (0). Therefore, if you'd like to select the second item in the list, you must set the ListIndex property to 1.

The UserForm_Initialize procedure calls the outside procedure (ListHardware) to populate its listbox control with the hardware items. The code of this procedure is shown in Step 5 below.

Notice that the UserForm_Initialize procedure ends with loading a picture into the image control. Make sure that the specified graphics file can be located in the indicated folder. If you don't have this file, enter the complete path of a valid picture file that you want to display.

5. Double-click the **ShowSurvey** module in the Project Explorer window and enter in the Code window the ListHardware procedure as shown below:

```
Sub ListHardware()
  With InfoSurvey.lboxSystems
      .AddItem "DVD Drive"
      .AddItem "Printer"
      .AddItem "Fax"
      .AddItem "Network"
      .AddItem "Joystick"
      .AddItem "Sound Card"
      .AddItem "Graphics Card"
      .AddItem "Modem"
      .AddItem "Monitor"
      .AddItem "Mouse"
      .AddItem "External Drive"
      .AddItem "Scanner"
  End With
End Sub
```

Now that you've prepared the UserForm_Initialize procedure and the ListHardware procedure, you can run the form to see how it displays with the initial settings.

6. Launch the form by clicking the **Survey** button in the Info Survey worksheet.
After the form is displayed, the user can select appropriate options or click the Cancel button. When the user clicks the Software option button, the listbox should display different items. At the same time, the image control should load a different picture. The next section explains how you can program these events.

Writing a Procedure to Populate the Listbox Control

In the preceding section, you prepared the ListHardware procedure to populate the lboxSystems listbox with the Hardware items. You can use the same method to load the Software items into the listbox.

Hands-On 17.1i Populating the Listbox Control (Step 9)

1. Activate the ShowSurvey module and enter the code of the ListSoftware procedure, as shown below:

```
Sub ListSoftware()
```

```
  With InfoSurvey.lboxSystems
      .AddItem "Spreadsheets"
      .AddItem "Databases"
      .AddItem "CAD Systems"
      .AddItem "Word Processing"
      .AddItem "Finance Programs"
      .AddItem "Games"
      .AddItem "Accounting Programs"
      .AddItem "Desktop Publishing"
      .AddItem "Imaging Software"
      .AddItem "Personal Information Managers"
  End With
End Sub
```

Writing a Procedure to Control Option Buttons

When you click the Software button in the Info Survey form, the hardware items from the listbox should be replaced with the software items and vice versa. Let's write procedures that will control the Hardware and Software buttons in the Main Interest frame.

Hands-On 17.1j Controlling Option Buttons (Step 10)

1. Activate the InfoSurvey form and double-click the **Software** option button located in the Main Interest frame.
2. When the Code window appears with the optSoft_Click procedure skeleton, highlight the code and press **Delete.**
3. Click the down arrow in the upper right-hand combo box and select the Change event procedure. Visual Basic will automatically enter the beginning and end of the optSoft_Change procedure for you.
4. Enter the code of the optSoft_Change procedure as shown below:

```
Private Sub optSoft_Change()
  Me.lboxSystems.Clear
  Call ListSoftware
  Me.lboxSystems.ListIndex = 0
  Me.picImage.Picture = _
       LoadPicture("C:\VBAExcel2021_ByExample\books.bmp")
End Sub
```

The optSoft_Change procedure begins with a statement that uses the `Clear` method to remove the current list of items from the lboxSystems listbox. The next statement calls the ListSoftware procedure to populate the listbox with software items. In other words, when the user clicks the Software button, the procedure removes the hardware items from the listbox and adds the software items. If you don't clear the listbox prior to adding new items, the new items will be appended to the current list. The statement `Me.lboxSystems.ListIndex = 0` selects the first item in the list. The final statement in this procedure loads a picture file to the image control. Be sure to replace the reference to this file with the complete path to a valid picture file that is in your computer. Because the user may want to reselect the Hardware button after selecting the Software button, you must create a similar Change event procedure for the optHard option button.

5. Enter the following optHard_Change procedure, just below the optSoft_Change procedure:

```
Private Sub optHard_Change()
  Me.lboxSystems.Clear
  Call ListHardware
  Me.lboxSystems.ListIndex = 0
  Me.picImage.Picture = _
LoadPicture("C:\VBAExcel2021_ByExample\cd.bmp")
End Sub
```

6. Launch the form by clicking the **Survey** button in the Info Survey worksheet and check the results.
   When you click the Software option button, you should see the software items display in the listbox below. At the same time, the image control should display the assigned picture. After clicking the Hardware option button, the listbox should display the appropriate hardware items. At the same time, the image control should display a different picture.
7. Close the form by clicking the **Close** button in the form's upper-right corner.

Writing Procedures to Synchronize the Text Box with the Spin Button

The Info Survey form has a text box in front of the spin button control. To indicate a percent of time that the selected Hardware or Software item is used, the user can type a value in a text box or use the spin button. The initial value of the text box is set to zero (0). Suppose the user entered 10 in the text box and now wants to increase this value to 15 by using the spin button. To enable this action, the text box and the spin button have to be synchronized. Each of these objects requires a separate Change event procedure.

Hands-On 17.1k Synchronizing the Text Box with the Spin Button (Step 11)

1. Right-click the spin button and choose **View Code** from the shortcut menu.
2. Enter the spPercent_Change procedure as shown below:

```
Private Sub spPercent_Change()
  txtPercent.Value = spPercent.Value
End Sub
```

   Using the spin buttons will cause the text box value to go up or down.

3. Working in the same Code window, enter the following txtPercent_Change procedure:

```
Private Sub txtPercent_Change()
  Dim entry As String

  On Error Resume Next

  entry = Me.txtPercent.Value
    If entry > 100 Then
        entry = 0
        Me.txtPercent.Value = entry
    End If
  spPercent.Value = txtPercent.Value
End Sub
```

   The txtPercent_Change procedure ensures that only values from 0 to 100 can be entered into the text box. The procedure uses the `On Error Resume Next` statement to ignore data entry errors. If the user enters a non-numeric value in the text box (or a number greater than 100), Visual Basic will reset the text box value to zero (0). Each time a spin button is pressed, a text box value is incremented or decremented by one.

Writing a Procedure that Closes the User Form

After displaying the form, you may want to cancel it by pressing the Esc key or clicking the Cancel button. To remove the form from the screen, let's prepare a simple procedure that uses the `Hide` method.

Hands-On 17.1l Writing a Procedure that Closes the Form (Step 12)

1. Double-click the **Cancel** button and enter the following cmdCancel_Click procedure:

```
Private Sub cmdCancel_Click()
  Me.Hide
End Sub
```

The `Hide` method hides the object but does not remove it from memory. This way, your VBA procedure can use the form's objects and properties behind the scenes when the form isn't visible to the user. Use the `Unload` method to remove the form both from the screen and from memory resources:

```
Unload Me
```

When the form is unloaded, all memory associated with it is reclaimed. The user can't interact with the form, and the form's objects can't be accessed by your VBA procedure until the form is placed in memory again by using the `Load` statement.

Transferring Form Data to the Worksheet

When you click the OK button, the form's selections should be written to the worksheet. You can quit using the form at any time by clicking the Cancel button. Let's write a procedure that will copy the form's data to the worksheet when the OK button is clicked.

Hands-On 17.1m Transferring Form Data to the Worksheet (Step 13)

1. In the Visual Basic Editor window, double-click the **InfoSurvey** form in the Project Explorer.
2. Double-click the **OK** button on the Info Survey form and enter the cmdOK_Click procedure shown below:

```
Private Sub cmdOK_Click()
  Dim r As Integer
  Me.Hide

  r = Application.CountA(Range("A:A"))
  Range("A1").Offset(r + 1, 0) = Me.lboxSystems.Value
```

```
  If Me.optHard.Value = True Then
      Range("A1").Offset(r + 1, 1) = "*"
  End If
  If Me.optSoft.Value = True Then
      Range("A1").Offset(r + 1, 2) = "*"
  End If
  If Me.chkIBM.Value = True Then
      Range("A1").Offset(r + 1, 3) = "*"
  End If
  If Me.chkNote.Value = True Then
      Range("A1").Offset(r + 1, 4) = "*"
  End If
  If Me.chkMac.Value = True Then
      Range("A1").Offset(r + 1, 5) = "*"
  End If
  Range("A1").Offset(r + 1, 6) = Me.cboxWhereUsed.Value
  Range("A1").Offset(r + 1, 7) = Me.txtPercent.Value

  If Me.optMale.Value = True Then
      Range("A1").Offset(r + 1, 8) = "*"
  End If
  If Me.optFemale.Value = True Then
      Range("A1").Offset(r + 1, 9) = "*"
  End If
  Unload Me
End Sub
```

The cmdOK_Click procedure begins by hiding the user form. The statement:

```
r = Application.CountA(Range("A:A"))
```

uses the Visual Basic `CountA` function to count the number of cells that contain data in column A. The result of the function is assigned to the variable `r`. The next statement:

```
Range("A1").Offset(r + 1, 0) = Me.lboxSystems.Value
```

enters the selected listbox item in a cell located one row below the last used cell in column A (`r` + 1).

Next, there are several conditional statements. The first one tells Visual Basic to place an asterisk in the appropriate cell in column B if the Hardware option button is selected. Column B is located one column to the right of column A; hence there's a 1 in the position of the second argument of the `Offset` method. The second `If` statement enters the asterisk in column C if the user selected the Software option button. Similar instructions record the actual checkbox values. In column G, the procedure will enter the item selected in the Used at combo box. Column H will show the value entered in the Percent (%) Used text box, and columns I and J will identify the gender of the person who submitted the survey.

Using the Info Survey Application

Your application is now ready for the final test. Take off your programming hat and enjoy the result of your work from the user's standpoint. As you work with the form, think of improvements you would like to make to enhance the user experience.

Hands-On 17.1n Using the Info Survey Application (Step 14)

1. Switch to the Microsoft Excel Info Survey worksheet and click the **Survey** button.
2. When the form appears, select appropriate options, and click **OK**.
3. Activate the form several times, each time selecting different options.
4. Save the changes made to the Chap17_Excel2021.xlsm workbook.

UserForm: Modal versus Modeless

By default, UserForm is *modal* which means that the user cannot interact with the parent application while the form is visible. The Info Survey application that you created in this chapter behaves exactly like that. Each time you click the Survey button, the form pops up and you are not allowed to interact with any other Excel screen until the form is dismissed. Sometimes, however, you may want to provide access to other parts of the application while the form is visible. For example, if you are creating a custom Search form, users may be required to perform specific operations in Excel outside of your form interface. The *modeless* form will allow you to do just that. To make a UserForm modeless is quite simple. Simply pass the `vbModeless` constant to the `Show` method:

```
Sub DoSurvey()
   InfoSurvey.Show vbModeless
End Sub
```

Run the modified DoSurvey procedure to observe the modeless form behavior. Notice that each time you click the OK button the form's data is written to the worksheet and the form is not dismissed. You have a full control over the worksheet; you can even delete rows of data and go back to the form to create new entries.

The `vbModal` constant passed to the `Show` method will make the form modal, however, you can omit it as this is the default.

SUMMARY

This chapter has shown you how you can program custom user forms. Let's quickly summarize what you've learned in this chapter's project:

- For custom VBA applications that require user input, you placed the desired controls on a custom form. You made sure the user could move around the form in a logical order by setting the tab order.
- For the form to respond to user actions, you wrote VBA procedures in a Form module. You set the initial values of controls by using the Properties window or writing the UserForm_Initialize procedure.
- To ensure that the data collected via the custom form is properly reported in Excel, you wrote VBA procedures that transferred Form data to a worksheet.

In the next chapter, you will learn how to format Excel worksheets with VBA.

Chapter 18 FORMATTING WORKSHEETS WITH VBA

Microsoft Excel has always provided users with a fairly comprehensive selection of formatting features. By applying different fonts, colors, borders, and patterns, or using conditional formatting and built-in styles, you can easily transform any raw and unfriendly worksheet data into a visually appealing and easy-to-understand document. Even if you don't care about cell appearance and your only desire is to provide a no-frills data dump, chances are that before you share your worksheet with others you will spend ample time formatting cell values. For your raw data to be understood, you will definitely want to control the format of your numerical values, dates, and times.

To better highlight important information, you can apply conditional formatting with a number of visual features such as data bars, color scales, and icon sets. The Sparkline feature allows you to place tiny charts in a cell to visually show trends alongside data. You can produce consistent-looking worksheets by using document themes and styles. When you select a theme, Excel automatically will make changes to text, charts, drawing objects, and graphics to reflect the theme you selected. By using Shape objects and SmartArt graphics layouts, you can bring different artistic effects to your worksheets.

This chapter assumes that you are already a master formatter and what really interests you is how the basic and advanced formatting features can be applied to your worksheets programmatically. So, let's get to work.

PERFORMING BASIC FORMATTING TASKS WITH VBA

This section focuses on cell value formatting that controls the relationship between the values that you enter in a worksheet cell and the cell's format. Cell *value* formatting should always be attempted prior to cell *appearance* formatting. Always begin your formatting tasks by checking that Excel correctly interprets the values you entered or copied over from an external data source, such as a text file, an SQL Server, or a Microsoft Access database.

When you enter data into a worksheet yourself, you are more likely to stop right away when Excel incorrectly interprets the data. When the data comes from an external source, it is much harder to pinpoint the cell formatting problems unless you run your custom VBA procedures that check for specific problems and automatically fix them when found. The meaning of your data largely depends on how Excel interprets your cell entries; therefore, to avoid confusing the end user you must take the cell formatting control into your own hands.

Formatting Numbers

Depending on how you have formatted the cell, the number that you actually see in a worksheet can differ from the underlying value stored by Excel. As you know, each new Excel worksheet will have its default cell format set to the built-in number format named "General." In this format, Excel removes the leading and trailing zeros. For example, if you entered 08.40, Excel displays 8.4. In VBA, you can write the following statement to have Excel retain both zeros:

```
ActiveCell.NumberFormat = "00.00"
```

The NumberFormat property of the CellFormat object is used to set or return the format for a specific cell or cell range. The format code is the string displayed in the Format Cells dialog box (see Figure 18.1) or your custom string.

If the number you entered has decimal places, Excel will only display as many decimal places as it can fit in the current column width. For example, if you enter 9.34512344443 in a cell that is formatted with the General format, Excel displays 9.345123 but keeps the full value you entered. When you widen the column, it will adjust the number of displayed digits. While determining the display of your number, Excel will also determine whether the last displayed digit needs to be rounded.

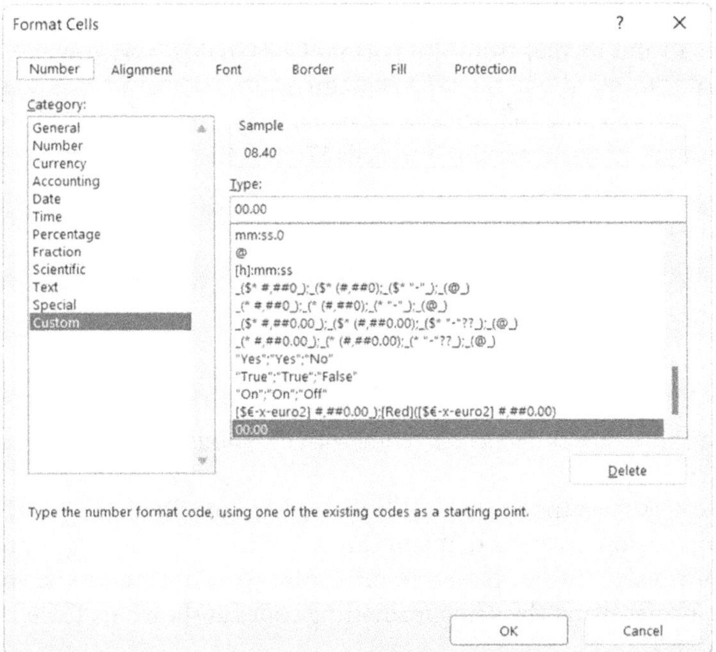

FIGURE 18.1 Format codes for your VBA procedures can be looked up in the Format Cells dialog box (choose Home | Format | Format Cells, or press Alt+H+O+E). The Custom category displays a list of ready-to-use number formats and allows you to create a new format or edit the existing format code to suit your particular needs, such as 00.00 as shown here.

You can use the NumberFormat property to determine the format that Excel applied to cells. For example, to find out the format in the third column of your worksheet, you can enter the following statement in the Immediate window:

```
?Columns(3).NumberFormat
```

If all cells in the specified column have the same format, Excel displays the name of the format, such as General, or the format code that has been applied, such as $#,##0.00. If different formatting is found in different cells of the specified column, Excel prints out Null in the Immediate window.

It is recommended that you apply the same number formatting for the entire column. Whether you are doing this programmatically or manually via the Excel user interface, the formatting can be applied before or after you enter the numbers. Excel will only apply number formatting to cells containing numeric values; therefore, you do not need to be concerned if the first cell in the selected column contains text that defines the column heading.

Because the `NumberFormat` property sets the cell's number format by assigning a string with a valid format from the Format Cells dialog box, you can use the macro recorder to get the exact VBA statement for the format you would like to apply. For example, the following statements were generated by the macro recorder to format the values entered in cells D1 and E1

```
Range("D1").Select
Selection.NumberFormat = "#,##0"
```

and display a large number with the thousands separator (a comma) and with no decimal places.

```
Range("E1").Select
Selection.NumberFormat = "$#,##0.00"
```

displays a large number formatted as currency with the thousands separator and two decimal places.

The Custom category in the Format Cells dialog box (see Figure 18.1 earlier) lists many built-in custom formats that you can use in the `NumberFormat` property to control how values are displayed in cells. Also, you can create your own custom number format strings by using formatting codes as shown in Table 18.1.

TABLE 18.1 Number formatting codes

Code	Description
0	Digit placeholder. Use it to force a zero. For example, to display .5 as 0.50, use the following VBA statement: `Selection.NumberFormat = "0.00"` or enter 0.00 in the Type box in the Format Cells dialog box.
#	Digit placeholder. Use it to indicate the position where the number can be placed. For example, the code #,### will display the number 2345 as 2,345.
.	Decimal placeholder. In the United States, a period is used as the decimal separator. In Germany, it is a comma.
,	Thousands separator (comma). In the United States, one thousand two hundred five is displayed as 1,205. In other countries, the thousands separator can be a period (e.g., Germany) or a space (e.g., Sweden). In the United States, placing a single comma after the number format indicates that you want to display numbers in thousands. To make it clear to the user that the number is in thousands, you may want to place the letter "K" after the comma: `Selection.NumberFormat = "#, ##0, K"` Use two commas at the end to display the number in millions: `Selection.NumberFormat = "#,##0.0,, "`

Code	Description

	To indicate that the number is in millions, add a backslash followed by "M":
	`Selection.NumberFormat = "#,##0.0,,\M"`
	Or surround the letter "M" with double quotes:
	`Selection.NumberFormat = "#,##0.0,,  ""M"""`
	This will cause the number 23093456 to appear as 23.1M.

/	Forward slash character. Used for formatting a number as a fraction. For example, to format 1.25 as 1¼, use the following statement: `Selection.NumberFormat = "# ?/?"`

_	The underscore character is used for aligning formatting codes. For example, to ensure that positive and negative numbers are aligned as shown below, apply the format as follows:
	`Selection.NumberFormat = "#,##0.00_);(#,##0.00)"`
	` 234.23`
	`(234.12)`

*	The asterisk in a number format allows you to fill in the cell with the character that follows the asterisk. For example, the following VBA statement produces the output shown below:
	`Selection.NumberFormat = "*_0000"`
	`_________1045`
	`________23455`

When working with cell formatting, keep in mind that number formats have four parts separated by semicolons. The first part is applied to positive numbers, the second to negative numbers, the third to zero, and the fourth to text. For example, take a look at the following VBA statement:

```
Range("A1:A4").NumberFormat = "#,##0;[red](#,#0);""zero"";@"
```

This statement tells Excel to format positive numbers with the thousands separator, display negative numbers in red and in parentheses, display the text "zero" whenever 0 is entered, and format any text entered in the cell as text. Make the following entries in cells A1:A4:

```
2870
-3456
0
Test text
```

When you apply the above format to cells A1:A4, you will see the cells formatted as shown below:

```
2,870
(3,456)
Zero
Test text
```

You can hide the content of any cell by using the following VBA statement:

```
Selection.NumberFormat = ";;;"
```

When the number format is set to three semicolons, Excel hides the display of the cell entry on the worksheet and in printouts. You can only see the actual value or text stored in the cell by taking a look at the Formula bar.

By using the number format codes, it is also possible to apply conditional formats with one or two conditions. Consider the following VBA procedure:

```
Sub FormatUsedRange()
  ActiveSheet.UsedRange.Select
  Selection.SpecialCells(xlCellTypeConstants, 1).Select
  Selection.NumberFormat = "[<150][Red];[>250][Green];[Yellow]"
End Sub
```

This procedure tells Excel to select all the values in the used range on the active sheet and display them as follows: values less than 150 in red, values over 250 in green, and all the other values in the range from 150 to 250 in yellow. Excel supports eight popular colors: [white], [black], [blue], [cyan], [green], [magenta], [red], and [yellow], as well as 56 colors from the predefined color palette that you can access by indicating a number between 1 and 56, such as [Color 11] or [Color 32]. Be sure to use closed brackets to enclose conditions and colors.

Later in this chapter we will learn how to use VBA to perform more advanced conditional formatting.

In addition to the NumberFormat property, Excel VBA has a `Format` function that you can use to apply a specific format to a variable. For example, take a look at the following procedure that formats a number prior to entering it in a worksheet cell:

```
Sub FormatVariable()
  Dim myResult, frmResult
  myResult = "1435.60"
  frmResult = Format(myResult, "Currency")
  Debug.Print frmResult
  ActiveSheet.Range("G1").FormulaR1C1 = frmResult
End Sub
```

When you run the FormatVariable procedure, cell G1 in the active worksheet will contain the entry $1,435.60. The `Format` function specifies the expression to format (in this case the expression is the name of the variable that stores a specified value) and the number format to apply to the expression. You can use one of the predefined number formats such as: "General," "Currency," "Standard," "Percent," and "Fixed," or you can specify your custom format using the formatting codes from Table 18.1. For example, the following statement will apply number formatting to the value stored in the `myResult` variable and assign the result to the `frmResult` variable:

```
frmResult = Format(myResult, "#.##0.00")
```

For more information about the `Format` function and the complete list of formatting codes, refer to the online help.

To check whether the cell value is a number, use the `IsNumber` function as shown below:

```
MsgBox Application.WorksheetFunction.IsNumber(ActiveCell.Value)
```

If the active cell contains a number, Excel returns True; otherwise, it returns False.

NOTE	*To use an Excel function in VBA, you must prefix it with "Application.WorksheetFunction." The* `WorksheetFunction` *property returns the* `WorksheetFunction` *object that contains functions that can be called from VBA.*

Formatting Text

To format a cell as a text string, use the following VBA statement:

```
Selection.NumberFormat = "@"
```

To find out if a cell value is a text string, use the following statement:

```
MsgBox Application.WorksheetFunction.IsText(ActiveCell.Value)
```

Use the `UCase` function to convert a cell entry to uppercase:

```
Range("K3").value = UCase(ActiveCell.Value)
```

Use the `LCase` function to convert a cell entry to lowercase if the cell is not a formula:

```
If not Range(ActiveWindow.Selection.Address).HasFormula then
  ActiveCell.Value = LCase(ActiveCell.Value)
End If
```

Use the `Proper` function to capitalize the first letter of each word in a text string:

```
ActiveCell.Value = Application.WorksheetFunction.
Proper(ActiveCell.Value)
```

Use the `Replace` function to replace a specified character within text. For example, the following statement replaces a space with an underscore (_) in the active cell:

```
ActiveCell.Value = Replace(ActiveCell.Value, " ", "_")
```

To ensure that the text entries don't have leading or trailing spaces, use the following VBA functions:

- `LTrim`—Removes the leading spaces
- `RTrim`—Removes the trailing spaces
- `Trim`—Removes both the leading and trailing spaces

For example, the following statement written in the Immediate window will remove the trailing spaces from the text found in the active cell:

```
ActiveCell.value = RTrim(ActiveCell.value)
```

Use the `Font` property to format the text displayed in a cell. For example, the following statement changes the font of the selected range to Verdana:

```
Selection.Font.Name = "Verdana"
```

You can also format parts of the text in a cell by using the `Characters` collection. For example, to display the first character of the text entry in red, use the following statement:

```
ActiveCell.Characters(1,1).Font.ColorIndex = 3
```

Formatting Dates

Microsoft Excel stores dates as serial numbers. In the Windows operating system, the serial number 1 represents January 1, 1900. If you enter the number 1 in a worksheet cell and then format this cell as Short Date using the Number Format drop-down in the Number section of the Ribbon's Home tab, Excel will display the date formatted as 1/1/1900 and will store the value of 1 (you can check this out by looking at the General category in the Format Number dialog box). By storing dates as serial numbers, Excel can easily perform date calculations.

To apply a date format to a particular cell or range of cells using VBA, use the `NumberFormat` property of the `Range` object, like this:

```
Range("A1").NumberFormat = "mm/dd/yyyy"
```

Formatting codes for dates and times are listed in Table 18.2.

TABLE 18.2 Date and time formatting codes

Code	Description
D	Day of the month. Single-digit number for days from 1 to 9.
Dd	Day of the month (two-digit). Leading zeros appear for days from 1 to 9.
ddd	A three-letter day of the week abbreviation (Mon, Tue, Wed, Thu, Fri, Sat, and Sun).
m	Month number from 1 to 12. Zeros are not used for single-digit month numbers.
mm	Two-digit month number.
mmm	Three-letter month name abbreviation (e.g., Jan, Jun, Sep).
yy	Two-digit year number (e.g., 13).
yyyy	Four-digit year number (e.g., 2016).
h	The hour from 0 to 23 (no leading zeros).
hh	The hour from 0 to 23 (with leading zeros).
:m	The minute from 0 to 59 (no leading zeros).
:mm	The minute from 0 to 59 (with leading zeros)
:s :s.0 :s.00	The second from 0 to 59 (no leading zeros). To add tenths of a second, follow this with a period and a zero (.0), and to add hundredths of a second, follow this code with a period and two zeros (.00).
:ss :ss.0 :ss.00	The second from 0 to 59 (with leading zeros). To add tenths of a second, follow this code with a period and a zero (.0), and to add hundredths of a second, follow this code with a period and two zeros (.00).
AM/PM am/pm A/P a/p	Use for a 12-hour clock, with AM or PM. Use for a 12-hour clock, with am or pm. Use for a 12-hour clock, with A or P. Use for a 12-hour clock, with a or p.
[ ]	Bracket the time component (hour, minute, second) to prevent Excel from rolling over hours, minutes, or seconds when they hit the 24-hour mark (hours become days) or the 60 mark (minutes become hours, seconds become minutes). For example, to display time as 25 hours, 59 minutes, and 12 seconds use the following format code: [hh]:[mm]:ss.

The following VBA procedure applies a date format to the Inspection Date column in Figure 18.2.

```
Sub FormatDateFields()
```

```
    Dim wks As Worksheet
    Dim cell As Range

    Set wks = ActiveWorkbook.ActiveSheet

    For Each cell In wks.UsedRange
      If cell.NumberFormat = "mm:ss.0" Then
          cell.NumberFormat = "m/dd/yyyy h:mm:ss AM/PM"
      End If
    Next
End Sub
```

	A	B	C
1	Room No	Floor No	Inspection Date
2	306	3	16:33.0
3	236	2	13:23.0
4	217	2	13:23.0
5	306	3	13:21.0
6	206	2	13:21.0
7	336	3	13:21.0
8	317	3	13:20.0
9	318	3	13:18.0
10	313	3	21:51.0
11	316	3	21:51.0
12	338	3	21:50.0
13	306	3	21:49.0

FIGURE 18.2 A worksheet with an unformatted Inspection Date column.

	A	B	C
1	Room No	Floor No	Inspection Date
2	306	3	2/04/2021 1:16:33 AM
3	236	2	2/03/2021 1:13:23 AM
4	217	2	2/03/2021 1:13:23 AM
5	306	3	2/03/2021 1:13:21 AM
6	206	2	2/03/2021 1:13:21 AM
7	336	3	2/03/2021 1:13:21 AM
8	317	3	2/03/2021 1:13:20 AM
9	318	3	2/03/2021 1:13:18 AM
10	313	3	1/22/2021 1:21:51 AM
11	316	3	1/22/2021 1:21:51 AM
12	338	3	1/22/2021 1:21:50 AM
13	306	3	1/22/2021 1:21:49 AM

FIGURE 18.3 The Inspection Date column has been formatted with a VBA procedure.

Formatting Columns and Rows

To speed up your worksheet formatting tasks you can apply formatting to entire rows and columns instead of single cells. The best way to find the required VBA statement is by using the macro recorder. Keep in mind that Excel will record more code than is necessary for your specific task and you'll need to clean it up before copying it to your VBA procedure. For example, here's the recorded code for setting the horizontal alignment of data in Row 7:

```
Rows("7:7").Select
  With Selection
      .HorizontalAlignment = xlRight
      .VerticalAlignment = xlBottom
      .WrapText = False
      .Orientation = 0
      .AddIndent = False
      .IndentLevel = 0
      .ShrinkToFit = False
      .ReadingOrder = xlContext
      .MergeCells = False
  End With
```

To set the horizontal alignment for Row 7, you can write a single VBA statement like this:

```
Rows(7).HorizontalAlignment = xlRight
```

You can use the macro recorder to help you find out the names of properties that should be used to turn on or off a specific formatting feature. Once you know the property and the required setting, you can write your own short statement to get the job done. Here are some VBA statements that can be used to format columns and rows:

Formatting Columns and Rows	VBA Statement
To format column D as a date using the NumberFormat property:	`Columns("D").NumberFormat = "mm/dd/yyyy"`
To format column G as currency:	`Columns("G").NumberFormat = "$###,##0.00"`
To format column G as currency using the Style property:	`Columns("G").Style = "Currency"`

(Contd.)

Formatting Columns and Rows	VBA Statement
To set column width or row height:	`Columns(2).ColumnWidth = 21.5` `Rows(2).RowHeight = 55.55`
To auto-fit column width or row height:	`Columns(2).AutoFit` `Rows(2).Autofit`
To apply bold font to the first row:	`Rows(1).Font.Bold = True`
To right-align data in row 1:	`Rows(1).HorizontalAlignment = xlRight`
To center data in column B:	`Columns("B").HorizontalAlignment = xlCenter`
To set the background of the column where the active cell is located to yellow:	`Columns(ActiveCell.Column).interior.color = vbYellow`
To check the width of a column, use the `ColumnWidth` method:	`MsgBox Columns(ActiveCell.Column).ColumnWidth`
To auto-fit all rows and columns:	`ActiveSheet.Cells.EntireRow.AutoFit` `ActiveSheet.Cells.EntireColumn.AutoFit`

Formatting Headers and Footers

Headers and footers are made of three sections each: LeftHeader, CenterHeader, and RightHeader, and LeftFooter, CenterFooter, and RightFooter. Using the special formatting codes shown in Table 18.3, you can customize your worksheet's header or footer according to your needs.

TABLE 18.3. Header and footer formatting codes

Format Code	Description
&D	Prints the current date
&T	Prints the current time
&F	Prints the name of the workbook
&A	Prints the name of the sheet tab
&P	Prints the page number
&P+number	Prints the page number plus the specified number
&P–number	Prints the page number minus the specified number
&N	Prints the total number of pages in the workbook
&Z	Prints the workbook's path
&G	Inserts an image
&&	Prints a single ampersand

Format Code	Description
&nn	Prints the characters that follow in the specified font size in points
&color	Prints the characters in the specified color using the hexadecimal color value
&"fontname"	Prints the characters that follow in the specified font
&L	Left-aligns the characters that follow
&C	Centers the characters that follow
&R	Right-aligns the characters that follow
&B	Turns bold printing on or off
&I	Turns italic printing on or off
&U	Turns underline printing on or off
&E	Turns double-underline printing on or off
&S	Turns strikethrough printing on or off
&X	Turns superscript printing on or off
&Y	Turns subscript printing on or off

Here are several VBA statements that demonstrate applying custom formatting to a header or footer:

Formatting Headers and Footers	VBA Statement (enter on one line)
To create a two-line header with bold text in the first line and italic text in the second line:	`ActiveSheet.PageSetup.LeftHeader = "&BYour Company Name" & Chr(13) & "&IYour Company Department"`
To place the workbook creation date in the footer:	`ActiveSheet.PageSetup.RightFooter = "Created on: " & ActiveWorkbook.BuiltinDocumentProperties ("Creation Date")`
To place a cell's contents in the header:	`ActiveSheet.PageSetup.CenterHeader = ActiveSheet.Cells(2,2).value`
To insert the filename and path in the footer:	`ActiveSheet.PageSetup.CenterFooter = ActiveWorkbook.FullName`
To place text in the header using Arial Narrow font and italic formatting, with the last word in bold, italic, and red:	`ActiveSheet.PageSetup.CenterHeader = "&""ArialNarrow""&IYour text goes here &I&B&KFF0000now."`
To remove the formatting and text entries from the center header:	`ActiveSheet.PageSetup.CenterHeader = ""`

NOTE	*If you need to use a different date format in your header or footer than the date format shown in the Regional settings of the Windows Control panel, use the* `Format` *function to specify the date format string you want to use:*
	`ActiveSheet.PageSetup.RightFooter =`
	`Format(Date, "mm-dd-yyyy")`
	The above statement inserts in the right footer a current system date returned by the `Date` *function. The date is formatted as a two-digit month number followed by a dash, two-digit day number followed by a dash, and four-digit year number (see Table 18.2 for the explanation of date and time formatting codes).*

Formatting Cell Appearance

As mentioned earlier, adding cosmetic touches to your worksheet such as fonts, color, borders, shading, and alignment should be undertaken after applying the required formatting to numbers, dates, and times. Formatting cell appearance makes your worksheet easier to read and interpret. By applying borders to cells, and with the clever use of font colors, background shading, and patterns, you can draw the reader's attention to particularly important information.

Use the `Font` object to change the font format in VBA. You can easily apply multiple format properties using the `With...End With` statement block shown below:

```
Sub ApplyCellFormat()
  With ActiveSheet.Range("A1").Font
    .Name = "Tahoma"
    .FontStyle = "italic"
    .Size = 14
    .Underline = xlUnderlineStyleDouble
    .ColorIndex = 3
  End With
End Sub
```

The `ColorIndex` property refers to the 56 colors that are available in the color palette. Number 3 represents red. The following procedure prints a color palette to the active sheet:

```
Sub ColorLoop()
  Dim r As Integer
  Dim c As Integer
  Dim k As Integer
```

```
  k = 0

  For r = 1 To 8
    For c = 1 To 7
        Cells(r, c).Select
        k = k + 1
        ActiveCell.Value = k
        With Selection.Interior
            .ColorIndex = k
            .Pattern = xlSolid
        End With
    Next c
  Next r
End Sub
```

To change the background color of a single cell or a range of cells, use one of the following VBA statements:

```
Selection.Interior.Color = vbBlue
Selection.Interior.ColorIndex = 5
```

To change the font color, use the following VBA statement:

```
Selection.Font.Color = vbMagenta
```

The font can be made bold, italic, or underlined or a combination of the three using the following `With...End With` block statement:

```
With Selection.Font
    .Italic = True
    .Bold = True
    .Underline = xlUnderlineStyleSingle
End With
```

To apply borders to your cells and ranges in VBA, use the following statement examples:

```
Selection.BorderAround Weight:=xlMedium, ColorIndex:=3
Selection.BorderAround Weight:=xlThin, Color:=vbBlack
```

The `BorderAround` method of the Range object places a border around all edges of the selected cells. The following `xlBorderWeightEnumeration` constants can be used to specify the thickness weight of the border: `xlHairline`, `xlMedium`, `xlThick`, and `xlDash`. When specifying border color, you can use either ColorIndex or Color but not both.

Instead of specifying the thickness of the border, you may want to use LineStyle as in the following example:

```
Selection.BorderAround LineStyle:=xlDashDotDot, Color:=vbBlack
```

You can use any of the following `xlLineStyle` enumeration constants:

- `xlContinuous`
- `xlDash`
- `xlDashDot`
- `xlDashDotDot`
- `xlDot`
- `xlDouble`
- `xlLineStyleNone`
- `xlSlantDashDot`

Use `xlLineStyleNone` to clear the border.

VBA has a `Borders` collection that contains the four borders of a `Range` or `Style` object. To set just a bottom border of cells A1:C1, use the following statement:

```
ActiveSheet.Range("A1:C1").Borders(xlEdgeBottom).Weight = xlThick
```

You may specify any of the following border types:

- `xlDiagonalDown`
- `xlDiagonalUp`
- `xlEdgeBottom`
- `xlEdgeLeft`
- `xlEdgeRight`
- `xlEdgeTop`
- `xlEdgeHorizontal`
- `xlEdgeVertical`

You can change the appearance of cells by specifying the horizontal or vertical alignment:

```
Selection.HorizontalAlignment = xlCenter
Selection.VerticalAlignment = xlTop
```

The value of the `HorizontalAlignment` property can be one of the following constants:

- `xlCenter`
- `xlDistributed`
- `xlJustify`

- `xlLeft`
- `xlRight`

The `VerticalAlignment` property can be one of the following constants:

- `xlBottom`
- `xlCenter`
- `xlDistributed`
- `xlJustify`
- `xlTop`

Removing Formatting from Cells and Ranges

To remove cell formatting, use the `ClearFormats` method of the `Range` object. This method restores the formatting to the original General format without removing the cell's content. To remove the content of the cell, use the `ClearContents` method.

PERFORMING ADVANCED FORMATTING TASKS WITH VBA

Let's focus on how you can use VBA with the enhanced formatting features that are available in the Styles group on the Ribbon's Home tab and in the Themes group of the Page Layout tab. We will work with the `FormatConditions` collection of the `Range` object and explore the conditional formatting tools: data bars, color scales, and icon sets. Then we'll look at how sparklines can be used to enhance your worksheets. We'll also take a look at document themes that can be applied to a workbook and see how they affect another formatting feature—styles.

Conditional Formatting Using VBA

To help you automatically highlight important parts of your worksheet, Excel provides a feature known as *conditional formatting*. This feature allows you to set a condition (a formatting rule), and specify the type of formatting that should be applied to cells and ranges when the condition is met. For example, you can use conditional formatting to apply different background colors, fonts, or borders to a cell based on its value. Conditional formatting provides users with various types of common rules and formatting tools such as data bars, color scales, and icon sets that make it easy to highlight certain worksheet data. For example, you can highlight the top or bottom 10% of values, locate duplicate or unique values, or indicate values above or below the average. You can specify an unlimited number of conditional formats and refer to ranges in other worksheets when using conditional formats. The Conditional Formatting Rules Manager shown in Figure 18.4 simplifies the creation, modification, and removal of conditional rules. All conditional formatting features that are available in the Excel application window can be accessed via VBA.

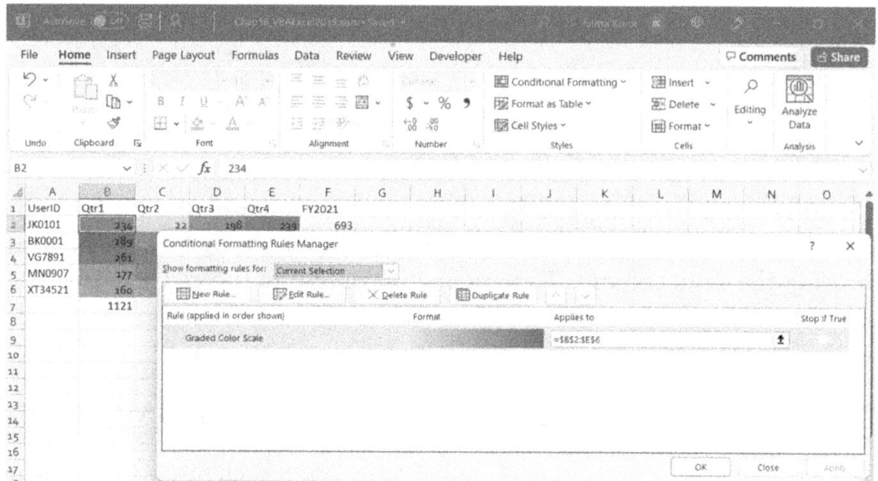

FIGURE 18.4 To activate the Conditional Formatting Rules Manager, choose Home | Conditional Formatting | Manage Rules.

To create a new conditional formatting rule, click the New Rule button in the Conditional Formatting Rules Manager dialog box. You will see the list of built-in rules that you can select from.

In VBA, use the `Add` method of the `FormatConditions` collection to create a new rule. For example, to format cells containing "Qtr" in the text string, enter the following procedure in a standard module and then run it:

```
Sub FormatQtrText()
  With ActiveSheet.UsedRange
       .FormatConditions.Delete
       .FormatConditions.Add Type:=xlTextString, String:="Qtr", _
          TextOperator:=xlContains
       .FormatConditions(1).Interior.Color = RGB(123, 130, 0)
  End With
End Sub
```

Notice that before creating and applying a new conditional format to a range of cells, it's a good idea to delete the existing format condition from the selection using the `Delete` method. The `Add` method that is used to add a new condition requires at least the `Type` argument that specifies whether the conditional format is based on a cell value or an expression. Use the `xlFormatConditionType` enumeration constants listed in Table 18.4 to set the condition type. For example, to format cells that contain dates, use the `xlTimePeriod` constant in the `Type` argument, and specify the DateOperator using one of the following constants: `xlToday`, `xlYesterday`, `xlTomorrow`, `xlLastWeek`, `xlThisWeek`, `xlNextWeek`, `xlLast7Days`, `xlLastMonth`, `xlThisMonth`, or `xlNextMonth`:

```
Selection.FormatConditions.Add Type:=xlTimePeriod,
    DateOperator:=xlLast7Days
```

TABLE 18.4 Conditional format Type settings (xlFormatConditionType enumeration)

Constant	Description

xlAboveAverageCondition	Above/below average condition:
	`With Selection`
	`    .FormatConditions.Delete`
	`    .FormatConditions.AddAboveAverage`
	`    .FormatConditions(1).AboveBelow =`
	`        xlAboveAverage`
	`    .FormatConditions(1).Font.Bold = True`
	`End With`

xlBlanksCondition	Format cells that contain blanks:
	`With Selection`
	`    .FormatConditions.Add _`
	`        Type:=xlBlanksCondition`
	`End With`

xlCellValue	Format a cell value:
	`With Selection`
	`.FormatConditions.Add Type:=xlCellValue,`
	`    Operator:=xlLess`
	`    Formula1:="=2000"`
	`.FormatConditions(1).NumberFormat = "#, ##0"`
	`End With`
	You can use the following constants in the `Operator` argument: `xlBetween`, `xlEqual`, `xlGreater`, `xlGreaterEqual`, `xl-Less`, `xlLessEqual`, `xlNotBetween`, or `xlNotEqual`.
	To specify the numeric value for the operator, use the `Formula1` argument. The `xlBetween` and `xlNotBetween` operators require that you also specify a second value in `Formula2`.

(Contd.)

<table>
<tr><th>Constant</th><th>Description</th></tr>
<tr><td>xlColorScale</td><td>Format color scale:
<pre>
If Selection.FormatConditions(1).Type = 3 Then
MsgBox "Formatted with " & _
    "ColorScale conditional format."
End If
</pre></td></tr>
<tr><td>xlDataBar</td><td>Format data bar:
<pre>
If Selection.FormatConditions(1).Type = 4 Then
MsgBox "Formatted with " & _
    "DataBar conditional format."
End If
</pre></td></tr>
<tr><td>xlErrorsCondition</td><td>Format cells that contain errors:
<pre>
Selection.FormatConditions.Add _
    Type:=xlErrorsCondition
</pre></td></tr>
<tr><td>xlExpression</td><td>Expression to specify a custom formula that identifies the cells that the conditional format applies to. For example, the following procedure changes the background color of alternate rows in the used range:
<pre>
Sub HighlightAltRows()
  With ActiveSheet.UsedRange
    .FormatConditions.Add Type:=xlExpression, _
        Formula1:="=MOD(ROW(),2)=0"
    .FormatConditions(1).Interior.ColorIndex = 6
  End With
End Sub
</pre>
To highlight every third row, use the formula:
<pre>
= MOD(ROW(),3)= 0
</pre></td></tr>
<tr><td>xlIconSet</td><td>Format icon set:
<pre>
If Selection.FormatConditions(1).Type = 6 Then
  MsgBox "Formatted with " & _
      "IconSet conditional format."
End If
</pre></td></tr>
<tr><td>xlNoBlanksCondition</td><td>Format cells that do not contain blanks:
<pre>
Sub HighlightNonEmptyCells()
  Range("A1:B12").Select
  Selection.FormatConditions.Add _
      Type:=xlNoBlanksCondition
    With Selection.FormatConditions(1).Interior
    .ThemeColor = xlThemeColorAccent4
    .TintAndShade = 0.399945066682943
  End With
End Sub
</pre></td></tr>
</table>

<table>
<tr><th>Constant</th><th>Description</th></tr>
<tr><td>xlNoErrorsCondition</td><td>Format cells that do not contain errors:

```
Sub HighlightCellsWithNoErrors()
  Range("F1:F7").Select
  Selection.FormatConditions.Add _
      Type:=xlNoErrorsCondition
  With Selection.FormatConditions(1).Interior
        .ThemeColor = xlThemeColorAccent4
        .TintAndShade = 0.399945066682943
  End With
End Sub
```

Before running the above procedure, enter any number in cell F1, and enter zero (0) in cell F2. In cell F3 enter the following formula: =F1/F2. Because there is no division by zero, Excel will display the following error code: #DIV/0! When you run the procedure, all cells in the selected range except for cell F2 will be shaded with the specified color.</td></tr>
<tr><td>xlTextString</td><td>Format cells that contain text:

```
With ActiveSheet.UsedRange
   .FormatConditions.Add Type:=xlTextString, _
       String:="es", TextOperator:=xlContains
   .FormatConditions(1).Font.Bold = True
End With
```

Other text operators you can use: `xlBeginsWith`, `xlDoesNot-Contain`, and `xlEndsWith`.</td></tr>
<tr><td>xlTimePeriod</td><td>Format cells that contain dates:

```
With ActiveSheet.UsedRange
   .FormatConditions.Add Type:=xlTimePeriod, _
       DateOperator:=xlLastMonth
   .FormatConditions(1).Interior.ColorIndex = 6
End With
```

Other date operators you can use: `xlToday`, `xlYesterday`, `xlTomorrow`, `xlLastWeekn`, `xlThisWeek`, `xlNextWeek`, `xlLast7Days`, `xlThisMonth`, and `xlNextMonth`.</td></tr>
<tr><td>xlTop10</td><td>Format 10 top values:

```
With Selection
   .FormatConditions.AddTop10
   .FormatConditions(1).TopBottom = xlTop10Top
   .FormatConditions(1).Value = 5
   .FormatConditions(1).Percent = False
   .FormatConditions(1).Interior.Color = _
       RGB(255,0,0)
End With
```
</td></tr>
</table>

(Contd.)

<table>
<tr><th>Constant</th><th>Description</th></tr>
<tr><td>xlUniqueValue</td><td>Format unique values:
<pre>With Selection
   .FormatConditions.AddUniqueValues
   .FormatConditions(1).DupeUnique = xlUnique
     Formula1:="=200"
End With</pre>By replacing the <code>xlUnique</code> constant with <code>xlDuplicate</code>, you can select duplicate values.</td></tr>
</table>

Conditional Formatting Rule Precedence

You can apply multiple conditional formats to a cell. For example, you can apply a conditional format to make the cell bold, and then another one to make a red border around the cell. Because these two formats do not conflict with one another, they can both be applied to the same cell. However, if you create another format that tells Excel to apply a blue border to the cell, this rule will not be applied because it conflicts with the previous rule that told Excel to apply the red border. In order to control multiple conditions applied to a range of cells, Excel uses rule precedence. When rules conflict with one another, Excel applies the rule that is higher in precedence. Rules are evaluated in order of precedence by how they are listed in the Conditional Formatting Rules Manager dialog box. In VBA, this is controlled by the `Priority` property of the `FormatConditions` object. For example, to assign a second priority to the first rule, use the following statement:

```
Range("B2:B17").FormatConditions(1).Priority = 2
```

You can make the rule the lowest priority with the following statement:

```
Range("B2:B17").FormatConditions(1).SetLastPriority
```

NOTE	*In cases where the same format is applied both manually and via conditional formatting to a range of cells, the conditional formatting rule takes precedence over the manual format. Formats applied manually are not considered when determining conditional formatting rule precedence and do not appear in the Conditional Formatting Rules Manager dialog box.*

Deleting Rules with VBA

You can use the following statement to delete all rules applied to a specific range of cells:

```
Range("B2:B17").FormatConditions.Delete
```

To delete a particular rule, refer to its index number before calling the `Delete` method of the `FormatConditions` collection:

```
Range("B2:B17").FormatConditions(2).Delete
```

Using Data Bars

The data visualization tool known as the data bar allows users to easily see how data values relate to each other. Data bars can be added via conditional formatting using the New Formatting Rule dialog box (choose Home | Conditional Formatting | Data Bars | More Rules) or by a VBA procedure.

Excel draws data bars proportionally according to their values. Thanks to this feature, data bars can be used to compare values. When you select the lowest value in the Type drop-down the data bar will not be drawn. When you select maximum value, Excel will draw a bar that covers the entire cell.

You can easily format the bar appearance with additional formatting options such as solid fills and borders. Thanks to this feature, you can see which cell has the highest value. However, keep in mind that applying a solid fill to a data bar may make some portions of the text harder to read, especially when using darker colors.

In VBA, you can create a data bar formatting rule by using the `AddDatabar` or `Add` method of the `FormatConditions` collection, as shown below:

```
Sub FormatWithDataBars()
  With Range("B2:E6").FormatConditions
  .AddDatabar
  .Add Type:=xlDatabar, _
      Operator:=xlGreaterEqual, Formula1:="200"
  End With
End Sub
```

This procedure will place a blue bar in the worksheet cells, as illustrated in Figure 18.5. Notice that the length of the data bar corresponds to the cell's value. If you change or recalculate the worksheet data, the data bar is automatically reapplied to the specified range. Instead of using the Lowest and Highest values to specify the Shortest and Longest bars, you can specify that the bar be based on numbers, percentages, formulas, or percentiles. For example, you can use the following statements to change the color, type, and threshold parameters of the data bar:

```
set mBar = Selection.FormatConditions.AddDatabar
mBar.MinPoint.Modify NewType:=xlConditionValuePercentile,
  NewValue:=20
```

```
mBar.MaxPoint.Modify NewType:=xlConditionValuePercentile,
  NewValue:=80
mBar.BarColor.ColorIndex = 7
```

In the previous statements, the MinPoint and MaxPoint properties of the DataBar object are used to set the values of the shortest and longest bars of a range of data, and the BarColor property is used to modify the color of the bars in the data bar conditional format.

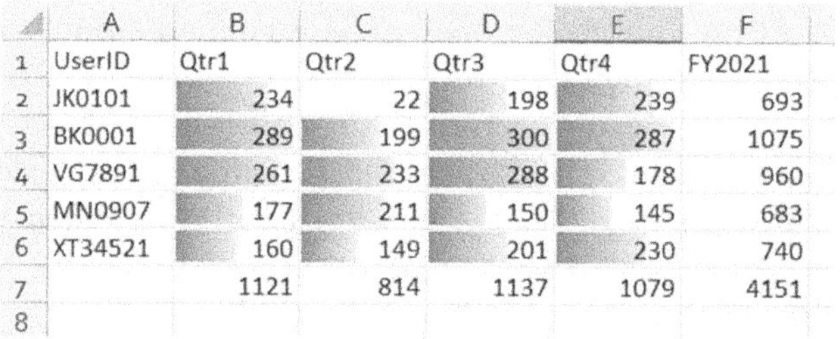

	A	B	C	D	E	F
1	UserID	Qtr1	Qtr2	Qtr3	Qtr4	FY2021
2	JK0101	234	22	198	239	693
3	BK0001	289	199	300	287	1075
4	VG7891	261	233	288	178	960
5	MN0907	177	211	150	145	683
6	XT34521	160	149	201	230	740
7		1121	814	1137	1079	4151
8						

FIGURE 18.5 A worksheet shown with the new data bar formatting.

Using Color Scales

You can create special visual effects in your worksheet by selecting a range of values and applying a color scale. Color scales use cell shading to help you understand variation in your data. When you apply a color scale conditional format via the user interface (Home | Conditional Formatting | Color Scales | More Rules) or from your VBA procedure, Excel uses the lowest, highest, and midpoint values in the range to determine the color gradients. You can apply a two-color or a three-color scale to your data, as shown in Figure 18.4.

To create a color scale conditional formatting rule in VBA, use the `AddColorScale` or `Add` method of the `FormatConditions` collection:

```
set cScale = Selection.FormatConditions.AddColorScale
   (ColorScaleType:=2)
```

The previous statement creates a two-color `ColorScale` object in the selected worksheet cells.

To change the minimum threshold to green and the maximum threshold to blue, use the following statements:

```
cScale.ColorScaleCriteria(1).FormatColor.Color = RGB(0, 255, 0)
cScale.ColorScaleCriteria(2).FormatColor.Color = RGB(0, 0, 255)
```

For darker color scales, it makes sense to change the font color to white:

```
Selection.Font.ColorIndex = 2
```

As with a data bar, you can change the type of threshold value for a color scale to a number, percent, formula, or percentile. To create striking visual effects, try applying both data bar and color scale conditional formatting to the same range of data.

Using Icon Sets

Icon sets are another visualization feature. By using icon sets, you can place icons in cells to make your data more comprehensive and visually appealing. Icon sets allow users to easily see the relationship between data values as well as recognize trends in the data.

To view the available icon choices, choose Home | Conditional Formatting | Icon Sets.

Each icon in an icon set represents a range of values. For example, in the three-icon set "3 Symbols (Circled)" shown in Figure 18.6, Excel uses the check mark symbol in a green circle for values that are greater than or equal to 67%, an exclamation point in an orange circle for values that are less than 67% and greater than or equal to 33%, and an X symbol in a red circle for values that are less than 33%.

Icon sets have become a very effective highlighting tool, thanks to the ability to apply icons only to specific cells instead of the entire range of cells. You can hide the icon for cells that meet the specified criteria by selecting No Cell Icon from the icon drop-down.

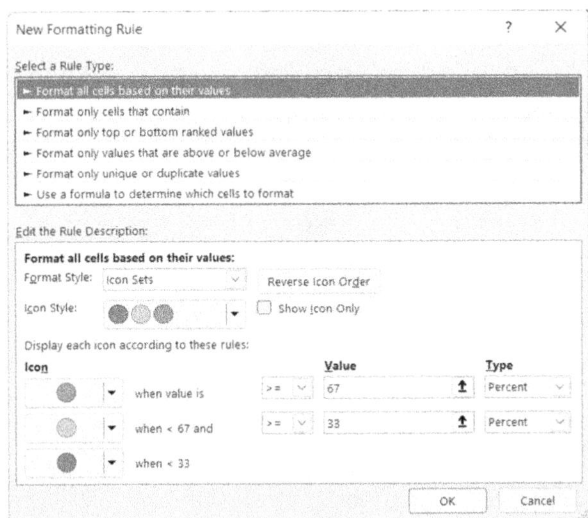

FIGURE 18.6 You can display each icon according to the rules set in the New Formatting Rule dialog box.

The Icon Style drop-down also allows you to select four- and five-icon sets. These sets display each icon according to which quartile or quintile the value falls into. You may change the default threshold value and its type (number, percent, formula, or percentile) for each icon in an icon set by editing the formatting rule or with a VBA procedure as demonstrated in Hands-On 18.1.

NOTE	*Icons can be made larger or smaller by increasing or decreasing the font size.*

In VBA, the `IconSet` object in the `IconSets` collection represents a single set of icons. To create a conditional formatting rule that uses icon sets, use the `IconSetCondition` object. You can add criteria for an icon set conditional formatting rule with the `IconCriteria` collection. The following VBA procedure applies an icon set conditional formatting rule to a range of cells. The result of this procedure is depicted in Figure 18.7.

NOTE	*Please note files for the "Hands-On" project may be found in the companion files.*

Hands-On 18.1 Using Icon Sets Programmatically

1. Copy the **Chap18_VBAExcel2021.xlsm file** from the Companion files to your **VBAExcel2021_ByExample** folder.
2. Open the **C:\VBAExcel2021_ByExample\Chap18_VBAExcel2021.xlsm** workbook and select **Sheet3.**
3. Switch to the Visual Basic Editor screen and insert a new module into VBAProject (Chap18_VBAExcel2021.xlsm).
4. In the module's Code window, enter the following IconSetRules procedure:

```
Sub IconSetRules()
  Dim iSC As IconSetCondition

  Columns("C:C").Select
  With Selection
    .SpecialCells(xlCellTypeConstants, 23).Select
    .FormatConditions.Delete
    .NumberFormat = "$#,##0.00"
    Set iSC = Selection.FormatConditions.AddIconSetCondition
    iSC.IconSet = ActiveWorkbook.IconSets(xl3Symbols)
  End With
End Sub
```

This procedure applies the currency format to the cell values in column C and clears the selected range from the conditional format that may have been applied earlier. Next, the `AddIconSetCondition` method is used to create an icon set conditional format for the selected range of cells.

In Step 5, when you run the procedure in step mode by pressing the F8 key, you will notice colored circles being applied to the cells. The next statement changes the default icon set to xl3Symbols as shown in Figure 18.7.

5. Place the insertion point anywhere inside the code of the IconSetRules procedure and press **F8** after each statement to execute the code in step mode.

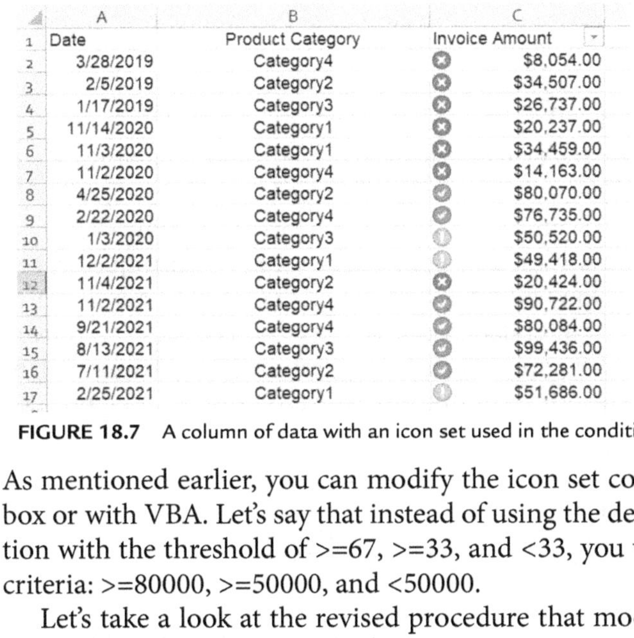

	A	B	C
1	Date	Product Category	Invoice Amount
2	3/28/2019	Category4	$8,054.00
3	2/5/2019	Category2	$34,507.00
4	1/17/2019	Category3	$26,737.00
5	11/14/2020	Category1	$20,237.00
6	11/3/2020	Category1	$34,459.00
7	11/2/2020	Category4	$14,163.00
8	4/25/2020	Category2	$80,070.00
9	2/22/2020	Category4	$76,735.00
10	1/3/2020	Category3	$50,520.00
11	12/2/2021	Category1	$49,418.00
12	11/4/2021	Category2	$20,424.00
13	11/2/2021	Category4	$90,722.00
14	9/21/2021	Category4	$80,084.00
15	8/13/2021	Category3	$99,436.00
16	7/11/2021	Category2	$72,281.00
17	2/25/2021	Category1	$51,686.00

FIGURE 18.7 A column of data with an icon set used in the conditional format.

As mentioned earlier, you can modify the icon set conditions using the dialog box or with VBA. Let's say that instead of using the default percentage distribution with the threshold of >=67, >=33, and <33, you want to use the following criteria: >=80000, >=50000, and <50000.

Let's take a look at the revised procedure that modifies the formatting rule and applies a filter by cell icon criteria:

```
Sub IconSetRulesRevised()
  Dim iSC As IconSetCondition

  Columns("C:C").Select
  Selection.SpecialCells(xlCellTypeConstants, 23).Select
  With Selection
     .FormatConditions.Delete
     .AutoFilter
     .NumberFormat = "$#,##0.00"
     Set iSC = Selection.FormatConditions.AddIconSetCondition
     iSC.IconSet = ActiveWorkbook.IconSets(xl3Symbols)
```

```
    With iSC.IconCriteria(2)
        .Type = xlConditionValueNumber
        .Value = 50000
        .Operator = xlGreaterEqual
    End With

    With iSC.IconCriteria(3)
        .Type = xlConditionValueNumber
        .Value = 80000
        .Operator = xlGreaterEqual
    End With

        .AutoFilter Field:=1, Criteria1:=iSC.IconSet.Item(3), _
            Operator:=xlFilterIcon
  End With
End Sub
```

Note that when changing the criteria for the icon set conditional format you do not need to specify the type, value, and operator for IconCriteria(1). This property is read-only. Excel determines on its own the threshold value of IconCriteria(1), and if you try to set it in your code as shown in the example procedure available in online help, you will get a runtime error. The Sort and Filter commands allow you to sort or filter data based on cell icon. The previous procedure demonstrates how you can apply the filter programmatically using an icon in the specified icon set. The results of this procedure are shown in Figure 18.8.

	A	B	C
1	Date	Product Category	Invoice Amount
8	4/25/2020	Category2	$80,070.00
13	11/2/2021	Category4	$90,722.00
14	9/21/2021	Category4	$80,084.00
15	8/13/2021	Category3	$99,436.00
18			

FIGURE 18.8 After running the IconSetRulesRevised procedure, a filter is applied to the Invoice Amount column to display only the cells with invoice values >=80000.

Let's say that you only want to highlight cells with values less than 50000. The following procedure creates a formatting rule that produces the output shown in Figure 18.9.

```
Sub IconSetHideIcons()
  Dim iSC As IconSetCondition

  Columns("C:C").Select
  Selection.SpecialCells(xlCellTypeConstants, 23).Select
  With Selection
```

```
        .FormatConditions.Delete
        .NumberFormat = "$#,##0.00"
        Set iSC = Selection.FormatConditions.AddIconSetCondition
        iSC.IconSet = ActiveWorkbook.IconSets(xl3Symbols)
      .FormatConditions(1).IconCriteria(1).Icon = xlIconRedCrossSymbol

        With iSC.IconCriteria(2)
            .Type = xlConditionValueNumber
            .Value = 50000
            .Operator = xlGreaterEqual
            .Icon = xlIconNoCellIcon
        End With

        With iSC.IconCriteria(3)
            .Type = xlConditionValueNumber
            .Value = 80000
            .Operator = xlGreaterEqual
            .Icon = xlIconNoCellIcon
        End With

    End With
End Sub
```

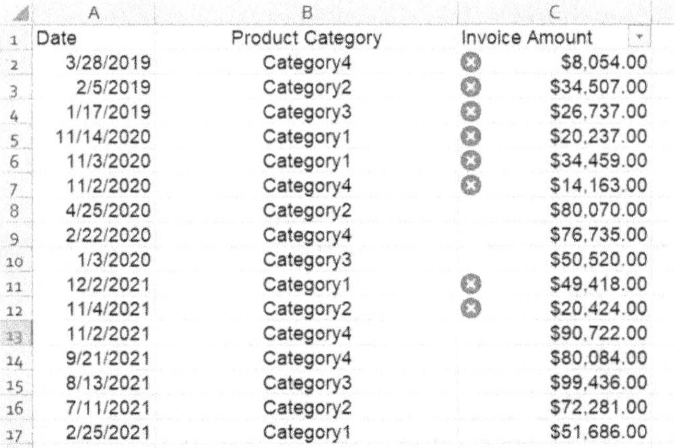

	A	B	C
1	Date	Product Category	Invoice Amount
2	3/28/2019	Category4	$8,054.00
3	2/5/2019	Category2	$34,507.00
4	1/17/2019	Category3	$26,737.00
5	11/14/2020	Category1	$20,237.00
6	11/3/2020	Category1	$34,459.00
7	11/2/2020	Category4	$14,163.00
8	4/25/2020	Category2	$80,070.00
9	2/22/2020	Category4	$76,735.00
10	1/3/2020	Category3	$50,520.00
11	12/2/2021	Category1	$49,418.00
12	11/4/2021	Category2	$20,424.00
13	11/2/2021	Category4	$90,722.00
14	9/21/2021	Category4	$80,084.00
15	8/13/2021	Category3	$99,436.00
16	7/11/2021	Category2	$72,281.00
17	2/25/2021	Category1	$51,686.00

FIGURE 18.9 In this scenario, we use the icon set to draw attention to cells with invoice amounts less than 50000. Notice that by not applying icons to other cells you can easily highlight the problem areas.

Formatting with Themes

If you need to change the look of the entire workbook, you ought to spend some time familiarizing yourself with document themes. A *document theme* consists of a predefined set of fonts, colors, and effects, such as lines and fills, that you can apply to the workbook and also share between other Office documents. It is important to note that a theme applies to the entire workbook, not just the active worksheet. There are numerous document themes available in the user interface (choose Page Layout | Themes) and you can also create custom themes by mixing and matching different theme elements using the three drop-down controls found in the Themes group on the Page Layout tab (Colors, Fonts, and Effects). Additional themes can also be downloaded from Office Online. When you change the theme, the font and color pickers on the Home tab, and other galleries such as Cell Styles or Table Styles, are automatically updated to reflect the new theme. Therefore, if you are looking to apply a cell background with a particular color, and that color is not listed in the color picker, apply a predefined theme that contains that color, or create your own custom color by choosing the More Colors option in the Font Color drop-down menu.

On the Page Layout tab, the Colors drop-down displays the color groups for each theme and gives you an option to create new theme colors. The Fonts drop-down shows a list of fonts for the theme. Theme fonts contain a heading font and a body text font, which can be changed using the Create New Theme Fonts option in the drop-down. The Effects drop-down displays the line and fill effects for each of the built-in themes and does not give you an option to create your own set of theme effects.

A theme color scheme consists of 12 base colors, as illustrated in Figure 18.10. When applying a color to a cell, the color is selected from the Fill Color drop-down as shown in Figure 18.11.

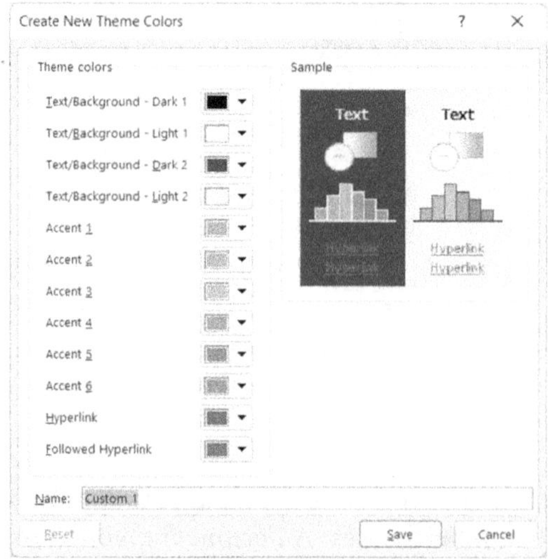

FIGURE 18.10 The theme colors consist of four text/ background colors, six accent colors, and two hyperlink colors. To display this dialog box, choose Page Layout | Colors | Customize Colors.

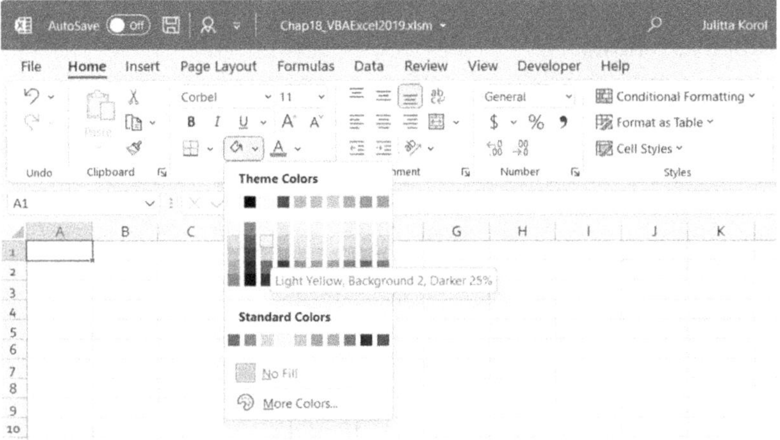

FIGURE 18.11 The Fill Color control is used to color the background of selected cells.

On the Home Tab in the Font area of the Ribbon there is a convenient Fill Color button that makes it easy to view the available theme colors (see Figure 18.11). When you click the drop-down arrow next to the Fill Color button, you will see a color palette. The top row in the palette displays 10 base colors in the current color theme (the two hyperlink colors shown in the Create New Theme Colors dialog box are not included). The five rows below show variations of the base color. A color can be lighter or darker. The color name is shown in the tooltip.

If you record a macro while applying the "Blue, Accent 1, Lighter 40%" color to the cell background, you will get the following VBA code:

```
Sub Macro1()
'
' Macro1 Macro
'

'
  Range("F4").Select
  With Selection.Interior
      .Pattern = xlSolid
      .PatternColorIndex = xlAutomatic
      .ThemeColor = xlThemeColorAccent1
      .TintAndShade = 0.399975585192419
      .PatternTintAndShade = 0
  End With
End Sub
```

The pattern properties refer to the cell patterns that can be set via the Format Cells dialog box (Home | Format | Format Cells | Fill). These properties can be ignored if all that's required is setting the cell background color. The above code can be modified as follows:

```
Sub Macro1()
'
' Macro1 Macro
'

'
  Range("F4").Select
  With Selection.Interior
    .ThemeColor = xlThemeColorAccent1
    .TintAndShade = 0.399975585192419
  End With
End Sub
```

The ThemeColor properties listed in Figure 18.12 specify the theme color to be used.

The TintAndShade property is used to modify the selected color. A tint (lightness) and a shade (darkness) is a value from –1 to 1. If you want a pure color, set the TintAndShade property to 0. The value of –1 will result in black, and the value of 1 will produce white. Negative values will produce darker colors, and positive values lighter colors. The TintAndShade value of 0.399975585192419 means a 40% tint (or 40% lighter than the base color). If you change this number to –0.399975585192419, you will get a 40% darker color.

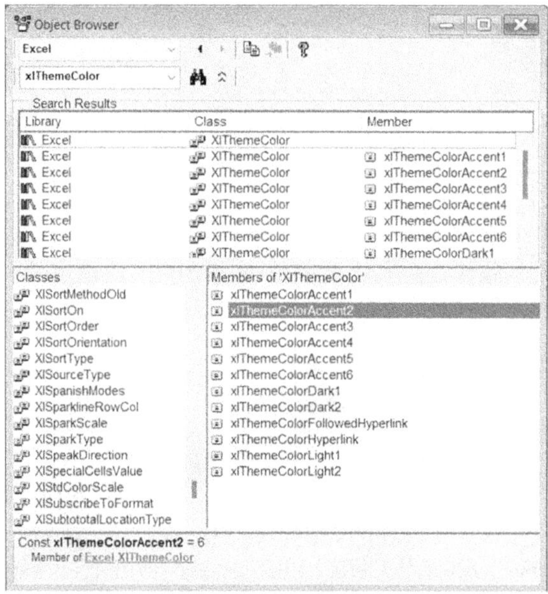

FIGURE 18.12 Theme color constants and values as shown in the Object Browser.

The following procedure loops through the colors in themes 4 through 10 and writes the color index and color variations to the range of cells shown in Figure 18.13.

```
Sub Themes4Thru10()
  Dim tintshade As Variant
  Dim heading As Variant
  Dim cell As Range
  Dim themeC As Integer
  Dim r As Integer
  Dim c As Integer
  Dim i As Integer

  heading = Array("ThemeColorIndex", "Neutral", "Lighter 80%", _
      "Lighter 60%", "Lighter 40%", "Darker 25%", "Darker 50%")
  tintshade = Array(0, 0.8, 0.6, 0.4, -0.25, -0.5)

  i = 0
  For Each cell In Range("A1:G1")
    cell.Formula = heading(i)
    i = i + 1
  Next

  For r = 2 To 8
    themeC = r + 2
      For c = 1 To 7
      If c = 1 Then
        Cells(r, c).Formula = themeC
      Else
        With Cells(r, c)
            With .Interior
              .ThemeColor = themeC
              .TintAndShade = tintshade(c - 2)
            End With
        End With
       End If
      Next c
   Next r
   ActiveSheet.Columns("A:G").AutoFit
End Sub
```

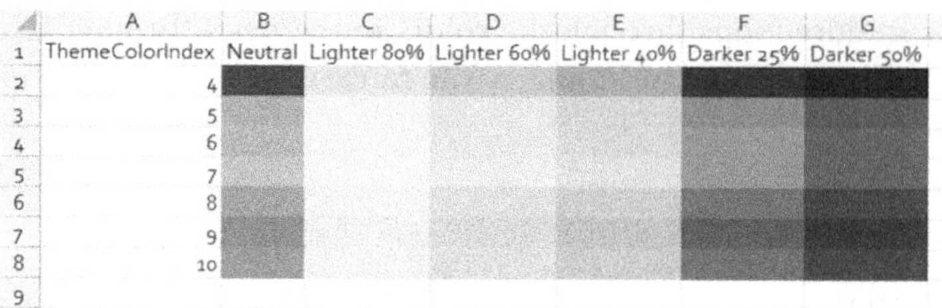

FIGURE 18.13 This worksheet was generated by a VBA procedure. When you apply a different document theme, the colors will be replaced by those from the new theme.

The following procedure applies the current theme colors to a range of cells in an active worksheet.

```
Sub GetThemeColors()
  Dim tColorScheme As ThemeColorScheme
  Dim colorArray(10) As Variant
  Dim i As Long
  Dim r As Long

  Set tColorScheme = ActiveWorkbook.Theme.ThemeColorScheme
  For i = 1 To 10
    colorArray(i) = tColorScheme.Colors(i).RGB
    ActiveSheet.Cells(i, 1).Value = colorArray(i)
  Next i
  i = 0
  For r = 1 To 10
    ActiveSheet.Cells(r, 2).Interior.Color = colorArray(i + 1)
    i = i + 1
  Next r
End Sub
```

In the above procedure, the ThemeColorScheme object represents the color scheme of a Microsoft Office theme. In the first `For Next` loop, the `Colors` method and the RGB property are used to return a specific color. The color value is then stored in the `colorArray` array variable and entered in the specified row of the first worksheet column. The second `For Next` loop applies background color to cells based on the color values stored in the `colorArray` variable.

The following procedure does more color work in the active sheet, this time using the Interior.ThemeColor property:

```
Sub ApplyThemeColors()
  Dim i As Integer

  For i = 1 To 10
```

```
    ActiveSheet.Cells(i, 3).Interior.ThemeColor = i
    ActiveSheet.Cells(i, 4).Value = i
  Next i
End Sub
```

In this procedure, we use the Interior.ThemeColor property to set the background color of cells in the third worksheet column using colors available in the current color scheme. The color scheme value is then written in the corresponding cell in the fourth column. The resulting worksheet (after running the GetThemeColors and ApplyThemeColors procedures) is shown in Figure 18.14.

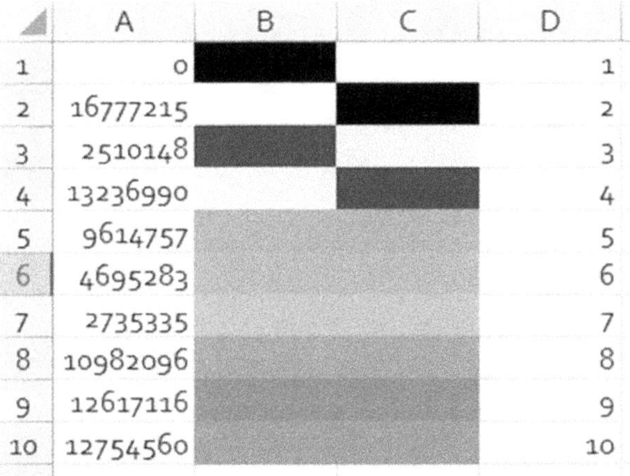

	A	B	C	D
1	0			1
2	16777215			2
3	2510148			3
4	13236990			4
5	9614757			5
6	4695283			6
7	2735335			7
8	10982096			8
9	12617116			9
10	12754560			10

FIGURE 18.14 The background color of the cells was applied with VBA. When you select a different color theme, the background color of these cells (C1:C10) will automatically adjust.

Each new workbook is created with a default theme named Office. The theme information is stored in a separate theme file with the extension .thmx. When you change the theme in the workbook, the workbook's theme file is automatically updated with the new settings. When you create a custom theme by selecting a new set of fonts, colors, or effects, save the theme in a file so that it can be used in any document in any Office application or shared with other users. You will find your custom theme file in the following location:

\Users\<user name>\AppData\Roaming\Microsoft\Templates\Document Themes

By default the Application Data (AppData) folder is hidden. To access this folder, you will need to modify the folder and search options in Windows Explorer.

To create a test theme named "MyTheme.thmx," choose Page Layout | Themes | Save Current Theme, change the name to MyTheme.thmx, and press

Save.

Now that you've created a custom theme, you can apply it programmatically to the workbook using the `ApplyTheme` method of the Workbook object. Try it out now by entering the following statement on one line in the Immediate window (revise the path as necessary to match the location of the theme file on your computer):

```
ActiveWorkbook.ApplyTheme  "C:\Users\<username>\AppData\Roaming\
Microsoft\Templates\Document Themes\MyTheme.thmx"
```

After you apply a custom theme to a workbook, the theme name should appear in the Custom group of the Themes control, as shown in Figure 18.15.

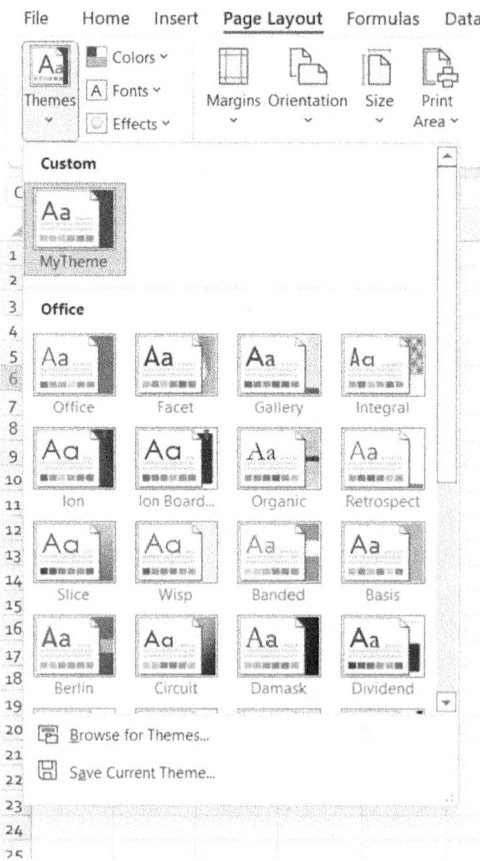

FIGURE 18.15 After applying a custom theme to a workbook, the theme name appears in the Custom group of the Themes control.

To programmatically load a color theme or font theme from a file, the following VBA statements can be used:

```
ActiveWorkbook.Theme.ThemeColorScheme.Load ("C:\Program Files\
Microsoft Office\root\Document Themes 16\Theme Colors\Paper.xml")

ActiveWorkbook.Theme.ThemeFontScheme.Load " C:\Program Files\
Microsoft Office\root\Document Themes 16\Theme Fonts\Calibri.xml")
```

In order to customize some theme components, you need to know how to work with document parts in the Office Open XML file format. You will find information on how to open, read, and modify data in Office XML files in Chapter 28, "Using XML in Excel 2021."

Formatting with Shapes

You can make your worksheets more interesting by adding various types of shapes, such as the cylinder in Figure 18.16. When formatting shapes, you can use document theme colors as shown in the following procedure:

```
Sub AddCanShape()
  Dim oShape As Shape

  Set oShape = ActiveSheet.Shapes.AddShape( _
    msoShapeCan, 54, 0, 54, 110)
  With oShape
      .Fill.ForeColor.ObjectThemeColor = msoThemeColorAccent4
      .Fill.Transparency = 0.5
      .Line.Visible = msoFalse
  End With
  Set oShape = Nothing
End Sub
```

In the above procedure, we declare an object variable of type Shape and then use the `AddShape` method of the ActiveSheet `Shapes` collection to add a new `Shape` object. This method has five required arguments. The first one specifies the type of the `Shape` object that you want to create. This can be one of the constants in the `msoAutoShapeType` enumeration (check out the online help). Excel offers a large number of shapes. The next two arguments tell Excel how far the object should be placed from the left and top corners of the worksheet. The last two arguments specify the width and height of the shape (in points). To specify the theme color of the Shape object, set the `ObjectThemeColor` property of the `ColorFormat` object to the required theme. To return the `ColorFormat` object, you must use the `ForeColor` property of the `FillFormat` object. The `FillFormat` object is returned by the `Fill` property of the `Shape` object:

```
oShape.Fill.ForeColor.ObjectThemeColor = msoThemeColorAccent4
```

Next, set the degree of transparency to make sure that the shape does not obstruct the data. The last line removes the border from the shape.

The previous procedure places a `Shape` object over the data in column B.

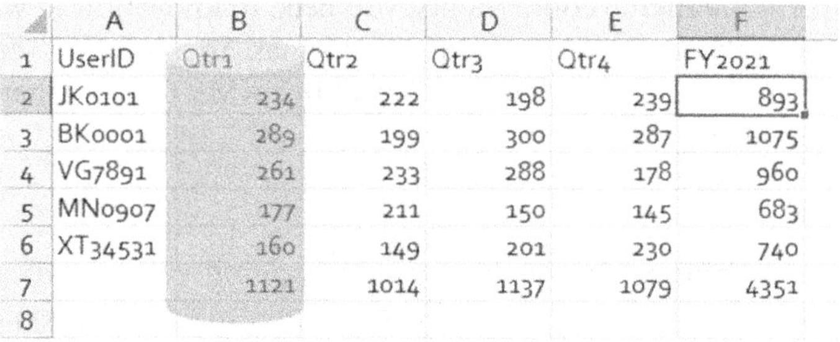

	A	B	C	D	E	F
1	UserID	Qtr1	Qtr2	Qtr3	Qtr4	FY2021
2	JK0101	234	222	198	239	893
3	BK0001	289	199	300	287	1075
4	VG7891	261	233	288	178	960
5	MN0907	177	211	150	145	683
6	XT34531	160	149	201	230	740
7		1121	1014	1137	1079	4351
8						

FIGURE 18.16 A Shape object placed on the worksheet uses the theme color scheme.

The following procedure can be run to programmatically remove shapes from the worksheet:

```
Sub RemoveShapes()
  Dim oShape As Shape
  Dim strShapeName As String
  With ActiveSheet
      For Each oShape In .Shapes
          strShapeName = oShape.Name
          oShape.Delete
          Debug.Print "The Shape Object named " _
          & strShapeName & " was deleted."
      Next oShape
  End With
End Sub
```

SIDEBAR ***Working with Shapes in VBA***

While you can look up the properties and methods of the `Shape` object in the online help, don't forget Excel's most useful programming tool—the macro recorder. Use `Shape` object recording to get a quick start in writing VBA code that inserts, positions, formats, and deletes shapes.

Formatting with Sparklines

Sparklines are tiny charts that can be inserted into a single cell to highlight important data trends and increase readers' comprehension. There are three types of sparklines in Excel: Line, Column, and Win/Loss. They can be inserted via the corresponding button in the Sparklines group on the Ribbon's Insert tab (Figure 18.17).

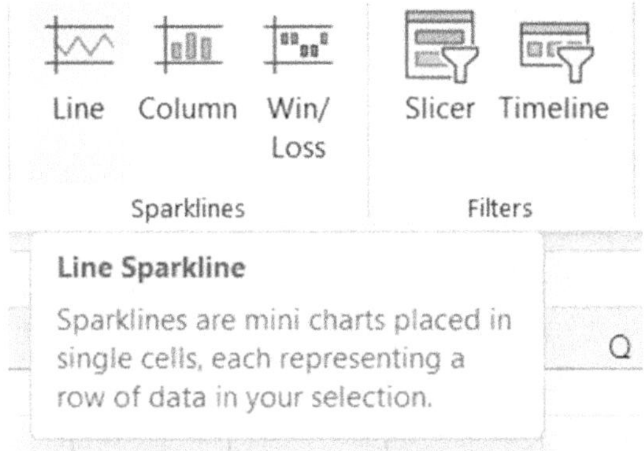

FIGURE 18.17 The Sparkline group on the Insert tab offers three buttons for inserting tiny charts into a cell.

To manually insert a sparkline graphic, click in the cell where you want the sparkline to appear and choose Insert. In the Sparklines group, click the type of sparkline you want to insert. At this point, Excel will pop up the Create Sparklines dialog box (Figure 18.18) where you can choose or enter the data range you want to include as the data source for the sparklines and the location range where you want them to be placed.

In Figure 18.18, we'd like to compare the performance of users during each quarter of fiscal year 2021. After making selections in the Create Sparklines dialog box and clicking OK, Excel activates the Sparkline Tools–Design context tab, where you can format the sparkline by showing points and markers, changing the sparkline or marker colors, switching between the types of sparklines, and more. Figure 18.19 displays the result of inserting and applying data point formatting to the sparklines.

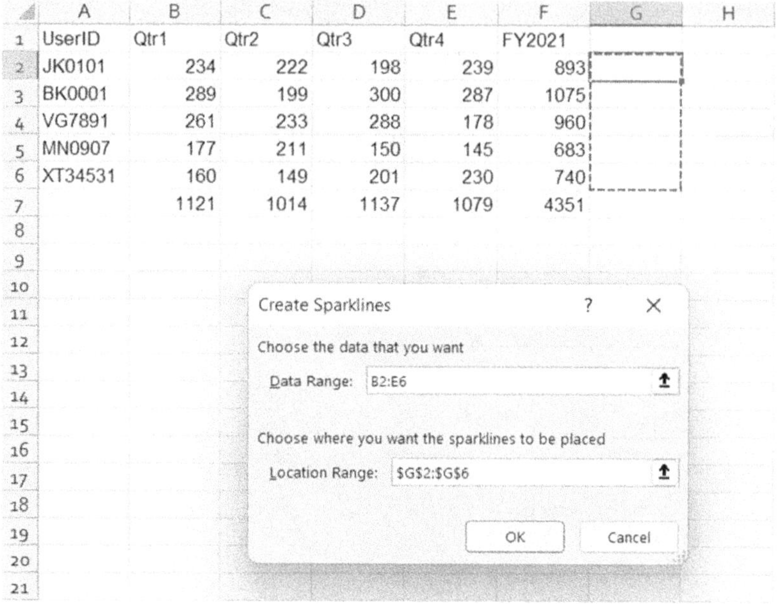

	A	B	C	D	E	F	G
1	UserID	Qtr1	Qtr2	Qtr3	Qtr4	FY2021	
2	JK0101	234	222	198	239	893	
3	BK0001	289	199	300	287	1075	
4	VG7891	261	233	288	178	960	
5	MN0907	177	211	150	145	683	
6	XT34531	160	149	201	230	740	
7		1121	1014	1137	1079	4351	

Create Sparklines

Choose the data that you want

Data Range: B2:E6

Choose where you want the sparklines to be placed

Location Range: $G$2:$G$6

OK Cancel

FIGURE 18.18 Selecting the location and data range for sparklines.

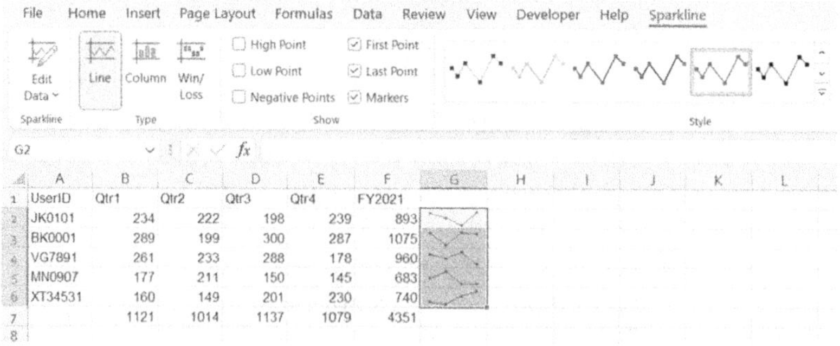

File Home Insert Page Layout Formulas Data Review View Developer Help Sparkline

Edit Data | Line Column Win/Loss | High Point, Low Point, Negative Points, First Point, Last Point, Markers | Style

	A	B	C	D	E	F	G
1	UserID	Qtr1	Qtr2	Qtr3	Qtr4	FY2021	
2	JK0101	234	222	198	239	893	
3	BK0001	289	199	300	287	1075	
4	VG7891	261	233	288	178	960	
5	MN0907	177	211	150	145	683	
6	XT34531	160	149	201	230	740	
7		1121	1014	1137	1079	4351	

FIGURE 18.19 Sparklines in column G make it easy to spot the trends in users' performance.

SIDEBAR *Handling Hidden Data and Empty Cells by Sparklines*

If you hide rows or columns that are used in a sparkline, the hidden data will not appear in the sparkline. You can specify how empty cells should be handled in the Hidden and Empty Cells Settings dialog box (choose Sparkline | Edit Data | Hidden and Empty Cells).

Sparklines are dynamic. They will automatically adjust whenever the data in the cells they are based on changes. Sparklines can be copied, cut, and pasted just like formulas. For bigger or wider sparklines, simply increase the width of the row or column. To get rid of the sparklines, use the Clear button in the Ribbon's Sparkline tab, and select Clear Selected Sparklines or Clear Selected Sparkline Groups. Because a sparkline is a part of a cell's background, you can display text or formulas in cells containing sparklines, as shown in Figure 18.20.

G2 fx =AVERAGE(B2:E2)

	A	B	C	D	E	F	G
1	UserID	Qtr1	Qtr2	Qtr3	Qtr4	FY2021	
2	JK0101	234	222	198	239	893	223.25
3	BK0001	289	199	300	287	1075	268.75
4	VG7891	261	233	288	178	960	240
5	MN0907	177	211	150	145	683	170.75
6	XT34531	160	149	201	230	740	185
7		1121	1014	1137	1079	4351	
8							

FIGURE 18.20 Sparklines can share a cell with text or formulas.

SIDEBAR ***Sparklines and Backward Compatibility***

When you open a workbook containing sparklines in older versions of Excel (2007/2003), you will see blank cells. When you edit a file with sparklines in Excel 2007 the sparklines will not be visible, but they will appear again if the file is loaded in more recent versions of Excel, provided that the cells with sparklines were not deleted.

Understanding Sparkline Groups

In Figure 18.18, we created multiple sparklines at once by choosing one data range (B2:E6). This caused the sparklines to be automatically grouped. When you click a grouped sparkline, you should see a thin blue line around the group. Each sparkline group contains the same formatting settings. You can format each sparkline separately by breaking the group. Simply select the sparkline you want to format differently, and choose Sparkline | Ungroup. The selected cell will be ungrouped from the group. Now you can format that sparkline as desired without affecting other sparklines. For example, in Figure 18.21 the sparkline in Row 4 was ungrouped and the type of sparkline was then changed to column type. To break the entire group, select all the cells containing sparklines and click Ungroup.

	A	B	C	D	E	F	G
1	UserID	Qtr1	Qtr2	Qtr3	Qtr4	FY2021	
2	JK0101	234	222	198	239	893	223.25
3	BK0001	289	199	300	287	1075	268.75
4	VG7891	261	233	288	178	960	240
5	MN0907	177	211	150	145	683	170.75
6	XT34531	160	149	201	230	740	185
7		1121	1014	1137	1079	4351	

FIGURE 18.21 Ungrouping sparklines allows you to format them independently of other sparklines.

Programming Sparklines with VBA

The Excel Object Model contains objects, properties, and methods that allow developers to use VBA to create and modify sparklines in their worksheets. To get an idea of how sparklines fit into the Object Model, take a look at Figure 18.22.

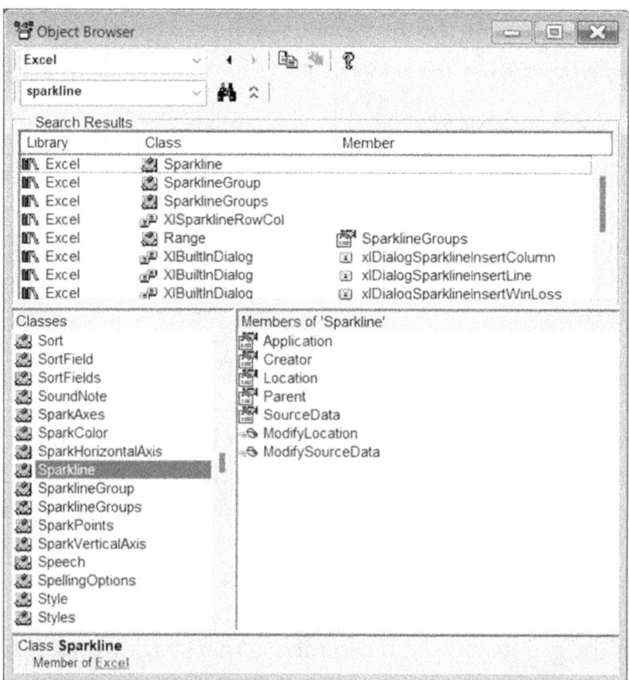

FIGURE 18.22 Choose the Object Browser from the VBE View menu (or press F2) to quickly locate objects, methods, and properties that can be used to program sparklines with VBA. Next, select the name of the object, property, or method that interests you, and click the question mark button at the top of the Object Browser to pop up the help topic.

Each sparkline is represented by a `Sparkline` object, which is a member of a `SparklineGroup` object. A `SparklineGroup` object can contain one or more `Sparkline` objects. You can have multiple `SparklineGroup` objects (collections of sparkline groups) in a worksheet. The `Range` object's `SparklineGroup` property returns a `SparklineGroups` object that represents an existing group of sparklines from the specified range.

Hands-On 18.2 demonstrates how to use VBA to read the information about sparklines contained in a worksheet.

Hands-On 18.2 Retrieving Information about Sparklines

1. Working with the **C:\VBAExcel2021_ByExample\Chap18_VBAExcel2021.xlsm** workbook, switch to the Visual Basic Editor screen and insert a new module.
2. In the module's Code window, enter the following GetSparklineInfo procedure:

```
Sub GetSparklineInfo()
  Dim spGrp As SparklineGroup
  Dim spCount As Long
  Dim i As Long

  spCount = Cells.SparklineGroups.count
  If spCount <> 0 Then
      For i = 1 To spCount
          Set spGrp = Cells.SparklineGroups(i)
          Debug.Print "Sparkline Group:" & i
          Select Case spGrp.Type
              Case 1
                  Debug.Print "Type:Line"
              Case 2
                  Debug.Print "Type:Column"
              Case 3
                  Debug.Print "Type:Win/Loss"
          End Select
          Debug.Print "Location:" & spGrp.Location.Address
          Debug.Print "Data Source: " & spGrp.SourceData
      Next i
  Else
      MsgBox "There are no sparklines in the active sheet."
  End If
End Sub
```

3. Activate the worksheet that contains sparklines and run the above procedure. Assuming you ran the procedure while the sheet displayed in Figure 18.21 was active, the following information was retrieved into the Immediate window.

```
Sparkline Group:1
Type:Column
Location:$G$4
Data Source: B4:E4
Sparkline Group:2
Type:Line
Location:$G$2,$G$3,$G$5,$G$6
Data Source: B2:E2,B3:E3,B5:E5,B6:E6
```

The next Hands-On you will create a sparkline Win/Loss report from scratch using VBA. The Win/Loss sparkline bar chart type is used to display Profit versus Loss or Positive versus Negative comparison.

Hands-On 18.3 Using VBA to Create Sparklines

1. In the **C:\VBAExcel2021_ByExample\Chap18_VBAExcel2021.xlsm** workbook, switch to the Visual Basic Editor screen and add the following procedures just below the GetSparklineInfo procedure that you created in the previous Hands-On:

```
Sub CreateSparklineReport()
  Dim spGrp As SparklineGroup
  Dim sht As Worksheet
  Dim cell As Range
  Dim spLocation As Range

  Workbooks.Add
  Set sht = ActiveSheet

  EnterData sht, 3, "Month", "Sales Quota", "Sales $", "Difference"
  EnterData sht, 4, "January", "234000", "250000", "=C4-B4"
  EnterData sht, 5, "February", "211000", "180000", "=C5-B5"
  EnterData sht, 6, "March", "304000", "370000", "=C6-B6"
  Range("B4:D6").Style = "Currency"

  Columns("A:D").AutoFit

  Range("A1").Value = "Win/Loss"
  Set spLocation = sht.Range("B1")
  Set spGrp = spLocation.SparklineGroups _
      .Add(xlSparkColumnStacked100, "D4:D6")
```

```
  spGrp.SeriesColor.ThemeColor = 2
  spLocation.SparklineGroups.Item(1) _
      .Axes.Horizontal.Axis.Visible = True
End Sub

Sub EnterData(sht As Worksheet, rowNum As Integer, _
  ParamArray myValues() As Variant)

  Dim j As Integer
  Dim count As Integer

  count = UBound(myValues()) + 1
  j = 1
  For j = j To count
     sht.Range(Cells(rowNum, 1), Cells(rowNum, count)) = myValues()
  Next
End Sub
```

2. Run the CreateSparklineReport procedure.
3. After running the procedure, you should see the Win/Loss report in a new workbook as depicted in Figure 18.23. Notice that the Win/Loss sparkline in cell B1 compares sales data during the first three months of the year with the sales quota for each month. The source range for the sparkline is located in column D, which contains the difference between monthly sales and the monthly quota. A quick glance at cell B1 reveals that the sales quota was not met in February.

	A	B	C	D
1	Win/Loss			
2				
3	Month	Sales Quota	Sales $	Difference
4	January	$234,000.00	$250,000.00	$ 16,000.00
5	February	$211,000.00	$180,000.00	$(31,000.00)
6	March	$304,000.00	$370,000.00	$ 66,000.00

FIGURE 18.23 This worksheet, including its Win/Loss sparkline in cell B1, was created programmatically in Hands-On 18.3.

Formatting with Styles

Most people use the Format Painter tool on the Ribbon's Home tab (the paint-brush icon) to quickly copy formatting to other cells of the same worksheet or from one worksheet to another. However, when you create complex worksheets with different types of formatting, it is a good idea to save all your formatting settings in a file so you can reuse them whenever you need them. This can be done via the Styles feature. Cell styles can contain format options such as Number, Alignment, Font, Border, Fill, and Protection. If you change the style after you have applied it to your worksheet, Excel will automatically update the cells that have been formatted using that style. Styles are easier to find and apply, thanks to the existence of galleries like those illustrated in Figure 18.24. To apply a style to a cell, simply select the cells you want to format with the style, and click on the appropriate style in the gallery (available by clicking Cell Styles). Styles are based on the current theme. You can also apply them to Excel tables, PivotTables, charts, and shapes. Excel offers a large number of built-in styles. You can modify, duplicate, or delete the existing styles and add your own—simply right-click the style in the gallery and select the option you need.

FIGURE 18.24 You can see the preview of how the style will look before you apply the style. If the built-in style does not suit your needs, you can create your own custom style.

To find out the number of styles in the active workbook, use the following statement:

```
MsgBox "Number of styles=" & ActiveWorkbook.Styles.Count
```

Excel tells us that there are 47 styles defined for a 2021 workbook. Use the `Styles` collection and the `Style` object to control the styles in a workbook. To get a list of style names, let's iterate through the `Styles` collection:

```
Sub GetStyleNames()
  Dim i As Integer

  For i = 1 To ActiveWorkbook.Styles.Count
    Debug.Print "Style " & i & ":" & _
        ActiveWorkbook.Styles(i).Name
  Next i
End Sub
```

The above procedure prints the names of all workbook styles into the Immediate window. The style names are listed alphabetically.

To add a style, use the `Add` method, as shown in the following example procedure:

```
Sub AddAStyle()
  Dim newStyleName As String
  Dim curStyle As Variant
  Dim i As Integer

  newStyleName = "SimpleFormat"
  i = 0

  For Each curStyle In ActiveWorkbook.Styles
      i = i + 1
      If curStyle.Name = newStyleName Then
          MsgBox "This style " & "(" & newStyleName & _
              ") already exists. " & Chr(13) & _
              "It's the " & i & " style in the Styles collection."
          Exit Sub
      End If
  Next

  With ActiveWorkbook.Styles.Add(newStyleName)
      .Font.Name = "Arial Narrow"
      .Font.Size = "12"
      .Borders.LineStyle = xlThin
      .NumberFormat = "$#,##0_);[Red]($#,##0)"
      .IncludeAlignment = False
  End With
End Sub
```

The above procedure adds a specified style to the workbook's `Styles` collection provided that the style name is unique. The procedure begins by checking whether the style name has already been defined. If the workbook has a style with the specified name, the procedure ends after displaying a message to the user. If the style name does not exist, then the procedure creates the style with the specified formatting. Notice that if you do not wish to include a specific formatting feature in the style, you can set the following properties to False: `IncludeAlignment`, `IncludeFont`, `IncludeBorder`, `IncludeNumber`, `IncludePatterns`, and `IncludeProtection`. For example, a setting of False omits the `HorizontalAlignment`, `VerticalAlignment`, `WrapText`, and `Orientation` properties in the style. The default setting for these properties is True.

The custom style is added to the `Styles` collection. To find out the index number of the newly added style, simply rerun this procedure.

To programmatically apply your custom style to a selected range, run the following code in the Immediate window:

```
Selection.Style = "SimpleFormat"
```

To check out the settings the specific style includes, select the formatted range of cells and choose Home | Cell Styles to display the gallery of styles. Right-click the name of the selected style and choose Modify. Excel displays the dialog box shown in Figure 18.25.

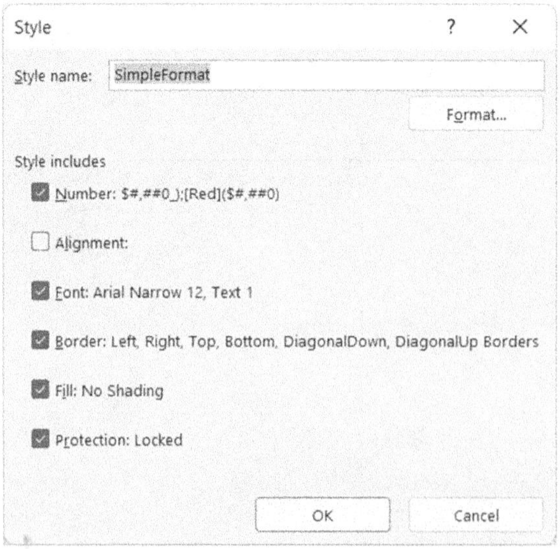

FIGURE 18.25 This dialog box displays the formatting settings of the SimpleFormat style that was created earlier by a VBA procedure.

The following code removes formatting applied to the selected range:

```
Selection.ClearFormats
```

The previous statement returns selection formats to the original state but does not remove the style from the `Styles` collection. To delete a style from a workbook, use the following statement:

```
ActiveWorkbook.Styles("SimpleFormat").Delete
```

If you have already applied formats to a cell, you can create a new style based on the active cell:

```
Sub AddSelectionStyle()
  Dim newStyleName As String

  newStyleName = "InvoiceAmount"
  ActiveWorkbook.Styles.Add Name:=newStyleName, _
      BasedOn:=ActiveCell
End Sub
```

By default Excel creates a new style based on the Normal style. However, if you have already applied formatting to a specific cell and would like to save the settings in a style, use the optional `BasedOn` argument of the Styles collection `Add` method to specify a cell on which to base the new style.

The custom styles you create can be reused in other workbooks. To do this you need to copy the style information from one workbook to another. In VBA, this can be done by using the `Merge` method of the Workbook object Styles collection:

```
ActiveWorkbook.Styles.Merge " Report2021.xlsx"
```

Assuming that you have defined some cool styles in the Report2021.xlsx workbook, the above statement copies the styles found in the specified workbook to the active workbook.

SUMMARY

In this chapter, you learned how to use VBA to apply basic formatting features to your worksheets to make your data easier to read and interpret. You also learned advanced formatting features such as conditional formatting and the utilization of tools such as data bars, icon sets, color scales, shapes, and sparklines, as well as themes and cell styles.

The next chapter focuses on the customization of the Ribbon interface and context menus in Excel.

Chapter 19

Context Menu Programming and Ribbon Customizations

Users have come to expect easy ways to select commands and options in any Windows application. Therefore, after you have written VBA procedures that provide solutions to specific worksheet automation dilemmas, you should spend additional time adding features that will make your application quick and easy to use. The most desired features of the user interface (UI) in Excel are customizations of the context menus and the Ribbon. While it is easy for users to get quick access to a specific command by placing it in the Quick Access toolbar located to the right of the Microsoft Office Menu button, your application's tools will need to appear either on the Ribbon or in a context menu. This chapter shows you how to work with the context menus and the Fluent Ribbon interface programmatically.

WORKING WITH CONTEXT MENUS

A *context* (also referred to as *shortcut*) *menu* appears when you right-click on an object in the Microsoft Excel application window. You can customize built-in context menus by using the `CommandBar` object or by applying Ribbon customizations as demonstrated later in this chapter. This section focuses on using the `CommandBar` object's properties and method to create, modify, or disable context menus depending on your application's needs.

Each object in the `CommandBars` collection is called `CommandBar`. The term `CommandBar` is used to refer to a context menu only. This object comes with a special Type property that can be used to return the specific type of the command bar (see Table 19.1).

TABLE 19.1 Types of CommandBar objects in the CommandBars collection

Type of Object	Index	Constant
Toolbar	0	msoBarTypeNormal
Menu Bar	1	msoBarTypeMenuBar
Context/Shortcut Menu	2	msoBarTypePopup

NOTE	*In versions of Excel prior to 2007, the* `CommandBar` *object was used to programmatically work with menu bars and toolbars. Since the introduction of the Ribbon interface, the* `CommandBar` *object can only be used with context menus. Later on in this chapter you will learn how to programmatically customize the RibbonX (Ribbon extensibility) model, which replaced the menus and toolbars found in Excel 2003 and earlier.*

Modifying a Built-In Context Menu

Microsoft Excel offers numerous context menus with different sets of frequently used menu options. Let's write a VBA procedure that prints the names of the context menus to the Immediate window.

NOTE	*Please note files for the "Hands-On" project may be found in the companion files.*

Hands-On 19.1 Enumerating Context Menus

1. Create a new workbook and save it as **C:\VBAExcel2021_ByExample\Chap19_VBAExcel2021.xlsm.**
2. Switch to the Visual Basic Editor screen and insert a new module into VBAProject (Chap19_VBAExcel2021.xlsm).
3. Use the Properties window to rename the module **ContextMenus.**
4. In the ContextMenus Code window, enter the ContextMenus procedure as shown below:

```
Sub ContextMenus()
  Dim myBar As CommandBar
  Dim counter As Integer
```

```
    For Each myBar In CommandBars
      If myBar.Type = msoBarTypePopup Then
        counter = counter + 1
        Debug.Print counter & ": " & myBar.Name
      End If
    Next
  End Sub
```

Notice the use of the `msoBarTypePopup` constant to identify the context menu in the collection of `CommandBars`.

5. Run the ContextMenus procedure.
   The result of this procedure is a list of context menus printed to the Immediate window.

Now that you know the exact names of Excel's context menus, you can easily add other frequently used commands to any of these menus. Let's add the Insert Picture command to the context menu activated when you right-click a worksheet cell.

Hands-On 19.2 Adding a New Item to a Context Menu

1. In the ContextMenus Code window that you created in the previous Hands-On, enter the following procedures:

```
Sub AddToCellMenu()
  With Application.CommandBars("Cell")
    .Reset
    .Controls.Add(Type:=msoControlButton, _
       Before:=2).Caption = "Insert Picture..."
    .Controls("Insert Picture...").OnAction = "InsertPicture"
  End With
End Sub

Sub InsertPicture()
  CommandBars.ExecuteMso ("PictureInsertFromFile")
End Sub
```

The `Reset` method of the `CommandBar` object used in the AddToCellMenu procedure prevents placing the same option in the context menu again when you run the procedure more than once.

To add a built-in or custom control to a context menu, use the `Add` method with the following syntax:

```
CommandBar.Controls.Add(Type, Id, Parameter, Before, Temporary)
```

`CommandBar` is the object to which you want to add a control. `Type` is a constant that determines the type of custom control you want to add. You may select one of the following types:

msoControlButton	1
msoControlPopup	10
msoControlEdit	2
msoControlDropDown	3
msoControlComboBox	4

`Id` is an integer that specifies the number of the built-in control you want to add. `Parameter` is used to send information to a Visual Basic procedure or to store information about the control.

The `Before` argument is the index number of the control before which the new control will be added. If omitted, Visual Basic adds the control at the end of the specified command bar.

The `Temporary` argument is a logical value (True or False) that determines when the control will be deleted. When you set this argument to `True`, the control will be automatically deleted when the Excel application is closed.

CommandBar controls have a number of properties that help you specify the appearance and functionality of a control. For example, the `Caption` property specifies the text displayed for the control. In the above procedure, you will see the "Insert Picture..." entry in the cell context menu. Note that it is customary to add an ellipsis (...) at the end of the menu option's text to indicate that the option will trigger a dialog box in which the user will need to make more selections. The `OnAction` property specifies the name of a VBA procedure that will execute when the menu option is selected. In this example, upon selecting the Insert Picture... option, the InsertPicture procedure will be called. This procedure uses the `ExecuteMso` method of the `CommandBar` object to execute the Ribbon's PictureInsertFromFile command.

2. Run the AddToCellMenu procedure.
3. Switch to the Microsoft Excel application window, right-click any cell in a worksheet, and select the **Insert Picture...** command (see Figure 19.1).

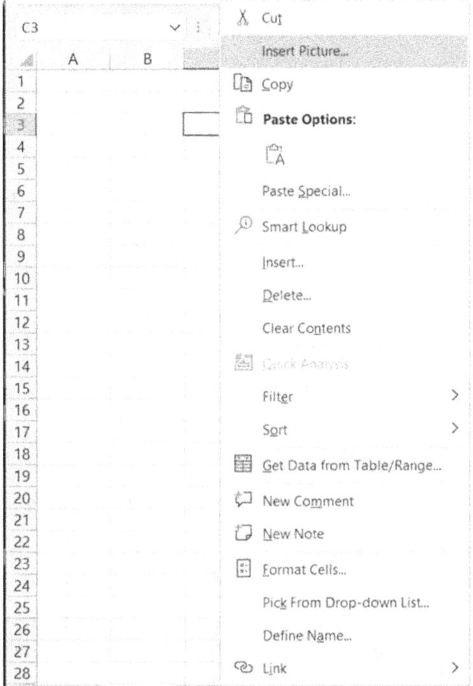

FIGURE 19.1 The built-in cell context menu displays a new item (Insert Picture...) that was added by a VBA procedure.

Excel displays the Insert Picture dialog box from which you can insert a picture from a file. The same dialog box is displayed when you click the Pictures button on the Ribbon's Insert tab.

NOTE	*Custom menu items added to Excel context menus are available in all open workbooks. It does not matter which workbook was used to add a custom item. For this reason, it's a good idea to ensure that the custom menu item is removed when the workbook is closed. (See the next section titled "Removing a Custom Item from a Context Menu.")*

Notice that some options in the context menu are preceded with a small graphic image. Let's write another version of the AddToCellMenu procedure to include an image next to the Insert Picture… command.

4. Enter the following procedure in the ContextMenus Code window:

```
Sub AddToCellMenu2()
  Dim ct As CommandBarButton
  With Application.CommandBars("Cell")
      .Reset
      Set ct = .Controls.Add(Type:=msoControlButton, _
          Before:=11, Temporary:=True)
  End With
  With ct
      .Caption = "Insert Picture..."
      .OnAction = "InsertPicture"
      .Picture = Application.CommandBars. _
          GetImageMso("PictureInsertFromFile", 16, 16)
      .Style = msoButtonIconAndCaption

  End With
End Sub
```

In this procedure code, we tell Visual Basic to add our custom menu item in the 11th position on the cell context menu. We also specify that this custom menu option is removed automatically when we exit Excel. This is accomplished by setting the value of the `Temporary` parameter to `True`. Next, we use the `With...End With` statement block to set a couple of properties for the newly created control object (`ct`). In addition to setting two standard properties (`Caption` and `OnAction`), we assign the `imageMso` image to the Picture property of our new control. To return the image, you must use the `CommandBars.GetImageMso` method and specify the name of the image and its size (width and height). The size of the image is specified as 16 x 16 pixels. The `Style` property is used here to specify that the control button should display both the icon and its caption.

5. Run the AddToCellMenu2 procedure.
6. Switch to the Microsoft Excel application window, right-click any cell in a worksheet, and look for the **Insert Picture...** command (see Figure 19.2). Notice that built-in context menu commands have a special hot key indicated by the underlined letter. To invoke a menu option, you simply press the underlined letter after opening the menu. Let's add a hot key to your custom menu option.
7. Modify the `Caption` property in the above procedure like this:

```
.Caption = "Insert Pict&ure..."
```

The "&" symbol in front of the letter "u" indicates that the lowercase "u" will serve as the hot key. Remember that hot keys are unique; you cannot use a letter that is already used by another menu item.

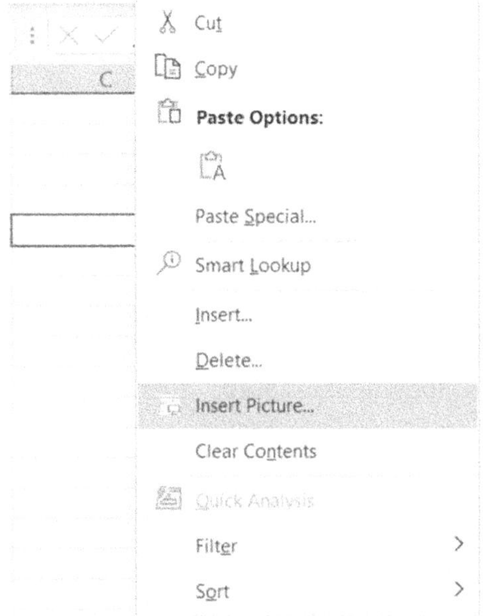

FIGURE 19.2 A custom Insert Picture... menu item is now identified by an icon and positioned just above the built-in Filter command.

8. Run the modified procedure.
9. Switch to the Microsoft Excel application window, right-click any cell in a worksheet, and then press the lowercase u. You should see the Insert Picture dialog box.

Removing a Custom Item from a Context Menu

When you modify context menus, your customizations will not go away when you close the workbook. Restarting Excel will remove your custom changes to the context menu only if you set the value of the `Temporary` parameter to `True` when adding your custom menu item. To ensure that the custom item is removed from the menu, consider writing a delete procedure similar to the one shown below:

```
Sub DeleteInsertPicture()
  Dim c As CommandBarControl
  On Error Resume Next
  Set c = CommandBars("Cell").Controls("Insert Pict&ure...")
  c.Delete
End Sub
```

For automatic cleanup, call the previous procedure from the Workbook_BeforeClose event procedure like this:

```
Private Sub Workbook_BeforeClose(Cancel As Boolean)
  Call DeleteInsertPicture
End Sub
```

The previous event procedure must be entered in the ThisWorkbook code module. The Workbook_BeforeClose procedure will be executed just before the workbook is closed.

To ensure that your custom menu option is in place when you open the workbook, call the procedure that adds a custom menu item from the Workbook_Open event procedure entered in the ThisWorkbook Code window:

```
Private Sub Workbook_Open()
  Call AddToCellMenu2
End Sub
```

Disabling and Hiding Items on a Context Menu

To disallow using a particular context menu item, you may want to disable it or hide it.

When a context menu item is disabled, its caption appears dimmed. When a menu item is hidden, it simply does not appear on the menu.

To disable a menu item, set the `Enabled` property of the control to False. For example, the following statement will disable the Insert Picture command that you've added earlier to the Cell context menu:

```
Application.CommandBars("Cell"). _
     Controls("Insert Pict&ure...").Enabled = False
```

To enable a disabled menu item, simply set the `Enabled` property of the desired control to True.

To hide a menu item, set the `Visible` property of the control to False:

```
Application.CommandBars("Cell"). _
     Controls("Insert Pict&ure...").Visible = False
```

And to unhide the hidden menu item set the `Visible` property of the control to True:

```
Application.CommandBars("Cell"). _
     Controls("Insert Pict&ure...").Visible = True
```

A good place to use the previous commands is in the `Worksheet_Activate` and `Worksheet_Deactivate` event procedures. For example, to disable the specific context menu item only when Sheet1 is active, write the following event procedures in the Sheet1 code module:

```
Private Sub Worksheet_Activate()
  Application.CommandBars("Cell").Controls("Sort").Enabled = False
End Sub

Private Sub Worksheet_Deactivate()
  Application.CommandBars("Cell").Controls("Sort").Enabled = True
End Sub
```

NOTE	*When writing code to control Excel context menus with the CommandBar object's properties and methods, you may find out that certain VBA statements will work in some but not all circumstances. Unless you need to write an application for Excel 2007 or earlier, you should move toward programming the RibbonX interface, which allows you to control commands in the context menus (see the section titled "Modifying Context Menus Using Ribbon Customizations" later in this chapter).*

Action Item 19.1

Excel has a SpeakCells command that allows Excel to read the contents of a cell, range of cells, or a worksheet. On your own, add the SpeakCells command to the Cells context menu. The solution can be found in the Chap19_SpeakCells.txt file.

Adding a Context Menu to a Command Button

When you design custom forms, you may want to add context menus to various controls placed on the form. The following set of VBA procedures demonstrates how right-clicking a command button can offer users a choice of options to select from.

Hands-On 19.3 Using Context Menus on User Forms

1. In the ContextMenus Code window, enter the Create_ContextMenu procedure as shown below:

```
Sub Create_ContextMenu()
  Dim sm As Object

  Set sm = Application.CommandBars.Add("MyComputer", msoBarPopup)
  With sm
```

```
    .Controls.Add(Type:=msoControlButton). _
        Caption = "Operating System"
    With .Controls("Operating System")
        .FaceId = 1954
        .OnAction = "OpSystem"
    End With
   .Controls.Add(Type:=msoControlButton).Caption = "Active Printer"
    With .Controls("Active Printer")
        .FaceId = 4
        .OnAction = "ActivePrinter"
    End With
   .Controls.Add(Type:=msoControlButton).Caption = "Active Workbook"
    With .Controls("Active Workbook")
        .FaceId = 247
        .OnAction = "ActiveWorkbook"
    End With
    .Controls.Add(Type:=msoControlButton).Caption = "Active Sheet"
    With .Controls("Active Sheet")
        .FaceId = 18
        .OnAction = "ActiveSheet"
    End With
  End With
End Sub
```

This procedure creates a custom context menu named MyComputer and adds four commands to it. Notice that each command is assigned an icon. When you select a command from this context menu, one of the procedures shown in Step 2 will run.

2. In the ContextMenus Code window, enter the following procedures that are called by the Create_ContextMenu procedure:

```
Sub OpSystem()
    MsgBox Application.OperatingSystem, , "Operating System"
End Sub

Sub ActivePrinter()
    MsgBox Application.ActivePrinter
End Sub

Sub ActiveWorkbook()
    MsgBox Application.ActiveWorkbook.Name
End Sub

Sub ActiveSheet()
    MsgBox Application.ActiveSheet.Name
End Sub
```

3. Run the Create_ContextMenu procedure.
   To test the custom context menu you just created, use the `ShowPopup` method, as shown in Step 4.
4. Type the following statement in the Immediate window and press Enter:

   ```
   CommandBars("MyComputer").ShowPopup 0, 0
   ```

   The `ShowPopup` method for the `CommandBar` object accepts two optional arguments (`x`, `y`) that determine the location of the context menu on the screen. In the above example, the MyComputer context menu that was added by running the Create_ContextMenu procedure will appear at the top left-hand corner of the screen.

   Let's make our context menu friendlier by attaching it to a command button placed on a user form.
5. In the Visual Basic Editor screen, choose **Insert | UserForm** to add a new form to the current VBA project.
   Using the CommandButton control in the Toolbox, place a button anywhere on the empty user form. Use the Properties window to change the `Caption` property of the command button to **System Information**. You may need to resize the button on the form to fit this text.
6. Switch to the Code window for the form by clicking the **View Code** button in the Project Explorer window or double-clicking the form background.
7. Enter the following procedure in the UserForm1 Code window:

   ```
   Private Sub CommandButton1_MouseDown(ByVal Button _
     As Integer, _
     ByVal Shift As Integer, _
     ByVal X As Single, _
     ByVal Y As Single)
     If Button = 2 Then
        Call Show_ShortMenu
     Else
        MsgBox "You must right-click this button."
     End If
   End Sub
   ```

   This procedure calls the Show_ShortMenu procedure (see Step 9) when the user right-clicks the command button placed on the form. Visual Basic has two event procedures that are executed in response to clicking a mouse button. When you click a mouse button, Visual Basic executes the `MouseDown` event procedure. When you release the mouse button, the `MouseUp` event occurs. The `MouseDown` and `MouseUp` event procedures require the following arguments:

- The `object` argument specifies the object. In this example, it's the name of the command button placed on the form.
- The `Button` argument is the Integer value that specifies which mouse button was pressed.

Value of Button Argument	Description
1	Left mouse button
2	Right mouse button
3	Middle mouse button

- The `Shift` argument determines whether the user was pressing the Shift, Ctrl, or Alt key when the event occurred.

Value of Shift Argument	Description
1	Shift key
2	Ctrl key
3	Shift and Ctrl keys
4	Alt key
5	Alt and Shift keys
6	Alt and Ctrl keys
7	Alt, Shift, and Ctrl keys

8. In the ContextMenus Code window, enter the code of the Show_ShortMenu procedure:

```
Sub Show_ShortMenu()
  Dim shortMenu As Object

  Set shortMenu = Application.CommandBars("MyComputer")
  With shortMenu
     .ShowPopup
  End With
End Sub
```

9. In the Project Explorer window, double-click **UserForm1** and press **F5** to run the form. Right-click the **System Information** button and select one of the options from the context menu.

Notice that the `ShowPopup` method used in this procedure does not include the optional arguments that determine the location of the context menu on the screen. Therefore, the menu appears where the mouse was clicked (see Figure 19.3).

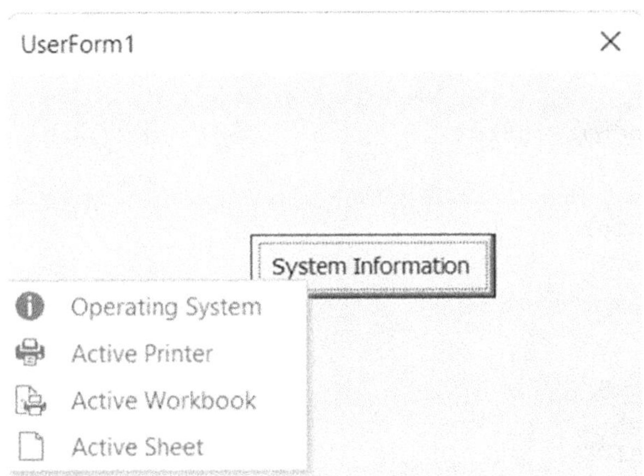

FIGURE 19.3 A custom context menu appears when you right-click an object.

10. To delete the context menu named MyComputer, enter and then run the following Delete_ShortMenu procedure in the ContextMenus Code window:

```
Sub Delete_ShortMenu()
   Application.CommandBars("MyComputer").Delete
End Sub
```

Finding a FaceID Value of an Image

When modifying context menus, you will most likely want to include an image next to the displayed text, as we did in Hands-On 19.3 (see Figure 19.3). The good news is that the `CommandBars` collection has hundreds of images that you can use. Each command bar control button has a `FaceID` that determines the look of a control. But how do you know which ID belongs to which control button? The `FaceID` property returns or sets the ID number of the icon on the control button's face. In most cases, the icon ID number (`FaceID`) is the same as the control's `ID` property. The icon image can be copied to the Windows clipboard using the `CopyFace` method. The Images procedure demonstrated below iterates through the `CommandBars` collection and writes to a new workbook a list of control buttons that have a FaceID number. If you'd like to see this procedure in action, enter the code shown below in the ContextMenus Code window in the Chap19_Excel2021.xlsm workbook and then run it.

```
Sub Images()
  Dim i As Integer
  Dim j As Integer
  Dim total As Integer
  Dim buttonId As Integer
  Dim buttonName As String
  Dim myControl As CommandBarControl
  Dim bar As CommandBar

  On Error GoTo ErrorHandler
  Workbooks.Add
  Range("A1").Select
  With ActiveCell
    .Value = "Image"
    .Offset(0, 1) = "Index"
    .Offset(0, 2) = "Name"
    .Offset(0, 3) = "FaceID"
    .Offset(0, 4) = "CommandBar Name (Index)"
  End With

  For j = 1 To Application.CommandBars.Count
      Set bar = CommandBars(j)
      total = bar.Controls.Count

      With bar
        For i = 1 To total
            buttonName = .Controls(i).Caption
            buttonId = .Controls(i).ID

            Set myControl = CommandBars.FindControl(ID:=buttonId)
            myControl.CopyFace ' error could occur here
            ActiveCell.Offset(1, 0).Select
            Sheets(1).Paste

            With ActiveCell
                .Offset(0, 1).Value = buttonId
                .Offset(0, 2).Value = buttonName
                .Offset(0, 3).Value = myControl.FaceID
                .Offset(0, 4).Value = bar.Name & " (" & j & ")"
            End With
StartNext:
        Next i
```

```
    End With
  Next j

  Columns("A:E").EntireColumn.AutoFit
  Exit Sub
ErrorHandler:
  Resume StartNext
End Sub
```

Because you cannot copy the image of an icon that is currently disabled, Visual Basic encounters an error when it attempts to copy the button's face to the clipboard. The procedure traps this error with the `On Error GoTo ErrorHandler` statement. This way, when Visual Basic encounters the error, it will jump to the `ErrorHandler` label and execute the instructions below this label. This will ensure that the problem control button is skipped and the procedure can continue without interruption. A partial result of the procedure is shown in Figure 19.4.

	A	B	C	D	E
1	Image	Index	Name	FaceID	CommandBar Name (Index)
2		1031	&WordArt...	1031	WordArt (3)
3		2094	Edit Te&xt...	2094	WordArt (3)
4		1606	&WordArt Gallery	1606	WordArt (3)
5		962	Format &Object...	962	WordArt (3)
6		1063	&WordArt Same Letter Heights	1063	WordArt (3)
7		1061	&WordArt Vertical Text	1061	WordArt (3)
8		2619	&From File...	2619	Picture (4)
9		1064	&More Contrast	1064	Picture (4)
10		1065	&Less Contrast	1065	Picture (4)
11		1066	&More Brightness	1066	Picture (4)
12		1067	&Less Brightness	1067	Picture (4)
13		732	&Crop	732	Picture (4)
14		199	Rotate &Left 90°	199	Picture (4)
15		6382	&Compress Pictures...	6382	Picture (4)
16		962	Format &Object...	962	Picture (4)
17		2827	&Set Transparent Color	2827	Picture (4)
18		1362	&Reset Picture	1362	Picture (4)
19		9524	&Stop Inking	9524	Ink Annotations (8)
20		451	Trace &Dependents	451	Circular Reference (9)
21		486	&Trace Precedents	486	Circular Reference (9)
22		453	Remove &All Arrows	453	Circular Reference (9)
23		2520	&New	2520	Standard (14)
24		23	Open	23	Standard (14)
25		3	&Save	3	Standard (14)
26		9004	Permission (Unrestricted Access)	9004	Standard (14)
27		3738	&Mail Recipient	3738	Standard (14)
28		2521	&Quick Print	2521	Standard (14)

FIGURE 19.4 A list of icon images and their corresponding FaceID values generated by the VBA procedure.

A QUICK OVERVIEW OF THE RIBBON INTERFACE

The Ribbon contains the title bar, the Quick Access toolbar, and the tabs. Each tab on the Ribbon provides access to features and commands related to a particular task. For example, you can use the Insert tab to quickly insert tables, illustrations, charts, links, or text (see Figure 19.5). Related commands within a tab are organized into groups. This type of organization makes it easy to locate a particular command.

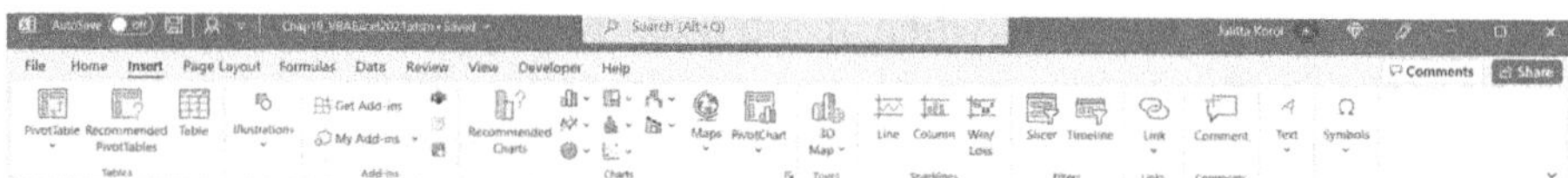

FIGURE 19.5 The rectangular area at the top of the Microsoft Excel window is called the Ribbon. Each tab on the Ribbon contains groups of related commands.

Various program commands are displayed as large or small buttons. A large button denotes a frequently used command, while a small button shows a specific feature of the main command that you may want to work with. Some large and small command buttons include drop-down lists of other specialized commands. For example, the small More Functions button drop-down in the Function Library group on the Formulas tab contains additional types of functions you can insert: Statistical, Engineering, Cube, Information, Compatibility, and Web.

Some controls that you find on the Ribbon do not display commands. Instead, they provide a visual clue of the output you might expect when a specific option is selected. These types of controls are known as *galleries*. The gallery control is often used to present various formatting options, such as the margin settings shown in Figure 19.6.

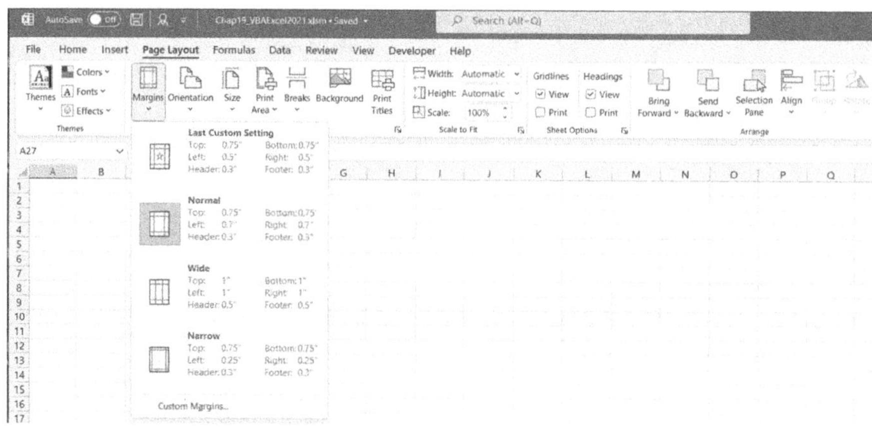

FIGURE 19.6 The margin layouts are displayed in a gallery control.

As mentioned earlier, the commands on the Ribbon tabs are organized into groups for easy browsing. Some tab groups have dialog box launchers in the bottom right-hand corner that display a dialog box where you can set several advanced options at once.

In addition to main Ribbon tabs, there are also contextual tabs that contain commands that apply to what you are doing. When a particular object is selected, the Ribbon displays a contextual tab that provides commands for working with that object. For example, when you select an image in a worksheet, the Ribbon displays a contextual tab called Picture Format, as shown in Figure 19.7.

Clicking on the Picture Format tab brings up commands for dealing with a Picture object. The contextual tab disappears when you cancel the selection of the object. In other words, if you select a different cell in a worksheet, the Picture Format tab will be gone.

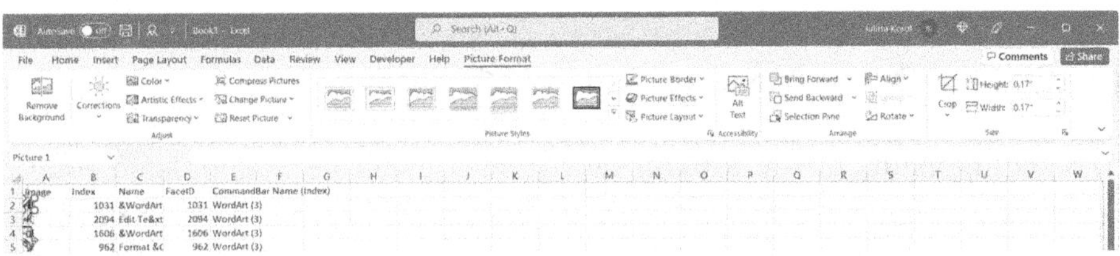

FIGURE 19.7 Contextual tabs will appear when you work with a particular object such as a picture, PivotTable, or chart.

The tooltips of the controls display the name of the command, the control keyboard context (where available), and a description of what the command does (see Figure 19.8).

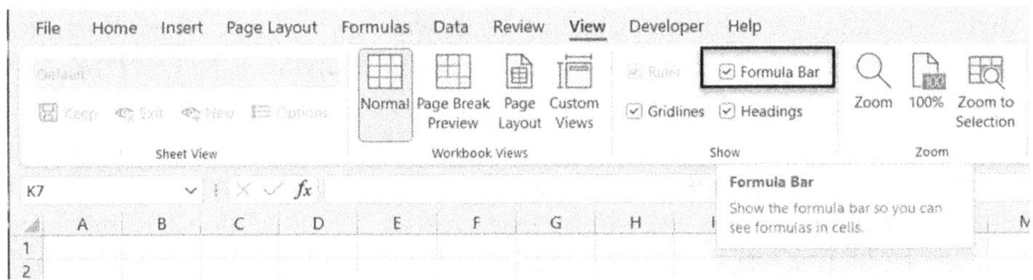

FIGURE 19.8 The enhanced tooltips, known as Super ToolTips, provide more information about the selected command.

All Ribbon commands and the Quick Access toolbar can be easily accessed via the keyboard. Simply press the Alt key on the keyboard to display small boxes with key tips. Every command has its own access key. For example, to access the

File tab, press Alt and then F. Within the menus you will see other key tips for every command. To view key tips for the commands on a particular tab, first select the access key for that tab. To remove the key tips, press the Alt key again. When you are working in command mode (after pressing the Alt key), you can also use the Tab key and arrow keys to move around the Ribbon.

Now that you've reviewed the main features of the Ribbon interface, let's look at how you can extend it with your own tabs and controls. The next section introduces you to Ribbon programming with XML and VBA.

SIDEBAR ***Ribbon Customizations via the User Interface***

In addition to customizing the Quick Access Toolbar (QAT), you can create custom Ribbon tabs and groups by choosing File | Options | Customize Ribbon. You can also rename and change the order of the built-in tabs and groups.

RIBBON PROGRAMMING WITH VBA AND XML

The components of the Ribbon user interface can be manipulated programmatically using *Extensible Markup Language (XML)* or other programming languages. All Microsoft 365 applications that use this interface rely on the programming model known as *Ribbon extensibility*, or *RibbonX.*

This section introduces you to customizing the Office Fluent user interface (UI) by using XML markup (refer to Chapter 28 for detailed information on using XML with Excel).

Custom UI XML Markup Specification specifies the markup used to implement UI customization in the context of ECMA-376 Office Open XML File Formats. You can review this specification by downloading it from the following site: *https://interoperability.blob.core.windows.net/files/MS-CUSTOMUI/%5bMS-CUSTOMUI%5d-210422.pdf.*

While no special tools are required to perform Ribbon customizations, it is much quicker and easier to work with a tool specifically designed for this purpose. In this chapter, we will be using a free Office RibbonX Editor created by Fernando Andreu. Download this tool from *https://github.com/fernandreu/office-ribbonx-editor/releases/latest.*

From the list of assets, click on the *OfficeRibbonXEditor-SelfContained-NET6-Binaries.zip* to download it, then unzip it. Find the *OfficeRibbonXEditor.exe* in the list of files, right-click on it and use the Send command from the context menu to send the shortcut to the desktop. Note that under Windows 11, the Send command is available after choosing Show More Options.

NOTE	*In the previous editions of this book, we used an older tool called Office CustomUI Editor. At the time of writing, this older tool can be downloaded from https://www.rondebruin.nl/win/winfiles/OfficeCustomUIEditorSetup.zip.* *If for any reasons, you cannot install any of the recommended tools, you can still customize the Microsoft 365 Fluent Ribbon by creating a customization file in any text editor and saving it with the name customUI.xml. For details, see the following article that describes adding a custom tab, a custom group, and a button using a Word document as an example: https://docs.microsoft.com/en-us/office/vba/library-reference/concepts/customize-the-office-fluent-ribbon-by-using-an-open-xml-formats-file.*

You can find out the names of the Ribbon controls by downloading the Office Fluent User Interface Control Identifiers from

http://www.microsoft.com/en-us/download/details.aspx?id=50745.

NOTE	*The identifier names can also be accessed in the QAT customization dialog box. Simply hover over control that interests you and look at Screen Tip of the control.* *To get the latest control identifiers for Office 365 applications, please visit: https://github.com/OfficeDev/office-fluent-ui-command-identifiers*

Creating the Ribbon Customization XML Markup

To make custom changes to the Ribbon user interface you need to prepare an XML markup file that specifies all your customizations. The contents of the XML markup file that we will use in Hands-On 19.4 is shown in Figure 19.9, and the resulting output appears in Figure 19.10.

FIGURE 19.9 This XML file defines a new tab with two groups for the existing Excel 2021 Ribbon. This file produces the output shown in Figure 19.10.

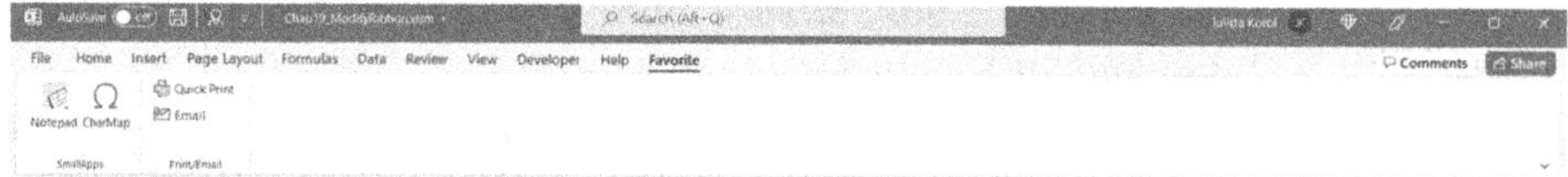

FIGURE 19.10 The custom Favorite tab is based on the custom XML markup file shown in Figure 19.9.

Hands-On 19.4 Creating an XML Document with Ribbon Customizations

This Hands-On and all the remaining Hands-On exercises in this chapter rely on the Office RibbonX Editor. See the instructions on how to get and install this free tool in the previous section.

1. Launch Microsoft Excel 2021 and create a new workbook. Save this workbook as **Chap19_ModifyRibbon.xlsm** in your **VBAExcel2021_ByExample** folder. Be sure to save the workbook as **Excel-Macro Enabled workbook (*.xlsm).**
2. Close the workbook and exit Excel.
3. Launch the **Office RibbonX Editor** using the shortcut you created on the desktop.
4. Choose **File | Open**.

5. Select the **C:\VBAExcel2021_ByExample\Chap19_ModifyRibbon.xlsm** workbook file you created in Step 1 above and click **Open**.
6. Make sure that name of the file is selected in the left pane of the Office RibbonX Editor, and choose **Insert | Office 2010+ Custom UI Part** as shown in Figure 19.11. This creates a **CustomUI14.xml** file in the workbook.

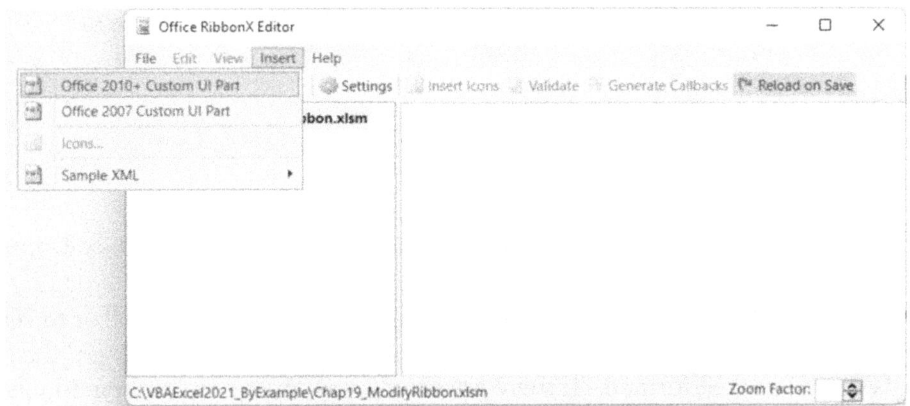

FIGURE 19.11 Use the Office RibbonX Editor to insert an Office 2010+ Custom UI Part into an Excel 2021 workbook you want to customize. This option works for Ribbon customizations in Excel 2010–2021. To customize the Ribbon in Excel 2007, you would choose the Office 2007 Custom UI Part instead.

7. Double-click the customUI14.xml file in the left pane to open it for edit.
8. In the right pane, enter the XML Ribbon customization markup as shown below (see also Figure 19.9 earlier). If you prefer, you can copy the code from the companion files. Look for the file named **CustomUI14_ver01.txt**.

```
<customUI xmlns="http://schemas.microsoft.com/office/2009/07/
customui">
  <ribbon startFromScratch="false">
    <tabs>
      <tab idMso="TabHome">
        <group idMso="GroupStyles" visible="false" />
      </tab>
      <tab id="TabJK1" label="Favorite">
        <group id="GroupJK1" label="SmallApps">
           <button id="btnNotes" label="Notepad" image=
                                            "Note1" size="large"
          onAction="OpenNotepad"  screentip=
                                          "Open Windows Notepad"
          supertip="It is recommended that you save your notes
                                                      about this
```

```
            worksheet in a simple text file."/>
          <button id="btnCharMap" label="CharMap"
            imageMso="SymbolInsert" size="large"
                                             onAction="OpenCharmap" />
        </group>
       <group id="GroupJK2" label="Print/Email" >
         <button idMso="FilePrintQuick" size="normal" />
         <button idMso="FileSendAsAttachment" size="normal" />
       </group>
     </tab>
   </tabs>
  </ribbon>
</customUI>
```

XML is case sensitive, so make sure you enter the statements exactly as shown above.

9. Click the **Validate** button ( ) on the Office RibbonX Editor Toolbar to verify that your XML does not contain errors. You should see the message "Custom UI XML is well formed." If there are errors, you must correct them to ensure that the XML is well formed.
   At this point, you should have a well-formed CustomUI14.xml document containing Ribbon customizations.

   Let's go over the XML document content. As you will learn in Chapter 28, every XML document consists of a number of elements, called *nodes*. In any XML document, there must be a root node, or a top-level element. In the Ribbon customization file, the root tag is <customUI>. The root's purpose is to specify the Office RibbonX XML namespace:

```
<customUI xmlns="http://schemas.microsoft.com/office/2009/07/
customui">
```

Namespaces are used to uniquely identify elements in the XML documents and avoid name collisions when elements with the same name are combined in the same document.

If you were to customize the Office 2007 Ribbon, you would use the following namespace instead:

```
<customUI xmlns="http://schemas.microsoft.com/office/2006/01/
customui">
```

The `xmlns` attribute of the <customUI> tag holds the name of the default namespace to be used in the Ribbon customization. Notice that the root element encloses all other elements of this XML document: ribbon, tabs, tab, group, and button. Each element consists of a beginning and ending tag. For example, <customUI> is the name of the beginning tag and </customUI> is the ending tag. The actual Ribbon definition is contained within the <ribbon> tag:

```
<ribbon startFromScratch="false">
  [Include xml tags to specify the required ribbon customization]
</ribbon>
```

The `startFromScratch` attribute of the <ribbon> tag defines whether you want to replace the built-in Ribbon with your own (true) or add a new tab to the existing Ribbon (false).

SideBar *Hiding the Elements of the Excel User Interface*

Setting `startFromScratch="true"` in the <ribbon> tag will hide the default Ribbon as well as the contents of the Quick Access toolbar. The File menu will be left with only three commands: New, Open, and Save.

To create a new tab in the Ribbon, use the <tabs> tag. Each tab element is defined with the <tab> tag. The `label` attribute of the tab element specifies the name of your custom tab. The name in the `id` attribute is used to identify your custom tab:

```
<tabs>
<tab id="TabJK1" label="Favorite">
```

Ribbon tabs contain controls organized in groups. You can define a group for the controls on your tab with the <group> tag. The example XML markup file defines the following two groups for the Favorite tab:

```
<group id="GroupJK1" label="SmallApps">
<group id="GroupJK2" label="Print/Email">
```

Like the tab node, the group nodes of the XML document also contain the `id` and `label` attributes. Placing controls in groups is easy. The group labeled SmallApps has two custom button controls, identified by the <button> elements. The group labeled Print/Email also contains two buttons; however, unlike the SmallApps group, the buttons placed here are built-in Office system controls rather than custom controls. You can quickly determine this by looking at the id attribute for the control. Any attribute that ends with "Mso" refers to a built-in Office item:

```
<button idMso="FilePrintQuick" size="normal" />
```

Buttons placed on the Ribbon can be large or small. You can define the size of the button with the size attribute set to "large" or "normal." Buttons can have additional attributes:

```
<button id="btnNotes" label="Notepad" image="Note1" size="large"
  onAction="OpenNotepad" screentip="Open Windows Notepad"
  supertip="
  It is recommended that you save your notes about this worksheet
  in a simple text file." />
<button id="btnCharMap" label="CharMap" imageMso="SymbolInsert"
  size="large" onAction="OpenCharmap" />
```

The `screentip` and `supertip` attributes allow you to specify the short and longer text that should appear when the mouse pointer is positioned over the button.

The `imageMso` attribute denotes the name of the existing Office icon. You can use images provided by any Office application. To provide your own image, use the image attribute as shown in this Hands-On, or use the `getImage` attribute in the XML markup (see more information in the section "Creating a Gallery Control," later in this chapter).

The controls that you specify in the XML markup perform their designated actions via callback procedures. For example, the `onAction` attribute of a button control contains the name of the callback procedure that is executed when the button is clicked. When that procedure completes, it calls back the Ribbon to provide the status or modify the Ribbon. You will write the callback procedures for the `onAction` attribute in Hands-On 19.5.

Buttons borrowed from the Office system do not require the `onAction` attribute. When clicked, these buttons will perform their default built-in action.

Before finishing off the XML Ribbon customization document, always make sure that you have included all the ending tags:

```
      </tab>
    </tabs>
  </ribbon>
</customUI>
```

Because our first Ribbon customization calls upon a custom image, let's add it to the file.

10. Copy the **Images** folder from the companion files to your **VBAExcel2021_ByExample** folder.
11. In the Office RibbonX Editor, select **CustomUI14.xml** in the left pane and choose **Insert | Icons....** or click the Insert Icons button in the toolbar.
12. Change the file filter to show all files in the **C:\VBAExcel2021_ByExample\Images** folder, then select **Note.gif** and click **Open**.
    A note image should appear just below the customUI14.xml file in the left pane.
13. In the left pane of the Office RibbonX Editor window, right-click the image and choose **Change ID**. Rename the image to **Note1** to match the name of the `image` attribute in the XML markup:

```
<button id="btnNotes" label="Notepad" image="Note1" size="large"
    onAction="OpenNotepad" screentip="Open Windows Notepad"
    supertip="It is recommended that you save your notes about this
    worksheet in a simple text file."/>
```

14. Click the Save button or press Ctrl+S to save the current document.
15. Choose **File | Exit** to exit Office RibbonX Editor.

The first part of the Ribbon customization is now completed. In the next part you will load the workbook file into Excel and view the custom tab you have just created. You will also write callback procedures that perform specific actions.

Loading Ribbon Customizations

Hands-On 19.5 walks you through the remaining steps that are necessary in order to integrate Ribbon customizations into your workbook.

Hands-On 19.5 Adding VBA Code for Use by the Ribbon Customizations

1. Open the **C:\VBAExcel2021_ByExample\Chap19_ModifyRibbon.xlsm** workbook in Excel 2021. Notice the Favorite tab at the end of the Ribbon (see Figure 19.10 earlier).
2. Switch to the Visual Basic Editor window and activate **VBAProject (Chap19_ModifyRibbon.xlsm)** in the Project Explorer window. Next, choose **Insert | Module** to add a new module to the selected project.

3. In the module's Code window, enter the following procedures:

```
Public Sub OpenNotepad(ctl As IRibbonControl)
  Shell "Notepad.exe", vbNormalFocus
End Sub

Public Sub OpenCharmap(ctl As IRibbonControl)
  Shell "Charmap.exe", vbNormalFocus
End Sub
```

OpenNotepad and OpenCharmap are the names of the callback procedures that were specified in the `onAction` attribute of the button (see Hands-On 19.4). As mentioned earlier, a callback procedure executes some action and then notifies the Ribbon that the task has been completed. The `onAction` callback is handled by a VBA procedure. The callback includes the `IRibbonControl` parameter, which is the control that was clicked. This control is passed to your VBA code by the Ribbon.

```
Sub OpenNotepad(ctl as IRibbonControl)
Sub OpenCharmap(ctl as IRibbonControl)
```

For VBA to recognize this parameter, you must make sure that the References dialog box (Tools | References) has a reference to the Microsoft Office 16.0 object library.

The OpenNotepad and OpenCharmap procedures tell Excel to use the `Shell` function to open Windows Notepad or the Charmap application. Notice that the program's executable filename is in double quotes. The second argument of the `Shell` function is optional. This argument specifies the window style, that is, how the program will appear once it is launched. The `vbNormalFocus` constant will open the application in a normal size window with focus. If the window style is not specified, the program will be minimized with focus (`vbMinimizedFocus`).

SIDEBAR ***The IRibbonControl Properties***

You can view the properties (Context, Id, and Tag) of the `IRibbonControl` object in the Object Browser. The `Context` property returns the active window that contains the Ribbon interface, in this case Microsoft Excel. The `Id` property contains the ID of the control that was clicked. The `Tag` property can be used to store additional information with the control. To use this property, you need to add a tag attribute to the Ribbon customization XML document. By using the `Tag` property, you can write a more generic procedure to handle the callbacks.

4. Switch to the Excel application window and test the Notepad and Charmap buttons on the Ribbon. These buttons should invoke the built-in Windows applications.
5. Save and close the **Chap19_ModifyRibbon.xlsm** workbook. Keep the Excel application window open. Proceed to Step 6 to make sure that Excel is set up to display the RibbonX errors.
6. Click **File | Options**. In the Excel Options dialog box, click the **Advanced** tab and scroll down to the **General** section. Make sure that the **Show Add-in User Interface Errors** checkbox is selected and click **OK**.
   When you enable Show Add-in User Interface Errors, Excel will display errors in your Ribbon customization when you load a workbook that contains errors in the custom RibbonX code. This is very helpful in the process of debugging. If you want to successfully use your customized Ribbon interface, you must make sure that Excel does not find any errors when loading your workbook.
7. Exit Microsoft Excel.

Errors on Loading Ribbon Customizations

If Excel finds any errors in the Ribbon customization markup, it displays an error message. For example, if the file is missing a matching opening or closing tag or you typed the name of an attribute in uppercase when lowercase was expected, you will see a message indicating a line and a column number, and the name of the attribute where the problem is located (see Figure 19.12). You should open the workbook file in the Office RibbonX Editor, find and correct the error, and then try again to open the workbook in Excel. The error messages will continue to pop up until the entire file is debugged.

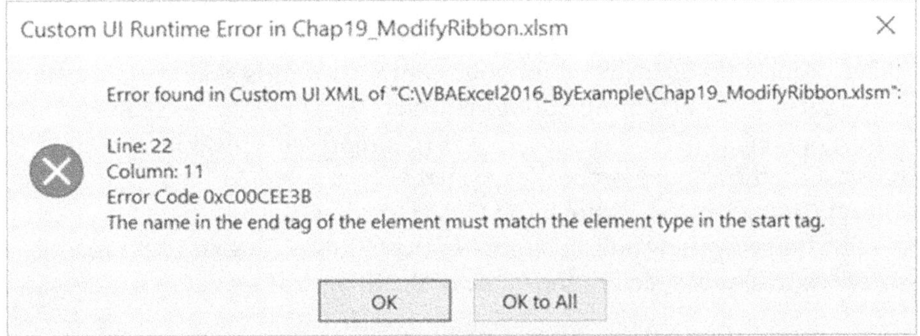

FIGURE 19.12 Excel displays an error message when it finds an error in the Custom UI XML code of the workbook file you are attempting to open.

Some problems found within the file may cause Excel to generate an error message about unreadable content and ask you if you want to recover the contents of the workbook. When you click Yes, Excel will try to repair the file and let you know whether it has succeeded. Sometimes the correction will be made for you, and other times you will have to locate and fix the problem yourself.

Using Images in Ribbon Customizations

So far in this chapter you have learned how to use built-in and custom images in your Ribbon customizations. You already know that to reuse an Office icon you must use the `imageMso` attribute of a control. You also know that to call your own BMP, GIF, and JPEG image files you should use the `image` attribute. Images can be added to the workbook file by using the Office RibbonX Editor (see Hands-On 19.4). You can also load the images at runtime when you open a workbook. To implement this particular scenario, use the `loadImage` callback procedure in the `loadImage` attribute for the `customUI` element.

```
<customUI    xmlns="http://schemas.microsoft.com/office/2009/07/
customui" loadImage="OnLoadImage">
```

The `loadImage` attribute specifies the following `OnLoadImage` callback procedure, which you must enter in a VBA code module of your Chap19_ModifyRibbon.xlsm workbook:

```
Public Sub OnLoadImage(imgName As String, ByRef image)
  Dim strImgFileName As String
  strImgFileName = "C:\VBAExcel2021_ByExample\Images\" & imgName
  Set image = LoadPicture(strImgFileName)
End Sub
```

You can load a picture from a file using the `LoadPicture` function. This function is a member of the stdole.StdFunctions library. The library file, which is called stdole2.tlb, is installed on your computer and is available to your VBA procedures without setting additional references. The `LoadPicture` function returns an object of type `IPictureDisp` that represents the image. You can view objects, methods, and properties available in the stdole library by using the Object Browser in the Visual Basic Editor window.

The following new button control in the CustomUI14.xml document has an image control that specifies the name of the image file:

```
<button id="btnCalc" label="Calculator"
  image="DownArrow.gif" onAction="OpenCalculator" />
```

This button, pictured in Figure 19.10 earlier, uses the following callback procedure entered in a VBA code module (Chap19_ModifyRibbon.xlsm):

```
Public Sub OpenCalculator(ctl As IRibbonControl)
  Shell "Calc.exe", vbNormalFocus
End Sub
```

The example XML markup can be found the CustomUI14_ver02.txt file in the companion files.

NOTE	*To update your Chap19_ModifyRibbon.xlsm file, perform the following steps:* • Open the Chap19_ModifyRibbon.xlsm workbook file in the Office RibbonX Editor (make sure the file is not open in Excel prior to loading it into the Editor application). • Replace the XML markup in the CustomUI14.xml part by entering or pasting the new XML markup. The new code should replace the code from the previous example. • Use the Validate icon in the Editor's toolbar to make sure that the revised XML is well formed. • Save the file and exit the Office RibbonX Editor. • Open the Chap19_ModifyRibbon.xlsm file in Excel to view Ribbon customizations. You may encounter errors due to the missing callbacks. • Continue with the explanations in the section below and enter any necessary callback procedures in the VBA module. Be sure to save the changes in the workbook. • Follow the same steps as you progress through the rest of the chapter. Whenever you see a revised Ribbon customization markup, you should enter it in the Office RibbonX Editor and then do the callbacks in Excel. ***Note:*** The required callbacks can be generated in the Office RibbonX Editor by clicking the Generate Callbacks button and then copied to VBE screen in Excel and completed with the required VBA code.

About Tabs, Groups, and Controls

Built-in tabs and groups can be made invisible by setting the visible property of the <tab> or <group> elements to "false." A built-in tab can contain a custom group. Built-in groups can also be added to other built-in or custom tabs. Some Ribbon tabs, called contextual tabs, appear only when certain objects are in focus. For example, inserting a table will bring up the Table Tools contextual tab that contains table-related options. You can add your custom groups to the built-in contextual tabs using the <tabSet> element within the <contextualTabs> element, like this:

```
<contextualTabs>
   <tabSet idMso="TabSetTableTools">
      <tab idMso="TabTableToolsDesign">
         <group id="CustomTools">
            <button id="btnID1"/>
         </group>
      </tab>
   </tabSet>
</contextualTabs>
```

Using Various Controls in Ribbon Customizations

By now, you should know how to go about creating the XML markup for your Ribbon customizations and applying the custom Ribbon to a workbook. Let's look at other types of controls you can show in the Ribbon.

Creating Toggle Buttons

A *toggle button* is a button that alternates between two states. Many formatting features such as Bold, Italic, or Format Painter are implemented as toggle buttons. When you click a toggle button, the button will stay down until you click it again. To create a toggle button, use the <toggleButton> XML tag as shown below:

```
<group id="GroupJK3" label="Various Controls">
 <toggleButton id="tglR1C1" label="Reference Style" size="normal"
          getPressed="onGetPressed" onAction="SwitchRefStyle" />
</group>
```

You will find the above Ribbon customization in the CustomUI14_ver03.txt file in the companion files. You can add a built-in image to the toggle button with the `imageMso` attribute or use a custom image as discussed earlier in this chapter. To find out whether or not the toggle button is pressed, include the `getPressed` attribute in your XML markup. The `getPressed` callback procedure provides two arguments: the control that was clicked and the pressed state of the toggle button.

```
Sub onGetPressed(control As IRibbonControl, ByRef pressed)
    If control.ID = "tglR1C1" Then
        pressed = False
    End If
End Sub
```

The previous callback procedure entered in a VBA code module of the Chap19_ModifyRibbon.xlsm workbook will ensure that the specified toggle button is not pressed when the Ribbon is loaded.

To perform an action when the toggle button is clicked, set the `onAction` attribute to the name of your custom callback procedure. This callback also provides two arguments: the control that was clicked and the state of the toggle button. The code below should be added to the VBA code module of the Chap19_ModifyRibbon.xlsm workbook:

```
Sub SwitchRefStyle(control As IRibbonControl, pressed As Boolean)
    If pressed Then
        Application.ReferenceStyle = xlR1C1
    Else
        Application.ReferenceStyle = xlA1
    End If
End Sub
```

If the toggle button is pressed, the value of the pressed argument will be True; otherwise, it will be False. Figure 19.13 in the next section shows a custom toggle button named Reference Style. When you click this button, the worksheet headings change to display letters or numbers. For more information on using R1C1 style references instead of A1 style, see the online help.

Creating Split Buttons, Menus, and Submenus

A *split button* is a combination of a button or toggle button and a menu. Clicking the button performs one default action, and clicking the drop-down arrow opens a menu with a list of related options to select from. To create the split button, use the <splitButton> tag. Within this tag, you need to define a <button> or a <toggleButton> control and the <menu> control, as shown in the following XML markup:

```
<splitButton id="btnSplit1" size="large">
   <button id="btnGoTo" label="Navigate To..." imageMso="GoTo" />
```

```
   <menu id="mnuGoTo" label="Spreadsheet Navigation"
itemSize="normal">
      <menuSeparator id="mnuDiv1" title="Formulas and Constants" />
         <button id="btnFormulas" label="Select Formulas"
           onAction="GoToSpecial" />
         <button id="btnNumbers" label="Select Numbers Only"
           onAction="GoToSpecial" />
         <button id="btnText" label="Select Text Only"
           onAction="GoToSpecial" />
      <menuSeparator id="mnuDiv2" title="Special Cells" />
         <button id="btnBlanks" label="Select blank cells"
           onAction="GoToSpecial" />
         <button id="btnLast" label="Select last cell"
           onAction="GoToSpecial" />
   </menu>
</splitButton>
```

You will find the above Ribbon customization in the CustomUI14_ver04.txt file in the companion files. You can specify the size of the items in the menu with the `itemSize` attribute. The <menuSeparator> tag can be used inside the menu node to break the menu into sections. Each menu segment can then be titled using the `title` attribute, as shown in the previous example. You can add the `onAction` attribute to each menu button to specify the callback procedure or macro to execute when the menu item is clicked. The above XML markup uses the following callback procedure entered in a VBA code module of the Chap19_ModifyRibbon.xlsm workbook:

```
Sub GoToSpecial(control As IRibbonControl)
    On Error Resume Next
    Range("A1").Select

    If control.id = "btnFormulas" Then
        Selection.SpecialCells(xlCellTypeFormulas, 23).Select
    ElseIf control.id = "btnNumbers" Then
        Selection.SpecialCells(xlCellTypeConstants, 1).Select
    ElseIf control.id = "btnText" Then
        Selection.SpecialCells(xlCellTypeConstants, 2).Select
    ElseIf control.id = "btnBlanks" Then
        Selection.SpecialCells(xlCellTypeBlanks).Select
    ElseIf control.id = "btnLast" Then
        Selection.SpecialCells(xlCellTypeLastCell).Select
    End If
End Sub
```

In addition to button controls, menus can contain toggle buttons, checkboxes, gallery controls, split buttons, and other menus.

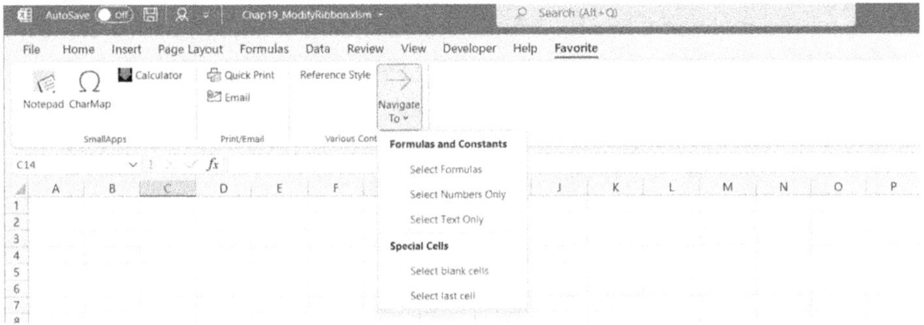

FIGURE 19.13 A toggle button (Reference Style) and a custom split button control (Navigate To) with a menu. See Chap19_ModifyRibbon_Fig13.xlsm in the companion files.

Creating Checkboxes

The checkbox control is used to show the state—either true (on) or false (off). It can be included inside a menu control or used as a separate control on the Ribbon. To create a checkbox, use the <checkBox> tag, as shown in the following XML:

```
<separator id="OtherControlsDiv1" />
    <labelControl id="TitleForBox1" label="Show or Hide Screen
     Elements" />
    <box id="boxLayout1">
        <checkBox id="chkGridlines" label="Gridlines"
                                           visible="true"
           getPressed="onGetPressed" onAction="DoSomething" />
        <checkBox id="chkFormulaBar" label="Formula Bar"
                                           visible="true"
           getPressed="onGetPressed" onAction="DoSomething" />
    </box>
```

You will find the previous Ribbon customization in the CustomUI14_ver05.txt file in the companion files. In the above XML markup, the <separator> tag will produce the vertical bar that visually separates controls within the same Ribbon group (see Figure 19.14). The <labelControl> tag can be used to display static text anywhere in the Ribbon. In this example, we use it to place a header over a set of controls. To control the layout of various controls (to display them horizontally instead of vertically), use the <box> tag. You can define whether a checkbox should be visible or hidden by setting the `visible` attribute to true or false. To disable a checkbox, set the `enabled` attribute to false; this will cause the checkbox to appear grayed out.

To get the checked state for a checkbox, add a callback procedure in the VBA Code window of the Chap19_ModifyRibbon.xlsm workbook. You can modify the onGetPressed procedure that we used earlier with the toggle button:

```
Sub onGetPressed(control As IRibbonControl, ByRef pressed)
    If control.id = "tglR1C1" Then
        pressed = False
    End If

    If control.id = "chkGridlines" And _
        ActiveWindow.DisplayGridlines = True Then
        pressed = True
    ElseIf control.id = "chkGridlines" And _
        ActiveWindow.DisplayGridlines = False Then
        pressed = False
    End If

    If control.id = "chkFormulaBar" And _
        Application.DisplayFormulaBar = True Then
        pressed = True
    ElseIf control.id = "chkFormulaBar" And _
        Application.DisplayFormulaBar = False Then
        pressed = False
    End If
End Sub
```

The action of the checkbox control is handled by the callback procedure in the `onAction` attribute. To make this checkbox example work, you need to enter the following procedure in a VBA code module of the Chap19_ModifyRibbon.xlsm workbook:

```
Sub DoSomething(ctl As IRibbonControl, pressed As Boolean)
    If ctl.id = "chkGridlines" And pressed Then
       ActiveWindow.DisplayGridlines = True
    ElseIf ctl.id = "chkGridlines" And Not pressed Then
        ActiveWindow.DisplayGridlines = False
    ElseIf ctl.id = "chkFormulaBar" And pressed Then
        Application.DisplayFormulaBar = True
    ElseIf ctl.id = "chkFormulaBar" And Not pressed Then
        Application.DisplayFormulaBar = False
    End If
End Sub
```

Similar to other controls, labels for checkboxes can contain static text in the `label` attribute as shown in the above XML, or they can be assigned dynamically using the callback procedure in the `getLabel` attribute.

NOTE	*Callback procedures don't need to be named the same as the attribute they are used with. Also, you may change the callback's argument names as desired.*

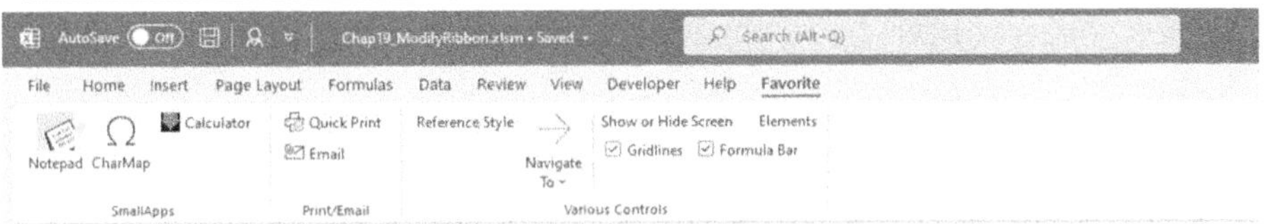

FIGURE 19.14 The checkbox controls (Gridlines and Formula Bar) are laid out horizontally. See Chap19_ModifyRibbon_Fig14.xlsm in the companion files.

Creating Edit Boxes

Use the <editBox> tag to provide an area on the Ribbon where users can type text or numbers:

```
<editBox id="txtFullName" label="First and Last Name:"
    sizeString="AAAAAAAAAAAAAAAA" maxLength="25"
    onChange="onFullNameChange" />
```

You will find the above Ribbon customization in the CustomUI14_ver06.txt file in the companion files. The `sizeString` attribute specifies the width of the edit box. Set it to a string that will give you the width you want. The `maxLength` attribute allows you to limit the number of characters and/or digits that can be typed in the edit box. If the text entered exceeds the specified number of characters (25 in this case), Excel automatically displays a balloon message on the Ribbon: "The entry may contain no more than 25 characters." When the entry is updated in an edit box control, the callback procedure specified in the `onChange` attribute is called:

```
Public Sub onFullNameChange(ctl As IRibbonControl, text As String)
  If text <> "" Then
    MsgBox "You've entered '" & text & _
        "' in the edit box."
  End If
End Sub
```

Enter the above procedure in the VBA code module of the Chap19_ModifyRibbon.xlsm workbook. When the user enters text in the edit box, the procedure will display a message box. The edit box control is shown in Figure 19.15.

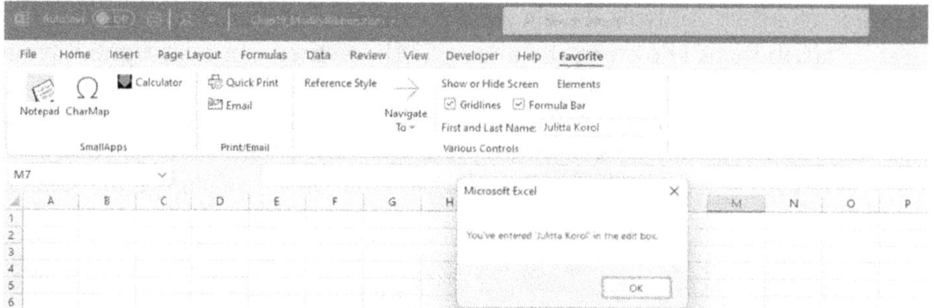

FIGURE 19.15 An edit box control allows data entry directly on the Ribbon. See Chap19_ModifyRibbon_Fig15.xlsm in the companion files.

Creating Combo Boxes and Drop-Downs

There are three types of drop-down controls that can be placed on the Ribbon: combo box, drop-down, and gallery.

These controls can be dynamically populated at runtime by writing callbacks for their `getItemCount`, `getItemID`, `getItemLabel`, `getItemImage`, `getItemScreentip`, or `getItemSupertip` attributes. The combo box and drop-down controls can also be made static by defining their drop-down content using the <item> tag, as shown below:

```
<separator id="OtherControlsDiv2" />
  <comboBox id="cboDepartment" label="Departments"
         supertip="Select  Department" onChange="onChangeDept">
        <item id="Marketing" label="Marketing" />
        <item id="Sales" label="Sales" />
        <item id="Personnel" label="Personnel" />
        <item id="ResearchAndDevelopment" label="Research and
          Development" />
  </comboBox>
```

You will find the combo box Ribbon customization in the CustomUI14_ver07.txt file in the companion files. To separate the combo box control from other controls in the same Ribbon group, the previous example uses the <separator> tag. Notice that each <item> tag specifies a new drop-down row.

NOTE	*A combo box is a combination of a drop-down list and a single-line edit box, allowing the user to either type a value directly into the control or choose from the list of predefined options. Use the* `sizeString` *attribute to define the width of the edit box.*

The combo box control does not have the `onAction` attribute. It uses the `onChange` attribute that specifies the callback to execute when the item selection changes:

```
Public Sub onChangeDept(ctl As IRibbonControl, text As String)
  MsgBox "You selected " & text & " department."
End Sub
```

Notice that the `onChange` callback provides only the text of the selected item; it does not give you access to the selected index. If you need the index of the selection, use the drop-down control instead, as shown below:

```
<dropDown id="drpBoro" label="City Borough"
    supertip="Select City Borough"
    onAction="onActionBoro">
    <item id="M" label="Manhattan" />
    <item id="B" label="Brooklyn" />
    <item id="Q" label="Queens" />
    <item id="I" label="Staten Island" />
    <item id="X" label="Bronx" />
</dropDown>
```

You will also find the dropDown Ribbon customization in the CustomUI14_ver8.txt file in the companion files.

The onAction callback of the drop-down control will give you both the selected item's ID and its index:

```
Public Sub onActionBoro(ctl As IRibbonControl, _
    ByRef SelectedID As String, _
    ByRef SelectedIndex As Integer)
  MsgBox "Index=" & SelectedIndex & " ID=" & SelectedID
End Sub
```

Be sure to enter the above callback procedures in the VBA code module of the Chap19_ModifyRibbon.xlsm workbook. The combo box and a drop-down control are shown in Figures 19.16 and 19.17.

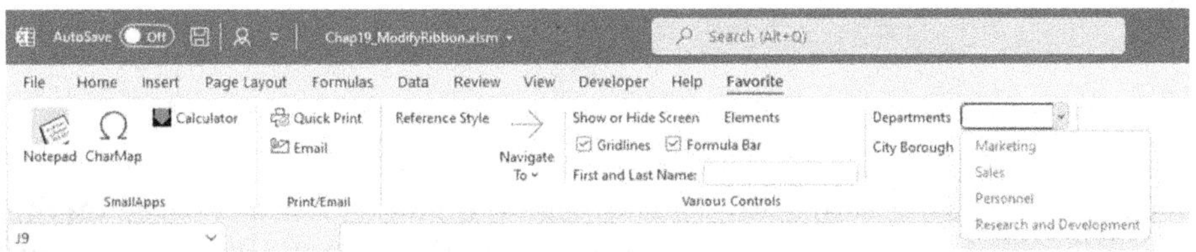

FIGURE 19.16 A combo box with a list of departments. See Chap19_ModifyRibbon_Fig16_Fig17.xlsm in the companion files.

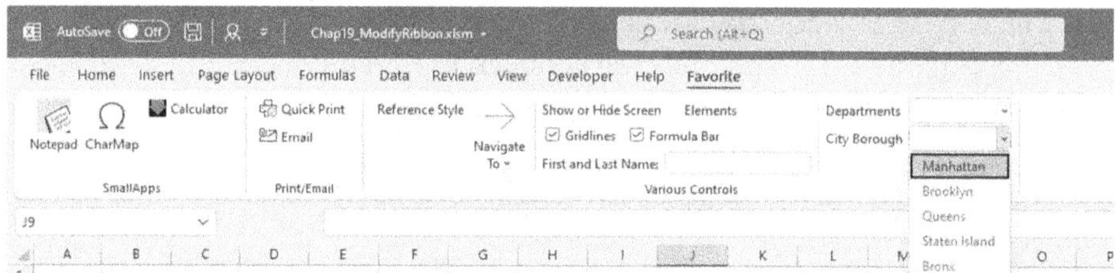

FIGURE 19.17 The City Borough combo box on the Ribbon lists the New York City boroughs. See Chap19_ModifyRibbon_Fig16_Fig17.xlsm in the companion files.

Creating a Gallery Control

A gallery control is a drop-down control that can display a grid of images with or without a label. Built-in galleries cannot be customized, but you can build your own using the <gallery> tag. The following XML markup dynamically populates a custom gallery control at runtime:

```
<gallery id="glHolidays" label="Holidays" columns="3" rows="4"
    getImage="onGetImage" getItemCount="onGetItemCount"
    getItemLabel="onGetItemLabel" getItemImage="onGetItemImage"
    getItemID="onGetItemID" onAction="onSelectedItem" />
```

You will find the Holidays gallery Ribbon customization in the CustomUI14_ver09.txt file in the companion files. In the above XML markup, the gallery control will perform the action specified in the `onSelectedItem` callback procedure. Notice that the gallery control has many attributes that contain static text or define callbacks. We will discuss them later. Right now, let's focus on the image loading process. The gallery control uses the `getImage` attribute with the `OnGetImage` callback procedure. This procedure entered in the VBA code module of the Chap19_ModifyRibbon.xlsm workbook will tell Excel to load the appropriate image to the Ribbon:

```
Public Sub onGetImage(ctl As IRibbonControl, ByRef image)
    Select Case ctl.ID
      Case "glHolidays"
         Set image = LoadPicture( _
         "C:\VBAExcel2021_ByExample\Images\Square0.gif")
    End Select
End Sub
```

Notice that the decision as to which image should be loaded is based on the ID of the control in the `Select Case` statement. The gallery control also uses the `OnGetItemImage` callback procedure (defined in the `getItemImage` attribute) to load custom images for its drop-down selection list (see Figure 19.18). Use the `columns` and `rows` attributes to specify the number of columns and rows in the gallery when it is opened. If you need to define the height and width of images in the gallery, use the `itemHeight` and `itemWidth` attributes (not used in this example due to the simplicity of the utilized images). The `getItemCount` and `getItemLabel` attributes contain callback procedures that provide information to the Ribbon on how many items should appear in the drop-down list and the names of those items. The `getItemImage` attribute contains a callback procedure that specifies the images to be displayed next to each gallery item. The `getItemID` attribute specifies the `onGetItemID` callback procedure that will provide a unique ID for each of the gallery items.

Now let's go over other VBA callbacks that are used by the gallery control. All the VBA procedures in this section need to be added to the VBA module for the previous XML markup to work:

```
Public Sub onGetItemCount(ctl As IRibbonControl, ByRef count)
  count = 12
End Sub
```

In the previous procedure, we use the `count` parameter to return to the Ribbon the number of items we want to have in the gallery control.

```
Public Sub onGetItemLabel(ctl As IRibbonControl, _
    index As Integer, ByRef label)
    label = MonthName(index + 1)
End Sub
```

The above procedure will label each of the gallery items. The VBA `MonthName` function is used to retrieve the name of the month based on the value of the index. The initial value of the index is zero (0). Therefore, `index + 1` will return January. To display an abbreviated form of the month's name (Jan, Feb, etc.), specify `True` as the second parameter to this function:

```
label = MonthName(index + 1, True)
```

If you are using a localized version of Microsoft Office (French, Spanish, etc.), the `MonthName` function will return the name of the month in the specified interface language.

The next callback procedure shows how to load images for each gallery item:

```
Public Sub onGetItemImage(ctl As IRibbonControl, _
    index As Integer, ByRef image)
  Dim imgPath As String

  imgPath = "C:\VBAExcel2021_ByExample\Images\square"
```

```
  Set image = LoadPicture(imgPath & index + 1 & ".gif")
End Sub
```

Each item in the gallery must have a unique ID, so the `onGetItemID` callback uses the `MonthName` function to use the month name as the ID:

```
Public Sub onGetItemID(ctl As IRibbonControl, _
    index As Integer, ByRef id)
  id = MonthName(index + 1)
End Sub
```

The last procedure you need to write for the Holidays gallery control should define the actions to be performed when an item in the gallery is clicked. This is done via the following `onSelectedItem` callback that was specified in the `onAction` attribute of the XML markup:

```
Public Sub onSelectedItem(ctl As IRibbonControl, _
    selectedId As String, selectedIndex As Integer)
    Select Case selectedIndex
        Case 6
            MsgBox "Holiday 1: Independence Day, July 4th", _
                vbInformation + vbOKOnly, _
                selectedId & " Holidays"
        Case 11
            MsgBox "Holiday 1: Christmas Day, December 25th", _
                vbInformation + vbOKOnly, _
                selectedId & " Holidays"
        Case Else
          MsgBox "Please program holidays for " & selectedId & ".", _
                vbInformation + vbOKOnly, _
                " Under Construction"
    End Select
End Sub
```

In the previous callback procedure, the `selectedId` parameter returns the name that was assigned to the label, while the `selectedIndex` parameter is the position of the item in the list. The first item in the list (January) is indexed with zero (0), the second one with 1, and so forth. In the previous procedure we have just coded two holidays: one for the month of July (`selectedIndex=6`) and one for December (`selectedIndex=11`). The `Case Else` clause in the `Select Case` statement provides a message when other months are selected.

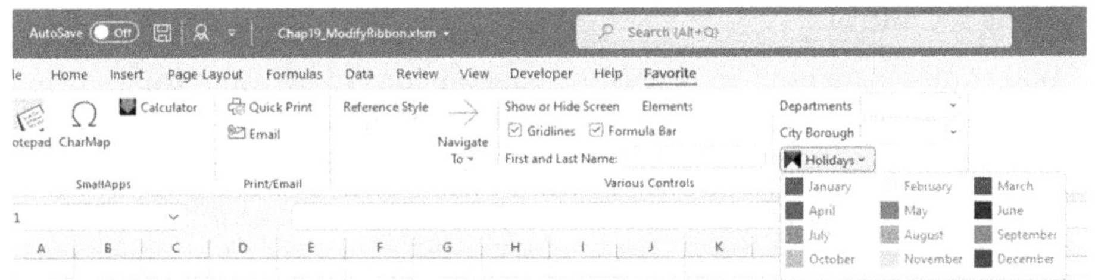

FIGURE 19.18 Customized Ribbon with the gallery control. See Chap19_ModifyRibbon_Fig18.xlsm in the companion files.

Creating a Dialog Box Launcher

On some Ribbon tabs you can see a small dialog box launcher button at the bottom-right corner of a group. You can use this button to open a special form that allows the user to set up many options at once, or you can display a form that contains specific information. To add a custom dialog box launcher button to the Ribbon, use the <dialogBoxLauncher> tag, as shown below:

```
<dialogBoxLauncher>
   <button id="Launch1" screentip="Show Auto Correct Dialog"
    onAction="onActionLaunch" />
</dialogBoxLauncher>
```

You will find the dialogBoxLauncher Ribbon customization in the CustomUI14_ver10.txt file in the companion files. The dialog box launcher control must contain a button. The `onAction` attribute for the button contains the callback procedure that will execute when the button is clicked:

```
Public Sub onActionLaunch(ctl As IRibbonControl)
  Application.Dialogs(xlDialogAutoCorrect).Show
End Sub
```

The dialog box launcher control must appear as the last element within the containing group element.

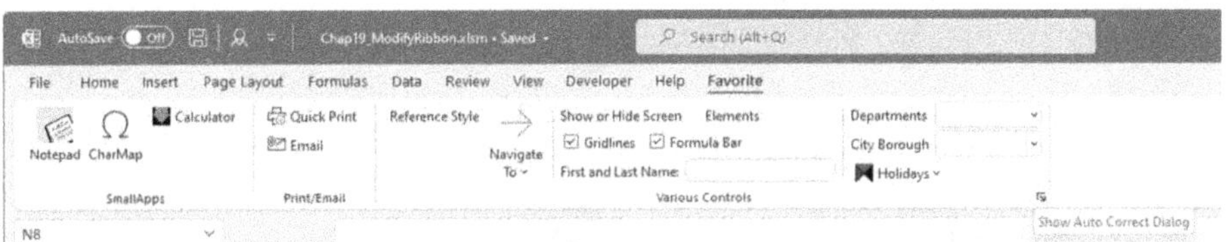

FIGURE 19.19 A dialog box launcher control on the Ribbon. See Chap19_ModifyRibbon_Fig19.xlsm in the companion files.

Disabling a Control

You can disable a built-in or custom Ribbon control by using the `enabled` or `getEnabled` attribute. The following XML markup uses the `enabled` attribute to disable our custom checkbox control that we created earlier:

```
<checkBox id="chkGridlines" label="Gridlines" visible="true"
 getPressed="onGetPressed" enabled="false" onAction="DoSomething" />
```

You can use the `getEnabled` attribute to disable a control based on some conditions. For example, the following XML markup uses the `getEnabled` attribute to disable the custom checkbox control named Formula Bar when Sheet3 is activated:

```
<checkBox id="chkFormulaBar" label="Formula Bar" visible="true"
   getPressed="onGetPressed" getEnabled="onGetEnabled"
   onAction="DoSomething" />
```

You will find the previous Ribbon customizations for checkboxes in the CustomUI14_ver11.txt file in the companion files.

The checkbox customization requires the following variable declaration at the top of the VBA module and a callback procedure in the module body:

```
Public blnEnabled As Boolean
Public Sub onGetEnabled(ctl As IRibbonControl, ByRef returnedVal)
    returnedVal = blnEnabled
End Sub
```

In addition to the previous procedure, you will need to implement the procedures and markup as explained in the "Refreshing the Ribbon" section later in this chapter.

The Sheet3 Code window of the Chap19_Ribbon.xlsm workbook should contain the following two event procedures and the declaration at the top of the VBA module (You may need to add the necessary sheets to the workbook):

```
' enter the declaration at the top of
' the Module1 code window
Public objRibbon As IRibbonUI

' enter these two procedures in Sheet3 code window
Private Sub Worksheet_Activate()
    blnEnabled = False
    objRibbon.Invalidate
    MsgBox "Formula bar checkmark is disabled in this sheet only."
End Sub
```

```
Private Sub Worksheet_Deactivate()
    blnEnabled = True
    objRibbon.Invalidate
End Sub
```

You can use a callback procedure to display a "not authorized" message when a Formulas | Name Manager Ribbon control is selected. The following XML code shows how to disable the built-in Name Manager button:

```
<!-- Built-in commands section -->
<commands>
    <command idMso="NameManager" onAction="DisableNameManager" />
</commands>
```

You will also find the NameManager command Ribbon customization in the CustomUI14_ver12.txt file in the companion files.

To make your XML code more readable, you can include comments between the <!-- and --> characters. The <command> tag can be used to refer to any built-in command. This tag must appear in the <commands> section of the XML code. To see how this works, simply add the above code fragment to the XML code shown in the previous section just before the line:

```
<ribbon startFromScratch="false">
```

The `onAction` attribute contains the following callback procedure that will display a message when the Name Manager button is clicked:

```
Sub DisableNameManager(ctl As IRibbonControl, ByRef cancelDefault)
  MsgBox "You are not authorized to use this function."
  cancelDefault = True
End Sub
```

You can add more code to the above procedure if you need to cancel the control's default behavior only when certain conditions have been satisfied. To ensure that the Ribbon customization introduced in this section works, be sure to enter all of the procedures in the VBA code module of the Chap19_ModifyRibbon.xlsm workbook.

Repurposing a Built-In Control

It is possible to change the purpose of a built-in Ribbon button. For example, when the user clicks the Picture button on the Insert tab when Sheet1 is active, you could display a Copy Picture dialog box instead of the default Insert Picture dialog box. To try this out, you need to add the following XML markup to your xml document (CustomUI14.xml):

```
<command idMso="PictureInsertFromFile" onAction="CopyPicture" />
```

You will find the previous Ribbon customization in the CustomUI14_ver13.txt file in the companion files.

The `onAction` attribute requires the following callback procedure in a VBA code module of the Chap19_ModifyRibbon.xlsm workbook:

```
Public Sub CopyPicture(ctl As IRibbonControl, _
    ByRef cancelDefault)
  If ActiveSheet.Name = "Sheet1" Then
    ' display the CopyPicture dialog box instead
    Application.Dialogs(xlDialogCopyPicture).Show
  Else
    cancelDefault = False
  End If
End Sub
```

Only simple controls that perform an action when clicked can be repurposed. You cannot repurpose advanced controls such as combo boxes, drop-downs, or galleries.

Refreshing the Ribbon

So far in this chapter you've seen how to use callback procedures to specify the values of control attributes at runtime. But what if you need to update your custom Ribbon or the controls placed in the Ribbon based on what the user is doing in your application? The good news is that you can change the attribute values at any time by using the `InvalidateControl` method of the `IRibbonUI` object. To use this object, start by adding the `onLoad` attribute to the `customUI` element in your Ribbon customization XML:

```
<customUI xmlns="http://schemas.microsoft.com/office/2009/07/
                customui"
  loadImage="OnLoadImage" onLoad="RefreshMe">
```

You will find the above Ribbon customization in the CustomUI14_ver14.txt file in the companion files.

NOTE	*When you open the Chap19_ModifyRibbon.xlsm workbook with the previous customization in Excel, you will get errors because of the missing procedures. Simply click OK to the error messages and then switch to the VBA window and enter the code as explained further in this section.*

The `onLoad` attribute points to the callback procedure that will give you a copy of the Ribbon that you can use to refresh anytime you want. In this example, the `onLoad` callback procedure name is RefreshMe. Let's say that upon entry you want the text of the edit box to appear in uppercase. Implementing the `onLoad` callback requires the Public module-level variable of type `IRibbonUI` declared earlier at the top of the VBA code module of the Chap19_ModifyRibbon.xlsm workbook:

```
Public objRibbon As IRibbonUI
```

To keep track of the state of the edit box control, declare a Private module-level variable:

```
Private strUserTxt As String
```

Next, enter the callback procedure that will store a copy of the Ribbon in the `objRibbon` variable:

```
'callback for the onLoad attribute of customUI
Public Sub RefreshMe(ribbon As IRibbonUI)
    Set objRibbon = ribbon
End Sub
```

When the Ribbon loads, you will have a copy of the IRibbonUI object saved for later use. Now let's take a look at the XML markup used in this scenario:

```
<editBox id="txtFullName" label="First and Last Name:"
   sizeString="AAAAAAAAAAAAAAAAAA" maxLength="25"
   getText="getEditBoxText" onChange="onFullNameChangeToUcase" />
```

You will find the editBox Ribbon customization in the CustomUI14_ver15.txt file in the companion files. Note that the edit box control was introduced earlier in this chapter (see Figure 19.17). You need to modify the original XML markup for the edit box by adding the `getText` attribute, which points to the following callback:

```
Public Sub getEditBoxText(control As IRibbonControl, ByRef text)
    text = UCase(strUserTxt)
End Sub
```

The above callback uses the VBA built-in `UCase` function to change the text that the user entered in the edit box to uppercase letters. When text is updated in the edit box, the procedure in the `onChange` attribute is called (be sure to change the procedure name in your original XML markup):

```
Public Sub onFullNameChangeToUcase(ByVal control As IRibbonControl, _
      text As String)
      If text <> "" Then
          strUserTxt = text
```

```
        objRibbon.InvalidateControl "txtFullName"
    End If
End Sub
```

The above callback begins by checking the value of the `text` parameter provided by the Ribbon. If this parameter contains a value other than an empty string (""), the text the user entered is stored in the `strUserTxt` variable. Before a change can occur in the Ribbon control, you need to mark the control as invalid. This is done by calling the `InvalidateControl` method of the `IRibbonUI` object that we have stored in the `objRibbon` variable:

```
objRibbon.InvalidateControl "txtFullName"
```

The above statement will tell the txtFullName control to refresh itself the next time it is displayed. When the control is invalidated, it will automatically call its callback functions. The `onFullNameChangeToUcase` callback procedure in the `onChange` attribute will execute, causing the text entered in the txtFullName edit box control to appear in uppercase letters.

NOTE	*The IRibbonUI object has only two methods:* `InvalidateControl` *and* `Invalidate`. *Use the* `InvalidateControl` *method to refresh an individual control. Use the* `Invalidate` *method to refresh all controls in the Ribbon.*

NOTE

If you find that some controls on the Favorite tab don't behave as programmed, make sure that the top of the VBA module contains the following three module-level variables and the RefreshMe procedure:

```
Public objRibbon As IRibbonUI
Private strUserTxt As String
Public blnEnabled As Boolean

'callback for the onLoad attribute of customUI
Public Sub RefreshMe(ribbon As IRibbonUI)
    Set objRibbon = ribbon
End Sub
```

Reload the Chap19_ModifyRibbon.xlsm workbook in Excel and check if the problem was resolved. All revisions we have so far implemented in this workbook are saved in Chap19_ModifyRibbon1.xslm in the companion files. You may want to check your work against this file.

The CommandBar Object and the Ribbon

You can make your custom Ribbon button match any built-in button by using the CommandBar object. This object has been extended with several get methods that expose the state information for the built-in controls: `GetEnabledMso`, `GetImageMso`, `GetLabelMso`, `GetPressedMso`, `GetScreentipMso`, `GetSupertipMso`, and `GetVisibleMso`. Use these methods in your callbacks to check the built-in control's properties. For example, the following statement will return False if the Ribbon's built-in Cut button is currently disabled (grayed out) or True if it is enabled (ready to use):

```
MsgBox Application.CommandBars.GetEnabledMso("Cut")
```

Notice that the `GetEnabledMso` method requires that you provide the name of the built-in control. To see the result of the above statement, simply type it in the Immediate window and press Enter.

The `GetImageMso` method is very useful if you'd like to reuse any of the built-in button images in your own controls. This method allows you to get the bitmap for any `imageMso` tag. For example, to retrieve the bitmap associated with the Cut button on the Ribbon, enter the following statement in the Immediate window:

```
MsgBox Application.CommandBars.GetImageMso("Cut", 16, 16)
```

The previous `GetImageMso` method uses three arguments: the name of the built-in control, and the width and height of the bitmap image in pixels. Because this method returns the `IPictureDisp` object, it is very easy to place the retrieved bitmap onto your own custom Ribbon control by writing a simple VBA callback for your control's `getImage` attribute.

In addition to the methods that provide information about the properties of the built-in controls, the `CommandBar` object also includes a handy `ExecuteMso` method that can be used to trigger the built-in control's default action. This method is quite useful when you want to perform a click operation for the user from within a VBA procedure or want to conditionally run a built-in feature.

Let's take a look at the example implementation of the `GetImageMso` and `ExecuteMso` methods. Here's the XML definition for a custom Ribbon button:

```
<button id="btnWordWizard" label="Use Thesaurus" size="normal"
   getImage="onGetBitmap" onAction="DoDefaultPlus" />
```

You will find the above Ribbon customization in the CustomUI14_ver16.txt file in the companion files. This XML code can be added to the custom Ribbon definition you've worked with in this chapter. Add it after the Reference Style toggle button.

Now let's look at the VBA part. You want the button to use the same image as the built-in button labeled ResearchPane. When the button is clicked, you'd like to display the built-in Research pane set to Thesaurus only when a certain condition is true. Here is the code you must add to your VBA module:

```
Sub onGetBitmap(ctl As IRibbonControl, ByRef image)
  Set image = Application.CommandBars.GetImageMso("ResearchPane",
     16, 16)
End Sub
```

When the Ribbon is loaded, the `onGetBitmap` callback automatically retrieves the image bitmap from the ResearchPane button's `imageMso` attribute and assigns it to the `getImage` attribute of your button. When your button is clicked and the active cell contains a text entry, the Thesaurus opens up in the Research pane; if the active cell is empty or it contains a number, the user will see a message box:

```
Sub DoDefaultPlus(ctl As IRibbonControl)
    If Not IsNumeric(ActiveCell.Value) Then
        Application.CommandBars.ExecuteMso "Thesaurus"
    Else
        MsgBox "To use Thesaurus, select a cell " & _
        "containing text.", vbOKOnly + vbInformation,
        "Action Required"
    End If
End Sub
```

Be sure to enter the above procedures in the VBA code module of the Chap19_ModifyRibbon.xlsm workbook. Figure 19.20 shows the Thesaurus button in the Various Controls group of the Favorite tab.

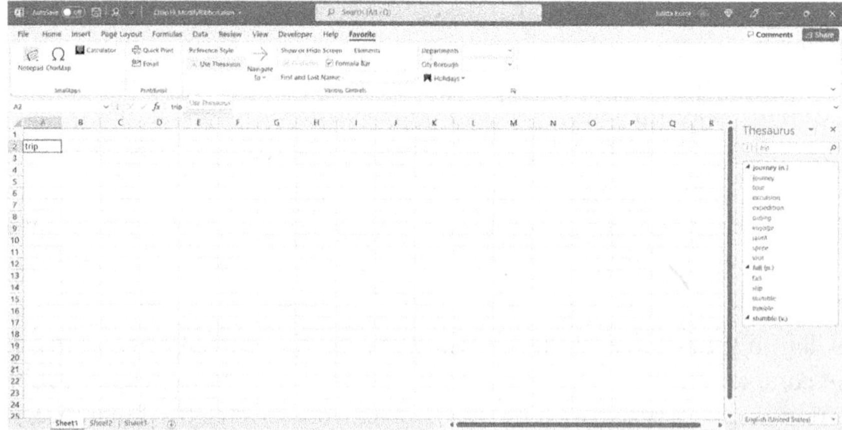

FIGURE 19.20 A custom button can conditionally trigger a built-in control's action. See Chap19_ModifyRibbon_Fig20.xlsm in the companion files.

Tab Activation and Group Auto-Scaling

Tab activation makes it possible to activate a specific tab in response to some event.

To activate a custom tab on the Excel Ribbon, use the `ActivateTab` method of the `IRibbonUI` object passing to it the ID of the custom string. For example, to activate the Favorite tab you created in this chapter, use the following statement:

```
objRibbon.ActivateTab "TabJK1"
```

Recall that `objRibbon` is the module-level Public variable we declared earlier for accessing the `IRibbonUI` object.

To activate a built-in tab, use the `ActivateTabMso` method. For example, the following statement activates the Data tab:

```
objRibbon.ActivateTabMso "TabData"
```

Finally, there is also a special `ActivateTabQ` method used to activate a tab shared between multiple add-ins. In addition to the tabID, this method requires that you specify the namespace of the add-in. The syntax is shown below:

```
expression.ActivateTabQ(tabID As String, namespace as String)
```

where `expression` returns an `IRibbonUI` object.

Keep in mind that tab activation applies only to tabs that are visible.

Group auto-scaling enables custom Ribbon groups to change their layout when the user resizes the window (see Figure 19.21).

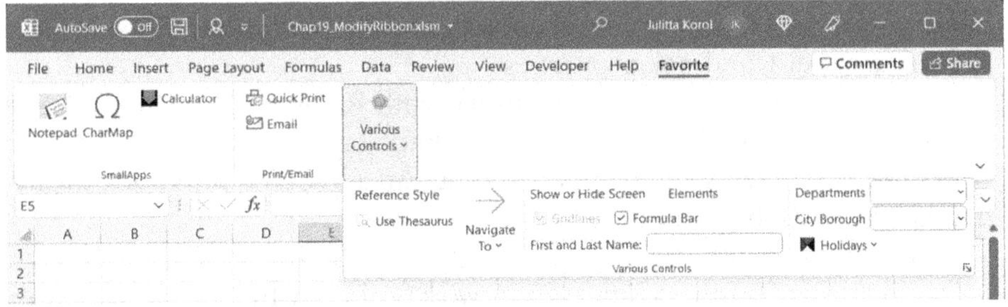

FIGURE 19.21 The commands in the Various Controls group are compressed to a single button when the Excel application window is made smaller. To change the icon that appears when the group is compressed, assign an image to the group itself.

You can enable auto-scaling by setting the `autoScale` attribute of the <group> tab to `true` as in the following:

```
<group id="GroupJK3" label="Various Controls" autoScale="true">
```

You will find the above Ribbon customization in the CustomUI14_ver17.txt file in the companion files. Notice that the value of the `autoScale` attribute is entered in lowercase. Auto-scaling is set on a per-group basis.

The completed workbook file with all Ribbon customizations that have been added up to this point can be found in the Chap19_RibbonCustomization1.xlsm workbook in the companion files.

CUSTOMIZING THE BACKSTAGE VIEW

The File tab provides an entry point to the Office UI known as Backstage View. This view is specifically designed for working with workbooks. It contains commands known as *Fast commands* that provide quick access to common functionality such as saving, opening, or closing workbooks. Here you also find the Exit command for exiting Microsoft Excel and the Options command for customizing numerous Excel features. In addition to Fast commands, the navigation bar on the left-hand side of the Backstage View includes several tabs that group related tasks. For example, clicking the Print tab in the navigation bar displays all the information related to the installed printers and allows you to easily access and change many of the print settings. A large area in the Print Backstage is used for the presentation of the workbook's Print Preview. The Info tab organizes tasks related to workbook permissions, versions, file sharing, and numerous other workbook properties.

As an Excel developer already familiar with Ribbon UI customization, you will feel very comfortable customizing the Backstage View. Like the Ribbon, the Backstage View uses XML markup that you can add to the workbook file by using the Office RibbonX Editor.

The Backstage View is a perfect place to include custom solutions that present summaries of business processes or workflows (see the sidebar with links to Microsoft documents that will walk you through the process of customizing the Office 2021 Backstage View).

In this section, you'll try a couple of simple things in the Backstage View to get your feet wet so that you can later move on to more advanced customizations with the downloads recommended in the sidebar.

SideBar ***Backstage View Development***

For an advanced introduction to the Backstage View, you may want to download the following Microsoft papers (note that 2010 versions of these docs are still applicable to the current 2021 version):

Customizing the Office 2010 Backstage View for Developers from
http://msdn.microsoft.com/en-us/library/ee815851(printer).aspx

Dynamically Changing the Visibility of Groups and Controls in the Office 2010 Backstage View
http://msdn.microsoft.com/en-us/library/ff645396(printer).aspx

The Backstage View XML markup should be entered between <backstage></backstage> elements within the <customui></customui> tags and below any Ribbon customization markup. The following XML markup adds a custom button named Synchronize and a custom tab named Endless Possibilities to the Backstage View:

```
<backstage>
    <button id="btnSync" label="Synchronize" imageMso="SyncNow"
       isDefinitive="true"
    insertBeforeMso="FileClose" onAction="onActionCopyToArchive" />
    <tab id="mySpecialTab" label="Endless Possibilities"
       insertAfterMso="TabRecent">
     <firstColumn>
      <group id="grp01" label="Home Group" helperText="This is group
         1 help text">
            <topItems>
               <button id="myButton1" label="My button" />
            </topItems>
      </group>
      <group id="gr02" label="Cheat Sheet">
            <topItems>
               <button id="myButton2" label="Cheat Ideas" />
            </topItems>
            <bottomItems>
           <layoutContainer id="set1" layoutChildren="horizontal" >
                 <editBox id="item1" label="Cheat Item 1"  />
                 <editBox id="item2" label="Cheat Item 2"  />
              </layoutContainer>
            </bottomItems>
      </group>
    </firstColumn>
    <secondColumn>
     <group id="grpHyperlinks" label="Frequently Accessed Websites"
```

```
        visible="true">
       <primaryItem>
        <button id="top1" label="Primary Button"
            imageMso="HyperlinkProperties" />
       </primaryItem>
     <topItems>
         <button id="msft" label="Microsoft" onAction="onActionE
           xecHyperlink" />
         <layoutContainer id="set2" layoutChildren="vertical" >
           <hyperlink id="YouTube" label="http://www.YouTube.com"
                onAction="onActionExecHyperlink" />
            <hyperlink id="amazon" label="http://www.amazon.com"
                onAction="onActionExecHyperlink" />
          <hyperlink id="merc" label="http://www.merclearning.com"
                onAction="onActionExecHyperlink" />
         </layoutContainer>
     </topItems>
    </group>
   </secondColumn>
 </tab>
</backstage>
```

You will find the previous Backstage View customization in the CustomUI14_ver18.txt file in the companion files. The resulting Backstage customization is shown in Figure 19.22.

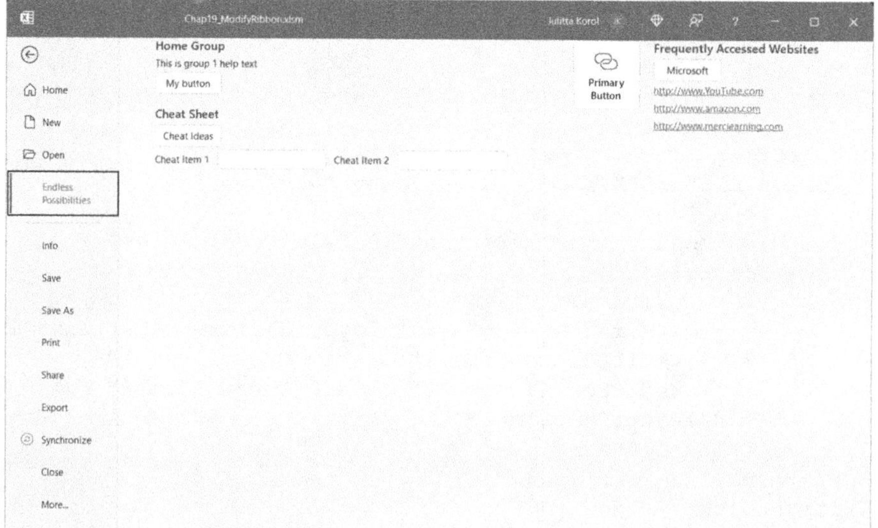

FIGURE 19.22 The Backstage View is highly customizable. The Synchronize button and the Endless Possibilities tab were created by adding some XML markup into the Ribbon customization file.

In the previous example XML markup, the <button> element is used to incorporate into the Backstage View navigation bar a custom command labeled Synchronize:

```
<button id="btnSync" label="Synchronize" imageMso="SyncNow"
isDefinitive="true"
   insertBeforeMso="FileClose" onAction="onActionCopyToArchive" />
```

The <button> element contains the `isDefinitive` attribute. When this attribute is set to `true`, clicking the button will trigger the callback procedure defined in the `onAction` attribute and then automatically close the Backstage View and return to the worksheet.

The `onAction` callback for the custom Synchronize button follows. Notice that the callback calls the CopyToArchive procedure. This procedure allows you to make a copy of the current workbook file in a folder of your choice. Be sure to enter the procedure code in the VBA code module of the Chap19_ModifyRibbon.xlsm workbook.

```
Sub onActionCopyToArchive(ctl As IRibbonControl)
    Archive
End Sub

Sub Archive()
    Dim folderName As String
    Dim MyDrive As String
    Dim BackupName As String

    Application.DisplayAlerts = False

    On Error GoTo ErrorHandler

    folderName = ActiveWorkbook.Path

    If folderName = "" Then
        MsgBox "You can't copy this file. " & Chr(13) _
            & "This file has not been saved.", _
        vbInformation, "File Archive"
    Else
        With ActiveWorkbook
            If Not .Saved Then .Save
            MyDrive = InputBox("Enter the Pathname:" & _
                Chr(13) & "(for example: D:\, " & _
                    "E:\MyFolder\, etc.)", _
                    "Archive Location?", "D:\")
```

```
                If MyDrive <> "" Then
                    If Right(MyDrive, 1) <> "\" Then
                        MyDrive = MyDrive & "\"
                    End If
                    BackupName = MyDrive & .Name
                    .SaveCopyAs Filename:=BackupName
                    MsgBox .Name & " was copied to: " _
                        & MyDrive, , "End of Archiving"
                End If
            End With
    End If
    GoTo ProcEnd
ErrorHandler:
    MsgBox "Visual Basic cannot find the " & _
        "specified path (" & MyDrive & ")" & Chr(13) & _
        "for the archive. Please try again.", _
        vbInformation + vbOKOnly, "Disk Drive or " & _
        "Folder does not exist"
ProcEnd:
    Application.DisplayAlerts = True
End Sub
```

The Backstage View XML markup also adds to the Backstage View navigation bar a custom tab labeled Endless Possibilities. Each <tab> element can have one or more columns. Our example contains two columns. Each tab can contain multiple <group> elements. Here we have two groups in the first column and one group in the second column. The Backstage group can contain different types of controls. You can group the controls into three types of sections listed as follows:

<primary item>	This element is used to specify the most important item in the group. The primary item control can be a button or a menu with buttons, toggle buttons, checkboxes, or another menu.
<topItems>	This element defines controls that will appear at the top of the group.
<bottomItems>	This element defines the controls that will appear at the bottom of the group.

The layout of controls in the Backstage View is defined using the <layoutContainer> element. This element's `layoutChildren` attribute can define the layout of controls as horizontal or vertical. The second column of our example XML markup uses the following callback procedure for the button labeled Microsoft and the three hyperlinks. Enter the following procedure in the VBA code module of the Chap19_ModifyRibbon.xlsm workbook.

```
Sub onActionExecHyperlink(ctl As IRibbonControl)
    Select Case ctl.id
        Case "YouTube"
            ThisWorkbook.FollowHyperlink Address:=
              "http://www.YouTube.com", _
                NewWindow:=True
        Case "amazon"
            ThisWorkbook.FollowHyperlink Address:=
              "http://www.amazon.com", _
                NewWindow:=True
        Case "merc"
            ThisWorkbook.FollowHyperlink Address:=
              "http://www.merclearning.com", _
                NewWindow:=True
        Case "msft"
            ThisWorkbook.FollowHyperlink Address:=
              "http://www.Microsoft.com", _
                NewWindow:=True
        Case Else
            MsgBox "You clicked control id " & ctl.id & _
              " that has not been programmed!"
    End Select
End Sub
```

SIDEBAR ***Hiding Backstage Buttons and Tabs***

The following XML will hide the Save button in the Backstage View navigation bar:

```
<button idMso="FileSave" visible="false" />
```

The Backstage View uses the following button IDs: `FileSave`, `FileSaveAs`, `FileOpen`, `FileClose`, `ApplicationOptionsDialog`, and `FileExit`.

To hide the Info tab in the Backstage, use this markup:

```
<tab idMso="TabInfo" visible="false" />
```

The Backstage View tab IDs are as follows: `TabInfo`, `TabRecent`, `TabNew`, `TabPrint`, `TabShare`, and `TabHelp`.

SIDEBAR ***Things to Remember while Customizing the Backstage View***

- The maximum number of allowed tabs is 255.
- You cannot reorder built-in tabs.
- You can add your custom tab before or after the built-in tab.
- You cannot modify the column layout of any built-in tab.

You cannot reorder built-in groups; however, you can specify the order of groups you create.

CUSTOMIZING THE QUICK ACCESS TOOLBAR (QAT)

The Quick Access toolbar that appears just above the File tab gives application users quick access to tools they use most frequently. These tools can be easily added to the toolbar by selecting More Commands from the Customize Quick Access Toolbar drop-down menu. The QAT can only be customized in the start from scratch mode by setting the `startFromScratch` attribute to `true` in the Ribbon XML customization file:

```
<ribbon startFromScratch="true">
```

When you load a workbook that contains this setting, Excel hides all built-in tabs. You must add your own custom tabs as demonstrated earlier in this chapter. QAT modifications are specified using the <qat> element. Within this element you should use the <sharedControls> element to include controls that are shared by all open workbooks, and the <documentControls> element to specify the controls that should appear in the Quick Access toolbar when the workbook has the focus. The following XML markup creates the custom Quick Access toolbar shown in Figure 19.23. You will find this code in the CustomUI_QAT.txt file located in the companion files.

```
<customUI xmlns="http://schemas.microsoft.com/office/2009/07/
               customui" >
<ribbon startFromScratch="true">
  <qat>
    <sharedControls>
      <button idMso="FilePrintQuick" />
    </sharedControls>
    <documentControls>
      <button id="btnCalc2" label="Calculator"
      imageMso="SadFace" onAction="OpenCalculator" />
```

```
    </documentControls>
  </qat>
</ribbon>
</customUI>
```

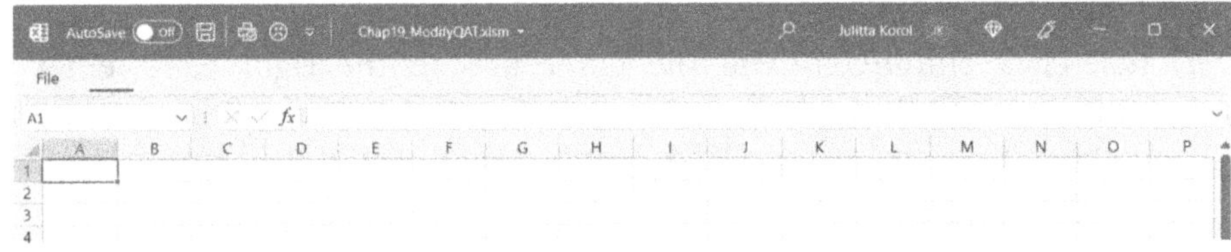

FIGURE 19.23 Customized Quick Access toolbar.

The button labeled Calculator that is represented by the SadFace image calls the OpenCalcuator procedure as shown below:

```
Public Sub OpenCalculator(ctl As IRibbonControl)
  Shell "Calc.exe", vbNormalFocus
End Sub
```

The above procedure can be found in the Chap19_ModifyQAT.xlsm file in the companion files.

MODIFYING CONTEXT MENUS USING RIBBON CUSTOMIZATIONS

You can modify context menus using the same XML markup and callbacks that you used earlier in this chapter to customize the Ribbon UI. By using the Ribbon extensibility you can add built-in and custom controls to menus and submenus as well as hide controls in built-in menus. When creating custom submenus, you can dynamically populate them with controls by using the dynamicMenu control. The following example XML markup will help you get acquainted with context menu extensibility.

Hands-On 19.6 Customizing a Context Menu

1. Launch Microsoft Excel and create a new workbook. Save this workbook as **Chap19_ContextMenu.xlsm** in your **VBAExcel2021_ByExample** folder. Be sure to save the workbook as **Excel Macro Enabled workbook (*.xlsm).**
2. Close the workbook and exit Excel.
3. Launch the **Office RibbonX Editor** that you installed and worked with earlier in this chapter.

4. Choose **File | Open.**
5. Select the **C:\VBAExcel2021_ByExample\Chap19_ContextMenu.xlsm** workbook file you created in Step 1 above and click **Open.**
6. Choose **Insert | Office 2010+ Custom UI Part.** This creates a CustomUI14.xml file in the workbook.
7. Double-click cutomUI14.xml file name and in the right pane, enter the context menu XML markup as shown in Figure 19.24. If you prefer, you can copy the code from **CustomUI14_ContextMenu.txt** in the companion files.

FIGURE 19.24 XML markup for customizing context menus.

8. Click the **Validate** button on the Office RibbonX Editor Toolbar to verify that your XML does not contain errors. You should see the message "Custom UI XML is well formed." If there are errors, you must correct them to ensure that the XML is well formed.
9. Save the file and close the Office RibbonX Editor.
10. Open the Chap19_ContextMenu.xlsm workbook in Excel and switch to the Visual Basic Editor window.
11. Choose **Insert | Module.**
12. In the Code window enter the callback procedures discussed below.
13. Switch to the Excel application window and right-click on any cell to view the custom commands added to the worksheet cell menu. Test each newly added command to ensure that it behaves as expected.

Notice that the context menu customization markup appears between the <contextMenus> </contextMenus> tags. The previous XML markup adds three new button controls and a menu control to the context menu that appears when you click on any worksheet cell. These controls are shown in Figure 19.25.

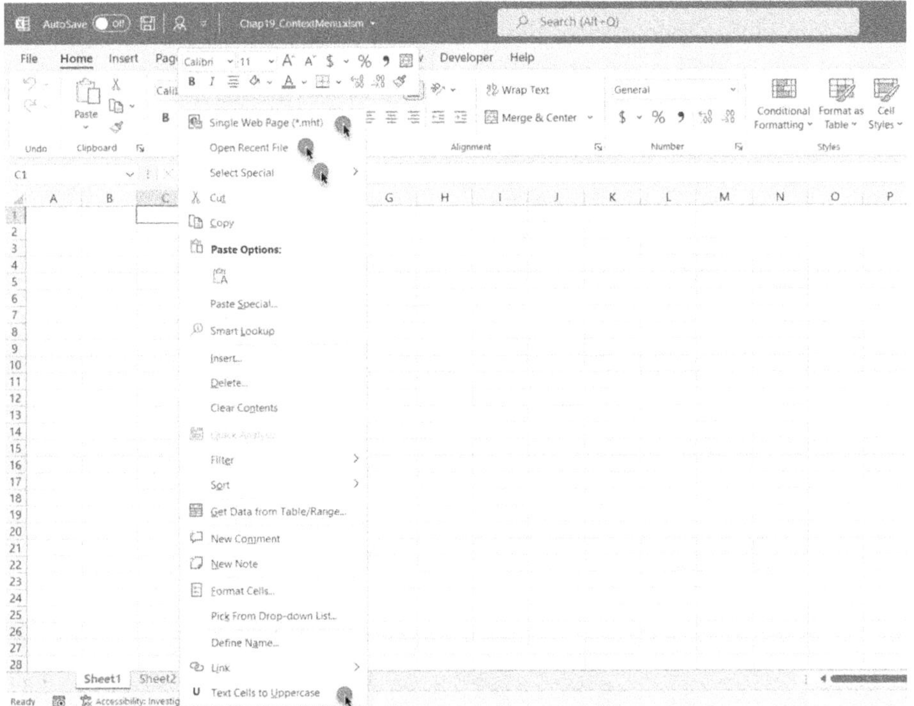

FIGURE 19.25 Standard worksheet cell context menu and the same context menu after applying the customization shown in Figure 19.24.

The first control added by the previous markup is a built-in Excel command with the `idMso` set to `FileSaveAsWebPage`. This command appears at the top of the context menu and is labeled Single Web Page (*.mht). Recall from earlier sections of this chapter that built-in commands use the `idMso` attribute while the custom commands use the `id` attribute. When clicked, this command will execute Excel's built-in action that will allow you to save the worksheet as a Web page. The second command in the previous markup adds a custom button labeled Open Recent File. When clicked, this command will run the following `onActionBuiltInCmd` callback procedure:

```
Sub onActionBuiltInCmd(ctl As IRibbonControl)
  CommandBars.ExecuteMso "FileOpenRecentFile"
End Sub
```

The onActionBuiltInCmd procedure uses the `ExecuteMso` method of the `CommandBars` object to run the built-in action assigned in Excel to the `FileOpenRecentFile` command.

The third button in the XML markup adds the custom control labeled Text Cells to Uppercase and designates the letter "U" as the keyboard accelerator. This command when clicked will convert any text cell found within the selection of cells to uppercase letters by running the following callback procedure:

```
Sub onActionUppercase(ctl As IRibbonControl)
    Dim cell As Variant
    For Each cell In Selection
      If WorksheetFunction.IsText(cell) Then
          cell.Value = UCase(cell.Value)
      End If
    Next
End Sub
```

The last command in the XML markup is a custom menu command labeled Select Special. This command when clicked displays a menu of options. When you select a menu option, the following callback procedure is executed:

```
Sub onActionSelSpec(ctl As IRibbonControl)
  Select Case ctl.ID
     Case "text"
         Selection.SpecialCells(xlCellTypeConstants, 2).Select
     Case "num"
         Selection.SpecialCells(xlCellTypeConstants, 1).Select
     Case "blank"
         Selection.SpecialCells(xlCellTypeBlanks).Select
     Case "zero"
         Dim cell As Variant
         Dim myRange As Range
         Dim foundFirst As Boolean

         foundFirst = True

         Selection.SpecialCells(xlCellTypeConstants, 1).Select
             For Each cell In Selection
                 If cell.Value = 0 Then
                     If foundFirst Then
                         Set myRange = cell
                         foundFirst = False
                     End If
                    Set myRange = Application.Union(myRange, cell)
                     End If
```

```
            Next
          myRange.Select
     Case Else
        MsgBox "Missing Case statement for control id=" & ctl.ID, _
          vbOKOnly + vbExclamation, "Check your VBA Procedure"
  End Select
End Sub
```

SUMMARY

In this chapter, you learned how to use VBA to work with built-in context menus and customize the Ribbon interface as well as the Backstage View using a combination of XML and VBA. While working with context menus, you learned about various properties and methods of the `CommandBar` object. Next, you learned how to use the Office RibbonX Editor to create XML Ribbon customization markup. You familiarized yourself with various controls that can be added to the Ribbon. You wrote VBA callback procedures in order to set your controls' attributes at runtime. You also learned how to modify the Backstage View and the Quick Access toolbar. Finally, you learned how to manipulate the context menus via XML and VBA callbacks.

The knowledge and experience you gained in this chapter can be used to make similar customizations in all of the Microsoft 365 applications that use the Ribbon interface.

In the next chapter, we focus on writing VBA code that handles printing and sending emails.

Chapter 20 Printing and Sending Email from Excel

After you set up your worksheet, you will want people to see it. Excel provides easy-to-use commands and buttons for printing and emailing your workbooks. In addition, programmers can control these tasks with VBA code. Excel provides easy access to all print features. From the user standpoint, all printing options can be accessed in the Backstage View by selecting File | Print. When the Print command is selected, the left side of the Backstage View shows all available options for printing as well as the Print button to execute printing. You automatically see the print preview of your worksheet in the right column of this window.

In this chapter, you will work with printing features as a developer. You will learn about methods of accessing and setting printing options and displaying print preview using VBA statements. These statements will allow you also to display the Print dialog box and Print Preview window as they were present in Excel 2007. You will use these statements to automatically set printers and printing options in your VBA programs. Similar to the Ribbon, the printing features displayed in the Backstage View cannot be modified with VBA. (See Chapter 19 for more information on Ribbon and Backstage View customizations.)

In addition to printing, this chapter also demonstrates how you can automate Excel's emailing features (including sending bulk emails) with VBA. To get the most out of this chapter, you should have a network or local printer connected to your computer.

CONTROLLING THE PAGE SETUP

You can control the look of your printed worksheet pages via the Page Layout tab on the Ribbon. The Page Layout tab, shown in Figure 20.1, is divided into groups that include settings related to page setup (margins, orientation, and size), scaling, and sheet options.

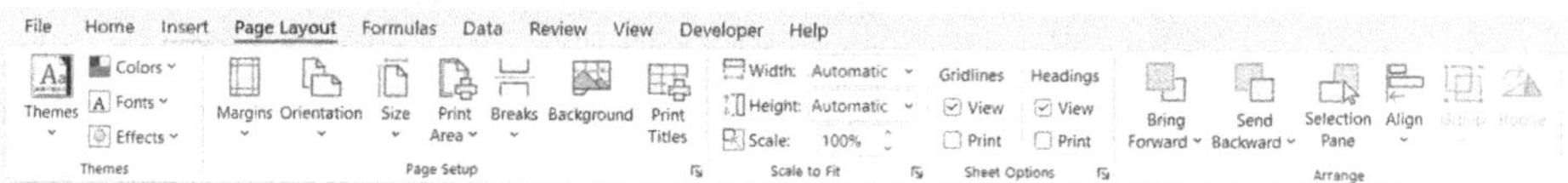

FIGURE 20.1 The Page Layout tab allows you to specify the page margins, orientation, paper size, and scaling and sheet options along with other settings.

You may programmatically access these settings via the Page Setup dialog box, using the properties of the `PageSetup` object. To display the Page Setup dialog box, type the following statement in the Immediate window and press Enter:

```
Application.Dialogs(xlDialogPageSetup).Show
```

The previous statement uses the `Show` method of the `Dialogs` object to display the built-in Page Setup dialog box. You can include a list of arguments after the `Show` method. To set initial values in the Page Setup dialog box, use the arguments in Table 20.1.

TABLE 20.1 Show method arguments for the Dialogs object

Argument Number	Argument Name
Arg1	Head
Arg2	Foot
Arg3	Left
Arg4	Right
Arg5	Top
Arg6	Bot
Arg7	Hdng
Arg8	Grid
Arg9	h_cntr
Arg10	v_cntr
Arg11	Orient
Arg12	paper_size

Argument Number	Argument Name
Arg13	Scale
Arg14	pg_num
Arg15	pg_order
Arg16	bw_cells
Arg17	Quality
Arg18	head_margin
Arg19	foot_margin
Arg20	Notes
Arg21	Draft

If you don't specify the initial settings, the Page Setup dialog box appears with its default settings. But how should you use the above arguments? If you wish to display the Page Setup dialog box with the page orientation set to landscape, use the following statement:

```
Application.Dialogs(xlDialogPageSetup).Show Arg11:=2
```

Excel uses 1 for portrait and 2 for landscape orientation.

The following statement displays the Page Setup dialog box in which the Center on page Horizontally setting is selected on the Margins tab (`Arg9:=1`), and the Page tab has the Orientation option set to Portrait (`Arg11:=1`):

```
Application.Dialogs(xlDialogPageSetup).Show Arg9:=1, Arg11:=1
```

You can also set the initial values in the Page Setup dialog box by using the `PageSetup` object with its appropriate properties. For example, to set the page orientation as landscape, type the following statements on one line in the Immediate window and press Enter:

```
ActiveSheet.PageSetup.Orientation = 2 :
   Application.Dialogs(xlDialogPageSetup).Show
```

These two statements are executed one after another. The colon indicates the end of the first statement and the beginning of another. This is a handy shortcut that can be used in the Immediate window to run a block of code.

The following sections describe various page settings (and the corresponding properties of the `PageSetup` object) you may want to specify prior to printing your worksheets.

Controlling the Settings on the Page Layout Tab

The settings on the Page Layout tab in Figure 20.1 are grouped into five main areas: Themes, Page Setup, Scale to Fit, Sheet Options, and Arrange. The Orientation settings in the Page Setup group indicate whether the page will be printed in portrait or landscape view (`Orientation` property). The Size setting lets you select one of the common paper sizes such as Letter, Legal, Executive, A4, and so on (`PaperSize` property). The options in the Scale to Fit group make it possible to adjust the printout according to your needs. You can reduce or enlarge the worksheet by using the Scale setting in the Scale to Fit group of the Page Layout tab. Excel can automatically scale a printout to fit a specified number of pages with the Width and Height settings.

To render this into VBA:	Use this statement:
Set Sheet1 to be printed in landscape orientation.	`Worksheets("Sheet1").PageSetup.Orientation = xlLandscape`
Scale Sheet1 for printing by 200%.	`Worksheets("Sheet1").PageSetup.Zoom = 200`

Scale the worksheet so it prints exactly one page tall and wide.	`With Worksheets("Sheet1").PageSetup`
	`.FitToPagesTall = 1`
	`.FitToPagesWide = 1`
	`End With`

Set the paper size to legal for Sheet1.	`Worksheets("Sheet1").PageSetup.PaperSize = xlPaperLegal`
Return current setting for the horizontal and vertical print quality.	`Debug.Print "Horizontal Print Quality = " & Worksheets("Sheet1").PageSetup.PrintQuality(1)` `Debug.Print "Vertical Print Quality = " & Worksheets("Sheet1").PageSetup.PrintQuality(2)`

Controlling the Settings on the Margins Tab

The settings available on the Margins tab of the Page Setup dialog box shown in Figure 20.2 allow you to specify the width of the top, bottom, left, and right margins (`TopMargin`, `BottomMargin`, `LeftMargin`, and `RightMargin` properties). The Header and Footer settings allow you to determine how far you'd like the header or footer to be printed from the top or bottom of the page (`HeaderMargin` and `FooterMargin` properties). The print area can be centered on the page horizontally and vertically (`CenterHorizontally` and `CenterVertically` properties).

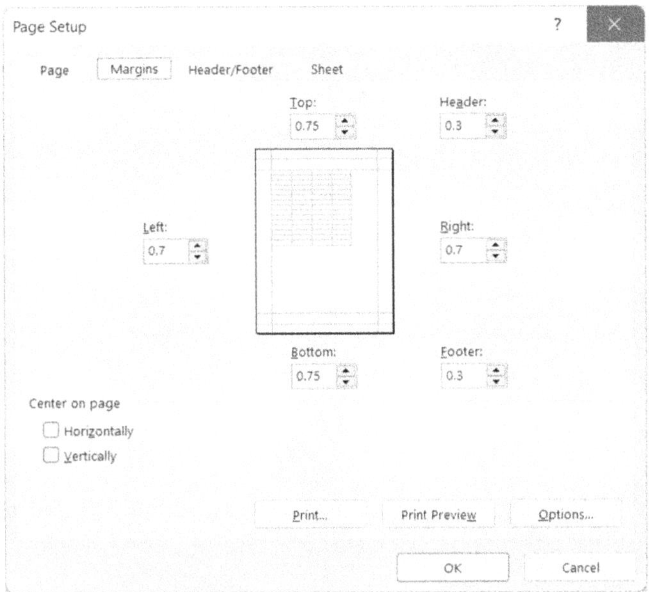

FIGURE 20.2 The settings on the Margins tab of the Page Setup dialog box determine the margins around the print area and the manner in which the print area should be centered on the printed page.

To render this into VBA:	Use this statement:

Set all page margins (left, right, top, and bottom) to 1.5 inches.	`With Worksheets("Sheet1").PageSetup`
	`    .LeftMargin = Application.InchesToPoints(1.5)`
	`    .RightMargin = Application.InchesToPoints(1.5)`
	`    .TopMargin = Application.InchesToPoints(1.5)`
	`    .BottomMargin = Application.InchesToPoints(1.5)`
	`End With`

Set header and footer margin to 0.5 inch.	`With Worksheets("Sheet1").PageSetup`
	`    .HeaderMargin = Application.InchesToPoints(0.5)`
	`    .FooterMargin =  Application.InchesToPoints(0.5)`
	`End With`

Center Sheet1 horizon-tally when it's printed.	`With Worksheets("Sheet1").PageSetup`
	`    .CenterHorizontally = True`
	`    .CenterVertically = False`
	`End With`

Controlling the Settings on the Header/Footer Tab

Figure 20.3 shows the settings on the Header/Footer tab that allow you to add built-in or custom headers and footers to your printed worksheets. You can use the Custom Header and Custom Footer buttons to design your own format for headers and footers.

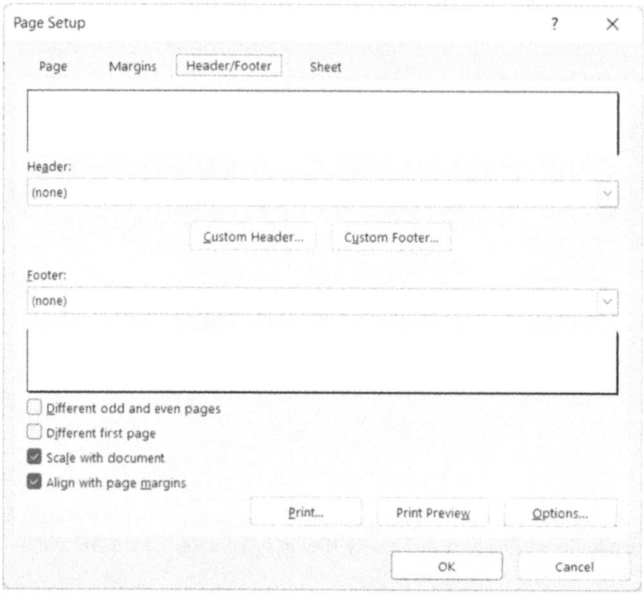

FIGURE 20.3 The Header/Footer tab of the Page Setup dialog box allows you to select one of the built-in headers or footers or create your own custom header and footer formats.

The `PageSetup` object has the following properties for setting up and controlling the creation of headers and footers: `RightHeader`, `LeftHeader`, `RightFooter`, `LeftFooter`, `CenterHeader`, `CenterFooter`, `RightHeaderPicture`, `RightFooterPicture`, `LeftHeaderPicture`, `LeftFooterPicture`, `CenterHeaderPicture`, and `CenterFooterPicture`.

The following settings are available on the Header/Footer tab of the Page Setup dialog box:

- Different odd and even pages—Use the `PageSetup.OddAndEvenPagesHeaderFooter` property. This property returns True if the specified `PageSetup` object has different headers and footers for odd-numbered and even-numbered pages.
- Different first page—Use the `PageSetup.DifferentFirstPageHeaderFooter` property. This property returns True if a different header or footer is used on the first page.

- Scale with document—Use the `PageSetup.ScaleWithDocHeaderFooter` property. This property returns True if the header and footer should use the same font size and scaling as the worksheet.
- Align with page margins—Use the `PageSetup.AlignMarginsHeaderFooter` property. This property returns True for Excel to align the header and the footer with the margins set in the page setup options.

Special formatting codes can be used in the header and footer text, as shown in Table 20.2.

TABLE 20.2 Formatting codes for headers and footers

Format Code	Description
`&L`	Left-aligns the characters that follow.
`&C`	Centers the characters that follow.
`&R`	Right-aligns the characters that follow.
`&E`	Turns double-underline printing on or off.
`&X`	Turns superscript printing on or off.
`&Y`	Turns subscript printing on or off.
`&B`	Turns bold printing on or off.
`&I`	Turns italic printing on or off.
`&U`	Turns underline printing on or off.
`&S`	Turns strikethrough printing on or off.
`&D`	Prints the current date.
`&T`	Prints the current time.
`&F`	Prints the name of the document.
`&A`	Prints the name of the workbook tab.
`&P`	Prints the page number.
`&P+number`	Prints the page number plus the specified number.
`&P-number`	Prints the page number minus the specified number.
`&&`	Prints a single ampersand.
`& "fontname"`	Prints the characters that follow in the specified font. Be sure to include the double quotation marks.
`&nn`	Prints the characters that follow in the specified font size. Use a two-digit number to specify a size in points.
`&N`	Prints the total number of pages in the document.
`&G`	Enables the image to show up in the header or footer.

To get some practice using the above codes, try the following statements:

1. Print the full path of the workbook in the upper-right corner of every page when Sheet1 is printed:

```
Worksheets("Sheet1").PageSetup.RightHeader = ActiveWorkbook.
FullName
```

2. Print the date, page number, and total number of pages on the left at the bottom of each page when Sheet1 is printed:

```
Worksheets("Sheet1").PageSetup.LeftFooter = "&D Page &P of &N"
```

3. Display a watermark in the center section of the header on Sheet1:

```
Sub ShowWaterMark()
  With Worksheets("Sheet1").PageSetup.CenterHeaderPicture
      .Filename = "C:\VBAExcel2021_ByExample\cd.bmp"
      .Height = 75
      .Width = 75
      .Brightness = 0.25
      .ColorType = msoPictureWatermark
      .Contrast = 0.45
  End With

  ' Display the picture in the center header.
    ActiveSheet.PageSetup.CenterHeader = "&G"
End Sub
```

Controlling the Settings on the Sheet Tab

The settings available on the Sheet tab of the Page Setup dialog box (shown in Figure 20.4) determine what types of data you would like to include in the printout and the order in which Excel should proceed to print data ranges if the printout will span multiple pages.

The print area is a special range that defines the cells you want to print. You can decide how much of the worksheet data you'd like to print. Excel prints the entire worksheet by default. You can print only what you actually want by defining a print area. You can specify the range address to print in the Print Area setting. If you do not specify a print area, Excel will print all the data in the current worksheet. If you specify the range of cells to print in the Print Area setting and then choose the Selection option in the Print dialog box, Excel will print the current selection of cells in the worksheet instead of the range of cells specified in the Print Area setting of the Print Setup dialog box. Use the `PrintArea` property of the `PageSetup` object to programmatically return or set the range of

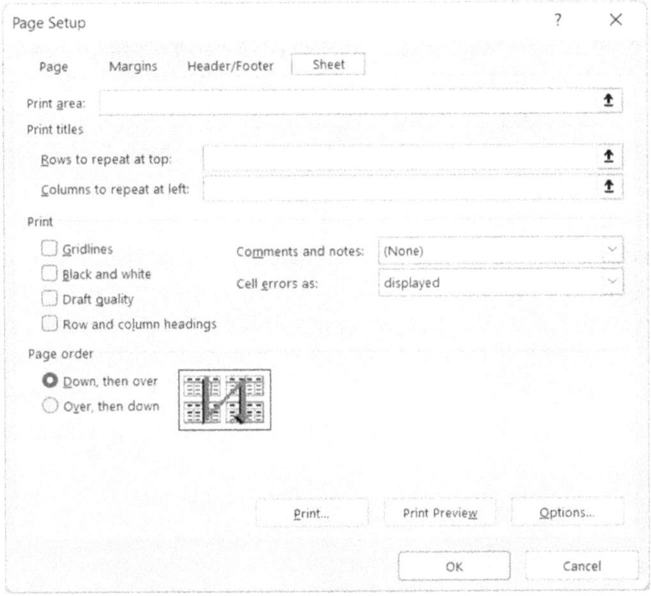

FIGURE 20.4 The Sheet tab of the Page Setup dialog box allows you to specify headings and ranges of data to appear on your printout and adjust the appearance of each page.

cells to be printed. Setting the `PrintArea` property to False or to an empty string ("") will set the print area to the entire sheet.

The Print titles area on the Sheet tab allows you to specify workbook rows that should be printed at the top of every page or workbook columns that should be printed on the left side of every page. These settings are especially useful for printing very large worksheets. By default, Excel prints your row and column titles only on the first page, making it very difficult to understand data on subsequent pages. To fix this problem, you can tell Excel to print the specified row and column headings on every page. Specify the rows that contain the cells to be repeated at the top of each page in the Rows to repeat at top setting (`PrintTitleRows` property), and specify the columns that contain cells to be repeated on the left side of each page in the Columns to repeat at left setting (`PrintTitleColumns` property). You should specify both of these settings for extremely large worksheets. To turn off the title rows or title columns, you may want to set the corresponding property (`PrintTitleRows` or `PrintTitleColumns`) to False or to an empty string ("").

The Print settings control the look of your printed pages. To print the worksheet with gridlines, check the Gridlines box (`PrintGridlines` property). To print colors as shades of gray, select the Black and white box (`BlackandWhite` property). Draft quality printing will be faster since Excel does not print gridlines and suppresses some graphics in this mode. To show row and column headings on the printed pages, check the Row and column headings box (`PrintHeadings` property). Excel will identify the rows with numbers and worksheet columns with letters or numbers, depending on the style setting in the Excel Options dialog box (choose File | Excel Options | Formulas, and see the R1C1 Reference style box). If your worksheet contains comments, you can indicate the position on the printed page where you would like to have them printed by choosing an option from the Comments drop-down box (`PrintComments` property). If the worksheet contains errors, you can suppress the display of error values when printing a worksheet by making a selection from the Cell errors as drop-down box (`PrintErrors` property). When using the `PrintErrors` property, specify how you would like errors to be displayed with one of the following constants:

- `xlPrintErrorsBlank`
- `xlPrintErrorsDash`
- `xlPrintErrorsDisplayed`
- `xlPrintErrorsNA`

The settings in the Page order area of the Sheet tab allow you to specify how Excel should print and number pages when printing large spreadsheets. The default printing order is from top to bottom. You may request this order to be changed to left to right, which is a convenient way to print wide tables. Use the `OrderProperty` of the `PageSetup` object to set or return the print order. The page order can be one of the following constants: `xlDownThenOver` or `xlOverThenDown`.

Again, here are some examples of actual statements:

1. Set the print area as cells A2:D10 on Sheet1:

```
Worksheets("Sheet1").PageSetup.PrintArea = "$A$2:$D$10"
```

2. Specify row 1 as the title row and columns A and B as title columns:

```
ActiveSheet.PageSetup.PrintTitleRows =
    ActiveSheet.Rows(1).Address
ActiveSheet.PageSetup.PrintTitleColumns = _
    ActiveSheet.Columns("A:B").Address
```

3. Print gridlines and column headings on Sheet1:

```
With Worksheets("Sheet1").PageSetup
  .PrintHeadings = True
```

```
   .PrintGridlines = True
End With
```

4. Number and print the worksheet starting from the first page to the pages to the right, and then move down and continue printing across the sheet:

```
Worksheets("Sheet1").PageSetup.Order = xlOverThenDown
```

Retrieving Current Values from the Page Setup Dialog Box

Now that you are familiar with the many settings available in the Page Setup dialog box and know the names of the corresponding properties that can be used in VBA to write code that sets up your worksheets for printing, it's time for a complete procedure. The following procedure prints some page setup settings to the Immediate window.

NOTE	*Please note files for the "Hands-On" project may be found in the companion files.*

Hands-On 20.1 Printing Page Setup Settings to the Immediate Window

1. Open a new workbook and save it as **C:\VBAExcel2021_ByExample\Chap20_VBAExcel2021.xlsm**.
2. On Sheet1, enter the data shown in Figure 20.5. The bonus values are calculated using the following formula: Months Employed * 3. Enter **=C2*3** in cell D2, **=C3*3** in cell D3, and so on.

	A	B	C	D
1	**First Name**	**Last Name**	**Months Employed**	**Bonus**
2	Kevin	Blanc	10	$30.00
3	Sylvia	Cohen	14	$42.00
4	Martha	Pilchman	34	$102.00
5	Robert	Almirez	27	$81.00
6	Mayumi	Nagasaki	18	$54.00
7	Mathew	Roder	60	$180.00
8	Myrna	Takum	16	$48.00
9				

FIGURE 20.5 Sample worksheet data.

3. Press **Alt+F11** to switch to the Visual Basic Editor. Select **VBAProject (Chap20_VBAExcel2021.xlsm)** in the Project Explorer window and choose **Insert | Module.**
4. In the Module1 Code window, enter the ShowPageSettings procedure as shown below.

```
Sub ShowPageSettings()
    With ActiveSheet.PageSetup
        Debug.Print "Orientation=" & .Orientation
        Debug.Print "Paper Size = " & .PaperSize
        Debug.Print "Print Gridlines = " & .PrintGridlines
        Debug.Print "Print Area = " & .PrintArea
    End With
End Sub
```

5. Run the ShowPageSettings procedure.
   The results of the procedure are printed to the Immediate window. Because we have not changed any settings in the Page Setup dialog box, the values you see after the equal signs are the default values.
6. Modify the ShowPageSettings procedure as follows:

```
Sub ShowPageSettings_Modified()
    With ActiveSheet.PageSetup
        Debug.Print "Orientation=" & .Orientation
        Debug.Print "Paper Size = " & .PaperSize
        Debug.Print "Print Gridlines = " & .PrintGridlines
        Cells(1, 1).Select
        .PrintArea = ActiveCell.CurrentRegion.Address
        Debug.Print "Print Area = " & .PrintArea
        .CenterHeader = Chr(10) & "Bonus Information Sheet"
    End With
    Application.Dialogs(xlDialogPrintPreview).Show
End Sub
```

7. Run the modified ShowPageSettings2 procedure.
   Now, in addition to writing selected settings to the Immediate window, the test worksheet is formatted and displayed in the Print Preview window.

When printing worksheets that contain a large number of rows, it is a good idea to separately set the print titles and print area so that each page is printed with the column titles. The following procedure demonstrates this particular scenario. Notice how the `CurrentRegion` property of the `Range` collection is used together with the Offset and Resize properties to resize the print area so that it does not include the header row (Row 1). The procedure sets the header row using the `PrintTitleRows` property of the `PageSetup` object.

```
Sub FormatSheet()
    Dim curReg As Range
    Set curReg = ActiveCell.CurrentRegion

    With ActiveSheet.PageSetup
        .PrintTitleRows = "$1:$1"
        Cells(1, 1).Select
        .PrintArea = curReg.Offset(1, 0).Resize _
            (curReg.Rows.Count - 1, curReg.Columns.Count).Address
        Debug.Print "Print Area = " & .PrintArea
        .CenterHeader = Chr(10) & "Bonus Information Sheet"
        .PrintGridlines = True
    End With
    Application.Dialogs(xlDialogPrintPreview).Show
End Sub
```

PREVIEWING A WORKSHEET

As you can see in Figure 20.6, the Page Layout view (View | Page Layout) makes it easy to see how the worksheet will print.

C:\VBAExcel2021_ByExample\Chap20_VBAExcel2021.xlsm
Bonus Information Sheet

First Name	Last Name	Months Employed	Bonus
Kevin	Blanc	10	$30.00
Sylvia	Cohen	14	$42.00
Martha	Pilchman	34	$102.00
Robert	Almirez	27	$81.00
Mayumi	Nagasaki	18	$54.00
Mathew	Roder	60	$180.00
Myrna	Takum	16	$48.00

FIGURE 20.6 To view the worksheet as it would look when printed, choose View | Page Layout.

To add a header, simply click the top area of the worksheet and type your text or click the appropriate buttons in the Design tab of the Header & Footer Tools on the Ribbon. For example, to add today's date, click the Current Date button. To add the footer, click the Go to Footer button in the Navigation group of the Header & Footer Tools Design tab.

Use the following VBA statement to activate the Page Layout view:

```
ActiveWindow.View =xlPageLayoutView
```

You can also display your worksheet in the Print Preview window by typing either one of the following statements in the Immediate window or in your VBA procedure:

```
Application.Dialogs(xlDialogPrintPreview).Show
```

or

```
Worksheets("Sheet1").PrintPreview
```

The above statements will not work if the worksheet has no data.

As you can see in Figure 20.7, there are buttons at the top of the Print Preview window that allow you to move between individual pages of your printout, make adjustments to the page setup and margins, get a closer look at the data or any part of the printout (Zoom button), and print your worksheet. If the worksheet has more than one page, you can display other pages in the Print Preview by clicking on the Next and Previous buttons or by using the keyboard (down arrow, up arrow, End, and Home keys).

You can use the Zoom button in the Print Preview window to change the Print Preview magnification, and you can adjust your page margins and column widths visually by using the mouse (to do this, select the Show Margins checkbox on the Preview area of the Ribbon). You can also print using the Print button and can easily access the Page Setup dialog box to make changes in the desired layout of your printout.

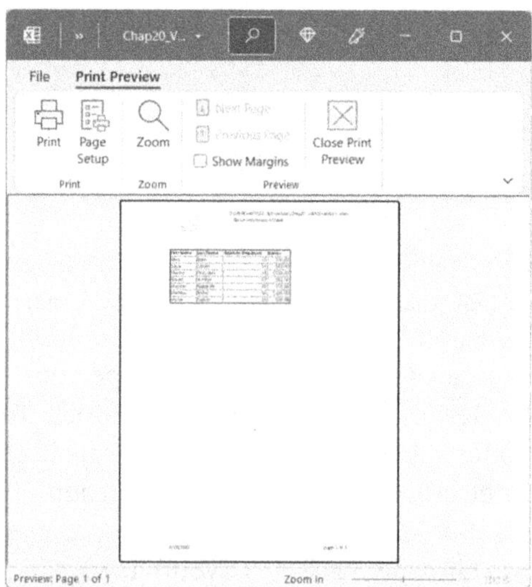

FIGURE 20.7 This Print Preview window displays a scaled-down version of the worksheet pages. Notice that this is an entirely different window from the one opened via the File | Print command or the Print Preview and Print button, which is available in the Quick Access Toolbar.

Sometimes you may want to prevent users from modifying the page setup or printing from the Print Preview window. This can be accomplished programmatically. You can disable the Show Margins and Page Setup buttons in the Print Preview window in one of the following ways:

```
Application.Dialogs(xlDialogPrintPreview).Show False
```

or

```
Worksheets("Sheet1").PrintPreview EnableChanges:=False
```

or

```
Worksheets("Sheet1").PrintPreview False
```

Figure 20.8 shows the Print Preview window with the Show Margins option and Page Setup button disabled.

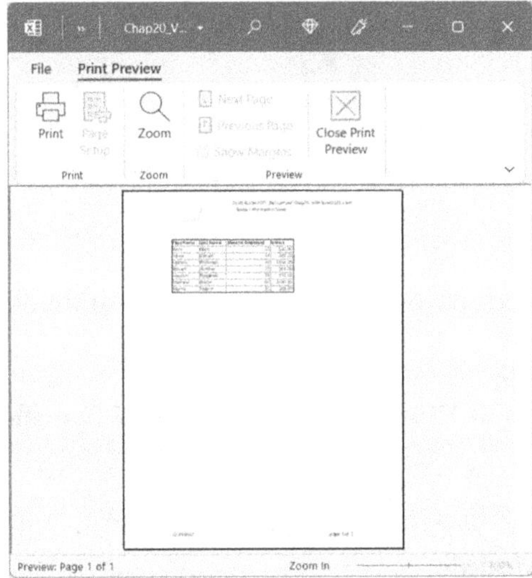

FIGURE 20.8 The Print Preview window with the disabled Page Setup and Show Margins options.

CHANGING THE ACTIVE PRINTER

Before printing, you may want to display a list of printers for the users to select from or force a print job to go to a specific printer. The Printer Setup dialog box is shown in Figure 20.9. This dialog box can be displayed with this statement:

```
Application.Dialogs(xlDialogPrinterSetup).Show
```

To find out the name of the active printer, use the ActivePrinter property of the Application object:

```
MsgBox Application.ActivePrinter
```

To change the active printer, use the following statement, replacing the printer name and port with your own:

```
Application.ActivePrinter = "Brother DCP-7065DN Printer on Ne08:"
```

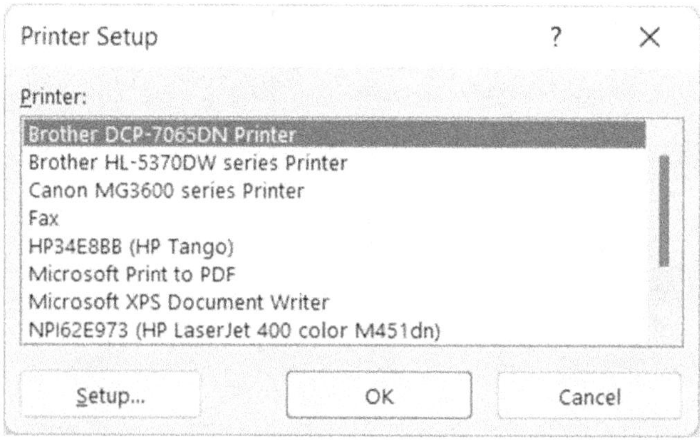

FIGURE 20.9 The Printer Setup dialog box.

You can tell Excel to set your default printer on opening a specific workbook by writing a simple Auto_Open macro.

Hands-On 20.2 Setting a Default Printer When Opening a Specific Workbook

1. In the Chap20_VBAExcel2021.xlsm workbook, switch to the Visual Basic Editor screen and choose **Insert | Module.**
2. In the module Code window, enter the Auto_Open procedure as shown below, replacing the printer's name with the name of your own printer:

```
Sub Auto_Open()
  Application.ActivePrinter = "Brother DCP-7065DN Printer on Ne08:"
  MsgBox Application.ActivePrinter
End Sub
```

   The printer needs to be connected for this code to execute.

3. Save the Chap20_VBAExcel2021.xlsm workbook and close it. Do not exit Excel.

4. Reopen the **Chap20_VBAExcel2021.xlsm** workbook.
   Excel will run the Auto_Open macro and display the active printer's name in the message box.

PRINTING A WORKSHEET WITH VBA

Prior to printing a worksheet you may want to set print options such as print ranges, collation, or the number of copies to print. This is easily done by setting appropriate options in the Print dialog box (Figure 20.10).

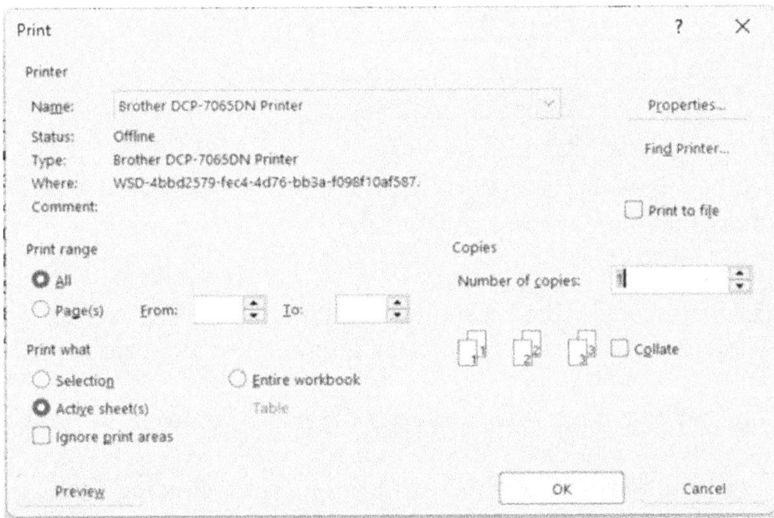

FIGURE 20.10 This Print dialog box allows you to specify various print options.

To display the Print dialog box programmatically, use the following statement:

```
Application.Dialogs(xlDialogPrint).Show
```

You can include a list of arguments after the `Show` method. To set initial values in the Print dialog box, use the arguments shown in Table 20.3.

TABLE 20.3 Show method arguments for the Print dialog

Argument Number	Argument Description
Arg1	range_num
Arg2	From
Arg3	To

(Contd.)

Argument Number	Argument Description
`Arg4`	Copies
`Arg5`	Draft
`Arg6`	Preview
`Arg7`	print_what
`Arg8`	Color
`Arg9`	Feed
`Arg10`	Quality
`Arg11`	y_resolution
`Arg12`	Selection
`Arg13`	printer_text
`Arg14`	print_to_file
`Arg15`	Collate

For example, the following statement will print pages 1 to 2 of the active worksheet (assuming that the worksheet consists of two or more pages):

```
Application.Dialogs(xlDialogPrint).Show Arg1:=2, Arg2:=1, Arg3:=2
```

The first argument specifies the Page(s) option button in the Print range area of the Print dialog box. To select the All option button in the Print range area, set `Arg1` to `1`.

The second and third arguments specify the pages you want to print (the beginning page number and the last page number to print should be specified).

To send your worksheet directly to the printer (without going through the Print dialog box), use the following statement:

```
ActiveSheet.PrintOut
```

The `PrintOut` method can take the following arguments:

TABLE 20.4 PrintOut method arguments

Argument Name	Argument Description
`From`	The number of the first page to print. If omitted, printing will start from the first page.
`To`	The number of the last page to print. If omitted, printing will end with the last page.
`Copies`	The number of copies to print. If omitted, one copy will be printed.
`Preview`	If set to `True`, Excel will display the Print Preview window before printing. If omitted or set to `False`, printing will begin immediately.

Argument Name	Argument Description
`ActivePrinter`	Sets the name of the active printer.
`PrintToFile`	If `True`, the worksheet is printed to a file. This is convenient when you want to print a worksheet on an offsite printer such as a PostScript printer. You should supply the filename in the `PrToFileName` argument.
`Collate`	Set this argument to `True` to collate multiple copies.
`PrToFileName`	Specifies the name of the file you want to print to if the `PrintToFile` argument is set to `True`.

DISABLING PRINTING AND PRINT PREVIEWING

At times you may not want to allow printing or print previewing the worksheet. You can remove these features by customizing the File tab. To disable the Print Preview window, write the Workbook_BeforePrint event procedure (see Figure 20.11 in the next section).

USING PRINTING EVENTS

Before the workbook is printed (and before the Print dialog box appears), Excel triggers the `Workbook_BeforePrint` event. You can use this event to perform certain formatting or calculating tasks prior to printing or to cancel printing and print previewing entirely when these features are requested. The code for the `Workbook_`BeforePrint event procedure must be placed in the ThisWorkbook Code window (Figure 20.11).

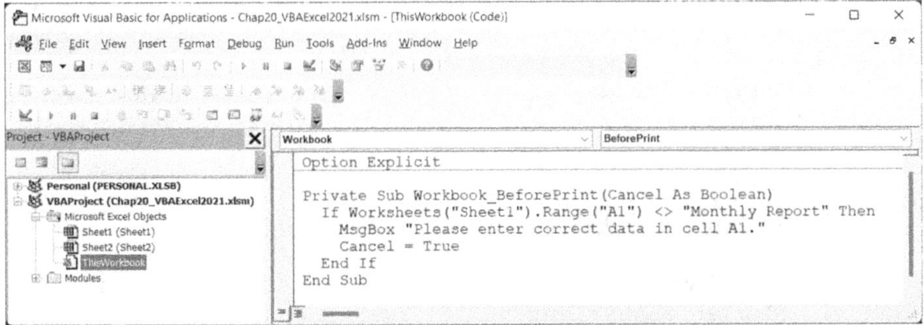

FIGURE 20.11 Writing the Workbook_BeforePrint event procedure in the ThisWorkbook Code window.

The ThisWorkbook Code window can be accessed by double-clicking the appropriate workbook name in the Project Explorer window of the Visual Basic

Editor screen and double-clicking the ThisWorkbook object. Next, at the top of the ThisWorkbook Code window, select Workbook from the Object drop-down list on the left. The Procedure drop-down list on the right will display the names of the events that the Workbook object can respond to. Select the `BeforePrint` event name; Excel will place the skeleton of this procedure in the Code window. Type your VBA code between the `Sub` and `End Sub` lines. The next time you print, Excel will run your code first and then proceed to print the worksheet. The Workbook_BeforePrint event code is triggered whether you have requested printing via Excel's built-in tools or have written your own VBA procedure to control printing.

The following tasks can be performed via the VBA code placed in the Workbook_BeforePrint event procedure:

- Disabling printing and print previewing

```
Private Sub Workbook_BeforePrint(Cancel As Boolean)
  If Weekday(Date, vbSunday) = 7 Then Cancel = True
End Sub
```

  When you set the `Cancel` argument to `True`, the worksheet isn't printed when the procedure ends. The above procedure disallows printing on Saturdays (the seventh day of the week). The `Weekday` function specifies that Sunday is the first day of the week.

- Placing the full workbook's name in the page footer
- Changing worksheet formatting prior to printing
- Validating data upon printing

```
Private Sub Workbook_BeforePrint(Cancel As Boolean)
   If Worksheets("Sheet1").Range("A1") <> "Monthly Report"
Then
    MsgBox "Please enter correct data in cell A1."
    Cancel = True
  End If
End Sub
```

- Calculating all worksheets in the active workbook

```
Private Sub Workbook_BeforePrint(Cancel As Boolean)
    Dim sh as Variant
    For Each sh in Worksheets
      sh.Calculate
    Next
End Sub
```

If you need to perform certain formatting tasks for all your workbooks prior to printing, you need to create the WorkbookBeforePrint event procedure for the Application object. You've already worked with Excel's application-level events in Chapter 15. The following example demonstrates how to have Excel automatically print in the footer the full path and filename of all existing and new workbooks.

Hands-On 20.3 Automatically Adding a Footer to Each Workbook

You will begin this Hands-On by creating the Personal.xlsb file. Macros and VBA procedures stored in this file are available each time you work with Excel. Personal Macro Workbook (Personal.xlsb) is stored in the XLStart folder. If this workbook does not already exist, Excel creates it when you record a macro and select the option to store it in the Personal Macro Workbook.

1. In the Excel Application window, choose **Developer | Record Macro.**
2. In the Record Macro dialog box, choose **Personal Macro Workbook** in the **Store macro in** drop-down list.
   The Personal macro workbook loads automatically in the background each time you start Excel.
3. Click **OK** to start recording.
   In this HandsOn you will not record anything.
4. Click the **Stop Recording** button to stop the Macro Recorder.
5. Switch to the Visual Basic Editor screen. In the Project Explorer window, select VBAProject (Personal.xlsb).
6. With the project selected, using the Properties window, rename the VBAProject **Personal**.
7. Double-click the **Personal (Personal.xlsb)** workbook.
8. In the Modules folder, right-click the **Module1** and choose **Remove Module1**. Click **No** when asked to export the module.
9. Choose **Insert | Class Module.**
   Excel inserts a module named Class1 in the Class Modules folder in the Personal (Personal.xlsb) workbook.
10. In the Properties window, rename Class1 **clsFooter**.
11. Enter the following declaration line and event procedure code in the clsFooter Code window:

```
Public WithEvents objApp As Application

Private Sub objApp_WorkbookBeforePrint(ByVal Wb As Workbook, _
```

```
    Cancel As Boolean)
  With Wb.ActiveSheet
    .PageSetup.RightFooter = Wb.FullName
  End With
End Sub
```

Recall from Chapter 15 that the `WithEvents` keyword is used in a class module to declare an object variable that points to the `Application` object. In this procedure, `objApp` is the variable name for the `Application` object. The `Public` statement before the `WithEvents` keyword allows the `objApp` variable to be accessed by all modules in the VBA project.

Once you've declared the object variable, you can select `objApp` in the Object drop-down list in the clsFooter module's Code window and select the WorkbookBeforePrint event in the Procedure drop-down list in the top-right corner of the Code window. When you start writing your event procedures using this technique (by choosing options from the Object and Procedure drop-down lists), Excel always inserts the procedure skeleton (the start and end of the procedure) in the Code window. This way you can be sure that you always start with the correct procedure structure and the definition of the parameters that the particular event can utilize. All that's left to do is write some VBA code to specify tasks that should be performed. The above procedure simply tells Excel to place the full path and filename in the right footer of the workbook's active sheet.

After writing the event procedure code in the class module, we need to write some code in the ThisWorkbook class module.

12. In the Project Explorer window, double-click the **ThisWorkbook** object located in the Microsoft Excel Objects folder under the Personal (Personal.xlsb) project.
13. Type the following declaration and event code in the ThisWorkbook Code window:

```
Dim clsFullPath As New clsFooter

Private Sub Workbook_Open()
  Set clsFullPath.objApp = Application
End Sub
```

The first line above declares a variable named `clsFullPath`, which points to the object (`objApp`) in the clsFooter class module. The `New` keyword indicates that a new instance of the object should be created the first time the object is referenced. We do this in the Workbook_Open event procedure by using the

`Set` keyword. This statement connects the object located in the clsFooter class module with the object variable `objApp` representing the `Application` object.

The code placed in the Workbook_Open event procedure is run whenever a workbook is opened. Therefore, when a workbook (an existing one or a new one) is opened, Excel will know that it must listen to the Application events; in particular, it must track events for the `objApp` object and execute the code of the WorkbookBeforePrint event procedure when a request for print or print preview is made through the Excel user interface or via the VBA code that is placed inside a custom printing procedure.

Before Excel can perform the programmed tasks, you must save the changes to the Personal.xlsb file and exit Excel.

14. Choose **Debug | Compile Personal** to ensure that Excel will be able to execute the VBA code you've added to the Personal.xlsb workbook. If Excel finds any errors, it will highlight the statement that you need to examine. Make the appropriate corrections and repeat the Debug | Compile Personal command. When there are no errors in the Personal.xlsb project, the Compile Personal command on the Debug menu is grayed out.
15. Close the **Chap20_VBAExcel2021.xlsm** workbook file and any other workbooks that you may have opened.
16. Exit Microsoft Excel. When Excel asks whether you'd like to save changes to the Personal.xlsb file, click **Yes**.
17. Restart Microsoft Excel. Open a new workbook and type anything in any cell on any sheet of this new workbook, then save the file as **TestFooter.xlsx**.
18. Click **File | Print**, select your printer, and click the **Print button**. When you click the Print button, Excel will execute the WorkbookBeforePrint event procedure, and your printout should include the file path in the right footer.
19. Close the **TestFooter.xlsx** workbook.
20. Open any existing workbook that did not have footers set up. Choose **File | Print**. When you print out the file, the hardcopy now includes a complete filename in the right footer.
21. Close the workbook you have opened.

NOTE	*You can modify the WorkbookBeforePrint event procedure to automatically perform other tasks as needed prior to printing. Save yourself time by delegating as many tasks as possible to Excel.*

SENDING EMAIL FROM EXCEL

You can share your Excel workbooks with others by emailing them. To send email from Excel, you need one of the following programs:

- Microsoft Outlook
- Microsoft Live Mail
- Microsoft Exchange Client
- Any MAPI-compatible email program (MAPI stands for Messaging Application Programming Interface)

Excel workbooks can be sent as attachments in PDF/XPS format or as faxes; or you can send a link to the file stored in a shared location. When you send an email with a workbook attachment, the file is larger but the recipient can open and edit the workbook in Excel. To share a file via email, choose File | Share. You should be presented with the Share window, as shown in Figure 20.12.

FIGURE 20.12 Share options allow you to send emails from Excel.

When you select to attach a copy of Excel Workbook, Excel displays an email message window as shown in Figure 20.13.

NOTE	*You may be notified that you need to create a Microsoft Outlook profile. Follow the instructions in the message to add a profile to Outlook.*

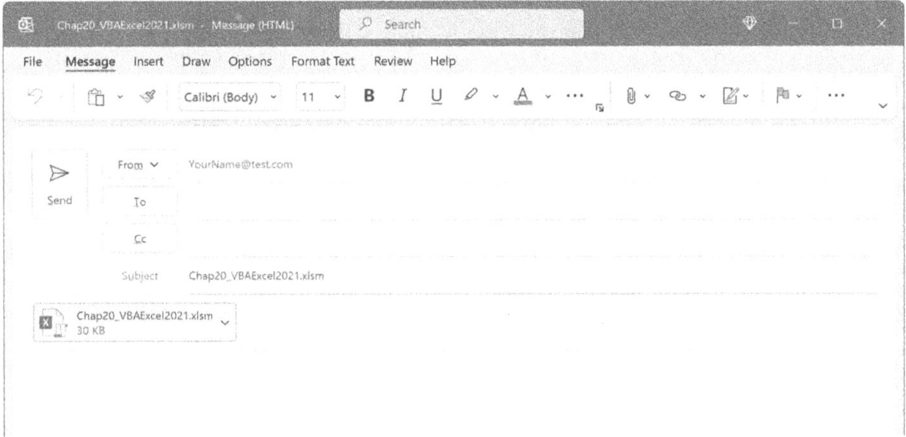

FIGURE 20.13 Sending a workbook as an email attachment from Excel.

You can invoke the email message window programmatically with the following statement:

```
Application.Dialogs(xlDialogSendMail).Show
```

You can include the arguments shown in Table 20.5 after the `Show` method.

TABLE 20.5 Show method arguments for the email message window

Argument Number	Argument Description
Arg1	Recipients
Arg2	Subject
Arg3	return_receipt

For example, the following statement displays the email message window with the recipient's email address filled in and the specified text in the subject line:

```
Application.Dialogs(xlDialogSendMail).Show
     Arg1:="SendToName@SendToProvider.com",
     Arg2:="New workbook file"
```

To check out the above statement, type the above statement on one line in the Immediate window and press Enter.

Sending Email Using the SendMail Method

Before you begin sending emails from your VBA procedures, it's a good idea to determine what email system is installed on your computer. You can do this with the `MailSystem` property of the `Application` object. This is a read-only property that uses the `xlMAPI`, `xlPowerTalk`, and `xlNoMailSystem` constants to determine the installed mail system. MAPI is used for interfacing with email systems. PowerTalk is a Macintosh email system.

The following Discover_EmailSystem procedure demonstrates how to use the MailSystem property.

```
Sub Discover_EmailSystem()
  Select Case Application.MailSystem
    Case xlMAPI
      MsgBox "You have Microsoft Mail installed."
    Case xlNoMailSystem
      MsgBox "No mail system installed on this computer."
    Case xlPowerTalk
      MsgBox "Your mail system is PowerTalk"
  End Select
End Sub
```

The easiest way to send an email from Excel is by using the `SendMail` method of the `Application` object. This method allows you to specify the email address of the recipient, the subject of your email, and whether you'd like a return receipt. Let's create an email and send it to ourselves.

Hands-On 20.4 Using the SendMail Method to Send Email

This Hands-On requires that you have a Microsoft Outlook account set up on your computer.

1. Open the **Chap20_VBAExcel2021.xlsm** workbook, switch to the Visual Basic Editor screen, and insert a new module in VBAProject (Chap20_VBAExcel2021.xlsm).
2. In the module's Code window, enter the following procedure:

```
Sub SendMailNow()
  Dim strEAddress As String

  On Error GoTo ErrorHandler

  strEAddress = InputBox("Enter e-mail address", _
      "Recipient's E-mail Address ")
```

```
  If IsNull(Application.MailSession) Then
    Application.MailLogon
  End If

  ActiveWorkbook.SendMail Recipients:=strEAddress, _
        Subject:="Test Mail"

  Application.MailLogoff
  Exit Sub

ErrorHandler:
  MsgBox "Some error occurred while sending e-mail."
End Sub
```

If Microsoft Mail isn't already running, you must use the `MailSession` property of the `Application` object to establish a mail session in Excel before sending emails. The `MailSession` property returns the MAPI mail session number as a hexadecimal string or Null if the mail session hasn't been established yet. The `MailSession` property isn't used on PowerTalk mail systems. To establish a mail session, use the `MailLogon` method of the Application object. To close a MAPI email session established by Microsoft Excel, use the `MailLogoff` method.

3. Run the SendMailNow procedure to email the active workbook. Type your email address when prompted and click **OK**.

When you see the message shown in Figure 20.14, click the **Allow** button to allow sending the email.

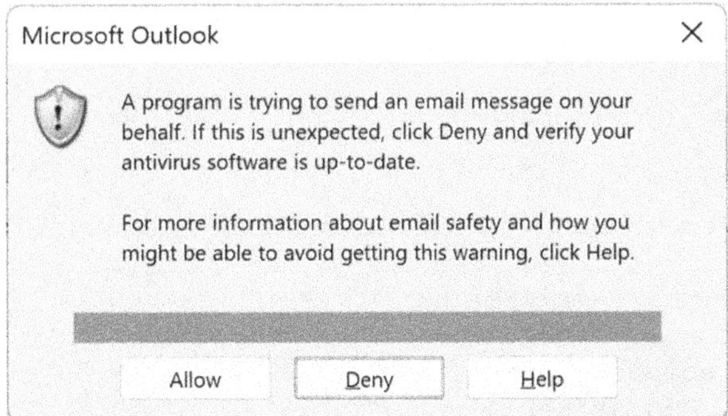

FIGURE 20.14. You will get a warning message when you try to send email from Excel.

4. Open your email program and check the received email.

When the recipient receives an email with an attached workbook, he or she will need Excel to open the file.

Sending Email Using the MsoEnvelope Object

You can send emails directly from Microsoft Excel and other Microsoft 365 applications via the `MsoEnvelope` object, which is included with the Microsoft Office 16.0 Object Library. To return an `MsoEnvelope` object, use the `MailEnvelope` property of the `Worksheet` object. You also need to set up a reference to the `MailItem` object in the Microsoft Outlook 16.0 Object Library to access its properties and methods that format the email message. The following procedure demonstrates sending email from Excel using the `MsoEnvelope` object. Instead of attaching the entire workbook, we will embed the data shown in Sheet1 (Figure 20.5 earlier in this chapter).

Hands-On 20.5 Sending Email Using the MsoEnvelope Object

1. Activate Sheet1 in the Chap20_VBAExcel2021.xlsm workbook file.
2. Press **Alt+F11** to switch to the Visual Basic Editor screen.
3. Set up a reference to the Microsoft Outlook 16.0 and Microsoft Office 16.0 object libraries using the **Tools | References** dialog box.
4. In the Visual Basic Editor screen, insert a new module in VBAProject (Chap20_VBAExcel2021.xlsm).
5. In the module's Code window, enter the following procedure:

```
Sub SendMsoMail(ByVal strRecipient As String)
' use MailEnvelope property of the Worksheet
' to return the msoEnvelope object

   ActiveWorkbook.EnvelopeVisible = True

   With ActiveSheet.MailEnvelope

        .Introduction = "Please see the list of  " & _
                   "employees who are to receive a bonus."
        With .Item
           ' Make sure the e-mail format is HTML
           .BodyFormat = olFormatHTML
           ' Add the recipient name
           .Recipients.Add strRecipient
           ' Add the subject
           .Subject = "Employee Bonuses"
           ' Send Mail
           .Send
        End With
   End With
End Sub
```

6. Run the SendMsoMail procedure by typing the following statement in the Immediate window (be sure to replace the email address with your own):

```
SendMsoMail("YourName@YourProvider.com")
```

When you press Enter, Excel calls the SendMsoMail procedure, passing to it the recipient's email address. The embedded worksheet is shown in Outlook in Figure 20.15.

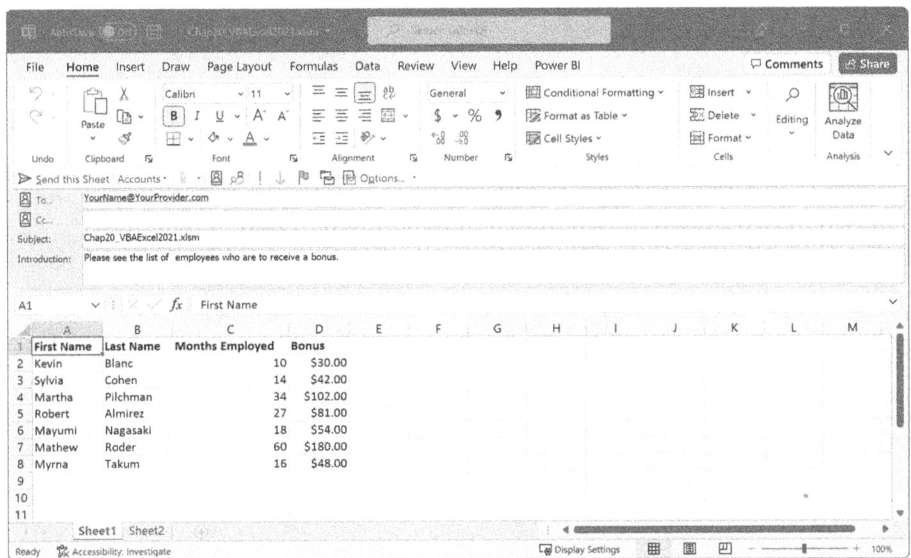

FIGURE 20.15 An email with an embedded worksheet generated by the VBA procedure in Hands-On 20.5.

Sending Bulk Email from Excel via Outlook

At times you may need to send individualized email messages to people whose email addresses and the information you want to send have been entered in a worksheet. The following procedure demonstrates how to process this kind of request from Excel via objects, properties, and methods provided by the Microsoft Outlook 16.0 Object Library.

Hands-On 20.6 Sending Bulk Email from Excel

1. Prepare the worksheet shown in Figure 20.16. Enter the valid email addresses of your own contacts in Column D. Type the names of your contacts in the Employee Name column.

	A	B	C	D
1	Employee Name	Expense Type	Amount	Email
2	Margaret Hicks	Education	$ 140.00	Mhicks@edomain.com
3	Terry Bergman	Medical	$ 234.00	Tbergman@edomain.com
4	Michael DeCastro	Transportation	$ 100.00	Mdecastro@edomin.com
5	Tony Bennet	Parking	$ 30.00	Tbennet@edomain.com
6				

FIGURE 20.16 Sample worksheet for bulk emailing demo.

2. Switch to the Visual Basic Editor screen and choose **Tools | References**. Ensure that there is a check mark next to **Microsoft Outlook 16.0 Object Library**. If the library is not yet selected, click the box next to its name. Click **OK** to close the References dialog box.
3. Choose **Insert | Module** to add a new module to VBAProject (Chap20_VBAExcel2021.xlsm).
4. In the module Code window, enter the code of the SendBulkMail procedure as shown below:

```
Sub SendBulkMail(EmailCol, BeginRow, EndRow, SubjCol, _
    NameCol, AmountCol)
  Dim objOut As Outlook.Application
  Dim objMail As Outlook.MailItem
  Dim strEmail As String
  Dim strSubject As String
  Dim strBody As String
  Dim r As Integer

  On Error Resume Next

  Application.DisplayAlerts = False

  Set objOut = New Outlook.Application

  For r = BeginRow To EndRow
      Set objMail = objOut.CreateItem(olMailItem)
      strEmail = Cells(r, EmailCol)
      strSubject = Cells(r, SubjCol) & " reimbursement"

      strBody = "Dear " & Cells(r, NameCol).Text & ":" & _
          vbCrLf & vbCrLf
      strBody = strBody & "We have approved your request for " & _
          LCase(strSubject)
      strBody = strBody & " in the amount of " & Cells(r, _
```

```
          AmountCol).Text & "."
      strBody = strBody & vbCrLf & "Please allow 3 business " & _
          "days for this"
     strBody = strBody & " amount to appear on your bank statement."
      strBody = strBody & vbCrLf & vbCrLf & " Employee Services"

      With objMail
          .To = strEmail
          .Body = strBody
          .Subject = strSubject
          .Send
      End With
  Next
  Set objOut = Nothing
  Application.DisplayAlerts = True
End Sub
```

The above procedure requires the following parameters: `EmailCol`, `BeginRow`, `EndRow`, `SubjCol`, `NameCol`, and `AmountCol`. The `EmailCol` parameter is the number of the column on the worksheet where the email address has been entered. In this example, it's the fourth column. The `BeginRow` and `EndRow` parameters specify the first and last rows of your data range. In this example, the first row we want to process is 2 and the last row is 5. `SubjCol` is the column number where the email subject is entered. In this example, it's the second column (Expense Type). `NameCol` contains the employee's name and is the first column here. `AmountCol` is the column number where the expense amount has been entered. In this example, it's the third column.

The statement `Application.DisplayAlerts = False` will cause Excel to stop displaying alert messages; however, this will not prevent Outlook's messages from appearing. Prior to specifying the details of the email, we must set up a reference to the Outlook application with the following statement:

```
Set objOut = New Outlook.Application
```

Next, we need to get data for each person to whom we need to send email. The procedure uses the `For...Next` loop to iterate through the worksheet data starting at row 2 and ending at row 5. Each time in the loop we set a reference to an Outlook `MailItem` and place the data we need for our email message in various variables. Once the procedure knows where the data is in the worksheet, we can go ahead and set the required properties of Microsoft Outlook:

```
With objMail
  .To = strEmail
```

```
  .Body = strBody
  .Subject = strSubject
  .Send
End With
```

The To property returns or sets a semicolon-delimited string list of display names for the To recipients for the Outlook item. In this example, we use one recipient for each email we send. The Body property returns or sets a string representing the text message we want to send in the email. The Subject property is used to specify the email subject. Finally, the Send method sends the email message. If you'd rather not send the email, you can view it by replacing the Send method with the Display method:

```
With objMail
  .To = strEmail
  .Body = strBody
  .Subject = strSubject
  .Display
End With
```

5. Enter Call_SendBulkMail in the same module where you entered the code of the SendBulkMail procedure:

```
Sub Call_SendBulkMail()
    SendBulkMail EmailCol:=4, _
        BeginRow:=2, _
        EndRow:=5, _
        SubjCol:=2, _
        NameCol:=1, _
        AmountCol:=3
End Sub
```

   The above procedure calls the SendBulkMail procedure and passes it the parameters indicating the column number of the recipient's address (4), the beginning and ending rows of the data (2, 5), the column where the email subject is located (2), the column containing the employee name (1), and the column number with the amount of reimbursement (3).

6. Run the Call_SendBulkMail procedure.
   Excel begins to execute the specified procedure. The first recipient listed in the worksheet should receive an email like the one shown in Figure 20.17.

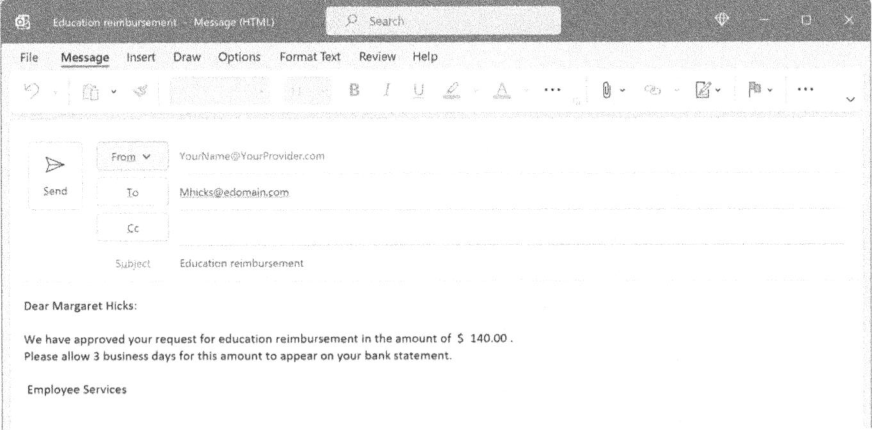

FIGURE 20.17 Sample email message viewed in Microsoft Outlook and sent by a VBA procedure in Hands-On 20.6.

SUMMARY

This chapter has shown you how to print and use various emailing techniques for the presentation and distribution of Excel workbooks. You learned how to programmatically set page and print options, set up printers, and use printing events to perform formatting or data calculation tasks prior to printing. You also practiced various methods of sending your workbooks through electronic email as attachments or embedded as the body of a message.

The next chapter focuses on using and programming Excel tables.

Part V

Excel Tools for Data Analysis

Microsoft Excel offers users powerful tools for organizing and presenting information from various sources. In this part of the book, you will learn how to work with Excel tables and how to analyze data from multiple perspectives using PivotTables and PivotCharts. In addition, you learn how to use the Get & Transform Data feature to clean, load, and shape your data.

Chapter 21 Using and Programming Excel Tables

Over the years people have used spreadsheets for storing and extracting data from databases. Currently a Microsoft Excel worksheet allows users to store as many as 1,048,576 rows by 16,384 columns. Furthermore, the data can be easily sorted, filtered, summarized, and validated. If you need to create any kind of a table and store it in a spreadsheet, this chapter's tour of Excel table management will be helpful. We will look at the user interface for the table ranges and learn how to access and work with the table feature programmatically.

UNDERSTANDING EXCEL TABLES

Tables are groups of cells that store related data and are managed separately from data in other cells on the worksheet. Tables aren't a new feature in Excel 2021; however, they were known as lists when they were first introduced in Excel 2003. You can have many tables in a worksheet, but a table cannot overlap another table. Each table is treated as a single entity and can be sorted, filtered, or shared. Tables can be easily recognized in worksheets as Excel automatically enables the filtering in the header row for each column, which you can see in Figure 21.1. You can use this feature to sort data in ascending or descending order or to create a custom view of your data.

When you create a table from a cell range and don't specify that your table contains column headers, Excel automatically adds column headers (Column1, Column2, etc.) to the range.

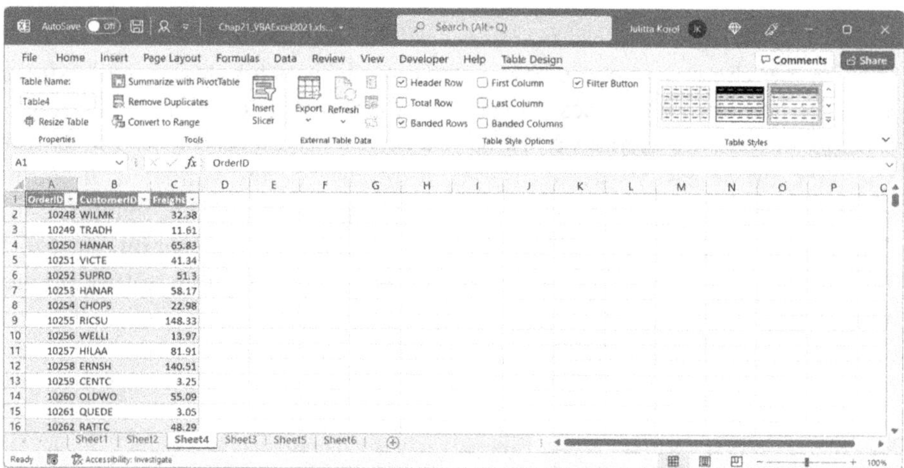

FIGURE 21.1 A table in an Excel worksheet.

To subtotal data in the table, take the following steps:

1. Convert an Excel table into a standard worksheet range. To do this, click the **Table Design** tab and select **Convert to Range** in the Tools group. Click **Yes** in the dialog box that appears.
2. Sort the data according to your needs. Select any cell in the column you want to sort by and click **Sort & Filter** in the Editing group on the Home tab. Select the desired option from the Sort & Filter menu.

3. Now to add a subtotal, click anywhere within the range, and then click **Subtotal** in the Outline group on the Data tab. You will see the Subtotal dialog box, as shown in Figure 21.2.

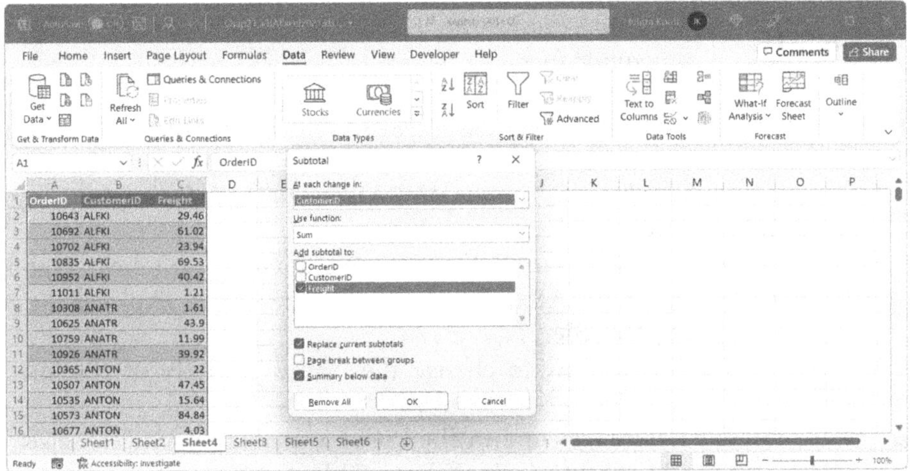

FIGURE 21.2 Use the Subtotal dialog box to subtotal Excel tables.

4. In the Subtotal dialog box, make appropriate selections:
    - In the At each change in drop-down box, choose the column by which you want to subtotal.
    - In the Use function drop-down, select a function that is appropriate for the type of summary you want to produce.
    - In the Add subtotal to drop-down, check the appropriate column.
5. Click **OK** to finish adding subtotals.

Excel cells belonging in the table can be formatted using the formatting options you are already familiar with (applying bold, underline, font color, pattern, shading, conditional formatting, and so on). Data in the table may be validated via the Data Validation button in the Data Tools group on the Data tab.

CREATING A TABLE USING BUILT-IN COMMANDS

To create a table in Excel, select a range of cells containing the data you want to include in the table and choose Insert | Table. Excel displays the Create Table dialog box shown in Figure 21.3, where you can accept the current selection of cells for the table or change the range of data for the table. To see how this is actually done, we will start by writing a VBA procedure that gets data from the Microsoft Access Northwind database (Northwind.mdb).

NOTE	*Please note files for the "Hands-On" project may be found in the companion files.*

Hands-On 21.1 Obtaining Data from a Microsoft Access Database

1. Open a new workbook and save it as **C:\VBAExcel2021_ByExample\Chap21_VBAExcel2021.xlsm**.
2. Press **Alt+F11** to switch to the Visual Basic Editor window, highlight **VBAProject (Chap21_VBAExcel2021.xlsm)** in the Project Explorer window, and choose **Insert | Module**.
3. Use the Properties window to change the Name property of Module1 to **Tables**.
4. Choose **Tools | References** and in the list of available references, select the checkbox next to **Microsoft ActiveX Data Objects Library** (6.1 or an earlier version). Next, click **OK** to exit the References dialog box.
5. In the Tables module Code window, enter the GetOrders procedure as shown below:

```
Sub GetOrders()
    Dim conn As New ADODB.Connection
    Dim rst As ADODB.Recordset
    Dim strPath As String
    Dim wks As Worksheet
    Dim j As Integer

    strPath = "C:\VBAExcel2021_ByExample\Northwind.mdb"
    Worksheets.Add
    Set wks = ThisWorkbook.ActiveSheet

    conn.Open "Provider=Microsoft.ACE.OLEDB.12.0;" _
              & "Data Source=" & strPath & ";"

    ' Create a Recordset from data in the Categories table

    Set rst = conn.Execute(CommandText:="Select OrderID," & _
               "CustomerID, Freight from Orders", _
               Options:=adCmdText)

    rst.MoveFirst
```

```
    ' transfer the data to Excel
    ' get the names of fields first

    With wks.Range("A1")
        .CurrentRegion.Clear
        For j = 0 To rst.Fields.Count - 1
            .Offset(0, j) = rst.Fields(j).Name
        Next j
        .Offset(1, 0).CopyFromRecordset rst
        .CurrentRegion.Columns.AutoFit
        .Cells(1, 1).Select
    End With
    rst.Close
    conn.Close

    Set rst = Nothing
    Set conn = Nothing

End Sub
```

6. Switch to the Microsoft Excel application window and select **Sheet1**.
7. Press **Alt+F8** to display the Macro dialog box. Highlight the **GetOrders** procedure and click **Run**.
   The data is retrieved from the Orders table and placed in a new sheet.
8. Choose **Insert | Table**.
   Microsoft Excel displays the Create Table dialog box and highlights the range of cells identified as a table, as shown in Figure 21.3. You may change the range by making your own range selection in the worksheet.

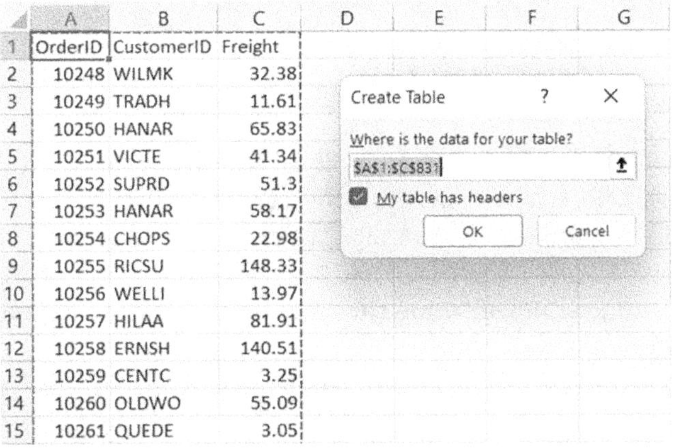

	A	B	C
1	OrderID	CustomerID	Freight
2	10248	WILMK	32.38
3	10249	TRADH	11.61
4	10250	HANAR	65.83
5	10251	VICTE	41.34
6	10252	SUPRD	51.3
7	10253	HANAR	58.17
8	10254	CHOPS	22.98
9	10255	RICSU	148.33
10	10256	WELLI	13.97
11	10257	HILAA	81.91
12	10258	ERNSH	140.51
13	10259	CENTC	3.25
14	10260	OLDWO	55.09
15	10261	QUEDE	3.05

Create Table
Where is the data for your table?
$A$1:$C$831
My table has headers
OK Cancel

FIGURE 21.3 Converting a range of cells into an Excel table.

9. Click **OK** to exit the Create Table dialog box.
   Your table is now ready to use or share with others (see Figure 21.1 earlier in this chapter).

CREATING A TABLE USING VBA

To programmatically create an Excel table, use the `ListObject` object, which represents a list object in a worksheet. The `ListObject` object is a member of the `ListObjects` collection. This collection contains all the list objects on the worksheet. As mentioned earlier, you can have one or more tables in a single worksheet.

In the previous section, you learned how to use VBA to retrieve data from Access and how to manually convert it into an Excel table using the built-in Ribbon commands. In this section, we will modify the GetOrders procedure you created in Hands-On 21.1 so that it automatically creates a table for us out of the Access data.

Hands-On 21.2 Creating a Table Using VBA

1. In the Tables module Code window, modify the GetOrders procedure as follows:
   - Add the following declaration to the procedure declaration section:

     ```
     Dim rng As Range
     ```

   - Type the following statements just before the `End Sub` keywords:

     ```
     'create a table in Excel

     Set rng = wks.Range(Range("A1").CurrentRegion.Address)
     wks.ListObjects.Add xlSrcRange, rng
     ```

   The first statement that follows the comment will set the object variable (`rng`) to point to the range of cells that we want to convert into a table. The second statement uses the Add method of the `ListObjects` collection to create a table out of a specified range of cells. The `xlSrcRange` constant specifies that the source of the table is an Excel range, while the rng object variable indicates a Range object representing the data source.

   The revised GetOrders procedure is shown below:

```
Sub GetOrders_2()
    Dim conn As New ADODB.Connection
```

```
    Dim rst As ADODB.Recordset
    Dim strPath As String
    Dim wks As Worksheet
    Dim j As Integer
    Dim rng As Range

    strPath = "C:\VBAExcel2021_ByExample\Northwind.mdb"
    Worksheets.Add
    Set wks = ThisWorkbook.ActiveSheet

    conn.Open "Provider=Microsoft.ACE.OLEDB.12.0;" _
              & "Data Source=" & strPath & ";"

    ' Create a Recordset from data in the Categories table

    Set rst = conn.Execute(CommandText:="Select OrderID," & _
               "CustomerID, Freight from Orders", _
               Options:=adCmdText)

    rst.MoveFirst

    ' transfer the data to Excel
    ' get the names of fields first
    With wks.Range("A1")
        .CurrentRegion.Clear
        For j = 0 To rst.Fields.Count - 1
            .Offset(0, j) = rst.Fields(j).Name
        Next j
        .Offset(1, 0).CopyFromRecordset rst
        .CurrentRegion.Columns.AutoFit
        .Cells(1, 1).Select
    End With
    rst.Close
    conn.Close

    Set rst = Nothing
    Set conn = Nothing

    'create a table in Excel

    Set rng = wks.Range(Range("A1").CurrentRegion.Address)
    wks.ListObjects.Add xlSrcRange, rng

End Sub
```

2. Switch to the Microsoft Excel application window.

3. Press **Alt+F8** to display the Macro dialog box. Highlight the **GetOrders_2** procedure and click **Run**.
   The data is retrieved from the Orders table and placed in a new sheet as an Excel table.

   When you use the `Add` method of the `ListObjects` collection to create an Excel table, you may specify the arguments as shown in Table 21.1.

TABLE 21.1 Arguments used with the Add method of the ListObjects collection

Argument Name	Description
SourceType (optional)	Indicates the type of data for the list. You can use one of the following source types: External data (xlSrcExternal) Excel range (xlSrcRange) XML data (xlSrcXML) If omitted, SourceType will default to xlSrcRange.
Source (optional when SourceType = xlSrcRange) (required when SourceType = xlSrcExternal)	This argument can be one of the following: An array of String values specifying a connection to the source: Use 0 to indicate the SharePoint URL. Use 1 to indicate the name of the list. Use 2 to indicate the ViewGUID (identifies the view for a list on SharePoint site). A Range object representing the data source. If this argument is omitted, Source is the range returned by list range detection code.
LinkSource (optional)	Indicates whether an external data source is to be linked to the ListObject object. The SourceType argument must be set to xlSrcExternal.
HasHeaders (optional)	Indicates whether the data to be used for the list has column labels. You can use one of the following constants for this argument: xlGuess, xlNo, or xlYes. If Source does not have column headings, Excel automatically generates headers as Column1, Column2, etc.

Argument Name	Description
Destination (required when SourceType = xlSrcExternal) (ignored when SourceType = xlSrcRange)	Indicates the top-left corner of the new list object. Use a Range object with a single-cell reference. You cannot reference more than one cell. If the destination range is not empty, new columns will be added to fit the new list (existing data will not be overwritten).

Notice that the arguments of the `ListObject` object's `Add` method are optional. If you omit the arguments, Excel will use its own logic to identify the range of cells for the table and will determine whether the table contains column headings. Contiguous cells containing data are always assumed to be a part of a table. If the first row of the identified data range contains text, Excel assumes that this is a header row.

Understanding Column Headings in the Table

When creating a table, Excel automatically adds column headings to the table. Depending on the type of data found in the first row of the data range, the first row may be designated as column headings or a new row may need to be inserted, causing other rows of data to shift down. Because you will not know exactly what Excel will do in a particular situation given a particular set of data, it is a good idea to supply the value for the `HasHeaders` argument in your VBA code, as shown in Table 21.1. Let's look at how we can control the location of the column headings in the Excel table.

Hands-On 21.3 Adding Headings to a Table

1. Insert a new sheet in the Chap21_VBAExcel2021.xlsm workbook and type the sample data shown in Figure 21.4.

	A	B	C
1			
2	EvanDeCastro	89	
3	Mathew Lambert	95	
4	Barbara O'Connor	91	
5	Lucy Moreno	83	
6			

FIGURE 21.4 Data in a spreadsheet prior to conversion into a table.

2. Switch to the Visual Basic Editor screen and enter the following procedure in the **Tables** module:

```
Sub List_Headers()
    Dim rng As Range
    Dim wks As Worksheet

    Set wks = ActiveSheet
    Set rng = wks.Range("A2:B5")

    wks.ListObjects.Add SourceType:=xlSrcRange, Source:=rng, _
      XlListObjectHasHeaders:=xlNo
End Sub
```

   Because the data in Figure 21.4 does not have column headings, we have specified `xlNo` for the `HasHeaders` argument. When Excel executes this procedure, it will add default headers (Column1, Column2) in row 2 and will shift the range down one row, as illustrated in Figure 21.5.

3. Position the insertion point anywhere within the List_Headers procedure and press **F5** to run it.
4. Switch to the Microsoft Excel application window to view the result of running the procedure.

	A	B	C
1			
2	Column1	Column2	
3	EvanDeCastro	89	
4	Mathew Lambert	95	
5	Barbara O'Connor	91	
6	Lucy Moreno	83	
7			

FIGURE 21.5 A range of data after conversion to an Excel table. Notice that Excel has added default column headings in row 2 and shifted the data range one row down.

   Sometimes you may not want Excel to shift data down when your table does not include column headings. To prevent this, it is recommended that you specify for your table a range of data in which the first row is blank. For example, to prevent Excel from shifting the data down one row, specify A1:B5 as the range and use `xlYes` for the `HasHeaders` parameter. Before trying this out, let's convert the Excel table we have just created back to a normal range.

5. Select any cell within the table on the worksheet and choose **Table Design | Convert to Range**. Click **Yes** when Excel displays a confirmation message.

Notice that after Excel creates a normal range out of a table, the default column headings are preserved.

6. Delete the headings row from this worksheet and save your changes.
7. Switch back to the Visual Basic Editor screen and, in the Tables module, enter the following List_Headers2 procedure:

```
Sub List_Headers2()
    Dim rng As Range
    Dim wks As Worksheet

    Set wks = ActiveSheet
    Set rng = wks.Range("A1:B5")

    wks.ListObjects.Add SourceType:=xlSrcRange, _
       Source:=rng, XlListObjectHasHeaders:=xlYes
End Sub
```

8. Run the List_Headers2 procedure. The results are shown in Figure 21.6.

	A	B	C
1	Column1	Column2	
2	EvanDeCastro	89	
3	Mathew Lambert	95	
4	Barbara O'Connor	91	
5	Lucy Moreno	83	
6			

FIGURE 21.6 A range of data after conversion to an Excel table. Notice that Excel has added default column headings in row 1, which was empty when we specified the range of data for the table.

Multiple Tables in a Worksheet

You have seen in the previous section how Excel shifts the cells down when the data range specified for your table does not have column headings. Because you may have more than one table in a worksheet, this behavior may cause problems when another table is placed right below the first table. Also, when you add new rows to the table, the table expands, so a conflict may occur if another table is placed in the rows below. Therefore, it is a good idea to avoid placing any data in the rows below a table.

When you have more than one table in a worksheet and want to manipulate these tables programmatically, it's a good practice to assign names to your tables so you can easily refer to them in your code. While you can always refer to a table by using its index number, names are more meaningful and easier to understand. By default Excel assigns the names Table1, Table2, Table3, etc., to the tables in a worksheet. To name a table or retrieve the name of an existing table, use the `Name` property of the `ListObject` object. For example, the following statement entered in the Immediate window returns the name of the table in the active sheet:

```
?ActiveSheet.ListObjects(1).Name
Table1
```

To rename Table1 (your table number may be different depending on how many tables you've already added to the workbook), we can simply type the following statement in the Immediate window and press Enter:

```
ActiveSheet.ListObjects(1).Name = "Student Scores"
```

Now you can refer to the first table in the active sheet as Student Scores.

The DefineTableName procedure shown below uses the `ListObjects` property to get a reference to the first table on the active sheet. Next, the Name property is used to assign a name to the referenced table.

```
Sub DefineTableName()
        Dim wks As Worksheet
        Dim lst As ListObject

        Set wks = ActiveWorkbook.Worksheets(ActiveSheet.Name)
        Set lst = wks.ListObjects(1)
        lst.Name = "1st Qtr. 2021 Student Scores"
End Sub
```

WORKING WITH THE EXCEL LISTOBJECT

The `ListObject` object represents a table on a worksheet. You can manipulate the table via the properties and methods of the `ListColumns` and `ListRows` collections.

- The `ListColumns` collection contains all the `ListColumn` objects in the specified ListObject object. Each ListColumn object is a column in the table.
- The `ListRows` collection contains all the `ListRow` objects in the specified `ListObject` object. Each `ListRow` object is a row in the table.

You can perform various operations on Excel tables using properties and methods of the `ListObject` object as shown in Tables 21.2 and 21.3.

TABLE 21.2 Properties of the ListObject object

Property Name	Description

Active	Indicates whether a list in a worksheet is currently active. Returns True or False. For example:
	`IsTblActive = ActiveSheet.ListObjects(1).active`
	`Debug.Print IsTblActive`
	There is no Activate method for the ListObject. To activate a table, you must activate a cell range within a table. For example:
	`ActiveSheet.ListObjects(1).Range.Activate`
	The above statement selects the entire range for the list.

DataBodyRange	Returns a Range object that represents the range of cells without the header row in a table. For example:
	`ActiveSheet.ListObjects(1).DataBodyRange.Select`
	or
	`dataRng = ActiveSheet.ListObjects(1). _ DataBodyRange.Address`
	`Debug.Print dataRng`

HeaderRowRange	Returns a Range object that represents the range of the header row for a table. For example, use the following statement to select the header row in the table: `ActiveSheet.ListObjects(1).HeaderRowRange.Select`
InsertRowRange	In Excel 2003, this property returns a Range object representing the insert row. This property is not supported in Excel 2007/ 2021: `ActiveSheet.ListObjects(1).InsertRowRange.Activate`

ListColumns	Returns a ListColumns collection that represents all the columns in a ListObject object. For example, the following procedure deletes the last column from the table:
	`Sub DeleteLastCol()`
	`    Dim myList As ListObject`
	`    Dim lastCol As Integer`
	
	`    Set myList = ActiveSheet.ListObjects(1)`
	`    lastCol = myList.ListColumns.Count`
	`    myList.ListColumns(lastCol).Delete`
	`End Sub`

Property Name	Description

ListRows	Returns a ListRows object that represents all the rows of data in the ListObject object. For example, the following procedure prints to the Immediate window the total number of rows in the table:
	`Sub CountListRows()`
	`  Dim objRows As ListRows`
	`  Set objRows = ActiveSheet.ListObjects(1).ListRows`
	`  Debug.Print objRows.Count`
	`End Sub`

Name	Returns or sets the name of the ListObject object. For example, use the following statement to assign a name to the first table in the active worksheet: `ActiveSheet.ListObjects(1).Name = "Student Scores"`
QueryTable	Returns the QueryTable object that provides a link for the ListObject object to the SharePoint site server.
Range	Returns a Range object that represents the range to which the specified list object applies. For example, the following statement prints to the Immediate window the range address of the entire list: `Debug.Print ActiveSheet.ListObjects(1).Range.Address`

SharePointURL	Returns a String representing the URL of the SharePoint list. Use it to find the address of the shared list after it has been published:
	`listURL = ActiveSheet.ListObjects(1).SharePointURL`
	`Debug.Print listURL`

ShowAutoFilter	Indicates whether the AutoFilter will be displayed in the header row (True or False). Use the following statement to turn off the AutoFilter mode for a given table: `ActiveSheet.ListObjects(1).ShowAutoFilter = False`
ShowTotals	Indicates whether the Total row is visible (True) or hidden (False). The following statement turns on the display of the Total row: `ActiveSheet.ListObjects(1).ShowTotals = True`
SourceType	Returns one of the XlListObjectSourceType constants indicating the current source of the table (xlSrcRange, xlSrcExternal, or xlSrcXML). Please see Table 21.1.

TotalsRowRange	Returns a range representing the Total row for the specified ListObject object:
	`Debug.Print ActiveSheet.ListObjects(1). _`
	`      TotalsRowRange.Address`

Property Name	Description
XmlMap	Returns an XmlMap object that represents the schema map used for the specified table. See Chapter 28 for more information.

TABLE 21.3 Methods of the ListObject object

Method Name	Description
Delete	Deletes the ListObject object and clears the cell data from the worksheet. If the list is linked to a SharePoint site, deleting it does not remove data on the server that is running Windows SharePoint Services. Any uncommitted changes not sent to the SharePoint list are lost when the list is deleted in Excel.
Publish	Publishes the ListObject object to a server that is running Microsoft Windows SharePoint Services. Returns a String indicating the URL of the published list on the SharePoint site. The Publish method requires two arguments: Target—This is a three-element string array that specifies the address of the SharePoint server (element 0), the name of the list (element 1), and an optional description of the list (element 2). LinkSource—A boolean value (True or False) If the ListObject object is not currently linked to a list on a SharePoint site: LinkSource = True (creates a new list on the specified SharePoint site) LinkSource = False (leaves the list object unlinked) If the ListObject object is currently linked to a SharePoint site: LinkSource = True (replaces the existing link—only one link to the list is allowed on the SharePoint site) LinkSource = False (keeps the ListObject object linked to the current SharePoint site)
Refresh	This method can be used only with tables that are linked to a SharePoint site. Retrieves the current data and schema for the table from the SharePoint server.
Resize	Allows a ListObject object to be resized over a new range. You must provide the range address as the argument to the Resize method. Assuming that the current table range is A1:B6, we can specify the new range for the table as: `ActiveSheet.ListObjects(1).Resize Range("A1:B3")`
Unlink	Removes the link to a SharePoint Services site from a list. For example: `ActiveSheet.ListObjects(1).Unlink`
Unlist	Converts an Excel table to a regular range of data. For example, the table on the active sheet is turned into a normal range like this: `ActiveSheet.ListObjects(1).Unlist`

(Contd.)

Method Name	Description

UpdateChanges	Updates the list on a Microsoft Windows SharePoint Services site with the changes made to a table in the worksheet. You can specify how list/table conflicts should be resolved by using one of the xlListConflict resolution constants:
	`xlListConflictDialog (default)`
	`xlListConflictRetryAllConflicts`
	`xlListConflictDiscardAllConflicts`
	`xlListConflictError`
	For example:
	`ActiveSheet.ListObjects(1).UpdateChanges xlListConflict-Dialog`

The following Hands-On demonstrates how to use selected properties from Table 21.2.

Hands-On 21.4 Defining Table Names

1. Enter the following procedure in the Tables module of VBAProject (Chap21_VBAExcel2021.xlsm):

```
Sub DefineTableName2()
    Dim wks As Worksheet
    Dim lst As ListObject
    Dim col As ListColumn
    Dim c As Variant

    Set wks = ActiveWorkbook.Worksheets(ActiveSheet.Name)

    Set lst = wks.ListObjects(1)
    With lst
        .Name = "1st Qtr. 2021 Student Scores"
        .ListColumns(1).Name = "Student Name"
        .ListColumns(2).Name = "Score"
        Set col = .ListColumns.Add
        col.Name = "Previous Score"
       Debug.Print "Header Address = " & .HeaderRowRange.Address
        Debug.Print "Data Range = " & .Range.Address
       Debug.Print "Data Body Range = " & .DataBodyRange.Address

        For Each c In wks.Range(.HeaderRowRange.Address)
            Debug.Print c
        Next
```

```
    End With
End Sub
```

2. Activate the sheet containing the data shown in Figure 21.6.
3. Press **Alt+F8** to display the Macro dialog box. Highlight the **DefineTable-Name2** procedure and click **Run**.
4. Check the Immediate window for the following procedure results:

```
Header Address = $A$1:$C$1
Data Range = $A$1:$C$5
Data Body Range = $A$2:$C$5
Student Name
Score
Previous Score
```

FILTERING DATA IN EXCEL TABLES USING AUTOFILTER

AutoFilter drop-down box has a great search capability (see Figure 21.7), making it easy to find data in large tables.

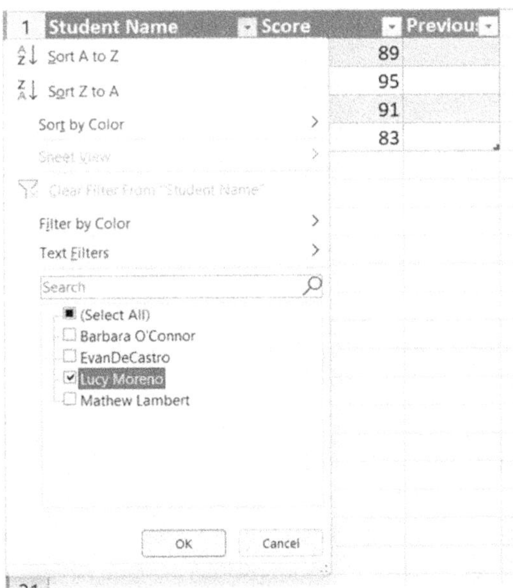

FIGURE 21.7 You can quickly navigate to specific data in the table by entering the required search criteria in the AutoFilter drop-down search box.

To find out how to use the AutoFilter feature programmatically, all you have to do is turn on the Macro Recorder and work with the AutoFilter drop-down. The following macro was recorded while searching for the record of Barbara O'Connor. To remove the filter, simply comment out the first statement in the macro code below, and uncomment the second statement.

```
Sub Macro1()
'
' Macro1 Macro
'
    ActiveSheet.ListObjects("1st Qtr. 2021 Student Scores"). _
        Range.AutoFilter Field:=1, Criteria1:="Barbara O'Connor"
   ' ActiveSheet.ListObjects("1st Qtr. 2021 Student Scores"). _
        Range.AutoFilter Field:=1
End Sub
```

To make the recorded macro more dynamic, modify it to pass a variable to the AutoFilter Criteria like this:

```
Sub Macro2()
    '
    ' Macro1 Macro
    '
    Dim strInput As String

    strInput = InputBox("Enter the search string:", "Find What")

    ActiveSheet.ListObjects("1st Qtr. 2021  Student Scores"). _
    Range.AutoFilter Field:=1, Criteria1:="=*" & strInput & "*"

  End Sub
```

FILTERING DATA IN EXCEL TABLES USING SLICERS

Slicers can be used on any Excel table. This makes filtering a table as simple as it can be. Because slicers are floating controls, they can be placed anywhere on the worksheet. The look and feel of your worksheets can be much improved by turning off the filter buttons on table headers and using colorful slicers instead to filter the data. With slicers used as your filtering controls, you can even hide columns you don't need and still be able to filter the data in the table.

To use slicers, simply select any cell in the table and click the Insert Slicers button on the Design tab of the Table Tools (Figure 21.8).

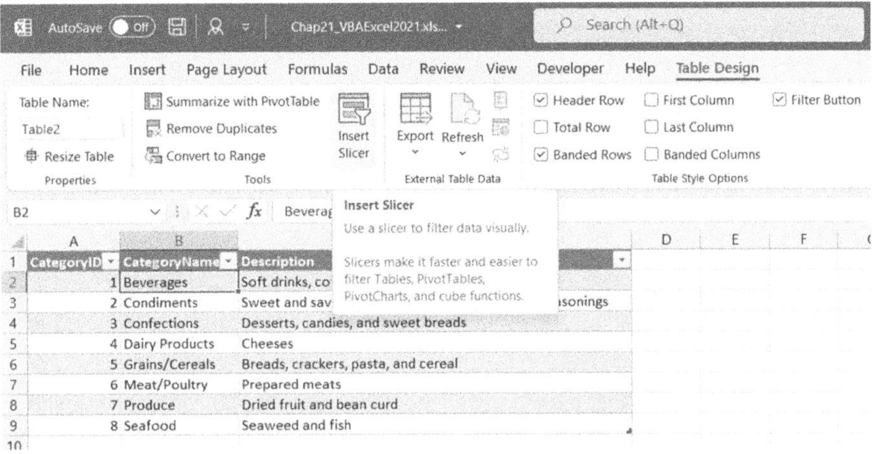

FIGURE 21.8 Inserting a slicer on a worksheet containing a table.

Excel displays the Insert Slicers dialog (Figure 21.9) where you can choose the columns you want to create slicers for. Each slicer is used to filter one column.

CategoryID	CategoryName	Description
1	Beverages	Soft drinks, coffees, teas, beers, and ales
2	Condiments	Sweet and savory sauces, relishes, spreads, and seasonings
3	Confections	Desserts, candies, and sweet breads
4	Dairy Products	Cheeses
5	Grains/Cereals	Breads, crackers, pasta, and cereal
6	Meat/Poultry	Prepared meats
7	Produce	Dried fruit and bean curd
8	Seafood	Seaweed and fish

Insert Slicers
- [ ] CategoryID
- [x] CategoryName
- [ ] Description

OK Cancel

FIGURE 21.9 Choosing columns for slicers.

When you make selections in the Insert Slicers dialog and click OK, the slicers are created and dropped on the worksheet (Figure 21.10). You can drag them anywhere you want.

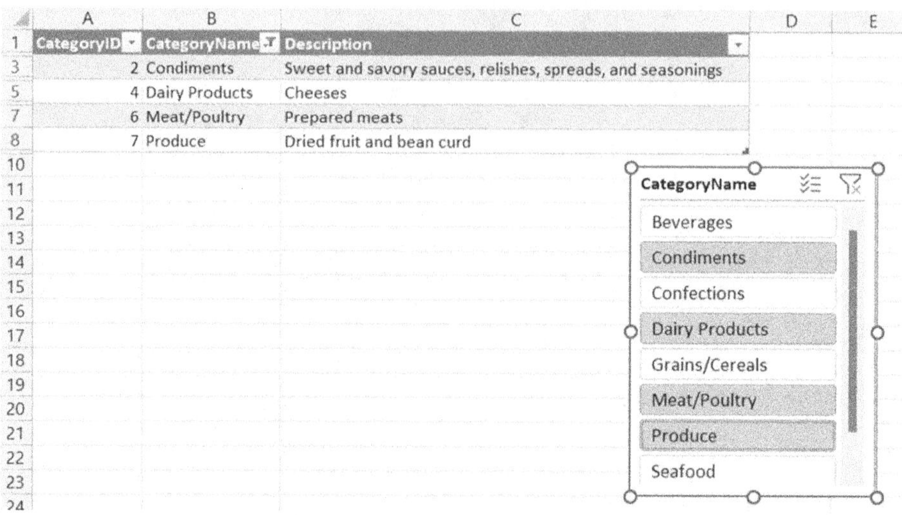

FIGURE 21.10 CategoryName Slicers used to filter an Excel table. You can select multiple buttons by holding the Shift or Ctrl key and clicking the button.

To clear the filtering from the table, click the Clear Filter icon on the top right of the slicer. This will return the table to the full view. You can change the Slicer header by typing new text in the Slicer Caption box on the Options tab. Slicer formatting styles are also controlled via buttons available on the Options tab.

You can easily control slicers with VBA. Here's an example macro created with the Excel macro recorder:

```
Sub Macro3()
'
' Macro3 Macro
'
'
    ActiveSheet.Shapes.Range(Array("CategoryName")).Select
    ActiveSheet.Shapes("CategoryName").IncrementLeft 0.75
    ActiveSheet.Shapes("CategoryName").IncrementTop 41.25
    With ActiveWorkbook.SlicerCaches("Slicer_CategoryName")
        .SlicerItems("Dairy Products").Selected = True
        .SlicerItems("Beverages").Selected = False
        .SlicerItems("Condiments").Selected = False
        .SlicerItems("Confections").Selected = False
        .SlicerItems("Grains/Cereals").Selected = False
        .SlicerItems("Meat/Poultry").Selected = False
        .SlicerItems("Produce").Selected = False
        .SlicerItems("Seafood").Selected = False
```

```
    End With
    ActiveWorkbook.SlicerCaches("Slicer_CategoryName").
ClearManualFilter
    With ActiveWorkbook.SlicerCaches("Slicer_CategoryName")
        .SlicerItems("Condiments").Selected = True
        .SlicerItems("Beverages").Selected = False
        .SlicerItems("Confections").Selected = False
        .SlicerItems("Dairy Products").Selected = False
        .SlicerItems("Grains/Cereals").Selected = False
        .SlicerItems("Meat/Poultry").Selected = False
        .SlicerItems("Produce").Selected = False
        .SlicerItems("Seafood").Selected = False
    End With
    With ActiveWorkbook.SlicerCaches("Slicer_CategoryName")
        .SlicerItems("Condiments").Selected = True
        .SlicerItems("Dairy Products").Selected = True
        .SlicerItems("Beverages").Selected = False
        .SlicerItems("Confections").Selected = False
        .SlicerItems("Grains/Cereals").Selected = False
        .SlicerItems("Meat/Poultry").Selected = False
        .SlicerItems("Produce").Selected = False
        .SlicerItems("Seafood").Selected = False
    End With
    ActiveSheet.Shapes("CategoryName").IncrementTop -23.25
End Sub
```

DELETING WORKSHEET TABLES

You can delete an Excel table using one of the following methods:

User Interface

- Select the table on the worksheet and choose Home | Cells | Delete | Delete Cells.
- If you don't need the sheet with the table, delete the entire worksheet.

VBA Code

- Use the `Delete` method to delete the worksheet table and its data.
- Use the `Unlist` method to convert the worksheet table to a normal data range.

- Use the `Unlink` method to remove the link between the worksheet table and the list on the SharePoint site. An unlinked list cannot be relinked. The SharePoint lists can only be deleted on the SharePoint site or by using the Lists Web service provided by SharePoint Services.

SUMMARY

This chapter introduced you to Excel tables. You have learned how to retrieve information from a Microsoft Access database, convert it into a table, and enjoy database-like functionality in the spreadsheet. You've also learned how tables are exposed through Excel's object model and manipulated via VBA.

In the next chapter, you will learn how to program two Microsoft Excel objects that are used for data analysis: the PivotTable and PivotChart.

Chapter 22 PROGRAMMING PIVOTTABLES AND PIVOTCHARTS

PivotTables serve millions of Microsoft 365 applications users as powerful tools for organizing and presenting information from various sources. If you are not familiar with this feature, now is the time to get your feet wet. Using PivotTables and PivotCharts, you can analyze your data from multiple perspectives. PivotTables make it possible to drag headings around a table to rearrange them so that your data is displayed dynamically any way you (or your users) want it. Similar to PivotTables, PivotCharts are interactive and allow you to view data in different ways by changing the position or detail of the PivotChart fields. Both PivotTables and PivotCharts allow you to focus on understanding your data rather than on organizing it.

CREATING A PIVOTTABLE REPORT

Before you can create a PivotTable, you need to prepare the data. You can get the data from one of the following sources:

- A range on an Excel worksheet (you can type in your data or paste it from other sources)
- An external data source (you can connect to a Microsoft Access file or an SQL Server database and get data directly)

Figure 22.1 displays the data that was dumped into a Microsoft Excel worksheet from an SQL Server database. The downloadable workbook file is named EquipmentList.xlsx. This file contains over 1,400 rows of data that would be difficult to summarize if it weren't for the built-in Excel PivotTable feature.

	A	B	C	D	E	F	G
1	Vendor	Equipment Type	Equipment Id	WarrStartDate	WarrYears	WarrParts	Warranty Type
2	Experts R Us	Scanner	11483	9/30/2016	1	NULL	Full Warranty
3	Experts R Us	Scanner	11487	9/27/2015	1	NULL	Full Warranty
4	Experts R Us	Scanner	11486	9/25/2018	1	NULL	Full Warranty
5	Expert Installers	Scanner	11481	9/24/2018	1	NULL	Full Warranty
6	Expert Installers	Scanner	11480	9/20/2018	1	NULL	Full Warranty
7	Expert Installers	Scanner	11485	9/17/2018	1	NULL	Full Warranty
8	Expert Installers	Scanner	11484	9/15/2018	1	NULL	Full Warranty
9	Expert Installers	Scanner	11479	9/11/2018	1	NULL	Full Warranty
10	Expert Installers	Scanner	11478	9/5/2018	1	NULL	Full Warranty
11	Expert Installers	Scanner	11477	8/31/2018	1	NULL	Full Warranty
12	Expert Installers	Scanner	11482	8/17/2015	1	NULL	Full Warranty
13	Expert Installers	Scanner	11476	8/7/2015	1	NULL	Full Warranty
14	ABC Hardware	Scanner	11475	8/3/2017	1	NULL	Full Warranty
15	ABC Hardware	Scanner	11474	7/31/2017	1	NULL	Full Warranty
16	ABC Hardware	Scanner	11473	7/27/2017	1	NULL	Full Warranty
17	ABC Hardware	Scanner	11471	7/18/2017	1	NULL	Full Warranty

FIGURE 22.1 Source data for the PivotTable.

Let's start our encounter with PivotTables by using built-in Ribbon commands.

NOTE	*Please note files for the "Hands-On" project may be found in the companion files.*

Hands-On 22.1 Creating a PivotTable

1. Copy the **EquipmentList.xlsx** workbook from the companion files to your **VBAExcel2021_ByExample** folder, and then open the copied file in Microsoft Excel.

   Select any cell anywhere in the data range. For example, select cell A2 in the Source Data worksheet.
2. Choose **Insert PivotTable**.

   The Create PivotTable dialog box appears, as shown in Figure 22.2.

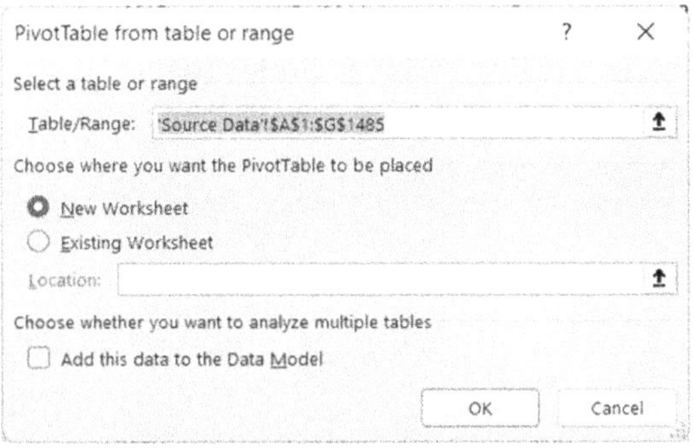

FIGURE 22.2 Create PivotTable dialog box.

Notice that there are three sections in the Create PivotTable dialog box. In the top section, you need to choose the data source for your report. This can be a table or range within a Microsoft Excel worksheet. The middle section of the Create PivotTable dialog box lets you choose between placing the PivotTable report in a new worksheet or in the existing worksheet. The bottom section allows you to create a data model based on multiple tables. This topic is discussed in the last section of this chapter.

3. Make sure the **Select a table or range** and **New Worksheet** option buttons are selected.
   Ensure that the range displayed in the Table/Range box incorporates all the data on which you want to report. The range will appear automatically if the active cell is within the data range. If the currently selected cell is outside of the data range, you will need to make your own selection.
4. Click **OK**.
   A blank PivotTable report is inserted in a new sheet and the PivotTable Field List pane is displayed, as shown in Figure 22.3.

   Notice that all the fields are listed in the PivotTable Field List pane to the right of the worksheet. Each field has a checkbox so you can easily indicate which fields to include in the report. The report is built as you make field selections. For example, when you check the box next to Vendor, you will notice that the Vendor field is automatically added to the Row Labels box at the bottom of the PivotTable Field List pane and the PivotTable updates to show your selection. By default, text fields are placed in the Row Labels list, and numeric fields appear in the Values list, as shown in Figure 22.4. You can specify the type of calculation you want to use to summarize data by clicking on the down arrow next to the field name in the Values area and selecting Value Field Settings. The default for the Values area is the Sum function. Figure 22.4 displays the pivot table using the Count function. You can easily adjust the position of the fields by dragging them between areas in the PivotTable Field List pane.

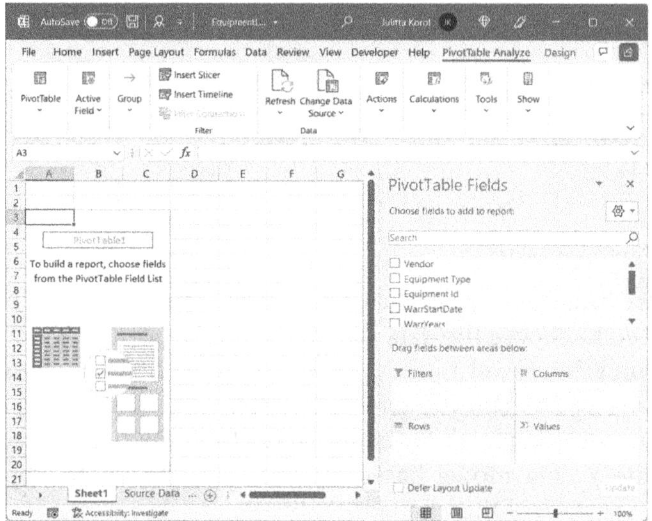

FIGURE 22.3 The PivotTable report waits for you to make field selections.

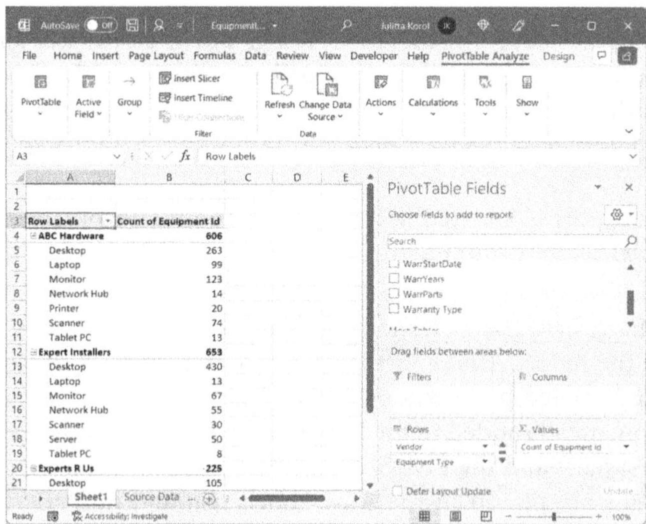

FIGURE 22.4 Adding fields to the PivotTable report.

Figure 22.5 shows the views made available in the PivotTable Field List pane by clicking on the button at the top of the pane.

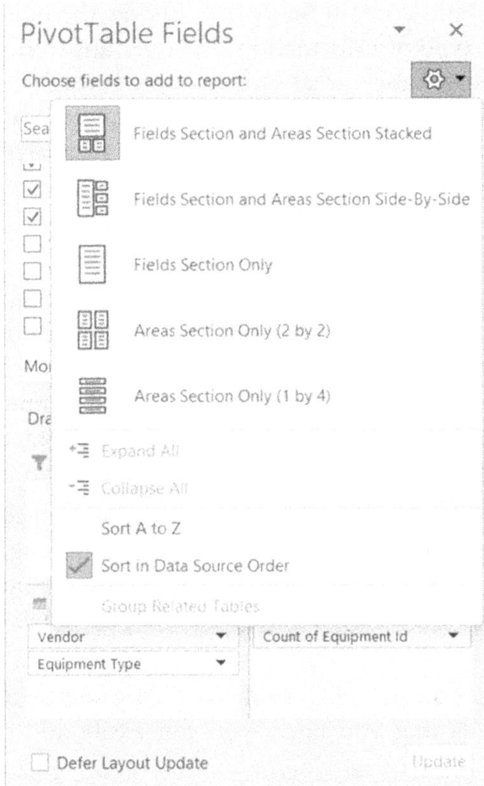

FIGURE 22.5 You can easily change the layout of the sections that are available in the PivotTable Field List pane on the right.

At the bottom of the PivotTable Field List pane, there are four areas where you can place the fields:

- The Row Labels area should contain the fields that you want to display your data "by." For example, if you want to produce the report by vendor, drag the Vendor field onto the Row Labels area. The Row Labels area can contain more than one field. In the example report that you will create, we also want to see the report by equipment type, so the Equipment Type field will be placed in the Row Labels area as well. If you position the Equipment Type field below the Vendor field in the Row Labels area, the data will be grouped first by vendor and then by equipment type within those vendors. Fields listed in the Row Labels area can be moved into desired position by dragging.

- The Column Labels area should contain fields that answer the question "what." For example: What type of information do you want to display for each of the fields in the Row Labels area? Our example PivotTable will report on the Warranty Type. Because we want to see all types of warranties for each vendor and equipment type, we will place the Warranty Type field in the Column Labels area. However, if you want to view your data from a different perspective, you can place the fields from the Row Labels area in the Column Labels area and vice versa. It is up to you.
- The Values area displays the data that you want to analyze. In our example, we want to find out the total number of units (equipment type) covered by each of the warranty types. The Values area must contain a field that has numeric data. Once we place the field containing numeric data in the Values area, we can choose what calculation (sum, count, average, and so on) we want to perform on the data.
- The Report Filter area is optional. Filter fields add a third dimension to your data analysis. Later in this chapter (see "Formatting, Grouping, and Sorting a PivotTable Report"), when you generate a PivotTable programmatically, you will add a field to the Report Filter area so you can experiment with the data.

Note that you do not have to place all the fields from your data source in the PivotTable. Place only those fields that you need; you can easily add other fields later.

5. Make the selections as shown in Figure 22.6.

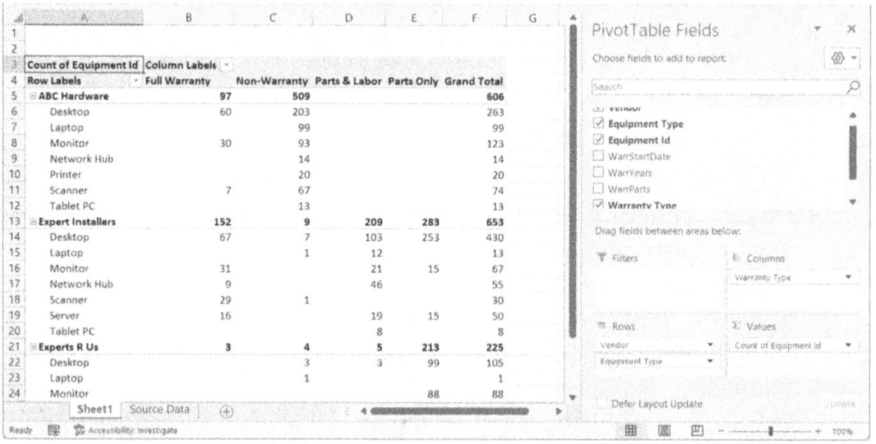

Count of Equipment Id	Column Labels				
Row Labels	Full Warranty	Non-Warranty	Parts & Labor	Parts Only	Grand Total
ABC Hardware	97	509			606
Desktop	60	203			263
Laptop		99			99
Monitor	30	93			123
Network Hub		14			14
Printer		20			20
Scanner	7	67			74
Tablet PC		13			13
Expert Installers	152	9	209	283	653
Desktop	67	7	103	253	430
Laptop		1	12		13
Monitor	31		21	15	67
Network Hub	9		46		55
Scanner	29	1			30
Server	16		19	15	50
Tablet PC			8		8
Experts R Us	3	4	5	213	225
Desktop		3	3	99	105
Laptop		1			1
Monitor				88	88

FIGURE 22.6 The completed PivotTable report.

While the PivotTable is selected, the PivotTable Field List pane is visible on the right-hand side so that you can easily modify the PivotTable by adding or removing fields. You can temporarily remove the PivotTable Field List pane by clicking outside the PivotTable selection in the worksheet. For example, if you click any cell in row 1 or 2, the pane will disappear. Click again anywhere in the area containing the pivot data and the pane reappears.

PivotTables are used for data analysis and presentation only. This means that you are not permitted to enter data directly into a PivotTable. You must make any changes or additions to the data in the underlying source data and then use the Refresh button on the PivotTable Analyze tab (see Figure 22.4) to update the PivotTable. If you added new rows to the source data, you must use the Change Data Source button in the Data group of the Options tab to expand the data range.

6. To see the data from a different point of view, reposition the selected fields in the PivotTable Field List as shown in Figure 22.7.

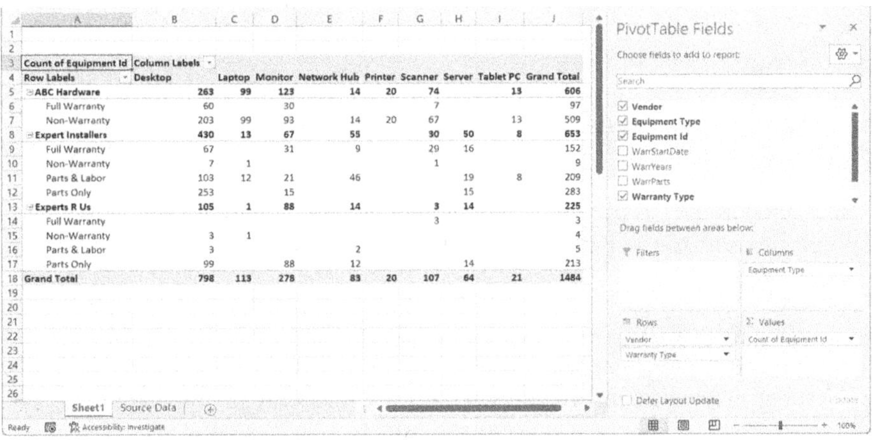

Count of Equipment Id	Column Labels								
Row Labels	Desktop	Laptop	Monitor	Network Hub	Printer	Scanner	Server	Tablet PC	Grand Total
ABC Hardware	263	99	123	14	20	74		13	606
Full Warranty	60		30			7			97
Non-Warranty	203	99	93	14	20	67		13	509
Expert Installers	430	13	67	55		30	50	8	653
Full Warranty	67		31	9		29	16		152
Non-Warranty	7	1				1			9
Parts & Labor	103	12	21	46			19	8	209
Parts Only	253		15				15		283
Experts R Us	105	1	88	14		3	14		225
Full Warranty						3			3
Non-Warranty	3	1							4
Parts & Labor	3			2					5
Parts Only	99		88	12			14		213
Grand Total	798	113	278	83	20	107	64	21	1484

FIGURE 22.7 The PivotTable report—another view of the source data.

You can examine the contributing data by double-clicking any cell in the Grand Total column.

7. Double-click cell **J13**.

Excel will add a new worksheet to the active workbook showing all the records that contributed to the selected total value (Figure 22.8).

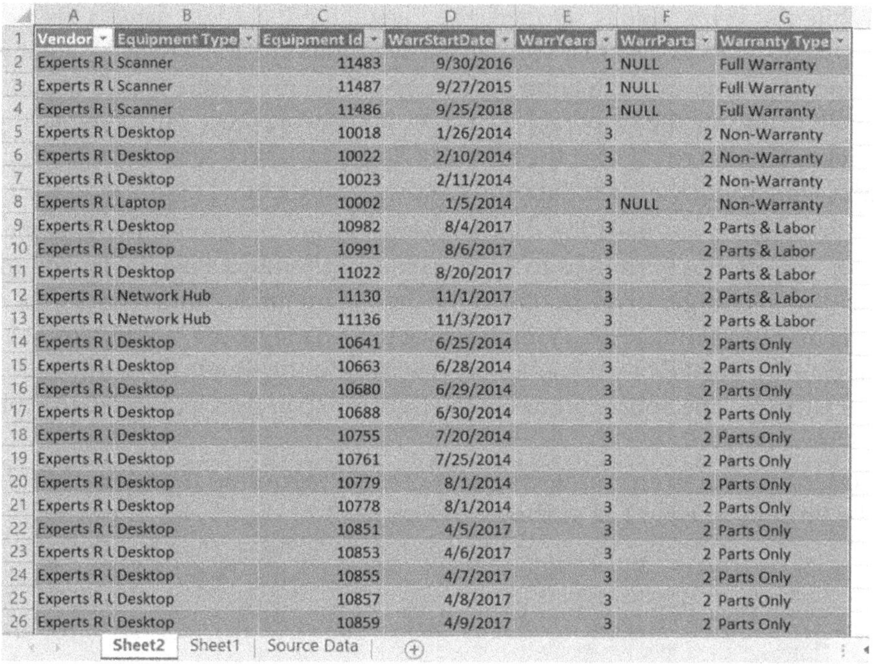

	A	B	C	D	E	F	G
1	Vendor	Equipment Type	Equipment Id	WarrStartDate	WarrYears	WarrParts	Warranty Type
2	Experts R U	Scanner	11483	9/30/2016	1	NULL	Full Warranty
3	Experts R U	Scanner	11487	9/27/2015	1	NULL	Full Warranty
4	Experts R U	Scanner	11486	9/25/2018	1	NULL	Full Warranty
5	Experts R U	Desktop	10018	1/26/2014	3	2	Non-Warranty
6	Experts R U	Desktop	10022	2/10/2014	3	2	Non-Warranty
7	Experts R U	Desktop	10023	2/11/2014	3	2	Non-Warranty
8	Experts R U	Laptop	10002	1/5/2014	1	NULL	Non-Warranty
9	Experts R U	Desktop	10982	8/4/2017	3	2	Parts & Labor
10	Experts R U	Desktop	10991	8/6/2017	3	2	Parts & Labor
11	Experts R U	Desktop	11022	8/20/2017	3	2	Parts & Labor
12	Experts R U	Network Hub	11130	11/1/2017	3	2	Parts & Labor
13	Experts R U	Network Hub	11136	11/3/2017	3	2	Parts & Labor
14	Experts R U	Desktop	10641	6/25/2014	3	2	Parts Only
15	Experts R U	Desktop	10663	6/28/2014	3	2	Parts Only
16	Experts R U	Desktop	10680	6/29/2014	3	2	Parts Only
17	Experts R U	Desktop	10688	6/30/2014	3	2	Parts Only
18	Experts R U	Desktop	10755	7/20/2014	3	2	Parts Only
19	Experts R U	Desktop	10761	7/25/2014	3	2	Parts Only
20	Experts R U	Desktop	10779	8/1/2014	3	2	Parts Only
21	Experts R U	Desktop	10778	8/1/2014	3	2	Parts Only
22	Experts R U	Desktop	10851	4/5/2017	3	2	Parts Only
23	Experts R U	Desktop	10853	4/6/2017	3	2	Parts Only
24	Experts R U	Desktop	10855	4/7/2017	3	2	Parts Only
25	Experts R U	Desktop	10857	4/8/2017	3	2	Parts Only
26	Experts R U	Desktop	10859	4/9/2017	3	2	Parts Only

Sheet2 | Sheet1 | Source Data

FIGURE 22.8 You can view the breakdown of the data by double-clicking on a data field in the PivotTable.

8. Save the changes in the EquipmentList.xlsx workbook. Do not close this file as it will be used in the next Hands-On.

Drilling down on the data is a nice feature except for the fact that if you do a lot of double-clicking you will end up with many additional and most likely unwanted worksheets in your workbook. You may want to delete the drill-down worksheet after examining the detail data. You can do this manually, or you can perform the cleanup programmatically by writing VBA event procedures as described in the next section.

REMOVING PIVOTTABLE DETAIL WORKSHEETS WITH VBA

In the previous Hands-On, Excel added to the EquipmentList.xlsx workbook a new worksheet that displays the detailed data included in the selected total. The following example demonstrates two event procedures that allow you to specify whether you want to keep the detailed worksheet or delete it automatically after you've examined the data. This exercise requires completion of the steps outlined in Hands-On 22.1.

Hands-On 22.2 Writing VBA Procedures to Remove a PivotTable Detail Worksheet

1. In the EquipmentList.xlsx workbook, rename the sheet with your PivotTable **PivotReport**.
   Save the workbook in the Excel macro-enabled format as **C:\VBAExcel2021_ByExample\EquipmentListPivot.xlsm.**
2. Press **Alt+F11** to switch to the Visual Basic Editor screen.
3. In the Project Explorer window, double-click the **ThisWorkbook** object in the Microsoft Excel object folder under VBAProject (EquipmentListPivot.xlsm).
4. In the EquipmentListPivot.xlsm – ThisWorkbook Code window, enter the global variable declaration and two event procedures as shown below:

```
' Global variables
Dim flag As Boolean           ' Boolean variable to indicate whether
                              ' to delete a drill-down worksheet
Dim strPivSheet As String     ' String to hold the name of the sheet
                              ' containing the PivotTable
Dim strDrillSheet As String   ' String to hold the name of the
                              ' drill-down sheet
Dim strPivSource As String    ' String to hold the name of the
                              ' worksheet with the PivotTable
                              ' source data

Private Sub Workbook_SheetActivate(ByVal Sh As Object)
    If strPivSheet = "" Then Exit Sub
    If Sh.Name <> strPivSheet Then
    If InStr(1, strPivSource, Sh.Name) = 0 Then
        If MsgBox("Do you want to Delete " & Sh.Name & _
            " from the workbook" & vbCrLf _
            & "upon returning to PivotTable report?", _
            vbYesNo + vbQuestion, _
            "Sheet: Delete or Keep") = vbYes Then
            flag = True
            strDrillSheet = Sh.Name
        Else
          flag = False
          Exit Sub
       End If
     End If
    End If
    If ActiveSheet.Name = strPivSheet And flag = True Then
        Application.DisplayAlerts = False
```

```
        Worksheets(strDrillSheet).Delete
        Application.DisplayAlerts = True
        flag = False
    End If
End Sub

Private Sub Workbook_SheetBeforeDoubleClick(ByVal Sh As Object, _
     ByVal Target As Range, Cancel As Boolean)
    With ActiveSheet
        If .PivotTables.Count > 0 Then
            strPivSource = ActiveSheet.PivotTables(1).SourceData
            If ActiveCell.PivotField.Name <> "" And _
                IsEmpty(Target) Then
                    MsgBox "Selected cell has no data " & _
                           "- cannot drill down."
                Cancel = True
                Exit Sub
            End If
            strPivSheet = ActiveSheet.Name
        End If
    End With
End Sub
```

The Workbook_SheetActivate event procedure will ask the user whether the drill-down worksheet should be deleted when the user returns to the worksheet containing the PivotTable report. If the user answers "Yes" in the message box, the Boolean variable `flag` will be set to `True`. Because by default Excel displays a confirmation message whenever the worksheet is about to be deleted, the procedure code turns off the application messages so the deletion can be performed without further user intervention. After the deletion, don't forget to turn the alerts back on.

The Workbook_SheetBeforeDoubleClick event procedure will disable the drill-down if the user clicks on a PivotTable cell that is empty. If the double-clicked cell is not empty, the name of the worksheet containing the PivotTable will be written to the global variable `strPivSheet`. Also, because we do not want to delete the worksheet containing the PivotTable source data, we will use the SourceData property of the PivotTables collection to store the name of the source data worksheet and the underlying data range in the global variable `strPivSource`.

To find out exactly how these two event procedures work together, use some of the debugging skills that you acquired in Chapter 9.

5. Press **Ctrl+S** to save changes you made in the Visual Basic Editor window.

6. Return to the Microsoft Excel application window, select the **PivotReport** worksheet and double-click cell **J9**.
   Excel will execute the code inside the Workbook_SheetBeforeDoubleClick event procedure and proceed to execute the code inside the Workbook_SheetActivate procedure. Because cell J9 is not empty, Excel will ask you whether you want to delete the drill-down worksheet upon returning to the PivotTable worksheet.
7. Click the **Yes** button in the message box.
   Nothing happens at this point. Excel simply has set the flag to delete this drill-down worksheet when you are done viewing it.
8. Click the **PivotReport** worksheet tab.
   At this point, Excel deletes the drill-down worksheet and activates the PivotReport worksheet.
9. Double click cell **B14** in the PivotReport worksheet.
   Excel displays the message that the drill-down is not allowed because there is no data in this cell. Recall that this message was coded inside the Workbook_SheetBeforeDoubleClick event procedure.
10. Save the EquipmentListPivot.xlsm workbook and then close it.

CREATING A PIVOTTABLE REPORT WITH VBA

Although the creation process of PivotTables has undergone many improvements in Excel, some users may still find the process of creating PivotTable reports confusing. For those users you may want to generate PivotTables via VBA code. Also with VBA, you can make many formatting changes to the existing PivotTables. This section demonstrates how to work with PivotTables programmatically. We will start by creating the PivotTable report shown earlier in Figure 22.6 using the data source presented in Figure 22.1.

Hands-On 22.3 Creating a PivotTable Report with VBA

1. Open the **C:\VBAExcel2021_ByExample\EquipmentList.xlsx** workbook. Right-click the **Source Data** sheet tab in the EquipmentList.xlsx workbook and choose the **Move or Copy** option from the pop-up menu.
2. In the Move or Copy dialog box, choose the **(new book)** entry from the **To book** drop-down list. Indicate that you want to make a copy of the selected sheet by clicking the checkbox next to **Create a copy label**. Click **OK** to proceed with the copy operation.

Excel creates a new workbook with one sheet named Source Data. This sheet has been copied from the EquipmentList.xlsx file.

3. Save this new workbook in the Excel macro-enabled format as **C:\VBAExcel2021_ByExample\Chap22_VBAExcel2021.xlsm.**
4. Insert three new sheets into the Chap22_VBAExcel2021.xlsm file and save the changes made to the workbook.
5. Close the **EquipmentList.xlsx** workbook. Leave **the Chap22_VBAExcel2021.xlsm** file open.
6. Press **Alt+F11** to switch to the Visual Basic Editor screen.
7. In the Project Explorer window, highlight **VBAProject (Chap22_VBAExcel2021.xlsm)** and choose **Insert | Module.**
8. In the Chap22_VBAExcel2021.xlsm – Module1 Code window, enter the CreateNewPivot procedure as shown below:

```
Sub CreateNewPivot()
    Dim wksData As Worksheet
    Dim rngData As Range
    Dim wksDest As Worksheet
    Dim pvtTable As PivotTable

    ' Set up object variables
    Set wksData = ThisWorkbook.Worksheets("Source Data")
    Set rngData = wksData.UsedRange
    Set wksDest = ThisWorkbook.Worksheets("Sheet2")

    ' Create a skeleton of a PivotTable

   Set pvtTable = wksData.PivotTableWizard(SourceType:=xlDatabase, _
       SourceData:=rngData, TableDestination:=wksDest.Range("B5"))

    ' Close the PivotTable Field List that appears automatically
    ActiveWorkbook.ShowPivotTableFieldList = False

    ' Add fields to the PivotTable
    With pvtTable
        .PivotFields("Vendor").Orientation = xlRowField
        .PivotFields("Equipment Type").Orientation = xlRowField
        .PivotFields("Warranty Type").Orientation = xlColumnField
        With .PivotFields("Equipment Id")
            .Orientation = xlDataField
            .Function = xlCount
        End With
        .PivotFields("Equipment Id").Orientation = xlPageField
    End With
```

```
    ' Autofit columns so all headings are visible
    wksDest.UsedRange.Columns.AutoFit
End Sub
```

The CreateNewPivot procedure shown above creates a new PivotTable report using the `PivotTableWizard` method of a Worksheet object. This method takes a few arguments that specify the type of the data source, its location, and the location where the PivotTable reports should be placed. All of these arguments are optional; however, it is a good idea to use them as we did in our example code. Because you can create a PivotTable from various sources of data by using the `xlDatabase` constant in the `SourceType` argument, the code specifically says that the data comes from an Excel range. If you want to create a PivotTable report from another PivotTable, use `xlPivotTable` for this argument. If your data is to be pulled from an external database (as shown in a later example), specify `xlExternal` as the `SourceType`. The `SourceData` argument in the above example procedure is a reference to the used range on the worksheet containing the source data. The `TableDestination` argument has a reference to cell B5 on Sheet2 in the current workbook. This is where the upper-left corner of the report will be placed.

The code assumes that Sheet2 exists in the workbook. If you don't have Sheet2, it's easy enough to add one via the VBA code prior to setting the reference. It is important to understand that when you call the `PivotTableWizard` method, you create a blank PivotTable report. All the fields from the data source are hidden. To make the fields visible, you need to add them to appropriate areas of the PivotTable Field List pane. As you recall, there are four such areas: Row Labels, Column Labels, Values, and Report Filter. While creating the PivotTable report, the PivotTable Field List pane appears automatically on the right-hand side of the worksheet. However, because you are creating a PivotTable programmatically, there is no need to display that list on the screen. By setting the ShowPivotTableFieldList property to `False`, the PivotTable Field List pane will not be displayed.

For each field that you want to display in the PivotTable report, set the Orientation property of the PivotField object. Use the following constants for the Orientation property: `xlRowField`, `xlColumnField`, `xlDataField`, and `xlPageField`. Note that for the Total Units field placed in the Values area, the procedure sets the Function property of the PivotField object to `xlSum`.

9. When you are creating a PivotTable report via code, you may need to check whether a PivotTable already exists in the destination worksheet. You can place the following code just below the code that sets up object variables (see the previous CreateNewPivot procedure):

```
' Check if PivotTable already exists
If wksDest.PivotTables.Count > 0 Then
    MsgBox "Worksheet " & wksDest.Name & _
        " already contains a pivot table."
    Exit Sub
End If
```

10. Run the CreateNewPivot procedure.
When you switch to the Microsoft Excel application window, Sheet2 should contain the PivotTable report shown in Figure 22.9.

Equipment Id	(All)					
Count of Equipment Id		**Warranty Type**				
Vendor	**Equipment Type**	**Full Warranty**	**Non-Warranty**	**Parts & Labor**	**Parts Only**	**Grand Total**
ABC Hardware	Desktop	60	203			263
	Laptop		99			99
	Monitor	30	93			123
	Network Hub		14			14
	Printer		20			20
	Scanner	7	67			74
	Tablet PC		13			13
ABC Hardware Total		97	509			606
Expert Installers	Desktop	67	7	103	253	430
	Laptop		1	12		13
	Monitor	31		21	15	67
	Network Hub	9		46		55
	Scanner	29	1			30
	Server	16		19	15	50
	Tablet PC			8		8
Expert Installers Total		152	9	209	283	653
Experts R Us	Desktop		3	3	99	105
	Laptop		1			1
	Monitor				88	88
	Network Hub			2	12	14
	Scanner	3				3
	Server				14	14

FIGURE 22.9 A PivotTable report created with VBA code.

CREATING A PIVOTTABLE REPORT FROM AN ACCESS DATABASE

You can use the same `PivotTableWizard` method of the Worksheet object (demonstrated in Hands-On 22.3) to create a PivotTable report from an external data source. Let's start by creating a PivotTable report from a Microsoft Access sample database. We will use a Microsoft Access driver to connect to the Northwind database (Northwind.mdb) and then call the `PivotTableWizard` method of the Worksheet object to create an empty PivotTable. We will populate the PivotTable report with the data by setting the Orientation property of the `PivotField` objects.

Hands-On 22.4 Creating a PivotTable Report from Access with VBA

1. Add a new module to VBAProject (Chap22_VBAExcel2021.xlsm) and enter the PivotTable_External1 procedure as shown below:

```
Sub PivotTable_External1()
    Dim strConn As String
    Dim strQuery_1 As String
    Dim strQuery_2 As String
    Dim myArray As Variant
    Dim destRange As Range
    Dim strPivot As String

   strConn = "Driver={Microsoft Access Driver (*.mdb, *.accdb)};" & _
       "DBQ=C:\VBAExcel2021_ByExample\Northwind.mdb;"

    strQuery_1 = "SELECT Customers.CustomerID, " & _
       "Customers.CompanyName," & _
       "Orders.OrderDate, Products.ProductName, Sum([Order " & _
       "Details].[UnitPrice]*[Quantity]*(1-[Discount])) " & _
           "AS Total " & _
      "FROM Products INNER JOIN ((Customers INNER JOIN Orders " & _
       "ON Customers.CustomerID = "

   strQuery_2 = "Orders.CustomerID) INNER JOIN [Order Details] " & _
       "ON Orders.OrderID = [Order Details].OrderID) ON " & _
       "Products.ProductID = [Order Details].ProductID " & _
      "GROUP BY Customers.CustomerID, Customers.CompanyName, " & _
       "Orders.OrderDate, Products.ProductName;"

    myArray = Array(strConn, strQuery_1, strQuery_2)
    Worksheets.Add

    Set destRange = ActiveSheet.Range("B5")
    strPivot = "PivotFromAccess"

    ActiveSheet.PivotTableWizard _
     SourceType:=xlExternal, _
     SourceData:=myArray, _
     TableDestination:=destRange, _
     TableName:=strPivot, _
     SaveData:=False, _
     BackgroundQuery:=False

    ' Close the PivotTable Field List that appears automatically
    ActiveWorkbook.ShowPivotTableFieldList = False
```

```
    ' Add fields to the PivotTable
    With ActiveSheet.PivotTables(strPivot)
    .PivotFields("ProductName").Orientation = xlRowField
    .PivotFields("CompanyName").Orientation = xlRowField
    With .PivotFields("Total")
        .Orientation = xlDataField
        .Function = xlSum
        .NumberFormat = "$#,##0.00"
    End With
    .PivotFields("CustomerID").Orientation = xlPageField
    .PivotFields("OrderDate").Orientation = xlPageField
    End With
    ' Autofit columns so all headings are visible
    ActiveSheet.UsedRange.Columns.AutoFit
End Sub
```

When using the `PivotTableWizard` method of the Worksheet object to create a PivotTable report from an external data source, you need to specify at a minimum the following arguments:

Name	Description
`SourceType`	Use the `xlExternal` constant to indicate that the data for the PivotTable comes from an external data source.
`SourceData`	Specify an array containing two or more elements. The first element of the array must be a connection string to the database. The second argument is the SQL statement for querying an external database. If the SQL statement is longer than 255 characters, break up the statement into several strings and pass each string as a separate element of the array. In the example procedure above, the SQL statement necessary for obtaining the required data from an external database is longer than 255 characters; therefore, the SQL string is broken into two strings: strQuery_1 and strQuery_2. Next, the connection string and the SQL statement are placed in an array like this: `myArray = Array(strConn, strQuery_1, strQuery_2)` `myArray` is then used as the `SourceData` argument of the `PivotTableWizard` method.
`TableDestination`	Specify a worksheet range where the PivotTable should be placed.
`TableName`	Specify the name of the PivotTable that you want to create.

In addition to the above arguments, the PivotTable_External1 example procedure uses the optional `SaveData` and `BackgroundQuery` arguments.

`SaveData`	This argument tells Visual Basic whether to save the PivotTable when the workbook file is saved. By setting the `SaveData` argument to `False`, the PivotTable will not be saved. This setting allows you to save space on disk.
`BackgroundQuery`	When set to `False`, this argument tells Visual Basic to refrain from executing other operations in Excel in the background until the query is complete.

After creating a PivotTable, the procedure specifies where the fields returned by the SQL statement should be placed in the PivotTable report.

2. Run the PivotTable_External1 procedure to generate the PivotTable. The resulting PivotTable report is illustrated in Figure 22.10.

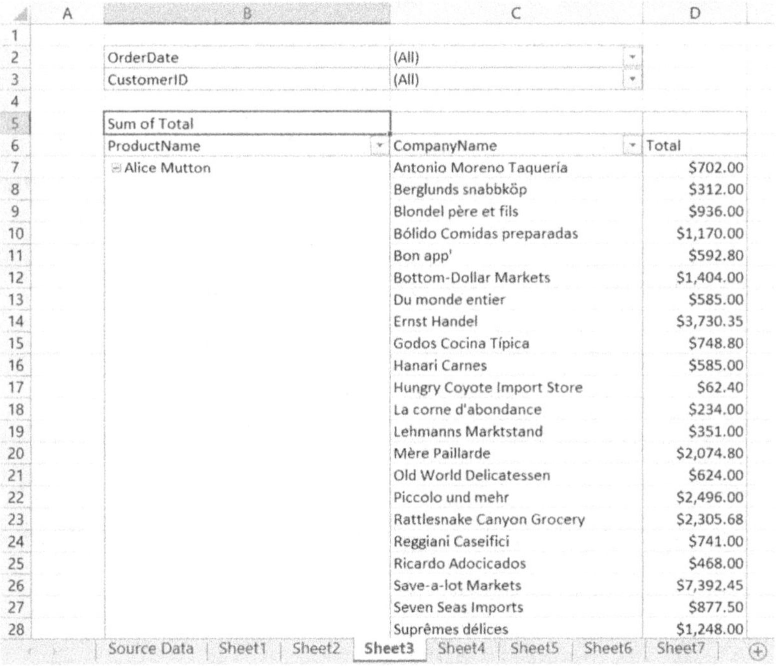

	A	B	C	D
1				
2		OrderDate	(All)	
3		CustomerID	(All)	
4				
5		Sum of Total		
6		ProductName	CompanyName	Total
7		⊟ Alice Mutton	Antonio Moreno Taquería	$702.00
8			Berglunds snabbköp	$312.00
9			Blondel père et fils	$936.00
10			Bólido Comidas preparadas	$1,170.00
11			Bon app'	$592.80
12			Bottom-Dollar Markets	$1,404.00
13			Du monde entier	$585.00
14			Ernst Handel	$3,730.35
15			Godos Cocina Típica	$748.80
16			Hanari Carnes	$585.00
17			Hungry Coyote Import Store	$62.40
18			La corne d'abondance	$234.00
19			Lehmanns Marktstand	$351.00
20			Mère Paillarde	$2,074.80
21			Old World Delicatessen	$624.00
22			Piccolo und mehr	$2,496.00
23			Rattlesnake Canyon Grocery	$2,305.68
24			Reggiani Caseifici	$741.00
25			Ricardo Adocicados	$468.00
26			Save-a-lot Markets	$7,392.45
27			Seven Seas Imports	$877.50
28			Suprêmes délices	$1,248.00

Source Data | Sheet1 | Sheet2 | Sheet3 | Sheet4 | Sheet5 | Sheet6 | Sheet7

FIGURE 22.10 A PivotTable report can be created programmatically from an external data source such as a Microsoft Access database.

USING THE CREATEPIVOTTABLE METHOD OF THE PIVOTCACHE OBJECT

When you use the macro recorder to generate VBA code for creating a PivotTable programmatically, Excel uses the `Add` method of the `PivotCaches` collection to create a new `PivotCache`. A `PivotCache` object represents the data behind a

PivotTable. It is an area in memory where data is stored and accessed as required from a data source. Use the `PivotCache` when you need to generate multiple PivotTables from the same data source. By using a `PivotCache`, you can gain a high level of control over your external data source. The `PivotCache` object can also be used to change and refresh data stored in the cache.

The example procedure in Hands-On 22.5 connects to the Microsoft Access Northwind 2007 database (Northwind 2007.accdb) using the Microsoft.ACE.OLEDB.12.0 provider. To use this type of connection, you must set up a reference to the Microsoft ActiveX Data Objects (ADO) in the References dialog box located in the Tools menu of the Microsoft Excel Visual Basic Editor screen.

Hands-On 22.5 Creating a PivotTable Report Using the PivotCache Object

1. In the Visual Basic Editor screen, choose **Tools | References**. In the Available References listbox, select the **Microsoft ActiveX Data Objects 6.1 Library** and click **OK**.
2. Add a new module to VBAProject (Chap22_VBAExcel2021.xlsm) and enter in the Code window the Pivot_External2 procedure as shown below:

```
Sub Pivot_External2()
    Dim objPivotCache As PivotCache
    Dim conn As New ADODB.Connection
    Dim rst As New ADODB.Recordset
    Dim dbPath As String
    Dim strSQL As String

    dbPath = "C:\VBAExcel2021_ByExample\Northwind 2007.accdb"

    conn.Open "Provider=Microsoft.ACE.OLEDB.12.0;" _
          & "Data Source=" & dbPath & _
          "; Persist Security Info=False;"

    strSQL = "SELECT Products.[Product Name], " & _
             "Orders.[Order Date], " & _
             "Sum([Unit Price]*[Quantity]) AS Amount " & _
             "FROM Orders INNER JOIN (Products INNER JOIN " & _
             "[Order Details] ON Products.ID = " & _
             "[Order Details].[Product ID]) ON " & _
             "Orders.[Order ID] = [Order Details].[Order ID] " & _
             "GROUP BY Products.[Product Name], " & _
             "Orders.[Order Date], Products.[Product Name]" & _
```

```
            "ORDER BY Sum([Unit Price]*[Quantity]) DESC , " & _
            "Products.[Product Name];"

    Set rst = conn.Execute(strSQL)

    ' Create a PivotTable cache and report
    Set objPivotCache = ActiveWorkbook.PivotCaches.Add( _
        SourceType:=xlExternal)
    Set objPivotCache.Recordset = rst

    Worksheets.Add
    With objPivotCache
        .CreatePivotTable TableDestination:=Range("B6"), _
            TableName:="Invoices"
    End With

    ' Add fields to the PivotTable
    With ActiveSheet.PivotTables("Invoices")
        .SmallGrid = False
        With .PivotFields("Product Name")
             .Orientation = xlRowField
             .Position = 1
        End With
        With .PivotFields("Order Date")
        .Orientation = xlRowField
            .Position = 2
            .Name = "Date"
        End With
        With .PivotFields("Amount")
             .Orientation = xlDataField
             .Position = 1
             .NumberFormat = "$#,##0.00"
        End With
    End With

    ' Autofit columns so all headings are visible
    ActiveSheet.UsedRange.Columns.AutoFit

    ' Clean up
    rst.Close
    conn.Close
    Set rst = Nothing
    Set conn = Nothing

    ' Obtain information about PivotCache
```

```
    With ActiveSheet.PivotTables("Invoices").PivotCache
        Debug.Print "Information about the PivotCache"
        Debug.Print "Number of Records: " & .RecordCount
        Debug.Print "Data was last refreshed on: " & .RefreshDate
        Debug.Print "Data was last refreshed by: " & .RefreshName
        Debug.Print "Memory used by PivotCache: " & .MemoryUsed & _
            " (bytes)"
    End With
End Sub
```

After establishing a connection with a database and executing the SQL statement to obtain the data, the procedure creates a PivotCache using the following line of code:

```
Set objPivotCache = ActiveWorkbook.PivotCaches.Add( _
        SourceType:=xlExternal)
```

The code then places the data from the external data source in the PivotCache by assigning a Recordset object to the PivotCache object, like this:

```
Set objPivotCache.Recordset = rst
```

Next, the code uses the `CreatePivotTable` method of the PivotCache object to create an empty PivotTable:

```
With objPivotCache
  .CreatePivotTable TableDestination:=Range("B6"), _
       TableName:="Invoices"
End With
```

Once the skeleton of the PivotTable is created, the code adds appropriate fields to the PivotTable. The last several lines of the example procedure demonstrate how to find out information about the PivotCache.

To force the PivotCache to refresh automatically when a workbook containing the PivotTable is opened, set the RefreshOnFileOpen property to `True`. To do this, you may want to add the following statement at the end of the Pivot_External2 procedure:

```
ActiveSheet.PivotTables("Invoices").PivotCache. _
 RefreshOnFileOpen = True
```

3. Run the Pivot_External2 procedure to generate the PivotTable. The resulting PivotTable report is illustrated in Figure 22.11.

	A	B	C	D
4				
5				
6		Sum of Amount		
7		Product Name	Date	Total
8		⊟Northwind Traders Almonds	5/24/2006	$200.00
9		Northwind Traders Almonds Total		$200.00
10		⊟Northwind Traders Beer	1/15/2006	$1,400.00
11			4/5/2006	$1,218.00
12			4/8/2006	$4,200.00
13		Northwind Traders Beer Total		$6,818.00
14		⊟Northwind Traders Boysenberry Spread	3/24/2006	$250.00
15			6/5/2006	$2,250.00
16		Northwind Traders Boysenberry Spread Total		$2,500.00
17		⊟Northwind Traders Cajun Seasoning	3/24/2006	$220.00
18			6/5/2006	$660.00
19		Northwind Traders Cajun Seasoning Total		$880.00
20		⊟Northwind Traders Chai	1/22/2006	$270.00
21			3/24/2006	$450.00
22		Northwind Traders Chai Total		$720.00
23		⊟Northwind Traders Chocolate	2/10/2006	$127.50
24			3/22/2006	$1,275.00
25			4/3/2006	$127.50
26			6/5/2006	$510.00
27			6/8/2006	$510.00
28		Northwind Traders Chocolate Total		$2,550.00
29		⊟Northwind Traders Chocolate Biscuits Mix	1/30/2006	$276.00
30			2/6/2006	$184.00
31			3/24/2006	$92.00

FIGURE 22.11 A PivotTable report created using the CreatePivotTable method of the PivotCache object.

FORMATTING, GROUPING, AND SORTING A PIVOTTABLE REPORT

You can modify the display and format of a PivotTable programmatically by using a number of different properties of the `PivotTable` object. For example, you may want to reposition the fields within the PivotTable report, sort the data by a specific field, or group your data by years, quarters, months, and so on. The example procedure below reformats the PivotTable report shown in Figure 22.10 to look like the one shown in Figure 22.12.

Hands-On 22.6 Formatting a PivotTable Report

1. Add a new module to VBAProject (Chap22_VBAExcel2021.xlsm) and enter the FormatPivotTable procedure as shown below:

```
Sub FormatPivotTable()
```

```
Dim pvtTable As PivotTable
Dim strPiv As String

If ActiveSheet.PivotTables.Count > 0 Then
    strPiv = ActiveSheet.PivotTables(1).Name
        Set pvtTable = ActiveSheet.PivotTables(strPiv)
Else
    Exit Sub
End If

With pvtTable
    .PivotFields("OrderDate").Orientation = xlRows
    .PivotFields("CompanyName").Orientation = xlHidden
    ' use this statement to group OrderDate by year
    .PivotFields("OrderDate").DataRange.Cells(1).Group _
        Start:=True, End:=True, _
        periods:=Array(False, False, False, False, False, _
        False, True)

    ' use this statement to group OrderDate both by quarter
    ' and year
    ' .PivotFields("OrderDate").DataRange.Cells(1).Group _
        Start:=True, End:=True, _
        periods:=Array(False, False, False, False, _
        False, True, True)

    .PivotFields("OrderDate").Orientation = xlColumns
    .TableRange1.AutoFormat Format:=xlRangeAutoFormatColor2
    .PivotFields("ProductName").DataRange.Select

    ' sort the Product Name field in descending order based
        ' on the
    ' Sum of Total
    .PivotFields("ProductName").AutoSort xlDescending, _
       "Sum of Total """
    Selection.IndentLevel = 2
    With Selection.Font
        .Name = "Times New Roman"
        .FontStyle = "Bold"
        .Size = 10
    End With
    With Selection.Borders(xlInsideHorizontal)
        .LineStyle = xlContinuous
        .Weight = xlThin
        .ColorIndex = xlAutomatic
    End With
```

```
    End With
End Sub
```

By studying the code of the procedure presented above, you can easily conclude that:

- To change the layout of a PivotTable, you should set the `Orientation` property of the required field to a different constant. The previous example code moves the OrderDate field from the Report Filter area to the Row Labels area of the PivotTable.
- To display a PivotTable without a particular field, you need to set the `Orientation` property of the required field to `xlHidden`.
- To group the OrderDate field by year, you should use the `Group` method of the `Range` object. For example, the code uses the following statement to group the data in the OrderDate field by year:

```
PivotFields("OrderDate").DataRange.Cells(1).Group Start:=True, _
    End:=True, periods:=Array(False, False, False, False, False, _
    False, True)
```

- The `Start` and `End` arguments specify the start and end date to be included in the grouping. By setting these arguments to `True`, all dates are included. The `periods` argument is an array of Boolean values that specifies the period for the group, as shown in the following table:

Array Element	Period
1	Seconds
2	Minutes
3	Hours
4	Days
5	Months
6	Quarters
7	Years

NOTE	*The following statement will ungroup the dates:* `ActiveSheet.PivotTables(1).PivotFields("OrderDate").LabelRange.Ungroup`

- You can apply automatic formatting to the entire PivotTable report by using the AutoFormat property of the Range object. The TableRange1 property returns a Range object that represents the range containing the entire PivotTable report without the page fields:

```
.TableRange1.AutoFormat Format:=xlRangeAutoFormatColor2
```

- You can select the data items in a particular field by using the DataRange property and the `Select` method, like this:

```
.PivotFields("ProductName").DataRange.Select
```

- You can sort a particular field in descending or ascending order. The example procedure uses the following statement to sort the ProductName field in descending order based on the Sum of Total:

```
.PivotFields("ProductName").AutoSort xlDescending, "Sum of Total"
```

- You can change the text indentation, font name, size, and style, as well as the borders of the selected range, as demonstrated in the last statements of the example procedure shown above.

2. Switch to the Microsoft Excel application window and activate the sheet containing the PivotTable report shown in Figure 22.10 earlier in this chapter.
3. Press **Alt+F8** to open the Macro dialog box. Highlight the Format-PivotTable procedure and click **Run**.
The resulting reformatted PivotTable report is illustrated in Figure 22.12.

CustomerID	(All)			
Sum of Total	OrderDate			
ProductName	1996	1997	1998	Grand Total
Alice Mutton	$6,962.28	$17,604.60	$8,131.50	$32,698.38
Aniseed Syrup	$240.00	$1,724.00	$1,080.00	$3,044.00
Boston Crab Meat	$2,778.30	$9,814.73	$5,317.60	$17,910.63
Camembert Pierrot	$9,024.96	$20,505.40	$17,295.12	$46,825.48
Carnarvon Tigers	$4,725.00	$15,950.00	$8,496.87	$29,171.87
Chai	$1,605.60	$4,887.00	$6,295.50	$12,788.10
Chang	$3,017.96	$7,038.55	$6,299.45	$16,355.96
Chartreuse verte	$3,558.24	$4,475.70	$4,260.60	$12,294.54
Chef Anton's Cajun Seasoning	$1,851.52	$5,214.88	$1,501.50	$8,567.90
Chef Anton's Gumbo Mix	$1,931.20	$373.62	$3,042.38	$5,347.20
Chocolade		$1,282.01	$86.70	$1,368.71
Côte de Blaye	$24,874.40	$49,198.08	$67,324.25	$141,396.73
Escargots de Bourgogne	$1,378.00	$2,076.27	$2,427.40	$5,881.67
Filo Mix	$246.40	$2,124.15	$862.40	$3,232.95
Flotemysost	$4,248.40	$8,438.75	$6,863.87	$19,551.02
Geitost	$385.50	$786.00	$476.62	$1,648.12
Genen Shonyu	$310.00	$1,474.82		$1,784.82
Gnocchi di nonna Alice	$2,763.36	$32,604.00	$7,225.70	$42,593.06
Gorgonzola Telino	$4,154.50	$7,300.75	$3,465.62	$14,920.87
Grandma's Boysenberry Spread	$720.00	$2,500.00	$3,917.00	$7,137.00
Gravad lax	$603.20	$629.20	$1,456.00	$2,688.40
Guaraná Fantástica	$556.74	$1,630.12	$2,317.50	$4,504.36

Source Data | Sheet1 | Sheet2 | Sheet11 | Sheet3 | Sheet4 | Sheet5 | Sheet6 | Sh ...

FIGURE 22.12 A PivotTable report was reformatted to view data from a different perspective.

HIDING ITEMS IN A PIVOTTABLE

In the previous example procedure, you grouped the data in the PivotTable by year based on the OrderDate field. To hide some of the grouped data, you can set the Visible property of the PivotItem object to `False`. For instance, the following procedure demonstrates how to hide the 1996 column of data in the PivotTable report presented in Figure 22.12.

```
Sub Hide1996Data()
    Dim myPivot As PivotTable
    Dim myItem As PivotItem
    Dim strFieldLabel As String

    strFieldLabel = "1996"

    Set myPivot = ActiveSheet.PivotTables(1)
     For Each myItem In myPivot.PivotFields("OrderDate")._
         PivotItems
         If myItem.Name <> strFieldLabel Then
             myItem.Visible = True
          Else
             myItem.Visible = False
          End If
     Next
End Sub
```

ADDING CALCULATED FIELDS AND ITEMS TO A PIVOTTABLE

You can customize a PivotTable report by defining calculated fields and items. Using the contents of other numeric fields in a PivotTable, you can create a calculated field that performs the required calculation. For example, let's create a procedure with two calculated fields named Change: 2010/2009 and Change: 2009/2008 to calculate the difference in number of products sold from year to year.

Hands-On 22.7 Creating a PivotTable Report with Calculated Fields

1. Save and close the Chap22_VBAExcel2021.xlsm workbook.
2. Copy the **Chap22b_VBAExcel2021.xlsm** workbook from the companion files to your **C:\VBAExcel2021_ByExample** folder.

3. Open the **C:\VBAExcel2021_ByExample\Chap22b_VBAExcel2021.xlsm** workbook (see Figure 22.13).

	A	B	C	D	E
1	**Product**	**2016**	**2017**	**2018**	
2	Prod1	904	614	694	
3	Prod2	456	139	755	
4	Prod3	1522	1009	1002	
5					

FIGURE 22.13 Sample data for the PivotTable report.

4. Switch to the Visual Basic Editor screen and highlight **VBAProject (Chap22b_VBAExcel2021.xlsm)** in the Project Explorer.
5. Choose **Insert | Module** to add a new module and enter the PivotWithCalcFields procedure as shown below:

```
Sub PivotWithCalcFields()
    ActiveWorkbook.PivotCaches.Add( _
        SourceType:=xlDatabase, _
        SourceData:="Sheet1!R1C1:R4C4").CreatePivotTable _
        TableDestination:="'[Chap22b_VBAExcel2021.xlsm]
        Sheet1'!R4C7", _
        TableName:="Piv1", _
        DefaultVersion:=xlPivotTableVersion10

    With ActiveSheet.PivotTables("Piv1").PivotFields("Product")
        .Orientation = xlRowField
        .Position = 1
    End With

    ActiveSheet.PivotTables("Piv1").AddDataField _
        ActiveSheet.PivotTables("Piv1").PivotFields("2018"), _
        "Sum of 2018", xlSum
    ActiveSheet.PivotTables("Piv1").AddDataField _
        ActiveSheet.PivotTables("Piv1").PivotFields("2017"), _
        "Sum of 2017", xlSum
    ActiveSheet.PivotTables("Piv1").AddDataField _
        ActiveSheet.PivotTables("Piv1").PivotFields("2016"), _
        "Sum of 2016", xlSum
    ActiveSheet.PivotTables("Piv1").CalculatedFields.Add _
        "Change: 2018/2017", "='2018' - '2017'", True
    ActiveSheet.PivotTables("Piv1").CalculatedFields.Add _
        "Change: 2017/2016", "='2017' - '2016'", True
    ActiveSheet.PivotTables("Piv1"). _
```

```
        PivotFields("Change: 2018/2017"). _
        Orientation = xlDataField
    ActiveSheet.PivotTables("Piv1"). _
        PivotFields("Change: 2017/2016"). _
        Orientation = xlDataField

End Sub
```

Notice that calculated fields are defined by using the `Add` method of the CalculatedFields object and supplying the name for the new field and a formula:

```
    ActiveSheet.PivotTables("Piv1").CalculatedFields.Add _
        "Change: 2018/2017", "='2018' - '2017'", True
    ActiveSheet.PivotTables("Piv1").CalculatedFields.Add _
        "Change: 2017/2016", "='2017' - '2016'", True
```

The third (optional) argument set to `True` indicates that the strings in field names will be interpreted as having been formatted in standard U.S. English instead of using local settings. The default setting is `False`.

A calculated field uses a formula that refers to other pivot fields that contain numeric data. This can be a simple formula, such as addition (+), subtraction (–), multiplication (*), or division (/), or an Excel function. In the procedure example above, we created the two calculated fields shown below:<TAB>

Calculated Field Name	Formula Used
Change: 2018/2017	='2018' - '2017'
Change: 2017/2016	='2017' - '2016'

"2018," "2017," and "2016" are the names of the fields placed in the Data area of the PivotTable. Figure 22.14 shows a new pivot field named Data, which Excel creates when you use multiple pivot fields in the Values area. The labels for the multiple pivot fields in the Data area can be displayed going down the rows or across the columns. You can specify the orientation of the labels by setting the Orientation property of the Data field to `xlRowField` or `xlColumnField`.

Once you define a calculated field, the field is added to the PivotTable Field List and maintained in the PivotTable cache.

NOTE	*You can add a calculated field manually by using the PivotTable Tools' Calculations tab on the context Ribbon. Click Fields, Items, & Sets. Then click Calculated Field to open the Insert Calculated Field dialog box.*

6. Run the PivotWithCalcFields procedure.
   The resulting PivotTable report is shown in Figure 22.14.

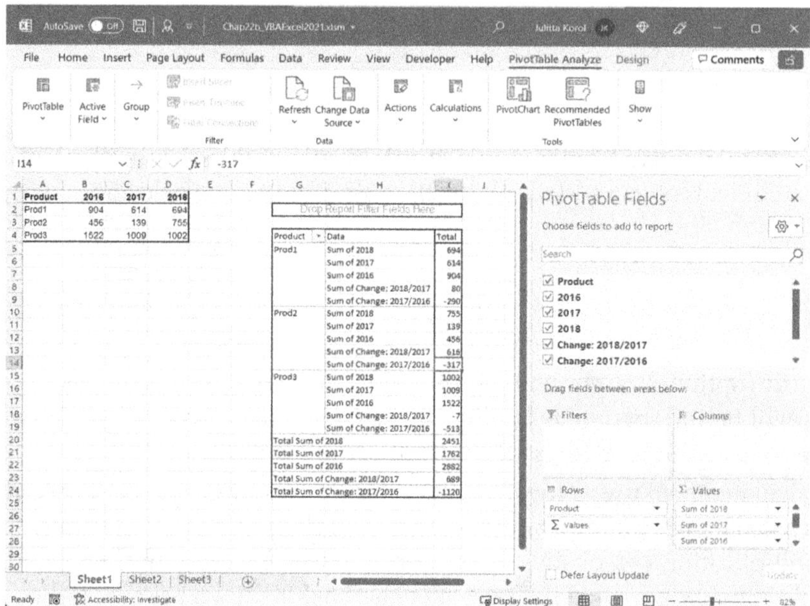

FIGURE 22.14 You can add additional calculations to a PivotTable by defining additional fields, such as Change: 2018/2017 and Change: 2017/2016 depicted here.

By adding the following statement at the end of the PivotWithCalcFields procedure, deleting columns G:I in Sheet1, and rerunning the procedure, the PivotTable depicted in Figure 22.14 will look like the one shown in Figure 22.15.

```
ActiveSheet.PivotTables("Piv1"). _
     PivotFields("Data").Orientation = xlColumnField
```

Product	2016	2017	2018
Prod1	904	614	694
Prod2	456	139	755
Prod3	1522	1009	1002

	Data				
Product	Sum of 2018	Sum of 2017	Sum of 2016	Sum of Change: 2018/2017	Sum of Change: 2017/2016
Prod1	694	614	904	80	-290
Prod2	755	139	456	616	-317
Prod3	1002	1009	1522	-7	-513
Grand Total	2451	1762	2882	689	-1120

FIGURE 22.15 Changing the orientation of the PivotTable data.

7. Save and close the Chap22b_VBAExcel2021.xlsm workbook.

You must not confuse a calculated item with a calculated field. A calculated item is a custom item you define in a PivotTable field to perform calculations using the contents of other fields and items in the PivotTable.

Let's say you have created a report showing the total product sales for each of your salespeople by country. Then you want to look at the data differently and show the sales made by each salesperson on three continents. You will need three new (calculated) items under the Country field. These items will be named North America, South America, and Europe. After you create these items, you can change the name of the Country field to Continent, as in Figure 22.16, to make your data easier to read. The following procedure retrieves the data for this demonstration example from the Microsoft Access sample Northwind database. The code of this procedure was generated by a macro recorder.

Hands-On 22.8 Creating a PivotTable Report with Calculated Items

1. Open a new workbook file and save it as **C:\VBAExcel2021_ByExample\Chap22c_VBAExcel2021.xlsm**.
   Switch to the Visual Basic Editor screen and select **VBAProject (Chap22c_VBAExcel2021.xlsm)** in the Project Explorer.
2. Choose **Insert | Module** to add a new module and enter the PivotWithCalcItems procedure as shown below:

```
Sub PivotWithCalcItems()
    Dim strConn As String
    Dim strSQL As String
    Dim myArray As Variant
    Dim destRng As Range
    Dim strPivot As String

   strConn = "Driver={Microsoft Access Driver (*.mdb, *.accdb)};" & _
           "DBQ=C:\VBAExcel2021_ByExample\" & _
           "Northwind.mdb;"

    strSQL = "SELECT Invoices.Customers.CompanyName, " & _
           "Invoices.Country, Invoices.Salesperson, " & _
           "Invoices.ProductName, Invoices.ExtendedPrice " & _
           "FROM Invoices ORDER BY Invoices.Country"

    myArray = Array(strConn, strSQL)
    Worksheets.Add

    Set destRng = ActiveSheet.Range("B5")
    strPivot = "PivotTable1"
```

```
    ActiveSheet.PivotTableWizard _
        SourceType:=xlExternal, _
        SourceData:=myArray, _
        TableDestination:=destRng, _
        TableName:=strPivot, _
        SaveData:=False, _
        BackgroundQuery:=False

  With ActiveSheet.PivotTables(strPivot).PivotFields("CompanyName")
        .Orientation = xlPageField
        .Position = 1
    End With

    With ActiveSheet.PivotTables(strPivot).PivotFields("Country")
        .Orientation = xlRowField
        .Position = 1
    End With

    ActiveSheet.PivotTables(strPivot).AddDataField _
   ActiveSheet.PivotTables(strPivot).PivotFields("ExtendedPrice"),
_
        "Sum of ExtendedPrice", xlSum

  With ActiveSheet.PivotTables(strPivot).PivotFields("Salesperson")
        .Orientation = xlRowField
        .Position = 1
    End With

  With ActiveSheet.PivotTables(strPivot).PivotFields("Salesperson")
        .Orientation = xlPageField
        .Position = 1
    End With

  With ActiveSheet.PivotTables(strPivot).PivotFields("Salesperson")
        .Orientation = xlColumnField
        .Position = 1
    End With

    ActiveSheet.PivotTables(strPivot).PivotFields("Country"). _
        CalculatedItems.Add "North America", "=USA+Canada", True
    ActiveSheet.PivotTables(strPivot).PivotFields("Country"). _
        CalculatedItems.Add "South America", _
        "=Argentina+Brazil+Venezuela ", True
    ActiveSheet.PivotTables(strPivot).PivotFields("Country"). _
        CalculatedItems("North America").StandardFormula = _
        "=USA+Canada+Mexico"
```

```
    ActiveSheet.PivotTables(strPivot).PivotFields("Country"). _
        CalculatedItems.Add "Europe", _
        "=Austria+Belgium+Denmark+Finland+" & _
        "France+Germany+Ireland+Italy+Norway+Poland+" & _
        "Portugal+Spain+Sweden+Switzerland+UK", True

    With ActiveSheet.PivotTables(strPivot).PivotFields("Country")
        .PivotItems("Argentina").Visible = False
        .PivotItems("Austria").Visible = False
        .PivotItems("Belgium").Visible = False
        .PivotItems("Brazil").Visible = False
        .PivotItems("Canada").Visible = False
        .PivotItems("Denmark").Visible = False
        .PivotItems("Finland").Visible = False
        .PivotItems("France").Visible = False
        .PivotItems("Germany").Visible = False
        .PivotItems("Ireland").Visible = False
        .PivotItems("Italy").Visible = False
        .PivotItems("Mexico").Visible = False
        .PivotItems("Norway").Visible = False
        .PivotItems("Poland").Visible = False
        .PivotItems("Portugal").Visible = False
        .PivotItems("Spain").Visible = False
        .PivotItems("Sweden").Visible = False
        .PivotItems("Switzerland").Visible = False
        .PivotItems("UK").Visible = False
        .PivotItems("USA").Visible = False
        .PivotItems("Venezuela").Visible = False
    End With

    ActiveSheet.PivotTables(strPivot). _
            PivotFields("Country").Caption = "Continent"

    With ActiveSheet.PivotTables(strPivot). _
      PivotFields("Sum of ExtendedPrice"). _
       NumberFormat = "$#,##0.00"
    End With

  With ActiveSheet.PivotTables(strPivot).PivotFields("ProductName")
        .Orientation = xlRowField
        .Position = 2
    End With

    ActiveSheet.PivotTables(strPivot). _
        PivotFields("ProductName").Orientation = xlHidden
End Sub
```

A calculated item uses a formula that refers to other items in the specified PivotTable field. For example, a PivotTable that contains a Country field listing a number of different country items (Austria, UK, Brazil, Argentina, etc.) could have a calculated item named "South America" defined as the sum of countries located on the South American continent:

Calculated Item	Formula
South America	`=Argentina+Brazil+Venezuela`

All of the calculated items in the specified PivotTable are members of the CalculatedItems collection. Calculated items are defined by using the `Add` method of the CalculatedItems object and supplying two arguments—the name for the new item and a formula as shown below:

```
ActiveSheet.PivotTables(strPivot).PivotFields("Country"). _
    CalculatedItems.Add "South America", _
    "=Argentina+Brazil+Venezuela", True
```

The third (optional) argument set to `True` indicates that the strings in field names will be interpreted as having been formatted in standard U.S. English instead of using local settings. The default setting is `False`.

3. Run the PivotWithCalcItems procedure.
   The resulting PivotTable report is shown in Figure 22.16.

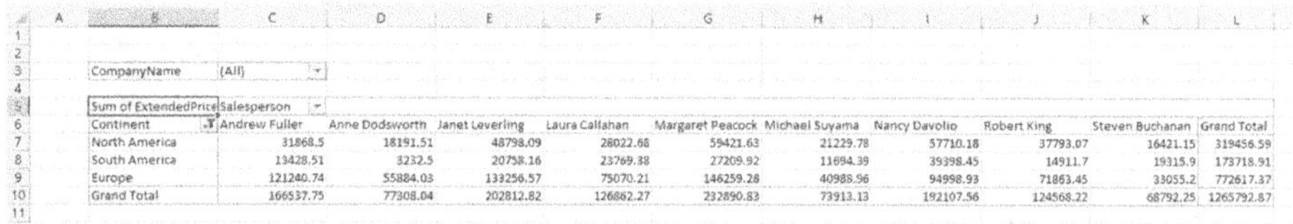

CompanyName (All)

Sum of ExtendedPrice	Salesperson									
Continent	Andrew Fuller	Anne Dodsworth	Janet Leverling	Laura Callahan	Margaret Peacock	Michael Suyama	Nancy Davolio	Robert King	Steven Buchanan	Grand Total
North America	31868.5	18191.51	48798.09	28022.68	59421.63	21229.78	57710.18	37793.07	16421.15	319456.59
South America	13428.51	3232.5	20758.16	23769.38	27209.92	11694.39	39398.45	14911.7	19315.9	173718.91
Europe	121240.74	55884.03	133256.57	75070.21	146259.28	40988.96	94998.93	71863.45	33055.2	772617.37
Grand Total	166537.75	77308.04	202812.82	126862.27	232890.83	73913.13	192107.56	124568.22	68792.25	1265792.87

FIGURE 22.16 By defining new items in a PivotTable report, you can present information summaries according to specific needs. Here the Country field has been renamed Continent to present information summarized by continent. North America, South America, and Europe are calculated items in this PivotTable report.

You can modify the PivotWithCalcItems procedure by defining new calculated items in the Salesperson PivotTable field to generate the output. For example, if you add the following code after the lines

```
ActiveSheet.PivotTables(strPivot). _
PivotFields("Country").Caption = "Continent"
```

in the PivotWithCalcItems procedure, you should see the modified table shown in Figure 22.17:

```
ActiveSheet.PivotTables(strPivot).PivotFields("Salesperson"). _
        CalculatedItems.Add "Male", _
        "=Michael Suyama+Andrew Fuller+Robert King+" & _
        "Steven Buchanan", True

ActiveSheet.PivotTables(strPivot).PivotFields("Salesperson"). _
    CalculatedItems.Add "Female", _
    "=Anne Dodsworth+Laura Callahan+Janet Leverling+" & _
    "Margaret Peacock+Nancy Davolio", True

With ActiveSheet.PivotTables("PivotTable1"). _
     PivotFields("Salesperson")
    .PivotItems("Andrew Fuller").Visible = False
    .PivotItems("Anne Dodsworth").Visible = False
    .PivotItems("Janet Leverling").Visible = False
    .PivotItems("Laura Callahan").Visible = False
    .PivotItems("Margaret Peacock").Visible = False
    .PivotItems("Michael Suyama").Visible = False
    .PivotItems("Nancy Davolio").Visible = False
    .PivotItems("Robert King").Visible = False
    .PivotItems("Steven Buchanan").Visible = False
End With
```

	A	B	C	D	E
1					
2					
3		CompanyName	(All)		
4					
5		Sum of ExtendedPrice	Salesperson		
6		Continent	Male	Female	Grand Total
7		North America	107312.5	212144.09	319456.59
8		South America	59350.5	114368.41	173718.91
9		Europe	267148.35	505469.02	772617.37
10		Grand Total	433811.35	831981.52	1265792.87
11					

FIGURE 22.17 By defining new calculated items in a PivotTable report, you can present information summaries according to specific needs. Here the Northwind employees are grouped by gender.

You can find out if the PivotField or PivotItem is calculated by using the `IsCalculated` property of the `PivotField` or `PivotItem` object. The procedure below prints a list of fields and items in the PivotTable to the Immediate window, indicating whether the field or item is calculated. In addition, this procedure prints the names of all calculated items and their formulas to Sheet2 of the current workbook.

4. To try it out, enter the ListCalcFieldsItems procedure code in the current module and then run it.

```
Sub ListCalcFieldsItems()
    Dim pivTable As PivotTable
    Dim fld As PivotField     ' field enumerator
    Dim itm As PivotItem     ' item enumerator
    Dim r As Integer    ' row number

    Set pivTable = Worksheets(1).PivotTables(1)

    On Error Resume Next

    ' print to the Immediate window the names of fields
    ' and calculated items
    For Each fld In pivTable.PivotFields
      If fld.IsCalculated Then
        Debug.Print fld.Name & ":" & _
        fld.Name & vbTab & "-->Calculated field"
      Else
        Debug.Print fld.Name
      End If
      For Each itm In pivTable. _
        PivotFields(fld.Name).CalculatedItems
          Debug.Print fld.Name & ":" & _
            itm.Name & vbTab & "--> Calculated item"
          ' enter information about Calculated items
          ' in a worksheet
          r = r + 1
          With Worksheets("Sheet2")
            .Cells(r, 1).Value = itm.Name
            .Cells(r, 2).Value = Chr(39) & itm.Formula
          End With
       Next
    Next
End Sub
```

CREATING A PIVOTCHART REPORT USING VBA

A PivotChart represents the data in a PivotTable report. Using VBA code you can create a PivotChart based on an existing PivotTable report, and you can change the layout and data displayed in a PivotChart just as easily as you can reformat a PivotTable report.

A PivotChart report is linked to a PivotTable report. This means that when you rearrange the data in a PivotTable report, the PivotChart report displays the same view of the data, and vice versa. The default chart type for a PivotChart is a stacked column chart. This type of chart is useful for comparing the contribution of each value to a total across categories. You can generate any type of PivotChart report except XY (Scatter), Stock, or Bubble.

You can create a PivotChart manually by choosing Insert | PivotChart. Creating a PivotChart report programmatically boils down to using the `SetDataSource` method of the PivotChart object and specifying a reference to the PivotTable range. The PivotTable object has the following two properties that return ranges representing part or all of the PivotTable report:

- TableRange1—Returns a range representing the PivotTable report without page fields
- TableRange2—Returns a range representing the entire PivotTable report

The procedures in Hands-On 22.9 generate a PivotTable report from the Microsoft Access sample Northwind database (Northwind.mdb). Another procedure in this Hands-On will set up a PivotChart based on the PivotTable's data.

Hands-On 22.9 Creating a PivotTable and PivotChart Reports

1. Save and close the Chap22c_VBAExcel2021.xlsm workbook file you created in the previous Hands-On.
2. Create a new workbook file and save it as **C:\VBAExcel2021_ByExample\Chap22d_VBAExcel2021.xlsm**.
3. Switch to the Visual Basic Editor screen and select **VBAProject (Chap22d_VBAExcel2021.xlsm)** in the Project Explorer.
4. Choose **Insert | Module** to add a new module and enter the GeneratePivotReport procedure as shown below:

```
Sub GeneratePivotReport()
    Dim strConn As String
    Dim strSQL As String
    Dim myArray As Variant
    Dim destRng As Range
    Dim strPivot As String

   strConn = "Driver={Microsoft Access Driver (*.mdb, *.accdb)};" & _
       "DBQ=C:\VBAExcel2021_ByExample\Northwind.mdb;"

    strSQL = "SELECT Invoices.Customers.CompanyName, " & _
        "Invoices.Country, Invoices.Salesperson, " & _
```

```
        "Invoices.ProductName, Invoices.ExtendedPrice " & _
        "FROM Invoices ORDER BY Invoices.Country"

    myArray = Array(strConn, strSQL)
    Worksheets.Add

    Set destRng = ActiveSheet.Range("B5")
    strPivot = "PivotTable1"

    ActiveSheet.PivotTableWizard _
        SourceType:=xlExternal, _
        SourceData:=myArray, _
        TableDestination:=destRng, _
        TableName:=strPivot, _
        SaveData:=False, _
        BackgroundQuery:=False

  With ActiveSheet.PivotTables(strPivot).PivotFields("ProductName")
        .Orientation = xlPageField
        .Position = 1
    End With


    With ActiveSheet.PivotTables(strPivot).PivotFields("Country")
        .Orientation = xlRowField
        .Position = 1
    End With

  With ActiveSheet.PivotTables(strPivot).PivotFields("Salesperson")
        .Orientation = xlColumnField
        .Position = 1
    End With

    ActiveSheet.PivotTables(strPivot).AddDataField _
   ActiveSheet.PivotTables(strPivot).PivotFields("ExtendedPrice"), _
    "Sum of ExtendedPrice", xlSum

    With ActiveSheet.PivotTables(strPivot). _
    PivotFields("Sum of ExtendedPrice").NumberFormat = "$#,##0.00"
    End With
End Sub
```

5. Run the GeneratePivotReport procedure.
   Excel adds a new worksheet with a PivotTable to the current workbook, as shown in Figure 22.18.

ProductName (All)

Sum of ExtendedPrice	Salesperson									
Country	Andrew Fuller	Anne Dodsworth	Janet Leverling	Laura Callahan	Margaret Peacock	Michael Suyama	Nancy Davolio	Robert King	Steven Buchanan	Grand Total
Argentina	477	944.5	319.2	2750.5	1329.4	76	686.7	1535.8		8119.1
Austria	16603.08	8967.8	23941.35	10970.59	17959.66	6728.93	17087.27	25745.15		128003.83
Belgium	2866.5	2808.37	295.38		13597.2	1209	732.6	4641.5	7674.3	33824.85
Brazil	9985.03	1910	9192.59	11118.58	17770.57	8444.87	29459.37	6200.2	14707.97	108789.18
Canada	9034.5	966.8	12156.73	1278.4	4826.05	3412.83	8801.41	9719.56		50196.28
Denmark	2345.7		1684.27	1814.35	17291.81	736	6674	2114.88		32661.01
Finland	5878.03	1590.56	957.86	4131.8	2117.7	270	1828.9	642	1833.2	19250.05
France	9434.28	3828.73	15471.13	5356	24340.8	4470.38	12487.44	2985.9	2543.65	80918.31
Germany	53627.17	15753.53	45978.81	26497.97	36836.67	7953.53	24611.38	7608.93	8048.54	226916.53
Ireland	10604.98	7403.9	16615.04	1313.82	1366.4	7558	2519	2598.76		49979.9
Italy	5422.05	583.8	88	2078.86	3686	55.2	1138.44	1025	1692.8	15770.15
Mexico	2190.65		3076.9	988.8	6706.1		5147.46	4223.06	1249.1	23582.07
Norway	622.35		2684.4				1728.4	700		5735.15
Poland				686	1019.1	808	858.85		160	3531.95
Portugal	1411	57.8	987.5	2893.4	4454.58		1519.24	285.12	1274.72	12883.36
Spain	977.5	224	3375.25	206	7729.89		1241	1861.1	2368.46	17983.2
Sweden	8036.7	4879.75	11520.4	9303.52	1826.3	3240.62	7491.18	6395.44	1801.23	54495.14
Switzerland		2949.24	5049.08	498.1	5282.06	3431.8	4135.5	9790.24	556.62	31692.64
UK	3411.4	6836.55	4608.1	9319.8	8751.11	4527.5	10945.73	5469.43	5101.68	58971.3
USA	20643.35	17224.71	33564.46	25755.48	47889.48	17816.95	43761.31	23850.45	15172.05	245678.24

FIGURE 22.18 This PivotTable report is used to graph data in the PivotChart report.

6. In the same code module where you entered the GeneratePivotReport procedure, enter the code of the CreatePivotChart procedure as shown below:

```
Sub CreatePivotChart()
    Dim shp As Shape
    Dim rngSource As Range
    Dim pvtTable As PivotTable
    Dim r As Integer

    Set pvtTable = Worksheets(ActiveSheet.Name).PivotTables(1)

    ' set the current page for the PivotTable report to the
    ' page named "Tofu"
    pvtTable.PivotFields("ProductName").CurrentPage = "Tofu"

    Set rngSource = pvtTable.TableRange2
    Set shp = ActiveSheet.Shapes.AddChart

    shp.Chart.SetSourceData Source:=rngSource
    shp.Chart.SetElement (msoElementChartTitleAboveChart)
    shp.Chart.ChartTitle.Caption = _
        pvtTable.PivotFields("ProductName").CurrentPage

    r = ActiveSheet.UsedRange.Rows.Count + 3

    With Range("B" & r & ":E" & r + 15)
        shp.Width = .Width
        shp.Height = .Height
        shp.Left = .Left
        shp.Top = .Top
    End With
End Sub
```

The CreatePivotChart procedure changes the current page for the PivotTable report to display information about the product named Tofu. The `AddChart` method of the Shapes collection is used to create a Chart object. The `SetSourceData` method of the Chart object is then used to specify the PivotTable range as the chart's data source. It's always a good idea to add a chart title, so the next two lines of code make sure that the title is positioned above the chart area and its text is set to the current product name in the PivotTable:

```
shp.Chart.SetElement (msoElementChartTitleAboveChart)
shp.Chart.ChartTitle.Caption = _
    pvtTable.PivotFields("ProductName").CurrentPage
```

To ensure that the chart appears just below the PivotTable report, we calculate the used range on the active worksheet and add to it three rows. The Top, Left, Width, and Height properties are used to position the chart over the specified range:

```
r = ActiveSheet.UsedRange.Rows.Count + 3

    With Range("B" & r & ":E" & r + 15)
        shp.Width = .Width
        shp.Height = .Height
        shp.Left = .Left
        shp.Top = .Top
    End With
```

7. Run the CreatePivotChart procedure.
   The resulting PivotChart report is shown in Figure 22.19.

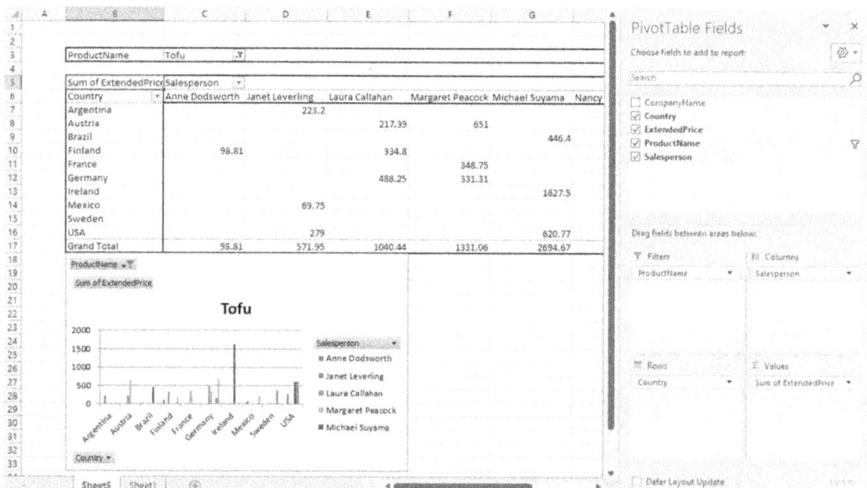

FIGURE 22.19 The PivotChart report is generated from the PivotTable report data embedded in the same worksheet.

To ensure that the chart title changes when you select a different product in the Product Name field of the PivotTable report, you must create the Worksheet_PivotTableUpdate event procedure in the Sheet5 module. If your sheet with the PivotChart has a different number, use it instead.

8. In the Project Explorer window, double-click the sheet number containing the PivotChart under VBAProject (Chap22d_VBAExcel2021.xlsm) and enter the following event procedure in the Code window:

```
Private Sub Worksheet_PivotTableUpdate(ByVal Target As PivotTable)
    Dim strPivotPage As String
    Dim r As Integer

    strPivotPage = Target.PivotFields("ProductName"). _
        CurrentPage.Value

    If ActiveSheet.ChartObjects.Count > 0 Then
        ActiveSheet.ChartObjects(1).Activate
        ActiveChart.ChartTitle.Text = strPivotPage

        r = ActiveSheet.UsedRange.Rows.Count + 3

        With Range("B" & r)
           ActiveSheet.ChartObjects(1).Top = .Top
    End With
    End If
End Sub
```

The above event procedure will be triggered automatically each time you update the PivotTable report.

9. In the Excel Application window in the sheet containing your PivotChart, select another product name from the PivotTable ProductName field.
   Notice that as you select a different product, the chart data and the chart title adjust to reflect your selection.
10. Save and close the **Chap22d_VBAExcel2021.xlsm** workbook.

UNDERSTANDING AND USING SLICERS

A *slicer* is a visual filter that allows you to easily interact with data. You worked with it when we discussed Excel tables. Slicers can also be applied to PivotTable and PivotChart reports. When you select values from the slicers, Excel automatically adjusts the pivot table or chart for you. Before you can start working with slicers, you need to create a PivotTable or PivotChart associated with a data source. Slicers are based on the row labels in your PivotTable. Depending on what sort of analysis you want to perform on your data, you can work with one or more slicers.

Creating Slicers Manually

In the next Hands-On, you will learn how slicers are applied to PivotTables using the Insert Slicer button available on the Ribbon's PivotTable Tools tab. We will reuse the EquipmentList.xlsx workbook that you worked with in Hands-On 22.1. This file already contains a PivotTable that's ready to go and is associated with the data stored in the Source Data sheet.

Hands-On 22.10 Creating a Slicer Using the Ribbon

1. Open the **EquipmentList.xlsx** workbook file and save it as **EquipmentListSlicers.xlsm** in the **VBAExcel2021_ByExample** folder.
2. Select **Row Labels** in the PivotTable report located on Sheet1 and then click **PivotTable Analyze | Insert Slicer** button in the Ribbon's Filter group as shown in Figure 22.20.

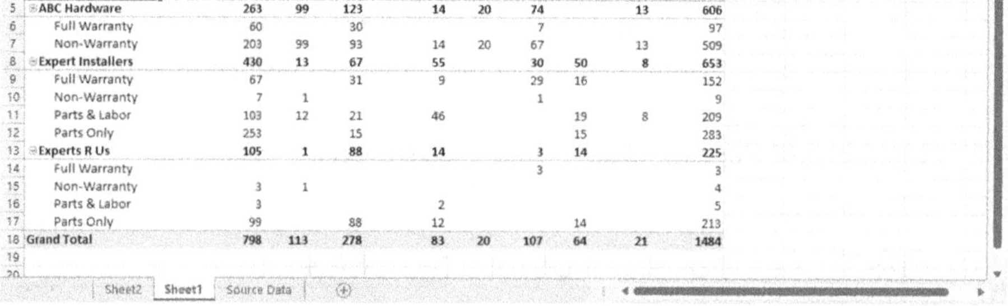

Count of Equipment Id	Column Labels								
Row Labels	Desktop	Laptop	Monitor	Network Hub	Printer	Scanner	Server	Tablet PC	Grand Total
ABC Hardware	**263**	**99**	**123**	**14**	**20**	**74**		**13**	**606**
Full Warranty	60		30			7			97
Non-Warranty	203	99	93	14	20	67		13	509
Expert Installers	**430**	**13**	**67**	**55**		**30**	**50**	**8**	**653**
Full Warranty	67		31	9		29	16		152
Non-Warranty	7	1				1			9
Parts & Labor	103	12	21	46			19	8	209
Parts Only	253		15				15		283
Experts R Us	**105**	**1**	**88**	**14**		**3**	**14**		**225**
Full Warranty						3			3
Non-Warranty	3	1							4
Parts & Labor	3			2					5
Parts Only	99		88	12			14		213
Grand Total	**798**	**113**	**278**	**83**	**20**	**107**	**64**	**21**	**1484**

FIGURE 22.20 Inserting a slicer using the Insert Slicer button.

The Insert Slicers dialog box appears (Figure 22.21) with the list of all the fields that are available in the PivotTable associated with the data source in the Source Data sheet.

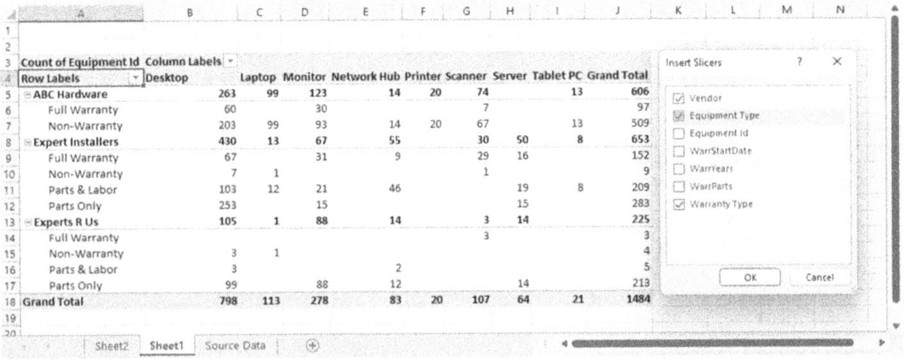

FIGURE 22.21 Selecting labels for slicers.

3. Select the labels as shown in Figure 22.21 (**Vendor**, **Equipment Type**, and **Warranty Type**) and click **OK**.
Excel creates a slicer for each label you selected (Figure 22.22).

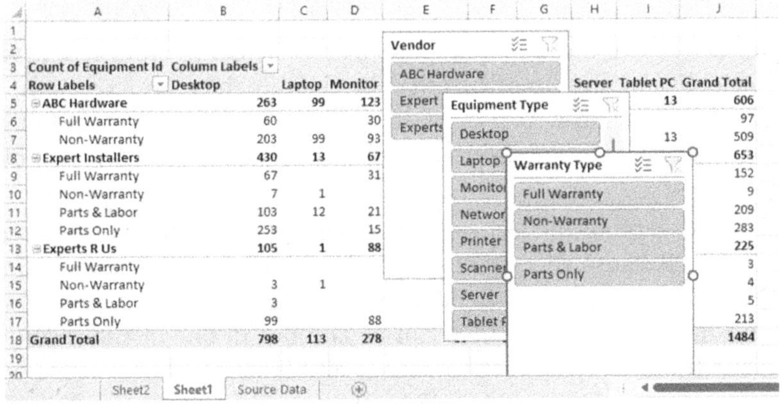

FIGURE 22.22 Each field label selected in the Insert Slicers dialog box (Figure 22.21) gets one slicer with a relevant list of values found in the data source.

4. Rearrange the slicers on the screen so you can easily view their content.
Suppose you want to analyze which equipment is covered by a full warranty. Now is the time to see how slicers work together to give you immediate feedback on the data.

5. In the Warranty Type slicer, select **Full Warranty**. Notice that not only does the PivotTable adjust automatically, but the other slicers (Equipment Type and Vendor) automatically disable values that don't meet the selected criteria. In

this case, the Equipment Type slicer tells us that we no longer have laptops, printers, and tablet PCs covered by a full warranty (see Figure 22.23).

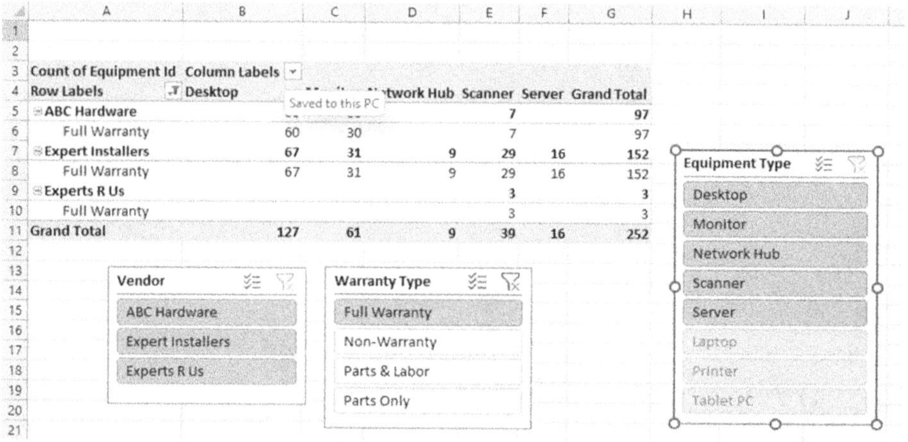

FIGURE 22.23 Using slicers to filter and analyze data.

You can continue drilling down on your data by clicking on different values shown in the slicers or remove the filters by clicking the filter icon in the top-right corner of each slicer. You can select nonconsecutive items in the slicer by holding down the Ctrl key or select a series of sequential items by holding down the Shift key.

You can also explore different options that are available in the Slicer tab on the Ribbon. Because slicers are shape objects, it's easy to move, resize, or delete them. You can change the look of slicers by applying different styles to each one. The items in the slicer can be laid out in one or more columns. Simply select the slicer you want to change and look for the Columns box in the Buttons group of the Slicer tab. You can control one or more PivotTables using the same set of slicers. You can also manage which PivotTables the slicer is connected to by clicking the Report Connections button in the Slicer tab (Figure 22.24).

6. Save the changes you made in the EquipmentListSlicers workbook and keep the file open for the next Hands-On.

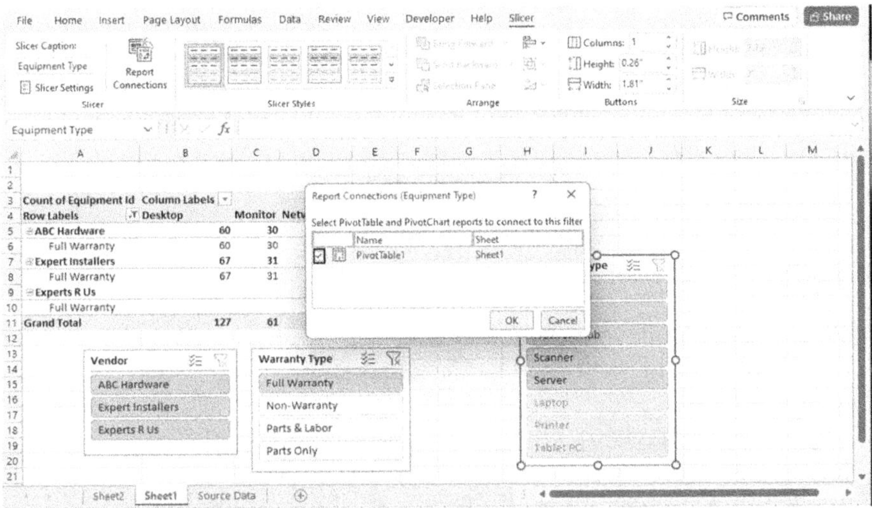

FIGURE 22.24 Working with the Slicer options on the Ribbon.

Working with Slicers Using VBA

To successfully program slicers with VBA, it's a good idea to take a look at the Object Browser for the types of objects that support this feature (Figure 22.25). In the previous Hands-On, you manually added three slicers to visually filter the PivotTable report. Each of the added slicers is represented by a `Slicer` object. Each `Slicer` object belongs to a workbook's Slicers object collection. Recall that before you were able to add slicers to your worksheet you had to have an existing PivotTable report associated with a data source.

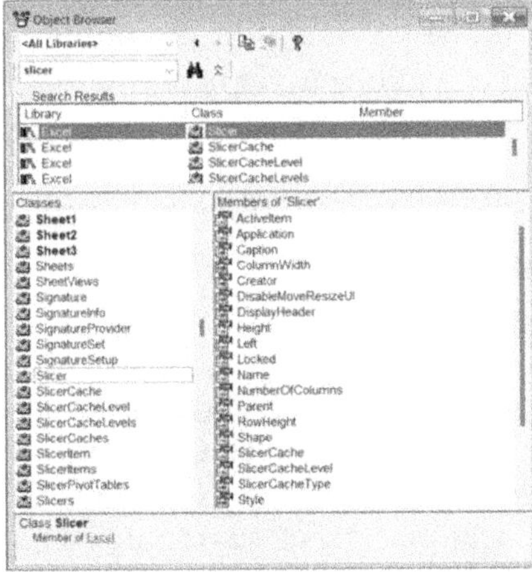

FIGURE 22.25 You can find the objects, properties, and methods for programming slicers with VBA in the Object Browser in the VBE window.

In VBA, before you can add a slicer, you must first define a slicer cache at the workbook level. Use the `Add` method of the SlicerCaches object collection to define a slicer cache. To do this, you need to specify the name of the PivotTable from which the slicer will be created and the name of the column header of the field the slicer will be based on as in the following code snippet:

```
Dim oSlicerCache As SlicerCache
Set oSlicerCache = ActiveWorkbook.SlicerCaches.
   Add(Source:=ActiveSheet. _
    PivotTables(1), SourceField:="WarrYears")
```

A slicer cache can have multiple slicers. Once you have defined a slicer cache, you are ready to add the slicer. Use the `Add` method of the Slicers object like this:

```
Dim oSlicer as Slicer
Set oSlicer = oSlicerCache.Slicers.Add( _
SlicerDestination:=ActiveSheet, _
    Name:="Warranty Years", Caption:="Warranty Years", _
    Top:=14.6551181102362, Left:=481.034409448819)
```

The first argument of the `Slicers.Add` method specifies the sheet where the slicer should be placed. All the other arguments listed in the above statement are optional. The `Name` argument specifies the name of the slicer. If this argument is omitted, Excel will automatically generate a name for the slicer. The name must be unique across all slicers within a workbook. The `Caption` argument is the name that appears in the header of the slicer. The `Top` argument (in points) specifies the initial vertical position of the slicer relative to the upper-left corner of cell A1 on the worksheet. The `Left` argument (in points) specifies the initial horizontal position of the slicer relative to the upper-left corner of cell A1 on the worksheet. You can also specify the initial width and height of the slicer by including the optional `Width` and `Height` arguments. To best position your slicer on the worksheet, record a macro to get the required settings for your statement.

By default, slicers are created with one column. However, you can easily change the number of columns like this:

```
oSlicer.NumberOfColumns = 3
oSlicer.Height = 50
```

When creating a slicer, you may want to specify which button in the slicer should be activated. To do this, you'll need to access the SlicerItem object. To access the SlicerItems collection that represents all the items in a slicer for a PivotTable, use the SlicerItems property of the SlicerCache object that is associated with the Slicer object. For example, the following code ensures that only items with the value of 3 are selected:

```
Dim oItem As SlicerItem

With ActiveWorkbook.SlicerCaches("Slicer_WarrYears")
    For Each oItem In .SlicerItems
        If oItem.Value = "3" Then
            oItem.Selected = True
        Else
            oItem.Selected = False
        End If
    Next
End With
```

To remove the filter from the Slicer object, use the following code:

```
ActiveWorkbook.SlicerCaches("Slicer_WarrYears").ClearManualFilter
```

Now let's put the above code snippets into a procedure that will add a fourth slicer to the PivotReport worksheet in the open EquipmentListSlicers workbook.

Hands-On 22.11 Creating a Slicer Using VBA

1. Switch to the VBE window and insert a new module into **VBAProject (EquipmentListSlicers.xlsm)**.
2. In the Code window, enter the AddSlicer procedure as shown in the following:

```
Sub AddSlicer()
    Dim oSlicerCache As SlicerCache
    Dim oSlicer As Slicer
    Dim oItem As SlicerItem

    Set oSlicerCache = ActiveWorkbook.SlicerCaches.Add( _
        Source:=ActiveSheet.PivotTables(1), _
        SourceField:="WarrYears")

    Set oSlicer = oSlicerCache.Slicers.Add( _
        SlicerDestination:=ActiveSheet, _
        Name:="Warranty Years", Caption:="Warranty Years", _
        Top:=14.6551181102362, Left:=481.034409448819)

    oSlicer.NumberOfColumns = 3
    oSlicer.Height = 50

     With ActiveWorkbook.SlicerCaches("Slicer_WarrYears")
        For Each oItem In .SlicerItems
            If oItem.Value = "3" Then
```

```
                oItem.Selected = True
            Else
                oItem.Selected = False
            End If
        Next
    End With
End Sub
```

3. Run the AddSlicer procedure and then switch to the Excel application window to view the result (see Figure 22.26).

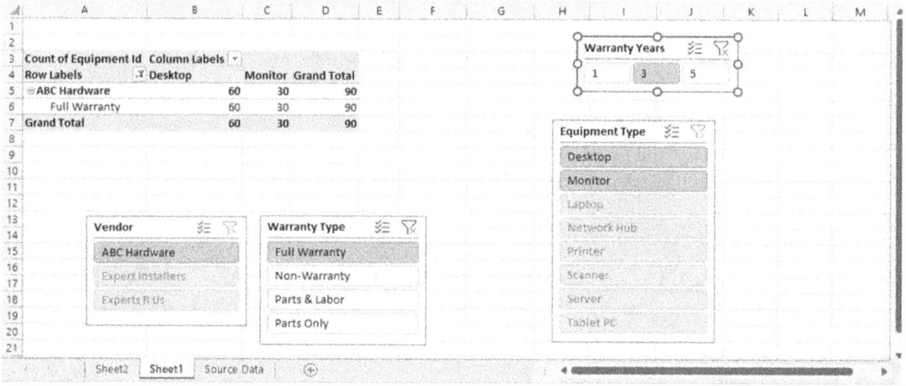

FIGURE 22.26 The Warranty Years slicer was added to this worksheet via a VBA procedure.

Let's proceed to Hands-On 22.12, which demonstrates a procedure that retrieves information about slicers.

Hands-On 22.12 Retrieving Information about Slicers

1. Switch to the VBE window and insert a new module into **VBAProject (EquipmentListSlicers.xlsm)**.
2. In the Code window, enter the ListSlicers procedure as shown below:

```
Sub ListSlicers()
    Dim oSlicerCache As SlicerCache
    Dim oSlicerCaches As SlicerCaches
    Dim oSlicer As Slicer
    Dim cnt As Integer

    Set oSlicerCaches = ActiveWorkbook.SlicerCaches
    cnt = oSlicerCaches.Count

    If cnt > 0 Then
        For Each oSlicerCache In oSlicerCaches
            Debug.Print "Slicer Cache Index|Name:" & _
```

```
  oSlicerCache.Index & "|" & oSlicerCache.Name
  Debug.Print "Source Type: " & oSlicerCache.SourceType
  For Each oSlicer In oSlicerCache.Slicers
    Debug.Print vbTab & "Name:" & oSlicer.Name
    Debug.Print vbTab & "Caption:" & oSlicer.Caption
    Debug.Print vbTab & "Cols:" & oSlicer.NumberOfColumns
    Debug.Print vbTab & "Col Width:" & oSlicer.ColumnWidth
    Debug.Print vbTab & "Height:" & oSlicer.Height
    Debug.Print vbTab & "Top:" & oSlicer.Top
    Debug.Print vbTab & "Left:" & oSlicer.Left
    Debug.Print vbTab & "Style:" & oSlicer.Style
    Debug.Print vbTab & "Cache level:" & _
      oSlicer.SlicerCache.CrossFilterType
  Next
Next
End If
End Sub
```

3. Run the ListSlicers procedure.
   Check the procedure output in the Immediate window.

   It's quite simple to delete a slicer you no longer need. For example, to remove the Warranty Years slicer that was added by the AddSlicer procedure in Hands-On 22.11, you would run the following code (try this out in the Immediate window):

   ```
   ActiveWorkbook.SlicerCaches("Slicer_WarrYears").Delete
   ```

   You can also delete the slicer by accessing the Shapes collection like this:

   ```
   ActiveSheet.Shapes.Range(Array("Warranty Years")).Delete
   ```

   You can move slicers to a different sheet altogether (see Step 4 below).

4. In the current module, enter the following procedure after the last procedure code:

   ```
   Sub MoveSlicers()
       ActiveSheet.Shapes.Range(Array("Vendor", _
           "Equipment Type", "Warranty Type")).Select
       Selection.Cut
       Sheets.Add
       Range("b3").Select
       With ActiveSheet
           .Name = "Slicers"
           .Paste
       End With
   ```

```
    'arrange windows
    With ActiveWindow
        .DisplayGridlines = False
        .DisplayHeadings = False
        .NewWindow
    End With
    Sheets("Sheet1").Select
    ActiveWorkbook.Windows.Arrange ArrangeStyle:=xlVertical
End Sub
```

The MoveSlicers procedure removes the remaining three slicers from Sheet1 and places them on another sheet of the current worksheet. Next, the procedure renames the newly inserted sheet and arranges the workbook sheets so that it is possible to view the changes in the PivotTable when slicing the data.

5. Run the MoveSlicers procedure.
6. After you run this procedure, slicers are no longer present in Sheet1. They can be found on the Slicers sheet added by the procedure.
7. Save and close the EquipmentListSlicers.xlsm workbook.

DATA MODEL FUNCTIONALITY AND PIVOTTABLES

An Excel feature called Data Model makes it possible to work with disparate data sources simultaneously in the same PivotTable and PivotChart reports. With the data model built directly into Excel, you can manage various data connections, import millions of rows from multiple data sources, and create relationships between multiple tables. When you use the built-in data model, the data is not only processed very fast, but it is highly compressed, so you don't need to worry about handling a large-size workbook file.

Hands-On 22.13 walks you through the steps required to create a data model. In this example, you will relate three tables from the Northwind 2007 database (Products, Orders, and Order Details) to analyze product sales by City.

Hands-On 22.13 Creating a Data Model and Exposing its Data through a Pivot Table

1. Open a new workbook and save it as **C:\VBAExcel2021_ByExample\Chap22_DataModel.xlsm**.
2. Choose **Insert** and click the **PivotTable** dropdown. Select **From External Data Source**.

The Create PivotTable dialog box appears, as shown in Figure 22.27.

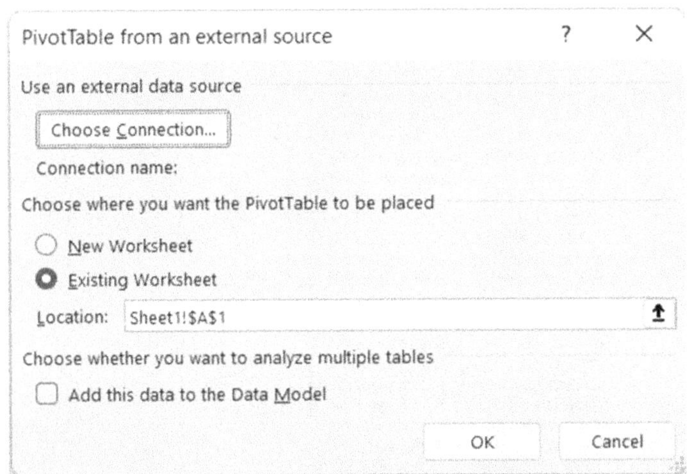

FIGURE 22.27 Using the External Data Source for a PivotTable.

3. Click the **Choose Connection…** button.
4. In the Existing Connections dialog box, click the **Browse for More…** button.
5. In the Select Data Source dialog box, choose **C:\VBAExcel2021_ByExample\Northwind 2007.accdb** from the File name drop down and click **Open**.
   Excel displays the Select Table dialog box listing all tables that are available in the selected database.
6. Click the **Enable selection of multiple tables** check box. Place a check next to **Order Details, Orders,** and **Products** tables and click **OK** (see Figure 22.28).
   When you click OK, you are returned to the PivotTable from external data source dialog box. Notice that Excel has placed the connection name **Northwind 2007** below the Choose Connection button and the setting **Add this data to the Data Model** is now checked (Figure 22.29).
7. Click **OK** to create a PivotTable.
   Excel displays the message *Loading data model and retrieving data* in the workbook's status bar. You should see a blank pivot table. You can start building your PivotTable based on the data model you have just created.

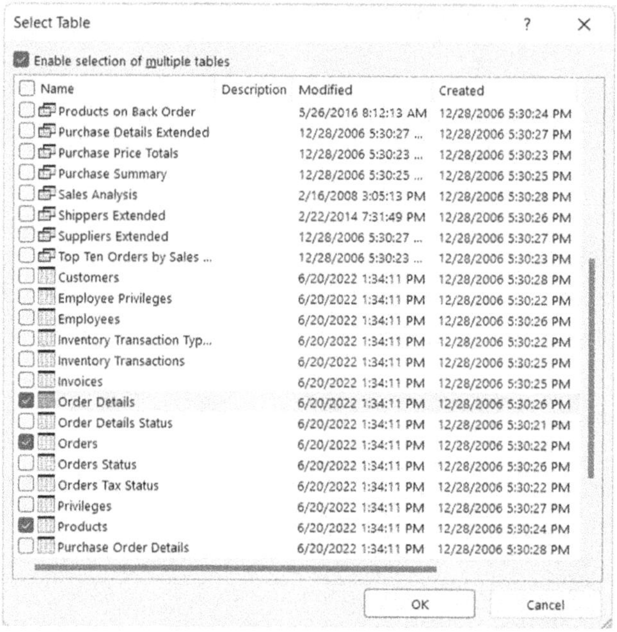

FIGURE 22.28 Selecting multiple tables in the Data Source.

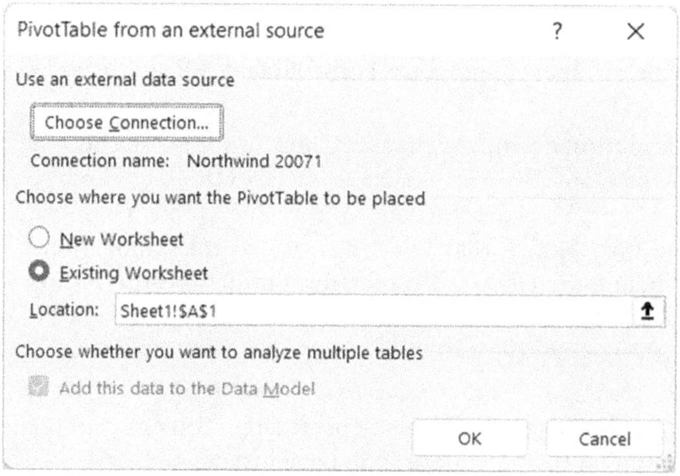

FIGURE 22.29 When you choose multiple tables or views in the Select Table dialog box (Figure 22.28) Excel adds the selected data to the Data Model. If you already have a data source connection with the same name, Excel adds a number to the end of the name to make it unique.

If Excel can detect the relationships between the selected tables, it automatically recreates these relationships in the data model when you import all the tables in a single operation.

If Excel fails to determine how your tables are related, you will need to explicitly define table relationships before Excel can handle the data in the data model. This is done via the Manage Relationships dialog box available by selecting Relationships in Ribbon's PivotTable Analyze tab. Let's create relationships between tables in the data model.

8. Click **Relationships** button on the Ribbon.
9. In the Manage Relationships dialog, click the **New** button.
10. In the Create Relationship dialog, make selections as shown in Figure 22.30 to define the relationship between the Order Details and Products tables.

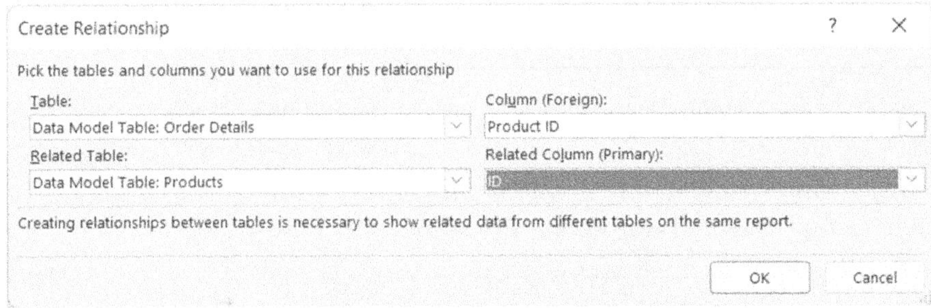

FIGURE 22.30 Defining a relationship between Order Details and Products tables.

11. Click **OK**.
    Excel lists the relationship to the Manage Relationships dialog.
12. Click the **New** button again to create another relationship.
13. In the Create Relationship dialog, make selections as shown in Figure 22.31 to define the relationship between the Orders and Order Details tables.

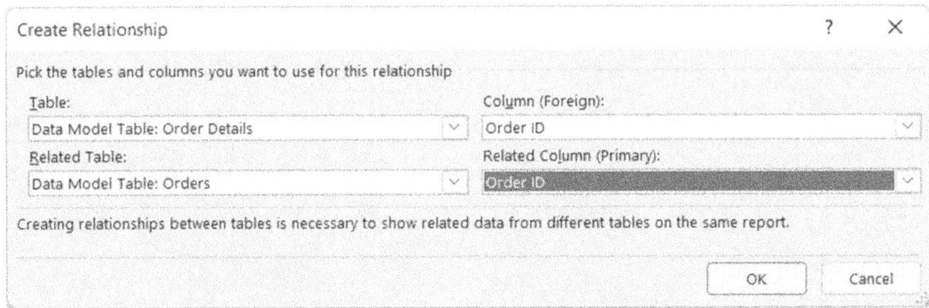

FIGURE 22.31 Defining a relationship between Orders and Order Details tables.

14. Click **OK**.
    Excel adds the relationship to the Manage Relationships dialog as shown in Figure 22.32.

15. Click **Close** to exit the Manage Relationship dialog.

Manage Relationships

Status	Table ▲	Related Lookup Table
Active	Order Details (Order ID)	Orders (Order ID)
Active	Order Details (Product ID)	Products (ID)

New... | Auto-Detect... | Edit... | Activate | Deactivate | Delete | Close

FIGURE 22.32 The relationships between tables in the data model are listed in the Manage Relationships dialog.

Finally, with the defined table relationships, you can proceed to build a pivot table. Let's choose fields from the PivotTable Field list.

16. In the PivotTable Fields panel, expand the **Products** table and drag the **Product Name** to the **Rows** area.
17. Expand the **Orders** table and drag the **Ship City** to the **Columns** area.
18. Expand the **Order Details** table and drag the **Quantity** to the **Values** area.
19. Make the formatting adjustments to your liking by using the buttons on the Design tab. The completed pivot table is shown in Figure 22.33.

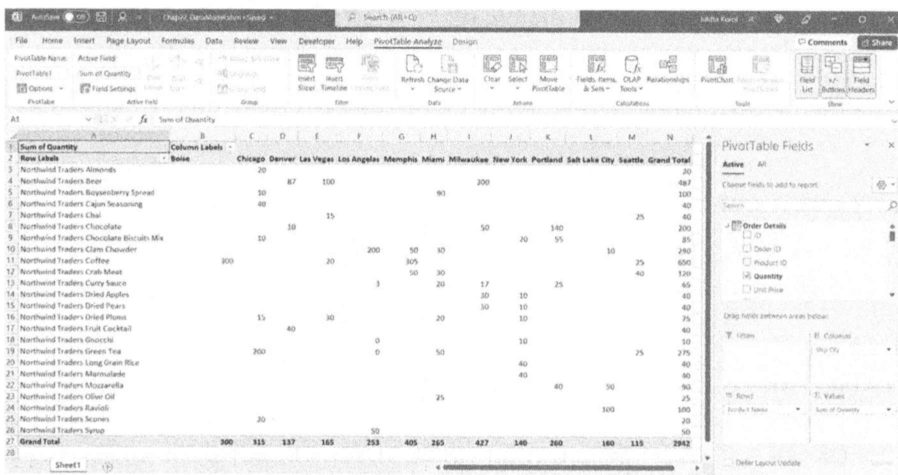

FIGURE 22.33 This pivot table summarizes product sales by City.

NOTE	*At any time, you can quickly add additional database tables to the data model by choosing PivotTable Analyze | Change Data Source | Connection Properties. Activate the Properties dialog box by right clicking on the Northwind 2007 database name. In the Connection Properties dialog box, modify Command text on the Definition tab (see Figure 22.34).* 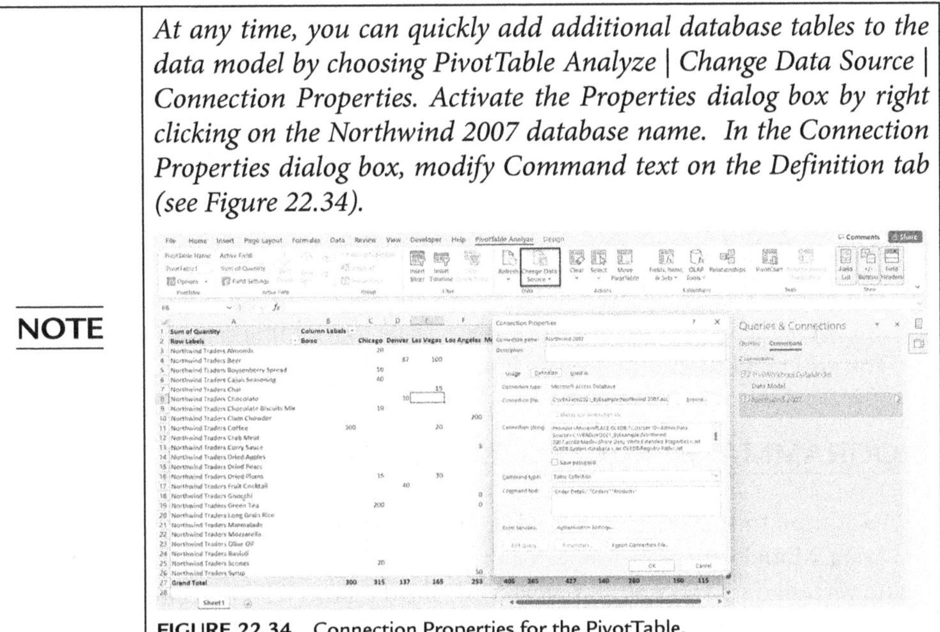 FIGURE 22.34 Connection Properties for the PivotTable.

SIDEBAR ***Deferring PivotTable Layout Updates***

If you take a close look at Figure 22.33 you will notice at the very bottom of the PivotTable Fields panel the Defer Layout Update checkbox. By placing a check in this box, you can prevent Excel from making real-time updates to your pivot table as you work with its fields. When you are ready to update your pivot table layout, click the Update button. When you are done building your pivot table, remove the check from the Defer Layout Update setting. You can also control this setting using VBA. Simply set the ManualUpdate property of the PivotTable object to true or false. For example, try out the following procedure:

```
Sub DeferLayoutUpdate()
    With Sheet1.PivotTables(1)
        .ManualUpdate = True
        With .CubeFields("[Products].[Category]")
             .Orientation = xlRowField
             .Position = 1
        End With
        .ManualUpdate = False
    End With
End Sub
```

You have now explored the basic data model built into Excel. If you require more advanced features that will allow you to enhance your data model, you will need to resort to the Power Pivot, which is available in Excel 2021 and Excel for Microsoft 365. See the following link for the details:

https://support.microsoft.com/en-us/office/power-pivot-overview-and-learning-f9001958-7901-4caa-ad80-028a6d2432ed

SIDEBAR ***Adding Calculated Fields to the Tables in the Data Model***

While Excel allows you to add calculated fields to pivot tables, this feature is not available when you link your pivot table to multiple tables in a data model. You will need to use the Power Pivot to create calculated fields.

PROGRAMMATIC ACCESS TO THE DATA MODEL

In addition to the existing Visual Basic for Application object model, Excel has a Data Model object model (OM) that can be used to programmatically load and refresh data sources and work with the data model. You can find many new objects in the Object Browser by searching for 'model' as shown in Figure 22.35.

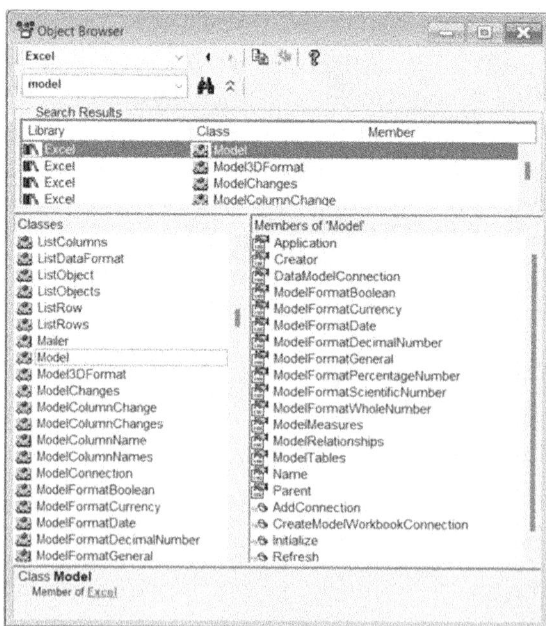

FIGURE 22.35 Using the Object Browser to locate new objects that support the new data model.

A large number of objects have been added to Excel to support programmatic access to the data model. The following VBA procedure shows how to use the Model property of the Workbook object to get some information about the data model you created in the previous section.

```
Sub GetDataModel_Info()
  Dim wkb As Workbook
  Dim tbl As Variant

  Set wkb = ActiveWorkbook

  Debug.Print "Model Name: " & wkb.Model.Name
  Debug.Print "Relationships: " & wkb.Model.ModelRelationships.Count
  Debug.Print "Number of Tables: " & wkb.Model.ModelTables.Count
  Debug.Print "--TABLE NAMES--"
  For Each tbl In wkb.Model.ModelTables
      Debug.Print tbl.Name
  Next
End Sub
```

When you run this procedure, the Immediate Window displays the following information:

```
Model Name: ThisWorkbookDataModel
Relationships: 2
Number of Tables: 3
--TABLE NAMES--
Order Details
Orders
Products
```

In Hands-On 22.14, you will work with the `ModelChanges` object that contains information about which changes were made to the data model when the `Workbook_ModelChange` event occurs. While various changes can be made to the data model, this exercise focuses on detecting whether any new tables were added to the existing data model.

Hands-On 22.14 Creating a Data Model and Exposing its Data through a Pivot Table

You must complete Hands-On 22.13 prior to working with this Hands-On.

1. In the Visual Basic Editor window, select **VBAProject (Chap22_DataModel.xlsm)** and choose **Insert | Module**.

2. In the Module code window, enter the following procedure:

```
Sub DataModel_TableChanges()
    Dim strCmdTxt_1 As String
    Dim strCmdTxt_2 As String

    strCmdTxt_1 = """Order Details"",""Orders"",""Products"""
    strCmdTxt_2 = strCmdTxt_1 & ",""Customers"",""Employees"""

    With ActiveWorkbook.Connections("Northwind 2007") _
        .OLEDBConnection
        .CommandText = strCmdTxt_2
        .Refresh
    End With
End Sub
```

This procedure modifies the CommandText property of the OLEDBConnection object to include two additional tables (Customers, Employees) in the data model. The Refresh method tells Excel to update the data model with the new data. After running this procedure the Customers and Employees tables should appear in the PivotTable Fields panel in the worksheet. To detect the change to the data model you will need to write the `Workbook_ModelChange` event procedure as instructed below.

3. In the Project Explorer double-click **ThisWorkbook** object of the VBAProject (Chap22_DataModel.xlsm).
4. In ThisWorkbook code window, enter the following event procedure:

```
Private Sub Workbook_ModelChange( _
    ByVal Changes As ModelChanges)

    Dim colTblNames As ModelTableNames
    Dim tblCount As Long
    Dim i As Integer

    Set colTblNames = Changes.TablesAdded
    tblCount = colTblNames.Count
    If tblCount > 0 Then
        Debug.Print tblCount & " tables were added."
    Else
       Debug.Print "There are no new tables in the data model."
    End If
    For i = 1 To tblCount
        Debug.Print colTblNames.Item(i)
    Next i
```

```
End Sub
```

This event procedure is triggered when Excel detects that changes were made to the data model. The `Changes` variable represents the `ModelChanges` object and denotes the type of change that was made. `Changes` can be such as:

- adding, changing, deleting columns (`ColumnsAdded`, `ColumnsChanged`, and `ColumnsDeleted` properties),
- adding, changing, deleting, renaming, and refreshing (recalculating) tables (`TablesAdded`, `TablesChanged`, `TablesDeleted`, `TableNamesChanged`, and `TablesModified` properties),
- changing one or more relationships in the model (`RelationshipChange` property),
- adding measures (`MeasuresAdded` property),
- making an unknown change (`UnknownChange` property)

When tables are added to the model as part of the model operation, we use `Changes.TablesAdded` property to find out the names of the tables that were added. This property returns a `ModelTableNames` Object (Excel) collection of table names as strings representing all tables which were added to the model as part of a model operation:

```
Set colTblNames = Changes.TablesAdded
```

You can count how many objects are in the `colTblNames` collection using the `Count` property of the `ModelTableNames` object:

```
tblCount = colTblNames.Count
```

We use the following code to obtain the names of tables that were added to the data model:

```
For i = 1 To tblCount
   Debug.Print colTblNames.Item(i)
Next i
```

5. Run the **DataModel_TableChanges** procedure.
This procedure will automatically trigger the Workbook_ModelChange procedure you wrote in the previous step. You should see the following output in the Immediate window when the procedure completes:

```
2 tables were added.
```

```
Customers
Employees
```

You should also see the Customers and Employees tables in the PivotTable Fields panel in the workbook on after activating the All tab (see Figure 22.36).

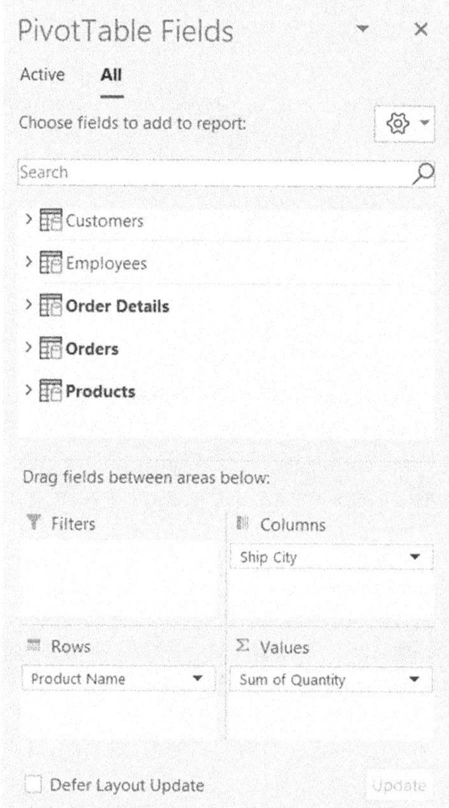

FIGURE 22.36 PivotTable Fields panel listing additional tables.

Modify the **CommandText** property in the DataModel_TableChanges procedure by inserting the following line of code:

```
.CommandText = strCmdTxt_1
```

Run the procedure again.

This will remove the Customers and Employees tables from the data model. You should see only the original three tables in the PivotTable Fields panel and the following text in the Immediate window:

```
There are no new tables in the data model.
```

SUMMARY

In this chapter, you have worked with two powerful Microsoft Excel objects that are used for data analysis: PivotTable and PivotChart. You have learned how to use VBA to manipulate these two objects to quickly produce reports that allow you or your users to easily examine large amounts of data pulled from an Excel worksheet range or from an external data source such as a Microsoft Access database. This chapter has also demonstrated the use of the slicer feature that makes it possible to visually filter PivotTable data. In the last two sections of this chapter, you learned how to use the Excel data model to load data from multiple tables, create relationships between tables, expose the data through a pivot table, and use several new VBA objects and properties to obtain information about the data model and specific changes that were made to it.

The next chapter features the data gathering, shaping, and modelling capabilities available in Excel.

Chapter 23

Getting and Transforming Data in Excel

If you need to deal with the data on a regular basis and need to automate the process of transforming, cleaning and loading of the data, there is a powerful feature in Excel that will assist you in this task.

The data import and transformation features that were once known as Power Query Add-In are now natively built into Excel. You can access these features under the Get & Transform section of the Ribbon's Data Tab (see Figure 23.1). With the Power Query technology integrated into Excel you can create powerful queries that will simplify the process of getting the data into Excel from both external and internal sources, as well as combining and transforming it.

This chapter provides a quick Hands-On introduction to the data analysis and transformation process with the Power Query.

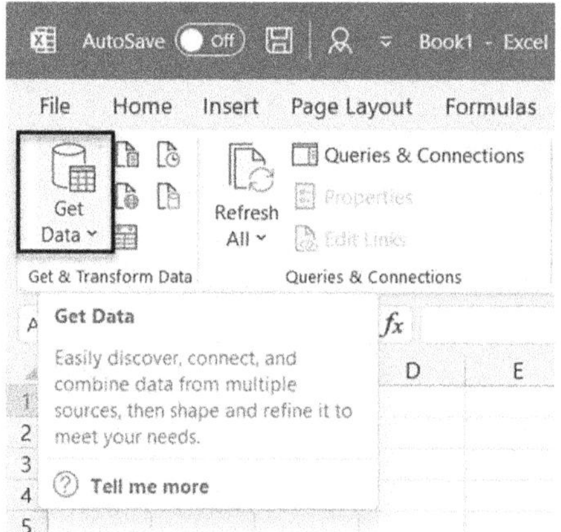

FIGURE 23.1 The Get Data button in the Get & Transform Data section of the Excel 2021 Ribbon is used for loading, shaping and refining data.

USING THE GET DATA BUTTON

When you click the Get Data button, Excel lists the types of data sources you can use for creating a query (see Figure 23.2).

NOTE	*Not all data sources shown in Figures 23.2-23.6 are available in all versions of Excel. Hands-On exercises in this chapter rely on sources that are available with the Microsoft 365 license.*

The **From File** category (see Figure 23.2) allows you to import data from a file such as Microsoft Excel workbook, text, csv, and xml and JSON. In addition, you can import data into a single consolidated file from a folder containing multiple files of the same type. The latter is very convenient when you need to create a report based on data spread over numerous files.

The **From Database** category (see Figure 23.3) allows you to import data from a database such as SQL Server, Microsoft Access, Analysis Services, Oracle, MySQL, and so on.

The **From Azure** category allows you to import data from Microsoft Azure data services such as SQL Server Azure database, Azure Marketplace, Azure HDInsight, Azure Blob and Table Storage. The Azure data source is not available if you have a Standard license.

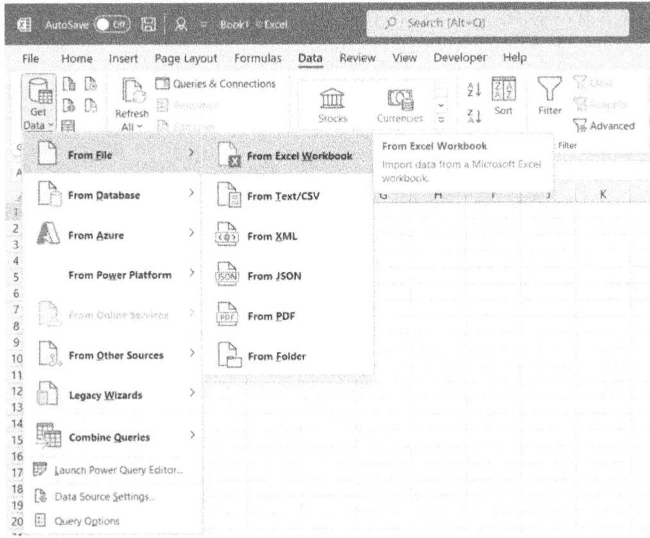

FIGURE 23.2 You can get data from various types of files including files of the same type located in a particular folder.

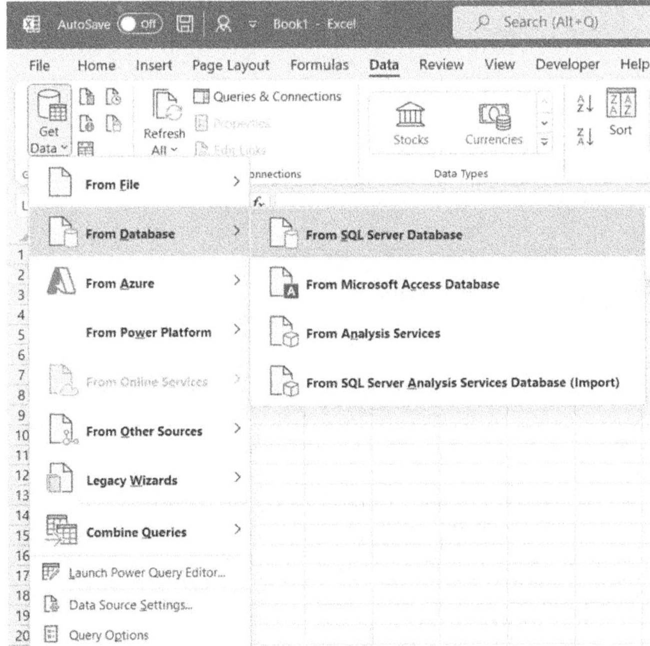

FIGURE 23.3 You can access data from various types of databases depending on the type of your Excel license.

- The **From Power Platform** category has an option to import data from Dataflows and Dataverse.
- The **From Online Services** category allows to import data from online services such as Facebook.
- The **From Other Sources** category (see Figure 23.4) lists all the other sources that can provide data for your query. You can even start with a clean slate by creating a blank query.

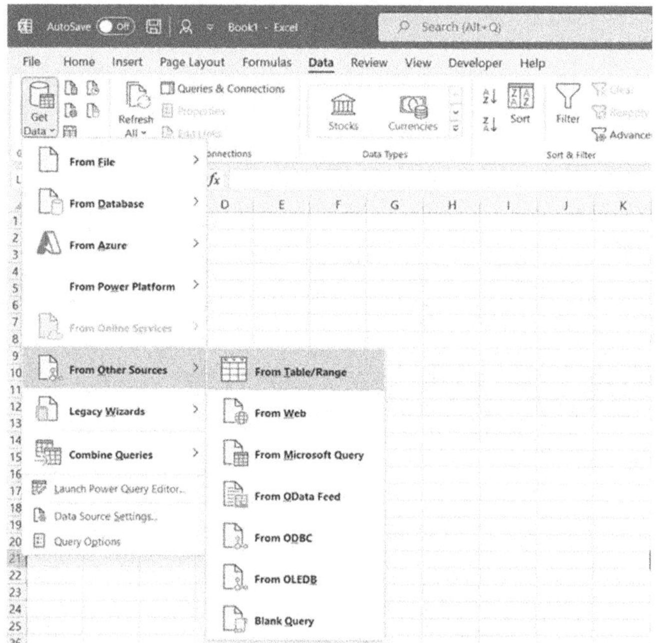

FIGURE 23.4 A query can be based on various other data sources depending on the type of Excel license you have purchased.

- **The Legacy Wizard**s category allows you to get data from the Web by using an older Excel feature known as Web query. For more information, and how to activate this feature, please see Chapter 27.
- **The Combine Queries** category (see Figure 23.5) has options for merging and appending queries which allow you to create complex queries.

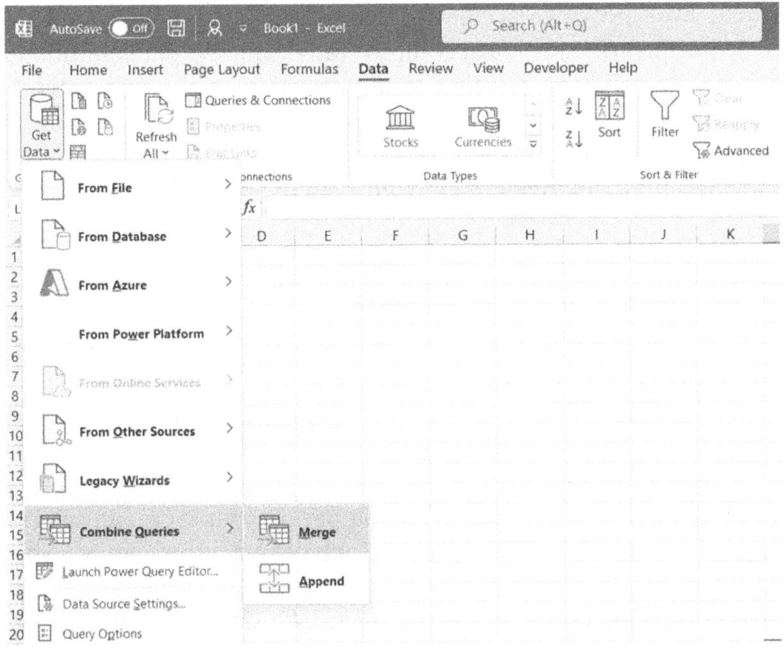

FIGURE 23.5 Queries can be combined by merging or appending.

At the bottom of the Get Data drop-down (see Figure 23.5) you will find options that will allow you to launch Power Query Editor, manage settings for your data sources, and view Query Options.

UNDERSTANDING POWER QUERIES

To create a query you begin by selecting a data source using the Get Data button (see Figure 23.2 earlier). The data can be a local file on your computer, or a file stored in the cloud, or a resource fetched via a web service. Your data source selection is recorded by the built-in Query Editor as a first step in your power query. After making a connection to your data you will be put in the Query Editor where you can shape your data to meet your needs (see Figure 23.6). The Query Editor Ribbon consists of the following tabs:

The Home tab – shows buttons for common query tasks, such as managing columns and rows, sorting, accessing the Advanced Editor and query properties, refreshing the preview, combining, transforming, and loading data as well as creating a new query.

The Transform tab– provides access to common data transformation tasks, such as working with various types of columns (any column, text column, number, and date & time column), splitting a column using a delimiter, extracting, parsing, and cleaning data. Here you will also find options for moving columns, pivoting and unpivoting columns and working with tables. The unpivot functionality is very useful if you need to get your data in a tabular form, instead of a matrix.

The Add Column tab – provides buttons for adding custom columns, formatting column data, merging and duplicating columns.

The View tab– enables turning on and off the display of various features in the Query Editor.

Using the Query Editor Ribbon buttons, you can remove columns and rows, add new columns, change the data type, change, and format values, perform calculations, merge, and append data.

The Query Editor will record each step you perform via its menu selections while keeping your original data unchanged. Each data transformation you perform is automatically labeled so it is easy to see at a glance what each step attempts to do (see Figure 23.6). You can also rename the steps to make then even more meaningful.

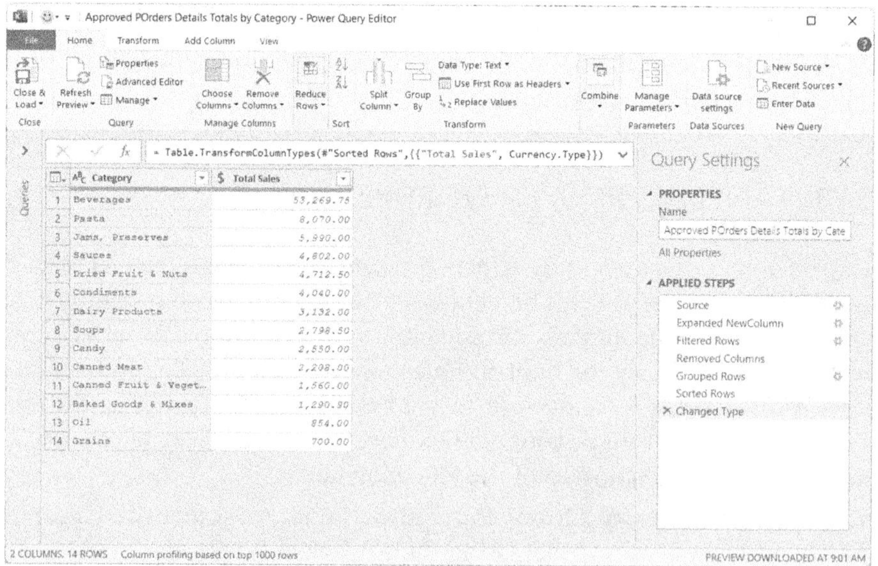

FIGURE 23.6 All Query Steps are listed in the Applied Steps section of the Query Settings Pane.

You can delete or modify a step, change the order of steps, and you can add new steps. A Query is simply a collection of steps arranged in a specific order, with the last step returning the final output to a worksheet or the Excel Data Model.

Power Query steps are written in the M expression language. You can view the scripting code of your query prepared in the M language in the Advanced Editor (see Figure 23.7) and in the Query Editor Formula Bar. You can edit the code manually to add transformations to your query that are not available via the menus. You can also create queries from scratch using the Advanced Editor.

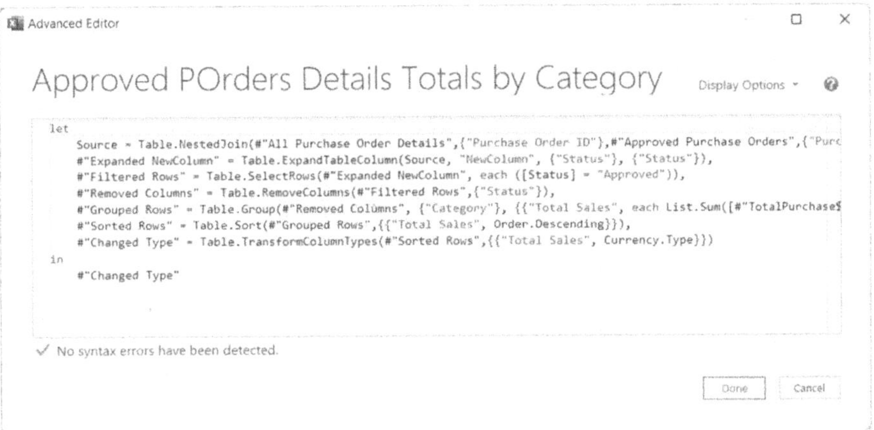

FIGURE 23.7 The query script code can be edited or written from scratch in the Advanced Editor.

Once the power query result is output to a worksheet, the query is saved automatically when you save the workbook. A workbook can contain multiple queries (see Figure 23.8). You can view all the queries in the workbook by selecting **Show Queries** from the **Get & Transform Data** section of the Ribbon's Data tab.

Power queries are very flexible. They can be easily duplicated if you need to change some of the transformations without changing the original query. You can also merge two queries together similar to joining two tables with an SQL statement, or you can append one query onto the end of another. The last two queries shown in Figure 23.8 have been created using the Merge option. Queries can also serve as data sources for other queries thus allowing you to build more complex data transformations.

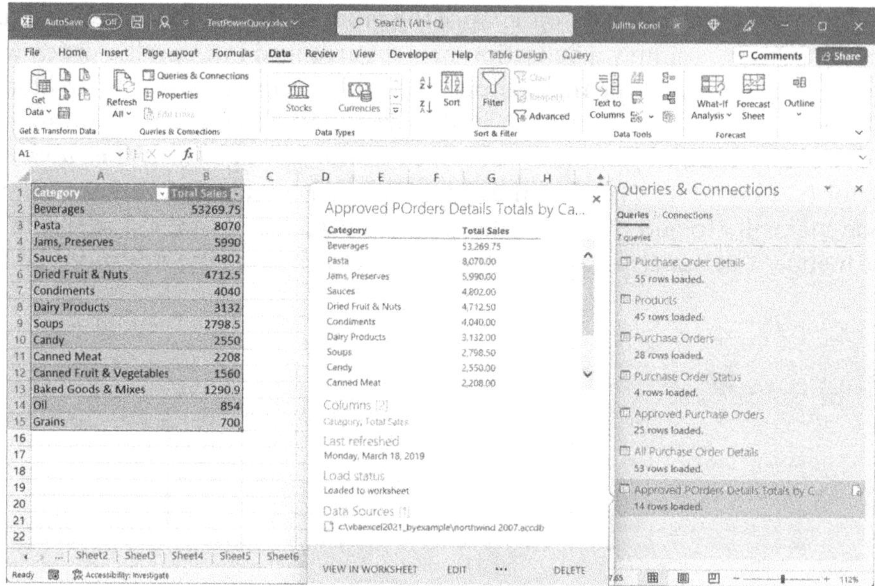

FIGURE 23.8 A workbook with multiple queries.

Let's get some hands-on experience with the Power Query user interface. In Custom Project 23.1 you are going to bring together data from the following:

- an Excel workbook (.XLSX) containing two worksheets
- a comma-separated value text file (.CSV)

These files hold information about post offices in Tri-State area (NY, NJ, and CT). The source data for each state was manually copied from the United States Postal Service Web resource at *http://webpmt.usps.gov/pmt010.cfm.*

The goal of this project is to combine and clean the data so that you can produce a summary of active and discontinued post offices by state. While this project can be easily performed by using the Copy & Paste operation, Excel formulas and built-in tools on the Excel Ribbon, the query option presented here is more powerful. Because queries are collections of steps, you will never have to perform the same tasks again if the data changes. Simply do the Refresh, and the data will be reprocessed without further work on your part.

NOTE	*Please note files for the "Hands-On" project may be found in the companion files.*

Custom Project 23.1 Creating a Query from Multiple Sources

1. Copy the **GetTransform** folder from the Companion files to your **VBAExcel2021_ByExample** folder.
2. Launch Excel and choose **New | Blank workbook.**
3. Save the empty workbook as **PostOffice_Queries.xlsx.**

Step 1: Get Data from an Excel Workbook

4. Choose **Get Data | From File | From Excel Workbook.**
5. Select the **PostOffice_NY_NJ.xlsx** workbook file from the **GetTransform** folder and click **Import.**
6. In the Navigator window, click the checkbox next to **Select Multiple Items** and select the checkboxes for **NY** and **NJ** as shown in Figure 23.9).

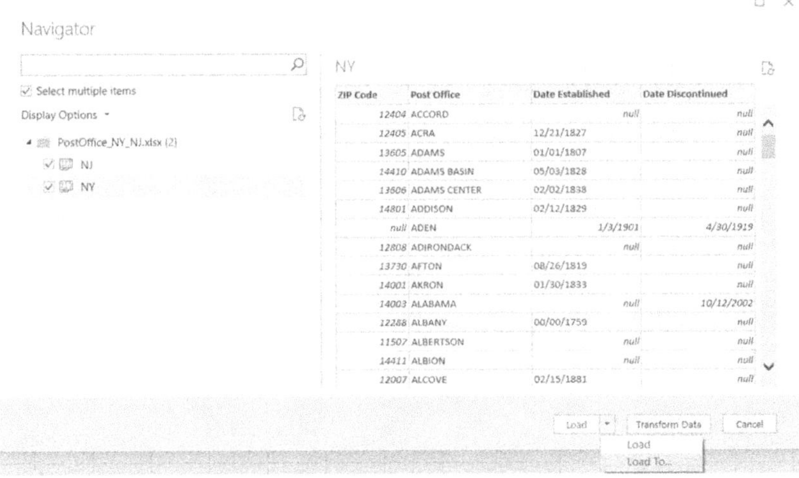

FIGURE 23.9 The Navigator Window is showing data that is available in the requested data source.

Notice that the right pane displays the contents of the selected item.

7. Click the drop-down arrow next to Load and choose **LoadTo** (see Figure 23.9).
8. In the Import Data window click the radio button next to **Table,** choose **New worksheet,** and check the **Add this data to the Data Model** (Figure 23.10).
9. Click the **OK** button in the Import Data dialog.
   Excel creates two tables based on the two worksheets that you selected. The right pane displays the Workbook Queries pane with a listing of queries (Figure 23.11). This list can be turned on and off using the Queries & Connections button on the Data tab.

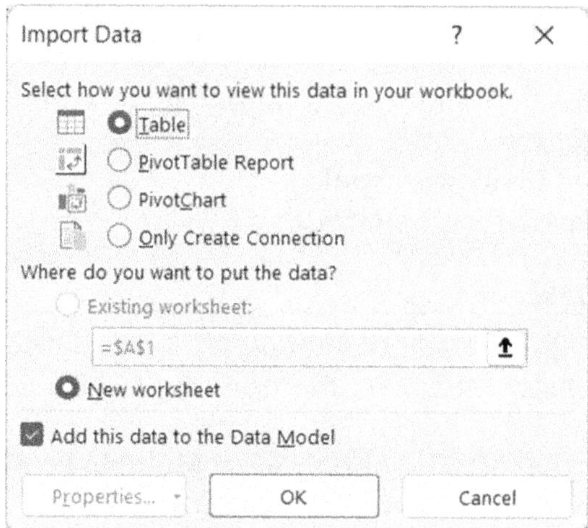

FIGURE 23.10 In the Load To dialog you can specify how you want to view the data and where it should be loaded.

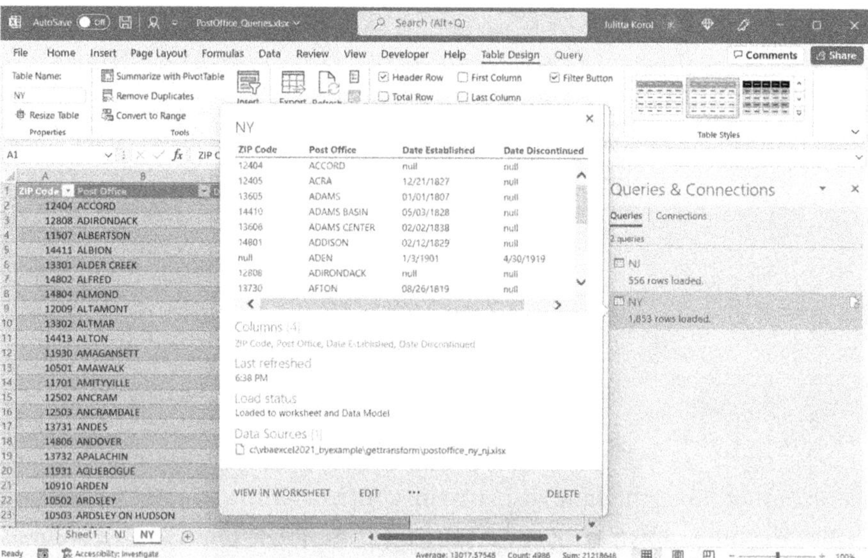

FIGURE 23.11 The Workbook with two Queries.

To see the information about each query, click on the query name to view the preview screen.

In the footer of the preview screen, you can find options that allow you to view the data in worksheet, delete the query from the workbook or edit the query. Notice that Excel displays the number of rows that were successfully loaded. If upon loading errors are encountered, the error count will be shown as hyperlink, so you can get more information about the error.

Looking at the initial data load in Figure 23.11, notice that the data has been converted to an Excel table for each worksheet found in the source file. The Ribbon shows the Table Design tab. At this point you could reformat your table or create a PivotTable, but we have more important tasks to perform. Currently there is no way to identify the data as belonging to NY or NJ other than looking at the query names. We need the State column in each table.

Step 2: Adding, Renaming, and Moving a New Column

10. In the Workbook Queries pane, right-click NJ query and choose **Edit**. The NJ - Query Editor window appears showing you the four transformation steps in the Applied Steps pane that Excel automatically created when you loaded the data (Figure 23.12).

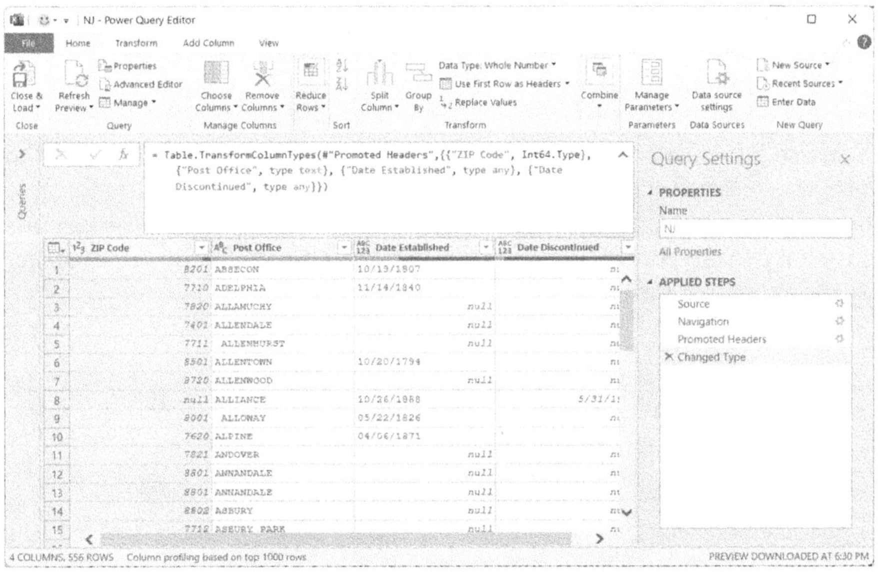

FIGURE 23.12 The NJ Query Editor Window displays the applied data transformation steps to NJ table.

A step can be deleted by clicking the button (x) in front of the step name. Keep in mind that there is no undo option. A deleted step must be recreated if you want it back. Some steps will show a Gears icon next to them (see Figures 23.12 and 23.13). These steps can be edited using the same dialog that was used to create it. Simply click this icon or right-click it and choose Edit settings. The Gears icon will disappear if you happen to make an invalid change in the formula for the step. Figure 23.13 shows the dialog used to edit the Source step.

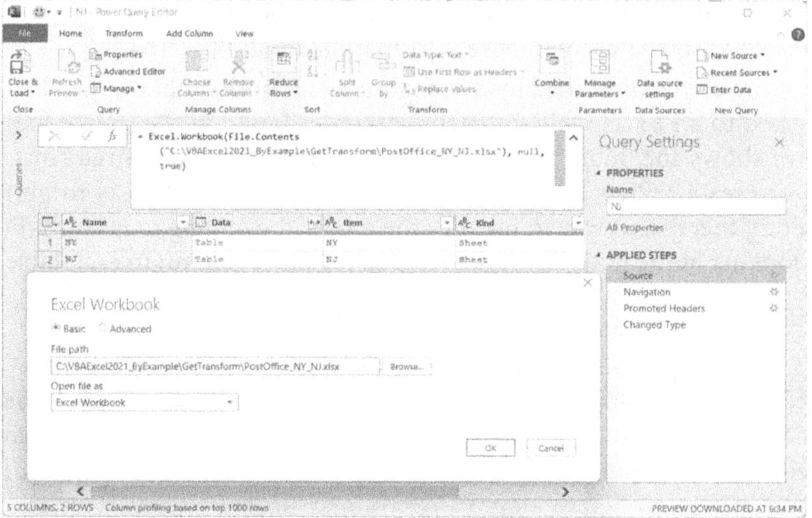

FIGURE 23.13 The Excel dialog provides a way to edit the source of the data.

11. Click the **Promoted Headers** step and choose **View | Formula Bar** (Figure 23.14).
    You can use Formula bar to check or edit the M expression that was used to perform the selected data transformation step. You can also use the formula bar to create a new step by clicking on the *fx* icon. You can expand the formula bar to see its entire contents by clicking the drop down. Figure 23.12 earlier shows the expanded formula bar.

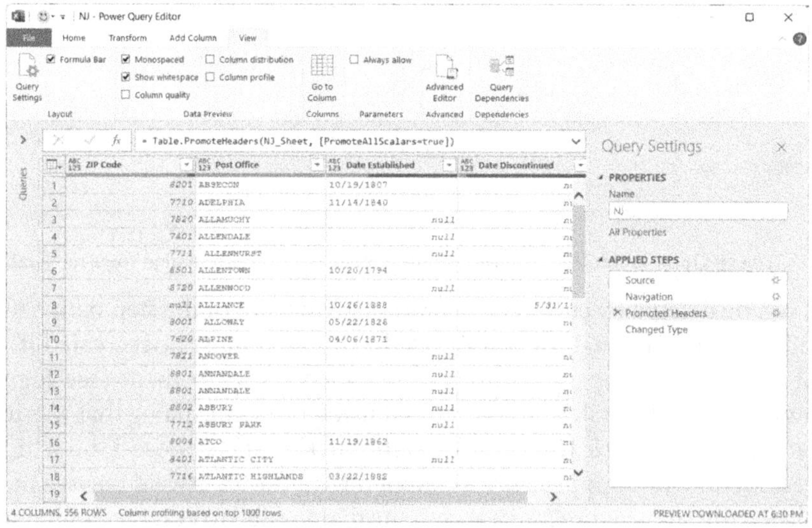

FIGURE 23.14 Examining the formula for the selected step.

12. Select the **Changed Type** step and notice that the formula references the previous step (Promoted Headers). See Figure 23.15.

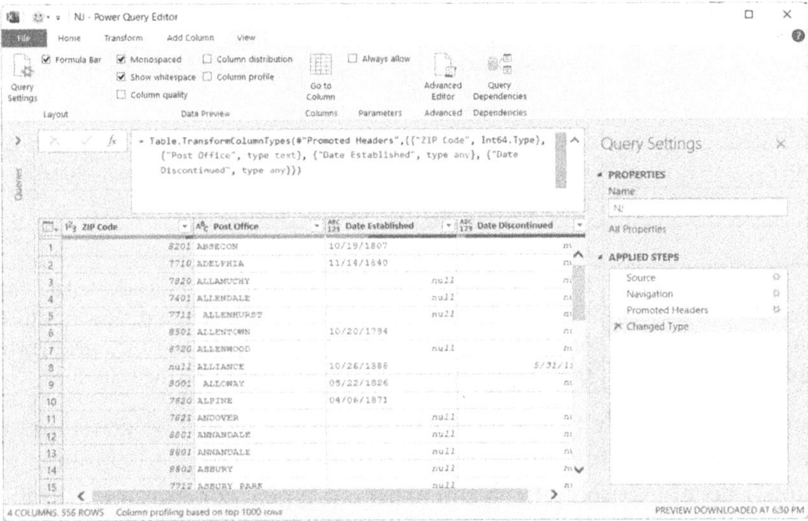

FIGURE 23.15 The Expanded Formula Bar.

The Changed Type step automatically applies a data type to each of the columns.

SIDEBAR *Referring to the Query Steps*

Steps or queries that have a space in the name must be referenced as #"query name".

SIDEBAR *Data Types*

Each column in the Power query has a specific data type. You do not need to declare data type of any value as the M language automatically determines this when you create a query. However, if you get an error because of an incorrect data type, there are commands on the Ribbon available for correcting this. The following data types can be used:

Data Type	Description
Binary	Used for storing images and the contents of files
Currency	Used for storing monetary values
Date	Used for storing dates between January 1, 0001 CE and December 31, 9999 CE in the Gregorian calendars.

Data Type	Description
Date/Time	Used for storing both date and time
Date/Time/Timezone	Used for storing date, time and time zone
Duration	Used for storing the difference between two times, date/times or date/time/time zones.
Logical	Used for storing False or True values
Number	Used for storing numeric values (integers and fractionals)
Text	Used for storing Unicode text. Text is case sensitive.
Time	Used for storing time of day values
Any (not available as a selection from the data type drop-down box)	Used for storing any type of value. Oftentimes selected automatically when you import the data. It is better to replace it with Text or Number so you can take advantage of the functionality which these types provide when replacing or filtering values.

M language is strongly typed. This means that errors will be generated if the arguments passed to functions (or the values you attempt to combine in expressions) do not closely match the expected type. For example, combining text with a number such as:

```
"This is example " & 1
```

by using the *&* operator will throw an error because text cannot be combined with a number without a conversion. To avoid the error, the function Number.ToText can be used to cast a number to text:

```
"This is example " & Number.ToText(1)
```

13. To add a new column to the current table, choose **Add Column | Add Custom Column**.
    Be sure to click out of the formula bar if you find that he Add Column button is disabled.
14. Enter the data as shown in Figure 23.16 and click **OK**.
    The Add Custom Column dialog specifies that you want to add a new column named State and fill it with the string NJ.

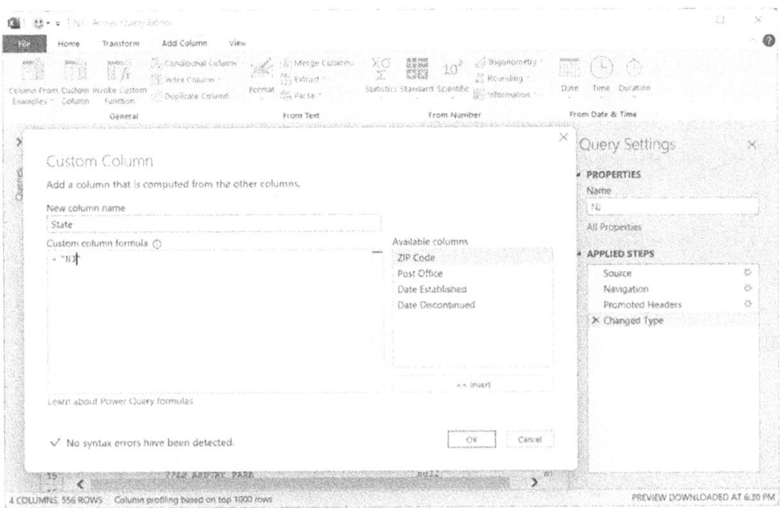

FIGURE 23.16 Adding a New Custom Column.

Excel adds a new State column and now we have a way to identify each zip code with the state of New Jersey (Figure 23.17).

NOTE	*Figure 23.17 shows four-digit zip codes which is incorrect. You can easily fix this by Choosing Transform | Format |Add Prefix and entering zero (0) in the dialog box.*

NJ - Power Query Editor

```
= Table.AddColumn(#"Changed Type", "State", each "NJ")
```

	ZIP Code	Post Office	Date Established	Date Discontinued	State
1	8201	ABSECON	10/19/1807	null	NJ
2	7710	ADELPHIA	11/14/1840	null	NJ
3	7820	ALLAMUCHY	null	null	NJ
4	7401	ALLENDALE	null	null	NJ
5	7711	ALLENHURST	null	null	NJ
6	8501	ALLENTOWN	10/20/1794	null	NJ
7	8720	ALLENWOOD	null	null	NJ
8	null	ALLIANCE	10/26/1888	5/31/1917	NJ
9	8002	ALLOWAY	05/22/1826	null	NJ
10	7620	ALPINE	04/06/1871		NJ
11	7821	ANDOVER	null	null	NJ
12	8801	ANNANDALE	null	null	NJ
13	8861	ANNANDALE	null	null	NJ
14	8602	ASBURY	null	null	NJ
15	7712	ASBURY PARK	null	null	NJ
16	8004	ATCO	11/19/1862	null	NJ
17	8401	ATLANTIC CITY	null	null	NJ
18	7716	ATLANTIC HIGHLANDS	03/22/1882	null	NJ
19	7822	AUGUSTA	05/15/1813	null	NJ

Query Settings: PROPERTIES, Name: NJ, All Properties; APPLIED STEPS: Source, Navigation, Promoted Headers, Changed Type, Added Custom

5 COLUMNS, 556 ROWS Column profiling based on top 1000 rows — PREVIEW DOWNLOADED AT 6:30 PM

FIGURE 23.17 The State column appears as a new transformation named Added Custom.

15. Right-click the **Added Custom** step in the Applied Steps pane and choose **Rename**. Type the new name for this step: **Added State Column.**
16. Right-click the **State** column in the data pane and choose **Move | To Beginning**. The State column should appear before the ZIP Code column.

    Now let's perform the same steps in the NY query.
17. Click the **Queries** Navigation Pane on the very left of the Query Editor window to expand the Navigation pane (Figure 23.17).
18. Select **NY** query to open it in the Query Editor.

    Notice that NY query contains the same steps as the NJ query in the Applied Steps pane except for the custom State column (Figure 23.18).

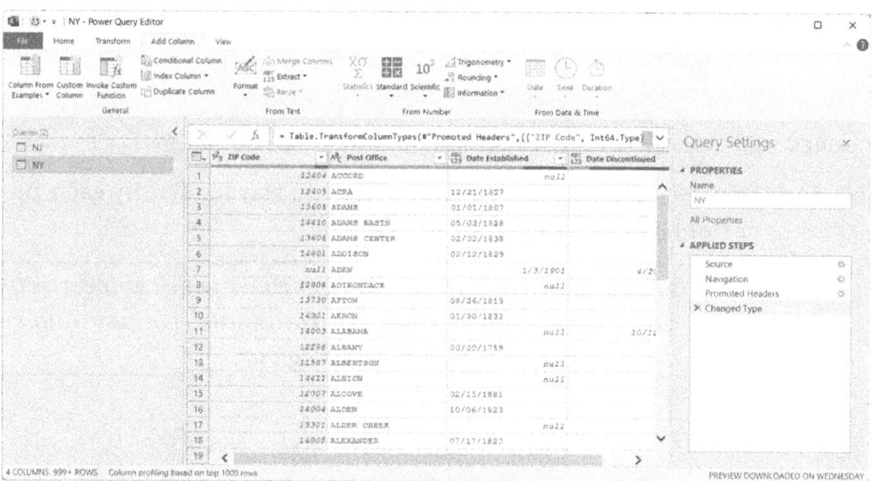

FIGURE 23.18 Loading the NY query into the Query Editor.

19. On your own add a State column to the NY query, rename the Query step and move the State column to the beginning (see Steps 13-16 above).

SIDEBAR *Adding New Steps to the Query*

The Query Editor allows you to add new steps at the end of the query or in between the existing steps. An inserted step may impact another step in the query. When you remove a step from the Applied Steps, subsequent steps may suddenly display errors. When you add a new step to the query pay attention to which step is currently selected. The Query Editor will warn you that adding a step could cause the query to break.

20. Choose **Home | Close & Load** to save the changes to the queries. This also closes the Editor window and loads the data in the default location.
Excel updates the tables to include the State Column (Figure 23.19).

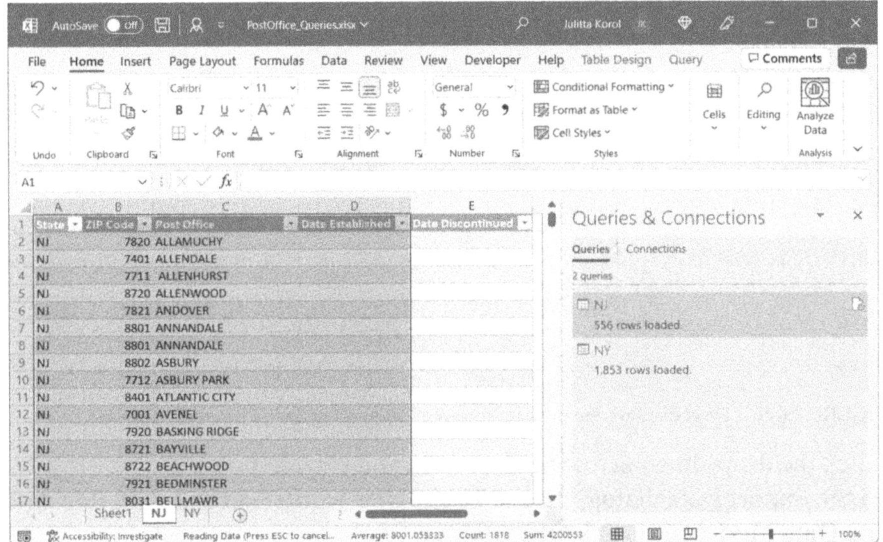

FIGURE 23.19 Excel table now contains the State column.

21. Save the **PostOffice_NY_NJ.xlsx** workbook but keep it open.
When you save the file, Excel also saves the queries you created. Make sure to save often while working with the queries as Excel may crash suddenly and you will lose your work.

Let's not forget that we still must pull the Connecticut data from another data source – a comma-separated value (CSV) file.

Step 3: Loading Data from a Text File

22. Choose **Data | From Text / CSV**.
23. Select the **PostOffice_CT.csv** file in the GetTransform folder and click **Import**. Excel displays the preview of the file as shown in Figure 23.20.

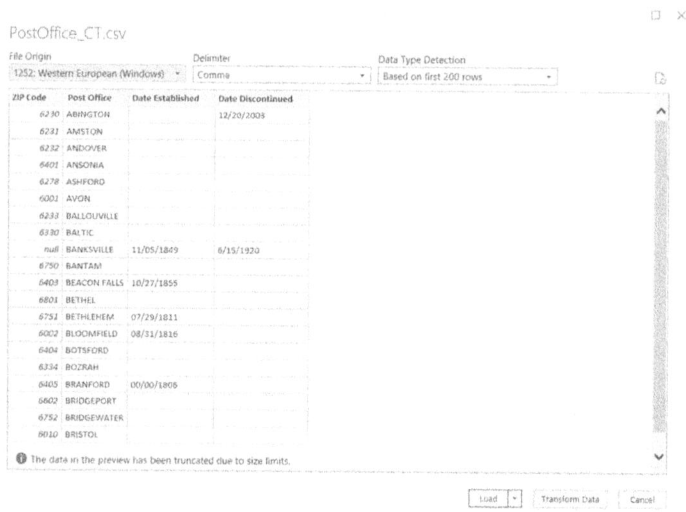

FIGURE 23.20 Excel displays the preview screen when loading data from text / csv files.

24. Click the drop-down arrow next to Load and choose **Load to.**
25. In the Import Data dialog, choose **Table, New worksheet** and **Add this data to the Data Model**, and click **OK.**

    Excel loads the data into a new worksheet and adds the query into the Queries & Connections pane (Figure 23.21).

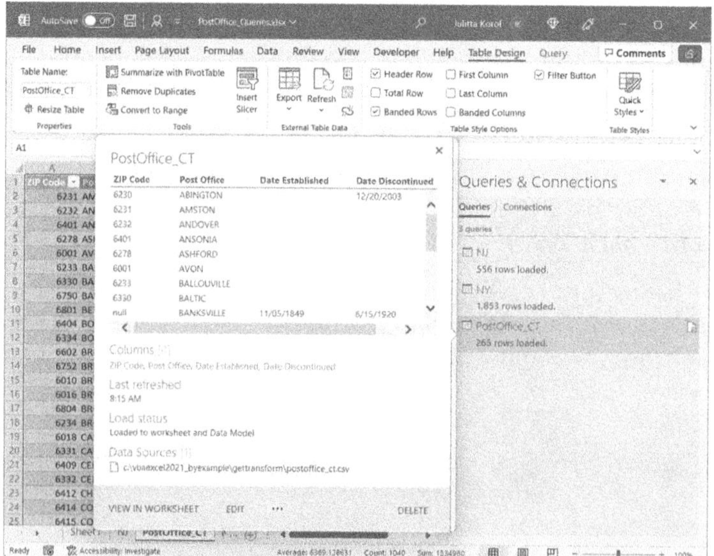

FIGURE 23.21 You can modify the query by clicking Edit in the preview window.

26. Highlight the PostOffice_CT query and click the Edit button in the preview window as shown in Figure 23.21 above.
    Excel loads the file into the Query Editor. It looks like the data is split correctly into four columns that we need. All that's missing is the custom column that will hold the state name.
27. On your own add a **State** column to the **PostOffice_CT** query as instructed in Steps 13-16 above.
28. In the Query Settings Properties Name box enter **CT** as the new name for your query. Click **Rename** button in the popup box to confirm.
    Figure 23.22 shows the Query Editor after changes made in Steps 27-28.

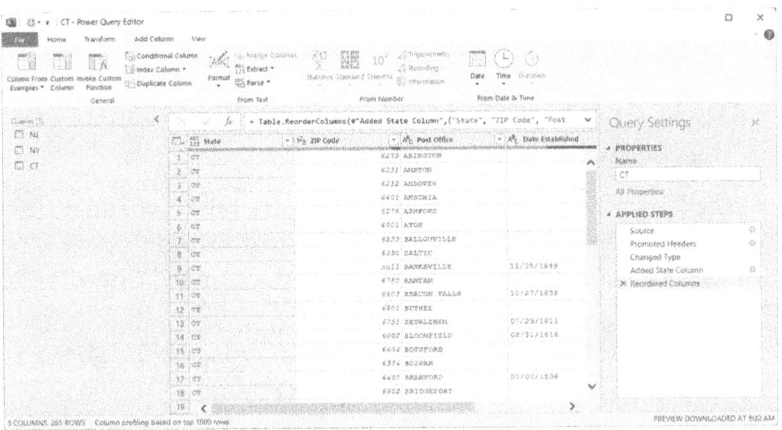

FIGURE 23.22 The CT query after modification.

29. Choose **File | Close & Load.**
    The PostOffice_Queries.xlsx workbook now contains three queries that we need for further data manipulation.
30. Press **Ctrl+S** to save the workbook file with the queries.

Step 4: Combining Data using Append Query

31. To combine the data for all three states, right-click **NJ** query name and choose **Append.**
    An Append dialog appears with two drop-down lists. The Primary table is already specified as NJ.
32. Click the **Three or more tables** radio button.
    Excel displays the Append dialog where you can select the tables you need to combine.

33. Enter the data as shown in Figure 23.23 and click **OK** to close the Append dialog.

Append

Concatenate rows from three or more tables into a single table.

○ Two tables ◉ Three or more tables

Available tables: NJ, NY, CT

Add >>

Tables to append: NJ, NY, CT

OK Cancel

FIGURE 23.23 Appending Multiple Tables.

Excel opens the Query Editor. You can see the result of the Append operation with one step in the Applied Steps section and a query named Append1. If the Query Settings pane is not visible, you can turn it back on by choosing View | Query Settings.

34. Change the query name to **Tri-State Data** as shown in Figure 23.24.

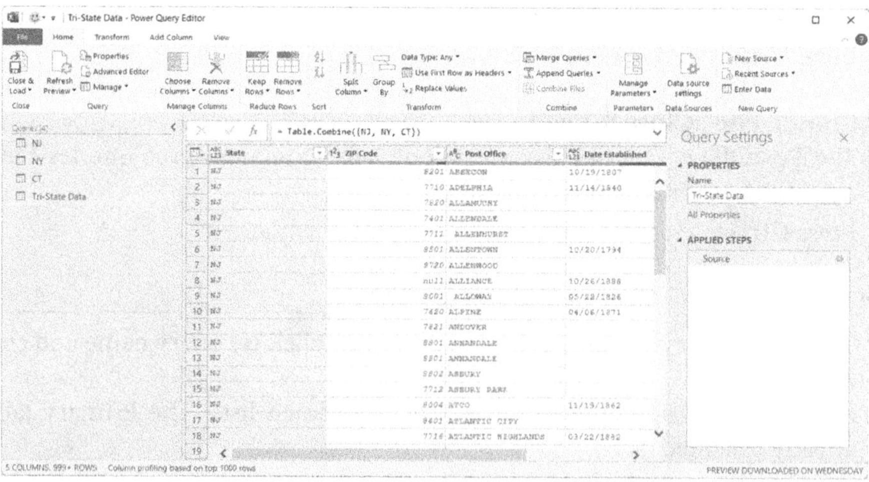

FIGURE 23.24 The Query Editor displays the result of the Append operation.

Notice that the formula bar shows the statement that combines three data sets:

```
= Table.Combine({CT, NJ, NY})
```

You could edit the `Table.Combine` formula to include more items if needed without having to open the Append dialog.

35. Choose **File | Close & Load.**
The Tri-State Data query now appears in the Workbook Queries pane and the active sheet displays Excel table with combined data for post offices in all three states.
36. Press **Ctr+S** to save the workbook.
Now that we have the data in one place, let's proceed with the cleanup of this data.

We will start by removing duplicate records.

Step 5: Data Cleanup

37. In the Queries & Connections pane, double-click the **Tri-State Data** query to open it in the Query Editor.
38. Select the **Post Office** column and click **Home | Remove Rows | Remove Duplicates.**
There are many blank entries in the Date Discontinued column. For consistency's sake, let's replace all blanks with null values.

NOTE	*Empty cells are shown as null in queries.*

39. Select the **Date Discontinued** column and choose **Home | Replace Values.**
Excel displays the Replace Values dialog.
40. Leave the **Value to Find** text box empty and enter **null** in the **Replace with** text box and click **OK.**
A Replaced Value step is added to the Applied Steps pane as shown in Figure 23.25.

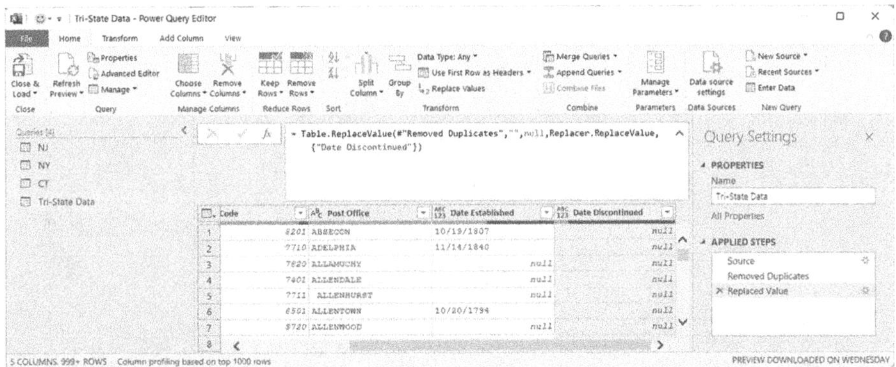

FIGURE 23.25 The Query Editor with a Replaced Value Step.

Before we can shape the data into its final output, we need to include a bit of logic into our query. To display the count of active and discontinued post offices, let's add a custom column to hold the category we need.

41. Choose **Add Column | Add Custom Column** and complete the dialog as shown in Figure 23.26. Press **OK** when done.

Custom Column

Add a column that is computed from the other columns.

New column name

Category

Custom column formula

```
= if [Date Discontinued] = null then "Active" else
  "Discontinued"
```

Available columns

State
ZIP Code
Post Office
Date Established
Date Discontinued

<< Insert

Learn about Power Query formulas

✓ No syntax errors have been detected.

OK Cancel

FIGURE 23.26 Entering a logical expression in a custom column formula.

The Query Editor now shows the Category column with Active and Discontinued values (Figure 23.27).

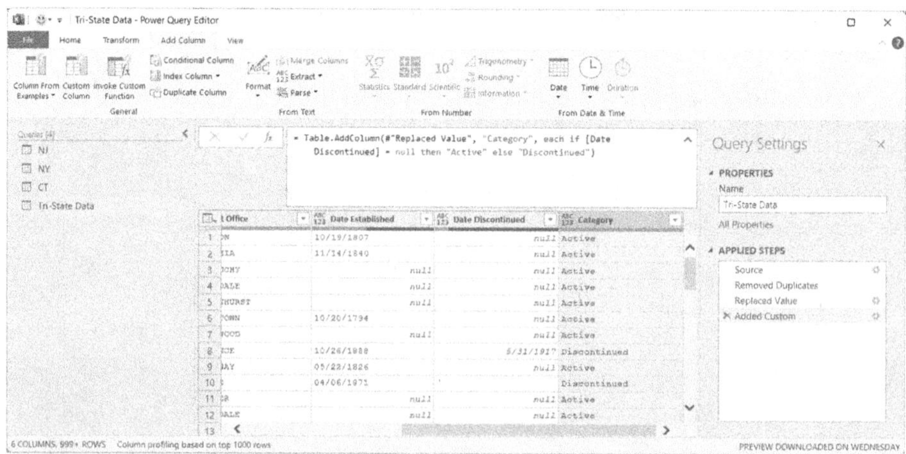

FIGURE 23.27 The Category Column data obtained via the logical expression.

SIDEBAR *Conditional Logic*

To add decisions in the M language, use the *if...then...else* expression. If the expression in the if clause returns *true* then the result of the expression in the then clause is returned, otherwise the result of the expression in the else clause is returned (see Figure 23.27 above).

M language does not have the Case statement. If you need decisions based on multiple conditions, you should use nested *if...then...else* expressions.

42. Rename the step **Added Custom** to **Added Category Column.**

Step 6: Shaping Data into Final Output

To produce the final report, we will need only two columns: State and Category. There are various ways to remove columns from a table. You can choose the Remove Columns option to remove the selected columns or the Remove Other Columns options to remove all but the selected columns. There is also a way to remove columns using the Choose Columns button on the Home tab of the Query Editor toolbar.

43. Select **Home | Choose Columns**, select **State** and **Category** and click **OK** (Figure 23.28).

FIGURE 23.28 Choosing the columns to keep.

Our table is now reduced to two columns. Let's shape the data into the final output by using the Group By option.

44. Choose **Transform | Group By** and complete the Group By dialog as shown in Figure 23.29. Click **OK** when done.

Group By

Specify the columns to group by and one or more outputs.

Basic Advanced

State

Category

Add grouping

New column name | Operation | Column

Count of Post Office Locations | Count Rows

Add aggregation

OK Cancel

FIGURE 23.29 Specifying the Grouping Criteria.

The Query Editor displays the grouping output as shown in Figure 23.30.

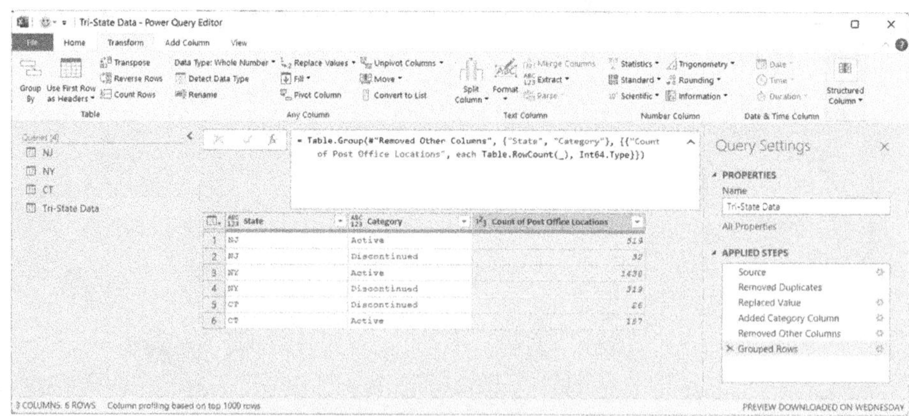

FIGURE 23.30 The Group By Output for this project.

SIDEBAR *Aggregating Data*

To aggregate and group data in the Query Editor, select the column you want to group by and click the Group By button in the Home tab. In the Group By window (Figure 23.29), you can group by multiple columns using the Advanced radio button. The Operation drop-down lets you choose from various aggregate functions such as Count Rows, Average, Min, Max, Sum, etc. If you require more than one grouping, click the Add grouping button. And if you need to remove a group, point to the group name, and notice the three-dot button to the right of the name. Click this button to reveal menu options: Delete, Move Up, and Move Down.

Let's add a final touch to the obtained summary of data by applying an ascending sort order to the State and Category columns.

45. Click the drop-down arrow in the **State** column and choose **Sort ascending**.
46. Click the drop-down arrow in the **Category** column and choose **Sort ascending**.
    The Query Editor displays the rearranged data (Figure 23.31).

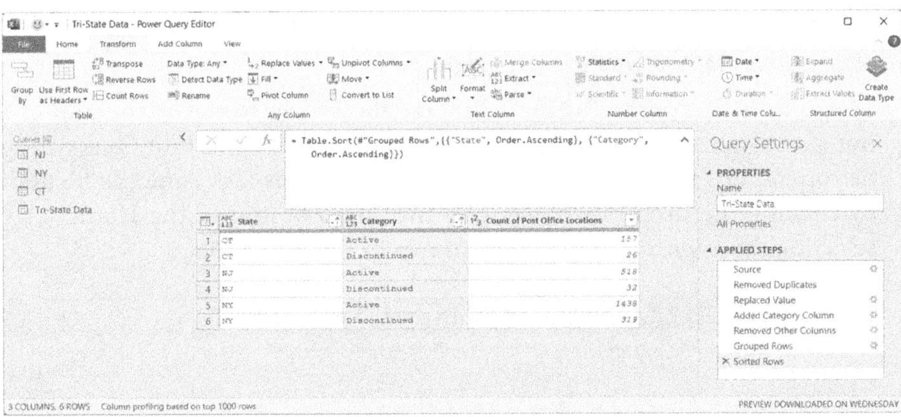

FIGURE 23.31 Query Editor showing the final output from the data manipulations performed in this Chapter's project.

47. Choose **File | Close & Load** to close the Query Editor and load the data into a worksheet.
    Figure 23.32 shows all the queries that you created and their output.
48. Save the workbook file.

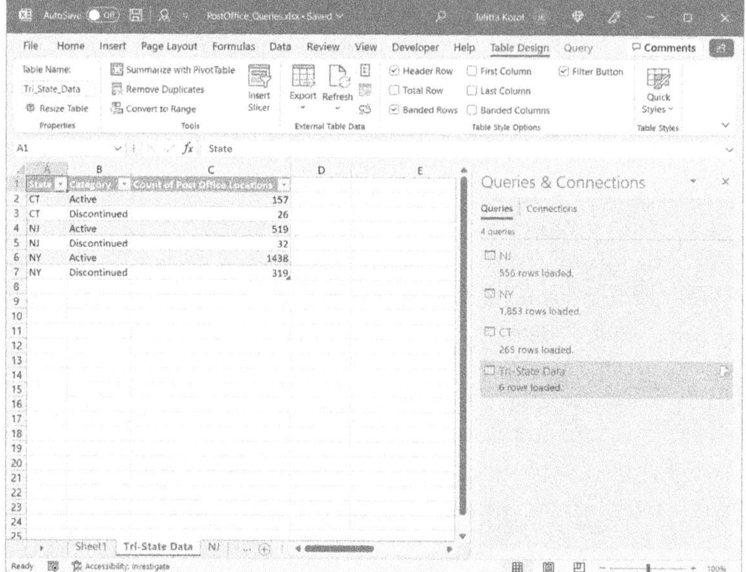

FIGURE 23.32 An Excel workbook showing the final output of data loading and transformation using the Power Query feature.

SIDEBAR *Repeatable Refresh and Undo Support*

The Refresh button on the Data Ribbon allows you to repeat the import and transformation of the data to the workbook. Refresh and Edit Query Properties operations performed in the Workbook Queries task pane can be undone by clicking the drop-down arrow in the Undo button in the Home tab and selecting the appropriate action as shown in Figure 23.33.

FIGURE 23.33 Undoing Refresh and Edit Query operations.

USING THE ADVANCED EDITOR

Now that you've created your first power queries, let's look at the M code that the Query Editor created for you. You can get a full view of the code by accessing the Advanced Editor. Simply double-click the Tri-State Data query in your workbook and choose Advanced Editor on the Power Query Editor's View tab. Figure 23.34 shows the M code for your query.

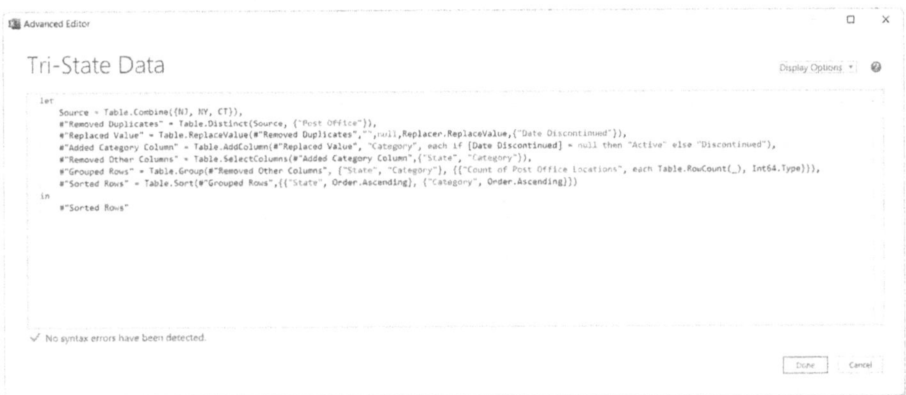

FIGURE 23.34 Reviewing the M code for the Tri-State Data query in the Advanced Editor.

SIDEBAR *Reusing an Output of one Query in Another*

A query can serve as a source for another query. If you right-click a query in the Workbook Queries pane and select Reference, a new query will be created and will produce the same output as the original query. For example, if Query1 already contains the data you need, you can reference this query. Query2 will be automatically created for you with the following M code:

```
let
  Source = Query1
in
  Source
```

Notice that the Query2 is using the name of Query1 in the source definition. You can then add specific steps to Query2 to transform the data obtained from Query1.

POWER QUERY VS EXCEL FORMULA LANGUAGE AND EXCEL VBA

Unfortunately, the "M" language used in Power Query formulas does not bear any resemblance to Excel formulas or VBA language. If you plan on building complex data solutions using the Get Data (Power Query) interface in Excel, you will need to invest time in becoming competent with it. The following link provides reference to the Power Query M Formula Language (informally known as "M"):

Power Query M formula language reference - PowerQuery M | Microsoft Docs

Table 23.1 shows examples of the M language formulas.

TABLE 23.1 Examples of M language Functions

Description	Functions
Create a new custom column in Excel	`= Excel.Workbook([Content)]`
Create a new custom column in a CSV file	`= Csv.Document([Content])`
Create a new column by concatenating values from two existing columns	`= [Column1Name] & " " & [Column2Name]`
Remove two first characters from the column entry	`= Text.Range([ColumnName], 2)`
Place a value in a column based on a condition	`= if[ColumnName]= "V" then "Vacation" else "Other"`
Rename the column to Employee	`= Table.RenameColumns(Source, {{"oldColumnName", "Employee"}})`
Get a list of Headers in your table	`= Table.ColumnNames(Source)`
Get the name of the second column Note: Lists in query are 0 based. 1 will get the second column.	`= Table.ColumnNames(Source){1}`

LEARNING ABOUT VARIOUS M LANGUAGE FUNCTIONS

You can learn about various M language functions in the Power Query Editor. Simply type a function in the Formula Bar and press Enter to see the syntax and examples of the function usage. For example, to find out how to use `Table.Combine`, type `=Table.Combine` in the Formula Bar. After pressing Enter you should see the output shown in Figure 23.35.

Important Note: The M language is case sensitive, therefore, to avoid errors caused by case sensitivity pay attention to lowercase and uppercase letters in the expressions.

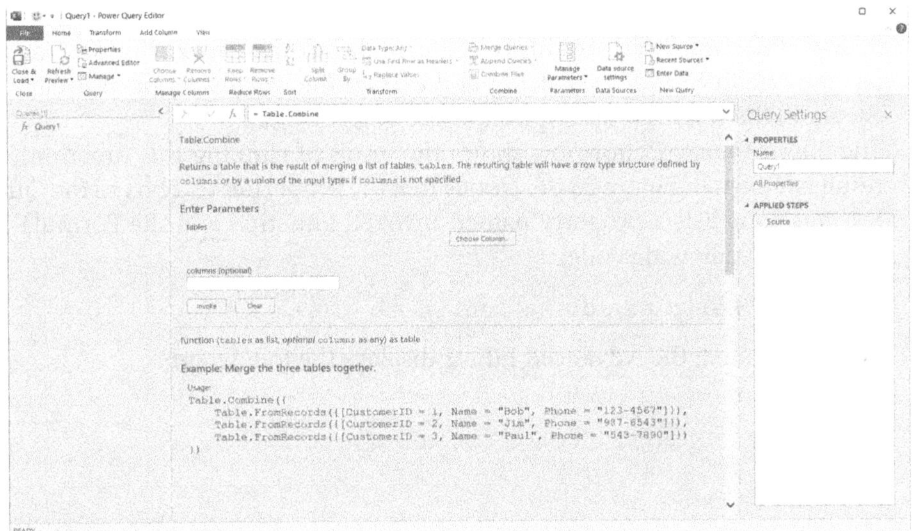

FIGURE 23.35 Looking up information about M language functions by using the Formula Bar in the Power Query Editor.

Let's take a couple of minutes now to look up information about some functions shown in Table 23.1. While you can use the Formula Bar in any query, in Hands-On 23.1 you will use a blank query for this purpose.

Hands-On 23.1 Using a Blank Query for trying out M functions

1. Open a new blank Excel workbook.
2. In the Excel Ribbon, choose **Data | Get Data | From Other Sources | Blank query**.

   The Power Query Editor appears with the insertion point in the Formula Bar ready for your input. The Applied Steps displays one step named Source which is currently empty as there is no formula for this step. If you open the Advanced Editor (View | Advanced Editor) at this time you will see the following script:

```
let
    Source = ""
```

```
in
    Source
```

3. In the Query Editor's Formula Bar, type `= Text.Range` and press **Enter.** The Data pane displays the information about the requested function. There is also an Invoke button below the function example that allows you to try it out for yourself.
4. Provide the parameters for this function and click the **Invoke** button. You can use the "Hello World" text string and extract the word starting at index 6 as shown in the function description or use your own text.
   The Power Query Editor now shows the result of running this function. The result is shown in Figure 23.36. Notice that the Properties text box in the Query Settings pane lists a property named Invoked Function and the Formula Bar displays the following code:

```
= Query1("Hello World", 6, null)
```

When activated, the Advanced Editor displays the following:

```
let
    Source = Query1("Hello World", 6, null)
in
    Source
```

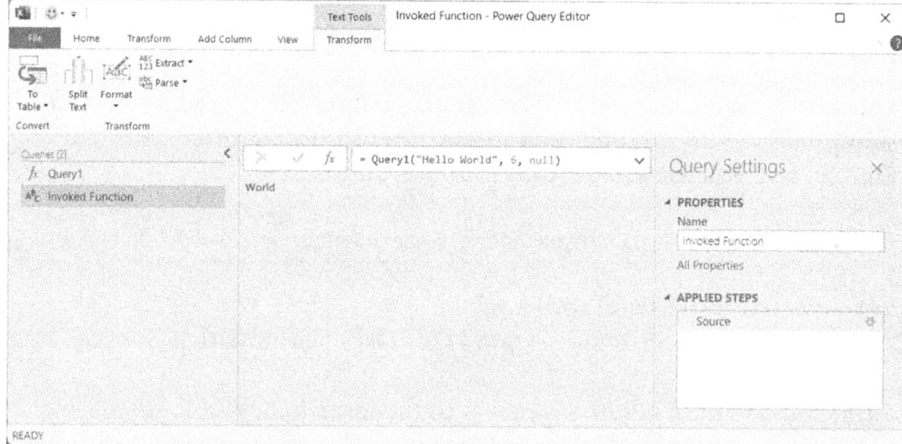

FIGURE 23.36 The result of invoking a function in the Power Query Editor.

You can continue testing other functions in the Formula Bar and invoking them to view the result. The blank query can be used as a scratch pad like the Immediate Window in Visual Basic Editor (VBE).

5. Select the blank query name (query1) in the Queries pane to the left of the Formula bar and then change the Name property of your query in the Query Settings pane to **TestFunctions**.
6. Use the **Close & Load** button to save your changes. Excel creates TestFunctions connection as shown in Figure 23.37.

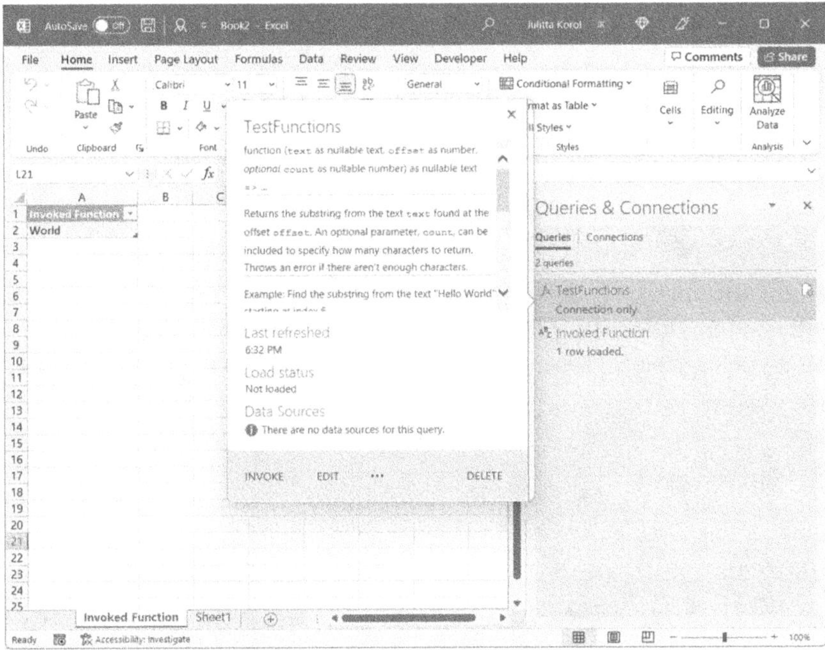

FIGURE 23.37 The blank query that you created has no data, so Excel created just a connection reference. This way the query will be saved with your workbook, and you can edit it anytime. Also, you can reference the query from other queries.

7. Save the workbook as **PowerQueries_Scratchpad.xlsx**.

CREATING A QUERY FROM A TABLE

In addition to creating queries from external data sources, you can use the Get Data button to work with a table of data in the currently open workbook. Simply choose Data | Get Data | From Other Sources | From Table / Range command to create a query linked to a selected Excel table. If a selected range is not part of a table, it will be converted into a table.

THE GET DATA AND VBA SUPPORT

To support the Get Data feature in the Get & Transform Data section of the Ribbon's Data tab, the VBA Object Model exposes the `Queries` and `WorkbookQuery` objects with their properties and methods (Figures 23.38 and 23.39). You can try out some of these properties in the Immediate window as shown below. Make sure that your workbook with the Post Office queries is active.

```
?ThisWorkbook.Queries.Count
4
?ThisWorkbook.Queries.Parent.Name
PostOffice_Queries.xlsx

?ThisWorkbook.Queries.Item(1).Name
NJ
```

In addition to Object Model support for the Get Data feature, you can also utilize the Macro Recording feature to automate the process of creating and refreshing your queries. However, you cannot record the actions performed in the Query Editor.

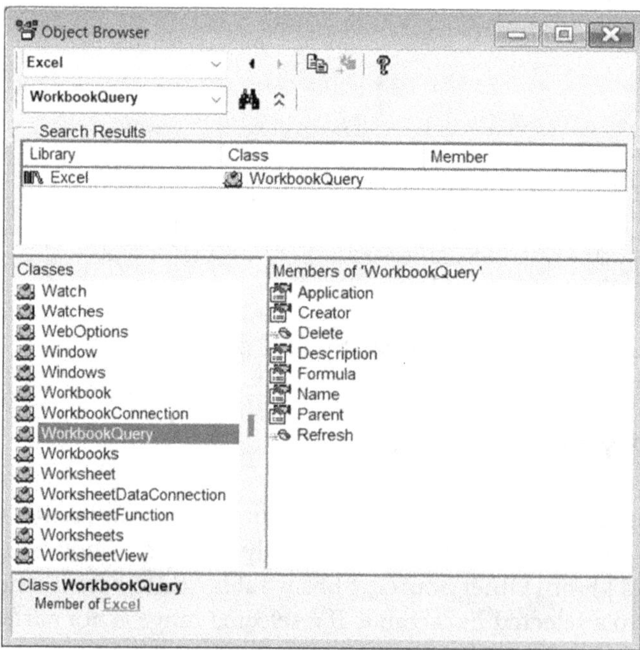

FIGURE 23.38 WorkbookQuery Object's properties and methods.

FIGURE 23.39 Queries Object's properties and methods.

Hands-On 23.2 walks you through the process of recording three queries obtained from a web data source.

Hands-On 23.2 Automating the Creation of Queries

1. Choose **File | New | Blank workbook.**
2. Choose **Developer | Record Macro.**
3. In the Record Macro dialog, type **CreateQuery** as the Macro Name and choose **ThisWorkbook** in the Store macro in dropdown, and then click **OK.**
4. Choose **Data | Get Data | From Other Sources | From Web.**
5. In the URL field, enter: **http://livingwage.mit.edu/states/06** and click **OK.**
6. In the Navigator, choose **Select multiple items** and choose all the tables as shown in Figure 23.40.
7. Select **Load | Load To.**
8. In the Import Data dialog, choose **Table** and uncheck **Add this data to the Data Model**, then click **OK.**
   All three tables are loaded into the workbook as shown in Figure 23.41.
9. Choose **Developer | Stop Recording** to end the macro recording session.
10. Save the workbook as **RecordedQueries.xlsm.**

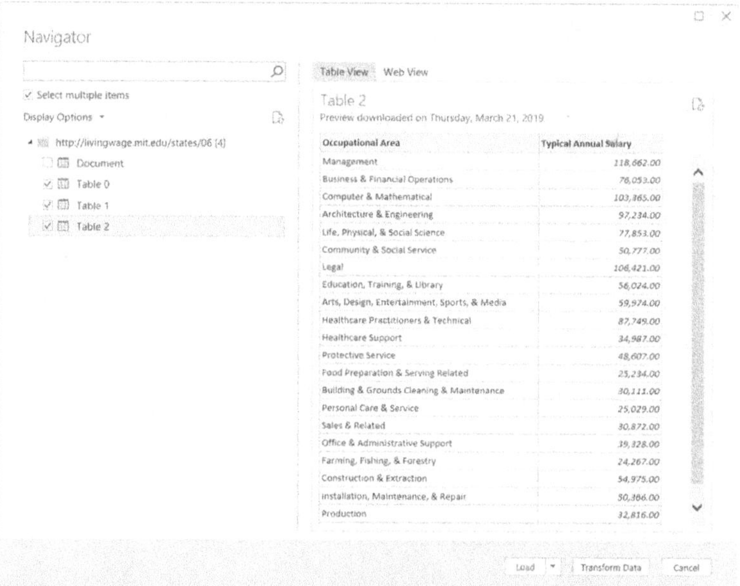

FIGURE 23.40 Selecting the data for a query (Macro Recording).

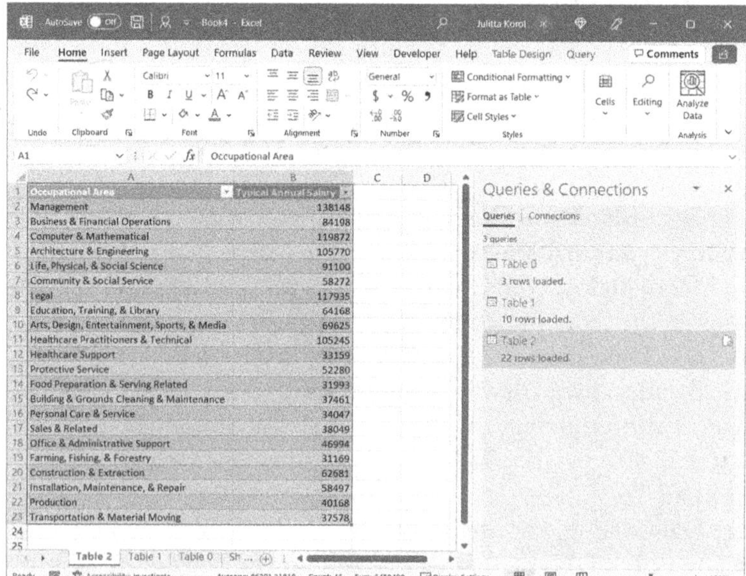

FIGURE 23.41 Three queries were generated after the selection process shown in Figure 23.40.

Let's open the VBE code window and examine the code that was recorded (see Figure 23.42).

FIGURE 23.42 Adding queries to the workbook was automated by using Excel macro recorder.

Notice that the `Queries.Add` method is used to add a new `WorkbookQuery` object to the `Queries` collection. This method requires that you provide the name of the query and the M formula for the query. You can also provide the description of the query, but this is optional. The `Web.Contents` function is used for downloading data from the web. This function expects the `URL` of the website as text string. The `Web.Page` function returns the contents of the HTML webpage as a table. The `Table.TransformColumnTypes` function transforms column types from a table using a specific data type.

The OLE DB Query connection uses the `Microsoft.Mashup.OleDb.1` Provider. In addition to the Provider name, the connection string includes `$Workbook` as the `Data Source` attribute and the name of the query in the `Location` attribute. The `QueryTable.Refresh` method updates the QueryTable. The optional argument `BackgroundQuery` specifies whether the query should be updated in the background. The `False` setting returns the control to the procedure only after all data has been fetched to the worksheet. With the `True` setting, the control is returned to the procedure as soon as a database connection is made, and the query is submitted.

By recording queries using different options you can discover other functions helpful in automating queries in Excel 2021.

ADDITIONAL LEARNING RESOURCES FOR USING THE GET DATA FEATURE

This chapter demonstrated only some of the simple capabilities of getting and transforming data in Excel. The advanced options need a separate book. If you'd like more Hands-On experience with building data mashup queries, be sure to check out the following tutorials:

- **Power Query 101**

  This tutorial will teach you how to connect to a Web data source, select tables for import, replace and filter values, and load the query into a worksheet.
  https://support.office.com/en-us/article/Power-Query-101-008B3F46-5B14-4F8B-9A07-D3DA689091B5

- **Combine Data from Multiple Data Sources**

  This tutorial will teach you how to combine a local Excel file with an OData feed, perform aggregations to produce a Total Sales per Product and Year report.
  https://support.office.com/en-us/article/Combine-data-from-multiple-data-sources-Power-Query-70cfe661-5a2a-4d9d-a4fe-586cc7878c7d

SUMMARY

This chapter provided a brief introduction to data import and shaping features of Excel 2021 known as Power Query. This feature was introduced in Excel 2016 as Get & Transform.

After importing and combing data from an Excel workbook and a CSV text file, you learned how to transform the raw data via a series of steps to produce a final aggregated Excel table. You learned how to use Power Query Editor to edit the query steps which were dynamically generated by various command buttons on the Power Query Editor's Ribbon. You saw how Power Query Editor's Formula Bar can be used to get information about and test M code expressions and functions, and how Advanced Editor shows and allows you to edit the entire query script. You discovered some M language features such as case sensitivity, data types, and logical expressions. Finally, you learned how macro recording and Excel Object Model can help you write VBA procedures that automate the process of creation and refreshing of queries.

The next chapter focuses on programming Visual Basic Editor.

Part VI TAKING CHARGE OF PROGRAMMING ENVIRONMENT

While VBA provides a very comprehensive Object Model for automating worksheet tasks, some of the processes and operations that you may need to program are integral part of the Windows operating system and cannot be controlled with VBA. In this part of the book, we start by learning how to programmatically work with VBA projects, modules, and procedures. Next, you are introduced to the Windows API library of functions that will come to your rescue when you need to overcome the limitations of the native VBA library.

Chapter 24 Programming the Visual Basic Editor (VBE)

Having worked through previous chapters of this book, you have already acquired a working knowledge of many tools available in the Visual Basic Editor (VBE) to create, modify, and troubleshoot Visual Basic for Applications (VBA) procedures. VBA also allows you to program its own development environment known as the Visual Basic Integrated Design Environment (VBIDE). For instance, you can:

- Control Visual Basic projects
  - Get or set project properties
  - Add or remove individual components
- Control Visual Basic code
  - Add, delete, and modify code
  - Save code to a file or insert code from a file
  - Search for specific information in the code
- Control UserForms
  - Programmatically design a UserForm
  - Dynamically add or remove controls from a form
- Work with references
  - Add a reference to an external object library
  - Check for broken references

- Control the VBIDE user interface
  - Control various windows
  - Add or change menus and toolbars

This chapter introduces you to objects, methods, and properties that you can use to automate the VBE.

THE VISUAL BASIC EDITOR OBJECT MODEL

To program and manipulate the VBE in code, you need to access objects contained in the Microsoft Visual Basic for Applications Extensibility 5.3 library. To ensure that you can run the procedures in this chapter, perform the steps as outlined below.

NOTE	*Please note files for the "Hands-On" project may be found in the companion files.*

Hands-On 24.1. Trusting Access to the VBA Project Object Model

1. Open a new workbook and save it as **C:\VBAExcel2021_ByExample\Chap24_VBAExcel2021.xlsm.**
2. To trust the Visual Basic project, click the **Developer** tab and then choose **Macro Security**. Excel displays the Trust Center dialog box with various macro settings (see Figure 24.1). Select the **Trust access to the VBA project object model** checkbox and click **OK**.

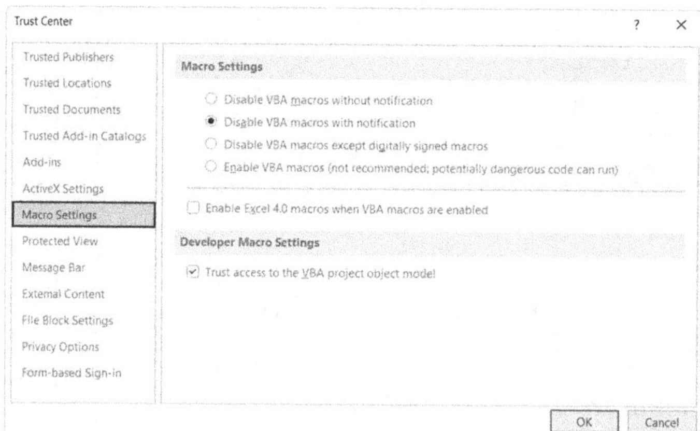

FIGURE 24.1 You must set access to the VBA project object model to allow for programming the Visual Basic Editor.

NOTE	*If access to the VBA project object model is not enabled, an attempt to run a VBA procedure that accesses objects from the Microsoft Visual Basic for Applications Extensibility 5.3 library results in the following runtime error message: "Programmatic access to Visual Basic Project is not trusted."*

3. Choose the **Visual Basic** button on the **Developer** tab to activate the Visual Basic Editor window. In the Properties window, rename the VBA project to **Chap24SourceCode**.
4. To create a reference to the Microsoft Visual Basic for Applications Extensibility 5.3 library, choose **Tools | References**. Check the **Microsoft Visual Basic for Applications Extensibility 5.3** reference, as shown in Figure 24.2, and click **OK**.

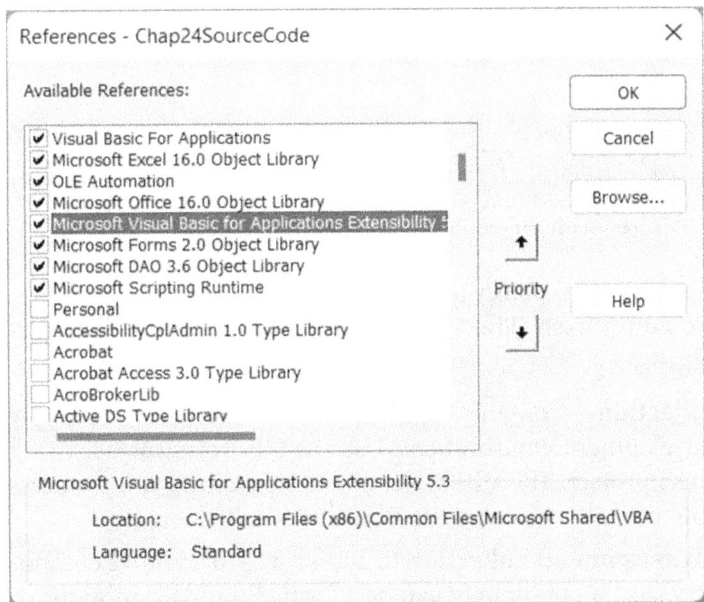

FIGURE 24.2 Setting a reference to the Microsoft Visual Basic for Applications Extensibility 5.3 library.

UNDERSTANDING THE VBE OBJECTS

In the Object Browser (Figure 24.3), the Microsoft Visual Basic for Applications Extensibility 5.3 library is referred to as VBIDE. You will use this name when referencing this library in code.

FIGURE 24.3 The Object Explorer lists all the members of the VBIDE object model.

The top-level object in the VBE object model is the VBE object, which represents the Visual Basic Editor itself. The VBE object model contains five collections of objects as follows:

- **VBProjects collection**—Contains each VBProject object that is currently open in the development environment. Use the VBProject object to set properties for the project. The VBProject object also allows you to access the VBComponents collection and the References collection.
  - Use the **VBComponents collection** to access, add, or remove components in a project. A component can be a form, a standard module, or a class module contained in a project.
  - Use the **References collection** to add or remove references in the VBA project. Each VBA project can reference one or more libraries or projects. Use the Reference object to find out what references are currently selected in the References dialog box for the specific VBA project.
- **AddIns collection**—Use this collection to access the AddIn objects. Add-ins are programs that add extended capabilities and features to Microsoft Excel or other Microsoft Office products.

- **Windows collection**—Use this collection to access window objects such as the Project Explorer window, Properties window, or currently open Code windows.
- **CodePanes collection**—Use this collection to access the open code panes in a project. A Code window can contain one or more code panes. A code pane contained in a Code window is used for entering and editing code.
- **CommandBars collection**—Contains all of the command bars in a project, including command bars that support shortcut menus.

ACCESSING THE VBA PROJECT

The only way to determine the current setting for Trust access to the VBA project object model in the Trust Center (see Figure 24.1) is via error trapping. The following procedure displays a message if access to the VBA project is not trusted. Instructions on how to change the security settings are then displayed in a text box placed in a new workbook.

Hands-On 24.2 Checking Access to the VBA Project Using VBA

NOTE	*All VBA code presented in this chapter will fail unless you followed the steps in Hands-On 24.1.*

1. Switch to the Visual Basic Editor window and insert a new module into **Chap24SourceCode(Chap24_VBAExcel2021.xlsm)**.
2. In the Code window, enter the AccessToVBProj procedure as shown below:

```
Sub AccessToVBProj()
    Dim objVBProject As VBProject
    Dim strMsg1 As String
    Dim strMsg2 As String
    Dim response As Integer

    On Error Resume Next

    If Application.Version >= "16.0" Then
        Set objVBProject = ActiveWorkbook.VBProject

       strMsg2 = "The access to the VBA "
       strMsg2 = strMsg2 + " project must be trusted for this "
       strMsg2 = strMsg2 + "procedure to work."
```

```
        strMsg2 = strMsg2 + vbCrLf + vbCrLf
        strMsg2 = strMsg2 + " Click 'OK' to view instructions,"
        strMsg2 = strMsg2 + "  or click 'Cancel' to exit."

        If Err.Number <> 0 Then
            strMsg1 = "Please change the security settings to "
            strMsg1 = strMsg1 & "allow access to the VBA project:"
            strMsg1 = strMsg1 & Chr(10) & "1. "
           strMsg1 = strMsg1 & "Choose Developer | Macro Security."
            strMsg1 = strMsg1 & Chr(10) & "2. "
            strMsg1 = strMsg1 & "Check the 'Trust access " _
                 & " to the project object model'. "
            strMsg1 = strMsg1 & Chr(10) & "3. Click OK."

            response = MsgBox(strMsg2, vbCritical + vbOKCancel, _
                        "Access to VB Project is not trusted")

                If response = 1 Then
                    Workbooks.Add
                    With ActiveSheet
                       .Shapes.AddTextbox _
                       (msoTextOrientationHorizontal, _
                          Left:=0, Top:=0, Width:=300, _
                          Height:=100).Select
                       Selection.Characters.Text = strMsg1
                       .Shapes(1).Fill.PresetTextured _
                            PresetTexture:=msoTextureBlueTissuePaper
                       .Shapes(1).Shadow.Type = msoShadow6
                    End With
                End If
            Exit Sub
        End If

        MsgBox "There are " & objVBProject.References.Count & _
            " project references in " & objVBProject.Name & "."
    End If
End Sub
```

The procedure begins by checking the application version currently in use. If the Trust access to the VBA project object model setting is turned off in the Trust Center dialog box's Developer Macro Settings area, the attempt to set the object variable `objVBProject` will cause an error. The procedure traps this error with the `On Error Resume Next` statement. If the error occurs, the Err object will return a nonzero value. At this point we can tell the user that security settings must be adjusted for the procedure to run. Instead of simply displaying the instructions in the message box, we print them to a worksheet so users can follow them easily while accessing the necessary options. They can also print them out if they want to make this change later (see Figure 24.4).

3. Run the above procedure.
   If the Trust access to the VBA project object model setting is turned on, the procedure displays the number of references that are set for the active workbook's VB project; otherwise, you get a message prompting you to click OK to view instructions on how to make the change.

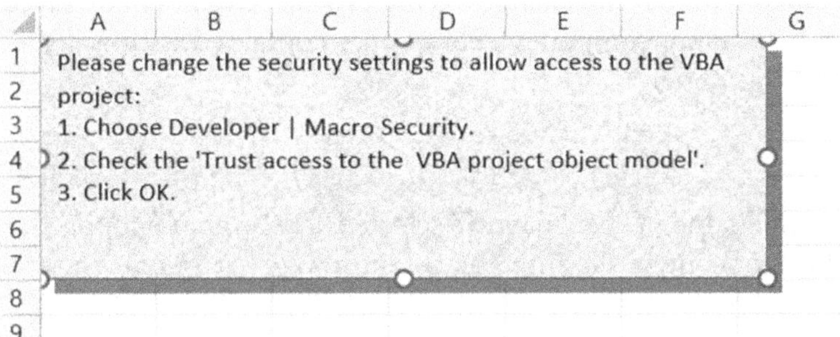

FIGURE 24.4 Instructions for allowing access to the VBA project object model are generated by the example procedure.

FINDING INFORMATION ABOUT A VBA PROJECT

As you already know, each new workbook in the Microsoft Excel user interface has a corresponding workbook project named VBAProject. You can change the project name to a more meaningful name by supplying a new value for the Name property in the Properties window or by accessing the VBAProject properties dialog box via the Tools menu in the Visual Basic Editor screen. You can also perform this change programmatically. If the project you want to edit is currently highlighted in the Project Explorer window, simply type the following statement in the Immediate window to replace the default VBA project name with your own:

```
Application.VBE.ActiveVBProject.Name = "Chap24SourceCode"
```

If the VBA project you want to change is not active, the following statement can be used:

```
Workbooks("Chap24_VBAExcel2021.xlsm").VBProject.Name =
    "Chap24SourceCode"
```

To change the description of the VBProject object, type the following statement on one line in the Immediate window:

```
Workbooks("Chap24_VBAExcel2021.xlsm").VBProject.Description =
        "Programming Visual Basic Editor"
```

You can find out if the project has been saved by using the `Saved` property of the `VBProject` object:

```
MsgBox Application.VBE.ActiveVBProject.Saved
```

Visual Basic returns `False` if the changes to the project have not been saved.

To find out how many component objects are contained within a specific VBA project, use this code:

```
MsgBox Workbooks("Chap24_VBAExcel2021.xlsm").VBProject.
                                             VBComponents.Count
```

And to find out the name of the currently selected VBComponent object, type the following lines of code in the Immediate window, pressing Enter after each statement:

```
Set objVBComp = Application.VBE.SelectedVBComponent
MsgBox objVBComp.Name
```

You can also quickly find out the number of references defined in the References dialog box by typing the following statement in the Immediate window:

```
?Application.VBE.ActiveVBProject.References.Count
```

VBA PROJECT PROTECTION

To prevent users from viewing code, you can lock each VBA project. To lock a VBA project, you will need to perform the following tasks:

1. In the Project Explorer, right-click the project you want to protect, and then click [**ProjectName**] **Properties** on the shortcut menu.
2. In the Project Properties dialog box, click the **Protection** tab and select the **Lock project for viewing** checkbox. Enter and confirm the password, and then click **OK**.

The next time you open the workbook file you will be prompted to enter the password when attempting to view code in the project. There is no way to programmatically specify a password for a locked VBA project. You should check whether the project is protected before you attempt to edit the project or run code that accesses information about the project's components. To determine if a VBA project is locked, check the `Protection` property of the `VBProject` object.

The following function procedure demonstrates how to check the `Protection` property of the VBA project in an Excel workbook.

Hands-On 24.3 Using VBA to Determine whether the VBA Project Is Protected

1. In the same module where you entered the procedure from Hands-On 24.2, enter the IsProjProtected function procedure as shown below:

```
Function IsProjProtected() As Boolean
    Dim objVBProj As VBProject

    Set objVBProj = ActiveWorkbook.VBProject

    If objVBProj.Protection = vbext_pp_locked Then
        IsProjProtected = True
    Else
        IsProjProtected = False
    End If
End Function
```

2. To test the above function, type **MsgBox IsProjProtected()** in the Immediate window and press **Enter**.
The `MsgBox` function displays `False` for a project that is not protected and `True` if protection is turned on.

NOTE	*If a project is protected and you attempt to run a procedure that needs to access information in this project without first checking whether the protection is turned on, runtime error 50289 appears with the following description: "Can't perform operation since the project is protected."*

WORKING WITH MODULES

All standard modules, class modules, code modules located behind worksheets and workbooks, as well as UserForms are members of the `VBComponents` collection of a `VBProject` object. To determine the type of the component object, use the `Type` property of the `VBComponent` object as shown in Figure 24.5.

The code of each `VBComponent` is stored in a CodeModule. The UserForm component has a graphical development interface called ActiveX Designer.

The **Type** property settings for the **VBComponent** object are described in the following table.

Constant	Value	Description
vbext_ct_StdModule	1	Standard module
vbext_ct_ClassModule	2	Class module
vbext_ct_MSForm	3	Microsoft Form
vbext_ct_ActiveXDesigner	11	ActiveX Designer
vbext_ct_Document	100	Document Module

FIGURE 24.5 Type property settings for the VBComponent object as shown in the online help at Properties (Visual Basic Add-In Model) | Microsoft Docs

The following sections demonstrate several procedures that access the `VBComponents` collection to perform the following tasks:

- Listing all modules in a workbook
- Adding a module
- Removing a module
- Removing all code from a module
- Removing empty modules
- Copying (exporting and importing) modules

Listing All Modules in a Workbook

The procedure below generates a list of all modules contained in the Chap24_VBAExcel2021.xlsm workbook. The name of each module and the description of the module type are placed in a two-dimensional array and then written to a worksheet. Because the `Type` property of the `VBComponent` object returns a constant or a numeric value containing the type of object (see Figure 24.5), the procedure uses a function to show the corresponding description of the object.

Hands-On 24.4 Listing All Workbook Modules

1. Insert a new module into the current VBA project in the Chap24_VBAExcel2021.xlsm workbook.

2. In the Code window, enter the following procedure and function:

```
Sub ModuleList()
    Dim objVBComp As VBComponent
    Dim listArray()
    Dim i As Integer


    If ThisWorkbook.VBProject.Protection = vbext_pp_locked Then
        MsgBox "Please unprotect the project to run this " & _
            "procedure."
        Exit Sub
    End If

    i = 2

    For Each objVBComp In ThisWorkbook.VBProject.VBComponents
        ReDim Preserve listArray(1 To 2, 1 To i - 1)
        listArray(1, i - 1) = objVBComp.Name
        listArray(2, i - 1) = GetModuleType(objVBComp)
        i = i + 1
    Next

    With ActiveSheet
        .Cells(1, 1).Resize(1, 2).Value = Array("Module Name", _
            "Module Type")
      .Cells(2, 1).Resize(UBound(listArray, 2), UBound(listArray, _
            1)).Value = Application.Transpose(listArray)
        .Columns("A:B").AutoFit
    End With

    Set objVBComp = Nothing
End Sub

Function GetModuleType(comp As VBComponent)
    Select Case comp.Type
        Case vbext_ct_StdModule
            GetModuleType = "Standard module"
        Case vbext_ct_ClassModule
            GetModuleType = "Class module"
        Case vbext_ct_MSForm
            GetModuleType = "Microsoft Form"
        Case vbext_ct_ActiveXDesigner
            GetModuleType = "ActiveX Designer"
        Case vbext_ct_Document
            GetModuleType = "Document module"
```

```
        Case Else
            GetModuleType = "Unknown"
    End Select
End Function
```

3. Run the ModuleList procedure and then switch to the Microsoft Excel application window to view the results.

   If the VBA project is protected when you execute this procedure, you will see a warning message.

Adding a Module to a Workbook

Use the `Add` method of the `VBComponents` collection to add a new module to ThisWorkbook. The CreateModule procedure shown below prompts the user for the module name and the type of module. When this information has been provided, the AddModule procedure is called.

Hands-On 24.5 Adding a Module to a Workbook

1. Insert a new module into the current VBA project in the Chap24_VBAExcel2021.xlsm workbook.
2. In the Code window, enter the following procedures:

```
Sub CreateModule()
    Dim modType As Integer
    Dim strName As String
    Dim strPrompt As String

   strPrompt = "Enter a number representing the type of module:"
    strPrompt = strPrompt & vbCr & "1 (Standard Module)"
    strPrompt = strPrompt & vbCr & "2 (Class Module)"
    modType = Val(InputBox(prompt:=strPrompt, _
        Title:="Insert Module"))
    If modType = 0 Then Exit Sub
   strName = InputBox("Enter the name you want to assign to " & _
              "new module", "Module Name")
    If strName = "" Then Exit Sub
    AddModule modType, strName
End Sub


Sub AddModule(modType As Integer, strName As String)
    Dim objVBProj As VBProject
    Dim objVBComp As VBComponent
```

```
    If InStr(1, "1, 2", modType) = 0 Then Exit Sub

    Set objVBProj = ThisWorkbook.VBProject
    Set objVBComp = objVBProj.VBComponents.Add(modType)
    objVBComp.Name = strName

    Application.Visible = True

    Set objVBComp = Nothing
    Set objVBProj = Nothing
End Sub
```

3. Run the CreateModule procedure. Enter **1** for a standard module when prompted and click **OK**. Enter **TestModule** as the module name and click **OK**. When the procedure finishes executing, you should see a new module named TestModule in the Project Explorer window. Do not delete this module, as you will need it for the next Hands-On.

Removing a Module

Use the following procedure to delete the module you added in the previous section.

Hands-On 24.6 Removing a Module from the Workbook

1. Insert a new module into the current VBA project in the Chap24_VBAExcel2021.xlsm workbook.
2. In the Code window, enter the following procedure:

```
Sub DeleteModule(strName As String)
    Dim objVBProj As VBProject
    Dim objVBComp As VBComponent

    Set objVBProj = ThisWorkbook.VBProject

    Set objVBComp = objVBProj.VBComponents(strName)

    objVBProj.VBComponents.Remove objVBComp

    Set objVBComp = Nothing
    Set objVBProj = Nothing
End Sub
```

3. Run the DeleteModule procedure by typing the following statement in the Immediate window and pressing **Enter** to execute:

```
DeleteModule "TestModule"
```

At this point, Chap24SourceCode (Chap24_VBAExcel2021.xlsm) should contain four standard modules with the VBA procedures entered so far in this chapter.

Deleting All Code from a Module

Use the `CountOfLines` property of the `CodeModule` object to return the number of lines of code in a code module. Use the `DeleteLines` method of the `CodeModule` object to delete a single line or a specified number of lines. The `DeleteLines` method can use two arguments. The first argument, which specifies the first line you want to delete, is required. The second argument is optional and specifies the total number of lines you want to delete. If you don't specify how many lines you want to delete, only one line will be deleted. The following procedure deletes all code from the specified module.

Hands-On 24.7 Deleting a Module's Code

1. Insert a new module into the current VBA project in the Chap24_VBAExcel2021.xlsm workbook.
2. In the Code window, enter the following procedure:

```
Sub DeleteModuleCode(strName As String)
    Dim objVBProj As VBProject
    Dim objVBCode As CodeModule
    Dim firstLn As Long
    Dim totLn As Long

    Set objVBProj = ThisWorkbook.VBProject
    Set objVBCode = objVBProj.VBComponents(strName).CodeModule
    With objVBCode
        firstLn = 1
        totLn = .CountOfLines
        .DeleteLines firstLn, totLn
    End With

    Set objVBProj = Nothing
    Set objVBCode = Nothing
End Sub
```

3. Insert a new module in the current VBA project and rename it **DeleteTest**.

4. Copy the first procedure you created in this chapter (in Hands-On 24.2) into the DeleteTest module.
5. In the Immediate window, enter the following statement:

   ```
   DeleteModuleCode "DeleteTest"
   ```

   When you press **Enter**, all the code in the DeleteTest module is removed. Do not delete the empty DeleteTest module. You will remove it programmatically in the next example.

Deleting Empty Modules

In the course of writing your VBA procedures you may have inserted a number of new modules in your VBA project. While most of these modules contain valid code, there are probably a couple of empty modules that were left behind. You can remove all the unwanted empty modules in one sweep with a VBA procedure. To remove a module, use the `Remove` method of the `VBComponents` collection. This method requires that you specify the type of component you want to remove. Use the enumerated constants shown in Figure 24.5 earlier in this chapter to indicate the type of component. The following procedure iterates through the `VBComponents` collection and checks whether the retrieved component is a standard module or a class module. If the module contains less than three lines, we assume that the module is empty and okay to delete. We write the information about the deleted modules into the Immediate window.

Hands-On 24.8 Deleting an Empty Module

1. Insert a new module into the current VBA project in the Chap24_VBAExcel2021.xlsm workbook.
2. In the Code window, enter the following procedure:

```
Sub DeleteEmptyModules()
    Dim objVBComp As VBComponent

    Const vbext_ct_StdModule As Long = 1
    Const vbext_ct_ClassModule As Long = 2

    For Each objVBComp In ActiveWorkbook.VBProject.VBComponents
      Select Case objVBComp.Type
        Case vbext_ct_StdModule, vbext_ct_ClassModule
          If objVBComp.CodeModule.CountOfLines < 3 Then
           Debug.Print "(deleted) " & objVBComp.Name & vbTab & _
                "declarations: " & objVBComp.CodeModule. _
```

```
                CountOfDeclarationLines & vbTab & _
                    "Total code Lines: " & _
                    objVBComp.CodeModule.CountOfLines
                ActiveWorkbook.VBProject.VBComponents. _
                    Remove objVBComp
            End If
        End Select
    Next
    Set objVBComp = Nothing
End Sub
```

3. Run the DeleteEmptyModules procedure.
   The DeleteTest module that we created in Hands-On 24.7 should now be removed from the current VBA project. Check the Immediate window for information about the deleted module.

Copying (Exporting/Importing) a Module

Sometimes you may want to copy modules between VBA projects. There is no single method to perform this task. To copy a module you must perform the following two steps:

1. Export a module to an external text file.
   The `Export` method of the `VBComponent` object saves the component as a separate text file. You must specify the name of the file to which you want to export the component. The filename must be unique, or an error will occur.
2. Import a module from an external text file.
   The `Import` method of the `VBComponent` object adds the component to a project from a file. You must specify the path and filename of the file from which you want to import the component. The workbook file that will receive the imported component must be open.

Let's assume that you want to copy Module1 from the Chap24_VBAExcel2021.xlsm workbook to another workbook file named Chap24b_VBAExcel2021.xlsm. The procedure that follows requires three arguments for the copy operation: the name of the workbook containing the module you want to copy, the name of the workbook that will receive the copied module, and the name of the module you will be copying.

Hands-On 24.9 Exporting/Importing a Module

1. Insert a new module into the current VBA project in the Chap24_VBAExcel2021.xlsm workbook.

2. In the Code window, enter the following procedure:

```
Sub CopyAModule(wkbFrom As String, wkbTo As String, _
                strFromMod As String)
    Dim wkb As Workbook
    Dim strFile As String

    Set wkb = Workbooks(wkbFrom)

    strFile = wkb.Path & "\vbCode.bas"
    wkb.VBProject.VBComponents(strFromMod).Export strFile

    On Error Resume Next
    Set wkb = Workbooks(wkbTo)
    If Err.Number <> 0 Then
        Workbooks.Open wkbTo
        Set wkb = Workbooks(wkbTo)
    End If

    wkb.VBProject.VBComponents.Import strFile
    wkb.Save

    Set wkb = Nothing
End Sub
```

3. Create a new workbook and save it as **Chap24b_VBAExcel2021.xlsm** in your **VBAExcel2021_ByExample** folder. You will use this workbook in the CopyAModule procedure.
4. In the Immediate window, type on one line the following statement and press **Enter** to run the procedure:
   `CopyAModule "Chap24_VBAExcel2021.xlsm", "Chap24b_VBAExcel2021.xlsm", "Module1"`
   When you execute the above statement, the CopyAModule procedure exports Module1 from Chap24_VBAExcel2021.xlsm to a file named vbCode.bas. Next, the vbCode.bas file is imported into the Chap24b_VBAExcel2021.xlsm workbook and the workbook is saved. You may want to add an additional statement to this procedure to remove the vbCode.bas file from your computer (use the `Kill` statement you learned earlier in this book).
5. Activate **VBAProject (Chap24b_VBAExcel2021.xlsm)** and notice Module1 in the Modules folder. Module1 should contain the same procedure as Module1 in the Chap24_VBAExcel2021.xlsm workbook.

NOTE	*When you copy a module to another workbook you may also need to add the necessary references to the VBA project so ensure that the code can be compiled and then run without errors. Please refer to Hands-On 24.18 and 24.19 to learn how you can add a reference programmatically.*

Copying (Exporting/Importing) All Modules

Sometimes you may want to transfer all your VBA code from one project to another. The procedure shown below exports all the modules in the specified workbook file to an external text file and then imports them into another workbook. An error occurs if the receiving workbook cannot be activated. The procedure traps this error by executing the code that opens the required workbook. If the text file with the same name already exists in the same folder, the procedure ensures that the file is deleted before the specified project modules are exported.

Hands-On 24.10 Exporting/Importing All Modules

This Hands-On assumes that the Chap24b_VBAExcel2021.xlsm workbook created in the previous Hands-On is open.

1. Insert a new module into the current VBA project in the Chap24_VBAExcel2021.xlsm workbook.
2. In the Code window, enter the following procedure:

```
Sub CopyAllModules(wkbFrom As String, _
                   wkbTo As String)

    Dim objVBComp As VBComponent
    Dim wkb As Workbook
    Dim strFile As String

    Set wkb = Workbooks(wkbFrom)

    On Error Resume Next
    Workbooks(wkbTo).Activate
    If Err.Number <> 0 Then Workbooks.Open wkbTo

    strFile = wkb.Path & "\vbCode.bas"
    If Dir(strFile) <> "" Then Kill strFile

    For Each objVBComp In wkb.VBProject.VBComponents
        If objVBComp.Type <> vbext_ct_Document Then
```

```
          objVBComp.Export strFile
         Workbooks(wkbTo).VBProject.VBComponents.Import strFile
        End If
    Next

    Set objVBComp = Nothing
    Set wkb = Nothing
End Sub
```

3. In the Immediate window, type the following statement and press **Enter** to run the procedure:

```
CopyAllModules "Chap24_VBAExcel2021.xlsm",
           "Chap24b_VBAExcel2021.xlsm"
```

When you execute the above statement, the CopyModules procedure will copy all the modules from the Chap24_VBAExcel2021.xlsm workbook to the Chap24b_VBAExcel2021.xlsm workbook that was created in Hands-On 24.9. Because a module with the same name may already exist in the receiving workbook, you may want to modify this procedure to only copy modules that do not have conflicting names. See the CopyAllModulesRevised.txt in the companion files.

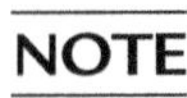

When you copy a module whose name is the same as the name of a module in the receiving workbook, Excel assigns a new name to the inserted module following its default naming conventions.

WORKING WITH PROCEDURES

Code modules contain procedures, and at times you may want to:

- List all the procedures contained in a module or in all modules
- Programmatically add or remove a procedure from a module
- Programmatically create an event procedure

The following sections demonstrate how to perform the above tasks.

Listing All Procedures in All Modules

Code modules contain declaration lines and code lines. You can obtain the number of lines in the declaration section of a module with the `CountOfDeclarationLines` property of the `CodeModule` object. Use the `CountOfLines` property of the `CodeModule` object to get the number of code lines in a module.

Each code line belongs to a specific procedure. Use the `ProcOfLine` property of the `CodeModule` object to return the name of the procedure in which the specified line is located. This property requires two arguments: the line number you want to check and the constant that specifies the type of procedure to locate. All subprocedures and function procedures use the `vbext_pk_Proc` constant. The following procedure prints to the Immediate window a list of all modules and all procedures within each module in the current VBA project.

Hands-On 24.11 Listing Procedures in Modules

1. Insert a new module into the VBA project in the Chap24_VBAExcel2021.xlsm workbook.
2. In the Code window, enter the following procedure:

```
Sub ListAllProc()
    Dim objVBProj As VBProject
    Dim objVBComp As VBComponent
    Dim objVBCode As CodeModule
    Dim strCurrent As String
    Dim strPrevious As String

    Dim x As Integer

    Set objVBProj = ThisWorkbook.VBProject

    For Each objVBComp In objVBProj.VBComponents
    If InStr(1, "1, 2", objVBComp.Type) Then
        Set objVBCode = objVBComp.CodeModule
        Debug.Print objVBComp.Name

        For x = objVBCode.CountOfDeclarationLines + 1 To _
                objVBCode.CountOfLines
           strCurrent = objVBCode.ProcOfLine(x, vbext_pk_Proc)

           If strCurrent <> strPrevious Then
              Debug.Print vbTab & objVBCode.ProcOfLine( _
                         x, vbext_pk_Proc)
              strPrevious = strCurrent
           End If
        Next
    End If
    Next
```

```
    Set objVBCode = Nothing

    Set objVBComp = Nothing
    Set objVBProj = Nothing
End Sub
```

3. Run the ListAllProc procedure.
   When this procedure finishes executing, the list can be seen in the Immediate window.

Adding a Procedure

It is fairly easy to write procedure code into a module. Use the `InsertLines` method of the `CodeModule` object to insert a line or lines of code at a specified location in a block of code. The `InsertLines` method requires two arguments: the line number at which you want to insert the code and the string containing the code you want to insert. The following example writes a simple procedure that opens a new workbook and renames it Sheet1. The procedure is inserted at the end of the specified module code.

Hands-On 24.12 Adding a Procedure to a Module Using VBA

1. Insert a new module into the VBA project in the Chap24_VBAExcel2021.xlsm workbook.
2. In the Code window, enter the following procedure:

```
Sub AddNewProc(strModName As String)
    Dim objVBCode As CodeModule
    Dim objVBProj As VBProject
    Dim strProc As String

    Set objVBProj = ThisWorkbook.VBProject

    Set objVBCode = objVBProj.VBComponents( _
        strModName).CodeModule

    strProc = "Sub CreateWorkBook()" & Chr(13)
    strProc = strProc & Chr(9) & "Workbooks.Add" & Chr(13)
    strProc = strProc & Chr(9)
    strProc = strProc & "ActiveSheet.Name = ""Test""" & Chr(13)
    strProc = strProc & "End Sub"

    Debug.Print strProc
```

```
    With objVBCode
        .InsertLines .CountOfLines + 1, strProc
    End With

    Set objVBCode = Nothing
    Set objVBProj = Nothing
End Sub
```

3. In the Immediate window, enter the following statement to run the above procedure and press **Enter**:

```
AddNewProc "Module6"
```

When the procedure finishes executing, Module6 will contain a new procedure named CreateWorkBook. The Immediate window will display the procedure code.

Deleting a Procedure

Use the `DeleteLines` method of the `CodeModule` object to delete a single line or a specified number of lines. The `DeleteLines` method has two arguments; one is required and the other is optional. You must specify the first line you want to delete. Specifying the total number of lines you want to delete is optional. Before deleting an entire procedure, you need to locate the line at which the specified procedure begins. This is done with the `ProcStartLine` property of the `CodeModule` object. This property requires two arguments: a string containing the name of the procedure and the kind of procedure to delete. Use the `vbext_pk_Proc` constant to delete a subprocedure or a function procedure.

The following procedure deletes a procedure from a specified module.

Hands-On 24.13 Deleting a Procedure from a Module Using VBA

1. Insert a new module into the current VBAProject in the Chap24_VBAExcel2021.xlsm workbook.
2. In the Code window, enter the following procedure:

```
Sub DeleteProc(strModName As String, strProcName As String)
    Dim objVBProj As VBProject
    Dim objVBCode As CodeModule
    Dim firstLn As Long
    Dim totLn As Long

    Set objVBProj = ThisWorkbook.VBProject
   Set objVBCode = objVBProj.VBComponents(strModName).CodeModule
```

```
    With objVBCode
      firstLn = .ProcStartLine(strProcName, vbext_pk_Proc)
      totLn = .ProcCountLines(strProcName, vbext_pk_Proc)
     .DeleteLines firstLn, totLn
    End With

    Set objVBProj = Nothing
    Set objVBCode = Nothing
End Sub
```

3. In the Immediate window, enter the following statement to run the above procedure and press **Enter**:

```
DeleteProc "Module6", "CreateWorkBook"
```

When the procedure finishes executing, Module6 will no longer contain the CreateWorkBook procedure that was created in the previous Hands-On.

Before attempting to delete a procedure from a specified module, it is recommended that you check whether the module and the procedure with the specified name exist. Consider creating two separate functions that return this information. You can call these functions whenever you need to test for the existence of a module or a procedure.

4. Enter the following function procedure in the Module6 Code window:

```
Function ModuleExists(strModName As String) As Boolean
    Dim objVBProj As VBProject

    Set objVBProj = ThisWorkbook.VBProject

    On Error Resume Next

   ModuleExists = Len(objVBProj.VBComponents(strModName).Name) <> 0
End Function
```

The above function will return True if the length of the module name is a number other than zero (0); otherwise, it will return False.

5. Enter the following function procedure in the Module6 Code window:

```
Function ProcExists(strModName As String, _
                    strProcName As String) As Boolean

    Dim objVBProj As VBProject

    Set objVBProj = ThisWorkbook.VBProject

    On Error Resume Next
```

```
    ' first find out if the specified module exists
    If ModuleExists(strModName) = True Then
        ProcExists = objVBProj.VBComponents(strModName) _
            .CodeModule.ProcStartLine(strProcName,
             vbext_pk_Proc) <> 0
    End If
End Function
```

6. On your own, modify the DeleteProc procedure in Step 2 so that it checks the existence of the procedure prior to its deletion. Include the call to the `ProcExists` function.

Creating an Event Procedure

While you could create an event procedure programmatically by using the `InsertLines` method of the `CodeModule` object as you've done earlier in the "Adding a Procedure" section, there is an easier way. Because event procedures have a specific structure and usually require a number of parameters, Visual Basic offers a special method to handle this task. The `CreateEventProc` method of the `CodeModule` object creates an event procedure with the required procedure declaration and parameters. All you need to do is specify the name of the event you want to add and the name of the object that is a source of the event. The `CreateEventProc` method returns the line at which the body of the event procedure starts. Use the `InsertLines` method of the `CodeModule` object to insert the code in the body of the event procedure.

The following procedure adds a new worksheet to the current workbook and writes the Worksheet_SelectionChange event procedure to its code module.

Hands-On 24.14 Creating an Event Procedure with VBA

1. Insert a new module into the VBA project in the Chap24_VBAExcel2021.xlsm workbook.
2. In the Code window, enter the following procedure:

```
Sub CreateWorkSelChangeEvent()
    Dim objVBCode As CodeModule
    Dim wks As Worksheet
    Dim firstLine As Long

    ' Add a new worksheet
    Set wks = ActiveWorkbook.Worksheets.Add

    ' create a reference to the code module of
    ' the inserted sheet
```

```
    Set objVBCode = wks.Parent.VBProject.VBComponents( _
        wks.Name).CodeModule

    ' create an event procedure and return the line at
    ' which the body of the event procedure begins

    firstLine = objVBCode.CreateEventProc( _
        "SelectionChange", "Worksheet")

    Debug.Print "Procedure first line: " & firstLine

    ' proceed to add code to the body of the event procedure
    objVBCode.InsertLines firstLine + 1, Chr(9) & _
        "Dim myRange As Range"
    objVBCode.InsertLines firstLine + 2, Chr(9) & _
        "On Error Resume Next"
    objVBCode.InsertLines firstLine + 3, Chr(9) & _
        "Set myRange = Intersect(Range(""A1:A10""),Target)"
    objVBCode.InsertLines firstLine + 4, _
        Chr(9) & "If Not myRange Is Nothing Then"
    objVBCode.InsertLines firstLine + 5, _
        Chr(9) & Chr(9) & _
        "MsgBox ""Data entry or edits are not permitted."""
    objVBCode.InsertLines firstLine + 6, _
        Chr(9) & "End If"

    Set objVBCode = Nothing
    Set wks = Nothing
End Sub
```

3. Run the CreateWorkSelChangeEvent procedure.
   As soon as the procedure finishes executing, the newly inserted sheet module is activated and displays the following event procedure code:

```
Private Sub Worksheet_SelectionChange(ByVal Target As Range)
    Dim myRange As Range
    On Error Resume Next
    Set myRange = Intersect(Range("A1:A10"), Target)
    If Not myRange Is Nothing Then
        MsgBox "Data entry or edits are not permitted."
    End If
End Sub
```

4. To test the newly inserted event procedure, switch to the sheet where the above procedure is located and click on any cell in the A1:A10 range. The event procedure will cause a message to appear.

WORKING WITH USERFORMS

Earlier in this book you learned how to create and work with UserForms. Creating UserForms is done most easily by utilizing the manual method; however, at times you may find it necessary to use VBA to create a quick form on the fly and display it correctly on the user's screen.

To programmatically add a UserForm to the active project, use the `Add` method of the `VBComponents` collection and specify `vbext_ct_MSForm` for the type of component to add:

```
Dim objVBComp As VBComponent
Set objVBComp = Application.VBE.ActiveVBProject. _
    VBComponents.Add(vbext_ct_MSForm)
```

To change the name of the UserForm, use the `Name` property of the `VBComponent` object. To change other properties of the UserForm, use the VBComponent's Properties collection. For example, to change the `Name` and `Caption` of the UserForm, use the following statement block:

```
With objVBComp
   .Name = "ReportGenerator"
   .Properties("Caption") = "My Report Form"
End With
```

Here's a complete procedure:

```
Sub ReportGeneratorForm()
    Dim objVBComp As VBComponent

    Set objVBComp = Application.VBE.ActiveVBProject. _
        VBComponents.Add(vbext_ct_MSForm)
    With objVBComp
        .Name = "ReportGenerator"
        .Properties("Caption") = "My Report Form"
    End With
    Set objVBComp = Nothing
End Sub
```

To delete the UserForm from the project, use the `Remove` method of the VBComponents collection:

```
Set objVBComp = Application.VBE.ActiveVBProject. _
    VBComponents("ReportGenerator")
Application.VBE.ActiveVBProject.VBComponents.Remove objVBComp
```

Creating and Manipulating UserForms

The procedure in Hands-On 24.15 creates a simple UserForm as shown in Figure 24.6 and writes procedures for each of the form's controls.

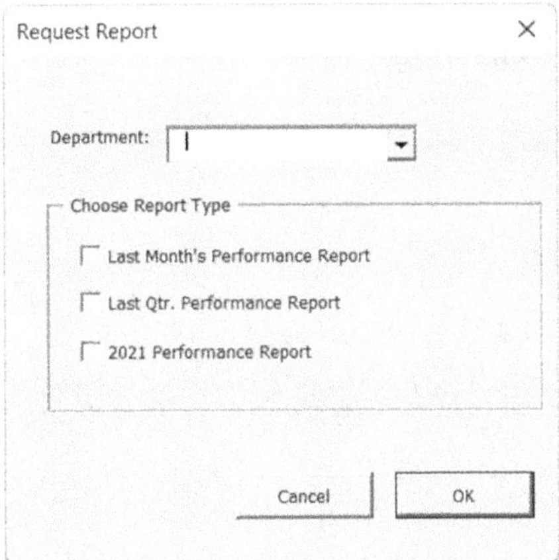

FIGURE 24.6 The UserForm, as well as all the controls and procedures used by this form, were created with VBA (see Hands-On 24.15).

Hands-On 24.15 Creating a Custom UserForm with VBA

1. Insert a new module into the VBA project in the Chap24_VBAExcel2021.xlsm workbook.
2. In the Code window, enter the following procedure:

```
Sub AddUserForm()
Dim objVBProj As VBProject
Dim objVBComp As VBComponent
Dim objVBFrm As UserForm
Dim objChkBox As Object
Dim x As Integer
Dim sVBA As String

Set objVBProj = Application.VBE.ActiveVBProject
Set objVBComp = objVBProj.VBComponents.Add(vbext_ct_MSForm)

With objVBComp
' read form's name and other properties
    Debug.Print "Default Name " & .Name
    Debug.Print "Caption: " & .DesignerWindow.Caption
    Debug.Print "Form is open in the Designer window: " & _
        .HasOpenDesigner
```

```
        Debug.Print "Form Name " & .Name
        Debug.Print "Default Width " & .Properties("Width")
        Debug.Print "Default Height " & .Properties("Height")

    ' set form's name, caption and size
        .Name = "ReportSelector"
        .Properties("Caption") = "Request Report"
        .Properties("Width") = 250
        .Properties("Height") = 250
    End With

    Set objVBFrm = objVBComp.Designer
    With objVBFrm
        With .Controls.Add("Forms.Label.1", "lbName")
            .Caption = "Department:"
            .AutoSize = True
            .Width = 48
            .Top = 30
            .Left = 20
        End With

        With .Controls.Add("Forms.Combobox.1", "cboDept")
            .Width = 110
            .Top = 30
            .Left = 70
        End With

        ' add frame control
        With .Controls.Add("Forms.Frame.1", "frReports")
            .Caption = "Choose Report Type"
            .Top = 60
            .Left = 18
            .Height = 96
        End With

        ' add three check boxes
        Set objChkBox = .frReports.Controls.Add("Forms.CheckBox.1")
        With objChkBox
            .Name = "chk1"
            .Caption = "Last Month's Performance Report"
            .WordWrap = False
            .Left = 12
            .Top = 12
            .Height = 20
            .Width = 186
        End With
```

```
        Set objChkBox = .frReports.Controls.Add("Forms.CheckBox.1")
        With objChkBox
            .Name = "chk2"
            .Caption = "Last Qtr. Performance Report"
            .WordWrap = False
            .Left = 12
            .Top = 32
            .Height = 20
            .Width = 186
        End With

        Set objChkBox = .frReports.Controls.Add("Forms.CheckBox.1")
        With objChkBox
             .Name = "chk3"
             .Caption = Year(Now) - 1 & " Performance Report"
             .WordWrap = False
             .Left = 12
             .Top = 54
             .Height = 20
             .Width = 186
        End With

        ' Add and position OK and Cancel buttons
        With .Controls.Add("Forms.CommandButton.1", "cmdOK")
              .Caption = "OK"
              .Default = "True"
              .Height = 20
              .Width = 60
              .Top = objVBFrm.InsideHeight - .Height - 20
              .Left = objVBFrm.InsideWidth - .Width - 10
        End With

        With .Controls.Add("Forms.CommandButton.1", "cmdCancel")
            .Caption = "Cancel"
            .Height = 20
            .Width = 60
            .Top = objVBFrm.InsideHeight - .Height - 20
            .Left = objVBFrm.InsideWidth - .Width - 80
        End With
    End With

    'populate the combo box
    With objVBComp.CodeModule
        x = .CountOfLines
        .InsertLines x + 1, "Sub UserForm_Initialize()"
        .InsertLines x + 2, vbTab & "With Me.cboDept"
```

```
.InsertLines x + 3, vbTab & vbTab & ".addItem ""Marketing"""
.InsertLines x + 4, vbTab & vbTab & ".addItem ""Sales"""
.InsertLines x + 5, vbTab & vbTab & ".addItem ""Finance"""
.InsertLines x + 6, vbTab & vbTab & _
    ".addItem ""Research & Development"""
.InsertLines x + 7, vbTab & vbTab & _
    ".addItem ""Human Resources"""
.InsertLines x + 8, vbTab & "End With"
.InsertLines x + 9, "End Sub"

' write a procedure to handle the Cancel button

Dim firstLine As Long
With objVBComp.CodeModule
     firstLine = .CreateEventProc("Click", "cmdCancel")
    .InsertLines firstLine + 1, "    Unload Me"
End With

' write a procedure to handle OK button
sVBA = "Private Sub cmdOK_Click()" & vbCrLf
sVBA = sVBA & " Dim ctrl As Control" & vbCrLf
sVBA = sVBA & " Dim chkflag As Integer" & vbCrLf
sVBA = sVBA & " Dim strMsg As String" & vbCrLf
sVBA = sVBA & " If Me.cboDept.Value = """" Then " & vbCrLf
sVBA = sVBA & "  MsgBox ""Select the Department.""" & _
                 vbCrLf
sVBA = sVBA & "   Me.cboDept.SetFocus " & vbCrLf
sVBA = sVBA & "   Exit Sub" & vbCrLf
sVBA = sVBA & "  End If" & vbCrLf
sVBA = sVBA & "  For Each ctrl In Me.Controls " & vbCrLf
sVBA = sVBA & "  Select Case ctrl.Name" & vbCrLf
sVBA = sVBA & "      Case ""chk1"", ""chk2"", ""chk3""" _
                       & vbCrLf
sVBA = sVBA & "  If ctrl.Value = True Then" & vbCrLf
sVBA = sVBA & "    strMsg = strMsg & vbCrLf & ctrl.Caption " _
                    & Chr(13) & vbCrLf
sVBA = sVBA & "     chkflag = 1" & vbCrLf
sVBA = sVBA & "    End If" & vbCrLf
sVBA = sVBA & "   End Select" & vbCrLf
sVBA = sVBA & " Next" & vbCrLf
sVBA = sVBA & " If chkflag = 1 Then" & vbCrLf
sVBA = sVBA & "  MsgBox ""Run the Report(s) for "" " & vbCrLf
sVBA = sVBA & " Me.cboDept.Value & "":"""
sVBA = sVBA & " & Chr(13) & Chr(13) & strMsg" & vbCrLf

sVBA = sVBA & " Else" & vbCrLf
```

```
    sVBA = sVBA & "  MsgBox ""Please select Report type.""" _
                        & vbCrLf
    sVBA = sVBA & " End If" & vbCrLf
    sVBA = sVBA & "End Sub"

    .AddFromString sVBA
End With
Set objVBComp = Nothing
End Sub
```

In the above procedure, the following statement creates a blank UserForm:

```
Set objVBComp = objVBProj.VBComponents.Add(vbext_ct_MSForm)
```

Next, the form's default name and other properties (`Caption`, `Width`, and `Height`) are written to the Immediate window and then reset with new values. Before we can access the content of the UserForm, we need a reference to the VBComponent's `Designer` object, like this:

```
Set objVBFrm = objVBComp.Designer
```

Several `With...End With` statement blocks are used to add controls (label, combo box, frame, checkboxes, and command buttons) to the blank UserForm and position them within the form by using the `Top` and `Left` properties. The `InsideHeight` and `InsideWidth` properties are used to move the OK and Cancel buttons to the bottom of the UserForm. These properties return the height and width, in points, of the space that's available inside the form.

The remaining code in the procedure creates various event procedures for the UserForm and its controls. The first one is the `UserForm_Initialize()` procedure that will populate the combo box control with department names before the form is displayed on a user's screen. Next, the event procedures for command buttons (OK and Cancel) are created. The `cmdCancel_Click()` event procedure unloads the form, and the `cmdOK_Click()` procedure displays a message box with information about the types of reports selected via the checkboxes. Code for the event procedure can be added with several techniques. One technique is using the `InsertLines` statement of the CodeModule. Another is creating a string to hold the code and adding this string to the code module with the `AddFromString` method. The code added by the `AddFromString` method is inserted on the line preceding the first procedure in the module. The `AddFromFile` method can be used for adding code that is stored in a text file.

NOTE	*The* `CreateEventProc` *method automatically adds the* `Private Sub` *and the* `End Sub` *statements and a space between these lines. All you need to do is add the actual code using the* `InsertLines` *statements. The* `CreateEventProc` *method returns the number of the line in the module where the* `Private Sub` *statement was added.*

3. Run the AddUserForm procedure.
   When the procedure finishes its execution, the Visual Basic Editor screen will display the form shown in Figure 24.6.
4. Choose **View | Code** or press **F7** and review the procedures that were programmatically created for the form by the AddUserForm procedure.
5. Choose **Run | Run Sub/UserForm** or press **F5** to display and work with the form.

If you'd like to display your custom UserForm in a specific location on the screen, consider adding the following event procedure to the AddUserForm procedure. You must code this procedure by using one of the techniques described earlier.

```
Private Sub UserForm_Activate()
  With ReportSelector
    .Top = 100
    .Left = 25
  End With
End Sub
```

Copying UserForms Programmatically

If you need to add an existing UserForm to another workbook, you can simply export the form to disk by choosing File | Export File in the Visual Basic Editor screen. Excel will create a form file (identified with a .frm extension) that you can then import to another VBA project by choosing the File | Import File command in the VBE screen.

You can also automate the export/import process of UserForms by writing VBA code. The following example procedure exports the form created in the previous section. After the form is imported, a procedure is written to a standard module of the Chap24b_VBAExcel2021.xlsm file (created earlier in this chapter) to display the form.

Hands-On 24.16 Copying a UserForm with VBA

1. Insert a new module into the VBA project in the Chap24_VBAExcel2021.xlsm workbook.

2. In the Code window, enter the following procedure:

```
Sub UserFormCopy(strFileName As String)
    Dim objVBComp As VBComponent
    Dim wkb As Workbook

    On Error Resume Next
    Set wkb = Workbooks(strFileName)
     If Err.Number <> 0 Then
        Workbooks.Open ActiveWorkbook.Path & "\" & strFileName
         Set wkb = Workbooks(strFileName)
     End If

    For Each objVBComp In ThisWorkbook.VBProject.VBComponents
        If objVBComp.Type = 3 Then   ' this is a UserForm
           ' export the UserForm to disk
           objVBComp.Export Filename:=objVBComp.Name
           ' import the UserForm to a specific workbook
           wkb.VBProject.VBComponents.Import _
               Filename:=objVBComp.Name
           ' delete two form files created by the Export method
           Kill objVBComp.Name
           Kill objVBComp.Name & ".frx"
        End If
    Next

    ' add a standard module to the workbook
    ' and write code to show the UserForm
    Set objVBComp = wkb.VBProject.VBComponents. _
        Add(vbext_ct_StdModule)

  objVBComp.CodeModule.AddFromString _
     "Sub ShowReportSelector()" & vbCrLf & _
     "    ReportSelector.Show" & vbCrLf & _
     "End Sub" & vbCrLf

 ' close the Code pane
   objVBComp.CodeModule.CodePane.Window.Close

 ' run the ShowReportSelector procedure to display the form
   Application.Run wkb.Name & "!ShowReportSelector"

   Set objVBComp = Nothing
   Set wkb = Nothing
End Sub
```

3. Run the UserFormCopy procedure by entering the following statement in the Immediate window and pressing Enter:

```
UserFormCopy "Chap24b_VBAExcel2021.xlsm"
```

Recall that the Chap24b_VBAExcel2021.xlsm workbook was created earlier in this chapter. When you execute the above statement, the UserForm is imported into this workbook and displayed on the user's screen.

WORKING WITH REFERENCES

When you write VBA procedures you often need to access objects that are stored in external object libraries. For example, so far in this chapter you have used objects defined in the Microsoft Visual Basic for Applications Extensibility 5.3 library. In other chapters of this book, you have worked with objects exposed by the Microsoft Word 16.0 object library or Microsoft Outlook 16.0 object library, Microsoft Access 16.0 object library, Microsoft ActiveX Data Objects 6.1 library, and so on.

Understanding Early Binding and Late Binding

There are two ways to expose an object model to your Excel application: *early binding* and *late binding*. Binding means exposing the client object model to the host application, in this case Microsoft Excel.

> You use early binding when you expose the object model at design time. This is done by choosing Tools | References in the Visual Basic Editor screen. The References dialog box lists files with which you can bind. To manipulate a specific application in your Excel VBA project, you must select the checkbox next to the name of the library you want to use.
>
> You perform late binding when you bind the object library in code at runtime. Instead of using the References dialog box, you use the `GetObject` or `CreateObject` functions.

By adding a reference to the external object library via the Tools | References dialog box (early binding), you are able to get on-the-fly programming assistance for the objects you need to include in your VBA code, consequently avoiding many syntax errors. You can also view the application's object model via the Object Browser and have access to the application's built-in constants. In addition, your code runs faster because the references to the external libraries are checked and compiled at design time. Problems arise, however, when you move your code to other computers that do not have the external libraries installed. The procedures that ran perfectly well on your computer suddenly begin to display compile-time errors that cannot be trapped using standard error-handling techniques. To ensure that the end users have the required references and object libraries, you must write code that checks not only whether these libraries are present but also that they are the correct version. This section shows how to:

- List references to the external object libraries that have been selected in the References dialog box
- Add a reference to a specific library on the fly
- Remove missing library references
- Check for broken references

Creating a List of References

The Reference object in the References collection represents a reference to a type library or a VBA project. You can use various properties of the Reference object to:

- Find out whether the reference is built in or added by a developer (`BuiltIn` property)
- Determine if the reference is broken (`IsBroken` property)
- Find out the reference version number (`Major` and `Minor` properties)
- Get the description of the reference as it appears in the Object Browser (`Description` property)
- Return the full path to the workbook, DLL, OCX, TLD, or OLB file that is a source of the reference (`FullPath` property)
- Return the globally unique identifier for the reference (`Guid` property)
- Determine the reference type (`Type` property)

The following procedure prints to the Immediate window the names of all VBA projects, the names and full paths of selected references for each VBA project, and the names of each project's components.

Hands-On 24.17 Listing VBA Project References and Components Using VBA

1. Insert a new module into the VBA project in the Chap24_VBAExcel2021.xlsm workbook.

2. In the Code window, enter the following procedure:

```
Sub ListPrjCompRef()
     Dim objVBPrj As VBIDE.VBProject
     Dim objVBCom As VBIDE.VBComponent
     Dim vbRef As VBIDE.Reference

    ' list VBA projects as well as references and
    ' component names they contain
          For Each objVBPrj In Application.VBE.VBProjects
       Debug.Print objVBPrj.Name
       Debug.Print vbTab & "References"
       For Each vbRef In objVBPrj.References
           With vbRef
             Debug.Print vbTab & vbTab & .Name & "---" & .FullPath
           End With
       Next
       Debug.Print vbTab & "Components"
       For Each objVBCom In objVBPrj.VBComponents
           Debug.Print vbTab & vbTab & objVBCom.Name
       Next
    Next
    Set vbRef = Nothing
    Set objVBCom = Nothing
    Set objVBPrj = Nothing
End Sub
```

3. Run the ListPrjCompRef procedure.
   When the procedure finishes executing, the Immediate window displays information about all the VBA projects that are currently open in Excel.
4. On your own, modify the ListPrjCompRef procedure to list procedures in each module. Refer to the "Listing All Procedures in All Modules" section earlier in this chapter for related code examples.

Adding a Reference

The `AddFromFile` method of the References collection is used to add a reference to a project from a file. You must specify the project library filename, including its path. The following procedure adds a reference to the Microsoft Scripting Runtime library, which is stored in the scrrun.dll (dynamic link library) file.

Hands-On 24.18 Adding a Project Reference with VBA

1. Insert a new module into the VBA project in the Chap24_VBAExcel2021.xlsm workbook.

2. In the Code window, enter the following procedure:

```
Sub AddRef()
    Dim objVBProj As VBProject

    Set objVBProj = ThisWorkbook.VBProject

    On Error GoTo ErrorHandle
    objVBProj.References.AddFromFile _
        "C:\Windows\System32\scrrun.dll"
    MsgBox "The reference to the Microsoft Scripting " _
        & "Runtime was set."
    Application.SendKeys "%tr"

ExitHere:
    Set objVBProj = Nothing
    Exit Sub
ErrorHandle:
    MsgBox "The reference to the Microsoft Scripting " & _
        " Runtime already exists."
    GoTo ExitHere
End Sub
```

3. Run the AddRef procedure. When a message box appears, click **OK**.
   If the reference to the Microsoft Scripting Runtime was set during the procedure execution, the References dialog box will appear with a check mark next to Microsoft Scripting Runtime.
4. Close the References dialog box if it is open.

Every type library has an associated *Globally Unique Identifier* (GUID) that is stored in the Windows registry. If you know the GUID of the reference, you can add a reference by using the `AddFromGuid` method. This method requires three arguments: a string expression representing the GUID of the reference, the major version number of the reference, and the minor version number of the reference. The `AddFromGuid` method searches the registry to find the reference you want to add.

The following procedure prints to the Immediate window the names, GUIDs, and version numbers of the libraries that are already installed in the active workbook's VBA project. The procedure also adds a reference to the Microsoft DAO 3.6 object library if this library has not yet been added.

Hands-On 24.19 Obtaining Information about Installed VBA Libraries from the Registry

1. In the Code window where you entered the previous procedure, enter the AddRef_FromGuid procedure as shown below:

```
Sub AddRef_FromGuid()
    Dim objVBProj As VBProject
    Dim i As Integer
    Dim strName As String
    Dim strGuid As String
    Dim strMajor As Long
    Dim strMinor As Long

    Set objVBProj = ActiveWorkbook.VBProject

    ' Find out what libraries are already installed
    For i = 1 To objVBProj.References.Count
          strName = objVBProj.References(i).Name
          strGuid = objVBProj.References(i).GUID
          strMajor = objVBProj.References(i).Major
          strMinor = objVBProj.References(i).Minor
          Debug.Print strName & " - " & strGuid & _
            ", " & strMajor & ", " & strMinor
    Next i

    ' reference the Microsoft DAO 3.6 Object library
    On Error Resume Next
    ThisWorkbook.VBProject.References.AddFromGuid _
       "{00025E01-0000-0000-C000-000000000046}", 5, 0
End Sub
```

2. Run the AddRef_FromGuid procedure.
   The procedure produces the following list of references in the Immediate window:

```
VBA - {000204EF-0000-0000-C000-000000000046}, 4, 2
Excel - {00020813-0000-0000-C000-000000000046}, 1, 8
stdole - {00020430-0000-0000-C000-000000000046}, 2, 0
Office - {2DF8D04C-5BFA-101B-BDE5-00AA0044DE52}, 2, 7
VBIDE - {0002E157-0000-0000-C000-000000000046}, 5, 3
MSForms - {0D452EE1-E08F-101A-852E-02608C4D0BB4}, 2, 0
Scripting - {420B2830-E718-11CF-893D-00A0C9054228}, 1, 0
```

   Notice that the reference to the Microsoft DAO 3.6 Object library is not listed because it was added after we already ran the `For...Next` loop. If some of the references are missing in your list, ensure that Chap24b_VBAExcel2021.xlsm is closed and run the procedure again.

Removing a Reference

To remove an unwanted reference from the VBA project, use the `Remove` method of the References collection. The following procedure removes the reference to the Microsoft DAO 3.6 object library that was added by the AddRef_FromGuid procedure in the previous section.

Hands-On 24.20 Removing a Reference Using VBA

1. In the Code window where you entered the previous procedure, enter the RemoveRef procedure as shown below:

```
Sub RemoveRef()
    Dim objVBProj As VBProject
    Dim objRef As Reference
    Dim sRefFile As String

    Set objVBProj = ActiveWorkbook.VBProject

    ' Loop through the references and delete
    ' the reference to DAO library
    For Each objRef In objVBProj.References
        If InStr(1, objRef.Description, "DAO 3.6") > 0 Then
            objVBProj.References.Remove objRef
            Exit For
        End If
    Next objRef
End Sub
```

2. Run the RemoveRef procedure. When the procedure finishes executing, open the References dialog box to verify that the reference to the Microsoft DAO 3.6 object library is no longer selected. Make sure that the Chap24_VBAExcel2021.xlsm workbook is active prior to running the procedure.

In addition to removing references to external object libraries, you can remove any existing references to other VBA projects. This is done by checking the `BuiltIn` property of the Reference object and removing the reference when the `BuiltIn` property is not True:

```
For Each objRef in objVBProjReferences
    If Not objRef.BuiltIn Then objVBProj.References.Remove objRef
Next objRef
```

The `BuiltIn` property of the `Reference` object returns False if the particular reference isn't a default reference. When a reference is not built in, it can be removed. Default references cannot be removed.

Checking for Broken References

If the required object libraries are not installed on a user's computer or aren't the correct version, the culprit references are marked as "missing" in the References dialog box. You can use the `IsBroken` property to find these invalid references. The `IsBroken` property returns a Boolean value True if the `Reference` object no longer points to a valid reference in the registry. If the reference is valid, False is returned. The code to check for broken references should be included or called from the Workbook_Open event procedure before attempting to add any new references via code.

The following example procedure checks for broken references.

Hands-On 24.21 Checking for Broken References in a VBA Project

1. In the ThisWorkbook module of Chap24SourceCode (Chap24_VBAExcel2021.xlsm), enter the following Workbook_Open event procedure:

```
Private Sub Workbook_Open()
    Dim objVBProj As VBProject
    Dim objRef As Reference
    Dim refBroken As Boolean

    Set objVBProj = ThisWorkbook.VBProject

    ' Loop through the selected references in
    ' the References dialog box
    For Each objRef In objVBProj.References
    ' If the reference is broken, get its name and its GUID
        If objRef.IsBroken Then
          Debug.Print objRef.Name
          Debug.Print objRef.GUID
          refBroken = True
       End If
    Next
    If refBroken = False Then
         Debug.Print "All references are valid."
    End If
End Sub
```

2. Save and close the Chap24_VBAExcel2021.xlsm workbook. Do not exit Microsoft Excel.
3. Reopen the **Chap24_VBAExcel2021.xlsm** workbook.
   When the workbook opens, Excel executes the code in the Workbook_Open event procedure.
4. Switch to the Visual Basic Editor window and activate the Immediate window. If broken references are found in the active project, you will see the reference name and its GUID; otherwise, a message is displayed that all references are valid.

If you'd like to test whether a specific reference is valid, insert a new module into the active VBA project and write a function procedure like this:

```
Function IsBrokenRef(strRef As String) As Boolean
    Dim objVBProj As VBProject
    Dim objRef As Reference

    Set objVBProj = ThisWorkbook.VBProject

    For Each objRef In objVBProj.References

    If strRef = objRef.Name And objRef.IsBroken Then
        IsBrokenRef = True
        Exit Function
    End If
    Next

    IsBrokenRef = False
End Function
```

To test the above function, you could enter the following statements in the Immediate window:

```
ref = IsBrokenRef("OLE Automation")
?ref
```

If True, the reference is invalid; if False, it is valid.

WORKING WITH WINDOWS

As you know, the VBE screen contains numerous windows. Each window (VBE main window, Project Explorer, Properties window, Immediate and Watch windows, open Code window, Designer windows, and so on) is represented by the `Window` object. Each `Window` object is a member of the VBIDE.Windows collection.

Use the `Type` property of the `Window` object to determine the window type. Available window types are listed in Table 24.1.

TABLE 24.1 Window types available in the VBA project

Window Description	Constant	Value
Code window	vbext_wt_CodeWindow	0
Designer	vbext_wt_Designer	1
Object Browser	vbext_wt_Browser	2
Watch window	vbext_wt_Watch	3
Locals window	vbext_wt_Locals	4
Immediate window	vbext_wt_Immediate	5
Project Explorer window	vbext_wt_ProjectWindow	6
Properties window	vbext_wt_PropertyWindow	7
Find dialog box	vbext_wt_Find	8
Search and Replace dialog box	vbext_wt_FindReplace	9
Toolbox	vbext_wt_Toolbox	10
Linked window frame	vbext_wt_LinkedWindowFrame	11
Main window	vbext_wt_MainWindow	12
Tool window	vbext_wt_ToolWindow	15

The following procedure loops through all the open windows in the VBE, closes the Immediate window, and displays a dialog box with the names of open windows.

Hands-On 24.22 Closing the Immediate Window and Listing All Open Windows in the VBE Screen

1. Insert a new module into the VBA project in the Chap24_VBAExcel2021.xlsm workbook.
2. In the Code window, enter the following procedure:

```
Sub Close_ImmediateWin()
    Dim objWin As VBIDE.Window
    Dim strOpenWindows As String

    strOpenWindows = "The following windows are open:" & _
           vbCrLf & vbCrLf

    For Each objWin In Application.VBE.Windows
        Select Case objWin.Type
```

```
            Case vbext_wt_Immediate
                MsgBox objWin.Caption & " window was closed."
                objWin.Close
            Case Else
                strOpenWindows = strOpenWindows & _
                    objWin.Caption & vbCrLf
        End Select
    Next
    MsgBox strOpenWindows
    Set objWin = Nothing
End Sub
```

3. Run the Close_ImmediateWin procedure.
   You should see the list of all open windows in a message box.

WORKING WITH VBE MENUS AND TOOLBARS

In Chapter 19, you learned how to write VBA code to create or modify shortcut menus. Using the same `CommandBar` object that you are already familiar with, you can now customize menus and toolbars in the Visual Basic Editor. To work with the `CommandBars` collection, you need to ensure that a reference to the Microsoft Office 16.0 object library is set in the References dialog box. If the reference to this library is not set, Excel displays a "User-defined type not defined" error message when the code attempts to access the `CommandBars` collection.

Generating a Listing of VBE CommandBars and Controls

The following procedure lists all the `CommandBars` that can be found in the Visual Basic Editor. Each command bar is defined as a menu bar, toolbar, or pop-up menu via the `Type` property of the `CommandBar` object. Each `CommandBar` object has a number of controls assigned to it. The procedure lists all these controls for each `CommandBar`, including the control IDs.

Hands-On 24.23 Listing VBE CommandBars and Controls

1. Insert a new module into the VBA project in the Chap24_VBAExcel2021.xlsm workbook.
2. In the Code window, enter the following procedure:

```
Sub ListVBECmdBars()
    Dim objCmdBar As CommandBar
```

```
    Dim strCmdType As String
    Dim c As Variant

    Workbooks.Add
    Range("A1").Select

    With ActiveCell
        .Offset(0, 0) = "CommandBar Name"
        .Offset(0, 1) = "Control Caption"
        .Offset(0, 2) = "Control ID"
    End With

    For Each objCmdBar In Application.VBE.CommandBars
        Select Case objCmdBar.Type
            Case 0
                strCmdType = "toolbar"
            Case 1
                strCmdType = "menu bar"
            Case 2
                strCmdType = "popup menu"
        End Select

        ActiveCell.Offset(1, 0) = objCmdBar.Name & _
            " (" & strCmdType & ")"

        For Each c In objCmdBar.Controls
            ActiveCell.Offset(1, 0).Select
            With ActiveCell
                .Offset(0, 1) = c.Caption
                .Offset(0, 2) = c.ID
            End With
        Next
    Next

    Columns("A:C").AutoFit

    Set objCmdBar = Nothing
End Sub
```

3. Run the ListVBECmdBars procedure.
   The procedure creates a new workbook and writes to it the information about all the CommandBars and controls found in the Visual Basic Editor (see the partial listing in Figure 24.7).

	A	B	C	D
1	CommandBar Name	Control Caption	Control ID	
2	Menu Bar (menu bar)	&File	30002	
3		&Edit	30003	
4		&View	30004	
5		&Insert	30005	
6		F&ormat	30006	
7		&Debug	30165	
8		&Run	30012	
9		&Tools	30007	
10		&Add-Ins	30038	
11		&Window	30009	
12		&Help	30010	
13	Standard (toolbar)	Microsoft Excel	106	
14		Insert Object	32806	
15		&Save Book3	3	
16		Cu&t	21	
17		&Copy	19	
18		&Paste	22	
19		&Find...	141	

FIGURE 24.7 You can list all the CommandBars available in the Visual Basic Editor by running the custom ListVBECmdBars procedure, as demonstrated in this section.

Adding a CommandBar Button to the VBE

The following procedure adds a new command button to the end of the Tools menu in the Visual Basic Editor.

Hands-On 24.24 Modifying the VBE Tools Menu

1. In the same module where you entered the ListVBECmdBars procedure (see the previous section), type the following procedure:

```
Sub AddCmdButton_ToVBE()
    Dim objCmdBar As CommandBar
    Dim objCmdBtn As CommandBarButton

   ' get the reference to the Tools menu in the VBE
    Set objCmdBar = Application.VBE.CommandBars.FindControl _
        (ID:=30007).CommandBar

    ' add a button to the Tools menu
    Set objCmdBtn = objCmdBar.Controls.Add(msoControlButton)

    ' set the new button's properties
    With objCmdBtn
        .Caption = "List VBE menus and toolbars"
```

```
        .onAction = "ListVBECmdBars"
    End With
End Sub
```

Please do not run this procedure yet, as it is not complete. To run a custom procedure assigned to any VBE menu item, you need to raise the `Click` event of the `CommandBarButton`. Use the `CommandBarEvents` object to trigger the `Click` event when a control on the `CommandBar` is clicked. This is done in a class module.

2. Choose **Insert | Class Module**.
3. In the Properties window, change the name of the Class1 module to **clsCmdBarEvents**.
4. In the clsCmdBarEvents module Code window, enter the following code:

```
Public WithEvents cmdBtnEvents As CommandBarButton

Private Sub cmdBtnEvents_Click( _
    ByVal Ctrl As Office.CommandBarButton, _
    CancelDefault As Boolean)
On Error Resume Next
MsgBox "inside class module"
' run the procedure specified in the onAction property
Application.Run Ctrl.OnAction

' specify that we already handled this event
CancelDefault = True
End Sub
```

Notice that the first statement in the class module uses the `WithEvents` keyword to declare an object called cmdBtnEvents of the type CommandBarButton whose events we want to handle. Next, we specify that this object (cmdBtnEvents) is to receive the `Click` event when the menu item is selected. The first statement in the cmdBtnEvents_Click event procedure will prevent an error message from appearing in case the procedure specified in the `onAction` property doesn't exist. The next statement will run the procedure specified in the control's `onAction` property. Because the `onAction` property of the controls located on the VBE CommandBars does not cause the specified procedure code to execute, you must call the required procedure with the `Run` method of the `Application` object.

Now that you've told Visual Basic that you'd like it to handle the `Click` event for the menu item, you need to connect the class module with the standard module containing the code of the AddCmdButton_ToVBE procedure that you created in Step 1.

5. Enter the following declaration line at the very top of the module that contains the AddCmdBtn_ToVBE procedure:

```
Dim myClickEvent As clsCmdBarEvents
```

In the previous declaration statement, the myClickEvent is a module-level variable defined by the class clsCmdBarEvents. This variable will serve as a link between the menu item and the clsCmdBarEvents class module.

The final step requires that you add additional code to the AddCmdButton_ToVBE procedure so that Visual Basic knows that it needs to handle the Click event for the menu item.

6. Enter the following code at the very end of the AddCmdButton_ToVBE procedure:

```
' create an instance of the clsCmdEvents class
Set myClickEvent = New clsCmdBarEvents

' hook up the class instance to the newly added button
Set myClickEvent.cmdBtnEvents = objCmdBtn

Set objCmdBtn = Nothing
Set objCmdBar = Nothing
```

The modified AddCmdButton_ToVBE procedure should look as follows:

```
Sub AddCmdButton_ToVBE()
    Dim objCmdBar As CommandBar
    Dim objCmdBtn As CommandBarButton

   ' get the reference to the Tools menu in the VBE
    Set objCmdBar = Application.VBE.CommandBars.FindControl _
            (ID:=30007).CommandBar

    ' add a button to the Tools menu
    Set objCmdBtn = objCmdBar.Controls.Add(msoControlButton)

    ' set the new button's properties
    With objCmdBtn
        .Caption = "List VBE menus and toolbars"
        .onAction = "ListVBECmdBars"
    End With
```

```
    ' create an instance of the clsCmdEvents class
    Set myClickEvent = New clsCmdBarEvents

    ' hook up the class instance to the newly added button
    Set myClickEvent.cmdBtnEvents = objCmdBtn

    Set objCmdBtn = Nothing
    Set objCmdBar = Nothing
End Sub
```

7. Run the AddCmdButton_ToVBE procedure.
   The procedure places a new menu item on the Tools menu (see Figure 24.8) and connects this item with the event handler located in the class module.
8. Choose **Tools | List VBE menus and toolbars.**
   Visual Basic triggers the Click event of the selected menu item and runs the procedure code specified in the `onAction` property. When you switch to the Microsoft Excel application window, you should see a new workbook with a complete listing of the VBE CommandBars and their controls.

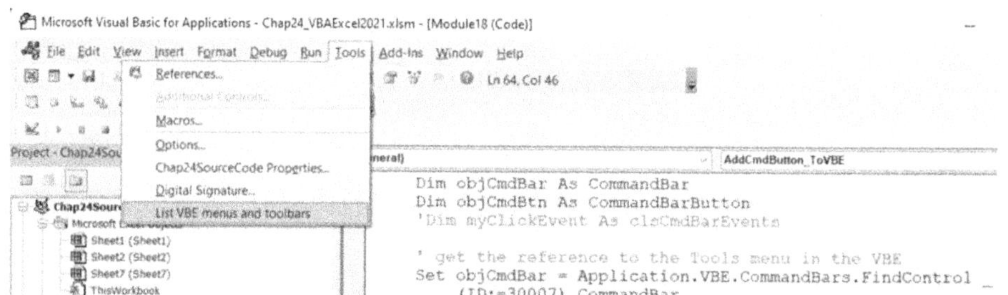

FIGURE 24.8 A custom menu option was added to the Visual Basic Editor's Tools menu by a VBA procedure.

Removing a CommandBar Button from the VBE

The following procedure removes the custom menu item that was added to the Tools menu by the procedure in the previous section.

Hands-On 24.25 Removing a Custom Option from the VBE Menu

1. In the same module where you entered the AddCmdButton_ToVBE procedure (see the previous section), type the following procedure:

```
Sub RemoveCmdButton_FromVBE()
    Dim objCmdBar As CommandBar
    Dim objCmdBarCtrl As CommandBarControl
```

```
    ' get the reference to the Tools menu in the VBE
    Set objCmdBar = Application.VBE.CommandBars("Tools")

    ' loop through the Tools menu controls
    ' and delete the control with the matching caption
    For Each objCmdBarCtrl In objCmdBar.Controls
       If objCmdBarCtrl.Caption = "List VBE menus and toolbars" Then
            objCmdBarCtrl.Delete
        End If
    Next

    Set objCmdBarCtrl = Nothing
    Set objCmdBar = Nothing
End Sub
```

2. Run the RemoveCmdButton_FromVBE procedure.
   Upon the procedure's completion, the Tools menu in the VBE screen no longer displays our custom item "List VBE menus and toolbars."

SUMMARY

In this chapter, you have used numerous objects, properties, and methods from the Microsoft Visual Basic for Applications Extensibility 5.3 Object Library to control the Visual Basic Editor (VBE).

In the next chapter, you learn how you can take advantage of the Windows API functions when programming VBA.

Chapter 25

CALLING WINDOWS API FUNCTIONS FROM VBA

While programming your Excel VBA applications, you may encounter a situation where VBA does not offer a method or property for performing a specific programming task, such as obtaining the user's screen resolution setting or changing the appearance of the UserForm. This is hardly a reason to give up. To ensure that all your program's specifications are implemented, look no further than the Windows operating system itself. A feature that is not directly supported by VBA might be supported by one of the thousands of functions that are exposed by the *Windows Application Programming Interface* (API). Therefore, overcoming many limitations of VBA boils down to learning how to locate the required Windows API function and then using it in your VBA procedure. This chapter shows you how functions found within the Windows API can help you extend your VBA procedures in areas where VBA does not provide desired functionality.

UNDERSTANDING THE WINDOWS API LIBRARY FILES

The Windows API is a collection of subroutines and functions located in files called *Dynamic Link Libraries* (DLLs). These files have a file extension of .dll and are located in the Windows System32 or SysWOW64 folder on every PC running Windows. The most popular dynamic link libraries are listed in Table 25.1.

The Windows API functions are written in the C language and can be accessed from Visual Basic for Applications by utilizing the `Declare` statement as discussed in the next section.

NOTE	*The following link provides a list of Windows API functions organized by category: http://msdn.microsoft.com/en-us/library/Aa383686.*

TABLE 25.1 Windows API library files. The first three files are known as the main (core) dlls. The remaining files are known as extension dlls.

API Library File	Description
USER32.DLL	This library file contains numerous functions that can be called upon whenever your VBA program needs to manage the Windows environment. For example, here you can find functions that relate to the use of windows such as setting or returning a window position, size, and state, or determining whether the window is active, or whether it's a parent window or a child window. Functions found in this library will also allow you to handle messages between various windows and dialog boxes, as well as manage menus, cursors, the keyboard, and the clipboard.
KERNEL32.DLL	This library contains functions that manage the low-level operating system functions such as memory management, resource management, computer drives, and file and folder management, as well as reading and writing to the Windows registry.
GDI32.DLL	This library has functions that will allow you to manage output to the screen. For example, you can manipulate fonts, drawings, graphics, bitmap images, and various display functions.
COMCTL32.DLL	Provides common GUI controls such as TreeView or ToolBar controls.
MAPI32.DLL	Includes functions for working with electronic mail.
NETAPI32. DLL	Provides functions for accessing and controlling networks.
ODBC32.DLL	Provides functions that allow applications to work with databases that are compliant with the Open Database Connectivity (ODBC).
TAPI32.DLL	Provides telephony functions used in managing voice mail and automated attendant phone systems.
WINMM.DLL	Allows access to multimedia capabilities.

HOW TO DECLARE A WINDOWS API FUNCTION

To access Windows API functions from VBA, you must use the `Declare` statement. This statement lets your program know where the function is located. The `Declare` statement must be added to the general declaration section of a standard module or a UserForm module. When added to the standard module, the function can be called from anywhere within your VBA application. If added to the general declaration section of the UserForm, the function will have a local scope, available only to the procedures of that form. To indicate that the function is local to the form, you must precede the `Declare` statement with the `Private` keyword.

The syntax of the `Declare` statement depends on whether or not the procedure returns a value.

If the procedure returns a value, it must be declared as a function, as shown in the syntax below:

```
[Public | Private] Declare Function name Lib "libname"
    [Alias "aliasname"] [[ByVal | ByRef] argument [As Type]
    [,[ByVal | ByRef] argument [As Type]…] [As Type]
```

If the procedure does not return a value, you must declare it as a subroutine, as shown in the syntax below:

```
[Public | Private] Declare Sub name Lib "libname"
   [Alias  "aliasname"] [[ByVal | ByRef] argument [As Type]
   [,[ByVal | ByRef]argument [As Type]…]
```

- The `Public` and `Private` keywords define the scope of the function or subroutine. Recall that a scope of Private will not allow the procedure to be used outside of the module in which it is declared.
- The `Declare` statement must be followed by the `Function` or `Sub` keyword, depending on whether or not the procedure returns a value.
- The name of the function or subroutine is followed by the name of the DLL library in which the function or subroutine is located.
- Some functions and subroutines have an *alias* that indicates that the function has another name in the library. Aliases make it possible to call the function or subroutine by any name you want, while providing a reference to the actual name of the function. An alias is particularly useful for those API functions that use characters that are illegal in VBA. For example, many Windows API functions have names that begin with the underscore character (_). Consider the Win API function `_lopen`, which opens an existing file. To have Excel VBA recognize this function's name as legal, use the `alias` keyword like this:

```
Declare Function lopen Lib "kernel32" Alias _
    "_lopen" (ByVal lpPathName As String, _
    ByVal iReadWrite As Long) As Long
```

- You should also alias the DLL function when its name conflicts with the VBA function of the same name. For example, use the following declaration when calling the `GetObject` function to let Excel know that you want to use the Win API `GetObject` function and not the Excel version of this function:

```
Public Declare Function GetObjectAPI Lib "gdi32" _
     Alias "GetObject" (ByVal hObject As Long, _
    ByVal nCount As Long, lpObject As Any) As Long
```

- Sometimes arguments need to be passed to functions and subroutines. Arguments can be passed by reference (default) or by value as explained in the next section.
- When declaring functions, you will need to define the type of value that is returned by including the `As Type` construct. Most functions return a long integer that can be indicated by appending `As Long` at the end of the function declaration. Or you can use a shortcut by specifying the function return type in the name of the function. For example, if the function returns a long integer, append the ampersand (&) to the function name as in the following:

```
Public Declare Function GetObjectAPI& Lib "gdi32" _
    Alias "GetObject" (ByVal hObject As Long, _
    ByVal nCount As Long, lpObject As Any)
```

  The `GetObjectAPI&` function indicates that the `GetObject` function which is located in the gdi32 library file (dll) returns a long integer.

The `Declare` statements that we've just discussed are for 32-bit operating systems. If used on a 64-bit system, they will fail. This topic is covered in detail later in this chapter.

Passing Arguments to the API Functions

When calling API functions you must know what type of arguments a function expects to receive. The functions in the Windows API library expect the arguments to be passed by reference or by value. Passing an argument by reference means that the function is passing a 32-bit or 64-bit pointer to the memory address where the value of the argument is stored. When the argument is passed by reference, it is possible for the function to change the value of the argument because it is working with the actual memory address where the argument is stored. You can use the `ByRef` keyword when passing arguments by reference or omit this keyword entirely from the `Declare` statement as passing arguments to function procedures by reference is the default in VBA.

When passing arguments by value, only a copy of the argument is sent to the function; therefore, the function cannot change the original value of the argument. If the API function expects to receive an argument by value and instead it receives the argument by reference, the function will not work properly. Strings are always passed by value (`ByVal`) to API functions. Always use the `ByVal` keyword when passing arguments by value.

Understanding the API Data Types and Constants

As mentioned earlier, the Windows API functions are written in C. Because there are differences between the data types used in the C language and the data types used in VBA, before you begin calling API functions from Excel you should familiarize yourself with the data types the different API functions expect and how you should declare them in VBA. The main data types that you will encounter when calling API functions are listed below.

Integer

The Integer data type (used for 16-bit numeric arguments) corresponds to the C data types known as short, unsigned short, and WORD. If the API function expects the Integer data type, you should pass it by value using the following syntax:

```
ByVal argumentname As Integer
```

The above Integer type declaration can also be written as:

```
ByVal argumentname%
```

Long

The Long data type (used for 32-bit numeric arguments) corresponds to the C data types known as int, unsigned int, unsigned long, BOOL, DWORD, and LONG. This is the most common data type in the Windows API functions. If the API function expects the Long data type, you should pass it by value using the following syntax:

```
ByVal argumentname As Long
```

The above Long type declaration can also be written as:

```
ByVal argumentname&
```

String

The Windows API functions expect string arguments to be passed in the LPSTR format. In the C language, the LPSTR data type is a memory pointer to an array of characters. Because VBA stores strings in a different way than the API functions expect, in order to handle textual data your VBA procedure will need to create a string buffer (a string filled with spaces or null characters) before calling the API function. In addition, because C uses 0-terminated strings and VBA does not, you will need to strip the 0-terminator from the end of the string returned by the API function (see Hands-On 25.1 later in this chapter). Strings are always passed to API functions by value (`ByVal`) even when the API function updates the string. Use the following syntax when declaring arguments with the String data type:

```
ByVal argumentname As String
```

The above String type declaration can also be written as:

```
ByVal argumentname$
```

Structure

In the C language, the Structure data type represents multiple variables and is an equivalent of a user-defined data type (UDT) in VBA. Before declaring and calling a Windows API function that uses a Structure argument, you must first define the structure using a `Type...End Type` construct. For example, the following API function called `GetCursorPos`, which retrieves the mouse cursor's position in screen coordinates, requires the `lpPoint` variable in the form of the POINTAPI structure:

```
Public Declare Function GetCursorPos Lib _
    "user32" (lpPoint As POINTAPI) As Long
```

Or (for the 64-bit systems)

```
Public Declare PtrSafe Function GetCursorPos Lib _
    "user32" (lpPoint As POINTAPI) As LongPtr
```

Adding the `PtrSafe` keyword after the `Declare` keyword will allow the above API declaration to work with 64-bit Excel. When writing VBA code in 32-bit Excel, this keyword should not be used.

Use the `Type...End Type` construct to declare the POINTAPI structure as shown below:

```
Private Type POINTAPI
    x as Long
    y as Long
End Type
```

By convention, the user-defined data type name is written in uppercase. The `x` and `y` are the coordinates of the cursor (relative to the screen).

Once the structure is declared as a user-defined data type in VBA, you must declare a variable of that type to use when you call the Windows API function:

```
Dim cPos As POINTAPI
```

You can give the variable any name you choose as long as the name does not conflict with any VBA reserved keywords. Next, to retrieve the coordinates of the mouse, all you need to do is write a VBA procedure that calls the `GetCursorPos` API function:

```
Sub getMouseCoordinates()
    Dim cPos As POINTAPI

    GetCursorPos cPos
    Debug.Print "x coordinate:" & cPos.x
    Debug.Print "y coordinate:" & cPos.y
End Sub
```

UDT arguments are passed to Windows API functions by reference (`ByRef`), as shown in Figure 25.1.

Any

The Any data type argument is used for those API functions that can accept more than one data type for the same argument. The Any data type is passed by reference (`ByRef`) and its syntax is:

```
argumentname As Any
```

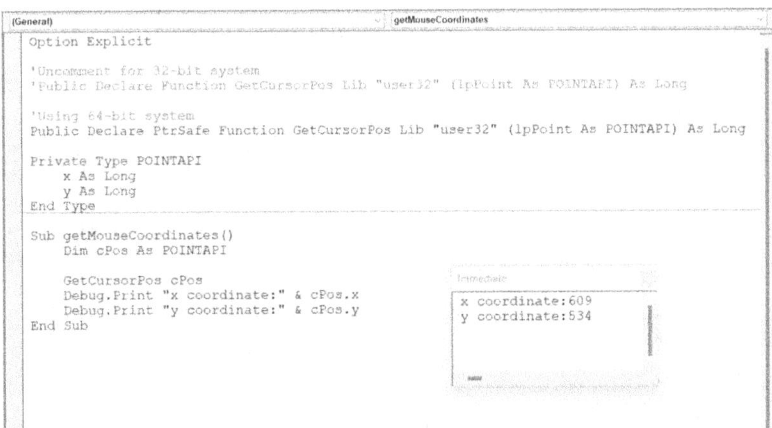

FIGURE 25.1 Passing the user-defined data type to a Windows API function.

Using Constants with Windows API Functions

Most of the Windows API functions rely on a number of predefined constants that have to be passed to them in specific arguments. Some functions can work with more than a dozen constants depending on what type of information you want to retrieve. For example, the following `GetSystemMetrics` function expects the `nIndex` argument that specifies the type of metric you want to return:

```
Public Declare Function GetSystemMetrics Lib "user32" _
    (ByVal nIndex As Long) As Long
```

Or (for the 64-bit systems)

```
Public Declare PtrSafe Function GetSystemMetrics Lib "user32" _
     (ByVal nIndex As Long) As Long
```

The `nIndex` argument must be passed to the `GetSystemMetrics` function as one of the number of predefined constants whose name begins with the letters SM followed by the underscore (_). For example, to return in pixels the width and height of the screen of the primary display monitor, you need to pass to the function the `SM_CXSCREEN` and `SM_CYSCREEN` constants as the `nIndex` argument. To do this, start by entering in the standard module the following constant declaration:

```
Public Const SM_CXSCREEN = 0  'defines the screen width
Public Const SM_CYSCREEN = 1  'defines the screen height
```

Next, enter the `Declare` statement to tell Excel that the external function is available:

```
Public Declare Function GetSystemMetrics Lib "user32" _
        (ByVal nIndex As Long) As Long
```

Or (for the 64-bit systems)

```
Public Declare PtrSafe Function GetSystemMetrics Lib "user32" _
        (ByVal nIndex As Long) As Long
```

Next, write a VBA procedure that calls the above function to retrieve the screen's dimensions:

```
Sub GetScreenResolution()
    Dim xSM As Long
    Dim ySM As Long

    xSM = GetSystemMetrics(SM_CXSCREEN)
```

```
    ySM = GetSystemMetrics(SM_CYSCREEN)

    Debug.Print "Your screen resolution is: " & _
        xSM & " x " & ySM
End Sub
```

Save the workbook file. You may also want to choose **Debug | CompileVBAProject** to ensure that there are no errors in the code you've entered.

Next, run the GetScreenResolution procedure. Assuming there were no run-time errors during the execution of your code, you should see your screen's resolution information in the Immediate window. The data retrieved should match the current setting of your screen resolution as displayed in the Control Panel. Figure 25.2 displays the code as entered in the Visual Basic standard module. The Immediate window shows the current screen resolution of the primary monitor.

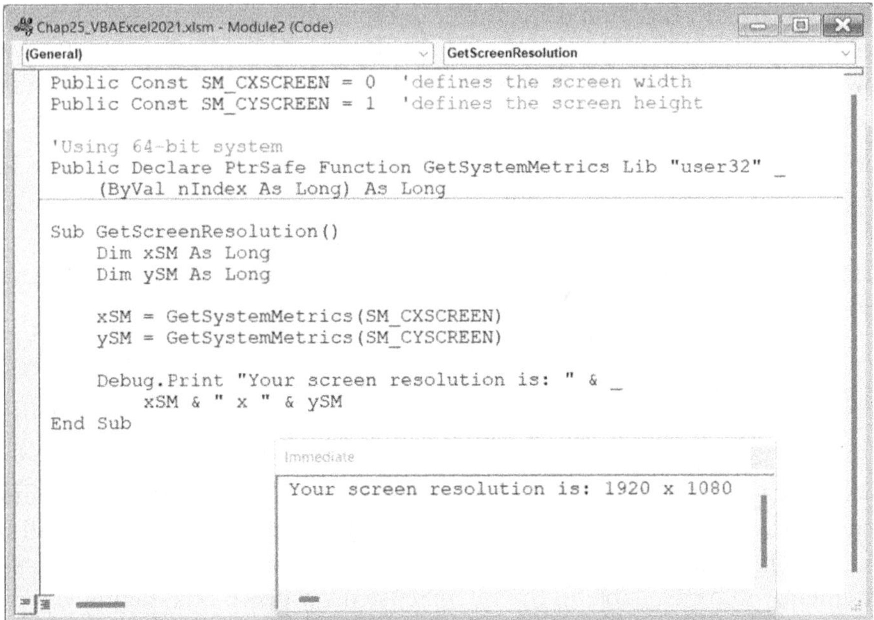

FIGURE 25.2 Retrieving information about screen resolution from a Windows API function using predefined constants.

When your application includes numerous calls to API functions and a great number of constants need to be declared in support of these functions, it is often difficult to know which constants are used with which function. To keep track of your constants and to make your code easier to write and comprehend, after declaring your constants with the `Const` keyword you can wrap them using an enumeration. An *enumeration* provides a listing of all its elements. For example, to keep the screen resolution constants together, use the `Enum` statement like this:

```
Enum SysMetConst
    x_screenWidth = SM_CXSCREEN
    y_screenHeight = SM_CYSCREEN
End Enum
```

The `Enum` statement declares a type for an enumeration. The `Enum` type is used to hold a collection of constants and make it easier to work with programs. The `Enum` statement can appear only at a module level. You can use any name for the `Enum` as long as it does not conflict with any of the VBA reserved keywords.

Next, write a VBA wrapper function that will pass the required constants to the Windows API function using the `Enum` type. The main purpose of a wrapper function is to use the functionality of another function, in this case the Windows API function, and pass to that function the required parameters via the `Enum` type like this:

```
Public Function ScreenRes(ByVal eIndex As SysMetConst) As Long
    ScreenRes = GetSystemMetrics(eIndex)
End Function
```

Next, you should write a VBA procedure that will display the result of the function to the user:

```
Sub WhatIsMyScreenResolution()
    MsgBox ScreenRes(x_screenWidth) & " x " & _
        ScreenRes(y_screenHeight)
End Sub
```

While encapsulating constants in an enumeration and writing wrapper functions may seem at first like much more coding to do, using this method will save you time in the long run. Also, the constants that are encapsulated in the `Enum` statement will be available in the IntelliSense drop-down box, saving you from typing them manually and possibly introducing errors into your code.

EXCEL 64-BIT AND WINDOWS API

To use the API functions with 64-bit Excel, you will need to modify the `Declare` statements to differentiate between 32-bit and 64-bit calls. To help avoid system crashes, truncation, and overflow errors when using API calls in 64-bit systems, Microsoft has introduced the `PtrSafe` keyword and two special data types: `LongLong` and `LongPtr`.

- The `PtrSafe` keyword indicates that the `Declare` statement is compatible with 64-bit systems. This keyword is mandatory on 64-bit systems.
- The `LongLong` data type is an 8-byte data type that is only available in 64-bit versions of Standalone Office 2021 and Microsoft 365.
- The `LongPtr` is a variable data type that is a 4-byte data type on 32-bit systems and an 8-byte data type on 64-bit versions of Microsoft 365 applications.

When making a call to an API function, you'll need to include the `PtrSafe` keyword in the `Declare` statement and also use `LongPtr` where the `Long` data type was used to return a handle or pointer (see the sidebar).

SIDEBAR *Understanding Pointers and Handles*

- A *pointer* is a reference to a specific location in physical memory where the application stores data or programming instructions. Versions of VBA prior to 2013 did not have a pointer data type (`LongPtr`). Pointers and handles were stored using 32-bit variables declared as `Long` data type. The `Long` data type cannot be used for pointers and handles on 64-bit systems because it is not large enough to store the 64-bit values returned by API functions.
- A *handle* is a unique identifier that Windows assigns to each window, dialog box, and control so that it can reference them. In 32-bit systems, handles were declared as `Long` data type. In 64-bit systems, they must be declared using the `LongPtr` data type.

To locate a window on a 64-bit system, declare the API `FindWindow` function as shown below:

```
Declare PtrSafe Function FindWindow Lib "user32" Alias _
    "FindWindowA" (ByVal lpClassName As String, _
    ByVal lpWindowName As String) As LongPtr
```

Notice that the `Declare` statement is followed by the `PtrSafe` keyword and the function's result is of the LongPtr data type. The Microsoft documentation states that `Declare` statements without the `PtrSafe` keyword are assumed not to be compatible with the 64-bit applications. Another important note specifies that the data types in the `Declare` statement will have to be updated to use `LongPtr` if they refer to handles and pointers. The above `FindWindow` API function returns a handle to the window; therefore its return value is declared `As LongPtr.`

In comparison, the `FindWindow` function on a 32-bit system is declared like this:

```
Declare Function FindWindow Lib "user32" Alias _
    "FindWindowA" (ByVal lpClassName As String, _
    ByVal lpWindowName As String) As Long
```

If the function requires a parameter that represents a handle or a pointer, in 64-bit Excel, this parameter data type will also need to be replaced with the `LongPtr` data type. For example, the following API function is used to retrieve a window's dimensions:

```
Declare PtrSafe Function GetWindowRect Lib "user32" _
 (ByVal hwnd As LongPtr, lpRect As RECT) As Long
```

In the above function, the first parameter is a handle and is therefore declared using the `LongPtr` data type.

The `GetWindowRect` function has the following syntax on a 32-bit system:

```
Declare Function GetWindowRect Lib "user32" _
 (ByVal hwnd As Long, lpRect As RECT) As Long
```

Similar changes need to be made to the Structure data type (UDT) if any member variable refers to a pointer or a handle. For example, the following API function allows the user to select a folder in 64-bit Excel:

```
Declare PtrSafe Function SHBrowseForFolder Lib "shell32" _
    Alias "SHBrowseForFolderA" (lpBrowseInfo As BROWSEINFO) _
    As Long
```

The above function requires that you pass it a structure (user-defined data type) named BROWSEINFO, declared as follows:

```
Public Type BROWSEINFO
    hwndOwner      As LongPtr
    pIDLRoot       As Long
    pszDisplayName As Long
    lpszTitle      As Long
    ulFlags        As Long
    lpfn           As LongPtr
    lParam         As LongPtr
    iImage         As Long
End Type
```

In the above user-defined data type declaration, some member variables reference handles or pointers and therefore are represented by the `LongPtr` data type.

The above UDT has the following format on 32-bit systems:

```
Type BROWSEINFO
    hwndOwner      As Long
    pIDLRoot       As Long
    pszDisplayName As Long
    lpszTitle      As Long
    ulFlags        As Long
    lpfn           As Long
    lParam         As Long
    iImage         As Long
End Type
```

If your VBA application utilizes Windows API functions and needs to be run in Excel 2021 or earlier, you should use the `VBA7` conditional compilation constant. The `VBA7` compilation constant allows you to determine the version of VBA being used so you can run the appropriate code segment for that version. For example:

```
#if VBA7 Then
```

' declare API function using the Declare statement with the PtrSafe keyword

```
#else
```

' declare API function without the PtrSafe keyword

```
#end if
```

Use the `Win64` compilation constant when you need to provide code for the 32-bit version of Excel as well as for the 64-bit version:

```
#if Win64 Then
```

' declare API function using the Declare statement with the `PtrSafe` keyword

```
#else
```

' declare API function without the `PtrSafe` keyword

```
#end if
```

NOTE	*For more information on compatibility between the 32-bit and 64-bit versions of Microsoft Office, please refer to Microsoft documentation at: http://msdn.microsoft.com/en-us/library/ee691831.aspx*

SIDEBAR *Using Conditional Compilation*

When you run a procedure for the first time, Visual Basic converts the VBA statements you used into the machine code understood by the computer. This process is called *compiling*. You can also perform the compilation of your entire VBA project manually before you run your procedure. To do this, simply choose Debug | Compile (your VBA project name) in the Visual Basic Editor window. You can tell Visual Basic to include or ignore certain blocks of code when compiling and running by using so-called *conditional compilation*.

To enable conditional compilation, use special expressions called *directives*. Use the `#Const` directive to declare a Boolean (True, False) constant. Next, check this constant inside the `#If...Then...#Else` directive. The portion of code that you want to compile conditionally must be surrounded by these directives. Notice that the If and Else keywords are preceded by a number sign (#). If a portion of code is to be run, the value of the conditional constant has to be set to True (–1). Otherwise, the value of this constant should be set to False (0). Declare the conditional constant in the declaration section of the module like this:

```
#Const User = True
```

This declares the conditional constant named User. Conditional compilation can be used to compile an application that will be run on different platforms (Windows or Macintosh, Win32-, Win64-bit). It is also useful in localizing an application for different languages or excluding certain debugging statements before the VBA application is sent off for distribution. The program code excluded during the conditional compilation is omitted from the final file; thus it has no effect on the size or performance of the program.

ACCESSING WINDOWS API DOCUMENTATION

Most of the Windows API `Declare` statements are rather long and require many parameters. Therefore, to save keystrokes and to avoid errors, many programmers prefer to resort to cutting and pasting the `Declare`s from the Win32API_PtrSafe.txt file that contains Windows API Declarations and Constants for Visual Basic, updated for 64-bit version of Office. This file replaces the original Win32API.txt file. For more information, and how to download and install the Win32API_PtrSafe.txt file, see the following link:

https://docs.microsoft.com/en-us/office/troubleshoot/office-suite-issues/win32api_ptrsafe-with-64-bit-support

You can find the Windows API Reference online at:

http://msdn.microsoft.com/en-us/library/aa383749(VS.85).aspx

USING WINDOWS API FUNCTIONS IN EXCEL

Now that we've discussed the steps involved in writing API functions and looked at the data types and parameters these functions expect, let's leave the theory behind and do some practical programming. The procedures in Hands-On 25.1 will teach you how you can make calls to API functions from a VBA code module. This particular example will introduce four API functions that you can use to return the following information:

- The current version number of Windows and information about the operating system platform (`GetVersionEx`)
- The path of your Windows directory (`GetWindowsDirectory`)
- The name of the user currently logged on (`GetUserName`)
- The user's computer name (`GetComputerName`)

NOTE	*Please note files for the "Hands-On" project may be found in the companion files.*

Hands-On 25.1 Retrieving Information about the Computer/User

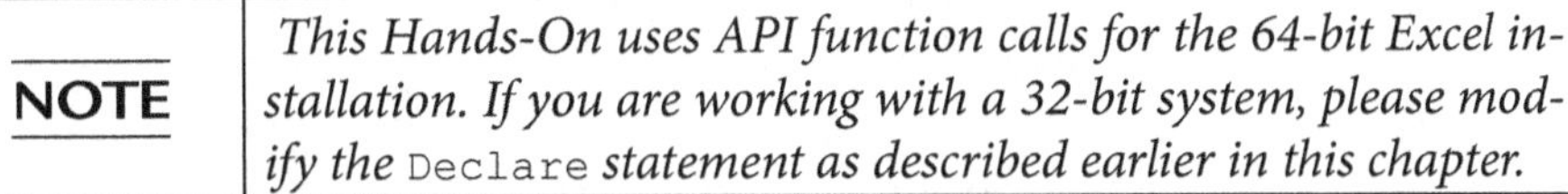

NOTE	*This Hands-On uses API function calls for the 64-bit Excel installation. If you are working with a 32-bit system, please modify the* `Declare` *statement as described earlier in this chapter.*

1. Open a new workbook in Excel and save it in a macro-enabled file format as **C:\VBAExcel2021_ByExample\Chap25_VBAExcel2021.xlsm**.
2. Switch to the Visual Basic Editor window and insert a new module.
3. In the module's Code window, enter the following four declarations of API functions:

```
Public Declare PtrSafe Function GetVersionEx Lib "kernel32" Alias _
    "GetVersionExA" (lpVersionInformation As OSVERSIONINFO) _
    As Long

Public Declare PtrSafe Function GetWindowsDirectory _
    Lib "kernel32" Alias "GetWindowsDirectoryA" _
```

```
    (ByVal lpBuffer As String, ByVal nSize As Long) _
    As Long

Public Declare PtrSafe Function GetUserName _
    Lib "advapi32.dll" Alias "GetUserNameA" _
    (ByVal lpBuffer As String, nSize As Long) As Long

Declare PtrSafe Function GetComputerName _
    Lib "kernel32.dll" Alias "GetComputerNameA" _
    (ByVal lpBuffer As String, nSize As Long) As Long
```

4. Below the last `Declare` statement, enter the following user-defined type definition:

```
Type OSVERSIONINFO
    dwOSVersionInfoSize As Long
    dwMajorVersion As Long
    dwMinorVersion As Long
    dwBuildNumber As Long
    dwPlatformId As Long
    szCSDVersion As String * 128
End Type
```

The OSVERSIONINFO data structure contains operating system version information. As mentioned earlier in this chapter, Structure data types are handled in VBA by user-defined data types.

The first member variable, `dwOSVersionInfoSize`, specifies the size, in bytes, of the data structure. Before calling the `GetVersionEx` function, it is necessary to set the size of `dwOSVersionInfoSize` to the size of the OSVERSIONINFO structure by using the `Len` function (see the procedure code in Step 5 below).

The `dwMajorVersion` and `dwMinorVersion` variables identify the major and minor version number of the operating system. The `dwBuildNumber` variable identifies the build number of the operating system. The `szCSDVersion` variable contains a null-terminated string that can provide additional information about the operating system such as the version of the service pack.

5. Enter the following OpSysInfo procedure that calls the `GetVersionEx` API function to retrieve information about the Windows platform:

```
Sub OpSysInfo()
    Dim os As OSVERSIONINFO
    Dim osVer As String

    os.dwOSVersionInfoSize = Len(os)
    GetVersionEx os
    osVer = os.dwMajorVersion & "." & os.dwMinorVersion
```

```
    Debug.Print "Windows Version = " & osVer
    Debug.Print "Windows Build Number = " & os.dwBuildNumber
    Debug.Print "Windows Platform ID = " & os.dwPlatformId
    Debug.Print "Additional info = " & os.szCSDVersion
End Sub
```

6. Save the changes to the Chap25_VBAExcel2021.xlsm workbook and then run the OpSysInfo procedure you entered in Step 5 above. After executing the above procedure on the machine running the Windows 10/11 Pro, the following information appears in the Immediate window:

```
Windows Version = 10.0
Windows Build Number = 22000
Windows Platform ID = 2
Additional info =
```

Procedure output on Windows 7 Home Premium:

```
Windows Version = 6.1
Windows Build Number = 7601
Windows Platform ID = 2
Additional info = Service Pack 1
```

7. Enter the PathToWinDir procedure in the code window just below the OpSysInfo procedure:

```
Sub PathToWinDir()
    Dim strWinDir As String
    Dim lngLen As Long

    strWinDir = String(255, 0)
    lngLen = GetWindowsDirectory(strWinDir, Len(strWinDir))
    strWinDir = Left(strWinDir, lngLen)
    MsgBox "Windows folder: " & strWinDir
End Sub
```

In the above procedure, we need to obtain textual data from the API function. This requires that you first create a string filled with spaces or null characters and then pass it to the function:

```
strWinDir = String(255, 0)
```

The VBA `String` function is used to return a string containing a repeating character string of the specified length. In this example, the string will be filled with null characters. You could also use the `Space` function to fill the string with 255 spaces like this:

```
strWinDir = Space(255)
```

In the next statement, we call the API function named `GetWindowsDirectory`, passing to it the required two arguments: the receiving string buffer (`strWinDir`) that we previously defined and the buffer's length (`Len(strWinDir)`). If the API function succeeds, it will return the length of the string copied to the buffer. If the function fails, the return value will be zero. Once we have the length of the returned string, we use the VBA `Left` function to extract the specified number of characters from the beginning of the buffer:

```
strWinDir = Left(strWinDir, lngLen)
```

8. Save the changes to the Chap25_VBAExcel2021.xlsm workbook and then run the PathToWinDir procedure in step mode by pressing F8. By stepping through the code, you can investigate the values of the individual variables that are passed to the API function to obtain the Windows path.
9. Enter the LoggedOnUserName function procedure in the Code window just below the PathToWinDir procedure:

```
Function LoggedOnUserName() As String
    Dim strBuffer As String * 255
    Dim strLen As Long

    strLen = Len(strBuffer)
    GetUserName strBuffer, strLen

    If strLen > 0 Then
        LoggedOnUserName = Left$(strBuffer, strLen - 1)
    End If

    MsgBox LoggedOnUserName
End Function
```

The above function procedure begins by declaring a `strBuffer` variable of fixed size (255 characters). This variable will be filled by the API function with the name of the logged-on user. The procedure also defines the `strLen` variable to hold the length of the buffer. The length of the buffer is set to the length of the `strBuffer` variable, which is initially 255 characters long. Next, to get the logged-on user name, the procedure calls the API function `GetUserName`, passing it two arguments as required by the function's `Declare` statement located at the top of the code module. If the length of the returned string is greater than zero (0), the function succeeded and the `strBuffer` variable should contain the name of the logged on user. However, before we return the user name to the VBA function, we need to extract the specified number of characters from the beginning of the `strBuffer` and strip off the terminating null character, which is also returned by the API function:

```
LoggedOnUserName = Left$(strBuffer, strLen - 1)
```

NOTE	*As mentioned earlier, the C language uses 0-terminated strings that are not recognized by VBA. Therefore, when calling a Windows API function that returns a string value, you must strip the 0-terminator from the end of the C string so VBA can recognize it correctly.*

10. Save the changes to the Chap25_VBAExcel2021.xlsm workbook and run the LoggedOnUserName function by typing its name in the Immediate window and then pressing **Enter**.
    When the function completes, you should see a message box with the name you used to log onto your computer.
11. Enter the GetUserComputerName procedure below the last procedure code:

```
Sub GetUserComputerName()
    Dim strCompName As String
    Dim retval As Long

    strCompName = Space(255)
    retval = GetComputerName(strCompName, 255)
    strCompName = Left(strCompName, _
        InStr(strCompName, vbNullChar) - 1)
    Debug.Print "Your computer name is: " _
        & strCompName
End Sub
```

12. Save the changes to the Chap25_VBAExcel2021.xlsm workbook and run the GetUserComputerName procedure.

Warnings and Precautions to Follow When Writing Procedures that Call the Windows API Functions

- Be sure to check all variable types, constants, and values that are required by the API function by checking the function documentation in the MSDN library.
- It is always better to specify the type of the variable explicitly rather than relying on the Any variable type.
- Be sure to pass strings to API functions by using the `ByVal` keyword.

- Before running the VBA procedure that calls the Windows API function, always save any changes made to the code module. Unexpected errors in the code may crash your system, and you will lose any unsaved work.

In the next Hands-On, you will work with the Excel VBA UserForm and learn how API functions can be used to change the appearance of the default UserForm that you create in Excel Visual Basic Editor. In particular, you will add an icon to the title bar, as well as include the missing maximize and minimize buttons. Next, you will make the form resizable and transparent. Finally, you will add the UserForm to the Windows task list. Figure 25.3 displays how the UserForm will look after you've completed Hands-On 25.2.

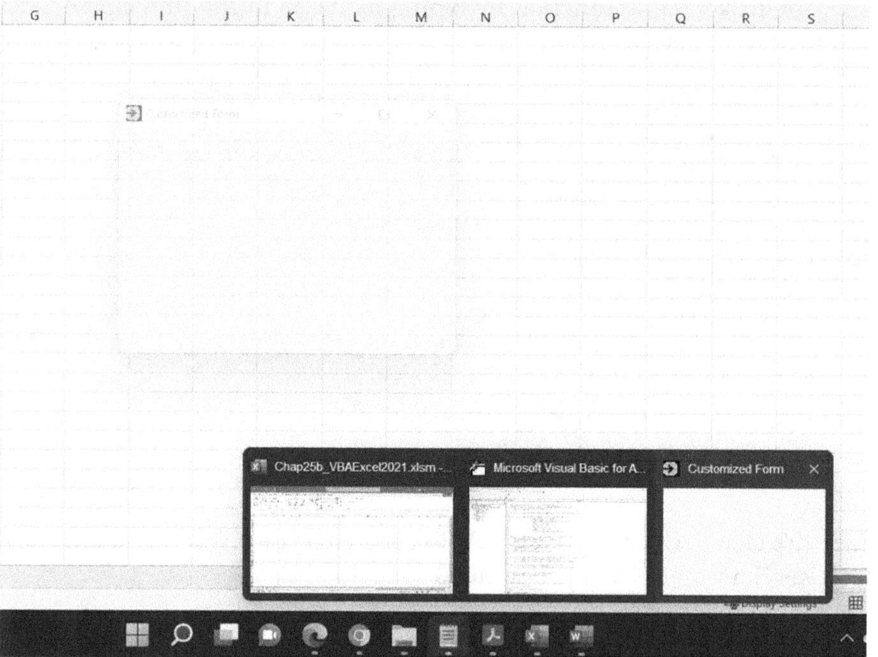

FIGURE 25.3 The Microsoft Excel UserForm can be customized by calling Windows API functions.

Hands-On 25.2 Enhancing a VBA UserForm by Calling Windows API Functions

NOTE	*This Hands-On uses API function calls for the 64-bit Excel installation. If you are working with a 32-bit system, please modify the* `Declare` *statement as described earlier in this chapter.*

1. Create a new workbook and save it in a macro-enabled file format as **C:\VBAExcel2021_ByExample\Chap25b_VBAExcel2021.xlsm**.
2. In the Visual Basic Editor window, insert a new module into the VBAProject (Chap25b_VBAExcel2021.xlsm) workbook.
3. In the module's Code window, enter the following API function, variable, and constant declarations:

```
' API FUNCTIONS DECLARATIONS

Declare PtrSafe Function FindWindow Lib "user32" Alias _
    "FindWindowA" (ByVal lpClassName As String, _
    ByVal lpWindowName As String) As LongPtr

Declare PtrSafe Function SendMessageA Lib "user32" _
    (ByVal hwnd As LongPtr, ByVal wMsg As Long, _
    ByVal wParam As LongPtr, ByVal lParam As LongPtr) As LongPtr

Declare PtrSafe Function ExtractIconA Lib "shell32.dll" _
(ByVal hInst As LongPtr, ByVal lpszExeFileName As String, _
    ByVal nIconIndex As Long) As Long

Declare PtrSafe Function GetActiveWindow Lib "user32" () As Long

Declare PtrSafe Function SetWindowPos Lib "user32" _
                    (ByVal hwnd As LongPtr, _
                     ByVal hWndInsertAfter As LongPtr, _
                     ByVal x As Long, _
                     ByVal y As Long, _
                     ByVal cx As Long, _
                     ByVal cy As Long, _
                     ByVal wFlags As Long) As Long

Declare PtrSafe Function GetWindowLong Lib "user32" Alias _
    "GetWindowLongA" (ByVal hwnd As LongPtr, _
    ByVal nIndex As Long) As Long

Declare PtrSafe Function SetWindowLong Lib "user32" Alias _
    "SetWindowLongA" (ByVal hwnd As LongPtr, _
    ByVal nIndex As Long, _
    ByVal dwNewLong As Long) As LongPtr

Declare PtrSafe Function SetLayeredWindowAttributes Lib "user32" _
    (ByVal hwnd As LongPtr, ByVal crey As Byte, _
    ByVal bAlpha As Byte, ByVal dwFlags As Long) As LongPtr
```

```
Declare PtrSafe Function FlashWindow Lib "user32" _
    (ByVal hwnd As LongPtr, ByVal bInvert As Long) As Long

Declare PtrSafe Sub Sleep Lib "kernel32" _
    (ByVal dwMilliseconds As Long)

' variable declarations

Public hwnd As Long  ' handle to the active window

' Constant declarations
Public Const GWL_EXSTYLE = (-20)
Public Const GWL_STYLE = (-16)
Public Const WS_EX_LAYERED = &H80000
Public Const WS_EX_APPWINDOW = &H40000
Public Const WS_MINIMIZEBOX = &H20000
Public Const WS_MAXIMIZEBOX = &H10000
Public Const WS_THICKFRAME = &H40000
Public Const SWP_NOMOVE = &H2
Public Const SWP_NOSIZE = &H1
Public Const SWP_NOACTIVATE = &H10
Public Const SWP_HIDEWINDOW = &H80
Public Const SWP_SHOWWINDOW = &H40
Public Const SW_SHOW = 5
Public Const HWND_TOP = 0
Public Const LWA_ALPHA = &H2&
Public Const WM_SETICON = &H80
```

4. Choose **Insert | UserForm** to add a new form to the VBAProject.
5. Right-click the UserForm and choose **View Code.**
6. In the UserForm1 Code window, enter the following three procedures:

```
Private Sub UserForm_Activate()
    CustomizeForm
End Sub

Private Sub UserForm_Initialize()
    With Me
        .Caption = "Customizing Form...Please Wait"
        .BackColor = RGB(255, 255, 51)
    End With
End Sub


Private Sub AddIcon_OnTitleBar(strIconBmpFile As String)
    Dim fLen As Long
```

```
    If Len(Dir(strIconBmpFile)) <> 0 Then
        'fLen = ExtractIconA(0, strIconBmpFile, 0)
         fLen = ExtractIconA(0, strIconBmpFile, 0)
        SendMessageA FindWindow(vbNullString, Me.Caption), _
            WM_SETICON, False, fLen

    Else
        Exit Sub
    End If
End Sub

Private Sub CustomizeForm()
    Dim wStyle As Long
    Dim xStyle As Long
    Dim bOpacity As Byte

    'get the handle of the active window
    hwnd = GetActiveWindow

    ' get user attention by flashing the window
    Call FlashThisWindow(hwnd)

    ' begin customization process
    AddIcon_OnTitleBar "C:\VBAExcel2021_ByExample\Images\arrow.bmp"

    bOpacity = 120 ' set opacity

    'retrieve the active window's styles
    wStyle = GetWindowLong(hwnd, GWL_STYLE)

    ' modify the window style settings
    wStyle = wStyle Or WS_MINIMIZEBOX   'add the minimize button
    wStyle = wStyle Or WS_MAXIMIZEBOX   'add the maximize button
    wStyle = wStyle Or WS_THICKFRAME    'add a sizing border

    'apply the revised style
    Call SetWindowLong(hwnd, GWL_STYLE, wStyle)

    'retrieve the active window's extended styles
    xStyle = GetWindowLong(hwnd, GWL_EXSTYLE)

    ' modify the window extended style settings
    xStyle = xStyle Or WS_EX_LAYERED     ' change opacity
    xStyle = xStyle Or WS_EX_APPWINDOW  ' add window to the task bar
```

```
    'apply the revised extended style
    Call SetWindowLong(hwnd, GWL_EXSTYLE, xStyle)

    Call SetLayeredWindowAttributes(hwnd, 0, bOpacity, LWA_ALPHA)

    Call SetWindowPos(hwnd, HWND_TOP, 0, 0, 0, 0, _
                           SWP_NOMOVE Or _
                           SWP_NOSIZE Or _
                           SWP_NOACTIVATE Or _
                           SWP_HIDEWINDOW)

    Call SetWindowPos(hwnd, HWND_TOP, 0, 0, 0, 0, _
                           SWP_NOMOVE Or _
                           SWP_NOSIZE Or _
                           SWP_NOACTIVATE Or _
                           SWP_SHOWWINDOW)

End Sub


Sub FlashThisWindow(myForm As Long)
    Dim counter As Integer
    ' declare return value used for flashing the window
    Dim retval As LongPtr

    For counter = 1 To 10
        ' toggle the look of the window
        retval = FlashWindow(myForm, 1)
        Sleep 500  ' wait for 5 seconds
    Next counter
    retval = FlashWindow(myForm, 0)
    UserForm1.Caption = "Customized Form"
End Sub
```

When you run the Sub/UserForm, Excel will look for the UserForm_Initialize procedure and will execute the code found therein. This code will tell Excel to replace the default caption with the specified text and change the form background color to a shade of yellow represented by the `RGB(255, 255, 51)` function. Next, the UserForm_Activate event will be triggered. Here we make a call to the CustomizeForm VBA procedure. The CustomizeForm procedure begins by obtaining a handle to the active window via the call to the `GetActiveWindow` API function. You'll need this handle for all the API functions used in this solution, hence the `hwnd` variable it is declared with the Public keyword in the standard module. After obtaining a window reference we want to get user's attention by flashing the form. This is done within the code of the FlashThisWindow VBA procedure which makes a direct call to the following Windows API functions:

```
Declare PtrSafe Function FlashWindow Lib "user32" _
    (ByVal hwnd As LongPtr, ByVal bInvert As Long) As Long


Declare PtrSafe Sub Sleep Lib "kernel32" _
    (ByVal dwMilliseconds As Long)
```

The `FlashWindow` function returns 0 if the window's look was inactive before flashing, or 1 if its look was active. The `hwnd` parameter is the handle to the window. The `bInvert` parameter specifies how to flash. Non-zero will switch the title bar from active to inactive or vice versa. Zero will restore window to its normal look.

The `Sleep` procedure pauses program execution for a specified amount of time. Sleep does not return any value. It requires that you specify the number of milliseconds to hold program execution for (see the `dwMilliseconds` parameter).

After flashing the UserForm1 window on and off, we again change the form's title using the `Caption` property and go on to perform form customizations. To put an icon on the form's title bar, we call the AddIcon_OnTitleBar procedure and pass to it the name and location of the bitmap image we want to use.

Before you can do anything with the image, you must ensure that it is indeed found in the specified pathname. Therefore, the AddIcon_OnTitleBar procedure begins by checking if the specified file exists, and if it does, we call upon three API functions that will allow us to extract the icon from the file (`ExtractIconA`) and then display it on the form's titlebar (`SendMessageA` and `FindWindow`). To find the UserForm1, you can use the `FindWindow` API function like this:

```
FindWindow(vbNullString, Me.Caption)
```

The `FindWindow` function finds a window handle based on the exact window title. A *window handle* is a unique identifier that Windows assigns to each window, dialog box, or control. Once you have a window handle, you can pass it to the API functions for all operations involving windows. In the above code snippet, the VBA statement Me.Caption will provide the title of our UserForm1 by using the `Caption` property of the form so that the `FindWindow` function will be able to locate the UserForm1 window and return the handle, which is a Long (4-byte) value.

NOTE	*If you want to find the handle of Microsoft Excel, keep in mind that VBA provides a special built-in property named* `hWnd` *for the Excel Application object; thus, it is not necessary to call the API function to retrieve the handle.*

The result of the `FindWindow` function (in this case the handle to the UserForm) is then fed along with other arguments to the `SendMessageA` function. This function tells Windows to perform the requested action, which is placing the icon image on the found form's titlebar. If the icon image is not found, the procedure does not do anything; you will end up with a UserForm that does not have the icon.

Before you can make modifications to the UserForm's titlebar, it is necessary to get the current style information of the active window. This is done by accessing the window's configuration memory by calling the `GetWindowLong` API function and passing it the `GWL_STYLE` constant that you defined in the standard code module. Once you have the `GWL_STYLE` setting in the `wStyle` variable, you can modify the setting by using the bitwise OR operator as shown below:

```
wStyle = wStyle Or WS_MINIMIZEBOX    'add the minimize button
wStyle = wStyle Or WS_MAXIMIZEBOX    'add the maximize button
wStyle = wStyle Or WS_THICKFRAME     'add a sizing border
```

To have Windows actually apply the new settings, the procedure goes on to call the `SetWindowLong` API function:

```
Call SetWindowLong(hWnd, GWL_STYLE, wStyle)
```

The parameters passed to the `SetWindowLong` API function inform Windows which window should be modified (`hWnd`), what settings need to be changed (`GWL_STYLE`), and what the replacement settings (`wStyle`) are.

You can follow the same logic to make modifications to the extended windows styles in order to make your form transparent and visible on the task bar:

```
'retrieve the active window's extended styles
xStyle = GetWindowLong(hWnd, GWL_EXSTYLE)

' modify the window extended style settings
xStyle = xStyle Or WS_EX_LAYERED     ' change opacity
xStyle = xStyle Or WS_EX_APPWINDOW   ' add window to the task bar

'apply the revised extended style
Call SetWindowLong(hWnd, GWL_EXSTYLE, xStyle)
```

Next you need to tell Windows the amount of transparency you want to apply to the form. This is done by calling the following function:

```
Call SetLayeredWindowAttributes(hWnd, 0, bOpacity, LWA_ALPHA)
```

The second argument in the above function, `0`, is the transparent color of the window; this argument is not used. The third argument is the amount of transparency you want. Zero (0) will make the form completely transparent and 255 will make it completely opaque. The procedure uses the setting of 120 stored in the `bOpacity` variable. The last parameter, `LWA_ALPHA`, tells the window that the form should be transparent.

The last two API function calls in the CustomizeForm procedure ensure that the name of the UserForm1 window appears in the top position on the window's task bar and the entry is removed when the form is closed.

7. Run the UserForm1 to examine the result of the applied customizations (see Figure 25.3 earlier in this chapter). Notice the presence of the icon on the title bar as well as Minimize and Maximize buttons to the left of the default Close (X) button. The minimize button will not be visible if the form is too small. Resize the form, dragging its borders to see all buttons. When you click on the icon in the upper-left corner, you should see a menu with options allowing you to move, size, minimize, maximize, and close the form. When you minimize the form, it will jump into the taskbar. You can activate the form directly from the task bar by right clicking it and choosing Restore.

SUMMARY

While VBA offers programmers a huge library of objects, properties, and methods, there are certain interface features supported by the Windows operating system that cannot be accessed by calling the native VBA library. The good news is that some of the VBA limitations can be directly dealt with by having your VBA procedure call a function from the Windows Application Programming Interface (API). This chapter introduced you to the basic Windows API concepts and showed you how you can call API functions from VBA. It also pointed you to resources you can use to find and research functions that should help you in extending your VBA programs by providing more functionality via Windows API.

In the next chapter, we will move into the next part of this book that will cover more advanced concepts in Excel VBA. You will learn about creating classes and programming in stand-alone class modules.

Part VII Advanced Concepts in Excel VBA

So far in this book, you learned that there are many ways to perform the same tasks in Excel. You've written many procedures and functions that contained programming code that you might want to reuse in other Excel applications. As your Excel VBA procedures become more complex, you may find that your code is scattered all over the place and is difficult to maintain. Copying code from place to place and modifying procedures to include more arguments and enhancements because of the changing requirements will eventually result in creating a coding mess that is difficult to manage. Before you go this route, you should know that Excel has a special feature known as a *class module* that allows you to create code that is self-contained and reusable.

Chapter 26 Creating Classes in VBA

The class helps you organize your code into more manageable objects that you can easily reuse and adjust when necessary. Classes also make it easier to share your programming code with others. The class hides its inner workings from the rest of the program. Any programmer can use the class without knowing how that class was put together. It's like driving a car. A driver does not need to know the intricate details of a car manufacture.

By getting acquainted with classes, you'll be able to move from the procedural programming that you're already familiar with into an object-oriented programming (OOP) where you program by creating objects, which may contain data defined as attributes or properties, and code, defined as procedures, or methods. Objects are the basic units of OOP and are created by adding class modules to your Excel VBA projects. A class is like a cookie cutter. Once you create it, you can make any number of cookies. In Excel, your cookies will be the custom objects you create from a class defined in a class module.

IMPORTANT TERMINOLOGY

In this chapter, you will work with advanced VBA concepts: VBA classes, class objects, and collection classes. Before diving into theory and this chapter's hands-on examples, let's review the following terms:

Object—An *object* is a logical representation of a thing. This thing can be a tangible, physical entity such as person, a car, a customer or an employee, or a logical entity such as an order, a transaction, or a report. It can also be something related to your specific Excel application, such as a process that simplifies data validation or manipulation of data. In other words, an object is basically anything you need to define.

Collection—An object that contains a set of related objects

Class—A definition of an object that includes its name, properties, methods, and events. The *class* acts as a sort of object template from which an instance of an object is created at runtime.

Instance—A specific object that belongs to a class is referred to as an *instance of the class*. When you create an instance, you create a new object that has the properties and methods defined by the class.

Class module—A module that contains the definition of a class, including its property and method definitions

Module—a module containing sub and function procedures that are available to other VBA procedures and are not related to any object in particular

Form module—a module that contains the VBA code for all event procedures triggered by events occurring in a user form or its controls. A form module is a type of class module.

Event—an action recognized by an object, such as a mouse click or a keypress, for which you can define a response. Events can be caused by a user action or a VBA statement or can be triggered by the system.

Event procedure—a procedure that is automatically executed in response to an event initiated by the user or program code or triggered by the system

CREATING AND USING CUSTOM OBJECTS

Visual Basic Editor's Insert menu has two Module options: Module and Class Module. So far, you've used standard modules to create subroutine and function procedures. You'll use the class module for the first time in this chapter to create a custom class named CAsset and learn how to define its properties and methods.

Before you can create custom objects, you need a basic understanding of what a class is. If you refer to the beginning of this chapter, you will see that we described a class as a sort of object template. A frequently used analogy is comparing an object class to a cookie cutter. Just as a cookie cutter defines what a cookie will look like, the definition of the class determines how an object should look and behave. Before you can use an object class, you must first create a new instance of that class. Object instances are the cookies. Each object instance has the characteristics (properties and methods) defined by its class. Just as you can cut out many cookies using the same cookie cutter, you can create multiple instances of a class. You can also change the properties of each instance of a class independently of any other instance of the same class.

A class module lets you define your own custom classes, complete with custom properties and methods. Recall that a property is an attribute of an object that defines one of its characteristics, such as shape, position, color, title, and so on. You can create the properties for your custom objects by writing property procedures in a class module. There are three types of property procedures (Property Get, Property Let, and Property Set). You will learn how to work with property procedures in Lab 26.1.

A *method* is an action that the object can perform. The object methods are also created in a class module by writing subroutines or function procedures.

Lab 26.1 will introduce you to the process of creating a custom object named CAsset. This object will contain information about a single computer hardware asset. It will have four properties to hold the information about AssetType, Manufacturer, Model, and Price. It will also have a method that will allow you to modify the price. The asset information that you will use in this project is provided in a text file in the companion files and depicted in Figure 26.1.

As you can see in Figure 26.1, the data file contains several lines (records). The data between the quotes is treated as a single field. Fields are delimited by a comma (,). This type of a text file is often called a *comma-delimited file* or a *sequential access file*. To successfully complete this lab, you need to know that in sequential access files the data is retrieved in the same order as it is stored. Sequential access files can be opened in Input, Output, or Append mode. In this project, you will use the Input mode, which will allow you to read the data from the file into your custom object's properties. Because the file contains data on several assets, you will also reinforce your understanding about collections by reading the data from the text file into a collection of CAsset objects and then manipulating these objects. So, let's get started.

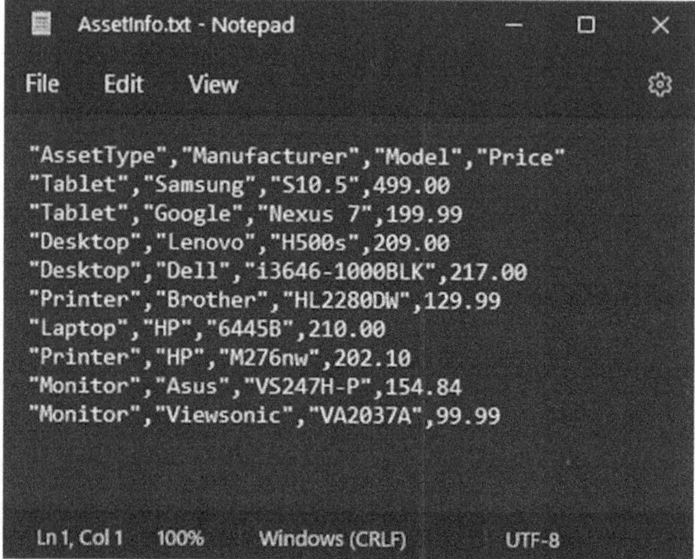


```
"AssetType","Manufacturer","Model","Price"
"Tablet","Samsung","S10.5",499.00
"Tablet","Google","Nexus 7",199.99
"Desktop","Lenovo","H500s",209.00
"Desktop","Dell","i3646-1000BLK",217.00
"Printer","Brother","HL2280DW",129.99
"Laptop","HP","6445B",210.00
"Printer","HP","M276nw",202.10
"Monitor","Asus","VS247H-P",154.84
"Monitor","Viewsonic","VA2037A",99.99
```

FIGURE 26.1 This text file (AssetInfo.txt) provides the data for the custom CAsset object class.

NOTE	*All figures and files for the hands-on projects can be found in the companion files.*

Lab 26.1a Creating a Class Module

1. Open a blank Excel workbook and save it as **C:\VBAExcel2021_ByExample\Chap26_VBAExcel2021.xlsm.**
2. Switch to the VBE Screen.
3. Select **VBAProject (Chap26_VBAExcel2021.xlsm)** in the Project Explorer window and choose **Insert | Class Module**.
4. Highlight the **Class 1** module in the Project Explorer window and use the Properties window to rename the class module **CAsset**.

SIDEBAR *Naming a Class Module*

Every time you create a new class module, give it a meaningful name. Set the name of the class module to the name you want to use in your VBA procedures that use the class. The name you choose for your class should be easily understood and identify the "thing" the object class represents. As a rule, the object class name is prefaced with an uppercase "C."

Member Variables in a Class Module

After adding and renaming the class module, the next step is to declare the variables that will hold the data you want to store in the object. Each item of data you want to store in an object should be assigned a variable. Variables in a class module are called *data members* and are declared with the `Private` keyword. This keyword ensures that the variables will be available only within the class module. Using the `Private` keyword instead of the familiar `Dim` statement hides the data members and prevents other parts of the application from referencing them. Only the procedures within the class module in which the variables were defined can modify the value of these variables.

Because the name of a variable also serves as a property name, use meaningful names for your object's data members. It's a common practice to preface the variable names with `m_` to indicate that they are data members of a class.

Let's continue with our Lab project by declaring data members for our CAsset class.

Lab 26.1b Declaring Members of the CAsset Class

1. Type the following declaration lines at the top of the CAsset class module:

```
'declarations
Private m_AssetType As String
Private m_Manufacturer As String
Private m_Model As String
Private m_Price As Currency
```

Notice that the name of each data member variable begins with the prefix `m_`.

Defining the Properties for the Class

Declaring the variables with the `Private` keyword guarantees that the variables cannot be directly accessed from outside the object. This means that the VBA procedures from outside the class module will not be able to set or read data stored in those variables. To enable other parts of your VBA application to set or retrieve the asset data, you must add special property procedures to the CAsset class module.

There are three types of property procedures:

- Property Let allows other parts of the application to set the value of a property.

- Property Get allows other parts of the application to get or read the value of a property.
- Property Set is used instead of Property Let when setting the reference to an object.

Property procedures are executed when an object property needs to be set or retrieved. The Property Get procedure can have the same name as the Property Let procedure.

You should create property procedures for each property of the object that can be accessed by another part of your VBA application. The easiest of the three types of property statements to understand is the Property Get procedure. Let's examine the syntax of the property procedures by taking a closer look at the Property Get AssetType procedure. As a rule, the property procedures contain the following parts:

- A procedure declaration line that specifies the name of the property and the data type:

  ```
  Property Get AssetType() As String
  ```

  AssetType is the name of the property and `As String` determines the data type of the property's return value.
- An assignment statement like the one used in a function procedure:

  ```
  AssetType = m_AssetType
  ```

  AssetType is the name of the property, and `m_AssetType` is the data member variable that holds the value of the property you want to retrieve or set. The `m_AssetType` variable should be defined with the `Private` keyword at the top of the class module.
- The `End Property` keywords that specify the end of the property procedure:

  ```
  Property Get AssetType() As String
      AssetType = m_AssetType
  End Property
  ```

Writing Property Procedures

The CAsset class has four properties (AssetType, Manufacturer, Model, and Price) that need to be exposed to a VBA procedure that you will write later. Because this procedure will need to read a data file and then write it into a collection of CAsset objects, the next step requires writing the necessary Property Get and Property Let procedures.

Lab 26.1c Writing Property Procedures for the CAsset Class

1. Type the following Property Get and Let procedures in the CAsset class module, just below the declaration section.

```
' Property procedures

Property Get AssetType() As String
    AssetType = m_AssetType
End Property

Property Let AssetType(ByVal aType As String)
    m_AssetType = aType
End Property

Property Get Manufacturer() As String
    Manufacturer = m_Manufacturer
End Property

Property Let Manufacturer(ByVal aMake As String)
    m_Manufacturer = aMake
End Property

Property Get Model() As String
    Model = m_Model
End Property

Property Let Model(ByVal aModel As String)
    m_Model = aModel
End Property

Property Get Price() As Currency
    Price = m_Price
End Property

Property Let Price(ByVal aPrice As Currency)
    m_Price = aPrice
End Property
```

Notice that each type of the needed asset information requires a separate Property Get procedure. Each of the Property Get procedures returns the current value of the property. The Property Get procedure is like a function procedure. Like function procedures, the Property Get procedures contain an assignment statement. As you recall from Chapter 4, to return a value from a function procedure, you must assign it to the function's name.

SIDEBAR ***Immediate Exit from Property Procedures***

Just like the `Exit Sub` and `Exit Function` keywords allow you to exit early from a subroutine or a function procedure, the `Exit Property` keywords give you a way to immediately exit from a property procedure. Program execution will continue with the statements following the statement that called the Property Get, Property Let, or Property Set procedure.

In addition to retrieving values stored in data members (private variables) with Property Get procedures, you wrote corresponding Property Let procedures to allow other parts of the application to change the values of these variables as needed. You can make a property read-only by not writing a corresponding property Let procedure.

The Property Let procedures require at least one parameter that specifies the value you want to assign to the property. This parameter can be passed by value (see the `ByVal` keyword in the Property Let Price procedure shown earlier) or by reference (`ByRef` is the default). If you need a refresher on the meaning of these keywords, see the section titled "Passing Arguments by Reference and Value" in Chapter 4.

The data type of the parameter passed to the Property Let procedure must have the same data type as the value returned from the Property Get procedure with the same name. Notice that the Property Let procedures have the same name as the Property Get procedures prepared in the preceding section.

SIDEBAR ***Defining the Scope of Property Procedures***

You can place the `Public`, `Private`, or `Static` keyword before the name of a property procedure to define its scope. For example, to indicate that the Property Get procedure is accessible to other procedures in all modules, use the following statement format:

```
Public Property Get AssetType() As String
```

To make the Property Get procedure accessible only to other procedures in the module where it is declared, use the following statement format:

```
Private Property Get Model() As String
```

To preserve the Property Get procedure's local variables between procedure calls, use the following statement format:

```
Static Property Get Manufacturer() As String
```

If not explicitly specified using either `Public` or `Private`, property procedures are public by default. Also, if the `Static` keyword is not used, the values of local variables are not preserved between the procedure calls.

Writing Class Methods

Apart from properties, objects usually have one or more methods. A *method* is an action that the object can perform. Methods allow you to manipulate data stored in a class object. Methods are created with the sub or function procedures. To make a method available outside the class module, use the `Public` keyword in front of the Sub or Function definition.

The CAsset class that you create in this lab has one method that allows you to calculate the new price. Assume that the asset's price can be decreased by a specific percentage or amount. Let's continue with our lab project by writing a class method that calculates the new price.

Lab 26.1d Writing a Method for the CAsset Class

1. Type the following `NewPrice` function procedure in the CAsset class module:

```
' function to calculate new price
Public Function NewPrice(discountType As Integer, _
                        currentPrice As Currency, _
                        amount As Long) As Currency

    If amount >= currentPrice Then
        NewPrice = currentPrice
        Exit Function
    End If
    Select Case discountType
       Case 1 ' by percent
        If amount > 50 Then
          amount = 50
        End If
          NewPrice = currentPrice - ((currentPrice * _
            amount) / 100)

        Case 2 ' by amount
```

```
            NewPrice = currentPrice - amount
    End Select
End Function
```

The NewPrice function defined with the Public keyword in a class module serves as a method for the CAsset class. To calculate a new price, a VBA procedure from outside the class module must pass three arguments: discountType, currentPrice, and amount. The discountType argument specifies the type of the calculation. Suppose you want to decrease the asset price by 5% or by $5. The first option will decrease the price by the specified percentage, and the second option will subtract the specified amount from the current price. The currentPrice argument is the current price figure for an asset, and amount determines the value by which the price should be changed. The other assumptions in the new price calculation that you might want to include can be specified with the conditional statements.

Creating an Instance of a Class

You have now completed the definition of the CAsset class. Every time you define a class, you must do this in a class module. In VBA, you can define only one class in a class module. The name of the class is the name of the module. A class is a template from which you can create objects. The class specifies the properties and methods that will be common for all objects created from that class.

After defining the class, you can create objects based on that class. This process takes place in a standard module. You start by declaring an object variable. If the name of the class module is CAsset, declare a variable of type CAsset and set that variable to a new instance of the class, like this:

```
Dim asset As CAsset
Set asset = New CAsset
```

It is also possible to combine the two statements into a single statement, like this:

```
Dim asset As New CAsset
```

The asset variable represents a reference to an object of the CAsset class. You can name your object variable anything you want except you cannot use any of the VBA reserved words. All the properties and methods defined in CAsset class will now be available in the asset variable. When you declare the object variable with the New keyword, VBA creates the object and allocates memory for it; however, the object isn't instanced until you refer to it in your procedure code by assigning a value to its property or running one of its methods.

Let's continue our hands-on lab project by writing the VBA procedure that reads the data from the text file into a collection of `CAsset` objects.

Lab 26.1e Writing Code

1. In the Visual Basic Editor screen, choose **Insert | Module** to add a standard module to the current VBA project.
2. In the Properties window, rename the module **AssetInfo**.
3. In the Project Explorer window, double-click the AssetInfo module to activate the Code window.
4. In the AssetInfo Code window, enter the Retrieve_AssetInfo procedure as shown here:

```
Sub Retrieve_AssetInfo()
    ' declare two object variables
    ' one for the object and the other
    ' for the collection of objects

Dim asset As CAsset
    Dim AssetsColl As Collection

    ' declare variables for reading the data file
    Dim strAssetType As String
    Dim strMake As String
    Dim strModel As String
    Dim itemPrice As String

    ' declare a variable to specify discount type
    ' in the calculation of new asset price
    Dim intDiscount As Integer

    ' declare variables used by the MsgBox function
    Dim strTitle As String
    Dim strPrompt As String

    ' declare variables to facilitate data
    ' entry in a worksheet and the Immediate window
    Dim strFilePath As String
    Dim strRecord As String
    Dim wRow As Integer

    ' declare variables used for collection purpose
    Dim counter As Integer
    Dim aKey As String
```

```
' declare variables for accessing an object
' in a collection via a key
Dim assetKey As String
'Dim m As Object

' if error occurs go to the next statement
On Error Resume Next

' initialize various variables
strFilePath = "C:\VBAExcel2021_ByExample\AssetInfo.txt"
counter = 0

wRow = 1

strPrompt = "Enter 1 for the percent discount or "
strPrompt = strPrompt + " 2 for the amount discount"

strTitle = "Price Discount Type"

' create an instance of the collection object
Set AssetsColl = New Collection

' open the text file for reading
Open strFilePath For Input As #1

'check is the file is available
If Err.Number <> 0 Then
    MsgBox "File not found!", vbCritical, "File Error"
    Exit Sub
End If

' ask the user the type of discount to apply
intDiscount = CInt(InputBox(strPrompt, strTitle, 1))

' add a new empty worksheet
ActiveWorkbook.Worksheets.Add

' -------------------------------------
' loop until end of file is encountered
' -------------------------------------
Do While Not EOF(1)

    'read data from the text file into four variables
    Input #1, strAssetType, strMake, strModel, itemPrice
```

```
        If strAssetType = "AssetType" Then
        ' ------------------------------------------------
        ' enter column headings in the worksheet 1st row
        ' 5th column is for new price calculation
        ' ------------------------------------------------
            With ActiveSheet
                .Cells(1, 1) = strAssetType
                .Cells(1, 2) = strMake
                .Cells(1, 3) = strModel
                .Cells(1, 4) = itemPrice
                .Cells(1, 5) = "New " & itemPrice
            End With
            ' skip lines of code following the if statement
            GoTo Label_SkipHeading
        End If

        '----------------------------------------
        ' create an instance of the CAsset class
        '----------------------------------------
        Set asset = New CAsset

        counter = counter + 1
        aKey = "record" & counter

        '------------------------------------
        ' set properties of the asset object
        '------------------------------------
        asset.AssetType = strAssetType
        asset.Manufacturer = strMake
        asset.Model = strModel
        asset.Price = itemPrice

        '----------------------------------------------
        ' add asset object to the AssetsColl collection
        ' and assign a custom key for that object
        '----------------------------------------------
        AssetsColl.Add asset, aKey

        Set asset = Nothing

Label_SkipHeading:
        Resume Next
    Loop

    'Close the text file
    Close #1
```

```
' display informational message
MsgBox "Asset Collection contains " & _
    AssetsColl.Count & " items.", _
    vbInformation, "Total Items"

'-------------------------------------------
' iterate through the collection and access
' each instance of the CAsset class
' printing the data to the Immediate window
'-------------------------------------------
For Each asset In AssetsColl
   Debug.Print asset.AssetType & vbTab & _
    asset.Manufacturer & vbTab & _
    asset.Model & vbTab & FormatNumber(asset.Price, 2)
Next asset

'-----------------------------------------------
' iterate through the collection to access
' each instance of the CAsset class
' this time entering data the active worksheet
'-----------------------------------------------
For Each asset In AssetsColl
 'set next row in the worksheet
    wRow = wRow + 1
    'write record to the worksheet
    With ActiveSheet
        .Cells(wRow, 1) = asset.AssetType
        .Cells(wRow, 2) = asset.Manufacturer
        .Cells(wRow, 3) = asset.Model
        .Cells(wRow, 4) = asset.Price
        ' calculate the discount
        .Cells(wRow, 5) = asset.NewPrice(intDiscount, _
                            asset.Price, 100)
    End With
Next asset
Selection.CurrentRegion.Columns.AutoFit

'retrieve the asset from a collection by a key
assetKey = InputBox("Enter key", "Retrieval", "record1")

Set asset = AssetsColl.Item(assetKey)
strRecord = "Asset Type" & vbTab & asset.AssetType & _
              vbCrLf
strRecord = strRecord & "Manufacturer" & vbTab & _
            asset.Manufacturer & vbCrLf
```

```
        strRecord = strRecord & "Model" & vbTab & vbTab & _
                    asset.Model & vbCrLf
        strRecord = strRecord & "Price" & vbTab & vbTab & _
                    Format(asset.Price, "Currency")

        MsgBox strRecord, vbInformation + vbOKOnly, _
                "Retrieving " & assetKey

    End Sub
```

5. Copy the **AssetInfo.txt** file from the companion files to your C:\VBAExcel 2021_ByExample folder.
6. Run the Retrieve_AssetInfo procedure. Reply to all the procedure prompts by accepting the default values.
   After running the procedure, you should see the asset data entered in a worksheet and in the Immediate window as shown in Figures 26.2 and 26.3.

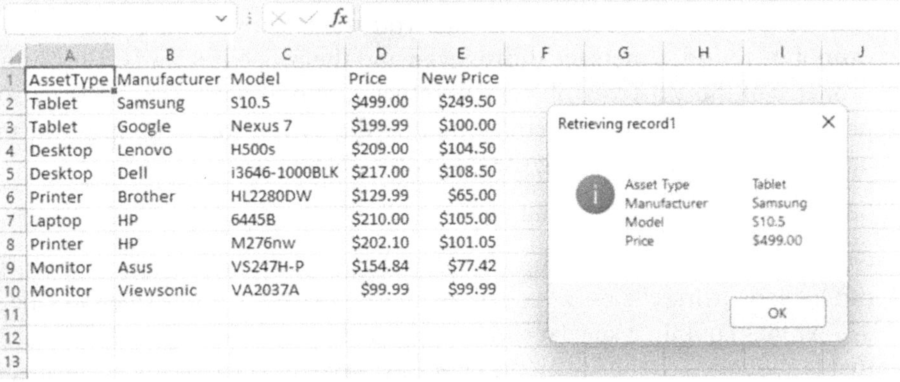

	A	B	C	D	E
1	AssetType	Manufacturer	Model	Price	New Price
2	Tablet	Samsung	S10.5	$499.00	$249.50
3	Tablet	Google	Nexus 7	$199.99	$100.00
4	Desktop	Lenovo	H500s	$209.00	$104.50
5	Desktop	Dell	i3646-1000BLK	$217.00	$108.50
6	Printer	Brother	HL2280DW	$129.99	$65.00
7	Laptop	HP	6445B	$210.00	$105.00
8	Printer	HP	M276nw	$202.10	$101.05
9	Monitor	Asus	VS247H-P	$154.84	$77.42
10	Monitor	Viewsonic	VA2037A	$99.99	$99.99

FIGURE 26.2 The asset data in the provided text file (see Figure 26.1) is stored in a collection of objects and written to the worksheet. The New Price column does not exist in the original file and was added by the VBA procedure to demonstrate the use of class methods.
The Retrieval input box demonstrates how a key can be used for accessing objects in a collection. The asset details for the specified record are displayed in a message box above.

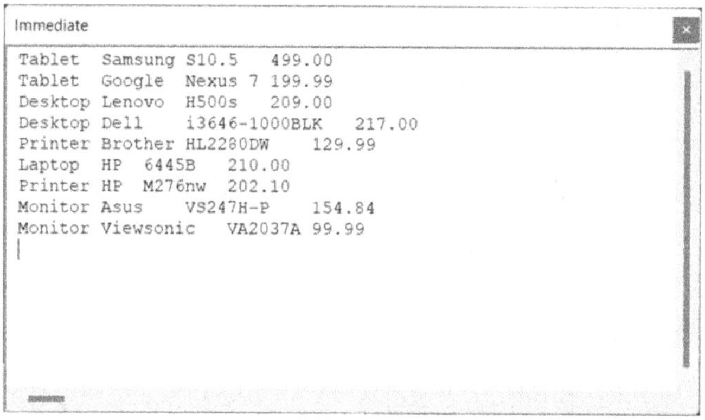

```
Immediate
Tablet  Samsung S10.5    499.00
Tablet  Google   Nexus 7 199.99
Desktop Lenovo   H500s    209.00
Desktop Dell     i3646-1000BLK    217.00
Printer Brother HL2280DW      129.99
Laptop  HP  6445B    210.00
Printer HP  M276nw  202.10
Monitor Asus     VS247H-P      154.84
Monitor Viewsonic    VA2037A 99.99
```

FIGURE 26.3 The asset data in the provided text file (see Figure 26.1) is written to the Immediate window.

The Retrieve_AssetInfo procedure starts off by declaring and initializing numerous variables that will be used by various sections of the code. Because you are dealing with an external file, you want to make sure that if the file cannot be found, a message is displayed and the procedure ends. The Number property of the VBA `Err` object will return a number other than zero if some problem was encountered while opening the file. To read the file, you must open it in `Input` mode using the following statement:

```
Open strFilePath For Input As #1
```

Once the file is open, you want to read it sequentially from top to bottom. This can be done using the `Do While` or `Do Until` loop that you learned in Chapter 6. Text files contain a special character known as an end-of-file (EOF) marker that is appended to the file by the operating system. When reading the file, you can use the `EOF` function to detect that marker and thus know if the end of file was reached. The statement

```
Do While Not EOF(1)
```

means that you want to keep executing the statements inside the loop until all data in the file has been read. This statement is equivalent to `Do Until EOF(1)`. The number between the parentheses is a number corresponding to the file number from which you want to read the data (the same number that was used in the `Open` statement).

Each time in the loop, we use the `Input #` statement to read the data from the file into four variables:

```
Input #1, strAssetType, strMake, strModel, itemPrice
```

After writing out the column names into the worksheet, we create our asset object and set its four properties (`AssetType`, `Manufacturer`, `Model`, and `Price`), using the values stored in the variables:

```
asset.AssetType = strAssetType
asset.Manufacturer = strMake
asset.Model = strModel
asset.Price = itemPrice
```

Each of the foregoing assignment statements is actually a call to the appropriate `Let procedure` in the `CAsset` class module. For example, to set the `AssetType` property of the asset object, the following procedure is executed:

```
Property Let AssetType(ByVal aType As String)
    m_AssetType = aType
End Property
```

You can execute the procedure line by line using the F8 key to gain a better understanding of what's going on when these statements are being executed.

At this point, the asset object contains the first record data, which is the second line in our text file. Before handling the next record's data, we use the `Add` method to add the asset object to the `AssetsColl` collection:

```
AssetsColl.Add asset, aKey
```

Each object in the collection is identified by a key that we create by concatenating a number and the word "*record*," obtaining "*record1*," "*record2*," "*record3*," and so on.

After adding the asset object to the collection, we release the memory by setting it to `Nothing` and we continue to the next record, executing the statements within the loop, skipping only those that were used for the preparation of the column headings. A new object is created, its properties are set, and the object is added to the collection. The same process repeats until the EOF is reached. When we are done looping, we close the file using the `Close#1` statement. We should now have 9 asset objects in the `AssetsColl` collection.

The remaining code in the procedure iterates through the collection of objects and prints the data to the Immediate window and to the worksheet. When we retrieve the objects from the collection, VBA goes on to execute the `Property Get` procedures that you wrote in the `CAsset` class module. When writing the New Price to the worksheet, we call the `NewPrice` method. This method uses the `intDiscount` variable whose value was obtained from the user earlier in the procedure. If you accepted the default value in the input box, then the Price is reduced by the specified percentage. The last parameter of the `NewPrice` method, which denotes `amount`, is hardcoded. Based on the entered amount, the `IF` statements included in the `NewPrice` method will execute or will be skipped. When entering prices, it is often necessary to appropriately format the data. The Retrieve_AssetInfo procedure uses the `FormatNumber` function to format the Price data in the Immediate window:

```
FormatNumber(asset.Price, 2)
```

The second argument of the `FormatNumber` function specifies how many places to the right of the decimal are displayed. To format the number as Currency, change the foregoing statement to

```
FormatCurrency(asset.Price, 2)
```

CREATING A CUSTOM APPLICATION

The next lab project in this chapter demonstrates the process of creating and working with a custom object called CEmployee. This object will represent an employee. The CEmployee object will have properties such as ID, FirstName, LastName, and Salary. It will also have a method for modifying the current salary. Be sure to perform all the exercises. Again, we'll start by creating a class module.

Lab 26.2a Creating a Class Module

1. In the Project Explorer window of the **VBAProject(Chap26_VBAExcel2021.xlsm)**, choose **Insert | Class Module.**
2. Highlight the **Class 1** module in the Project Explorer window and use the Properties window to rename the class module **CEmployee.**

Lab 26.2b Declaring Members of the CEmployee Class

1. Type the following declaration lines at the top of the CEmployee class module:

```
' declarations
Private m_LastName As String
Private m_FirstName As String
Private m_Salary As Currency
Private m_ID As String
```

Notice that the name of each data member variable begins with the prefix `m_`.

Lab 26.2c Writing Property Get Procedures for the CEmployee Class

1. Type the following Property Get procedures in the CEmployee class module, just below the declaration section.

```
Property Get ID() As String
  Id = m_ID
End Property

Property Get LastName() As String
  LastName = m_LastName
End Property

Property Get FirstName() As String
  FirstName = m_FirstName
End Property

Property Get Salary() As Currency
  Salary = m_Salary
End Property
```

Let's continue with our lab project and write the required Property Let procedures for our custom CEmployee object. The CEmployee class will only have three properties (`LastName`, `FirstName`, and `Salary`). Each of these properties will require a separate Property Let procedure. To make the ID property read-only, we will not write a Property Let procedure for it.

Lab 26.2d Writing Property Let Procedures for the CEmployee Class

1. Type the following Property Let procedures in the CEmployee class module:

```
Property Let LastName(L As String)
  m_LastName = L
End Property

Property Let FirstName(F As String)
  m_FirstName = F
End Property

Property Let Salary(ByVal dollar As Currency)
  m_Salary = dollar
End Property
```

The CEmployee object has one method that allows you to calculate the new salary. Assume that the employee salary can be increased or decreased by a specific percentage or amount.

Let's continue with our lab project by writing a class method that calculates the employee salary.

Lab 26.2e Writing Methods for the CEmployee Class

1. Type the following CalcNewSalary function procedure in the CEmployee class module:

```
Public Function CalcNewSalary(choice As Integer, _
  curSalary As Currency, amount As Long) As Currency
  Select Case choice
    Case 1 ' by percent
      CalcNewSalary = curSalary + ((curSalary + amount)/100)
    Case 2 ' by amount
      CalcNewSalary = curSalary + amount
  End Select
End Function
```

The `CalcNewSalary` function defined with the `Public` keyword in a class module serves as a method for the CEmployee class. To calculate a new salary, a VBA procedure from outside the class module must pass three arguments: `choice`, `curSalary`, and `amount`. The `choice` argument specifies the type of the calculation. Suppose you want to increase the employee salary by 5% or by $5. The first option will increase the salary by the specified percentage, and the second option will add the specified amount to the current salary. The `curSalary` argument is the current salary figure for an employee, and `amount` determines the value by which the salary should be changed.

EVENT PROCEDURES IN THE CLASS MODULE

An event is basically an action recognized by an object. Custom classes recognize only two events: `Initialize` and `Terminate`. These events are triggered when an instance of the class is created and destroyed, respectively. The `Initialize` event is generated when an object is created from a class (see the preceding section on creating an instance of a class). In the CEmployee class example, the `Initialize` event will also fire the first time that you use the `emp` variable in code. Because the statements included inside the `Initialize` event are the first ones to be executed for the object before any properties are set or any methods are executed, the `Initialize` event is a good place to perform initialization of the objects created from the class.

As you recall, the ID is read-only in the CEmployee class. You can use the `Initialize` event to assign a unique five-digit number to the `m_ID` variable.

Let's continue with our lab project by adding the `Initialize` event procedure to our CEmployee class.

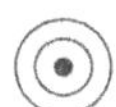

Lab 26.2f Writing the Initialize Event Procedure for the CEmployee Class

1. In the CEmployee class module, enter the following `Class_Initialize` procedure:

```
Private Sub Class_Initialize()
  Randomize
  m_ID = Int((99999 - 10000) * Rnd + 10000)
End Sub
```

The `Class_Initialize` procedure initializes the CEmployee object by assigning a unique five-digit number to the variable `m_ID`. To generate a random integer between two given integers where `ending_number = 99999` and `beginning_number = 10000`, the following formula is used:

```
=Int((ending_number - beginning_number) * Rnd + beginning_number)
```

The `Class_Initialize` procedure also uses the `Randomize` statement to reinitialize the random number generator. For more information on using the `Rnd` and `Int` functions, as well as the `Randomize` statement, see the online help.

The `Terminate` event occurs when all references to an object have been released. This is a good place to perform any necessary cleanup tasks. The `Class_Terminate` procedure uses the following syntax:

```
Private Sub Class_Terminate()
  [cleanup code goes here]
End Sub
```

To release an object variable from an object, use the following syntax:

```
Set objectVariable = Nothing
```

When you set the object variable to `Nothing`, the `Terminate` event is generated. If you have written a `Terminate` event procedure, any code in this event is executed then.

CREATING A FORM FOR DATA COLLECTION

Implementing your custom CEmployee object requires that you design a custom form. We will create the form shown in Figure 26.4 and later connect it with our custom CEmployee object.

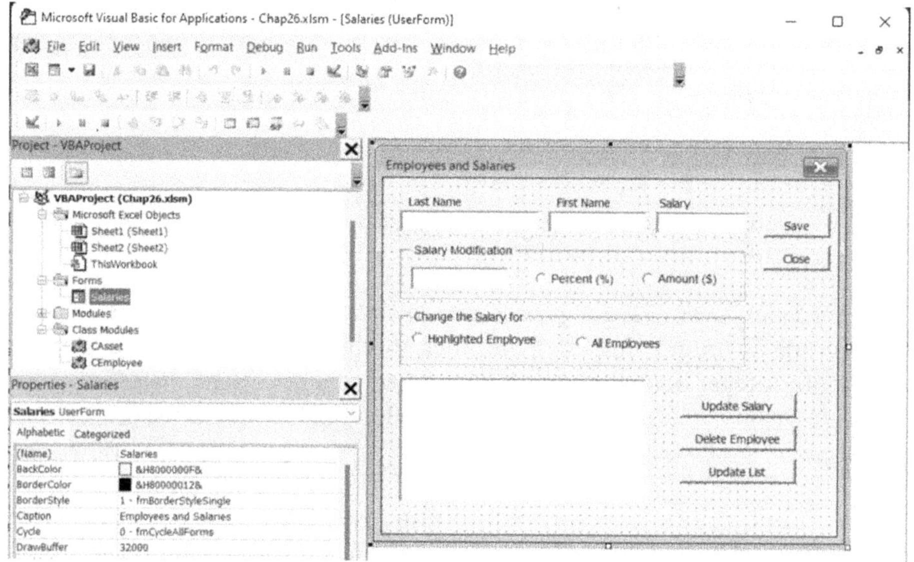

FIGURE 26.4 This form demonstrates the use of the CEmployee custom object.

Lab 26.2g Creating a User Form for the CEmployee Object

1. Highlight the current VBA project in the Project Explorer window and choose **Insert | UserForm.**
   A blank form should appear with UserForm1 in its title bar.
2. Make the form larger by positioning the mouse on the selection handle in the bottom right-hand corner and dragging it to the right and down. Make the form big enough to hold all the controls and labels shown in Figure 26.4.
3. Choose **View | Toolbox.**
   A small toolbox should appear on the screen with standard Visual Basic buttons that can be placed on the user form.
4. Click the **Text Box** control in the toolbox and drag it to the form. Drop it at the position shown in Figure 26.4. Use the same technique to add all the remaining controls and labels to the form.

5. Now that all the controls and labels are placed on the form, you need to set the form and control properties listed in Table 26.1. To set each of these properties:
   1. On the form, click on the object listed in the Object column in Table 26.1.
   2. In the VBE Properties window, locate the object's property name listed in the Property column in Table 26.1.
   3. In the VBE Properties window, replace the property setting in the second column with the value stated in the Settings column in Table 26.1.

TABLE 26.1 Setting the properties for the custom form.

Object	Property	Settings
UserForm1	Name Caption	Salaries Employees and Salaries
label1	Caption	Last Name
text box below the Last Name label	Name	txtLastName
label2	Caption	First Name
text box below the First Name label	Name	txtFirstName
label3	Caption	Salary
text box below the Salary label	Name	txtSalary
frame1	Caption	Salary Modification
text box in the frame titled Salary Modification	Name	txtRaise
option button 1	Name Caption	optPercent Percent (%)
option button 2	Name Caption	optAmount Amount ($)
frame2	Caption	Change the Salary for
option button 3	Name Caption	optHighlighted Highlighted Employee
option button 4	Name Caption	optAll All Employees
list box	Name Height Width	lboxPeople 91.45 180.75
command button 1	Name Caption	cmdSave Save
command button 2	Name Caption	cmdClose Close

(Contd.)

Object	Property	Settings
command button 3	Name Caption	cmdUpdate Update Salary
command button 4	Name Caption	cmdDelete Delete Employee
command button 5	Name Caption	cmdEmployeeList Update List

CREATING A WORKSHEET FOR DATA OUTPUT

Now that the user form is ready, the next step requires the preparation of the data entry worksheet shown in Figure 26.5.

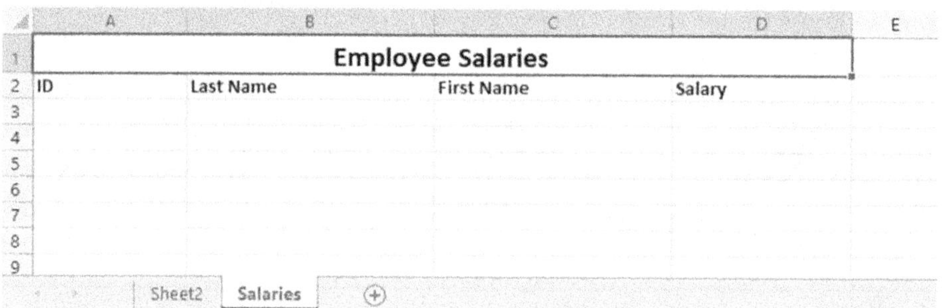

FIGURE 26.5 Data entered on the Employees and Salaries form will be transferred to the Salaries worksheet.

Lab 26.2h Creating a Worksheet for Data Transfer

1. Insert a new worksheet to the current workbook and rename it **Salaries.**
2. Prepare a Salaries data entry worksheet as shown in Figure 26.5.

WRITING CODE BEHIND THE USERFORM

With the form and worksheet ready, all that is left to do for the CEmployee class implementation is writing the necessary procedures in the form class module. We will need an event procedure to initialize the controls on the form and several click event procedures that will run when a user clicks the form's buttons. We also need to write a function to locate employee data in a worksheet.

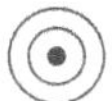

Lab 26.2i Writing Code for the UserForm

1. Switch back to the Visual Basic Editor window and double-click the form background to activate the form module. You can also click the **View Code** button in the Project Explorer window when the form is selected.
2. Enter the following variable declarations at the top of the Code window of the Salaries form just below the `Option Explicit` statement.

```
' Global declarations
Dim emp As New CEmployee
Dim CEmployees As New Collection
Dim index As Integer
Dim ws As Worksheet
Dim extract As String
Dim cell As Range
Dim lastRow As Integer
Dim empLoc As Integer
Dim startRow As Integer
Dim endRow As Integer
Dim choice As Integer
Dim amount As Long
```

The first statement declares the variable `emp` as a new instance of the CEmployee class. The second statement declares a custom collection. The CEmployees collection will be used to store employee data. Other variables declared here will be used by VBA procedures assigned to various controls on the form.

3. Type the following `UserForm_Initialize` procedure to enable or disable controls on the form:

```
Private Sub UserForm_Initialize()
  ' enable or disable firm controls
  txtLastName.SetFocus
  cmdEmployeeList.Visible = False
  lboxPeople.Enabled = False
  Frame1.Enabled = False
  txtRaise.Value = ""
  optPercent.Value = False
  optAmount.Value = False
  txtRaise.Enabled = False
  optPercent.Enabled = False
  optAmount.Enabled = False
  Frame2.Enabled = False
  optHighlighted.Enabled = False
  optAll.Enabled = False
```

```
    cmdUpdate.Enabled = False
    cmdDelete.Enabled = False
End Sub
```

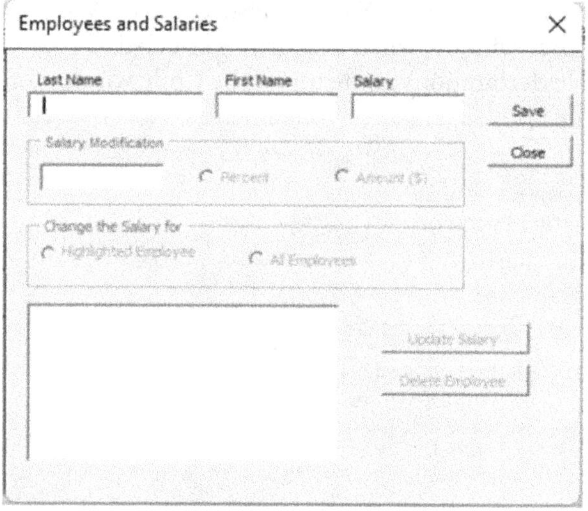

FIGURE 26.6 The UserForm_Initialize procedure disables certain controls so they cannot be used when the form is first loaded.

Figure 26.6 shows the result of the statements inside the UserForm_Initialize procedure that enable only the desired controls when the form is first loaded.

4. Enter the following cmdSave_Click procedure to transfer the data entered on the form to the spreadsheet:

```
'transfer form data to spreadsheet
Private Sub cmdSave_Click()
  If txtLastName.Value = "" Or txtFirstName.Value = "" Or _
    txtSalary.Value = "" Then
      MsgBox "Enter Last Name, First Name and Salary."
      txtLastName.SetFocus
      Exit Sub
  End If

  If Not IsNumeric(txtSalary) Then
    MsgBox "You must enter a value for the Salary."
    txtSalary.SetFocus
    Exit Sub
  End If
```

```
    If txtSalary < 0 Then
      MsgBox "Salary cannot be a negative number."
      Exit Sub
    End If

    Worksheets("Salaries").Select
    index = ActiveSheet.UsedRange.Rows.Count + 1
    lboxPeople.Enabled = True

    ' set and enter data into the CEmployees collection
    With emp
      Cells(index, 1).Formula = emp.ID
      .LastName = txtLastName
      Cells(index, 2).Formula = emp.LastName
      .FirstName = txtFirstName
      Cells(index, 3).Formula = emp.FirstName
      .Salary = CCur(txtSalary)
      If .Salary = 0 Then Exit Sub
      Cells(index, 4).Formula = emp.Salary
      CEmployees.Add emp
    End With

    ' delete data from text boxes
    txtLastName = ""
    txtFirstName = ""
    txtSalary = ""

    ' enable hidden controls
    cmdEmployeeList.Value = True
    cmdUpdate.Enabled = True
    cmdDelete.Enabled = True
    Frame1.Enabled = True
    txtRaise.Enabled = True
    optPercent.Enabled = True
    optAmount.Enabled = True
    Frame2.Enabled = True
    optHighlighted.Enabled = True
    optAll.Enabled = True
    txtLastName.SetFocus
End Sub
```

The cmdSave_Click procedure starts off with validating the user's input in the Last Name, First Name, and Salary text boxes. If the user entered correct data, VBA assigns to the variable `index` the number of the first empty row on the Employee Salaries worksheet. The next statement enables the form's list box control. When the program reaches the `With emp ...` construct, a new instance of the CEmployee class is created. The `LastName`, `FirstName`, and `Salary` properties are set based on the data entered in the corresponding text boxes, and the ID property is set with the number generated by the `Class_Initialize` event procedure. Each time VBA sees the reference to the instanced `emp` object, it will call the appropriate Property Let procedure in the class module.

The last section of this chapter demonstrates how to walk through this procedure step by step to see exactly when the property procedures are executed. After setting the object property values, VBA transfers the employee data to the Employee Salaries worksheet. The last statement inside the `With emp...` construct adds the user-defined object `emp` to a custom collection called CEmployees.

Next, Visual Basic clears the form's text boxes and enables command buttons that were turned off by the UserForm_Initialize procedure. Notice the first instruction in this block: `cmdEmployeeList.Value = True`. This statement causes the automatic execution of the cmdEmployeeList_Click procedure attached to the Update List command button. (This is the only control that the user never sees.) The code for this procedure is shown in Step 21.

5. Type the cmdEmployeeList_Click procedure, as shown here:

```
Private Sub cmdEmployeeList_Click()
  ' add new employee data to list box
  lboxPeople.Clear
  For Each emp In CEmployees
    lboxPeople.AddItem emp.ID & ", " & _
    emp.LastName & ", " & emp.FirstName & ", $" & _
    Format(emp.Salary, "0.00")
 Next emp
End Sub
```

The cmdEmployeeList_Click procedure is attached to the Update List command button. This button is controlled by the cmdSave_Click procedure and causes the new employee data to be added to the list box control. As we will see when we run our project later, the cmdEmployeeList_Click procedure begins by clearing the contents of the list box and then populates it with the items stored in the custom collection CEmployees, as shown in Figure 26.7.

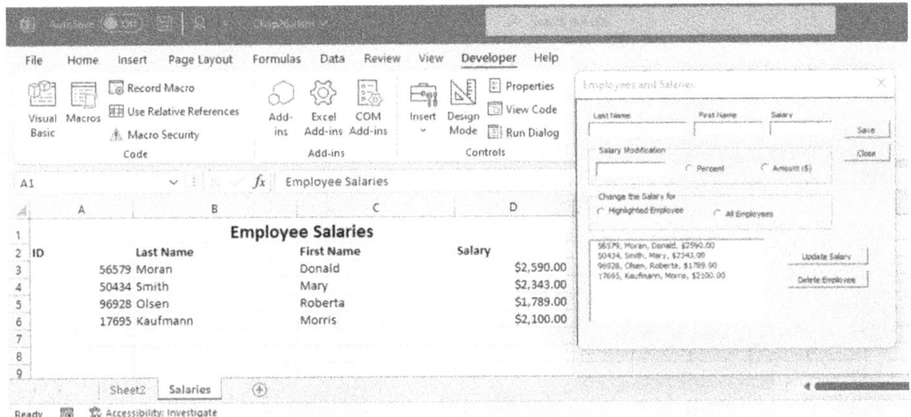

FIGURE 26.7 The list box control displays employee data as entered in the custom collection CEmployees.

6. Type the following cmdClose_Click procedure:

```
Private Sub cmdClose_Click()
  ' remove the user form from the screen
  Unload Me
End Sub
```

The cmdClose_Click procedure allows you to remove the user form from the screen and finish working with the custom collection of employees. When you run the form again, the employees you enter will become members of a new CEmployees collection.

7. Type the following cmdDelete_Click procedure:

```
Private Sub cmdDelete_Click()
  ' remove an employee from the CEmployees custom collection
  ' make sure that an employee is highlighted in the
  ' list control

  If lboxPeople.ListIndex > -1 Then
    MsgBox "Selected item number: " & lboxPeople.ListIndex
    extract = CEmployees.Item(lboxPeople.ListIndex + 1).ID
    MsgBox extract
    Call FindId
    MsgBox empLoc
    Range("A" & empLoc).Delete (3)
    MsgBox "There are " & CEmployees.Count & _
        " items in the CEmployees collection. "
```

```
      CEmployees.Remove lboxPeople.ListIndex + 1
      MsgBox "The CEmployees collection has now " & _
          CEmployees.Count & " items."
      cmdEmployeeList.Value = True
      If CEmployees.Count = 0 Then
        Call UserForm_Initialize
      End If
    Else
      MsgBox "Click the item you want to remove."
    End If
  End Sub
```

The cmdDelete_Click procedure lets you remove an employee from the CEmployees custom collection. To delete an employee, you must click the appropriate item in the list box. When you click a list item, the cmdEmployeeList_Click procedure is automatically executed. This procedure makes sure that the list box contents are refreshed. The employee is removed from both the collection and the list box. If the list box contains only one employee, VBA calls the UserForm_Initialize procedure to disable certain form controls after removing the last employee from the collection.

The cmdDelete_Click procedure contains several `MsgBox` statements that allow you to examine the contents of the list box control as you make deletions. In addition to removing the employee from the custom collection, the cmdDelete_Click procedure must also remove the corresponding row of employee information from the worksheet. Locating the employee data in the worksheet is handled by the `FindId` function. (The code of this procedure is in Step 24.) This function returns to the cmdDelete_Click procedure the row number that has to be deleted.

8. Type the following function procedure:

```
Private Function FindId()
  ' return number of list box selected row
  Set ws= ActiveWorkbook.Sheets("Salaries")
  startRow = ActiveSheet.UsedRange.Rows.Count + _
    1 - CEmployees.Count
  endRow = ActiveSheet.UsedRange.Rows.Count
  For Each cell In ws.Range(Cells(startRow, 1), _
    Cells(endRow, 1))
    If cell.Value = extract Then
      empLoc = cell.Row
      FindId = empLoc
      Exit Function
    End If
```

```
  Next
End Function
```

The `FindId` function procedure returns to the calling procedure the row number of the employee selected in the form's list box. The search for the data in the worksheet is based on the contents of the variable `extract` that stores the unique employee number. The search for the employee ID is limited to the first worksheet column and begins with the row containing the first collection item. This approach makes the search faster. You don't want to search the entire used area of the worksheet.

9. Type the following cmdUpdate_Click procedure:

```
Private Sub cmdUpdate_Click()
 If optHighlighted.Value = False And optAll.Value = False Then
   MsgBox "Click the 'Highlighted Employee' or " _
     & " 'All Employees' option button."
   Exit Sub
  End If
  If Not IsNumeric(txtRaise) Then
   MsgBox "This field requires a number."
   txtRaise.SetFocus
   Exit Sub
  End If
  If optHighlighted.Value = True And _
   lboxPeople.ListIndex = -1 Then
     MsgBox "Click the name of the employee."
     Exit Sub
  End If
  If lboxPeople.ListIndex <> -1 And _
   optHighlighted.Value = True And _
   optAmount.Value = True And _
   txtRaise.Value <> "" Then
     extract = CEmployees.Item(lboxPeople.ListIndex + 1).ID
     MsgBox extract
     Call FindId
     MsgBox empLoc
     choice = 2
     amount = txtRaise
     CEmployees.Item(lboxPeople.ListIndex + 1).Salary = _
       emp.CalcNewSalary(choice, _
     CEmployees.Item(lboxPeople.ListIndex + 1).Salary, amount)
     Range("D" & empLoc).Formula = CEmployees. _
       Item(lboxPeople.ListIndex + 1).Salary
     cmdEmployeeList.Value = True
  ElseIf lboxPeople.ListIndex <> -1 And _
```

```
    optHighlighted.Value = True And _
    optPercent.Value = True And _
    txtRaise.Value <> "" Then
      extract = CEmployees.Item(lboxPeople.ListIndex + 1).ID
      MsgBox extract
      Call FindId
      MsgBox empLoc
      CEmployees.Item(lboxPeople.ListIndex + 1).Salary = _
        CEmployees.Item(lboxPeople.ListIndex + 1).Salary _
        + (CEmployees.Item(lboxPeople.ListIndex + _
        1).Salary * txtRaise / 100)
      Range("D" & empLoc).Formula = CEmployees. _
        Item(lboxPeople.ListIndex + 1).Salary
      cmdEmployeeList.Value = True
  ElseIf optAll.Value = True And _
    optPercent.Value = True And _
    txtRaise.Value <> "" Then
      For Each emp In CEmployees
        emp.Salary = emp.Salary + ((emp.Salary * _
            txtRaise) / 100)
        extract = emp.ID
        MsgBox extract
        Call FindId
        MsgBox empLoc
        Range("D" & empLoc).Formula = emp.Salary
      Next emp
      cmdEmployeeList.Value = True
  ElseIf optAll.Value = True And _
    optAmount.Value = True And _
    txtRaise.Value <> "" Then
      For Each emp In CEmployees
        emp.Salary = emp.Salary + txtRaise
        extract = emp.ID
        MsgBox extract
        Call FindId
        MsgBox empLoc
        Range("D" & empLoc).Formula = emp.Salary
      Next emp
      cmdEmployeeList.Value = True
  Else
    MsgBox "Enter data or select an option."
  End If
End Sub
```

With the cmdUpdate_Click procedure, you can modify the salary by the specified percentage or amount. The update can be done for the selected employee, or all the employees listed in the list box control and collection. The cmdUpdate_Click procedure checks whether the user selected the appropriate option buttons and entered the increase value in the text box. Depending on which options are specified, the Salary amount is updated for one employee or all the employees, either by a percentage or amount. The salary modification is also reflected in the worksheet.

Figure 26.8 displays a new value for the salary of Roberta Olsen, which has been increased by 10%. By entering a negative number in the text box, you can decrease the salary by the specified percentage or dollar amount.

Updating the employee information in the form also updates the worksheet, as shown in Figure 26.9.

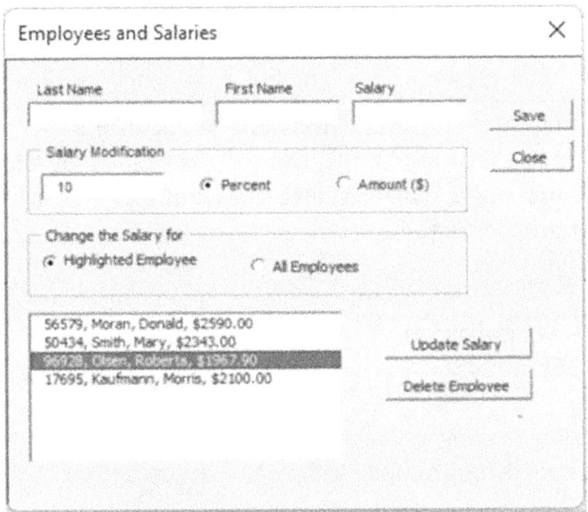

FIGURE 26.8 The employee salary can be increased or decreased by the specified percentage or dollar amount.

	A	B	C	D
1		Employee Salaries		
2	ID	Last Name	First Name	Salary
3	56579	Moran	Donald	$2,590.00
4	50434	Smith	Mary	$2,343.00
5	96928	Olsen	Roberta	$1,967.90
6	17695	Kaufmann	Morris	$2,100.00
7				

FIGURE 26.9 When you update the employee information in the form, the relevant data is also updated in the worksheet.

WORKING WITH THE CUSTOM CEMPLOYEE CLASS

The application using a custom CEmployee class is now ready. To make it easy to work with the user form, we'll write a one-line procedure in the standard module that displays the form.

Lab 26.2j Writing a Procedure to Display the User Form

1. Insert a standard module into the current project by choosing **Insert | Module**. Rename this module **WorkAndPay**.
2. Type the following procedure in the WorkAndPay module to display the Employees and Salaries form:

```
Sub ClassDemo()
  Salaries.Show
End Sub
```

In the next section, we'll step through the ClassDemo procedure to see what happens when you run the code. Until then, you can view your form by clicking the form's background and pressing F5, or you can place a button in a worksheet and assign the ClassDemo procedure to it.

WATCHING THE EXECUTION OF YOUR CUSTOM APPLICATION

To help you understand what's going on when your code runs and how your custom object works, let's step through the cmdSave_Click procedure.

Lab 26.2k Walking through the CEmployee Application Code

1. In the Project Explorer window, select the **Salaries** form and click the **View Code** button at the top of this window.
2. When the Salaries (Code) window appears, select the **cmdSave** procedure from the combo box at the top left-hand side of the window.
3. Set a breakpoint by clicking in the left margin next to the following line of code, as shown in Figure 26.10.

```
If txtLastName.Value = "" Or txtFirstName.Value = "" Or _
  txtSalary.Value = "" Then
```

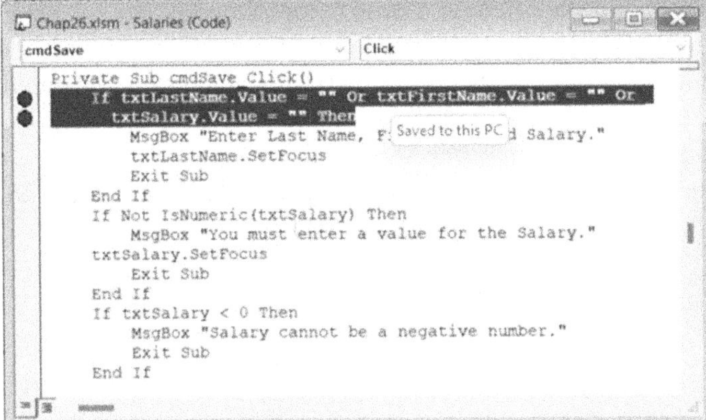

FIGURE 26.10 A red circle in the margin indicates a breakpoint. When VBA encounters the statement with a breakpoint, it automatically switches to the Code window and displays the text of the line as white on a red background.

4. In the Project Explorer window, highlight the **WorkAndPay** module and click the **View Code** button.
5. Place the cursor anywhere inside the ClassDemo procedure (in the WorkAndPlay module) and press **F5** or choose **Run | Run Sub/UserForm**.
6. When the form appears, enter data in the Last Name, First Name, and Salary text boxes, and click the **Save** button on the form. Visual Basic should now switch to the Code window because it encountered the breakpoint in the first line of the cmdSave_Click procedure, as shown in Figure 26.11.

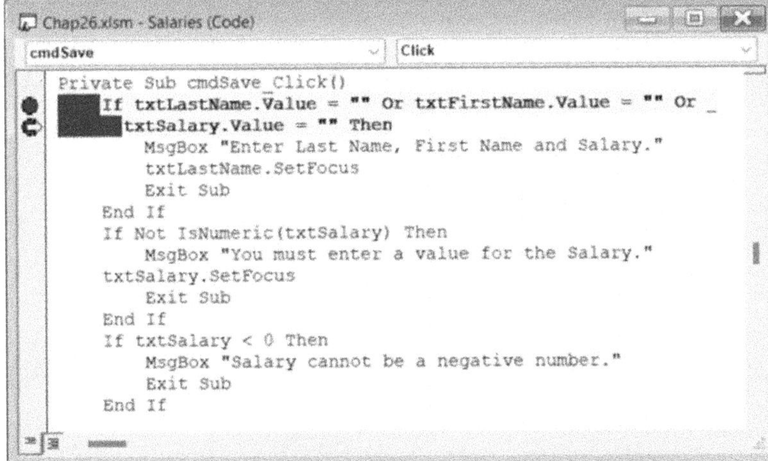

FIGURE 26.11 When Visual Basic encounters a breakpoint while running a procedure, it switches to the Code window and displays a yellow arrow in the margin to the left of the statement at which the procedure is suspended and highlights the statement in yellow.

7. Step through the code one statement at a time by pressing **F8**.
   Visual Basic runs the current statement and then automatically advances to the next statement and suspends execution. The current statement is indicated by a yellow arrow in the margin and a yellow background. Keep pressing **F8** to execute the procedure step by step. When Visual Basic encounters the `With emp` statement, it switches to the Class_Initialize procedure, as shown in Figure 26.12.

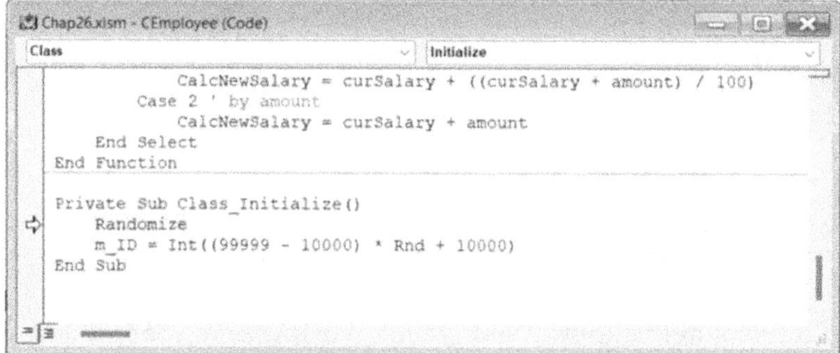

FIGURE 26.12 When Visual Basic encounters the reference to the object variable emp, it goes out to execute the Class_Initialize procedure. After executing the statements inside this procedure, VBA returns to the cmdSave_Click procedure.

   When Visual Basic encounters the statement `Cells(Index, 1).Formula = emp.ID`, it executes the Property Get ID procedure in the CEmployee class module, as shown in Figure 26.13.

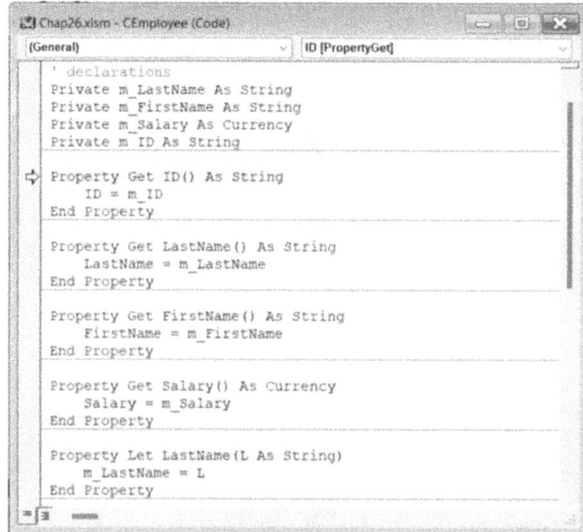

FIGURE 26.13 Reading properties of your custom object is accomplished through the Property Get procedures.

8. Using the **F8** key, trace the execution of the cmdSave_Click procedure to the end.
9. When VBA encounters the end of the procedure (`End Sub`), the yellow highlight is turned off. At this time, press **Alt+F11** to return to the active form. Enter data for a new employee and click the **Save** button.
10. When Visual Basic displays the Code window, choose **Debug | Clear All Breakpoints**. Now press **F5** to run the rest of the procedure without stepping through it.
11. Click the **Close** button on the Salaries form to exit the application.
12. Save and close the **Chap26_VBAExcel2021.xlsm** workbook.

SUMMARY

In this chapter, you used class modules in the Visual Basic Editor screen to create two custom objects. You saw how to define your objects' properties by using Property Get and Property Let procedures. You wrote custom methods for your objects, learned how to create an instance of a class and were introduced to using event procedures in a class module. Next, you created a custom form for your object, wrote code behind the User Form and learned how to debug your application.

This chapter completes Part VII of this book, which focused on introducing advanced concepts in Excel VBA. The next chapter covers the topics of HTML programming and using Web Queries.

Part VIII Working Together: VBA, HTML, XML, and the REST API

Thanks to the Internet and intranets, your worksheet data can be easily accessed and shared with others 24/7. Excel is capable of both capturing data from the Web and publishing it to the Web.

In this part of the book, you are introduced to using Excel VBA with HTML (the Hypertext Markup Language), XML (the Extensible Markup Language) and calling a new type of a Web service, known as the REST API.

Chapter 27 HTML Programming and Web Queries

The dramatic growth of the Internet made it possible to gain access to enormous knowledge archives scattered all over the world. Thanks to the Internet, we now have at our fingertips databases covering various industries and fields of knowledge, dictionaries and encyclopedias, stock quotes, maps, weather forecasts, and a great deal of other types of information stored on millions of Web servers. Often, the information retrieved from Web pages becomes a subject of further analysis by computer programs. Because of its file structure (rows and columns), Microsoft Excel is a preferred tool for working with table data found on the Internet. From Chapter 23, you already know how to use the Power Query feature in Excel to get data from the Web. This chapter demonstrates other built-in tools available in Excel for retrieving data from the Web and publishing Excel spreadsheets on the Web. You will find many Visual Basic statements here that will allow you to obtain and publish data using custom Visual Basic procedures. To maximize your benefit from this chapter, you should have a connection to the Internet.

CREATING HYPERLINKS USING VBA

Excel, like other applications in Microsoft 365, allows you to create hyperlinks in your worksheets. After clicking on a cell that contains a hyperlink, you can open a document located on a network server, an intranet, or the Internet. Hyperlinks can be created manually via the Insert Hyperlink dialog (choose Insert | Link | Insert Link) as shown in Figure 27.1 or programmatically using VBA.

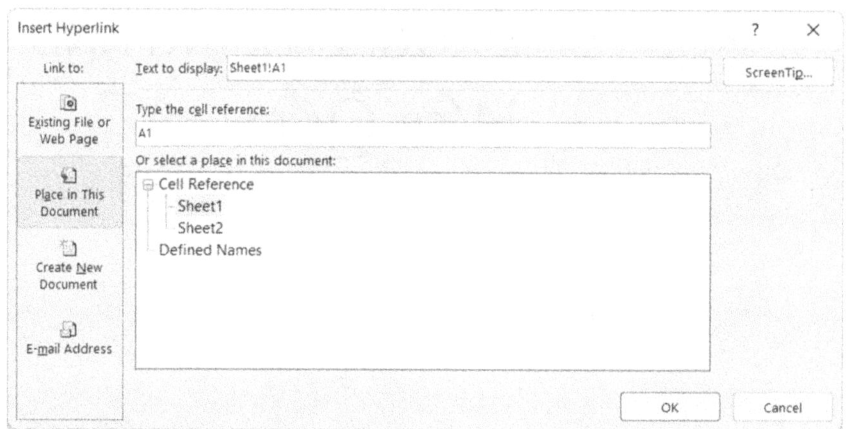

FIGURE 27.1 The Insert Hyperlink dialog box is used to insert a hyperlink in a Microsoft Excel spreadsheet.

In VBA, each hyperlink is represented by a `Hyperlink` object. To create a hyperlink to a Web page, use the `Add` method of the `Hyperlinks` collection. The syntax of this method is as follows:

```
Expression.Hyperlinks.Add(Anchor, Address, [SubAddress],
    [ScreenTip], [TextToDisplay])
```

The arguments in square brackets are optional. `Expression` denotes a worksheet or range of cells where you want to place the hyperlink. `Anchor` is an object to be clicked. This can be either a `Range` or `Shape` object. `Address` points to a local network or a Web page. `SubAddress` is the name of a range in the Excel file. `ScreenTip` allows the display of a screen label. `TextToDisplay` is the name that you'd like to display in a spreadsheet cell for a specific hyperlink.

Let's programmatically place a hyperlink in a worksheet cell. The hyperlink should take you to the Yahoo!® site when clicked.

NOTE	*Please note files for the "Hands-On" project may be found in the companion files.*

Hands-On 27.1 Using VBA to Place a Hyperlink in a Worksheet Cell

1. Open a new workbook and save it as **C:\VBAExcel2021_ByExample\Chap27_VBAExcel2021.xlsm**.

2. Switch to the Visual Basic Editor screen and insert a new module into VBAProject (Chap27_VBAExcel2021.xlsm).
3. In the Code window, enter the code of the FollowMe procedure:

```
Sub FollowMe()
    Dim myRange As Range
    Set myRange = Sheets(1).Range("A1")

    myRange.Hyperlinks.Add Anchor:=myRange, _
       Address:="http://search.yahoo.com/", _
       ScreenTip:="Search Yahoo", _
       TextToDisplay:="Click here"
End Sub
```

4. Run the FollowMe procedure.
   When you run the FollowMe procedure, cell A1 in the first worksheet will contain a hyperlink titled "Click here" with the screen tip "Search Yahoo" (see Figure 27.2). If you are now connected to the Internet, clicking on this hyperlink will activate your browser and load the Yahoo! search engine.

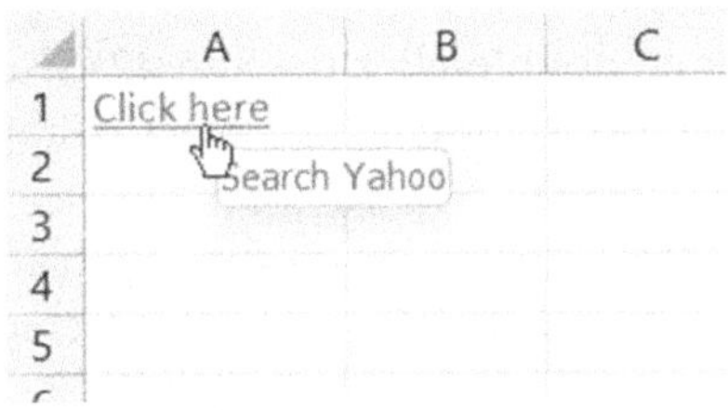

FIGURE 27.2 This hyperlink was placed in a worksheet by a VBA procedure.

If you'd rather not place hyperlinks in a worksheet but want to make it possible for a user to reach the required Internet pages directly from an Excel worksheet, you can use the `FollowHyperlink` method. This method allows you to open the required Web page without the need to place a hyperlink object in a worksheet. The `FollowHyperlink` method looks like this:

```
Expression.FollowHyperlink(Address, [SubAddress], [NewWindow],
     [AddHistory], [ExtraInfo], [Method], [HeaderInfo])
```

Again, the arguments in square brackets are optional. `Expression` returns a `Workbook` object. `Address` is the address of the Web page that you want to activate. `SubAddress` is a fragment of the object to which the hyperlink address points. This can be a range of cells in an Excel worksheet. `NewWindow` indicates whether you want to display the document or page in a new window; the default setting is `False`. The next argument, `AddHistory`, is not currently used and is reserved for future use. `ExtraInfo` gives additional information that allows jumping to the specific location in a document or on a Web page. For example, here you can specify the text for which you want to search. `Method` specifies the method in which the additional information (`ExtraInfo`) is attached. This can be one of the following constants: `msoMethodGet` or `msoMethodPost`. When you use `msoMethodGet`, `ExtraInfo` is a string that's appended to the URL address. When using `msoMethodPost`, `ExtraInfo` is posted as a string or byte array. The last optional argument, `HeaderInfo`, is a string that specifies header information for the HTTP request. The default value is an empty string.

Let's use the `FollowHyperlink` method in a VBA procedure. The purpose of this procedure is to use the Bing search engine to find pages containing the text entered in a worksheet cell.

Hands-On 27.2 Using a Search Engine to Find Text Entered in a Worksheet Cell

1. Insert a new sheet into the current workbook.
2. Switch to the Visual Basic Editor window and double-click the **Sheet2 (Sheet2)** object in the Microsoft Excel Objects folder located in VBAProject (Chap27_VBAExcel2021.xlsm).
3. In the Sheet2 Code window, enter the Worksheet_BeforeDoubleClick event procedure that follows (you may want to review Chapter 15 on creating and using event procedures in Excel):

```
Private Sub Worksheet_BeforeDoubleClick(ByVal Target As Range, _
            Cancel As Boolean)
    Dim strSearch As String

    strSearch = Sheets(2).Range("C3").Formula
    If Target = Range("C3") Then
        Cancel = True
        ActiveWorkbook.FollowHyperlink _
        Address:="https://www.bing.com/search?q=" & strSearch
    End If

End Sub
```

4. Switch to the Microsoft Excel application window. In cell C3 on Sheet2, enter any word or term about which you want to find information (see Figure 27.3).

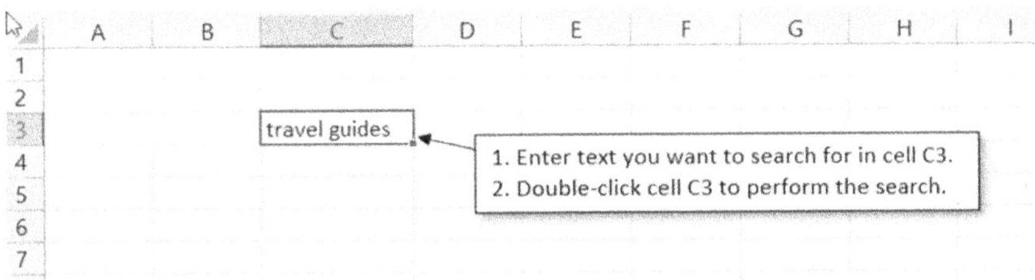

FIGURE 27.3 A Microsoft Excel worksheet can be used to send search parameters to any search engine on the Internet.

5. Make sure that you are connected to the Internet. Double-click cell **C3**. This will cause the text entered in cell C3 to be sent to the Bing search engine. The screen should show the index to found topics with the specified criteria (see Figure 27.4).

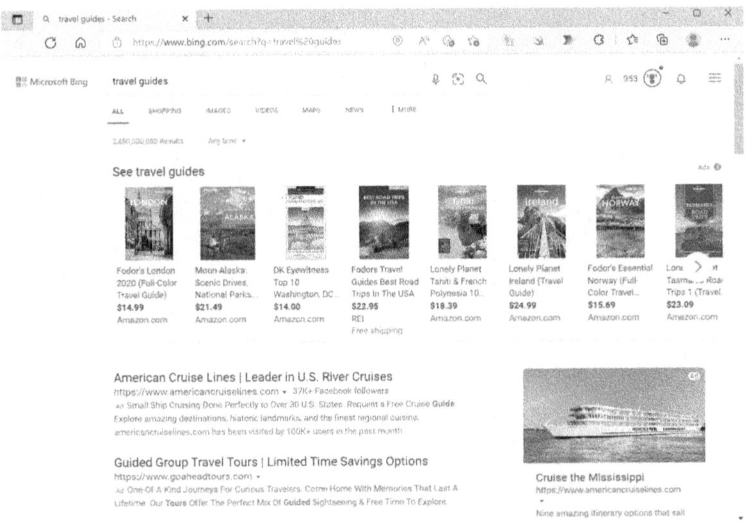

FIGURE 27.4 A Web page opened from a Microsoft Excel worksheet lists topics that were found based on the criteria entered in a worksheet cell (see Figure 27.4).

CREATING AND PUBLISHING HTML FILES USING VBA

Excel allows you to save files in the Hypertext Markup Language (HTML) format using .htm or .html file extensions. When you save an Excel file as html, you can view your worksheets using your favorite Web browser. You can save your HTML files directly to the Web server, a network server, or a local computer. To do this, click File | Save As. Select the folder for the file location, and in the Save as type drop-down box, choose Web Page. Working with nothing other than the user interface (see Figures 27.5 and 27.6), you can place an entire workbook or selected sheets on the Web page. Detailed instructions on how to go about placing an entire workbook or any worksheet (or its elements, such as charts or PivotTables) on a Web page can be found in the Excel online help. Because this book is about programming, we will focus only on the way these tasks are performed via VBA code.

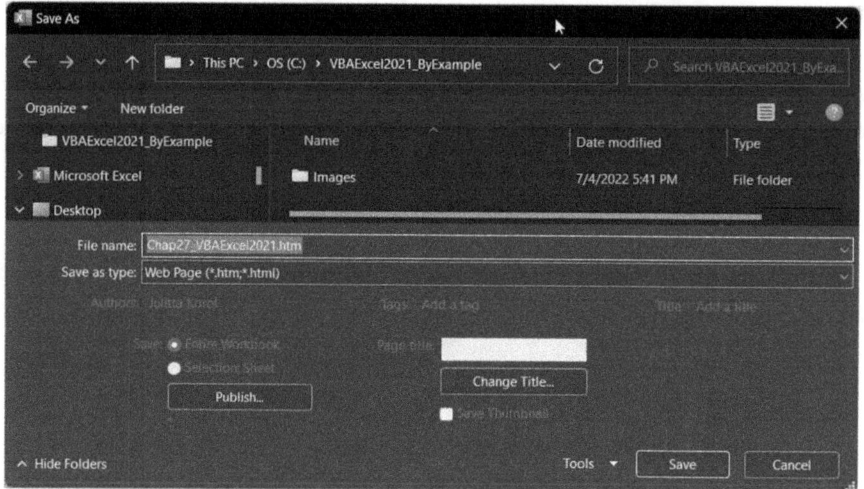

FIGURE 27.5 The Save As dialog box allows users to save their workbook as a Web page.

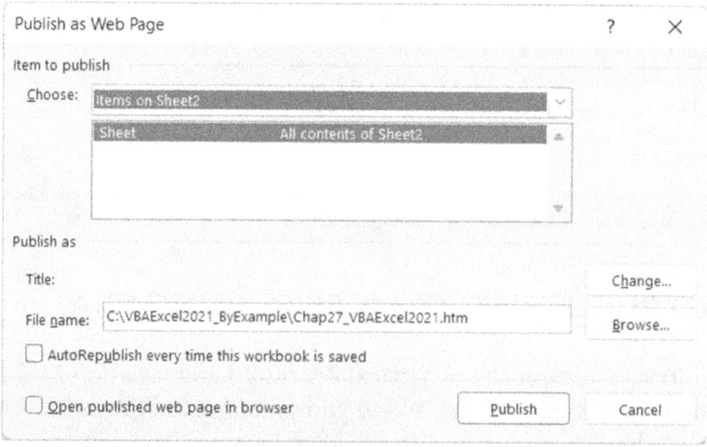

FIGURE 27.6 The Publish as Web Page dialog box appears after clicking the Publish button on the Save As dialog box (see Figure 27.5).

The VBA object library offers objects for publishing worksheets on Web pages. To programmatically create and publish Excel files in the HTML format, you should become familiar with the `PublishObject` object and the `PublishObjects` collection.

`PublishObject` represents a worksheet element that was saved on a Web page, while `PublishObjects` is a collection of all `PublishObject` objects of a specific workbook. To add a worksheet element to the `PublishObjects` collection, use its `Add` method. This method will create an object representing a specific worksheet element that was saved as a Web page.

The format of the `Add` method is as follows:

```
Expression.Add(SourceType, Filename, Sheet, Source, HtmlType,
    [DivID], [Title])
```

The arguments in square brackets are optional. `Expression` returns an object that belongs to the `PublishObjects` collection. `SourceType` specifies the source object using one of the following constants:

SourceType Constants	Value	Description
`xlSourceAutoFilter`	3	An AutoFilter range
`xlSourceChart`	5	A chart
`xlSourcePivotTable`	6	A PivotTable report
`xlSourcePrintArea`	2	A range of cells selected for printing
`xlSourceQuery`	7	A query table (an external data range)
`xlSourceRange`	4	A range of cells
`xlSourceSheet`	1	An entire worksheet
`xlSourceWorkbook`	0	A workbook

`Filename` is a string specifying the location where the source object (`SourceType`) was saved. This can be a *Uniform Resource Locator* (URL) or the path to a local or network file. `Sheet` is the name of the worksheet that was saved as a Web page. `Source` is a unique name that identifies a source object. This argument depends on the `SourceType` argument. `Source` is a range of cells or a name applied to a range of cells when the `SourceType` argument is the `xlSourceRange` constant. If the `SourceType` argument is a constant such as `xlSourceChart`, `xlSourcePivotTable`, or `xlSourceQuery`, `Source` specifies the name of a chart, PivotTable report, or query table. `HtmlType` specifies whether the selected worksheet element is saved as static (non-interactive) HTML or an interactive Microsoft Office Web Component (this feature was depreciated in Excel 2007 and is used only for backward compatibility. See the side note for more information.). `HtmlType` constants are listed in the following table.

HtmlType Constants	Description
`xlHTMLCalc` (depreciated)	Use the Spreadsheet component. This component makes it possible to view, analyze, and calculate spreadsheet data directly in an Internet browser. This component also has options that allow you to change the formatting of fonts, cells, rows, and columns.
`xlHTMLChart` (depreciated)	Use the Chart component. This component allows you to create interactive charts in the browser.
`xlHTMLList` (depreciated)	Use the PivotTable component. This component allows you to rearrange, filter, and summarize information in a browser. This component is also able to display data from a spreadsheet or a database (for instance, Microsoft Access, SQL Server, or OLAP servers).
`XlHTMLStatic` (default)	(default value) Use static (non-interactive) HTML for viewing only. The data published in an HTML document does not change.

NOTE

The Office Web Components (OWC) are ActiveX controls that provide four components: Spreadsheet, Chart, PivotTable, and Data Source Control (DSC). In the Office releases prior to 2007 (XP/2003/2000), these components made it possible to use Excel analytical options in an Internet browser. The Office Web Components were discontinued in Office 2007. If you need OWC to support older applications, you will need to reinstall these components or allow users to download and install them on the fly when the document that requires their use is opened in a browser.

`DivID` is a unique identifier used in the HTML DIV tag to identify the item on the Web page. `Title` is the title of the Web page.

Before we look at how you can use the `Add` method from a VBA procedure, you also need to learn how to use the `Publish` method of the `PublishObject` object. This method allows publishing an element or a collection of elements in a particular document on the Web page. This method is quite simple and looks like this:

```
Expression.Publish([Create])
```

`Expression` is an expression that returns a `PublishObject` object or `PublishObjects` collection. The optional argument, `Create`, is used only with a `PublishObject` object. If the HTML file already exists, setting this argument to `True` will overwrite the file. Setting this argument to `False` inserts the item or items at the end of the file. If the file does not yet exist, a new HTML file is created, regardless of the value of the `Create` argument.

Now that you've been introduced to VBA objects and methods used for creating and publishing an Excel workbook in HTML format, let's get back to programming. In the following Hands-On, you will create an Excel worksheet with an embedded chart and publish it as static HTML.

Hands-On 27.3 Creating and Publishing an Excel Worksheet with an Embedded Chart

1. Create a new workbook and save it as **C:\VBAExcel2021_ByExample\PublishExample.xlsm.**
2. Right-click **Sheet1** and choose **Rename**. Type **Help Desk,** and press **Enter**.
3. In the Help Desk worksheet, enter data as shown in Figure 27.7. To create the chart, select cells **A1:B10** and choose the **Insert** tab. In the Charts group, click the **Column** drop-down and select **2-D Column**. Add Data labels to columns in the plot area and set other chart elements as depicted in Figure 27.7.
4. Activate the Visual Basic Editor window and insert a new module into VBAProject (PublishExample.xlsm).

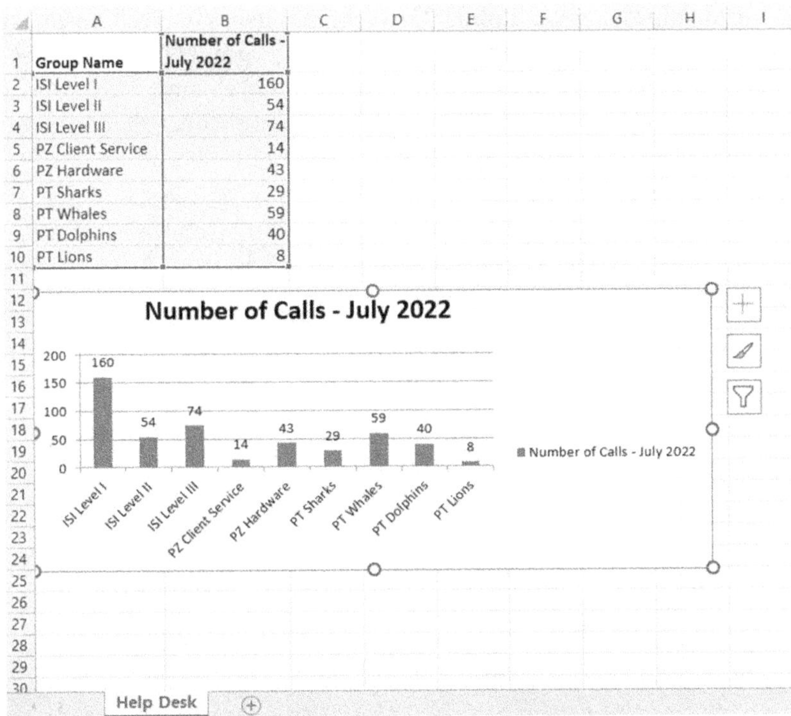

FIGURE 27.7 A worksheet with an embedded chart can be placed on a Web page by using Save As and choosing Web Page as the file format or via a VBA procedure.

5. In the Code window, enter the following two procedures:

```
' The procedure below will publish a worksheet
' with an embedded chart as static HTML

Sub PublishOnWeb(strSheetName As String, _
                 strFileName As String)

    Dim objPub As Excel.PublishObject
    Set objPub = ThisWorkbook.PublishObjects.Add( _
       SourceType:=xlSourceSheet, _
       Filename:=strFileName, Sheet:=strSheetName, _
       HtmlType:=xlHtmlStatic, Title:="Calls Analysis")
    objPub.Publish True
End Sub

Sub CreateHTMLFile()
    Call PublishOnWeb("Help Desk", _
         "C:\VBAExcel2021_ByExample\WorksheetWithChart.htm")
End Sub
```

   The first procedure above, PublishOnWeb, publishes a Web page with a worksheet containing an embedded chart as static HTML. The second procedure, CreateHTMLFile, calls the PublishOnWeb procedure and feeds it the two required arguments: the name of the worksheet that you want to publish and the name of the HTML file where the data should be saved.

6. Run the CreateHTMLFile procedure.
   When this procedure finishes, a new file called C:\VBAExcel2021_ByExample\WorksheetWithChart.htm is created on your hard drive. Also, there will be a folder named WorksheetWithChart_files for storing supplemental files.

7. Locate the **C:\VBAExcel2021_ByExample\WorksheetWithChart.htm** file and open it in your Internet browser (see Figure 27.8).

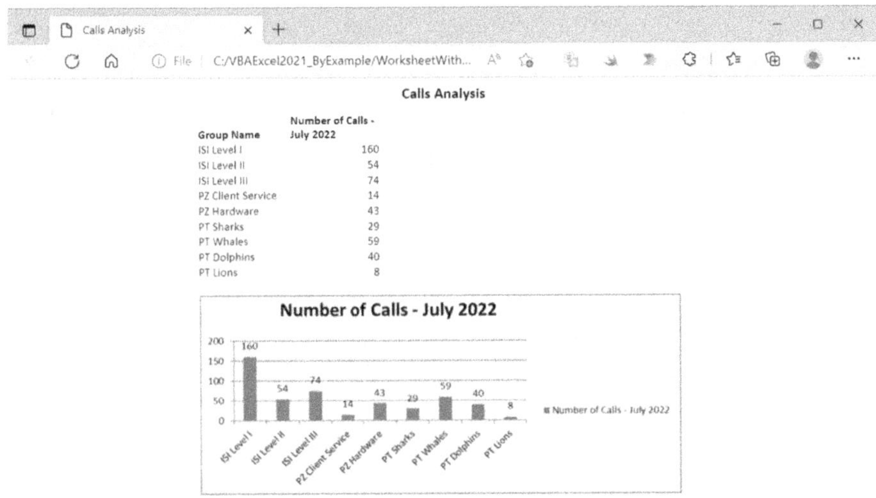

FIGURE 27.8 An Excel worksheet published as a static (non-interactive) Web page.

WEB QUERIES

Over a decade ago, Microsoft introduced in Excel a feature known as Web Query. This feature allowed users to retrieve data from a Web page for use and analysis in Excel. While Web Query is still present in the 2021 version as one of the many Legacy Wizards, the Web page layouts have undergone so many changes in recent years that there are fewer and fewer pages that can be accessed using the Web Query. In this section, we will look at a simple Web query so that you are familiar with this concept.

To pull data from the Web via Web queries, you must have an active Internet connection. You also need to know the address (URL) of the Web page that contains some data in tabular format.

To enable the Web Query in the current version of Excel, choose File | Options | Data, check the box next to From Web (Legacy) and click OK as shown in Figure 27.9.

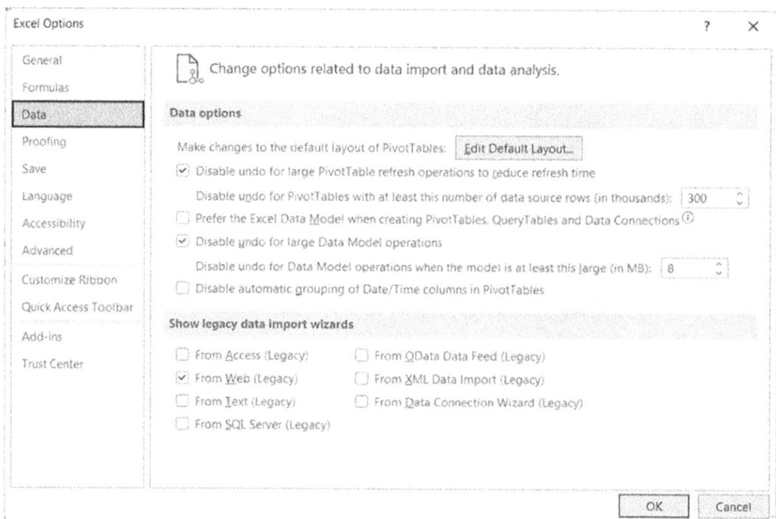

FIGURE 27.9 The Legacy Data import features are now disabled by default. You can enable them by checking appropriate boxes in the Show legacy import wizards' section as displayed here.

After activating the From Web (Legacy) wizard, you will notice that the Get Data button on the Ribbon's Data tab now includes the Legacy Wizard command with the command that you activated (see Figure 27.10).

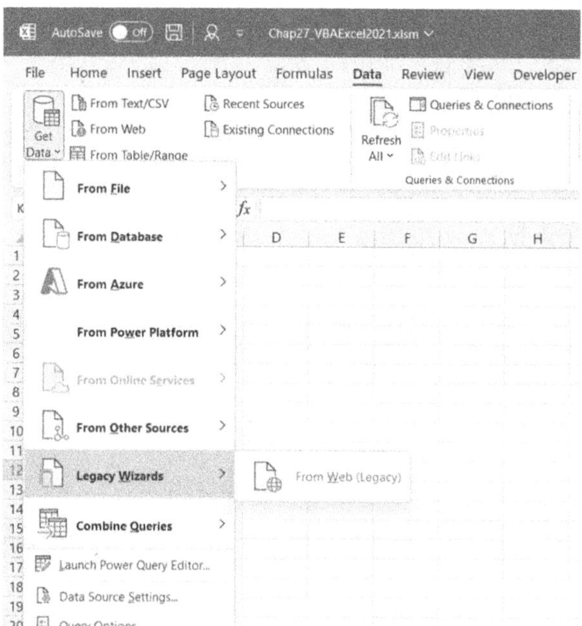

FIGURE 27.10 Older data import commands are shown in Excel 2021 under the Legacy Wizards command and you need to enable them via the Options dialog (see Figure 27.9).

When you select the From Web (Legacy) command, Excel will display the New Web Query dialog box. By default, Excel will try to read data from your home page. To load a specific Web page, simply type its URL in the address bar, as shown in Figure 27.11.

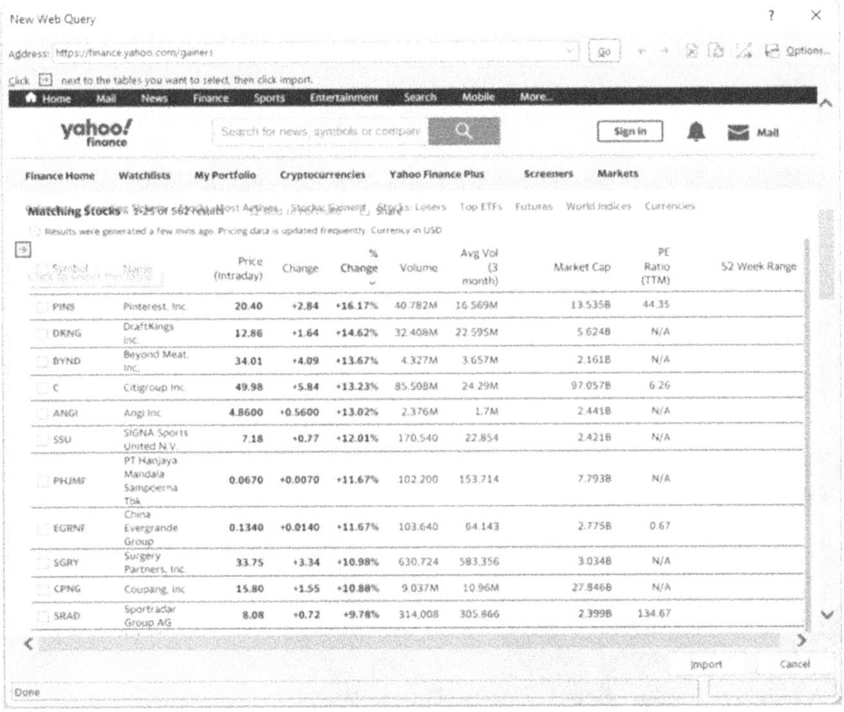

FIGURE 27.11 The New Web Query dialog box provides a special user interface for obtaining data from Web pages.

Web queries allow you to retrieve data from the Web directly into Microsoft Excel without having to know anything about programming. After placing data in a worksheet, you can use Excel tools to perform data analysis. A single table, several tables, or all the text that a website contains can be retrieved into a worksheet. Simply click the arrow next to the table you want to select and click Import (see Figure 27.11). You can get the data with or without formatting by choosing the Options button located in the top right corner of the New Web Query dialog (see Figure 27.11). Figure 27.12 shows the Excel worksheet after the retrieval of the table data.

You can save the underlying Web query using the Save button in the New Web Query dialog. This button is located immediately before the Options button. Web queries are stored in text files with the .iqy extension. The content of the .iqy file can be viewed by opening the file in any text editor (for example, Windows Notepad), as shown in Figure 27.13. Web queries can be also created manually by entering the required commands in a text file and saving the file with the .iqy extension.

Symbol	Name	Price (Intraday)	Change	% Change	Volume	Avg Vol (3 month)	Market Cap	PE Ratio (TTM)	52 Week Range
PINS	Pinterest, Inc.	20.4	2.84	16.17%	40.782M	16.569M	13.535B	44.35	
DKNG	DraftKings Inc.	12.86	1.64	14.62%	32.408M	22.595M	5.624B	N/A	
BYND	Beyond Meat, Inc.	34.01	4.09	13.67%	4.327M	3.657M	2.161B	N/A	
C	Citigroup Inc.	49.98	5.84	13.23%	85.508M	24.29M	97.057B	6.26	
ANGI	Angi Inc.	4.86	0.56	13.02%	2.376M	1.7M	2.441B	N/A	
SSU	SIGNA Sports United N.V.	7.18	0.77	12.01%	170,540	22,854	2.421B	N/A	
PHJMF	PT Hanjaya Mandala Sampoerna Tbk	0.067	0.007	11.67%	102,200	153,714	7.793B	N/A	
EGRNF	China Evergrande Group	0.134	0.014	11.67%	103,640	64,143	2.775B	0.67	
SGRY	Surgery Partners, Inc.	33.75	3.34	10.98%	630,724	583,356	3.034B	N/A	
CPNG	Coupang, Inc.	15.8	1.55	10.88%	9.037M	10.96M	27.846B	N/A	
SRAD	Sportradar Group AG	8.08	0.72	9.78%	314,008	305,866	2.399B	134.67	
IBA	Industrias Bachoco, S.A.B. de C.V.	44.62	3.97	9.77%	19,930	15,856	2.231B	9.07	
STT	State Street Corporation	65.67	5.83	9.74%	7.685M	3.01M	24.108B	8.89	
ACSAY	ACS, Actividades de Construcción y Servicios, S.A.	4.56	0.4	9.62%	36,964	37,990	6.526B	1.99	
MQ	Marqeta, Inc.	8.5	0.72	9.25%	7.053M	10.972M	4.628B	N/A	
BKBSY	PT Berkah Beton Sadaya Tbk	14.15	1.1	8.43%	206,800	121,540	2.863B	283	
BCH	Banco de Chile	17.33	1.32	8.24%	293,175	170,280	8.753B	7.53	
NFLX	Netflix, Inc.	189.11	14.33	8.20%	16.319M	14.265M	84.017B	16.03	
CELH	Celsius Holdings, Inc.	80.87	6.02	8.04%	1.596M	1.073M	6.095B	622.08	
MNSO	MINISO Group Holding Limited	7.1	0.51	7.74%	992,310	978,548	2.248B	23.67	
LFST	LifeStance Health Group, Inc.	5.99	0.43	7.73%	1.067M	814,370	2.242B	N/A	
OSH	Oak Street Health, Inc.	23.96	1.72	7.73%	1.559M	1.679M	5.776B	N/A	
PENN	Penn National Gaming, Inc.	31.4	2.25	7.72%	3.684M	4.293M	5.238B	13.14	

Sheet1 Sheet3 Sheet2

FIGURE 27.12 Web data retrieved into a Microsoft Excel worksheet using the New Web Query dialog box (see Figure 27.11).

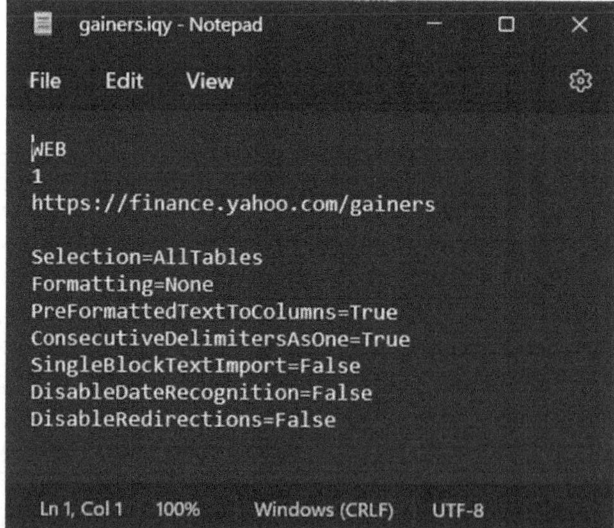

FIGURE 27.13 This Web query file was created by clicking the Save button in the New Web Query dialog (see the button to the left of the Options button in Figure 27.11).

The .iqy files contain the following parts:

Section Name	Description / Example
Query Type (Optional section)	Set to WEB when you use Version Section: WEB
Query Version (optional section)	Allows you to set the version number of a Web query. For example: 1
URL (required)	The URL of the Web page where you will get your data. For example: *https://finance.yahoo.com/gainers* You can send parameters by attaching them to the URL address using the question mark, as follows: *https://finance.yahoo.com/quote/CELH?p=CELH* *https://www.x-rates.com/historical/?from=USD&amount=1&da te=2022-07-16* "*from*," "*amount*," and "*date*" are parameter names. The values USD, 1, and 2022-07-16 that follow the equal signs are parameter settings you want to retrieve from the specified URL. Parameters are separated from one another with the ampersand symbol (&). If a parameter requires multiple values, you must separate them with a plus sign (+). You can send parameters to the Web server using the POST or GET method.

Web queries can be static or dynamic. Static queries always return the same data, while dynamic queries allow the user to specify different parameters to narrow down the data returned from the Web page.

Creating and Running Web Queries with VBA

In the previous section, you learned that a Web query can be created by using the From Web (Legacy) option or typing special instructions in a text editor such as Notepad. The third method of creating a Web query is through a VBA statement.

To programmatically create a Web query, use the `Add` method of the `QueryTables` collection. This collection belongs to the `Worksheet` object and contains all the `QueryTable` objects for a specific worksheet. The `Add` method returns the `QueryTable` object that represents a new query. The format of this method is as follows:

```
Expression.Add(Connection, Destination,[Sql])
```

`Expression` is an expression that returns the `QueryTable` object. `Connection` specifies the data source for the query table. The data source can be one of the following:

- A string containing the address of the Web page in the form "URL; <url>". For example:

  ```
  "URL;http://www.usa.gov/"
  ```

  See Hands-On 27.4 for a procedure example that uses the URL connection.

- A string indicating the path to the existing Web query file (.iqy) using the form "FINDER; <data finder file path>". For instance:

  ```
  "FINDER;C:\VBAExcel2021_ByExample\www.gainers.iqy"
  ```

- A string containing an OLEDB or ODBC connection string. The ODBC connection string has the form "ODBC; <connection string>". For instance:

  ```
  "ODBC;DSN=MyNorthwind;UID=;PWD=;" & _
    "Database=Northwind 2007"
  ```

  Here's how this could be used to retrieve data from the Northwind 2007.accdb file:

  ```
  Sub GetAccessData()
      Dim strSQL As String
      Dim strConn As String

      strSQL = "Select * from Shippers"
      strConn = "ODBC;DSN=MyNorthwind;UID=;PWD=;" & _
          "Database=Northwind 2007"
      Sheets.Add
      With ActiveSheet.QueryTables.Add(Connection:=strConn, _
          Destination:=Range("B1"), Sql:=strSQL)
          .Refresh
      End With
  End Sub
  ```

  To try out this procedure, start by creating the MyNorthwind data source name. You can do this by accessing the ODBC Data Source Administrator dialog box from the Start menu. In the ODBC Data Source Administrator dialog (the User DSN tab), click the Add button. Next, select the Microsoft Access Driver (*.mdb, *.accdb) and click the Finish button. Enter MyNorthwind in the Data Source Name text box, then click the Select button, and choose the C:\VBAExcel2021_ByExample\Northwind 2007.accdb file. Click OK to confirm your selection. Next, click OK to exit. MyNorthwind should appear in the list of the User Data Sources. Click OK to close the ODBC Data Source Administrator dialog. Enter the procedure in a standard module of any workbook and then run it.

- An ADO or DAO `Recordset` object. Microsoft Excel retains the `Recordset` until the query table is deleted or the connection is changed. The resulting query table cannot be edited.
- A string indicating the path to a text file in the form "TEXT; <text file path and name>". For instance:

```
"TEXT;C:\VBAExcel2021_ByExample\ProductsOver50.txt"
```

The following example procedure opens the comma-separated file in Excel:

```
Sub GetDelimitedText()
    Dim qtblOutput As QueryTable

    Sheets.Add
    Set qtblOutput = ActiveSheet.QueryTables.Add( _
    Connection:="TEXT;C:\VBAExcel2021_ByExample\
      ProductsOver50.txt", _
      Destination:=ActiveSheet.Cells(1, 1))
    With qtblOutput
        .TextFileParseType = xlDelimited
        '.TextFileCommaDelimiter = True
        .TextFileOtherDelimiter = "Tab"
        .Refresh
    End With
End Sub
```

`Destination` is the cell in the upper-left corner of the query table destination range (this is where the resulting query table will be placed). This cell must be in the worksheet containing the `QueryTable` object used in the expression. The optional argument, `Sql`, is not used when a `QueryTable` object is used as the data source.

NOTE	*Be careful not to include spaces in the connection strings as this will cause runtime error 1004 during the execution of a VBA procedure.*

The following example procedure creates a new Web query in the active workbook. The data retrieved from a Web page is placed in a worksheet as static text.

Hands-On 27.4 Creating a Web Query in an Active Workbook

1. Open a new workbook and save it as **C:\VBAExcel2021_ByExample\MyWebQueries.xlsm.**
2. Switch to the Visual Basic Editor window and insert a new module in VBAProject (MyWebQueries.xlsm).
3. In the Code window, enter the GetTrendingTickers procedure, which retrieves to Excel trending stocks from the Yahoo investing site.

```
Sub GetTrendingTickers()
    ' create a web query in the current worksheet
    ' connect to the web, retrieve data, and paste it
    ' in the worksheet as static text

  Sheets.Add
  With ActiveSheet.QueryTables.Add _
    (Connection:="URL;http://finance.yahoo.com/trending-tickers", _
          Destination:=Range("A2"))
         .Name = "yfin-list"
         .BackgroundQuery = True
         .WebFormatting = xlWebFormattingNone
         .Refresh BackgroundQuery:=False
         .SaveData = True
  End With
End Sub
```

4. Switch to the Microsoft Excel application window and choose **Developer | Macros.**
5. In the **Macros** dialog box, highlight the **GetTrendingTickers** procedure and click **Run.**

   While the procedure executes, the following tasks occur: (a) a connection is established with the specified Web page, (b) data from a Web page is retrieved, and (c) data is placed in a worksheet. When the procedure finishes executing, the active worksheet displays data as shown in Figure 27.14.

	A	B	C	D	E	F	G	H	I
1									
2	Symbol	Name	Last Price	Market Time	Change	% Change	Volume	Market Cap	Intraday High/Low
3	BTC-USD	Bitcoin USD	21,168.76	10:10PM UTC	239.89	1.15%	24.034B	404.227B	
4	ETH-USD	Ethereum USD	1,342.16	10:09PM UTC	88.02	7.02%	18.05B	163.172B	
5	ETH-CAD	Ethereum CAD	1,749.18	10:10PM UTC	105.65	6.43%	23.524B	212.656B	
6	DOGE-USD	Dogecoin USD	0.063912	10:10PM UTC	0.00057	0.90%	280.536M	8.479B	
7	XRP-USD	XRP USD	0.352187	10:10PM UTC	0.016947	5.06%	1.298B	17.026B	
8	BTC-CAD	Bitcoin CAD	27,588.40	10:10PM UTC	161.44	0.59%	31.323B	526.813B	
9	SOL-USD	Solana USD	39.36	10:09PM UTC	1.51	3.99%	1.129B	13.598B	
10	SHIB-USD	SHIBA INU USD	0.000011	10:09PM UTC	0	-0.01%	278.756M	6.015B	
11	ADA-USD	Cardano USD	0.4547	10:09PM UTC	0.009419	2.12%	640.244M	15.341B	
12	TSLQ		49.41	4:00PM EDT	-0.3	-0.61%	288,992	N/A	
13	XRP-CAD	XRP CAD	0.458992	10:10PM UTC	0.019665	4.48%	1.691B	22.189B	
14	MATIC-USD	Polygon USD	0.723046	10:09PM UTC	0.008033	1.12%	709.52M	5.789B	
15	STOR	STORE Capital Corporation	26.86	4:00PM EDT	0.67	2.56%	3.233M	7.536B	
16	FPI	Farmland Partners Inc.	13.73	4:00PM EDT	0.29	2.16%	327,000	706.643M	
17	EURUSD=X	EUR/USD	1.0088	10:29PM BST	0.0067	0.67%	0	N/A	
18	ETH-EUR	Ethereum EUR	1,331.42	10:10PM UTC	78.39	6.26%	17.906B	161.867B	
19	LUNA1-USD	Terra USD	0.000105	10:10PM UTC	-0.000002	-1.71%	134.897M	688.628M	

FIGURE 27.14 This data was retrieved from a Web page using the Web query in a VBA procedure.

Notice that this worksheet does not contain any hyperlinks because we set the `WebFormatting` property of the query table to `xlWebFormattingNone` in the procedure code. This property determines how much formatting from a Web page, if any, is applied when you import the page into a query table. You can use one of the following constants: `xlWebFormattingAll`, `xlWebFormattingNone` (this is the default setting), or `xlWebFormattingRTF`.

Setting the `BackgroundQuery` property of the `QueryTable` object to `True` allows you to perform other operations in the worksheet while the data is being retrieved from the Web page. After retrieving data from the Web page, you must use the `Refresh` method of the `QueryTable` object in order to display the data in a worksheet. If you omit this method in your procedure code, the data retrieved from the Web page will be invisible.

By setting the `SaveData` property to `True`, the table retrieved from the Web page will be saved with the workbook.

6. Right-click anywhere within the data placed by the Web query in the worksheet. Choose **Edit Query** from the shortcut menu.
   You will see the Edit Web Query window (Figure 27.15). You may need to click No multiple times to dismiss the Script Error window. Microsoft has abandoned the Legacy Web Query so there is no chance this error will ever get fixed.
7. Click the **Options** button located on the Edit Web Query window's toolbar to access the Web Query Options dialog box, as shown in Figure 27.15.
   Notice that the option button None is selected in the Formatting area. This option button represents the `xlWebFormattingNone` setting of the `WebFormatting` property in the procedure code.

8. Press **Cancel** to close the Web Query Options dialog box and then click Cancel to exit the Edit Web Query window.

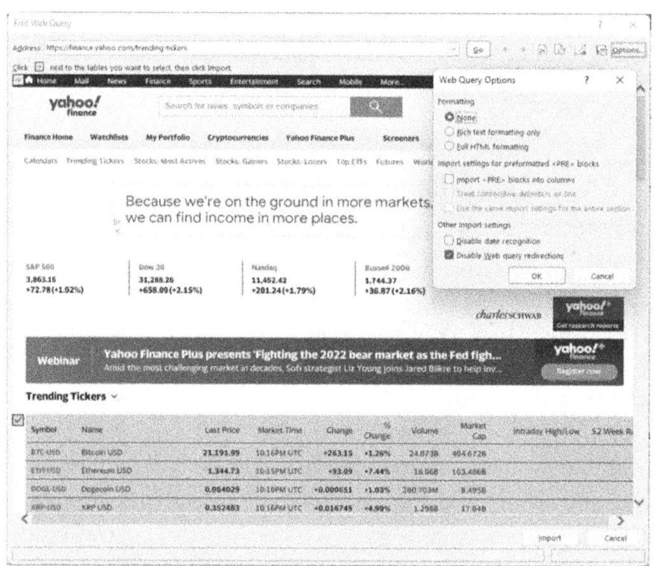

FIGURE 27.15 The Web Query Options dialog box.

NOTE	*Web pages undergo frequent modifications. It's not uncommon to find out that a Web query you prepared a while ago suddenly stops working because the Web page address or parameters required to process the data have changed. If you plan on using Web queries in your applications, you must watch for any changes introduced on Web sites that supply you with critical information. Particularly watch for table references. A reference to table "4" from a while ago could now be a totally different number or name, causing your Web query to retrieve data that you don't care about or no data at all.*

Dynamic Web Queries

Instead of hardcoding the parameter values in the code of your VBA procedures, you can create a dynamic query that will prompt the user for the parameter settings when the query is run. The Portfolio2 procedure next uses the `GET` method for sending dynamic parameters. This procedure displays a dialog box prompting the user to enter stock symbols separated by spaces.

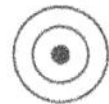

Hands-On 27.5 Using the GET Method for Sending Dynamic Parameters

1. In the Code window of VBAProject (MyWebQueries.xlsm), enter the following Hist_Exchange_OnDate procedure below the code of the Portfolio procedure:

```
Sub Hist_Exchange_OnDate()
    Dim sht As Worksheet
    Dim qryTbl As QueryTable

    ' insert a new worksheet in the current workbook
    Set sht = ThisWorkbook.Worksheets.Add
    ' create a new web query in a worksheet
    Set qryTbl = sht.QueryTables.Add _
    (Connection:="URL;https://www.x-rates.com/historical/?" & _
     "from=USD&Amount=1&Date=[""Enter the date in the format
        YYYY-MM-DD""]", _
      Destination:=sht.Range("A1"))

    ' retrieve data from web page and specify formatting
    ' paste data in a worksheet
    With qryTbl
        .BackgroundQuery = True
        .WebSelectionType = xlSpecifiedTables
        .WebTables = "1, 2"
        .WebFormatting = xlWebFormattingAll
        .Refresh BackgroundQuery:=False
        .SaveData = True
    End With
End Sub
```

2. Switch to the Microsoft Excel application window and choose **Developer | Macros**.
3. In the Macro dialog box, highlight the **Hist_Exchange_OnDate** procedure and click **Run**.

   When the Web query is activated, the Enter Parameter Value dialog box appears.
4. Enter the date in the dialog box as shown in Figure 27.16 and click OK.

   The data is retrieved from the specified Web page and placed in a worksheet.

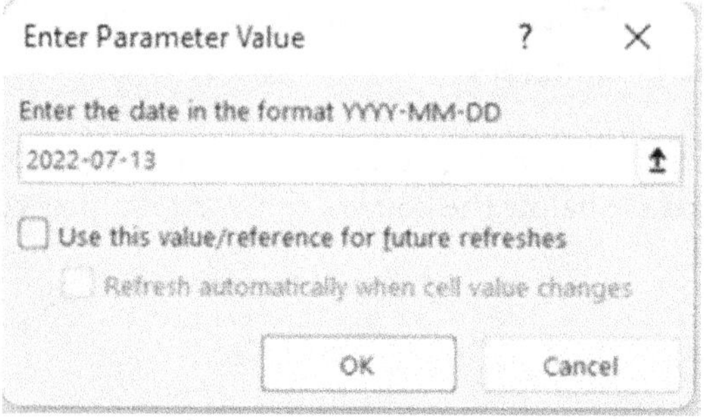

FIGURE 27.16 Dynamic Web queries request parameter values from the user.

You can revise the above procedure to save the date entered by the user in a variable so that you can enter the date in the worksheet when the data is retrieved (see the following code example).

```
Sub Hist_Exchange_OnDate2()
    Dim sht As Worksheet
    Dim qryTbl As QueryTable
    Dim strDate As String

    strDate = Application.InputBox("Enter the date in the
      format YYYY-MM-DD")
    ' insert a new worksheet in the current workbook
    Set sht = ThisWorkbook.Worksheets.Add
    ' create a new web query in a worksheet
    Set qryTbl = sht.QueryTables.Add _
    (Connection:="URL;https://www.x-rates.com/historical/?" & _
     "from=USD&Amount=1&Date=" & strDate, _
      Destination:=sht.Range("A2"))

    sht.Range("A1").Formula = "US Dollar Rates on " & strDate
    ' retrieve data from web page and specify formatting
    ' paste data in a worksheet
    With qryTbl
        .BackgroundQuery = True
        .WebSelectionType = xlSpecifiedTables
        .WebTables = "1, 2"
        .WebFormatting = xlWebFormattingAll
        .Refresh BackgroundQuery:=False
        .SaveData = True
    End With
End Sub
```

REFRESHING DATA

You can refresh data retrieved from a Web page by using the Refresh option on the shortcut menu. To access this menu, right-click any cell in the range where the data is located.

The Refresh option is also available from the Ribbon's Data tab. Data can be refreshed in the background while you are performing other tasks in the worksheet, when the file is being opened, or at specified time intervals. You can specify when the data should be refreshed in the External Data Range Properties dialog box; right-click anywhere in the data range and choose Data Range Properties from the shortcut menu to bring up the dialog box shown in Figure 27.17.

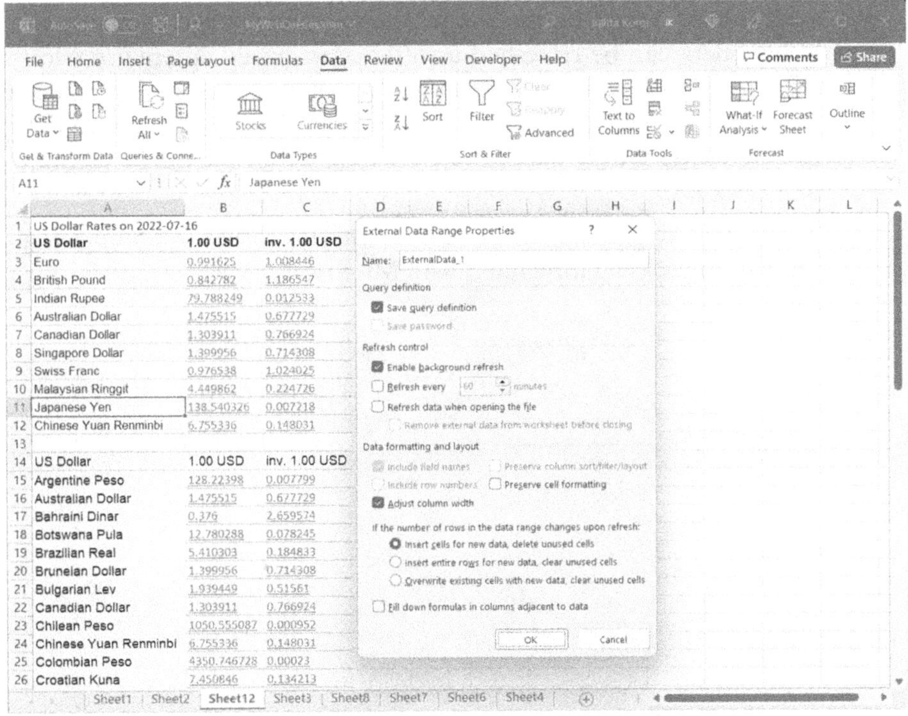

FIGURE 27.17 After retrieving data from a particular Web page using the Web query, you can use the External Data Range Properties dialog box to control when data is refreshed and how it is formatted.

SUMMARY

In this chapter, you were introduced to using Excel with the Internet. Let's quickly summarize the information we've covered here:

- Hyperlinks allow you to activate a specified Web page from a worksheet cell.
- HTML files can be created and published from Excel by selecting the Web Page (*.htm; *.html) format type in the Save As dialog box or via VBA procedures.
- Web queries allow you to retrieve "live" data from a Web page into a worksheet. These queries can be created using the From Web (Legacy) command or programmatically with VBA. Web queries let you retrieve an entire Web page or specific tables that a Web page contains. The retrieved data can be refreshed as often as required. There are two types of Web queries: static and dynamic. Web query is an old technology and should not be used in new Excel applications. It is recommended that you use the Power Query instead (see Chapter 23 for the quick introduction to this topic).

In the next chapter, you are introduced to the Extensible Markup Language (XML) and learn how it is integrated with Microsoft Excel.

Chapter 28 USING XML IN EXCEL 2021

This chapter introduces you to the Extensible Markup Language (XML). The XML functionality is not new; it was added to Excel in version 2000 and has been much improved since. We will look at the XML file format in detail later on in this chapter after we've learned what XML is and how it is used in Excel.

WHAT IS XML?

XML is a standard that provides a mechanism for designing your own custom markup language and using that language for describing the data in your own documents. Although XML was designed specifically for delivering information over the World Wide Web, it is being utilized in other areas, such as storing, sharing, and exchanging data. Like HTML, XML is a markup language; however, HTML and XML serve different functions. HTML describes Web page layout by using a set of fixed non-customizable tags, while XML lets you describe data content using custom tags.

The main goal of XML is the separation of content from presentation. Because XML documents are text files, XML is independent of operating system platform, software vendor, and natural or programming language. XML makes it easy to describe any data (structured or unstructured) and send it anywhere across the Web using common protocols, such as HTTP or FTP. As long as any two organizations can agree on the XML tag set to be used to represent the data being exchanged, the data can be interpreted and easily exchanged no matter what back-end systems these organizations run or databases they use. Although anyone can describe the data by creating a set of custom tags, the representatives of many industry groups have defined and published XML schemas that dictate how XML documents are formatted to represent data for their industry. XML schemas define the structure and data types that are allowed within an XML document and enforce the document's conformity to the rules.

Let's take a look at the following XML document (Courses1.xml) that was created using Windows Notepad:

```
<?xml version = "1.0"?>
<Courses>
    <Course ID = "VBA1EX">
        <Title>Beginning VBA in Excel</Title>
        <Startdate>3/4/2022</Startdate>
        <Sessions>6</Sessions>
    </Course>
    <Course ID = "VBA2EX">
        <Title>Intermediate VBA in Excel</Title>
        <Startdate>4/13/2022</Startdate>
        <Sessions>8</Sessions>
    </Course>
    <Course ID = "VBA3EX">
        <Title>Advanced VBA in Excel</Title>
        <Startdate>9/7/2022</Startdate>
        <Sessions>12</Sessions>
    </Course>
</Courses>
```

The first line of an XML document is called the XML declaration:

```
<?xml version = "1.0"?>
```

The above instruction identifies the file as an XML file. Recent versions of Excel can easily open the structured data file even if you omit this instruction. The declaration line is also known as a processing instruction. This instruction begins and ends with a question mark (?) and contains the name of the application (in this example "xml") to which the instruction is directed, as well as additional information that needs to be passed to the XML processor, such as the version number and optional `encoding` and `standalone` attributes:

```
<?xml version = "1.0" encoding = "UTF-8" standalone = "Yes"?>
```

The `encoding` attribute specifies the character style to be applied. When the `standalone` attribute is set to `Yes`, it tells the XML processor that the document does not reference an external file.

You can include other processing instructions in the XML file if you need the processing application to take a specific action. For example, you can specify that the file be opened by Excel by adding the following instruction to the above XML markup:

```
<?mso-application progid = "Excel.Sheet"?>
```

Notice the simple structure of XML. Similar to HTML, XML uses tags for data markup. However, unlike HTML, XML tags are not predefined. You can change the name of the tag to anything you want. For example, <Courses> and </Courses> can become <Classes> and </Classes>. You can create custom tags that best describe data in your document. To do this right, you'll need to follow some simple XML rules so that your document is well-formed. This is explained in the next section of this chapter.

An XML document contains one or more elements, data attributes, and text. The top element, in this example the element marked with the <Courses> tag, is called a root node. Every XML file must have a start root node and an end root node. There can be only one root node in the file. The start tag is represented by left and right angle brackets (< >), and the end tag has a left angle bracket, forward slash, and a right angle bracket (< / >). The names of the tags are case-sensitive. The name of the start tag and the name of the corresponding end tag must match exactly.

Elements may contain text and other elements. For example, the <Courses> element is defined to contain one or more <Course> elements. Notice that in the previous example, the data for the <Course> element is provided by the `ID` attribute:

```
<Course ID = "VBA1EX">
```

The values of attributes must be surrounded by double or single quotation marks.

Notice that the <Course> element has three other elements: <Title>, <Startdate>, and <Sessions>. The second and third <Course> elements have exactly the same structure. The structure of the XML document is very logical and easy to follow. You can quickly add more data to the file by following the same pattern.

SIDEBAR ***Character Encodings in XML***

When you type an XML document into Notepad and save it, you can choose from one of several supported character encodings, including ANSI, Unicode (UTF-16), Unicode (Big Endian), or UTF-8. The encoding declaration in the XML document identifies which encoding is used to represent the characters in the document. UTF-8 encoding allows the use of non-ASCII characters, regardless of the language of the user's operating system and browser or the language version of Office. When you use UTF-8 or UTF-16 character encoding, an encoding declaration is optional. XML parsers can determine automatically if a document uses UTF-8 or UTF-16 Unicode encoding.

WELL-FORMED XML DOCUMENTS

When you create or modify an XML document, you must make sure that your XML file is well-formed. Here's what makes a document well-formed:

- An XML document must have one root element. In HTML the root element is always <HTML>, but in the XML document you can name your root element anything you want. Element names must begin with a letter or underscore character. The root element must enclose all other elements. Elements must be properly nested. The XML data must be hierarchical; the beginning and ending tags cannot overlap.

```
<Employee>
  <Employee ID>090909</Employee ID>
</Employee>
```

- All element tags must be closed. A begin tag must be followed by an end tag:

```
<Sessions>5</Sessions>
```

- You can use shortcuts, such as a single slash (/), to end the tag so you don't have to type the full tag name. For example, if the current <Sessions> element is empty (does not have a value), you could use the following tag:

```
<Sessions />
```

- Tag names are case sensitive. The tags <Title> and </Title> aren't equivalent to <TITLE> and </TITLE>. For example, the following line:

```
<Title>Beginning VBA Programming</Title>
```

is not the same as:

```
<TITLE>Beginning VBA Programming</TITLE>
```

- All attributes must be in quotation marks:

```
<Course Id = "VBAEX1"/>
```

- You cannot have more than one attribute with the same name within the same element.

If the <Course> element has two ID attributes, they must be written separately, as shown below:

```
<Course ID = "VBAEX1"/>
<Course ID = "VBAEX2"/>
```

Checking that an XML document is well-formed is similar to syntax checking in VBA. When you try to open an XML file in Excel that is not well-formed, you will receive an error message similar to the one in Figure 28.1. You can force this error by removing the ending "s" from the tag <Courses> in the Courses1.xml file while it is open in Notepad. When you do this, the beginning <Course> tag will not match the ending </Courses> tag; thus, an error will occur when you try to open the file with Excel. Notice that the error message specifies the type of error that was found and the name of the source file. To help you troubleshoot the error, the XML Import Error dialog box includes the Details button.

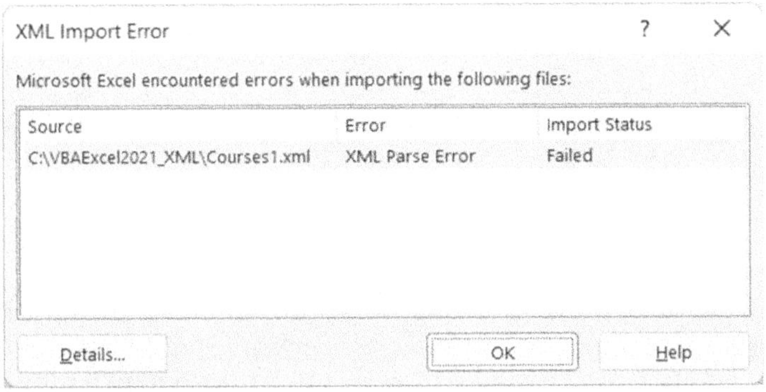

FIGURE 28.1 When the XML document is not well-formed, Excel displays an XML Import Error dialog box when you try to open the file.

To investigate the error, select the error in the XML Import Error dialog box (Figure 28.1) and click the Details button. This brings up a dialog box that details the error, as shown in Figure 28.2. You must fix all the errors before you can successfully open the file in Excel.

XML Error ? ×

An XML error has occurred. Please correct the problem and try again.

Click the Details button for a more specific description of the problem.

OK Details <<<

Details

Error Code : -1072896659
URL : <not-supplied>
Reason : End tag 'Courses' does not match the start tag 'Course'.
Line : 35
Column : 3
File Offset : 991

FIGURE 28.2 XML Error dialog box with error details.

You do not need to wait for Excel to discover errors in XML files. To verify that the document is well-formed, it's a good idea to open it in the browser before attempting this task with Excel. Double-click the XML filename, and it should open up in your default browser (Figure 28.3).

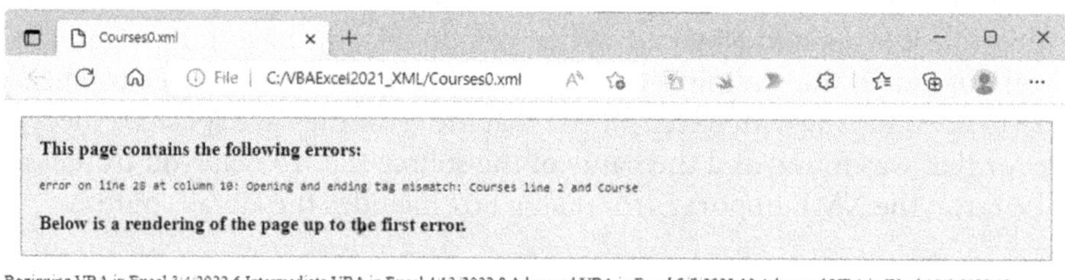

FIGURE 28.3 The Microsoft Edge browser depicted here notifies you about the error in the XML file.

SIDEBAR *What Is a Parser?*

If you want to read, update, create, or manipulate any XML document, you will need an XML parser. A *parser* is a software engine, usually a dynamic link library (DLL), that can read and extract data from XML. Microsoft Internet Explorer and Edge browsers has a built-in XML parser (MSXML*.DLL) that can read and detect all non-well-formed documents. MSXML has its own object model, known as DOM (Document Object Model), that you can use from VBA to quickly and easily extract information from an XML document (see "The XML Document Object Model" later in this chapter).

VALIDATING XML DOCUMENTS

There are two types of validation in XML. One is checking whether the document is well-formed (see the previous section). The other type of validation requires that you create a Document Type Definition (DTD) or a set of rules known as a *schema* to determine the type of elements and attributes an XML document should contain, how these elements and attributes should be named, and how the elements should be related.

Creating DTD or schema for an XML document is optional. Create either one only if you are planning to validate data. In XML, data validation is accomplished by comparing the document with the DTD or schema. When you open the XML document in a parser, the parser compares the DTD to the data and raises an error if the data is invalid. This book does not explore the creation and use of DTDs or schemas. These topics alone would require a separate chapter. What you should remember from this section is that a valid XML document is not the same as a well-formed XML document. A valid XML document conforms to a structure outlined in the DTD or schema, while well-formed documents follow the basic formatting rules mentioned in the previous section titled "Well-Formed XML Documents."

EDITING AND VIEWING AN XML DOCUMENT

To make changes in an XML document, you should open it in a text editor such as Notepad or an XML editor. There are many XML editors that you can purchase or download free from the Internet. Figure 28.4 shows an xml file open in Notepad ++ and in the XML Copy Editor Store Edition downloaded from Microsoft Store.

The advantage of using XML editors is that they come with special features that organize your XML data into an easy-to-read format and allow you to create well-formed documents. They also provide validation features.

You can make your XML documents legible and clear by using comments. The XML processor ignores all commented text. A comment begins with the <! -- characters and ends with the --> characters. Within your comment you can use any characters except for a double hyphen (--). A comment can be placed anywhere within an XML document provided that it's outside (not within) other markup tags. Let's add a comment to the Courses1.xml document that we discussed earlier.

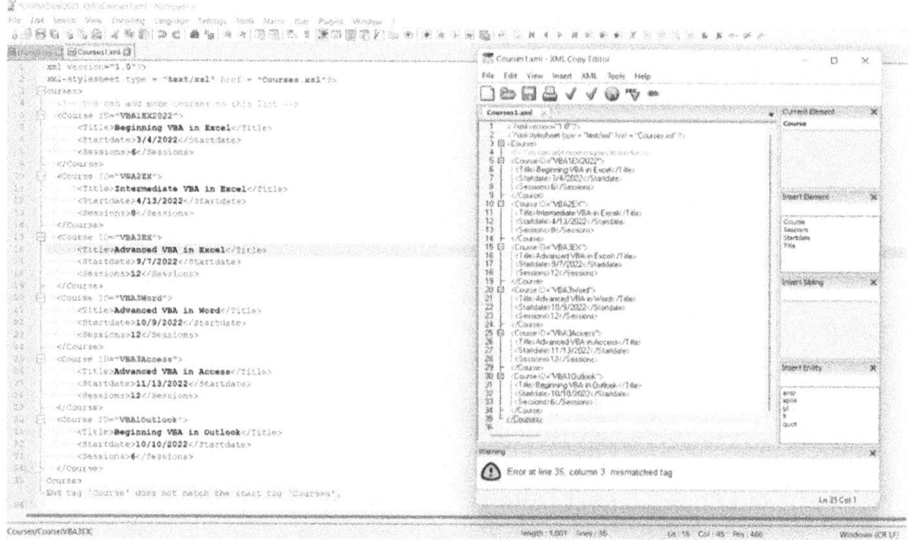

FIGURE 28.4 The example Courses1.xml file opened in two different editors.

NOTE	*Please note files for the "Hands-On" project may be found in the companion files.*

Hands-On 28.1 Adding a Comment to an XML Document

1. In Windows Explorer, create a new folder named **VBAExcel2021_XML.**
2. Copy the Courses0.xml file from the companion files to your VBAExcel2021_XML folder.
3. Right-click the **Courses0.xml** file, choose **Open with** and then select **Notepad.** If Notepad is not listed, select **Choose Program,** and then locate and select **Notepad** in the list.
4. Type the following comment between the <Courses> and <Course ID = "VBA1EX"> tags:

```
<!-- You can add more courses to this list -->
```

   The beginning of the file should now look like this:

```
<Courses>
<!-- You can add more courses to this list -->
   <Course ID = "VBA1EX">
```

5. Save the file as **Courses1.xml** file and exit Notepad.

Comments can also be used to disable a particular processing instruction or an XML node. For example, you could prevent the display of the information about a specific course by commenting out the section of XML markup like this:

```
<!--
  <Course ID = "VBA2EX">
    <Title>Intermediate VBA in Excel</Title>
      <Startdate>4/13/2018</Startdate>
      <Sessions>8</Sessions>
  </Course>
-->
```

Now that you've edited the file, let's open it in the browser to ensure that you have a well-formed XML document.

Hands-On 28.2 Viewing an XML Document in the Internet Browser

1. Open the **Courses1.xml** file in your browser.
2. Figure 28.5 shows what the file looks like when it is opened in an internet browser. Here you can see the hierarchical layout of an XML document very clearly. Microsoft Edge automatically places a down arrow to the left of each element so you can expand and collapse the XML data layout.

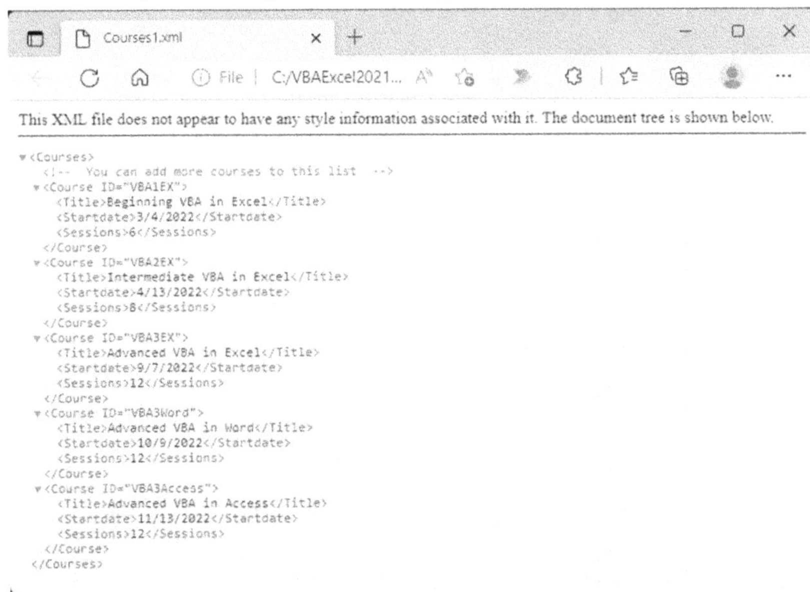

FIGURE 28.5 An XML data file opened in the Microsoft Edge browser.

3. Close the browser.

OPENING AN XML DOCUMENT IN EXCEL

Once you've checked that you have a well-formed XML document by opening it with your browser, let's open it in Excel.

Hands-On 28.3 Opening an XML Document in Excel

1. Start Excel and open the **C:\VBAExcel2021_XML\Courses1**.xml file.
   Excel displays the Open XML dialog box like the one shown in Figure 28.6.
2. In the Open XML dialog box, select the **As an XML table** option button and click **OK**.
   When you select the first option button, Excel tells you that it could not find the schema for the XML document (see Figure 28.7). A schema will be automatically created for you when you click OK.

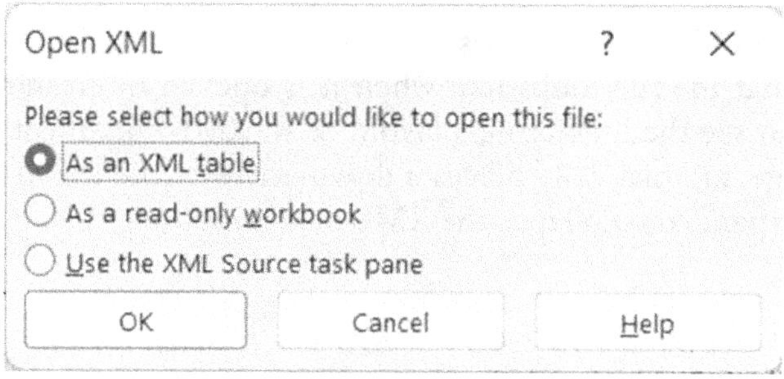

Open XML ? ×

Please select how you would like to open this file:

As an XML table

As a read-only workbook

Use the XML Source task pane

OK Cancel Help

FIGURE 28.6 Excel displays the Open XML dialog box when you open an XML document that does not have a stylesheet associated with it.

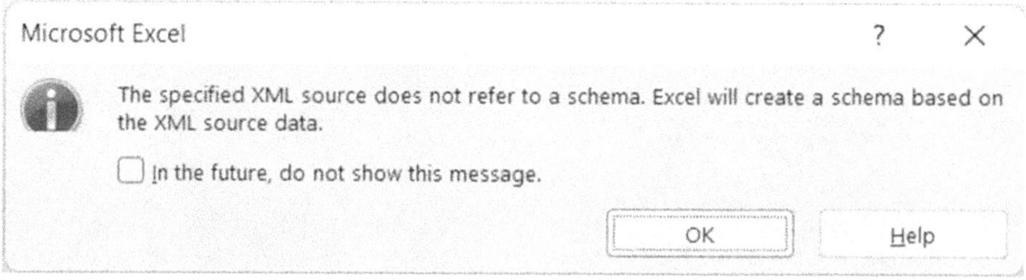

Microsoft Excel ? ×

The specified XML source does not refer to a schema. Excel will create a schema based on the XML source data.

In the future, do not show this message.

OK Help

FIGURE 28.7 A schema file provides the rules for the XML document. If it is missing, Excel will infer the schema from the XML data file.

NOTE	*If you are trying to open a very complex XML document, a schema file created by Excel may be incorrect or insufficient for your needs. If this is the case, you will need to create your own XML Schema Description file (XSD) or have someone else create it for you.*

3. Click **OK** to have Excel create a schema and open the file.
Excel imports the contents of the XML document into an XML table. The cells in the worksheets are mapped to the XML elements in the source file and can be refreshed at any time by clicking the Refresh button on the Design tab (Figure 28.8).

	A	B	C	D
1	ID	Title	Startdate	Sessions
2	VBA1EX	Beginning VBA in Excel	3/4/2022	6
3	VBA2EX	Intermediate VBA in Excel	4/13/2022	8
4	VBA3EX	Advanced VBA in Excel	9/7/2022	12
5	VBA3Word	Advanced VBA in Word	10/9/2022	12
6	VBA3Access	Advanced VBA in Access	11/13/2022	12
7				

FIGURE 28.8 An XML document opened in Excel.

When Excel creates a schema based on the contents of your XML document, your XML source file becomes read-only. This means that you cannot make changes to the file by editing the XML table in Excel. Excel refers to the schema files it creates as XML maps. Only by creating your own XML map can you write back to your XML document from Excel. The next section of this chapter demonstrates how to work with XML maps.

4. Leave Excel open with the data as shown in Figure 28.8 and open the **Courses1.xml** in Notepad.
5. Modify the file by adding the following information about another course to the end of the file just before the end </Courses> tag:

```
<Course ID = "VBA1Outlook">
  <Title>Beginning VBA in Outlook</Title>
  <Startdate>10/10/2022</Startdate>
  <Sessions>6</Sessions>
</Course>
```

6. Save the file and close Notepad.
7. In Excel, click the **Refresh** button on the Table Design tab.
Notice that Excel adds a new row of data to the XML table.
8. Save the workbook as **C:\VBAExcel2021_ByExample\Chap28_VBAExcel2021.xlsm** in the macro-enabled format, and then close it.

WORKING WITH XML MAPS

XML schemas in Excel are called *XML maps*. You can associate one or more schemas with a workbook and then map all or some of the schema elements to various cells or ranges on a worksheet. Using XML mapping makes it relatively easy to import and export data into and out of Excel. In the following Hands-On, you will learn how to:

- Work with the XML Source task pane
- Add a schema to your workbook
- Map cells to elements in an XML map
- Populate the XML map with XML data

Hands-On 28.4 Mapping Schema Elements to Worksheet Cells

1. Copy the **Employees.xml** and **Employees.xsd** files from the companion files into your **VBAExcel2021_XML** folder.
2. Open a new workbook in Microsoft Excel.
3. Click the **Source** button in the XML group on the **Developer** tab. Excel displays the XML Source task pane, as shown in Figure 28.9.

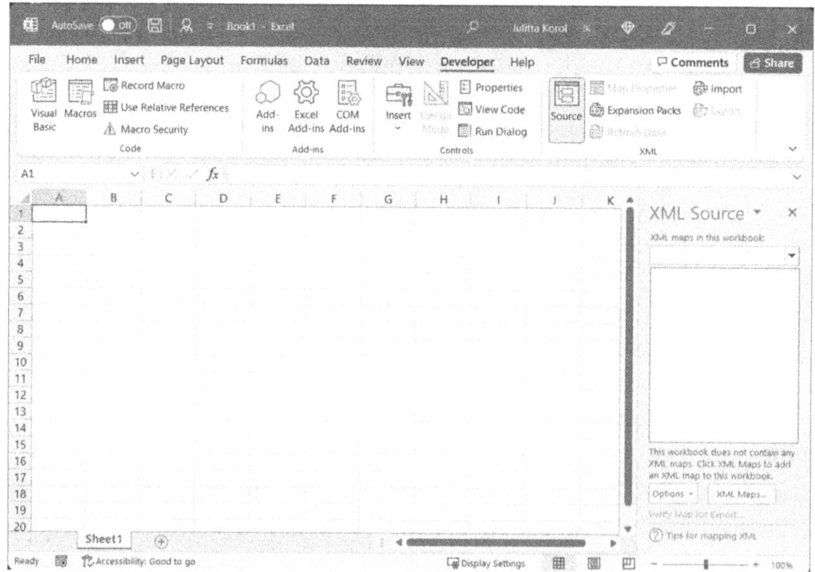

FIGURE 28.9 The XML Source task pane.

The XML Source task pane is used for displaying XML maps found in the XML data or schema documents, and mapping XML elements to cells or ranges on a worksheet. If the current worksheet doesn't have any XML maps associated with it, the XML Source task pane is blank. The XML Source task pane includes two buttons (Options and XML Maps) and one hyperlink (Verify Map for Export).

4. In the XML Source task pane, click the **XML Maps** button.
   Excel displays the XML Maps dialog box shown in Figure 28.10.

FIGURE 28.10 Use the XML Maps dialog box to add, delete, or rename an XML map associated with the workbook.

5. Click the **Add** button in the XML Maps dialog box.
6. In the Select XML Source dialog box, switch to the **VBAExcel2021_XML** folder, select the **Employees.xsd** schema file, and click **Open**.
   Excel displays the Multiple Roots dialog box shown in Figure 28.11.

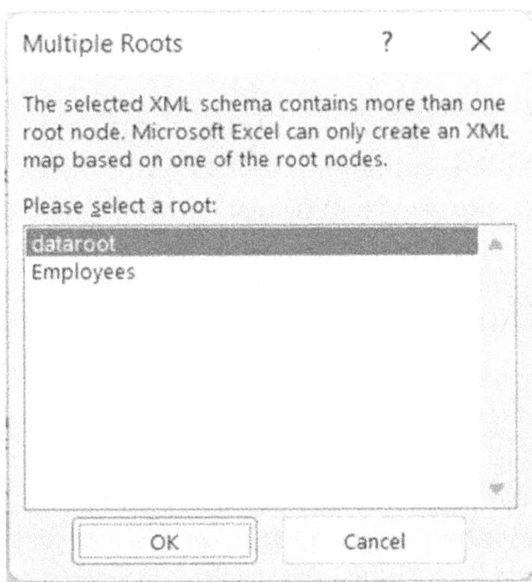

FIGURE 28.11 If the XML data or schema file contains more than one root node, you must indicate which root node should be used.

7. In the Multiple Roots dialog box, select **dataroot** and click **OK**.
   Excel displays the XML map name in the XML Maps dialog box shown in Figure 28.12. The name of the map consists of the schema's root element followed by an underscore and the word "Map." You can change the map name by clicking the Rename button.

   You cannot update an existing XML map. Excel only allows you to create new maps or delete existing ones using the XML Maps dialog box. Because of this, you must recreate the XML table created from an XML map any time the source XML schema changes.

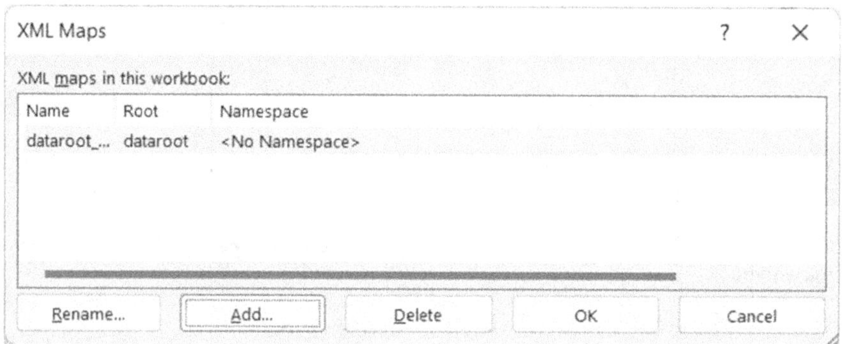

FIGURE 28.12 The XML Maps dialog box now displays the XML map (dataroot_Map) that was added to the workbook.

8. Click **OK** to close the XML Maps dialog box and return to Excel.
   The XML Source task pane now displays the structure of the XML map, as shown in Figure 28.13.
   Notice that the name of the XML map appears in the listbox at the top of the XML Source task pane. If the workbook contains more than one XML map, you will use this listbox to select the map you want to work with. Excel obtains the map information from the schema that the XML file references; when the schema is not available, the map is generated based on the content of the XML data file, as you have seen earlier in this chapter while opening the Courses1.xml document.

   The XML map is displayed as a tree and can be expanded or collapsed by clicking the plus and minus buttons to the left of the element names. Elements in the tree are represented by different icons. For example, in Figure 28.13, the folder icon with a red asterisk in front of the dataroot element represents a required parent element. An icon that looks like a sheet of paper with a corner

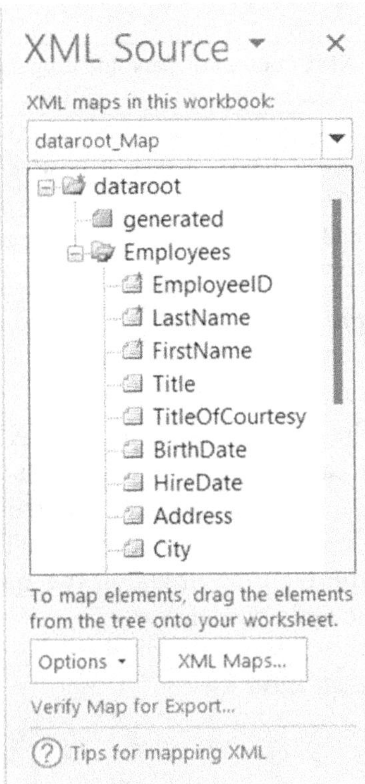

FIGURE 28.13 The XML Source task pane displays the XML map generated from the XML schema file (Employees.xsd).

folded down in front of the element name indicates a child element. The child element labeled "generated" stores the date the schema was generated. The folder icon in front of the Employees element tells us that this is the repeating parent element with children. The elements below the Employees element are child and required child elements. Required elements have a red asterisk in the icon image. To get the list and images of all the icons that can appear in the XML map, click on Tips for mapping XML at the bottom of the XML Source task pane.

Now that you've got the XML map, you can use it to map XML elements to your worksheet. Mapping is done by selecting the elements or entire nodes in the XML map and then dragging them onto a worksheet. You can drag mapped cells anywhere on the worksheet in any order you require. You can only map one schema element to one location in a workbook at a time.

XML Mapping	Follow This Procedure...
Single element	Drag the desired element from the XML Source task pane and drop it in the desired location on a worksheet.
Multiple elements	Select the first desired element in the XML Source task pane and hold down the Ctrl key while selecting other elements. Next, drag the selection to the desired location on a worksheet.
Entire node	Click on the parent node. All the child items will be highlighted. Drag the selection to the desired location on a worksheet.

9. In the XML Source task pane, select the **Employees** folder and drag it to cell **A1** on the worksheet.

   Excel maps XML elements to a range of cells, as you can see in Figure 28.14. Notice that the XML elements are laid out in the order they appear in the XML Source task pane. Excel generates a structure called an XML table when you drag the repeating elements from the XML Source task pane to a worksheet. At this point, the generated table contains a header row with the AutoFilter option enabled. You can adjust the size of the table by dragging the resize handle found at the bottom-right corner of the table border.

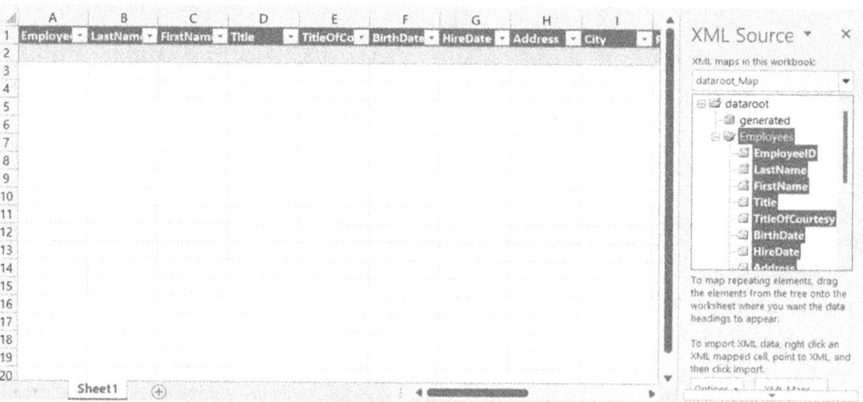

FIGURE 28.14 Mapping XML elements to cells in a worksheet.

In this example we have placed all of the XML elements on the worksheet by dragging them from the XML Source task pane and dropping them at a specific cell. When you don't require all the elements, simply drag those you need and leave out those you do not need. Mapped elements appear in bold type in the XML Source task pane.

NOTE	*Recall that you've already been introduced to the table feature in Chapter 24. XML tables are described in the next section.*

10. To populate the table with data, right-click anywhere within the table and choose **XML | Import** (or click the **Import** button on the Developer tab).
11. In the Import XML dialog box, select **Employees.xml** and click **Import**.
12. The table on the worksheet is now populated with the data from the selected XML document, as shown in Figure 28.15.

	A	B	C	D	E	F	G
1	EmployeeID	LastName	FirstName	Title	TitleOfCourtesy	BirthDate	HireDate
2	1	Davolio	Nancy	Sales Representative	Ms.	12/8/1968 0:00	5/1/1
3	2	Fuller	Andrew	Vice President, Sales	Dr.	2/19/1952 0:00	8/14/1
4	3	Leverling	Janet	Sales Representative	Ms.	8/30/1963 0:00	4/1/1
5	4	Peacock	Margaret	Sales Representative	Mrs.	9/19/1958 0:00	5/3/1
6	5	Buchanan	Steven	Sales Manager	Mr.	3/4/1955 0:00	10/17/1
7	6	Suyama	Michael	Sales Representative	Mr.	7/2/1963 0:00	10/17/1
8	7	King	Robert	Sales Representative	Mr.	5/29/1960 0:00	1/2/1
9	8	Callahan	Laura	Inside Sales Coordinator	Ms.	1/9/1958 0:00	3/5/1
10	9	Dodsworth	Anne	Sales Representative	Ms.	7/2/1969 0:00	11/15/1
11							
12							
13							

Sheet1

FIGURE 28.15 A table populated with the data from the XML document.

13. Save the workbook in the macro-enabled format as **C:\VBAExcel2021_XML\Employees.xlsm**.

SIDEBAR *Understanding the XML Schemas*

Schema files describe XML data using the XML Schema Definition (XSD) language and allow the XML parser to validate the XML document. An XML document that conforms to the structure of the schema is said to be valid. The Employees.xsd schema file that we worked with in Hands-On 28.4 was generated in Microsoft Access using built-in menu options. Here are some examples of types of information that can be found in an XML schema file:

- Elements that are allowed in a given XML document
- Data types of allowed elements
- Number of occurrences of a given element that are allowed
- Attributes that can be associated with a given element
- Default values for attributes
- Elements that are child elements of other elements
- Sequence and number of child elements

If you open the Employees.xsd file in Notepad, you will notice a number of declarations and commands that begin with the <xsd> tag followed by a colon and the name of the command. You will also notice the names of the elements and attributes that are allowed in the Employees.xml file as well as the data types for each element. The names of the data types are preceded with the "od" prefix followed by a colon. For example:

od:jetType ="text"	Defines the Jet data type for an element.
od:sqlSType ="nvarchar"	Defines the Microsoft SQL Server data type for an element.
od:autounique = "yes"	Defines a Boolean data type for an auto-incremented identity column.
od:nonNullable ="yes"	Indicates whether or not a column can contain a null value.

The schema file also specifies the number of times an element can be used in a document based on the schema. This is done via the `minOccurs` and `maxOccurs` attributes.

WORKING WITH XML TABLES

An XML table is a table in Excel that has been mapped to one or more XML elements. In other words, each column in the XML table represents an element in your XML document. In this chapter you've already created two XML tables based on the Courses1.xml and Employees.xml documents (see Hands-On 28.3 and 28.4).

After placing your XML data in an XML table in a workbook, you can work with this data just like any other Excel workbook file. This means you can add new columns and rows to your data, include formulas and functions, create charts, and perform various formatting tasks. You can even change the column headings that were automatically created from the XML element names. It is important to keep in mind that even when you change the column headings in the worksheet, the original XML element names will be used to export data from the mapped cells.

The changes you make to the data in the XML table will not affect the XML data that is stored in the original XML data file. Once you are done working with the XML table, you can save it as a standard Excel workbook (.xlsx) or in any other file format that is available in the Save As dialog box. You can also export the contents of mapped cells. The XML export feature is explained in the next section.

If the original XML data file has changed, you can easily update the data in your XML table by clicking the Refresh Data button on the Developer tab.

When you use the Refresh command, the data is read from the original XML document into the mapped locations on the worksheet. If you have another XML file that uses the same mapping, you can import the data from that file into your XML table by clicking the Import button on the Developer tab. Simply said, refreshing updates the XML table with the most current data from the original XML file, while importing gets the data from another XML file that follows the same schema.

When refreshing or importing data you can:

- Overwrite existing data with new data
- Append new data to an existing XML table

These options can be specified via the XML Map Properties dialog box, shown in Figure 28.16.

The XML Map Properties dialog box allows you to set certain properties that relate to working with XML maps. This dialog can be accessed using any of the techniques listed below:

- Click the Map Properties button on the Developer tab.
- Right-click anywhere in the XML table and choose XML | XML Map Properties.

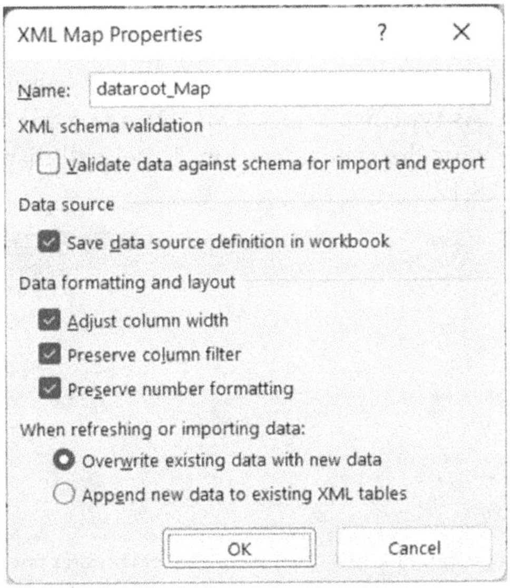

FIGURE 28.16 The XML Map Properties dialog box.

Each XML table in a workbook can be independently manipulated via the XML Map Properties dialog. The following properties can be set:

XML Property	Description
Name	The name of the active XML map.
Validate data against schema for import and export	Excel will validate XML data against its schema while importing and exporting.
Save data source definition in workbook	Specifies whether your table is dynamic or static. If selected, the XML data is linked to the XML file and can be refreshed. If not selected, the data is static and cannot be refreshed.
Adjust column width	Excel will automatically adjust the width of table columns to fit the data.
Preserve column filter	Excel will preserve the selected column sorting, filtering, and layout.
Preserve number formatting	If selected, Excel will preserve the specified formatting of numbers in the table.
Overwrite existing data with new data	New data from the XML file will replace old data during a refresh or import.
Append new data to existing XML tables	New data from the XML file will be added at the bottom of the XML table during a refresh or import.

Exporting an XML Table

You can preserve the data in your XML table in two ways:

- Save your data to an XML data file.

  To do this, click the File | Save As. In the File name box, type a name for the XML data file. In the Save As type list, select XML Data (*.xml) and click Save. Before proceeding with the save operation, Excel will display the message shown in Figure 28.17.

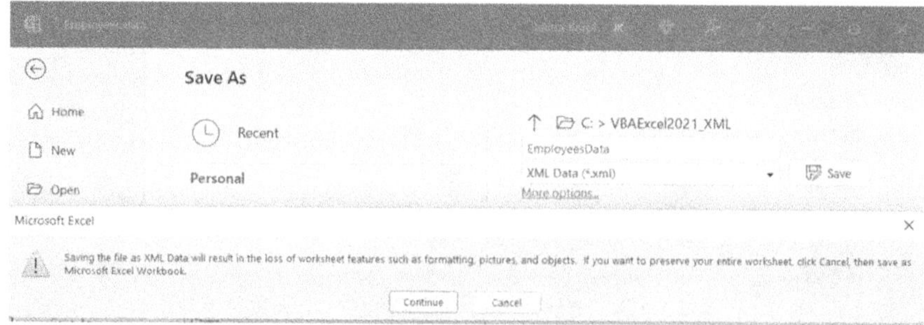

FIGURE 28.17 Excel displays a message about the loss of certain worksheet features prior to saving data in an XML data file.

To save the data as an XML document, click Continue. If you keep working with this file and make any data and formatting changes, only the data will be saved during subsequent save operations.

- Save your data by exporting it through the XML map.

  We will see how this feature is used in the following Hands-On. You should be working with the XML table that was created in Figure 28.15 earlier in this chapter.

Hands-On 28.5 Exporting XML Data in Mapped Worksheet Cells

1. Make sure that the **Employees.xlsm** file you created in Hands-On 28.4 is open in Microsoft Excel. The XML Source task pane should be visible on the right side of the worksheet. If it is missing, click the **Source** button on the Developer tab.
2. Click the **Verify Map for Export** hyperlink at the bottom of the XML Source task pane.
   If the map is valid for export, Excel displays the message that the map is exportable. If the map is invalid for export, a message is displayed with information about why the map isn't exportable. A map is invalid for export when:
   - It contains more than one level of data. Although Excel can import data using multilevel maps, only single-level maps can be exported, such as the dataroot_Map in Figure 28.13 that you've worked with in prior sections.
   - It is denormalized. A map becomes denormalized when nonrepeating items from an XML map are included in the XML table on the worksheet. Denormalized elements appear multiple times on the worksheet. If the user changes a nonrepeating item in one row, that item will become inconsistent with other rows that should be showing the same data. Because Excel does not know how to reconcile the differences, the table can't be exported. To avoid denormalization of data, always create separate XML tables for nonrepeating and repeating nodes.
3. Click **OK** when Excel displays the message that the dataroot_Map is exportable.
4. Click the **Export** button in the XML section on the Developer tab.
   If the workbook contains more than one XML map, you will be prompted to select the map to use. You can export data using only one XML map at a time. Excel proceeds to display the Export XML dialog box.
5. In the Export XML dialog box, specify the name for your XML file and the folder where it should be saved. Select your **VBAExcel2021_XML** folder and

enter **Northwind_Employees.xml** in the File name box. Click the **Export** button to complete the export operation.

6. Open the Northwind_Employees.xml document in Notepad to view its contents.
7. Close Notepad.

NOTE	*After exporting XML data in mapped cells to an XML data file, the name of your active workbook does not change. You can continue working with the data in this workbook. However, if you make changes to existing data or add new rows of data, you should re-export the data to the Northwind_Employees.xml file.*

XML Export Precautions

When exporting data, be aware of the fact that only the data included in the XML table will be saved; XML elements that were not mapped will not be exported. If you don't want to lose any content during export, always place all the elements from the XML map on the worksheet.

If the XML table contains a formula, the result of the formula (and not the formula itself) will be exported with the other data in the XML table. Formulas that you place in an XML table column must reference XML data elements that contain either a number, time, or date value.

If you add a new column to your XML table and then export the data, the data from this new unmapped column will not be saved. The reason for this is that Excel exports a table as XML using the schema stored in the workbook. The generated XML file must match the XML source file from which the XML table was created. Because the added column is not in the XML source file, Excel cannot save it. Therefore, if you need to add data to the existing XML table, do the following:

- Open the appropriate schema file in Notepad and add a new element with the name for your new column.
- Save the modified schema file and close Notepad.
- Because the XML schema has changed, and Excel does not allow you to modify an existing XML map, you will need to create a new XML map and drag the required XML elements to your worksheet. You are already familiar with this process, as it was a part of the Hands-On in the section titled "Working with XML Maps" earlier in this chapter. After mapping your XML elements to cells in a worksheet, simply refresh your XML table. There will be no data in the optional column that you've added to

the schema file. You can now proceed to enter the data or formula you need in this empty column. Formulas can be copied as required. When you export your data to the XML file, the data in the new column will be exported together with the other data in your XML table.

VALIDATING XML DATA

To have Excel validate XML data upon import or export, you need to follow these steps:

1. Select any cell within your XML table on the worksheet and click the **Map Properties** button on the Developer tab.
   Excel displays the XML Map Properties dialog box shown earlier in Figure 28.16.
2. Select **Validate data against schema for import and export.**
3. Click **OK** to close the dialog box.

If you enter an invalid value in any column of your XML table, Excel will not automatically validate your entry. However, all of the entries will be validated when you click the Export button on the Developer tab to export the data. If any data is found to be invalid, Excel displays an error message similar to the one shown in Figure 28.18.

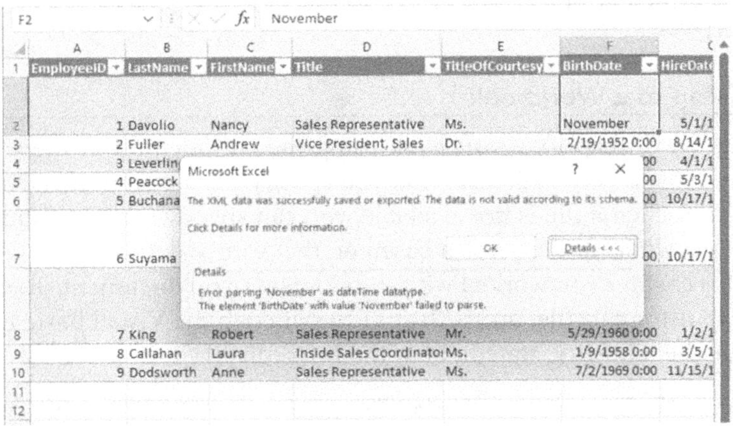

FIGURE 28.18 Excel displays a message when data is found to be invalid according to its schema during the export or a refresh operation.

Notice that the error in validating the data does not prevent Excel from saving or exporting. The Details section in the error message dialog box will give you a hint why data is invalid, so that you can correct the data and re-export it. You may want to define your own data validation rules that comply with the XML schema by using the Data Validation button on the Data tab. Then Excel will validate your data as you work in the worksheet.

PROGRAMMING XML MAPS

Earlier in this chapter you learned that a workbook can contain more than one XML map. These maps can be from the same schema or different schemas. When mapping XML elements to cells and ranges on the worksheet, keep in mind that mapped cell ranges cannot overlap.

In this section, we will add another XML map to the current workbook, but instead of using a manual method we'll perform this task programmatically. Excel provides specific objects to deal with programming its XML features such as the `XmlMap` object in the `XmlMaps` collection and the `XmlNamespace` object in the `XmlNamespaces` collection.

The `XmlMaps` collection contains the `XmlMap` object, which can be used to perform the programming tasks described in the following subsections. You can try out the example code in the Immediate window. Be sure that you have the Employees.xlsm workbook open and your active worksheet contains the XML table displaying Northwind employees. This table was created earlier in this chapter from the dataroot_Map based on the Employees.xsd schema (see Hands-On 28.4).

Adding an XML Map to a Workbook

You can add an XML map to a workbook using the `Add` method of the `XmlMaps` collection. This method requires that you specify the location of an XML schema file. If the schema file is not available, you can specify the XML source data file and Excel will create a schema based on that source data.

Earlier in this chapter you worked with the Courses1.xml document. To create an XML map using this file, press Alt+F11 to switch to the Visual Basic Editor screen. Type the following statement in the Immediate window:

```
ActiveWorkbook.XmlMaps.Add("C:\VBAExcel2021_XML\Courses1.xml")
```

When you press Enter, Excel will display the message shown earlier in this chapter in Figure 28.7. Click OK to the message. When you switch back to the Excel application window, you will notice that the Courses_Map is added to the XML maps in the drop-down list at the top of the XML Source task pane (see Figure 28.19).

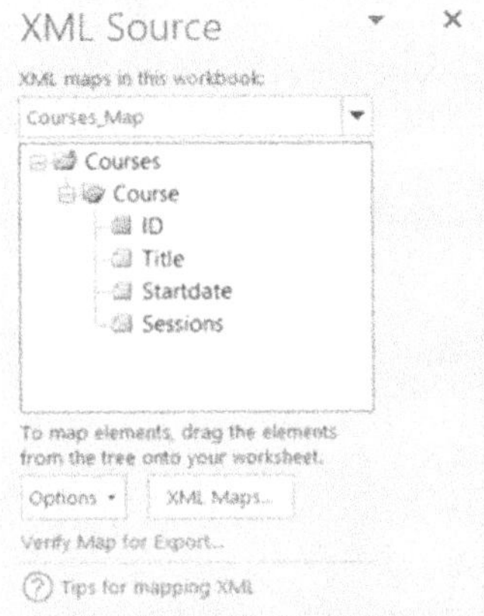

FIGURE 28.19 Adding another XML map to a workbook.

When Excel creates a new map, it uses the name of the root node for its name, followed by an underscore and the word "Map." Sometimes a newly added map may have the same root node name as an existing map. To differentiate one map from another, Excel will add a number following the word "Map." So, if you already have a dataroot_Map in the workbook and you are adding another map whose root node is also named dataroot, Excel will assign the name "dataroot_Map2" to the new map.

Deleting Existing XML Maps

To delete an existing XML map from the workbook, use the `Delete` method of the `XmlMap` object. The `Delete` method requires that you specify the name of the map to delete. Let's delete the Courses_Map that you added in the previous section. Type the following statement in the Immediate window:

```
ActiveWorkbook.XmlMaps("Courses_Map").Delete
```

When you press Enter, Excel deletes the specified map. This map's name no longer appears in the XML Source task pane's drop-down list.

NOTE	*When you delete the map using the Delete button in the XML Maps dialog box, shown in Figure 28.12 earlier, Excel displays a message informing you "If you delete the specified XML map, you will no longer be able to import or export XML data using this XML map." You do not get this warning message when you delete the XML map programmatically.*

Exporting and Importing Data via an XML Map

Use the `XmlMap` object to export and import XML data. Use the `XmlMap` object's `Export` method for exporting and the `Import` method for importing. For example, to export the XML table data through the dataroot_Map that the Northwind employees XML table is mapped to, type the following statement on one line in the Immediate window:

```
ActiveWorkbook.XmlMaps("dataroot_Map").Export
    "C:\VBAExcel2021_XML\InternalContacts.xml"
```

When you press Enter, Excel creates the specified XML document in your VBAExcel2021_XML folder. If the file with the same name already exists in the destination folder, Excel displays an Automation error.

Excel also offers the `ExportXML` method for those situations when you'd rather export your XML data to a String variable instead of to a file as is done with the simple `Export` method. The following procedure demonstrates this:

```
Sub ExportToString()
  Dim strEmpData As String

  ActiveWorkbook.XmlMaps("dataroot_Map").ExportXml _
    Data: = strEmpData
  Debug.Print strEmpData
End Sub
```

To import new XML data into an XML map, copy the **Davolio.xml** document from the companion files to your VBAExcel2021_XML folder, and then in the Immediate window, enter the following statement on one line:

```
ActiveWorkbook.XmlMaps("dataroot_Map").Import
    URL: = "C:\VBAExcel2021_XML\Davolio.xml", Overwrite: = True
```

The `Overwrite` parameter specifies whether or not the newly imported data should overwrite existing data. The Davolio.xml file holds data for only one Northwind employee named Nancy Davolio. After running the above statement, the XML table in the Employees.xlsm workbook will contain only one record.

Binding an XML Map to an XML Data Source

Each XML map is bound to an XML data source. Use the `DataBinding` property of the `XMLMap` object to find out the name of the data source that is used in the XML map. For example, when you type the following statement in the Immediate window:

```
Debug.Print ActiveWorkbook.XmlMaps("dataroot_Map").DataBinding
```

Excel returns the following data source: C:\VBAExcel2021_XML\Davolio.xml. If you haven't run the statement in the previous section, you should see C:\VBA-Excel2021_XML\ Employees.xml as the data source.

It is possible to change the data source used by the XML map with the `LoadSettings` method of the `DataBinding` property as shown below. Be sure to enter this on one line in the Immediate window.

```
ActiveWorkbook.XmlMaps("dataroot_Map").DataBinding.LoadSettings
    ("C:\VBAExcel2021_XML\Employees.xml")
```

After changing the data source used by the XML map, you should refresh the data in your XML table (Employees.xlsm workbook) either via the user interface by clicking the Refresh Data button on the Developer tab, Refresh All button on the Data tab, or from code using the `Refresh` method (as shown in the next section).

Refreshing XML Tables from an XML Data Source

Use the `Refresh` method of the `DataBinding` property of the `XmlMap` object to refresh the XML table in your worksheet. The following statement can be used:

```
ActiveWorkbook.XmlMaps("dataroot_Map").DataBinding.Refresh
```

After running the above statement, the XML table in the worksheet should display all of the Northwind employee records.

VIEWING THE XML SCHEMA

To see the schema that is used by an XML map, use the `Schemas` collection of the `XmlMap` object. The `Schemas` property of the `XmlMap` object is used to return the `XmlSchemas` collection. The `XmlSchemas` collection contains `XmlSchema` objects. By using the `XML` property of the `XmlSchema` object, it is possible to return the string representing the content of the specified schema. Try out this code in the Immediate window:

```
Set objMap = ActiveWorkbook.XmlMaps(1)
Debug.Print objMap.Name
Debug.Print objMap.Schemas(1).Xml
```

If you'd like to use the above code fragment inside a VBA procedure, don't forget to declare the `objMap` variable with the following statement:

```
Dim objMap As XmlMap
```

NOTE	*By saving the text of the generated schema in a file, you can create a schema file for future use. To do this, open Notepad and paste the data returned by the* `Debug.Print objMap.Schemas(1).Xml` *statement. Next, save the Notepad file using any name you wish, but be sure to use the .xsd file extension.*

Now that you've acquired a useful vocabulary for programming tasks related to XML maps, let's write a full-fledged VBA procedure that will add an XML map to the current workbook, perform the mapping, and refresh the data. You can work with the current Employees.xlsm workbook that already has the dataroot_Map.

Hands-On 28.6 Using VBA to Program XML Maps

1. In the Visual Basic Editor screen, insert a new module in VBAProject (Employees.xlsm).
2. In the module's Code window, enter the AddNew_XMLMap procedure as shown below:

```
Sub AddNew_XMLMap()
    Dim lstCourses As ListObject
    Dim lstCol As ListColumn
    Dim objMap As XmlMap
    Dim mapName As String
    Dim strXPath As String

    On Error GoTo ErrorHandler

    ' Create a new XML map
    ActiveWorkbook.XmlMaps.Add _
        ("C:\VBAExcel2021_XML\Courses1.xml ", _
        "Courses").Name = "Courses_Map"

    'location for the new XML table
    Set objMap = ActiveWorkbook.XmlMaps("Courses_Map")
    Range("B20").Select

    ' Create a new List object
    Set lstCourses = ActiveSheet.ListObjects.Add

    ' Bind the first XML element to the first table column
    strXPath = "/Courses/Course/@ID"
    With lstCourses.ListColumns(1)
```

```
            .XPath.SetValue objMap, strXPath
            .Name = "ID"
        End With

        ' Add a column to the table
        ' and bind it to an XML node
        Set lstCol = lstCourses.ListColumns.Add
        strXPath = "/Courses/Course/Title"
        With lstCol
            .XPath.SetValue objMap, strXPath
            .Name = "Title"
        End With

        ' Add a column to the table
        ' and bind it to an XML node
        Set lstCol = lstCourses.ListColumns.Add

        strXPath = "/Courses/Course/Startdate"
        With lstCol
            .XPath.SetValue objMap, strXPath
            .Name = "Start Date"
        End With

        ' Add a column to the table
        ' and bind it to an XML node
        Set lstCol = lstCourses.ListColumns.Add

        strXPath = "/Courses/Course/Sessions"
        With lstCol
            .XPath.SetValue objMap, strXPath
            .Name = "Sessions"
        End With

        ' Set some XML properties
        With ActiveWorkbook.XmlMaps("Courses_Map")
            .ShowImportExportValidationErrors = False
            .AdjustColumnWidth = True
            .PreserveColumnFilter = True
            .PreserveNumberFormatting = True
            .AppendOnImport = False
        End With

        ' Refresh the XML table in the worksheet
        ActiveWorkbook.XmlMaps("Courses_Map").DataBinding.Refresh
    Exit Sub
```

```
ErrorHandler:
    MsgBox "The following error has occurred: " & vbCrLf _
    & Err.Description
End Sub
```

The above code begins by creating the XML map named "Courses_Map" using the Courses1.xml data file. Next, a new XML table is created in a worksheet. At this time, the table will contain just one column with the default name "Column1." We bind this column with the first item in the XML map—ID. The `XPath` object's `SetValue` method is used to bind data from an XML map to a table column. This method has two required arguments, `Map` and `XPath`. `Map` is the XML map that has been added to the workbook. In this example, it's the object variable named `objMap`. `XPath` is the `XPath` statement in the form of a String variable (`strXPath`) that specifies the XML map data you want to bind to the specified table column. Because the `ID` is an attribute, you must precede it with the "@" character. Once the ID is mapped to the table column, we replace the default column name with our own (ID), using the `Name` property of the `ListColumn` object:

```
strXPath = "/Courses/Course/@ID"
With lstCourses.ListColumns(1)
    .XPath.SetValue objMap, strXPath
    .Name = "ID"
End With
```

Next, we proceed to add another column to the table using the `Add` method of the ListColumns collection:

```
Set lstCol = lstCourses.ListColumns.Add
```

This column is then bound to the next item in the XML map—Title. Again, we use the `SetValue` method of the `XPath` object to do the binding:

```
strXPath = "/Courses/Course/Title"
With lstCol
    .XPath.SetValue objMap, strXPath
    .Name = "Title"
End With
```

In the same manner, we add two more columns to our table and bind each column to the remaining elements in the XML map. Next, we set some XML map properties and proceed to refresh the list. The empty table is now populated with the data from the source XML file (Courses1.xml).

3. Switch to the Microsoft Excel application window and choose **Developer | Macros** to open the Macro dialog box.

4. In the Macro dialog box, select **AddNew_XMLMap** and click the **Run** button.
5. Excel displays a message informing you that the specified XML source document does not have a schema and Excel will create one on the fly using the XML source data, as in Figure 28.7 earlier in this chapter.
6. Click **OK** to the message.
7. Excel adds the specified columns and performs the required data mappings; however, it stops and displays the message about incompatible formatting shown in Figure 28.20 when it gets to the mapping of the <Sessions> element.

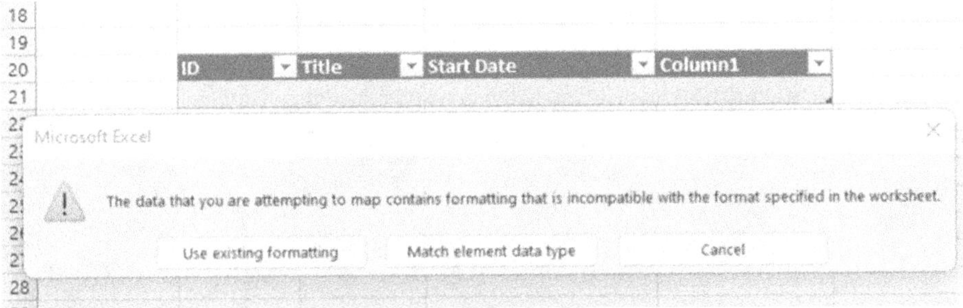

FIGURE 28.20 This warning message appears when the data type of the data being mapped is not compatible with the cell formatting.

When Excel determines that the cell formatting is not compatible with the data type specified in the XSD for the requested data element, you receive a warning message as shown in Figure 28.20. This dialog box contains the following buttons:

Use existing formatting	Click this button to ignore the data type in the XSD file.
Match element data type	Click this button to change the cell formatting to the appropriate type.
Cancel	Click this button to cancel mapping of this data element.

8. Click the **Match element data type** button to proceed with the data mapping. The resulting XML table and XML map are shown in Figure 28.21.

SIDEBAR *What Is XPath?*

XML Path Language (XPath) is a query language used to create expressions for finding data in the XML file. These expressions can manipulate strings, numbers, and Boolean values (true, false). They can also be used to navigate an XML tree structure and process its elements with XSL Transformations (XSLT) instructions. With XPath expressions, you can easily identify and extract from the XML document specific elements (nodes) based on their type, name, values, or the relationship of a node to other nodes (this is covered later in this chapter).

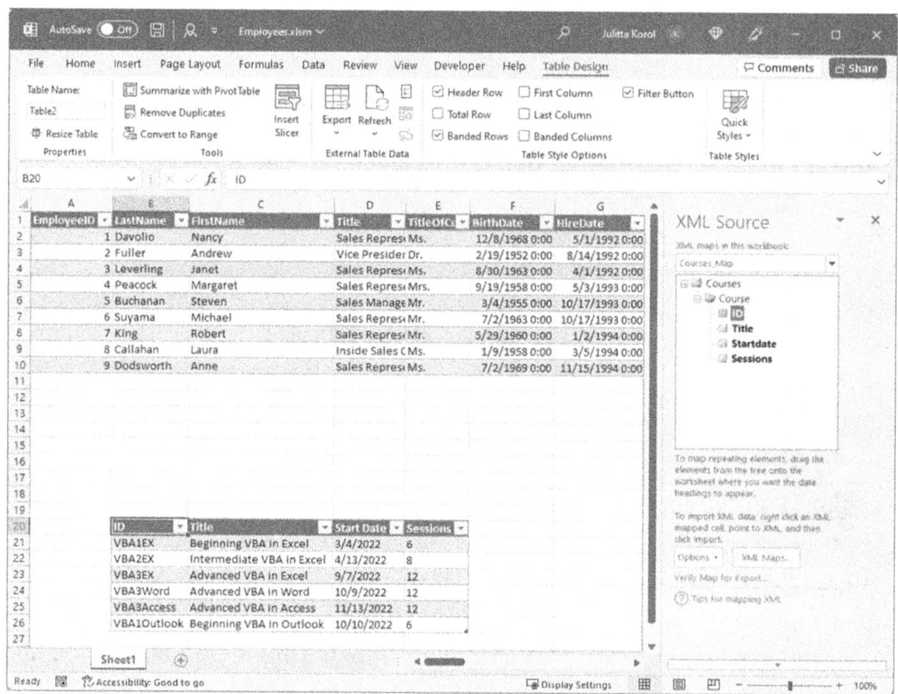

FIGURE 28.21 The Excel worksheet with two XML tables. The upper table was created via the user interface; the one at the bottom was generated programmatically. The XML Source task pane displays the Courses_Map with mapped data elements.

CREATING XML SCHEMA FILES

When you request that Excel create an XML map based on the specified XML data file, Excel informs you that the specified XML source data does not refer to a schema and therefore Excel will create a schema based on the XML source data. To obtain the schema information that Excel has generated during the XML mapping process, do the following:

1. Open the Immediate window and type the following statement:

```
? ThisWorkbook.XMLMaps(1).Schemas(1).xml
```

When you press **Enter**, the content of the schema appears in the Immediate window in the form of a very long string.

2. Highlight the retrieved schema text in the Immediate window, and press Ctrl+C to copy it to the clipboard.
3. Open Windows Notepad and press Ctrl+V to paste the data from the clipboard. You may want to format the data as shown in Figure 28.22 to make it easier to understand.
4. Save the file using any name but be sure to specify the .xsd file extension.
5. Close Notepad.

FIGURE 28.22 This XML schema was generated by Excel during the XML mapping of the XML data file.

USING XML EVENTS

Chapter 15 of this book focused on event-driven programming. This section expands your knowledge of Excel events by introducing you to events that occur before and after data is exported, imported, or refreshed via the XML map.

The `Workbook` object provides the following events: `AfterXMLExport`, `AfterXMLImport`, `BeforeXMLExport`, and `BeforeXMLImport`. By writing code for these events in the ThisWorkbook code module, you can fully control what happens before and after import, export, and refresh operations.

EventName: **AfterXMLExport**
This event applies to the `Workbook` object. It occurs after Microsoft Excel saves or exports XML data from the specified workbook. The following parameters are required:

- **Map**—The schema map that was used to save or export data
- **Url**—The location of the XML file that was exported
- **Result**—A constant indicating the result of the save or export operation. Use one of the following `xlXmlExportResult` constants:
  - `xlXmlExportSuccess`—Specifies that the XML data file was successfully exported
  - `xlXmlExportValidationFailed`—Specifies that the content of the XML data file does not match the specified schema map

```
Private Sub Workbook_AfterXMLExport _
    (ByVal Map As XmlMap, _
    ByVal Url As String, _
    ByVal Result As XlXmlExportResult)
    If Result = xlXmlExportSuccess Then
       MsgBox ("XML export succeeded.")
    Else
       MsgBox ("XML export failed.")
    End If
End Sub
```

Event Name: **AfterXMLImport**
This event applies to the `Workbook` object. It occurs after an existing XML data connection is refreshed or after new XML data is imported into the specified Microsoft Excel workbook.

The following parameters are required:

- **Map**—The XML map that will be used to import data
- **IsRefresh**—A Boolean value (True/False): `True` if the event was triggered by refreshing an existing connection to XML data; `False` if the event was triggered by importing from a different data source
- **Result**—A constant indicating the result of the refresh or import operation. Use one of the following `xlXmlImportResult` constants:
  - `xlXmlImportElementsTruncated`—Specifies that the content of the specified XML data file has been truncated because the XML data file is too large for the worksheet
  - `xlXmlImportSuccess`—Specifies that the XML data file was successfully imported
  - `xlXmlImportValidationFailed`—Specifies that the content of the XML data file does not match the specified schema map

```
Private Sub Workbook_AfterXMLImport _
    (ByVal Map As XmlMap, _
    ByVal IsRefresh As Boolean, _
    ByVal Result As XlXmlImportResult)
    If Result = xlXmlImportSuccess Then
        MsgBox ("XML import succeeded.")
        ActiveSheet.ListObjects(1).Range.Select
     Selection.Interior.ColorIndex = 35
     ActiveCell.Select
    Else
        MsgBox ("XML import failed.")
    End If
End Sub
```

Event Name: **BeforeXMLExport**
This event applies to the `Workbook` object. It occurs before Microsoft Excel saves or exports XML data from the specified workbook. This event occurs only when saving to an XML data file format; it does not occur when you are saving to the XML spreadsheet file format.

The following parameters are required:

- **Map**—The XML map that will be used to save or export data
- **Url**—The location where you want to export the resulting XML file
- **Cancel**—A Boolean value (True/False). Set to `True` to cancel the save or export operation

```
Private Sub Workbook_BeforeXMLExport _
    (ByVal Map As XmlMap, _
    ByVal Url As String, _
    Cancel As Boolean)

    If (Map.IsExportable) Then
        If MsgBox("Excel is about" & _
        " to export XML from the" & _
        Map.Name & "." & vbCrLf & "Do" & _
        " you want to continue?", _
        vbYesNo + vbQuestion, _
        "XML Export Process") = 7 Then
        Cancel = True
        End If
    End If
End Sub
```

Event Name: **BeforeXMLImport**

This event applies to the `Workbook` object. It occurs before an existing XML data connection is refreshed or before new XML data is imported into a Microsoft Excel workbook. The following parameters are required:

- **Map**—The XML map that will be used to import data
- **Url**—The location of the XML file to be imported
- **IsRefresh**—A Boolean value (True/False). `True` if the event was triggered by refreshing an existing connection to XML data; `False` if the event was triggered by importing from a different data source
- **Cancel**—A Boolean value (True/False). Set to `True` to cancel the import or refresh operation

```
Private Sub Workbook_BeforeXMLImport _
    (ByVal Map As XmlMap, _
    ByVal Url As String, _
    ByVal IsRefresh As Boolean, _
    Cancel As Boolean)

    If MsgBox("Excel is about " & _
       " to import XML into the" & _
       " workbook. Continue with" & _
       " importing?", _
       vbYesNo + vbQuestion, _
       "XML Import Process") = 7 Then
       Cancel = True
    End If
End Sub
```

The XML events are also available for the `Application` object. These events are listed below. Recall from Chapter 15 that event procedures for the `Application` object require that you create a new object using the `WithEvents` keyword in a class module.

- **WorkbookBeforeXmlExport**—Occurs before Microsoft Excel saves or exports XML data from the specified workbook. Use this event if you want to capture XML data that is being exported or saved from a particular workbook.
- **WorkbookAfterXmlExport**—Occurs after Microsoft Excel saves or exports XML data from the specified workbook. Use this event if you want to perform an operation after XML data has been exported from a particular workbook.
- **WorkbookBeforeXmlImport**—Occurs before an existing XML data connection is refreshed or new XML data is imported into any open Microsoft Excel workbook. Use this event if you want to capture XML data that is being imported or refreshed to a particular workbook.
- **WorkbookAfterXmlImport**—Occurs after an existing XML data connection is refreshed or new XML data is imported into any open Microsoft Excel workbook. Use this event if you want to perform an operation after XML data has been imported into a particular workbook.

THE XML DOCUMENT OBJECT MODEL

You can create, access, and manipulate XML documents programmatically via the XML Document Object Model (DOM). The DOM has properties and methods for interacting with XML documents. The XML DOM is supplied free with the browser. To use the XML DOM from your VBA procedures, you need to set up a reference to the MSXML Object library.

Hands-On 28.7 Setting up a Reference to DOM

1. In the Visual Basic Editor window of VBAProject (Empoyees.xlsm), choose **Tools | References.**
2. In the References dialog box, locate and select **Microsoft XML 6.0** as shown in Figure 28.23.
3. Click **OK** to close the References dialog box.
4. Now that you have the reference set, open the Object Browser, and examine the XML DOM's objects, methods, and properties, as shown in Figure 28.24.

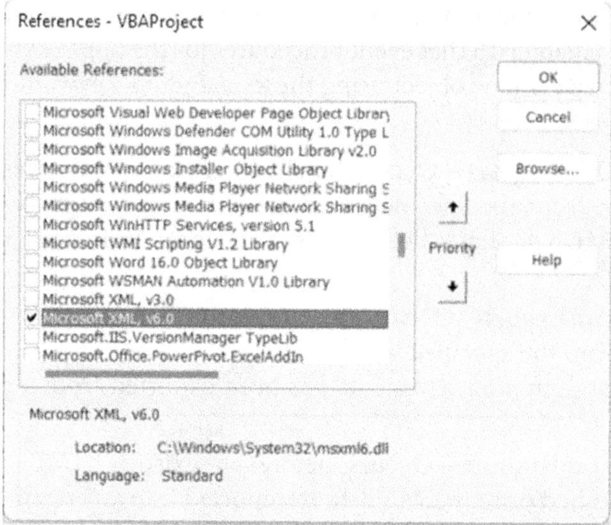

FIGURE 28.23 To work with XML documents programmatically, you need to establish a reference to the Microsoft XML type library.

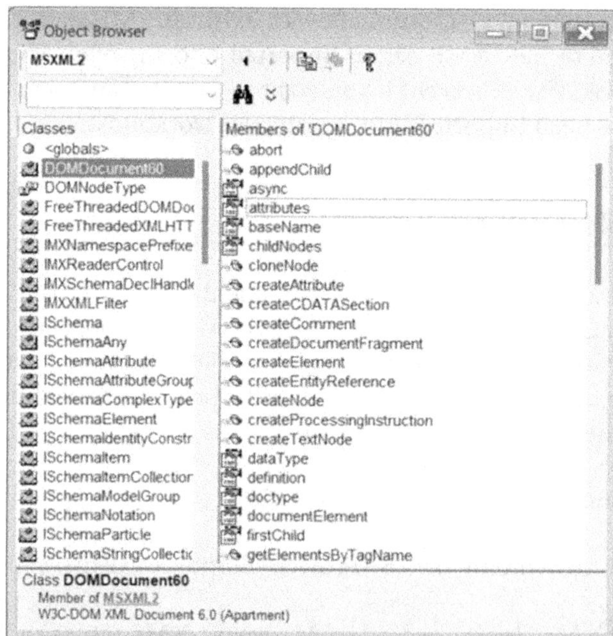

FIGURE 28.24 To see objects, properties, and methods exposed by the DOM, open the Object Browser after setting up a reference to the Microsoft XML type library, as shown in Figure 28.23.

5. Close the Object Browser.

The `DOMDocument60` object is the top level of the XML DOM hierarchy. This object represents a tree structure composed of nodes. You can navigate through this tree structure and manipulate the data contained in the nodes by using various methods and properties. The `DOMDocument60` object is the parent for all other elements in the DOM hierarchy. Because every XML object is created and accessed from the document, the `DOMDocument60` object must be created first.

To work with an XML document, you must create an instance of the `DOMDocument60` object, as in the following example:

```
Dim myXMLDoc As MSXM2.DOMDocument60
Set myXMLDoc = New MSXML2.DOMDocument60
```

To make the instantiated `DOMDocument60` object useful, you should load it with some data. The following Hands-On demonstrates how to get started with the XML DOM. You will perform the following tasks:

- Create an instance of the `DOMDocument60`.
- Load XML information from a file using the `Load` method.
- Use the `DOMDocument60` object's `XML` property to retrieve the raw data.
- Use the `DOMDocument60` object's `Text` property to retrieve the text stored in nodes.

Hands-On 28.8 Reading an XML Document with DOM

1. Enter the following Load_ReadXMLDoc procedure in a new module of VBAProject (Employees.xlsm):

```
Sub Load_ReadXMLDoc()
    Dim xmldoc As MSXML2.DOMDocument60

    ' Create an instance of the DOMDocument60
    Set xmldoc = New MSXML2.DOMDocument60

    ' Disable asynchronous loading
    xmldoc.async = False

    ' Load XML information from a file
    If xmldoc.Load("C:\VBAExcel2021_XML\Courses1.xml") Then
        ' Use the DOMDocument60 object's XML property to
        ' retrieve the raw data
        Debug.Print xmldoc.XML
        ' Use the DOMDocument60 object's Text property to
```

```
        ' retrieve the actual text stored in nodes
        Sheets.Add
        ActiveSheet.Range("A1").Value = xmldoc.Text
    End If
End Sub
```

The XML DOM has two methods for loading XML information: `Load` and `LoadXML`. Use the `Load` method to load XML information from a text file. Use the `LoadXML` method when loading from a string in memory.

MSXML uses an *asynchronous* loading mechanism by default for working with documents. Asynchronous loading allows you to perform other tasks during long database operations, such as providing feedback to the user as MSXML parses the XML file or giving the user the chance to cancel the operation. Before calling the `Load` method, however, it's a good idea to set the `Async` property of the `DOMDocument60` object to `False` to ensure that when the load returns, the entire document has finished loading. The `Load` method returns True if it successfully loaded the data and False otherwise.

Having loaded the data into a `DOMDocument60` object, you can use the `XML` property to retrieve the raw data or use the `Text` property to obtain the text stored in document nodes.

2. Run the Load_ReadXMLDoc procedure and examine its results in the Immediate window and in Sheet2 of the Employees.xlsm workbook. Cell A1 in Sheet2 should contain the entire string of data.

WORKING WITH XML DOCUMENT NODES

As you already know, the XML DOM represents a tree-based hierarchy of nodes. An XML document can contain nodes of different types. Some nodes represent comments and processing instructions in the XML document, and others hold the text content of a tag. To determine the type of node, use the `nodeType` property of the `IXMLDOMNode` object. Node types are identified by either a text string or a constant. For example, the node representing an element can be referred to as NODE_ELEMENT or 1, while the node representing the comment is named NODE_COMMENT or 8. See the MSXML2 library in the Object Browser shown in Figure 28.24 in the previous section for the names of other node types.

In addition to node types, nodes can have parent, child, and sibling nodes. The `hasChildNodes` method lets you determine if a `DOMDocument60` object has child nodes. There's also a `childNodes` property for retrieving a collection of child nodes. Before you start looping through the collection of child nodes, it's a good idea to use the `Length` property of the `IXMLDOMNode` to determine how many elements the collection contains.

The LearnAboutNodes procedure shown below will get you working with nodes programmatically in no time. The following example demonstrates how to experiment with XML document nodes.

Hands-On 28.9 Working with XML Document Nodes

1. In the Visual Basic Editor window of VBAProject (Employees.xlsm), insert a new module and enter the LearnAboutNodes procedure, as shown below:

```
Sub LearnAboutNodes()
    Dim xmldoc As MSXML2.DOMDocument60
    Dim xmlNode As MSXML2.IXMLDOMNode

    ' Create an instance of the DOMDocument60
    Set xmldoc = New MSXML2.DOMDocument60

    xmldoc.async = False

    ' Load XML information from a file
    xmldoc.Load ("C:\VBAExcel2021_XML\Courses1.xml")

    ' find out the number of child nodes in the document
    If xmldoc.hasChildNodes Then
        Debug.Print "Number of Child Nodes: " & _
        xmldoc.childNodes.Length

        ' iterate through the child nodes to gather information
        For Each xmlNode In xmldoc.childNodes
            Debug.Print "Node Name: " & xmlNode.nodeName
            Debug.Print vbTab & "Type: " & _
            xmlNode.nodeTypeString & _
            "(" & xmlNode.nodeType & ")"
            Debug.Print vbTab & "Text: " & xmlNode.Text
        Next xmlNode
    End If
End Sub
```

2. Run the LearnAboutNodes procedure in step mode by pressing **F8**.
   The LearnAboutNodes procedure prints to the Immediate window the information about child nodes found in the Courses1.xml document. Notice

that the `Text` property of a node returns all the text from all the node's children in one string (see the text for the Courses node below).

```
Number of Child Nodes: 2
Node Name: xml
    Type: processinginstruction(7)
    Text: version="1.0"
Node Name: Courses
    Type: element(1)
    Text: Beginning VBA in Excel 3/4/2022 6 Intermediate VBA in
Excel 4/13/2022 8 Advanced VBA in Excel 9/7/2022 12 Advanced
VBA in Word 10/9/2022 12 Advanced VBA in Access 11/13/2022 12
Beginning VBA in Outlook 10/10/2022 6
```

RETRIEVING INFORMATION FROM ELEMENT NODES

Let's assume that you want to read only the information from the text element nodes and place it in an Excel worksheet. Use the `getElementsByTagName` method of the `DOMDocument60` object to retrieve an `IXMLDOMNodeList` object containing all the element nodes.

The `getElementsByTagName` method takes one argument specifying the tag name to search for. You should use "*" as the tag to search for all the element nodes as illustrated in Hands-On 28.10. The following example demonstrates how to obtain data from an XML document's element nodes.

Hands-On 28.10 Obtaining Data from Element Nodes

1. In the Visual Basic Editor window of VBAProject (Employees.xlsm), insert a new module and enter the IterateThruElements procedure, as shown below:

```
Sub IterateThruElements()
    Dim xmldoc As MSXML2.DOMDocument60
    Dim xmlNodeList As MSXML2.IXMLDOMNodeList
    Dim xmlNode As MSXML2.IXMLDOMNode
    Dim myNode As MSXML2.IXMLDOMNode

    ' Create an instance of the DOMDocument60
    Set xmldoc = New MSXML2.DOMDocument60
    xmldoc.async = False

    ' Load XML information from a file
    xmldoc.Load ("C:\VBAExcel2021_XML\Courses1.xml")
```

```
    ' Find out the number of child nodes in the document
    Set xmlNodeList = xmldoc.getElementsByTagName("*")

    ' Open a new workbook and paste the data
    Workbooks.Add
    Range("A1:B1").Formula = Array("Element Name", "Text")
    For Each xmlNode In xmlNodeList
        For Each myNode In xmlNode.ChildNodes
            If myNode.nodeType = NODE_TEXT Then
             ActiveCell.Offset(0, 0).Formula = xmlNode.nodeName
                ActiveCell.Offset(0, 1).Formula = xmlNode.Text
            End If
        Next myNode
        ActiveCell.Offset(1, 0).Select
    Next xmlNode
    Columns("A:B").AutoFit
End Sub
```

2. Run the above procedure in step mode by pressing **F8**.
The IterateThruElements procedure fills in two worksheet columns with the XML element name and the corresponding text for all the text elements in the Courses1.xml document. The procedure result is shown in Figure 28.25. Notice that this procedure uses two `For Each...Next` loops. The first one (outer `For Each...Next` loop) iterates through the entire collection of element nodes. The second one (inner `For Each...Next` loop) uses the nodeType property to find only those element nodes that contain a single text node.

	A	B
1	Element Name	Text
2		
3	Title	Beginning VBA in Excel
4	Startdate	3/4/2022
5	Sessions	6
6		
7	Title	Intermediate VBA in Excel
8	Startdate	4/13/2022
9	Sessions	8
10		
11	Title	Advanced VBA in Excel
12	Startdate	9/7/2022
13	Sessions	12
14		
15	Title	Advanced VBA in Word
16	Startdate	10/9/2022
17	Sessions	12
18		
19	Title	Advanced VBA in Access
20	Startdate	11/13/2022
21	Sessions	12
22		
23	Title	Beginning VBA in Outlook
24	Startdate	10/10/2022
25	Sessions	6

FIGURE 28.25 You can programmatically retrieve information about element nodes from the XML document. The IterateThruElements procedure was used to create this worksheet.

To list all the nodes that match a specified criterion, use the `selectNodes` method. In the next example you will see how you can return to the Immediate window the text found in all Title nodes in the Courses1.xml file.

Hands-On 28.11 Obtaining Data from an Element Node Based on a Condition

1. In the Visual Basic Editor window of VBAProject (Employees.xlsm), insert a new module and enter the SelectNodes_SpecifyCriterion procedure, as shown below:

```
Sub SelectNodes_SpecifyCriterion()
    Dim xmldoc As MSXML2.DOMDocument60
    Dim xmlNodeList As MSXML2.IXMLDOMNodeList
    Dim myNode As Variant

    ' Create an instance of the DOMDocument60
    Set xmldoc = New MSXML2.DOMDocument60
    xmldoc.async = False

    ' Load XML information from a file
    xmldoc.Load ("C:\VBAExcel2021_XML\Courses1.xml")

    ' Retrieve all the nodes that match the specified criterion
    Set xmlNodeList = xmldoc.selectNodes("//Title")
    If Not (xmlNodeList Is Nothing) Then
        For Each myNode In xmlNodeList
            Debug.Print myNode.Text
        Next myNode
    End If
End Sub
```

   In the SelectNodes_SpecifyCriterion procedure, the `"//Title"` criterion of the `selectNodes` method looks for the element named "Title" at any level within the tree structure of the nodes.

2. Run the above procedure in step mode by pressing **F8**.
   Excel prints to the Immediate window only the names of the courses:

```
Beginning VBA in Excel
Intermediate VBA in Excel
Advanced VBA in Excel
Advanced VBA in Word
Advanced VBA in Access
Beginning VBA in Outlook
```

The criterion in the `selectNodes` method can be more complex. Let's assume that you are only interested in the title for the Course element with an ID of "VBA2EX." To retrieve this information, use the following statement:

```
Set xmlNodeList = xmldoc.selectNodes("//Course[@ID =
    'VBA2EX']//Title")
```

The above statement tells the XML processor to search for an element named "Course" at any level within the tree structure of nodes, find only the course element whose ID attribute contains the value of "VBA2EX," and return the Title element. To retrieve only the first node that meets the specified criterion, use the `selectSingleNode` method of the XML document. As the argument of this method, specify the string representing the node that you'd like to find. In the next example you will find the first node that matches the criterion `"//Title"` in the Courses1.xml document.

Hands-On 28.12 Finding a Specific Node

1. In the Visual Basic Editor window of VBAProject (Employees.xlsm), insert a new module and enter the Select_SingleNode procedure, as shown below:

```
Sub Select_SingleNode()
    Dim xmldoc As MSXML2.DOMDocument60
    Dim xmlSingleN As MSXML2.IXMLDOMNode

    ' Create an instance of the DOMDocument60
    Set xmldoc = New MSXML2.DOMDocument60
    xmldoc.async = False

    ' Load XML information from a file
    xmldoc.Load ("C:\VBAExcel2021_XML\Courses1.xml")

    ' Retrieve the reference to a particular node
    Set xmlSingleN = xmldoc.selectSingleNode("//Title")
    Debug.Print xmlSingleN.Text
End Sub
```

2. Run the above procedure in step mode by pressing **F8**.
   The result of this procedure is the text "Beginning VBA in Excel" written to the Immediate window.

   The following statements will retrieve the first Course node with the `ID` attribute:

```
Set xmlSingleN = xmldoc.selectSingleNode("//Course//@ID")
Debug.Print xmlSingleN.Text
```

If you replace the last two lines in the Select_SingleNode procedure with the above statements and run the procedure again, you should see the text "VBA1EX" in the Immediate window.

Once you find the correct node to work with, you can easily modify its value. For example, to change the text of the first Course element with the `ID` attribute, use the following lines of code:

```
Set xmlSingleN = xmldoc.selectSingleNode("//Course//@ID")
xmlSingleN.Text = "VBA1EX2010"
xmldoc.Save "C:\VBAExcel2021_XML\Courses1.xml"
```

Notice that to make a permanent change in the XML document, you must save it using the `Save` method.

When using the `selectSingleNode` method, you should use the `Is Nothing` conditional expression to determine whether a matching element was found in the loaded XML document, as demonstrated in the next example.

Hands-On 28.13 Using a Conditional Expression with an Element Node

1. In the Visual Basic Editor window of VBAProject (Employees.xlsm), insert a new module and enter the Select_SingleNode_2 procedure, as shown below:

```
Sub Select_SingleNode_2()
    Dim xmldoc As MSXML2.DOMDocument60
    Dim xmlSingleN As MSXML2.IXMLDOMNode

    ' Create an instance of the DOMDocument60
    Set xmldoc = New MSXML2.DOMDocument60
    xmldoc.async = False

    ' Load XML information from a file
    xmldoc.Load ("C:\VBAExcel2021_XML\Courses1.xml")

    ' Retrieve the reference to a particular node
    Set xmlSingleN = xmldoc.SelectSingleNode("//Course//@ID")
    If xmlSingleN Is Nothing Then
        Debug.Print "No nodes selected."
    Else
        Debug.Print xmlSingleN.Text
```

```
            xmlSingleN.Text = "VBA1EX2023"
            Debug.Print xmlSingleN.Text
            xmldoc.Save "C:\VBAExcel2021_XML\Courses1.xml"
        End If
    End Sub
```

2. Run the procedure in step mode by pressing **F8**.
   Excel prints to the Immediate window the text of the node before and after modification.
3. Replace the XPath expression `"//Course//@ID"` with **"//Cours//@ID"** and run the procedure again.
   You should see the text "No nodes selected" in the Immediate window.

SIDEBAR ***Using the built-in FilterXML Function to Retrieve Data from XML***

If you are planning to work a lot with XML, you will be thrilled to find out that Excel offers a powerful function called `FilterXML`. This function returns specific data from XML content by using the specified XPath expression:

```
FilterXML(xml, xpath)
```

`Xml` is a string in valid XML format. If xml is not valid, `FilterXML` will return #VALUE! error. `Xpath` is a string in standard XPath format.

The `FilterXML` function can be entered directly in a worksheet, or it can be called from VBA using the `WorksheetFunction` property of the Application object. To quickly learn how this function works, insert a new module in the Employees.xlsm workbook and enter the following VBA procedure:

```
Sub Load_ReadXMLDoc_FilterXML()
    Dim xmlDoc As MSXML2.DOMDocument60
    Dim retval As String

    ' Create an instance of the DOMDocument60
    Set xmlDoc = New MSXML2.DOMDocument60

    ' Disable asynchronous loading
    xmlDoc.async = False

    ' Load XML information from a file
    If xmlDoc.Load("C:\VBAExcel2021_XML\Courses1.xml") Then
        ' Use the DOMDocument60 object's XML property to
        ' retrieve the raw data to the worksheet
        Sheets.Add
        ActiveSheet.Range("A1").Value = xmlDoc.XML
        Columns("A:A").ColumnWidth = 65
```

```
        ' Use the built-in function FilterXML to
        ' retrieve data stored in a specific node
        ActiveSheet.Range("A4").Value = _
          WorksheetFunction.FilterXML( _
          Range("A1").Value, "//Course[@ID='VBA2EX']//Title")
    End If
End Sub
```

When you run this procedure, Excel loads the Courses1.xml file and adds a new worksheet to the Employees.xlsm workbook. The entire XML string is then placed in cell A1. Next, the specific data is retrieved from XML using the `FilterXML` function. Notice that the first argument of this function points to cell A1 containing the xml data and the second argument specifies that we want to retrieve the title element with the Course ID set to VBA2Ex. Cell A4 in the added worksheet should now contain the text *Intermediate VBA in Excel.*

NOTE	*Excel currently limits the number of characters per cell to 32,767 characters. While that seems like a lot, some XML files you may need to work with will exceed this limit and you will see the #Value! error value when you attempt to retrieve the data. You can overcome this limitation by writing additional procedures or functions to clean unnecessary characters from the XML to avoid exceeding the 32K character limit.*

NOTE	*XML DOM provides a number of other methods that make it possible to programmatically add or delete elements. Covering all of the details of the XML DOM is beyond the scope of this chapter. When you are ready for more information on this subject, please visit the following Web sites:* *http://www.w3.org/DOM/* *http://www.w3.org/XML/*

XML VIA ADO

Earlier in this book you learned how to retrieve external data using the ActiveX Data Objects (ADO). This section will show you what you can do with XML and ADO. You can save all types of recordsets as XML to a file on your computer. You can also save any type of ADO recordset to XML in memory using the ADO `Stream` object; however, that is not covered here.

Saving an ADO Recordset to Disk as XML

To save an ADO recordset as XML to a file, use the `Save` method of the `Recordset` object with the `adPersistXML` constant. The following example procedure demonstrates how to create XML files from ADO recordsets.

Hands-On 28.14 Saving an ADO Recordset as an XML Document

1. In the Visual Basic Editor window of VBAProject (Employees.xlsm), insert a new module.
2. Choose **Tools | References**. In the References dialog box, find and select the reference to the **Microsoft ActiveX Data Objects 6.1 Library** or earlier.
3. Click **OK** to close the References dialog box.
4. In the Code window of the new module, you added in Step 1, enter the SaveRst_ADO procedure, as shown below:

```
Sub SaveRst_ADO()
    Dim rst As ADODB.Recordset
    Dim conn As New ADODB.Connection
    Const strConn = "Provider = Microsoft.ACE.OLEDB.12.0;" _
    & "Data Source = C:\VBAExcel2021_ByExample\Northwind.mdb"

    ' Open a connection to the database
    conn.Open strConn

    ' Execute a select SQL statement against the database
    Set rst = conn.Execute("SELECT * FROM Products")

    ' Delete the file if it exists
    On Error Resume Next
    Kill "C:\VBAExcel2021_XML\Products.xml"

    ' Save the recordset as an XML file
    rst.Save "C:\VBAExcel2021_XML\Products.xml", adPersistXML

    rst.Close
    conn.Close
End Sub
```

The previous procedure establishes a connection to the sample Northwind.mdb database using the ADO Connection object. Next, it executes a `select` SQL statement against the database to retrieve all of the records from the Products table. Once the records are placed in a recordset, the `Save` method is called to store the recordset to a disk file. If the disk file already exists, the procedure deletes the existing file using the VBA `Kill` statement. The `On Error Resume Next` statement allows bypassing the `Kill` statement if the file that you are going to create does not yet exist.

5. Run the **SaveRst_ADO** procedure.
6. Use Notepad to open the **C:\VBAExcel2021_XML\Products.xml** file created by the SaveRst_ADO procedure.
   The file content is depicted in Figure 28.26.

XML files can be element-based or attribute-based. The XML files produced by ADO 2.5 or higher are all attribute-based. XML files generated by ADO are self-describing objects that contain data and metadata (information about the data). If you take a look at the Products.xml file in Figure 28.26, you will notice that below the XML document's root tag there are two children nodes: <s:Schema> and <rs:data>. The schema node describes the structure of the recordset, while the data node holds the actual data.

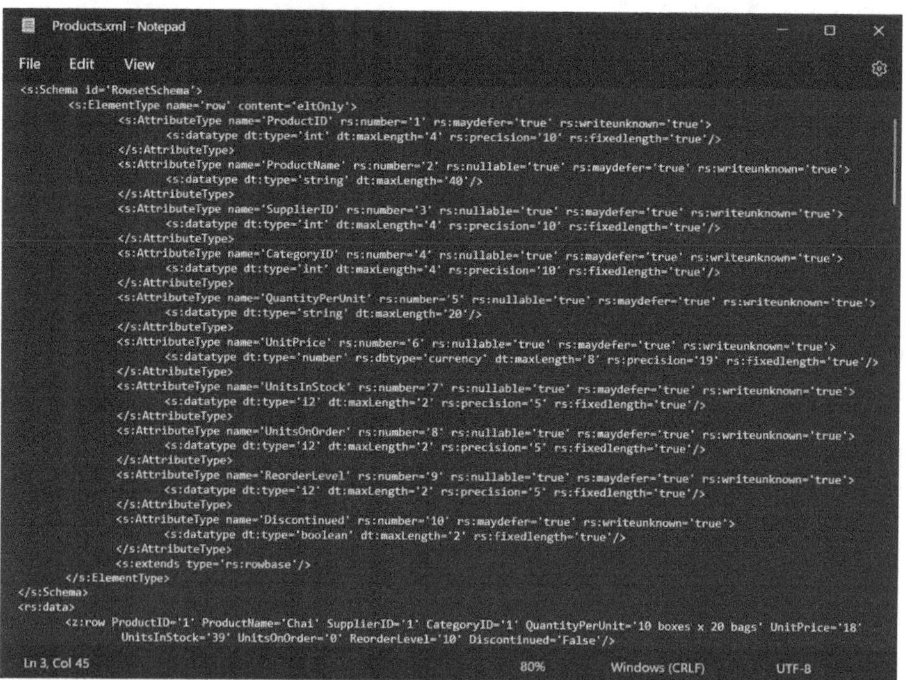

FIGURE 28.26 Saving a recordset to an XML file with the ADO produces an attribute-based XML file.

Between the <s:Schema id ="RowsetSchema"> and </s:Schema> tags, ADO places information about each column, including field name, position, data type and length, nullability, and whether the column is writable.

Notice that each field is represented by the <s:AttributeType> element. The value of the name attribute is the field name. The <s:AttributeType> element also has a child element, <s:datatype>, which holds information about its data type (integer, number, string, etc.) and the maximum field length.

Below the schema definition, you will find the actual data. The ADO schema represents each record using the <z:row> tag. The fields in a record are expressed as attributes of the <z:row> element. Every XML attribute is assigned a value that is enclosed in a pair of single or double quotation marks; however, if the value of a field in a record is NULL, the attribute on the <z:row> is not created. Notice that each record is written out in the following format:

```
<z:row ProductID='1' ProductName='Chai' SupplierID='1' CategoryID='1'
QuantityPerUnit='10 boxes x 20 bags' UnitPrice='18' UnitsInStock='39'
UnitsOnOrder='0' ReorderLevel='10' Discontinued='False'/>
```

The above code fragment is an attribute-based XML document. However, you may want to have each record written out as follows:

```
<Product>
   <ProductID>1</ProductID>
   <ProductName>Chai</ProductName>
   <SupplierID>1</SupplierID>
   <CategoryID>1</CategoryID>
   <QuantityPerUnit>10 boxes x 20 bags</QuantityPerUnit>
   <UnitPrice>18</UnitPrice>
   <UnitsInStock>39</UnitsInStock>
   <UnitsOnOrder>0</UnitsOnOrder>
   <ReorderLevel>10</ReorderLevel>
   <Discontinued>False</Discontinued>
</Product>
```

The above code fragment represents an element-based XML. Each record is wrapped in a <Product> tag, and each field is an element under the <Product> tag. You can write a stylesheet to transform attribute-based XML into element-based XML. Writing stylesheets and using XSL transformations are not covered in this book.

7. Close the Products.xml file and exit Notepad.

Loading an ADO Recordset

After saving an ADO recordset to an XML file, you can load it back and read it as if it were a database. To gain access to the records saved in the XML file, use the `Open` method of the `Recordset` object and specify the filename including its path and the persisted recordset service provider as `"Provider=MSPersist"`. Let's look at an example that demonstrates opening a persisted recordset.

Hands-On 28.15 Opening a Persisted Recordset with XML Data

1. In the Visual Basic Editor window of VBAProject (Employees.xlsm), insert a new module and enter the procedure OpenAdoFile, as shown below:

```
Sub OpenAdoFile()
    Dim rst As ADODB.Recordset
    Dim StartRange As Range
    Dim h As Integer

    ' Create a recordset and fill it with
    ' the data from the XML file
    Set rst = New ADODB.Recordset
    rst.Open "C:\VBAExcel2021_XML\Products.xml", _
    "Provider=MSPersist"

    ' Display the number of records
    MsgBox rst.RecordCount

    ' Open a new workbook
    Workbooks.Add

    ' Copy field names as headings to the first row
    ' of the worksheet
    For h = 1 To rst.fields.Count
        ActiveSheet.Cells(1, h).Value = rst.fields(h - 1).Name
    Next

    ' Specify the cell range to receive the data (A2)
    Set StartRange = ActiveSheet.Cells(2, 1)

    ' Copy the records from the recordset
    ' beginning in cell A2
    StartRange.CopyFromRecordset rst

    ' Autofit the columns to make the data fit
    Range("A1").CurrentRegion.Select
    Columns.AutoFit

    ' Close the workbook and save the file
    ActiveWorkbook.Close SaveChanges:=True, _
    Filename:="C:\VBAExcel2021_ByExample\Products.xlsx"
End Sub
```

The example procedure shown above creates a `Recordset` object and fills it with the data from the Products.xml file. After displaying the number of records in the file, the procedure opens a new workbook and fills the first worksheet row with field names. Next, the `CopyFromRecordset` method is used to retrieve all the records into the worksheet. After adjusting the size of the columns to fit the data, the workbook is saved using the default Excel 2021 file format (.xlsx).

2. Run the **OpenAdoFile** procedure.
3. Open the **Products.xlsx** file that was created by the OpenAdoFile procedure in your VBAExcel2021_ByExample folder.
4. You should see all of the records from the Products.xml document nicely arranged in rows and columns and therefore easy to analyze and make changes to.
5. Close the **Products.xlsx** file. Do not close the Employees.xlsm workbook as we will continue to use it in the next section.

Saving an ADO Recordset into the DOMDocument60 Object

You can save an ADO recordset directly into an XML `DOMDocument60` object using the following code:

```
Set xmlDoc = New MSXML2.DOMDocument60
rst.Save xmlDoc, adPersistXML
```

The next Hands-On exercise demonstrates how to use DOM to modify XML data in the recordset generated by the ADO `Save` method.

Hands-On 28.16 Modifying a Recordset Saved into the XML DOMDocument Object

1. In the Visual Basic Editor window of VBAProject (Employees.xlsm), insert a new module and enter the SaveToDOM procedure, as shown below:

```
Sub SaveToDOM()
    Dim conn As ADODB.Connection
    Dim rst As ADODB.Recordset
    Dim xmlDoc As MSXML2.DOMDocument60
    Dim myNode As IXMLDOMNode
    Dim strCurValue As String

    ' Declare constant used as database connection string
    Const strConn = "Provider=Microsoft.ACE.OLEDB.12.0;" _
    & "Data Source=C:\VBAExcel2021_ByExample\Northwind.mdb"
```

```
    ' Open a connection to the database
    Set conn = New ADODB.Connection
    conn.Open strConn

    ' Open the Shippers table
    Set rst = New ADODB.Recordset
    rst.Open "Shippers", conn, adOpenStatic, adLockOptimistic

    ' Create a new XML DOMDocument60 object
    Set xmlDoc = New MSXML2.DOMDocument60

    ' Add the default namespace declaration
    ' to the Namespace names of the DOMDocument60 object
    ' using the setProperty method of the DOMDocument60 object

    xmlDoc.setProperty "SelectionNamespaces", _
    "xmlns:rs='urn:schemas-microsoft-com:rowset'" & _
    " xmlns:z='#RowsetSchema'"


    ' Save the recordset directly into
    ' the XML DOMDocument60 object
    rst.Save xmlDoc, adPersistXML
    Debug.Print xmlDoc.XML

    ' Modify shipper's phone
    Set myNode = xmlDoc.selectSingleNode( _
    "//z:row[@CompanyName='Speedy Express']/@Phone")
    strCurValue = myNode.Text
    Debug.Print strCurValue
    myNode.Text = "(508)" & Right(strCurValue, 9)
    Debug.Print myNode.Text

    xmlDoc.Save "C:\VBAExcel2021_XML\Shippers_Modified.xml"

    ' Cleanup
    Set xmlDoc = Nothing
    Set conn = Nothing
    Set rst = Nothing
    Set myNode = Nothing
End Sub
```

After saving the recordset into the XML DOMDocument60 object, the procedure locates a node matching a specified search string by using the `selectSingleNode` method. Notice that the XPath expression used as an argument of this method searches for the `Phone` attribute in the z:row element nodes that have a `CompanyName` attribute set to `"Speedy Express"`:

```
Set myNode = xmlDoc.selectSingleNode( _
    "//z:row[@CompanyName='Speedy Express']/@Phone")
```

Once the required phone number is located, the procedure modifies the area code, as follows:

```
strCurValue = myNode.Text
myNode.Text = "(508)" & Right(strCurValue, 9)
```

If you'd rather remove the Phone entry completely, you could use the following code:

```
Set myNode = xmlDoc.selectSingleNode( _
    "//z:row[@CompanyName='Speedy Express']")
myNode.Attributes.removeNamedItem "Phone"
```

The `removeNamedItem` method removes an attribute from the attributes of a given node. This method requires one parameter: a string specifying the name of the attribute to remove from the collection.

2. Run the procedure in step mode by pressing **F8**. Make sure the Immediate window is open so you can see at once the results of various `Debug.Print` statements that the example procedure contains.
3. Use Notepad to open the **C:\VBAExcel2021_XML\Shippers_Modified.xml** file created by the **SaveToDOM** procedure.
   Notice the modified phone number for the Speedy Express record.
4. Close the Shippers_Modified.xml file and exit Notepad.
5. Close the **Employees.xlsm** workbook, saving changes when prompted.

UNDERSTANDING NAMESPACES

As mentioned earlier, XML is a markup language that uses custom tags. Because XML allows you to invent your own tag names to describe your data, how can you ensure that your tags will not conflict with someone else's tags when two or more XML documents are combined? The <TABLE> tag will certainly have a different meaning and content in an Excel XML document than the <TABLE> element used to describe different types of tables listed in a catalog for a furniture store. Fortunately, there is a way to differentiate elements and attributes that have the same name. The XML Namespaces specification ensures that element names do not conflict with one another and are unique within a particular set of names (a namespace).

A *namespace* is a collection of names in which all names are unique. The namespace is identified by a *Uniform Resource Identifier* (URI)—either a *Uniform Resource Locator* (URL) or a *Uniform Resource Name* (URN). Usually the namespace declaration is placed at the beginning of the XML document. There is no requirement for the specified URI to be valid or for it to conform to any sort of specification. Most namespaces use URIs for the namespace names because URIs are guaranteed to be unique.

Take a look at the following lines in the Shippers_Modified.xml file that was created in Hands-On 28.16:

```
<xml xmlns:s="uuid:BDC6E3F0-6DA3-11d1-A2A3-00AA00C14882"
xmlns:dt="uuid:C2F41010-65B3-11d1-A29F-00AA00C14882"
xmlns:rs="urn:schemas-microsoft-com:rowset"
xmlns:z="#RowsetSchema">
```

Namespaces can be declared in any element by using the `xmlns` attribute. A namespace whose `xmlns` attribute is not followed by a prefix is referred to as a *default namespace.* Therefore, elements or attributes with no prefix will be assumed to be part of the default namespace. In the above example, there are four namespaces, each of which is associated with a particular prefix ("s", "dt", "rs", and "z"). In the XML document, these prefixes are used in front of element and attribute names to indicate which namespace they are referencing. In other words, anything with an "s" in front of it applies to the uuid:BDC6E3F0-6DA3-11d1-A2A3-00AA00C14882 namespace, and anything marked with the "z" prefix references the RowsetSchema namespace.

What you should remember from this section is that namespaces don't really exist. They are arbitrary names that allow you to distinguish between tags with the same names that need to be processed differently. Namespaces prevent naming conflicts that might arise in XML documents.

UNDERSTANDING OPEN XML FILES

Since the release of Excel 2007, all workbook files are saved in an XML file format by default. This file format known as *Open XML* uses four-letter file extensions (.xlsx, .xlsm, .xltx, .xltm, and .xlam).

The first two letters of the file extension refer to the application, in this case, xl=Excel. The third letter (s/t/a) indicates the specific file type: s=spreadsheet;

t=template; and a=add-in. The last letter (x/m) specifies whether the file format supports macros: x=macro-free file; m=macro-enabled file.

The Open XML file is actually a compressed zip file. A zip file contains one or more files that have been compressed to reduce their file size. By changing the Excel file extension to .zip, you can take a look inside the zip container using WinZip or another zip-aware tool, or use the built-in compressed folders feature in Windows.

The Open XML file format gives developers the ability to directly edit the workbook without the need to open Excel. This means that you can work with the file content without having an Excel application installed on your computer. The same applies to Word and PowerPoint documents that follow the same Open Packaging Conventions (OPC) specification. You can easily insert new data, edit existing data, modify document properties, and add or remove specific XML parts.

This section takes a detailed look inside the compressed file, known as a *package*. Figure 28.27 shows the contents of the Chap28_VBAExcel2021.xlsm workbook file you created in this chapter.

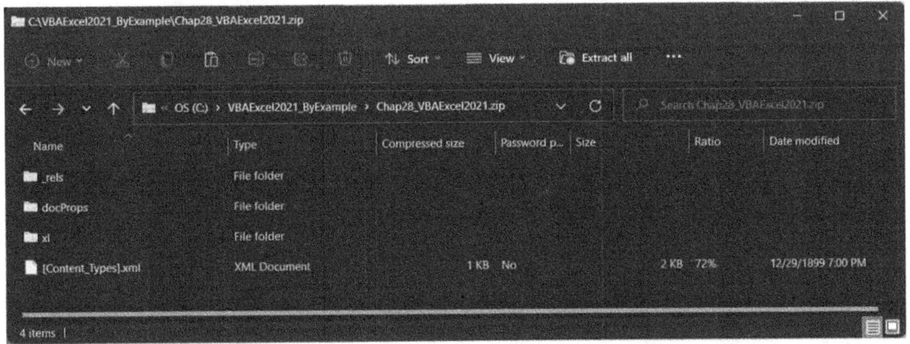

FIGURE 28.27 A sample Excel 2021 workbook is shown here after renaming the file with a .zip extension and opening it with Compressed folders in File Explorer.

The package file contains a number of documents called "parts" grouped into various folders. Every part has a defined content type that describes whether it's a worksheet, image, sound, or other binary object. Some types of parts are shared across all Office applications; others are unique to the application. For example, a worksheet part can only be found in an Excel file. While most parts are XML documents, some parts such as images, VBA projects, or embedded OLE objects are stored in their native format as binary files. Every part within a container package is connected to at least one other part using a special part referred to as a relationship. A relationship file is an XML document with a .rels extension.

At the root level in Figure 28.27, you will notice three folders named _rels, docProps, and xl, and an XML file called [Content_Types].xml.

- The [Content_Types].xml file—This XML file lists the types of files that are included in the package. The example Excel file package contains the following content types:

```
<Types xmlns="http://schemas.openxmlformats.org/package/2006/
content-types">
<Default Extension="rels" ContentType="application/vnd.
openxmlformats-package.relationships+xml"/>
<Default Extension="xml" ContentType="application/xml"/>
<Override PartName="/xl/workbook.xml" ContentType="application/
vnd.ms-excel.sheet.macroEnabled.main+xml"/>
<Override PartName="/xl/worksheets/sheet1.
xml" ContentType="application/vnd.openxmlformats-officedocument.
spreadsheetml.worksheet+xml"/>
<Override PartName="/xl/theme/theme1.
xml" ContentType="application/vnd.openxmlformats-officedocument.
theme+xml"/>
<Override PartName="/xl/connections.
xml" ContentType="application/vnd.openxmlformats-officedocument.
spreadsheetml.connections+xml"/>
<Override PartName="/xl/styles.xml" ContentType="application/
vnd.openxmlformats-officedocument.spreadsheetml.styles+xml"/>
<Override PartName="/xl/sharedStrings.
xml" ContentType="application/vnd.openxmlformats-officedocument.
spreadsheetml.sharedStrings+xml"/>
<Override PartName="/xl/tables/table1.
xml" ContentType="application/vnd.openxmlformats-officedocument.
spreadsheetml.table+xml"/>
<Override PartName="/docProps/core.
xml" ContentType="application/vnd.openxmlformats-package.core-
properties+xml"/>
<Override PartName="/docProps/app.xml" ContentType="application/
vnd.openxmlformats-officedocument.extended-properties+xml"/>
</Types>
```

- The _rels folder—The parts listed in the Excel package are linked together via relationships. The .rels file in the _rels folder defines the package relationships. You will see here relationships between document properties files, docProps/app.xml and docProps/core.xml, and the xl/workbook.

xml file. Parts that are related to other parts contain a _rels subfolder. Within this subfolder you will find a .rels file that describes the relationships. The name of the relationship consists of the filename of the original part and the .rels extension. For example, for the Workbook.xml file in the xl folder there is a relationship file named Workbook.xml.rels in the xl_rels folder.

```
<?xml version="1.0" encoding="UTF-8" standalone="yes"?>
<Relationships xmlns="http://schemas.openxmlformats.org/package/2006/relationships"> <Relationship Id="rId3" Type="http://schemas.openxmlformats.org/officeDocument/ 2006/ relationships/extended-properties" Target="docProps/app.xml"/><Relationship Id="rId2" Type="http://schemas.openxmlformats.org/package/2006/relationships/metadata/core-properties" Target="docProps/core.xml"/><Relationship Id="rId1" Type="http://schemas.openxmlformats.org/officeDocument/2006/relationships/officeDocument" Target="xl/workbook.xml"/></Relationships>
```

- The docProps folder—This folder contains two document properties files that were referenced in the .rels file: app.xml and core.xml. These properties files store information that you enter in Excel when you click the File tab and choose Info and then Properties. The core.xml part consists of properties such as the document title, subject, and author. The app.xml part stores application-specific properties such as the name and the version of the application, company name, and others, as shown below:

```
<Properties xmlns="http://schemas.openxmlformats.org/
officeDocument/2006/extended-properties" xmlns:vt="http://
schemas.openxmlformats.org/officeDocument/2006/docPropsVTypes">
<Application>Microsoft Excel</Application>
<DocSecurity>0</DocSecurity>
<ScaleCrop>false</ScaleCrop>
<HeadingPairs>
<vt:vector size="2" baseType="variant">
<vt:variant>
<vt:lpstr>Worksheets</vt:lpstr>
</vt:variant>
<vt:variant>
<vt:i4>1</vt:i4>
</vt:variant>
</vt:vector>
</HeadingPairs>
```

```
<TitlesOfParts>
<vt:vector size="1" baseType="lpstr">
<vt:lpstr>Sheet1</vt:lpstr>
</vt:vector>
</TitlesOfParts>
<LinksUpToDate>false</LinksUpToDate>
<SharedDoc>false</SharedDoc>
<HyperlinksChanged>false</HyperlinksChanged>
<AppVersion>16.0300</AppVersion>
</Properties>
```

- The xl folder—This is the application folder for the program that was used to create the file, in this case, Excel. This folder contains application-specific document files organized in various subfolders. Figure 28.28 shows the root level of the xl folder containing the workbook part, sharedStrings part, vbaProject part, and the styles part. The sharedStrings.xml part stores all of the strings used in the entire workbook. If you change a string in this file, the change will be applied to every occurrence of the string in your workbook.

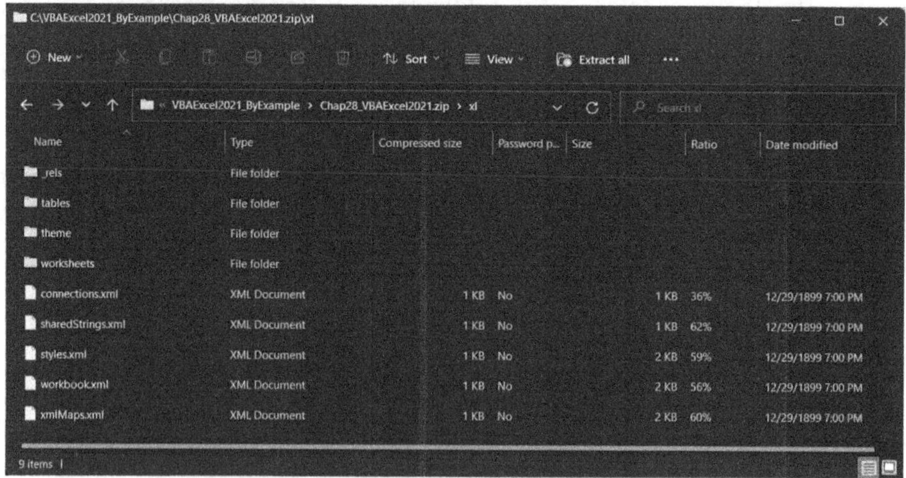

FIGURE 28.28 The contents of the xl folder.

The worksheets folder within the xl folder contains a separate XML part for every worksheet; in this case, sheet1.xml (Figure 28.29).

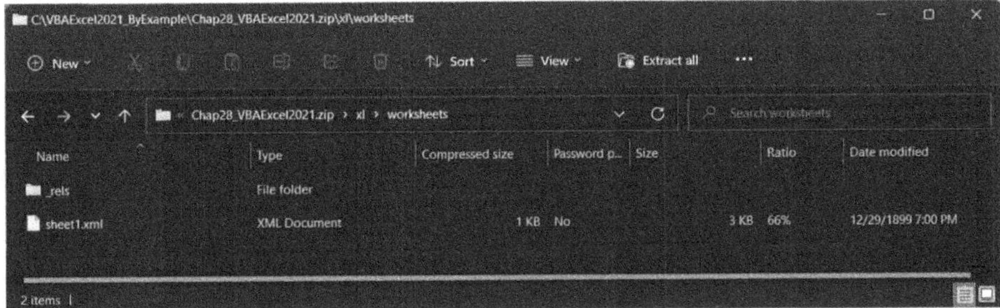

FIGURE 28.29 The contents of the worksheets folder.

Figure 28.30 shows the contents of the sheet1.xml part.

```
▼<worksheet xmlns="http://schemas.openxmlformats.org/spreadsheetml/2006/main" xmlns:r="http://schemas.openxmlformats.org/officeDocument/2006/relationships"
 xmlns:mc="http://schemas.openxmlformats.org/markup-compatibility/2006" xmlns:x14ac="http://schemas.microsoft.com/office/spreadsheetml/2009/9/ac"
 xmlns:xr="http://schemas.microsoft.com/office/spreadsheetml/2014/revision" xmlns:xr2="http://schemas.microsoft.com/office/spreadsheetml/2015/revision2"
 xmlns:xr3="http://schemas.microsoft.com/office/spreadsheetml/2016/revision3" mc:Ignorable="x14ac xr xr2 xr3" xr:uid="{00000000-0001-0000-0000-000000000000}">
  <dimension ref="A1:D7"/>
 ▼<sheetViews>
    <sheetView tabSelected="1" workbookViewId="0"/>
  </sheetViews>
  <sheetFormatPr defaultRowHeight="14.4" x14ac:dyDescent="0.3"/>
 ▼<cols>
    <col min="1" max="1" width="11.88671875" bestFit="1" customWidth="1"/>
    <col min="2" max="2" width="22.21875" bestFit="1" customWidth="1"/>
    <col min="3" max="3" width="11" bestFit="1" customWidth="1"/>
    <col min="4" max="4" width="10.21875" bestFit="1" customWidth="1"/>
  </cols>
 ▼<sheetData>
  ▼<row r="1" spans="1:4" x14ac:dyDescent="0.3">
   ▼<c r="A1" t="s">
      <v>0</v>
    </c>
   ▼<c r="B1" t="s">
      <v>1</v>
    </c>
   ▼<c r="C1" t="s">
      <v>2</v>
    </c>
   ▼<c r="D1" t="s">
      <v>3</v>
    </c>
   </row>
  ►<row r="2" spans="1:4" x14ac:dyDescent="0.3">
   ...
   </row>
  ►<row r="3" spans="1:4" x14ac:dyDescent="0.3">
   ...
   </row>
  ►<row r="4" spans="1:4" x14ac:dyDescent="0.3">
   ...
   </row>
  ►<row r="5" spans="1:4" x14ac:dyDescent="0.3">
   ...
   </row>
  ►<row r="6" spans="1:4" x14ac:dyDescent="0.3">
   ...
   </row>
  ►<row r="7" spans="1:4" x14ac:dyDescent="0.3">
   ...
   </row>
  </sheetData>
  <pageMargins left="0.7" right="0.7" top="0.75" bottom="0.75" header="0.3" footer="0.3"/>
 ▼<tableParts count="1">
    <tablePart r:id="rId1"/>
  </tableParts>
</worksheet>
```

FIGURE 28.30 The contents of the sheet1.xml file in the Chap28_VBAExcel2021.xlsm workbook.

Notice that all the sheet data is contained within the <sheetData> element. Each data row has its own <row> element and an index (`r` attribute). Rows use a `span` attribute to indicate the number of cells occupied. Other attributes may be used to indicate row style or custom formatting. Cell values are stored in the `c` element. The `r` attribute holds the cell address using the A1 reference style notation (e.g., "A2", "B2"); the `s` attribute indicates which style was used.

The numbers used in the `style` attribute are described in the xl/styles.xml part. The `t` attribute indicates a data type (String, Number, or Boolean). For example, t="s" denotes that the underlying value is a string, not a number. String values are not stored in cells unless they are the result of a calculation. They are stored in the sharedStrings.xml part. Each unique text value found within a workbook is listed only once in this part. This prevents duplication of information, saves space, and speeds up loading and saving workbooks. If the cell value is textual, then the numeric value inside the `v` element is an index to a particular string in the sharedStrings.xml document.

You can easily replace the sharedStrings file in the package with a file containing strings from another language, thus providing multiple language support for your spreadsheet users.

After this short overview of the internals of the Open XML file format, let's spend some time putting this newfound knowledge to practical use. The next section will introduce you to working with XML document parts programmatically.

MANIPULATING OPEN XML FILES WITH VBA

Earlier in this chapter you learned how to work with XML document nodes using the XML DOM. In this section, you will learn how to use the DOM objects, properties, and functions, and XPath expressions to augment some of the XML parts found in the Excel workbook. Working with the XML document parts requires that you first learn how to programmatically zip and unzip Excel workbook files.

Hands-On 28.17 Unzipping an Excel Workbook with VBA

1. Copy the **SupportedEquipment.xlsx** workbook from the companion files to your **VBAExcel2021_ByExample** folder.
2. Open a new Microsoft Excel workbook and save it in a macro-enabled format as **C:\VBAExcel2021_ByExample\ManipulateXMLParts.xlsm**.
3. Press **Alt+F11** to activate the Visual Basic Editor and select **VBAProject (ManipulateXMLParts.xlsm)** in the Project Explorer window.
4. Choose **Insert | Module.**
5. Choose **Tools | References**. In the Available References listbox, select **Microsoft XML, v6.0** or earlier object library, and click **OK** to exit the References dialog box.

6. In the Code window of VBAProject (ManipulateXMLParts.xlsm), enter the variable declaration and the UnizpExcelFile procedure code that follows:

```
' Declare a module-level variable
Public blnIsFileSelected As Boolean

Sub UnzipExcelFile()
    Dim objShell As Object
    Dim strZipFile, strZipFolder, strSourceFile, objFile
    Dim strStartDir As String

    strStartDir = "C:\VBAExcel2021_ByExample"
    'change folder
    If ActiveWorkbook.Path <> strStartDir Then
        ChDir strStartDir
    End If

    ' get Excel file to unzip
    strSourceFile = Application.GetOpenFilename _
    (FileFilter:="Excel Files (*.xlsx; *.xlsm), *.xlsx; *.xlsm", _
    Title:="Select Excel file you want to unzip")

    'exit if file was not selected
    If strSourceFile = False Then
        blnIsFileSelected = False
        Exit Sub
    End If

    blnIsFileSelected = True
    strZipFile = strSourceFile & ".zip"

    'create the zip file
    FileCopy strSourceFile, strZipFile

    'Create new folder to store unzipped files
    strZipFolder = "C:\VBAExcel2021_ByExample\ZipPackage"
    On Error Resume Next
    MkDir strZipFolder

    'Copy package files to the ZipPackage folder
    Set objShell = CreateObject("Shell.Application")

    For Each objFile In objShell.Namespace(strZipFile).items
        objShell.Namespace(strZipFolder).CopyHere (objFile)
    Next objFile
```

```
    'Activate Windows Explorer
    Shell "Explorer.exe /e," & strZipFolder, vbNormalFocus

    'remove the zip file and release resources
    Kill strZipFile
    Set objShell = Nothing
End Sub
```

The above example procedure asks the user for an Excel file to unzip using the `GetOpenFilename` method of the Application object. After the file is selected, the `FileCopy` statement copies this file to another file with a .zip extension. This way, you can work with the temporary zip file without changing the original file. Next, the procedure uses the `MkDir` statement to create a destination folder named ZipPackage for the zip archive. A Shell.Application object is then created and used for accessing the Windows filesystem. Its `CopyHere` method copies files to the zip folder returned by the `Namespace` method. Once all the files have been copied, the procedure activates the File Explorer. The "`/e`" parameter of the `Shell` function is used to display the files in the list view. The procedure ends by deleting the temporary zip file using the VBA `Kill` statement.

7. Run the **UnzipExcelFile** procedure. When prompted to select the file to unzip, choose the **SupportedEquipment.xlsx** workbook from your C:\VBAExcel2021_ByExample folder. The File Explorer window will pop up automatically when the unzip process is complete.

After making changes to the XML parts (as shown in subsequent Hands-On exercises), you will need to zip the files back into the Excel container before you can open the modified file in Excel.

The next Hands-On demonstrates how you can perform the zip operation with VBA.

Hands-On 28.18 Zipping Files to Create an Excel 2021 Package Container

1. In the same module where you entered the UnzipExcelFile procedure in the previous Hands-On, enter the following two procedures: CreateEmptyZipFile and ZipToExcel:

```
Sub CreateEmptyZipFile(strFileName As String)
    Dim strHeader As String
    Dim fso As Object
```

```
    strHeader = Chr$(80) & Chr$(75) & Chr$(5) & Chr$(6) & _
        String(18, 0)

    ' delete the file if it already exists
    If Len(Dir(strFileName)) > 0 Then
        Kill strFileName
    End If

    ' add a required header
    Set fso = CreateObject("Scripting.FileSystemObject")
    fso.CreateTextFile(strFileName).Write strHeader
End Sub
```

The above procedure uses the `CreateTextFile` method of the Scripting. FileSystemObject to create an empty zip container. The `Write` method is used to add a required header to the file so Windows can recognize the file as a zip archive. The following procedure (ZipToExcel) will fill the file with the files found in the specified folder.

```
Sub ZipToExcel()
    Dim objShell As Object
    Dim strZipFile, strZipFolder, objFile
    Dim strStartDir As String
    Dim strExcelFile As String
    Dim mFlag As Boolean

    strZipFolder = "C:\VBAExcel2021_ByExample\ZipPackage"
   strZipFile = "C:\VBAExcel2021_ByExample\PackageModified.zip"
    mFlag = False

    'check if folder is empty
    If Len(Dir(strZipFolder & "\*.*")) < 1 Then
        MsgBox "There are no files to zip."
        Exit Sub
    End If

    ' check if a VBA project exists
    If Len(Dir(strZipFolder & "\xl\vbaProject.bin")) > 0 Then
        mFlag = True
    End If

    'Create an empty zip file
    CreateEmptyZipFile (strZipFile)

    'Copy files from strZipFolder to the strZipFile
```

```
    On Error Resume Next
    Set objShell = CreateObject("Shell.Application")

    For Each objFile In objShell.Namespace(strZipFolder).items
        objShell.Namespace(strZipFile).CopyHere (objFile)
        Application.Wait (Now + TimeValue("0:00:10"))
    Next objFile

    'Create Excel file name
    If mFlag Then
        strExcelFile = Replace(strZipFile, ".zip", ".xlsm")
    Else
        strExcelFile = Replace(strZipFile, ".zip", ".xlsx")
    End If

    'Rename the strZipFile
    Name strZipFile As strExcelFile

    Set objShell = Nothing
    Set objFile = Nothing

    MsgBox "Zipping process completed."
End Sub
```

The above procedure starts by designating ZipPackage as the zip folder name and PackageModified.zip as the target zip file. Before we go ahead with the copy operation, we perform two checks. First, we want to exit the procedure if there are no files in the zip folder. Second, we check for the existence of the vbaProject.bin file in the xl folder of the zip folder. Based on this test we will assign a macro-free or macro-enabled Excel format to the destination file later in the procedure when we rename the zip archive. If there are files in the zip folder, we call the CreateEmptyZipFile procedure to create an empty zip container. Next, we use the `CopyHere` method of the Shell.Application object (discussed in Hands-On 28.17) to copy files into the zip archive. Copying and compressing files can take some time, so we use the `Application.Wait` statement to wait 10 seconds between each copy operation. If the procedure ends before the files are copied, you may end up with a corrupt file when you try to open it in Excel. When the files have been copied into a zip container, we rename the file with the .xlsx or .xlsm extension.

2. Run the **ZipToExcel** procedure.
   When the procedure has executed, you should see the PackageModified.xlsx workbook file in your VBAExcel2021_ByExample folder. Because we have not

yet made any changes to the XML parts contained in the SupportedEquipment.xlsx file that was unzipped in Hands-On 28.17, the PackageModified.xlsx file should contain the same content as this file.

3. Open **PackageModified.xlsx** in Microsoft Excel to ensure that the file is not corrupted. If you get a message indicating file corruption, you must modify the procedure to pause the ZipToExcel procedure for a couple of seconds longer to allow each file to be completely compressed and saved.
4. Close the **PackageModified.xlsx** workbook.
5. Delete the **PackageModified.xlsx** workbook from your VBAExcel2021_ByExample folder.

In the next three Hands-On examples, we will utilize both the zip and unzip procedures from Hands-On 28.17 and 28.18 to modify some XML parts in the Excel zip archive. The procedure in Hands-On 28.19 demonstrates how to retrieve to a worksheet the unique text values that are stored in the sharedStrings.xml part shown in Figure 28.31.

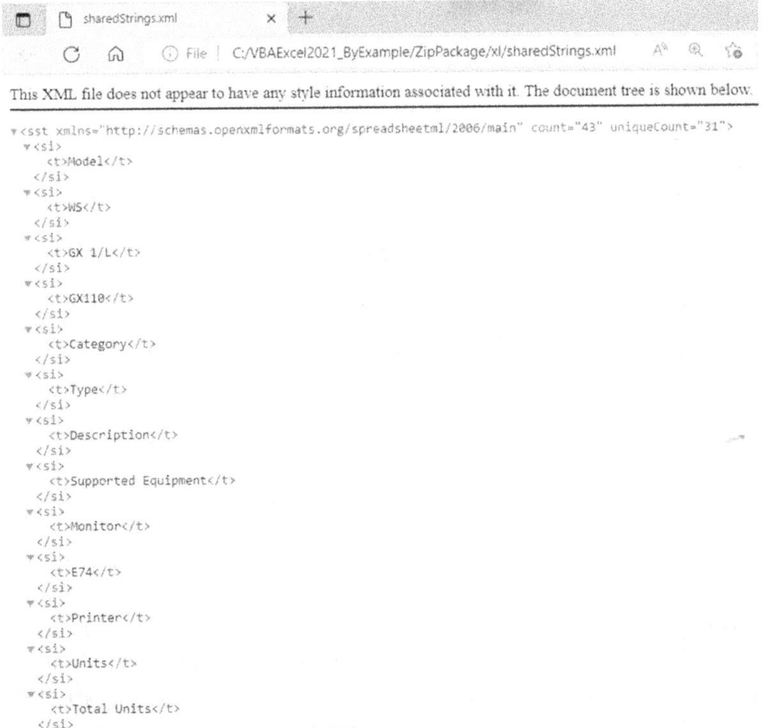

FIGURE 28.31 Partial content of the sharedStrings.xml part in the SupportedEquipment.xlsx workbook.

Hands-On 28.19 Retrieving Unique Text Values from the sharedStrings XML File

1. Insert a new module in VBAProject (ManipulateXMLParts.xlsm), and in the Code window, enter the following ListUniqueValues procedure:

```
Sub ListUniqueValues()
    Dim xmlDoc As MSXML2.DOMDocument60
    Dim myNodeList As MSXML2.IXMLDOMNodeList
    Dim i As Integer
    Dim strFile As String
    Dim strFolder As String
    Dim xNode As Variant
    Dim cNode As Variant

    i = 1
    strFolder = "C:\VBAExcel2021_ByExample\ZipPackage\xl\"
    strFile = "sharedStrings.xml"

    Set xmlDoc = New MSXML2.DOMDocument60
    xmlDoc.async = False
    xmlDoc.Load strFolder & strFile
    Set myNodeList = xmlDoc.ChildNodes

    Worksheets(1).Activate
    'Iterate over the elements and print their Text property
    For Each xNode In xmlDoc.ChildNodes
     '  only look at type=NODE_ELEMENT
        If xNode.NodeType = 1 Then
            For Each cNode In xNode.ChildNodes
                ActiveSheet.Cells(i, 1).Value = cNode.Text
                i = i + 1
            Next
        End If
    Next
    Columns("A").AutoFit
    Set myNodeList = Nothing
    Set xmlDoc = Nothing
End Sub
```

The above procedure uses the `Load` method of the `DOMDocument60` object to open the sharedStrings.xml file. For this procedure to run, you must set a reference to the Microsoft XML object library as you already did in Hands-On 29-17. The procedure retrieves the text property of all the child nodes and writes them into a worksheet.

2. Ensure that the VBAExcel2021_ByExample folder contains the folder named ZipPackage with XML parts. If this folder is missing, run the procedure in Hands-On 28.17.
3. Run the **ListUniqueValues** procedure.
   The result of the procedure is the list of unique text values that were originally entered in the SupportedEquipment.xlsx workbook and stored in the sharedStrings.xml part shown in Figure 28.32.

	A
1	Model
2	WS
3	GX 1/L
4	GX110
5	Category
6	Type
7	Description
8	Supported Equipment
9	Monitor
10	E74
11	Printer
12	Units
13	Total Units
14	Optra S 1620N
15	Optra T614N
16	Lexmark B/W Laser Printer

FIGURE 28.32 Partial contents of the sharedStrings.xml part for the SupportedEquipment.xlsx workbook.

Now that you retrieved text values stored in the sharedStrings.xml part, let's proceed to editing this file. In the next Hands-On we will replace the worksheet's text entry "Monitor" with "Flat Panel Monitor" without opening the Excel application.

Hands-On 28.20 Modifying the sharedString XML File

1. Insert a new module in VBAProject (ManipulateXMLParts.xlsm), and in the Code window, enter the following Text_Replace procedure:

```
Sub Text_Replace()
    Dim xmlDoc As MSXML2.DOMDocument60
    Dim myNode As MSXML2.IXMLDOMNode
```

```
    Dim srchStr As String
    Dim newStr As String
    Dim strFile As String
    Dim strFolder As String
    Dim strFileToEdit As String

    strFolder = "C:\VBAExcel2021_ByExample\ZipPackage\xl\"
    strFile = "sharedStrings.xml"
    strFileToEdit = strFolder & strFile

    Call UnzipExcelFile
    If blnIsFileSelected = False Then Exit Sub

    Set xmlDoc = New DOMDocument60
    xmlDoc.async = False
    xmlDoc.validateOnParse = False
    xmlDoc.setProperty "SelectionNamespaces", _
 "xmlns:a='http://schemas.openxmlformats.org/spreadsheetml/2006/
main'"
    xmlDoc.setProperty "SelectionLanguage", "XPath"
    xmlDoc.Load (strFileToEdit)

    srchStr = InputBox("Please enter the string to find:", _
            "Search for String")

    If srchStr <> "" Then
        ' find the text that needs to be replaced
       Set myNode = xmlDoc.SelectSingleNode("//a:t[text()='" + _
            srchStr + "']")
        If myNode Is Nothing Then GoTo ExitHere
    Else
        GoTo ExitHere
    End If

    ' replace text
   newStr = InputBox("Please enter the replacement string for " _
    & srchStr, "Replace with String")
    If newStr <> "" Then
        myNode.Text = newStr
        xmlDoc.Save strFileToEdit
    Else
        Exit Sub
    End If
ExitHere:
    ' zip the files in the package
    Call ZipToExcel
```

```
    Set xmlDoc = Nothing
    Set myNode = Nothing
End Sub
```

In the above procedure, we use the `InputBox` function to prompt the user to enter the string to search for. If text was specified, then we use the following statement to find the node with the specified text entry:

```
Set myNode = xmlDoc.SelectSingleNode("//a:t[text()='" + _
            srchStr + "']")
```

The XPath `text()` function is used to retrieve the text value of a node. The XPath expression tells the XML parser to look at the single element node and select the t node, shown earlier in Figure 28.31, where the text content is equal to the value of the `srchStr` variable. Instead of using the XPath `text()` function, you can examine the t node using the dot operator, like this:

```
Set myNode = xmlDoc.SelectSingleNode("//a:t[.='" + srchStr + "']")
```

Note that the "a:" string before the node name is the alias that was assigned to the namespace using the `SetProperty` property of the `XMLDocument` object.

If the node with the text entry was not found, we go to the Exit Here label and perform the final tasks before exiting the procedure. If the node was found, we prompt the user for the replacement text. When we get the new string, we write it to the node and save the file:

```
myNode.Text = newStr
xmlDoc.Save strFileToEdit
```

Next, we need to zip the files back into an Excel container, so we call the ZipToExcel procedure that we created earlier.

2. In the File Explorer, delete the **ZipPackage** folder that was created in Hands-On 28.17.
3. Run the **Text_Replace** procedure. When prompted for the filename to unzip, select **SupportedEquipment.xlsx**. When prompted for the string to find, enter **Monitor** and click **OK**. When prompted for the new text, enter **Flat Panel Monitor** and click **OK**.
4. When the procedure completes, open the **PackageModified.xlsx** file in Excel. Each cell entry that previously had "Monitor" as the underlying text value in column B should now show "Flat Panel Monitor."
5. Close the **PackageModified.xlsx** workbook.
6. Delete the **PackageModified.xlsx** workbook from your VBAExcel2021_ByExample folder.

The next Hands-On demonstrates how to change the size of the left margin and remove the entire pageSetup node from the sheet1.xml part.

Hands-On 28.21 Changing and Removing Elements in an XML Part

1. Insert a new module in VBAProject (ManipulateXMLParts.xlsm), and in the Code window, enter the following ChangeLeftMargin_RemovePageSetup procedure:

```
Sub ChangeLeftMargin_RemovePageSetup()
    Dim xmlDoc As DOMDocument60
    Dim myNode As MSXML2.IXMLDOMNode
    Dim strSrchNode As String

    Set xmlDoc = New DOMDocument60
    xmlDoc.async = False
    xmlDoc.validateOnParse = False

    xmlDoc.Load ("C:\VBAExcel2021_ByExample\ZipPackage\xl\" _
        & "worksheets\Sheet1.XML")

    xmlDoc.SetProperty "SelectionNamespaces", _
        "xmlns:x14ac='http://schemas.openxmlformats.org/" & _
            "spreadsheetml/2006/main'"

    strSrchNode = "/x14ac:worksheet/x14ac:pageMargins/@left"

    Set myNode = xmlDoc.SelectSingleNode(strSrchNode)

    Debug.Print "previous left margin = " & myNode.Text

    myNode.Text = "0.50"

    Set myNode = xmlDoc.SelectSingleNode("//x14ac:pageSetup")

    On Error Resume Next
    myNode.ParentNode.RemoveChild myNode
    xmlDoc.Save ("C:\VBAExcel2021_ByExample\ZipPackage\xl\" _
        & "worksheets\Sheet1.XML ")

    Set myNode = Nothing
    Set xmlDoc = Nothing
End Sub
```

In the above procedure, we begin by loading the sheet1.xml part into the DOMDocument60 object.

To change the left margin, we must read the value of the `left` attribute of the <pageMargins> element, which is a child of the <worksheet> element. However, before we can write the correct XPath expression, we also have to consider whether our XML elements are under any namespaces. If you open the Sheet1.xml document, you will notice that the root element <worksheet> has four namespace declarations as shown in Figure 28.33.

Because the elements we want to access are not in 'no namespace' but rather in the namespace http://schemas.microsoft.com/office/spreadsheetml/2009/9/ac, in order to select them with XPath, we will need to bind a prefix (x14ac) to the namespace URI and use that prefix in our XPath expression. This can easily be achieved in MSXML by using the `setProperty` property of the `XMLDocument60` object:

```
xmlDoc.setProperty "SelectionNamespaces", _
        "xmlns:x14ac='http://schemas.openxmlformats.org/" & _
            "spreadsheetml/2006/main'"
```

```
<worksheet xmlns="http://schemas.openxmlformats.org/spreadsheetml/2006/main"
xmlns:r="http://schemas.openxmlformats.org/officeDocument/2006/relationships"
xmlns:mc="http://schemas.openxmlformats.org/markup-compatibility/2006"
xmlns:x14ac="http://schemas.microsoft.com/office/spreadsheetml/2009/9/ac"
xmlns:xr="http://schemas.microsoft.com/office/spreadsheetml/2014/revision"
xmlns:xr2="http://schemas.microsoft.com/office/spreadsheetml/2015/revision2"
xmlns:xr3="http://schemas.microsoft.com/office/spreadsheetml/2016/revision3"
mc:Ignorable="x14ac xr xr2 xr3" xr:uid="{00000000-0001-0000-0000-000000000000}">
```

FIGURE 28.33 Examining Namespaces in an XML document.

Having specified the namespace prefix, we can now use it in the XPath expression and successfully access the required node:

```
strSrchNode = "/x14ac:worksheet/x14ac:pageMargins/@left"
Set myNode = xmlDoc.selectSingleNode(strSrchNode)
```

Once we have located the node with the specified attribute, we set the node's text to the new value:

```
myNode.Text = "0.50"
```

The remaining part of the procedure locates the <pageSetup> element inside the sheet1.xml part and uses the `RemoveChild` method to remove this node:

```
Set myNode = xmlDoc.SelectSingleNode("//x14ac:pageSetup")
```

```
On Error Resume Next
myNode.ParentNode.RemoveChild myNode
```

In case the node is not found (for example, you may have mistyped the element name in the XPath expression), `On Error Resume Next` will skip over the node removal statement. The last statement will save the changes in the sheet1.xml part.

NOTE	*You may want to add to this procedure statements that call the zipping and unzipping procedures that you created in this chapter.*

2. Run the **ChangeLeftMargin_RemovePageSetup** procedure.
3. After running the procedure, open the **C:\VBAExcel2021_ByExample\ZipPackage\xl\worksheets\sheet1.xml** file in your browser and verify that the left margin is now set to 0.50 and the file no longer contains the <pageSetup> element.
4. Close the **sheet1.xml** file.
5. Delete the **ZipPackage** folder from the **VBAExcel2021_ByExample** folder.
6. Save and close the ManipulateXMLParts.xlsm workbook.

SUMMARY

This chapter has only scratched the surface of what's possible with XML. You learned here what XML is and how it is structured. While HTML consists of markup tags that define how the information should be formatted for display in a Web browser, XML allows you to invent your own tags in order to define and describe data stored in a wide range of documents.

This chapter has shown you how to perform many tasks using XML and Excel together. You learned how to view and edit XML documents and open them in Excel. You also used XML maps and XML tables and learned how to program these features with VBA. You were introduced to working with the Document Object Model in your VBA procedures and wrote procedures that saved XML data in an ADO recordset. Finally, this chapter has shown you how you can read and manipulate Open XML files with VBA.

In the next chapter, you will learn about REST APIs, the newest and the most flexible method of integrating applications.

Chapter 29 EXCEL AND REST API

We've almost reached the end of this book. In this last chapter, we will focus on expanding your VBA skillset by covering topics such as working with a VBA Dictionary Object, using regular expressions, and calling a new type of a Web service, known as the REST API.

INTRODUCTION TO A VBA DICTIONARY OBJECT

After you've learned how arrays and collections can help you store values while your program is running, you may be surprised to learn that there is still another way to manipulate your data. An object known as *VBA dictionary* operates like a collection object but offers more flexibility and speed. It works in a similar way to a normal dictionary, allowing you to look up values based on a key you provide. A dictionary is a collection of key-value pairs, and each key must be unique. Unlike an array, its size does not need to be predefined. Its data type is a Variant so you can enter any type of data you want to keep track of (text, numbers, dates, arrays, or any other objects).

The dictionary object is not part of standard VBA. It is a part of the Microsoft Scripting Runtime library (scrrun.dll).

Accessing the VBA Dictionary

There are two ways in which you can access the VBA dictionary in your VBA code. One is referred to as *early binding* and the other is called *late binding*.

- Early Binding

  To use the early binding, you need to add a reference to the *Microsoft Scripting Runtime* library as described in the next section. With early binding, your code is compiled before it runs, so your procedures can run much faster. Once the reference is added to the required library, you can write the following code to define your dictionary object:

  ```
  Dim myDict As New Scripting.Dictionary
  ```

  With early binding you can count on the *Intellisense* to help you with syntax and programming assistance.

- Late Binding

  With the late binding, your object will be compiled while your code runs, therefore it will be slower. You are not required to set up a library reference. To define the dictionary object, specify the `Scripting.Dictionary` using the `CreateObject` method as shown here:

  ```
  Dim myDict As Object
  Set myDict = CreateObject("Scripting.Dictionary")
  ```

Adding a Reference to the Microsoft Scripting Runtime Library

You add the reference to the Microsoft Scripting Runtime library in the same way you added references to other libraries that were introduced in this book. Simply select **Tools | References** in the Visual Basic Editor (VBE) screen and scroll down in the References window until you locate the library. Select it and click OK. Figure 29.1 shows this selection. After you've added the library reference, it's a good idea to examine the content of this library by using the Object Browser. In the VBE screen, press **F2** or choose **View | Object Browser**. Choose **Scripting** in the first drop-down as shown in Figure 29.2. Notice the available types of objects, one of them being the Dictionary. By clicking on each Dictionary member, you can find out the type of the member (method, property) and its function. For example, the `Item` property is the default member of Scripting. Dictionary and is used to set or get the item for a given key, while the `Add` is a method used to add a new key and item to the dictionary.

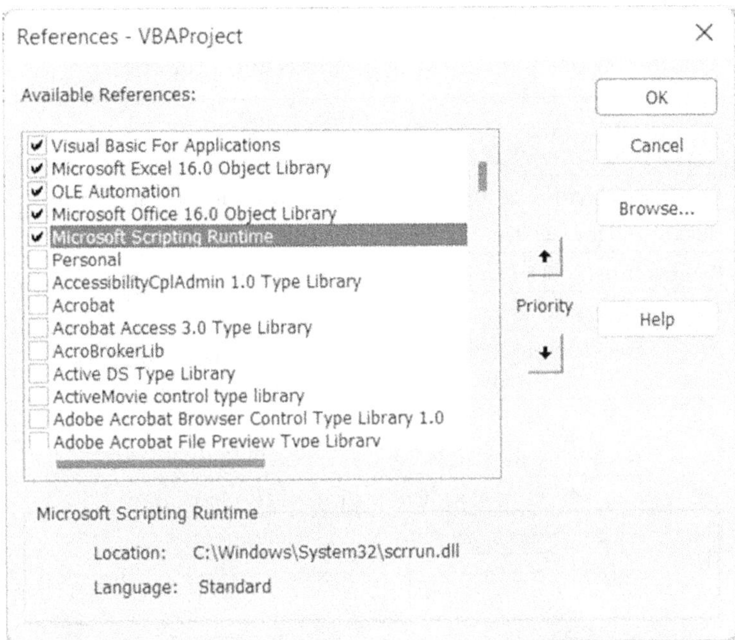

FIGURE 29.1 Adding a reference to the Microsoft Scripting Runtime library.

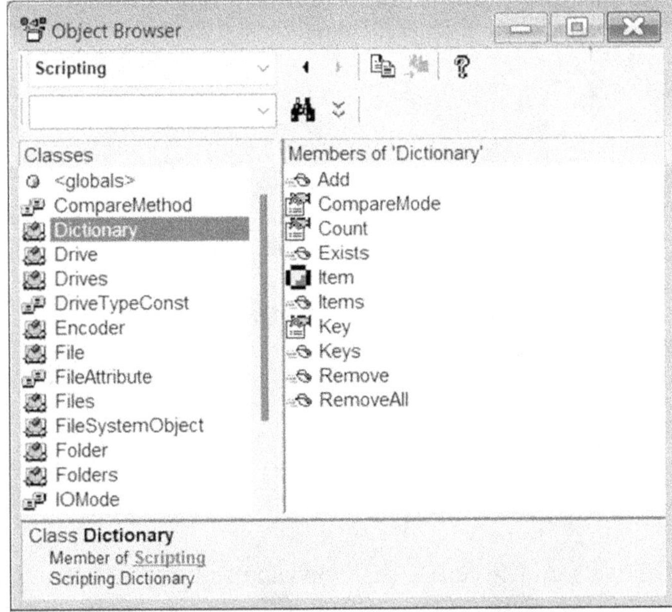

FIGURE 29.2 Examining the content of the Microsoft Scripting Runtime library.

Working with the Dictionary Object's Properties and Methods

The Scripting Dictionary has the following methods and Properties:

Methods	
Add	Adds a new key/item pair to a Dictionary object.
Remove	Removes a specified key/item pair from the Dictionary object.
RemoveAll	Removes all the key/item pairs in the Dictionary object.
Items	Returns an array of all the items in a Dictionary object.
Keys	Returns an array of all the keys in a Dictionary object.
Exists	Returns a Boolean value (true/false) that indicates whether a specified key exists in a Dictionary object.
Properties	
Key	Sets a new key value for an existing key value in the Dictionary object.
Item	Sets or returns the value of an item in a Dictionary object.
Count	Returns the number of key/value pair in a Dictionary object.
CompareMode	Sets or returns the comparison mode for comparing keys in a Dictionary object.

Let's assume that you need to create a dictionary of world capital cities. Using the Add method of the Scripting.Dictionary, you can fill your dictionary like this:

```
Sub FillDictionary()
'declare a dictionary object
'uses early binding
'requires the reference to the Microsoft Scripting Runtime
Library
Dim objDict As New Scripting.Dictionary

'add items to the dictionary
objDict("USA") = "Washington D.C."
objDict("Canada") = "Ottawa"
objDict("France") = "Paris"
objDict("England") = "London"
objDict("Hungary") = "Budapest"
objDict("Italy") = "Rome"
objDict("Japan") = "Tokyo"
objDict.Add "Germany", "Berlin"
objDict.Add key:="China", item:="Beijing"
```

In the code snippet above, you will notice that you can use three different ways to add an item to a dictionary. Use whatever method feels more comfortable to you.

After filling in the dictionary, you will want to read its keys / values. You can use the `Keys` method to return an array of all the keys like this:

```
'iterate through the dictionary to read its keys
Dim i As Long
For i = LBound(objDict.Keys) To UBound(objDict.Keys)
    Debug.Print i & "--> " & objDict.Keys(i)
Next i
```

In this code, we utilize the Upper and Lower Bound methods (`UBound`, `LBound`) of an array to list the keys.

The following code will retrieve a specific key:

```
'retrieve 3rd key
Debug.Print "3rd key=" & objDict.Keys()(2)
```

Recall that arrays are zero-based. You can place all keys into an array like this:

```
Dim aKeys() As Variant
aKeys = objDict.Keys
Debug.Print "Dictionary contains " & UBound(aKeys) + 1 & "
keys."
Debug.Print "The first key is " & aKeys(0)
```

It is easy to remove a key from a dictionary, but before removal always check if the key exists using the `Exists` method. This method is what makes the dictionary object easier to manipulate than collections and arrays. The keys are case-sensitive, so pay attention to the case when checking for the key existence.

```
'remove the key if it exists
If objDict.Exists("France") Then
    objDict.Remove "France"
Else
    Debug.Print "This key does not exist"
End If
```

The `Count` property returns the total items in dictionary and the `Item` property is used to set the value of a dictionary item. In the following example, we replace the value for Germany.

```
'count the items in the dictionary
Debug.Print "Now the dictionary contains " & objDict.Count & " keys."
objDict.item("Germany") = "Frankfurt"
Debug.Print objDict("Germany") & " is a city in Germany."
```

Using the `for each` loop, you can list all the items or keys in the dictionary, like this:

```
' list all the items in the dictionary
Dim item As Variant
For Each item In objDict.Items
    Debug.Print item
Next
' List all keys in the dictionary
Dim key As Variant
For Each key In objDict.Keys
    Debug.Print key & " --> " & objDict.item(key)
Next
```

To clear your dictionary of all items, use the `RemoveAll` method:

```
' remove all key/item pairs
objDict.RemoveAll
' verify that dictionary is empty
Debug.Print objDict.Count
End Sub
```

NOTE	*The complete FillDictionary procedure can be found in the Chap29_VBAExcel2021.xlsm workbook in the companion files.*

Recall that key searches are case sensitive by default. However, you can use the `CompareMode` property to change this behavior. The mode change must be specified right after creation of the dictionary object, before adding any data to the dictionary. Let's look at some code.

```
Sub CaseNotSensitive()
    Dim objDict As New Scripting.Dictionary
    objDict.CompareMode = TextCompare
    objDict.Add "Math", 89
    objDict.Add "English", 70
    objDict.Add "Chemistry", 90
    Debug.Print objDict.Exists("math")
End Sub
```

In this example, we set the `CompareMode` to `TextCompare` to allow for searches that are not case sensitive. So instead of typing "Math" for the key name, we can simply enter "math" in lower case and the `Exists` method is able to locate the key. The `CompareMode` can also be set to two other settings: `BinaryCompare` and `DatabaseCompare`. `BinaryCompare` performs binary comparisons; it is case sensitive, so "EventName" is not the same as "eventName" or eventname." The `DatabaseCompare` performs a comparison based on information in the database. The latter only exists in Microsoft Access (it's not available in Excel and other VBA capable office applications).

Dictionary versus Collection

The following table shows several advantages of the dictionary object over the native VBA collection object. In your programming endeavors, you should always pick the object that is most suitable for a particular task.

Dictionary	Collection
Retrieving items in a dictionary is faster than in a collection.	Retrieving items is slower than in a dictionary.
Easier to search for a given item	Harder to search for a given item
The Item value can be changed directly.	The item value must be first removed and then the changed item can be added back.
Uses keys to locate a particular item; keys can be checked for existence.	The keys are used to look up data but cannot be retrieved. Uses index values that are harder to work with.
Offers compare mode for changing case-sensitivity	Collections are case-sensitive, and sensitivity cannot be changed.
Key values can be any data type.	Key values must be strings.
Items can be easily removed using the Remove-All method.	Removing items from a collection requires re-defining the Collection object.
Cannot store a reference to a custom collection	Can store a reference to a custom collection
Requires a reference to the Microsoft Scripting Runtime Library or an object created using the late binding	Collection is an object available in the VBA library.

INTRODUCTION TO REGULAR EXPRESSIONS

As you know, the VBA has many useful functions that apply to strings. You can use the `Len` function to return the number of characters in a string, for example,

```
?Len("Today is Sunday")
```

returns the number 15.

You can use the `Left`, `Right`, and `Mid` functions to return a portion of a string. For example,

```
?Left("Today is Sunday", 5)
```

returns the string `Today`. Replace `Left` with `Right`, and you return the five rightmost characters from that string. If you need to return a string starting from a particular character in the string, you can use `Mid` function to extract the required portion of the string. For example, let's extract "is" from our test string:

```
?Mid("Today is Sunday", 7, 2)
```

This returns the following string: `is`.

If you instead want to find the position of the first occurrence of one string within another string, you can call the `InStr` function like this:

```
?InStr("Today is Sunday and it's a holiday", "Sunday")
```

This will display the number 10, indicating that the string was found starting at character 10. If you don't need to search from the beginning of the string, specify the position to search from in the first argument, like this:

```
?InStr(5, "Today is Sunday and it's a holiday", "o")
```

This searches for the letter "o," starting from the fifth character in the specified string. The "o" is found in the 29th position.

As you can see, using string manipulation functions in VBA is quite straightforward. However, there will be many situations in your VBA programs where these methods will not be enough. You may need to match a certain pattern of characters in various expressions. A pattern match can involve a character, a word, a group of words, or an entire sentence. This is where a working knowledge of regular expressions can come to your rescue. Simply put, a *Regular Expression (often referred to as RegEx or RegExp)* is a sequence of characters that specifies a search pattern in text. Regular expressions are commonly used in search engines, Find/Replace dialogs in text editors, and word processing applications. Before you can try out some pattern matching in VBA, let's go over a few basic concepts.

Character Matching in RegExp Patterns

The *Pattern* is basically a schema that you put together to match character combinations in strings. Patterns are composed of simple characters such as /abc/, or a combination of simple and special characters such as /ab*c/. The latter indicates that we want to match a single "a" followed by zero or more "b" characters followed by "c." The * after "b" means zero or more occurrences of the preceding item. The following table shows some examples of special characters used in regular expressions patterns. For more detailed information, you will need to look to other sources. This section supplies just a bare minimum of the regex knowledge for you to complete a specific VBA programming task that will be introduced later in this chapter.

Pattern	Description	Example	Found Matches
. (a single dot)	Matches any single character except vbNewLine	d.g	deg, dig, dog
[characters]	Matches any single character between brackets []	[jv]	Would match j and v in "java"
[^characters]	Matches any single character that is not between brackets []	[^jv]	Would match "a" in "java"
[start-end]	Matches any character that is part of the range in brackets []	[0-9] [A-Z]	Matches any number in the range 0 to 9 Matches any character in the range "A" to "Z"
\	Escapes special characters so that special characters can be searched for	\[	Escaped character. Matches a "[" character.
\n	New line	\n	Matches a new line (vbNewLine)
\r	Carriage Return	\r	Matches a carriage return (vbCr)
\t	Tab	\t	Matches a tab character (vbTab)
\w	Matches any word character alphanumeric and underscore.	\w	Would match "morning" in "morning"
\W	Matches any non-alphanumeric characters and the underscore	\W	Would match "@" in your email address
\s	Matches any white space character (spaces, tabs, line breaks)	\s	Would match the space in "good morning"
\S	Matches any non-white space character	\S	Would match "good" and "morning" in "good morning"
\d	Matches any decimal digit	\d	Would match "7" in "7Eleven"
\D	Matches any character that is not a digit character (0-9)	\D	Would match "Eleven" in "7Eleven"

Quantifiers in RegExp Patterns

Regular expression patterns can include quantifiers that allow you to control how many times a match occurs.

Quantifier	Description	Example	Found Matches
*	Matches zero or more of preceding characters/digits	b\w*	Matches a "b" character Matches any word character (alphanumeric & underscore) Matches 0 or more of the preceding items

(Contd.)

Quantifier	Description	Example	Found Matches
+	Matches 1 or more of the preceding characters/digits	b\w+	Same as above, but matches 1 or more
?	Matches zero or one	colou?r	Matches color, colour
{n}	Matches "n" many times	c{2}	Matches a "c" character twice. Case sensitive. Will match the second and third letter "c" in "Cecilia is sick."
{n,}	Matches at least "n" occurrences of the preceding item	a{3,}	Matches all of the "a" characters in "baaarber" and "baaaarber"
{n,m}	Matches the specified quantity of the previous character/digit	a{1,3}	Will match 1 to 3 of the previous items. It will match the "a" in "barber", the two "a's" in "barber" and the three "a's" in "baaarber"

You can use parentheses () to group multiple items in your pattern together. You can also indicate the beginning and ending of lines and words and other patterns indicating that a match is possible. These topics are beyond the scope of this book. Numerous books have been devoted to the subject of regular expression pattern matching operations. Also, hundreds of websites offer useful tools that will help you decipher an unknown regex pattern and help you understand its building elements. While regex can take some time to learn, once mastered, these skills can be reused in many other programming languages for validating, replacing, and extracting data from strings.

Using the RegExp Object in VBA

Many programming languages provide built-in support for working with regexes. To use regexes in your VBA programs and take advantage of the built-in programming assistance (Intellisense), you will need to add a reference to an external library. In your VBE screen, choose the Tools | References dialog box (see Figure 29.3), scroll down and select the *Microsoft VBScript Regular Expressions 5.5,* then click OK. Once you've added this library to your VBA project, the Object Browser (press F2) will display all available properties and methods of the RegExp object (see Figure 29.4).

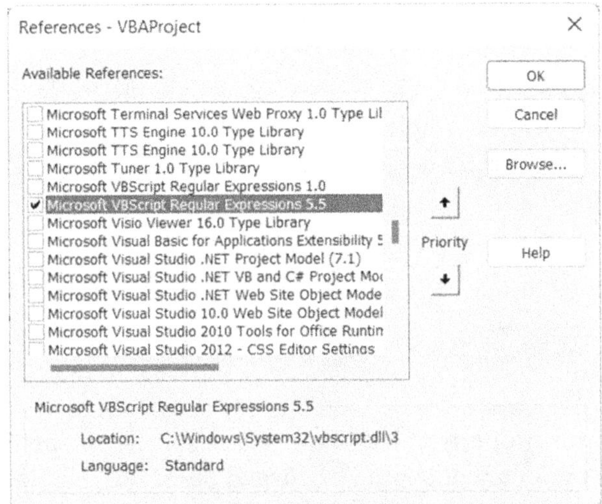

FIGURE 29.3 Setting a Reference to the Microsoft VBScript Regular Expressions 5.5 Object Library

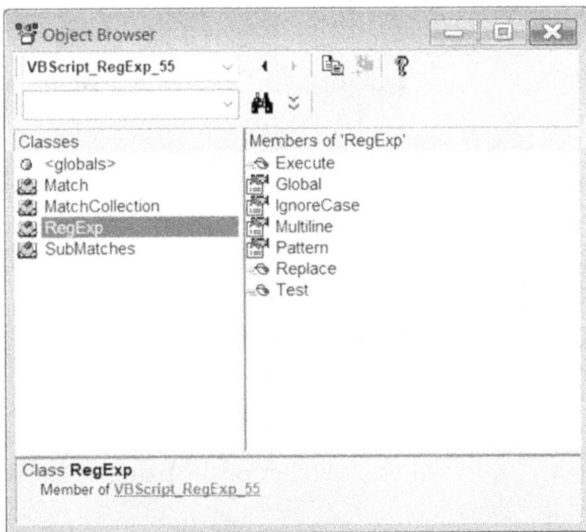

FIGURE 29.4 Regular Expressions can be used via the VBScript Regular Expressions 5.5 library displayed as VBScript_RegExp_55 in the Object Browser.

The RegExp Object Declaration

If you already set up the reference to the *Microsoft VBScript Regular Expressions 5.5 library*, you can declare the RegExp object using the following early-binding syntax:

```
Dim oRegExp As RegExp
Set oRegExp = New RegExp
```

If you don't want to add the reference to the `RegExp` object via the References dialog box, use any of the following examples:

```
Dim oRegExp As Object
Set oRegExp = CreateObject("VBScript.RegExp")
```

Or

```
Dim oRegExp As Object
Set oRegExp = New VBScript_RegExp_55.RegExp
```

The RegExp Object's Properties

The `RegExp` object offers four properties that allow you to specify the pattern to be matched and various options that should be turned on or off. The most important property is the `Pattern` property. This is where you specify the pattern that you are going to use for matching against the string.

The `Global` property can be set to `True` or `False`. Set it to `True` to find all matches in the pattern. If set to `False` only the first match will be found.

The `IgnoreCase` property set to `True` will make the matching case insensitive.

The `Multiline` property should be set to `True` if your string consists of multiple lines and you want to run the same pattern through all the lines.

The RegExp Object's Methods

To work with the `RegExp` object, you can use the following methods:

Use the `Test` method to search for a pattern in a string. When a match is found, `True` is returned.

Use the `Replace` method to replace the occurrences of the pattern with a replacement string.

Use the `Execute` method to return all the matches of the pattern that were found in the provided string.

Writing VBA procedures using the RegExp Object

Let's create example procedures that use some of the methods and properties of the RegExp object. The first procedure will use the `Test` method to check whether the supplied text string contains a correctly formatted phone number. Assume we want to ensure that phone numbers are in the following US format: (999) 999-9999.

NOTE	*All code files and figures for the hands-on projects may be found in the companion files.*

Hands-On 29.1 Testing for a Pattern Match

1. Copy the **Chap29_VBAExcel2021.xlsm** workbook from the companion files to your **C:\VBAExcel2021_ByExample** folder.
2. In the VBE screen, add a new Module and rename it **RegExpressions**.
3. Enter the following VBA procedure and run it.

```
Sub RegExp_TestDemo()
    Dim oRegExp As RegExp
    Dim strToSearch As String
    Set oRegExp = New RegExp
    strToSearch = "Customer phone number: (201) 234-7899."
    ' match US Phone numbers in the format: (999) 999-9999
    oRegExp.Pattern = "\(\d{3}\) \d{3}-\d{4}"
    MsgBox oRegExp.Test(strToSearch)
End Sub
```

   When this procedure executes, you should see "True" in the message box.

4. Remove the parentheses surrounding the area code and run the procedure again.
   The phone number will no longer match the pattern we defined, so the Test method will return False.

   Let's look at the pattern expression we defined for the phone:

```
\(\d{3}\) \d{3}-\d{4}
```

Element	Explanation
\(	Escaped character. Matches a "(" character.
\d	Matches any digit character (0-9).
{3}	Quantifier. Matches 3 of the preceding digits.
\)	Escaped character. Matches a ")" character.
	Matches a space character (empty space)
\d	Matches any digit character (0-9).
-	Dash character. Matches a "-" character.
{4}	Quantifier. Matches 4 of the preceding digits.

In the next Hands-On exercise, we will write a procedure that will search for all occurrences of characters provided in the pattern and replace them with nothing, meaning that they will be removed from the search string.

Hands-On 29.2 Replacing All Occurrences of the Pattern Match

1. In the VBE window, enter the code of the procedure as shown in Figure 29.5.

```
Sub RegExp_ReplaceDemo()
Dim oRegExp As RegExp
Set oRegExp = New RegExp

Dim strToSearch As String
strToSearch = "{""userId"":1,""Title"":""Account Manager"",""TaskCompleted"":false}"

'Find all matches in the pattern
oRegExp.Global = True

'Match any character in this set
oRegExp.Pattern = "[\{\}""]"
MsgBox oRegExp.Replace(strToSearch, "")

End Sub
```

FIGURE 29.5 This VBA procedure uses the Replace method of the RegExp object to remove characters specified in the pattern from the searched string.

2. Execute the RegExp_ReplaceDemo procedure.
   Figure 29.6 displays the message box with the resulting string.

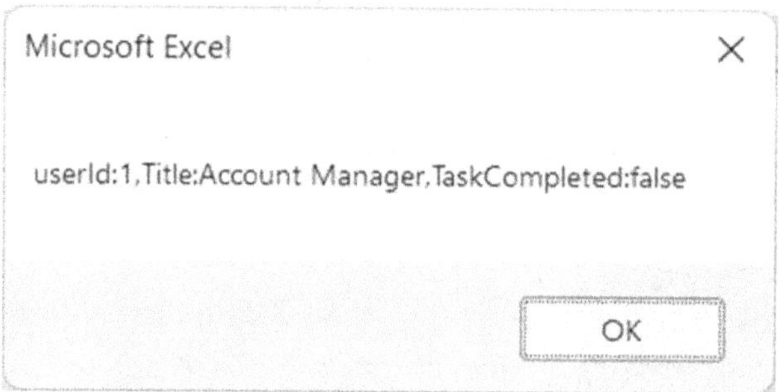

FIGURE 29.6 The Replace method of the RegExp object has successfully removed all occurrences of { } “” characters from the original string.

   Note that prior to defining the pattern, we used the `Global` property of the `RegExp` object to ensure that all the characters specified in the `Pattern` are removed, not just their first occurrence.

3. Comment out the line of code that sets the Global property to True and run the procedure again.
   This time, the message box should display partially cleaned up string; only the first occurrence of each character in the pattern was removed, giving you the following text string:

```
"userId":1,"title":"Account Manager","TaskCompleted":false}
```

Finally, let's create a procedure that uses the `Execute` method of the `RegExp` object to display all the matches for the pattern that was found in the search string. We will use the same pattern and search string as in the previous procedure.

Hands-On 29.3 Obtaining a List of all the Matches in the Pattern

1. Create a copy of the procedure from Hands-On 29.2 and rename it **RegExp_ExecuteDemo**.
2. Add the following two declaration statements:

```
Dim matches As Object
Dim itm As Variant
```

3. Uncomment the statement that sets the `Global` property to True.
4. Comment out the statement that displays the message box. We will not be making any replacements in this procedure.
5. Add the following code before the `End Stub` statement:

```
Set matches = oRegExp.Execute(strToSearch)
For Each itm In matches
    Debug.Print itm
Next
```

6. Run the completed RegExp_ExecuteDemo procedure.
   After running the procedure, you should see all the matches that were found, listed on separate lines like this:

```
{
"
"
"
"
"
"
"
"
}
```

Now you've learned the basics of using the `RegExp` object in your VBA procedures. We will revisit this object in a later Hands-On project when we need to locate and extract specific strings from a JSON response obtained from an external resource. If you've never heard about JSON, read on. The next section introduces you to communicating with Web servers: sending requests and processing responses.

INTRODUCTION TO THE REST API

Over the past few years, the method which developers use to connect to external resources and share information between various computer systems frequently includes a mysterious initialism: API. This vastly popular term is formed from the initial letters of *Application Programming Interface*.

Application Programming Interfaces (known as APIs) allow programs and scripts to communicate with each other. These programming interfaces expose certain data, services, and functionality of an application so other developers can use them. This allows one product to interact with other products. In other words, the APIs are specifically built to be consumed by another application programmatically. APIs allow you to automate many tasks, and create user-friendly dashboards and client applications both for mobile and Web use. More than that, they allow you to extend your product functionality by grabbing the required resource from somewhere else. Basically, APIs make things easier. Think of how many times you have seen a Google map embedded in some website. That map came from the Google Maps API! Many popular websites such as YouTube, Twitter, and Facebook, as well as multitude of commercial and government websites, provide APIs that allow you to get and update their data. To use these APIs, you don't need to know how they were created internally. All you need is to get acquainted with their documentation, find out how to ask for what you need, and how to process the response. Some APIs are free, others require that you pay for the service. Some will ask you to create a developer account to obtain an API key for the authentication purposes. This key consists of a set of letters and numbers that uniquely identify you to the application. An API key is like a password; it is important to keep it secure.

There are different types of APIs. The one that everyone is using and talking about right now is called *Representational State Transfer (REST)*. The REST API, also referred to as a RESTful API, was created by computer scientist Roy Fielding. REST is a set of rules (also known as architectural style) that developers must follow to create programs on a server that allow communication with various client applications. In a RESTful system, a client application sends a request to the server, usually over the HTTP protocol. This request might be to fetch data (GET request), alter the state of the data (PUT request), create data

(POST request), delete some data (DELETE request), or modify some details about the resource (PATCH request). POST, GET, PUT, and DELETE are special verbs that specify a CRUD (Create, Read, Update, Delete) action that needs to be performed on the server. After the server completes the action, it sends a response back to the client application, often in the form of a representation of the requested resource. A very important fact in the REST API is that all client requests are stateless. This means that each request must contain all the necessary information for the server to process the request. In other words, the client cannot depend on the server to remember prior requests. Server responses can be formatted in plain text/HTML, XML, or JSON.

In this section, you learn how to use VBA to use a GET method to fetch data from some free APIs that you can access without applying for a developer account or using authentication. There is a lot to know about the REST API and, unfortunately, there isn't enough room in this chapter to cover all methods of using it. Even the simple GET method can get quite complex when you need to pass parameters to the service and authenticate yourself. Thus, for simplicity's sake, we will focus on the basic syntax that should provide you with enough understanding of the topic, so you are ready to dive deeper into it the next time you encounter it.

Accessing REST APIs with VBA

VBA does not have a special method for accessing REST APIs. However, there is a special `XMLHTTPRequest` object that allows you to use external API from your VBA code. You must declare the `XMLHttpRequest` object by using an early or late binding.

As mentioned earlier in this chapter, to use an early binding, you must set up a reference to an external library. In this case, the library you need is called *Microsoft XML, vb6.0.* Figure 29.7 shows the selection of this library in the References dialog box. You will need to scroll down in the list of Available References to find it.

Once the library is selected in the References dialog box, you can view the object's properties and methods (see Figure 29.8) using the Object Browser (View | Object Browser or Press F2).

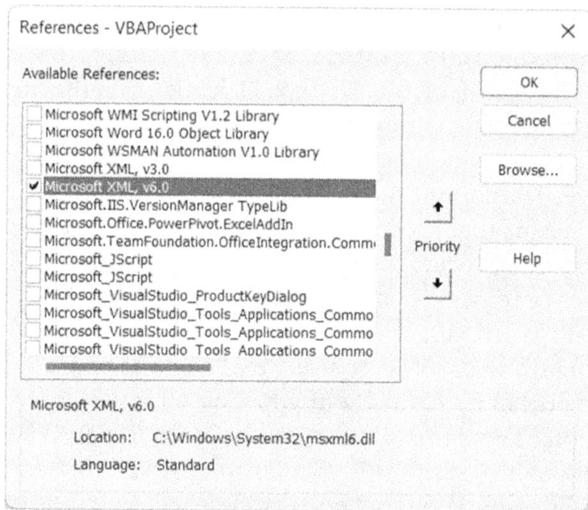

FIGURE 29.7 Activating the Microsoft XML, vb.60 Object Library

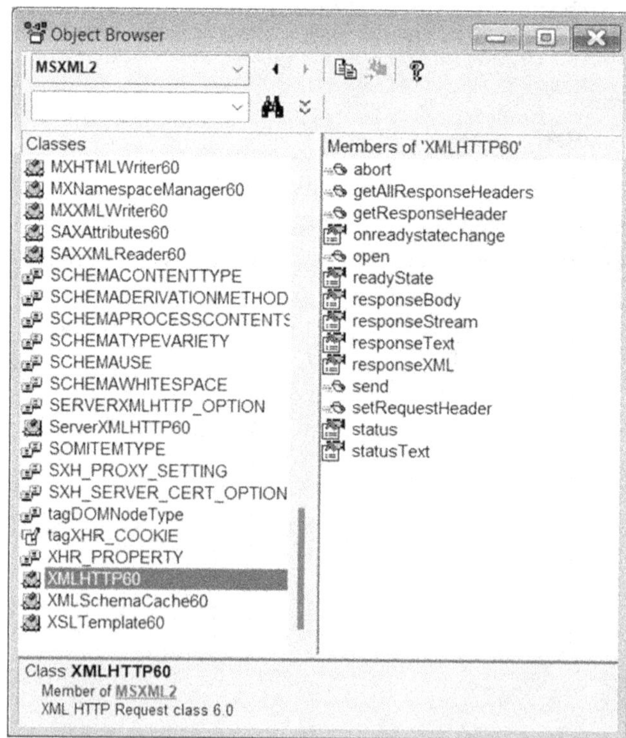

FIGURE 29.8 Exploring the Microsoft XML, vb.60 Object Library using the Object Browser.

To use this object, declare it like this in your VBA code:

```
Dim httpReq As MSXML2.XMLHTTP60
Set httpReq = New MSXML2.XMLHTTP60
```

Or put everything in the declaration line:

```
Dim httpReq As New MSXML2.XMLHTTP60
```

Note that the `httpReq` is the name of the object variable; here, you can specify any name you like. Some people prefer to call it `xmlhttp`; others use `xhr`. Use the name that you feel most comfortable with.

With the late binding, you can skip selecting a reference. Simply declare the object variable of the generic object type and use `CreateObject` function like this:

```
Dim httpReq As Object
Set httpReq = CreateObject("MSXML2.ServerXMLHttp")
```

In this chapter's examples, we will be using the early binding so we can rely on the built-in programming assistance while writing our code.

Methods and Properties of the XMLHTTPRequest Object

Let's look at the methods and properties that we need to be familiar with to make successful requests to any external API.

The most important methods are `Open` and `Send`. Use the `Open` method to initialize a request. You will need to provide the two required arguments. The first argument is a method which can be either GET, POST, or PUT. The second argument is the URL of the resource you are calling. You may optionally pass a Boolean value (TRUE/FALSE) to indicate whether the API call is meant to be asynchronous (TRUE is default) or synchronous (FALSE). If you pass False, processing waits until the response is returned from the server.

Using the `httpReq` object variable defined earlier, here is how you would set up a basic GET request:

```
httpReq.Open "GET","strURL ", False
```

where the `strURL` is the URL address of the server you want to access.

The actual request to the server is made using the `Send` method. If the request was declared asynchronous (TRUE) then this method returns immediately, otherwise it waits until the response is received. You can pass additional optional arguments with the `Send` method. The simple syntax of this method is as follows:

```
httpReq.send
```

The `Send` method will send the request to the resource you indicated in the second parameter of the `Open` method.

The `Abort` method is handy for aborting the current request. You will use it when you want to stop the request.

Any problems and issues with an API can often be resolved by examining API headers, and we have three methods to deal with headers: `setRequestHeader`, `getResponseHeader`, and `getAllResponseHeaders`. Headers provide extra information about each API call and response. The most common API headers are listed in the following table.

Authorization	This header contains the authentication credentials for HTTP authentication.
WWW-Authenticate	The server may send this header if it needs some form of authentication before sending the response for the requested resource. It may include an error code 401, which means "unauthorized."
Accept_Charset	The client may send this header with a request to let the server know which character sets (such as UTF-8, ISO-8859-1, and Windows-1251) are acceptable by the client.
Content-Type	This header tells the client what media type (e.g., application/xml and application/json) the response is sent in. This helps client to correctly process the response received from the server.
Cache-Control	This header contains caching directives (instructions) defined by the server for the response. These directives determine how a resource is cached, where it's cached and its maximum age before expiring. The no-cache entry in the Cache-Control header indicates that returned responses can't be used for subsequent requests to the same URL before checking if server responses have changed.

To get all the response headers from the HTTP request, use the `getAllResponseHeaders` method. This method must be used after you've set up the `Send` method to send the request. For example,

```
httpReq.Send
Debug.Print httpReq.getAllResponseHeaders
```

The second statement above should print to the Immediate window the string containing response headers. What you get in the response headers depends on the server. Here is an example of the headers obtained from the resource we'll be querying in Hands-On 29.4:

```
content-type: application/xml
expires: -1
server: Microsoft-IIS/10.0
x-aspnet-version: 4.0.30319
request-context: appId=cid-v1:39f1cd0a-de7e-435f-bf7d-39de930d88c6
```

```
access-control-expose-headers: Request-Context
x-powered-by: ASP.NET
date: Thu, 14 Apr 2022 21:48:23 GMT
strict-transport-security: max-age=31536000 ; includeSubDomains ;
preload
```

As you can see from this example, the headers are key/value pairs in text format separated by a colon.

To find out a specific header value you want, use the `getResponseHeader` method, providing it with the argument denoting the specific header value you want. For example, to get the value of the content-type header, use the following line of code:

```
Debug.Print HttpReq.getResponseHeader("content-type")
```

The `setRequestHeader` method is used by the client to provide information to the server about the types of content that are acceptable for the response, the acceptable character sets, list of acceptable encoding etc. For a full list of standard request fields see the article at *https://en.wikipedia.org/wiki/List_of_HTTP_header_fields#Requests.* It is the responsibility of the server to consider the sent-in client requirements. The `setRequestHeader` method has two required arguments that specify the name of the header and its value. You must call it after calling `Open` method, but before calling `Send`. Here is an example:

```
httpReq.Open "GET", strURL, False
httpReq.setRequestHeader("Accept", "text/xml")
httpReq.Send
```

The above example will tell the server that the client is looking for a response in text/xml format.

NOTE

Before sending a request to the server you may want to query the server to find out if the server is operational and what server resources are available. By sending a HEAD request, instead of GET or POST, the server will send back its response headers. Here is a short VBA procedure that demonstrates how to query the server:

```
Sub GetOnlyHeaders()
Dim xhr As New MSXML2.XMLHTTP60
xhr.Open "HEAD", "https://itunes.apple.com/search?term=
                  celine+dion", False
xhr.send

If xhr.ReadyState = 4 Then
    Debug.Print xhr.getAllResponseHeaders
End If
End Sub
```

With the methods covered, let's look at the `XMLHTTPRequest` object's properties.

The `readyState` property specifies the state of the request. There are five possible values:

0 = uninitialized
1 = loading
2 = loaded
3 = interactive
4 = complete

Every time the `readyState` change, the `onreadystatechange` event is fired. When `readyState` is `4` and status is `200`, the response is ready.

The `status` property returns the HTTP status code from the server. The most common status is `200`, which means "OK," signifying that the request was successful. The `403` status means that the access is forbidden. The `404` denotes that the requested page/resource was not found. For a complete list of statuses, go to *https://en.wikipedia.org/wiki/List_of_HTTP_status_codes*.

The `statusText` property returns the text version of the HTTP status code. It is useful for programming error messages. You will see the example of using `status` and `statusText` in the Hands-On 29.4.

Finally, the last four properties `responseText`, `responseXML`, `responseStream`, and `responseBody` specify the form in which the HTTP response can be returned. Use the `responseXML` property if you know that the response body is an XML formatted text. If you need the response body as a string, use the `responseText` property. The `responseStream` property will return the server response in the form of binary-encoded data (such as UTF-8, UCS-2, UCS-3, and Shift_JIS). The `responseBody` property is useful when the response body is binary. This property returns the response content as a byte stream.

Making a Basic GET Request

You may be wondering how exactly you can put this newfound knowledge to use. Here again, the best learning occurs from working through an example.

In the first Hands-On example on calling the REST API, we will access the NHTSA (National Highway Traffic Safety Administration) Product Information Catalog and Vehicle Listing (vPIC) API Programming Interface. The following is a direct link: *https://vpic.nhtsa.dot.gov/api/* .

It describes API methods that can be used to get various types of data in XML, CSV, and JSON format. We will get a list of all the makes available in vPIC dataset. We will get this list in XML format and will push it into an Excel worksheet. Let's get started.

Hands-On 29.4 Requesting Data from REST API

1. In the VBE screen, insert a new standard module to your **Chap29_VBAExcel2021.xlsm** workbook. Use the Properties box to rename the module **APIRequest_XML**.
2. In the APIRequest_XML module code window, enter the following procedure:

```
' set up a reference to the following Library
' --->Microsoft XML, v6.0
' using the References dialog box

Sub RequestData_XML_toExcel()

Dim URL As String
Dim httpReq As Object
Dim Resp As New MSXML2.DOMDocument60
Dim wkb As Workbook
Dim ws As Worksheet
Dim Header As Boolean
Dim n As Integer
Dim i As Integer
Dim c As Integer
Dim startTime As Single
Dim endTime As Single
Dim strExcelFile As String

On Error GoTo ErrorHandler

URL = "https://vpic.nhtsa.dot.gov/api/vehicles/
       getallmakes?format=xml"

strExcelFile = "C:\VBAExcel2021_ByExample\MakesList.xlsx"

' delete Excel file if it exists
If Dir(strExcelFile) <> "" Then Kill strExcelFile

Set httpReq = CreateObject("MSXML2.ServerXMLHttp")
httpReq.Open "GET", URL, False

httpReq.send
' check if we sucessfully made the request
If httpReq.status <> 200 Then
    Debug.Print httpReq.status & ":" & httpReq.statusText
    Set httpReq = Nothing
    Exit Sub
```

```
End If

'Assume we got through to the API
Debug.Print httpReq.responseText

Resp.LoadXML httpReq.responseText

' set up an Excel workbook for our data
Set wkb = Workbooks.Add
Set ws = wkb.Sheets(1)
ws.Activate

Header = False
i = 1

ws.UsedRange.Clear

Dim NodeList As MSXML2.IXMLDOMNodeList
Dim iNode As MSXML2.IXMLDOMNode

startTime = Timer() ' start the timer

Set NodeList = Resp.getElementsByTagName("AllVehicleMakes")
If NodeList.length <> 0 Then
    For c = 0 To NodeList.length - 1
        For n = 0 To NodeList.item(c).childNodes.length - 1
            Set iNode = NodeList.item(c).childNodes(n)

            If Header = False Then
                ws.[A1].Offset(0, n).Value = iNode.baseName
            End If
            ws.[A1].Offset(i, n).Value = iNode.Text
        Next n
    i = i + 1
    ' this will get only the first 100 items from the response
    ' and will shorten the processing time
     ' comment it out to get all records (processing may take over
5 minutes)
    If i = 101 Then Exit For
    Next

    'autofit columns
    ws.Columns.AutoFit

    'save and close the workbook
```

```
    wkb.SaveAs strExcelFile
    wkb.Close

    endTime = Timer() ' end the timer

    Debug.Print "Processing completed in " & _
       Format(Round(endTime - startTime, 2), "#0.00") & " seconds."

    MsgBox "Processing completed in " & _
        Int((endTime - startTime) / 60) & " minutes, " & _
        Round(endTime - startTime, 2) Mod 60 & " seconds.", _
        vbInformation

   Debug.Print "Excel worksheet with All Vehicle Makes is completed."
Else
     Debug.Print "There was nothing to process. Please check for
errors."
End If

ExitHere:
'cleanup
    Set httpReq = Nothing
    Set ws = Nothing
    Set wkb = Nothing
    Exit Sub
ErrorHandler:
    Debug.Print Err.Number & ":" & Err.Description
    Resume ExitHere
End Sub
```

3. Click in the selection bar next to the `httpReq.send` statement in the procedure to put a breakpoint on this line of code and press **F5** to run the procedure.
4. When the break mode is activated and you see the yellow selection in the code window, keep pressing **F8** to debug the code line by line. Keep the Immediate window open while debugging the procedure so you can see the output of the Debug statements. Activate the Immediate window by pressing **Ctrl+G**.

   The first debug statement in this procedure should return the contents of the headers as shown earlier in this chapter. Notice that we are asking for the headers after we have sent the request to the server. This statement is for demonstration purposes only. Most of the time you don't need to look at headers unless problems arise, and you need to troubleshoot some issues. After sending the request, the server gives you back a status code: 200 means that the request was successful, and the server produced the response. Only then should we proceed with the rest of the code. There is no point of asking for a response when an error code was returned in the server `status` property. If the `status` is not 200, we will output to the Immediate window the status code and the equivalent text error message using the `status` and `statusText` properties discussed earlier. If the request was successful, we use the `responseText` property to get the response and print it to the Immediate window. Debug statements help you understand the output from the server. Now that we have the output, we also want to save it so we can use it for a specific purpose. In this procedure, we use the `LoadXML` method of the `XMLDocument` object to load the server response into an XML document, which we declared at the top of the procedure in the `Resp` object variable. Note that we have extensively covered working with XML in Chapter 28. After the XML data is retrieved to the Immediate Window, we write some VBA code to read the XML nodes and output their contents to an Excel workbook.

5. When you have reached the end of the procedure by pressing the **F8** key, switch to the main Excel application window to view the result. Figure 29.9 illustrates the contents of XML data retrieval in the Immediate Window. Figure 29.10 shows the same data written to an Excel worksheet.

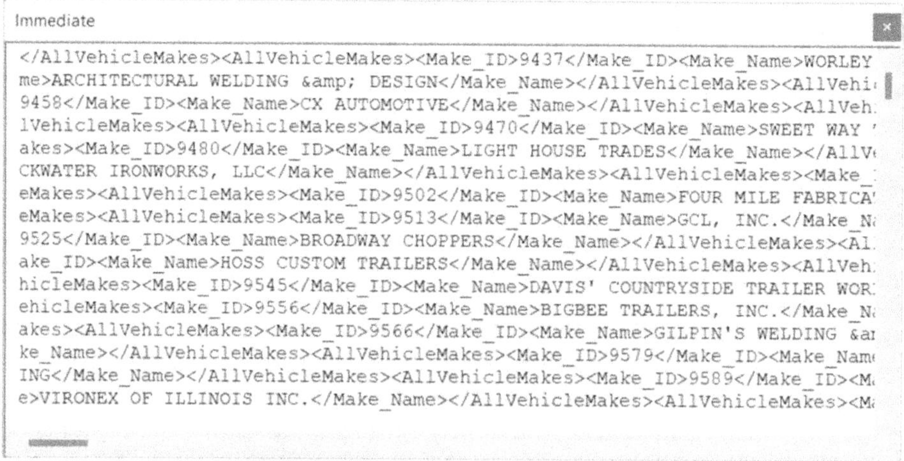

Immediate


```
</AllVehicleMakes><AllVehicleMakes><Make_ID>9437</Make_ID><Make_Name>WORLEY
me>ARCHITECTURAL WELDING &amp; DESIGN</Make_Name></AllVehicleMakes><AllVehi
9458</Make_ID><Make_Name>CX AUTOMOTIVE</Make_Name></AllVehicleMakes><AllVeh
lVehicleMakes><AllVehicleMakes><Make_ID>9470</Make_ID><Make_Name>SWEET WAY
akes><Make_ID>9480</Make_ID><Make_Name>LIGHT HOUSE TRADES</Make_Name></AllV
CKWATER IRONWORKS, LLC</Make_Name></AllVehicleMakes><AllVehicleMakes><Make_
eMakes><AllVehicleMakes><Make_ID>9502</Make_ID><Make_Name>FOUR MILE FABRICA
eMakes><AllVehicleMakes><Make_ID>9513</Make_ID><Make_Name>GCL, INC.</Make_N
9525</Make_ID><Make_Name>BROADWAY CHOPPERS</Make_Name></AllVehicleMakes><Al
ake_ID><Make_Name>HOSS CUSTOM TRAILERS</Make_Name></AllVehicleMakes><AllVeh
hicleMakes><Make_ID>9545</Make_ID><Make_Name>DAVIS' COUNTRYSIDE TRAILER WOR
ehicleMakes><Make_ID>9556</Make_ID><Make_Name>BIGBEE TRAILERS, INC.</Make_N
akes><AllVehicleMakes><Make_ID>9566</Make_ID><Make_Name>GILPIN'S WELDING &a
ke_Name></AllVehicleMakes><AllVehicleMakes><Make_ID>9579</Make_ID><Make_Nam
ING</Make_Name></AllVehicleMakes><AllVehicleMakes><Make_ID>9589</Make_ID><M
e>VIRONEX OF ILLINOIS INC.</Make_Name></AllVehicleMakes><AllVehicleMakes><M
```


FIGURE 29.9 The AllVehicleMakes list was created from the REST API response and written to the Immediate Window.

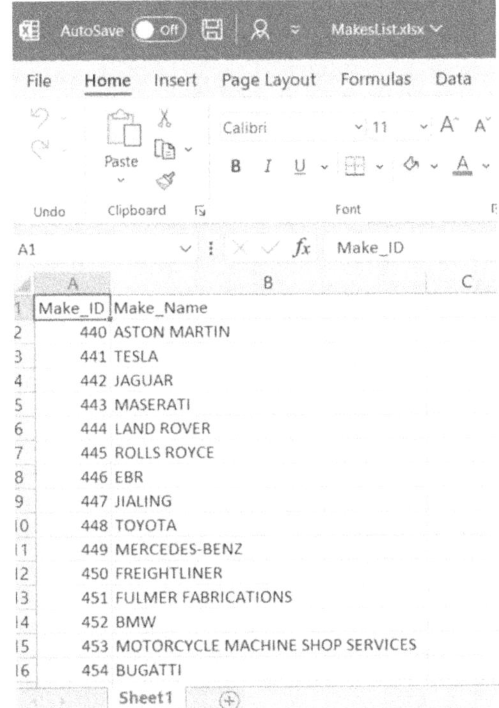

FIGURE 29.10 The XML data returned from the REST API written to an Excel worksheet.

The Overview of JSON

Using XML with REST API requests and responses requires the knowledge of the XML language and a good understanding of the process of generating and modifying XML structures. In recent years, a new text format, known as *JSON* (pronounced "JASON") has become an alternative to XML. JSON, which stands for *JavaScript Object Notation*, is a language-independent data format often used for data interchange between disparate system due to its lightweight format. JSON format is a human-readable text that consists of name/value pairs.

Figure 29.11 displays the sample of the JSON file obtained from the free fake API that is available for testing and prototyping (*https://jsonplaceholder.typicode.com/users*).

FIGURE 29.11 Example of the JSON file format.

The JSON format can include

- An object which is an unordered set of name/value pairs

  Objects begin with { *left brace* and end with } *right brace*. Each name is followed by a : *colon*, and the name / value pairs are separated by , *comma*.

- An array, which is an ordered collection of values

  Arrays begin with [*left bracket* and end with] *right bracket*. Values are separated by a , *comma*. A value can be a string enclosed in double quotes, a number, a true or false, an object or an array. Values can be nested so you can create very elaborate JSON structures to fit all your needs.
- A string, which is a sequence of zero or more Unicode characters, wrapped in double quotes using backslash escapes
- A number (e.g., digits 1-9, fractions, and exponents)
- Whitespace (e.g., space, linefeed, carriage return, or horizontal tab)

In the following example, the JSON object represents three courses in an array called `courses`. Notice that the array starts and ends with square brackets. Within the array are three objects, one for each course:

```
{
"courses": [
{
"courseID": 1001,
"title": "Access 2021 / Microsoft 365 Programming by Example",
"dateOffered": "September 14",
"location": "virtual"
},
{
"courseID": 1002,
"title": "Excel 2021 / Microsoft 365 Programming by Example",
"dateOffered": "September 18",
"location": "New York, Hilton"
},
{
"courseID": 1003,
"title": "PowerPoint VBA Programming by Example",
"dateOffered": "December 5-7",
"location": "Unspecified"
}
]
}
```

Because JSON is a simple text format, you can use Windows Notepad to create, save, and view JSON files. The above snippet can be found in the companion files as Courses.json.

The JSON format is supported by virtually all modern browsers, and because it is smaller than the XML encoding, JSON can provide bigger performance gains when sending large amounts of data over a network. The format you should use for data exchange (plain text /HTML, XML, or JSON) will depend on your specific situation and your project requirements.

SIDEBAR ***Getting JSON data from a server in a different domain***

When working with JSON data, you may come across another term – *JSONP* or *Jason with Padding*. JSONP allows you to get JSON data from a server in a different domain. This will help you get around the cross-domain security policy that modern browsers implement.

A more detailed description and examples of JSON formatting can be found at *www.json.org*.

Loading JSON Data into Excel

In the next Hands-On example, we will access another free REST API resource, but this time, we will receive the response formatted as JSON. The direct link to that resource is *https://api.zippopotam.us*. The website shows how the API can be used to autocomplete the City and State text boxes based on the zip code you enter. We will build a similar form in Excel (see Figure 29.12) that obtains the zip code data through that API.

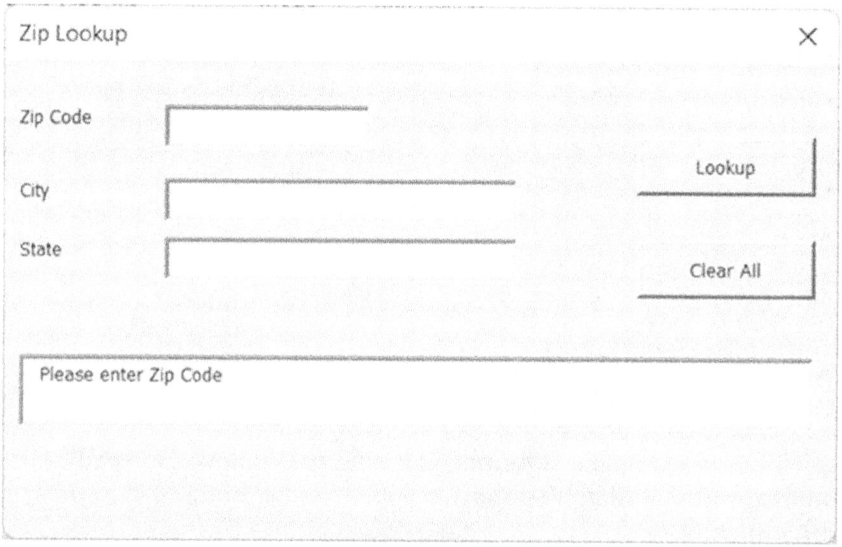

FIGURE 29.12 Excel Form used in Zip Code Demo REST API - JSON

If you enter *api.zippopotam.us/us/90210* in your favorite browser, you should see the JSON response shown in Figure 29.13.

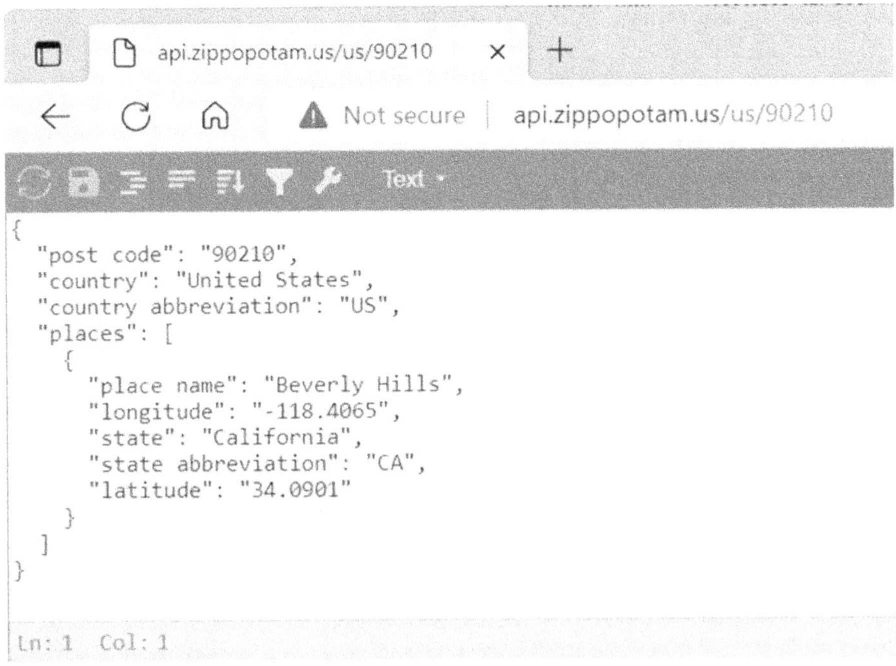

FIGURE 29.13 JSON structure returned from Zippopotam API

To work with the JSON format in VBA, we don't have a method that can help us easily extract individual key values from the JSON string. For simple structures like the one shown in Figure 29.13, we can use the basic string functions discussed earlier in this chapter, or we can use what we've learned so far about Regular Expressions. Let's take the latter route to gain more experience.

Hands-On 29.5 Requesting Data from REST API (JSON Example)

1. In the **Chap29_VBAExcel2021.xlsm** workbook, choose Insert | UserForm to create a new form as shown in Figure 29.12 earlier.

   This form should include the following:

   - Three unbound text boxes with caption properties set to **Zip Code**, **City**, and **State** and name properties set to **txtZip**, **txtCity**, and **txtState**
   - Two command buttons with caption properties set to **Lookup** and **Clear All**, and name properties set to **cmdRequest** and **cmdClearAll**
   - One unbound text box without a label. The name property of the text box is **txtStatus**. This box is used to return any errors received during the lookup process.

2. Rename the UserForm1 to **ZipLookup**.
3. Double-click the form's Lookup button.
4. In the ZipLookup code module, enter the following VBA procedure, which will run when the Lookup button is clicked:

```
Private Sub cmdRequest_Click()
    ClearFields

    If Me.txtZip = "" Or IsNull(Me.txtZip) Then
        With Me
            .txtStatus.Visible = True
            .txtStatus = "Please enter Zip Code"
            .txtZip.SetFocus
        End With
        Exit Sub
    End If
    If Len(Me.txtZip) <> 5 Or Not IsNumeric(Me.txtZip) Then
        Me.txtStatus.Visible = True
        Me.txtStatus = "Zip code must be 5-digit long."
        Exit Sub
    End If
    RequestData Me.txtZip
End Sub
```

This procedure will make sure that the Zip Code text box is not empty and is entered in the correct format. In the first line of this procedure, we will call a ClearFields procedure that will clear the existing entries in the City, State, and Status text boxes and will set the visibility of the Status box to False when it is empty. In the last procedure statement, we will call the RequestData procedure and pass it the current value from the Zip text box. The RequestData procedure will make a call to the REST API. We will enter it later in the standard code module.

5. Enter the following two procedures in the same Form_ZipLookup Code module. The first of these procedures will handle the form's Clear All button click.

```
Private Sub cmdClearAll_Click()
    Me.txtZip = ""
    ClearFields
    Me.txtZip.SetFocus
End Sub
Sub ClearFields()
    With Me
        .txtCity = ""
```

```
            .txtState = ""
            .txtStatus = ""
            .txtStatus.Visible = False
        End With
    End Sub
```

6. Save the changes you've made in the ZipLookup Code module.
7. Choose **Insert | Module** to add a new standard module to your VBAProject (Chap29_VBAExcel2021.xlsm). Use the properties window to rename it **APIRequest_JSON**.
8. In the **APIRequest_JSON** module, enter the code of the **RequestData** procedure as follows:

```
Sub RequestData(ByVal postcode As String)
Dim httpReq As MSXML2.XMLHTTP60
Dim oRegExp As Object
Dim rec As Variant
Dim aRecords As Variant
Dim aRecord As Variant
Dim fld As Variant
Dim fldName As String
Dim fldContent As String
Dim strAObj As String
Dim webResponse As String

Set httpReq = New MSXML2.XMLHTTP60
httpReq.Open "GET", "https://api.zippopotam.us/us/" + postcode,
False
httpReq.send
If httpReq.status <> "200" Then
    ZipLookup.txtStatus.Visible = True
    ZipLookup.txtStatus = "Error Code: " & _
        httpReq.status & " - " & httpReq.statusText
    Exit Sub
End If
'get the entire JSON string
webResponse = httpReq.responseText

Debug.Print "Below is raw web response json" & vbCrLf
Debug.Print webResponse
'convert json string to an array
Set oRegExp = New RegExp

oRegExp.Global = True
oRegExp.Pattern = "[\[\]\{\}""]+"
```

```
    strAObj = "[{"

    If InStr(1, webResponse, strAObj) > 0 Then
        webResponse = Replace(webResponse, strAObj, ", ")
    End If

    Debug.Print webResponse
    webResponse = oRegExp.Replace(webResponse, "")
    Debug.Print webResponse

    aRecords = Split(webResponse, ", ")
    For Each rec In aRecords
        aRecord = Split(rec, ", ")
            For Each fld In aRecord
                fldName = Split(fld, ":")(0)
                    fldContent = Split(fld, ":")(1)
                     If fldName = "place name" Then
                        ZipLookup.txtCity = fldContent
                    End If
                    If fldName = "state" Then
                        ZipLookup.txtState = fldContent
                    End If
            Next
        Debug.Print fldName & vbTab & vbTab & fldContent
    Next
    Set httpReq = Nothing
    End Sub
```

9. Save the changes in the module.
10. In the Project Explorer, double-click the ZipLookup form and choose **Run | Sub/UserForm**.
11. Click the Lookup button. You should see the error message shown earlier in Figure 29.12.
12. Click the Clear All button. The error message box should disappear.
13. Enter your zip code or any valid zip code you can recall and click the Lookup button.
    If the Zip code exists, you should see both the City and State text boxes populated. If the zip code is invalid, for example you've entered 11345, you should see "Error Code: 404."

To retrieve the zip code data, we pass the value from the Zip Code text box to the RequestData procedure in the string type variable called `postcode`. Notice that we then add this value to the URL string like this:

```
httpReq.Open "GET", "https://api.zippopotam.us/us/" + postcode, False
```

We send the request to the server in the same way we did it in the previous Hands-On. Our code will stop executing when the status of the response is not equal to 200. Any value but successful execution (200) will not provide us with a response, so we make the Status box visible on the form and load it with the error message. If the server response code is 200, our procedure continues, and we store the server response in the `webResponse` string variable. We print the response string to the Immediate window so we can examine its format. To get individual values from the JSON string, we will convert it to an array using the `RegExp` object discussed earlier in this chapter. We define the pattern that we want to match as the following:

```
oRegExp.Pattern = "[\[\]\{\}""]+"
```

The `Global` property of the `oRegExp` object will ensure that all occurrences of the characters specified in our pattern will be removed when we apply the `Remove` method. But prior to that, we want to find and replace the character string "[{" that follows the "places" key in the returned JSON string. These characters indicate that the next section of JSON is an array containing an object. We clean up our string of the characters we don't need by using the VBA `InStr` and `Replace` functions like this:

```
strAObj = "[{"
If InStr(1, webResponse, strAObj) > 0 Then
    webResponse = Replace(webResponse, strAObj, ", ")
End If
```

After this code is completed, we print the revised string to the Immediate window:

```
{"post code": "90210", "country": "United States", "country abbreviation": "US", "places": , "place name": "Beverly Hills", "longitude": "-118.4065", "state": "California", "state abbreviation": "CA", "latitude": "34.0901"}]}
```

Notice that `"places":` is now followed with a space and a comma.

Next, we use the pattern matching and replace with a comma all the braces and brackets that are remaining in the previous string. As a result, we get the following string:

```
post code: 90210, country: United States, country abbreviation: US, places: , place name: Beverly Hills, longitude: -118.4065, state: California, state abbreviation: CA, latitude: 34.0901
```

Now all that's left to do is split the above string into the name/value pairs so we can get access to individual items. We can use the VBA `Split` function to break the string each time we encounter a comma and a space:

```
aRecords = Split(webResponse, ", ")
```

The `aRecords` variable is an array and we can count the number of items we have in it using the `UBound` function. If you enter `?Ubound(aRecords)` in the Immediate window during the break mode (while your code is running), you should see 8 as a return value. If you type `?aRecords(0)`, you will get back the first name/value pair like this:

```
?aRecords(0)
post code: 90210
```

We use the `For Each` loop to iterate through the array. To make the process easier, we split each of the name/value pairs into individual fields using the colon separating the name from the value. The first (0) item will be a field name and the second (1) item will be the field content (value). We use the `If` statement to find the value for the place name field that we put in the `txtCity` text box on our form, and then look for the state to get the state. The looping process continues until we find the values we are searching for.

To gain more understanding of how this code performs its magic trick parsing the JSON string using the VBA string functions and regular expressions, set a breakpoint on the first Debug statement in the RequestData procedure, then go back to your form, enter a valid zip code, and click the Lookup button. When the VBA encounters the break statement and the code window appears, you can use the Step Into (**F8**) to step through the entire code line by line asking questions and checking responses in the Immediate window. You can also try to set up some watch expressions that were introduced in Chapter 9.

Figure 29.14 shows the Zip Lookup form populated with the zip code data retrieved from the Web service.

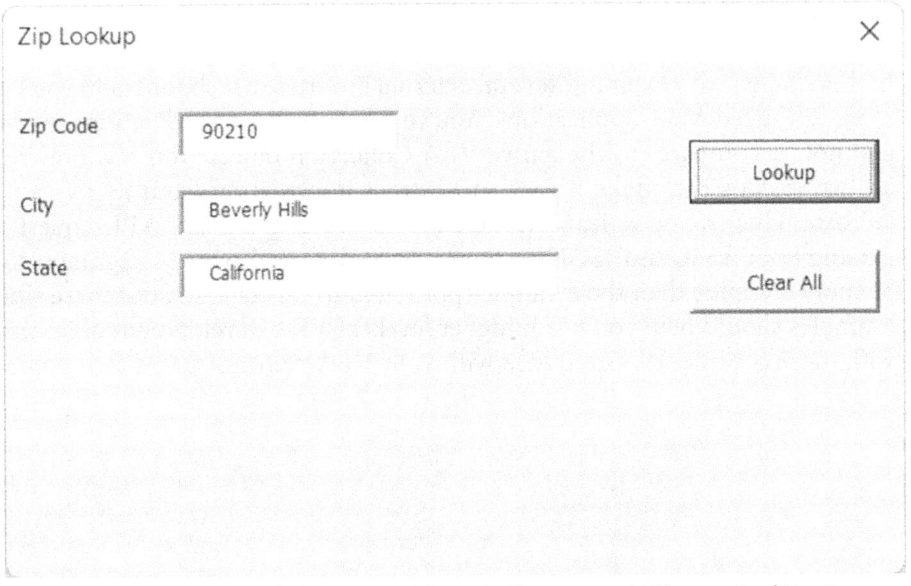

FIGURE 29.14 JSON zip code data returned from the Zippopotam API into an Excel UserForm.

Parsing JSON with Third-Party Libraries

Parsing REST API responses, especially the complex ones, will not be as straightforward as the example you've tried here. You may need a custom VBA library written specifically to help you handle the intricate JSON format your response can be returned in. Search the Web for this topic and you're bound to find a great set of VBA-JSON tools created by Tim Hall and available via *https://github.com/VBA-tools*. It contains the JSON conversion and parsing for VBA (Windows/Mac Excel, Access, and other Office applications). I have successfully used it in several of my own VBA projects and it made the task of dealing with the JSON output so much easier. There are other tools that you may also like and find useful in your work if you keep on searching. These tools may not work 100% of the time, but they are certainly better than having nothing that's built-into VBA to handle all your data parsing issues that you will come across while making REST API requests. Getting a response and not being able to turn it into the format you can further work with can be a painful and time-consuming effort. Do your own research; find the tool you like, read its documentation, and be ready to use it in your project. Now that you know how to program in VBA (you've learned about classes, dictionaries, arrays, and collections), you can create your own tool or improve one that already exists.

SUMMARY

In this chapter, you explored several external libraries that should help you build more advanced VBA applications. You've learned about the Dictionary object and how it compares to the native VBA Collection object. You saw how regular expressions can make it easier to extract information from JSON formatted data. Finally, you've learned the basics of making a REST API request and parsing both XML and JSON response data. Your real-world assignments will be more complex than the examples presented in this chapter, but these simple examples should help you reach higher levels of VBA development quicker and with more confidence. Good luck with your VBA coding!

INDEX

Q

R

S

T

W

www.ingramcontent.com/pod-product-compliance
Lightning Source LLC
Chambersburg PA
CBHW082100220326
41598CB00066BA/4484

* 9 7 8 1 6 8 3 9 2 8 8 6 7 *